STREET

Hertfordshire

Hemel Hempstead, Luton, St Albans, Stevenage, Watford

www.philips-maps.co.uk

First published in 1986 by

Philip's, a division of
Octopus Publishing Group Ltd
www.octopusbooks.co.uk
2-4 Heron Quays, London E14 4JP
An Hachette Livre UK Company
www.hachettelivre.co.uk

Fourth colour edition 2008
First impression 2008
HERDA

ISBN 978-0-540-09269-7 (spiral)

Data for the speed cameras provided by PocketGPSWorld.com Ltd.

Printed by Toppan, China

Contents

II **List of mobile speed cameras**

III **Key to map symbols**

IV **Key to map pages**

VI **Route planning**

VIII **Administrative and Postcode boundaries**

1 **Street maps** at 3½ inches to 1 mile

177 **Index** of towns, villages, streets, hospitals, industrial estates, railway stations, schools, shopping centres, universities and places of interest

Digital Data

The exceptionally high-quality mapping found in this atlas is available as digital data in TIFF format, which is easily convertible to other bitmapped (raster) image formats.

The index is also available in digital form as a standard database table. It contains all the details found in the printed index together with the National Grid reference for the map square in which each entry is named.

For further information and to discuss your requirements, please contact james.mann@philips-maps.co.uk

On-line route planner

For detailed driving directions and estimated driving times visit our free route planner at www.philips-maps.co.uk

Mobile speed cameras

The vast majority of speed cameras used on Britain's roads are operated by safety camera partnerships. These comprise local authorities, the police, Her Majesty's Court Service (HMCS) and the Highways Agency.

This table lists the sites where each safety camera partnership may enforce speed limits through the use of mobile cameras or detectors. These are usually set up on the roadside or a bridge spanning the road and operated by a police or civilian enforcement officer. The speed limit at each site (if available) is shown in red type, followed by the approximate location in black type.

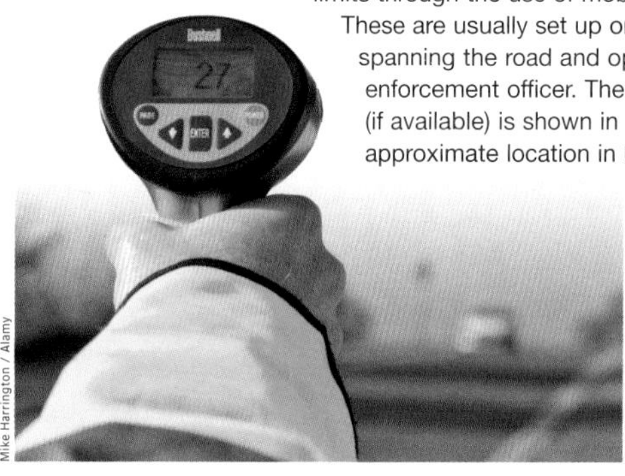

Mike Harrington / Alamy

A119
30 Hertford, North Rd

A409
30 Bushey, Heathbourne Rd

A411
30 Bushey, London Rd
30 Elstree, Barnet Lane
30 Watford, Hempstead Rd

A414
40 Hemel Hempstead, St Albans Rd
40 Hertford, Hertingfordbury Rd

A505
70 Royston Rd between Baldock and Royston near Slip End farm
30 Hitchin, Cambridge Rd

A600
30 Hitchin, Bedford Rd

A602
40 Hitchin, Stevenage Rd
40 Stevenage, Broadhall Way
40 Stevenage, Monkswood Way

A1000
40 Potters Bar, Barnet Rd

A1057
40 Hatfield, St Albans Rd West
30 St Albans, Hatfield Rd

A1170
30 Wormley, High Rd
30 Turnford, High Rd

A4125
40 South Oxhey, Sandy Lane
30 Watford, Eastbury Rd

A4145
30 Watford, Tolpits Lane

A4147
30 Hemel Hempstead, Leverstock Green Rd

A4251
30 Bourne End, London Rd

A5183
30 Elstree, Elstree Hill South
30 St Albans, Frogmore Rd

A6141
60 Letchworth, Letchworth Gate

B156
30 Cheshunt, Goffs Lane

B176
30 Cheshunt, High Street

B197
30 Baldock, London Rd
30 Stevenage, North Rd

B462
30 Bushey, Aldenham Rd

B487
30 Harpenden, Hatching Green, Redbourn Lane
40 Hemel Hempstead, Queensway

B488
40 Tring, Icknield Way

B556
30 Potters Bar, Mutton Lane

B1004
30 Bishops Stortford, Windhill

B1197
30 Hertford, London Rd

B1502
30 Hertford, Stansted Rd

B4505
30 Bovingdon, Chesham Rd

B4630
30 St Albans, Watford Rd

B5378
30 Elstree, Borehamwood, Allum Lane
40 London Colney, Shenleybury

B6426
30 Hatfield, Cavendish Way

UNCLASSIFIED
30 Cheshunt, Hammond St Rd
30 Hemel Hempstead, Bennetts End Rd
30 Hemel Hempstead, High Street Green
30 Hemel Hempstead, Long Chaulden
30 Hoddesdon, Essex Rd
30 Letchworth, Pixmore Way
30 Royston, Old North Rd
30 South Oxhey, Hayling Rd
30 St Albans, Sandpit Lane
30 Stevenage, Clovelly Way
30 Stevenage, Grace Way
40 Stevenage, Gresley Way
40 Stevenage, Monkswood Way
30 Watford, Radlett Rd
30 Welwyn Garden City, Heronswood Rd
30 Welwyn Garden City, Howlands

Key to map symbols

- **Motorway** with junction number
- **Primary route** – dual/single carriageway
- **A road** – dual/single carriageway
- **B road** – dual/single carriageway
- **Minor road** – dual/single carriageway
- **Other minor road** – dual/single carriageway
- **Road under construction**
- **Tunnel, covered road**
- **Speed cameras - single, multiple**
- **Rural track, private road or narrow road in urban area**
- **Gate or obstruction to traffic** (restrictions may not apply at all times or to all vehicles)
- **Path, bridleway, byway open to all traffic, road used as a public path**
- **Pedestrianised area**
- **Postcode boundaries**
- **County and unitary authority boundaries**
- **Railway, tunnel, railway under construction**
- **Tramway, tramway under construction**
- **Miniature railway**
- **Railway station**
- **Private railway station**
- **London Underground station**
- **Tram stop, tram stop under construction**
- **Bus, coach station**

- **Ambulance station**
- **Coastguard station**
- **Fire station**
- **Police station**
- **Accident and Emergency entrance to hospital**
- **Hospital**
- **Place of worship**
- **Information Centre** (open all year)
- **Shopping Centre**
- **Parking**
- **Park and Ride**
- **Post Office**
- **Camping site**
- **Caravan site**
- **Golf course**
- **Picnic site**
- **Important buildings, schools, colleges, universities and hospitals**
- **Built up area**
- **Woods**
- **Water name**
- **River, weir, stream**
- **Canal, lock, tunnel**
- **Water**
- **Tidal water**
- **Non-Roman antiquity**
- **Roman antiquity**
- **Adjoining page indicators**

Acad	**Academy**	Inst	**Institute**	Recn Gd	**Recreation Ground**
Allot Gdns	**Allotments**	Ct	**Law Court**	Resr	**Reservoir**
Cemy	**Cemetery**	L Ctr	**Leisure Centre**	Ret Pk	**Retail Park**
C Ctr	**Civic Centre**	LC	**Level Crossing**	Sch	**School**
CH	**Club House**	Liby	**Library**	Sh Ctr	**Shopping Centre**
Coll	**College**	Mkt	**Market**	TH	**Town Hall/House**
Crem	**Crematorium**	Meml	**Memorial**	Trad Est	**Trading Estate**
Ent	**Enterprise**	Mon	**Monument**	Univ	**University**
Ex H	**Exhibition Hall**	Mus	**Museum**	W Twr	**Water Tower**
Ind Est	**Industrial Estate**	Obsy	**Observatory**	Wks	**Works**
IRB Sta	**Inshore Rescue Boat Station**	Pal	**Royal Palace**	YH	**Youth Hostel**
		PH	**Public House**		

■ The small numbers around the edges of the maps identify the 1 kilometre National Grid lines

■ The dark grey border on the inside edge of some pages indicates that the mapping does not continue onto the adjacent page

The scale of the maps on the pages numbered in blue is 5.52 cm to 1 km • 3½ inches to 1 mile • 1: 18103

0 ¼ ½ ¾ 1 mile

0 250 m 500 m 750 m 1 kilometre

Key to map pages

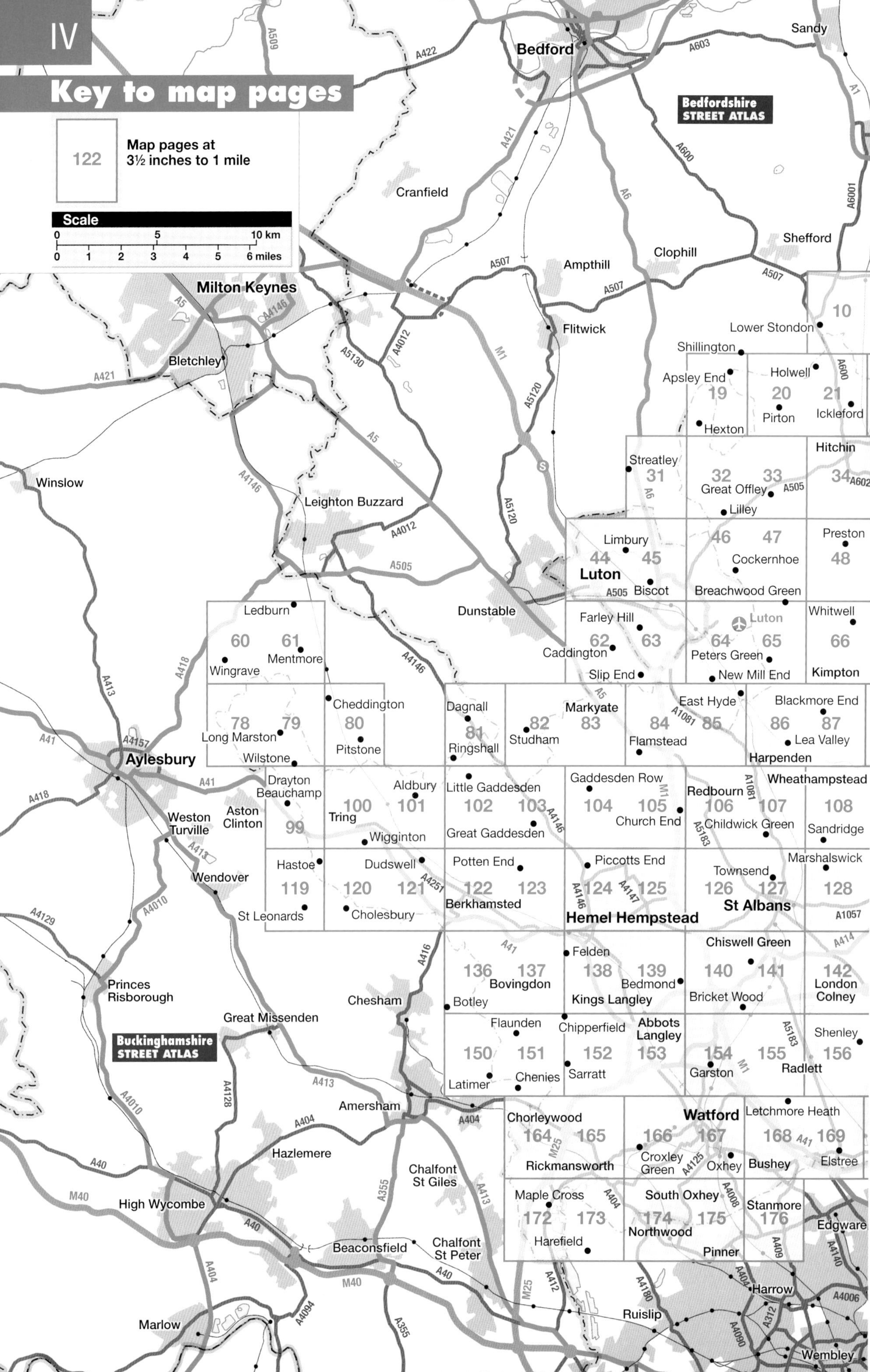

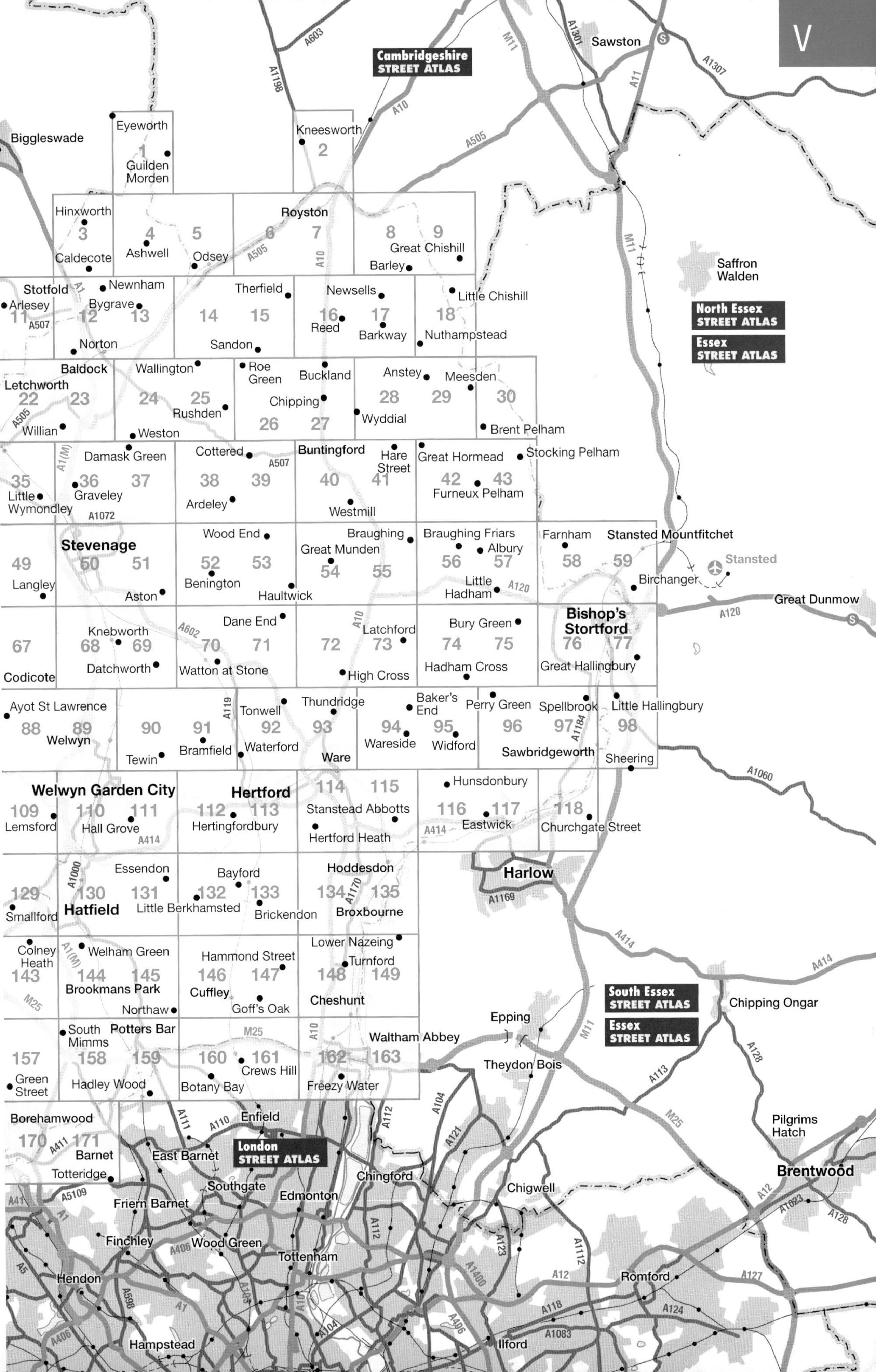
Cambridgeshire STREET ATLAS
North Essex STREET ATLAS
Essex STREET ATLAS
South Essex STREET ATLAS
Essex STREET ATLAS
London STREET ATLAS
Sawston
Biggleswade
Eyeworth
Guilden Morden
Kneesworth
Hinxworth
Caldecote
Ashwell
Odsey
Royston
Great Chishill
Barley
Saffron Walden
Stotfold
Arlesey
Newnham
Bygrave
Norton
Therfield
Sandon
Newsells
Reed
Barkway
Little Chishill
Nuthampstead
Baldock
Letchworth
Willian
Wallington
Rushden
Weston
Roe Green
Buckland
Chipping
Anstey
Meesden
Wyddial
Brent Pelham
Damask Green
Graveley
Little Wymondley
Cottered
Ardeley
Buntingford
Hare Street
Westmill
Great Hormead
Furneux Pelham
Stocking Pelham
Stevenage
Langley
Aston
Wood End
Benington
Haultwick
Braughing
Great Munden
Braughing Friars
Albury
Little Hadham
Farnham
Stansted Mountfitchet
Birchanger
Stansted
Great Dunmow
Bishop's Stortford
Knebworth
Datchworth
Codicote
Dane End
Watton at Stone
Latchford
High Cross
Bury Green
Hadham Cross
Great Hallingbury
Ayot St Lawrence
Welwyn
Tewin
Bramfield
Tonwell
Waterford
Thundridge
Ware
Baker's End
Wareside
Widford
Perry Green
Spellbrook
Sawbridgeworth
Little Hallingbury
Sheering
Welwyn Garden City
Lemsford
Hall Grove
Hertford
Hertingfordbury
Stanstead Abbotts
Hertford Heath
Hunsdonbury
Eastwick
Churchgate Street
Harlow
Essendon
Bayford
Hoddesdon
Smallford
Hatfield
Little Berkhamsted
Brickendon
Broxbourne
Colney Heath
Welham Green
Hammond Street
Lower Nazeing
Turnford
Brookmans Park
Cuffley
Goff's Oak
Cheshunt
Northaw
Chipping Ongar
Epping
South Mimms
Potters Bar
Waltham Abbey
Theydon Bois
Crews Hill
Green Street
Hadley Wood
Botany Bay
Freezy Water
Borehamwood
Enfield
Barnet
East Barnet
Totteridge
Southgate
Chingford
Chigwell
Pilgrims Hatch
Brentwood
Friern Barnet
Edmonton
Finchley
Wood Green
Tottenham
Hendon
Romford
Hampstead
Ilford
1 2 3 4 5 6 7 8 9
11 12 13 14 15 16 17 18
22 23 24 25 26 27 28 29 30
35 36 37 38 39 40 41 42 43
49 50 51 52 53 54 55 56 57 58 59
67 68 69 70 71 72 73 74 75 76 77
88 89 90 91 92 93 94 95 96 97 98
109 110 111 112 113 114 115 116 117 118
129 130 131 132 133 134 135
143 144 145 146 147 148 149
157 158 159 160 161 162 163
170 171
A603 A1198 A10 M11 A1301 A11 A1307 A505 A1 A507 A1(M) A1072 A120 A602 A119 A1184 A1060 A414 A1000 A1170 A1169 M25 A113 A128 A104 A121 A112 A111 A110 A411 A5109 A41 A5 A406 A598 A105 A1010 A123 A1400 A1112 A12 A118 A1083 A124 A127 A1023

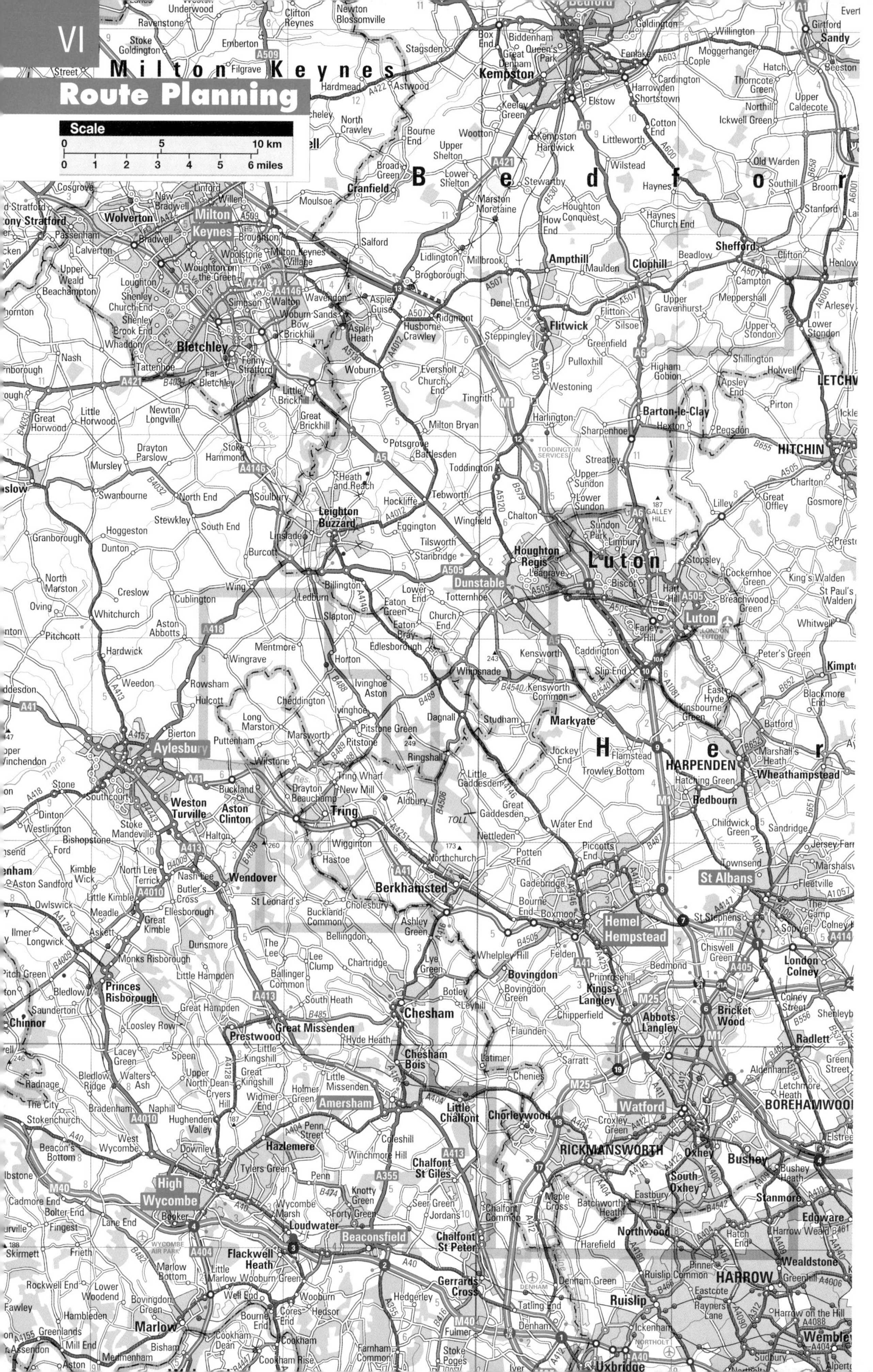
Milton Keynes
Route Planning
Scale
0 5 10 km
0 1 2 3 4 5 6 miles
Bedford
Hertfordshire
Milton Keynes
Wolverton
Bletchley
Fenny Stratford
Newport Pagnell
Kempston
Bedford
Cranfield
Ampthill
Flitwick
Clophill
Shefford
Barton-le-Clay
Hitchin
Leighton Buzzard
Dunstable
Houghton Regis
Luton
Harpenden
Wheathampstead
St Albans
Hemel Hempstead
Berkhamsted
Tring
Aylesbury
Wendover
Princes Risborough
Chesham
Amersham
Great Missenden
Prestwood
Hazlemere
High Wycombe
Beaconsfield
Marlow
Chalfont St Giles
Chalfont St Peter
Gerrards Cross
Little Chalfont
Chorleywood
Rickmansworth
Watford
Bushey
Radlett
Borehamwood
London Colney
Kings Langley
Abbots Langley
Bricket Wood
Northwood
Ruislip
Harrow
Wealdstone
Stanmore
Edgware
Wembley
Uxbridge
Denham
Woburn
Toddington
Markyate
Redbourn
Stotfold
Sandy
Letchworth
Weston Turville
Stokenchurch
Chinnor
Loudwater
Flackwell Heath
Bourne End
Cookham
Tatling End
Fulmer
Stoke Poges
Farnham Common

VII
Arrington
Orwell
New Wimpole
Barrington
Harston
Newton
Little Shelford
Babraham
Sawston
Little Abington
Great Abington
Hildersham
Pampisford
Whittlesford
Shepreth
Foxton
Thriplow
Duxford
Linton
Horseheath
Bartlow
East Hatley
Cockayne Hatley
Potton
Croydon
Wrestlingworth
Tadlow
Wendy
Sutton
Eyeworth
Whaddon
Meldreth
Chiswick End
Fowlmere
Hinxton
Ickleton
Stump Cross
Great Chesterford
Little Chesterford
Hadstock
Shudy Camps
Ashdon
Church End
Biggleswade
Dunton
Guilden Morden
Abington Pigotts
Kneesworth
Bassingbourn
Melbourn
Litlington
Steeple Morden
Edworth
Hinxworth
Royston
Heydon
Great Chishill
Chrishall
Strethall
Elmdon
Littlebury
Saffron Walden
Little Walden
Astwick
Ashwell
Caldecote
Church End
Stotfold
Newnham
Baldock Services
Bygrave
Slip End
Therfield
Kelshall
Barley
Little Chishill
Littlebury Green
Wendens Ambo
Sewards End
Radwinter
Wimbish
Radwell
Norton
Baldock
Reed
Barkway
Nuthampstead
Duddenhoe End
Bridge Green
Langley Upper Green
Langley Lower Green
Arkesden
Newport
Tye Green
Wimbish Green
Howlett End
Sandon
Roe Green
Mill End
Buckland
Wallington
Chipping
Anstey
Meesden
Clavering
Wicken Bonhunt
Rickling
Debden
Widdington
Debden Cross
Thaxted
Letchworth
Clothall
William
Rushden
Wyddial
Hare Street
Brent Pelham
Starlings Green
Berden
Quendon
Hamperden End
Cutlers Green
Walsworth
Weston
Throcking
Great Wymondley
Little Wymondley
Hall's Green
Cromer
Cottered
Buntingford
Great Hormead
Stocking Pelham
Ugley
Henham
Monk Street
Graveley
Aspenden
Ardeley
Furneaux Pelham
East End
Manuden
Ugley Green
Elsenham
Broxted
Duton Hill
St Ippollitts
Walkern
Westmill
Hay Street
Farnham Green
Molehill Green
Brick End
Great Easton
Stevenage
Wood End
Braughing
Gravesend
Clapgate
Farnham
Stansted Mountfitchet
Butcher's Pasture
Aston End
Benington
Nasty
Great Munden
Albury
Albury End
Stansted Airport
London Stansted
Shephall
Langley
Haultwick
Levens Green
Puckeridge
Little Hadham
Birchanger
Little Easton
Bambers Green
Great Dunmow
Aston
Broadwater
Wellpond Green
Standon
Hadham Ford
Bishop's Stortford
Takeley
Takeley Street
Bragbury End
Dane End
Whempstead
Collier's End
Latchford
Bury Green
Birchanger Green Services
Smith's Green
Hope End Green
Dunmow Services
Old Knebworth
Knebworth
Datchworth
Watton at Stone
Much Hadham
Thorley Street
Thorley
Gt. Hallingbury
Bacon End
Codicote
Datchworth Green
Sacombe
Barwick
High Cross
Hadham Cross
Perry Green
Bishop's Green
Ayot St Lawrence
Woolmer Green
Bull's Green
Wadesmill
Baker's End
Allens Green
Spellbrook
Lit. Hallingbury
Great Canfield
High Roding
Welwyn
Oakland
Burnham Green
Stapleford
Tonwell
Thundridge
Wareside
Sawbridgeworth
Hatfield Heath
Hatfield Broad Oak
Ayot St Peter
Harmer Green
Bramfield
Chapmore End
Widford
Aythorpe Roding
High Easter
Welwyn Garden City
Digswell Park
Tewin
Waterford
Hertford
Ware
Hunsdon
High Wych
Sheering
Leaden Roding
Panshanger
Great Amwell
Stanstead Abbotts
Eastwick
Gilston
Matching
White Roding
Margaret Roding
Woodhall
Hatfield Hyde
Hall Grove
Cole Green
Hertingfordbury
St Margarets
Hertford Heath
Hailey
Matching Tye
Abbess Roding
Churchgate Street
Netteswell
Harlow
Stanborough
Hatfield Garden Village
Letty Green
Hoddesdon
Rye Park
Roydon
Gt. Parndon
Tye Green
Potter Street
Foster Street
Matching Green
Beauchamp Roding
The Ryde
Hatfield
Essendon
Bayford
Brickendon
Broxbourne
Roydon Hamlet
Nazeing
Broadley Common
Latton Bush
Hastingwood
Magdalen Laver
High Laver
Little Laver
Shellow Bowells
South Hatfield
Wildhill
Little Berkhamsted
Epping Green
Wormley West End
Lower Nazeing
Thornwood Common
Fyfield
Moreton
Willingale
Woodside
Bell Bar
Welham Green
Newgate Street
Hammond Street
Wormley
Turnford
Bumble's Green
Epping Green
Epping Upland
Bovinger
Bobbingworth
Norton Mandeville
Cooksmill Green
Water End
Brookmans Park
Flamstead End
Goff's Oak
Cheshunt
Coopersale Common
Epping
North Weald Bassett
Toot Hill
Greensted
Shelley
High Ongar
Chipping Ongar
Nine Ashes
Norton Heath
Northaw
Cuffley
South Mimms
Potters Bar
Waltham Cross
Waltham Abbey
Ivy Chimneys
Fiddlers Hamlet
Stanford Rivers
Blackmore
South Mimms Services
Upshire
Theydon Bois
Little End
Stondon Massey
Fryerning
Botany Bay
Forty Hill
Enfield Wash
High Beach
Stapleford Tawney
Kelvedon Hatch
Doddinghurst
Swallows Cross
Sewardstone
Debden
Navestock Heath
Navestock Side
Mountnessing
Barnet
Monken Hadley
Enfield
Sewardstonebury
Loughton
Abridge
Stapleford
Lambourne End
Stapleford Abbotts
Pilgrims Hatch
Arkley
Cockfosters
Winchmore Hill
Ponders End
Epping Forest
London Gateway Services
Totteridge
East Barnet
Chigwell
Chigwell Row
South Weald
Shenfield
Brentwood
Friern Barnet
Southgate
Edmonton
Chingford
Buckhurst Hill
Grange Hill
Havering-atte-Bower
Noak Hill
Mill Hill
Finchley
Wood Green
Tottenham
Woodford
Woodford Bridge
Hainault
Harold Hill
Great Warley
Little Warley
Hornsey
Collier Row
Barkingside
Gidea Park
Harold Wood
Romford
Cranham
West Horndon
Hendon
Walthamstow
Wanstead
Newbury Park
Golders Green
Highgate
Hampstead
Stoke Newington
Leytonstone
Leyton
Seven Kings
Ilford
Becontree
Hornchurch
Rush Green
Elm Park
Upminster
Cricklewood
Hackney
Forest Gate
Manor Park
Dagenham
Granta
Cam or Rhee
Quin
Rib
Stort
Lea
Fourwentways Services
A1
A1(M)
A10
A11
A12
A14
A41
A120
A127
A406
A414
A505
A507
A602
A1400
M1
M11
M25
B1039
B1368
B1038
B1004
B1042
B1383
B183
B184
d
t
f
o
r
d

Major administrative and Postcode boundaries

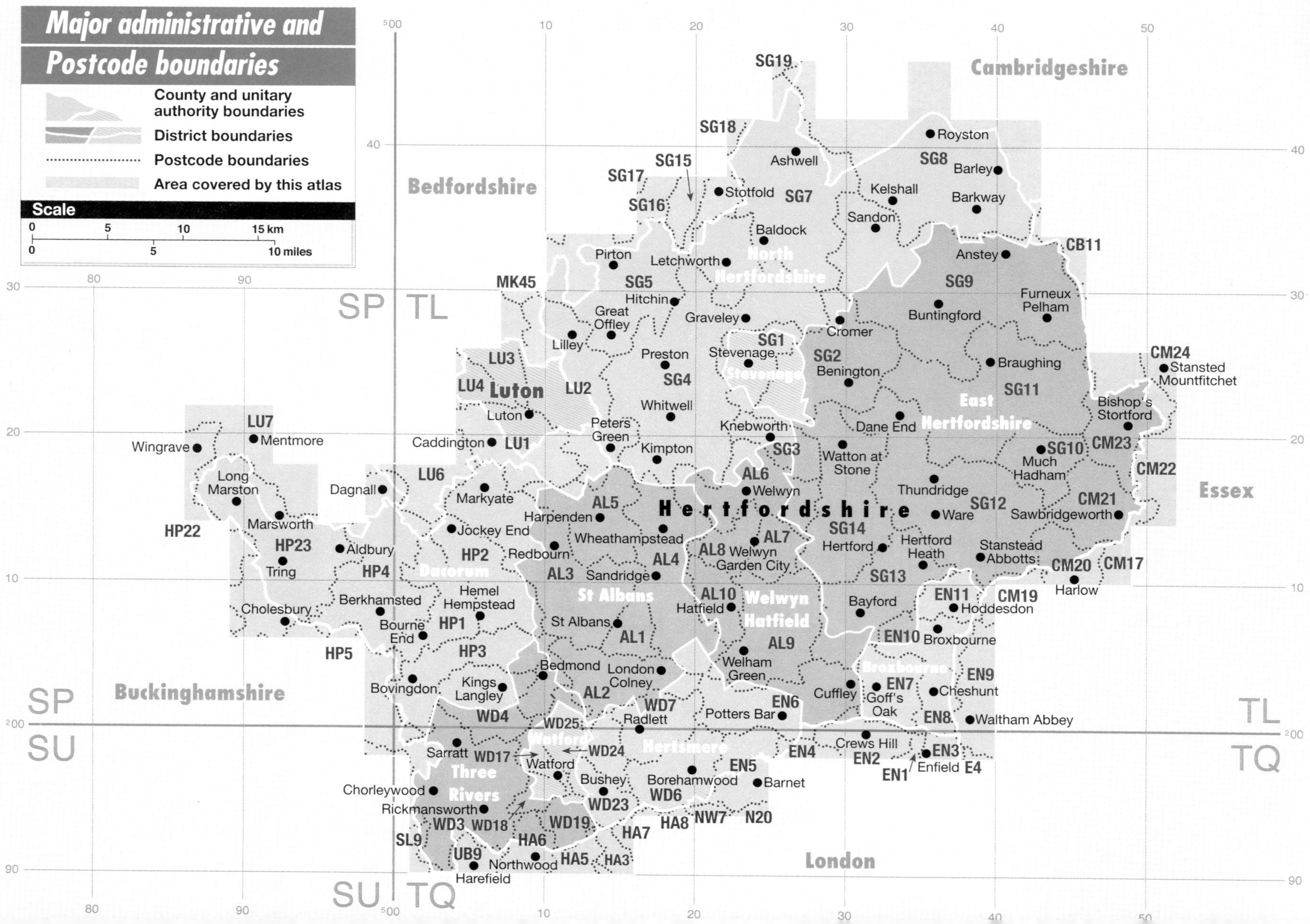

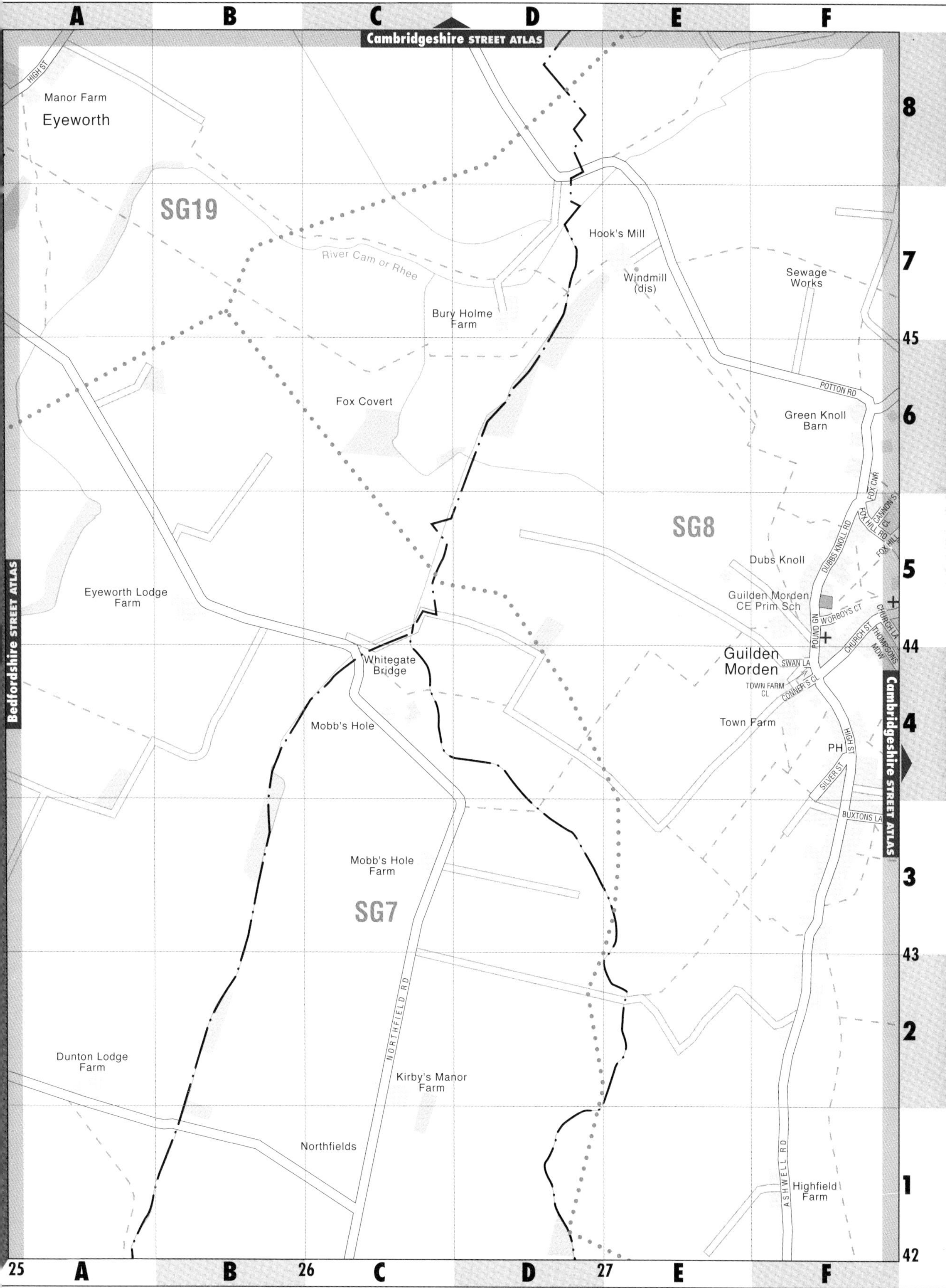
A
B
C
D
E
F
Cambridgeshire STREET ATLAS
Bedfordshire STREET ATLAS
HIGH ST
Manor Farm
Eyeworth
SG19
River Cam or Rhee
Hook's Mill
Windmill
(dis)
Sewage
Works
Bury Holme
Farm
Fox Covert
POTTON RD
Green Knoll
Barn
SG8
FOX CNR
CANNON ST
FOX HILL RD
CL
FOX HILL
DUBBS KNOLL RD
Dubs Knoll
Eyeworth Lodge
Farm
Guilden Morden
CE Prim Sch
WORBOYS CT
CHURCH LA
POUND GN
CHURCH ST
THOMPSONS MDW
Whitegate
Bridge
Guilden
Morden
SWAN LA
TOWN FARM
CL
CONNER'S CL
Mobb's Hole
Town Farm
PH
HIGH ST
SILVER ST
BUXTONS LA
Mobb's Hole
Farm
SG7
NORTHFIELD RD
Dunton Lodge
Farm
Kirby's Manor
Farm
Northfields
ASHWELL RD
Highfield
Farm
8
7
45
6
5
44
4
3
43
2
1
42
25
26
27

4

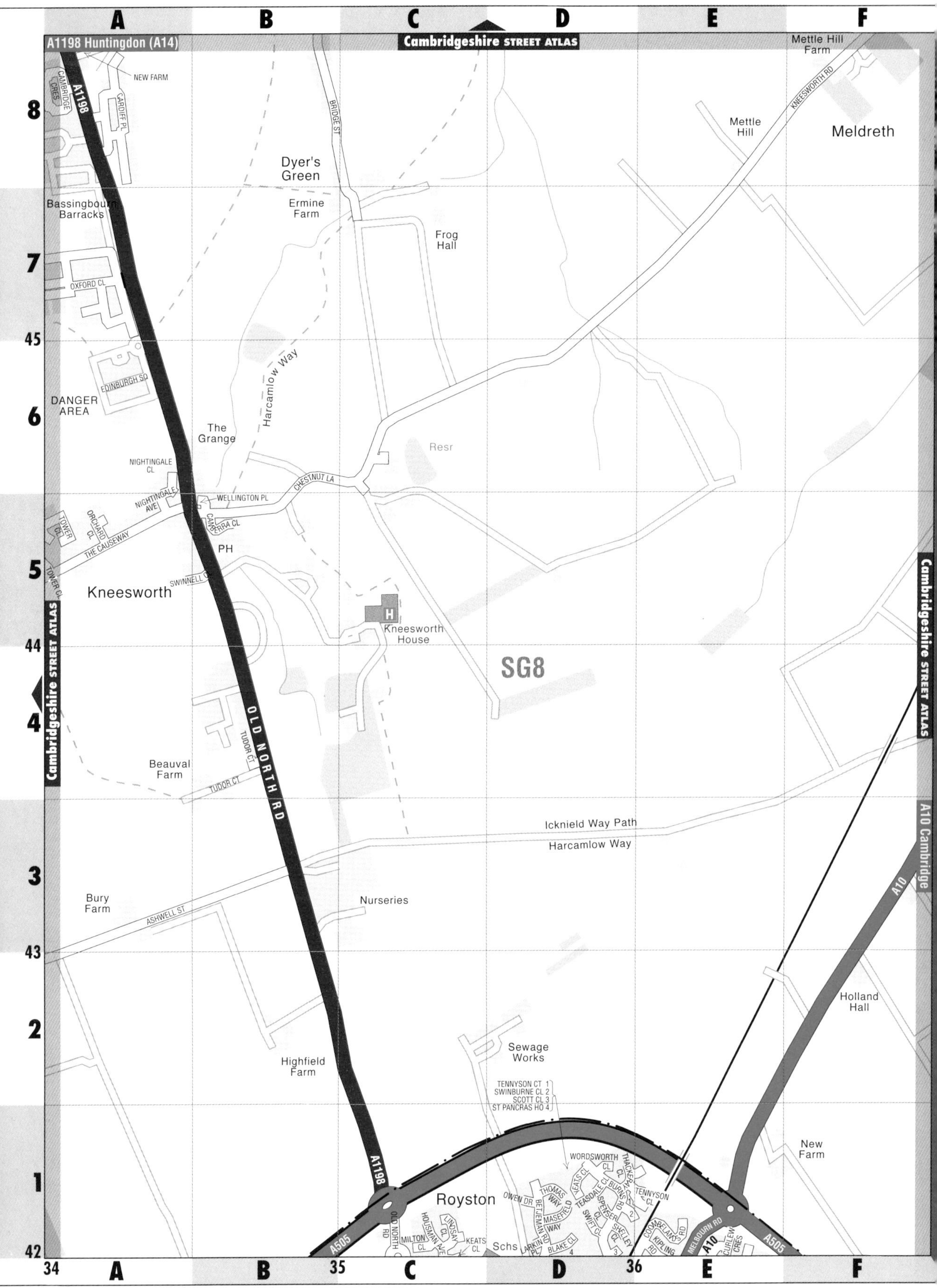
A1198 Huntingdon (A14)
Cambridgeshire STREET ATLAS
Mettle Hill Farm
NEW FARM
CAMBRIDGE CRES
CARDIFF PL
BRIDGE ST
KNEESWORTH RD
Mettle Hill
Meldreth
Dyer's Green
Bassingbourn Barracks
Ermine Farm
Frog Hall
OXFORD CL
Harcamlow Way
EDINBURGH SQ
DANGER AREA
The Grange
Resr
NIGHTINGALE CL
CHESTNUT LA
NIGHTINGALE AVE
WELLINGTON PL
TOWER CL
ORCHARD CL
CANBERRA CL
THE CAUSEWAY
PH
TOWER CL
SWINNELL CL
Kneesworth
Kneesworth House
SG8
OLD NORTH RD
TUDOR CT
Beauval Farm
TUDOR CT
Icknield Way Path
Harcamlow Way
A10 Cambridge
Bury Farm
ASHWELL ST
Nurseries
A10
Holland Hall
Sewage Works
Highfield Farm
TENNYSON CT 1
SWINBURNE CL 2
SCOTT CL 3
ST PANCRAS HO 4
New Farm
WORDSWORTH CL
THACKERAY
TENNYSON CL
A1198
Royston
OWEN DR
THOMAS WAY
KEATS CL
BURNS RD
TEASDALE CL
BETJEMAN RD
MASEFIELD WAY
SPENSER CL
SWIFT CL
SHELLEY CL
COOMBELANDS RD
KIPLING RD
MELBOURN RD
A10
CURLEW CRES
A505
A505
OLD NORTH RD
HOUSMAN AVE
LINDSAY CL
MILTON CL
KEATS CL
Schs
LARKIN PL
BLAKE CL
34
35
36
A B C D E F
8 7 45 6 5 44 4 3 43 2 1 42

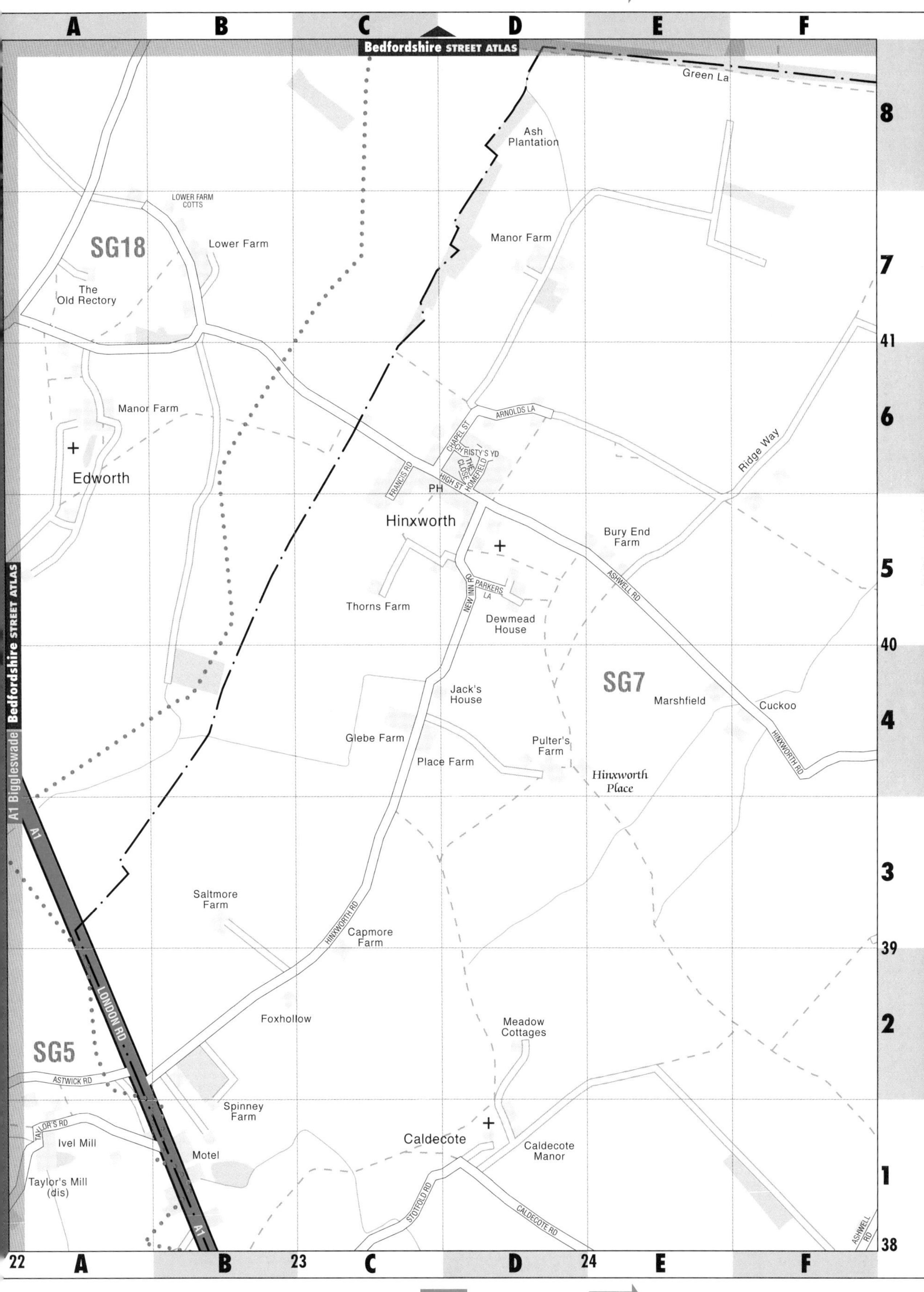
4
A
B
C
D
E
F
Bedfordshire STREET ATLAS
Green La
8
Ash
Plantation
LOWER FARM
COTTS
Lower Farm
SG18
Manor Farm
7
The
Old Rectory
41
Manor Farm
ARNOLDS LA
6
CHAPEL ST
CHRISTY'S YD
THE CLOSE
HOMEFIELD
FRANCIS RD
HIGH ST
PH
Ridge Way
Edworth
Hinxworth
Bury End
Farm
5
Thorns Farm
NEW INN RD
PARKERS LA
ASHWELL RD
Dewmead
House
40
Jack's
House
SG7
Marshfield
Cuckoo
4
Glebe Farm
Pulter's
Farm
HINXWORTH RD
Place Farm
Hinxworth
Place
A1 Biggleswade
A1
3
Saltmore
Farm
HINXWORTH RD
Capmore
Farm
39
LONDON RD
Foxhollow
Meadow
Cottages
2
SG5
ASTWICK RD
Spinney
Farm
TAYLOR'S RD
Ivel Mill
Caldecote
Caldecote
Manor
Motel
1
Taylor's Mill
(dis)
STOTFOLD RD
CALDECOTE RD
ASHWELL RD
A1
38
22
A
B
23
C
D
24
E
F
12
4

3
1

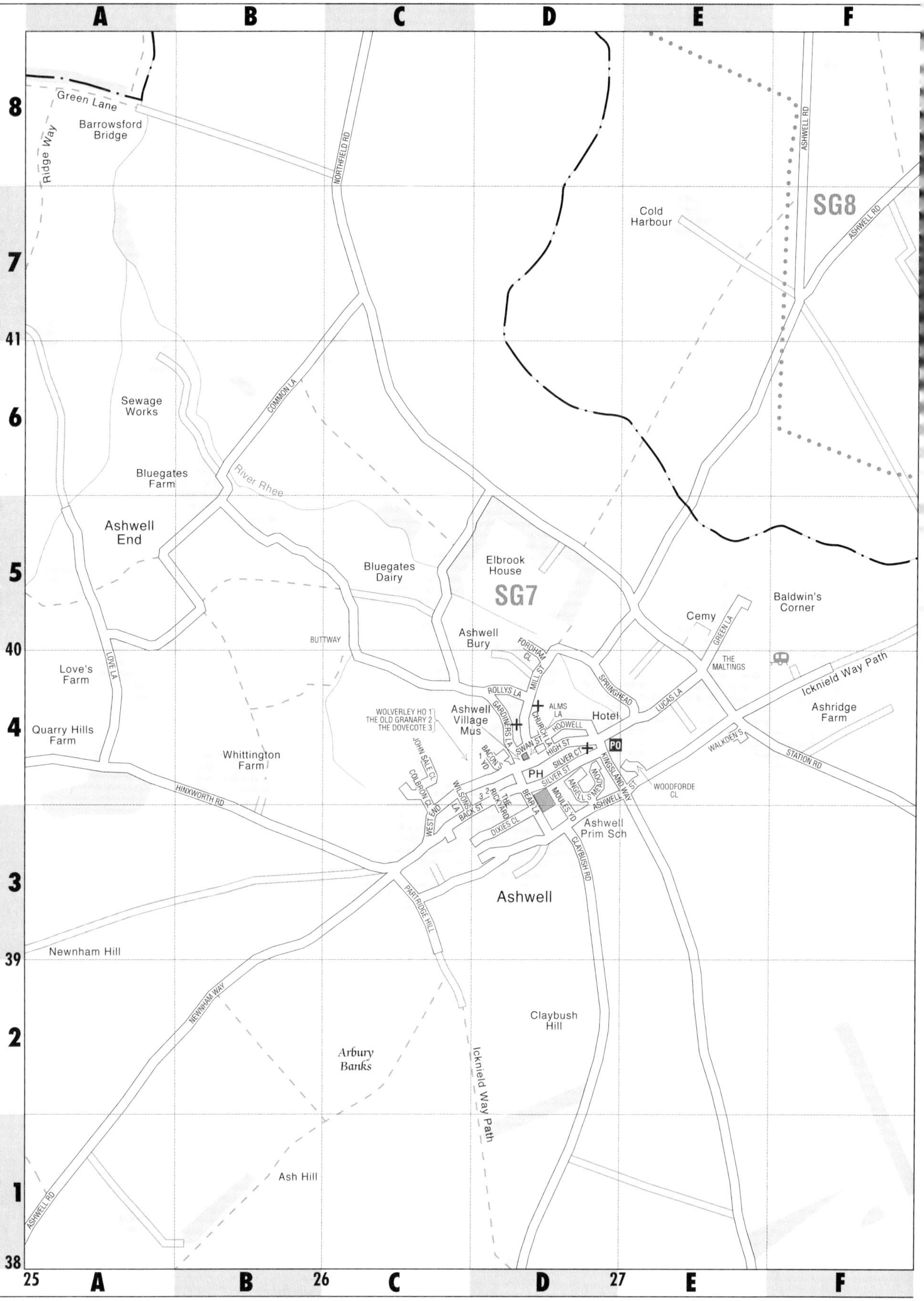

A B C D E F

8 7 41 6 5 40 4 3 39 2 1 38

Green Lane
Barrowsford Bridge
Ridge Way
NORTHFIELD RD
ASHWELL RD
Cold Harbour
SG8
ASHWELL RD
Sewage Works
COMMON LA
Bluegates Farm
River Rhee
Ashwell End
Bluegates Dairy
Elbrook House
SG7
Baldwin's Corner
Cemy
GREEN LA
Ashwell Bury
BUTTWAY
FORDHAM CL
THE MALTINGS
Icknield Way Path
Love's Farm
LOVE LA
ROLLYS LA
MILL ST
SPRINGHEAD
LUCAS LA
Ashwell Village Mus
ALMS LA
Hotel
Ashridge Farm
WOLVERLEY HO 1
THE OLD GRANARY 2
THE DOVECOTE 3
GARDINERS LA
CHURCH LA
HODWELL
Quarry Hills Farm
JOHN SALE CL
SWAN ST
HIGH ST
PO
WALKDEN'S
STATION RD
Whittington Farm
BACON'S YD
SILVER CT
KINGSLAND WAY
PH
SILVER ST
MOO MEAD
WOODFORDE CL
COLBRON CL
ANGEL'S
HINXWORTH RD
WILSONS LA
THE RICKYARD
BEAR LA
MOULES YD
ASHWELL ST
WEST END
BACK ST
DIXIES CL
Ashwell Prim Sch
CLAYBUSH RD
PARTRIDGE HILL
Ashwell
Newnham Hill
NEWNHAM WAY
Claybush Hill
Arbury Banks
Icknield Way Path
Ash Hill
ASHWELL RD

25 A B 26 C D 27 E F

3
13

6

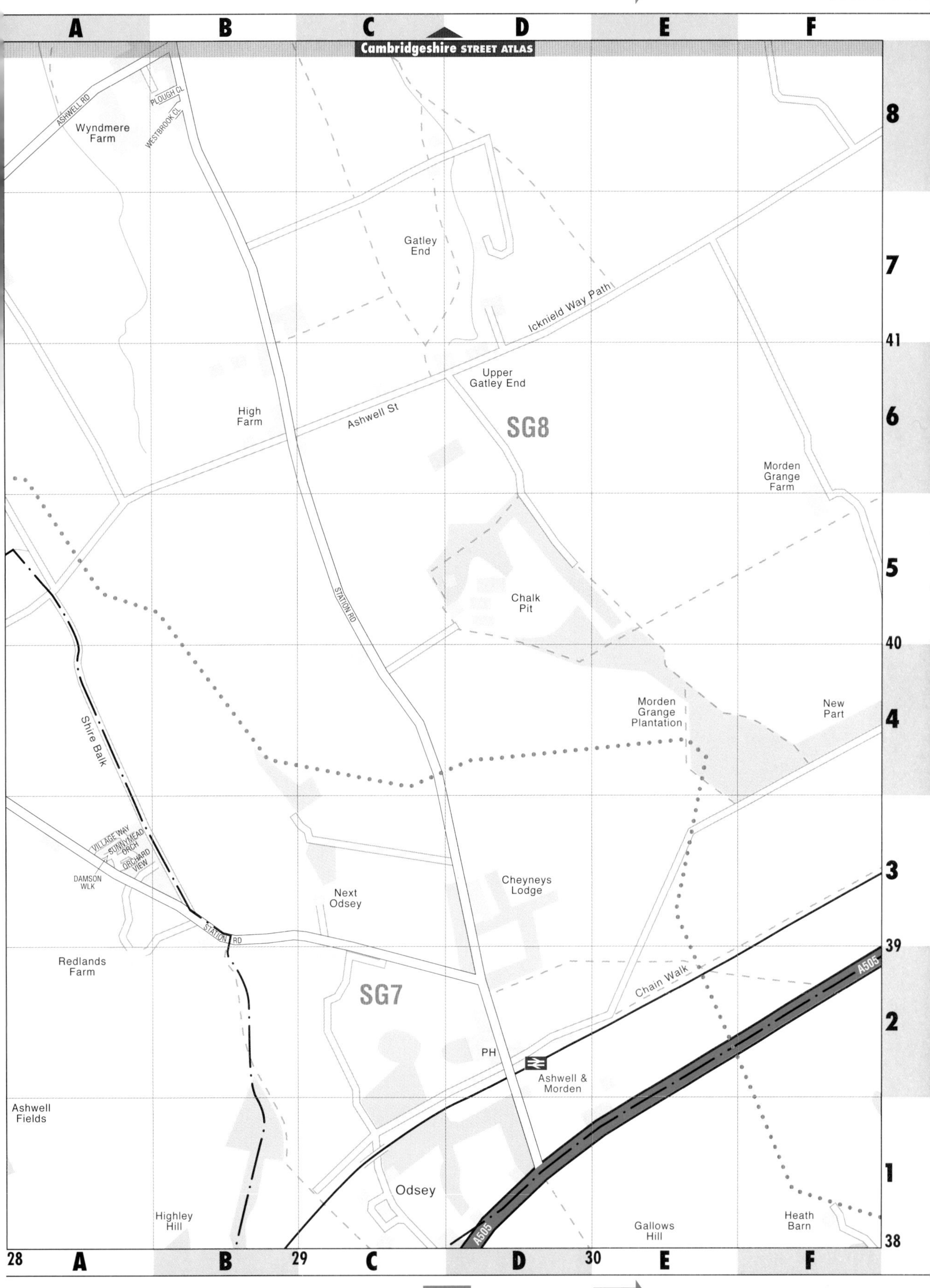
A
B
C
D
E
F
Cambridgeshire STREET ATLAS
8
7
41
6
5
40
4
3
39
2
1
38
28
29
30
ASHWELL RD
Wyndmere Farm
PLOUGH CL
WESTBROOK CL
Gatley End
Icknield Way Path
Upper Gatley End
High Farm
Ashwell St
SG8
Morden Grange Farm
STATION RD
Chalk Pit
Morden Grange Plantation
New Part
Shire Balk
VILLAGE WAY
SUNNYMEAD
ORCH
ORCHARD VIEW
DAMSON WLK
Next Odsey
Cheyneys Lodge
STATION RD
Redlands Farm
SG7
Chain Walk
A505
PH
Ashwell & Morden
Ashwell Fields
Odsey
A505
Highley Hill
Gallows Hill
Heath Barn

14

6

5

A B C D E F

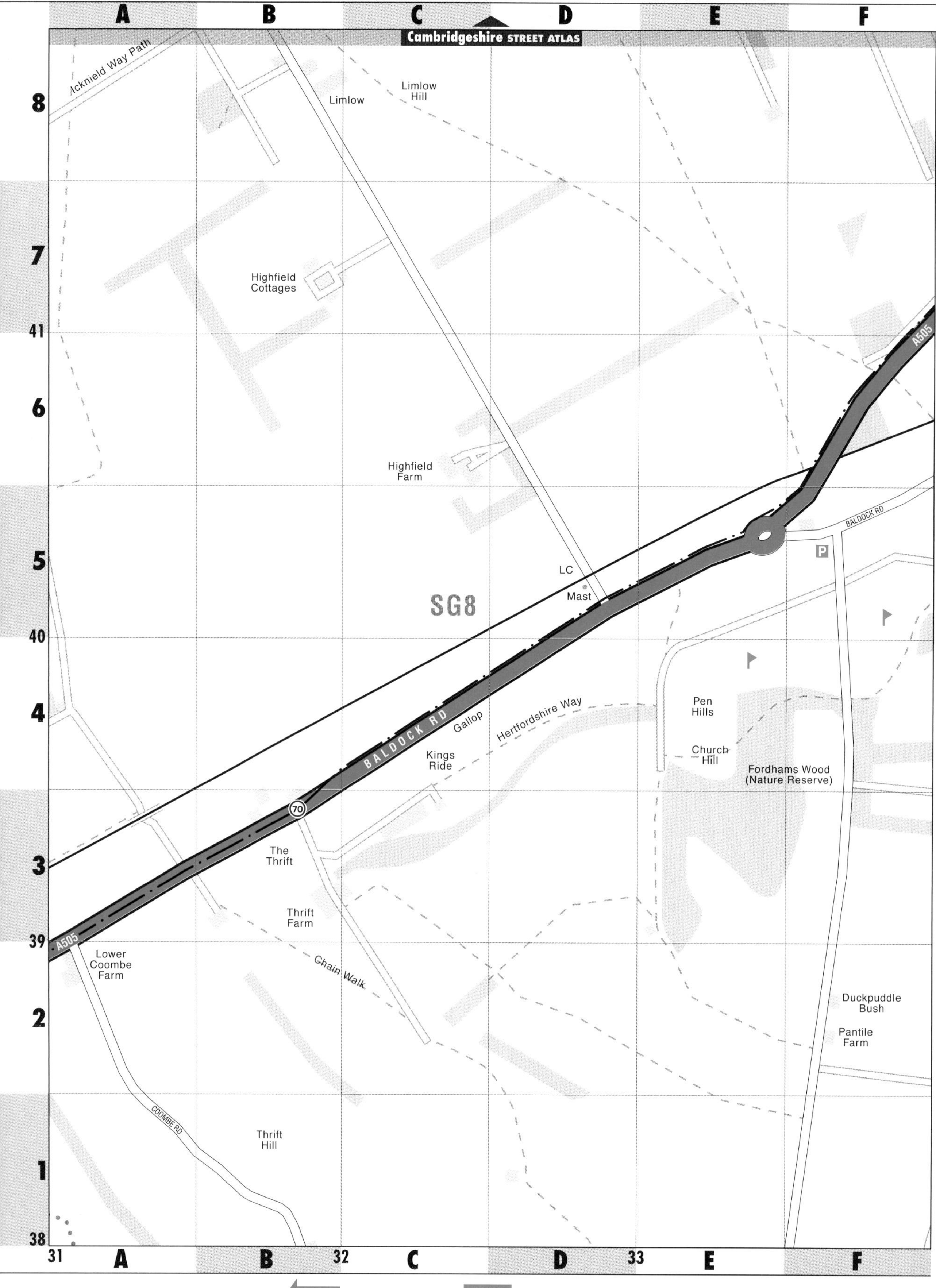

A B C D E F

5
15

2
8

A B C D E F

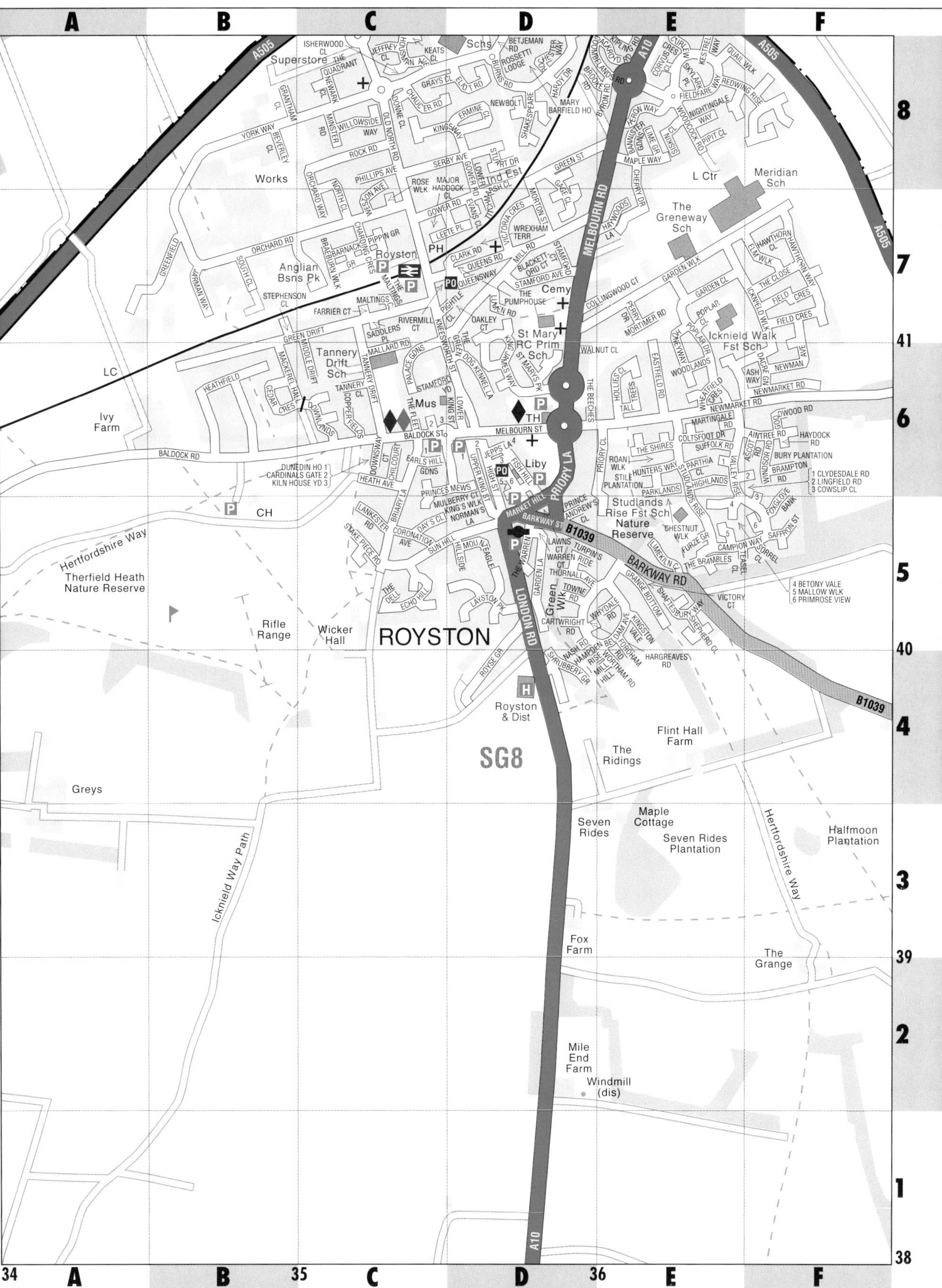

A B C D E F

D6
1 ABBOTTS YD
2 KING ST
3 JOHN ST
4 CHURCH LA
5 GEORGE LA
6 MARKET HILL
7 ANGEL PAVEMENT

16
8

7

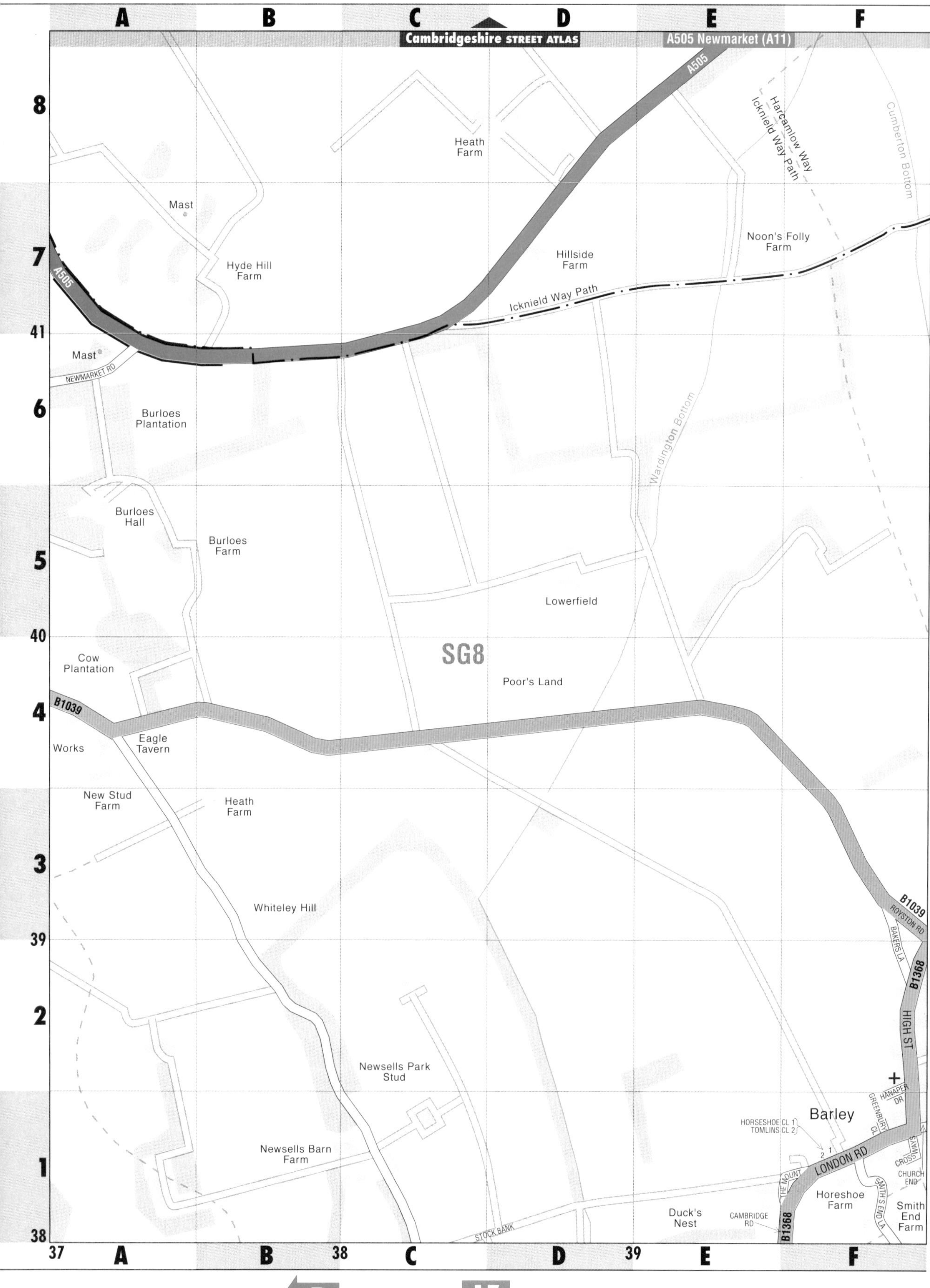

A
B
C
D
E
F
Cambridgeshire STREET ATLAS
A505 Newmarket (A11)
8
7
41
6
5
40
4
3
39
2
1
38
37
38
39
A505
Heath Farm
Harcamlow Way
Icknield Way Path
Cumberton Bottom
Mast
Noon's Folly Farm
Hillside Farm
Hyde Hill Farm
Icknield Way Path
Mast
NEWMARKET RD
Burloes Plantation
Wardington Bottom
Burloes Hall
Burloes Farm
Lowerfield
Cow Plantation
SG8
Poor's Land
B1039
Eagle Tavern
Works
New Stud Farm
Heath Farm
Whiteley Hill
B1039
ROYSTON RD
BAKERS LA
B1368
HIGH ST
Newsells Park Stud
HANAPER DR
GREENBURY CL
Barley
HORSESHOE CL 1
TOMLINS CL 2
Newsells Barn Farm
LONDON RD
CROSS
CHURCH END
THE MOUNT
SMITH'S END LA
Horeshoe Farm
Duck's Nest
CAMBRIDGE RD
Smith End Farm
B1368
STOCK BANK

7
17

A
B
C
D
E
F
Cambridgeshire STREET ATLAS
North Hall Farm
B1368
Harcamlow Way
Icknield Way Path
Sells Close Farm
BARLEY RD
Icknield Way Path
FOWLMERE RD
Harcamlow Way
Icknield Way Path
Green Ditch
New Buildings Farm
Clay Hill
NEW RD
Rectory Farm
SG8
Cumberton Bottom
Cambridgeshire STREET ATLAS
Lynchets Farm
CHISHILL RD
Lime Farm
New Hill
CAMBRIDGE RD
HEYDON RD
REEVES PIGHTLE
THE PUDGELL
BARLEY RD
PLAISTOW WAY
PH
Great Chishill
PICKNAGE RD
Chishill Windmill
Hill Farm
CHISHILL RD
B1039
MALTINGS LA
COLTS CROFT
HALL LA
MAY ST
WALLER'S CL
B1039
Barley CE Fst Sch
PO
PICKNAGE CNR
CHURCH END
SCHOOL LA
PUDDING LA
WARREN COTTS
CHURCHFIELD
SHAFTENHOE END RD
Standard Hill
May Street Farm
The Hall
BOGMOOR RD
LITTLE CHISHILL RD
8
7
41
6
5
40
4
3
39
2
1
38
40
41
42

18

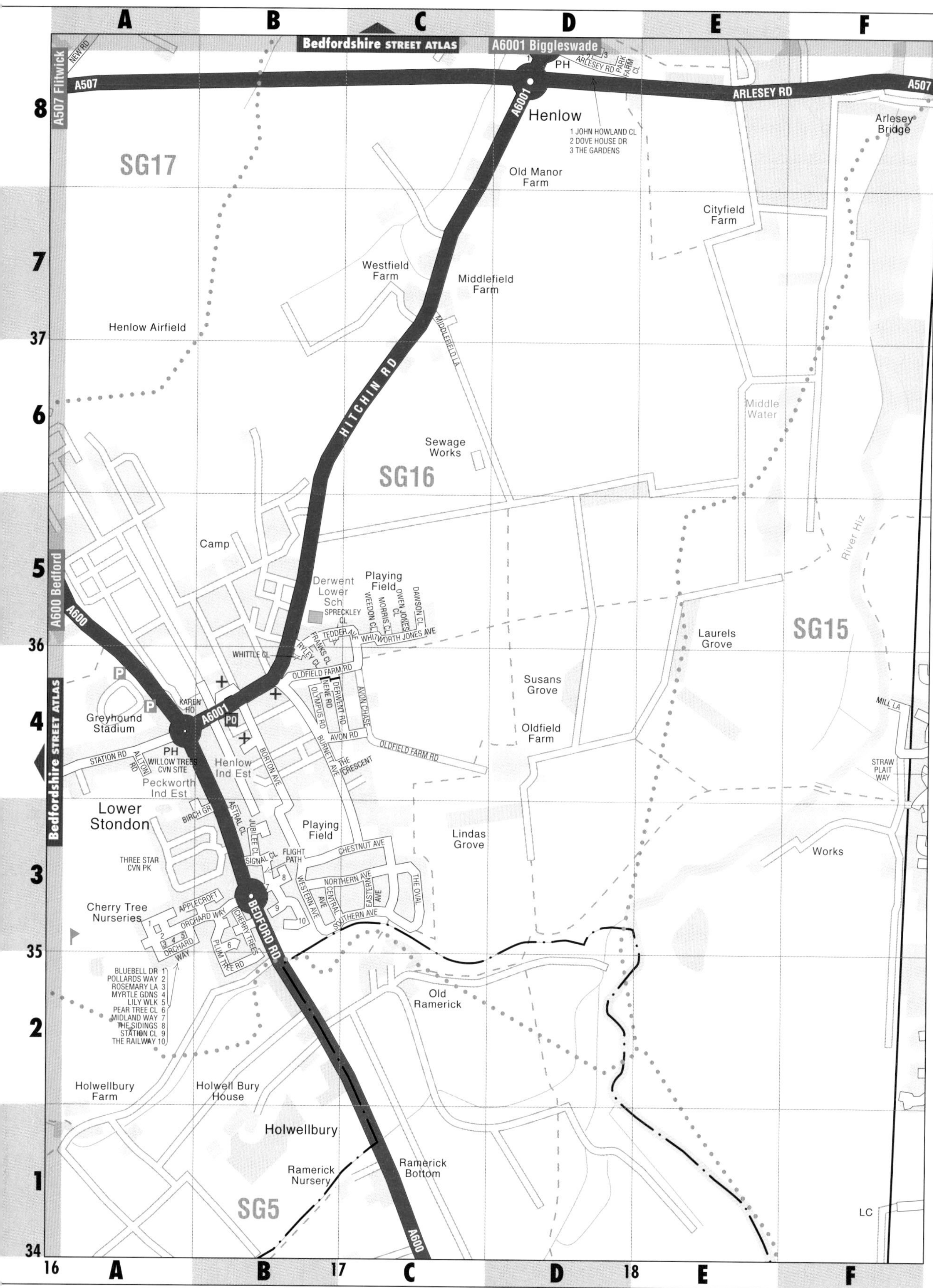

A
B
C
D
E
F
Bedfordshire STREET ATLAS
A6001 Biggleswade
A507 Flitwick
A507
ARLESEY RD
A6001
Henlow
PH
ARLESEY RD
PARK FARM CL
1 JOHN HOWLAND CL
2 DOVE HOUSE DR
3 THE GARDENS
Arlesey Bridge
SG17
Old Manor Farm
Cityfield Farm
Westfield Farm
Middlefield Farm
MIDDLEFIELD LA
Henlow Airfield
HITCHIN RD
Middle Water
Sewage Works
SG16
Camp
River Hiz
A600 Bedford
A600
Derwent Lower Sch
Playing Field
SPRECKLEY CL
WEEDON CL
MORRIS CL
OWEN JONES CL
DAWSON CL
TEDDER AVE
WHITWORTH JONES AVE
Laurels Grove
SG15
WHITTLE CL
FRANKS CL
OLDFIELD FARM RD
Susans Grove
MILL LA
KAREN HO
Greyhound Stadium
A6001
PO
NENE RD
OLYMPUS RD
DERWENT RD
AVON CHASE
Oldfield Farm
PH
STATION RD
ALLTON RD
WILLOW TREES CVN SITE
Henlow Ind Est
BORTON AVE
AVON RD
BURNETT AVE
THE CRESCENT
OLDFIELD FARM RD
STRAW PLAIT WAY
Peckworth Ind Est
Lower Stondon
BIRCH GR
ASTRAL CL
JUBILEE CL
Playing Field
Lindas Grove
THREE STAR CVN PK
SIGNAL CL
FLIGHT PATH
CHESTNUT AVE
Works
NORTHERN AVE
WESTERN AVE
CENTRAL AVE
EASTERN AVE
THE OVAL
SOUTHERN AVE
Cherry Tree Nurseries
APPLECROFT
ORCHARD WAY
CHERRY TREES
BEDFORD RD
PLUM TREE RD
BLUEBELL DR 1
POLLARDS WAY 2
ROSEMARY LA 3
MYRTLE GDNS 4
LILY WLK 5
PEAR TREE CL 6
MIDLAND WAY 7
THE SIDINGS 8
STATION CL 9
THE RAILWAY 10
Old Ramerick
Holwellbury Farm
Holwell Bury House
Holwellbury
Ramerick Nursery
Ramerick Bottom
SG5
LC
8
7
37
6
5
36
4
3
35
2
1
34
16
17
18

12

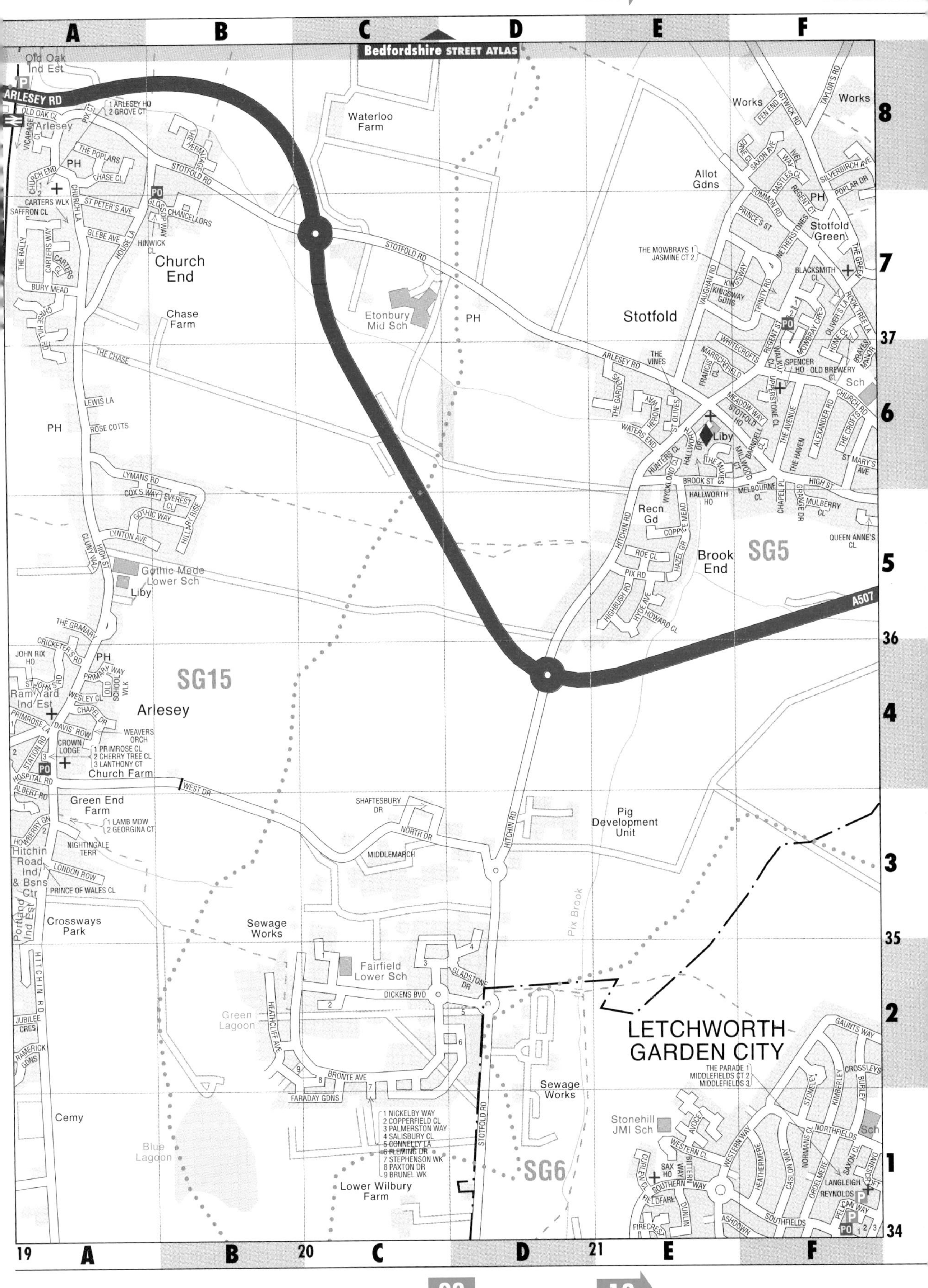

Bedfordshire STREET ATLAS
A
B
C
D
E
F
Old Oak Ind Est
ARLESEY RD
OLD OAK CL
Arlesey
1 ARLESEY HO
2 GROVE CT
PIX CT
THE HERMITAGE
STOTFOLD RD
Waterloo Farm
Works
Works
Allot Gdns
THE POPLARS
CHASE CL
PH
CARTERS WLK
SAFFRON CL
ST PETER'S AVE
GLOSSOP WAY
CHANCELLORS
HINWICK CL
GLEBE AVE
HOUSE LA
CHURCH LA
Church End
THE RALLY
CARTERS WAY
BURY MEAD
Chase Farm
Etonbury Mid Sch
PH
STOTFOLD RD
Stotfold
Stotfold Green
THE MOWBRAYS 1
JASMINE CT 2
BLACKSMITH CL
THE CHASE
ARLESEY RD
THE VINES
LEWIS LA
ROSE COTTS
PH
Sch
Liby
BROOK ST
HALLWORTH HO
MELBOURNE CL
HIGH ST
MULBERRY CL
QUEEN ANNE'S CL
LYMANS RD
COX'S WAY
EVEREST CL
GOTHIC WAY
LYNTON AVE
HILLARY RISE
Recn Gd
COPPICE MEAD
ROE CL
PIX RD
Brook End
SG5
A507
Gothic Mede Lower Sch
Liby
THE GRANARY
CRICKETERS RD
JOHN RIX HO
PH
SG15
Arlesey
Ram Yard Ind Est
WEAVERS ORCH
CROWN LODGE
1 PRIMROSE CL
2 CHERRY TREE CL
3 LANTHONY CT
Church Farm
HOSPITAL RD
ALBERT RD
WEST DR
Green End Farm
1 LAMB MDW
2 GEORGINA CT
NIGHTINGALE TERR
Hitchin Road Ind/ & Bsns Ctr
LONDON ROW
PRINCE OF WALES CL
Portland Ind Est
Crossways Park
SHAFTESBURY DR
NORTH DR
MIDDLEMARCH
HITCHIN RD
Pig Development Unit
Pix Brook
Sewage Works
Fairfield Lower Sch
GLADSTONE DR
DICKENS BVD
Green Lagoon
HEATHCLIFF AVE
BRONTE AVE
FARADAY GDNS
1 NICKELBY WAY
2 COPPERFIELD CL
3 PALMERSTON WAY
4 SALISBURY CL
5 CONNELLY LA
6 FLEMING DR
7 STEPHENSON WK
8 PAXTON DR
9 BRUNEL WK
Lower Wilbury Farm
STOTFOLD RD
Sewage Works
SG6
LETCHWORTH GARDEN CITY
THE PARADE 1
MIDDLEFIELDS CT 2
MIDDLEFIELDS 3
Stonehill JMI Sch
JUBILEE CRES
Cemy
Blue Lagoon
HITCHIN RD
8
7
37
6
5
36
4
3
35
2
1
34
19
20
21

22
12

11
3

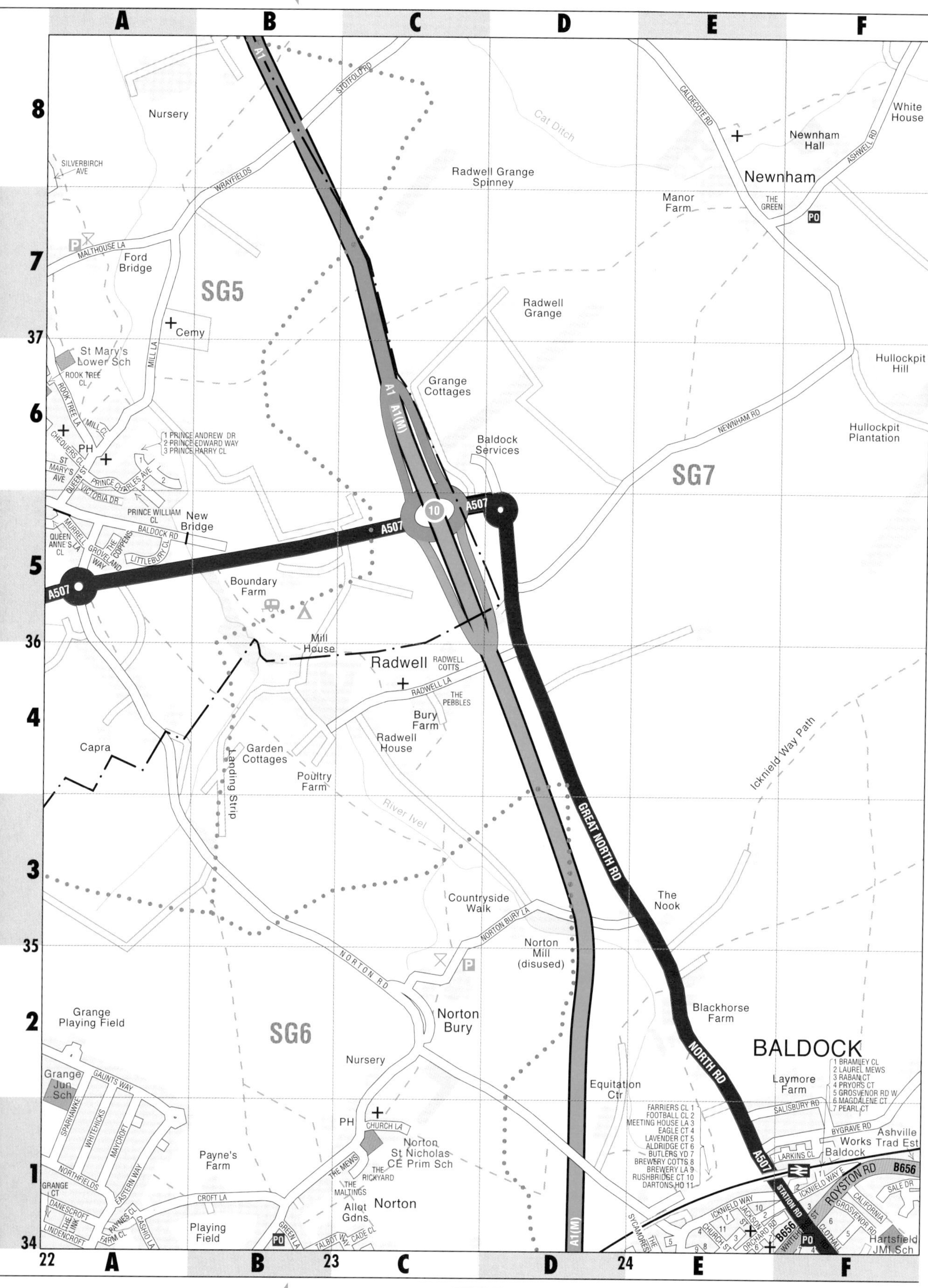
A
B
C
D
E
F
8
7
37
6
5
36
4
3
35
2
1
34
22
23
24
A1
STOTFOLD RD
Nursery
SILVERBIRCH AVE
WRAYFIELDS
Cat Ditch
Radwell Grange Spinney
CALDECOTE RD
Newnham Hall
White House
ASHWELL RD
Newnham
THE GREEN
Manor Farm
PO
MALTHOUSE LA
Ford Bridge
SG5
Radwell Grange
Cemy
St Mary's Lower Sch
MILL LA
ROOK TREE CL
ROOK TREE LA
Grange Cottages
Hullockpit Hill
A1
A1(M)
MILL CL
1 PRINCE ANDREW DR
2 PRINCE EDWARD WAY
3 PRINCE HARRY CL
CHEQUERS CL
PH
ST MARY'S AVE
QUEEN ST
VICTORIA DR
PRINCE CHARLES AVE
Baldock Services
NEWNHAM RD
Hullockpit Plantation
SG7
PRINCE WILLIAM CL
New Bridge
10
A507
MURRELL LA
QUEEN ANNE'S CL
THE COPPENS
BALDOCK RD
GROVELAND WAY
LITTLEBURY CL
Boundary Farm
Mill House
Radwell
RADWELL COTTS
RADWELL LA
THE PEBBLES
Bury Farm
Radwell House
Capra
Garden Cottages
Landing Strip
Poultry Farm
Icknield Way Path
River Ivel
GREAT NORTH RD
Countryside Walk
The Nook
NORTON BURY LA
Norton Mill (disused)
NORTON RD
Norton Bury
Blackhorse Farm
Grange Playing Field
SG6
NORTH RD
BALDOCK
Nursery
Grange Jun Sch
GAUNTS WAY
SPARHAWKE
WHITEHICKS
MAYCROFT
Equitation Ctr
Laymore Farm
1 BRAMLEY CL
2 LAUREL MEWS
3 RABAN CT
4 PRYORS CT
5 GROSVENOR RD W
6 MAGDALENE CT
7 PEARL CT
SALISBURY RD
PH
CHURCH LA
FARRIERS CL 1
FOOTBALL CL 2
MEETING HOUSE LA 3
EAGLE CT 4
LAVENDER CT 5
ALDRIDGE CT 6
BUTLERS YD 7
BREWERY COTTS 8
BREWERY LA 9
RUSHBRIDGE CT 10
DARTONS HO 11
BYGRAVE RD
Ashville Works Trad Est
Baldock
Payne's Farm
Norton St Nicholas CE Prim Sch
THE MEWS
THE RICKYARD
NORTHFIELDS
EASTERN WAY
LARKINS CL
ROYSTON RD
B656
GRANGE CT
THE MALTINGS
Norton
Allot Gdns
CROFT LA
DANESCROFT
THE LINK
LINDENCROFT
PAYNES CL
FARM CL
CASHIO LA
Playing Field
GREEN LA
TALBOT WAY
CADE CL
A1(M)
SYCAMORES
ICKNIELD WAY
JACKSON ST
CHURCH ST
ORCHARD RD
STATION RD
WHITEHORSE ST
CLOTHALL RD
GROSVENOR RD
CALIFORNIA
SALE DR
Hartsfield JMI Sch

11
23

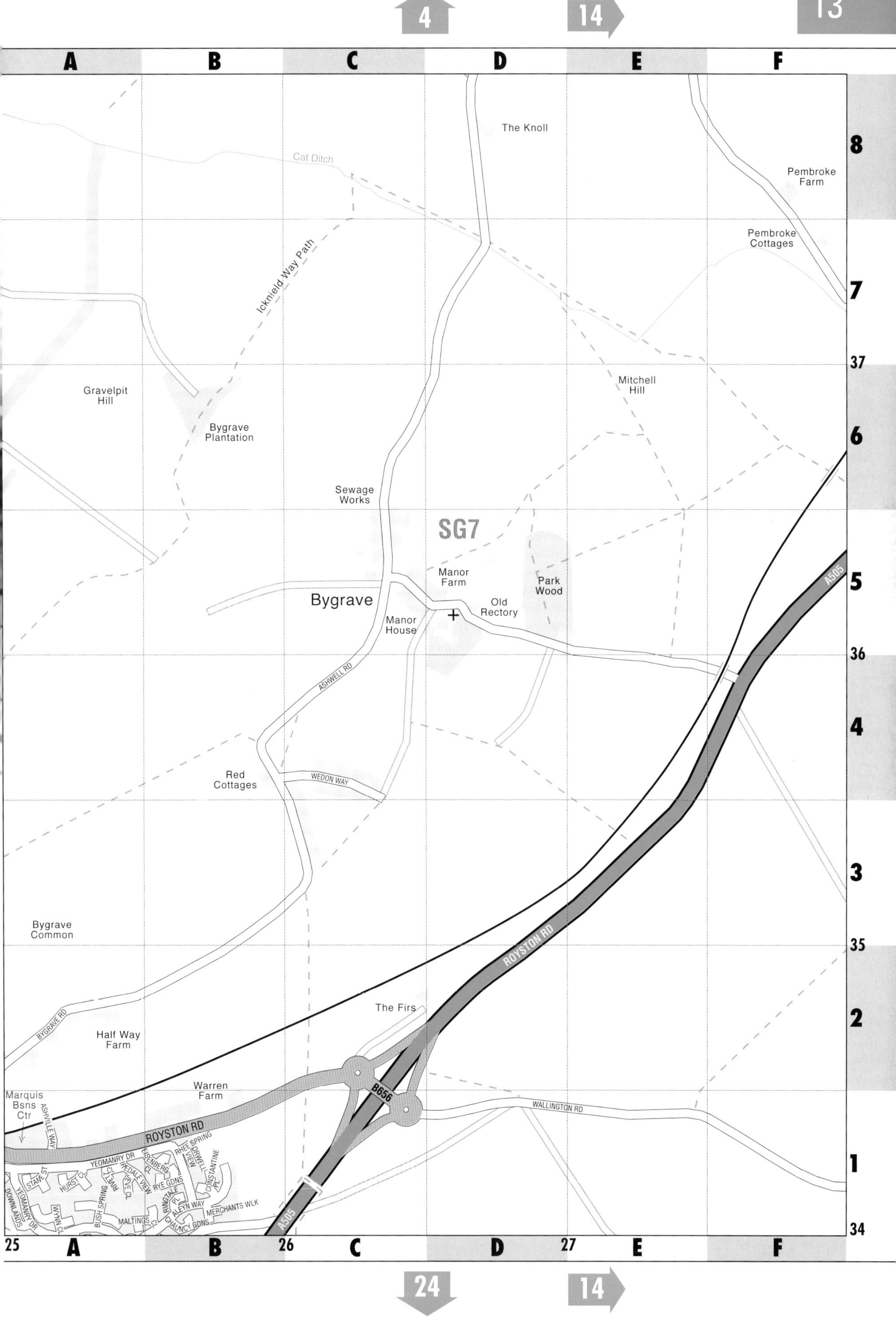
A
B
C
D
E
F
The Knoll
Cat Ditch
Pembroke Farm
Pembroke Cottages
Icknield Way Path
Gravelpit Hill
Bygrave Plantation
Mitchell Hill
Sewage Works
SG7
Manor Farm
Park Wood
Bygrave
Manor House
Old Rectory
A505
ASHWELL RD
Red Cottages
WEDON WAY
Bygrave Common
ROYSTON RD
The Firs
BYGRAVE RD
Half Way Farm
Warren Farm
Marquis Bsns Ctr
ASHVILLE WAY
B656
WALLINGTON RD
ROYSTON RD
YEOMANRY DR
EISENBERG CL
RHEE SPRING
VIEW
ORWELL VIEW
CONSTANTINE PL
STANE ST
HURST CL
RIVETT CL
IREDALE VIEW
JEVE CL
RYE GDNS
RINGTALE PL
ALEYN WAY
MERCHANTS WLK
DOWNLANDS
YEOMANRY DR
WYNN CL
BUSH SPRING
MALTINGS CL
CHAUNCY GDNS
8
7
37
6
5
36
4
3
35
2
1
34
25
26
27

13
5

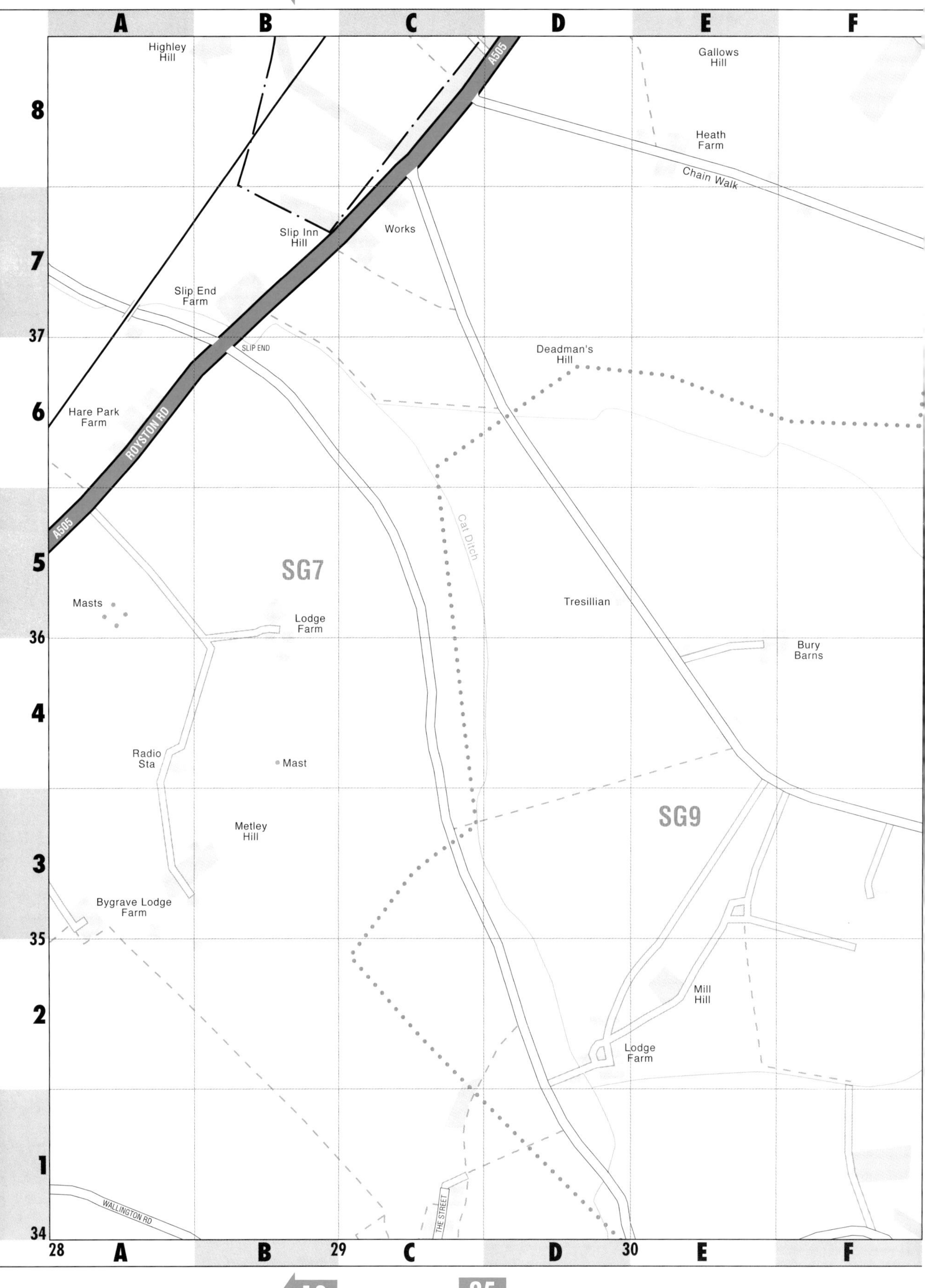
A
B
C
D
E
F
8
7
37
6
5
36
4
3
35
2
1
34
28
29
30
Highley Hill
Gallows Hill
Heath Farm
Chain Walk
A505
Slip Inn Hill
Works
Slip End Farm
SLIP END
Deadman's Hill
Hare Park Farm
ROYSTON RD
A505
Cat Ditch
SG7
Masts
Lodge Farm
Tresillian
Bury Barns
Radio Sta
Mast
Metley Hill
SG9
Bygrave Lodge Farm
Mill Hill
Lodge Farm
WALLINGTON RD
THE STREET

13
25

6
16
A B C D E F
8 7 37 6 5 36 4 3 35 2 1 34
31 32 33
Coombe Farm
COOMBE RD
Chain Walk
Hertfordshire Way
Park Farm
MILL LA
Hill Farm
Slipes Wood
Therfield
FORDHAMS TERR
THE CAUSEWAY
Therfield Fst Sch
The Fox & Duck (PH)
Horseshoe Wood Farm
TUTHILL CT
PEDLARS LA
Mast
Tuthill Farm
FOX LA
Wtr Twr
Hall
CHURCH LA
POLICE ROW
Hay Farm
Crouch Hill
Chain Walk
SG8
STUMP CROSS
North End
Recn Gd
THE GRANGE
Hay Green
HOOPS LA
HAY GN
Mount Hill
Fox Hall
The Grange
Hay Green Farm
Duck's Gn
Hagger's Farm
KELSHALL ST
Manor Farm
Pott's Hill
Kelshall
Chain Walk
Rain Hill
Chain Walk
Hertfordshire Way
Woodcotes
Kelshall La
Wheat Hill
Gannock Farm
Lords Wood
Gannock Green
SG9
Little Sark
Philpott's Wood
Drift Way
Hertfordshire Way
Icknield Way Path
Hawkins Wood
Chestnut Hill
Partridge Hall Farm
Notley La
The Mount
Park Lane
Churchend Green
PAYNE END
Sandon Bury
Sandon
DARK LA
Notley Green
Roe Wood
The Chequers (PH)
RUSHDEN RD
PO
Sandon Jun Mix & Inf Sch
Icknield Way Path
Cock's Lodge
26
16

15
7

A
B
C
D
E
F
8
7
37
6
5
36
4
3
35
2
1
34
Icknield Way Path
A10
Hatchpen
Hertfordshire Way
Washingditch Green
MEADOW WAY
HAYWOOD LA
River Rib
Mardlebury
Mast
Reed End
SG8
THE JOINT
BRICKYARD LA
JACKSON'S LA
WILLOW CL
BLACKSMITH'S LA
HOBBS HAYES
CROW LA
Reed Fst Sch
NICHOLLS YD
Reed
Wisbridge Farm
ROOKS NEST LA
Holborn Farm
CHURCH LA
HIGH ST
The Cabinet (PH)
Southview
DRIFTWAY
Queenbury
Dane End
Rooksnest Farm
CHURCH CL
Reed Hall
DANE END
Gannock Grove
Kelshall La
Icknield Way Path
Gannock Green
Chapel Green
Reed Wood
River Rib
Hilly Wood
Sewage Works
Brandish Wood
Southfield Grove
SG9
Slate Hall Farm
34
35
36

15
27

A B C D E F
8 7 37 6 5 36 4 3 35 2 1 34
STOCK BANK
Ducks Nest
B1368
SMITH'S END LA
Newsells Park Stud
Cooper Green
Newsells
CAMBRIDGE RD
East Wood
Newsells Park
THE PENNS
BOGMOOR RD
Obelisk
BARKWAY HILL
Barkway Hill
THE JOINT
Mast
SG8
Mast
MILL COTTS
Sallow Wood
CAMBRIDGE RD
Walk Wood
ROYSTON RD
Periwinkle Hill
WINDMILL CL
PERIWINKLE CL
Cokenach
Rokey Wood
Bush Wood
WHITEHOUSE CT
Earl's Wood Cottage
CHURCH LA
Manor Farm
Barkway
Barkway CE Fst Sch
River Quin
BURRS LA
HIGH ST
Earl's Wood
Ashgrove
Rushing Wells
TOWNSEND CL
ASH MILL
Hertfordshire Way
Strawberry Grove
GAS LA
Sewage Works
Howlet's Farm
PH
NUTHAMPSTEAD RD
CH
LONDON RD
Barkway Equestrian Ctr
B1368
SG9
SG9
37 A B 38 C D 39 E F

17
9

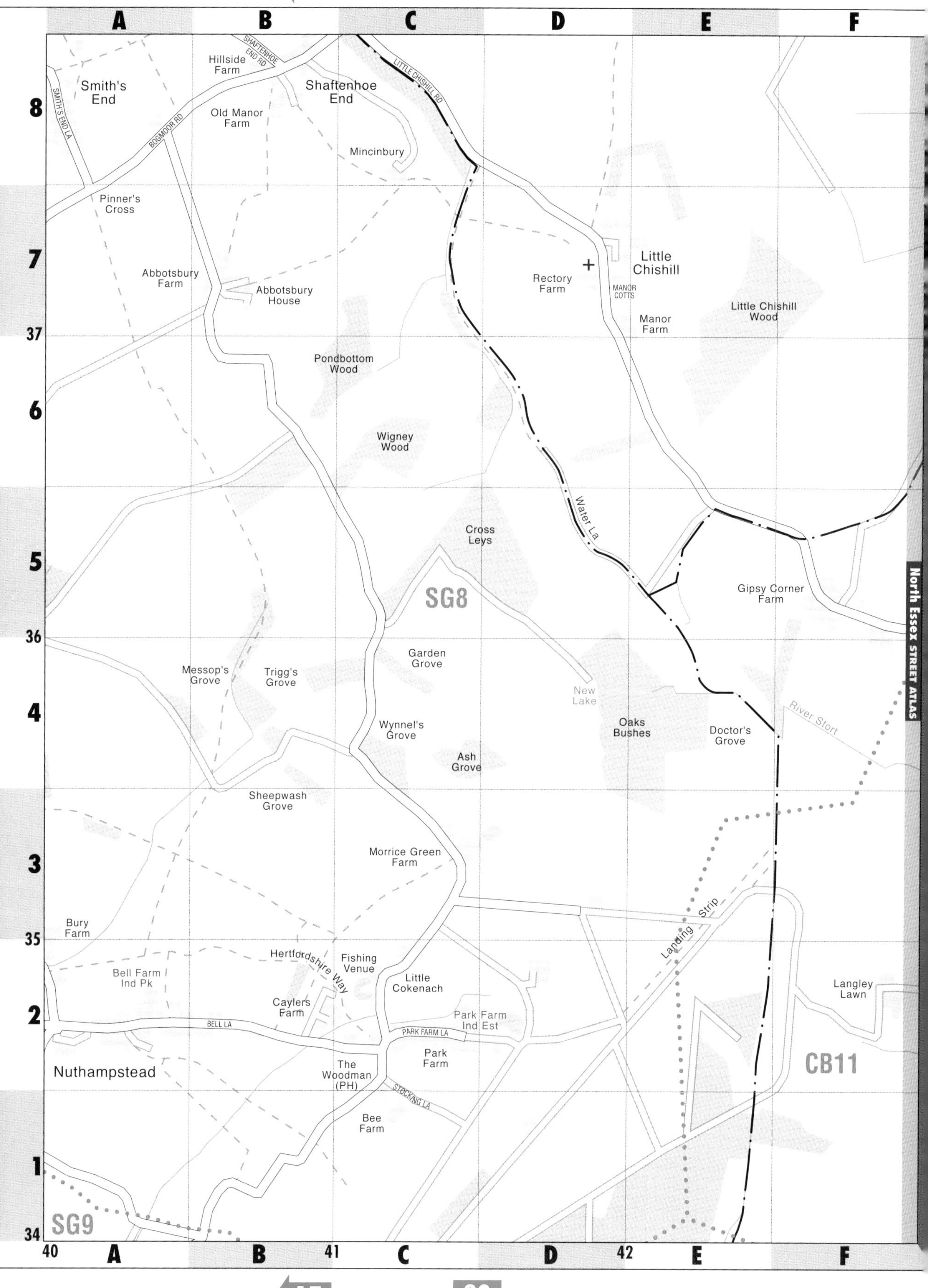
A
B
C
D
E
F
8
7
37
6
5
36
4
3
35
2
1
34
40
41
42
Smith's End
SMITH'S END LA
Hillside Farm
SHAFTENHOE END RD
Shaftenhoe End
LITTLE CHISHILL RD
BOGMOOR RD
Old Manor Farm
Mincinbury
Pinner's Cross
Little Chishill
Rectory Farm
MANOR COTTS
Manor Farm
Little Chishill Wood
Abbotsbury Farm
Abbotsbury House
Pondbottom Wood
Wigney Wood
Water La
Cross Leys
SG8
Gipsy Corner Farm
North Essex STREET ATLAS
Garden Grove
Messop's Grove
Trigg's Grove
New Lake
Oaks Bushes
Doctor's Grove
River Stort
Wynnel's Grove
Ash Grove
Sheepwash Grove
Morrice Green Farm
Landing Strip
Bury Farm
Hertfordshire Way
Fishing Venue
Bell Farm Ind Pk
Little Cokenach
Langley Lawn
Caylers Farm
Park Farm Ind Est
BELL LA
PARK FARM LA
Nuthampstead
The Woodman (PH)
Park Farm
CB11
STOCKING LA
Bee Farm
SG9

17
29

20

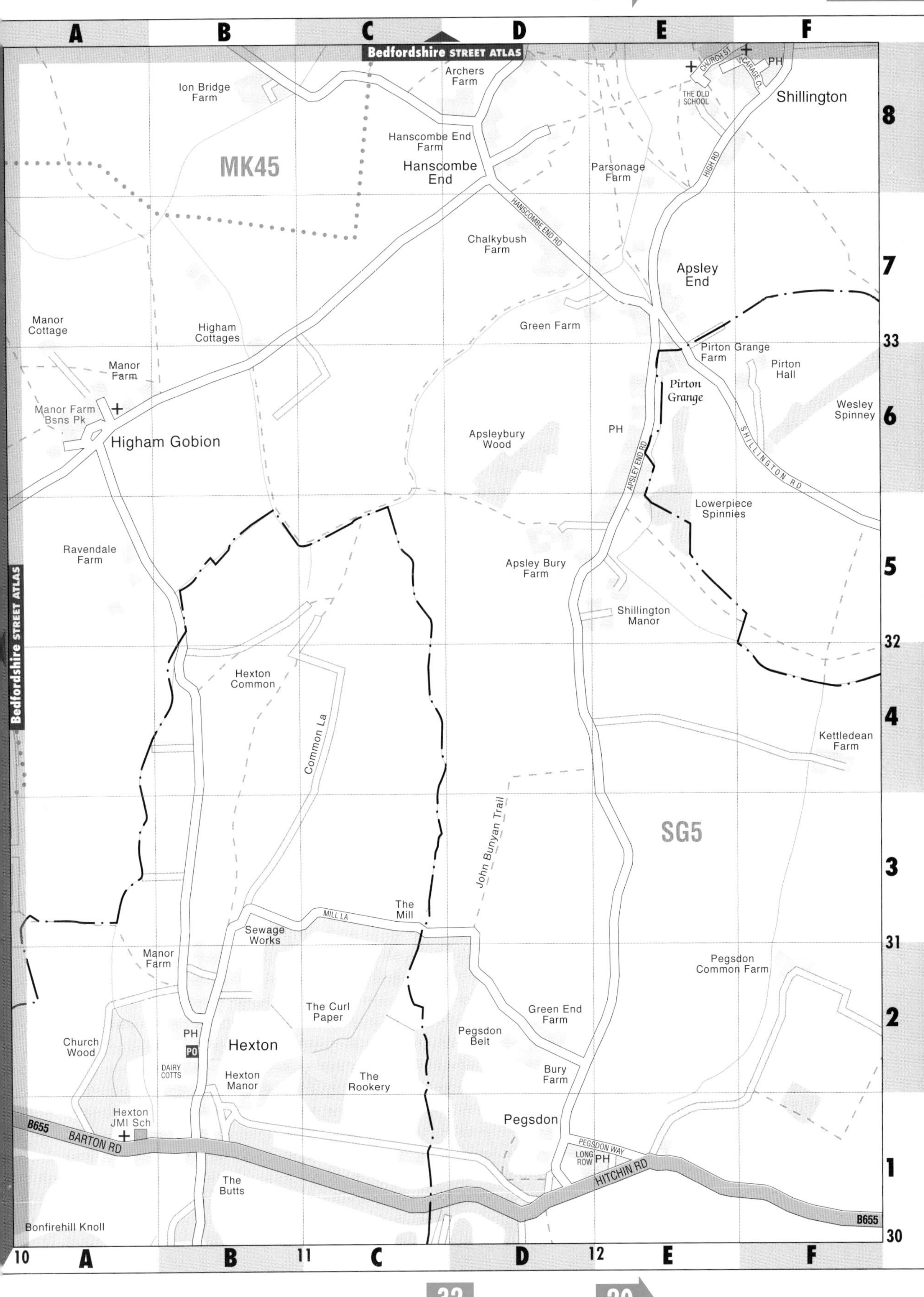

Bedfordshire STREET ATLAS
A
B
C
D
E
F
Archers Farm
Ion Bridge Farm
Shillington
CHURCH ST
VICARAGE CL
PH
THE OLD SCHOOL
8
Hanscombe End Farm
Hanscombe End
MK45
Parsonage Farm
HIGH RD
HANSCOMBE END RD
Chalkybush Farm
7
Apsley End
Manor Cottage
Higham Cottages
Green Farm
33
Pirton Grange Farm
Pirton Hall
Manor Farm
Pirton Grange
Manor Farm Bsns Pk
Wesley Spinney
6
Higham Gobion
Apsleybury Wood
PH
SHILLINGTON RD
APSLEY END RD
Lowerpiece Spinnies
Ravendale Farm
5
Apsley Bury Farm
Shillington Manor
Bedfordshire STREET ATLAS
32
Hexton Common
4
Kettledean Farm
Common La
John Bunyan Trail
SG5
3
The Mill
MILL LA
Sewage Works
31
Manor Farm
Pegsdon Common Farm
2
The Curl Paper
Green End Farm
Church Wood
PH
PO
Pegsdon Belt
Hexton
DAIRY COTTS
Hexton Manor
The Rookery
Bury Farm
Hexton JMI Sch
Pegsdon
B655
BARTON RD
PEGSDON WAY
LONG ROW
PH
HITCHIN RD
1
The Butts
B655
Bonfirehill Knoll
30
10
A
B
11
C
D
12
E
F

32

20

19

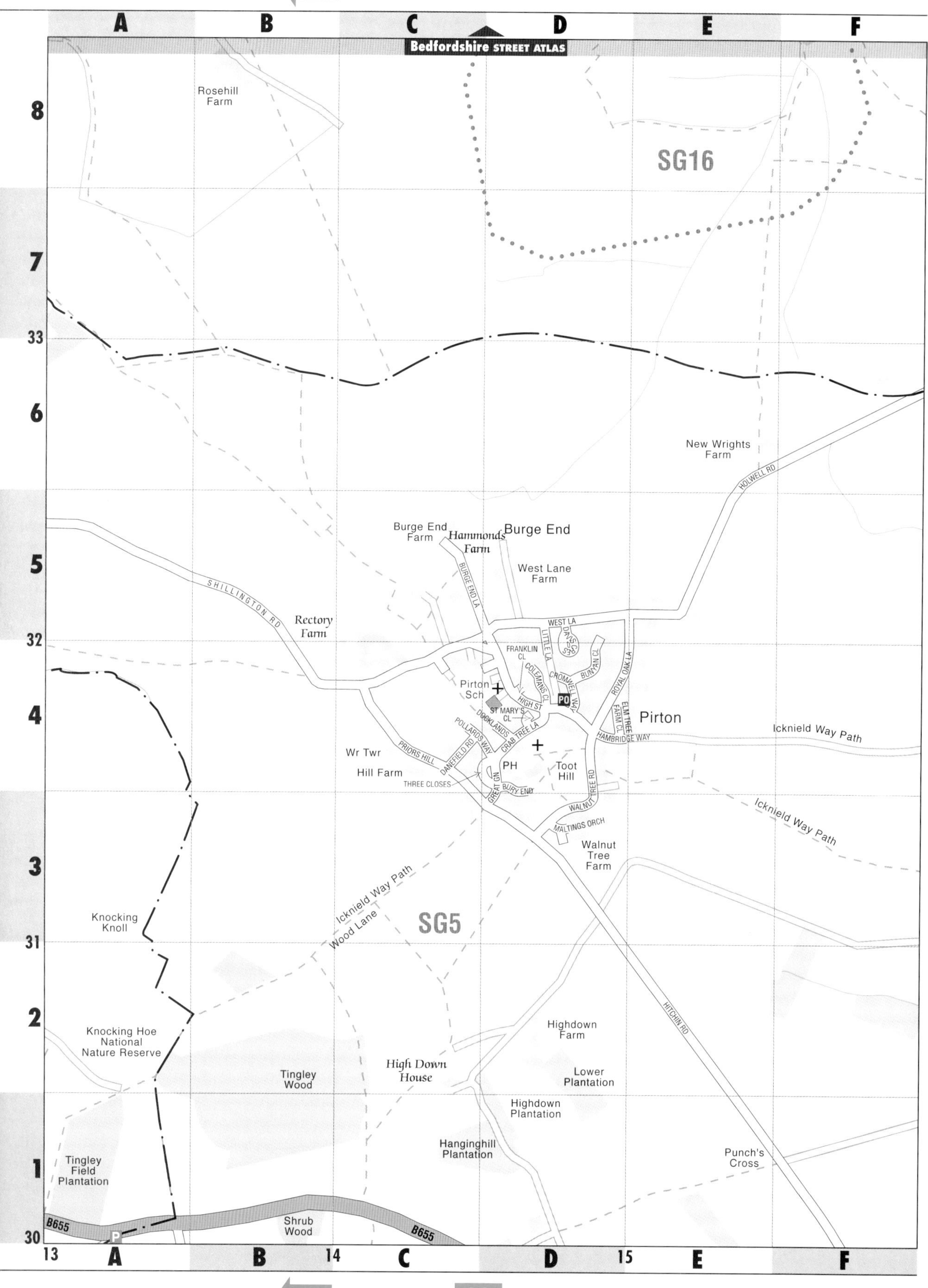
A
B
C
D
E
F
Bedfordshire STREET ATLAS
8
7
33
6
5
32
4
3
31
2
1
30
13
14
15
Rosehill Farm
SG16
New Wrights Farm
HOLWELL RD
Burge End Farm
Hammonds Farm
Burge End
West Lane Farm
BURGE END LA
SHILLINGTON RD
Rectory Farm
WEST LA
DAVIS CRES
FRANKLIN CL
LITTLE LA
BUNYAN CL
COLEMANS CL
CROMWELL WAY
ROYAL OAK LA
Pirton Sch
HIGH ST
PO
ST MARY'S CL
DOCKLANDS
CRAB TREE LA
FARM CL
ELM TREE
Pirton
HAMBRIDGE WAY
Icknield Way Path
POLLARDS WAY
PRIORS HILL
DANEFIELD RD
Wr Twr
Hill Farm
THREE CLOSES
PH
Toot Hill
GREAT GN
BURY END
WALNUT TREE RD
MALTINGS ORCH
Walnut Tree Farm
Icknield Way Path
Icknield Way Path
Wood Lane
SG5
Knocking Knoll
HITCHIN RD
Knocking Hoe National Nature Reserve
Highdown Farm
Tingley Wood
High Down House
Lower Plantation
Highdown Plantation
Hanginghill Plantation
Punch's Cross
Tingley Field Plantation
B655
P
Shrub Wood
B655

19
33

10
22

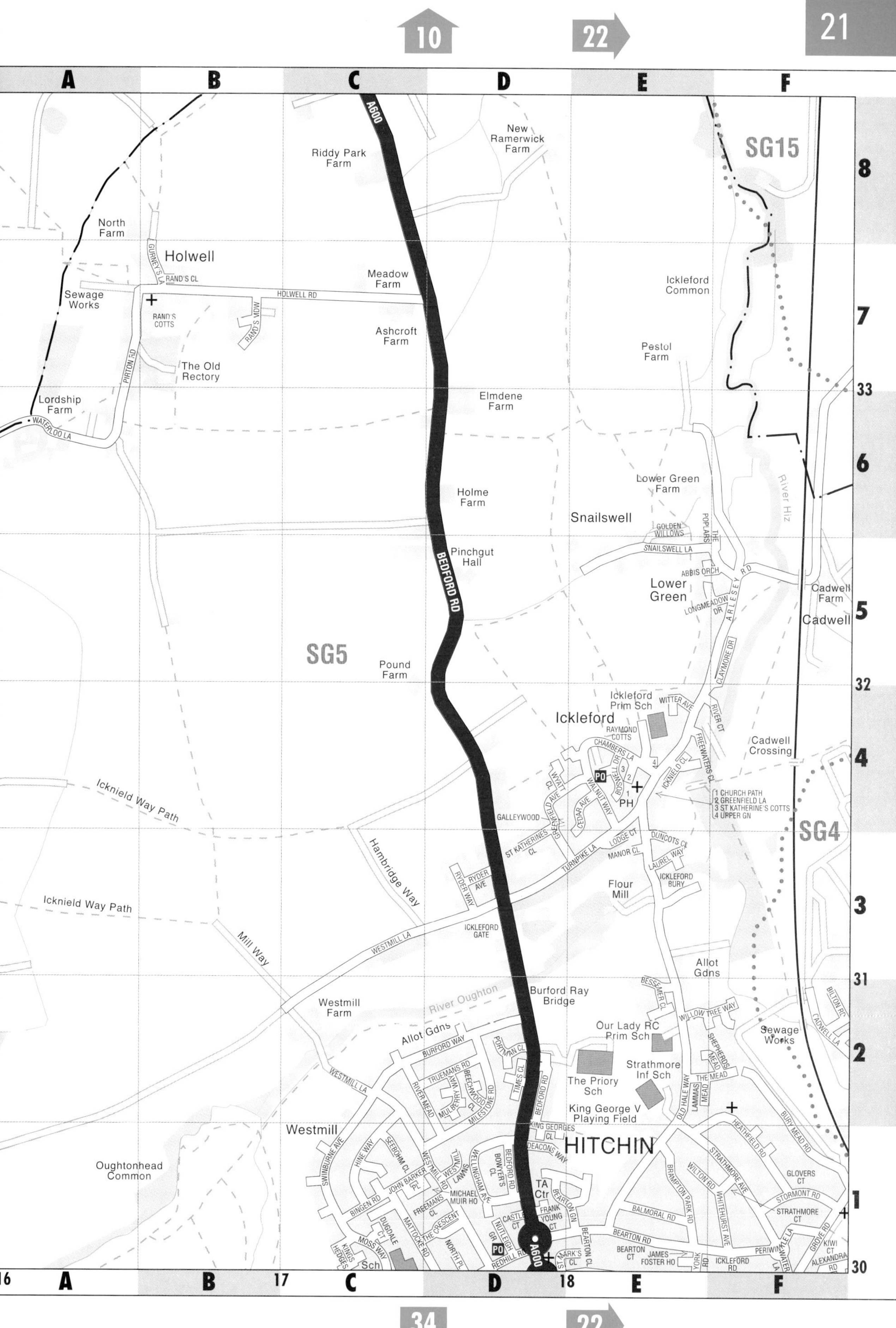
A
B
C
D
E
F
A600
New Ramerwick Farm
Riddy Park Farm
SG15
North Farm
Holwell
Meadow Farm
Sewage Works
RAND'S CL
HOLWELL RD
Ickleford Common
RAND'S COTTS
Ashcroft Farm
The Old Rectory
Pestol Farm
Lordship Farm
Elmdene Farm
WATERLOO LA
Lower Green Farm
River Hiz
Holme Farm
Snailswell
GOLDEN WILLOWS
POPLARS
SNAILSWELL LA
Pinchgut Hall
BEDFORD RD
ABBIS ORCH
Lower Green
Cadwell Farm
Cadwell
SG5
Pound Farm
Ickleford Prim Sch
WITTER AVE
Ickleford
RAYMOND COTTS
CHAMBERS LA
Cadwell Crossing
Icknield Way Path
GALLEYWOOD
PH
1 CHURCH PATH
2 GREENFIELD LA
3 ST KATHERINE'S COTTS
4 UPPER GN
SG4
Hambridge Way
ST KATHERINES CL
LODGE CT
DUNCOTS CL
MANOR CL
LAUREL WAY
TURNPIKE LA
RYDER AVE
Flour Mill
ICKLEFORD BURY
Icknield Way Path
ICKLEFORD GATE
Mill Way
WESTMILL LA
Allot Gdns
Burford Ray Bridge
Westmill Farm
River Oughton
Allot Gdns
Our Lady RC Prim Sch
Sewage Works
BURFORD WAY
Strathmore Inf Sch
The Priory Sch
King George V Playing Field
Westmill
HITCHIN
Oughtonhead Common
TA Ctr
16
17
18
30
31
32
33
8
7
6
5
4
3
2
1

34
22

21 11

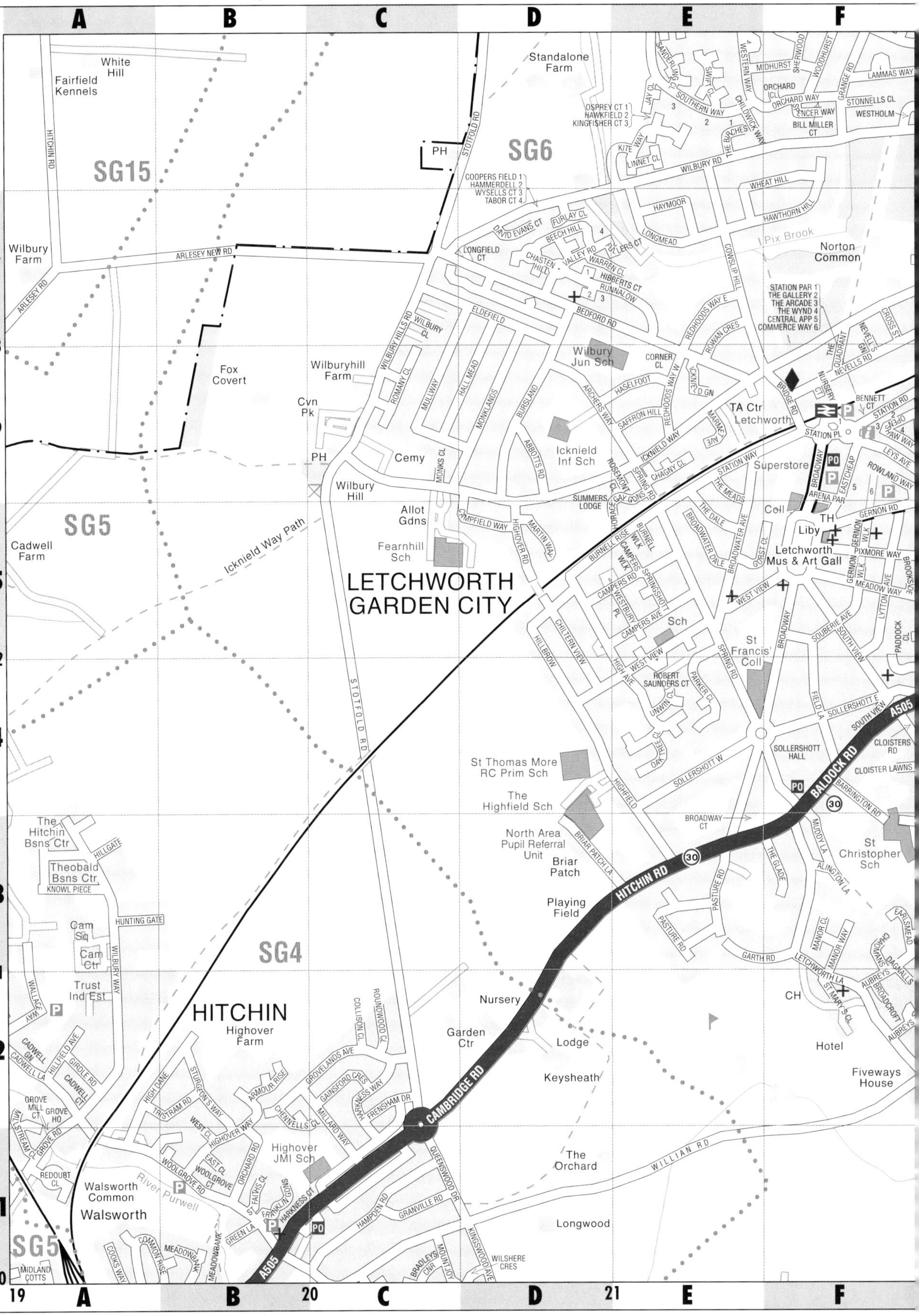

A B C D E F
8 7 33 6 5 32 4 3 31 2 1 30
SG15
SG6
SG5
SG4
White Hill
Fairfield Kennels
Standalone Farm
Wilbury Farm
Fox Covert
Wilburyhill Farm
Cvn Pk
PH
Cemy
Wilbury Hill
Allot Gdns
Fearnhill Sch
Cadwell Farm
Icknield Way Path
LETCHWORTH GARDEN CITY
Wilbury Jun Sch
Icknield Inf Sch
TA Ctr Letchworth
Superstore
Coll
Liby
TH
Letchworth Mus & Art Gall
Sch
St Francis' Coll
Norton Common
Pix Brook
St Thomas More RC Prim Sch
The Highfield Sch
North Area Pupil Referral Unit
Briar Patch
Playing Field
SOLLERSHOTT HALL
St Christopher Sch
HITCHIN RD
BALDOCK RD
A505
CAMBRIDGE RD
HITCHIN
Highover Farm
Highover JMI Sch
Nursery
Garden Ctr
Lodge
Keysheath
The Orchard
Longwood
CH
Hotel
Fiveways House
The Hitchin Bsns Ctr
Theobald Bsns Ctr
Cam Sq
Cam Ctr
Trust Ind Est
Walsworth Common
Walsworth
River Purwell
WILLIAN RD
STOTFOLD RD
ARLESEY NEW RD
HITCHIN RD
WILBURY RD
BEDFORD RD
ICKNIELD WAY
STATION WAY
BROADWAY
SOLLERSHOTT W
SOLLERSHOTT E
HIGHFIELD
SPRING RD
PASTURE RD
GARTH RD
LETCHWORTH LA
WILBURY WAY
HIGHOVER WAY
QUEENSWOOD DR
KINGSWOOD AVE
GRANVILLE RD
HAMPDEN RD
WILSHERE CRES
OSPREY CT 1
HAWKFIELD 2
KINGFISHER CT 3
COOPERS FIELD 1
HAMMERDELL 2
WYSELLS CT 3
TABOR CT 4
STATION PAR 1
THE GALLERY 2
THE ARCADE 3
THE WYND 4
CENTRAL APP 5
COMMERCE WAY 6
19 20 21

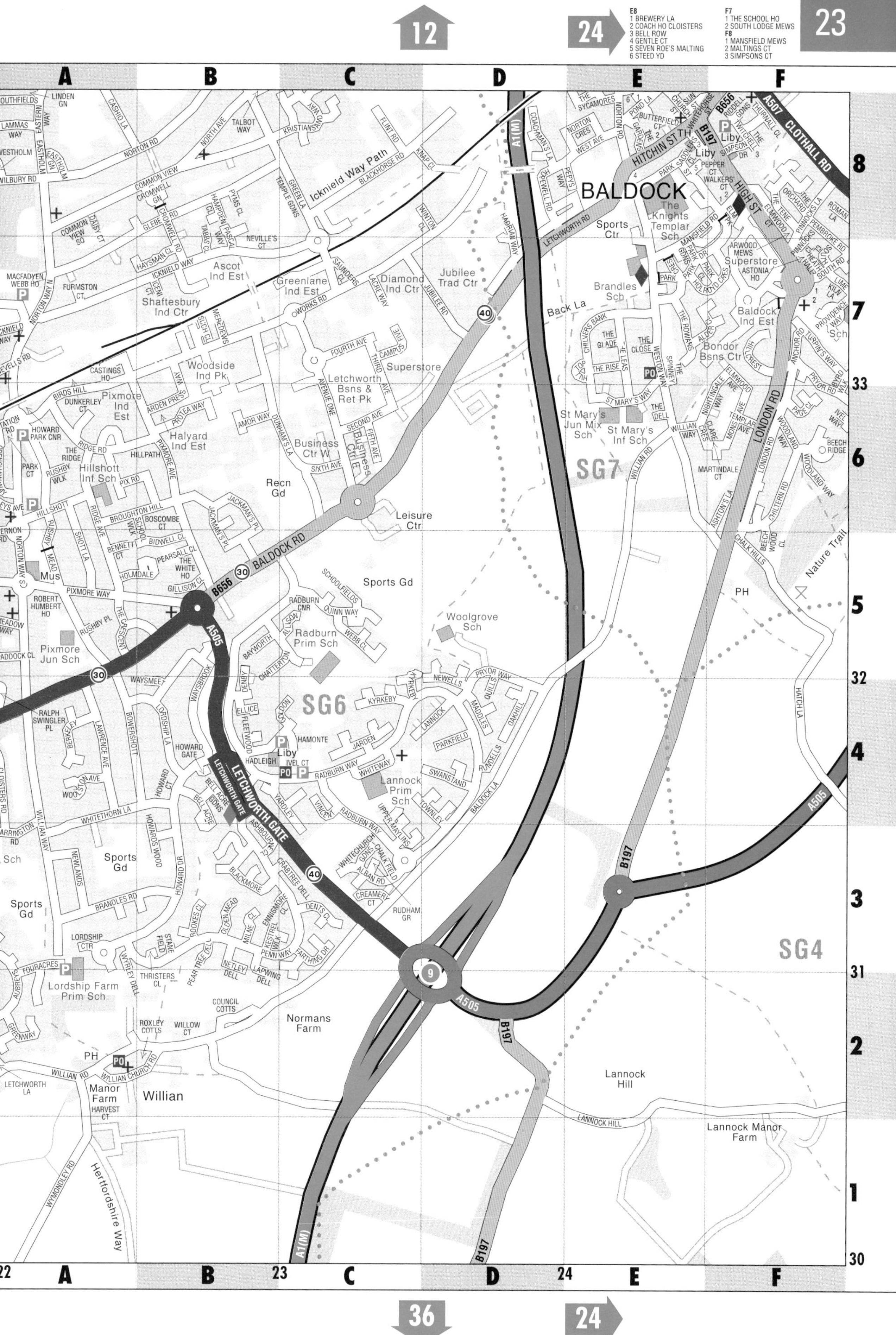
A
B
C
D
E
F
8
7
33
6
5
32
4
3
31
2
1
30
22
23
24
BALDOCK
SG7
SG6
SG4
Icknield Way Path
Nature Trail
Hertfordshire Way
The Knights Templar Sch
Sports Ctr
Brandles Sch
Back La
Baldock Ind Est
Bondor Bsns Ctr
Superstore
Liby
St Mary's Jun Mix Sch
St Mary's Inf Sch
Jubilee Trad Ctr
Diamond Ind Ctr
Greenlane Ind Est
Ascot Ind Est
Shaftesbury Ind Ctr
Woodside Ind Pk
Pixmore Ind Est
Halyard Ind Est
Letchworth Bsns & Ret Pk
Business Ctr W
Business Ctr E
Recn Gd
Leisure Ctr
Sports Gd
Hillshott Inf Sch
Mus
Pixmore Jun Sch
Radburn Prim Sch
Woolgrove Sch
Lannock Prim Sch
Lordship Farm Prim Sch
Lordship Ctr
Normans Farm
Manor Farm
Willian
Lannock Hill
Lannock Manor Farm
PH
PO
BALDOCK RD
LETCHWORTH GATE
LONDON RD
CLOTHALL RD
HITCHIN ST
HIGH ST
LETCHWORTH RD
PIXMORE WAY
RADBURN WAY
ICKNIELD WAY
NORTON RD
NORTON WAY N
NORTON WAY S
WILLIAN WAY
WILLIAN RD
LANNOCK HILL
BALDOCK LA
WYMONDLEY RD
LETCHWORTH LA
A1(M)
A505
A507
B656
B197
30
40
9

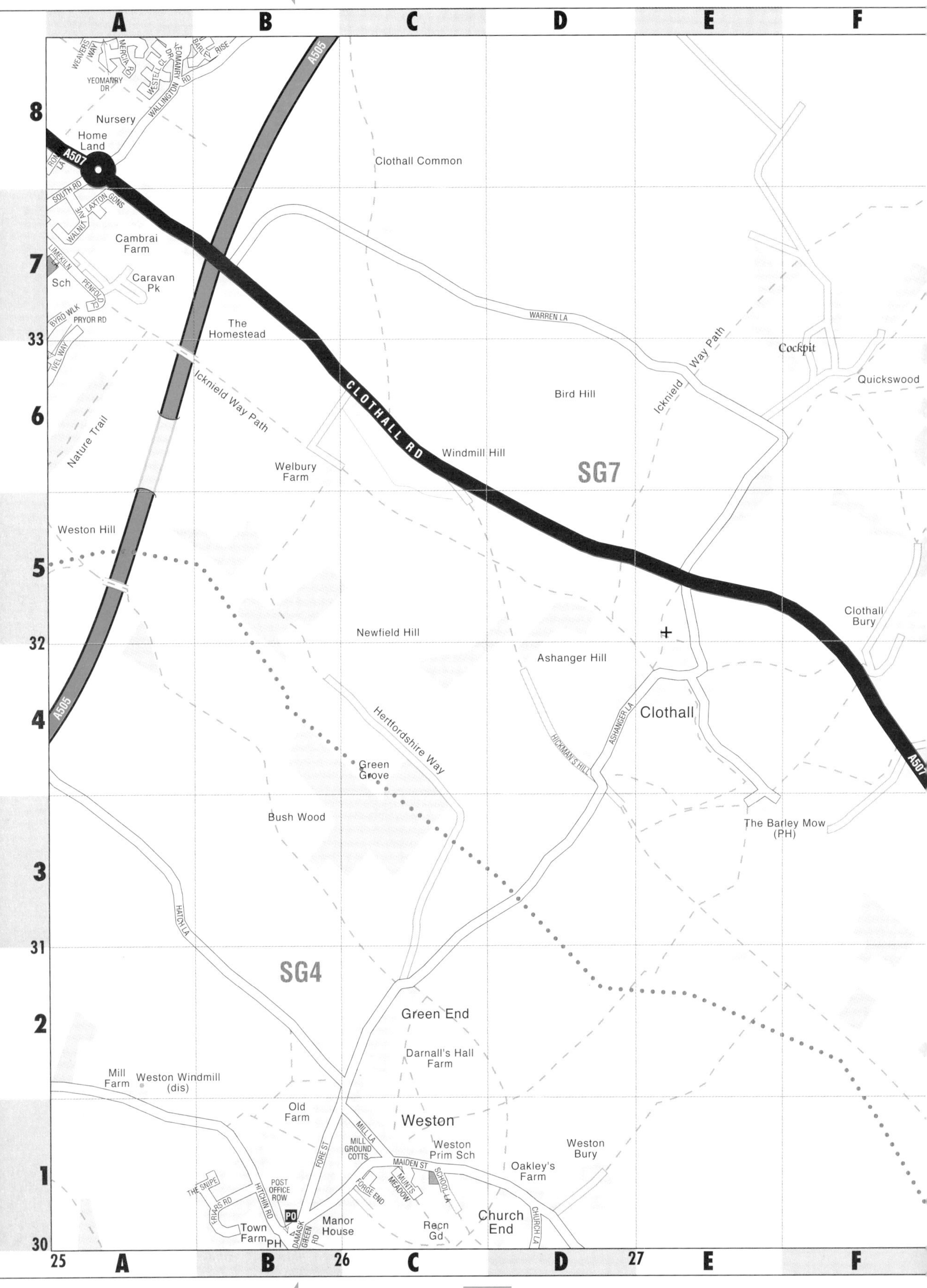
23
13
A
B
C
D
E
F
8
7
33
6
5
32
4
3
31
2
1
30
25
26
27
A505
A507
WEAVERS WAY
MERCIA RD
YEOMANRY DR
WESTELL CL
YEOMANRY DR
WALLINGTON RD
BARLEY RISE
Nursery
Home Land
SOUTH RD
LAXTON GDNS
WALNUT AVE
Cambrai Farm
LIMEKILN LA
Sch
PENFOLD CL
Caravan Pk
BYRD WLK
PRYOR RD
IVEL WAY
The Homestead
Clothall Common
WARREN LA
Icknield Way Path
CLOTHALL RD
Windmill Hill
Welbury Farm
Nature Trail
Bird Hill
SG7
Cockpit
Quickswood
Weston Hill
Newfield Hill
Ashanger Hill
Clothall Bury
Clothall
ASHANGER LA
HICKMAN'S HILL
Hertfordshire Way
Green Grove
Bush Wood
The Barley Mow (PH)
HATCH LA
SG4
Green End
Darnall's Hall Farm
Mill Farm
Weston Windmill (dis)
Old Farm
Weston
MILL LA
MILL GROUND COTTS
FORE ST
Weston Prim Sch
Weston Bury
MAIDEN ST
SCHOOL LA
MUNTS MEADOW
FORGE END
Oakley's Farm
THE SNIPE
FRIARS RD
HITCHIN RD
POST OFFICE ROW
PO
Manor House
Recn Gd
Church End
CHURCH LA
Town Farm
PH
DAMASK GREEN RD
23
37

14
26

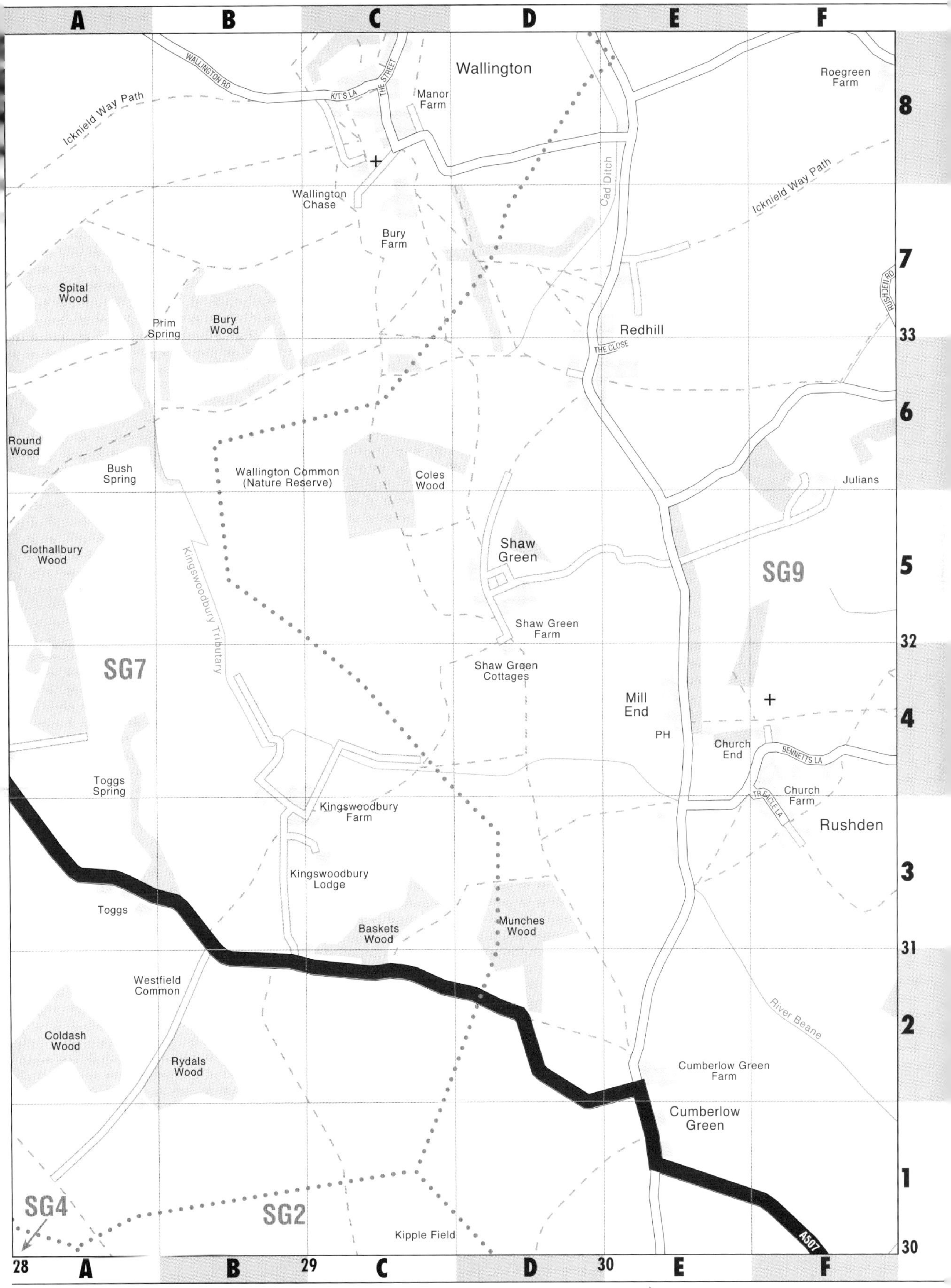

A B C D E F

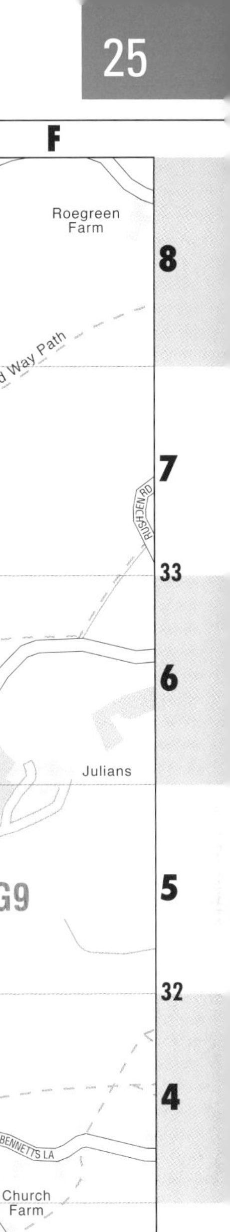

Wallington
WALLINGTON RD
KIT'S LA
THE STREET
Manor Farm
Icknield Way Path
Wallington Chase
Roegreen Farm
8
Cad Ditch
Icknield Way Path
Bury Farm
7
RUSHDEN RD
Spital Wood
Prim Spring
Bury Wood
Redhill
THE CLOSE
33
6
Round Wood
Bush Spring
Wallington Common (Nature Reserve)
Coles Wood
Julians
Clothallbury Wood
Shaw Green
SG9
5
Kingswoodbury Tributary
Shaw Green Farm
32
SG7
Shaw Green Cottages
Mill End
4
PH
Church End
BENNETTS LA
Toggs Spring
Kingswoodbury Farm
TREACLE LA
Church Farm
Rushden
Kingswoodbury Lodge
3
Toggs
Baskets Wood
Munches Wood
31
Westfield Common
River Beane
2
Coldash Wood
Rydals Wood
Cumberlow Green Farm
Cumberlow Green
1
SG4
SG2
Kipple Field
A507
30

28 A B 29 C D 30 E F

38
26

25
15

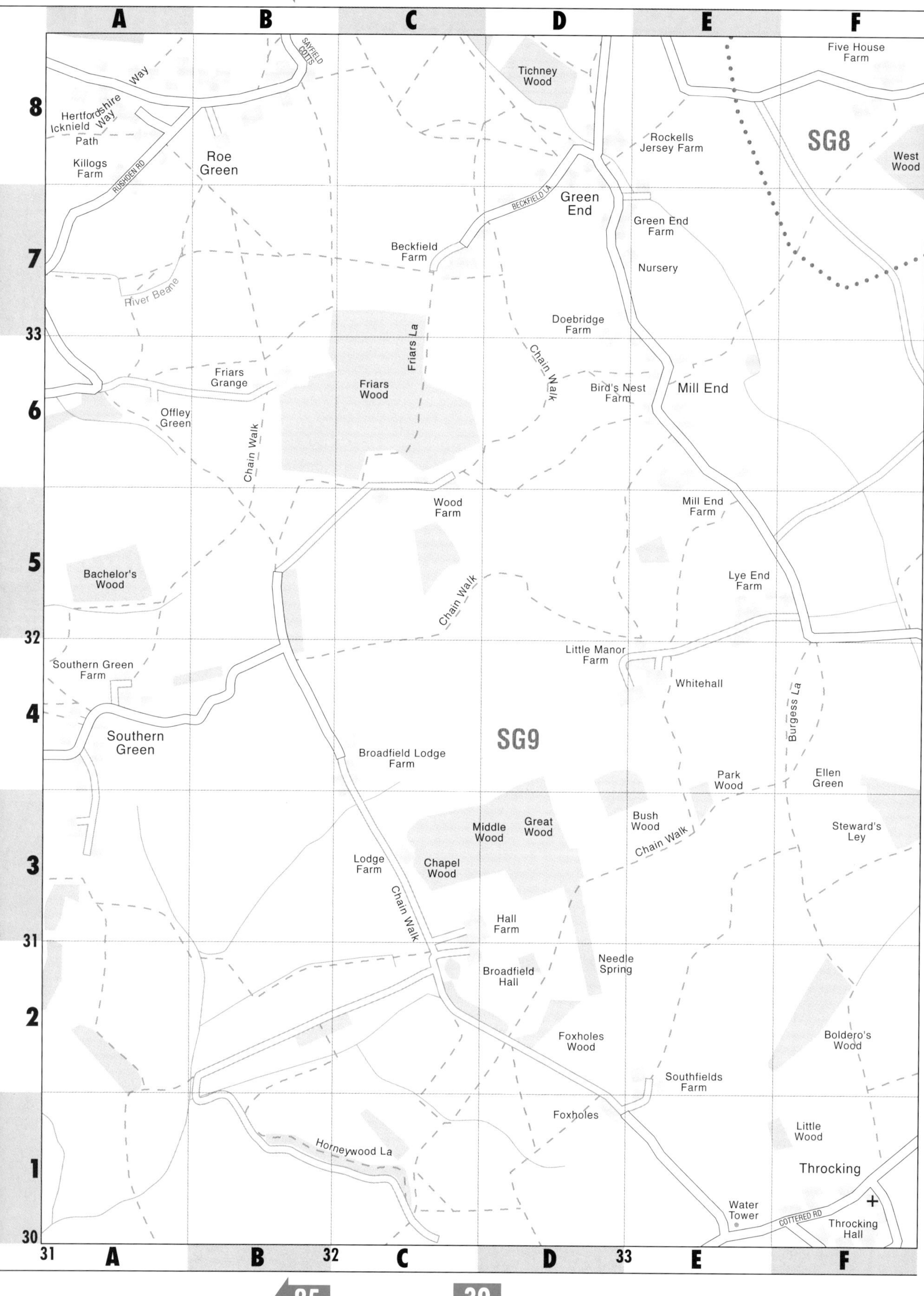
A
B
C
D
E
F
8
7
33
6
5
32
4
3
31
2
1
30
31
32
33
Hertfordshire Way
Icknield Way Path
Killogs Farm
RUSHDEN RD
SAYFIELD COTTS
Roe Green
Tichney Wood
Five House Farm
Rockells Jersey Farm
SG8
West Wood
BECKFIELD LA
Green End
Green End Farm
Beckfield Farm
Nursery
River Beane
Doebridge Farm
Friars La
Friars Grange
Friars Wood
Chain Walk
Bird's Nest Farm
Mill End
Offley Green
Chain Walk
Wood Farm
Mill End Farm
Bachelor's Wood
Chain Walk
Lye End Farm
Little Manor Farm
Southern Green Farm
Whitehall
Burgess La
Southern Green
SG9
Broadfield Lodge Farm
Park Wood
Ellen Green
Middle Wood
Great Wood
Bush Wood
Steward's Ley
Chain Walk
Lodge Farm
Chapel Wood
Chain Walk
Hall Farm
Needle Spring
Broadfield Hall
Foxholes Wood
Boldero's Wood
Southfields Farm
Foxholes
Little Wood
Horneywood La
Throcking
Water Tower
COTTERED RD
Throcking Hall

25
39

A
B
C
D
E
F
Slate Hall Farm
SG8
West Wood
Hodenhoe Manor
BRICK COTTS
A10
HILL VIEW
BACK LA
Buckland
WHITELEY LA
THE LIMES
Dades's Wood
River Rib
Buckland Bottom
Chipping Hill
ERMINE ST
Hyde Hall Farm
Capons Wood
Bush Wood
Burhill Wood
SG9
THE SQUARE
BROOKSIDE
Chipping
ROYAL OAK CL
Mill Hill
Chipping Bridge
Chipping Hall
CHIPPING HALL COTTS
PH
Four Acre Wood
Dalefield Spring
Brick Bridge
Blunt's Wood
BROWN'S CNR
PARKSIDE
River Rib
Parkhill Plantation
Middle Farm
Lower Farm
Corney Bury
THROCKING LA
Thistley Vale Brook
Freman Coll
VICARAGE RD
VICARAGE RD
Cemy
THE CAUSEWAY
8
7
33
6
5
32
4
3
31
2
1
30
34
35
36

27
17

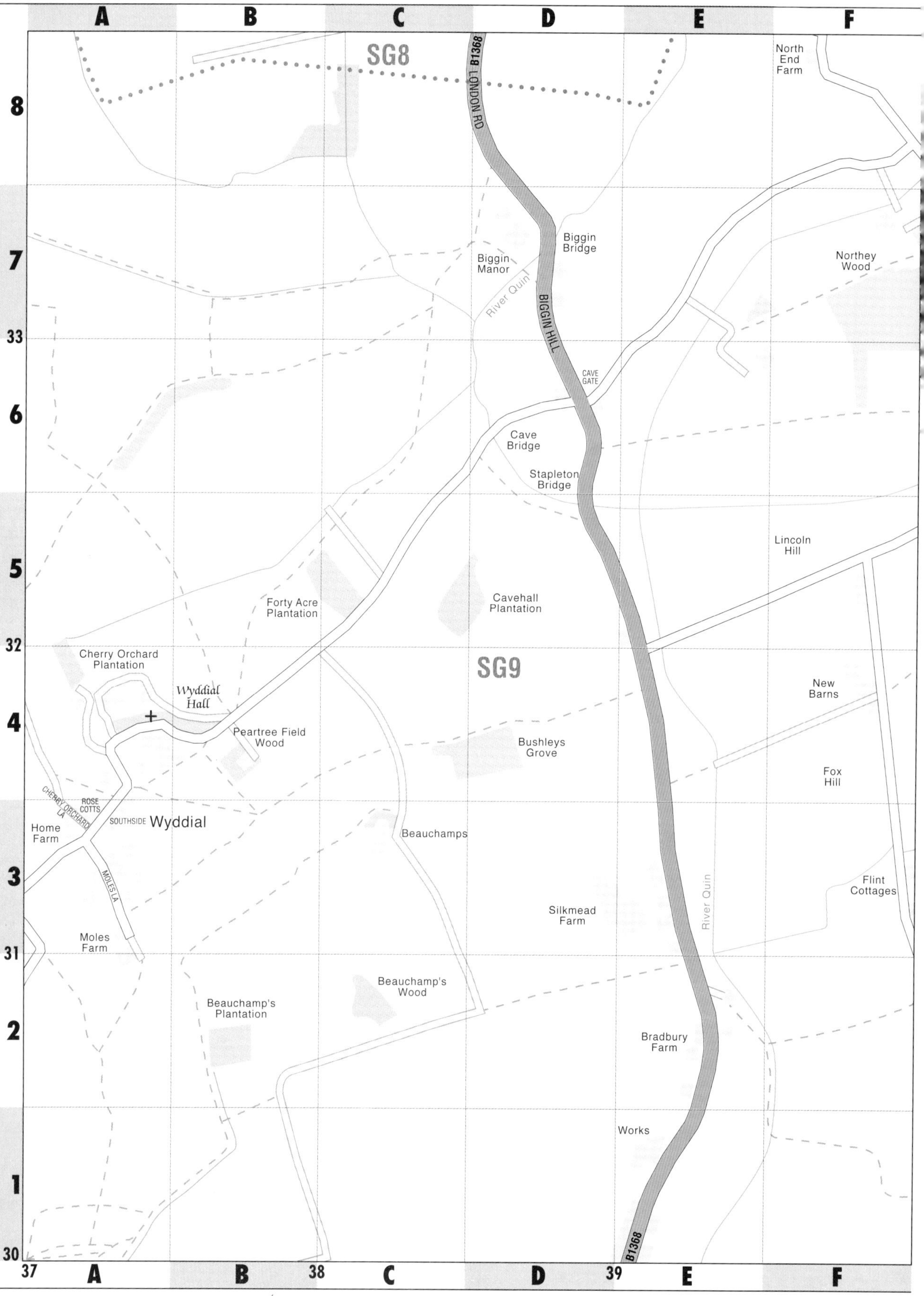

A B C D E F

8
7
33
6
5
32
4
3
31
2
1
30

SG8
B1368
LONDON RD
North End Farm
Biggin Bridge
Biggin Manor
River Quin
BIGGIN HILL
Northey Wood
CAVE GATE
Cave Bridge
Stapleton Bridge
Lincoln Hill
Forty Acre Plantation
Cavehall Plantation
Cherry Orchard Plantation
SG9
Wyddial Hall
Peartree Field Wood
New Barns
Bushleys Grove
Fox Hill
CHERRY ORCHARD LA
ROSE COTTS
SOUTHSIDE
Wyddial
Home Farm
Beauchamps
MOLES LA
Flint Cottages
Silkmead Farm
River Quin
Moles Farm
Beauchamp's Wood
Beauchamp's Plantation
Bradbury Farm
Works
B1368

37 A B 38 C D 39 E F

27
41

18
30

SG8
Scales Park
CB11
Bandons
Pain's End
Two Acres Farm
Northey Wood
Anstey Castle
DIMSDALE COTTS
Cheapside
CASTLE COTTS
The Blind Fiddler (PH)
MOATSIDE
BURY FIELD
White Hill
Lower Green
The Hale
ST GEORGES END
Anstey
Anstey Fst Sch
ELM COTTS
Meesden
Snow End
ROGER S LA
LINCOLN HILL
Daw's End
Coltsfoot Farm
Manor Farm
SILVER ST
Anstey Bury
River Ash
Hertfordshire Way
Puttock's End
SG9
Cole Green
Mill Mound
Brick House Farm
B1038
Borley Green Cottage
ANDERSON'S LA
Hormead Hall
Three Acre Wood
Black Ditch
HALL LA
HALL COTTS
CONDUIT LA
Dane End House
A
B
C
D
E
F
8
7
33
6
5
32
4
3
31
2
1
30
40
41
42

42
30

29

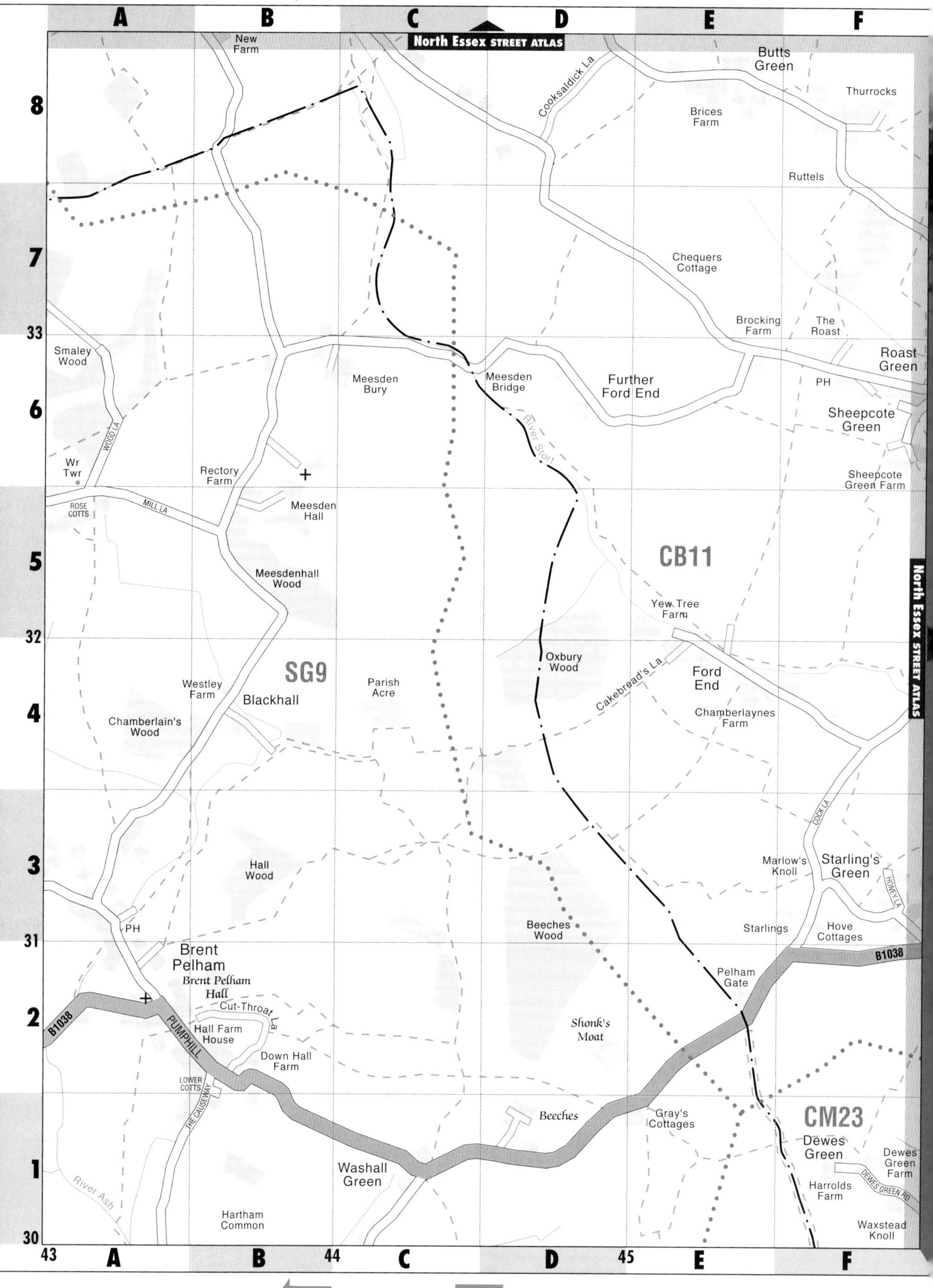
A
B
C
D
E
F
North Essex STREET ATLAS
8
7
33
6
5
32
4
3
31
2
30
1
43
44
45
New Farm
Butts Green
Cooksaldick La
Thurrocks
Brices Farm
Ruttels
Chequers Cottage
Brocking Farm
The Roast
Roast Green
Smaley Wood
Meesden Bury
Meesden Bridge
Further Ford End
PH
Sheepcote Green
River Stort
WOOD LA
Wr Twr
Rectory Farm
Sheepcote Green Farm
ROSE COTTS
MILL LA
Meesden Hall
CB11
Meesdenhall Wood
Yew Tree Farm
SG9
Oxbury Wood
Westley Farm
Parish Acre
Cakebread's La
Ford End
Blackhall
Chamberlain's Wood
Chamberlaynes Farm
COCK LA
Hall Wood
Marlow's Knoll
Starling's Green
HONEY LA
Beeches Wood
Starlings
Hove Cottages
PH
Brent Pelham
B1038
Brent Pelham Hall
Pelham Gate
Cut-Throat La
B1038
PUMPHILL
Hall Farm House
Shonk's Moat
Down Hall Farm
LOWER COTTS
THE CAUSEWAY
Beeches
Gray's Cottages
CM23
Dewes Green
Dewes Green Farm
Washall Green
DEWES GREEN RD
River Ash
Harrolds Farm
Hartham Common
Waxstead Knoll

32

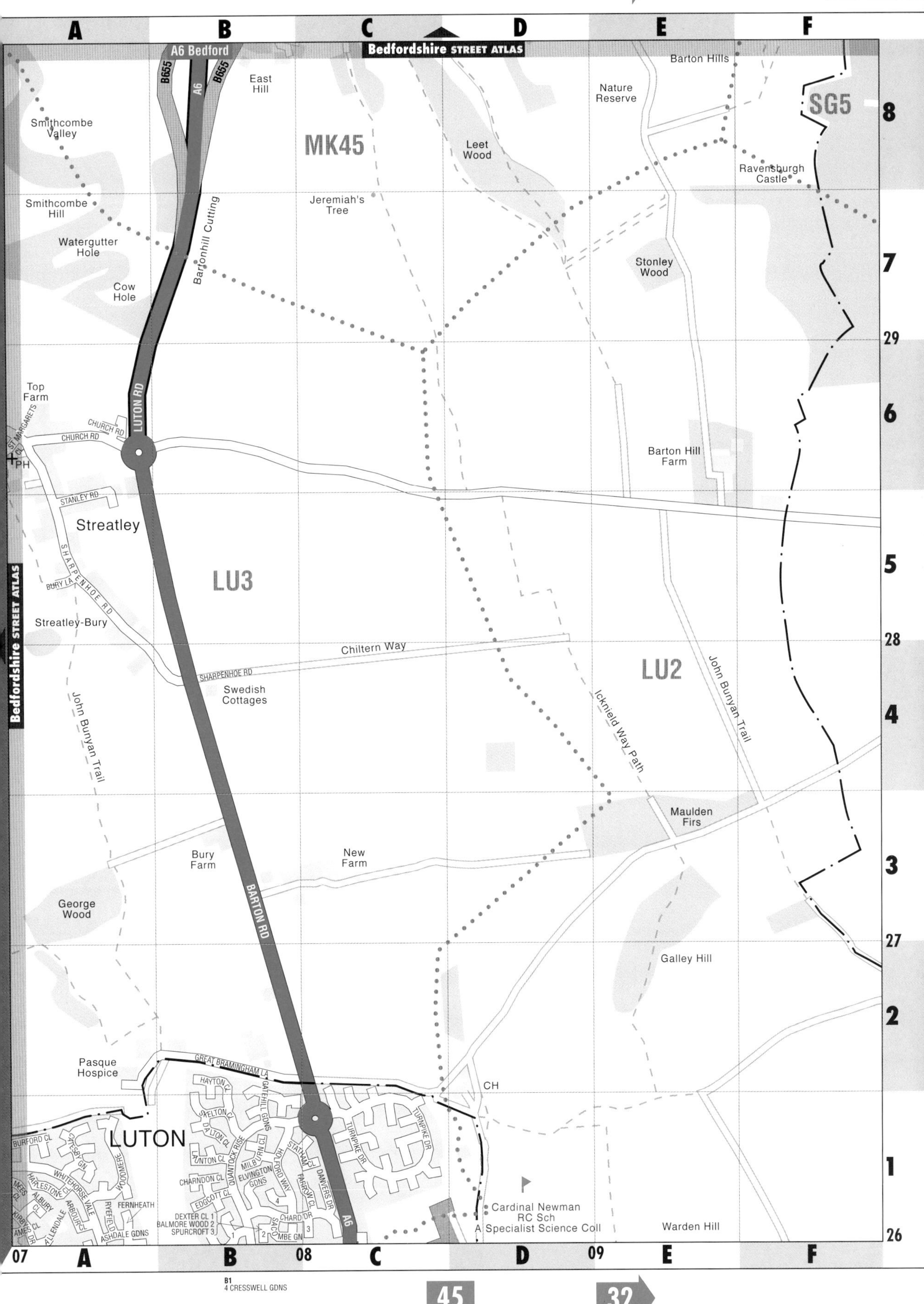

A B C D E F
Bedfordshire STREET ATLAS
A6 Bedford
B655
A6
East Hill
MK45
Smithcombe Valley
Smithcombe Hill
Watergutter Hole
Cow Hole
Bartonhill Cutting
Jeremiah's Tree
Leet Wood
Nature Reserve
Barton Hills
SG5
Ravensburgh Castle
Stonley Wood
Top Farm
LUTON RD
CHURCH RD
ST MARGARETS CL
PH
STANLEY RD
Streatley
Barton Hill Farm
LU3
SHARPENHOE RD
BURY LA
Streatley-Bury
Chiltern Way
SHARPENHOE RD
Swedish Cottages
LU2
John Bunyan Trail
Icknield Way Path
Maulden Firs
Bury Farm
New Farm
BARTON RD
George Wood
Galley Hill
Pasque Hospice
GREAT BRAMINGHAM LA
CH
LUTON
HAYTON CL
SKELTON CL
DALTON CL
GATEHILL GDNS
TURNPIKE DR
BURFORD CL
CATESBY GN
WHITEHORSE VALE
WOODMERE
AUNTON CL
QUANTOCK RISE
MILBURN CL
ELVINGTON GDNS
FORD WAY
STATHAM CL
DANVERS DR
FARROW CL
CHARNDON CL
EDGCOTT CL
FERNHEATH
RYEFIELD
ASHDALE GDNS
ARBOUR CL
ALLENDALE
ALBURY CL
HARLESTONE CL
KIRBY DR
DEXTER CL 1
BALMORE WOOD 2
SPURCROFT 3
CHARD DR
SACO
AMBE GN
Cardinal Newman RC Sch
A Specialist Science Coll
Warden Hill
8 7 29 6 5 28 4 3 27 2 1 26
07 08 09

31
19

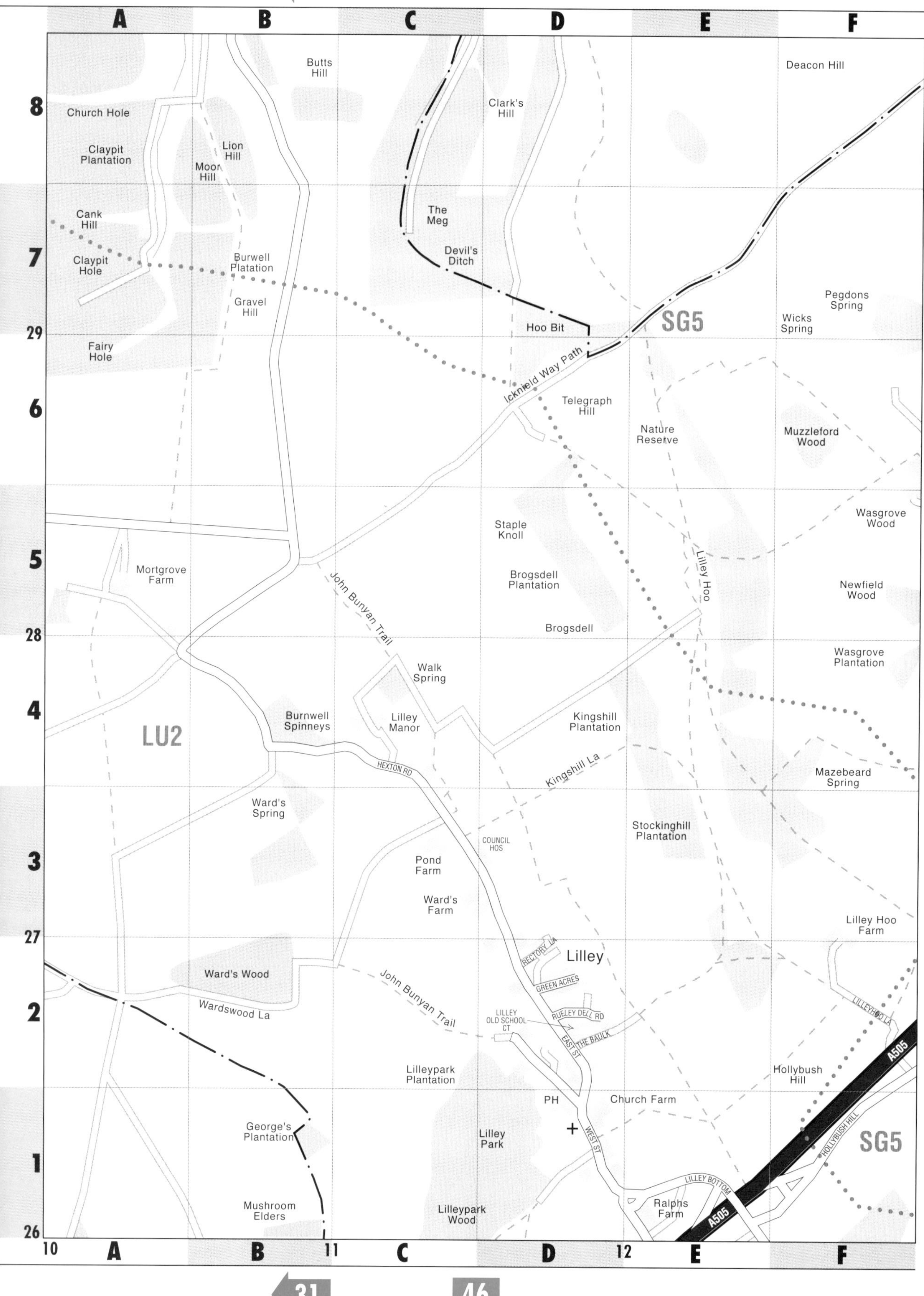
A
B
C
D
E
F
8
7
29
6
5
28
4
3
27
2
1
26
10
11
12
Butts Hill
Deacon Hill
Church Hole
Clark's Hill
Claypit Plantation
Lion Hill
Moor Hill
The Meg
Cank Hill
Devil's Ditch
Burwell Platation
Claypit Hole
Pegdons Spring
Gravel Hill
Wicks Spring
Hoo Bit
SG5
Fairy Hole
Icknield Way Path
Telegraph Hill
Nature Reserve
Muzzleford Wood
Staple Knoll
Wasgrove Wood
Mortgrove Farm
Brogsdell Plantation
Lilley Hoo
Newfield Wood
John Bunyan Trail
Brogsdell
Wasgrove Plantation
Walk Spring
Burnwell Spinneys
Lilley Manor
Kingshill Plantation
LU2
HEXTON RD
Kingshill La
Mazebeard Spring
Ward's Spring
Stockinghill Plantation
COUNCIL HOS
Pond Farm
Ward's Farm
Lilley Hoo Farm
RECTORY LA
Lilley
Ward's Wood
GREEN ACRES
John Bunyan Trail
LILLEYHOO LA
Wardswood La
RUELEY DELL RD
LILLEY OLD SCHOOL CT
THE BAULK
EAST ST
A505
Lilleypark Plantation
Hollybush Hill
PH
Church Farm
George's Plantation
Lilley Park
WEST ST
HOLLYBUSH HILL
SG5
LILLEY BOTTOM
Mushroom Elders
Lilleypark Wood
Ralphs Farm
A505

31
46

20
34

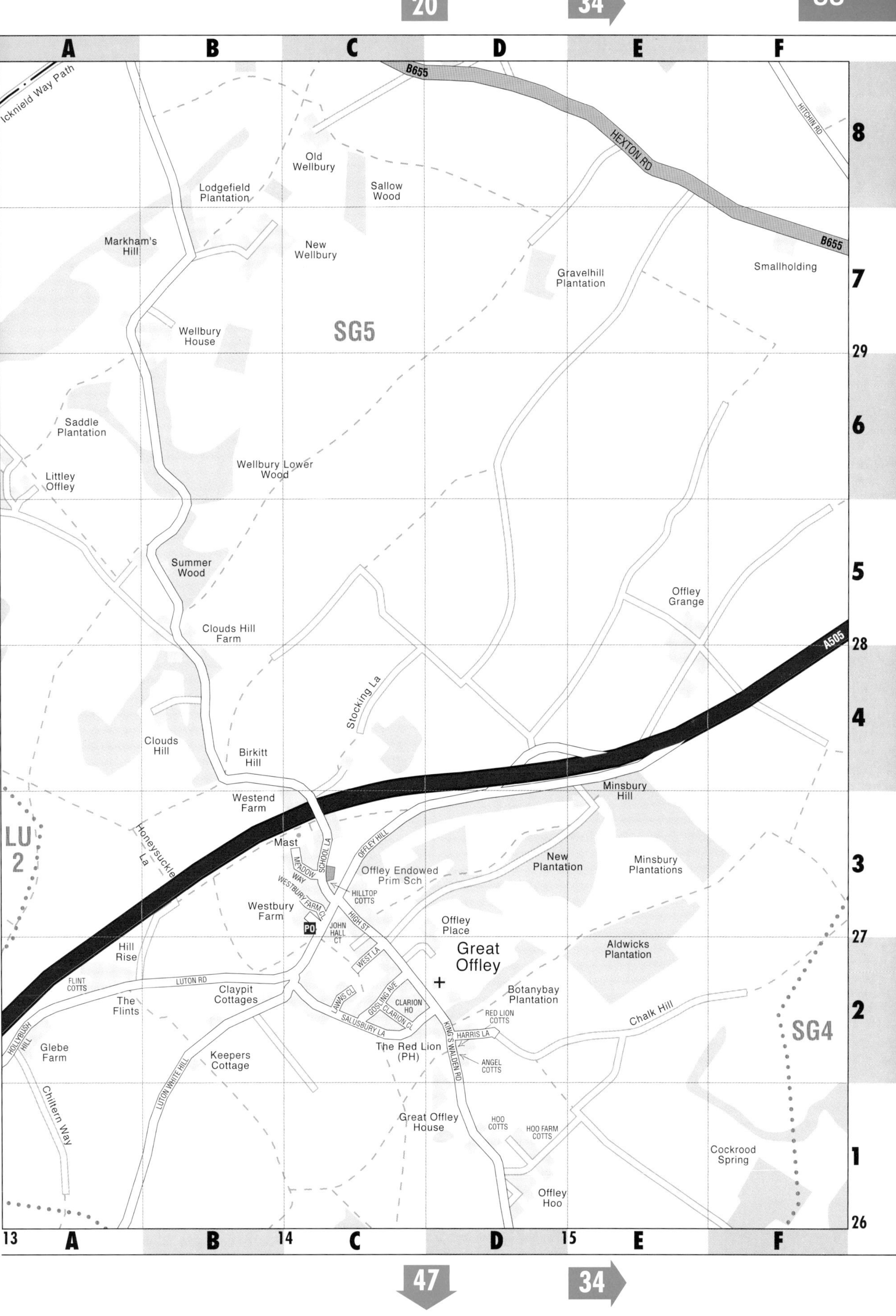
A
B
C
D
E
F
Icknield Way Path
B655
HEXTON RD
HITCHIN RD
Old Wellbury
Sallow Wood
Lodgefield Plantation
Markham's Hill
New Wellbury
Gravelhill Plantation
Smallholding
Wellbury House
SG5
Saddle Plantation
Littley Offley
Wellbury Lower Wood
Summer Wood
Offley Grange
Clouds Hill Farm
A505
Stocking La
Clouds Hill
Birkitt Hill
Westend Farm
Minsbury Hill
LU 2
Honeysuckle La
Mast
MEADOW WAY
SCHOOL LA
OFFLEY HILL
Offley Endowed Prim Sch
New Plantation
Minsbury Plantations
WESTBURY FARM CL
HILLTOP COTTS
Westbury Farm
PO
JOHN HALL CT
HIGH ST
Offley Place
Great Offley
Aldwicks Plantation
Hill Rise
WEST LA
FLINT COTTS
LUTON RD
Claypit Cottages
The Flints
LAWNS CL
GOSLING AVE
CLARION HO
CLARION CL
Botanybay Plantation
RED LION COTTS
SALUSBURY LA
Chalk Hill
SG4
HOLLYBUSH HILL
Glebe Farm
The Red Lion (PH)
KING'S WALDEN RD
HARRIS LA
ANGEL COTTS
Keepers Cottage
LUTON WHITE HILL
Chiltern Way
Great Offley House
HOO COTTS
HOO FARM COTTS
Cockrood Spring
Offley Hoo
8
7
29
6
5
28
4
3
27
2
1
26
13
14
15

47
34

33 21

D8
1 MATTOCKE RD
2 NORTH PL
3 BEAUMONT CL
4 CHESTNUT CT
5 SPELLBROOKE
6 BERKELEY CL
7 FOSMAN CL
8 CHALKDELL PATH
9 VICTORIA TERR

E7
1 MAPLES CT
2 BRAHAM CT
3 WEST ALLEY
4 ARCADE WLK
5 ARCADE
6 CHURCHYARD WLK
7 CHURCHGATE

F6
1 CANNON HO
2 WILSHERE CT
3 ST ANDREWS HO
4 ST ANDREW'S PL
5 KENDALE RD
6 WALTHAM RD
7 JEEVES YD

F7
1 WOODCOTE HO
2 GARRISON CT
3 HARRISON CL
4 CALDICOTT CT
5 ROSEMARY LODGE
6 ELDERFLOWER CT
7 RANSOM YD

F8
1 ST AUGUSTINE CL
2 WATER LA
3 ANDERSON'S HO
4 ROYAL QUARTER
5 FORGE CL
6 GARDEN ROW
7 ST ANNE'S CT
8 WHINBUSH GR
9 OSIER CT
10 WALLACE CT

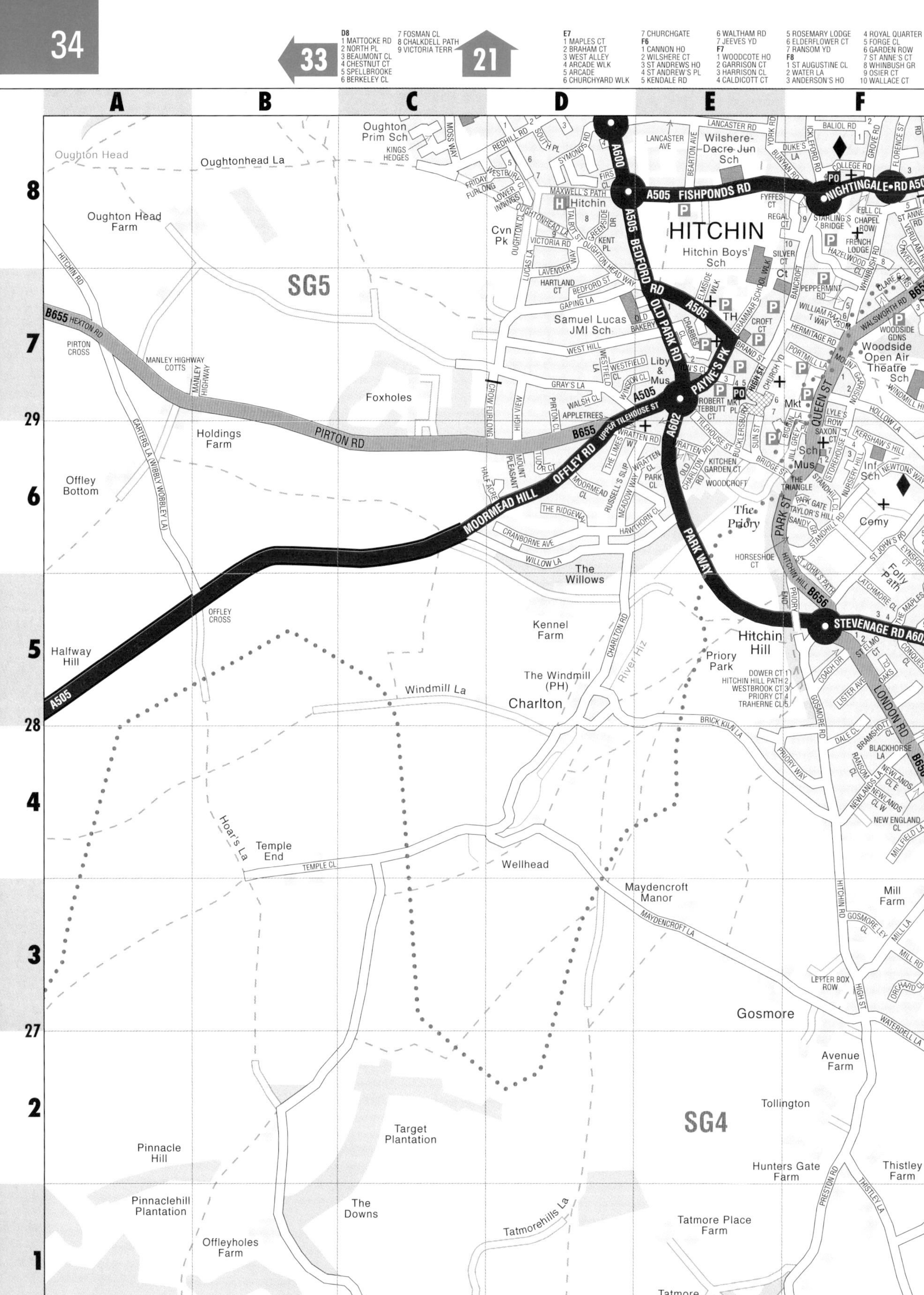

33 48

A8
1 ORIENT LODGE
2 ATLANTIC LODGE
3 PACIFIC LODGE

22
36

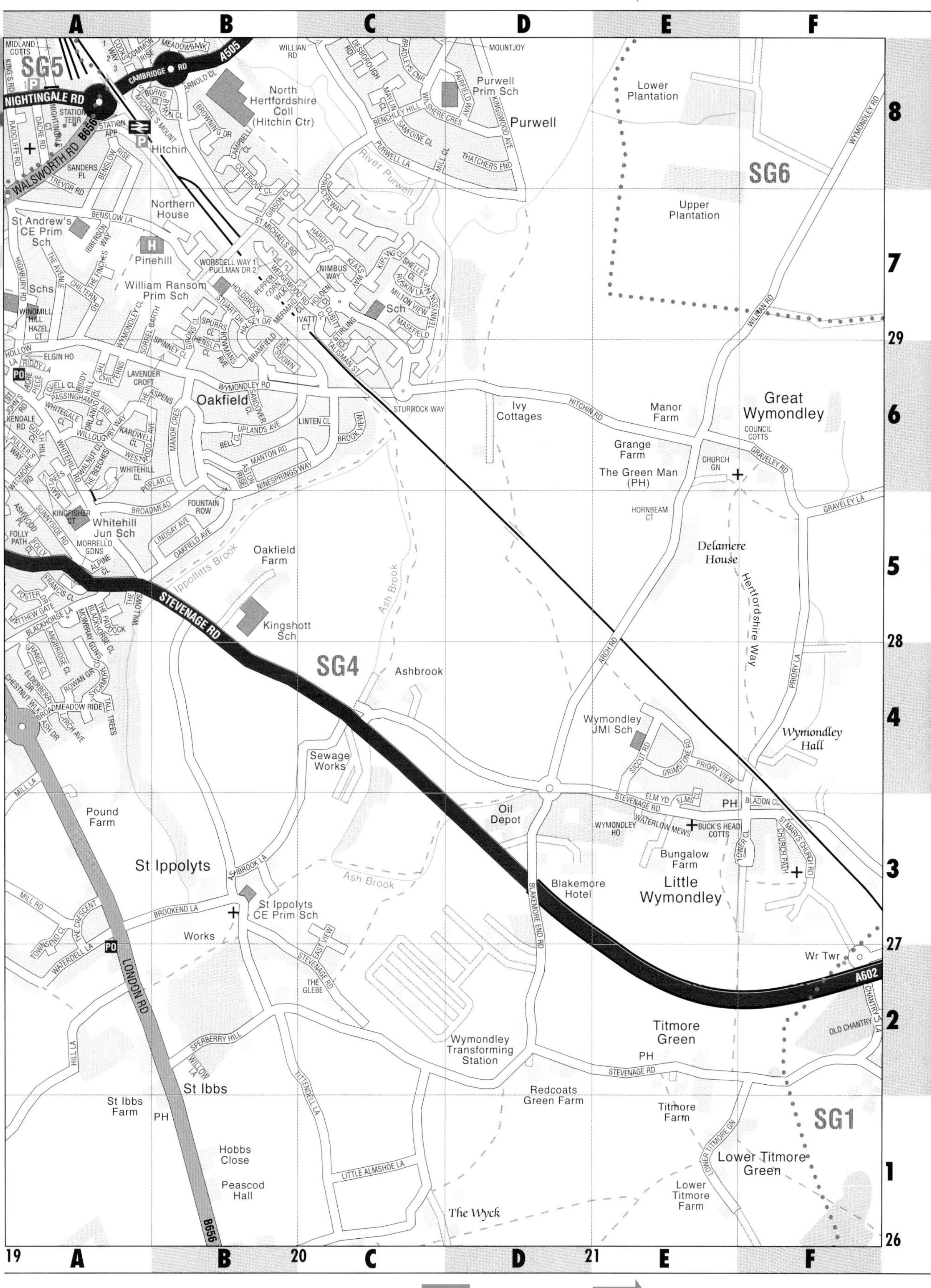

49
36

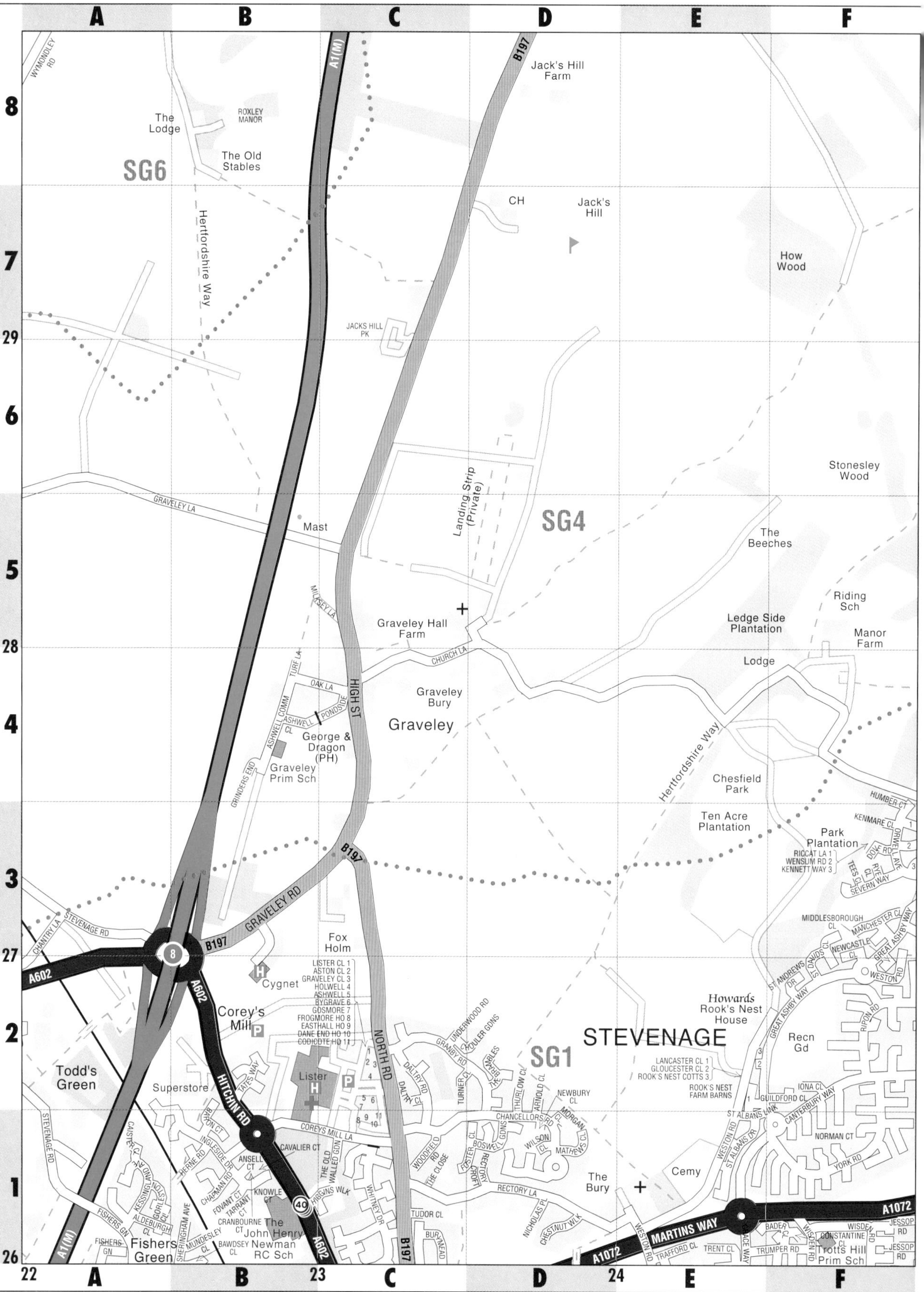

35
23

A B C D E F
8 7 29 6 5 28 4 3 27 2 1 26
WYMONDLEY RD
A1(M)
B197
Jack's Hill Farm
The Lodge
ROXLEY MANOR
The Old Stables
SG6
Hertfordshire Way
CH
Jack's Hill
How Wood
JACKS HILL PK
Stonesley Wood
GRAVELEY LA
Landing Strip (Private)
SG4
Mast
The Beeches
MILTSEY LA
Riding Sch
Graveley Hall Farm
Ledge Side Plantation
Manor Farm
CHURCH LA
Lodge
TURF LA
OAK LA
HIGH ST
Graveley Bury
ASHWELL COMM
ASHWELL CL
PONDSIDE
Graveley
George & Dragon (PH)
Hertfordshire Way
GRINDERS END
Graveley Prim Sch
Chesfield Park
HUMBER CT
Ten Acre Plantation
KENMARE CL
Park Plantation
ORWELL AVE
RICCAT LA 1
WENSUM RD 2
KENNETT WAY 3
DOVE RD
RYE CL
TEES CL
SEVERN WAY
GRAVELEY RD
CHANTRY LA
STEVENAGE RD
MIDDLESBOROUGH CL
MANCHESTER CL
B197
Fox Holm
NEWCASTLE CL
GREAT ASHBY WAY
ST DAVIDS CL
A602
8
LISTER CL 1
ASTON CL 2
GRAVELEY CL 3
HOLWELL 4
ASHWELL 5
BYGRAVE 6
GOSMORE 7
FROGMORE HO 8
EASTHALL HO 9
DANE END HO 10
CODICOTE HO 11
ST ANDREWS DR
WESTON RD
Cygnet
Howards
Rook's Nest House
Corey's Mill
UNDERWOOD RD
FOWLER GDNS
GRANBY RD
NORTH RD
RIPON RD
Recn Gd
STEVENAGE
SG1
THE BRAMBLES
TAITS WAY
DALTRY RD
DALTRY CL
Todd's Green
Lister
THURLOW CL
ARNOLD CL
LANCASTER CL 1
GLOUCESTER CL 2
ROOK'S NEST COTTS 3
Superstore
HITCHIN RD
TURNER CL
NEWBURY CL
ROOK'S NEST FARM BARNS
IONA CL
GUILDFORD CL
BARON CT
CHANCELLORS RD
MORGAN CL
ST ALBANS LINK
CANTERBURY WAY
STEVENAGE RD
COREYS MILL LA
CAISTER CL
INGLESIDE DR
CAVALIER CT
THE OLD WALLED GDN
WOODFIELD RD
BOSWELL GDNS
WILSON CL
MATHEWS CL
NORMAN CT
HERNE RD
ANSELL CT
THE CLOSE
FOSTER CL
RECTORY CROFT
ST ALBANS DR
WESTON RD
YORK RD
KESSINGLAND AVE
GORLESTON CL
CHAPMAN RD
Cemy
FOVANT CT
TARRANT CT
KNOWLE CT
HIGGINS WLK
WHITNEY DR
RECTORY LA
The Bury
ALDEBURGH CL
40
NICHOLAS PL
A1072
FISHERS GN
SHERINGHAM AVE
CRANBOURNE CT
The John Henry Newman RC Sch
TUDOR CL
CHESTNUT WLK
MARTINS WAY
BADER CL
WISDEN RD
JESSOP RD
CONSTANTINE CL
Fishers Green
MUNDESLEY CL
BAWDSEY CL
BURYMEAD
TRAFFORD CL
TRENT CL
GRACE WAY
TRUMPER RD
Trotts Hill Prim Sch
A1(M)
A602
B197
A1072
22 A B 23 C D 24 E F

35
50

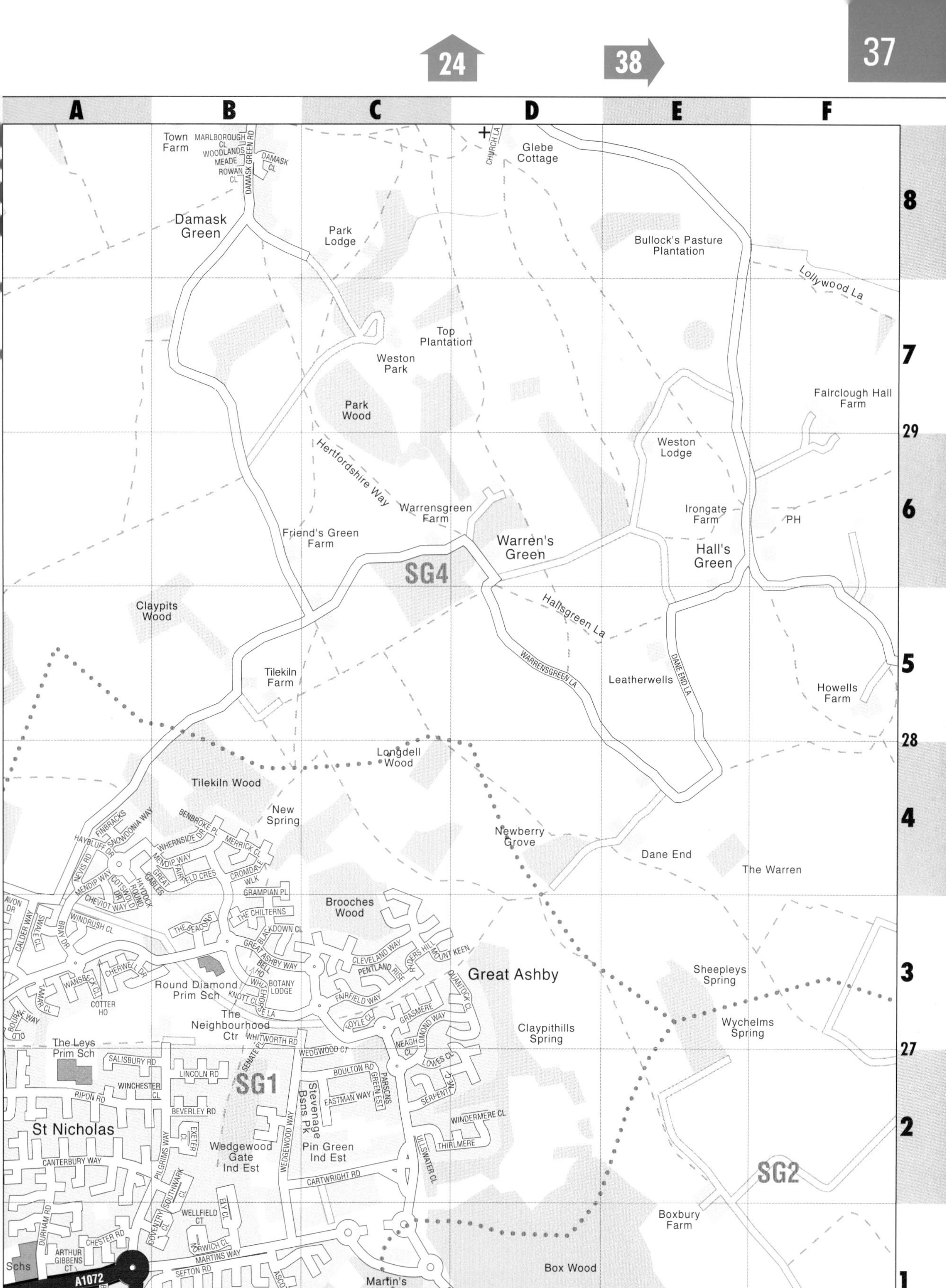
A
B
C
D
E
F
Town Farm
MARLBOROUGH CL
WOODLANDS
MEADE
ROWAN CL
DAMASK GREEN RD
DAMASK CL
CHURCH LA
Glebe Cottage
Damask Green
Park Lodge
Bullock's Pasture Plantation
Lollywood La
Top Plantation
Weston Park
Park Wood
Fairclough Hall Farm
Weston Lodge
Hertfordshire Way
Warrensgreen Farm
Irongate Farm
PH
Friend's Green Farm
Warren's Green
Hall's Green
SG4
Hallsgreen La
Claypits Wood
WARRENSGREEN LA
DANE END LA
Tilekiln Farm
Leatherwells
Howells Farm
Longdell Wood
Tilekiln Wood
New Spring
Newberry Grove
Dane End
The Warren
Brooches Wood
Great Ashby
Sheepleys Spring
Round Diamond Prim Sch
The Neighbourhood Ctr
Claypithills Spring
Wychelms Spring
The Leys Prim Sch
SG1
Stevenage Bsns Pk
St Nicholas
Wedgewood Gate Ind Est
Pin Green Ind Est
SG2
Boxbury Farm
Box Wood
Martin's Wood
Martins Wood Prim Sch
Boxwood Lodge
Schs
A1072
VERITY WAY
A1155
THE OVAL
PO
8
7
29
6
5
28
4
3
27
2
1
26
25
26
27

37 25

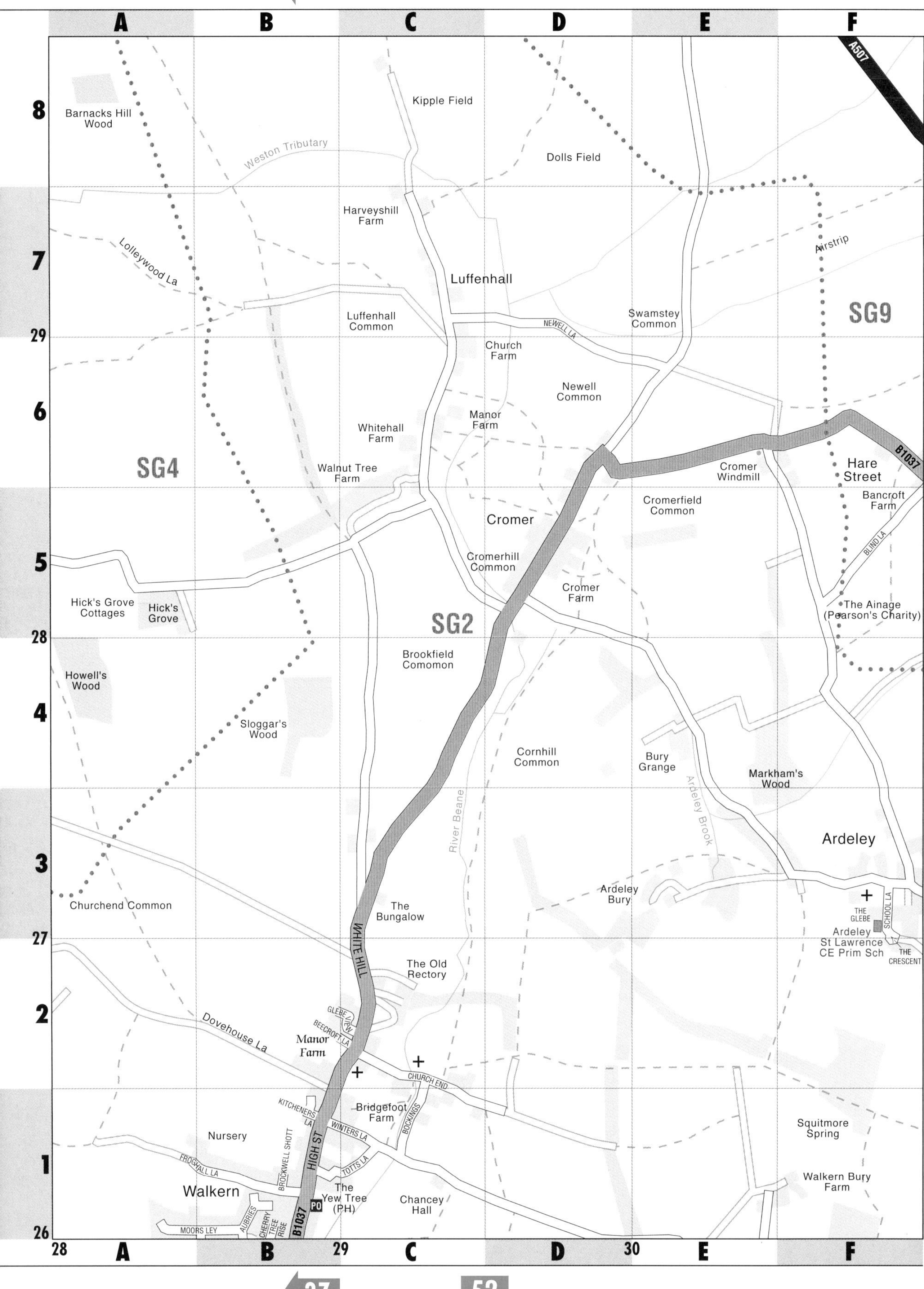

A B C D E F
8 7 29 6 5 28 4 3 27 2 1 26
28 29 30
Barnacks Hill Wood
Kipple Field
Weston Tributary
Dolls Field
A507
Harveyshill Farm
Lolleywood La
Luffenhall
Airstrip
Luffenhall Common
NEWELL LA
Swamstey Common
SG9
Church Farm
Newell Common
Manor Farm
Whitehall Farm
SG4
Walnut Tree Farm
Cromer Windmill
Hare Street
B1037
Cromerfield Common
Bancroft Farm
Cromer
BLIND LA
Cromerhill Common
Cromer Farm
Hick's Grove Cottages
Hick's Grove
The Ainage (Pearson's Charity)
SG2
Brookfield Comomon
Howell's Wood
Sloggar's Wood
Cornhill Common
Bury Grange
Markham's Wood
Ardeley Brook
River Beane
Ardeley
Ardeley Bury
Churchend Common
The Bungalow
THE GLEBE
SCHOOL LA
Ardeley St Lawrence CE Prim Sch
THE CRESCENT
WHITE HILL
The Old Rectory
Dovehouse La
GLEBE VIEW
BEECROFT LA
Manor Farm
CHURCH END
KITCHENERS LA
Bridgefoot Farm
BOCKINGS
WINTERS LA
Squitmore Spring
Nursery
BROCKWELL SHOTT
HIGH ST
FROGHALL LA
TOTTS LA
Walkern Bury Farm
Walkern
The Yew Tree (PH)
PO
Chancey Hall
B1037
MOORS LEY
AUBRIES
CHERRY TREE RISE

37 52

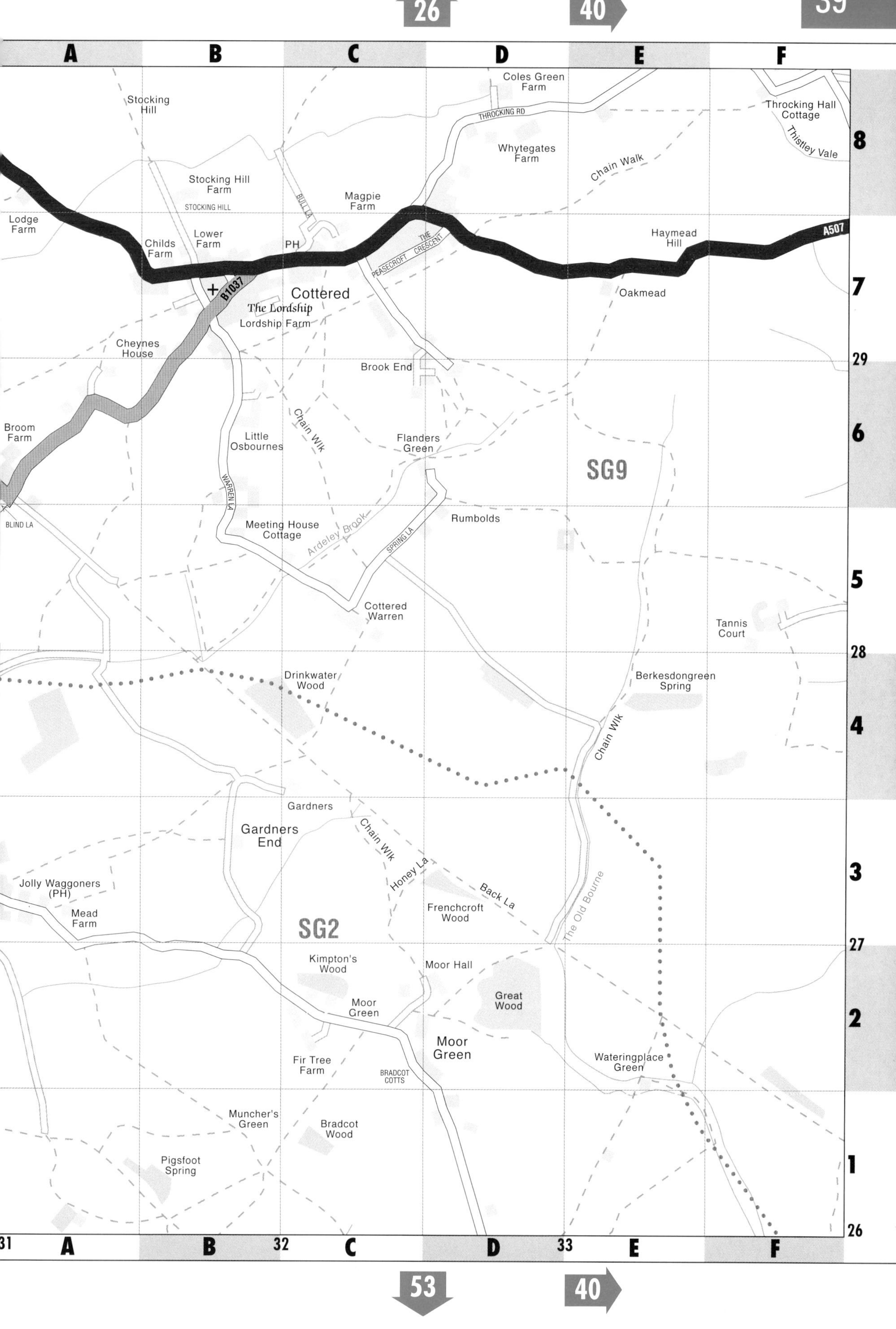
26
40
A
B
C
D
E
F
8
7
29
6
5
28
4
3
27
2
1
26
31
32
33
53
Coles Green Farm
Stocking Hill
Throcking Hall Cottage
THROCKING RD
Thistley Vale
Whytegates Farm
Stocking Hill Farm
STOCKING HILL
BULL LA
Magpie Farm
Chain Walk
Lodge Farm
Childs Farm
Lower Farm
PH
THE CRESCENT
PEASECROFT
Haymead Hill
A507
B1037
Cottered
The Lordship
Lordship Farm
Oakmead
Cheynes House
Brook End
Broom Farm
Little Osbournes
Chain Wlk
Flanders Green
SG9
WARREN LA
BLIND LA
Meeting House Cottage
Ardeley Brook
SPRING LA
Rumbolds
Cottered Warren
Tannis Court
Drinkwater Wood
Berkesdongreen Spring
Chain Wlk
Gardners
Gardners End
Chain Wlk
Honey La
Back La
Jolly Waggoners (PH)
Mead Farm
Frenchcroft Wood
The Old Bourne
SG2
Kimpton's Wood
Moor Hall
Great Wood
Moor Green
Moor Green
Fir Tree Farm
BRADCOT COTTS
Wateringplace Green
Muncher's Green
Bradcot Wood
Pigsfoot Spring

39
27

A B C D E F

8
7
29
6
5
28
4
3
27
2
1
26

Park Farm Ind Est
Freman Coll
A10
VICARAGE RD
BRIDGE END
HONEY LA
AYLOTTS CL
BROAD BAULK
FREMAN DR
CHEQUERS CL
PORTERS CL
WYDDIAL RD
1 JACKSONS CT
2 BAKEHOUSE CT
3 ERMINE CT
4 ASHFORDS
THE CAUSEWAY
Edwinstree CE Mid Sch
BOWLING GREEN LA
NORFOLK RD
HIGH ST
Layston CE Fst Sch
Buntingford Bsns Pk
GREENWAYS
Liby
WHITE HART CL
BRIDEWELL CL
RIVER GN
PADDOCK RD
Tire Hill
THE WILLOWS
THE PYGHTLE
CHURCH ST
GARDEN RD
ARCHERS
Newtown
ANVIL CT
GATEHOUSE MEWS
DELL SPRING
A507
BALDOCK RD
BOWLERS MEAD
DIXON PL
THE TANNERY
RIVERSIDE
SUNNY HILL
B1038
HARE STREET RD
TYLERS CL
LONGMEAD
THE FOLLY
PO
MARKET HILL
UNION TERR
BRIDGEFOOT
Buttermilk Farm
The Thicket
MEETING HOUSE LA
CHAPEL END
Buntingford
MONKS WLK
RUB WAY
STATION RD
Millfield Fst Sch
SNELLS MEAD
OAK END
CAMPBELL CL
DOWNHALL LEY
MILL CL
NUT SLIP
LAYSTON MDW
Thistley Vale
MEADOW VIEW
PEASMEAD
LUYNES RISE
KNIGHTS CL
BARLEY CROFT
PH
PLASHES DR
OWLES LA
The Watermill
Watermill Ind Est
FAIRFIELD
Sewage Wks
ST FRANCIS CL
LONDON RD
WINDMILL HILL
Tudor Stud
Depot
Aspenden Hall
ASPENDEN RD
Aspenden Bridge
Home Farm
JUBILEE COTTS
QUEEN'S CT
JUBILEE COTTS
The Old Rectory
ASPENDEN HO
MALTING COTTS
Aspenden
The Fox (PH)
SG9
Pine Hill Farm
Westmill
THE ROOKERY
PILGRIMS ROW
PH
PO
Whatbarns Farm
Wakeley Spring
CHERRY GREEN LA
Gaylors Farm
Westmill Green
Wakeley
THE TERRACE
Button Snap
Thrift Wood
Graves Wood
Back La
Cherry Green
CHERRY GREEN BARNS
Cherry Green

34 A B 35 C D 36 E F

39
54

28
42

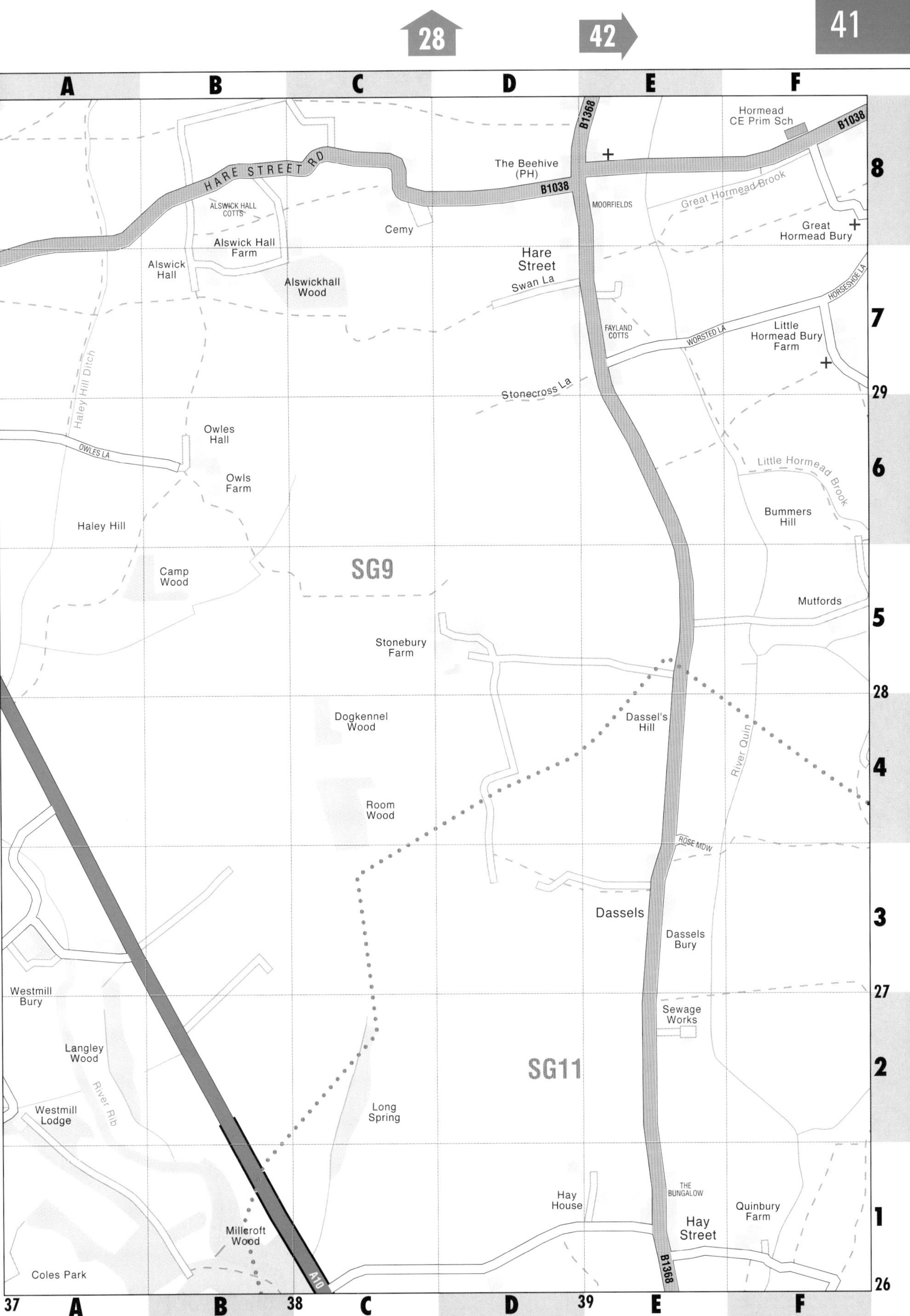
A
B
C
D
E
F
Hormead CE Prim Sch
B1038
B1368
HARE STREET RD
The Beehive (PH)
ALSWICK HALL COTTS
Alswick Hall Farm
Alswick Hall
Alswickhall Wood
Cemy
MOORFIELDS
Great Hormead Brook
Great Hormead Bury
Hare Street
Swan La
FAYLAND COTTS
WORSTED LA
HORSESHOE LA
Little Hormead Bury Farm
Haley Hill Ditch
Stonecross La
Owles Hall
OWLES LA
Owls Farm
Haley Hill
Little Hormead Brook
Bummers Hill
Camp Wood
SG9
Mutfords
Stonebury Farm
Dogkennel Wood
Dassel's Hill
River Quin
Room Wood
ROSE MDW
Dassels
Dassels Bury
Westmill Bury
Sewage Works
Langley Wood
SG11
River Rib
Westmill Lodge
Long Spring
Hay House
THE BUNGALOW
Quinbury Farm
Hay Street
Millcroft Wood
Coles Park
A10
8
7
29
6
5
28
4
3
27
2
1
26
37
38
39

55
42

41
29

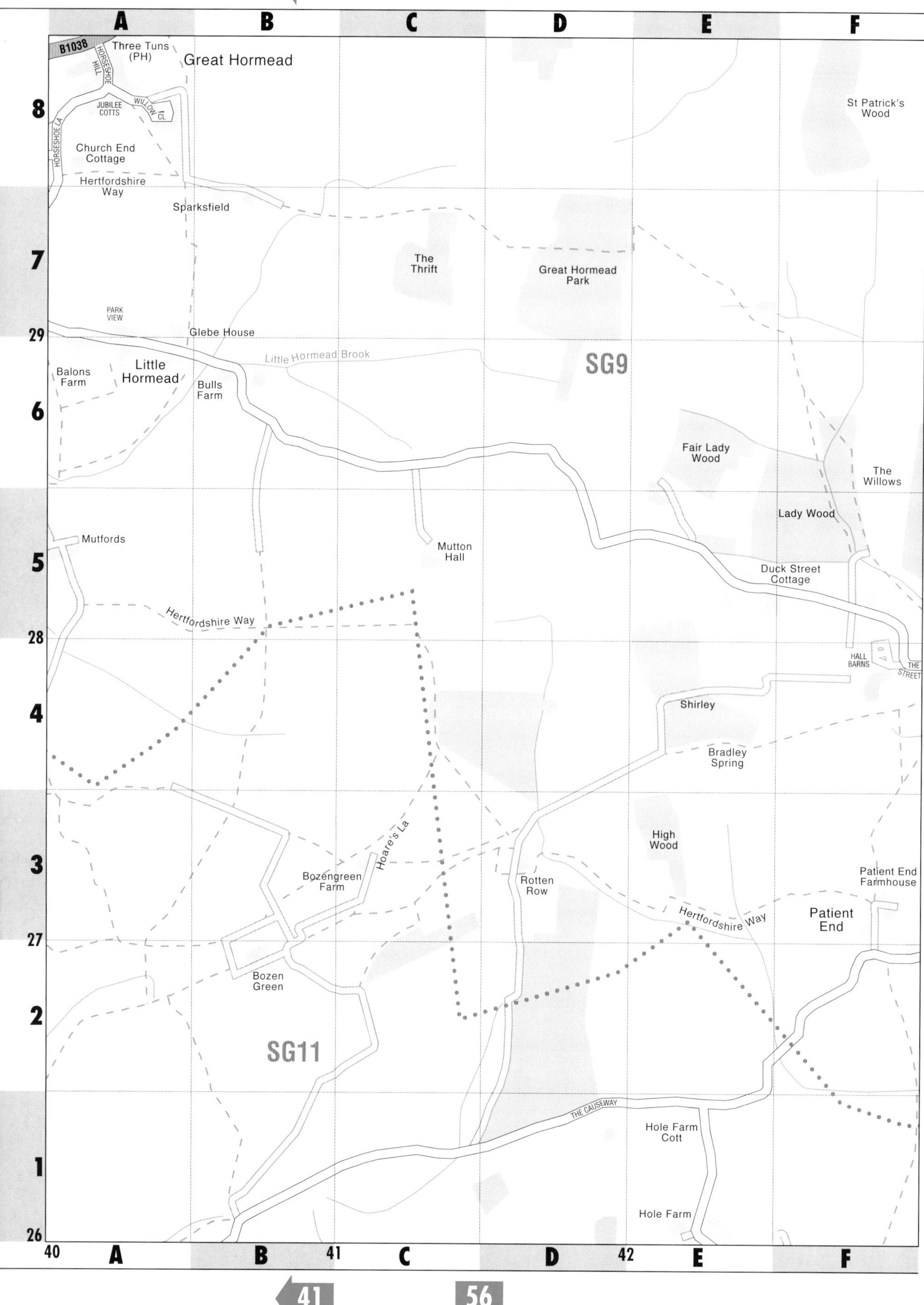
A
B
C
D
E
F
B1038
HORSESHOE HILL
Three Tuns (PH)
Great Hormead
JUBILEE COTTS
WILLOW CL
HORSESHOE LA
Church End Cottage
Hertfordshire Way
Sparksfield
St Patrick's Wood
The Thrift
Great Hormead Park
PARK VIEW
Glebe House
Little Hormead Brook
SG9
Balons Farm
Little Hormead
Bulls Farm
Fair Lady Wood
The Willows
Lady Wood
Mutfords
Mutton Hall
Duck Street Cottage
Hertfordshire Way
HALL BARNS
THE STREET
Shirley
Bradley Spring
High Wood
Hoare's La
Bozengreen Farm
Rotten Row
Patient End Farmhouse
Hertfordshire Way
Patient End
Bozen Green
SG11
THE CAUSEWAY
Hole Farm Cott
Hole Farm
8
7
29
6
5
28
4
3
27
2
1
26
40
41
42

41
56

30

A
B
C
D
E
F
CM23
8
Hall Wood
Stocking Farm
Stocking Pelham Hall
Violets Spring
7
The Cock (PH)
Stocking Pelham
White Hart Farm
Whitebarns
29
MEAD VIEW
WHITEBARNS LA
CRABB'S LA
Sports Ground
Crabb's Green
6
GINNS RD
Crabb's Green Farm
Silla Farm
Whitebarns Cottages
The Willows
El Sub Sta
Willows Farm
North Essex STREET ATLAS
5
SG9
THE WASH
WHITEBARNS
VIOLETS LA
Furneux Pelham
GINNS RD
28
PO
THE STREET
Lower Farm
East End
Green's Farm
Furneux Pelham CE Sch
The Brewery Tap (PH)
LAKE VILLAS
THE OLD COMMON
Old Mill House
Eastend Farm
4
BROOKSIDE
Barleycroft End
Recn Gd
Clay Chimneys
The Brook
THE CAUSEWAY
Pheasant Hall
3
Sewage Works
River Ash
27
Hixham Cottages
Kings Cottage
Hixham Hall
2
Kings
CM23
1
SG11
Oaken Spring
Heath Farm
26
43
A
B
44
C
D
45
E
F

57

C5
1 CHAWORTH GN
2 ACWORTH CT
3 MOSSDALE CT
4 WOLFSBURG CT
5 THORNTONDALE
6 GREEN CT
7 AIREDALE
8 WHARFEDALE

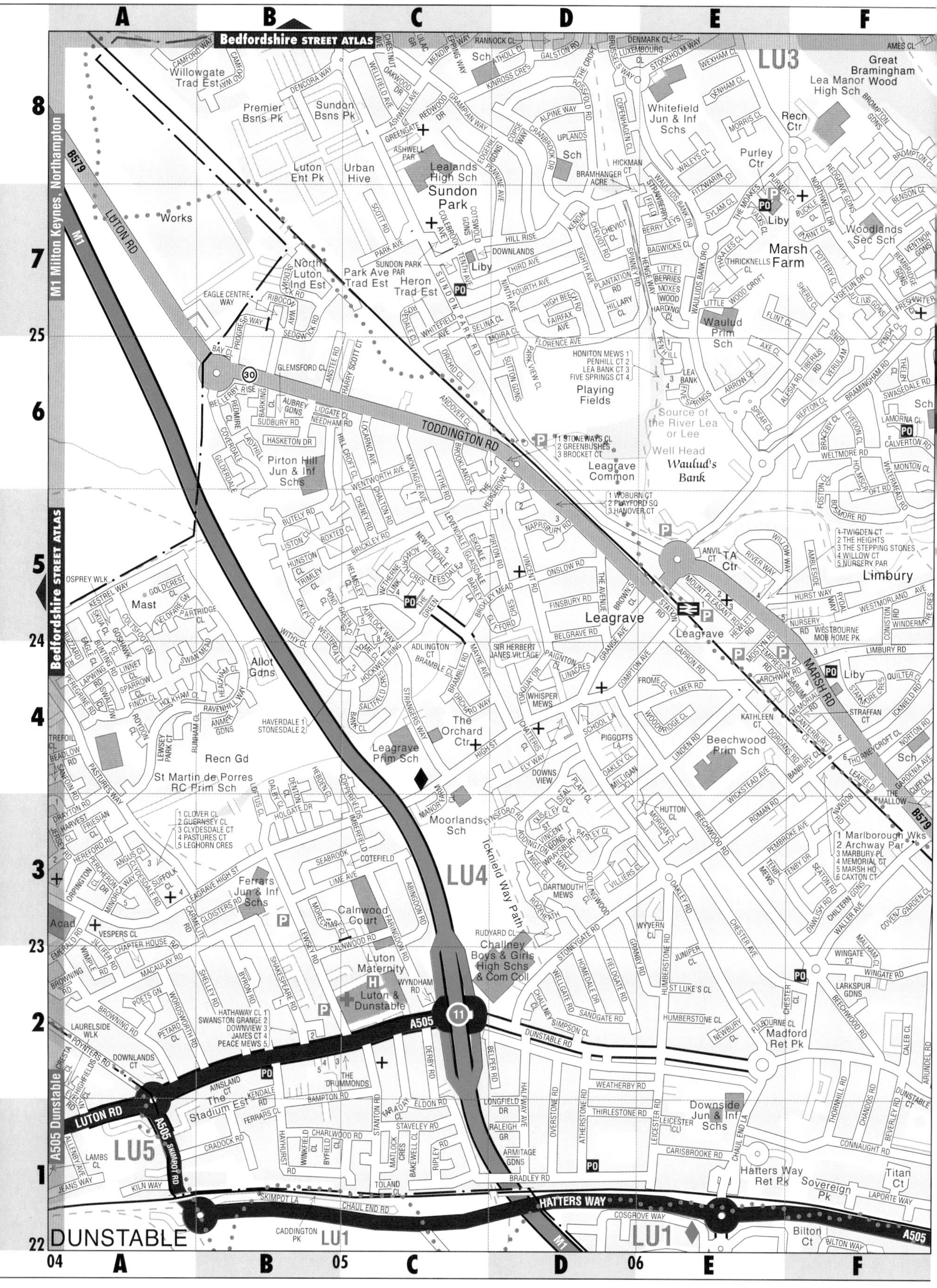

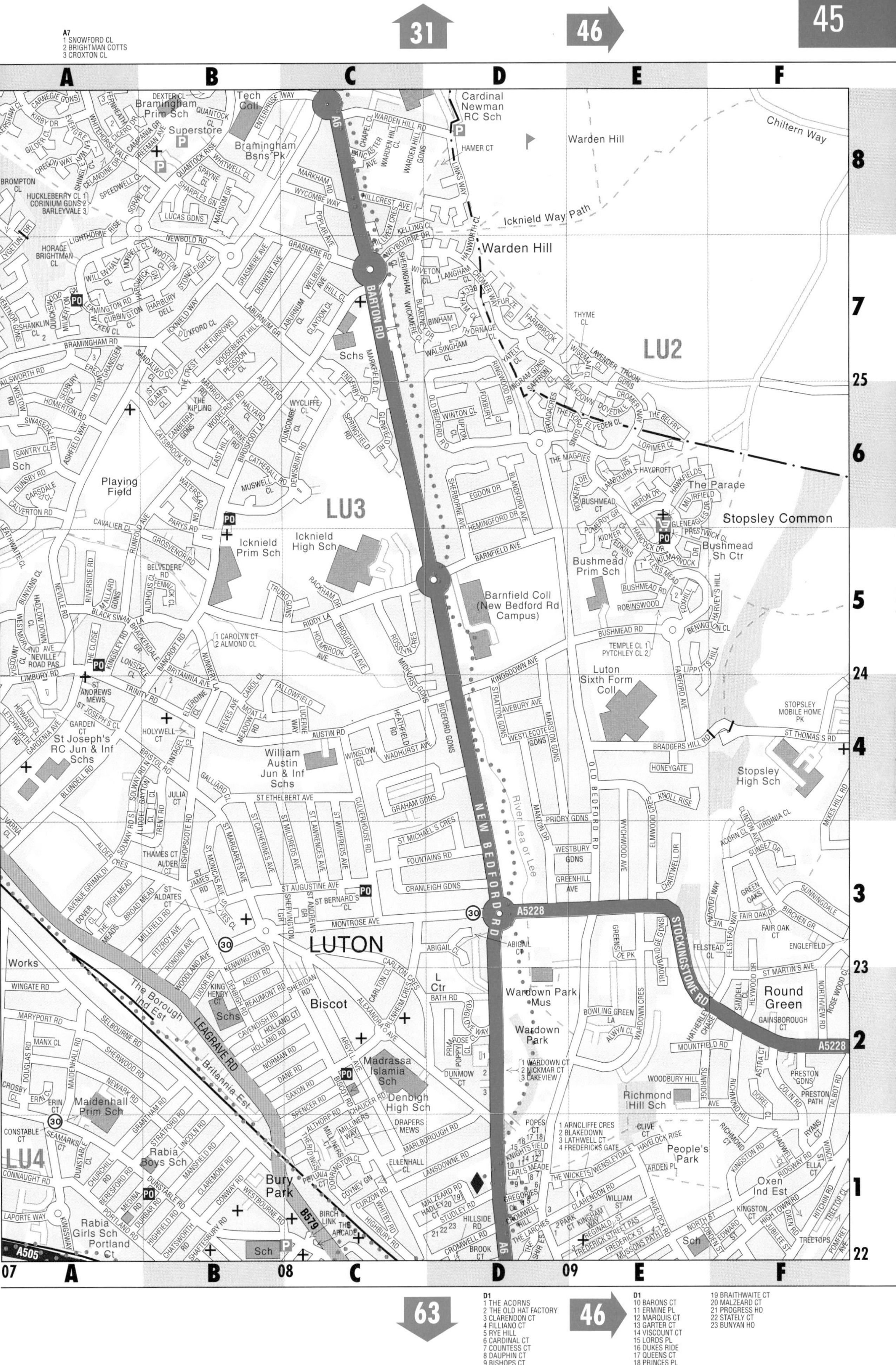
45
31
46
63
46
A7
1 SNOWFORD CL
2 BRIGHTMAN COTTS
3 CROXTON CL
A
B
C
D
E
F
8
7
25
6
5
24
4
3
23
2
1
22
07
08
09
Cardinal Newman RC Sch
Warden Hill
Chiltern Way
Icknield Way Path
Bramingham Prim Sch
Tech Coll
Superstore
Bramingham Bsns Pk
LU2
LU3
LU4
LUTON
Schs
Playing Field
Icknield Prim Sch
Icknield High Sch
Barnfield Coll (New Bedford Rd Campus)
Bushmead Prim Sch
Bushmead Sh Ctr
The Parade
Stopsley Common
Luton Sixth Form Coll
Stopsley High Sch
STOPSLEY MOBILE HOME PK
St Joseph's RC Jun & Inf Schs
William Austin Jun & Inf Schs
River Lea or Lee
Round Green
Wardown Park Mus
Wardown Park
L Ctr
Biscot
Madrassa Islamia Sch
Denbigh High Sch
Richmond Hill Sch
People's Park
Oxen Ind Est
Works
The Borough Ind Est
Britannia Est
Maidenhall Prim Sch
Rabia Boys Sch
Rabia Girls Sch
Portland Ct
Bury Park
Sch
BARTON RD
NEW BEDFORD RD
LEAGRAVE RD
STOCKINGSTONE RD
A6
A5228
A505
B579
D1
1 THE ACORNS
2 THE OLD HAT FACTORY
3 CLARENDON CT
4 FILLIANO CT
5 RYE HILL
6 CARDINAL CT
7 COUNTESS CT
8 DAUPHIN CT
9 BISHOPS CT
D1
10 BARONS CT
11 ERMINE PL
12 MARQUIS CT
13 GARTER CT
14 VISCOUNT CT
15 LORDS PL
16 DUKES RIDE
17 QUEENS CT
18 PRINCES PL
19 BRAITHWAITE CT
20 MALZEARD CT
21 PROGRESS HO
22 STATELY CT
23 BUNYAN HO

45
32

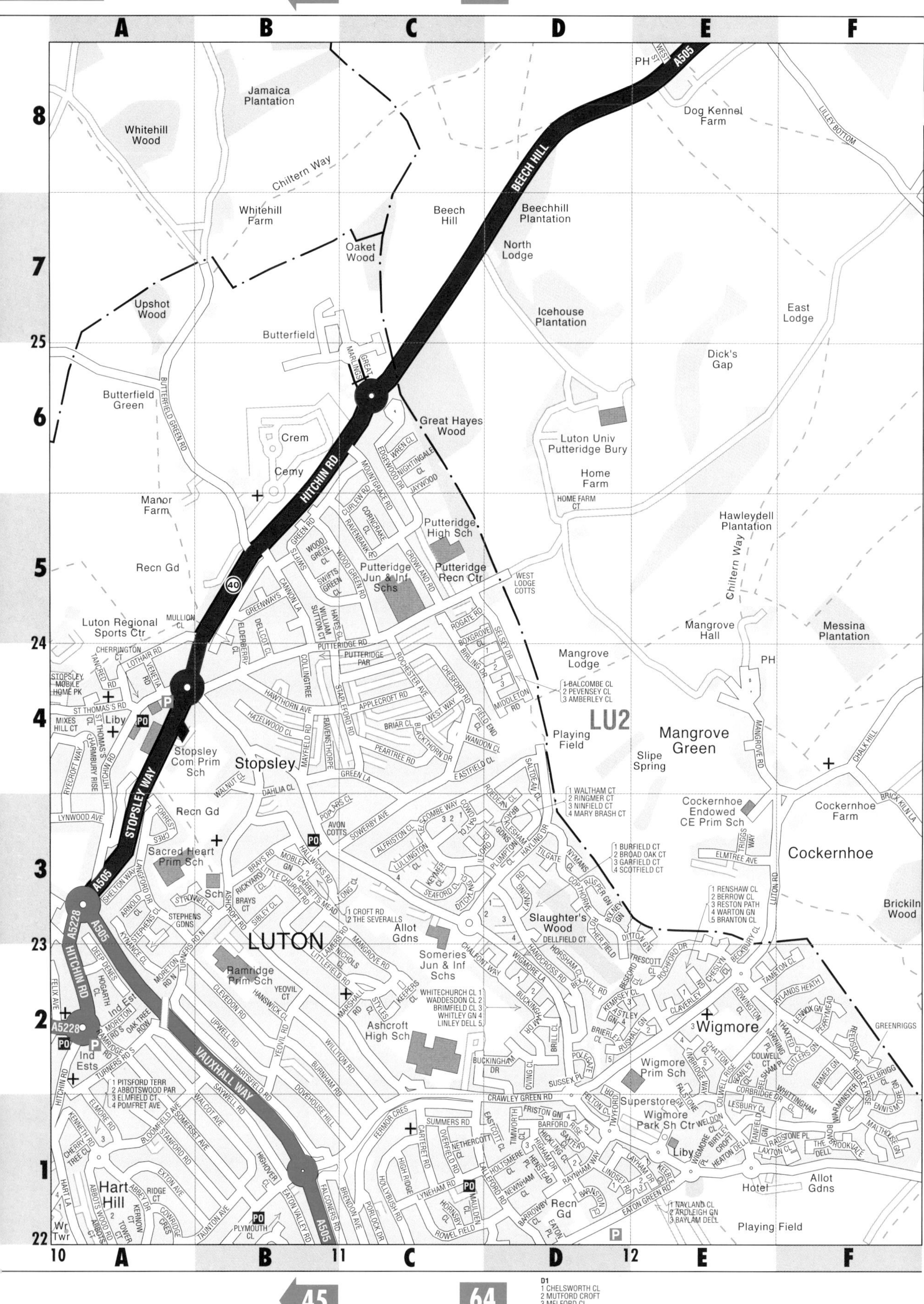

45
64

D1
1 CHELSWORTH CL
2 MUTFORD CROFT
3 MELFORD CL
4 PINFORD DELL
5 ALDERTON CL

33
48

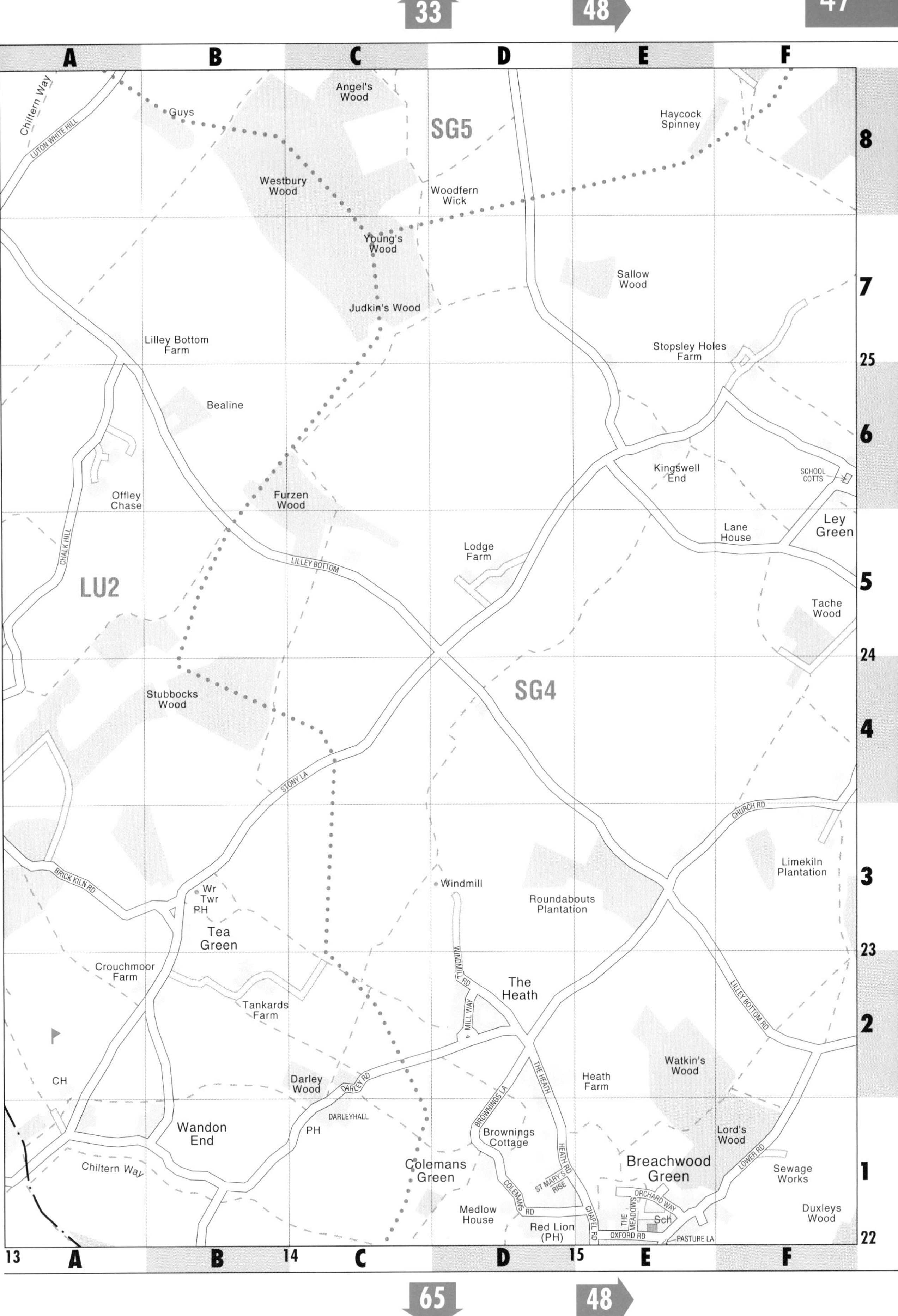
A
B
C
D
E
F
Chiltern Way
LUTON WHITE HILL
Guys
Angel's Wood
SG5
Haycock Spinney
Westbury Wood
Woodfern Wick
Young's Wood
Sallow Wood
Judkin's Wood
Lilley Bottom Farm
Stopsley Holes Farm
Bealine
Kingswell End
SCHOOL COTTS
Offley Chase
Furzen Wood
Lane House
Ley Green
CHALK HILL
Lodge Farm
LILLEY BOTTOM
LU2
Tache Wood
Stubbocks Wood
SG4
STONY LA
CHURCH RD
Limekiln Plantation
BRICK KILN RD
Windmill
Wr Twr
PH
Roundabouts Plantation
Tea Green
Crouchmoor Farm
WINDMILL RD
The Heath
Tankards Farm
MILL WAY
LILLEY BOTTOM RD
CH
Darley Wood
DARLEY RD
THE HEATH
Heath Farm
Watkin's Wood
DARLEYHALL
BROWNINGS LA
Wandon End
PH
Brownings Cottage
HEATH RD
Lord's Wood
Breachwood Green
Colemans Green
Chiltern Way
ST MARY'S RISE
LOWER RD
Sewage Works
ORCHARD WAY
COLEMANS RD
Medlow House
THE MEADOWS
Sch
Duxleys Wood
Red Lion (PH)
CHAPEL RD
OXFORD RD
PASTURE LA
8
7
25
6
5
24
4
3
23
2
1
22
13
14
15

65
48

47
34

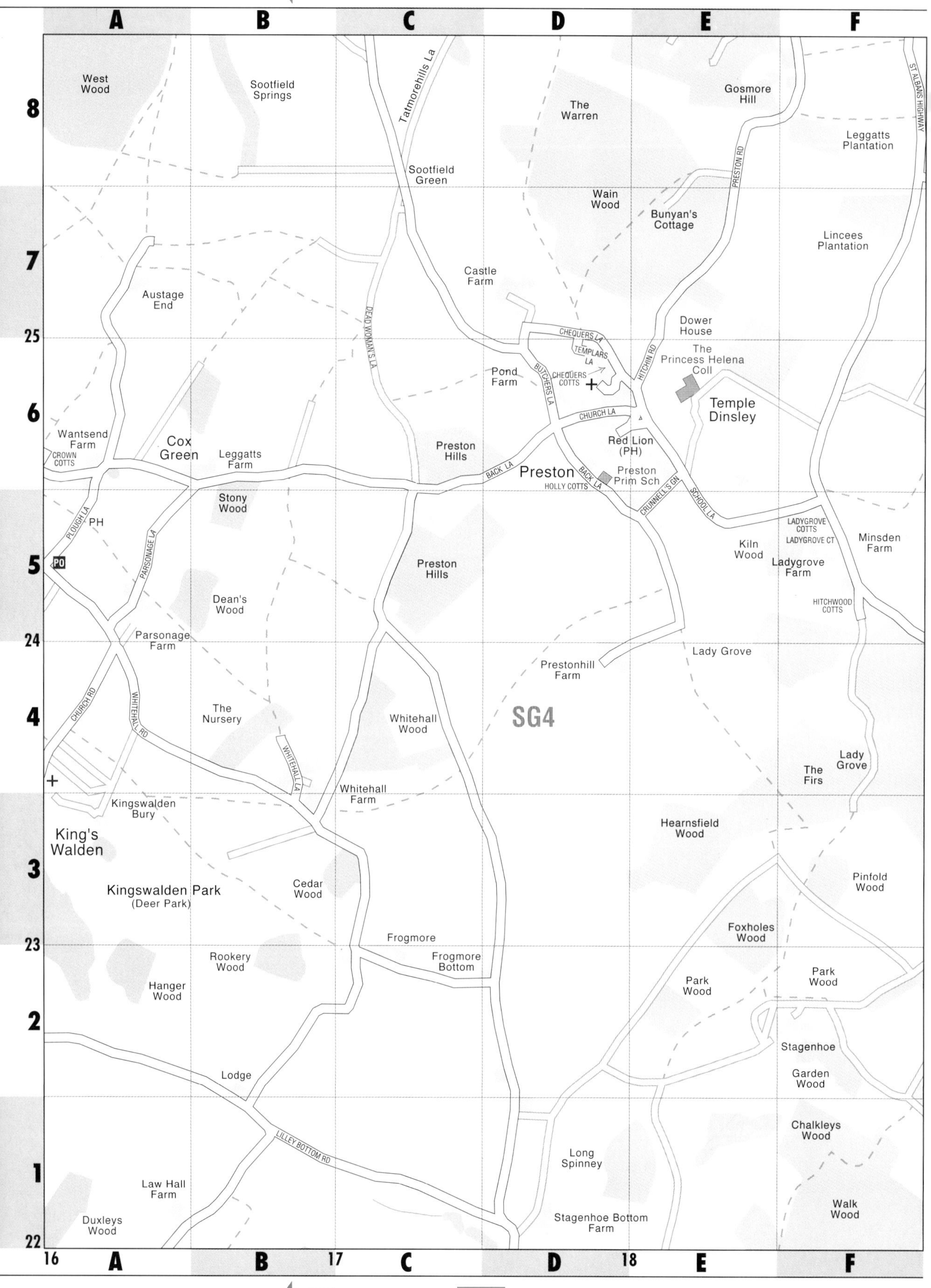
A
B
C
D
E
F
8
7
25
6
5
24
4
3
23
2
1
22
16
17
18
West Wood
Sootfield Springs
Tatmorehills La
The Warren
Gosmore Hill
ST ALBANS HIGHWAY
Leggatts Plantation
Sootfield Green
PRESTON RD
Wain Wood
Bunyan's Cottage
Lincees Plantation
Castle Farm
Austage End
DEAD WOMAN'S LA
CHEQUERS LA
TEMPLARS LA
Dower House
HITCHIN RD
The Princess Helena Coll
Pond Farm
BUTCHERS LA
CHEQUERS COTTS
Temple Dinsley
CHURCH LA
Wantsend Farm
CROWN COTTS
Cox Green
Leggatts Farm
Preston Hills
Red Lion (PH)
BACK LA
Preston
Preston Prim Sch
HOLLY COTTS
CRUNNELL'S GN
SCHOOL LA
Stony Wood
PLOUGH LA
PH
PO
PARSONAGE LA
LADYGROVE COTTS
LADYGROVE CT
Kiln Wood
Minsden Farm
Ladygrove Farm
Preston Hills
Dean's Wood
HITCHWOOD COTTS
Parsonage Farm
Lady Grove
Prestonhill Farm
CHURCH RD
WHITEHALL RD
The Nursery
Whitehall Wood
SG4
WHITEHALL LA
Lady Grove
The Firs
Whitehall Farm
Kingswalden Bury
King's Walden
Hearnsfield Wood
Kingswalden Park
(Deer Park)
Cedar Wood
Pinfold Wood
Foxholes Wood
Frogmore
Rookery Wood
Frogmore Bottom
Hanger Wood
Park Wood
Park Wood
Stagenhoe
Lodge
Garden Wood
Chalkleys Wood
LILLEY BOTTOM RD
Long Spinney
Law Hall Farm
Walk Wood
Duxleys Wood
Stagenhoe Bottom Farm

47
66

35
50
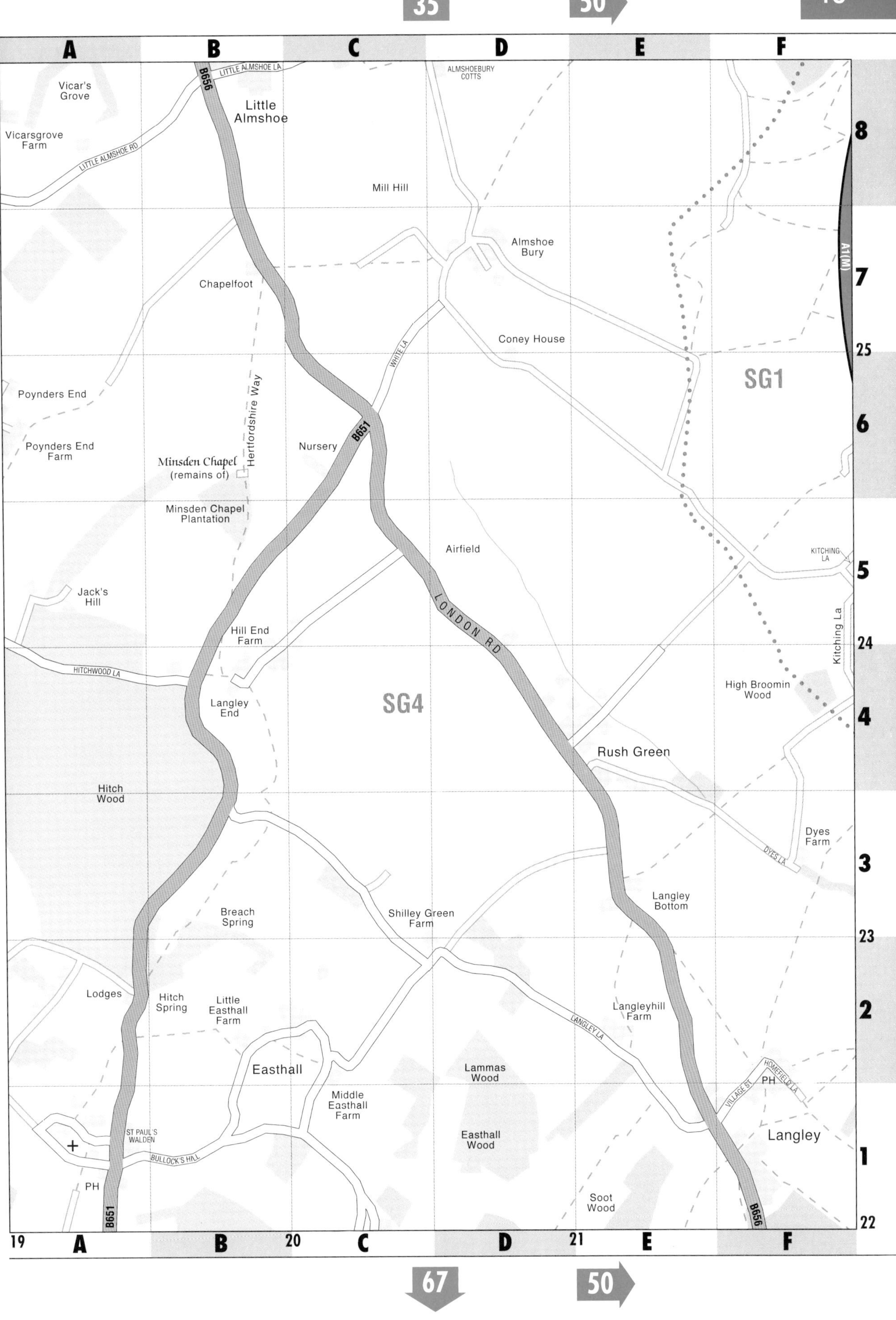
A
B
C
D
E
F
8
7
25
6
5
24
4
3
23
2
1
22
19
20
21
LITTLE ALMSHOE LA
B656
ALMSHOEBURY COTTS
Vicar's Grove
Little Almshoe
Vicarsgrove Farm
LITTLE ALMSHOE RD
Mill Hill
Almshoe Bury
A1(M)
Chapelfoot
Coney House
WHITE LA
SG1
Poynders End
Hertfordshire Way
B651
Poynders End Farm
Nursery
Minsden Chapel (remains of)
Minsden Chapel Plantation
Airfield
KITCHING LA
Jack's Hill
LONDON RD
Kitching La
Hill End Farm
HITCHWOOD LA
High Broomin Wood
Langley End
SG4
Rush Green
Hitch Wood
Dyes Farm
DYES LA
Breach Spring
Shilley Green Farm
Langley Bottom
Lodges
Hitch Spring
Little Easthall Farm
Langleyhill Farm
LANGLEY LA
Easthall
Lammas Wood
HOMEFIELD LA
VILLAGE ST
PH
Middle Easthall Farm
Easthall Wood
Langley
ST PAUL'S WALDEN
BULLOCK'S HILL
PH
Soot Wood
67
50

B8
1 BAWDSEY CL
2 SHERINGHAM AVE
3 BOURNEMOUTH RD
49
C7
1 MIDDLE ROW
2 BAKER ST
36
E6
1 JOWITT HO
2 SHARP CT
3 CHAUNCY HO
4 WILCOX CT
F5
1 LINKWAYS CT

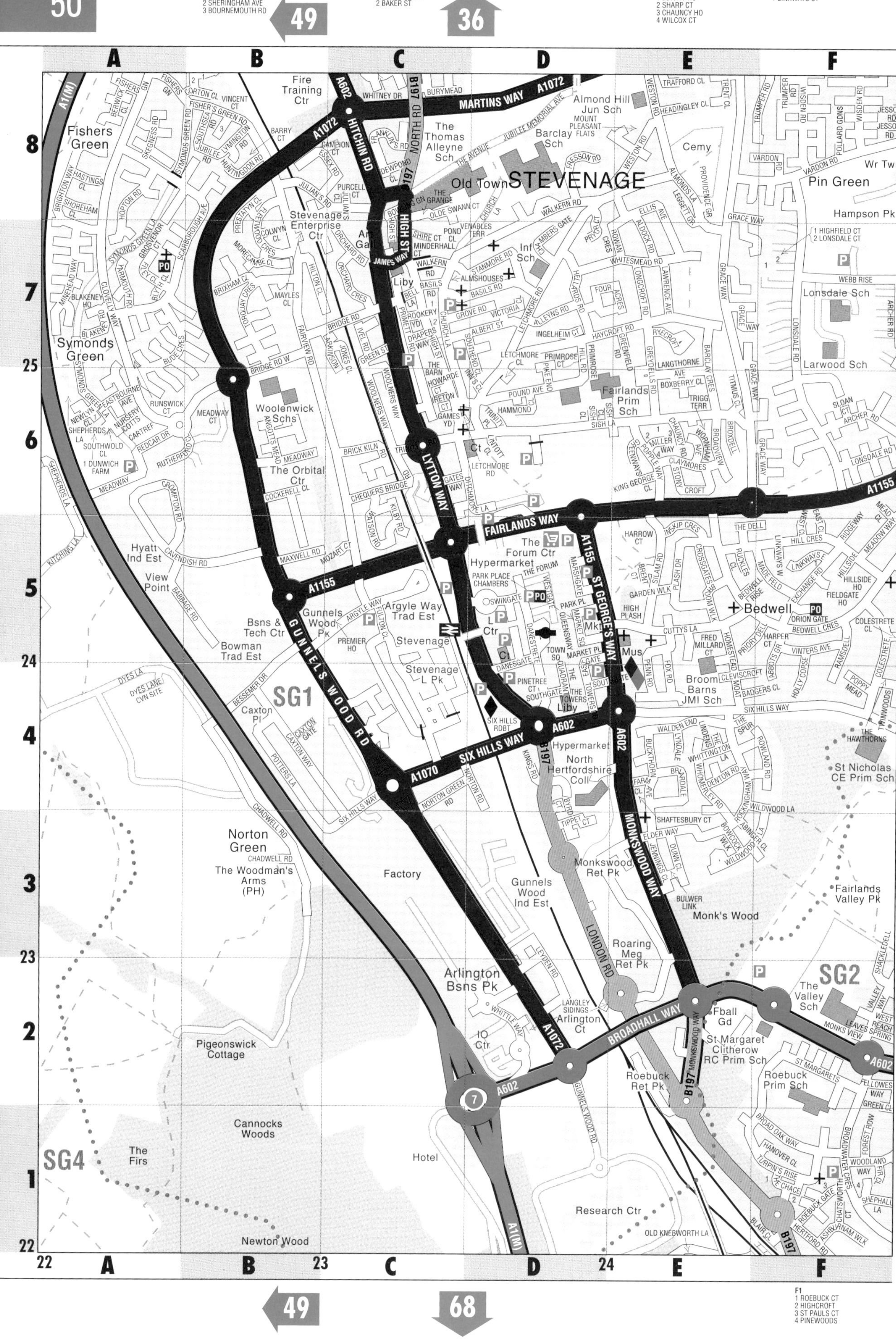

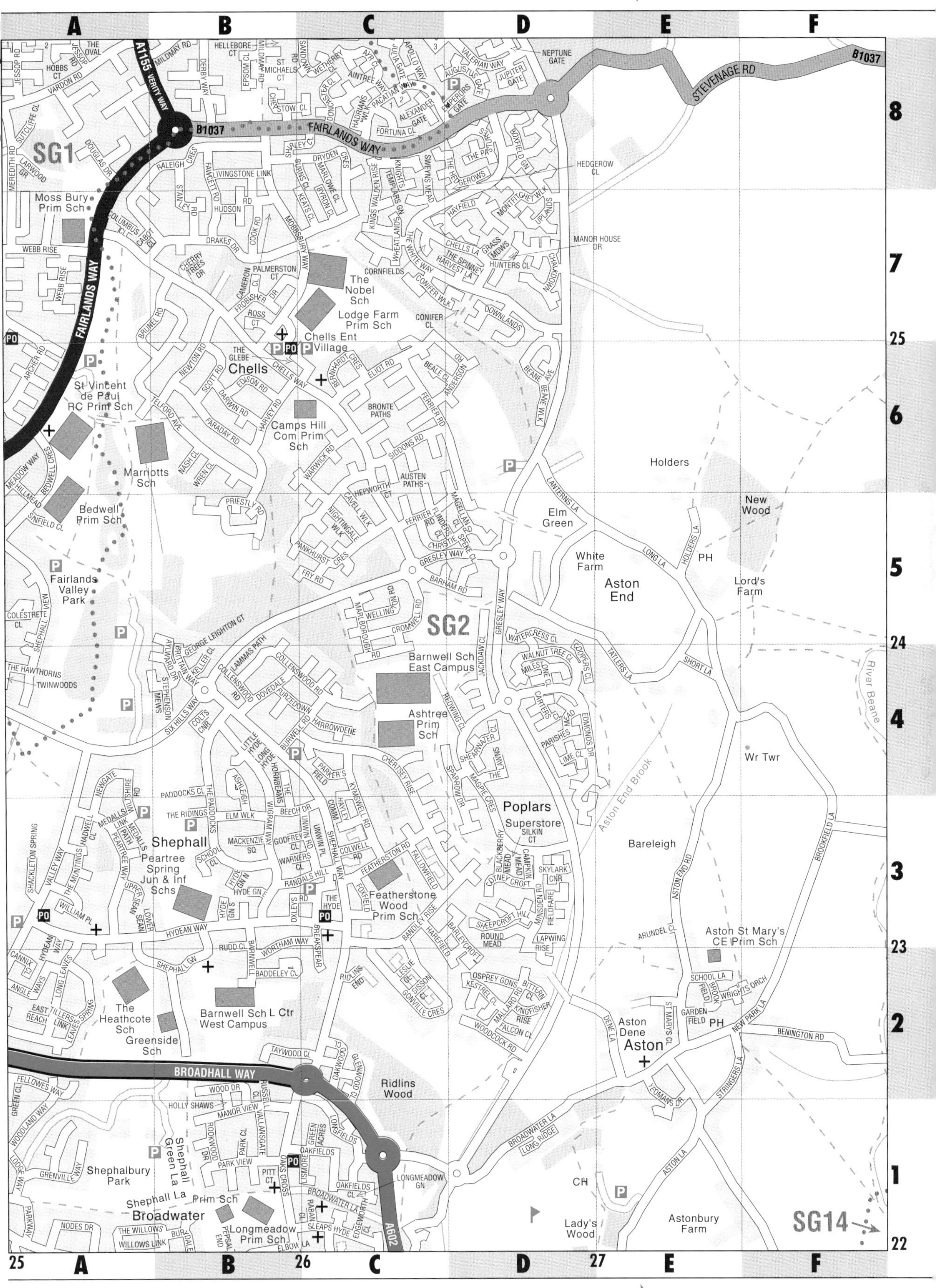
A
B
C
D
E
F
8
7
25
6
5
24
4
3
23
2
1
22
25
26
27
SG1
SG2
SG14
A1155
VERITY WAY
B1037
FAIRLANDS WAY
STEVENAGE RD
NEPTUNE GATE
HEDGEROW CL
MANOR HOUSE DR
Moss Bury Prim Sch
WEBB RISE
The Nobel Sch
Lodge Farm Prim Sch
Chells Ent Village
THE GLEBE
Chells
St Vincent de Paul RC Prim Sch
Camps Hill Com Prim Sch
Marriotts Sch
Bedwell Prim Sch
Fairlands Valley Park
Holders
New Wood
Elm Green
White Farm
Aston End
PH
Lord's Farm
River Beane
Barnwell Sch East Campus
Ashtree Prim Sch
Wr Twr
Aston End Brook
Poplars
Superstore
Bareleigh
Shephall
Peartree Spring Jun & Inf Schs
Featherstone Wood Prim Sch
Aston St Mary's CE Prim Sch
The Heathcote Sch
Greenside Sch
Barnwell Sch L Ctr West Campus
Aston Dene
Aston
BROADHALL WAY
Ridlins Wood
Shephalbury Park
Shephall Green La
Shephall La
Prim Sch
Broadwater
Longmeadow Prim Sch
A602
CH
Lady's Wood
Astonbury Farm
BENINGTON RD
BROOKFIELD LA
ASTON END RD
LONG LA
SHORT LA
TATLERS LA
GRESLEY WAY
STRINGERS LA
ASTON LA
BROADWATER LA

51
38

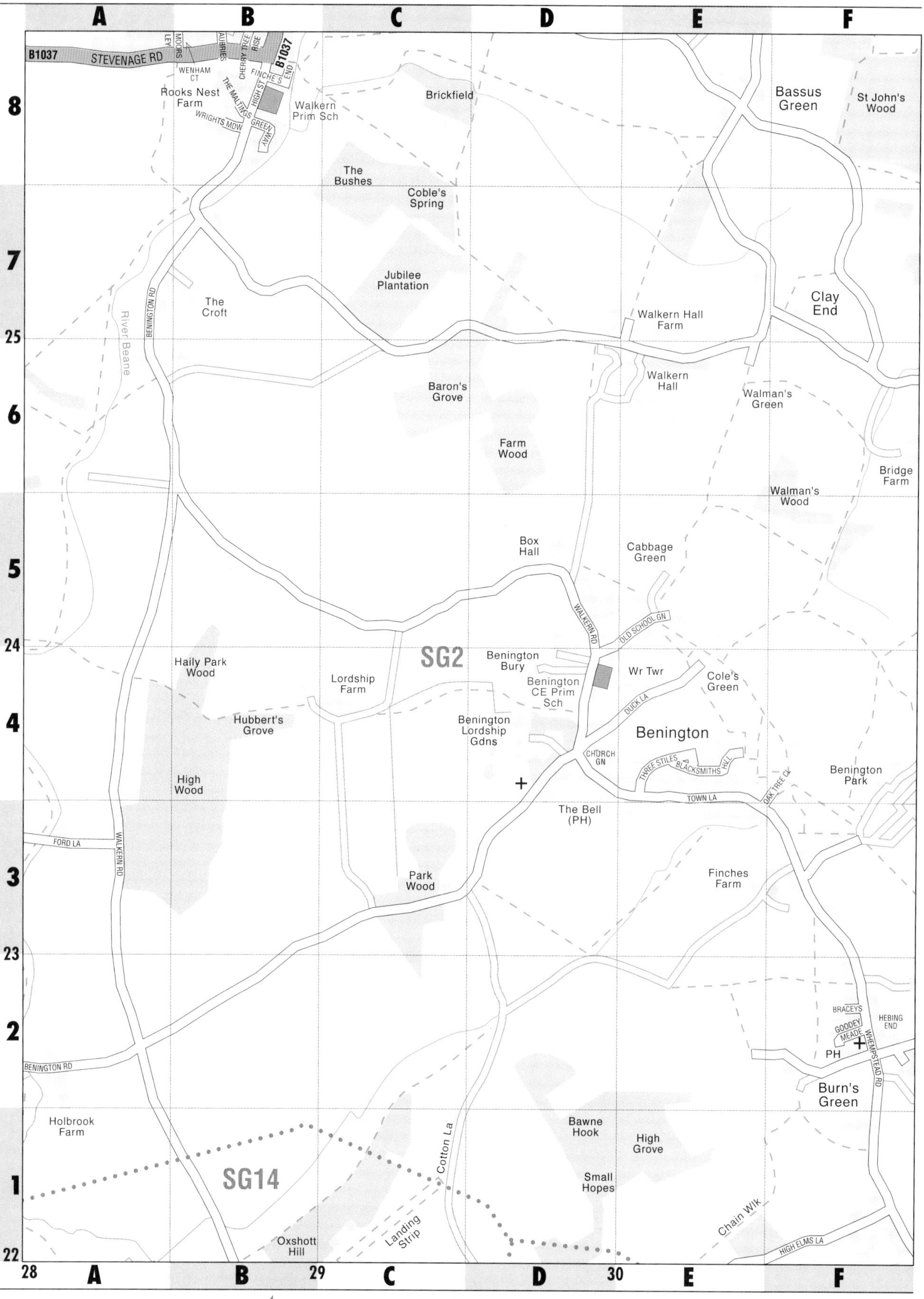

A B C D E F
8 7 25 6 5 24 4 3 23 2 22 1
B1037
STEVENAGE RD
LEY
MOORS
AUBRIES
CHERRY TREE
RISE
B1037
WENHAM CT
FINCHE'S END
Rooks Nest Farm
THE MALTINGS
HIGH ST
WRIGHTS MDW
GREEN WAY
Walkern Prim Sch
Brickfield
Bassus Green
St John's Wood
The Bushes
Coble's Spring
Jubilee Plantation
The Croft
BENINGTON RD
River Beane
Walkern Hall Farm
Clay End
Baron's Grove
Walkern Hall
Walman's Green
Farm Wood
Bridge Farm
Walman's Wood
Box Hall
Cabbage Green
WALKERN RD
OLD SCHOOL GN
SG2
Haily Park Wood
Lordship Farm
Benington Bury
Wr Twr
Cole's Green
Benington CE Prim Sch
DUCK LA
Hubbert's Grove
Benington Lordship Gdns
Benington
CHURCH GN
THREE STILES
BLACKSMITHS HILL
OAK TREE CL
Benington Park
High Wood
TOWN LA
The Bell (PH)
FORD LA
WALKERN RD
Park Wood
Finches Farm
BRACEYS
HEBING END
GOODEY MEADE
PH
WHEMPSTEAD RD
BENINGTON RD
Burn's Green
Holbrook Farm
Bawne Hook
High Grove
Cotton La
SG14
Small Hopes
Chain Wlk
Landing Strip
Oxshott Hill
HIGH ELMS LA
28 A B 29 C D 30 E F

51
70

39
54

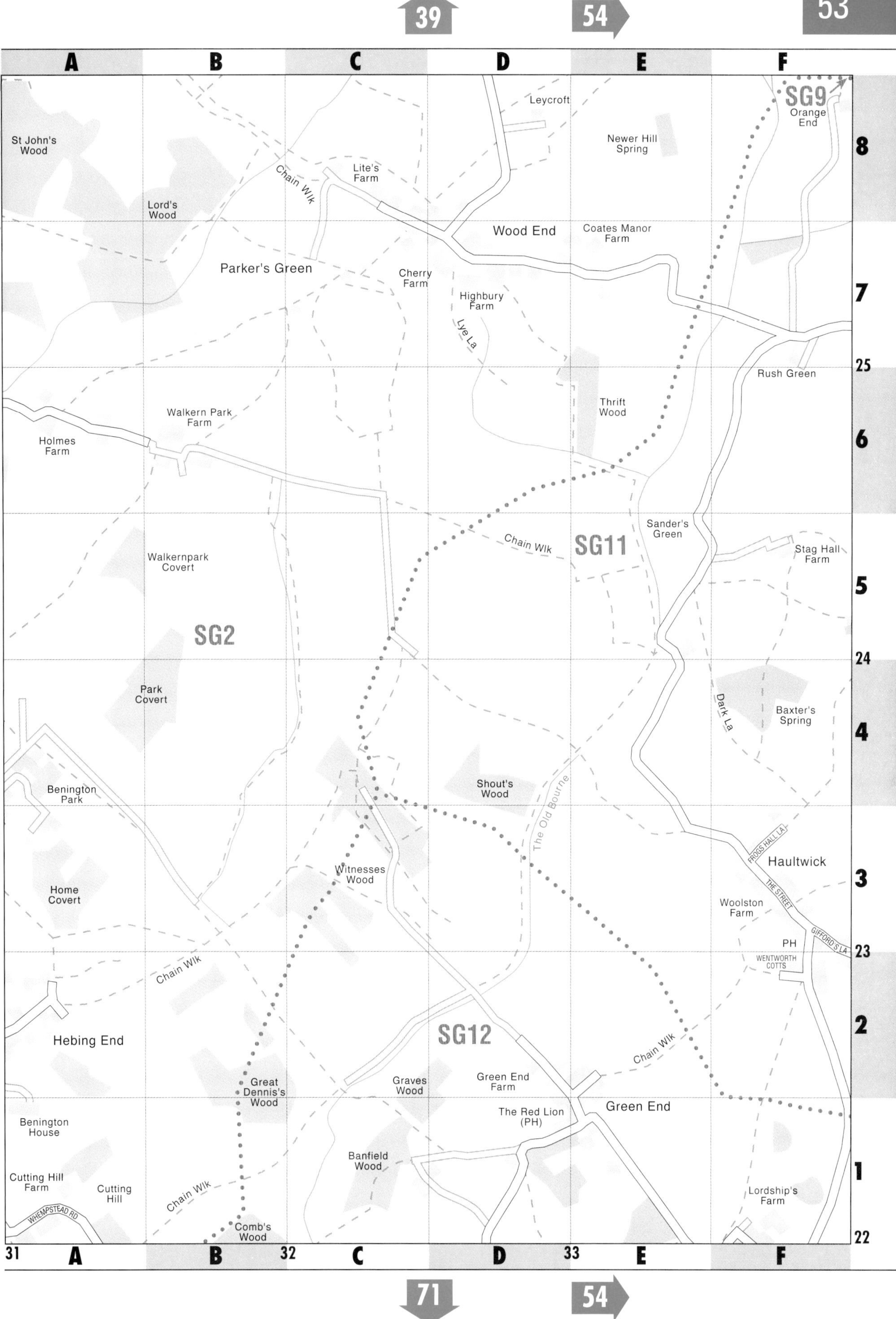
A
B
C
D
E
F
St John's Wood
Lord's Wood
Chain Wlk
Lite's Farm
Leycroft
Newer Hill Spring
SG9
Orange End
8
Wood End
Coates Manor Farm
Parker's Green
Cherry Farm
Highbury Farm
7
Lye La
Rush Green
25
Walkern Park Farm
Thrift Wood
Holmes Farm
6
Chain Wlk
SG11
Sander's Green
Stag Hall Farm
Walkernpark Covert
5
SG2
24
Park Covert
Dark La
Baxter's Spring
4
Benington Park
Shout's Wood
The Old Bourne
FROGS HALL LA
Haultwick
Home Covert
Witnesses Wood
THE STREET
Woolston Farm
3
GIFFORD'S LA
PH
WENTWORTH COTTS
23
Chain Wlk
Hebing End
SG12
Chain Wlk
2
Great Dennis's Wood
Graves Wood
Green End Farm
Green End
The Red Lion (PH)
Benington House
Banfield Wood
1
Cutting Hill Farm
Cutting Hill
Chain Wlk
Lordship's Farm
WHEMPSTEAD RD
Comb's Wood
22
31
32
33

71
54

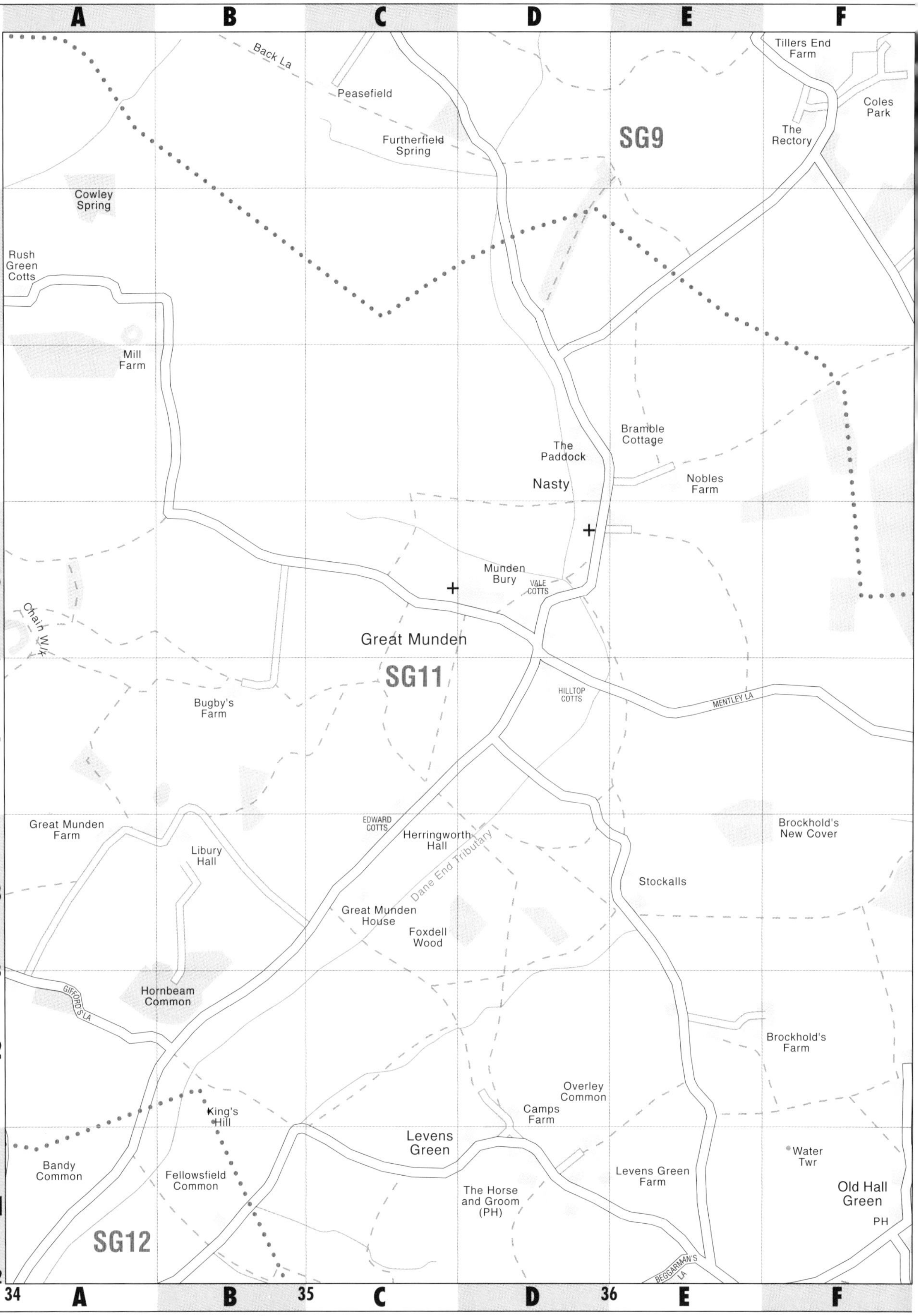

53 40

A B C D E F

8 7 25 6 5 24 4 3 23 2 1 22

Back La
Peasefield
Furtherfield Spring
Tillers End Farm
Coles Park
The Rectory
SG9
Cowley Spring
Rush Green Cotts
Mill Farm
Bramble Cottage
The Paddock
Nasty
Nobles Farm
Munden Bury
VALE COTTS
Chain Wlk
Great Munden
SG11
HILLTOP COTTS
MENTLEY LA
Bugby's Farm
Great Munden Farm
EDWARD COTTS
Herringworth Hall
Dane End Tributary
Brockhold's New Cover
Libury Hall
Stockalls
Great Munden House
Foxdell Wood
GIFFORD'S LA
Hornbeam Common
Brockhold's Farm
Overley Common
Camps Farm
King's Hill
Levens Green
Water Twr
Bandy Common
Fellowsfield Common
The Horse and Groom (PH)
Levens Green Farm
Old Hall Green
PH
SG12
BEGGARMAN'S LA

34 A B 35 C D 36 E F

53 72

A B C D E F

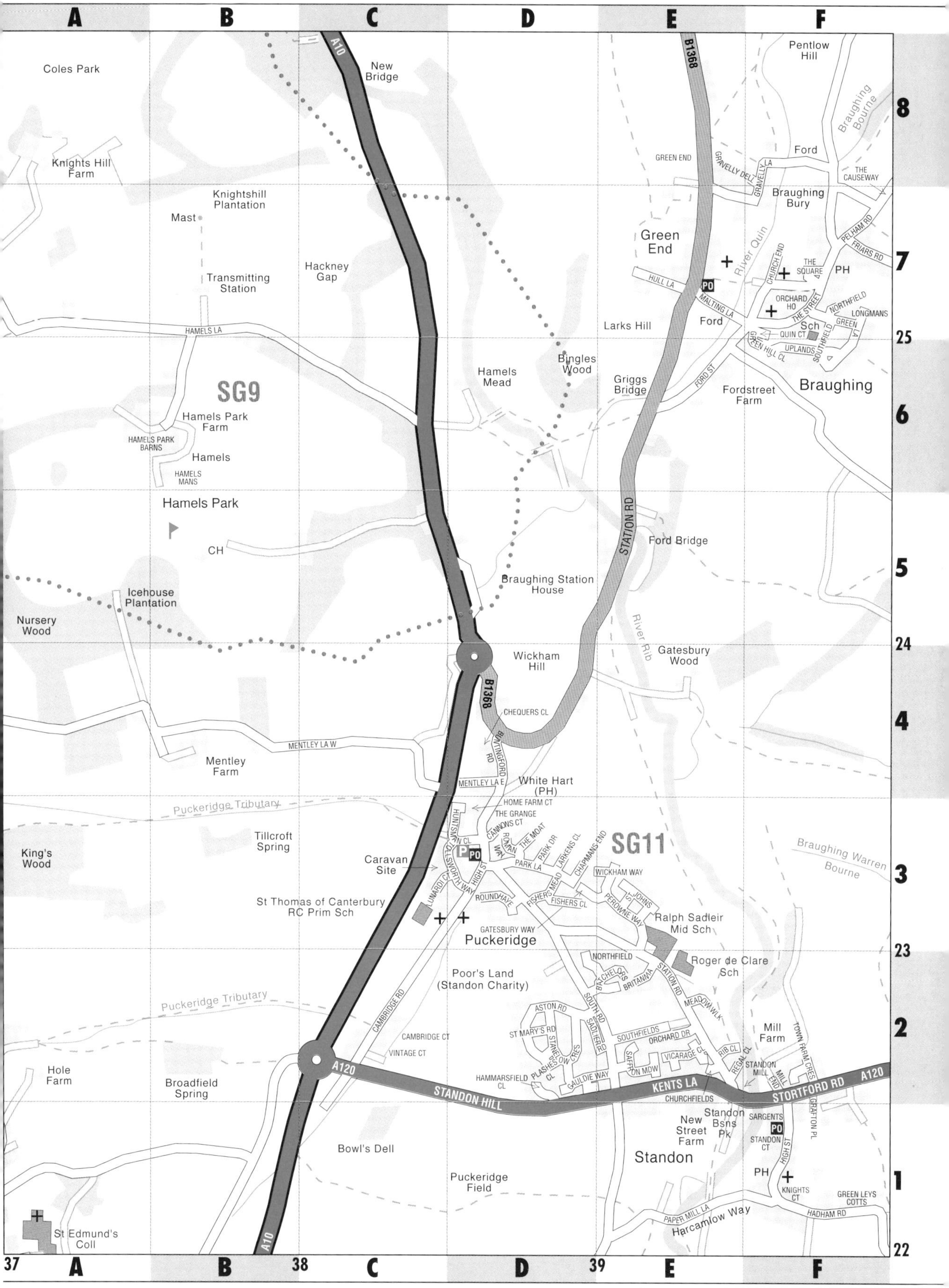

Coles Park
New Bridge
A10
B1368
Pentlow Hill
Braughing Bourne
8
Knights Hill Farm
Ford
GREEN END
GRAVELLY DELL
GRAVELLY LA
THE CAUSEWAY
Knightshill Plantation
Braughing Bury
Mast
Green End
PELHAM RD
FRIARS RD
River Quin
CHURCH END
THE SQUARE
PH
7
Transmitting Station
Hackney Gap
HULL LA
PO
ORCHARD HO
THE STREET
NORTHFIELD
LONGMANS
MALTING LA
Larks Hill
Ford
Sch
GREEN LA
QUIN CT
SOUTHFIELD
HAMELS LA
GREEN HILL CL
UPLANDS
25
Bingles Wood
Hamels Mead
Griggs Bridge
FORD ST
Fordstreet Farm
Braughing
SG9
Hamels Park Farm
6
HAMELS PARK BARNS
Hamels
HAMELS MANS
Hamels Park
STATION RD
CH
Ford Bridge
5
Braughing Station House
Icehouse Plantation
Nursery Wood
River Rib
Gatesbury Wood
Wickham Hill
24
B1368
CHEQUERS CL
4
BUNTINGFORD RD
MENTLEY LA W
Mentley Farm
MENTLEY LA E
White Hart (PH)
HOME FARM CT
Puckeridge Tributary
THE GRANGE
CANNONS CT
Tillcroft Spring
ROWAN WAY
THE MOAT
PARK DR
LARKENS CL
CHAPMANS END
SG11
Braughing Warren Bourne
King's Wood
HUNTSMAN CL
P
PO
PARK LA
WICKHAM WAY
Caravan Site
3
TOLLSWORTH WAY
HIGH ST
LUNARDI CT
ROUNDHAYE
FISHERS MEAD
FISHERS CL
ST JOHNS
PEROWNE WAY
St Thomas of Canterbury RC Prim Sch
Ralph Sadleir Mid Sch
GATESBURY WAY
Puckeridge
23
NORTHFIELD
Roger de Clare Sch
Poor's Land (Standon Charity)
BUTCHERS
BRITANNIA
STATION RD
CAMBRIDGE RD
Puckeridge Tributary
ASTON RD
SOUTH RD
MEADOW WLK
2
ST MARY'S RD
SADLEIR RD
SOUTHFIELDS
ORCHARD DR
Mill Farm
TOWN FARM CRES
CAMBRIDGE CT
STANELOW CRES
VICARAGE CL
RIB CL
VINTAGE CT
SAFFRON MDW
REGAL CL
STANDON MILL
MILL END
Hole Farm
A120
HAMMARSFIELD CL
PLASHES CL
GAULDIE WAY
KENTS LA
STORTFORD RD
A120
Broadfield Spring
STANDON HILL
CHURCHFIELDS
New Street Farm
Standon Bsns Pk
SARGENTS
STANDON CT
PO
GRAFTON PL
Bowl's Dell
Standon
HIGH ST
1
Puckeridge Field
PH
KNIGHTS CT
GREEN LEYS COTTS
PAPER MILL LA
Harcamlow Way
HADHAM RD
St Edmund's Coll
A10
22

37 A B 38 C D 39 E F

55
42

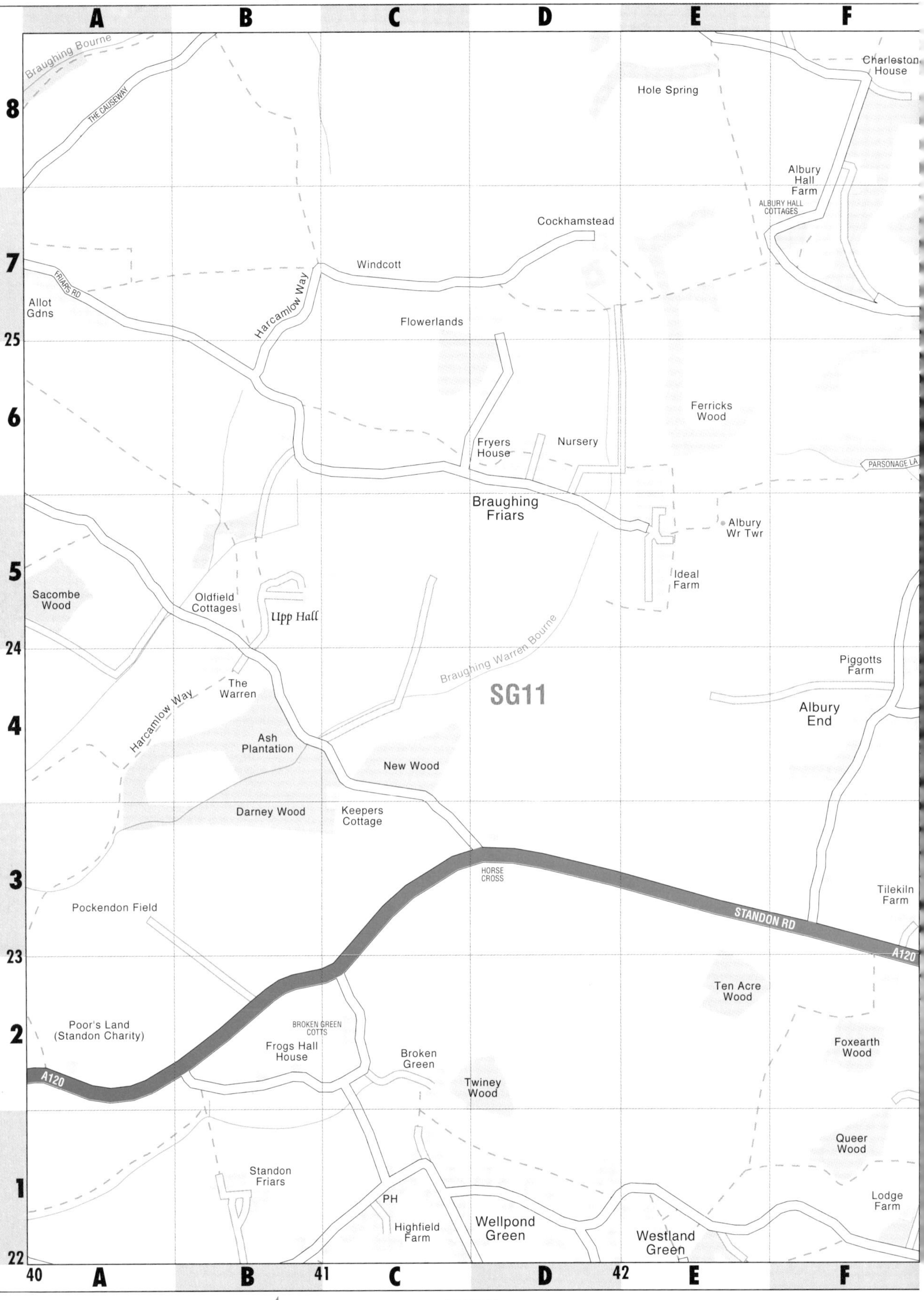

A B C D E F

8
7
25
6
5
24
4
3
23
2
1
22

Braughing Bourne
THE CAUSEWAY
Charleston House
Hole Spring
Albury Hall Farm
ALBURY HALL COTTAGES
Cockhamstead
Windcott
FRIARS RD
Allot Gdns
Harcamlow Way
Flowerlands
Ferricks Wood
Fryers House
Nursery
PARSONAGE LA
Braughing Friars
Albury Wr Twr
Ideal Farm
Sacombe Wood
Oldfield Cottages
Upp Hall
Braughing Warren Bourne
Piggotts Farm
The Warren
SG11
Albury End
Harcamlow Way
Ash Plantation
New Wood
Darney Wood
Keepers Cottage
HORSE CROSS
Tilekiln Farm
Pockendon Field
STANDON RD
A120
Ten Acre Wood
Poor's Land (Standon Charity)
BROKEN GREEN COTTS
Frogs Hall House
Broken Green
Foxearth Wood
A120
Twiney Wood
Queer Wood
Standon Friars
PH
Lodge Farm
Highfield Farm
Wellpond Green
Westland Green

40 A B 41 C D 42 E F

55
74

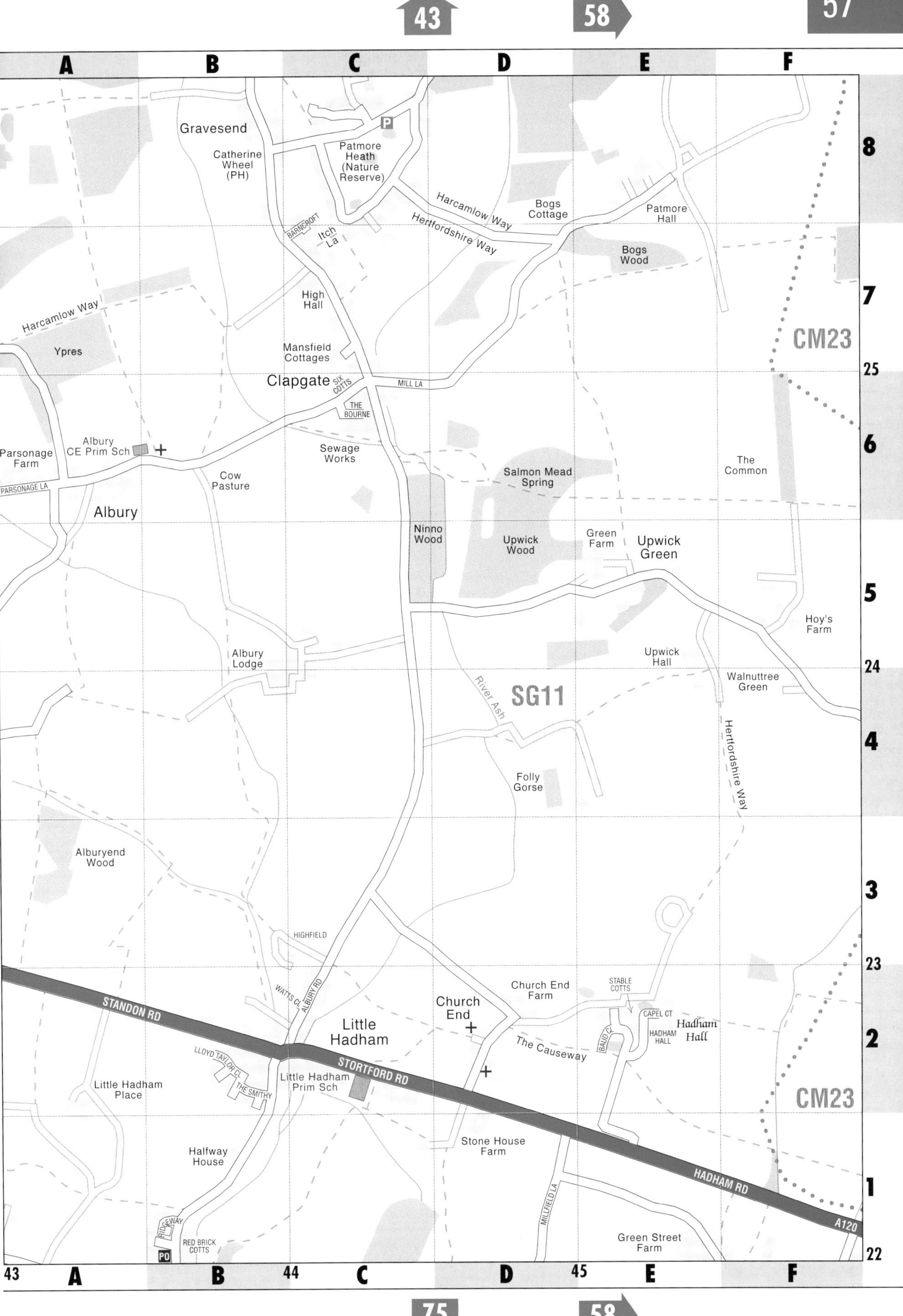
A
B
C
D
E
F
Gravesend
Catherine Wheel (PH)
Patmore Heath (Nature Reserve)
Harcamlow Way
Hertfordshire Way
Bogs Cottage
Patmore Hall
Bogs Wood
BARNCROFT
Itch La
High Hall
Harcamlow Way
Ypres
Mansfield Cottages
Clapgate
SIX COTTS
MILL LA
THE BOURNE
CM23
Albury CE Prim Sch
Parsonage Farm
PARSONAGE LA
Sewage Works
Cow Pasture
Salmon Mead Spring
The Common
Albury
Ninno Wood
Upwick Wood
Green Farm
Upwick Green
Hoy's Farm
Albury Lodge
Upwick Hall
Walnuttree Green
River Ash
SG11
Hertfordshire Way
Folly Gorse
Alburyend Wood
HIGHFIELD
WATTS CL
ALBURY RD
STANDON RD
Church End Farm
STABLE COTTS
Church End
CAPEL CT
Hadham Hall
HADHAM HALL
BAUD CT
Little Hadham
The Causeway
LLOYD TAYLOR CL
THE SMITHY
STORTFORD RD
Little Hadham Prim Sch
Little Hadham Place
CM23
Halfway House
Stone House Farm
MILFIELD LA
HADHAM RD
RIDGEWAY
A120
RED BRICK COTTS
PO
Green Street Farm
8
7
25
6
5
24
4
3
23
2
1
22
43
44
45

57

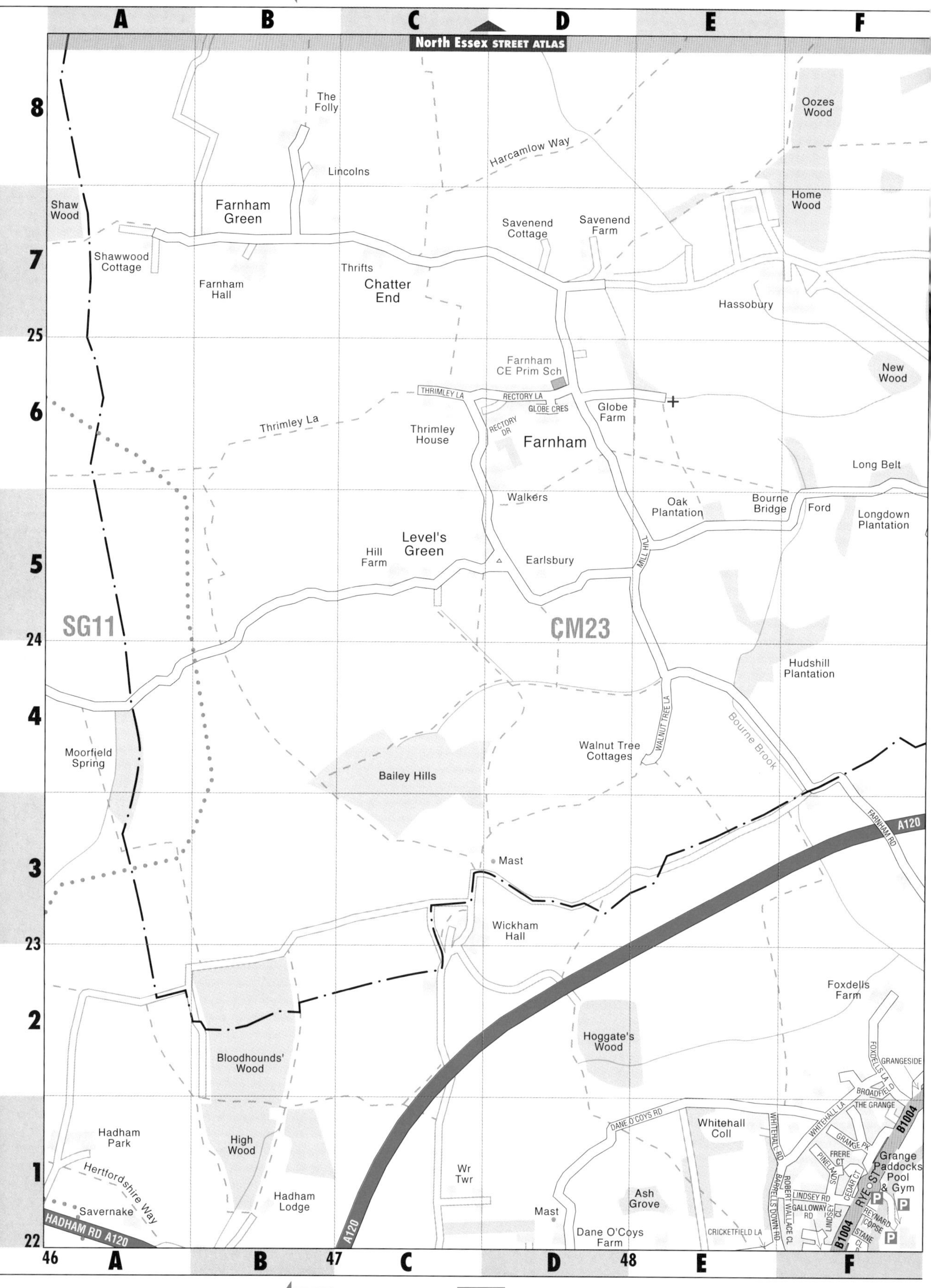
North Essex STREET ATLAS
A
B
C
D
E
F
8
7
6
5
4
3
2
1
25
24
23
22
46
47
48
The Folly
Lincolns
Harcamlow Way
Oozes Wood
Shaw Wood
Farnham Green
Home Wood
Savenend Cottage
Savenend Farm
Shawwood Cottage
Farnham Hall
Thrifts
Chatter End
Hassobury
Farnham CE Prim Sch
New Wood
THRIMLEY LA
RECTORY LA
GLOBE CRES
Globe Farm
RECTORY DR
Thrimley La
Thrimley House
Farnham
Long Belt
Walkers
Oak Plantation
Bourne Bridge
Ford
Longdown Plantation
Hill Farm
Level's Green
Earlsbury
MILL HILL
SG11
CM23
Hudshill Plantation
Bourne Brook
WALNUT TREE LA
Moorfield Spring
Walnut Tree Cottages
Bailey Hills
FARNHAM RD
A120
Mast
Wickham Hall
Foxdells Farm
Hoggate's Wood
Bloodhounds' Wood
FOXDELLS LA
GRANGESIDE
BROADFIELD
THE GRANGE
DANE O'COYS RD
Whitehall Coll
WHITEHALL RD
WHITEHALL LA
B1004
GRANGE PK
Hadham Park
High Wood
FRERE CT
PINELANDS
Grange Paddocks Pool & Gym
Hertfordshire Way
Wr Twr
Ash Grove
CEDAR CT
RYE ST
BARRELLS DOWN RD
ROBERT WALLACE CL
LINDSEY RD
GALLOWAY RD
LINDSEY CL
Hadham Lodge
REYNARD COPSE
Savernake
Mast
HADHAM RD A120
A120
Dane O'Coys Farm
CRICKETFIELD LA
STANE CL
P

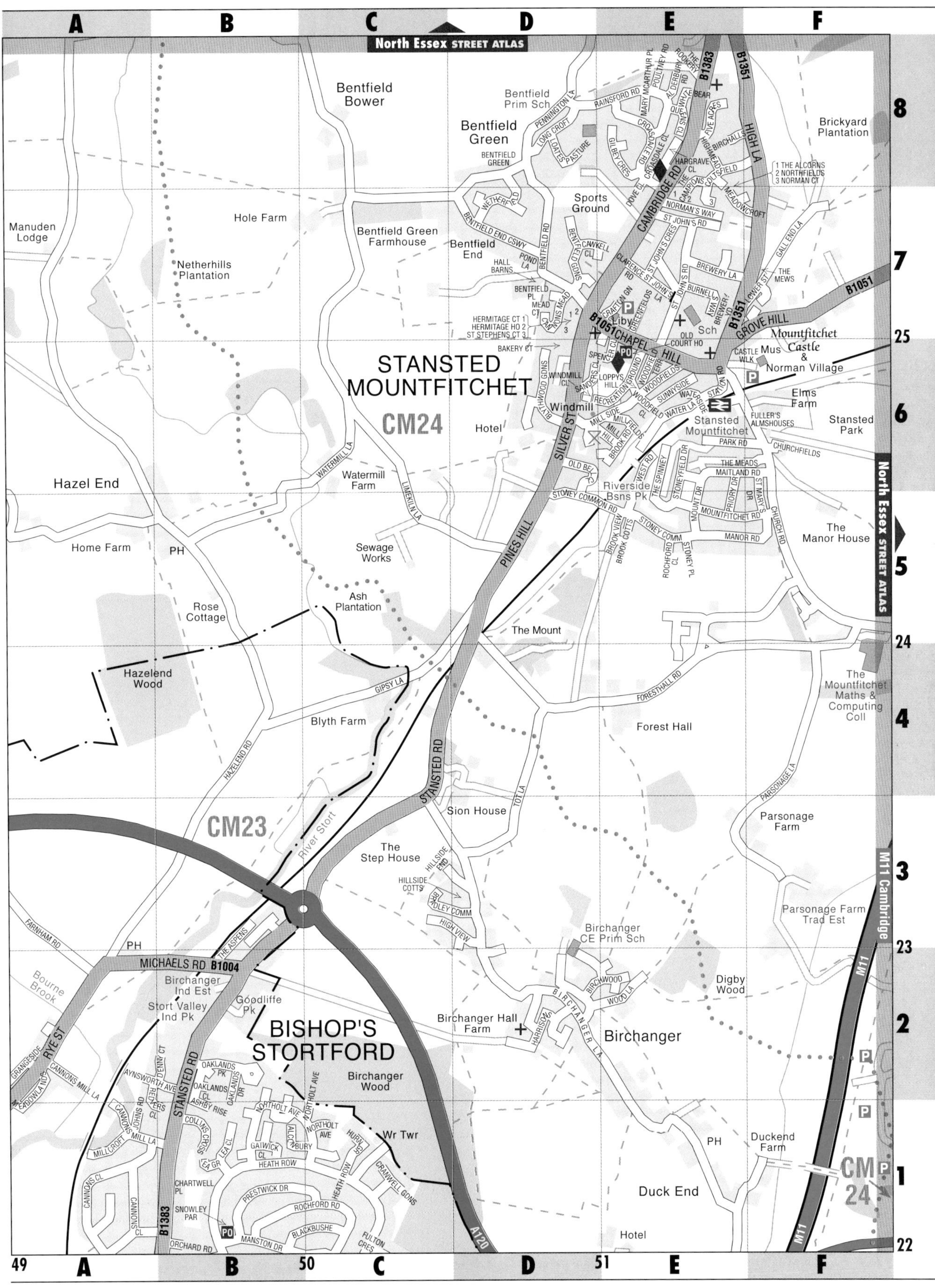
North Essex STREET ATLAS
A
B
C
D
E
F
8
7
25
6
5
24
4
3
23
2
1
22
49
50
51
Bentfield Bower
Bentfield Prim Sch
Bentfield Green
Brickyard Plantation
Manuden Lodge
Hole Farm
Bentfield Green Farmhouse
Bentfield End
Sports Ground
Netherhills Plantation
STANSTED MOUNTFITCHET
CM24
Hotel
Windmill
Mountfitchet Castle & Norman Village
Mus
Elms Farm
Stansted Park
Stansted Mountfitchet
Hazel End
Watermill Farm
Riverside Bsns Pk
The Manor House
Home Farm
PH
Sewage Works
Rose Cottage
Ash Plantation
The Mount
Hazelend Wood
Blyth Farm
Forest Hall
The Mountfitchet Maths & Computing Coll
CM23
Sion House
Parsonage Farm
The Step House
River Stort
Parsonage Farm Trad Est
Birchanger CE Prim Sch
Digby Wood
Birchanger Hall Farm
Birchanger
Birchanger Ind Est
Goodliffe Pk
Stort Valley Ind Pk
BISHOP'S STORTFORD
Birchanger Wood
Bourne Brook
Wr Twr
Duckend Farm
Duck End
Hotel
M11 Cambridge
B1383
B1351
B1051
B1004
A120
M11
SILVER ST
PINES HILL
STANSTED RD
CAMBRIDGE RD
HIGH LA
CHAPEL HILL
GROVE HILL
MICHAELS RD
HAZELEND RD
FORESTHALL RD
BIRCHANGER LA
GIPSY LA
WATERMILL LA
LIMEKILN LA
TOT LA
PARSONAGE LA
CHURCH RD
FARNHAM RD
RYE ST
CANNONS MILL LA
NORTHOLT AVE
HEATH ROW
PRESTWICK DR
ROCHFORD RD
BLACKBUSHE
MANSTON DR
ORCHARD RD
CRANWELL GDNS
FULTON CRES
1 THE ALCORNS
2 NORTHFIELDS
3 NORMAN CT
HERMITAGE CT 1
HERMITAGE HO 2
ST STEPHENS CT 3
BAKERY CT
CM 24
77

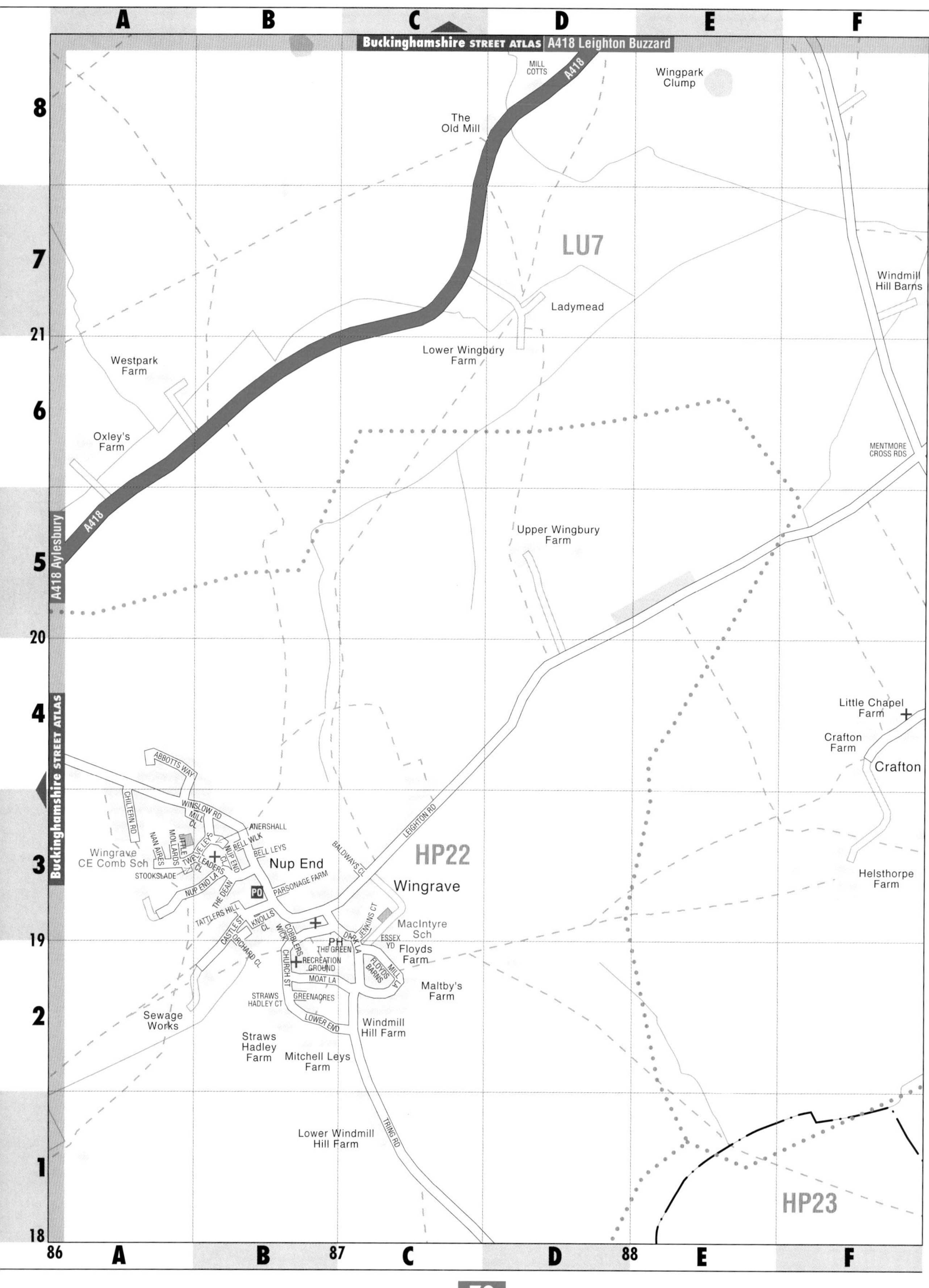
A
B
C
D
E
F
Buckinghamshire STREET ATLAS
A418 Leighton Buzzard
MILL COTTS
A418
Wingpark Clump
The Old Mill
LU7
Windmill Hill Barns
Ladymead
Westpark Farm
Lower Wingbury Farm
Oxley's Farm
MENTMORE CROSS RDS
A418
A418 Aylesbury
Upper Wingbury Farm
Little Chapel Farm
Crafton Farm
Crafton
ABBOTTS WAY
WINSLOW RD
CHILTERN RD
ANERSHALL
BELL WLK
BELL LEYS
LEIGHTON RD
BALDWAYS CL
HP22
Wingrave CE Comb Sch
Nup End
STOOKSLADE
NUP END LA
PO
PARSONAGE FARM
Wingrave
TATTLERS HILL
KNOLLS CL
JENKINS CT
MacIntyre Sch
ESSEX YD
Floyds Farm
Helsthorpe Farm
THE GREEN
RECREATION GROUND
MOAT LA
Maltby's Farm
STRAWS HADLEY CT
GREENACRES
LOWER END
Windmill Hill Farm
Sewage Works
Straws Hadley Farm
Mitchell Leys Farm
TRING RD
Lower Windmill Hill Farm
HP23
8
7
21
6
5
20
4
3
19
2
1
18
86
87
88
Buckinghamshire STREET ATLAS

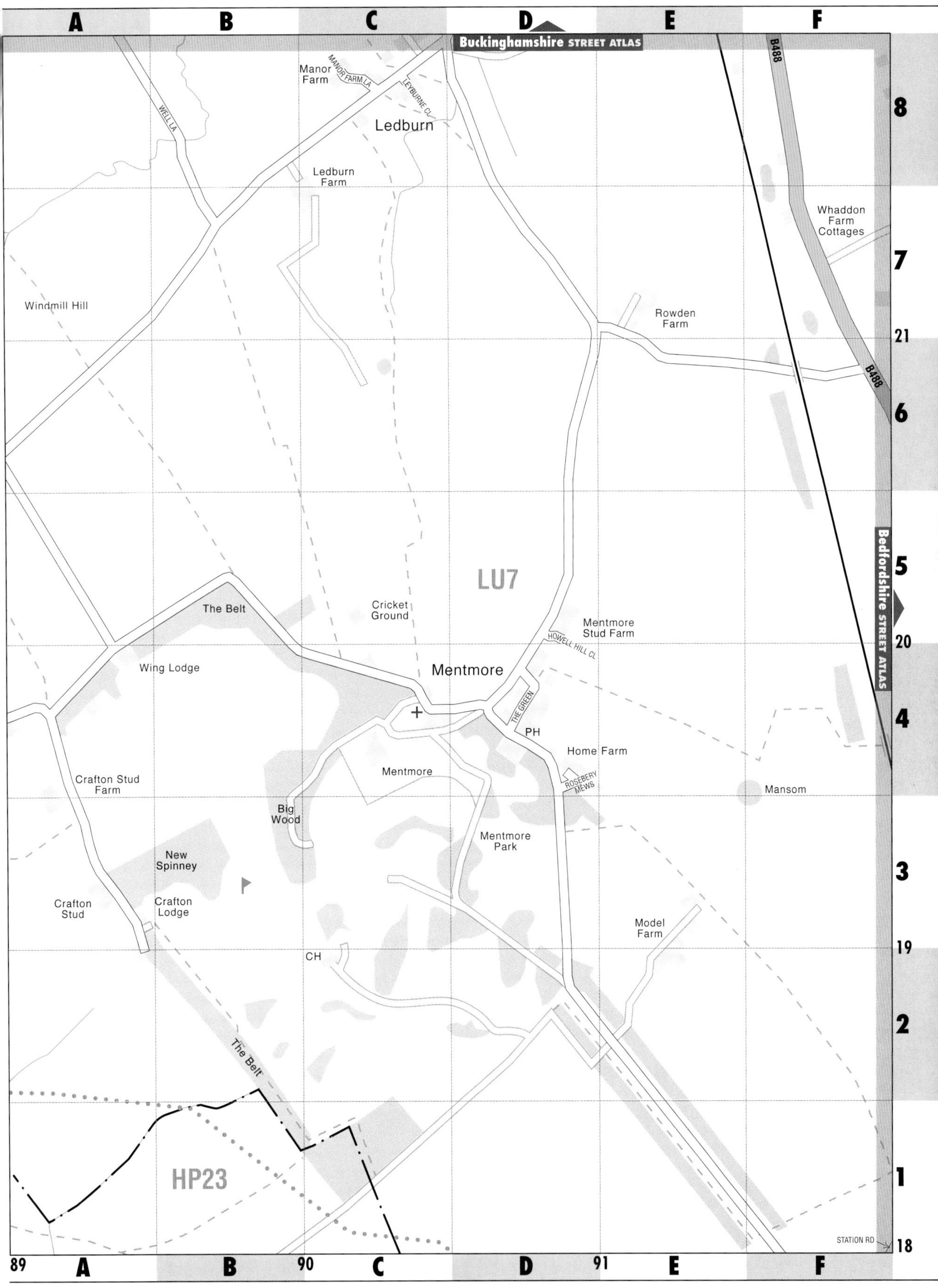
A
B
C
D
E
F
Buckinghamshire STREET ATLAS
B488
Manor Farm
MANOR FARM LA
LEYBURNE CL
WELL LA
Ledburn
Ledburn Farm
8
Whaddon Farm Cottages
7
Windmill Hill
Rowden Farm
21
B488
6
LU7
5
Bedfordshire STREET ATLAS
Cricket Ground
The Belt
Mentmore Stud Farm
HOWELL HILL CL
20
Wing Lodge
Mentmore
THE GREEN
4
PH
Home Farm
Mentmore
ROSEBERY MEWS
Crafton Stud Farm
Mansom
Big Wood
Mentmore Park
New Spinney
3
Crafton Stud
Crafton Lodge
Model Farm
19
CH
2
The Belt
HP23
1
STATION RD
18
89
A
B
90
C
D
91
E
F

44

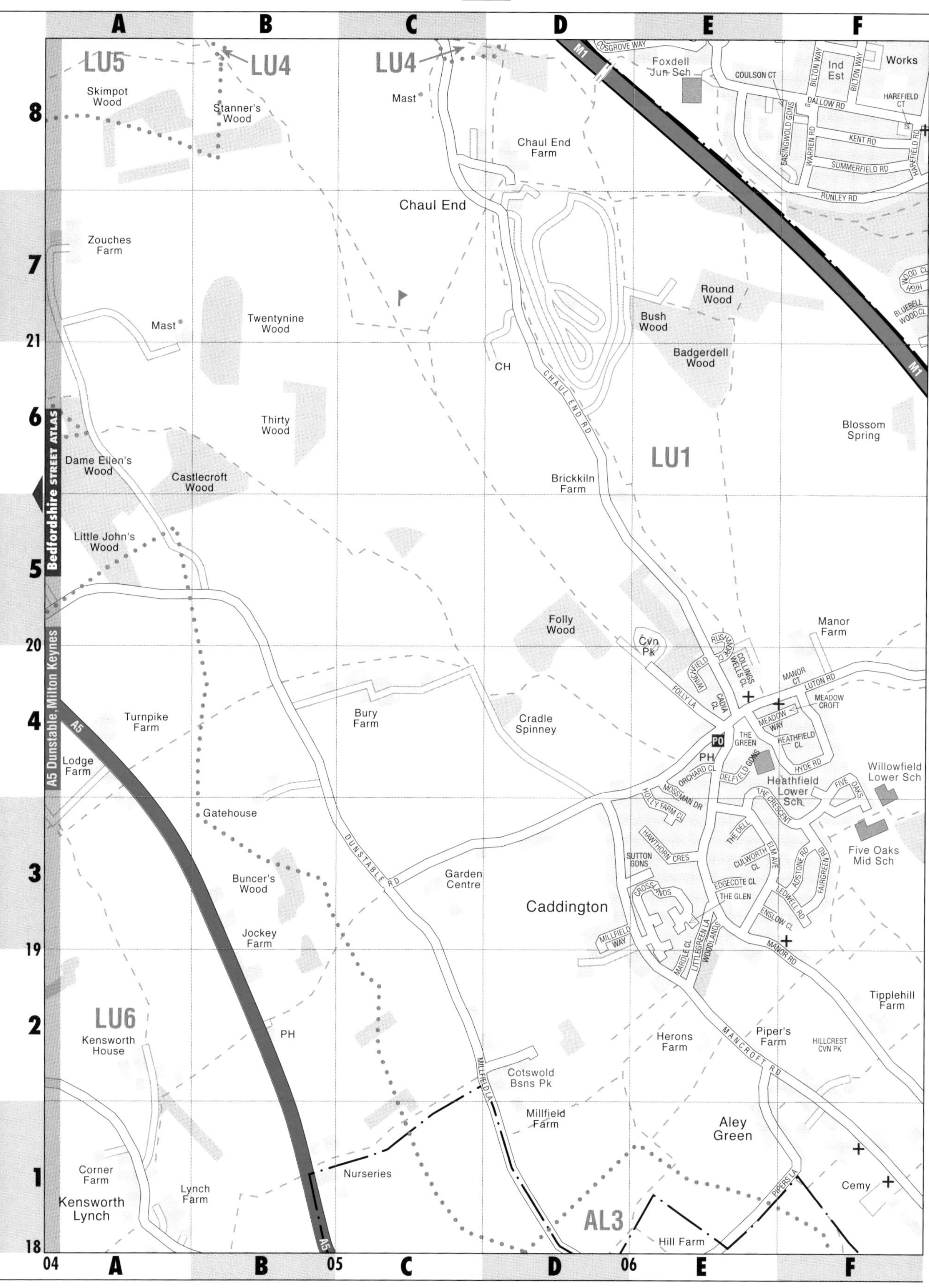

LU5
LU4
LU4
Skimpot Wood
Stanner's Wood
Mast
Chaul End Farm
Foxdell Jun Sch
Ind Est
Works
COULSON CT
BILTON WAY
DALLOW RD
HAREFIELD CT
KENT RD
SUMMERFIELD RD
RUNLEY RD
WARREN RD
EASINGWOLD GDNS
HAREFIELD RD
M1
Chaul End
Zouches Farm
Round Wood
Bush Wood
Twentynine Wood
Mast
Badgerdell Wood
CH
CHAUL END RD
BLUEBELL WOOD CL
Thirty Wood
Blossom Spring
Dame Ellen's Wood
Castlecroft Wood
LU1
Brickkiln Farm
Bedfordshire STREET ATLAS
Little John's Wood
Folly Wood
Cvn Pk
Manor Farm
A5 Dunstable, Milton Keynes
Turnpike Farm
Bury Farm
Cradle Spinney
FOLLY LA
CADIA CL
COLLINGS WELLS CL
MANOR CT
LUTON RD
MEADOW CROFT
MEADOW WAY
HEATHFIELD CL
THE GREEN
PO
PH
Lodge Farm
ORCHARD CL
DELFIELD GDNS
HYDE RD
Heathfield Lower Sch
Willowfield Lower Sch
FIVE OAKS
MOSSMAN DR
HOLLY FARM CL
THE CRESCENT
Gatehouse
HAWTHORN CRES
THE DELL
CULWORTH CL
ELM AVE
SUTTON GDNS
ADSTONE RD
FAIRGREEN RD
Five Oaks Mid Sch
DUNSTABLE RD
Garden Centre
Buncer's Wood
CROSSLANDS
EDGECOTE CL
THE GLEN
LEDWELL RD
Caddington
ENSLOW CL
Jockey Farm
MILLFIELD WAY
MARDLE CL
LITTLEGREEN LA
WOODLANDS
MANOR RD
LU6
Kensworth House
PH
Herons Farm
Piper's Farm
HILLCREST CVN PK
Tipplehill Farm
MANCROFT RD
MILLFIELD LA
Cotswold Bsns Pk
Millfield Farm
Aley Green
Corner Farm
Nurseries
Cemy
Kensworth Lynch
Lynch Farm
AL3
PIPERS LA
Hill Farm
A5
A
B
C
D
E
F
8
7
21
6
5
20
4
3
19
2
1
18
04
05
06

83

C8
1 NIGHTINGALE CT
2 BENTLEY CT
3 HAZELBURY CT
4 Bury Park Ind Est

D7
1 MERSEY PL
2 CHARLOTTES CT
3 ALMA LINK
4 ALDWYCK HO
5 DUNSTABLE PL
6 PEEL PL
7 STUART ST PAS
8 STUART PL
9 COOPERS MEWS
10 PRINCESS LODGE
11 FAITH HO
12 GROVE HO
13 MARLBOROUGH CT
14 CROWN CT

D8
1 THE BARLEYCORN
2 BROOK CT
3 DOWNTON CT
4 BEDFORD GDNS
5 THE MOUNT
6 VILLA CT
7 DEACONS CT
8 ST NINIAN'S CT
9 LANGHAM HO
10 COLLINGDON CT
11 CARDIGAN CT
12 CARDIGAN GDNS

E7
1 WILLIAMSON ST
2 BARBERS LA
3 WALLER STREET MALL
4 CHEAPSIDE SQ
5 SMITHS LANE MALL
6 SMITHS SQ

45

E7
7 THE GALLERY
8 MELSON SQ
9 WAYNES CT
10 AUCTION HOUSE CTYD
11 LAWRENCE HALL

64

E8
1 BUTTERWORTH PATH
2 BERKELEY PATH
3 WELBECK RD
4 ALBION CT
5 WARDEN CT
6 LIDDELL HALL

F8
1 High Town Ent Ctr
2 SOUTHLYNN HO
3 MOULTON CT
4 LINDEN CT
5 HYDE HO
6 The Abbeygate Bsns Ctr

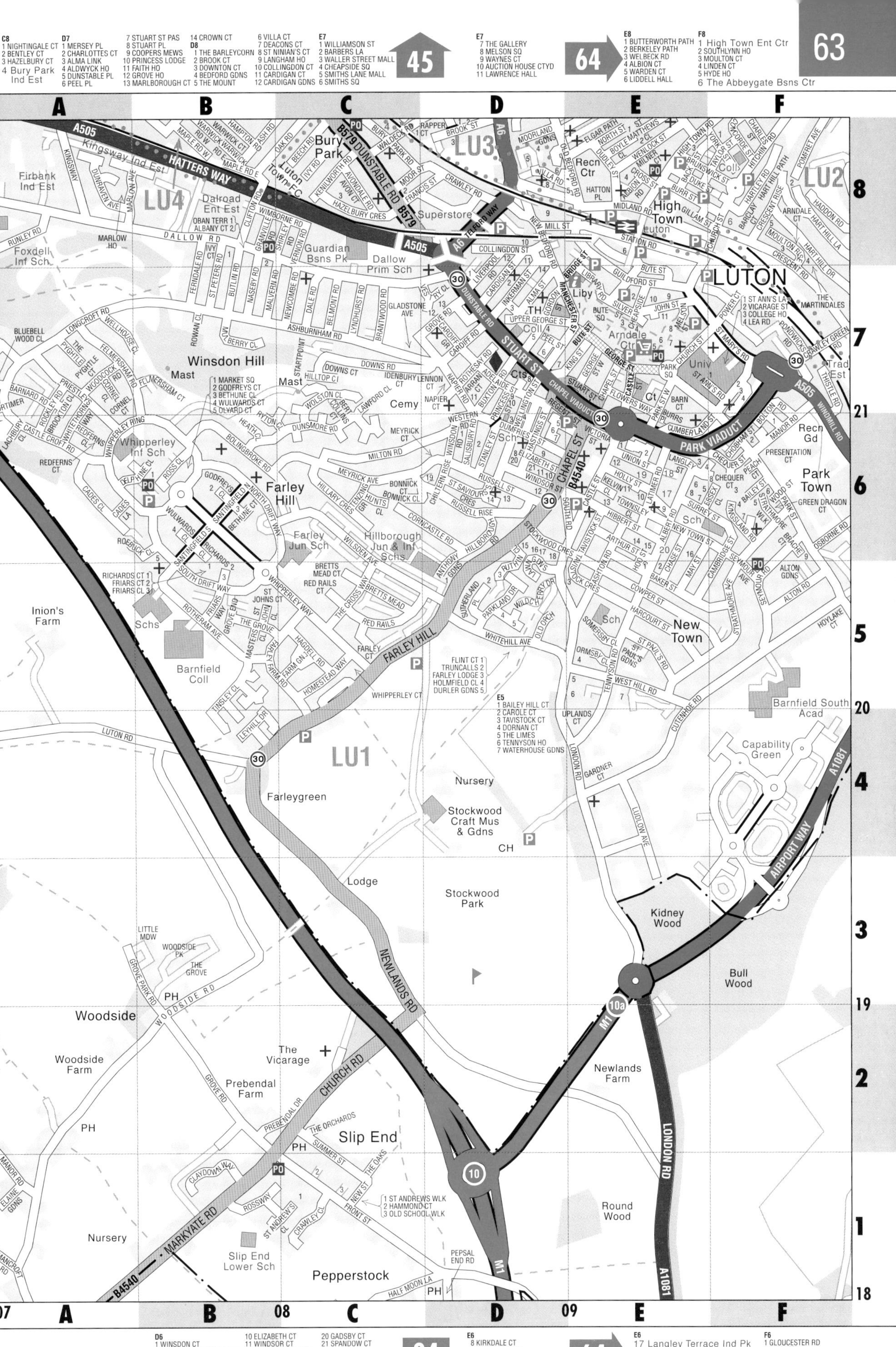

A
B
08
C
D
09
E
F

D6
1 WINSDON CT
2 STANLEY LIVINGSTONE CT
3 WELLINGTON CT
4 DUKES CT
5 NEW ST
6 SPRING PL
7 EBENEZER ST
8 WINDSOR WLK
9 DUMFRIES CT
10 ELIZABETH CT
11 WINDSOR CT
12 HOUGHTON MEWS
13 BLYTH PL
14 BRECON CL
15 HIGH POINT
16 ALPINE TERR
17 MAPLE CT
18 STOCKWOOD CT
19 THE CONIFERS
20 GADSBY CT
21 SPANDOW CT

E6
1 UNION CHAPEL HO
2 OXFORD RD
3 ROBERT ALLEN CT
4 QUEENS CL
5 CHOBHAM WLK
6 ROCHDALE CT
7 ESSEX CT

84

E6
8 KIRKDALE CT
9 NEW TOWN RD
10 JEPHSON CT
11 THE ACADEMY
12 TRIUMPH CT
13 HIBBERT STREET ALMSHOUSES
14 JAMES CT
15 TRACEY CT
16 CHESFORD CT

64

E6
17 Langley Terrace Ind Pk
18 Flowers Ind Est
19 Holly Street Trad Est
20 Telmere Ind Est

F6
1 GLOUCESTER RD
2 PARK TERR
3 DES FULLER CT
4 DORSET CT
5 HESWALL CT
6 PARKMEAD
7 KINGSLAND CT
8 CHOBHAM CT
9 OSBORNE CT

63
46

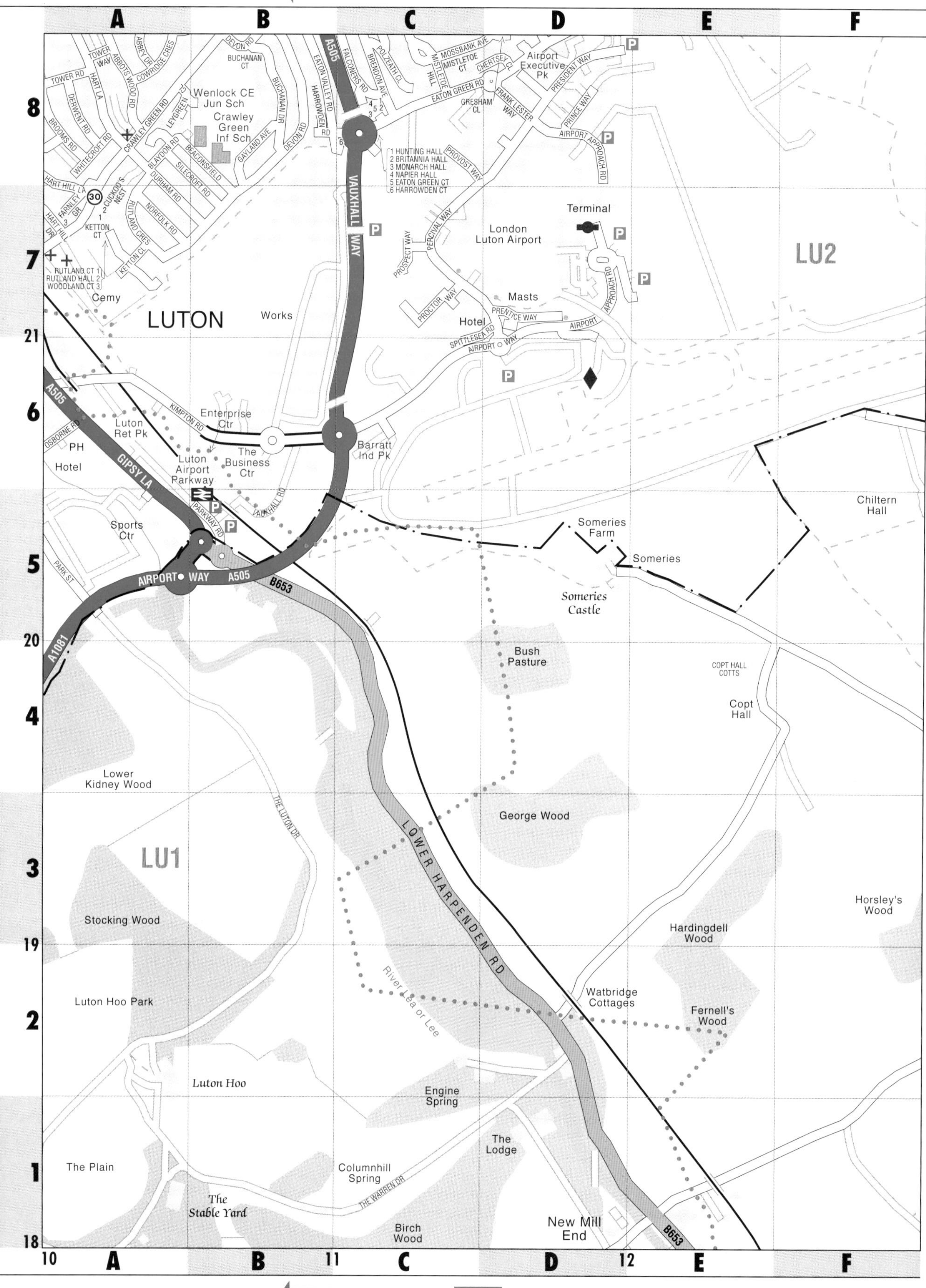
A
B
C
D
E
F
8
7
21
6
5
20
4
3
19
2
1
18
10
11
12
LUTON
LU2
LU1
Wenlock CE Jun Sch
Crawley Green Inf Sch
Airport Executive Pk
Terminal
London Luton Airport
Masts
Hotel
Works
Cemy
Enterprise Ctr
Luton Ret Pk
PH
Hotel
Luton Airport Parkway
The Business Ctr
Barratt Ind Pk
Sports Ctr
Someries Farm
Someries
Someries Castle
Chiltern Hall
Bush Pasture
COPT HALL COTTS
Copt Hall
Lower Kidney Wood
George Wood
Stocking Wood
Horsley's Wood
Hardingdell Wood
Watbridge Cottages
Fernell's Wood
Luton Hoo Park
Luton Hoo
Engine Spring
The Lodge
The Plain
Columnhill Spring
The Stable Yard
Birch Wood
New Mill End
River Lea or Lee
VAUXHALL WAY
AIRPORT WAY
GIPSY LA
LOWER HARPENDEN RD
THE LUTON DR
THE WARREN DR
A505
A1081
B653
1 HUNTING HALL
2 BRITANNIA HALL
3 MONARCH HALL
4 NAPIER HALL
5 EATON GREEN CT
6 HARROWDEN CT
RUTLAND CT 1
RUTLAND HALL 2
WOODLAND CT 3
EATON GREEN RD
MOSSBANK AVE
MISTLETOE CT
MISTLETOE HILL
CHERTSEY CL
GRESHAM CL
FRANK LESTER WAY
PRESIDENT WAY
PRINCE WAY
AIRPORT APPROACH RD
PROVOST WAY
PERCIVAL WAY
PROSPECT WAY
PROCTOR WAY
PRENTICE WAY
SPITTLESEA RD
KIMPTON RD
OSBORNE RD
PARK ST
PARKWAY RD
VAUXHALL RD
EATON VALLEY RD
HARROWDEN RD
FALCONERS RD
BRENDON AVE
POLZEATH CL
DEVON RD
BUCHANAN CT
BUCHANAN DR
GAYLAND AVE
BEACONSFIELD
SILECROFT RD
DURHAM RD
NORFOLK RD
RUTLAND CRES
KETTON CL
KETTON CT
BLAYDON RD
LEYGREEN CL
CRAWLEY GREEN RD
COWRIDGE CRES
ABBEY DR
ABBOTS WOOD RD
TOWER WAY
TOWER RD
HART LA
DERWENT RD
BROOMS RD
WHITECROFT RD
HART HILL LA
HART HILL DR
FARNLEY GR
CUCKOO'S NEST

63
85

47
66

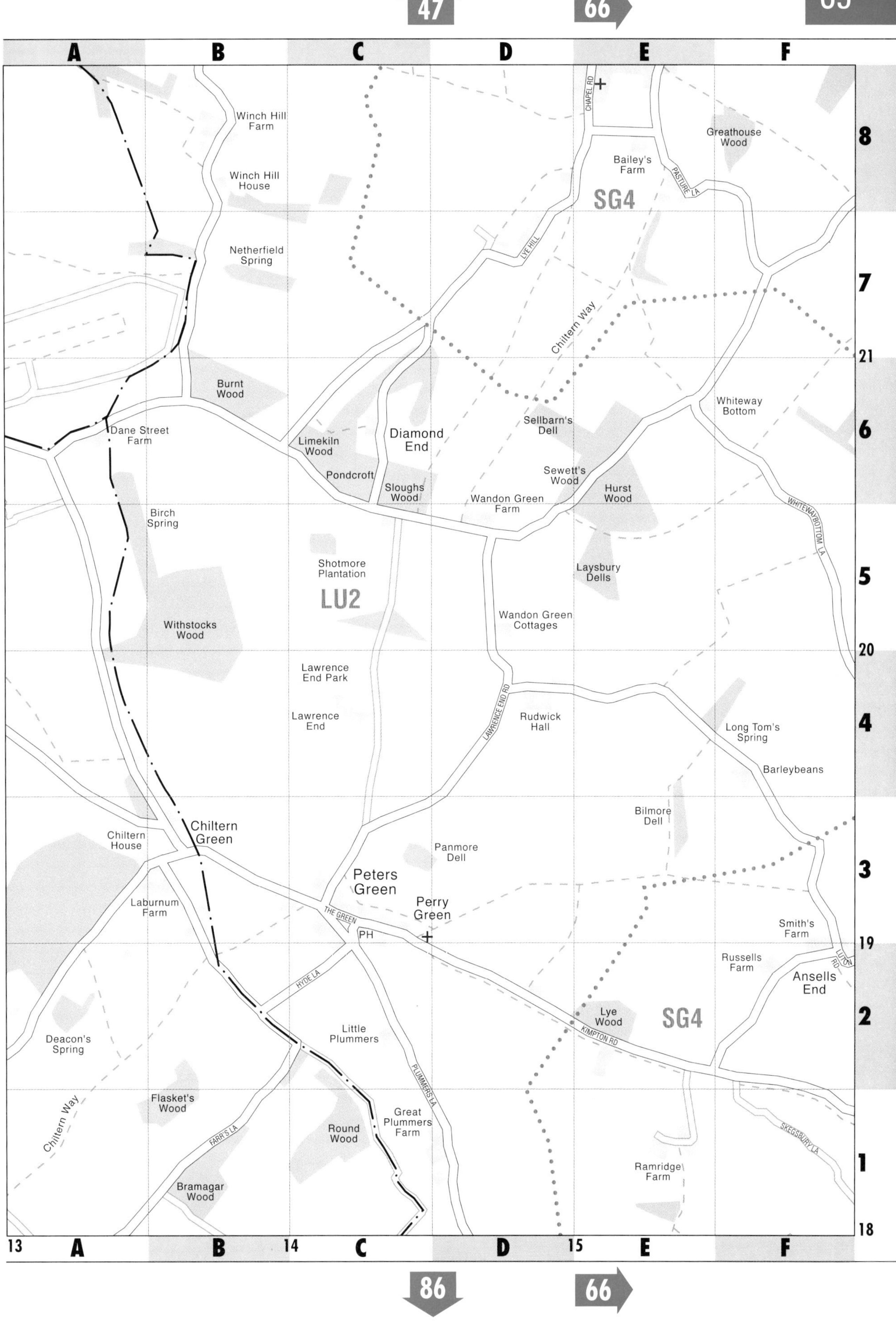
A
B
C
D
E
F
8
7
21
6
5
20
4
3
19
2
1
18
13
14
15
Winch Hill Farm
Winch Hill House
Netherfield Spring
Burnt Wood
Dane Street Farm
Birch Spring
Withstocks Wood
Chiltern House
Chiltern Green
Laburnum Farm
Deacon's Spring
Chiltern Way
Flasket's Wood
Bramagar Wood
FARR'S LA
Limekiln Wood
Pondcroft
Diamond End
Sloughs Wood
Shotmore Plantation
LU2
Lawrence End Park
Lawrence End
Peters Green
Perry Green
THE GREEN
PH
HYDE LA
Little Plummers
PLUMMERS LA
Round Wood
Great Plummers Farm
Panmore Dell
CHAPEL RD
Bailey's Farm
SG4
LYE HILL
Chiltern Way
Sellbarn's Dell
Sewett's Wood
Wandon Green Farm
Hurst Wood
Laysbury Dells
Wandon Green Cottages
LAWRENCE END RD
Rudwick Hall
Bilmore Dell
Lye Wood
KIMPTON RD
SG4
Ramridge Farm
Greathouse Wood
PASTURE LA
Whiteway Bottom
WHITEWAYBOTTOM LA
Long Tom's Spring
Barleybeans
Smith's Farm
Russells Farm
Ansells End
LUTON RD
SKEGSBURY LA

86
66

65
48

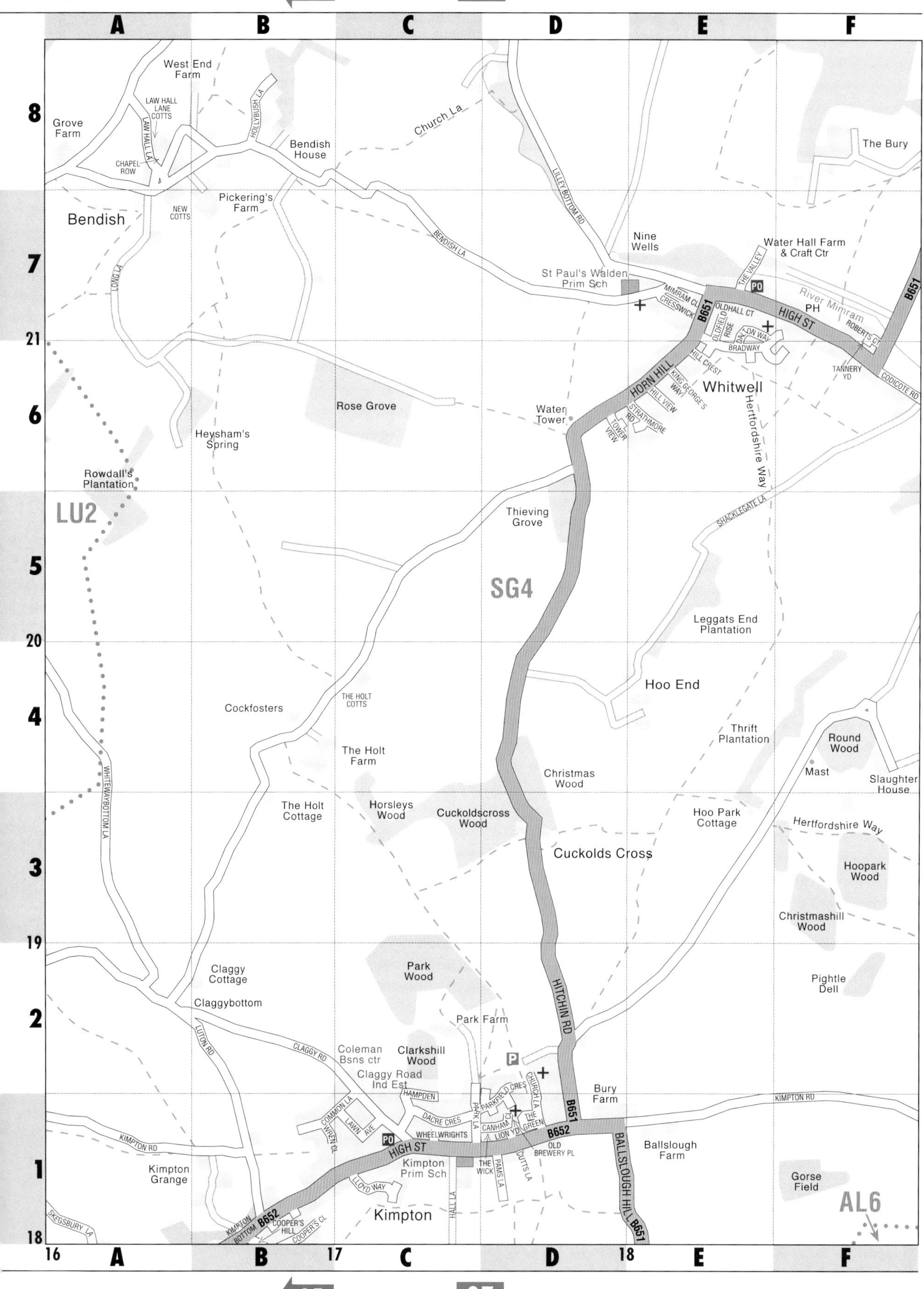
A
B
C
D
E
F
8
7
21
6
5
20
4
3
19
2
1
18
16
17
18
West End Farm
Grove Farm
LAW HALL LANE COTTS
LAW HALL LA
CHAPEL ROW
HOLLYBUSH LA
Bendish House
Church La
The Bury
Bendish
NEW COTTS
Pickering's Farm
BENDISH LA
LILLEY BOTTOM RD
Nine Wells
Water Hall Farm & Craft Ctr
THE VALLEY
PO
St Paul's Walden Prim Sch
MIMRAM CL
CRESSWICK
B651
OLDHALL CT
HIGH ST
PH
River Mimram
ROBERTS CT
LONG LA
OLDFIELD RISE
BRADWAY
HILL CREST
TANNERY YD
CODICOTE RD
HORN HILL
KING GEORGE'S WAY
HILL VIEW
Whitwell
Hertfordshire Way
Rose Grove
Water Tower
STRATHMORE RD
TOWER VIEW
Heysham's Spring
Rowdall's Plantation
LU2
Thieving Grove
SHACKLEGATE LA
SG4
Leggats End Plantation
Hoo End
THE HOLT COTTS
Cockfosters
Thrift Plantation
Round Wood
The Holt Farm
Christmas Wood
Mast
Slaughter House
WHITEWAYBOTTOM LA
The Holt Cottage
Horsleys Wood
Cuckoldscross Wood
Hoo Park Cottage
Hertfordshire Way
Cuckolds Cross
Hoopark Wood
Christmashill Wood
Claggy Cottage
Park Wood
HITCHIN RD
Pightle Dell
Claggybottom
Park Farm
LUTON RD
CLAGGY RD
Coleman Bsns ctr
Clarkshill Wood
P
Claggy Road Ind Est
HAMPDEN
PARKFIELD CRES
CHURCH LA
Bury Farm
KIMPTON RD
COMMON LA
LAWN AVE
DACRE CRES
PARK LA
CANHAM CL
THE GREEN
B651
WREN CL
WHEELWRIGHTS
LION YD
B652
KIMPTON RD
PO
HIGH ST
OLD BREWERY PL
BALLSLOUGH HILL
Ballslough Farm
Kimpton Grange
Kimpton Prim Sch
THE WICK
PAMS LA
CUTTS LA
Gorse Field
LLOYD WAY
AL6
HALL LA
Kimpton
SKEGSBURY LA
KIMPTON BOTTOM
B652
COOPER'S HILL
COOPER'S CL
B651

65
87

49
68

A B C D E F
8 7 21 6 5 20 4 3 19 2 1 18
19 20 21
Michael's Hope
B651
Reynolds Wood
Easthall Farm
EASTHALL COTTS
Peartree Wood
Roundwood Dell
Briary Spring
B656
LONDON RD
Claggdell Spring
The Fussens
Rusling End
Rusling End Farm
Graffridge Wood
NORTON STREET LA
Rose Farm
CODICOTE RD
Warren Wood
Rough Bushes
Holl Lays Wood
Winter Wood
Tower Lodges
Crouch Green
Hoo Cotts
Pannmill Cotts
Dumb Hills
SG4
THREE HOUSES LA
The Node
Troopers Stables
Hoo Farm
Three Houses Farm
Node Wood
Nursery
Lygraves Wood
The Cottage
DRIVER'S END LA
Chalkdale Wood
Hoo Park
River Mimram
Luckswarren Wood
Ealing Lodge
Bigg's Grove
Mansells Farm
MANSELLS LA
Rye-end Cotts
High Heath Farm
Rye-end Farm
Hertfordshire Way
Wr Twr
Sch
Coronation Plantation
The Grove
TOWER RD
BURY LA
CHURCH CL
Hogg Wood
Codicote Heath
THE ELMS
ST GILES RD
BENTICK WAY
THE CHESTNUTS
THE BURY
The Kennels
Kimpton Mill
GOMER CL
OLD SCHOOL CL
KIMPTON RD
Green La
Codicote
HILLSIDE
GRANGE RISE
LODGE FARM
HIGH ST
POND GDNS
THE PADDOCKS
PORTER'S MEWS
THE RIDGEWAY
VALLEY RD
Codicote Lodge
PH
THE CLOSE
HEATH HILL
HEATH LA
GLENBOURNE
PO
HEATH LA
THE GREEN
ST ALBANS RD
BAKER'S LA
HILL RD
MEADOW WAY
FARRIERS
OLD CHAPEL MEWS
NEW TOWN
MAYFLOWER CL
THE ORCHARD
TITHE CL
DOLLIMORE CL
AL6
TANYARD LA
Codicote CE Prim Sch
B656

67
50

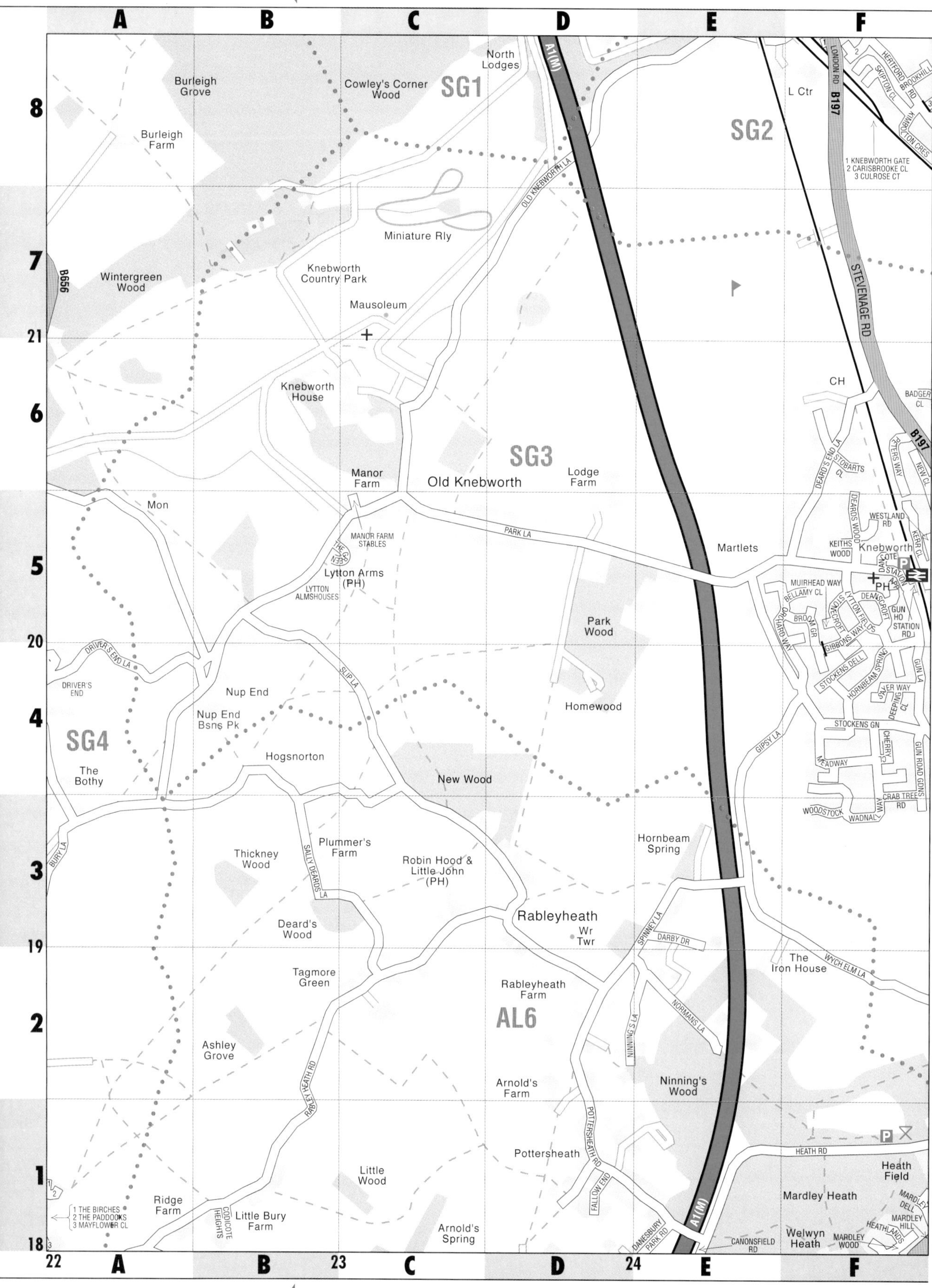
A
B
C
D
E
F
8
7
21
6
5
20
4
3
19
2
1
18
22
23
24
Burleigh Grove
Cowley's Corner Wood
North Lodges
SG1
SG2
L Ctr
Burleigh Farm
Miniature Rly
Knebworth Country Park
Wintergreen Wood
Mausoleum
Knebworth House
SG3
Manor Farm
Old Knebworth
Lodge Farm
Mon
PARK LA
MANOR FARM STABLES
Lytton Arms (PH)
LYTTON ALMSHOUSES
Martlets
Knebworth
Park Wood
DRIVER'S END LA
DRIVER'S END
Nup End
Nup End Bsns Pk
SLIP LA
Homewood
SG4
The Bothy
Hogsnorton
New Wood
GIPSY LA
Thickney Wood
Plummer's Farm
Robin Hood & Little John (PH)
Hornbeam Spring
SALLY DEARDS LA
Rableyheath
Wr Twr
Deard's Wood
SPINNEY LA
DARBY DR
The Iron House
WYCH ELM LA
Tagmore Green
Rableyheath Farm
AL6
NORMANS LA
NINNING'S LA
Ashley Grove
Arnold's Farm
Ninning's Wood
RABLEY HEATH RD
POTTERSHEATH RD
Pottersheath
HEATH RD
Heath Field
Little Wood
Mardley Heath
Ridge Farm
Little Bury Farm
CODICOTE HEIGHTS
FALLOW END
Arnold's Spring
DANESBURY PARK RD
A1(M)
CANONSFIELD RD
Welwyn Heath
MARDLEY WOOD
1 THE BIRCHES
2 THE PADDOCKS
3 MAYFLOWER CL
1 KNEBWORTH GATE
2 CARISBROOKE CL
3 CULROSE CT
B197
B656
LONDON RD
STEVENAGE RD
OLD KNEBWORTH LA
CH
BADGER CL
STOBARTS CL
DEARD'S END LA
DEARDS WOOD
WESTLAND RD
KEITHS WOOD
MUIRHEAD WAY
BELLAMY CL
ORCHARD WAY
STATION RD
GUN LA
GIBBONS WAY
STOCKENS DELL
HORNBEAM SPRING
STOCKENS GN
MEADWAY
CHERRY CL
GUN ROAD GDNS
CRAB TREE RD
WOODSTOCK
WADNAL WAY
BURY LA
HERTFORD RD
SKIPTON CL
BROOKHILL
KIMBOLTON CRES
NEW CL
KERR CL
MARDLEY DELL
MARDLEY HILL
HEATHLANDS
PH

67
89

51
70

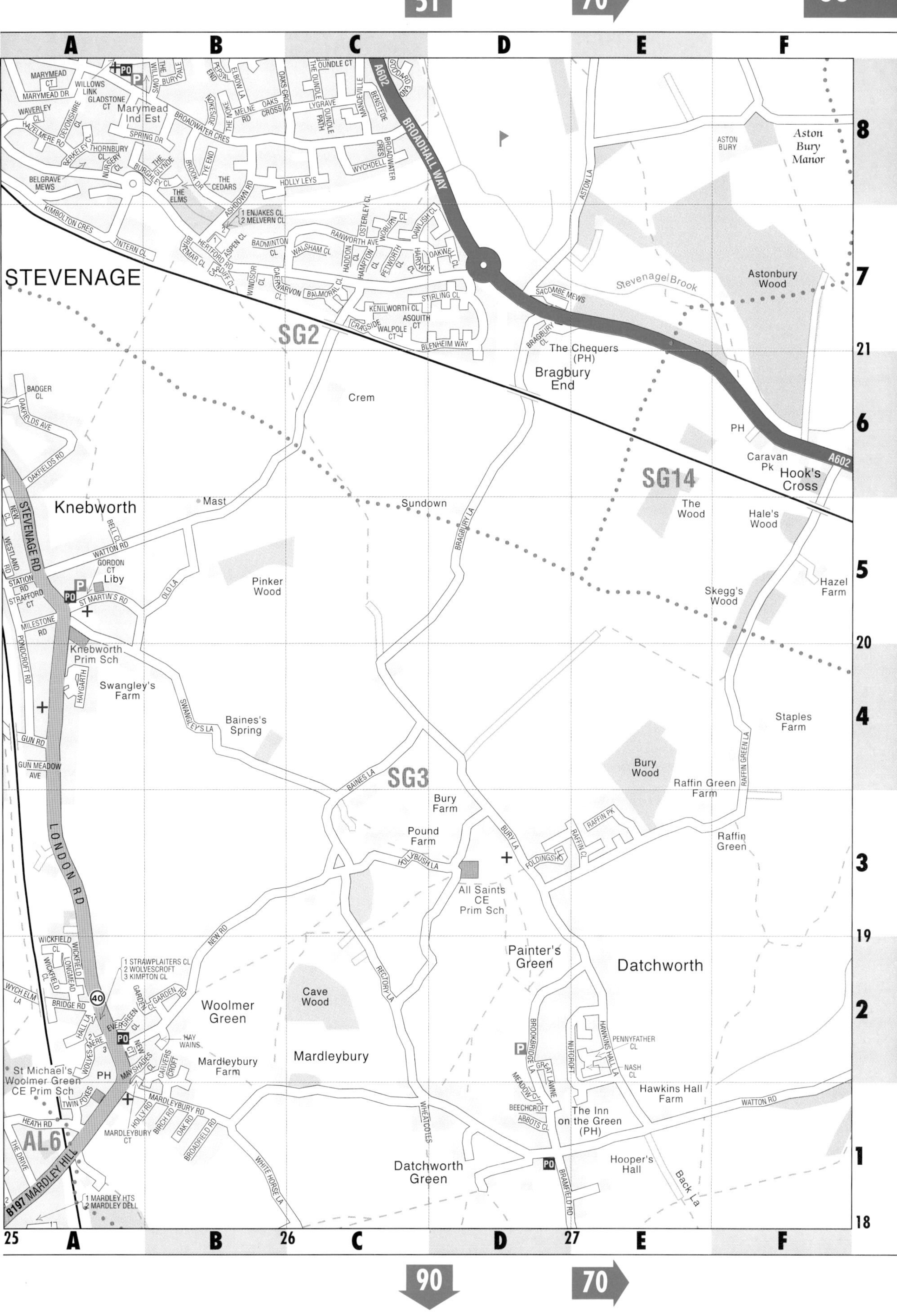
STEVENAGE
Knebworth
Marymead Ind Est
SG2
SG14
SG3
Crem
Bragbury End
The Chequers (PH)
Stevenage Brook
Astonbury Wood
Aston Bury Manor
ASTON BURY
BROADHALL WAY
A602
Hook's Cross
Caravan Pk
PH
The Wood
Hale's Wood
Sundown
Mast
Pinker Wood
Liby
Skegg's Wood
Hazel Farm
Knebworth Prim Sch
Swangley's Farm
Baines's Spring
Staples Farm
Bury Wood
Raffin Green Farm
Raffin Green
Bury Farm
Pound Farm
All Saints CE Prim Sch
Painter's Green
Datchworth
Woolmer Green
Cave Wood
Mardleybury
Mardleybury Farm
St Michael's Woolmer Green CE Prim Sch
Hawkins Hall Farm
The Inn on the Green (PH)
Hooper's Hall
Datchworth Green
AL6
B197 MARDLEY HILL
LONDON RD
STEVENAGE RD
WATTON RD
BRAGBURY LA
BAINES LA
BURY LA
HOLLYBUSH LA
RECTORY LA
NEW RD
WHITE HORSE LA
WHEATCOTES
BRAMFIELD RD
Back La
RAFFIN GREEN LA
SWANGLEY'S LA
ASTON LA

90
70

69
52

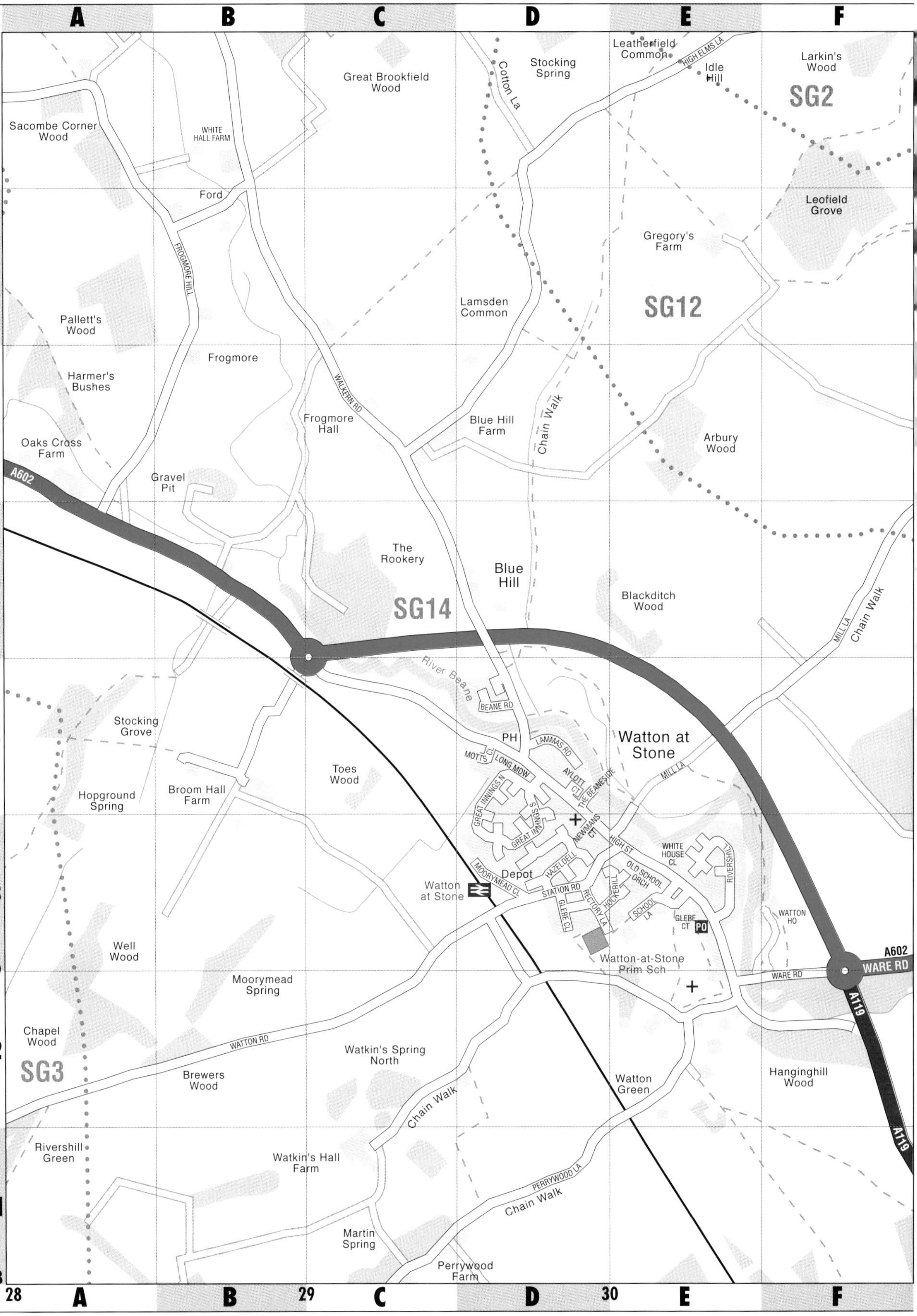

A B C D E F

8 7 21 6 5 20 4 3 19 2 1 18

Great Brookfield Wood
Stocking Spring
Leatherfield Common
High Elms La
Idle Hill
Larkin's Wood
SG2
Cotton La
Sacombe Corner Wood
White Hall Farm
Ford
Frogmore Hill
Leofield Grove
Gregory's Farm
SG12
Lamsden Common
Pallett's Wood
Frogmore
Harmer's Bushes
Walkern Rd
Frogmore Hall
Blue Hill Farm
Chain Walk
Arbury Wood
Oaks Cross Farm
A602
Gravel Pit
The Rookery
Blue Hill
Blackditch Wood
SG14
Mill La
Chain Walk
River Beane
Beane Rd
Stocking Grove
PH
Lammas Rd
Watton at Stone
Motts Cl
Long Mdw
Aylott Ct
The Beaneside
Mill La
Toes Wood
Great Innings N
Great Innings S
Newmans Ct
Hopground Spring
Broom Hall Farm
High St
White House Cl
Rivershill
Hazeldell
Old School Orch
Depot
Moorymead Cl
Station Rd
Watton at Stone
Rectory La
Hockerill
School La
Glebe Cl
Glebe Ct
PO
Watton Ho
Well Wood
A602
Watton-at-Stone Prim Sch
Ware Rd
Ware Rd
Moorymead Spring
A119
Chapel Wood
Watton Rd
Watkin's Spring North
SG3
Brewers Wood
Watton Green
Hanginghill Wood
Chain Walk
A119
Rivershill Green
Watkin's Hall Farm
Perrywood La
Chain Walk
Martin Spring
Perrywood Farm

28 A B 29 C D 30 E F

69
91

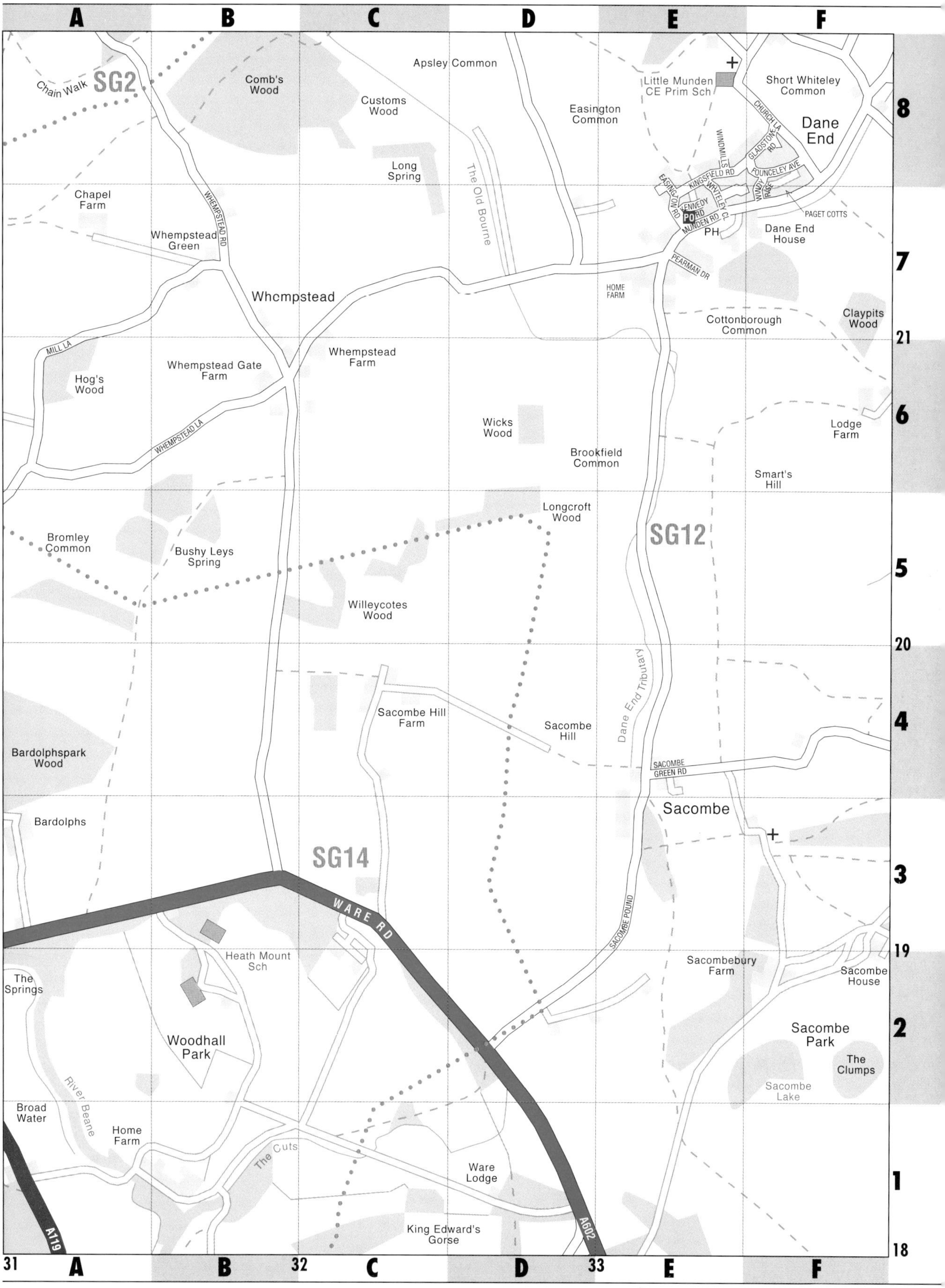

A B C D E F

8
7
21
6
5
20
4
3
19
2
1
18

31 32 33

SG2
Chain Walk
Comb's Wood
Customs Wood
Apsley Common
Long Spring
The Old Bourne
Easington Common
Little Munden CE Prim Sch
Short Whiteley Common
Dane End
CHURCH LA
GLADSTONE RD
WINDMILLS
KINGSFIELD RD
POUNCELEY AVE
WHITELEY CL
WINDY RISE
EASINGTON RD
KENNEDY RD
PO
MUNDEN RD
PH
PAGET COTTS
Dane End House
PEARMAN DR
Chapel Farm
WHEMPSTEAD RD
Whempstead Green
Whempstead
HOME FARM
Cottonborough Common
Claypits Wood
MILL LA
Hog's Wood
Whempstead Gate Farm
Whempstead Farm
WHEMPSTEAD LA
Wicks Wood
Brookfield Common
Lodge Farm
Smart's Hill
Longcroft Wood
SG12
Bromley Common
Bushy Leys Spring
Willeycotes Wood
Dane End Tributary
Sacombe Hill Farm
Sacombe Hill
Bardolphspark Wood
SACOMBE GREEN RD
Sacombe
Bardolphs
SG14
WARE RD
SACOMBE POUND
Heath Mount Sch
The Springs
Sacombebury Farm
Sacombe House
Woodhall Park
Sacombe Park
The Clumps
Sacombe Lake
River Beane
Broad Water
Home Farm
The Cuts
Ware Lodge
King Edward's Gorse
A119
A602

71
54

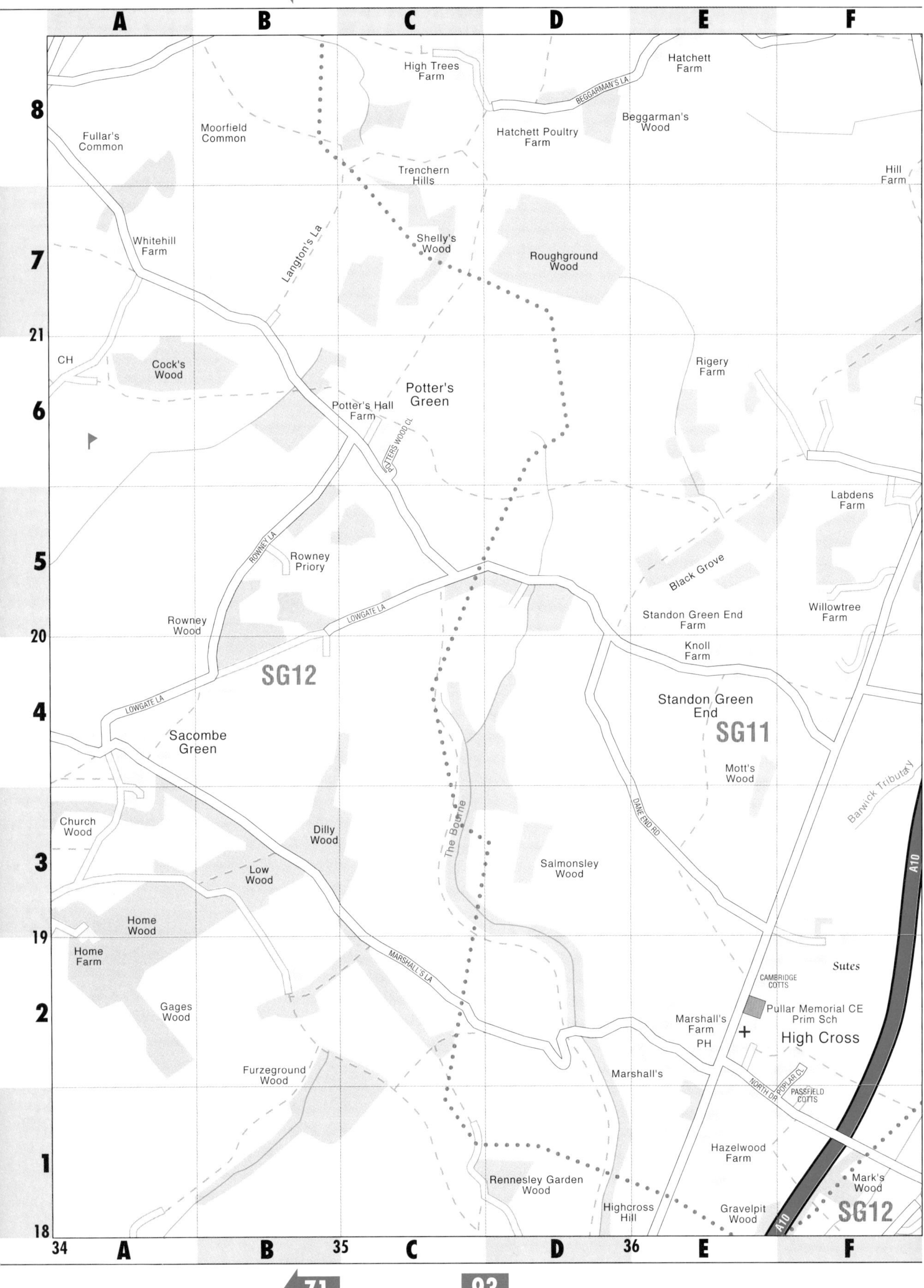
A
B
C
D
E
F
8
7
21
6
5
20
4
3
19
2
1
18
34
35
36
High Trees Farm
Hatchett Farm
BEGGARMAN'S LA
Beggarman's Wood
Fullar's Common
Moorfield Common
Hatchett Poultry Farm
Trenchern Hills
Hill Farm
Whitehill Farm
Langton's La
Shelly's Wood
Roughground Wood
CH
Cock's Wood
Rigery Farm
Potter's Green
Potter's Hall Farm
POTTERS WOOD CL
Labdens Farm
ROWNEY LA
Rowney Priory
Black Grove
Willowtree Farm
Rowney Wood
LOWGATE LA
Standon Green End Farm
Knoll Farm
SG12
LOWGATE LA
Standon Green End
SG11
Sacombe Green
Mott's Wood
Barwick Tributary
Church Wood
Dilly Wood
The Bourne
DANE END RD
A10
Low Wood
Salmonsley Wood
Home Wood
Home Farm
MARSHALL'S LA
Sutes
CAMBRIDGE COTTS
Pullar Memorial CE Prim Sch
Gages Wood
Marshall's Farm
High Cross
PH
Furzeground Wood
Marshall's
NORTH DR
POPLAR CL
PASSFIELD COTTS
Hazelwood Farm
Rennesley Garden Wood
Mark's Wood
Highcross Hill
Gravelpit Wood
A10
SG12

71
93

55
74

A
B
C
D
E
F
FARM LA
Sch
GARDEN COTTS
Ryders Grove
A10
Kitchencroft Wood
Sewage Works
New Plantation
Nurseries
WELLINGTON COTTS
The Lordship
RIGERY LA
Dowsett's Farm
Harcamlow Way
Fisher's Farm
WEST VIEW
PH
Colliers End
PARKINS CL
Plashes Wood
Ford
Latchford Farm
Latchford
Plashes Farm
Hangingwood Plantation
SG11
ARCHES HALL COTTS
Arches Hall
FB
River Rib
Hanging Wood
Ford
Barwick Tributary
Blackey Mead Wood
Badger's Eye Plantation
Wellington House
Cook's Wood
BARWICK LA
ASHLEIGH CVN PK
Denvers Yd
Biggin's Wood
Barwick
Furzeground Wood
GORE LA
Sutes Wood
Round Wood
Heathfield Wood
Biggin's Farm
Barwick Ford
Great Barwick
Ash Plantation
Tyler's Hill
Little Barwick Farm
New Plantation
SG10
Gutteridge Lye
Great Southey Wood
Harcamlow Way
Round Wood
Sawtrees Wood
SG12
Aldeck Spring
Steere Wood
Rush Green
8
7
21
6
5
20
4
3
19
2
1
18
37
38
39

94
74

73
56

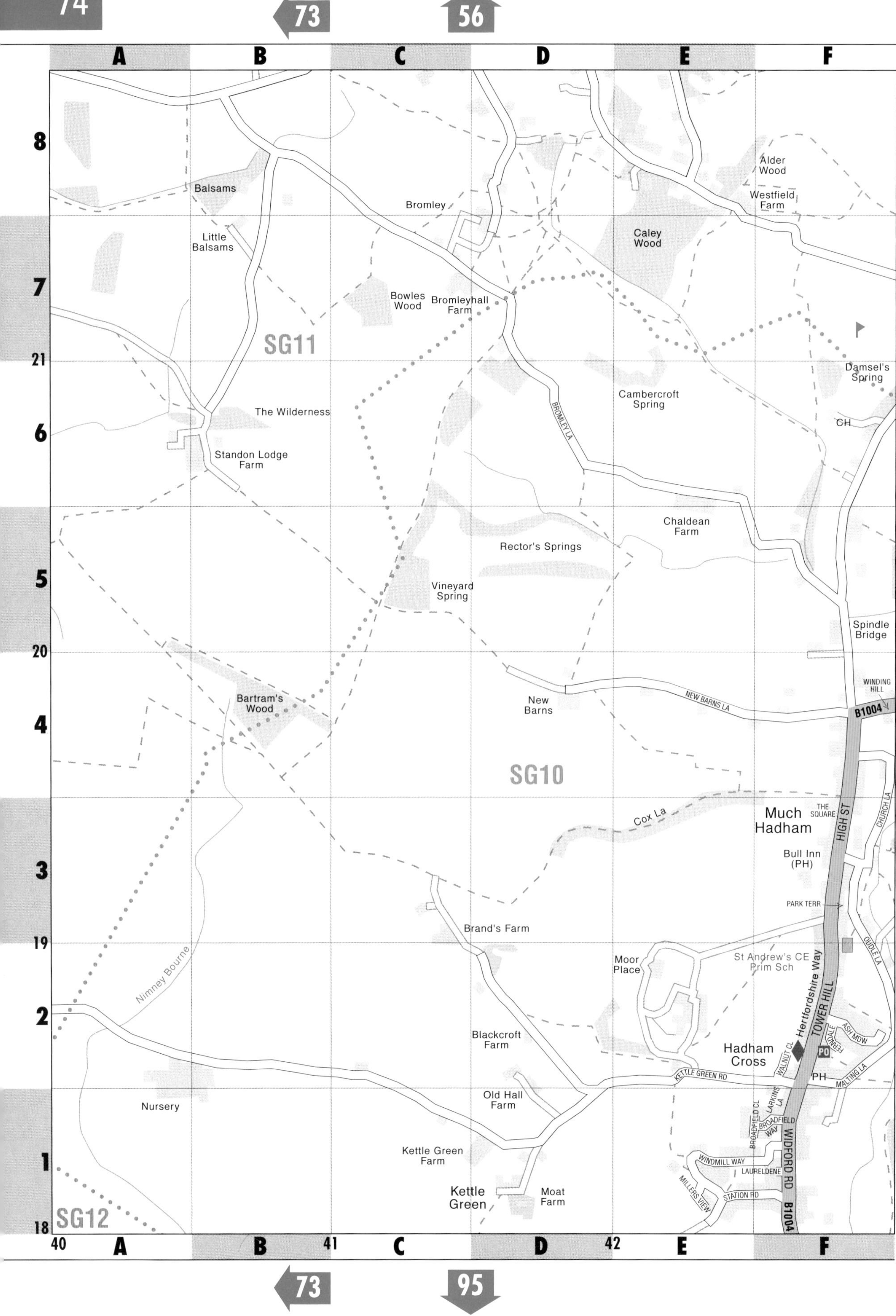
A
B
C
D
E
F
8
7
21
6
5
20
4
3
19
2
1
18
40
41
42
Balsams
Little Balsams
Bromley
Alder Wood
Westfield Farm
Caley Wood
Bowles Wood
Bromleyhall Farm
SG11
Damsel's Spring
The Wilderness
Cambercroft Spring
BROMLEY LA
CH
Standon Lodge Farm
Chaldean Farm
Rector's Springs
Vineyard Spring
Spindle Bridge
WINDING HILL
Bartram's Wood
New Barns
NEW BARNS LA
B1004
SG10
Cox La
Much Hadham
THE SQUARE
HIGH ST
CHURCH LA
Bull Inn (PH)
PARK TERR
Brand's Farm
Moor Place
St Andrew's CE Prim Sch
Hertfordshire Way
TOWER HILL
OUDLE LA
Nimney Bourne
ASH MDW
FERNDALE
Blackcroft Farm
Hadham Cross
WALNUT CL
PO
PH
MALTING LA
KETTLE GREEN RD
Nursery
Old Hall Farm
LARKINS LA
BROADFIELD CL
BROADFIELD WAY
WIDFORD RD
Kettle Green Farm
WINDMILL WAY
LAURELDENE
MILLERS VIEW
STATION RD
Kettle Green
Moat Farm
SG12

73
95

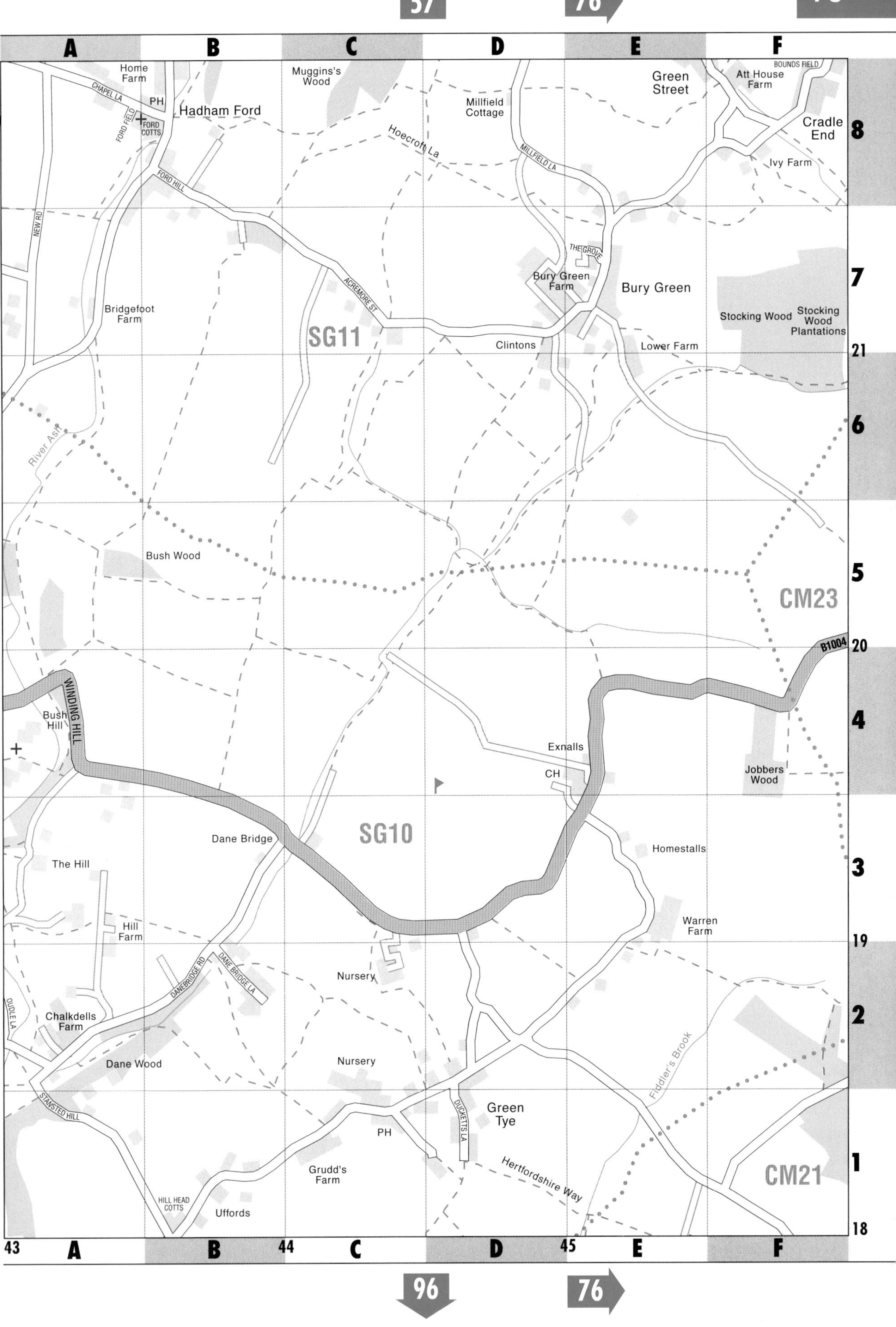
57
76
A
B
C
D
E
F
Home Farm
CHAPEL LA
PH
FORD FIELD
FORD COTTS
Hadham Ford
Muggin's's Wood
Millfield Cottage
Green Street
Att House Farm
BOUNDS FIELD
Cradle End
Ivy Farm
Hoecroft La
MILLFIELD LA
FORD HILL
NEW RD
THE GROVE
Bury Green Farm
Bury Green
ACREMORE ST
Bridgefoot Farm
SG11
Clintons
Lower Farm
Stocking Wood
Stocking Wood Plantations
River Ash
Bush Wood
CM23
B1004
WINDING HILL
Bush Hill
Exnalls
CH
Jobbers Wood
SG10
Dane Bridge
Homestalls
The Hill
Hill Farm
Warren Farm
DANEBRIDGE RD
DANE BRIDGE LA
Nursery
OUDLE LA
Chalkdells Farm
Nursery
Fiddler's Brook
Dane Wood
STANSTED HILL
Green Tye
DUCKETTS LA
PH
Hertfordshire Way
Grudd's Farm
CM21
HILL HEAD COTTS
Uffords
8
7
21
6
5
20
4
3
19
2
1
18
43
44
45
96
76

E5
1 BENHOOKS PL
2 MERRILL PL
3 BRITANNIA PL
4 MARGRAVE GDNS
5 OSBOURNE GDNS
6 SANDRINGHAM GDNS

F6
1 South St Commercial Ctr
2 SWAN CT
3 CHAPEL ROW
4 TUCKER'S ROW
5 MIDDLE ROW
6 ROYAL OAK GDNS

75

F6
7 APTON FIELDS
8 BARTHOLOMEW RD
9 STACEY CT
10 DUCKETTS WHARF
11 CYGNET CT
12 WHARF RD

58

F6
13 BRIDGEFORD HO
14 BOWLING CL
15 SANDPIPER CT
16 STARLING CT
17 ROBIN JEFFREY CT

F7
1 KING STREET MEWS
2 BASBOW LA
3 SWORDERS YD
4 NORTH ST
5 BARRETT LA
6 MARKET SQ
7 MARKET ST
8 PALMERS LA
9 DEVOILS LA
10 Jackson Sq
11 THE DELLS
12 MASTERMAN WHARF
13 DORSET HO
14 OAKTREE CL
15 NAILS LA
16 RIVERSIDE WLK
17 PORTLAND PL
18 VICARAGE CL
19 GROVE PL
20 SHERWOOD CT
21 CARELESS CT
22 PARK VIEW
23 NAVIGATION HO
24 JACKSON WHARF

F8
1 GALLOWAY CL
2 SQUIRRELS CL
3 BROOKHOUSE PL
4 ALPHA PL
5 NORTH TERR
6 THE CHANTRY
7 CONIFER CT
8 FLORENCE WLK
9 WATSONS YD

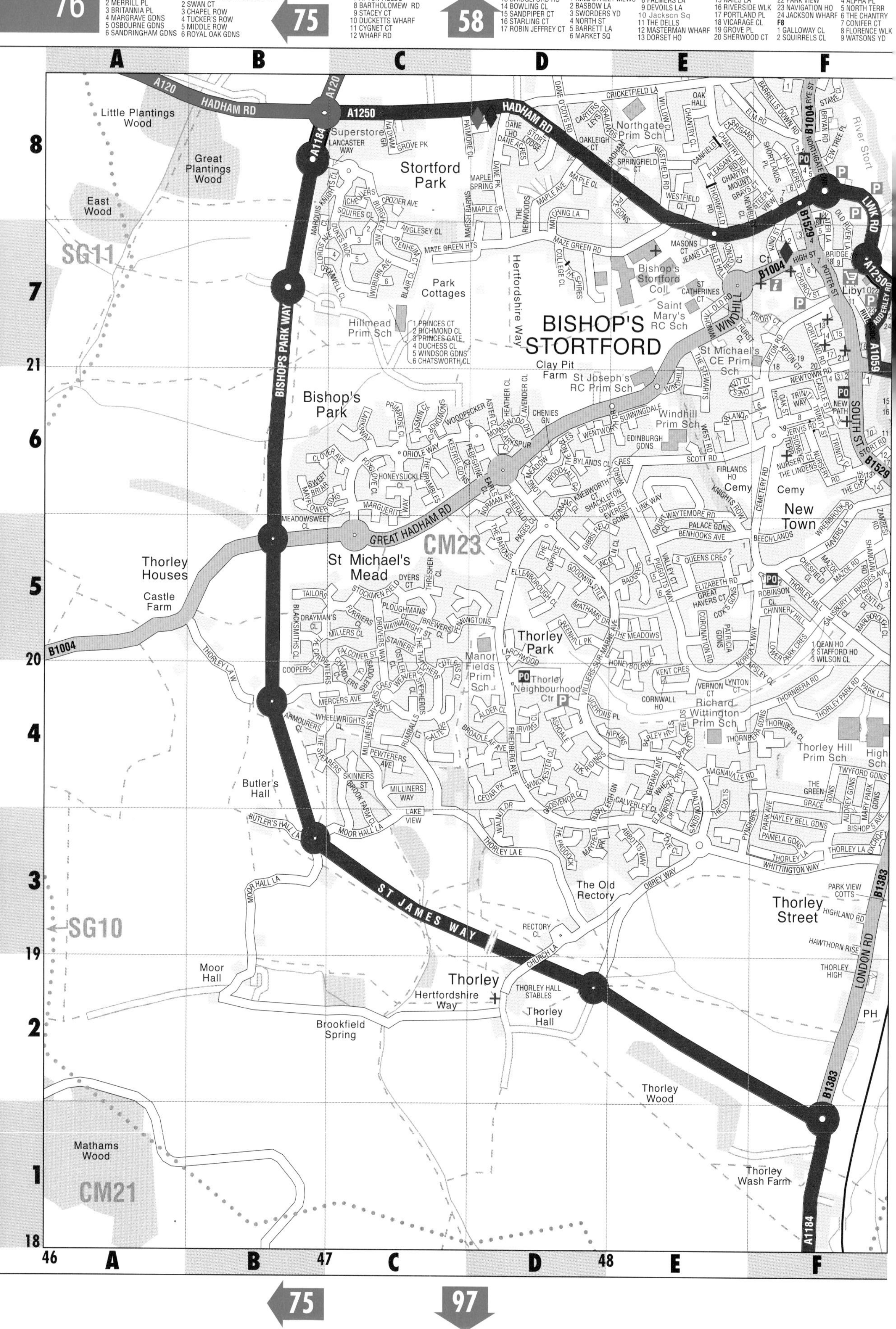

75
97

A6
1 EIDER CT
2 JOHN DYDE CL
3 MALLARD CT
4 SWALLOW CT

A7
1 THE CAUSEWAY
2 THE OLD MALTINGS
3 FULLER CT
4 LIMES CRES
5 RED LION CT
6 BAKERS CT
7 HOCKERILL CT
8 HARRINGTON CL
9 PRIORS
10 CLIFFORD CT
11 THOMAS HESKIN CT
12 THE PUMP HO
13 JUBILEE COTT
14 JOSCELYN'S YD

B8
1 BOYD CL
2 HEATH ROW
3 STORTFORD HALL RD
4 GROSVENOR HO
5 EATON HO
6 BELGRAVE HO

59

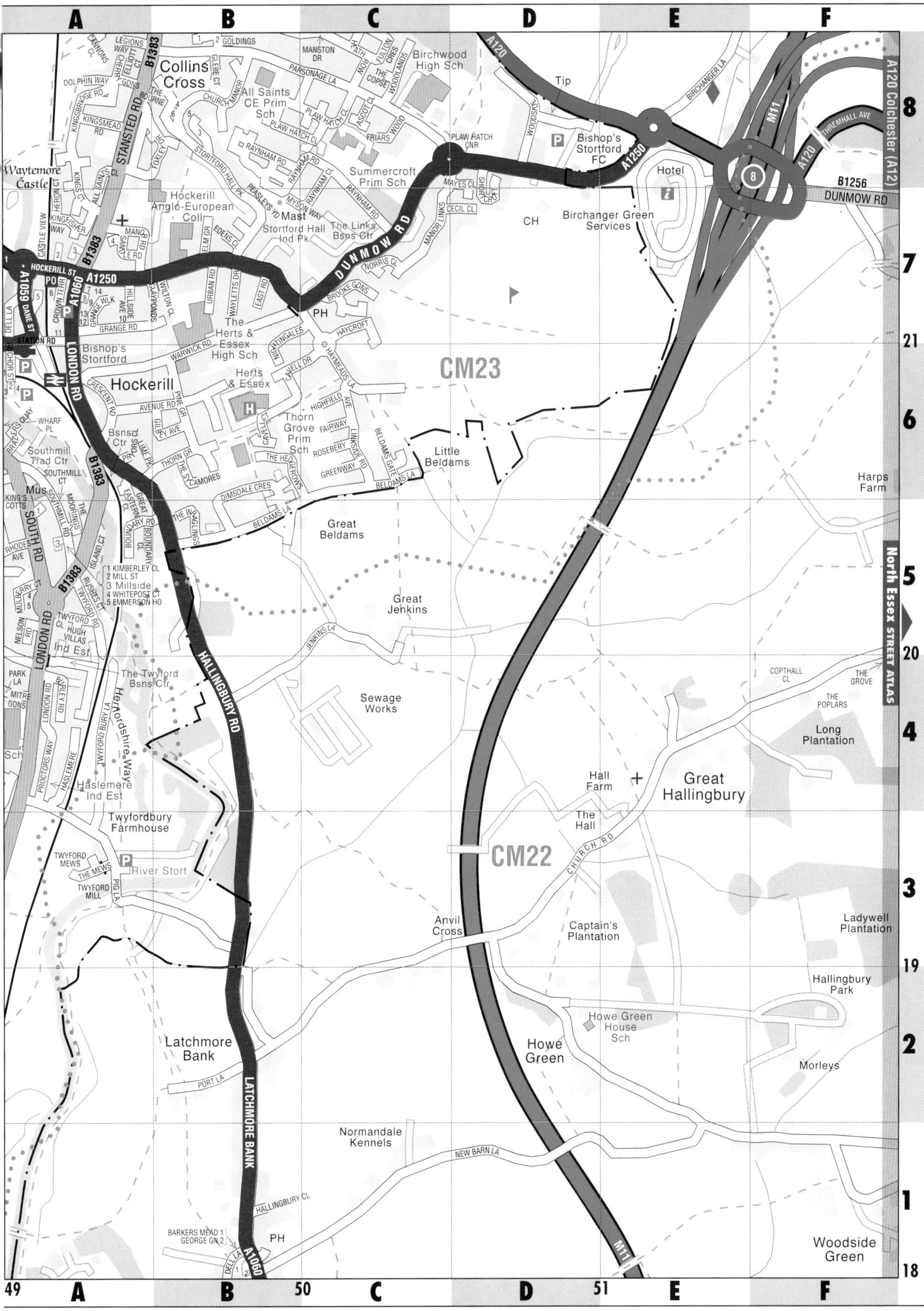

A
B
C
D
E
F
8
7
21
6
5
20
4
3
19
2
1
18
49
50
51
Collins Cross
Birchwood High Sch
All Saints CE Prim Sch
Summercroft Prim Sch
Tip
Bishop's Stortford FC
Hotel
Birchanger Green Services
Waytemore Castle
Hockerill Anglo-European Coll
Mast
Stortford Hall Ind Pk
The Links Bsns Ctr
CH
PH
The Herts & Essex High Sch
Bishop's Stortford
Hockerill
Herts & Essex
CM23
Thorn Grove Prim Sch
Little Beldams
Bsns Ctr
Southmill Trad Ctr
Mus
Great Beldams
Great Jenkins
Harps Farm
1 KIMBERLEY CL
2 MILL ST
3 Millside
4 WHITEPOST CT
5 EMMERSON HO
Ind Est
The Twyford Bsns Ctr
Sewage Works
Hertfordshire Way
Haslemere Ind Est
Long Plantation
Hall Farm
Great Hallingbury
The Hall
Twyfordbury Farmhouse
CM22
River Stort
Anvil Cross
Captain's Plantation
Ladywell Plantation
Hallingbury Park
Howe Green House Sch
Latchmore Bank
Howe Green
Morleys
Normandale Kennels
Woodside Green
BARKERS MEAD 1
GEORGE GN 2
A120 Colchester (A12)
North Essex STREET ATLAS
A120
A1250
M11
B1256
DUNMOW RD
B1383
A1060
A1059
STANSTED RD
HOCKERILL ST
LONDON RD
SOUTH RD
HALLINGBURY RD
LATCHMORE BANK
CHURCH RD
NEW BARN LA
PORT LA
HALLINGBURY CL
JENKINS LA
BELDAMS LA
THREMHALL AVE
BIRCHANGER LA
PLAW HATCH CNR
GOLDINGS
PARSONAGE LA
MANSTON DR
DOLPHIN WAY
KINGSBRIDGE RD
KINGSMEAD RD
STORTFORD HALL PK
RAYNHAM RD
MYSON WAY
NORRIS CL
BROOKE GDNS
HAYCROFT
HAYMEADS LA
NIGHTINGALES
WARWICK RD
CRESCENT RD
AVENUE RD
HIGHFIELD AVE
FAIRWAY
ROSEBERY
GREENWAY
LINKSIDE RD
BELDAMS GATE
DIMSDALE CRES
THE HEDGEROWS
CAVELL DR
THORN GR
STATION RD
DANE ST
WHARF PL
SOUTHMILL RD
TWYFORD RD
HUGH VILLAS
PARK LA
MITRE GDNS
BURLEY RD
PROCTORS WAY
HASLEMERE
TWYFORD BURY LA
TWYFORD MEWS
THE MEWS
TWYFORD MILL
PIG LA
COPTHALL CL
THE GROVE
THE POPLARS
MAYES CL
CECIL CL
MANOR LINKS
WOODSIDE

98

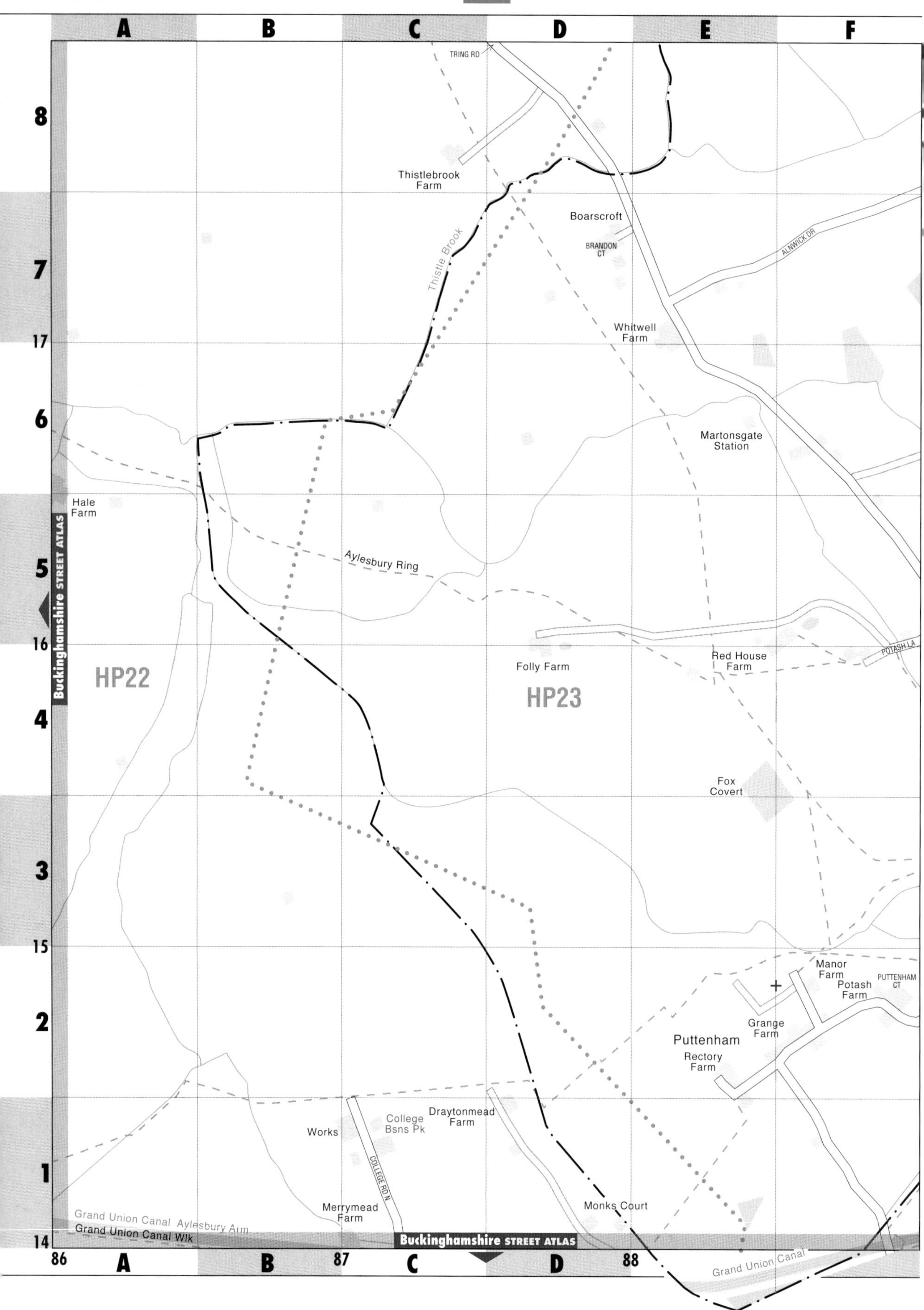
60
A
B
C
D
E
F
8
7
17
6
5
16
4
3
15
2
1
14
TRING RD
Thistlebrook Farm
Boarscroft
BRANDON CT
ALNWICK DR
Thistle Brook
Whitwell Farm
Martonsgate Station
Hale Farm
Aylesbury Ring
Buckinghamshire STREET ATLAS
HP22
Folly Farm
HP23
Red House Farm
POTASH LA
Fox Covert
Manor Farm
PUTTENHAM CT
Potash Farm
Grange Farm
Puttenham
Rectory Farm
Draytonmead Farm
College Bsns Pk
Works
COLLEGE RD N
Merrymead Farm
Monks Court
Grand Union Canal Aylesbury Arm
Grand Union Canal Wlk
Buckinghamshire STREET ATLAS
Grand Union Canal
86
A
B
87
C
D
88

61
80

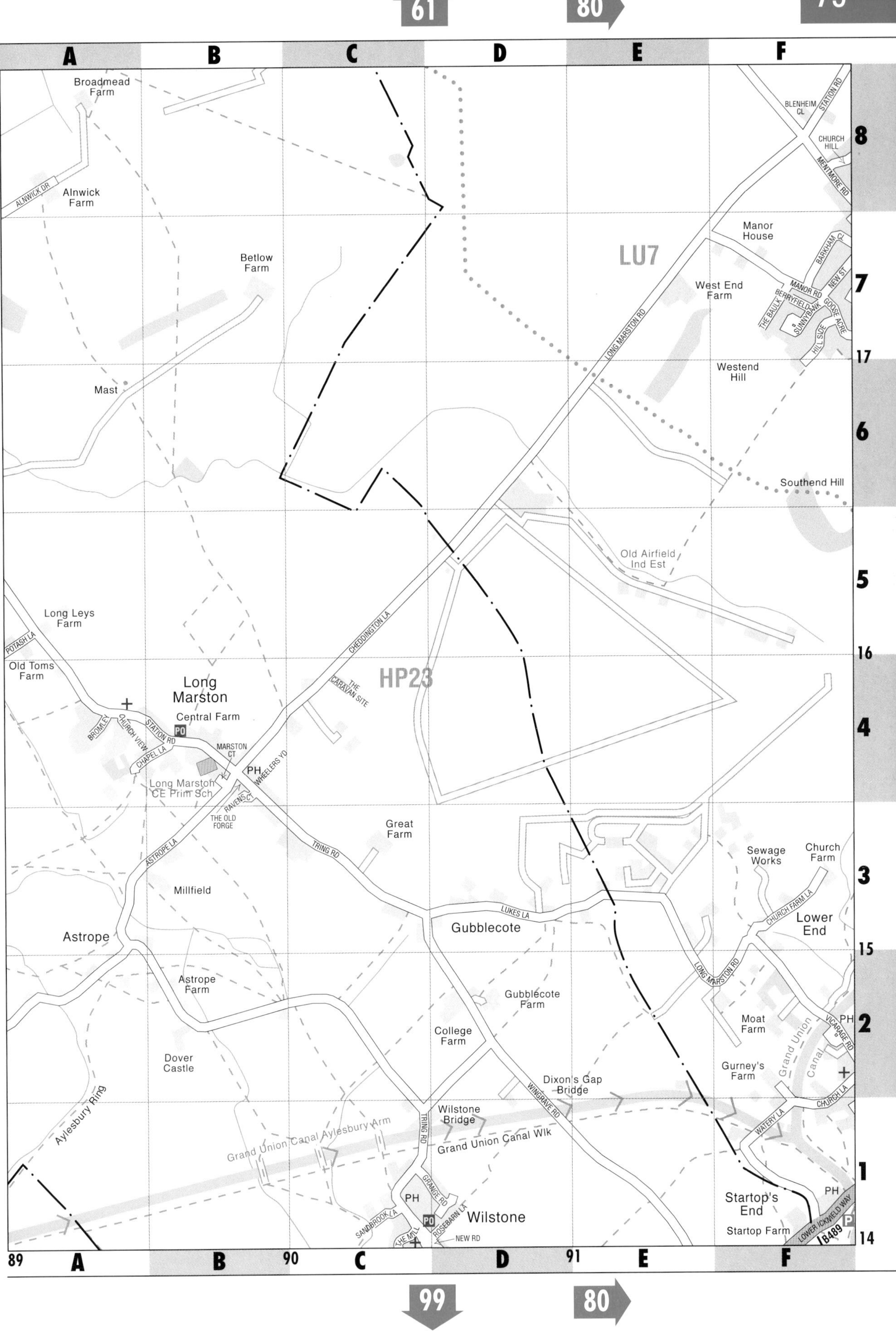
A
B
C
D
E
F
Broadmead Farm
Alnwick Farm
ALNWICK DR
Betlow Farm
Mast
LU7
BLENHEIM CL
STATION RD
CHURCH HILL
MENTMORE RD
Manor House
BARKHAM CL
West End Farm
MANOR RD
NEW ST
BERRYFIELD
THE BAULK
SUNNYBANK
GOOSE ACRE
HILL SIDE
LONG MARSTON RD
Westend Hill
Southend Hill
Old Airfield Ind Est
Long Leys Farm
POTASH LA
Old Toms Farm
CHEDDINGTON LA
HP23
THE CARAVAN SITE
Long Marston
Central Farm
BROMLEY
CHURCH VIEW
STATION RD
PO
CHAPEL LA
MARSTON CT
PH
WHEELERS YD
Long Marston CE Prim Sch
RAVENS CT
THE OLD FORGE
ASTROPE LA
TRING RD
Great Farm
Millfield
LUKES LA
Gubblecote
Sewage Works
Church Farm
CHURCH FARM LA
Lower End
Astrope
LONG MARSTON RD
Astrope Farm
Gubblecote Farm
Moat Farm
PH
VICARAGE RD
Grand Union Canal
College Farm
Dover Castle
Gurney's Farm
Aylesbury Ring
Dixon's Gap Bridge
WINGRAVE RD
CHURCH LA
Wilstone Bridge
TRING RD
WATERY LA
Grand Union Canal Aylesbury Arm
Grand Union Canal Wlk
PH
GRANGE RD
SANDBROOK LA
PO
Wilstone
ROSEBARN LA
THE MILL
NEW RD
Startop's End
PH
Startop Farm
LOWER ICKNIELD WAY
B489
P
8
7
17
6
5
16
4
3
15
2
1
14
89
90
91

99
80

79

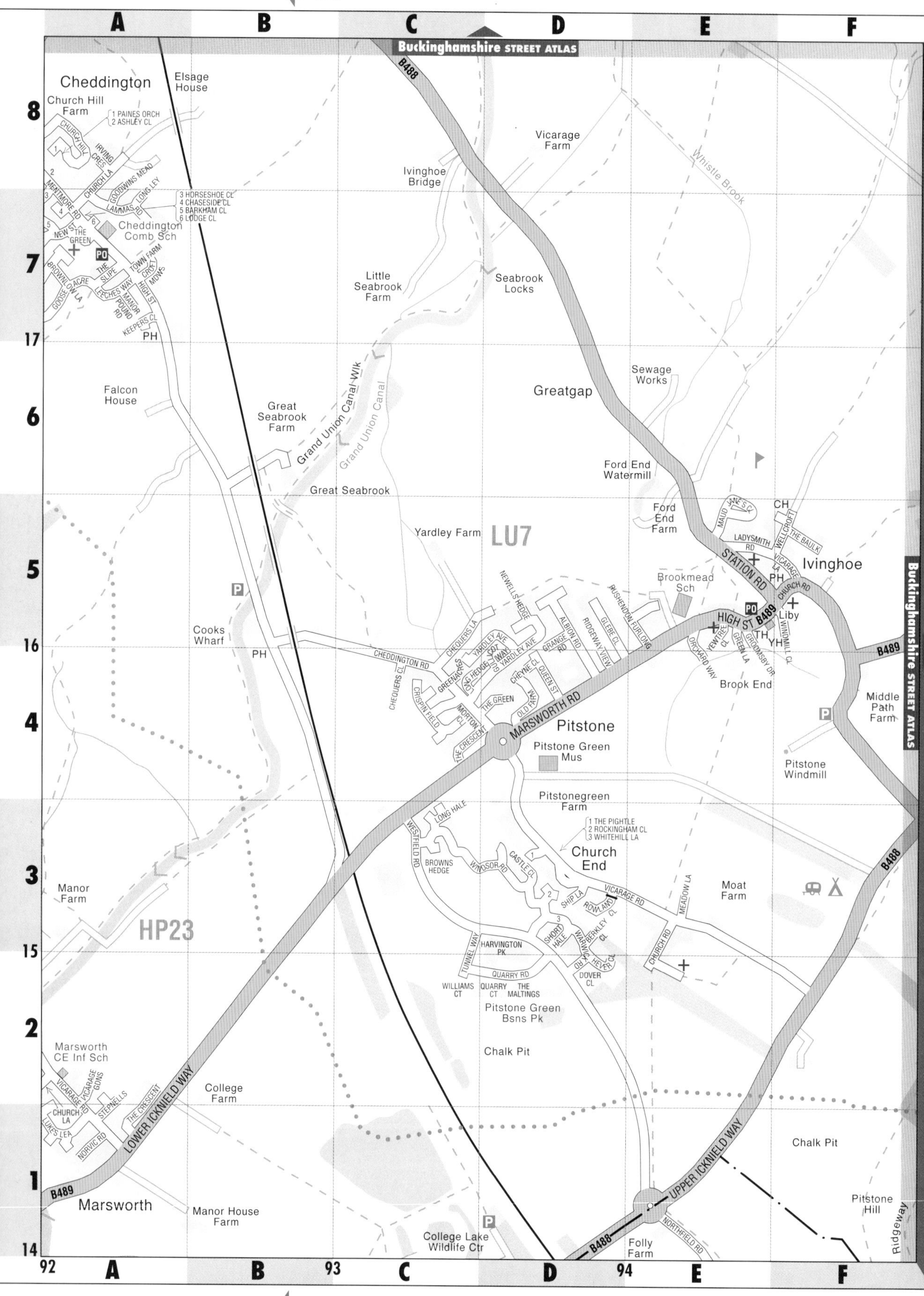
Buckinghamshire STREET ATLAS
Cheddington
Church Hill Farm
Elsage House
1 PAINES ORCH
2 ASHLEY CL
3 HORSESHOE CL
4 CHASESIDE CL
5 BARKHAM CL
6 LODGE CL
Cheddington Comb Sch
Vicarage Farm
Ivinghoe Bridge
Whistle Brook
Little Seabrook Farm
Seabrook Locks
Falcon House
Great Seabrook Farm
Grand Union Canal Wlk
Grand Union Canal
Greatgap
Sewage Works
Ford End Watermill
Great Seabrook
Ford End Farm
Yardley Farm
LU7
STATION RD
Ivinghoe
Brookmead Sch
Cooks Wharf
HIGH ST
B489
Liby
CHEDDINGTON RD
MARSWORTH RD
Brook End
Middle Path Farm
Pitstone
Pitstone Green Mus
Pitstone Windmill
Pitstonegreen Farm
1 THE PIGHTLE
2 ROCKINGHAM CL
3 WHITEHILL LA
Church End
Manor Farm
Moat Farm
HP23
B488
Pitstone Green Bsns Pk
Chalk Pit
Marsworth CE Inf Sch
College Farm
LOWER ICKNIELD WAY
UPPER ICKNIELD WAY
Marsworth
Manor House Farm
College Lake Wildlife Ctr
Folly Farm
Pitstone Hill
Ridgeway

79
100

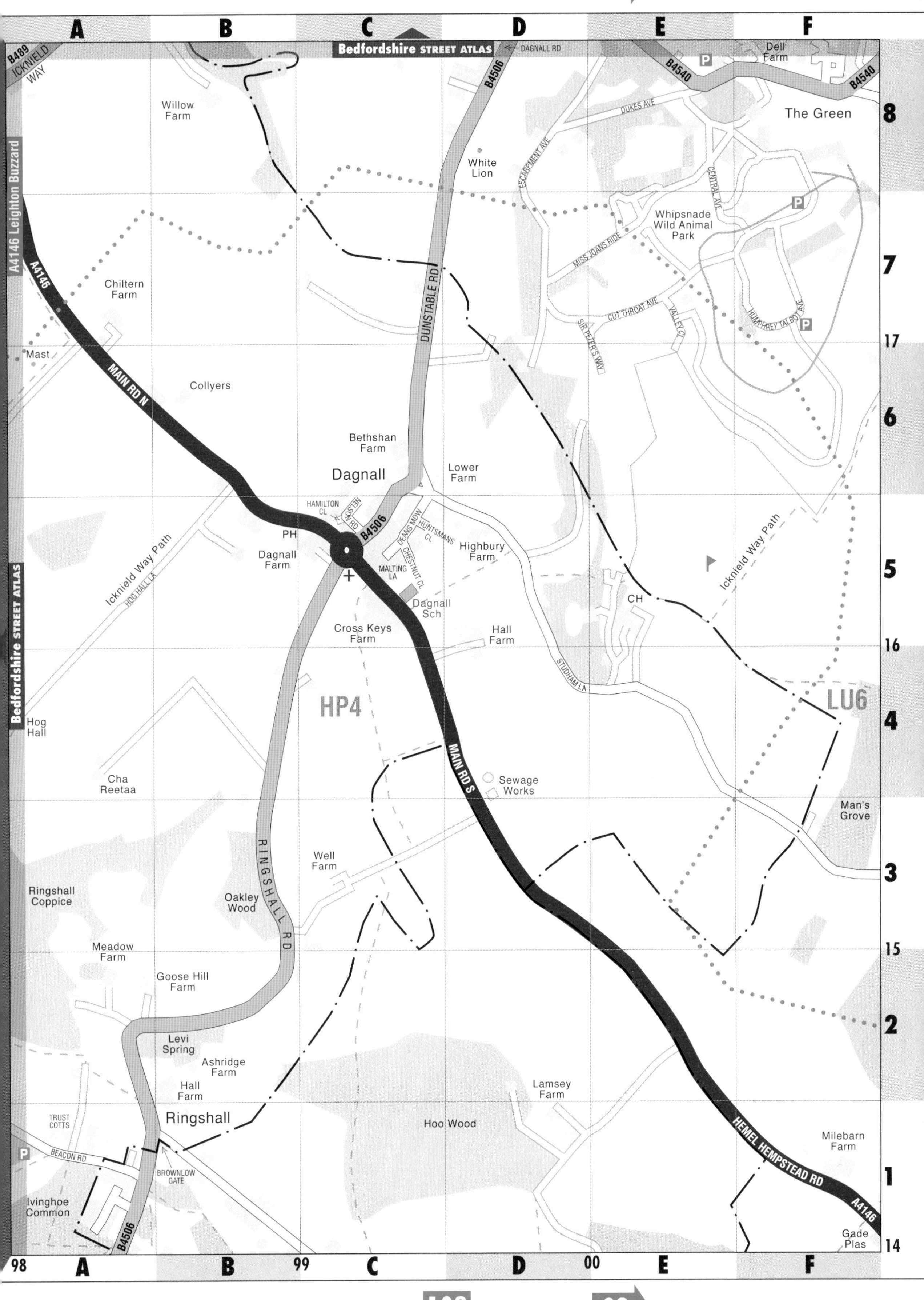
A
B
C
D
E
F
Bedfordshire STREET ATLAS
DAGNALL RD
B489
ICKNIELD WAY
Willow Farm
B4506
B4540
Dell Farm
The Green
DUKES AVE
White Lion
ESCARPMENT AVE
CENTRAL AVE
Whipsnade Wild Animal Park
MISS JOANS RIDE
A4146 Leighton Buzzard
A4146
Chiltern Farm
DUNSTABLE RD
CUT THROAT AVE
VALLEY CL
SIR PETER'S WAY
HUMPHREY TALBOT AVE
Mast
MAIN RD N
Collyers
Bethshan Farm
Dagnall
Lower Farm
HAMILTON CL
NELSON RD
DEANS MDW
HUNTSMANS CL
CHESTNUT CL
MALTING LA
PH
Dagnall Farm
Highbury Farm
Icknield Way Path
HOG HALL LA
Dagnall Sch
CH
Cross Keys Farm
Hall Farm
STUDHAM LA
HP4
LU6
Bedfordshire STREET ATLAS
Hog Hall
Cha Reetaa
MAIN RD S
Sewage Works
Man's Grove
RINGSHALL RD
Well Farm
Ringshall Coppice
Oakley Wood
Meadow Farm
Goose Hill Farm
Levi Spring
Ashridge Farm
Hall Farm
Lamsey Farm
TRUST COTTS
Ringshall
Hoo Wood
HEMEL HEMPSTEAD RD
Milebarn Farm
BEACON RD
BROWNLOW GATE
Ivinghoe Common
Gade Plas
8
7
17
6
5
16
4
3
15
2
1
14
98
99
00

81

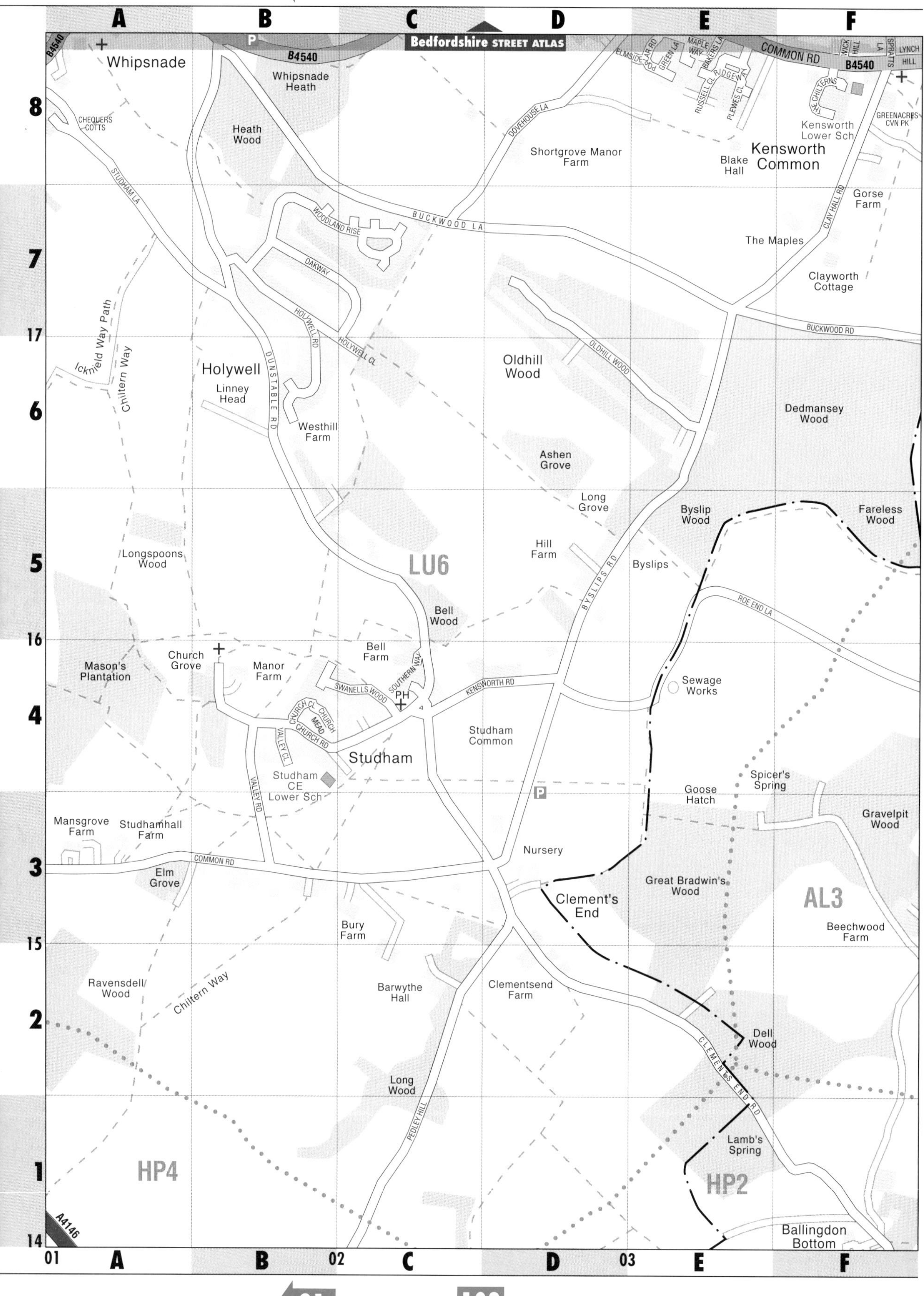

Bedfordshire STREET ATLAS
A
B
C
D
E
F
Whipsnade
Whipsnade Heath
B4540
Heath Wood
CHEQUERS COTTS
STUDHAM LA
Shortgrove Manor Farm
DOVEHOUSE LA
ELMSIDE
POPLAR RD
GREEN LA
MAPLE WAY
BAKERS LA
RUSSELL CL
RIDGEWAY
PLEWES CL
COMMON RD
LYNCH HILL
GREENACRES CVN PK
THE CHILTERNS
Kensworth Lower Sch
Kensworth Common
Blake Hall
Gorse Farm
CLAY HALL RD
The Maples
Clayworth Cottage
WOODLAND RISE
BUCKWOOD LA
OAKWAY
HOLYWELL RD
HOLYWELL CL
BUCKWOOD RD
Icknield Way Path
Chiltern Way
Holywell
Linney Head
DUNSTABLE RD
Westhill Farm
Oldhill Wood
OLDHILL WOOD
Dedmansey Wood
Ashen Grove
Long Grove
Byslip Wood
Fareless Wood
Longspoons Wood
LU6
Hill Farm
BYSLIPS RD
Byslips
Bell Wood
ROE END LA
Bell Farm
Church Grove
Mason's Plantation
Manor Farm
SWANELLS WOOD
SOUTHERN WAY
PH
KENSWORTH RD
Sewage Works
CHURCH CL
CHURCH MEAD
CHURCH RD
VALLEY CL
Studham
Studham Common
Studham CE Lower Sch
Spicer's Spring
Goose Hatch
Mansgrove Farm
Studhamhall Farm
VALLEY RD
Gravelpit Wood
Nursery
COMMON RD
Elm Grove
Clement's End
Great Bradwin's Wood
AL3
Bury Farm
Beechwood Farm
Ravensdell Wood
Chiltern Way
Barwythe Hall
Clementsend Farm
Dell Wood
CLEMENTS END RD
Long Wood
PEDLEY HILL
Lamb's Spring
HP4
HP2
A4146
Ballingdon Bottom
8
7
17
6
5
16
4
3
15
2
1
14
01
02
03

81
103

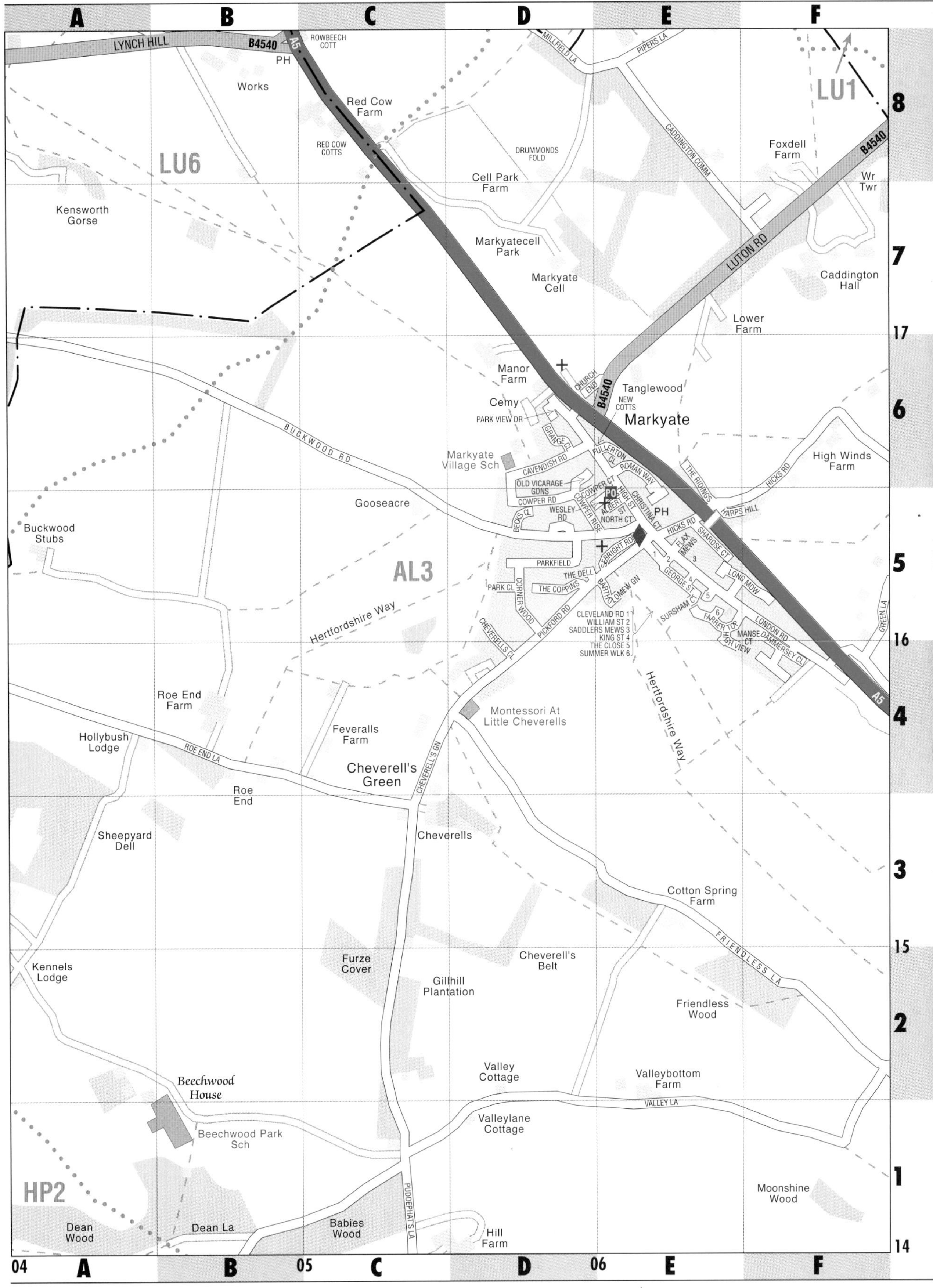
A
B
C
D
E
F
LYNCH HILL
B4540
A5
PH
ROWBEECH COTT
MILLFIELD LA
PIPERS LA
LU1
8
Works
Red Cow Farm
LU6
RED COW COTTS
DRUMMONDS FOLD
CADDINGTON COMM
Foxdell Farm
B4540
Wr Twr
Kensworth Gorse
Cell Park Farm
Markyatecell Park
LUTON RD
7
Caddington Hall
Markyate Cell
Lower Farm
17
Manor Farm
CHURCH END
B4540
Tanglewood
Cemy
NEW COTTS
Markyate
6
PARK VIEW DR
GRANGE CL
BUCKWOOD RD
FULLERTON CL
High Winds Farm
Markyate Village Sch
CAVENDISH RD
ROMAN WAY
THE RIDINGS
HICKS RD
OLD VICARAGE GDNS
COWPER CT
PO
HIGH ST
CHRISTINA CT
COWPER RD
ALBERT ST
PH
HARPS HILL
Gooseacre
WESLEY RD
BECKS CL
COWPER RISE
NORTH CT
HICKS RD
Buckwood Stubs
SEBRIGHT RD
FLAX MEWS
SHAROSE CT
5
AL3
PARKFIELD
THE DELL
LONG MDW
PARK CL
CORNER WOOD
THE COPPINS
BARTHOLOMEW GN
GEORGE ST
SURSHAM CT
Hertfordshire Way
CLEVELAND RD 1
WILLIAM ST 2
SADDLERS MEWS 3
KING ST 4
THE CLOSE 5
SUMMER WLK 6
FARRER TOP
LONDON RD
GREEN LA
CHEVERELLS CL
PICKFORD RD
HIGH VIEW
MANSE CT
DAMMERSEY CL
16
Hertfordshire Way
Roe End Farm
A5
4
Montessori At Little Cheverells
Hollybush Lodge
Feveralls Farm
ROE END LA
Cheverell's Green
CHEVERELL'S GN
Roe End
Sheepyard Dell
Cheverells
3
Cotton Spring Farm
15
FRIENDLESS LA
Kennels Lodge
Furze Cover
Cheverell's Belt
Gillhill Plantation
Friendless Wood
2
Valley Cottage
Valleybottom Farm
Beechwood House
VALLEY LA
Valleylane Cottage
Beechwood Park Sch
1
Moonshine Wood
HP2
PUDDEPHAT'S LA
Dean Wood
Dean La
Babies Wood
Hill Farm
14
04
05
06

83
63

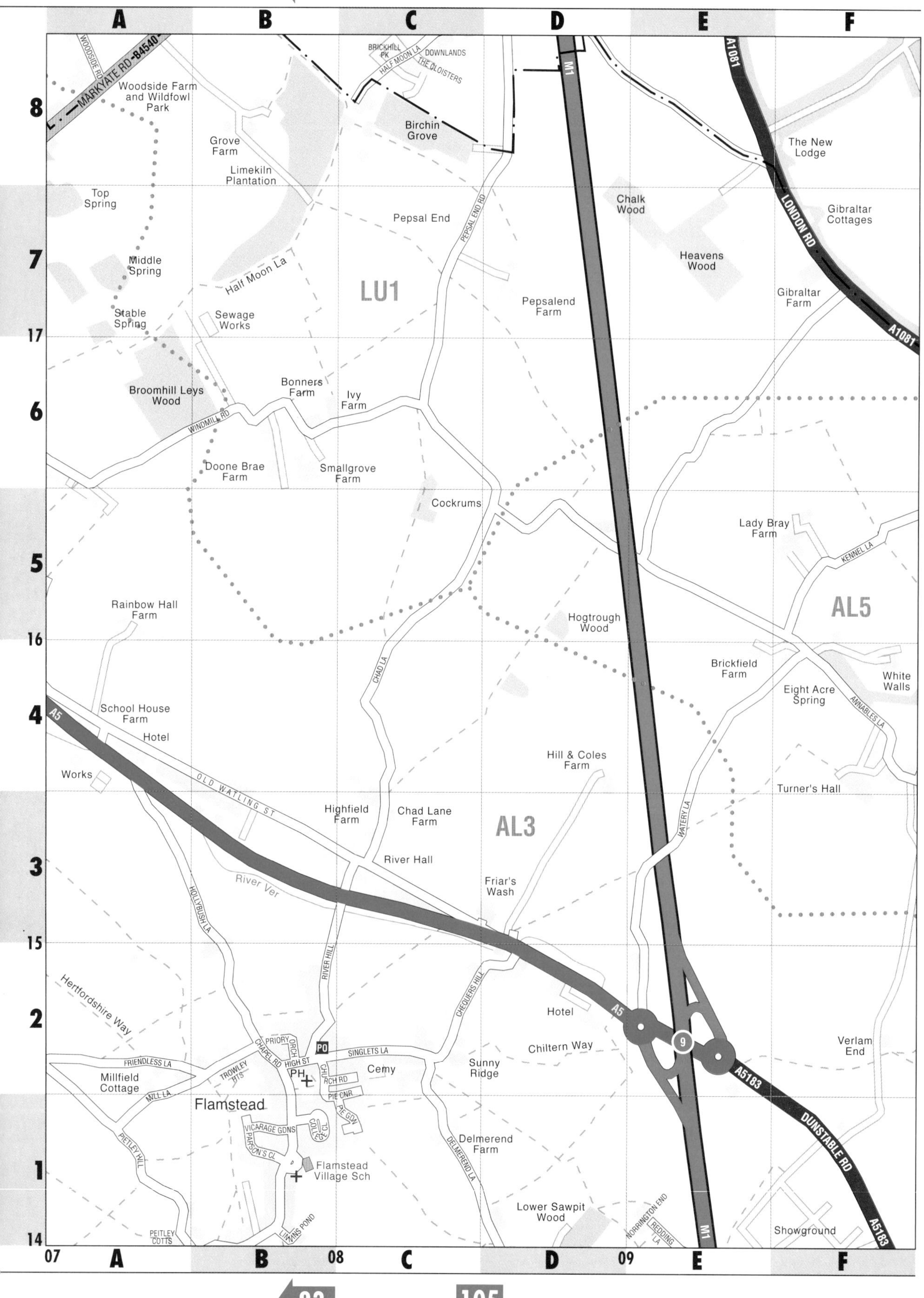
A
B
C
D
E
F
8
7
17
6
5
16
4
3
15
2
1
14
07
08
09
WOODSIDE RD
MARKYATE RD B4540
Woodside Farm
and Wildfowl
Park
BRICKHILL PK
HALF MOON LA
DOWNLANDS
THE CLOISTERS
Birchin
Grove
M1
A1081
The New
Lodge
Grove
Farm
Limekiln
Plantation
Top
Spring
Pepsal End
PEPSAL END RD
Chalk
Wood
LONDON RD
Gibraltar
Cottages
Middle
Spring
Half Moon La
LU1
Heavens
Wood
Stable
Spring
Sewage
Works
Pepsalend
Farm
Gibraltar
Farm
Broomhill Leys
Wood
Bonners
Farm
Ivy
Farm
WINDMILL RD
Doone Brae
Farm
Smallgrove
Farm
Cockrums
Lady Bray
Farm
KENNEL LA
AL5
Rainbow Hall
Farm
Hogtrough
Wood
Brickfield
Farm
White
Walls
CHAD LA
Eight Acre
Spring
School House
Farm
A5
Hotel
ANNABLES LA
Works
Hill & Coles
Farm
OLD WATLING ST
Turner's Hall
Highfield
Farm
Chad Lane
Farm
AL3
WATERY LA
River Hall
HOLLYBUSH LA
River Ver
Friar's
Wash
RIVER HILL
CHEQUERS HILL
Hertfordshire Way
Hotel
9
Verlam
End
Chiltern Way
PRIORY
ORCH
CHAPEL RD
PO
SINGLETS LA
FRIENDLESS LA
HIGH ST
PH
CHURCH RD
Cemy
Sunny
Ridge
A5183
Millfield
Cottage
TROWLEY HTS
MILL LA
PIE CNR
PIE GDN
Flamstead
VICARAGE GDNS
COLLEGE CL
PARSON'S CL
DUNSTABLE RD
PIETLEY HILL
Delmerend
Farm
DELMEREND LA
Flamstead
Village Sch
Lower Sawpit
Wood
NORRINGTON END
REDDING LA
PEITLEY COTTS
LINTONS POND
Showground

83
105

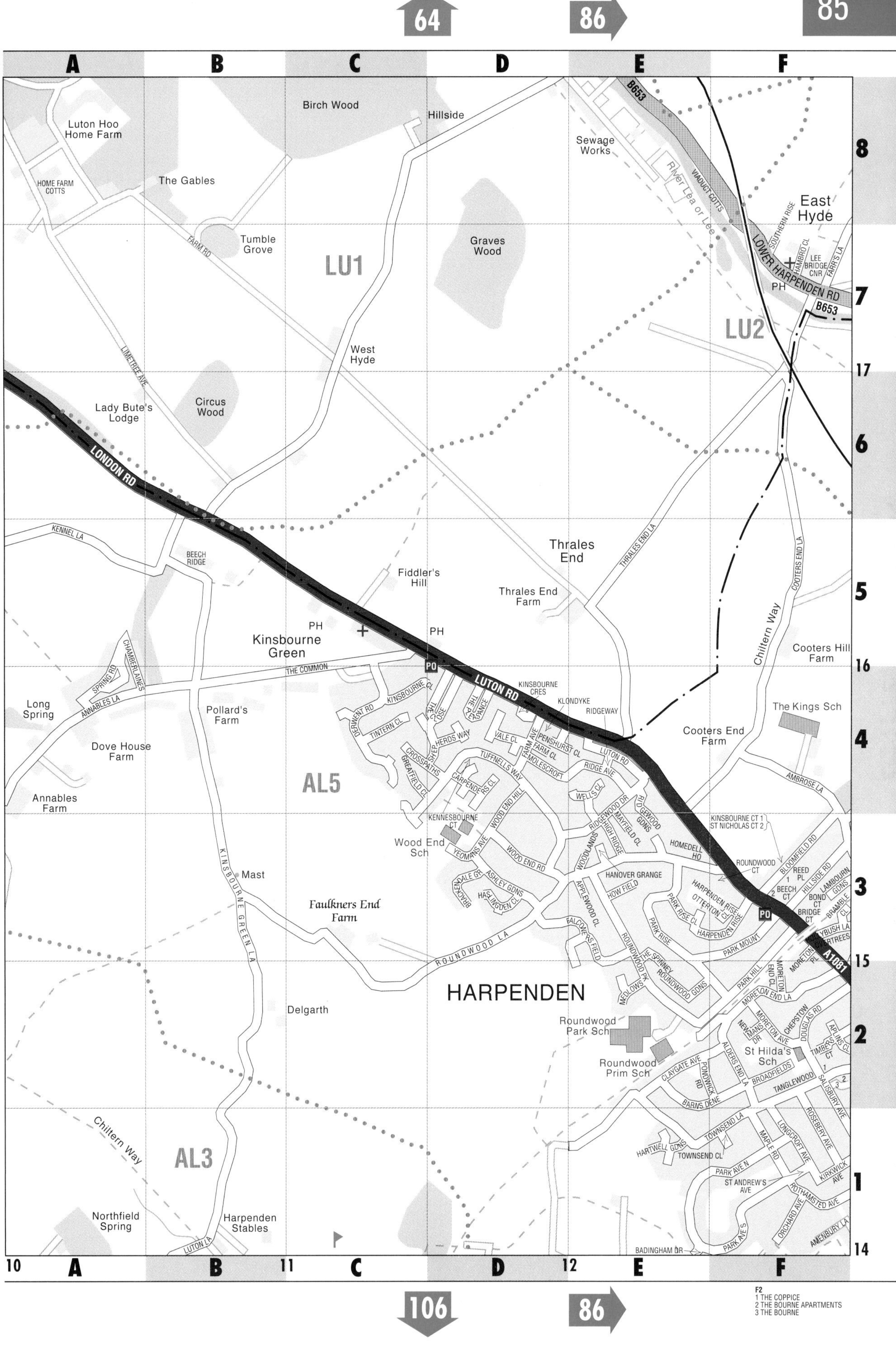

F2
1 THE COPPICE
2 THE BOURNE APARTMENTS
3 THE BOURNE

85
65

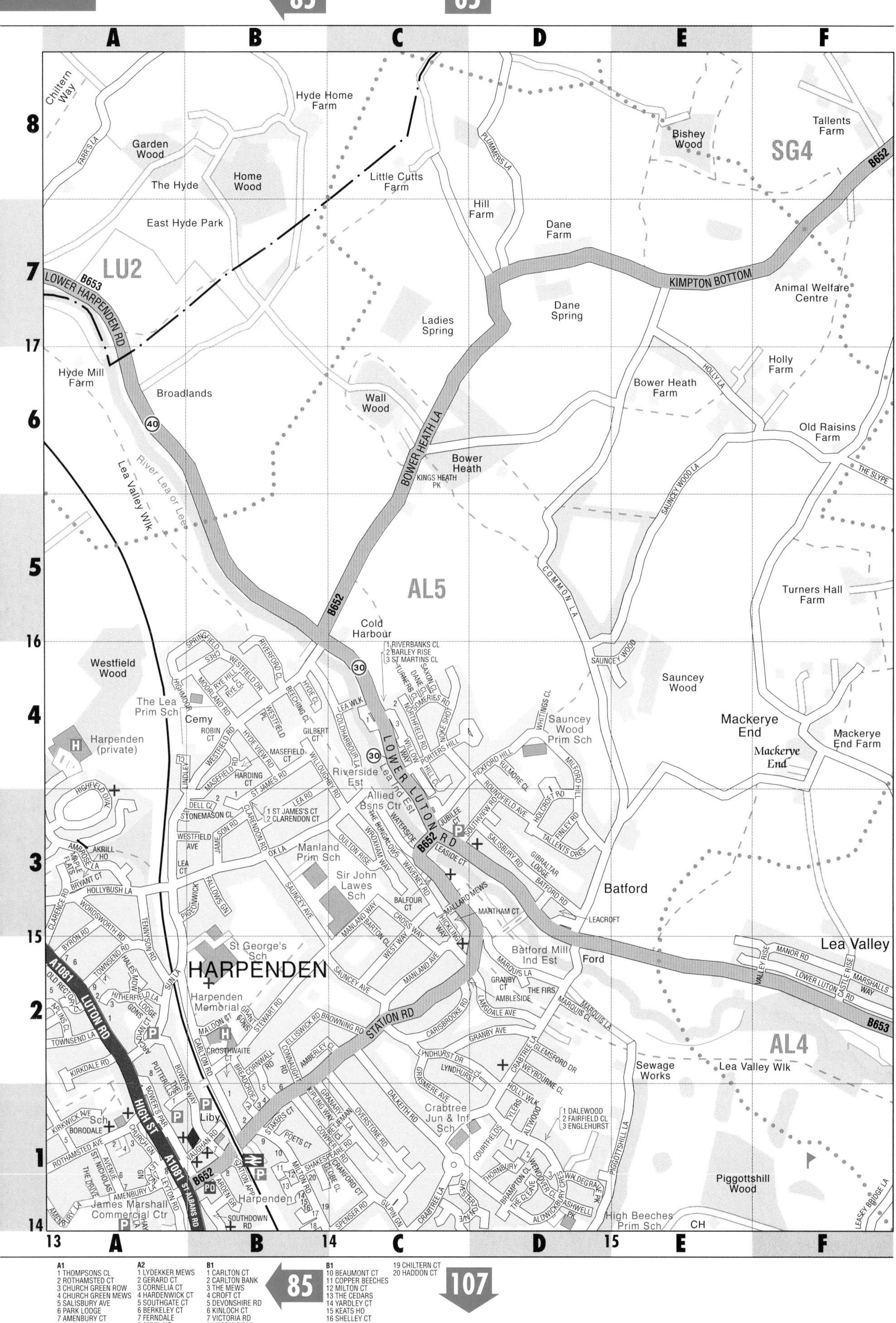

A1
1 THOMPSONS CL
2 ROTHAMSTED CT
3 CHURCH GREEN ROW
4 CHURCH GREEN MEWS
5 SALISBURY AVE
6 PARK LODGE
7 AMENBURY CT
8 POPPY CT

A2
1 LYDEKKER MEWS
2 GERARD CT
3 CORNELIA CT
4 HARDENWICK CT
5 SOUTHGATE CT
6 BERKELEY CT
7 FERNDALE
8 ANVIL HO
9 ST HELENAS CT

B1
1 CARLTON CT
2 CARLTON BANK
3 THE MEWS
4 CROFT CT
5 DEVONSHIRE RD
6 KINLOCH CT
7 VICTORIA RD
8 HARDING PAR
9 COLERIDGE CT

B1
10 BEAUMONT CT
11 COPPER BEECHES
12 MILTON CT
13 THE CEDARS
14 YARDLEY CT
15 KEATS HO
16 SHELLEY CT
17 AVON CT
18 FURZEDOWN CT
19 CHILTERN CT
20 HADDON CT

85
107

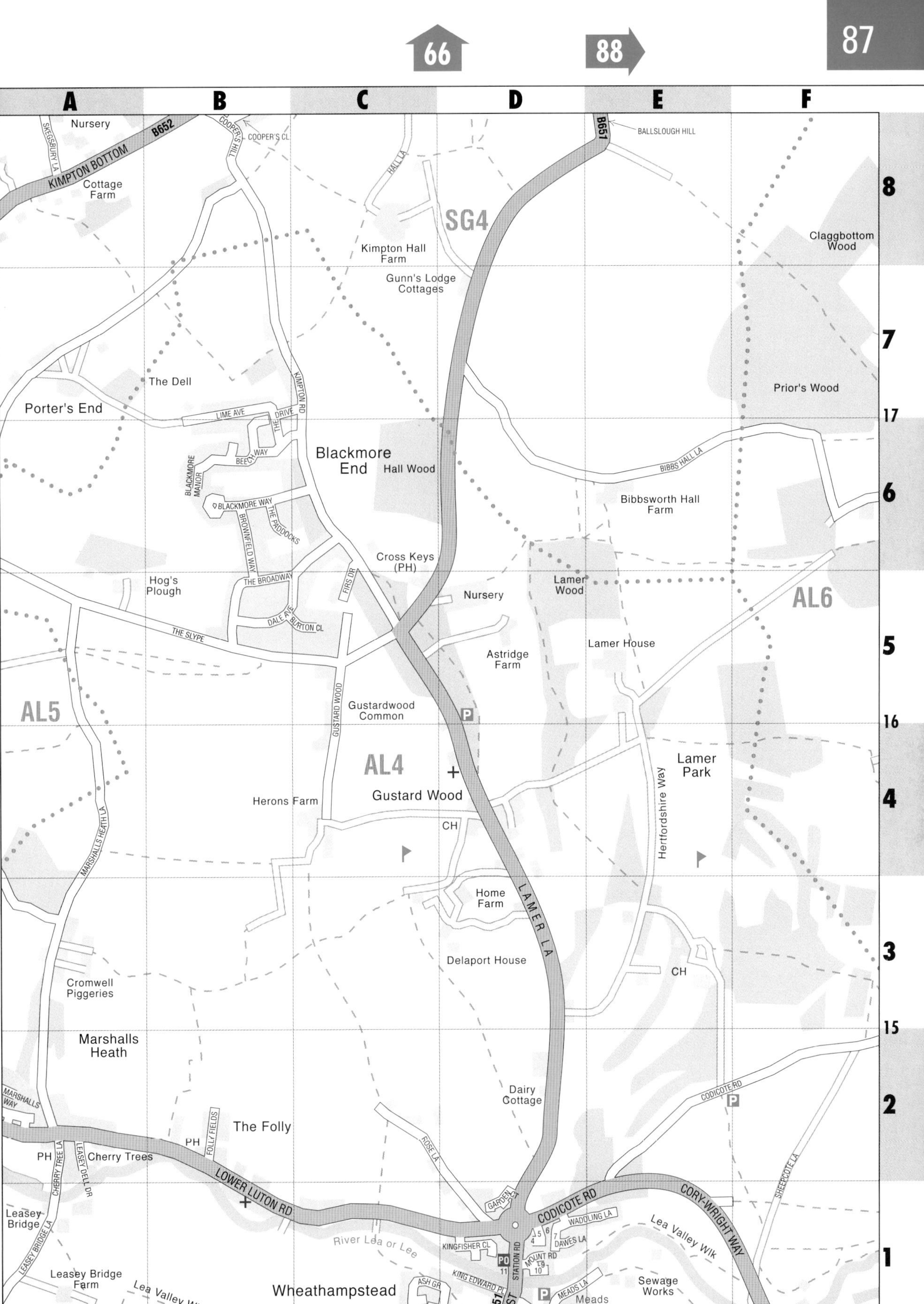

108

88

D1
1 OLD RECTORY GDNS
2 EAST MOUNT
3 BROCKET VIEW
4 ABBOT JOHN MEWS
5 OLD WADDLING LA
6 PIKES LEAP
7 PALMERSTON DR
8 LATCHFORD MEWS
9 THE BARN

D1
10 PLACE FARM
11 MILL WLK

87
67

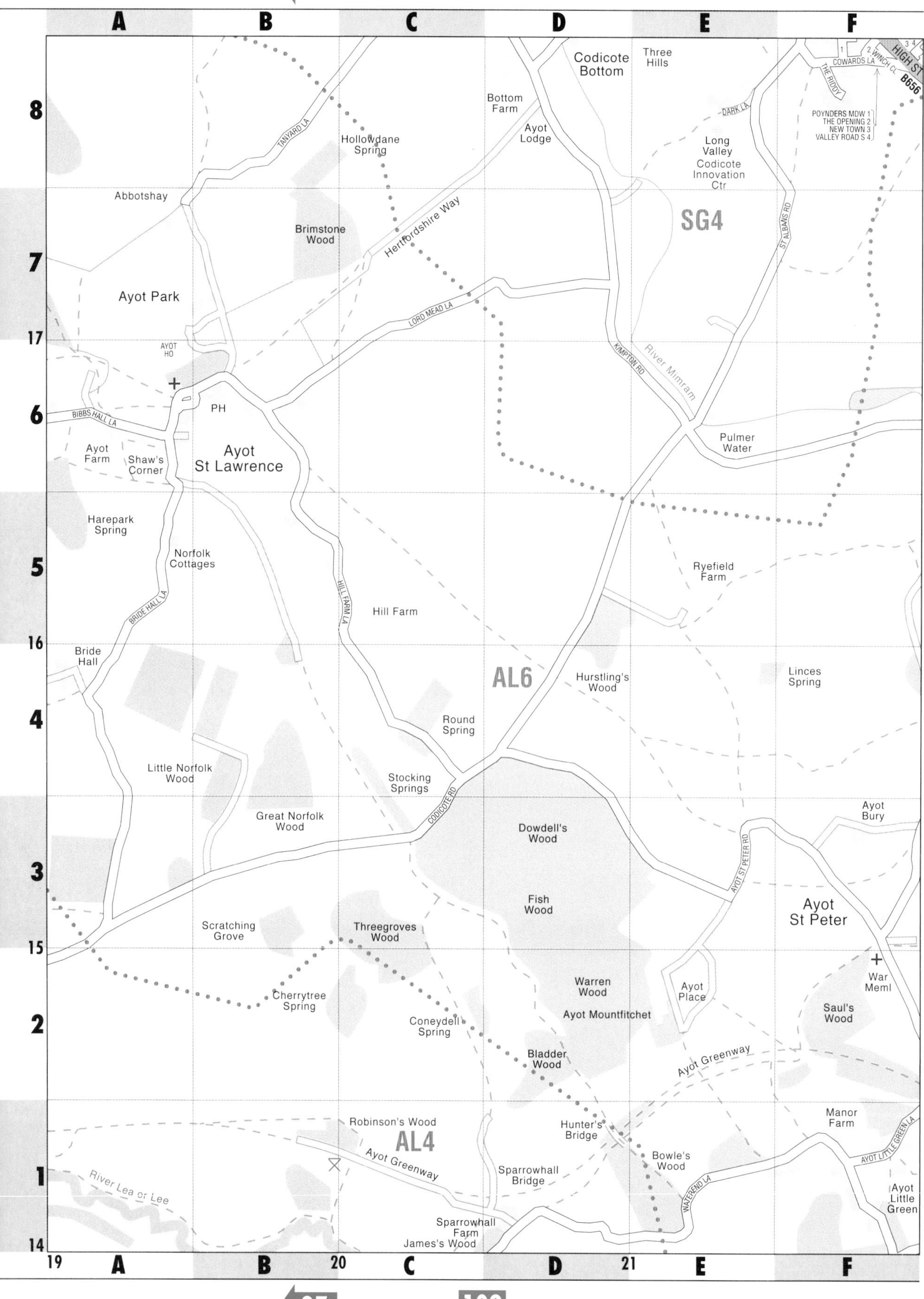
A
B
C
D
E
F
8
7
17
6
5
16
4
3
15
2
1
14
19
20
21
Codicote Bottom
Three Hills
Bottom Farm
Ayot Lodge
Hollowdane Spring
TANYARD LA
DARK LA
COWARDS LA
HIGH ST
B656
THE RIDDY
WINCH CL
POYNDERS MDW 1
THE OPENING 2
NEW TOWN 3
VALLEY ROAD S 4
Long Valley
Codicote Innovation Ctr
SG4
Abbotshay
Brimstone Wood
Hertfordshire Way
ST ALBANS RD
Ayot Park
LORD MEAD LA
AYOT HO
KIMPTON RD
River Mimram
PH
BIBBS HALL LA
Ayot Farm
Shaw's Corner
Ayot St Lawrence
Pulmer Water
Harepark Spring
Norfolk Cottages
Ryefield Farm
HILL FARM LA
Hill Farm
BRIDE HALL LA
Bride Hall
AL6
Hurstling's Wood
Linces Spring
Round Spring
Little Norfolk Wood
Stocking Springs
CODICOTE RD
Great Norfolk Wood
Dowdell's Wood
Ayot Bury
AYOT ST PETER RD
Fish Wood
Ayot St Peter
Scratching Grove
Threegroves Wood
Cherrytree Spring
Warren Wood
Ayot Place
War Meml
Ayot Mountfitchet
Saul's Wood
Coneydell Spring
Bladder Wood
Ayot Greenway
Robinson's Wood
Hunter's Bridge
Manor Farm
AL4
AYOT LITTLE GREEN LA
Bowle's Wood
River Lea or Lee
Sparrowhall Bridge
WATEREND LA
Ayot Little Green
Sparrowhall Farm
James's Wood

87
109

68
90

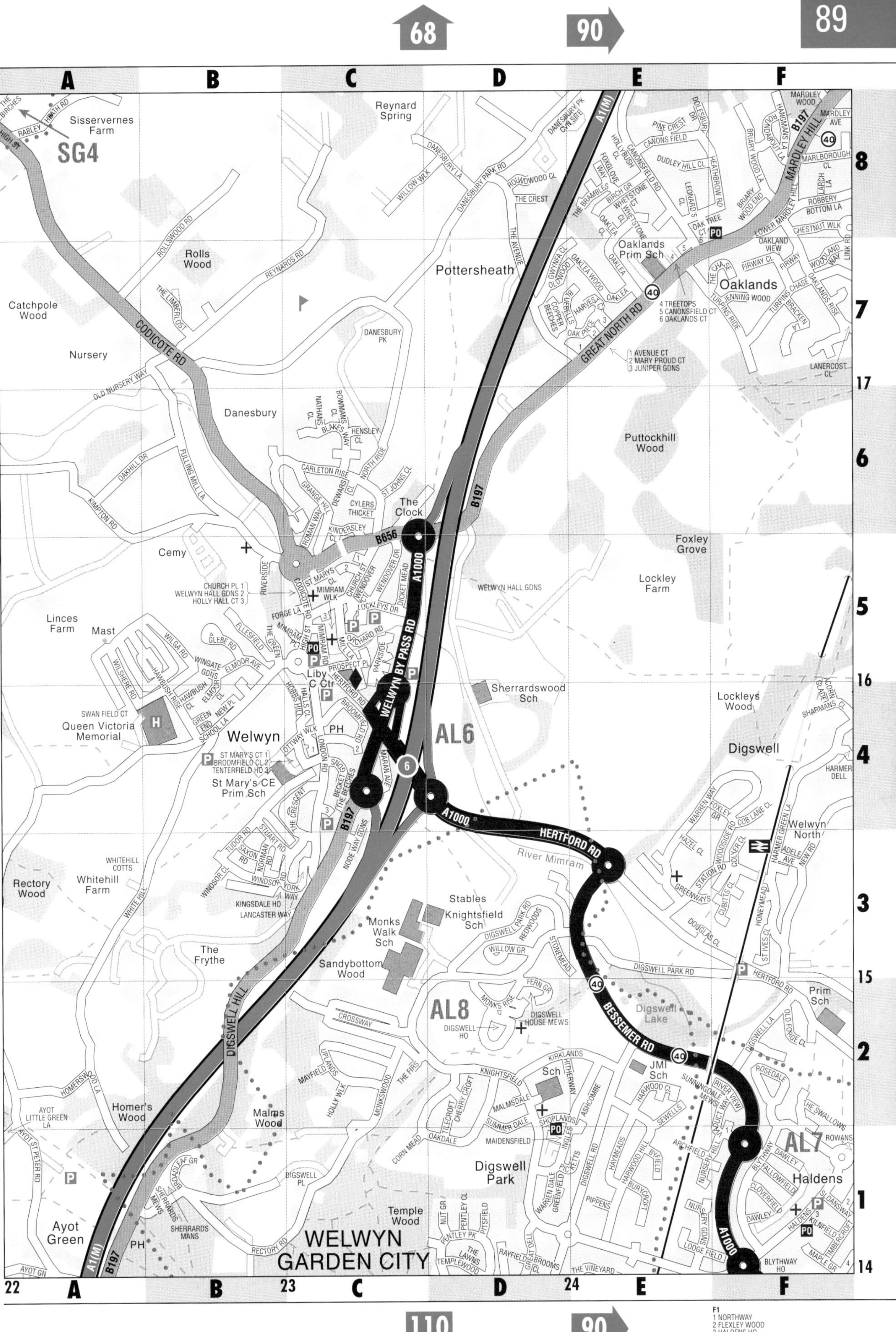

110
90

F1
1 NORTHWAY
2 FLEXLEY WOOD
3 HALDENS HO
4 RUNSLEY

89
69

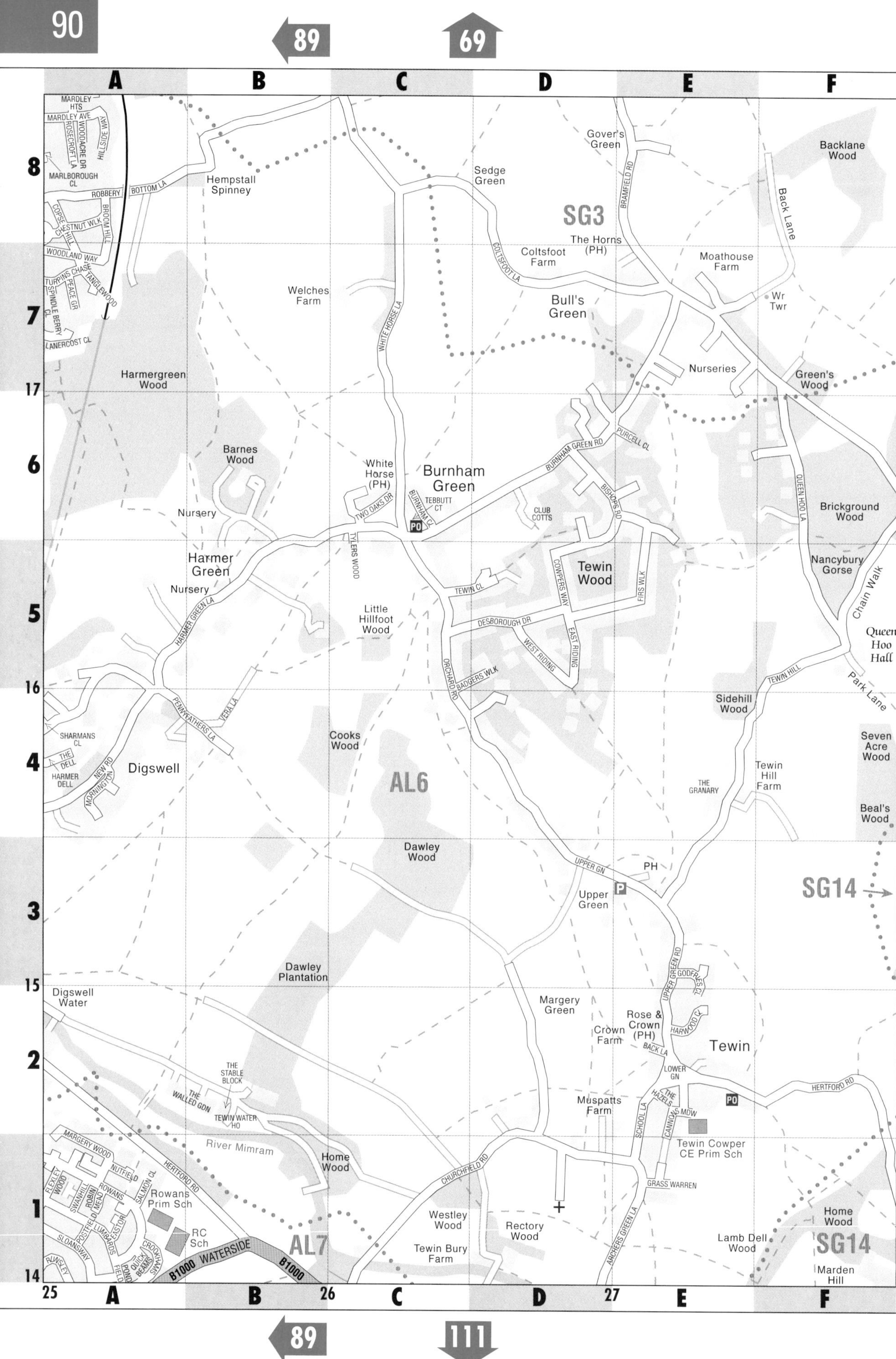
A
B
C
D
E
F
8
7
17
6
5
16
4
3
15
2
1
14
25
26
27
MARDLEY HTS
MARDLEY AVE
ROSECROFT LA
WOODACRE DR
HILLSIDE WAY
MARLBOROUGH CL
ROBBERY
BOTTOM LA
BROOM HILL
CHESTNUT WLK
WOODLAND WAY
TURPINS CHASE
TANGLEWOOD
PEACE GR
LANERCOST CL
Hempstall Spinney
Sedge Green
Gover's Green
BRAMFIELD RD
Backlane Wood
Back Lane
SG3
The Horns (PH)
Coltsfoot Farm
COLTSFOOT LA
Moathouse Farm
Welches Farm
WHITE HORSE LA
Bull's Green
Wr Twr
Nurseries
Green's Wood
Harmergreen Wood
Barnes Wood
White Horse (PH)
Burnham Green
BURNHAM GREEN RD
PURCELL CL
TEBBUTT CT
BURNHAM CL
TWO OAKS DR
PO
CLUB COTTS
BISHOPS RD
QUEEN HOO LA
Brickground Wood
Nursery
Harmer Green
TYLERS WOOD
Tewin Wood
COWPERS WAY
FIRS WLK
Nancybury Gorse
Chain Walk
Nursery
TEWIN CL
Little Hillfoot Wood
HARMER GREEN LA
DESBOROUGH DR
WEST RIDING
EAST RIDING
Queen Hoo Hall
ORCHARD RD
BADGERS WLK
TEWIN HILL
Park Lane
Sidehill Wood
PENNYFATHERS LA
VERA LA
SHARMANS CL
THE DELL
HARMER DELL
NEW RD
MORNINGTON
Digswell
Cooks Wood
AL6
Seven Acre Wood
Tewin Hill Farm
THE GRANARY
Beal's Wood
Dawley Wood
UPPER GN
PH
P
Upper Green
SG14
Dawley Plantation
UPPER GREEN RD
GODFREYS CL
Digswell Water
Margery Green
Rose & Crown (PH)
Crown Farm
HARWOOD CL
BACK LA
Tewin
LOWER GN
THE STABLE BLOCK
THE WALLED GDN
TEWIN WATER HO
Muspatts Farm
THE HAZELS
SCHOOL LA
CANNONS MDW
HERTFORD RD
River Mimram
Home Wood
Tewin Cowper CE Prim Sch
CHURCHFIELD RD
GRASS WARREN
MARGERY WOOD
NUTFIELD
FLEXLEY WOOD
SWANHILL
ROBIN MEAD
ROWANS
SALMON CL
HERTFORD RD
Rowans Prim Sch
POSTFIELD
LUMBARDS
EASTOR
Westley Wood
Rectory Wood
ARCHERS GREEN LA
Home Wood
SLOANSWAY
CROOKHAMS
QUICKBEAMS
POND FIELD
RUMSLEY
RC Sch
B1000 WATERSIDE
B1000
AL7
Tewin Bury Farm
Lamb Dell Wood
SG14
Marden Hill

89
111

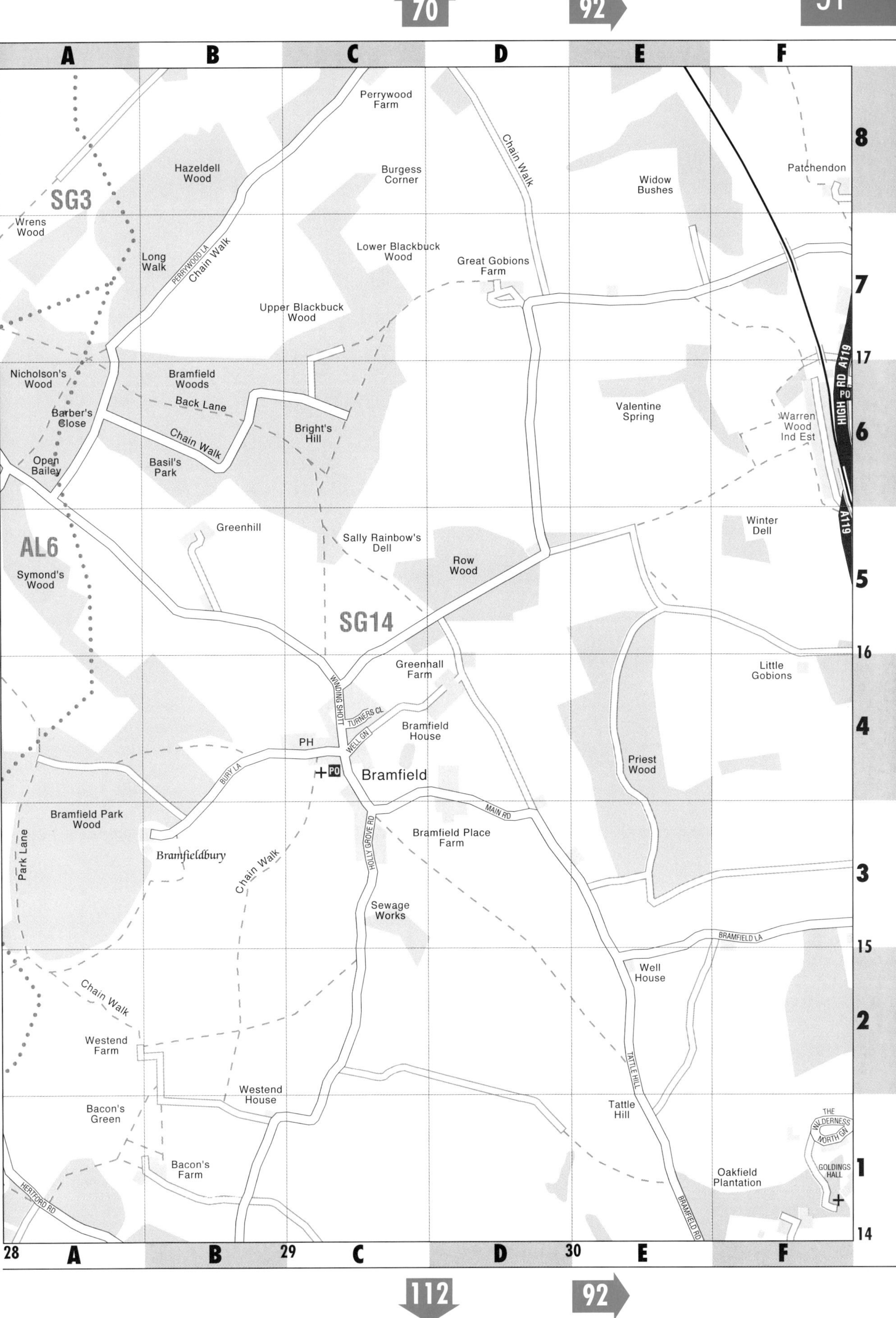
A
B
C
D
E
F
8
7
17
6
5
16
4
3
15
2
1
14
28
29
30
Perrywood Farm
Burgess Corner
Chain Walk
Widow Bushes
Patchendon
Hazeldell Wood
SG3
Wrens Wood
Long Walk
PERRYWOOD LA
Lower Blackbuck Wood
Great Gobions Farm
Upper Blackbuck Wood
Nicholson's Wood
Bramfield Woods
Back Lane
Barber's Close
Bright's Hill
Valentine Spring
Warren Wood Ind Est
HIGH RD
PO
A119
Open Bailey
Basil's Park
Greenhill
Sally Rainbow's Dell
Row Wood
Winter Dell
AL6
Symond's Wood
SG14
Greenhall Farm
Little Gobions
WINDING SHOTT
TURNERS CL
WELL GN
Bramfield House
PH
Priest Wood
BURY LA
Bramfield
MAIN RD
Bramfield Park Wood
HOLLY GROVE RD
Bramfield Place Farm
Bramfieldbury
Park Lane
Sewage Works
BRAMFIELD LA
Well House
Westend Farm
Westend House
TATTLE HILL
Tattle Hill
Bacon's Green
THE WILDERNESS
NORTH GN
GOLDINGS HALL
Bacon's Farm
Oakfield Plantation
HERTFORD RD
BRAMFIELD RD

91
71

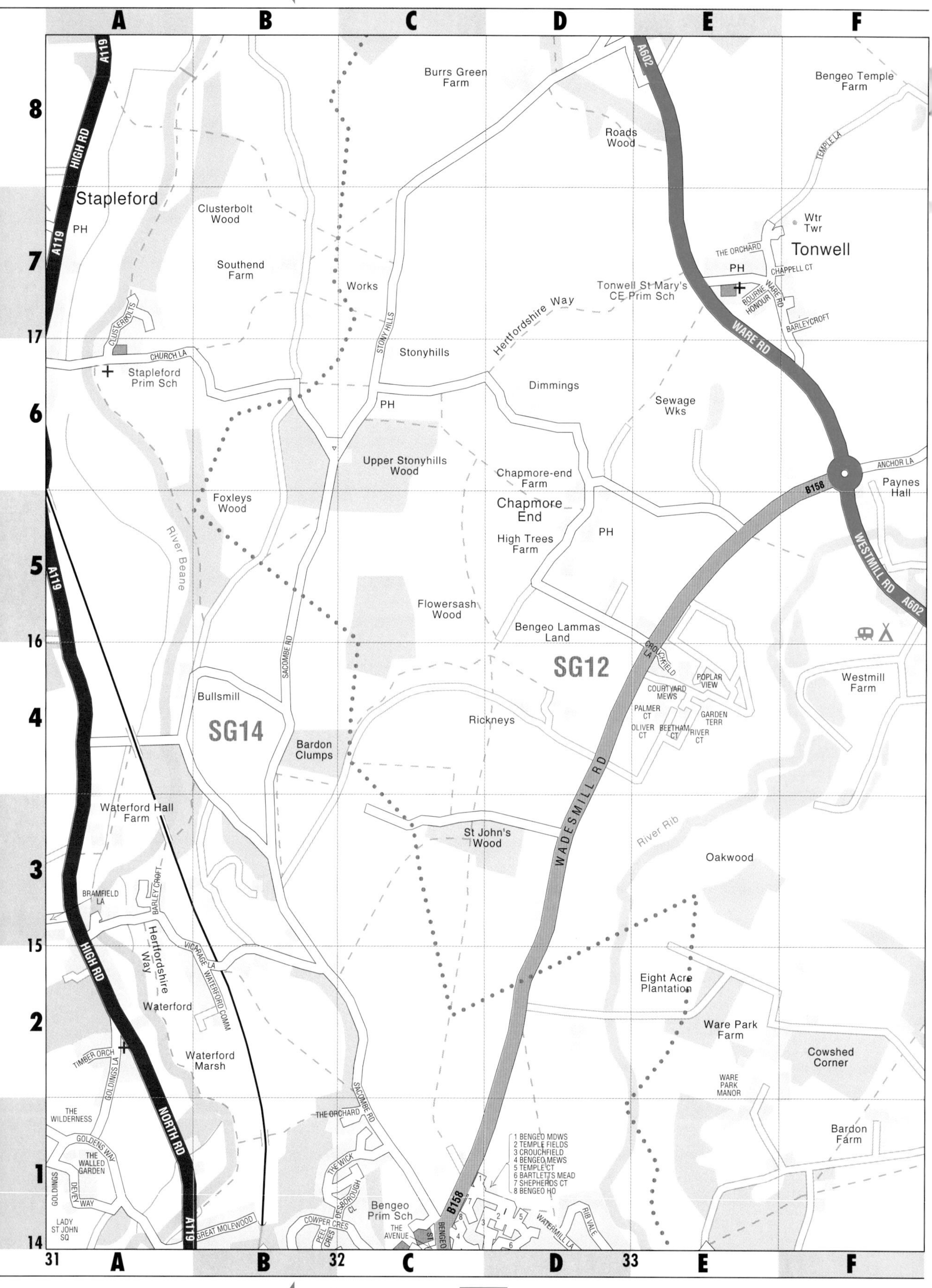
A
B
C
D
E
F
8
7
17
6
5
16
4
3
15
2
1
14
31
32
33
Stapleford
PH
Clusterbolt Wood
Southend Farm
Works
Burrs Green Farm
Roads Wood
Bengeo Temple Farm
TEMPLE LA
Wtr Twr
Tonwell
THE ORCHARD
CHAPPELL CT
Tonwell St Mary's CE Prim Sch
BOURNE HONOUR
WARE RD
BARLEYCROFT
Hertfordshire Way
STONY HILLS
Stonyhills
CHURCH LA
CLUSTERBOLTS
Stapleford Prim Sch
Dimmings
Sewage Wks
Upper Stonyhills Wood
Chapmore-end Farm
Chapmore End
High Trees Farm
ANCHOR LA
Paynes Hall
B158
Foxleys Wood
River Beane
A119
HIGH RD
A602
WESTMILL RD
Flowersash Wood
Bengeo Lammas Land
SG12
SG14
SACOMBE RD
Bullsmill
Bardon Clumps
Rickneys
CROUCHFIELD
LA
POPLAR VIEW
COURTYARD MEWS
PALMER CT
OLIVER CT
BEETHAM CT
RIVER CT
GARDEN TERR
Westmill Farm
Waterford Hall Farm
St John's Wood
WADESMILL RD
River Rib
Oakwood
BRAMFIELD LA
BARLEY CROFT
Hertfordshire Way
VICARAGE LA
WATERFORD COMM
Waterford
Eight Acre Plantation
Ware Park Farm
Cowshed Corner
WARE PARK MANOR
TIMBER ORCH
GOLDINGS LA
Waterford Marsh
NORTH RD
THE WILDERNESS
GOLDENS WAY
THE WALLED GARDEN
GOLDINGS
DEVEY WAY
LADY ST JOHN SQ
GREAT MOLEWOOD
THE ORCHARD
THE WICK
DESBOROUGH CL
COWPER CRES
PEEL CRES
Bengeo Prim Sch
THE AVENUE
BENGEO
1 BENGEO MDWS
2 TEMPLE FIELDS
3 CROUCHFIELD
4 BENGEO MEWS
5 TEMPLE CT
6 BARTLETTS MEAD
7 SHEPHERDS CT
8 BENGEO HO
WATERMILL LA
RIB VALE
Bardon Farm

91
113

72
94

A B C D E F

8 7 17 6 5 16 4 3 15 2 1 14

SG11
A10
Youngsbury
Lord's Wood
Chelsing Farm
Bourne Wood
Chelsing Cottages
Hertfordshire Way
Wadesmill
Upper Millfield Wood
Rennesley Farm
ANCHOR COTTS
DELLFIELD
MILLFIELD
YOUNGSBURY LA
PH
PO
OLD CHURCH LA
Wade's Wood
Thundridge CE Prim Sch
ERMINE ST
River Rib
Thundridge Bsns Pk
Thundridge
ELEANOR'S CL
DUCKETTS WOOD
WOODLANDS RD
WINDMILL COTTS
Thundridge Hill
ANCHOR LA
COLD CHRISTMAS LA
Chelsing Lodge
The Sow & Pigs (PH)
Cowards
POLES LA
POLES PK
HANBURY DR
HANBURY MEWS
DOWNFIELD CT
CH
Hanbury Manor (Hotel)
Mole's Wood
Moles Farm
FARM COTTS
Gravel Pit
Tip
Jubilee Plantation
SG12
A1170
Wodson Park Sports & L Ctr
Little Fanhams
South Lodge
Round House
THE LARCHES
QUINCEY RD
AMBERLEY GN
SALMONS CL
CHILTERN CL
DOVEDALE
WICKEN FIELDS
THE CREST
HEATH DR
St Mary's CE Jun Sch
Great Cozens
Ermine Point Bsns Pk
GENTLEMENS FIELD
WESTMILL RD
A602
GREYFRIARS
WHEATSHEAF DR
THE HAWTHORNS
BRIARDALE
THE BLAKES
THE BRAMBLES
GREENHILLS
CRANBROOK CL
ROCKFIELD AVE
Kingshill Inf Sch
HORROCKS CL
FANHAMS HALL RD
Dark La
THE PASTURES
POLES LA
MAPLEWOOD
THE RIDGEWAY
THE CHAUNCY
POPES ROW
VALLANS CL
THE GREEN
Gravel Pit
RICHMOND CL
Cemy
DEMONTFORT RISE
WULFRATH WAY
ALDWYKE RISE
LOWER BOURNE GDNS
HIGHMILL
BRYCE CL
KINGSWAY
CLARKS CL
GRASMERE RD
HITHER FIELD
LARKSFIELD
COLTSFOOT RD
ST JOHNS CT
LOWER MARGARET GDNS
EVERGREEN RD
LINWOOD RD
RUSHFIELD RD
ELDER RD
CHESTNUT AVE
COZENS RD
CHURCH FIELD
WESTMILL RD
B1001
ROLLESTON CL
DELCROFT
WARD CL
CROFT RD
WADESMILL RD
CHEYNE CL
CLIFTON WAY
HIGH OAK RD
REDAN RD
MUSLEY HILL
QUAKER RD
Tower Prim Sch
SELWYN CT
TOWER RD
BEAZLEY CL
SELLS RD
BEECHFIELD RD
THE HYDE
WENGEO LA
RAGE HILL
THUNDERCOURT
MILTON RD
SOUTHALL CL
HOMEFIELD RD
Western House
SANDEMAN GDNS
PARNEL RD
JUBILEE AVE
The Chauncy Sch
CANONS RD
BERKELEY CL
ORCHARD CL
BOURNE
GOLDSTONE CL
THE OCTAGON
LIME CL
TRINITY RD
FANHAMS RD
QUEENS RD
GROVE RD
WOODLEY RD
RENDLESHAM CL
WENGEO LA
VALLEY CL
STRAWBERRY FIELDS
Fanshawe Pool (L Ctr)
WATTON RD
BALDOCK ST
THE BOURNE
COLLETT RD
KING GEORGE RD
PO
COBHAM RD
St Catherine's CE Prim Sch
BRICKFIELDS
TRAPSTYLE RD
FANSHAWE CRES
GLADSTONE RD
CENTURY RD
CRIB ST
PRINCES ST
CORONATION RD
FRANCIS RD
MILL RD
KILN HOUSE CL
MUSLEY LA
POPIS GDNS
HAMPDEN HILL CL
HAMPDEN HILL
CROMWELL RD
UPPER CLABDENS
COZENS RD
WARE
PARK RD
B1001
A1170
BURYFIELD MALTINGS
BURYFIELD WAY
DEERFIELD CL
KING EDWARD'S RD
GRANTHAM GDNS
UPLANDS
Monastery
Works
HARRIS'S LA
Works
Ind Est
CHURCH ST
BLUECOAT YD
NEW RD
HANBURY CL
Sch
BOWLING RD
NURSERY GDNS
VICARAGE RD
GARLAND RD
JEFFRIES RD
MUSLEY LA
BELLE VUE RD
WINTON RD
LOWER CLABDENS
BARLEY PONDS CL
BARLEY PONDS RD
BURYFIELD TERR
MAPLETHORPE CT
MILL CL
WEST ST
HIGH ST
EAST ST
KIBES LA
THE CLOSE
STAR HOLME CT
CLEMENTS ST
CROSS ST
CAYNSFORD RD
LITTLE WIDBURY LA
LITTLE WIDBURY
PRIORY ST
Ware Mus
Liby
BURGAGE LA
River Lea or Lee
River Lea Navigation
Sacred Heart RC Prim Sch
Lea Valley Wlk
BRIDGE FOOT
COMMON WHARF
B1004
STAR ST
WIDBURY GDNS
MUSLEIGH MANOR
WIDBURY HILL
B1004
A119
A1170
VIADUCT RD
AMWELL END
WICKHAMS WHARF
RIVER ST
LYGEAN AVE
HOLLYCROSS RD
BROADMEADS
A119
HERTFORD RD
LC
STATION RD
CRANE
LOXLEY CT
A10

34 A B 35 C D 36 E F

C3
1 PEREGRINE HO
2 FALCON CT
3 OSPREY HO
4 KESTREL CT
5 LOWER BOURNE CL

D1
1 BLACK SWAN CT
2 CHURCH ROW MEWS
3 ST MARY'S CTYD
4 OMEGA CT
5 FRENCH HORN CT
6 LEASIDE WLK
7 DOLPHIN YD
8 WELLS YD
9 GEORGE WLK
10 RIVERSIDE MEWS
11 WATER ROW
12 BURGAGE CT
13 CHRISTOPHER CT
14 BECKETS WLK
15 STATION CT
16 YORKES MEWS
17 TUDOR WLK
18 TUDOR SQ
19 DICKENSON WAY

114

D1
20 CATHERINE WHEEL MEWS
21 FRENCH'S YD

94

D2
1 THUNDER HALL
2 THE BAKERY
3 ROKEWOOD MEWS
4 WAGGONERS YD
5 ST EVROUL CT
6 HARTFIELD CT
7 MONKS ROW
8 CAMERON CT
9 THE ALBION
10 CHURCH CT
11 VINE CT

E1
1 MILLACRES
2 OMEGA MALTINGS
3 ALBANY MEWS
4 STEWART PL
5 BOWSHER CT
6 Mill Studio Bsns Ctr

93
73

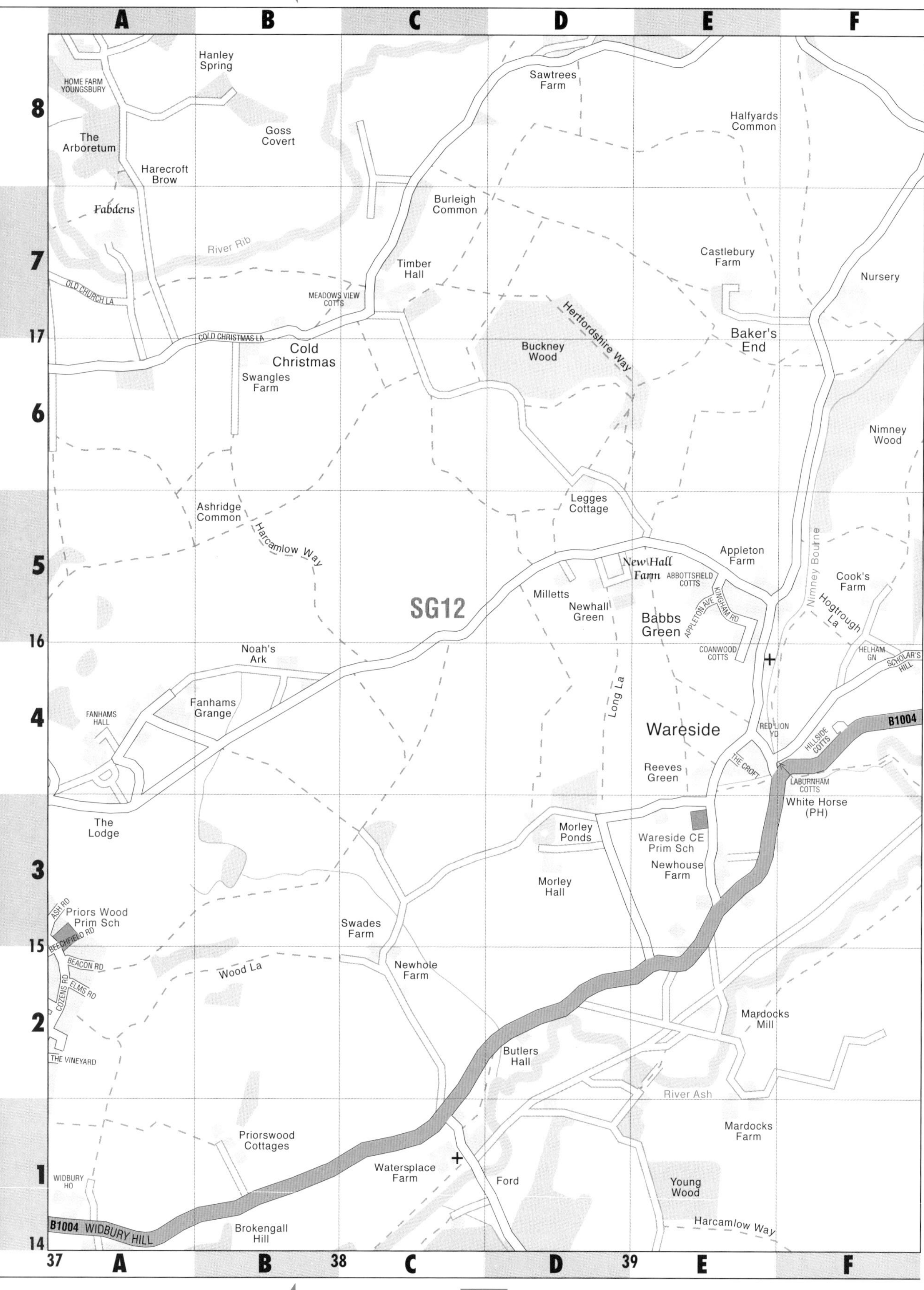
A
B
C
D
E
F
8
7
17
6
5
16
4
3
15
2
1
14
37
38
39
Hanley Spring
HOME FARM YOUNGSBURY
The Arboretum
Goss Covert
Harecroft Brow
Fabdens
River Rib
OLD CHURCH LA
MEADOWS VIEW COTTS
COLD CHRISTMAS LA
Cold Christmas
Swangles Farm
Sawtrees Farm
Halfyards Common
Burleigh Common
Timber Hall
Castlebury Farm
Nursery
Hertfordshire Way
Buckney Wood
Baker's End
Nimney Wood
Legges Cottage
Ashridge Common
Harcamlow Way
Appleton Farm
New Hall Farm
ABBOTTSFIELD COTTS
Cook's Farm
Nimney Bourne
Hogtrough La
Milletts
Newhall Green
Babbs Green
APPLETON AVE
KINGHAM RD
SG12
COANWOOD COTTS
HELHAM GN
SCHOLAR'S HILL
Noah's Ark
Fanhams Grange
FANHAMS HALL
Long La
Wareside
RED LION YD
HILLSIDE COTTS
B1004
THE CROFT
Reeves Green
LABURNHAM COTTS
White Horse (PH)
The Lodge
Morley Ponds
Wareside CE Prim Sch
Newhouse Farm
Morley Hall
ASH RD
Priors Wood Prim Sch
BEECHFIELD RD
BEACON RD
Swades Farm
Wood La
Newhole Farm
COZENS RD
ELMS RD
Mardocks Mill
THE VINEYARD
Butlers Hall
River Ash
Priorswood Cottages
Mardocks Farm
WIDBURY HO
Watersplace Farm
Ford
Young Wood
B1004 WIDBURY HILL
Brokengall Hill
Harcamlow Way

93
115

74
96

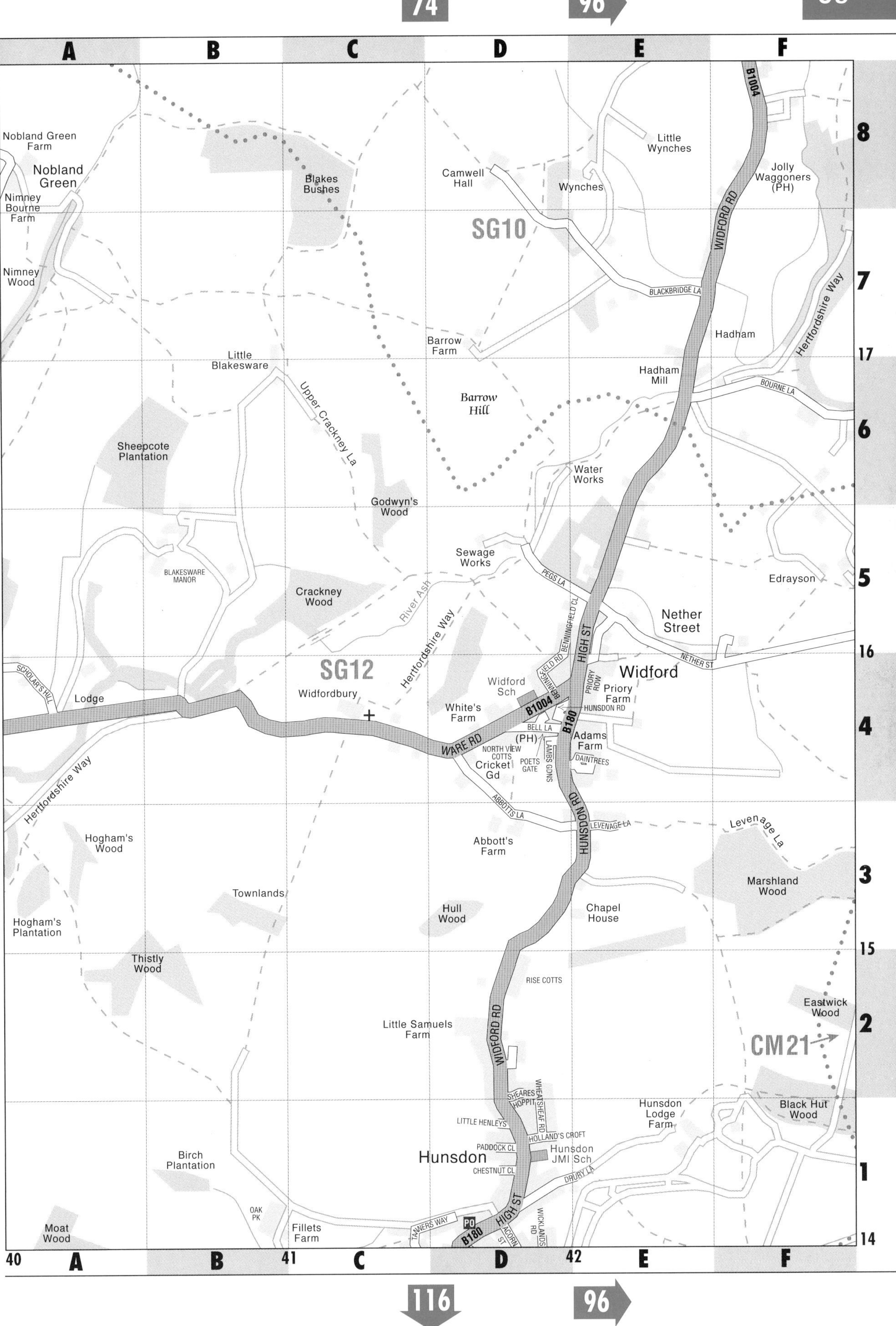
A
B
C
D
E
F
8
7
17
6
5
16
4
3
15
2
1
14
40
41
42
Nobland Green Farm
Nobland Green
Nimney Bourne Farm
Nimney Wood
Blakes Bushes
Camwell Hall
Wynches
Little Wynches
Jolly Waggoners (PH)
SG10
WIDFORD RD
B1004
BLACKBRIDGE LA
Hertfordshire Way
Barrow Farm
Hadham
Hadham Mill
BOURNE LA
Little Blakesware
Upper Crackney La
Barrow Hill
Sheepcote Plantation
Water Works
Godwyn's Wood
Sewage Works
BLAKESWARE MANOR
PEGS LA
Edrayson
Crackney Wood
River Ash
Hertfordshire Way
BENNINGFIELD CL
HIGH ST
Nether Street
NETHER ST
SG12
Widford Sch
PRIORY ROW
Widford
Priory Farm
SCHOLAR'S HILL
Lodge
Widfordbury
White's Farm
B1004
HUNSDON RD
B180
BELL LA
(PH)
WARE RD
Adams Farm
NORTH VIEW COTTS
Cricket Gd
POETS GATE
LAMBS GDNS
DAINTREES
Hertfordshire Way
ABBOTTS LA
LEVENAGE LA
Levenage La
HUNSDON RD
Hogham's Wood
Abbott's Farm
Marshland Wood
Townlands
Hull Wood
Chapel House
Hogham's Plantation
Thistly Wood
RISE COTTS
Eastwick Wood
Little Samuels Farm
WIDFORD RD
CM21
SHEARES HOPPIT
WHEATSHEAF RD
Hunsdon Lodge Farm
Black Hut Wood
LITTLE HENLEYS
HOLLAND'S CROFT
PADDOCK CL
Hunsdon JMI Sch
Hunsdon
Birch Plantation
CHESTNUT CL
DRURY LA
OAK PK
TANNERS WAY
PO
HIGH ST
B180
ACORN ST
WICKLANDS RD
Fillets Farm
Moat Wood

116
96

95
75

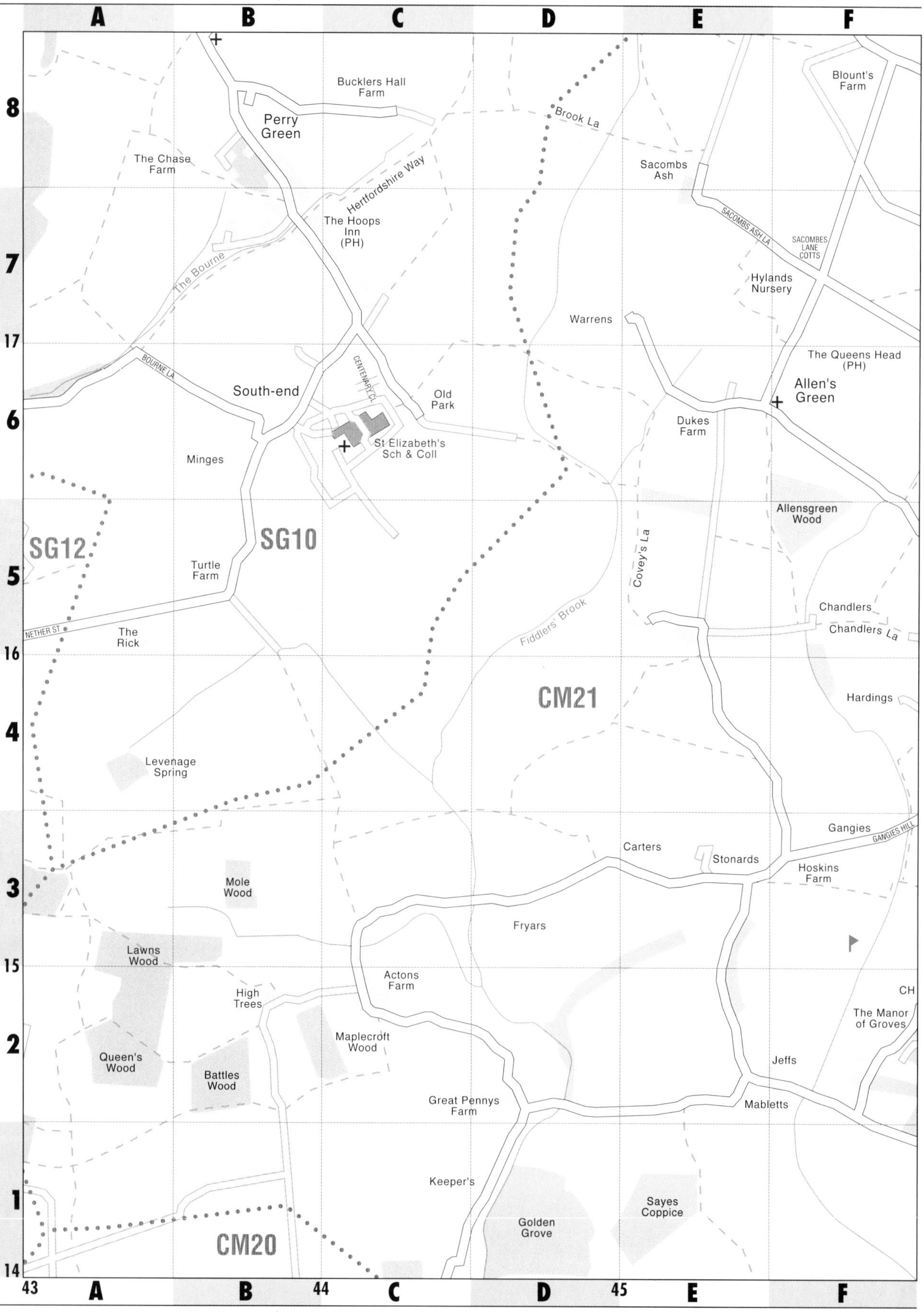

A
B
C
D
E
F
8
7
17
6
5
16
4
3
15
2
1
14
Bucklers Hall Farm
Perry Green
Brook La
Blount's Farm
The Chase Farm
Hertfordshire Way
Sacombs Ash
SACOMBS ASH LA
SACOMBES LANE COTTS
The Hoops Inn (PH)
The Bourne
Hylands Nursery
Warrens
BOURNE LA
CENTENARY CL
The Queens Head (PH)
South-end
Old Park
Allen's Green
Dukes Farm
St Elizabeth's Sch & Coll
Minges
Allensgreen Wood
SG12
SG10
Covey's La
Turtle Farm
Chandlers
Chandlers La
NETHER ST
The Rick
Fiddlers' Brook
CM21
Hardings
Levenage Spring
Gangies
GANGIES HILL
Carters
Stonards
Hoskins Farm
Mole Wood
Fryars
Lawns Wood
Actons Farm
High Trees
CH
The Manor of Groves
Maplecroft Wood
Queen's Wood
Jeffs
Battles Wood
Great Pennys Farm
Mabletts
Keeper's
Sayes Coppice
Golden Grove
CM20
43
44
45

95
117

76
98

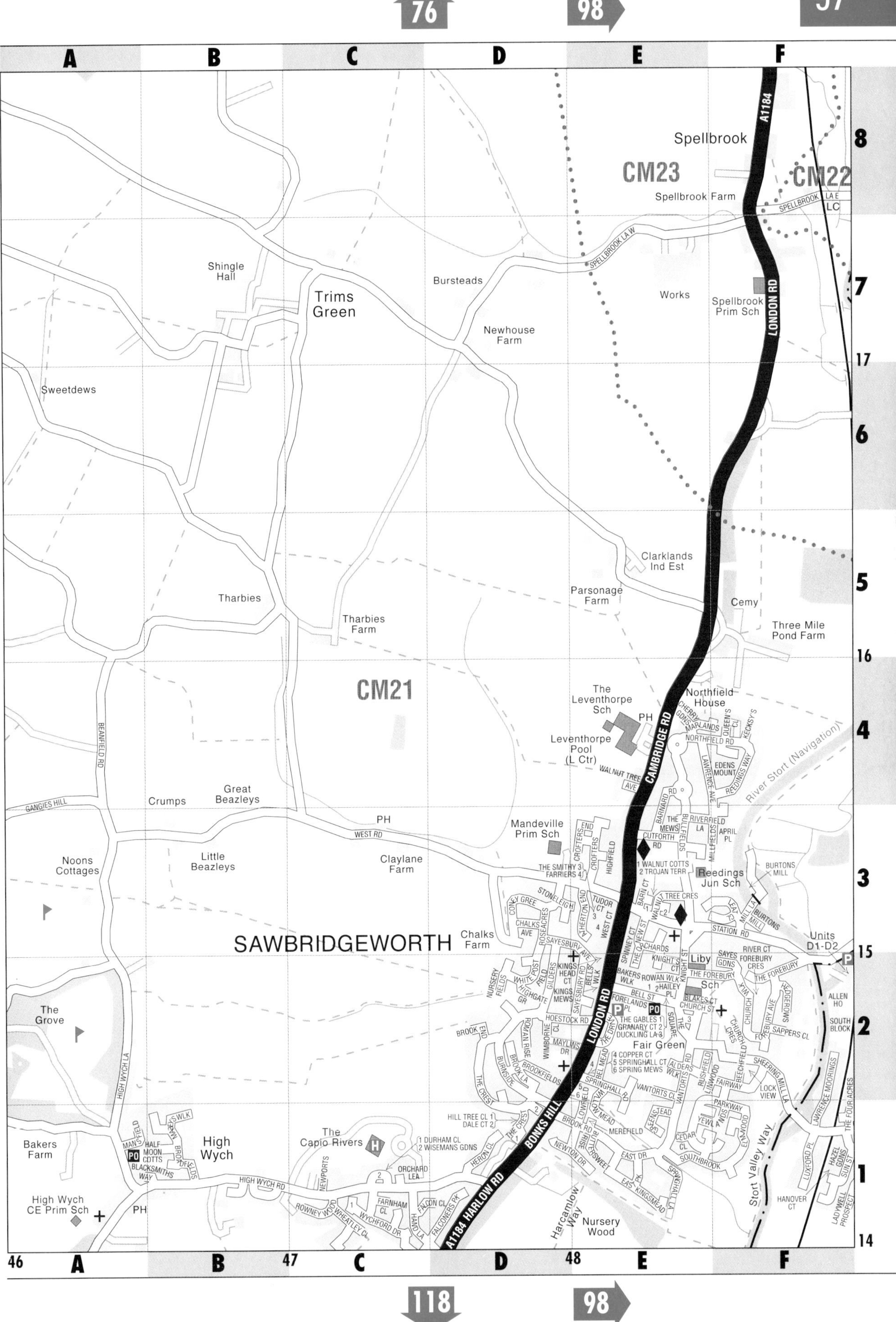
Spellbrook
CM23
CM22
Spellbrook Farm
SPELLBROOK LA E
LC
SPELLBROOK LA W
A1184
Shingle Hall
Trims Green
Bursteads
Works
Spellbrook Prim Sch
LONDON RD
Newhouse Farm
Sweetdews
Clarklands Ind Est
Parsonage Farm
Tharbies
Tharbies Farm
Cemy
Three Mile Pond Farm
CM21
The Leventhorpe Sch
Northfield House
PH
Leventhorpe Pool (L Ctr)
CAMBRIDGE RD
River Stort (Navigation)
BEANFIELD RD
GANGIES HILL
Crumps
Great Beazleys
WEST RD
Mandeville Prim Sch
Noons Cottages
Little Beazleys
Claylane Farm
Reedings Jun Sch
BURTONS MILL
SAWBRIDGEWORTH
Chalks Farm
Units D1-D2
Liby
Sch
Fair Green
The Grove
ALLEN HO
SOUTH BLOCK
HIGH WYCH LA
Bakers Farm
High Wych
The Capio Rivers
HIGH WYCH RD
BONKS HILL
A1184 HARLOW RD
Harcamlow Way
Nursery Wood
Stort Valley Way
High Wych CE Prim Sch
PH
HANOVER CT
A
B
C
D
E
F
8
7
17
6
5
16
4
3
15
2
1
14
46
47
48

118
98

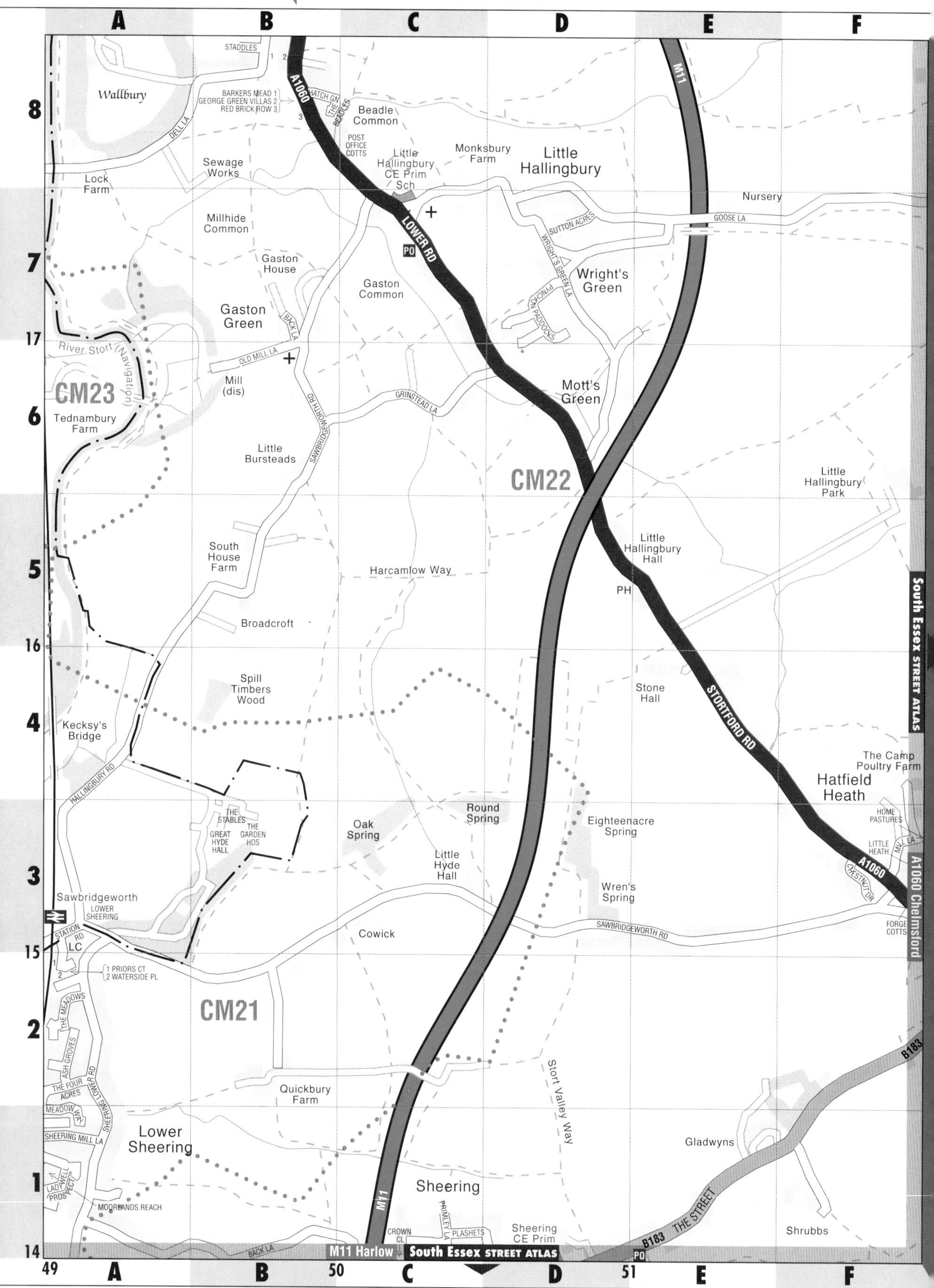
97
77
A
B
C
D
E
F
8
7
17
6
5
16
4
3
15
2
1
14
49
50
51
STADDLES
Wallbury
BARKERS MEAD 1
GEORGE GREEN VILLAS 2
RED BRICK ROW 3
HATCH GN
THE BEADLES
Beadle Common
A1060
M11
DELL LA
POST OFFICE COTTS
Little Hallingbury CE Prim Sch
Monksbury Farm
Little Hallingbury
Sewage Works
Lock Farm
Nursery
GOOSE LA
SUTTON ACRES
Millhide Common
LOWER RD
PO
WRIGHT'S GREEN LA
Gaston House
Gaston Common
Wright's Green
PYNCHON PADDOCKS
Gaston Green
BACK LA
River Stort (Navigation)
OLD MILL LA
Mill (dis)
CM23
Mott's Green
GRINSTEAD LA
Tednambury Farm
SAWBRIDGEWORTH RD
Little Bursteads
CM22
Little Hallingbury Park
South House Farm
Little Hallingbury Hall
Harcamlow Way
PH
Broadcroft
Spill Timbers Wood
Stone Hall
STORTFORD RD
Kecksy's Bridge
The Camp Poultry Farm
Hatfield Heath
HALLINGBURY RD
HOME PASTURES
THE STABLES
GREAT HYDE HALL
THE GARDEN HOS
Round Spring
Oak Spring
Eighteenacre Spring
LITTLE HEATH
MILL LA
Little Hyde Hall
CHESTNUT DR
Wren's Spring
Sawbridgeworth
LOWER SHEERING
STATION RD
LC
Cowick
SAWBRIDGEWORTH RD
FORGE COTTS
1 PRIORS CT
2 WATERSIDE PL
CM21
THE MEADOWS
ASH GROVES
THE FOUR ACRES
MEADOW WALK
SHEERING LOWER RD
Quickbury Farm
Stort Valley Way
B183
SHEERING MILL LA
Lower Sheering
Gladwyns
LADYWELL PROSPECT
Sheering
THE STREET
MOORLANDS REACH
PRIMLEY LA
CROWN CL
PLASHETS
Sheering CE Prim
Shrubbs
BACK LA
M11 Harlow
South Essex STREET ATLAS
A1060 Chelmsford

97

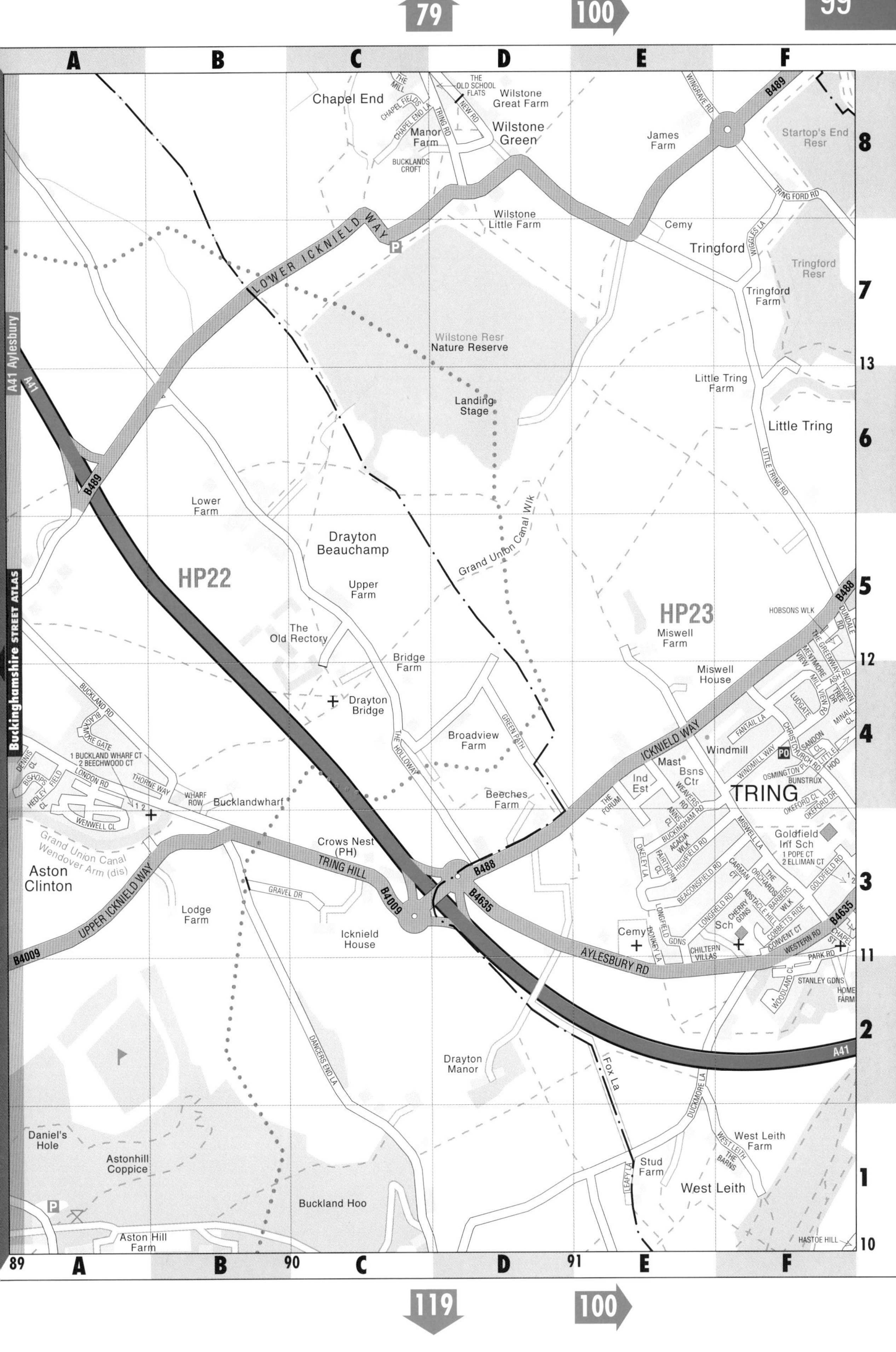
79
100
Chapel End
Wilstone Great Farm
Wilstone Green
Manor Farm
James Farm
Startop's End Resr
Wilstone Little Farm
Cemy
Tringford
Tringford Resr
Tringford Farm
LOWER ICKNIELD WAY
Wilstone Resr
Nature Reserve
Little Tring Farm
Little Tring
Landing Stage
A41 Aylesbury
Lower Farm
Drayton Beauchamp
HP22
Grand Union Canal Wlk
Upper Farm
HP23
Miswell Farm
The Old Rectory
Bridge Farm
Miswell House
Drayton Bridge
Broadview Farm
ICKNIELD WAY
Windmill
Mast
Bsns Ctr
Ind Est
TRING
Bucklandwharf
Beeches Farm
Goldfield Inf Sch
Aston Clinton
Grand Union Canal Wendover Arm (dis)
Crows Nest (PH)
TRING HILL
UPPER ICKNIELD WAY
Lodge Farm
Icknield House
Cemy
Sch
AYLESBURY RD
Drayton Manor
Fox La
Daniel's Hole
Astonhill Coppice
West Leith Farm
Stud Farm
West Leith
Buckland Hoo
Aston Hill Farm
Buckinghamshire STREET ATLAS
89
90
91
A
B
C
D
E
F
1
2
3
4
5
6
7
8
10
11
12
13
119
100

99
80

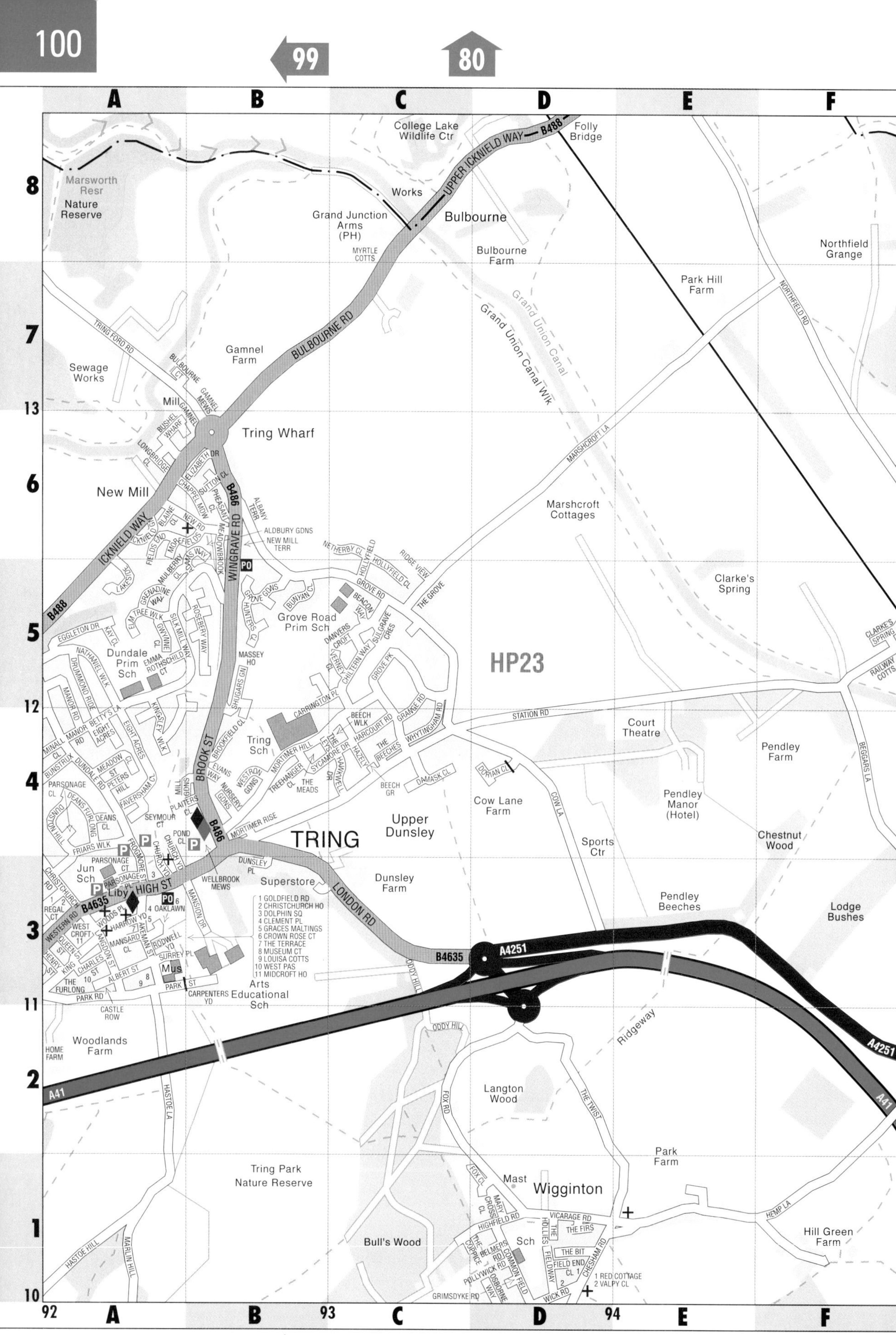
A
B
C
D
E
F
8
7
13
6
5
12
4
3
11
2
1
10
92
93
94
College Lake
Wildlife Ctr
Folly
Bridge
Marsworth
Resr
Nature
Reserve
Works
UPPER ICKNIELD WAY
B488
Grand Junction
Arms
(PH)
MYRTLE
COTTS
Bulbourne
Bulbourne
Farm
Northfield
Grange
Park Hill
Farm
NORTHFIELD RD
Grand Union Canal
Grand Union Canal Wlk
TRING FORD RD
Gamnel
Farm
BULBOURNE RD
Sewage
Works
BULBOURNE CT
GAMNEL MEWS
Mill
BUSHEL WHARF
LONGBRIDGE CL
Tring Wharf
ELIZABETH DR
New Mill
MARSHCROFT LA
Marshcroft
Cottages
ICKNIELD WAY
B486
WINGRAVE RD
ALBANY TERR
ALDBURY GDNS
NEW MILL TERR
PO
NETHERBY CL
HOLLYFIELD
HOLLYFIELD CL
RIDGE VIEW
THE GROVE
GROVE RD
BEACON WAY
Clarke's
Spring
B488
EGGLETON DR
Grove Road
Prim Sch
HP23
CLARKE'S SPRING
RAILWAY COTTS
Dundale
Prim
Sch
MASSEY HO
CARRINGTON PL
STATION RD
Court
Theatre
Pendley
Farm
BEGGARS LA
Tring
Sch
BEECH WLK
HARCOURT RD
WHYTINGHAM RD
DAMASK CL
Cow Lane
Farm
COW LA
Pendley
Manor
(Hotel)
Chestnut
Wood
BROOK ST
Upper
Dunsley
TRING
Sports
Ctr
MORTIMER RISE
DUNSLEY PL
Superstore
Dunsley
Farm
Pendley
Beeches
Lodge
Bushes
HIGH ST
B4635
Liby
PO
LONDON RD
1 GOLDFIELD RD
2 CHRISTCHURCH HO
3 DOLPHIN SQ
4 CLEMENT PL
5 GRACES MALTINGS
6 CROWN ROSE CT
7 THE TERRACE
8 MUSEUM CT
9 LOUISA COTTS
10 WEST PAS
11 MIDCROFT HO
4 OAKLAWN
WELLBROOK MEWS
Jun
Sch
Mus
Arts
Educational
Sch
CARPENTERS YD
A4251
B4635
ODDY HILL
CASTLE ROW
PARK RD
THE FURLONG
Woodlands
Farm
HOME FARM
Ridgeway
A4251
A41
HASTOE LA
Langton
Wood
FOX RD
THE TWIST
A41
Park
Farm
Tring Park
Nature Reserve
Mast
Wigginton
FOX CL
MARY CROSS CL
HIGHFIELD RD
VICARAGE RD
THE FIRS
HEMP LA
Hill Green
Farm
Bull's Wood
Sch
THE BIT
FIELD END
CHESHAM RD
1 RED COTTAGE
2 VALPY CL
WICK RD
GRIMSDYKE RD
HASTOE HILL
MARLIN HILL

99
120

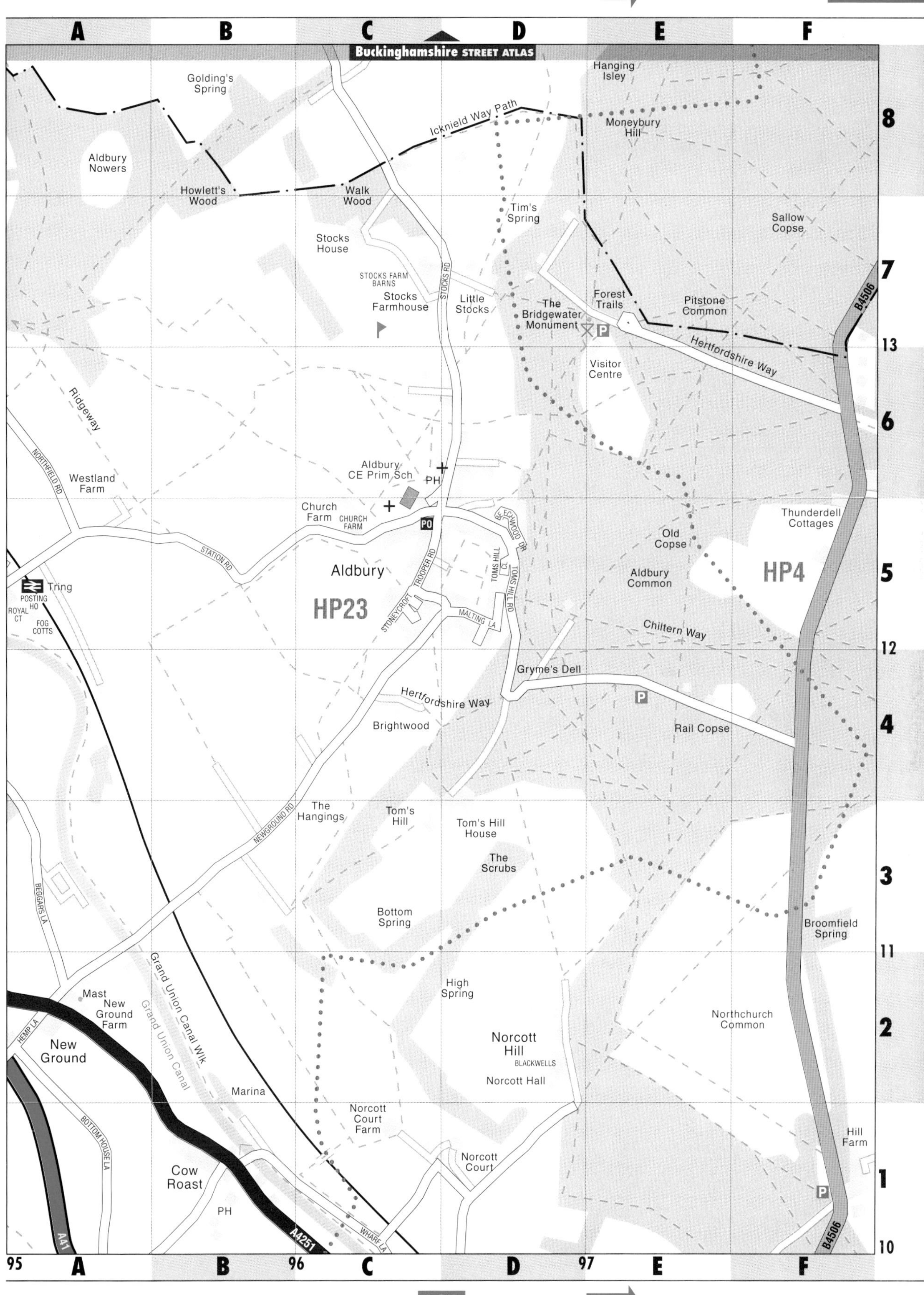
A
B
C
D
E
F
Buckinghamshire STREET ATLAS
Golding's Spring
Hanging Isley
Icknield Way Path
Moneybury Hill
Aldbury Nowers
Howlett's Wood
Walk Wood
Tim's Spring
Sallow Copse
Stocks House
STOCKS FARM BARNS
Stocks Farmhouse
STOCKS RD
Little Stocks
The Bridgewater Monument
Forest Trails
Pitstone Common
B4506
Hertfordshire Way
Visitor Centre
Ridgeway
NORTHFIELD RD
Westland Farm
Aldbury CE Prim Sch
PH
Church Farm
CHURCH FARM
PO
BEECHWOOD DR
Thunderdell Cottages
Old Copse
STATION RD
Aldbury
TROOPER RD
TOMS HILL
TOMS HILL RD
Aldbury Common
HP4
Tring
POSTING HO
ROYAL CT
FOG COTTS
HP23
STONEYCROFT
MALTING LA
Chiltern Way
Gryme's Dell
Hertfordshire Way
Brightwood
Rail Copse
NEWGROUND RD
The Hangings
Tom's Hill
Tom's Hill House
The Scrubs
BEGGARS LA
Bottom Spring
Broomfield Spring
Grand Union Canal Wlk
Grand Union Canal
Mast
New Ground Farm
High Spring
Northchurch Common
HEMP LA
New Ground
Norcott Hill
BLACKWELLS
Norcott Hall
Marina
Norcott Court Farm
BOTTOM HOUSE LA
Hill Farm
Cow Roast
Norcott Court
PH
A41
A4251
WHARF LA
8
7
13
6
5
12
4
3
11
2
1
10
95
96
97

101
81

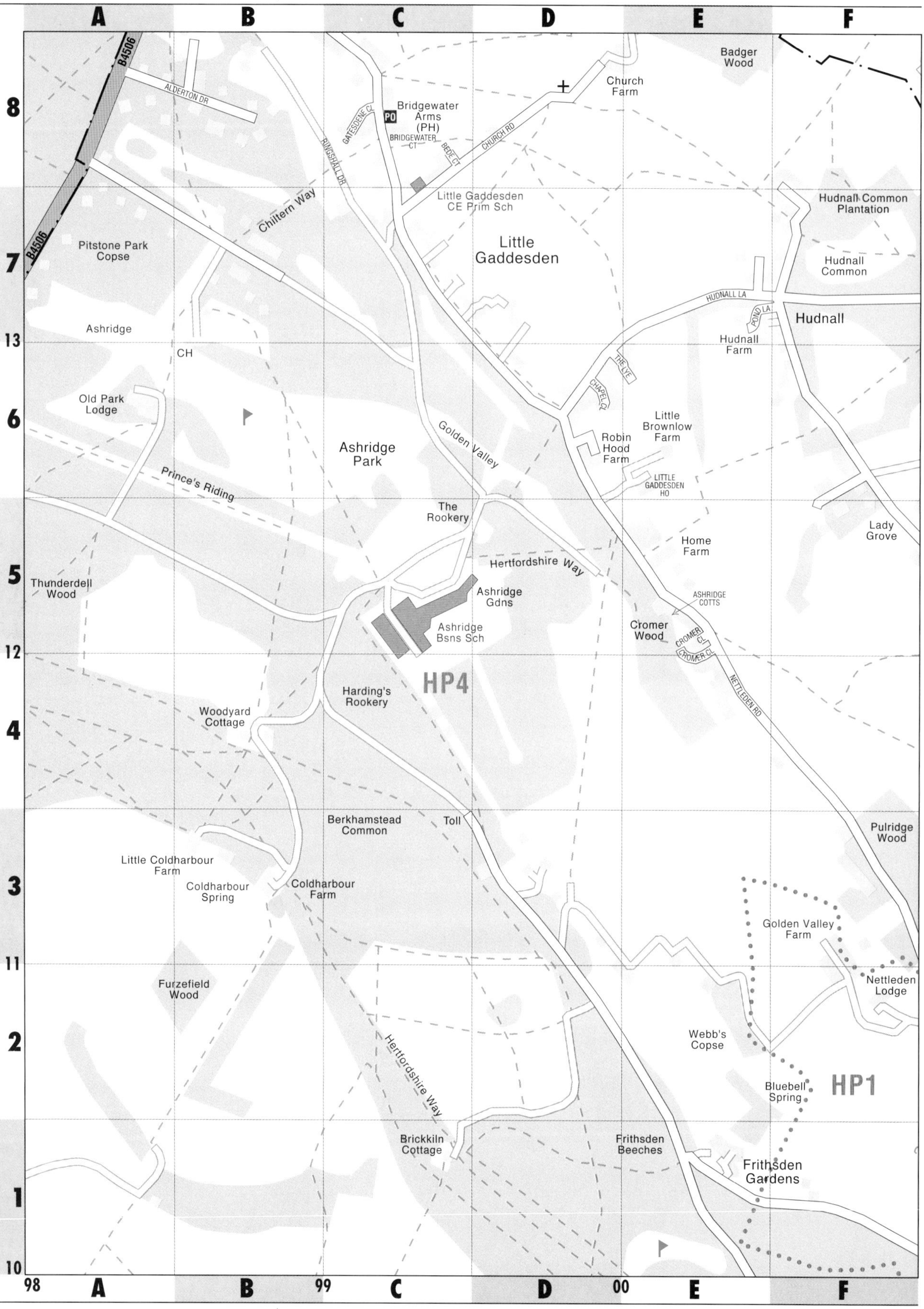

A B C D E F

8 7 13 6 5 12 4 3 11 2 1 10

Badger Wood
Church Farm
Bridgewater Arms (PH)
PO
GATESDENE CL
BRIDGEWATER CT
BEDE CT
CHURCH RD
ALDERTON DR
B4506
RINGSHALL DR
Chiltern Way
Little Gaddesden CE Prim Sch
Little Gaddesden
Hudnall Common Plantation
Hudnall Common
HUDNALL LA
POND LA
Hudnall
Hudnall Farm
Pitstone Park Copse
Ashridge
CH
Old Park Lodge
THE LYE
CHAPEL CL
Little Brownlow Farm
Robin Hood Farm
LITTLE GADDESDEN HO
Ashridge Park
Golden Valley
Prince's Riding
The Rookery
Home Farm
Lady Grove
Hertfordshire Way
Thunderdell Wood
Ashridge Gdns
ASHRIDGE COTTS
Ashridge Bsns Sch
Cromer Wood
CROMER CL
NETTLEDEN RD
HP4
Harding's Rookery
Woodyard Cottage
Berkhamstead Common
Toll
Pulridge Wood
Little Coldharbour Farm
Coldharbour Spring
Coldharbour Farm
Golden Valley Farm
Nettleden Lodge
Furzefield Wood
Webb's Copse
Hertfordshire Way
Bluebell Spring
HP1
Brickkiln Cottage
Frithsden Beeches
Frithsden Gardens

98 99 00

101
122

82
104

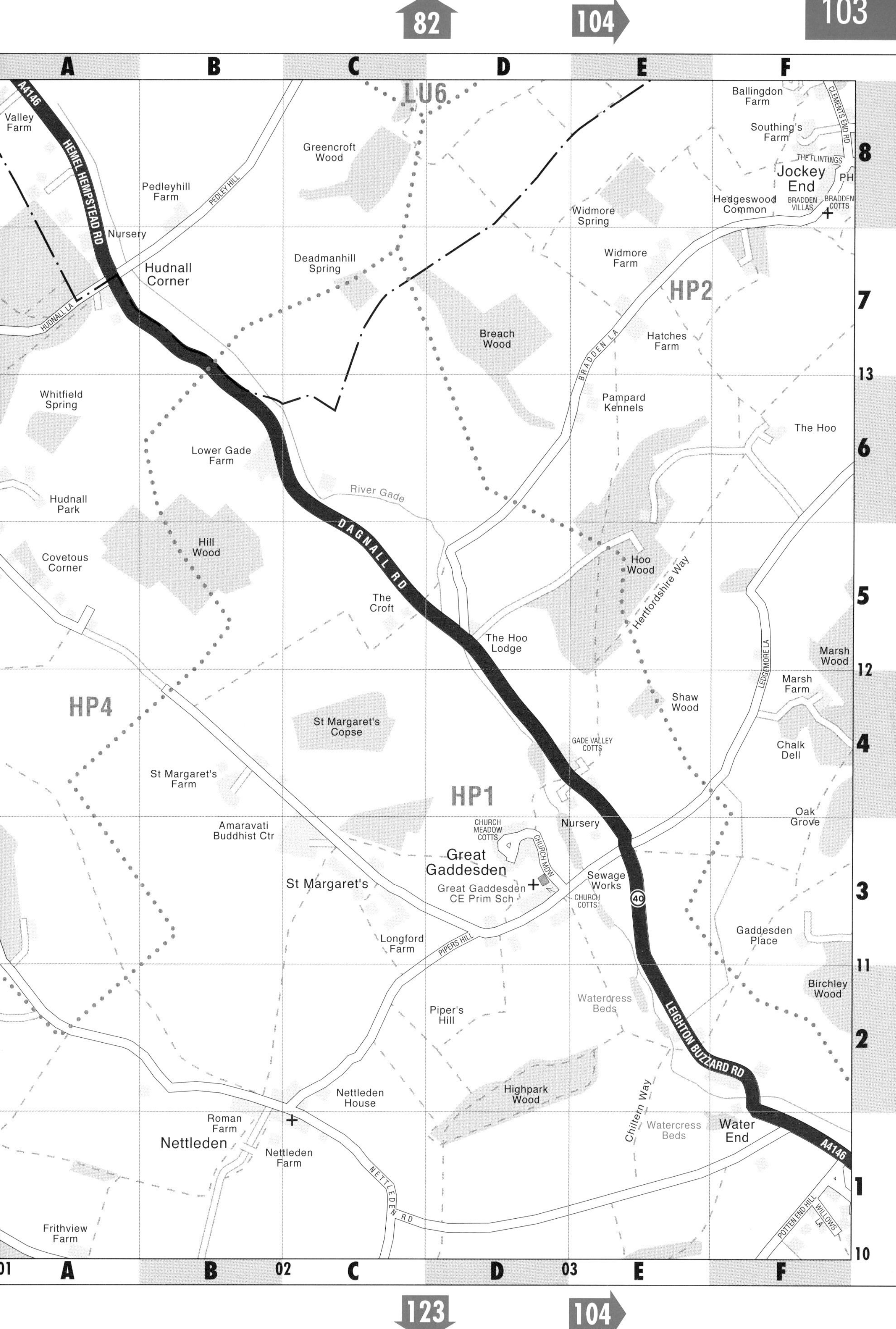

123
104

103
83
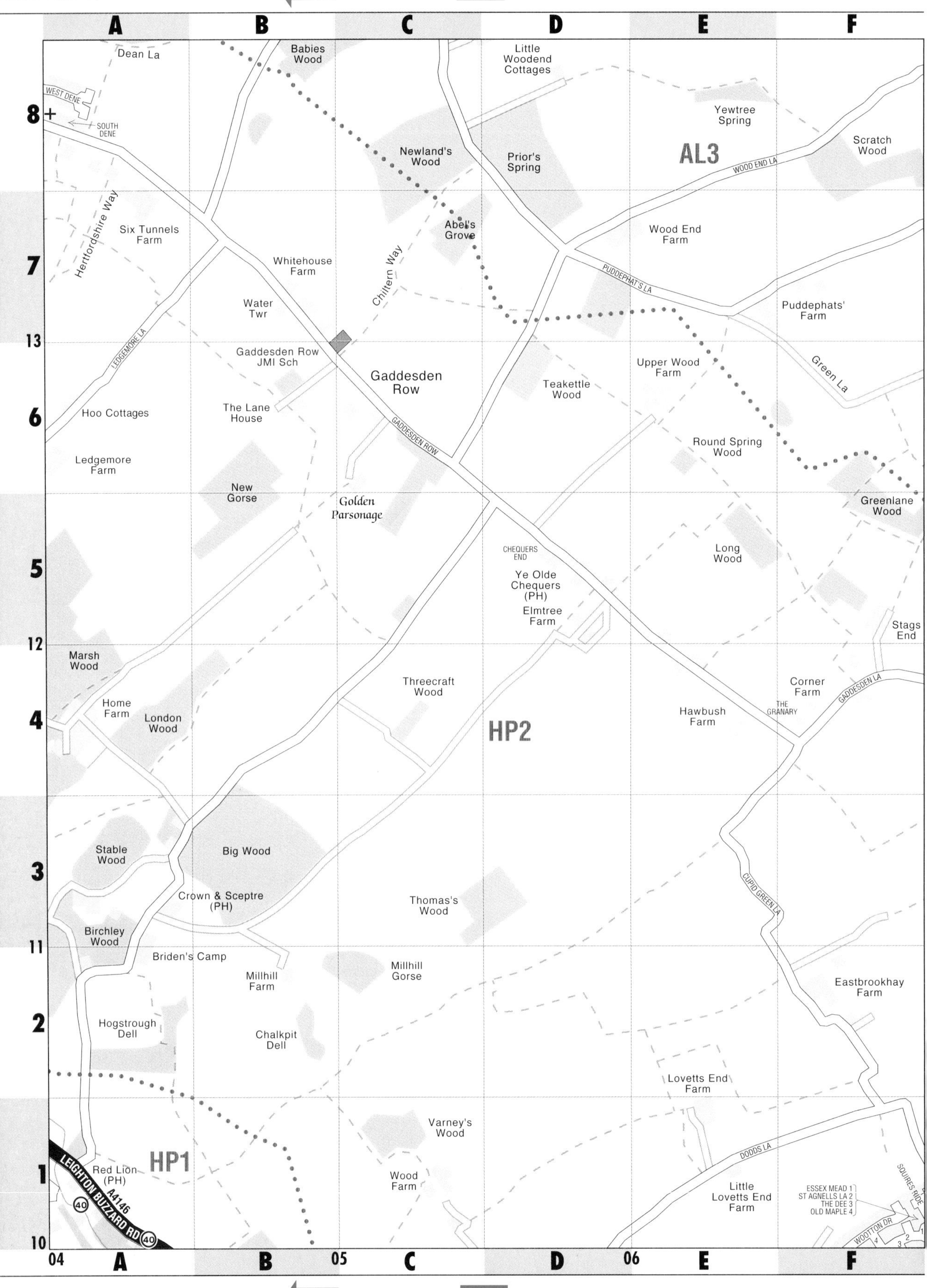

103
124

A
B
C
D
E
F
PH
Trowley Bottom
WOOD END LA
TROWLEY BOTTOM
WHITE HILL
Trowley Bottom Farm
PUDDEPHAT'S LA
Grove Farm
DELMEREND LA
St Agnells Farm
Wr Twr
Redding Wood
REDDING LA
DUNSTABLE RD
A5183
M1
8
7
Nursery
LYBURY LA
Nicholls Farm
13
Green La
Hertfordshire Way
Nicholl's Great Wood
Rabbitfield Spring
Nirvana
6
HILLTOP
TASSELL HALL
THE SQUARE
ROSE ACRE
NICHOLLS CL
DOWN EDGE
Greenlane Farm
New Wood
5
Flamsteadbury Farm
BURY COTTS
Bury Wood
ST STEPHENS WAY
12
MANSDALE RD
AL3
Church End
4
GADDESDEN LA
SABERTON CL
Hay Wood
HEMEL HEMPSTEAD RD
B487
The Aubreys
Woodside
3
Holtsmore End Farm
Holtsmore End
Great Revel End Farm
Pantake Wood
Hotel
AUBREY LA
11
HP2
Smallholding
The Beeches
2
Little Revelend Farm
HEMEL HEMPSTEAD RD
1 ASHBY CT
2 EVERSDEN CT
3 LONGSTANTON CT
4 SEDGEWICK CT
5 HADDENHAM CT
6 MILTON CT
YEOMANS CT
HIGH WYCH WAY
ASTON VIEW
BRAEMAR
BLAIR CL
VALLEY GN
HOLTSMERE END LANE
Nicky Way
Brockswood Prim Sch
1
WIDFORD TERR
ELSTREE RD
BRAMFIELD PL
ROYDON CT
TATTERSHALL DR
SHENLEY RD
GLAMIS CL
CUPID GREEN LA
WARESIDE
SANDRIDGE CL
HORTON GDNS
ESSEX MEAD
YEOMANS RIDE
KIPLING GR
KEATS CL
BRONTE CRES
DARWIN CL
BYRON PL
BERKELEY SQ
NIGHTINGALE WLK
PERRY GN
CODICOTE ROW
DICKENS CT
CHAUCER WLK
COLERIDGE CRES
B487
M1
10
07
08
09

105
85

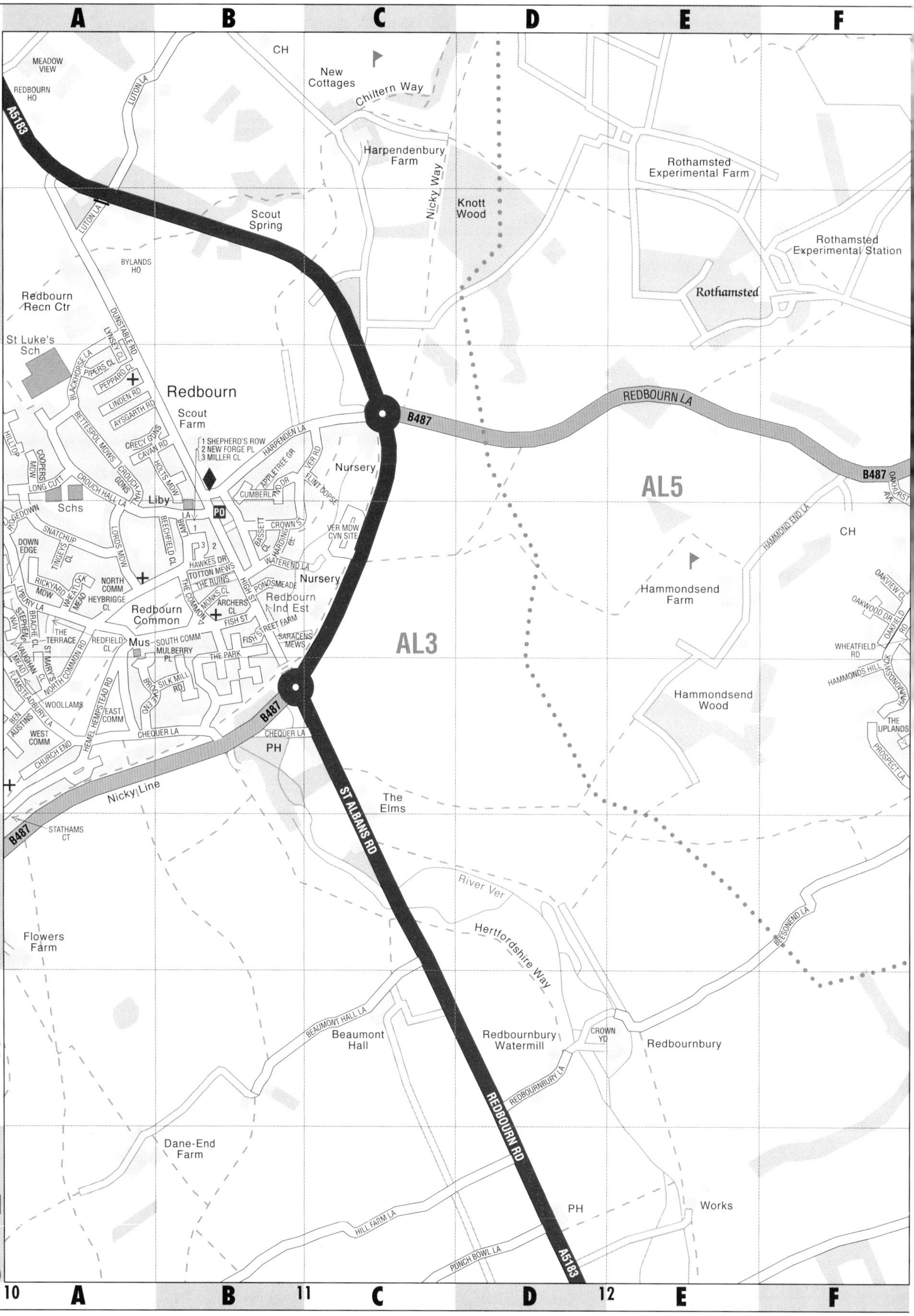

A B C D E F

8
7
13
6
5
12
4
3
11
2
1
10

MEADOW VIEW
REDBOURN HO
A5183
LUTON LA
CH
New Cottages
Chiltern Way
Harpendenbury Farm
Nicky Way
Knott Wood
Rothamsted Experimental Farm
Rothamsted Experimental Station
Rothamsted
Scout Spring
BYLANDS HO
Redbourn Recn Ctr
St Luke's Sch
DUNSTABLE RD
LYNSEY CL
BLACKHORSE LA
PIPERS CL
PEPPARD CL
LINDEN RD
AYSGARTH RD
Redbourn
Scout Farm
BETTESPOL MDWS
CRECY GDNS
CAVAN RD
HOLTS MDW
1 SHEPHERD'S ROW
2 NEW FORGE PL
3 MILLER CL
HARPENDEN LA
APPLETREE GR
VER RD
FLINT COPSE
CUMBERLAND DR
Nursery
B487
REDBOURN LA
AL5
B487
OAKHURST AVE
HILLTOP
COOPERS MDW
LONG CUTT
CROUCH HALL GDNS
CROUCH HALL LA
Liby
PO
RIDGEDOWN
Schs
SNATCHUP
DOWN EDGE
TINGEYS CL
LORDS MDW
BEECHFIELD CL
LAMB LA
BASSETT CL
CROWN ST
HARDING CL
VER MDW CVN SITE
WATEREND LA
HAMMOND END LA
CH
HAWKES DR
TOTTON MEWS
THE RUINS
MONKS CL
PONDSMEADE
Nursery
RICKYARD MDW
WHEATLOCK MEAD
NORTH COMM
HEYBRIGGE CL
Redbourn Common
THE COMMON
ARCHERS CL
HIGH ST
Redbourn Ind Est
Hammondsend Farm
OAKVIEW CL
OAKWOOD DR
OAKFIELD RD
LYBURY LA
STEPHENS WAY
BRACHE CL
THE TERRACE
REDFIELD CL
Mus
SOUTH COMM
FISH ST
STREET FARM
SARACENS MEWS
AL3
WHEATFIELD RD
HAMMONDS HILL
VAUGHAN MEAD
ST MARY'S CL
NORTH COMMON RD
MULBERRY PL
THE PARK
SILK MILL RD
BROOKEND
Hammondsend Wood
FLAMSTEAD
BURY LA
WOOLLAMS
HEMEL HEMPSTEAD RD
EAST COMM
B487
BEN AUSTINS
WEST COMM
CHEQUER LA
CHEQUER LA
THE UPLANDS
PROSPECT LA
CHURCH END
PH
Nicky Line
ST ALBANS RD
The Elms
B487
STATHAMS CT
River Ver
Hertfordshire Way
BEESONEND LA
Flowers Farm
BEAUMONT HALL LA
Beaumont Hall
Redbournbury Watermill
CROWN YD
Redbournbury
REDBOURNBURY LA
REDBOURN RD
Dane-End Farm
PH
Works
HILL FARM LA
PUNCH BOWL LA
A5183

10 A B 11 C D 12 E F

105
126

86
108

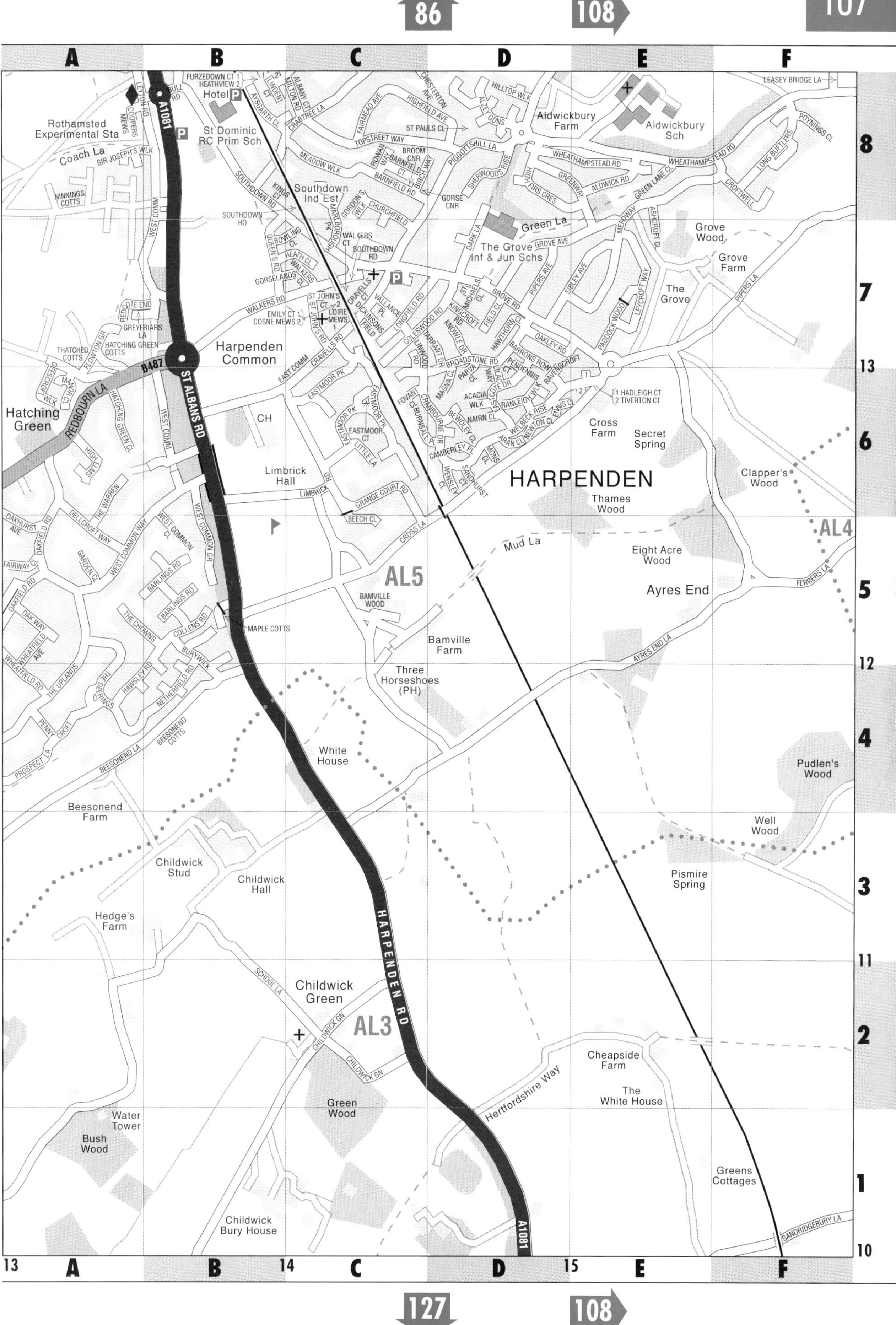

127
108

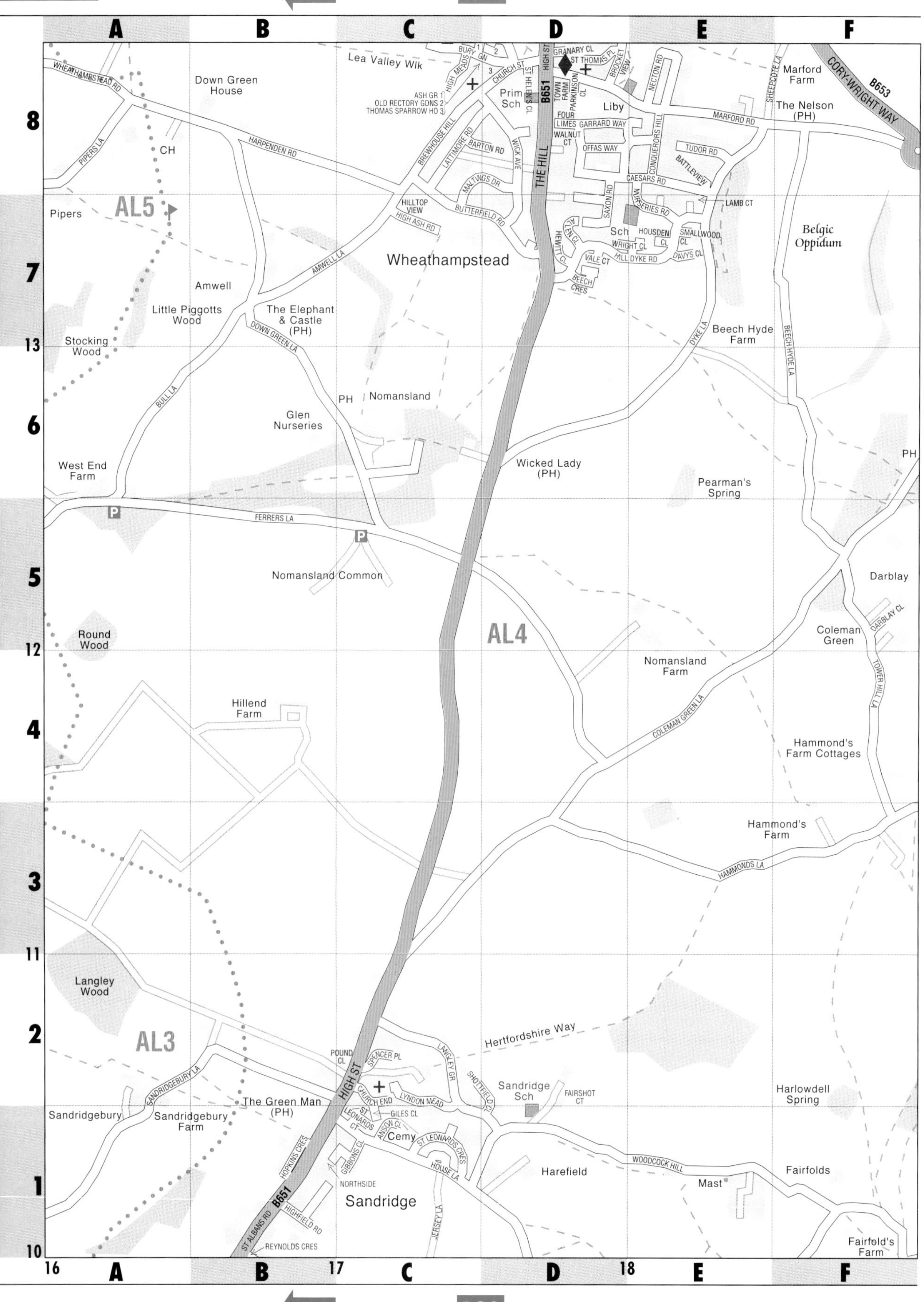
A
B
C
D
E
F
8
7
13
6
5
12
4
3
11
2
1
10
16
17
18
Lea Valley Wlk
WHEATHAMPSTEAD RD
Down Green House
HARPENDEN RD
PIPERS LA
CH
Pipers
AL5
Amwell
Little Piggotts Wood
Stocking Wood
The Elephant & Castle (PH)
DOWN GREEN LA
AMWELL LA
HILLTOP VIEW
HIGH ASH RD
Wheathampstead
BULL LA
PH
Nomansland
Glen Nurseries
West End Farm
Wicked Lady (PH)
FERRERS LA
Nomansland Common
Round Wood
AL4
Hillend Farm
Langley Wood
AL3
SANDRIDGEBURY LA
Sandridgebury
Sandridgebury Farm
The Green Man (PH)
HIGH ST
POUND CL
SPENCER PL
CHURCH END
LYNDON MEAD
ST LEONARDS CT
GILES CL
ANSON CL
Cemy
ST LEONARDS CRES
HOUSE LA
GIBBONS CL
HOPKINS CRES
NORTHSIDE
Sandridge
JERSEY LA
HIGHFIELD RD
ST ALBANS RD
B651
REYNOLDS CRES
LANGLEY GR
SHOTTFIELD CL
Sandridge Sch
FAIRSHOT CT
Hertfordshire Way
Harefield
WOODCOCK HILL
Mast
Fairfolds
Fairfold's Farm
Harlowdell Spring
HAMMONDS LA
Hammond's Farm
Hammond's Farm Cottages
COLEMAN GREEN LA
Nomansland Farm
Coleman Green
TOWER HILL LA
DARBLAY CL
Darblay
PH
Pearman's Spring
BEECH HYDE LA
Beech Hyde Farm
DYKE LA
Belgic Oppidum
Marford Farm
The Nelson (PH)
B653
CORY-WRIGHT WAY
MARFORD RD
SHEEPCOTE LA
BURY GN
HIGH MEADS
CHURCH ST
ASH GR 1
OLD RECTORY GDNS 2
THOMAS SPARROW HO 3
Prim Sch
ST HELENS CL
HIGH ST
THE HILL
BREWHOUSE HILL
LATTIMORE RD
BARTON RD
WICK AVE
MALTINGS DR
BUTTERFIELD RD
GRANARY CL
ST THOMAS PL
BROCKET VIEW
NECTON RD
TOWN FARM
PARKINSON CL
FOUR LIMES
Liby
GARRARD WAY
WALNUT CT
OFFAS WAY
CONQUERORS HILL
TUDOR RD
BATTLEVIEW
CAESARS RD
SAXON RD
NURSERIES RD
LAMB CT
Sch
HOUSDEN CL
SMALLWOOD CL
WRIGHT CL
HALL DYKE RD
DAVYS CL
ALLEN CL
HEWITT CL
VALE CT
BEECH CRES

88
110

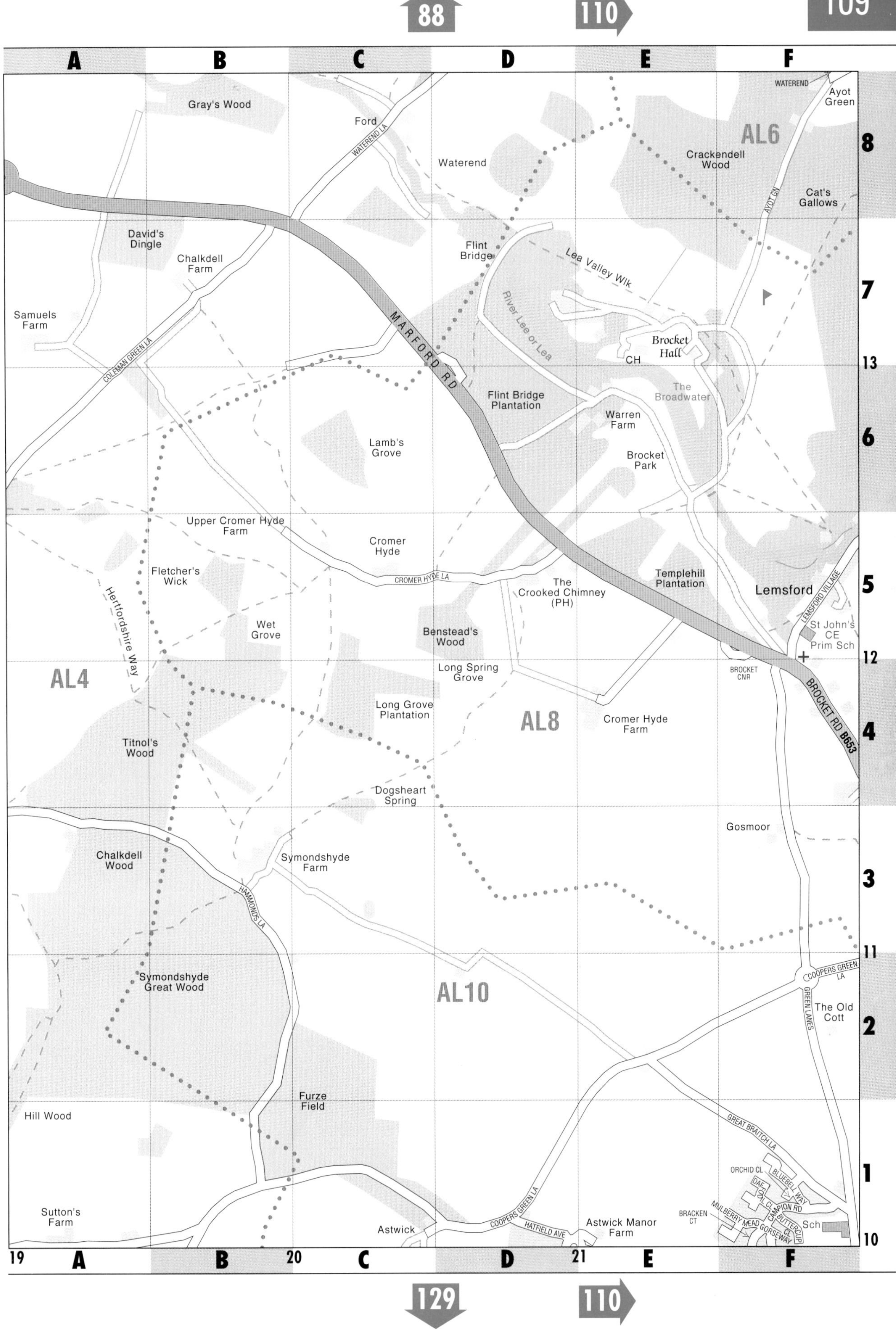

129
110

109
89

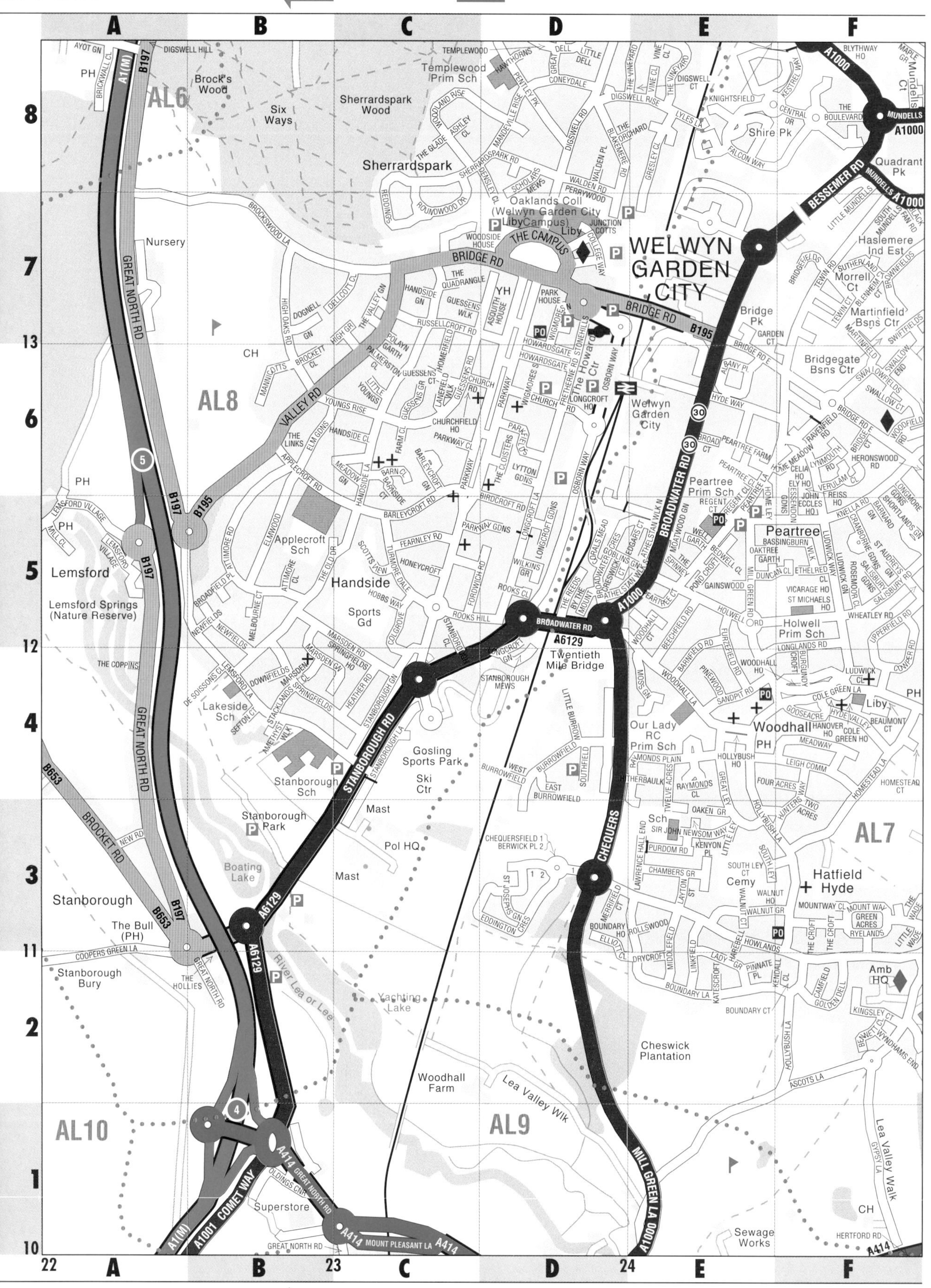

109
130

90
112

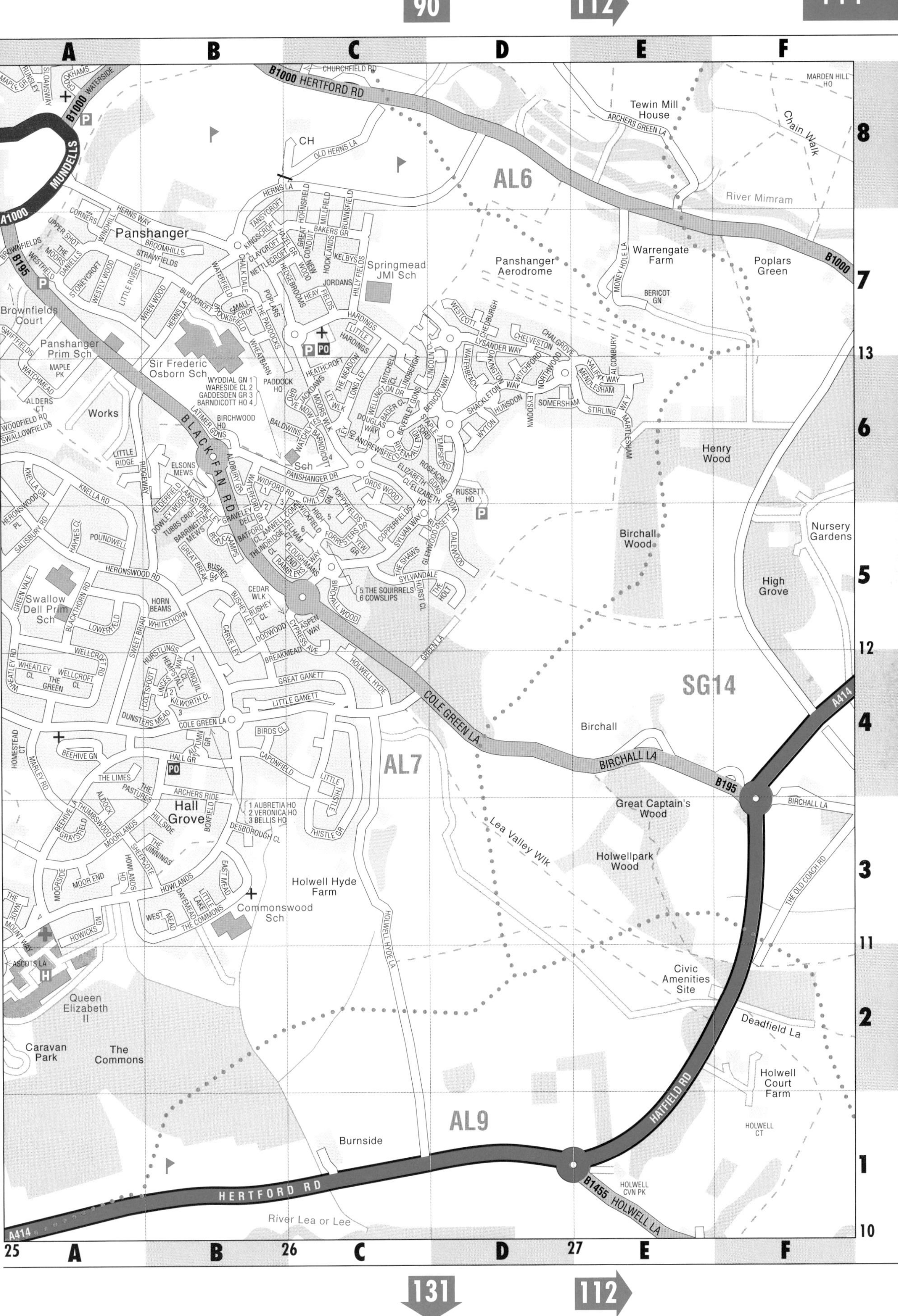

131
112

111
91

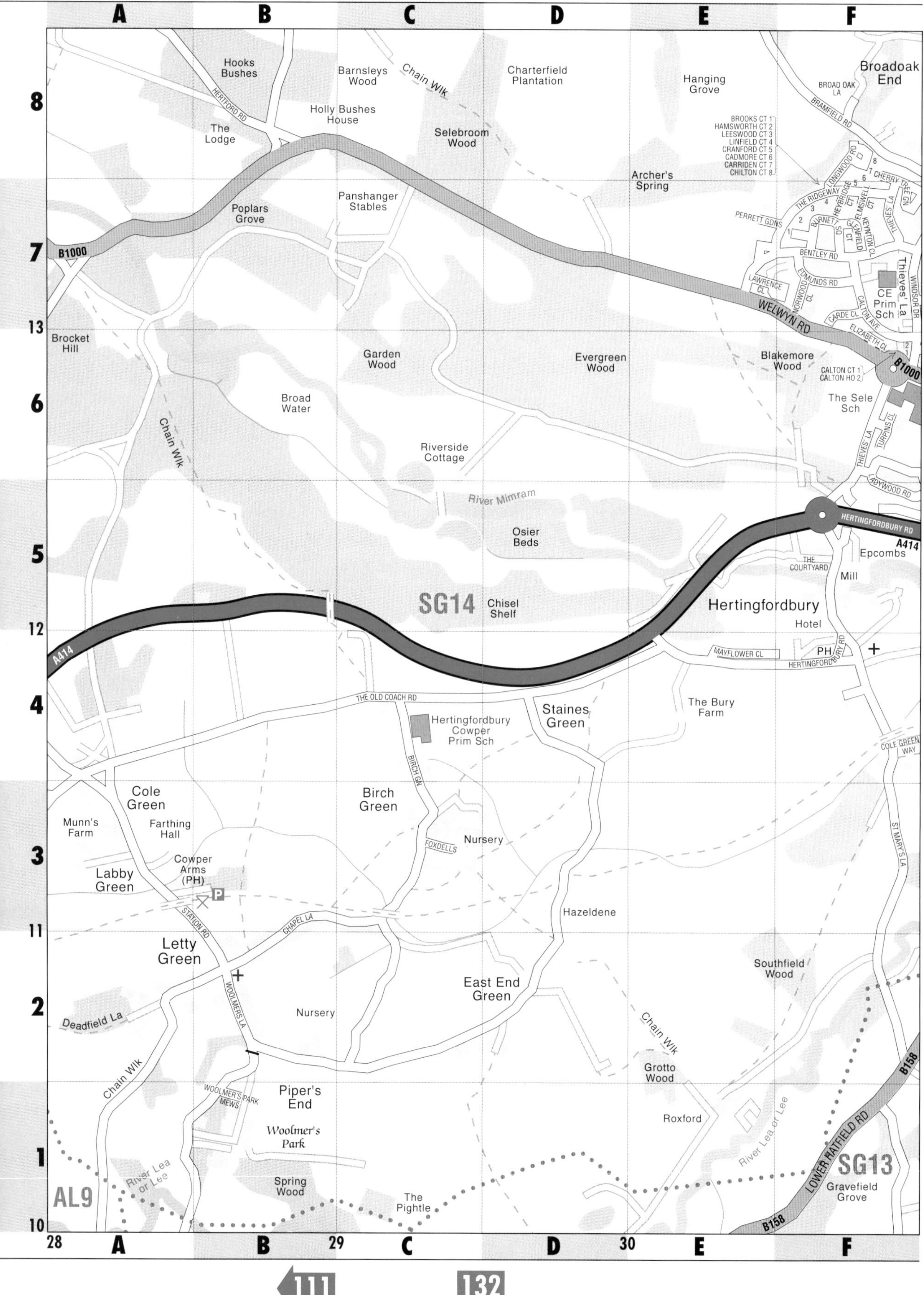

111
132

C6
1 ST ANDREW MEWS
2 MILLBRIDGE MEWS
3 TOWN MILL MEWS
D6
1 ADAM'S YD
2 DOLPHIN YD
3 MAIDENHEAD ST
4 EVRON PL
5 HONEY LA
6 MARKET PL
7 SALISBURY SQ
8 POST OFFICE WLK
9 The Bircherley Green Ctr
10 ODDFELLOWS CT
11 SHAFTESBURY QUAY
12 PRIORY WHARF
13 PRIORY CT
14 BIRCHERLEY CT
15 THE MALTHOUSE
16 WARREN PL
17 PROVIDENCE PL
18 BLUECOAT CT
19 CHAUNCY CT
20 MITRE CT
21 ST JOHN'S CT
22 THE WATERFRONT
23 NORRIS WORKS
D6
24 BRIDEWELL MEWS
25 OLD CROSS WHARF
26 NICHOLAS LA
27 OLD LIBRARY LA
F7
1 STANTS VIEW
2 ROWLEY'S RD
3 STANSTEAD RD

92
114

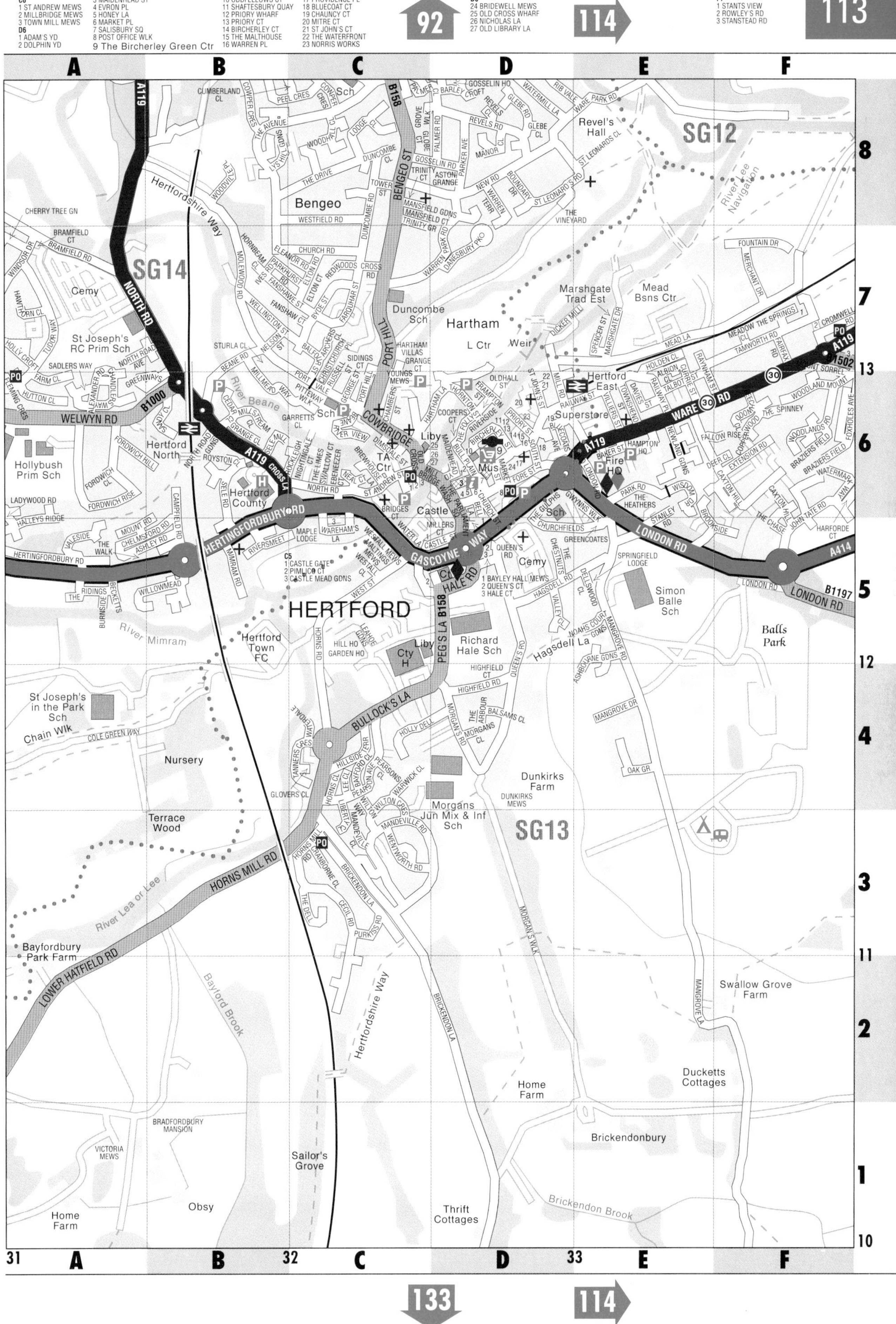

133
114

113
93

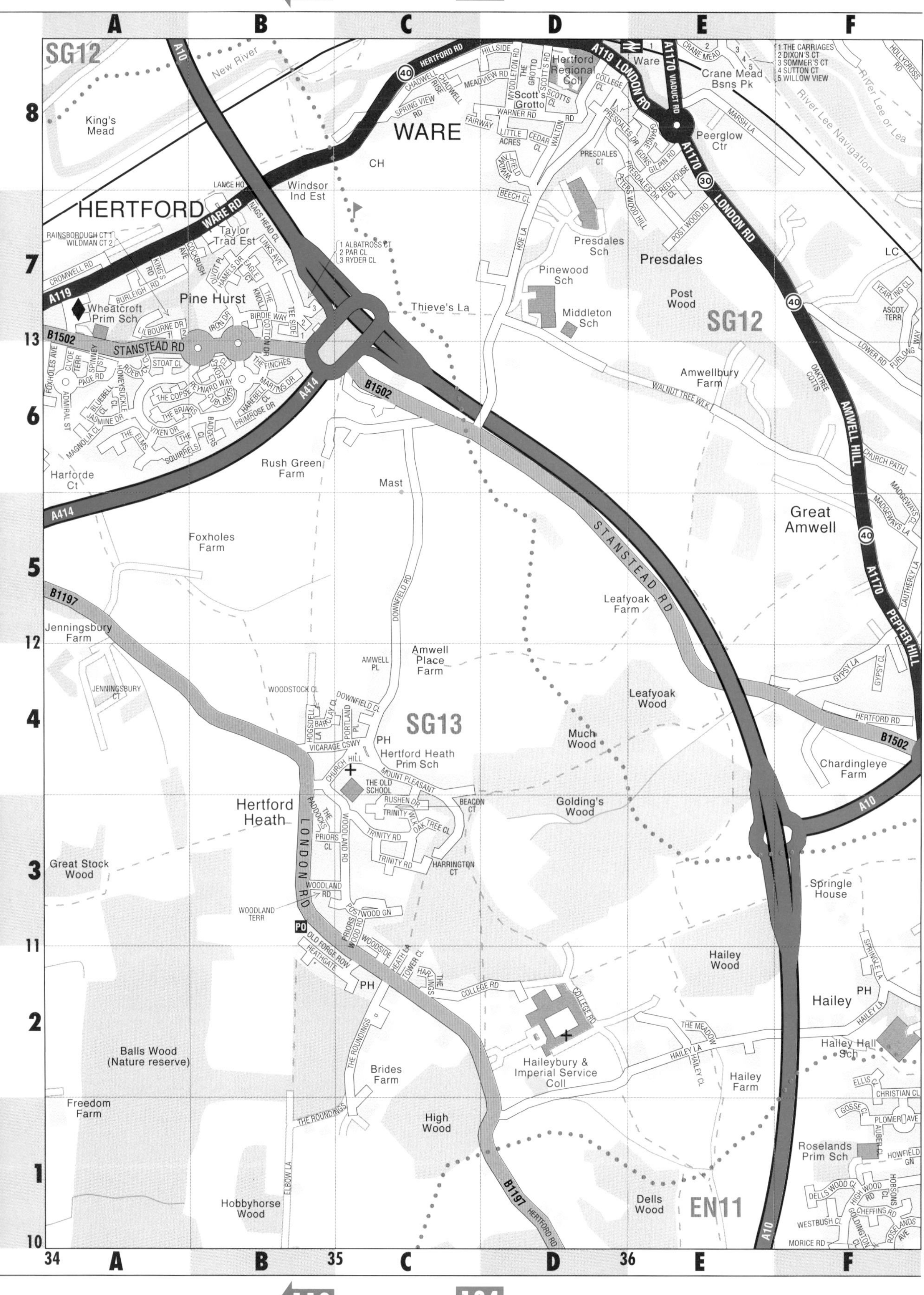

113
134

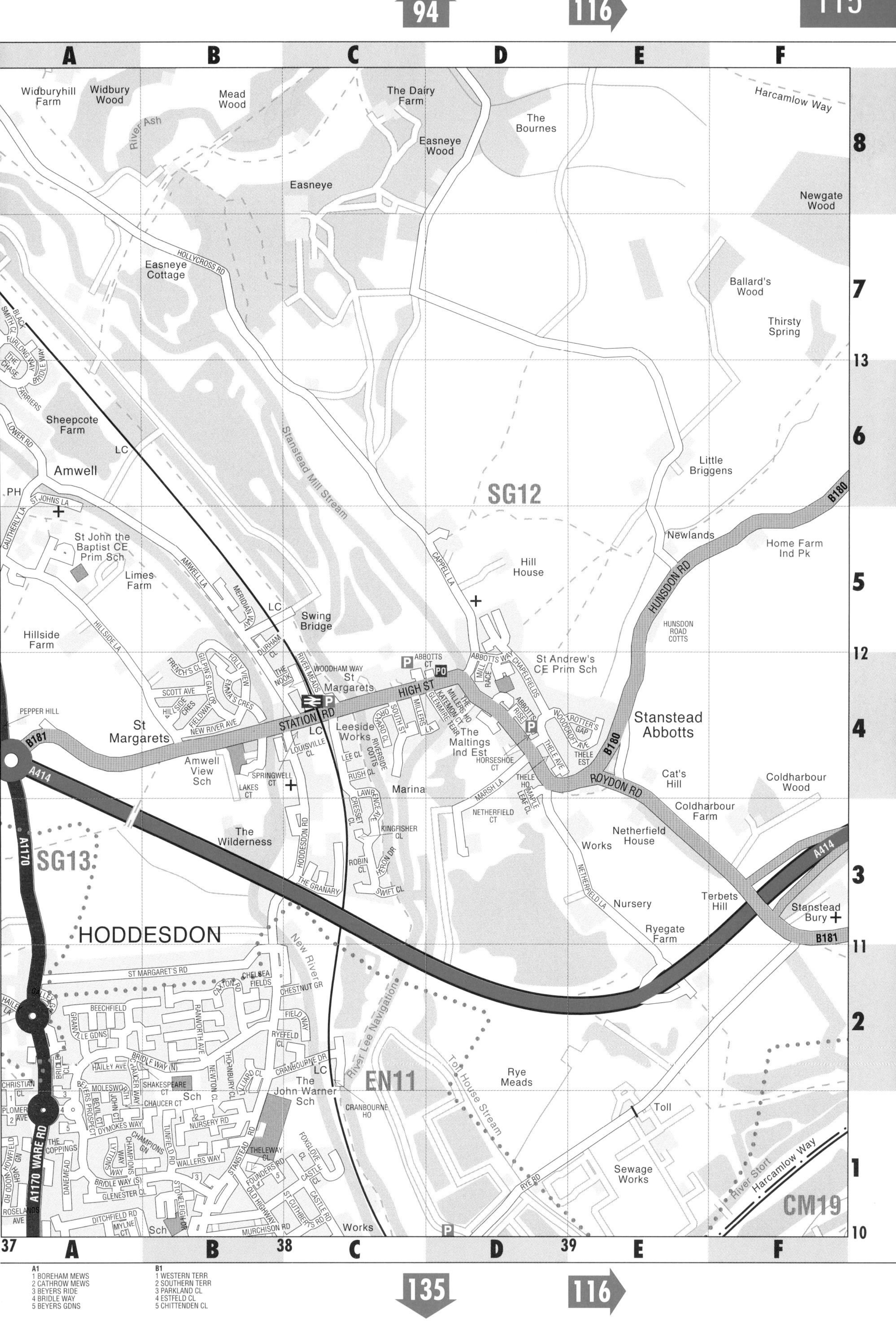

A1
1 BOREHAM MEWS
2 CATHROW MEWS
3 BEYERS RIDE
4 BRIDLE WAY
5 BEYERS GDNS

B1
1 WESTERN TERR
2 SOUTHERN TERR
3 PARKLAND CL
4 ESTFELD CL
5 CHITTENDEN CL

115
95

Moat Wood
Newfield Plantation
The Wilderness
Little Spellers
Spellers
Nine Ashes Farmhouse
Black Bushes
Bonningtons
Hunsdonbury
Copt Hall
Halfway House
HUNSDON RD
B180
Hunsdon House
Olives Farm
Bury Plantation
Cemy
Hunsdon Brook
Square Spring
SG12
Lord's Wood
Long Spring
Harcamlow Way
Pogden's Wood
Brickhouse Farm
Stone Basin Spring
Tuck's Spring
Eastwick Hall Farm
CM20
A414
Briggens Home Farm
Mead Lodge
Hunsdon Mill House
Eastwick Mead
The Grove
Stanstead Lodge
Briggens Park
Briggens (Hotel)
Stanstead Bury Farm
Hunsdon Mead
Oak Pollard
B181
Three Forests Way
Stort Valley Way
Roydon Mead
Roydon Lea
River Stort
Roydon
LC
River Stort (Navigation)
ROYDON LODGE CHALET EST
CM19
Harlow Stadium (Greyhounds)
Eastend
Roydon
Temple Farm
HIGH ST
HARLOW RD
Mount Pleasant
East End Farm
EASTEND COTTS
ROYDON RD
STADIUM WAY
Scimitar Pk
Barrows Farm
Mast
A1169
PH
PO
WICKLANDS RD
RECTORY CL
ST DUNSTAN'S RD
THE HOMESTEADS
TANNERS WAY
WHITEHALL COTTS
ACORN ST
NINE ASHES
1 ROYDON MILL LEISURE PK
CYGNET WAY
MALLARD WAY
MOORHEN WAY
MILL CNR
1 SWAN WAY
2 KINGFISHER WAY
3 HERON WAY
THE GRANARY
DUCKETTS MEAD
FARM CL
CHURCH MEAD
TEMPLE MEAD

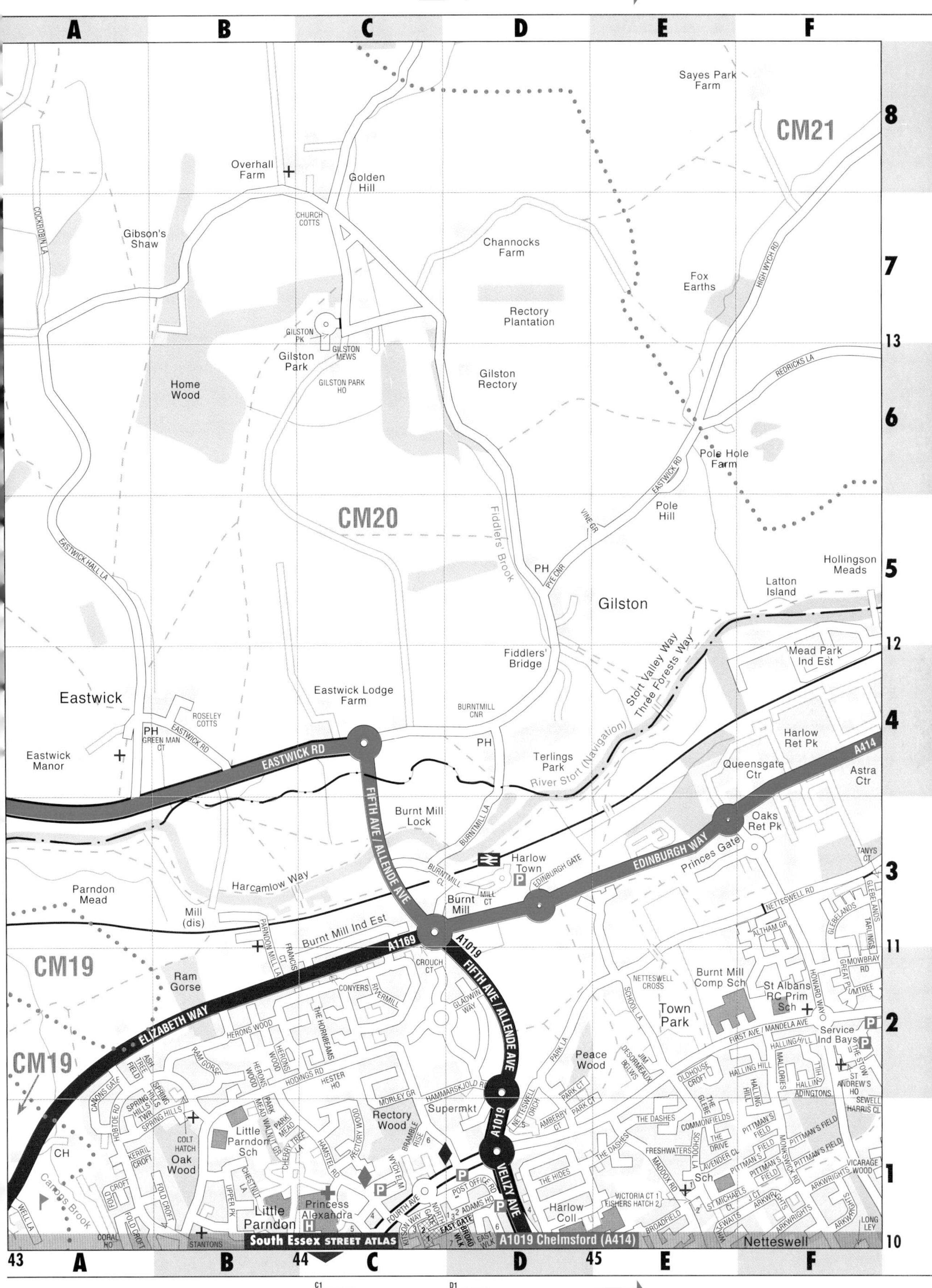

C1
1 WEST GATE
2 WEST SQ
3 MITRE BLDGS
4 BENTHAM HO
5 THE ANGLE
6 AMHERST LODGE

D1
1 THE ROWS
2 MARKET HO
3 STONE CROSS
4 HUGH'S TWR
5 NETTESWELL TWR
6 TERMINUS ST
7 LITTLE WLK

117
97

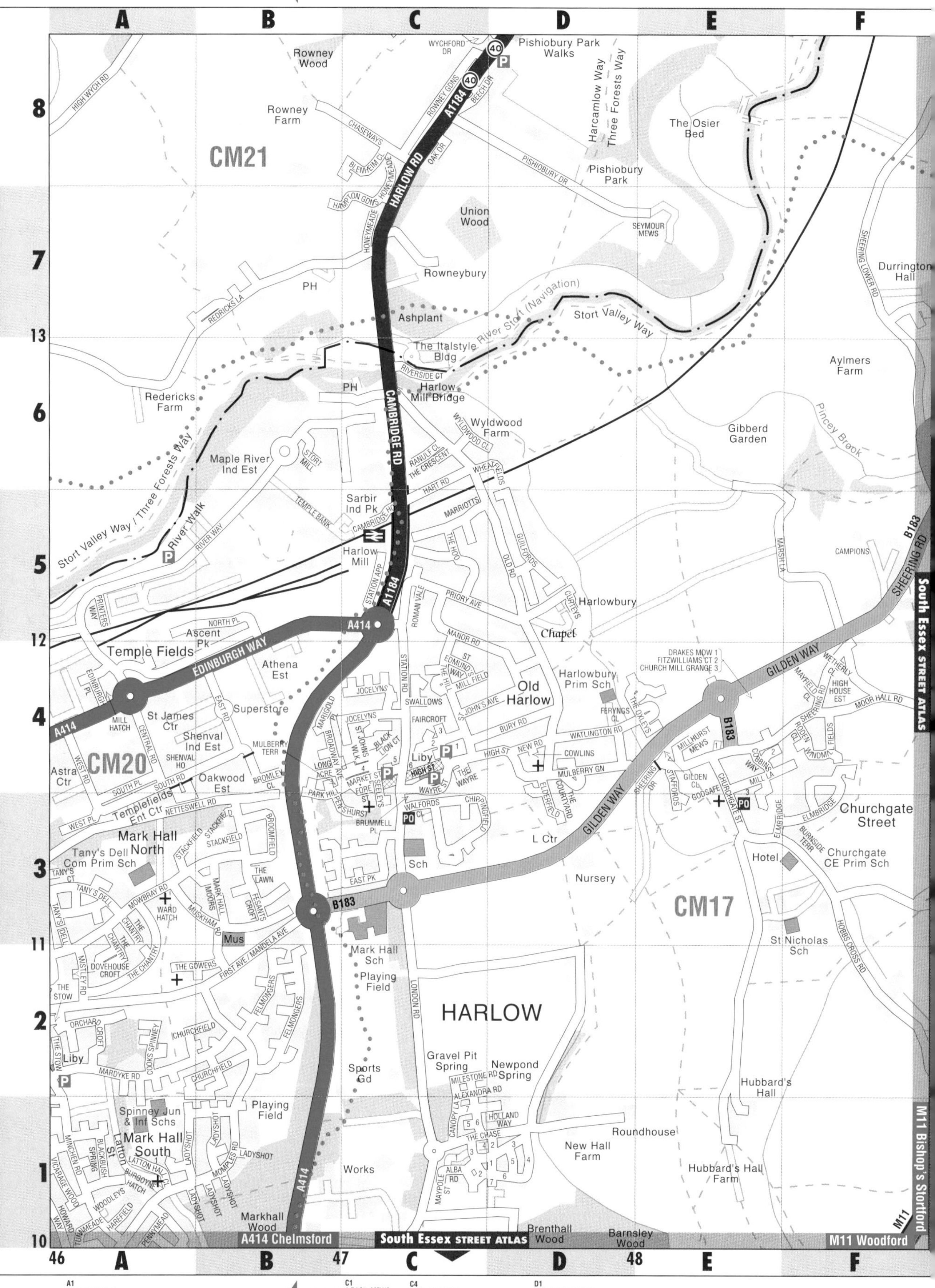

A1
1 THE SPINNEY

117

C1
1 BASIL MEWS
2 SOPER SQ
3 SQUARE ST
4 REGINALD MEWS
5 ALLIS MEWS
6 TATTON ST
7 HARROWBAND RD

C4
1 ROSEMARY CL
2 GARDEN TERRACE RD
3 CHERRY BLOSSOM CL
4 DELLFIELD CT
5 OAKWOOD MEWS
6 DARLINGTON CT

D1
1 ST NICHOLAS GN
2 GREEN ST
3 CROSS WAY
4 GREAT AUGUR ST
5 RAMBLERS LA
6 SIMPLICITY LA
7 HONOR ST

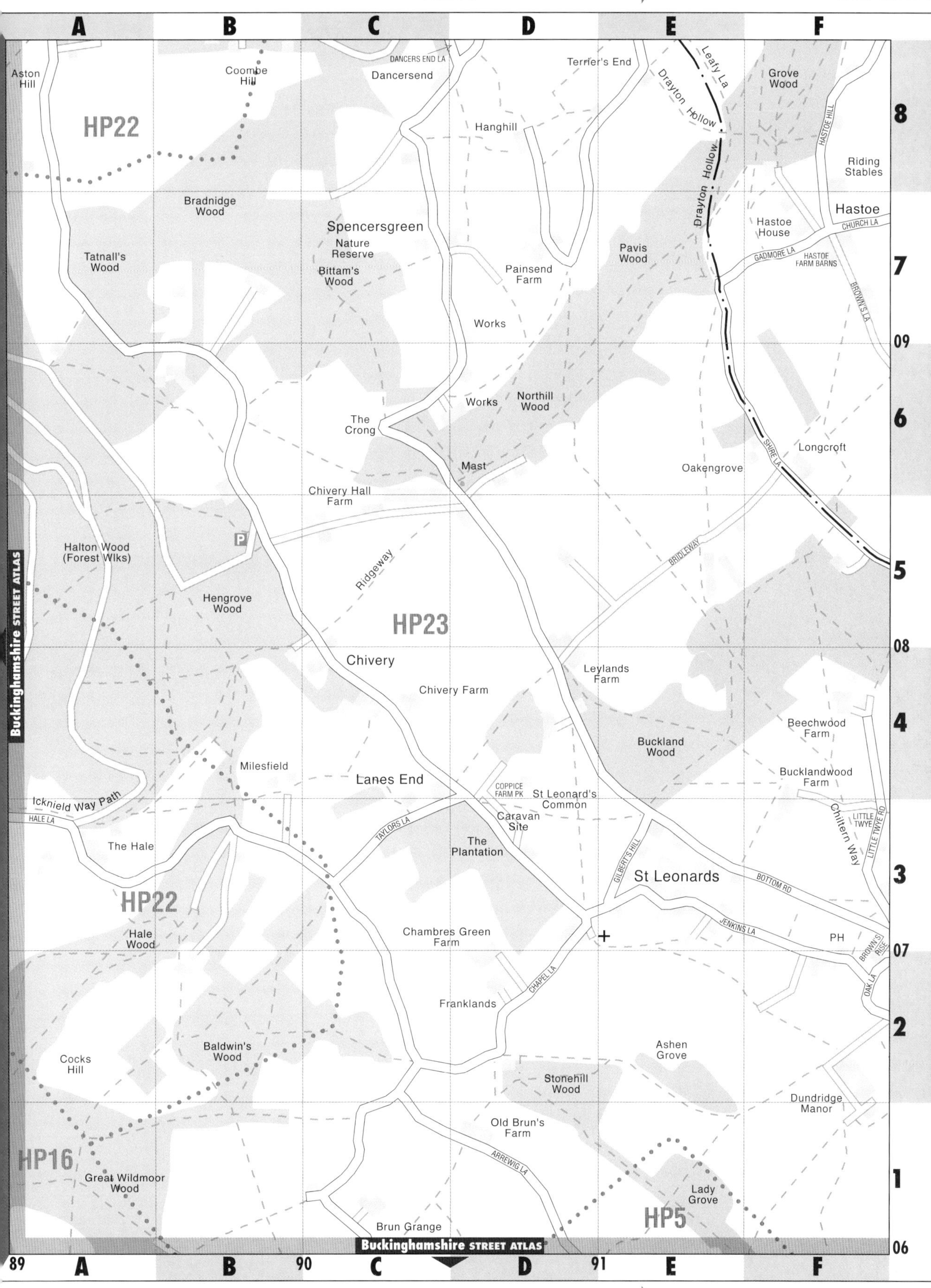
A
B
C
D
E
F
Aston Hill
Coombe Hill
DANCERS END LA
Dancersend
Terrier's End
Leafy La
Drayton Hollow
Grove Wood
HP22
Hanghill
HASTOE HILL
Riding Stables
Bradnidge Wood
Drayton Hollow
Hastoe
Hastoe House
CHURCH LA
Spencersgreen
Nature Reserve
Tatnall's Wood
Bittam's Wood
Painsend Farm
Pavis Wood
GADMORE LA
HASTOE FARM BARNS
BROWN'S LA
Works
Works
Northill Wood
The Crong
Longcroft
SHIRE LA
Mast
Oakengrove
Chivery Hall Farm
Halton Wood (Forest Wlks)
Ridgeway
BRIDLEWAY
Hengrove Wood
HP23
Chivery
Leylands Farm
Chivery Farm
Beechwood Farm
Buckland Wood
Milesfield
Lanes End
Bucklandwood Farm
COPPICE FARM PK
St Leonard's Common
Icknield Way Path
HALE LA
Caravan Site
Chiltern Way
LITTLE TWYE
LITTLE TWYE RD
TAYLORS LA
The Hale
The Plantation
GILBERT'S HILL
St Leonards
BOTTOM RD
HP22
Chambres Green Farm
JENKINS LA
PH
BROWN'S RISE
Hale Wood
OAK LA
CHAPEL LA
Franklands
Ashen Grove
Cocks Hill
Baldwin's Wood
Stonehill Wood
Dundridge Manor
Old Brun's Farm
HP16
ARREWIG LA
Great Wildmoor Wood
Lady Grove
HP5
Brun Grange
8
09
7
6
5
08
4
3
07
2
1
06
89
90
91
Buckinghamshire STREET ATLAS

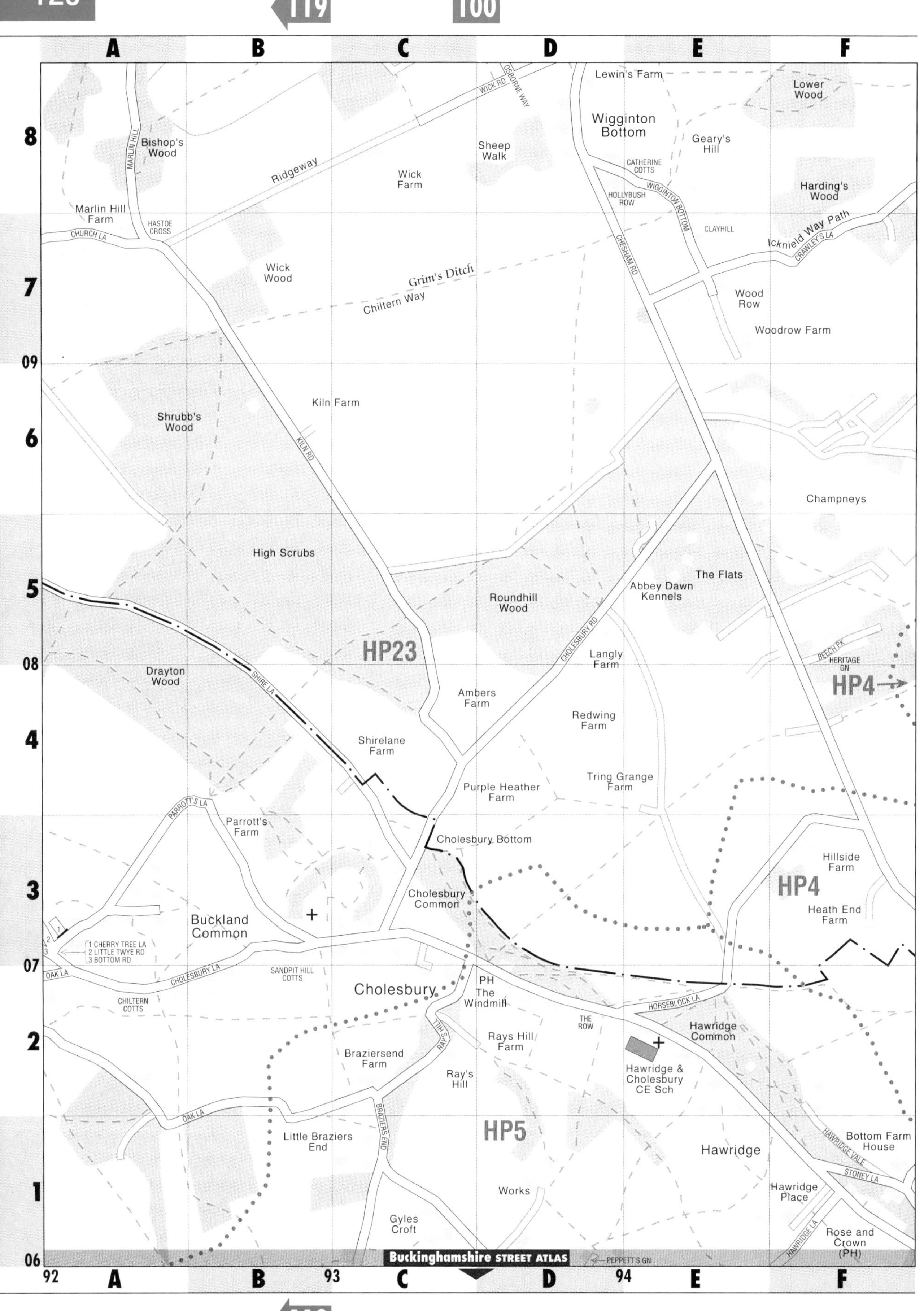
119
100
A
B
C
D
E
F
8
7
09
6
5
08
4
3
07
2
1
06
92
93
94
Lewin's Farm
Lower Wood
Wigginton Bottom
Geary's Hill
Bishop's Wood
MARLIN HILL
WICK RD
OSBORNE WAY
Sheep Walk
Wick Farm
Ridgeway
CATHERINE COTTS
HOLLYBUSH ROW
WIGGINTON BOTTOM
Harding's Wood
Marlin Hill Farm
CHURCH LA
HASTOE CROSS
CLAYHILL
Icknield Way Path
CRAWLEY'S LA
CHESHAM RD
Wick Wood
Grim's Ditch
Chiltern Way
Wood Row
Woodrow Farm
Kiln Farm
Shrubb's Wood
KILN RD
Champneys
High Scrubs
The Flats
Abbey Dawn Kennels
Roundhill Wood
HP23
CHOLESBURY RD
Langly Farm
BEECH PK
HERITAGE GN
HP4
Drayton Wood
SHIRE LA
Ambers Farm
Redwing Farm
Shirelane Farm
Tring Grange Farm
Purple Heather Farm
PARROTT'S LA
Parrott's Farm
Cholesbury Bottom
Hillside Farm
Cholesbury Common
HP4
Buckland Common
Heath End Farm
1 CHERRY TREE LA
2 LITTLE TWYE RD
3 BOTTOM RD
OAK LA
CHOLESBURY LA
SANDPIT HILL COTTS
Cholesbury
PH
The Windmill
HORSEBLOCK LA
CHILTERN COTTS
THE ROW
Hawridge Common
RAY'S HILL
Rays Hill Farm
Braziersend Farm
Hawridge & Cholesbury CE Sch
Ray's Hill
OAK LA
BRAZIERS END
HP5
Little Braziers End
Hawridge
Bottom Farm House
HAWRIDGE VALE
STONEY LA
Hawridge Place
Works
Gyles Croft
HAWRIDGE LA
Rose and Crown (PH)
PEPPETT'S GN

101
122

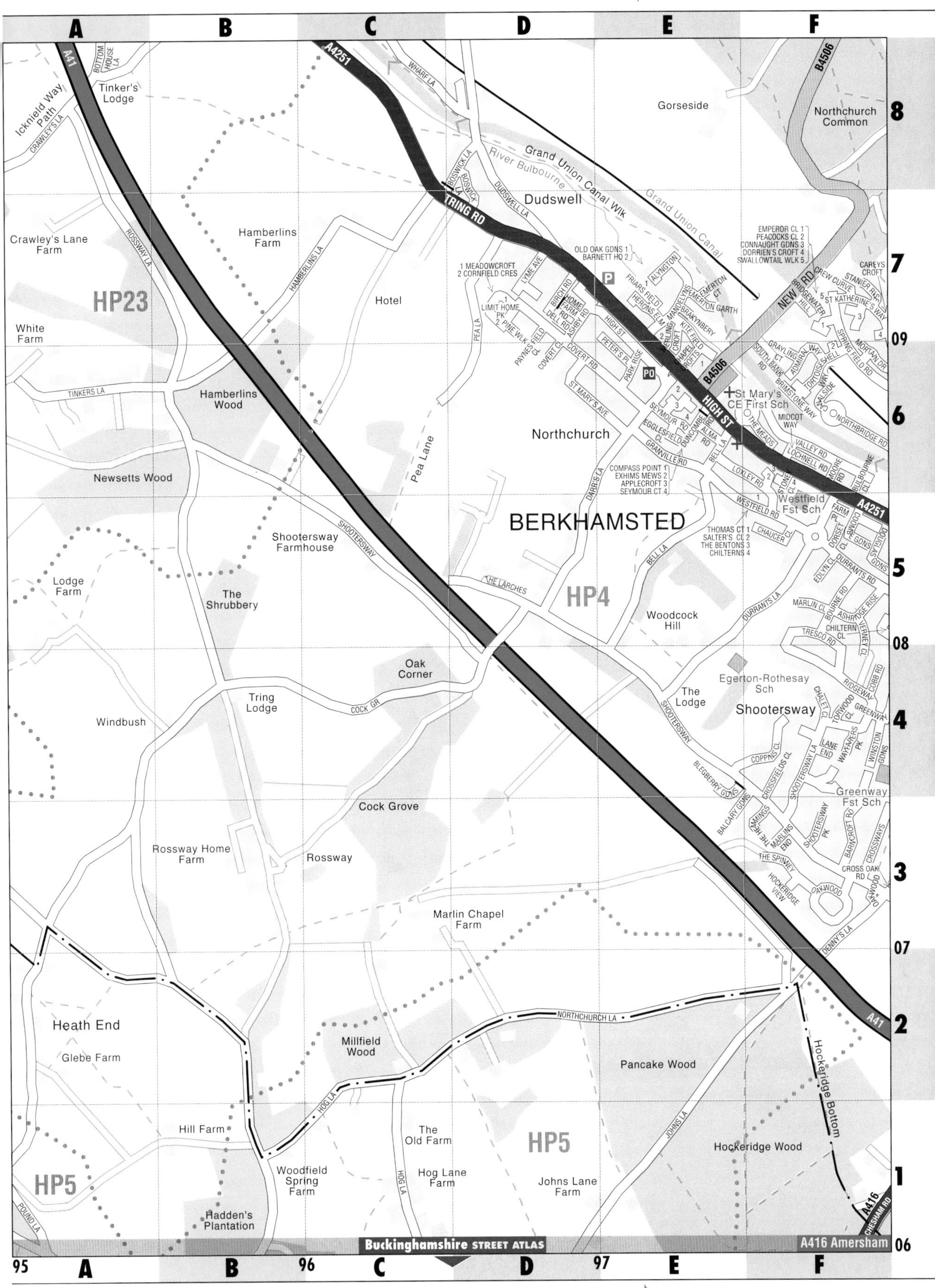
A
B
C
D
E
F
8
7
09
6
5
08
4
3
07
2
1
06
95
96
97
A41
A4251
B4506
A416
Icknield Way Path
CRAWLEY'S LA
BOTTOM HOUSE LA
Tinker's Lodge
WHARF LA
Gorseside
Northchurch Common
Grand Union Canal Wlk
River Bulbourne
Grand Union Canal
BOSWICK LA
Dudswell
DUDSWELL LA
TRING RD
Crawley's Lane Farm
ROSSWAY LA
Hamberlins Farm
HAMBERLINS LA
HP23
Hotel
EMPEROR CL 1
PEACOCKS CL 2
CONNAUGHT GDNS 3
DORRIEN'S CROFT 4
SWALLOWTAIL WLK 5
CAREYS CROFT
OLD OAK GDNS 1
BARNETT HO 2
1 MEADOWCROFT
2 CORNFIELD CRES
LYME AVE
ALYNGTON
EMERTON CT
EMERTON GARTH
NEW RD
BRIDGEWATER HILL
CREW CURVE
STANIER RISE
ST KATHERINE'S WAY
White Farm
LIMIT HOME PK
PINE WLK
PEA LA
BIRCH RD
HOME FARM RD
DELL RD
ASHBY RD
FRIARS FIELD
HERONS ELM
MANDELYNS
BRAKYNBERY
KITE FIELD
HIGH ST
PETER'S PL
PARK RISE
PAYNES FIELD CL
COVERT CL
COVERT RD
SOUTH BANK RD
GRAYLING CT
ADMIRAL WAY
TORTOISESHELL WAY
SPRING FIELD RD
MORTAIN DR
BRIMSTONE WAY
CANALSIDE
Hamberlins Wood
TINKERS LA
ST MARY'S AVE
SEYMOUR RD
St Mary's CE First Sch
THE MEADS
MIDCOT WAY
NORTHBRIDGE RD
Northchurch
EGGLESFIELD CL
DUNCOMBE
ALMA RD
BELL LA
VALLEY RD
LOCHNELL RD
MOORE RD
BULBOURNE CL
Pea Lane
Newsetts Wood
GRANVILLE RD
COMPASS POINT 1
EXHIMS MEWS 2
APPLECROFT 3
SEYMOUR CT 4
DARR'S LA
LOXLEY RD
STONEY CL
Westfield Fst Sch
WESTFIELD RD
BERKHAMSTED
Shootersway Farmhouse
SHOOTERSWAY
THOMAS CT 1
SALTER'S CL 2
THE BENTONS 3
CHILTERNS 4
CHAUCER CL
FARM PL
DORSET CL
ASHWOOD
GDNS
DOUGLAS GDNS
Lodge Farm
EDLYN CL
DURRANTS RD
THE LARCHES
HP4
The Shrubbery
DURRANTS LA
MARLIN CL
BOURNE RD
ASHRIDGE RISE
Woodcock Hill
CHILTERN CL
TRESCO RD
VERNEY CL
Oak Corner
Egerton-Rothesay Sch
COBB RD
RIDGEWAY
The Lodge
CHALET CL
TORWOOD CL
GREENWAY
Tring Lodge
COCK GR
Shootersway
Windbush
WAYFARERS PK
LANE END
WINSTON GDNS
COPPINS CL
CROSSFIELDS CL
BLEGBERRY GDNS
Greenway Fst Sch
Cock Grove
BALCARY GDNS
THE HEMMINGS
MARLINS END
SHOOTERSWAY PK
BARNCROFT RD
CROSSWAYS
Rossway Home Farm
Rossway
THE SPINNEY
CROSS OAK RD
HOCKERIDGE VIEW
OAKWOOD
Marlin Chapel Farm
DENNY'S LA
Heath End
NORTHCHURCH LA
Glebe Farm
Millfield Wood
Pancake Wood
Hockeridge Bottom
Hill Farm
HOG LA
The Old Farm
HP5
JOHNS LA
Hockeridge Wood
Woodfield Spring Farm
Hog Lane Farm
Johns Lane Farm
HP5
POUND LA
Hadden's Plantation
CHESHAM RD
Buckinghamshire STREET ATLAS
A416 Amersham

122

121
102

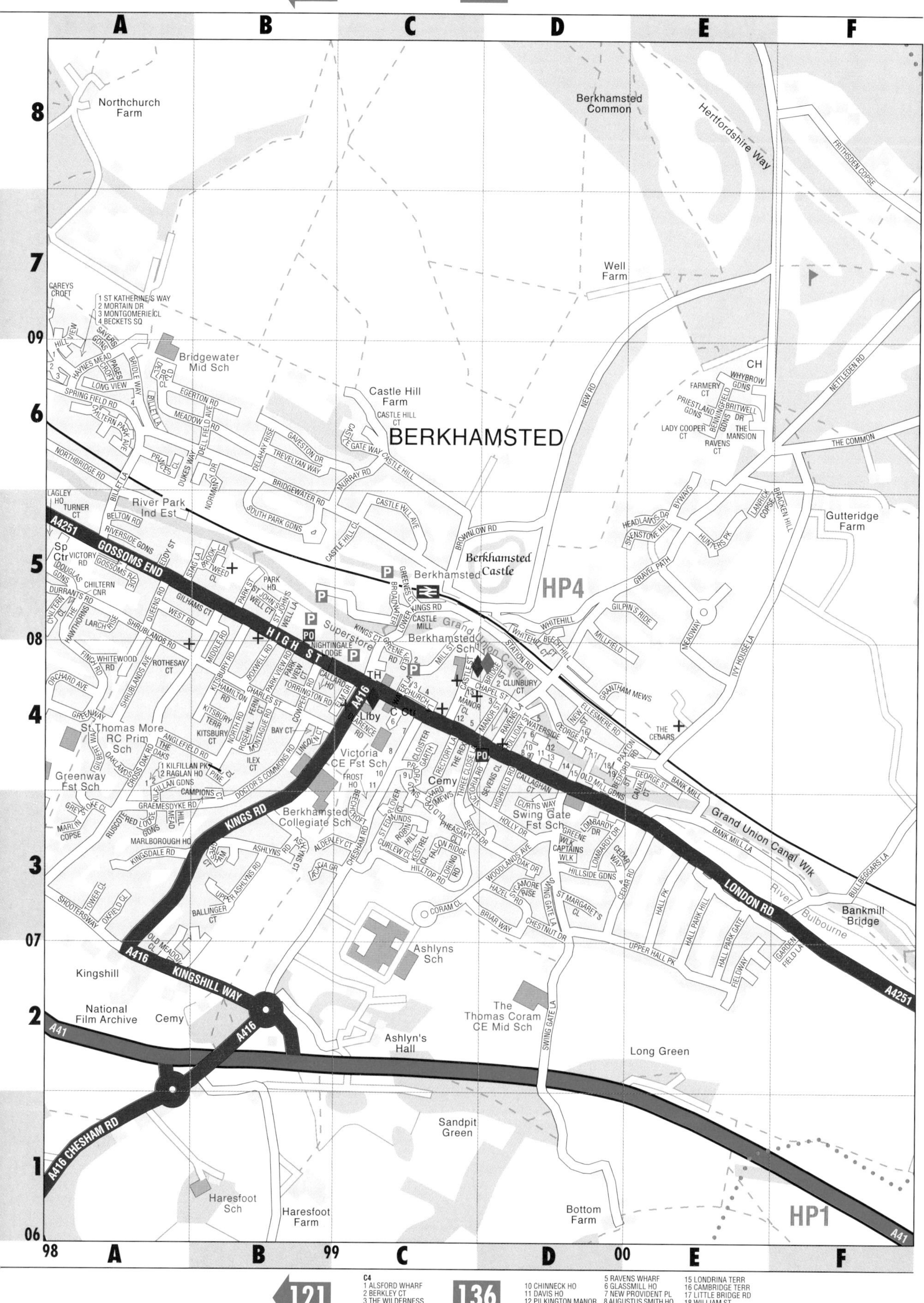

121
136

C4
1 ALSFORD WHARF
2 BERKLEY CT
3 THE WILDERNESS
4 CHURCH GATES
5 DOWER MEWS
6 PRINCE EDWARD ST
7 CAVALIER CT
8 DEANS LAWN
9 PRIORY CT
10 CHINNECK HO
11 DAVIS HO
12 PILKINGTON MANOR
13 WILLIAM FISKE HO

D4
1 BRIDGE CT
2 MASON'S YD
3 CASTLE MEWS
4 BARTRUM VILLAS
5 RAVENS WHARF
6 GLASSMILL HO
7 NEW PROVIDENT PL
8 AUGUSTUS SMITH HO
9 THOMAS BOURNE HO
10 COOPER WAY
11 ROBERTSON RD
12 COSTINS WLK
13 McDOUGALL RD
14 LONDRINA CT
15 LONDRINA TERR
16 CAMBRIDGE TERR
17 LITTLE BRIDGE RD
18 WILLIAM ST
19 UNION CT

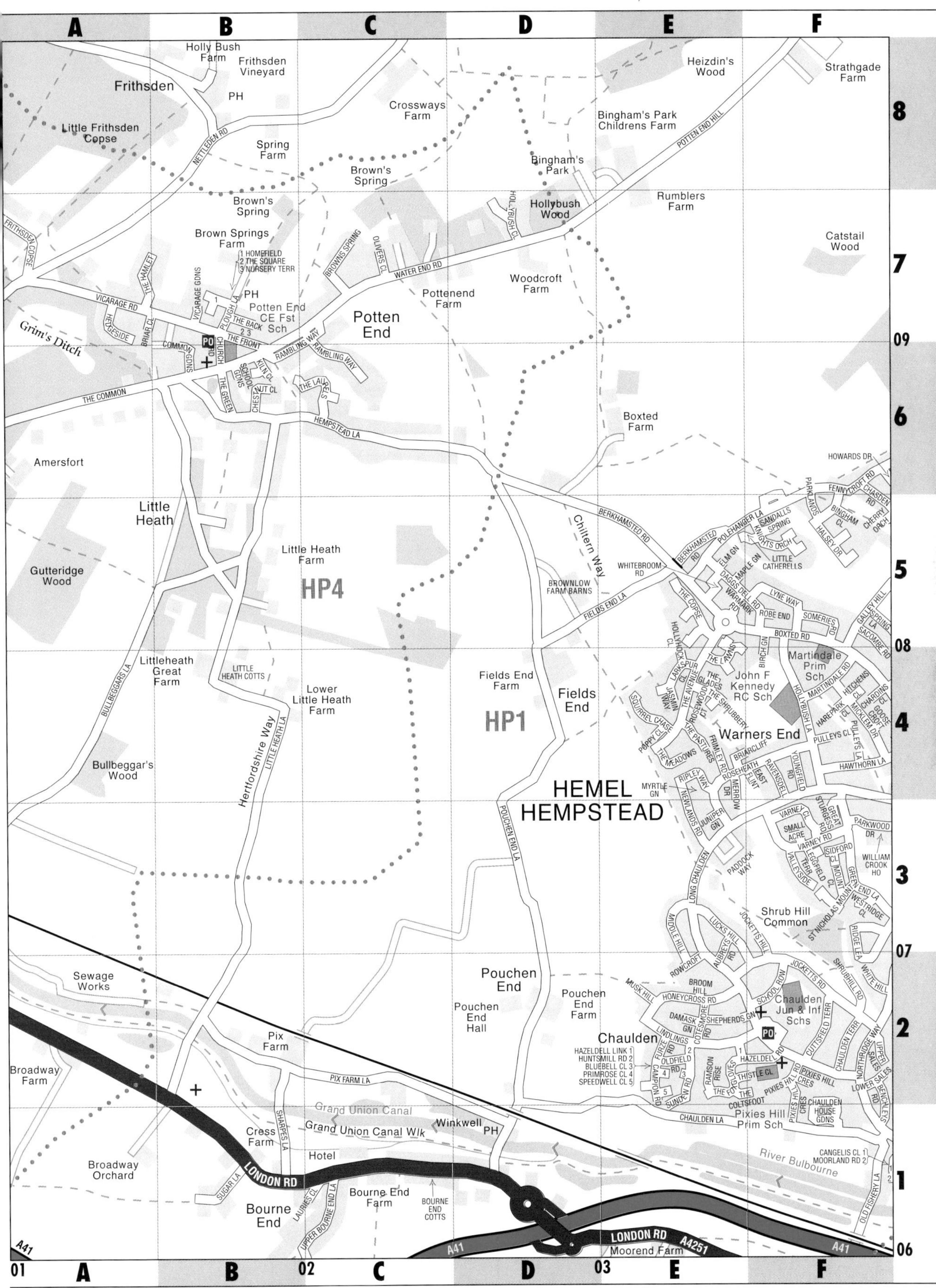
A
B
C
D
E
F
Holly Bush Farm
Frithsden Vineyard
Frithsden
PH
Little Frithsden Copse
Spring Farm
Crossways Farm
Heizdin's Wood
Strathgade Farm
Bingham's Park Childrens Farm
Brown's Spring
Bingham's Park
Brown's Spring
Hollybush Wood
Rumblers Farm
Brown Springs Farm
Catstail Wood
Woodcroft Farm
Pottenend Farm
Potten End
Potten End CE Fst Sch
PH
Grim's Ditch
HEMPSTEAD LA
Boxted Farm
Amersfort
Little Heath
Little Heath Farm
HP4
Gutteridge Wood
Chiltern Way
BROWNLOW FARM BARNS
Littleheath Great Farm
Lower Little Heath Farm
Fields End Farm
Fields End
HP1
John F Kennedy RC Sch
Martindale Prim Sch
Warners End
Bullbeggar's Wood
Hertfordshire Way
HEMEL HEMPSTEAD
Shrub Hill Common
Sewage Works
Pouchen End
Pouchen End Hall
Pouchen End Farm
Chaulden Jun & Inf Schs
Chaulden
Pix Farm
Broadway Farm
Grand Union Canal
Grand Union Canal Wlk
Winkwell
PH
Cress Farm
Hotel
Pixies Hill Prim Sch
Broadway Orchard
River Bulbourne
LONDON RD
Bourne End
Bourne End Farm
BOURNE END COTTS
Moorend Farm
A41
A4251
8
7
09
6
5
08
4
3
07
2
1
06
01
02
03

123

104

D5
1 SHARPCROFT
2 BROADCROFT
3 BOXHILL
4 PHYLLIS COURTNAGE HO
5 HELENA PL
6 BOWYERS

E6
1 WATLING CL
2 LANGDALE CT
3 ESKDALE CT
4 BORROWDALE CT
5 COTSWOLD
6 BARMOUTH ROW

F5
1 TANNSFIELD DR
2 TANNSMORE CL
3 WIDMORE DR

F6
1 MERCURY WLK
2 IONIAN WAY
3 PHOEBE RD

F7
1 SHERWOOD PL
2 PETERLEE CT

F8
1 TRESLIAN SQ
2 TORRIDGE WLK
3 THE DART
4 MARION WLK

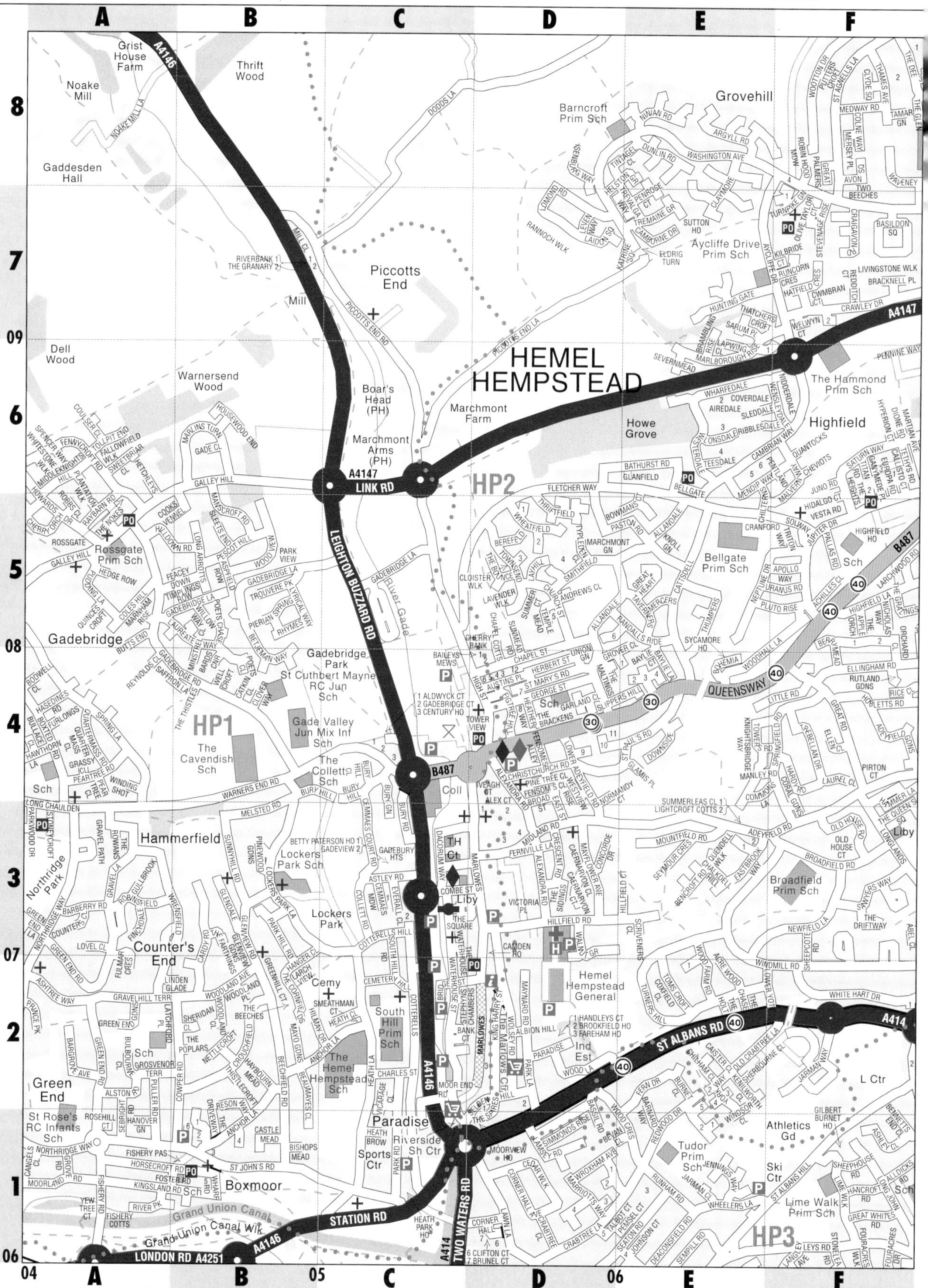

HEMEL HEMPSTEAD

B1
1 HALWICK CL
2 VEYSEY CL
3 ST JOHNS CL
4 CLEMENTINE WAY
5 WHARF VILLAS
6 THORNE CL

123

D1
1 PANXWORTH RD
2 RANWORTH CL
3 STUARTS CL
4 CHARLESWORTH CL
5 FOREST AVE

D3
1 MAITLAND HO
2 ALBYN HO
3 ROSETTA HO

138

D3
4 REGENCY CT

D4
1 ARMSTRONG PL
2 SUN SQ
3 THE GABLES
4 SHEPPARDS YD
5 MULBERRY CT
6 AUSTIN MEWS
7 KING'S MEWS
8 ST MARY'S CT
9 HARKNESS RD
10 GILROY RD
11 DAVIDSON HO
12 ELIZABETH HO

E1
1 SATINWOOD CT
2 EVERGREEN WLK
3 CRABTREE CT
4 WOODMAN RD

E2
1 FURTHERGROUND
2 DENBIGH CL
3 MORPETH CL
4 CORFE CL
5 PINETREE GDNS

E4
1 CLARENDON CL
2 LITTLE MIMMS
3 LONG MIMMS
4 EAST MIMMS

F2
1 WADLEY CL
2 BENNETTS END RD

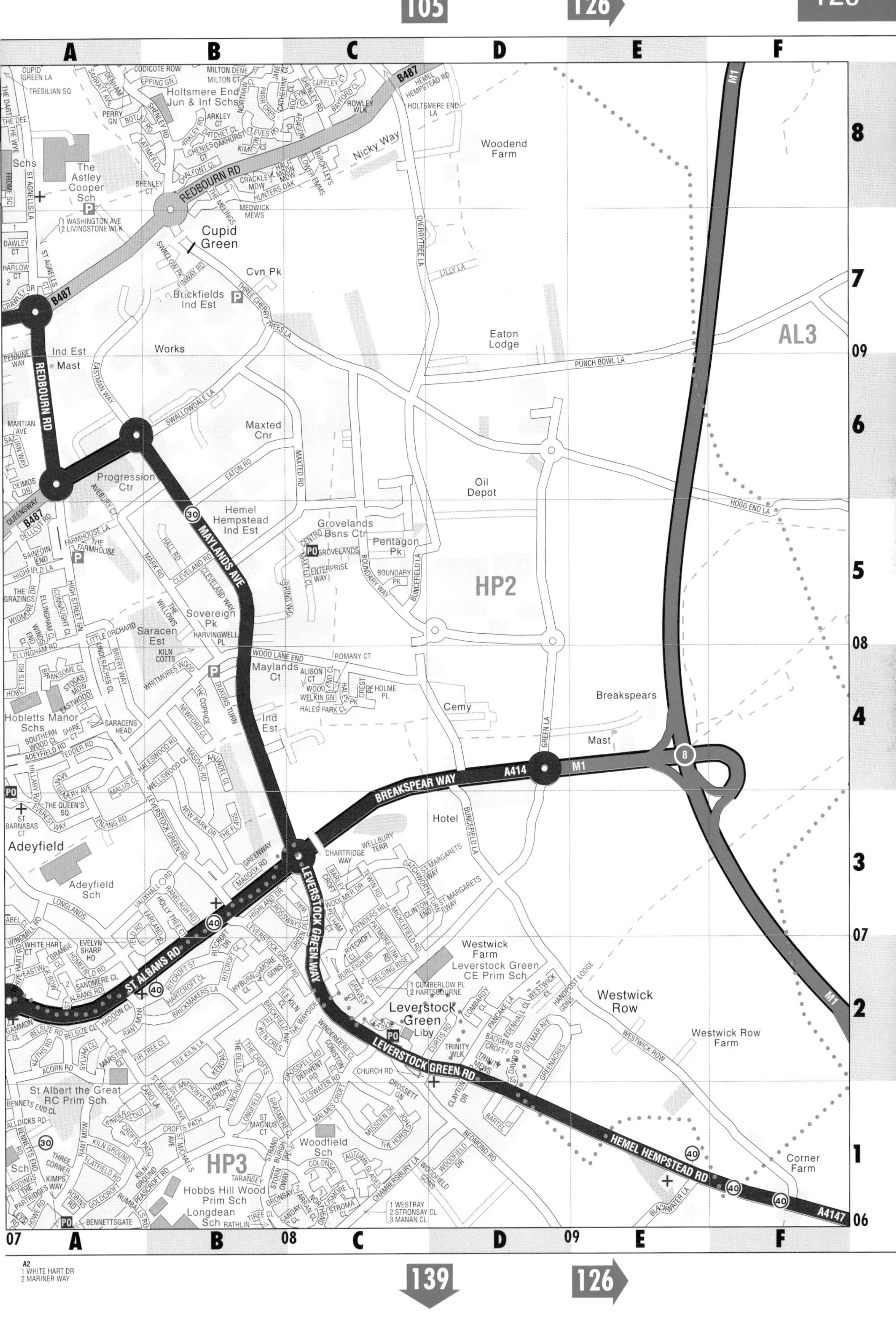

A2
1 WHITE HART DR
2 MARINER WAY

125
106

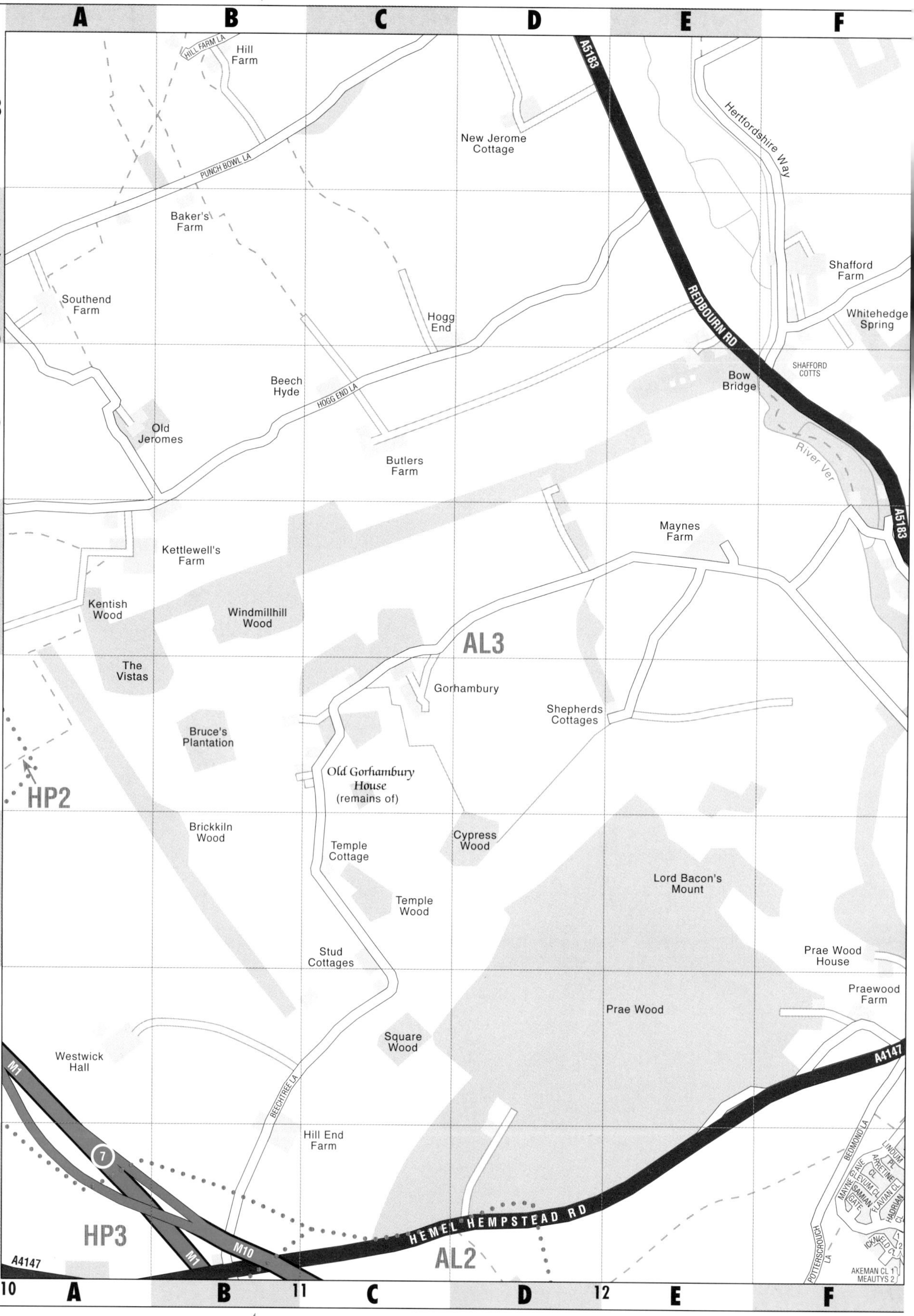

125
140

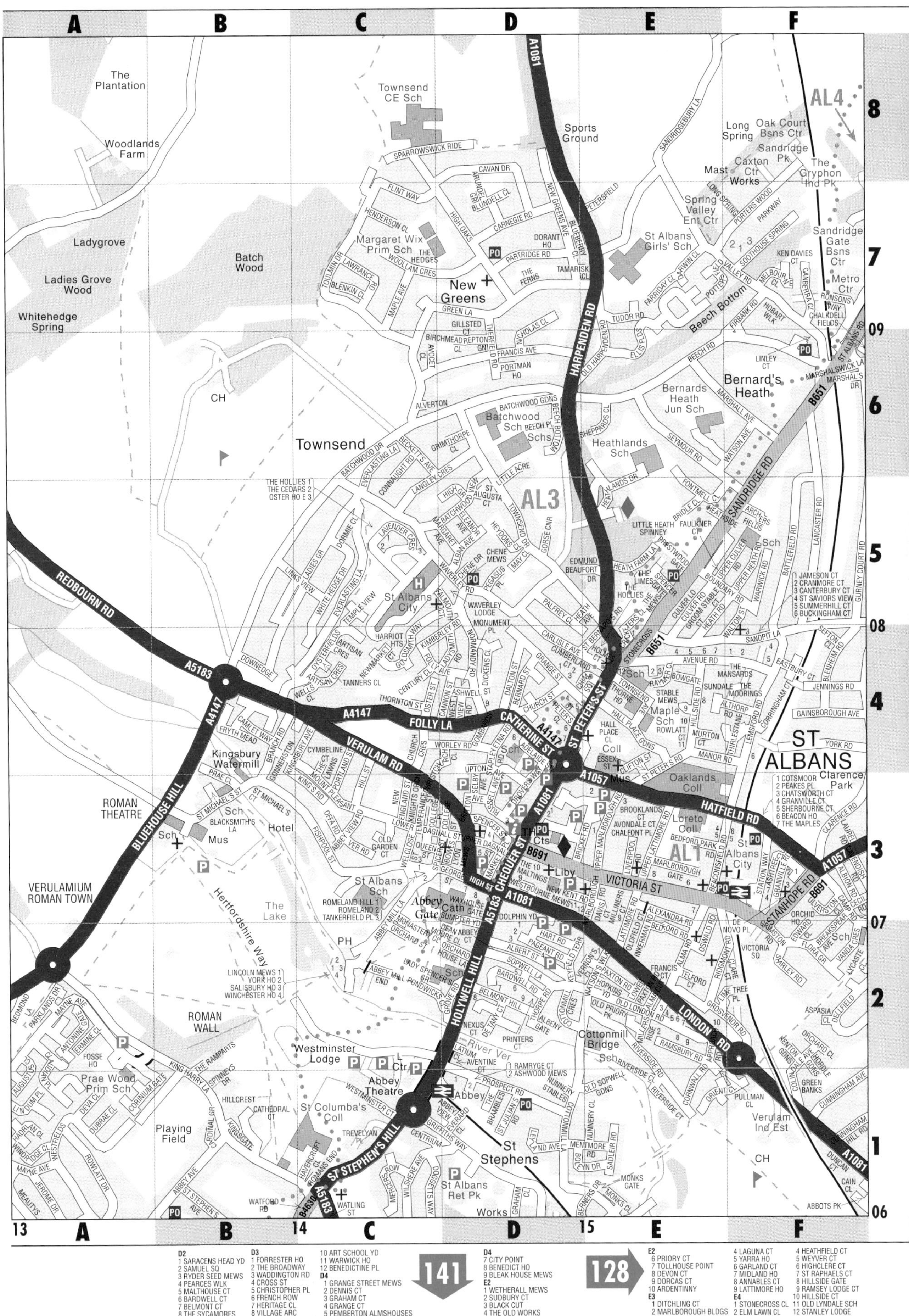

D2
1 SARACENS HEAD YD
2 SAMUEL SQ
3 RYDER SEED MEWS
4 PEARCES WLK
5 MALTHOUSE CT
6 BARDWELL CT
7 BELMONT CT
8 THE SYCAMORES
9 PAT LARNER HO

D3
1 FORRESTER HO
2 THE BROADWAY
3 WADDINGTON RD
4 CROSS ST
5 CHRISTOPHER PL
6 FRENCH ROW
7 HERITAGE CL
8 VILLAGE ARC
9 HALF MOON MEWS
10 ART SCHOOL YD
11 WARWICK HO
12 BENEDICTINE PL

D4
1 GRANGE STREET MEWS
2 DENNIS CT
3 GRAHAM CT
4 GRANGE CT
5 PEMBERTON ALMSHOUSES
6 ST PETERS MEWS

D4
7 CITY POINT
8 BENEDICT HO
9 BLEAK HOUSE MEWS

E2
1 WETHERALL MEWS
2 SUDBURY CT
3 BLACK CUT
4 THE OLD WORKS
5 WINTON TERR

E2
6 PRIORY CT
7 TOLLHOUSE POINT
8 DEVON CT
9 DORCAS CT
10 ARDENTINNY

E3
1 DITCHLING CT
2 MARLBOROUGH BLDGS
3 BEAUMONDS
4 LAGUNA CT
5 YARRA HO
6 GARLAND CT
7 MIDLAND HO
8 ANNABLES CT
9 LATTIMORE HO

E4
1 STONECROSS CL
2 ELM LAWN CL
3 RAYMER CT
4 HEATHFIELD CT
5 WEYVER CT
6 HIGHCLERE CT
7 ST RAPHAELS CT
8 HILLSIDE GATE
9 RAMSEY LODGE CT
10 HILLSIDE CT
11 OLD LYNDALE SCH
12 STANLEY LODGE

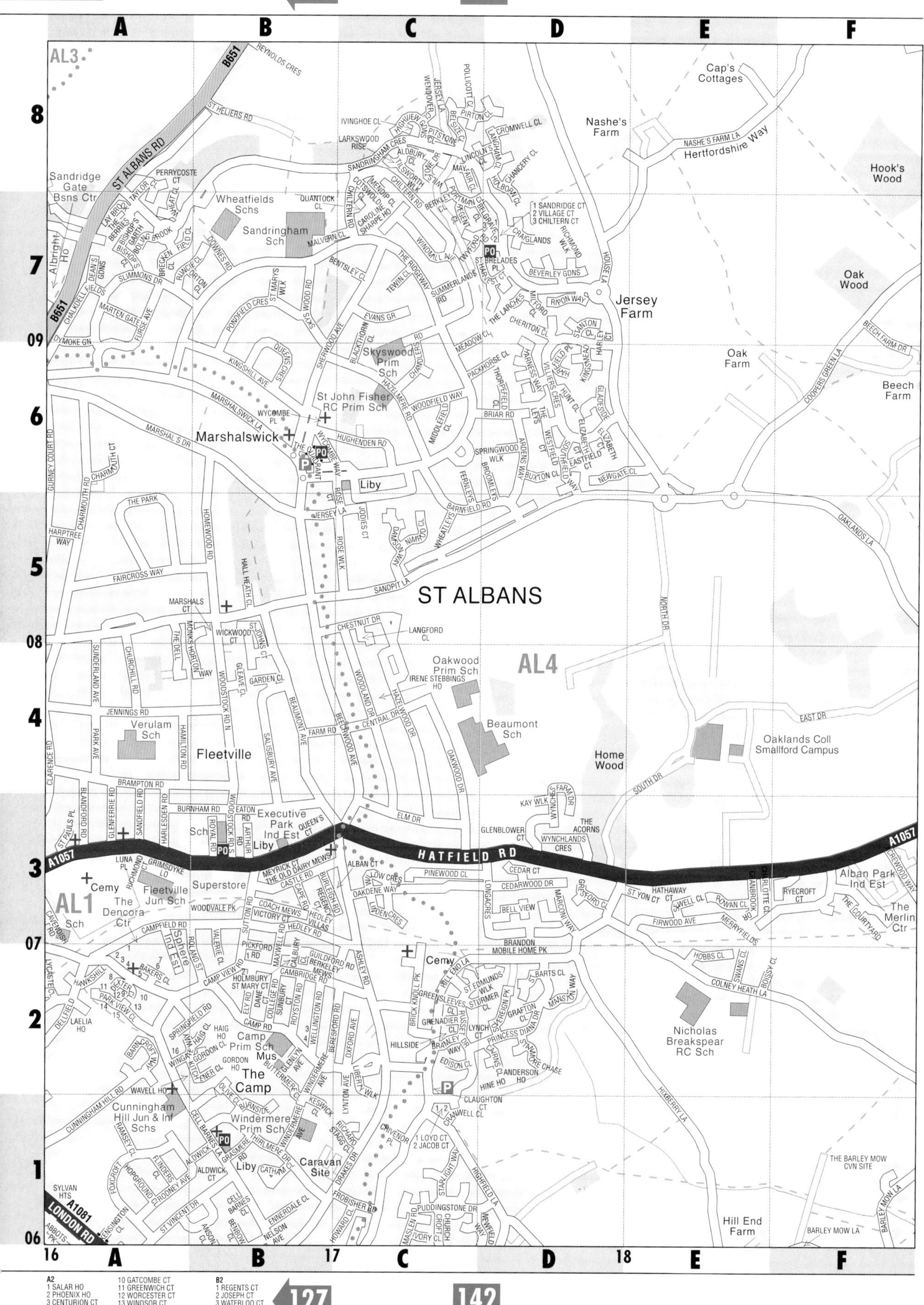

A2
1 SALAR HO
2 PHOENIX HO
3 CENTURION CT
4 ALBANIAN CT
5 MISTRAL CT
6 DAWN CT
7 CLEMENT CT
8 DORCHESTER CT
9 CHELTENHAM CT
10 GATCOMBE CT
11 GREENWICH CT
12 WORCESTER CT
13 WINDSOR CT
14 SYON CT
15 ST JAMES CT
16 WINGATE HO

B2
1 REGENTS CT
2 JOSEPH CT
3 WATERLOO CT
4 ST LUKES PL

127
142

109
130

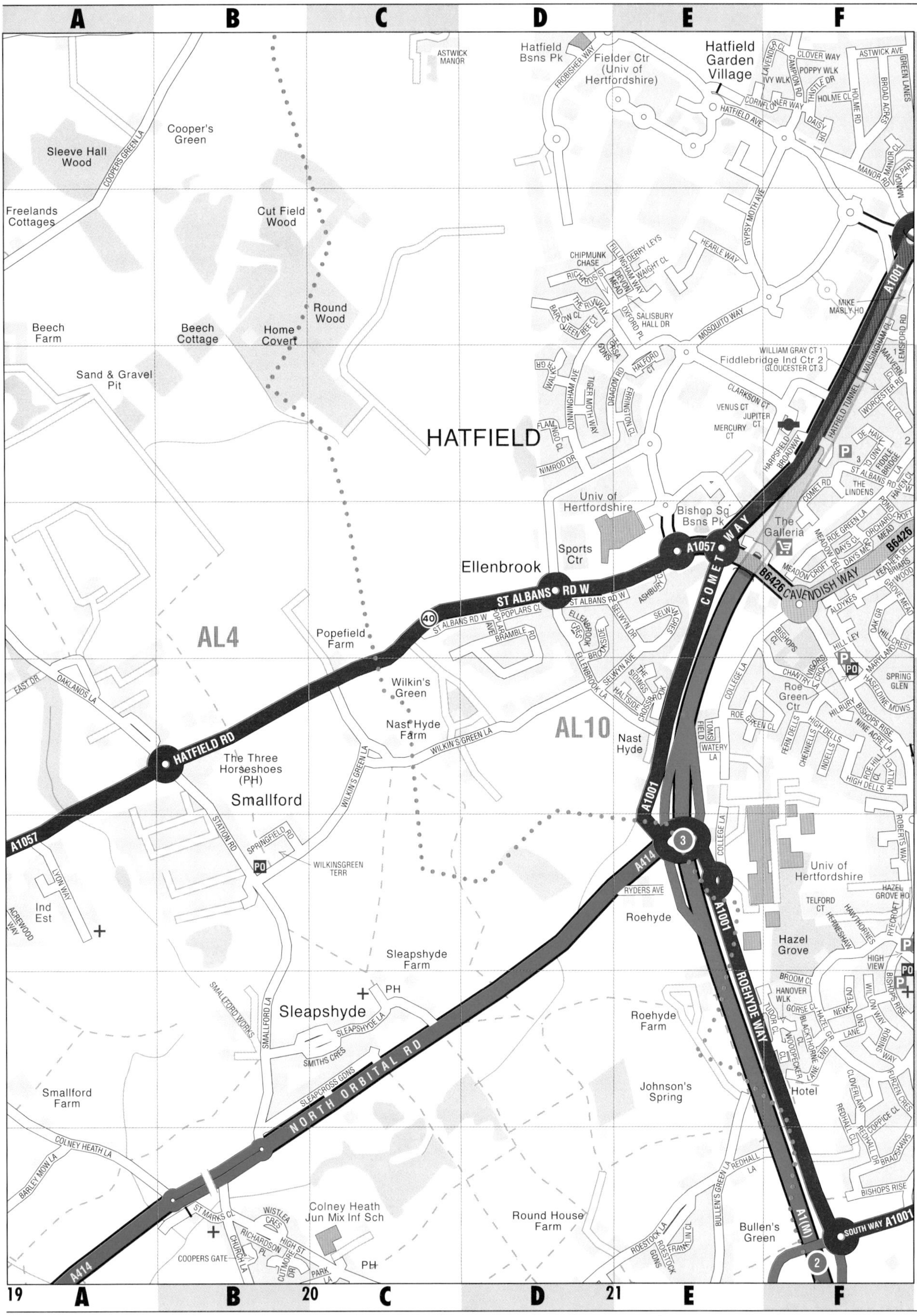

143
130

A6
1 QUEENSWAY HO
2 BROOMFIELD CT
3 LOTHAIR CT
4 GALLEYCROFT CT
5 WHITE LION HO

129
110

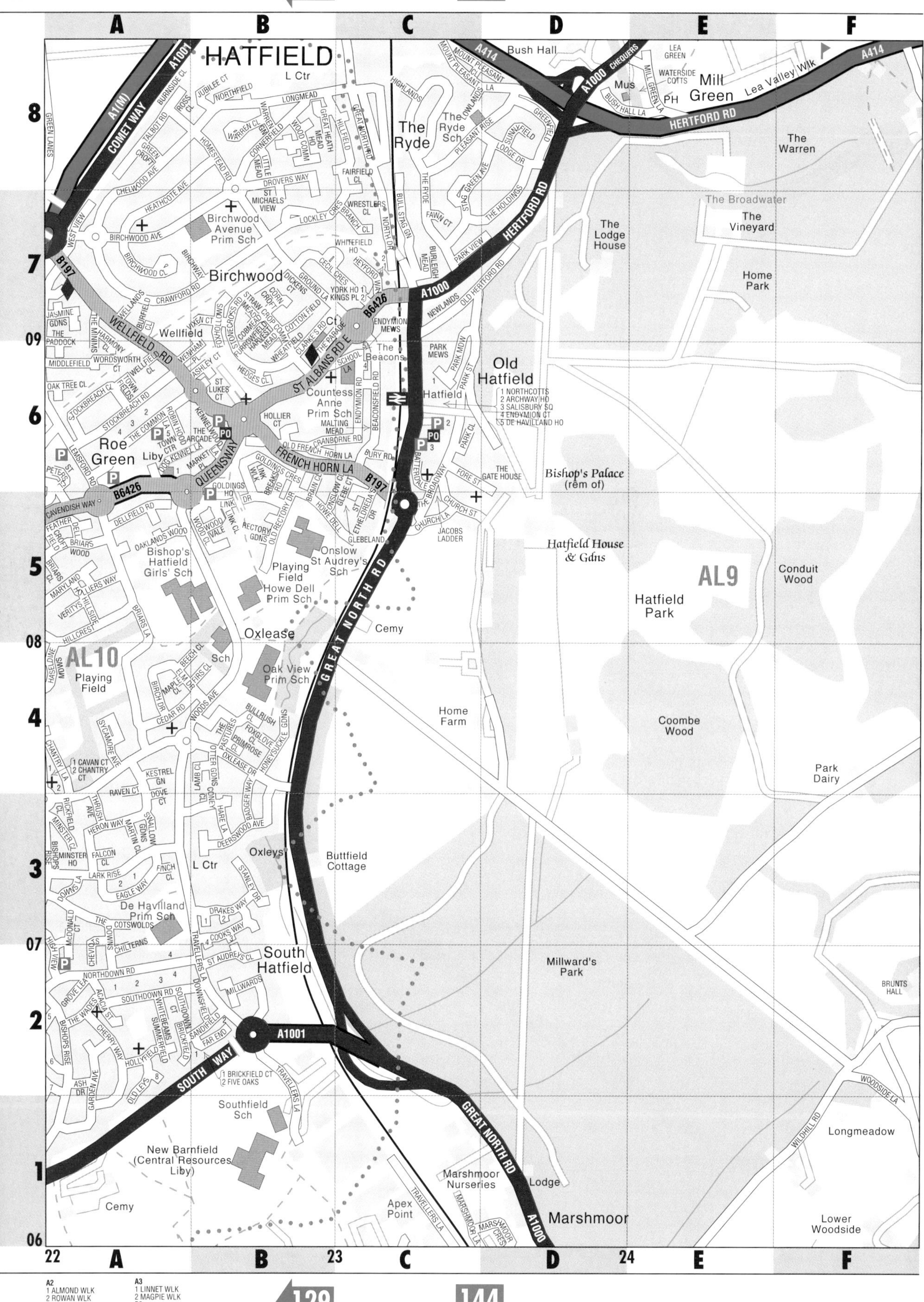

A2
1 ALMOND WLK
2 ROWAN WLK
3 GEAN WLK
4 SCHOLARS WLK
5 HAZEL GR
6 SHALLCROSS CRES
7 FURZEN CRES
8 STRAWBERRY FIELD

A3
1 LINNET WLK
2 MAGPIE WLK

B3
1 KINGSMILL CT
2 ALLEN CT
3 HAMILTON CT
4 RICHMOND CT

129
144

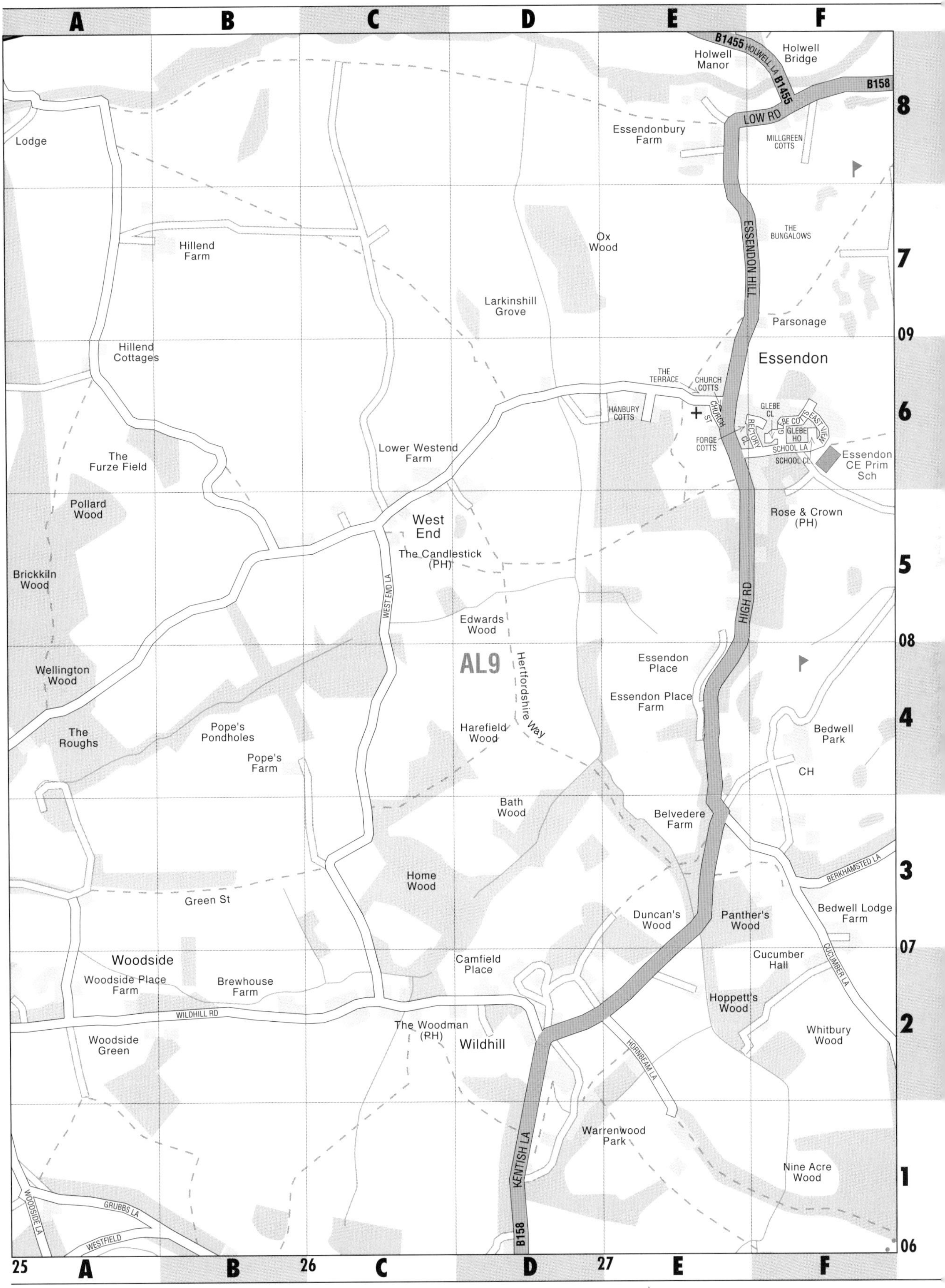

A B C D E F
Holwell Manor
Holwell Bridge
B1455
HOLWELL LA
B158
LOW RD
Lodge
Essendonbury Farm
MILLGREEN COTTS
8
Hillend Farm
Ox Wood
THE BUNGALOWS
ESSENDON HILL
7
Larkinshill Grove
Parsonage
09
Hillend Cottages
Essendon
THE TERRACE
CHURCH COTTS
HANBURY COTTS
GLEBE CL
CHURCH ST
RECTORY CL
GLEBE COTTS
EAST VIEW
GLEBE HO
FORGE COTTS
SCHOOL LA
SCHOOL CL
6
Lower Westend Farm
The Furze Field
Essendon CE Prim Sch
Pollard Wood
Rose & Crown (PH)
West End
The Candlestick (PH)
Brickkiln Wood
5
WEST END LA
Edwards Wood
HIGH RD
08
AL9
Hertfordshire Way
Essendon Place
Wellington Wood
Essendon Place Farm
The Roughs
Pope's Pondholes
Harefield Wood
Bedwell Park
4
Pope's Farm
CH
Bath Wood
Belvedere Farm
BERKHAMSTED LA
3
Home Wood
Green St
Duncan's Wood
Panther's Wood
Bedwell Lodge Farm
07
Woodside
Camfield Place
Cucumber Hall
CUCUMBER LA
Woodside Place Farm
Brewhouse Farm
Hoppett's Wood
WILDHILL RD
The Woodman (PH)
Wildhill
Whitbury Wood
2
Woodside Green
HORNBEAM LA
Warrenwood Park
KENTISH LA
Nine Acre Wood
1
WOODSIDE LA
GRUBBS LA
WESTFIELD
B158
06
25 A B 26 C D 27 E F

131
112

131
146

113
134

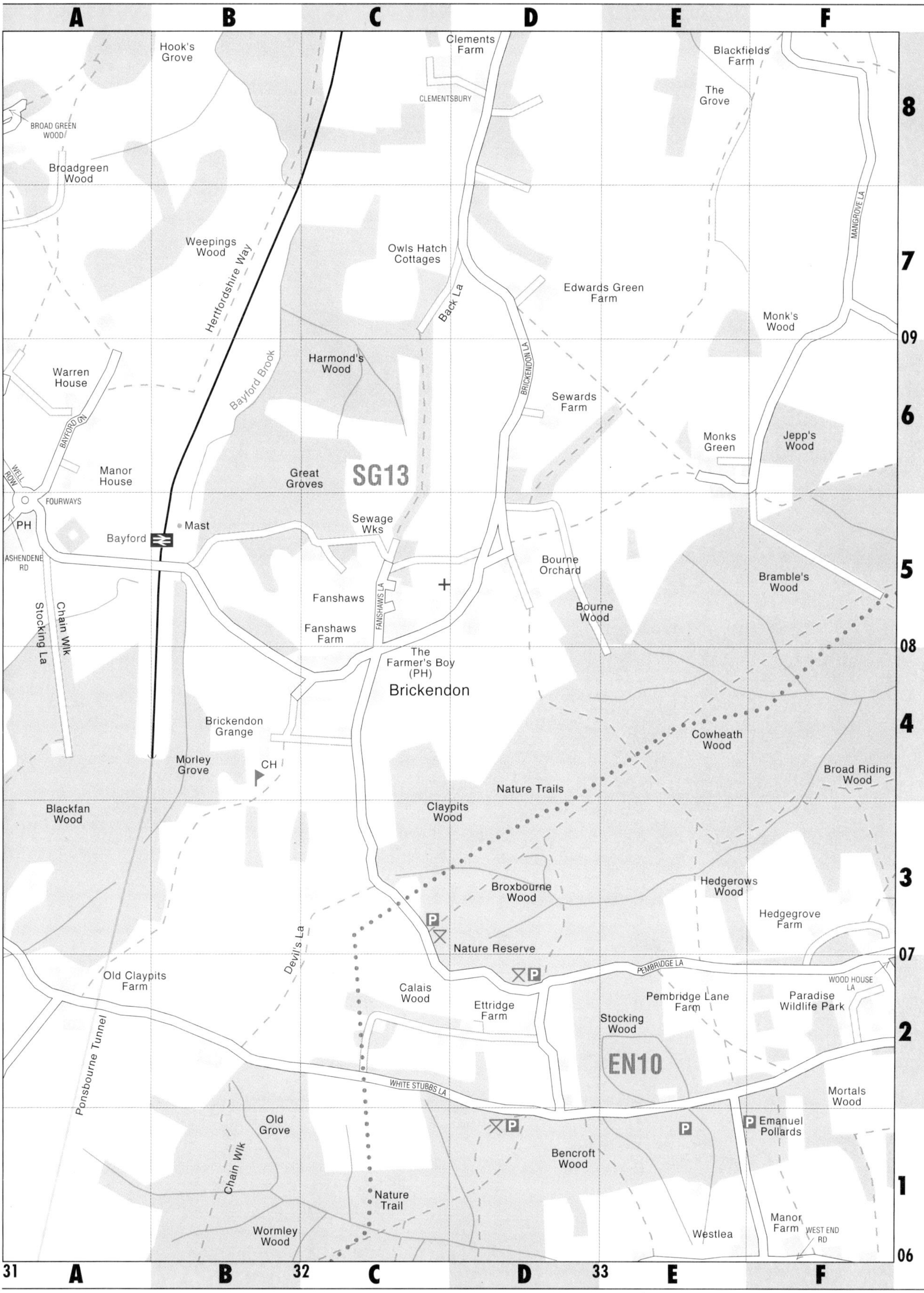

147
134

133 114

A B C D E F
8
7
09
6
5
08
4
3
07
2
1
06
34 35 36
Mast
Elbowlane Farm
SG13
Dalmonds
Dalmond's Wood
Wr Twr
Goose Green
Box Wood
The Huntsman (PH)
The Woodman (PH)
The Chalet
Woollensbrook
B1197
Hertford Rd
Cutthroat La
Bramble La
Westfield Com Prim Sch
Woollens Brook
Lanthorn's Wood
A10
EN11
High Leigh Barns
High Leigh Farm
High Leigh
Box La
Mangrove La
Highfield Farm
Lord St
Beech Wlk
Kennedy Ave
Rosehill Cl
Highfield Wood
Red Hills
Hoddesdonpark Wood
Hoddesdon Lodge
Spital Brook
Recn Gd
Sheredes Sch
Sheredes Prim Sch
Danemead Wood
Cock La
Nursery Grove
Chestnut Grove
Great Grove
Broxbournebury Mews
Icehouse Grove
Broxbournebury Mansion
CH
Broxbourne
EN10
Pembridge La
Edgewood Farm
Lower White Stubbs
Wood House La
White Stubbs La
Cold Hall
Baas Hill
Sports Gd
Broxbourne CE Prim Sch
High Rd
A1170
B194
Station Rd
White Stubbs Farm
Spring Wlk
Church La
Baas Manor Farm
Carneles Green
Cozens Grove
The Broxbourne Sch
New River
Wentworth Cotts
Tudor Farm
West End Rd
Manor House
Bury Farm
Ley Park Prim Sch
A B C D E F

A6
1 Tower Ctr
2 HIGHBOURNE CT
3 THE OLD MALTINGS CT
4 HOPPS HO
5 CHRISTIES CT
6 BUCKINGHAM LODGE
7 SANDRINGHAM LODGE
8 CLARENCE LODGE
9 BENSTEDE CT
10 PEARL CT
11 EVERSLEY LODGE
12 ACACIAS CT
13 COMROSTON
14 LOWFIELD CT
15 BROCKET CT
16 HOGGES CL
17 LIMES CT
18 PORTLAND CT

A7
1 FOURWAYS CT
2 CUMBERLAND CT
3 WESTFIELD RD
4 NORRIS RISE
5 WINTERSCROFT RD
6 BELCHER RD
7 ROMAN MEWS
8 ROMAN ST
9 BURFORD MEWS
10 TOWER HTS
11 BURFORD PL

115

D8
1 NECTAR CT
2 BARLEY CT
3 MEAD LODGE
4 PEPYS CT
5 TEALE HO
6 LEASIDE LODGE
7 PLOTTERS CT
8 CHARLES HO
9 MALTSTERS LODGE

A B C D E F

Rye House Gatehouse
Stadium
Rye House
Parkside Bsns Ctr
Hoddesdon Ind Ctr
Rye Park Ind Est
Rye Park
Impresa Pk
Spurling Wks
HODDESDON
New England Est
Optima Bsns Pk
Trident Ind Est
Power Sta
GLEN FABA
The Grove
Knights Properties
Liby
Superstore
Sch
Maple Pk
Nicholson Ct
Belcon Ind Est
Francis Works
Mast
The Haslemere Est
Waterside Ind Est
Hailes Farm
Burles Farm
CM19
Netherhall (rems of)
Dobb's Weir
Dobb's Weir Bridge
PH
Civic Hall
Mus
Spitalbrook
EN11
Harcamlow Way
Lea Valley Walk
River Lynch
River Lea or Lee Navigation
Lee Valley Country Park
Broxbourne & Hoddesdon
Nurseries
Meadgate
Nazeing Mead
Shottentons Farm
CARTHAGENA EST
L Ctr
Cvn Site
Nazeing Glass Works
Meridian House
EN9
Keysers Estate
Lower Nazeing
Hillgrove Bsns Pk
Brook Farm
EN10
River Stort
River Stort (Navigation)
Three Forests Way
Stort Valley Way
Toll House Stream
A1170 WARE RD
A10 DINANT LINK RD
B1197 HERTFORD RD
CHARLTON WAY
HIGH ST
STATION RD
NAZEING NEW RD
B194 NAZEING RD
GLEN FABA RD
LOW HILL RD
HAMLET HILL
NETHERHALL RD
SEDGE GN
PECK'S HILL
NORTH ST
NURSERY RD
DOBB'S WEIR RD
ESSEX RD

1 BRICKENDON CT
2 ESDAILE HALL
3 BRUNSWICK CT
4 ASHLEIGH CT
5 WOODGRANGE CT
6 THE GRANGE
7 KNOWLE HO
8 SQUIRES CT
9 GILLIFLOWER HO
10 BELVEDERE CT

1 LANSDOWNE CT
2 STAFFORD HO
3 CHURCH CT
4 STAFFORD CT

1 THE AVENUE
2 WESTCROFT CT
3 ST CATHARINE'S RD

1 THURGOOD RD
2 MIDDLEFIELD CL

LANGLEY GN 1
NAZEINGBURY PAR 2
NAZEINGBURY CL 3

8 7 6 5 09 4 08 3 07 2 1 06

37 38 39

South Essex STREET ATLAS

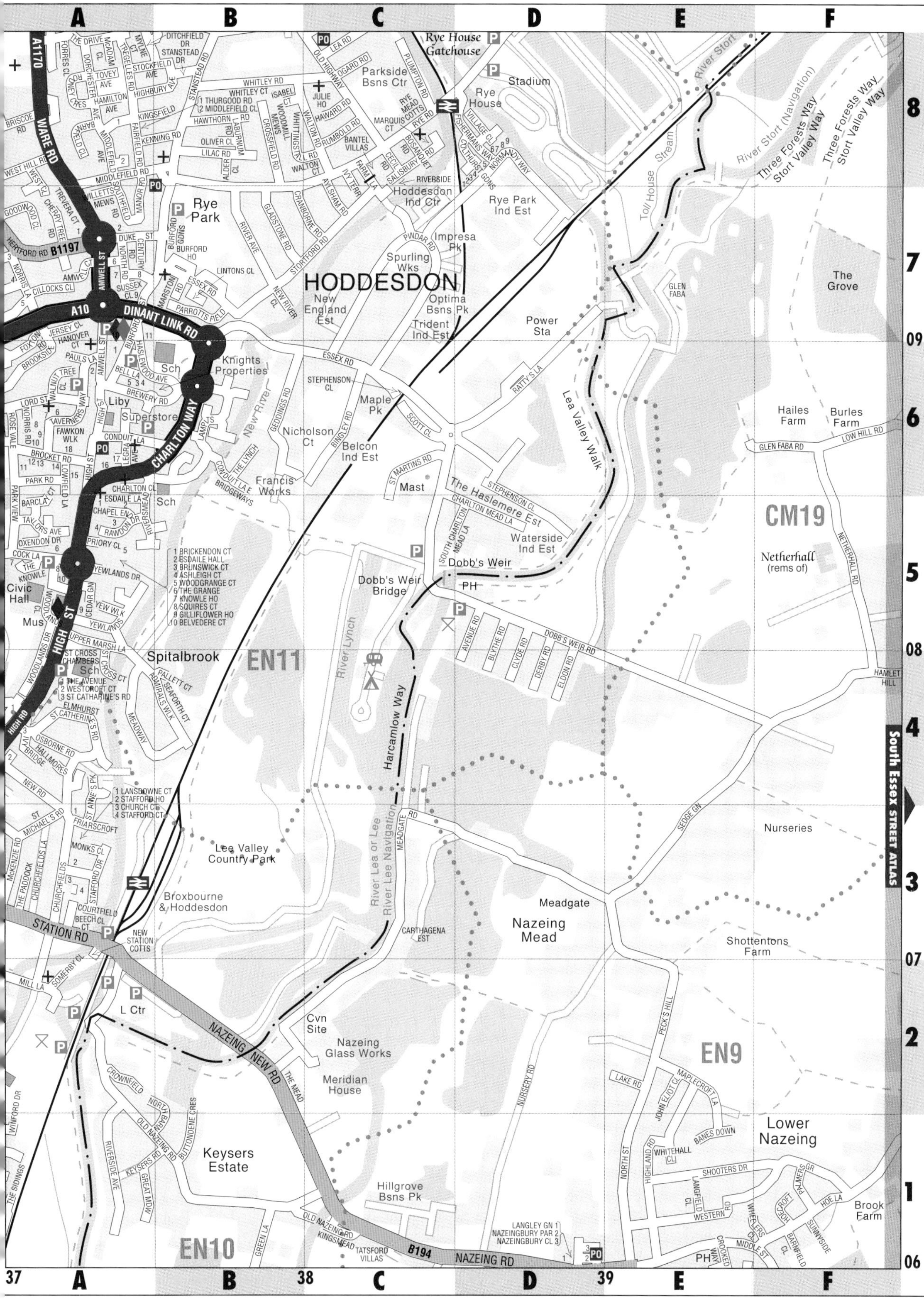

149

122

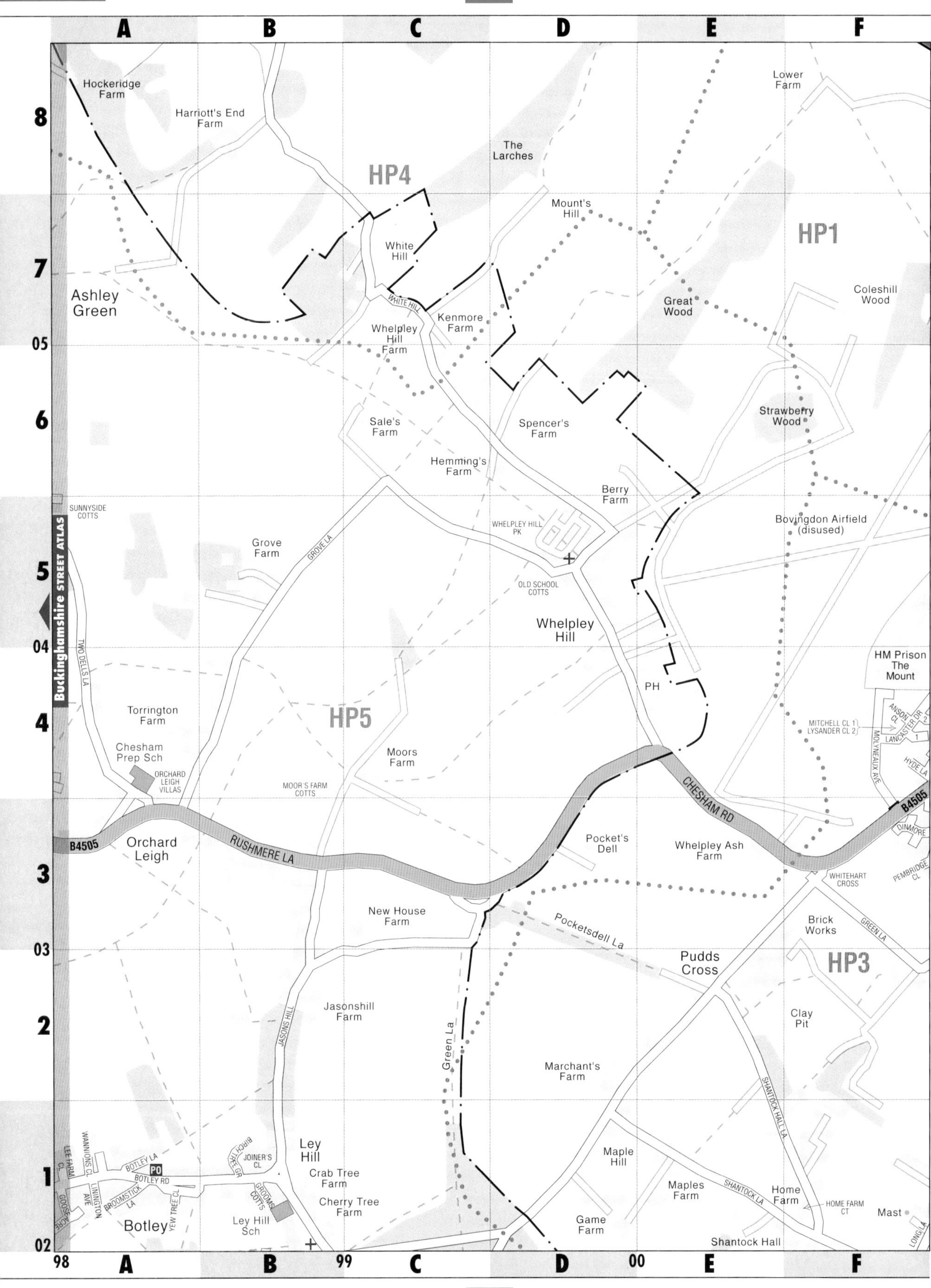
A
B
C
D
E
F
8
7
05
6
5
04
4
3
03
2
1
02
98
99
00
Hockeridge Farm
Harriott's End Farm
The Larches
HP4
Lower Farm
Mount's Hill
White Hill
HP1
Ashley Green
WHITE HILL
Kenmore Farm
Great Wood
Coleshill Wood
Whelpley Hill Farm
Sale's Farm
Spencer's Farm
Strawberry Wood
Hemming's Farm
Berry Farm
SUNNYSIDE COTTS
WHELPLEY HILL PK
Bovingdon Airfield (disused)
Grove Farm
GROVE LA
OLD SCHOOL COTTS
Buckinghamshire STREET ATLAS
Whelpley Hill
TWO DELLS LA
HM Prison The Mount
PH
Torrington Farm
HP5
ANSON CL
LANCASTER DR
MITCHELL CL 1
LYSANDER CL 2
Chesham Prep Sch
Moors Farm
MOLYNEAUX AVE
HYDE LA
ORCHARD LEIGH VILLAS
MOOR'S FARM COTTS
CHESHAM RD
B4505
B4505
Orchard Leigh
RUSHMERE LA
Pocket's Dell
Whelpley Ash Farm
DINMORE
WHITEHART CROSS
PEMBRIDGE CL
New House Farm
Pocketsdell La
Brick Works
GREEN LA
Pudds Cross
HP3
Jasonshill Farm
JASONS HILL
Clay Pit
Green La
Marchant's Farm
SHANTOCK HALL LA
WANNIONS CL
LEE FARM CL
BIRCH TREE GR
Ley Hill
JOINER'S CL
BOTLEY LA
PO
BOTLEY RD
Crab Tree Farm
Maple Hill
Maples Farm
SHANTOCK LA
Home Farm
HOME FARM CT
Mast
GOOSE ACRE
LININGTON AVE
BROOMSTICK LA
YEW TREE CL
GROOMS COTTS
Cherry Tree Farm
Botley
Ley Hill Sch
Game Farm
Shantock Hall
LONG LA

150

123
138

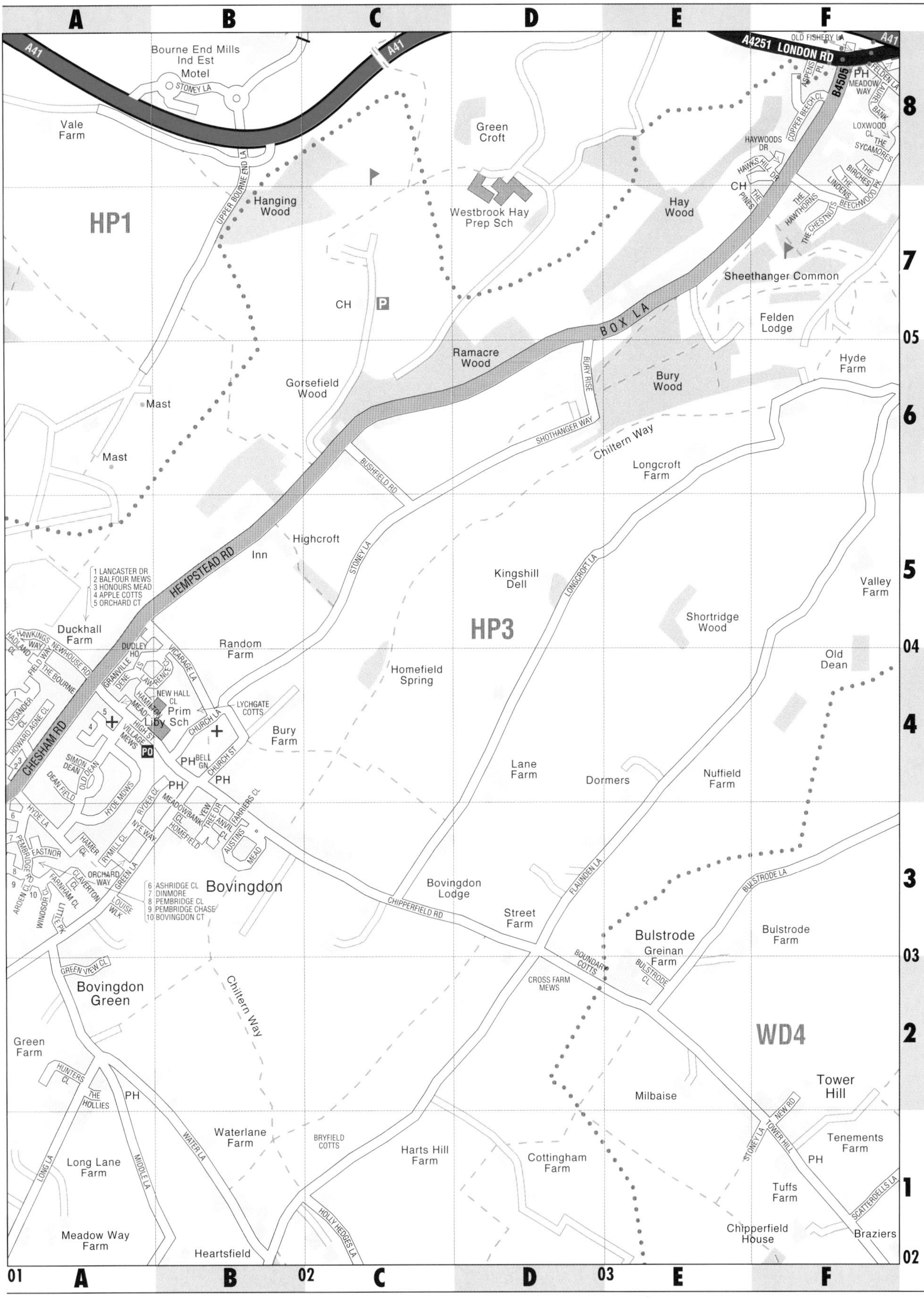
A
B
C
D
E
F
A41
Bourne End Mills
Ind Est
Motel
STONEY LA
Vale
Farm
OLD FISHERY LA
A4251 LONDON RD
B4505
PH
MEADOW WAY
Green
Croft
HAYWOODS DR
HAWKS HILL DR
COPPER BEECH CL
LOXWOOD CL
THE SYCAMORES
THE BIRCHES
THE LINDENS
BEECHWOOD PK
CH
THE PINES
THE HAWTHORNS
THE CHESTNUTS
HP1
UPPER BOURNE END LA
Hanging
Wood
Westbrook Hay
Prep Sch
Hay
Wood
Sheethanger Common
CH
BOX LA
Felden
Lodge
Ramacre
Wood
BURY RISE
Bury
Wood
Hyde
Farm
Gorsefield
Wood
Mast
Mast
SHOTHANGER WAY
Chiltern Way
Longcroft
Farm
BUSHFIELD RD
Highcroft
Inn
HEMPSTEAD RD
STONEY LA
Kingshill
Dell
LONGCROFT LA
Valley
Farm
1 LANCASTER DR
2 BALFOUR MEWS
3 HONOURS MEAD
4 APPLE COTTS
5 ORCHARD CT
Duckhall
Farm
HP3
Shortridge
Wood
Random
Farm
Old
Dean
Homefield
Spring
HAWKINGS WAY
HADLAND CL
NEWHOUSE RD
FIELD WAY
THE BOURNE
DUDLEY HO
GRANVILLE DENE
VICARAGE LA
NEW HALL CL
Prim
Sch
Liby
LYCHGATE COTTS
CHURCH LA
Bury
Farm
CHESHAM RD
LYSANDER CL
HOWARD AGNE CL
HIGH ST
VILLAGE MEWS
PO
PH
BELL GN
CHURCH ST
PH
SIMON DEAN
OLD DEAN
DEAN FIELD
HYDE MDWS
RYDER CL
PH
Lane
Farm
Dormers
Nuffield
Farm
HYDE LA
MEADOWBANK CL
YEW TREE DR
ANVIL CL
FARRIERS CL
AUSTINS MEAD
NYE WAY
HOMEFIELD
EASTNOR
HAMER CL
RYMILL CL
PEMBRIDGE RD
ORCHARD WAY
GREEN LA
CLAVERTON CL
FARNHAM CL
ARDEN CL
WINDSOR CL
LITTLE PK
LOUISE WLK
6 ASHRIDGE CL
7 DINMORE
8 PEMBRIDGE CL
9 PEMBRIDGE CHASE
10 BOVINGDON CT
Bovingdon
Bovingdon
Lodge
CHIPPERFIELD RD
Street
Farm
FLAUNDEN LA
BULSTRODE LA
Bulstrode
Greinan
Farm
Bulstrode
Farm
BOUNDARY COTTS
BULSTRODE CL
CROSS FARM MEWS
GREEN VIEW CL
Bovingdon
Green
Chiltern Way
WD4
Green
Farm
HUNTERS CL
THE HOLLIES
PH
Milbaise
Tower
Hill
NEW RD
TOWER HILL
STONEY LA
Tenements
Farm
PH
WATER LA
Waterlane
Farm
BRYFIELD COTTS
Harts Hill
Farm
Cottingham
Farm
Long Lane
Farm
LONG LA
MIDDLE LA
Tuffs
Farm
SCATTERDELLS LA
HOLLY HEDGES LA
Meadow Way
Farm
Heartsfield
Chipperfield
House
Braziers
8
7
05
6
5
04
4
3
03
2
1
02
01
02
03

151
138

137
124

E7
1 RUSHMERE CT
2 WATERSIDE CT
3 WILLOW CT

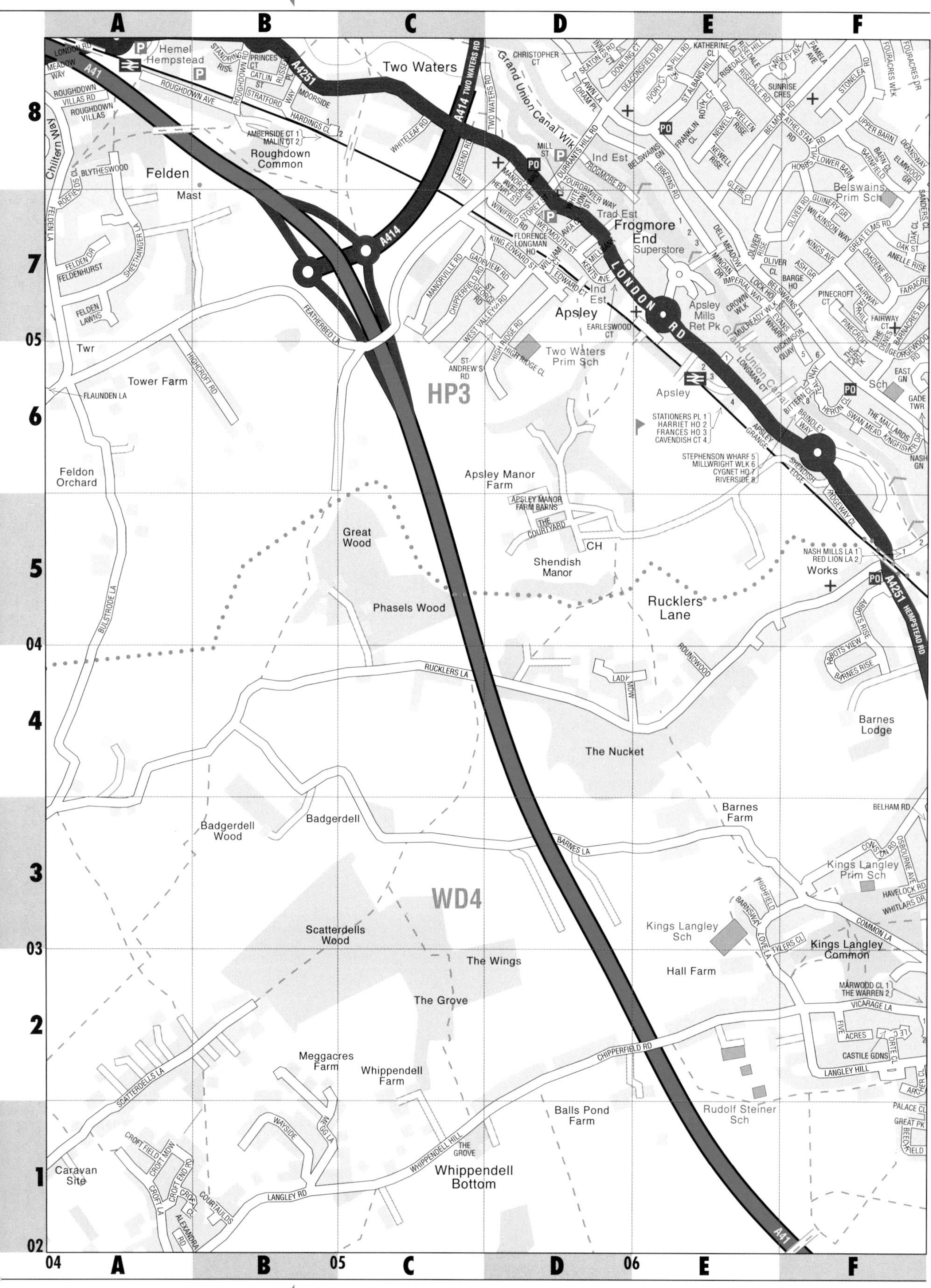

137
152

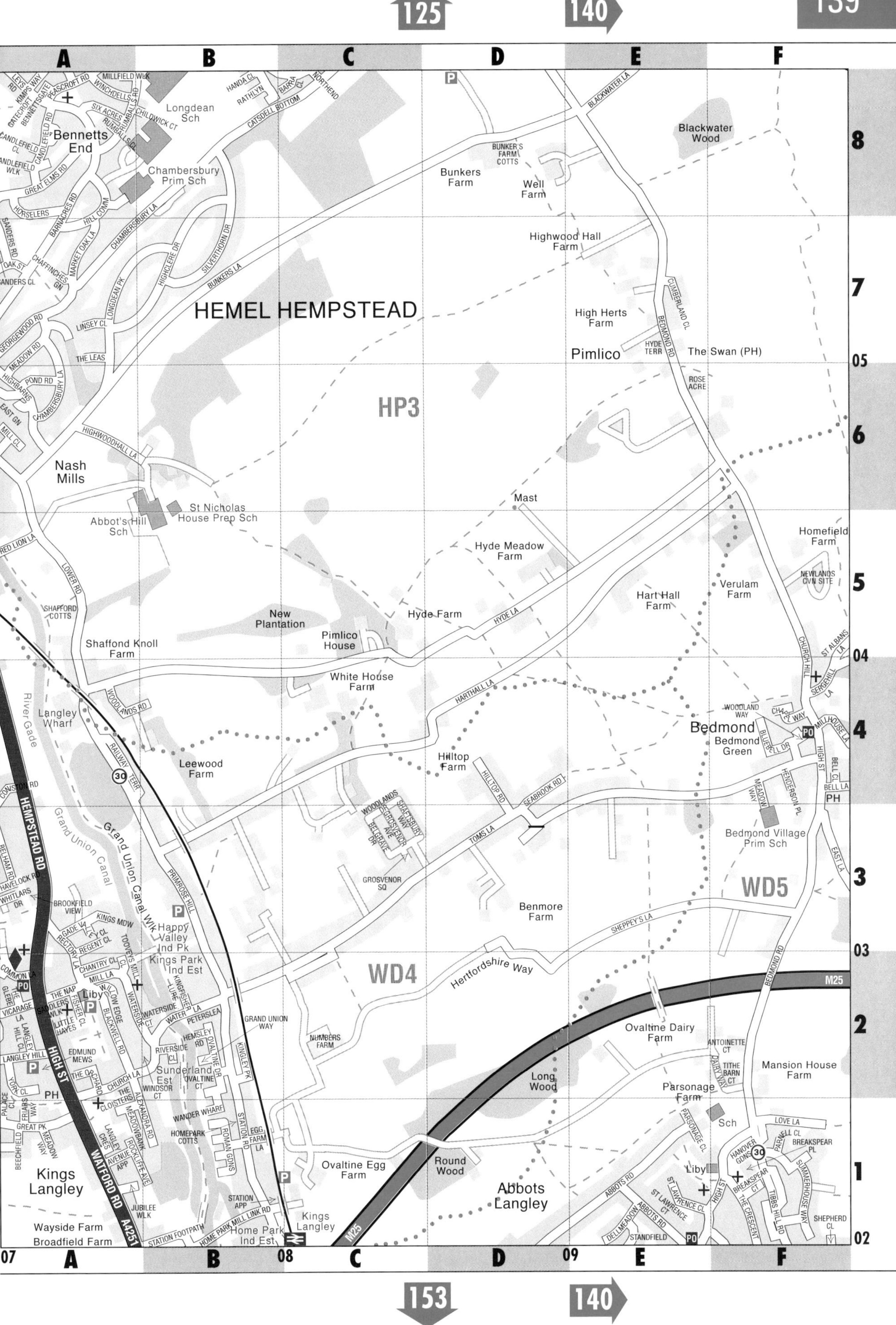
A
B
C
D
E
F
HEMEL HEMPSTEAD
Bennetts End
Longdean Sch
Chambersbury Prim Sch
Bunkers Farm
Well Farm
Blackwater Wood
Highwood Hall Farm
High Herts Farm
Pimlico
The Swan (PH)
HP3
Nash Mills
St Nicholas House Prep Sch
Abbot's Hill Sch
Mast
Hyde Meadow Farm
Homefield Farm
Verulam Farm
Hart Hall Farm
Hyde Farm
New Plantation
Pimlico House
Shaffond Knoll Farm
White House Farm
Langley Wharf
River Gade
Leewood Farm
Hilltop Farm
Bedmond
Bedmond Green
Bedmond Village Prim Sch
Grand Union Canal
Grand Union Canal Wlk
Happy Valley Ind Pk
Kings Park Ind Est
Benmore Farm
WD5
WD4
Hertfordshire Way
M25
Ovaltine Dairy Farm
Mansion House Farm
Long Wood
Parsonage Farm
Sunderland Est
Kings Langley
Ovaltine Egg Farm
Round Wood
Abbots Langley
Wayside Farm
Broadfield Farm
Home Park Ind Est
HEMPSTEAD RD
HIGH ST
WATFORD RD
A4251
BUNKERS LA
HYDE LA
HARTHALL LA
TOMS LA
SHEPPEY'S LA
BEDMOND RD
CHURCH HILL
BLACKWATER LA
LOWER RD
RED LION LA
HIGHWOODHALL LA
CHAMBERSBURY LA
8
7
6
5
4
3
2
1
05
04
03
02
07
08
09

139
126

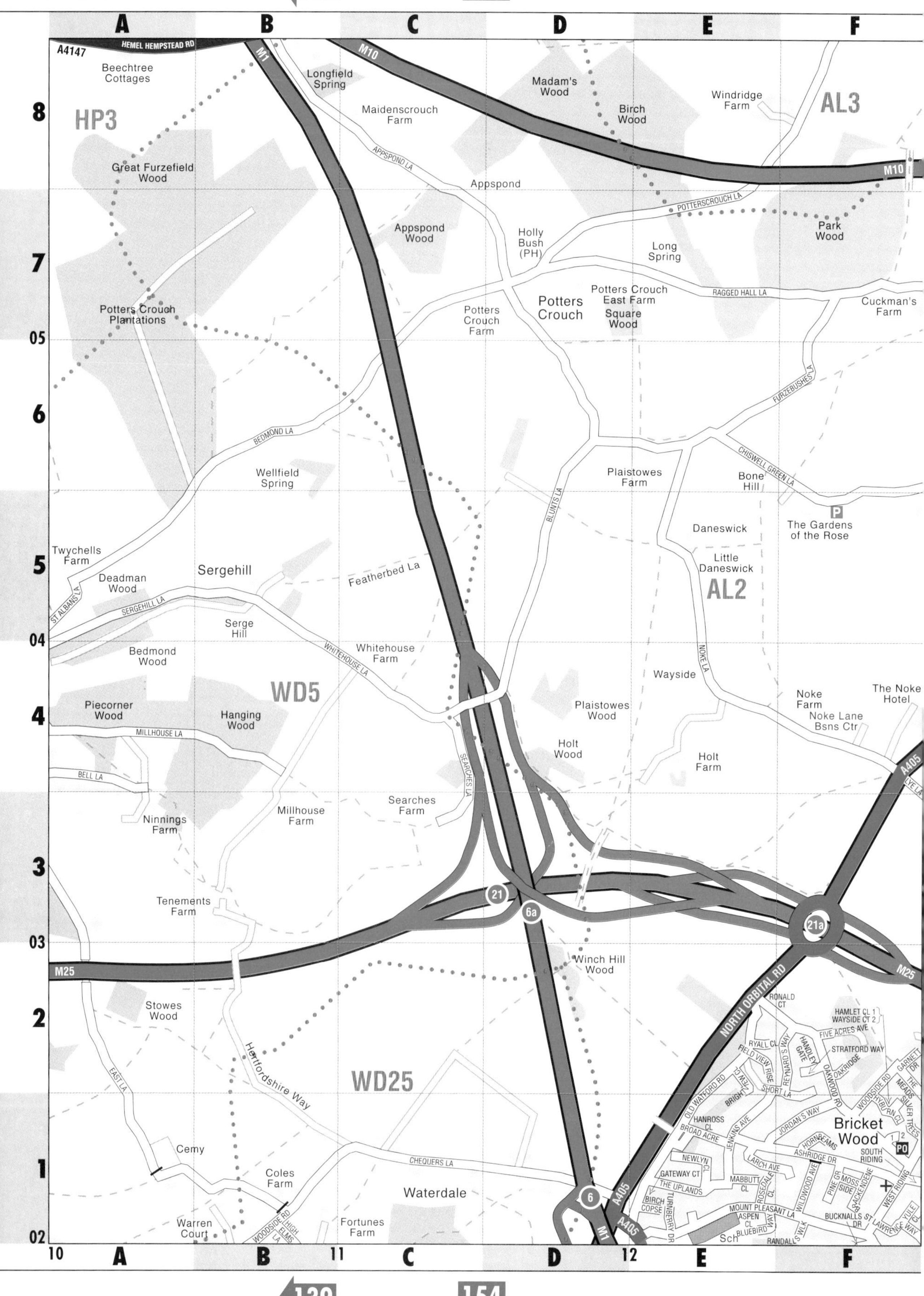

139
154

A B C D E F

8 7 05 6 5 04 4 3 03 2 1 02

ST ALBANS
AL3
AL1
AL2
Marlborough Sch
St Julians
Sch
Mandeville Prim Sch
Sopwell
Sopwell House Farm
Sopwell House Hotel
Westfield's Farm
Watling View Sch
St Julian's Wood
Killigrew Inf Sch
Killigrew Jun Sch
Greenwood Park L Ctr
Hedges Farm
River Ver
Mill Stream
Chiswell Green
Park Street
Park Street
Park Ind Est
Stroud Wood Bsns Ctr
Frogmore
Burton Manor Farm
Birchwood Bungalow
Birch Wood
How Wood
How Wood Prim Sch
Park Street CE Prim Sch
How Wood
Tenterden House
Frogmore Bsns Pk
Homewood Ind Sch
Blackgreen Wood
Smug Oak Bsns Ctr
Horseshoe Bsns Pk
Smug Oak
The Gate (PH)
Bricket Wood
Hotel
Colney Street Farm
Colney Street

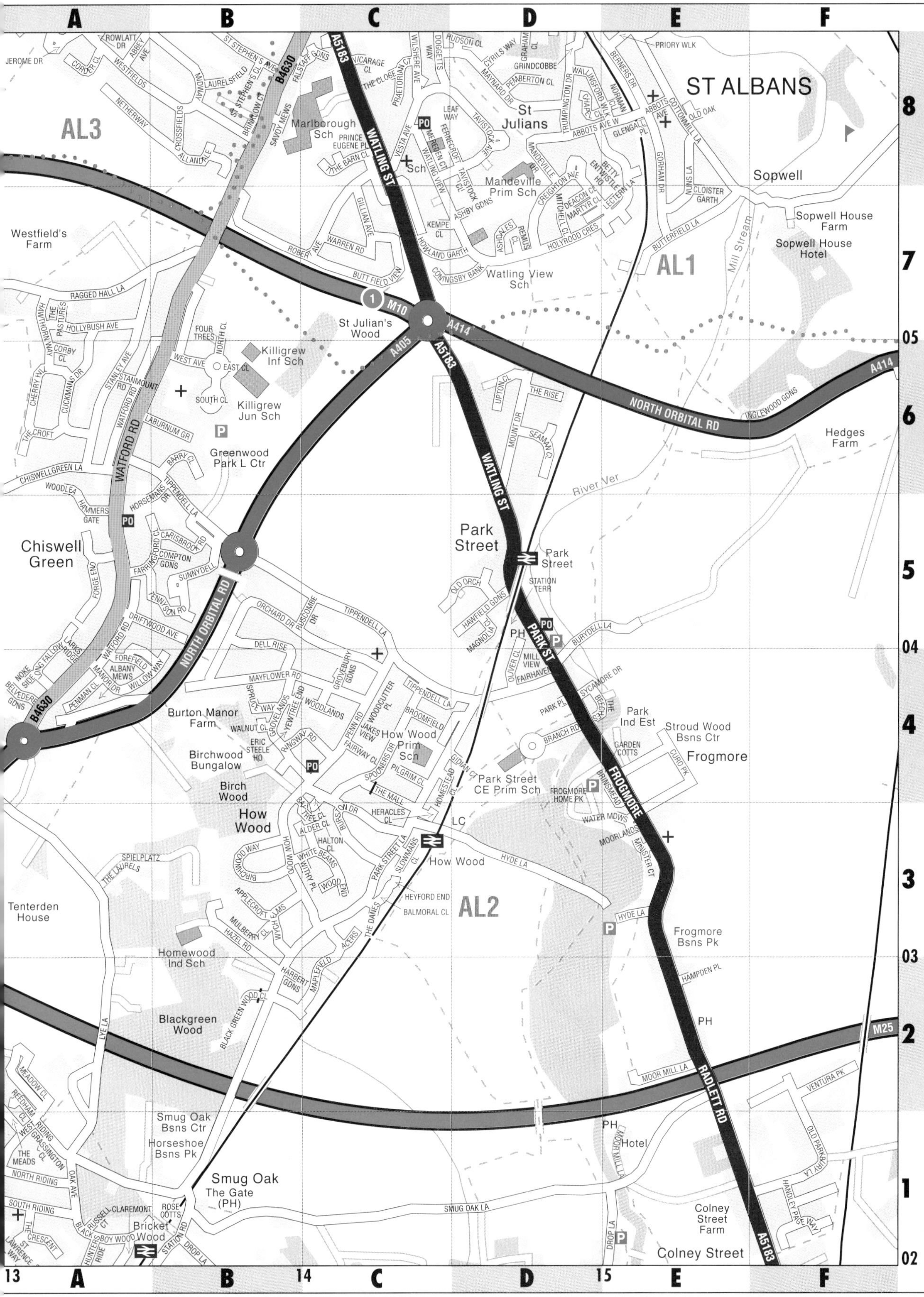

WATLING ST
A5183
PARK ST
FROGMORE
RADLETT RD
NORTH ORBITAL RD
A414
A405
M10
M25
B4630
WATFORD RD
SMUG OAK LA
MOOR MILL LA
HYDE LA
TIPPENDELL LA
RAGGED HALL LA
CHISWELLGREEN LA
BURYDELL LA
VENTURA PK
OLD PARKBURY LA

13 A B 14 C D 15 E F

141
128

141
156

129
144

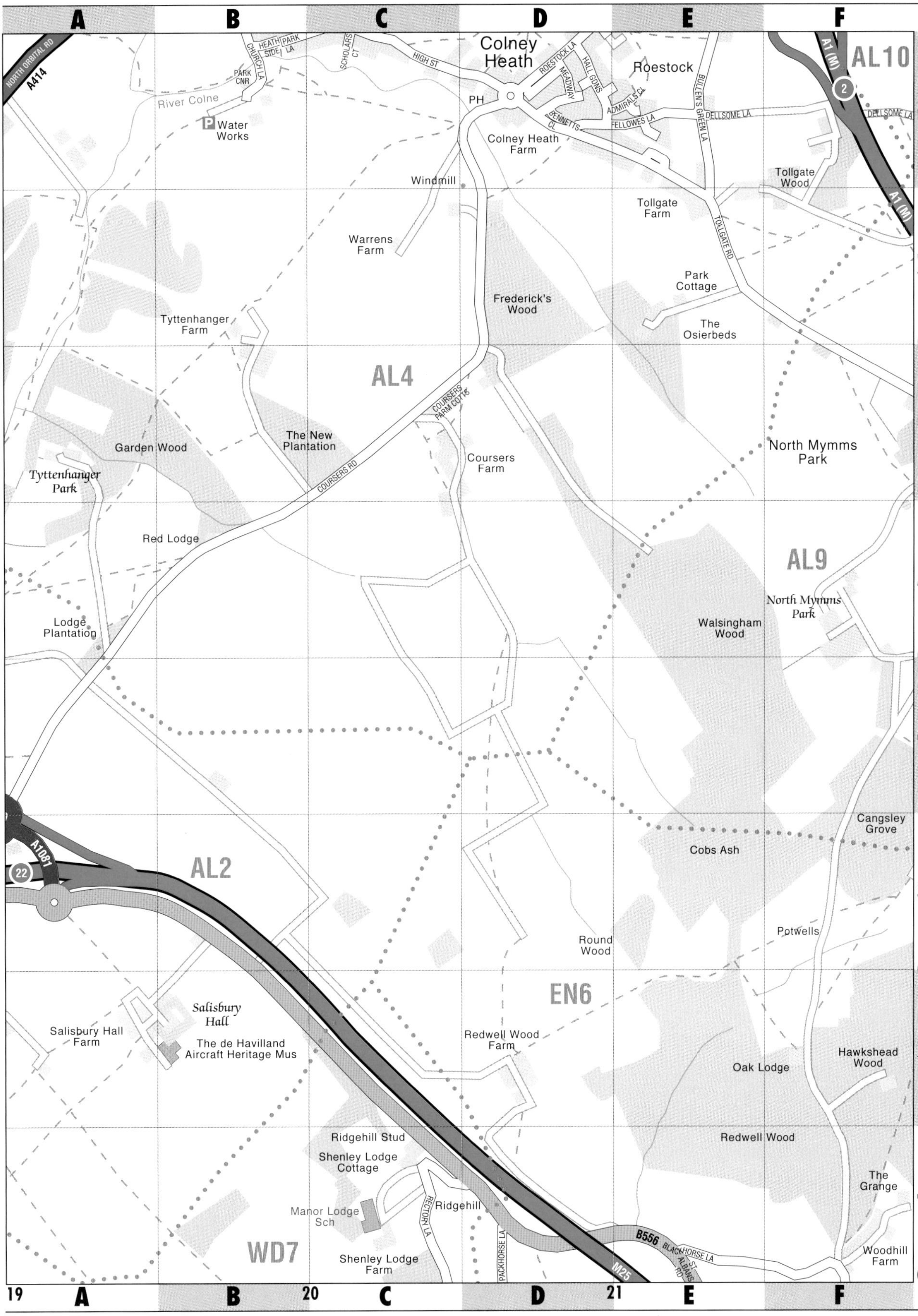

A B C D E F

A B C D E F

157
144

143
130

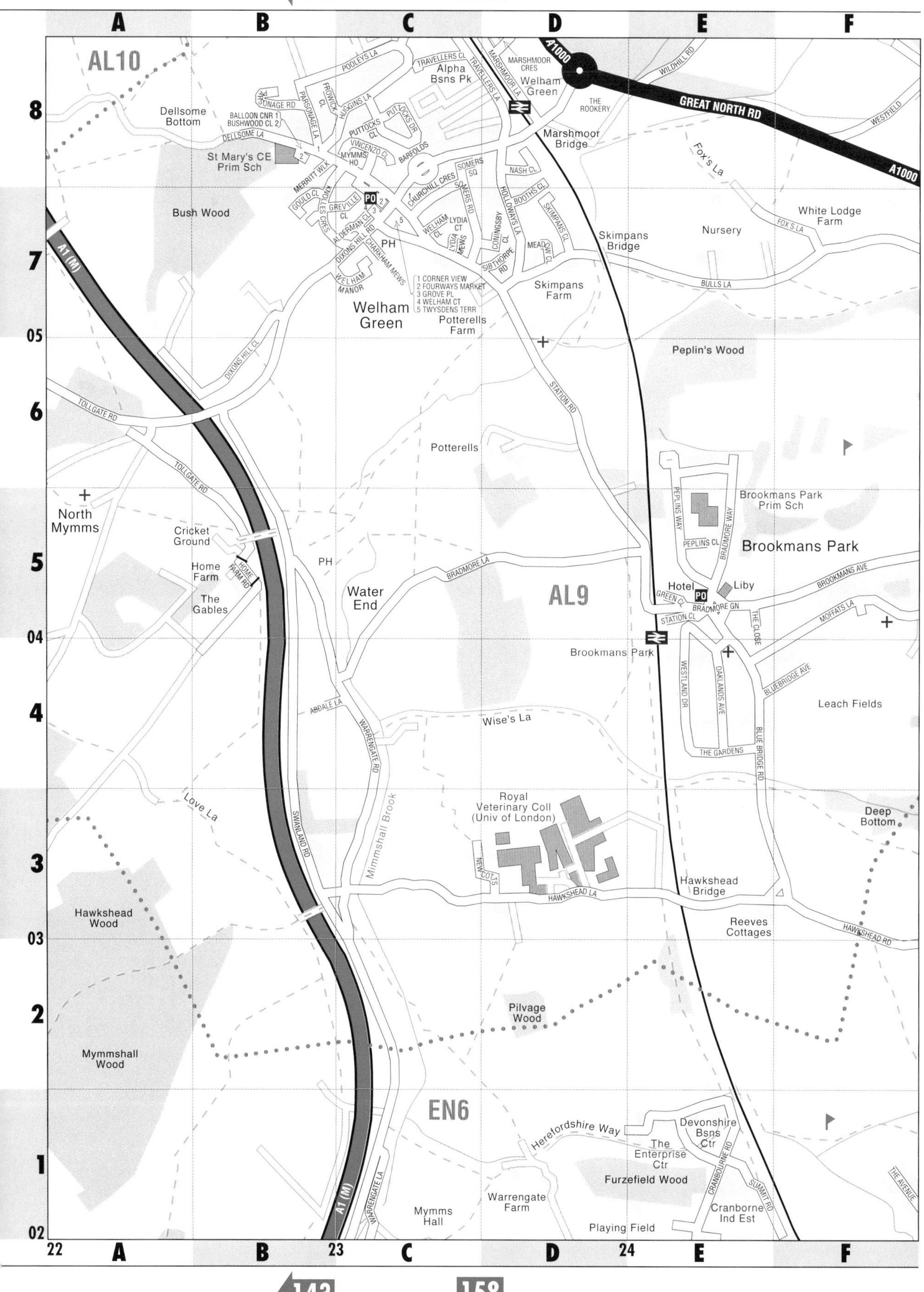

143
158

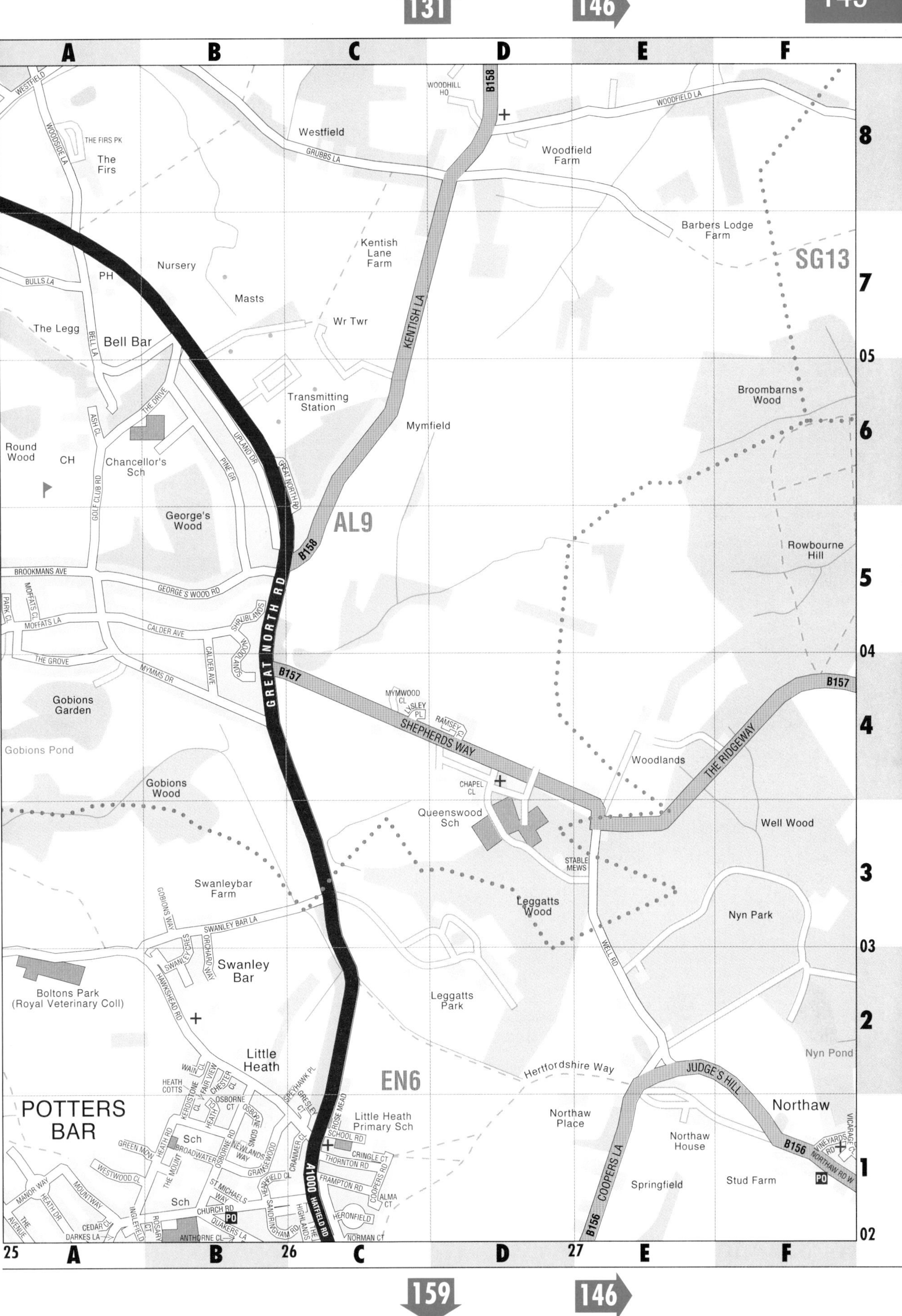
A
B
C
D
E
F
WESTFIELD
WOODSIDE LA
THE FIRS PK
The Firs
Westfield
GRUBBS LA
WOODHILL HO
B158
WOODFIELD LA
Woodfield Farm
Barbers Lodge Farm
SG13
BULLS LA
PH
Nursery
Kentish Lane Farm
Masts
Wr Twr
The Legg
BELL LA
Bell Bar
KENTISH LA
Transmitting Station
THE DRIVE
ASH CL
UPLAND DR
Mymfield
Broombarns Wood
Round Wood
CH
Chancellor's Sch
PINE GR
GREAT NORTH RD
GOLF CLUB RD
George's Wood
AL9
Rowbourne Hill
B158
BROOKMANS AVE
GEORGE'S WOOD RD
MOFFATS CL
PARK CL
MOFFATS LA
CALDER AVE
SHRUBLANDS
WOODLANDS
THE GROVE
MYMMS DR
CALDER AVE
B157
GREAT NORTH RD
MYMWOOD CL
LYSLEY PL
RAMSEY CL
SHEPHERDS WAY
B157
THE RIDGEWAY
Gobions Garden
Gobions Pond
Woodlands
Gobions Wood
CHAPEL CL
Queenswood Sch
Well Wood
STABLE MEWS
Swanleybar Farm
Leggatts Wood
Nyn Park
GOBIONS WAY
SWANLEY BAR LA
SWANLEY CRES
ORCHARD WAY
Swanley Bar
WELL RD
Boltons Park (Royal Veterinary Coll)
HAWKSHEAD RD
Leggatts Park
Little Heath
Nyn Pond
Hertfordshire Way
JUDGE'S HILL
EN6
Northaw
POTTERS BAR
Little Heath Primary Sch
Northaw Place
Northaw House
SCHOOL RD
Sch
COOPERS LA
B156
Springfield
Stud Farm
A1000 HATFIELD RD
B156
NORTHAW RD W
VICARAGE CL
VINEYARDS RD
PO
8
7
05
6
5
04
4
3
03
2
1
02
25
26
27

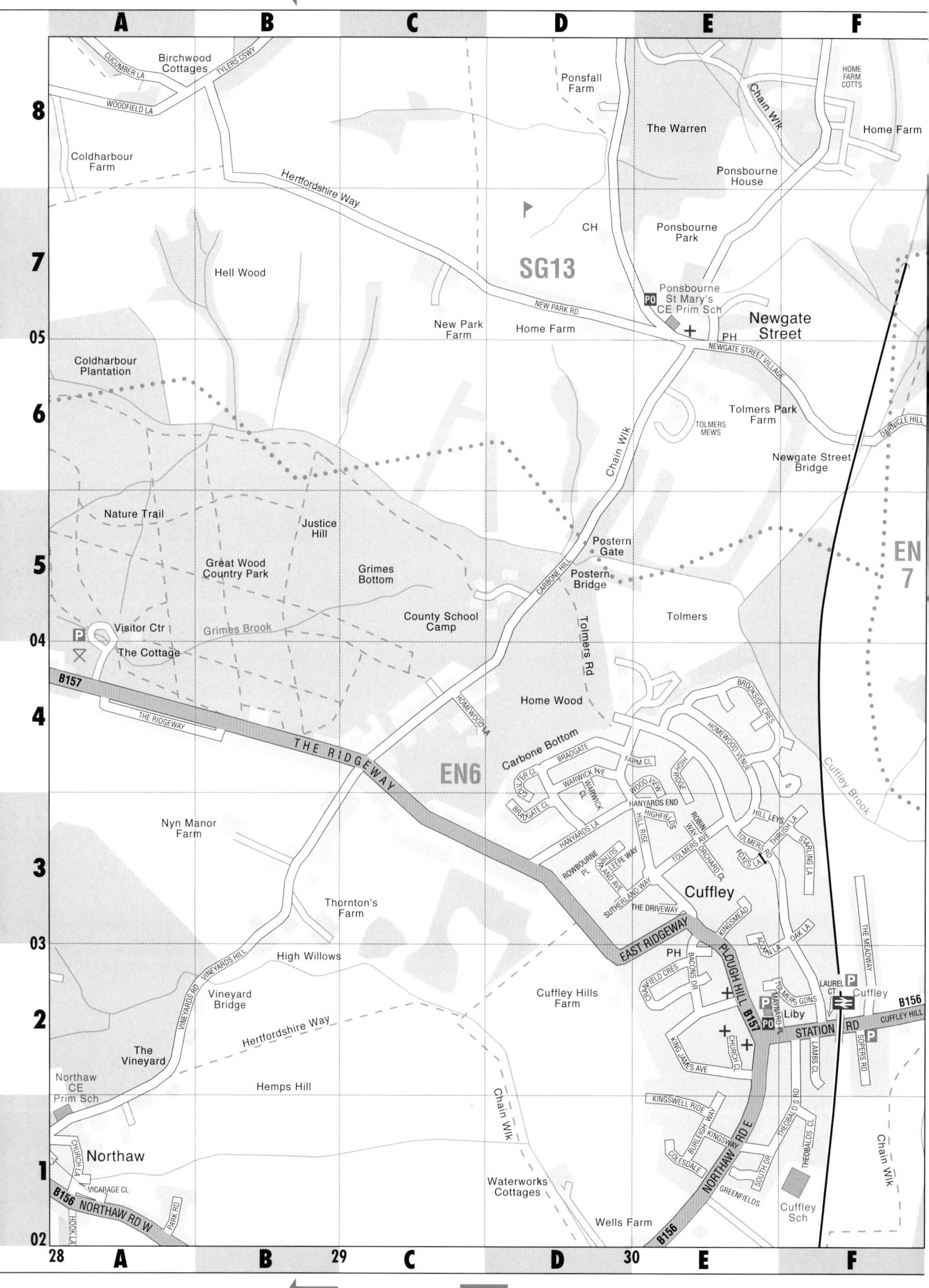
A
B
C
D
E
F
8
7
05
6
5
04
4
3
03
2
1
02
28
29
30
Birchwood Cottages
CUCUMBER LA
TYLERS CSWY
WOODFIELD LA
Coldharbour Farm
Hertfordshire Way
Hell Wood
Ponsfall Farm
The Warren
Chain Wlk
HOME FARM COTTS
Home Farm
Ponsbourne House
CH
Ponsbourne Park
SG13
NEW PARK RD
Ponsbourne St Mary's CE Prim Sch
PO
PH
Newgate Street
New Park Farm
Home Farm
NEWGATE STREET VILLAGE
Coldharbour Plantation
TOLMERS MEWS
Tolmers Park Farm
DARNICLE HILL
Newgate Street Bridge
Nature Trail
Justice Hill
Postern Gate
Great Wood Country Park
Grimes Bottom
Postern Bridge
CARBONE HILL
EN 7
County School Camp
Tolmers
Visitor Ctr
Grimes Brook
The Cottage
Tolmers Rd
B157
THE RIDGEWAY
HOMEWOOD LA
Home Wood
BROOKSIDE CRES
HOMEWOOD AVENUE
Carbone Bottom
BRADGATE
FARM CL
THE RIDGEWAY
EN6
Cuffley Brook
Nyn Manor Farm
HANYARDS END
HANYARDS LA
HIGHFIELDS
HILL RISE
ROBIN WAY
HILL LEYS
THRUSH LA
STARLING LA
TOLMERS AVE
ORCHARD CL
FOXES LA
Cuffley
Thornton's Farm
THE DRIVEWAY
SUTHERLAND WAY
KINGSMEAD
EAST RIDGEWAY
OAK LA
THE MEADWAY
PH
High Willows
PLOUGH HILL
VINEYARDS HILL
VINEYARDS RD
Vineyard Bridge
BACONS DR
CRANFIELD CRES
Cuffley Hills Farm
LAUREL CT
Cuffley
B156
CUFFLEY HILL
Liby
STATION RD
Hertfordshire Way
TOLMERS GDNS
SOPERS RD
The Vineyard
KING JAMES AVE
CHURCH CL
LAMBS CL
Northaw CE Prim Sch
Hemps Hill
KINGSWELL RIDE
Chain Wlk
BURLEIGH WAY
KINGSWAY
THEOBALDS RD
THEOBALDS CL
Northaw
CHURCH LA
COLESDALE
NORTHAW RD E
SOUTH DR
Waterworks Cottages
Cuffley Sch
VICARAGE CL
B156 NORTHAW RD W
PARK RD
HOOK LA
GREENFIELDS
Wells Farm
B156

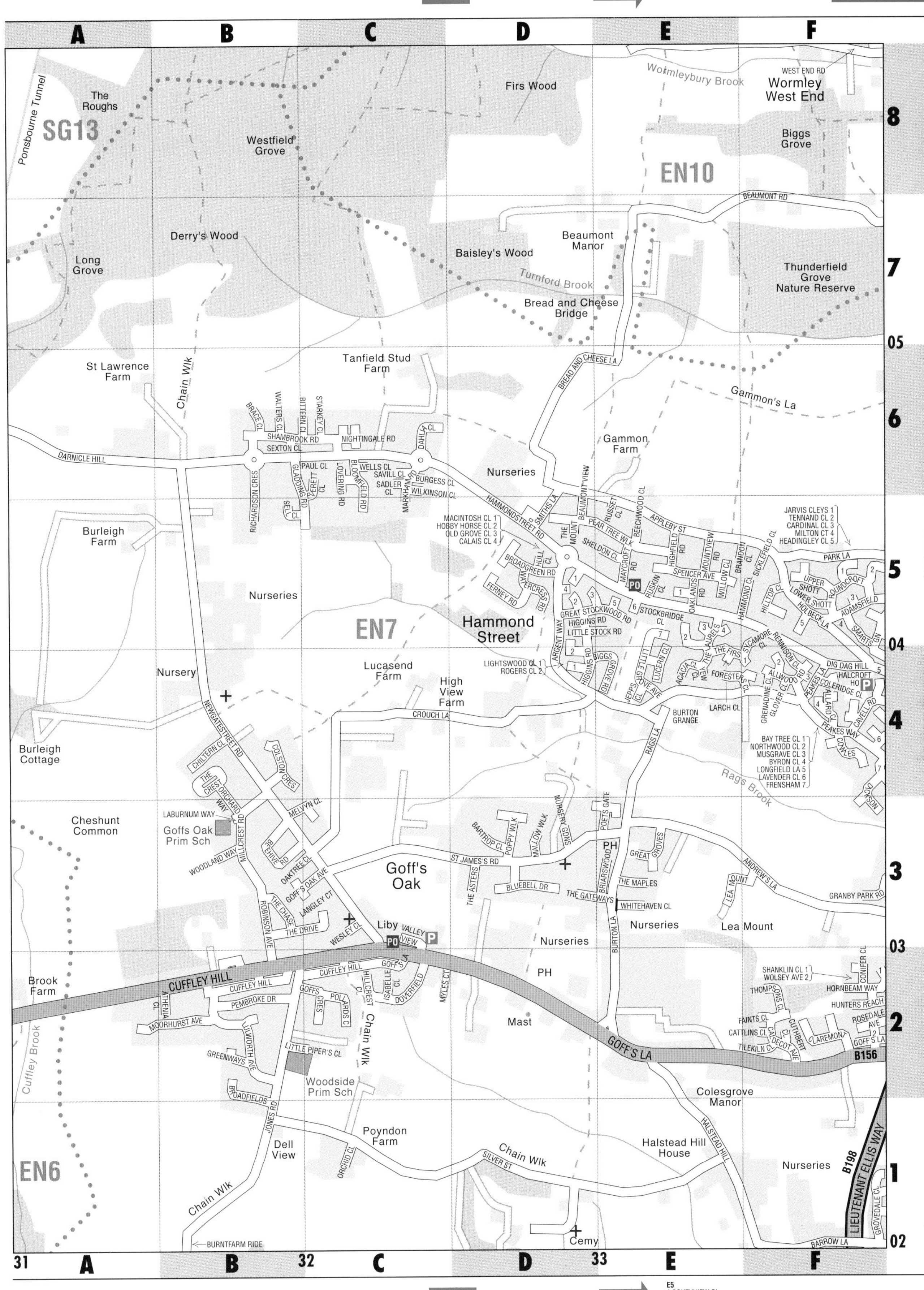

133
148
161
148
Firs Wood
Wormley West End
Biggs Grove
The Roughs
SG13
Westfield Grove
EN10
Derry's Wood
Long Grove
Baisley's Wood
Beaumont Manor
Thunderfield Grove Nature Reserve
Bread and Cheese Bridge
Turnford Brook
Wormleybury Brook
St Lawrence Farm
Tanfield Stud Farm
Gammon Farm
Gammon's La
Nurseries
Burleigh Farm
EN7
Hammond Street
Lucasend Farm
High View Farm
Nursery
Burleigh Cottage
Cheshunt Common
Goffs Oak Prim Sch
Goff's Oak
Lea Mount
Brook Farm
Woodside Prim Sch
Poyndon Farm
Dell View
Colesgrove Manor
Halstead Hill House
Mast
Cemy
EN6
Chain Wlk
CUFFLEY HILL
GOFF'S LA
B156
B198
LIEUTENANT ELLIS WAY
DARNICLE HILL
CROUCH LA
RAGS LA
BURTON LA
ST JAMES'S RD
Rags Brook
Cuffley Brook
Ponsbourne Tunnel
E5
1 SOUTHVIEW CL
2 THE POPLARS
3 HAZEL CL
4 WHITEBEAM CL
5 NUTWOOD GDNS
6 FRIERN CL
7 CONY CL

147 134

F5
1 CONNEMARA CT
2 ARCKLE HO
3 TURNFORD COTTS
4 QUEEN ELIZABETH CT
5 BROOK HO
6 CONVENT HO

F6
1 HAYES WLK
2 CLYDESDALE WLK
3 FARMHOUSE CL
4 NURSERY RD

A B C D E F

8 7 05 6 5 04 4 3 03 2 1 02

EN10
EN7
EN8

Rectory
Wormleybury
Wormley
Wormley Prim Sch
New Plantation
Nursery Wood
Factory Farm
Priests Osiers
Spring Wood
Watercress Trot
Hell Wood
Turnford Brook
Doggett Hill
Cromwell Wood
Paradise House
Gammon's La
Park Lane Paradise
Holy Cross Hill
West End Rd
Beaumont Rd
Cheshunt Park Farm
Candlestick La
Chesthunt Park
Smartsgreen
Hertford Regional Coll
Longlands Prim Sch
Turnford Marsh
Turnford
Hotel
Travellers Encampment
Brookfield Ret Pk
New River
New River Trad Est
Brookfield Ctr
Halfhide La
Great Cambridge Rd
High Road Turnford
High Road Wormley
Cheshunt Wash
St Clement's CE Jun Sch
Mayfield Inf Sch
Flamstead End Prim Sch
St Pauls RC Prim Sch
Flamstead End
Fairfields Prim Sch
Rosedale
Brookfield La W
Flamstead End Rd
Churchgate Rd
Goffs La
Goffs Sch
Churchgate
Bonneygrove Prim Sch
St Mary's CE High Sch
CHESHUNT
Cheshunt Sch
Cemy
Burleigh Prim Sch
Turner's Hill
High St
College Rd
Turnford Sch
Dacre Ind Est
Brookland Inf & Jun Schs
Youth Sail Training & Canoeing Ctr
YH
Cheshunt
Small River Lee or Lea
L Ctr
A10 A1170 B176 B156 B198

34 35 36

A B C D E F

147 162

D1
1 SOUTHGATE HO
2 ALEXANDER CT
3 ROWLANDS CT
4 ANCIENT ALMHOS
5 NEWNHAM PAR
6 MANORCROFT PAR
7 CLAYTON PAR
8 CHAPMAN CTYD

D3
1 CAMPINE CL
2 SOUTHBROOK DR
3 THE SPUR
4 CRAIGS WLK
5 BREEZE TERR
6 THE WHITE HO
7 THE COLONNADE
8 CEDAR LODGE
9 BLAXLAND TERR
10 COOPERS WLK
11 DOUGLAS HO
12 CADMORE CT
13 SYMONDS CT
14 CLIFF RICHARD CT
15 CAIN CT

E3
1 BAKERSCROFT
2 GRANDMILL PL
3 BRAY LODGE
4 CUNNINGHAM CT
5 GUIVER CT
6 HUDSCROFT CT
7 GOODMAN CT
8 BEECHOLM MEWS
9 FAIRFIELD WLK

135

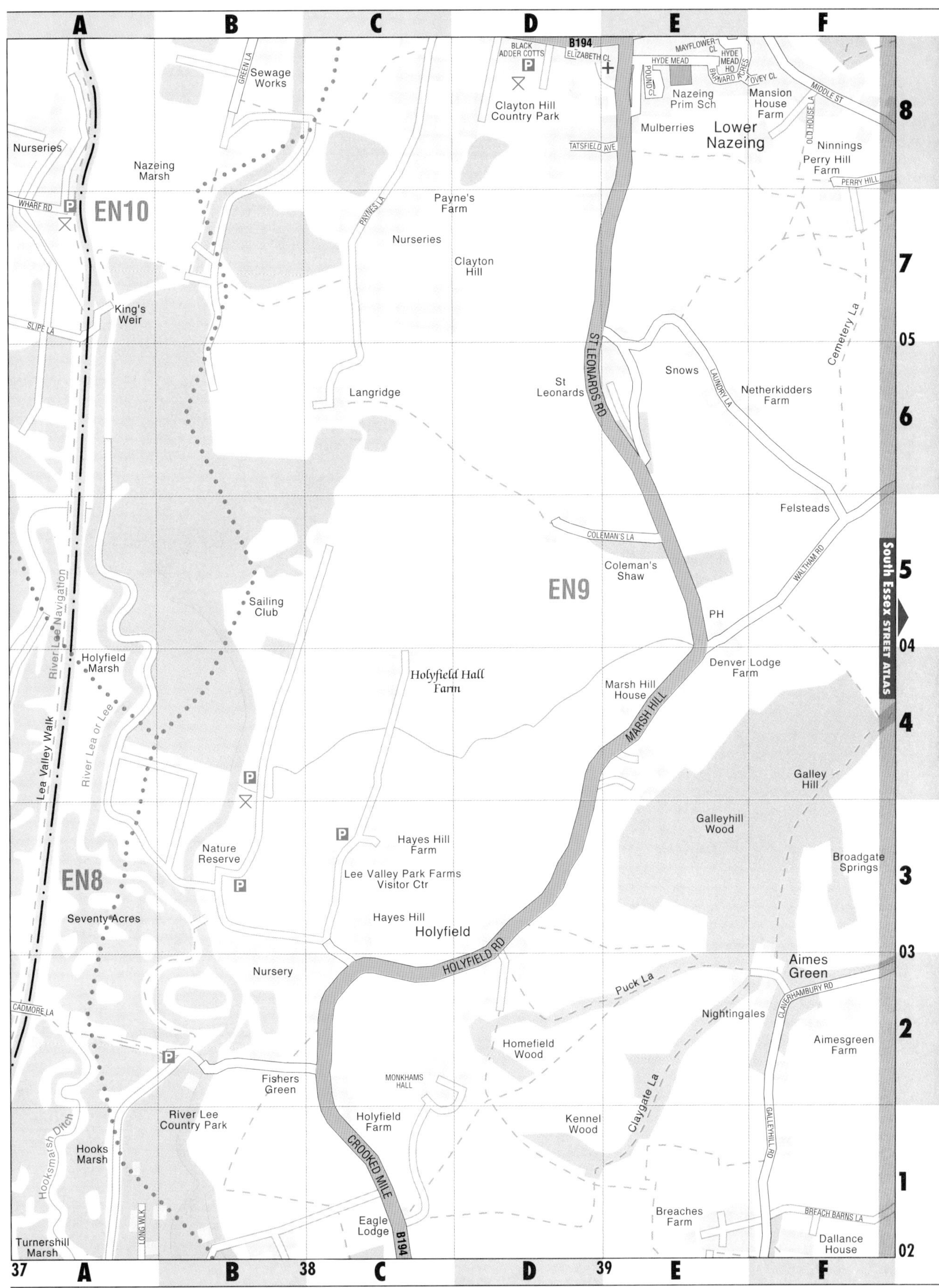

A
B
C
D
E
F
B194
BLACK ADDER COTTS
ELIZABETH CL
MAYFLOWER CL
HYDE MEAD
HYDE MEAD HO
BARNARD ACRES
POUND CL
OVEY CL
Sewage Works
GREEN LA
Clayton Hill Country Park
Nazeing Prim Sch
Mansion House Farm
MIDDLE ST
8
Nurseries
Nazeing Marsh
TATSFIELD AVE
Mulberries
Lower Nazeing
OLD HOUSE LA
Ninnings
Perry Hill Farm
PERRY HILL
WHARF RD
EN10
Payne's Farm
PAYNES LA
Nurseries
Clayton Hill
7
King's Weir
SLIPE LA
Cemetery La
05
ST LEONARDS RD
Snows
LAUNDRY LA
Langridge
St Leonards
Netherkidders Farm
6
Felsteads
COLEMAN'S LA
Coleman's Shaw
WALTHAM RD
5
EN9
Sailing Club
PH
04
Holyfield Marsh
River Lee Navigation
Holyfield Hall Farm
Denver Lodge Farm
Marsh Hill House
MARSH HILL
4
River Lea or Lee
Lea Valley Walk
Galley Hill
Galleyhill Wood
Hayes Hill Farm
Nature Reserve
Broadgate Springs
Lee Valley Park Farms Visitor Ctr
3
EN8
Seventy Acres
Hayes Hill
Holyfield
HOLYFIELD RD
03
Aimes Green
Nursery
Puck La
CLAVERHAMBURY RD
CADMORE LA
Nightingales
2
Aimesgreen Farm
Homefield Wood
Fishers Green
MONKHAMS HALL
Claygate La
River Lee Country Park
Holyfield Farm
Kennel Wood
Hooksmarsh Ditch
Hooks Marsh
GALLEYHILL RD
CROOKED MILE
1
Breaches Farm
BREACH BARNS LA
Eagle Lodge
LONG WLK
Turnershill Marsh
B194
Dallance House
02
37
38
39
South Essex STREET ATLAS

163

136

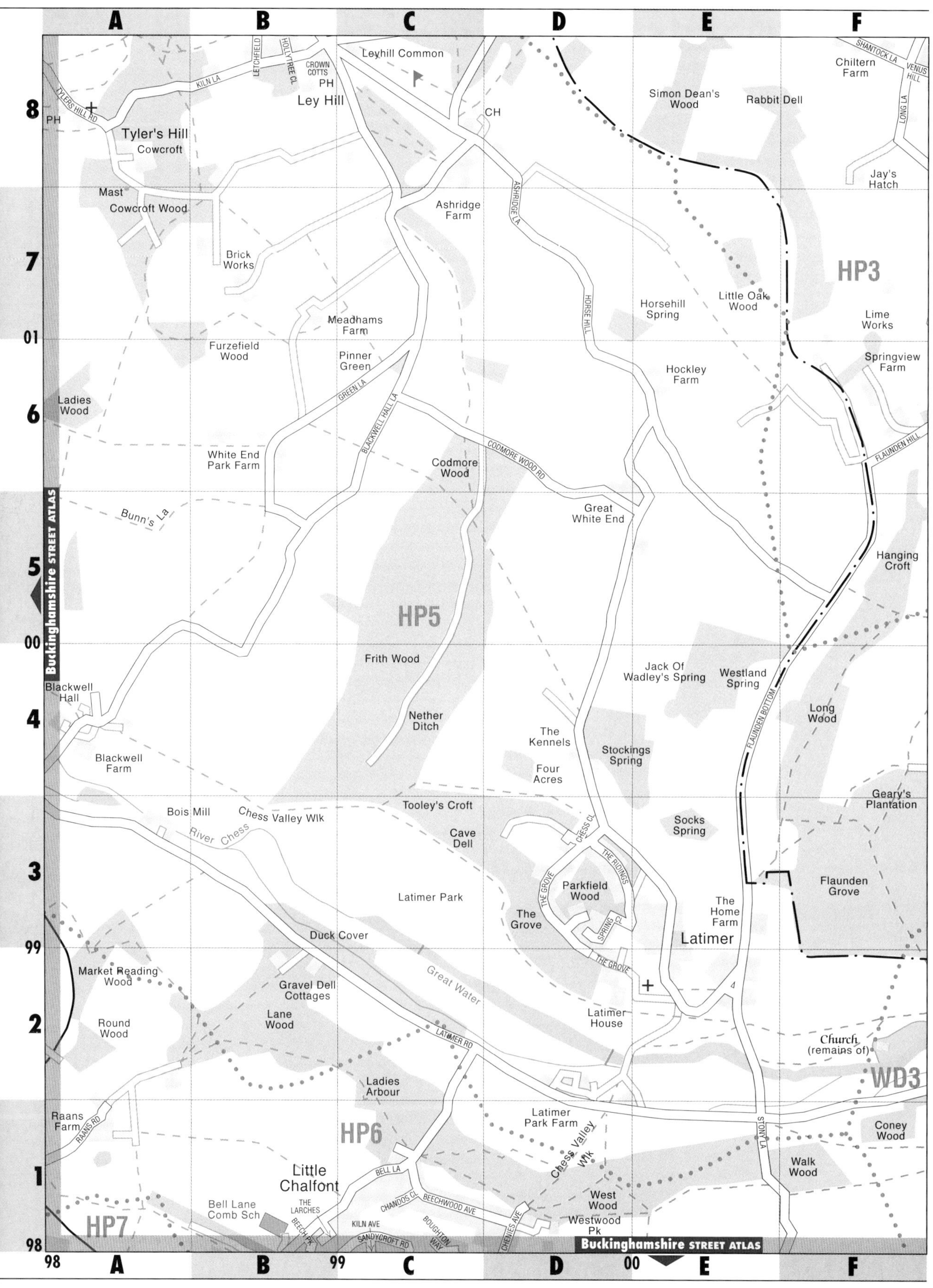
A
B
C
D
E
F
8
7
01
6
5
00
4
3
99
2
1
98
98
99
00
Leyhill Common
Ley Hill
PH
CROWN COTTS
LETCHFIELD
HOLLYTREE CL
KILN LA
TYLERS HILL RD
Tyler's Hill
Cowcroft
Mast
Cowcroft Wood
CH
Ashridge Farm
ASHRIDGE LA
Simon Dean's Wood
Rabbit Dell
Chiltern Farm
SHANTOCK LA
VENUS HILL
LONG LA
Jay's Hatch
HP3
Brick Works
Meadhams Farm
Furzefield Wood
Pinner Green
GREEN LA
BLACKWELL HALL LA
HORSE HILL
Horsehill Spring
Little Oak Wood
Lime Works
Springview Farm
Hockley Farm
Ladies Wood
White End Park Farm
Codmore Wood
CODMORE WOOD RD
FLAUNDEN HILL
Great White End
Bunn's La
Hanging Croft
HP5
Frith Wood
Jack Of Wadley's Spring
Westland Spring
Blackwell Hall
Nether Ditch
The Kennels
Stockings Spring
FLAUNDEN BOTTOM
Long Wood
Blackwell Farm
Four Acres
Bois Mill
Chess Valley Wlk
Tooley's Croft
Geary's Plantation
River Chess
Cave Dell
Socks Spring
CHESS CL
THE RIDINGS
Parkfield Wood
THE GROVE
Latimer Park
The Grove
SPRING CL
The Home Farm
Flaunden Grove
Duck Cover
Latimer
Market Reading Wood
Gravel Dell Cottages
Great Water
Lane Wood
Latimer House
Round Wood
LATIMER RD
Church (remains of)
Ladies Arbour
WD3
Raans Farm
RAANS RD
HP6
Latimer Park Farm
STONY LA
Coney Wood
Chess Valley Wlk
Walk Wood
Little Chalfont
BELL LA
CHANDOS CL
BEECHWOOD AVE
West Wood
Bell Lane Comb Sch
THE LARCHES
BEECH PK
KILN AVE
SANDYCROFT RD
BOUGHTON WAY
CHENIES AVE
Westwood Pk
HP7
Buckinghamshire STREET ATLAS

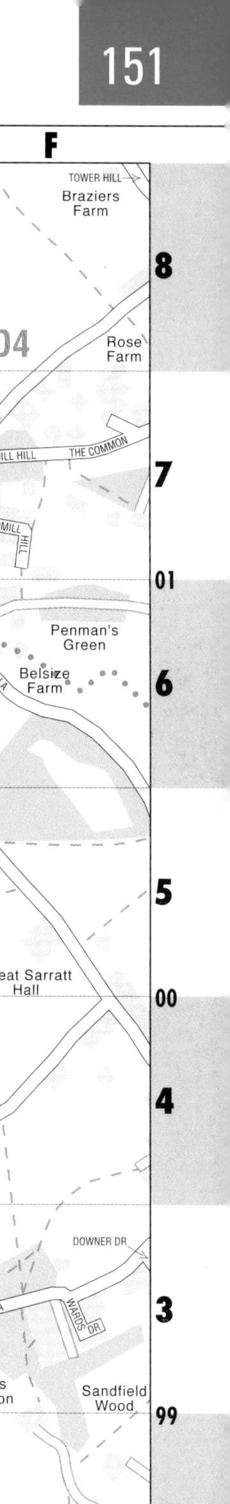
A
B
C
D
E
F
Oxgate Farm
Venus Hill
Venus Hill Farm
MIDDLE LA
VENUS HILL
HOLLY HEDGES LA
TOWER HILL
Braziers Farm
8
New Maulden Farm
FLAUNDEN LA
FLAUNDEN PK
Woodman's Wood
Woodman's Farm
WD4
Rose Farm
LONG LA
Hogpits Bottom
HOGPITS BOTTOM
Bricklayers Arms (PH)
Hertfordshire Way
OLLEBERRIE LA
DUNNY LA
WINDMILL HILL
THE COMMON
7
Lower Plantation
Cherry Trees Farm
WINDMILL HILL
LITTLE WINDMILL HILL
BIRCH LA
Sharlowe's Farm
Holly Hedges Farm
01
Green Dragon (PH)
Dale Farm
Olleberrie Farm
BELSIZE COTTS
PH
Penman's Green
FLAUNDEN HILL
Whitedell Farm
FLAUNDEN LA
Belsize
PLOUGH LA
Belsize Farm
6
Flaunden
HP3
Newhouse Farm
BRAGMANS LA
POLES HILL
Bragman's Farm
Rosehall Farm
Rosehall Wood
5
Hollin's Hall
Moonshine Farm
Chiltern Way
Mast
Great Sarratt Hall
00
Oldcroft Wood
WD3
4
Martin Top Farm
Hanginglane Wood
Bramble Croft
Oldfield Spring
HP5
Limeshill Wood
DOWNER DR
MOOR LA
3
Baldwin's Wood
Wallace's Wood
Valley Farm
DAWES LA
WARDS DR
Dawes Common
Sandfield Wood
Chess Valley Wlk
99
Ford
Mill Farm
River Chess
Chenies Bottom
HOLLOWAY LA
Mount Wood
Sarratt Bottom
2
Chenies Place
CHURCH LA
Chenies
Chenies Manor Ho
Mountwood Farm
Church End
CHURCH END COTTS
Bedford Arms (PH)
Goldingtons
Chenies Sch
Nicholas Spring
1
Greathouse Farm
BEDFORD CL
Turveylane Wood
NEW RD
Wyburn Wood
98
01
A
B
02
C
D
03
E
F

151
138

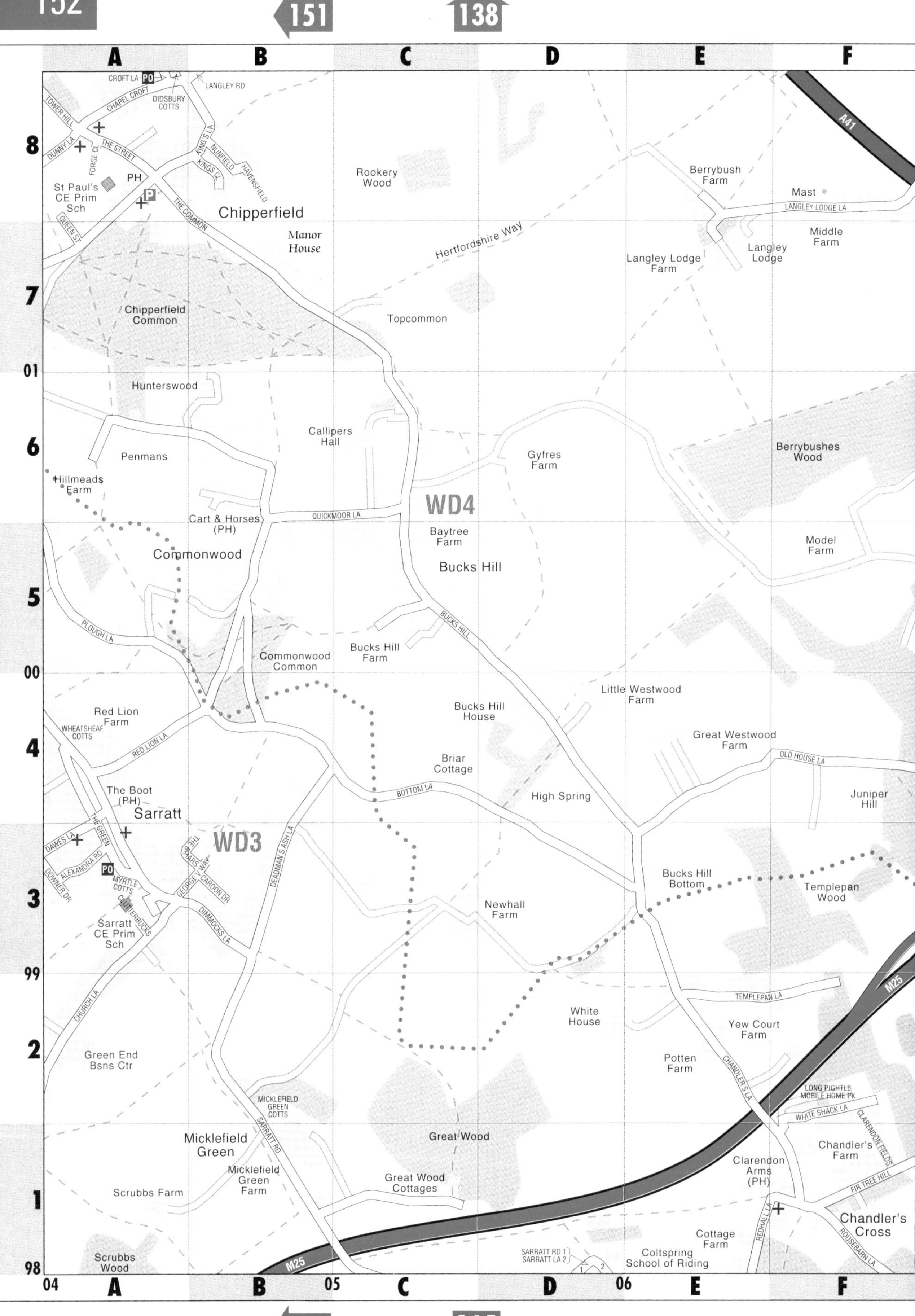

151
165

139

154

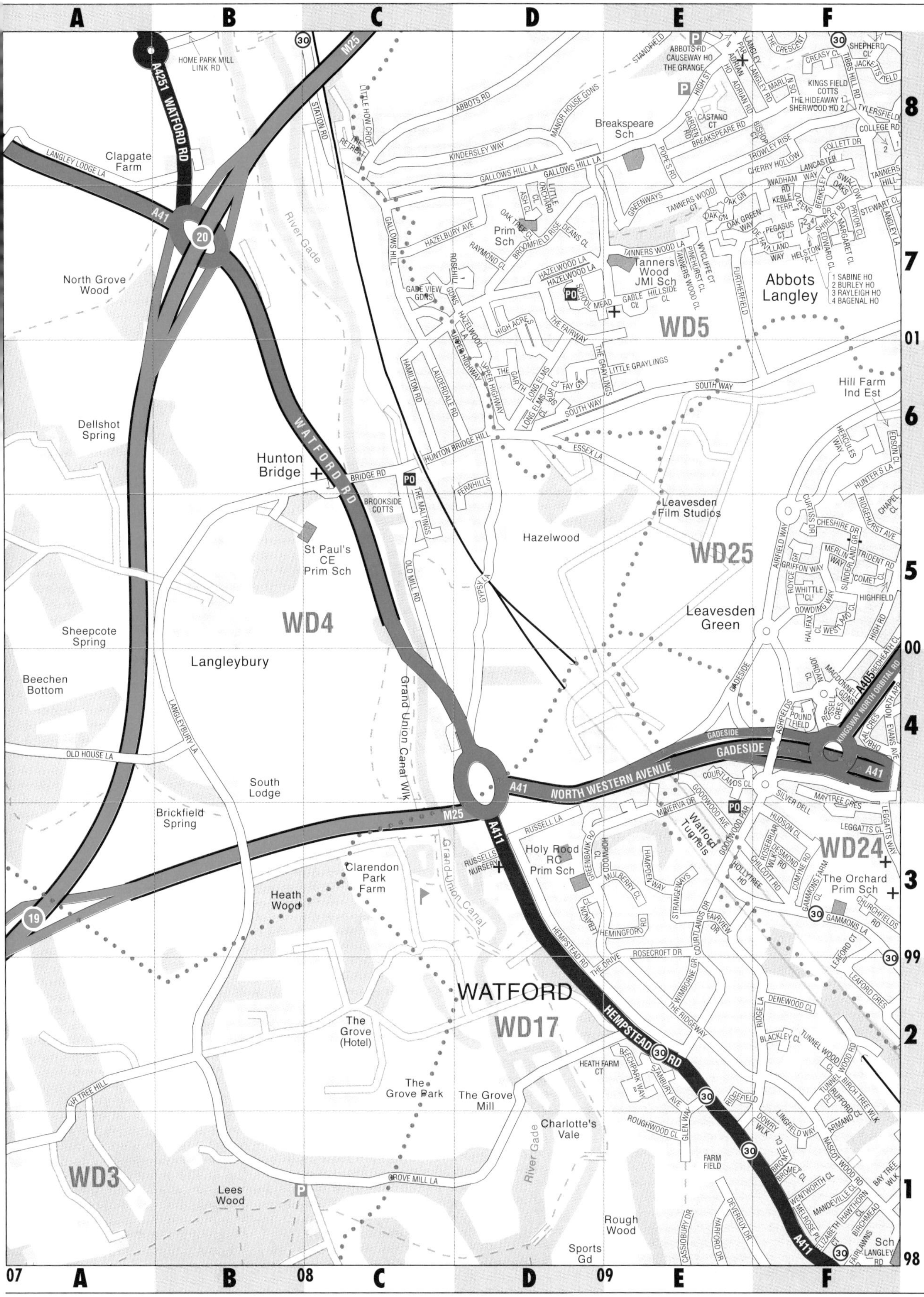

A B C D E F

8 7 01 6 5 00 4 3 99 2 1 98

07 08 09

HOME PARK MILL LINK RD
A4251 WATFORD RD
STATION RD
M25
LITTLE HOW CROFT
THE RETREAT
ABBOTS RD
MANOR HOUSE GDNS
STANDFIELD
ABBOTS RD
CAUSEWAY HO
THE GRANGE
HIGH ST
ADRIAN HO
ADRIAN RD
LANGLEY RD
PARK HO
THE CRESCENT
CREASY CL
SHEPHERD CL
JACKETTS FIELD
KINGS FIELD COTTS
THE HIDEAWAY 1
SHERWOOD HO 2
TIBBS HILL RD
TYLERSFIELD
COLLEGE RD
MARLIN SQ
BISHOP CL
CASTANO CT
GARDEN RD
BREAKSPEARE RD
Breakspeare Sch
KINDERSLEY WAY
GALLOWS HILL LA
POPES RD
TROWLEY RISE
CHERRY HOLLOW
FOLLETT DR
LANCASTER WAY
TANNERS HILL
Clapgate Farm
LANGLEY LODGE LA
A41
20
LITTLE ORCHARD CL
ASH CL
OAK TREE CL
GREENWAYS
TANNERS WOOD CT
OAK GN
OAK GREEN WAY
WADHAM RD
KEBLE TERR
QUEENS CT
BERKELEY CL
SWALLOW OAKS
PRYOR CL
STEWART CL
LANGLEY LA
PEGASUS CT
DE HAVILLAND WAY
HELSTON PL
SHIRLEY RD
EDWARD CL
MARGARET CL
GALLOWS HILL
HAZELBURY AVE
Prim Sch
BROOMFIELD RISE
DEANS CL
RAYMOND CL
TANNERS WOOD LA
WYCLIFFE CT
PINEHURST CL
TANNERS WOOD CL
FURTHERFIELD
Abbots Langley
1 SABINE HO
2 BURLEY HO
3 RAYLEIGH HO
4 BAGENAL HO
North Grove Wood
River Gade
ROSEHILL GDNS
HAZELWOOD LA
Tanners Wood JMI Sch
SCHOOL MEAD
GABLE CL
HILLSIDE CL
GADE VIEW GDNS
HAZELWOOD RD
HIGH ACRES
THE FAIRWAY
WD5
HAMILTON RD
LAUDERDALE RD
LOWER HIGHWAY
UPPER HIGHWAY
THE GARTH
LONG ELMS
FAY GN
THE GRAYLINGS
LITTLE GRAYLINGS
SOUTH WAY
Hill Farm Ind Est
LONG ELMS CL
SUR CL
Dellshot Spring
WATFORD RD
HUNTON BRIDGE HILL
ESSEX LA
HERCULES WAY
EDSON CL
HUNTER'S LA
Hunton Bridge
BRIDGE RD
PO
BROOKSIDE COTTS
THE MALTINGS
FERNHILLS
Leavesden Film Studios
CURTISS DR
CHESHIRE DR
RIDGEHURST AVE
CHAPEL CL
St Paul's CE Prim Sch
Hazelwood
WD25
AIRFIELD WAY
GRIFFON WAY
MERLIN WAY
TRIDENT RD
SUNDERLAND GR
COMET CL
OLD MILL RD
GYPSY LA
ROYCE GR
WHITTLE CL
DOWDING WAY
HIGHFIELD
WD4
Leavesden Green
HALIFAX CL
WESTLAND CL
HIGH RD
Sheepcote Spring
Langleybury
JORDAN CL
MACDONNELL GDNS
A405 NORTH ORBITAL RD
Beechen Bottom
GADESIDE
ASHFIELDS
POUND FIELD
RUSSELL CRES
KINGSWAY NORTH ORBITAL RD
NORTH APPROACH
EVANS AVE
ORBITAL CRES
LANGLEYBURY LA
Grand Union Canal Wlk
GADESIDE
A41
OLD HOUSE LA
NORTH WESTERN AVENUE
COURTLANDS CL
SILVER DELL
MAYTREE CRES
LEGGATTS WAY
South Lodge
MINERVA DR
GOODWOOD AVE
GOODWOOD PAR
Watford Tunnels
HUDSON CL
LEGGATTS CL
Brickfield Spring
M25
A411
RUSSELL LA
Holy Rood RC Prim Sch
GREENBANK RD
HOPWOOD CL
HAMPDEN WAY
ROSEBRIAR WLK
DESMOND RD
COMYNE RD
GAMMONS FARM CL
WD24
The Orchard Prim Sch
CHURCHFIELDS RD
RUSSELLS NURSERY
Clarendon Park Farm
Grand Union Canal
MULBERRY CL
STRANGEWAYS
HOLLYTREE HO
CHILCOTT RD
GAMMONS LA
Heath Wood
NORTON RD
HEMINGFORD RD
COURTLANDS DR
FAIRVIEW DR
LEAFORD CT
19
HEMPSTEAD RD
THE DRIVE
ROSECROFT DR
LEAFORD CRES
WATFORD
WIMBORNE GR
THE RIDGEWAY
RIDGE LA
DENEWOOD CL
WD17
The Grove (Hotel)
HEMPSTEAD RD
BLACKLEY CL
TUNNEL WOOD RD
TUNNEL WOOD CL
HEATH FARM CT
BEECHPARK WAY
STANBURY AVE
RIDGEFIELD
BIRCH TREE WLK
RUFFORD CL
ARMAND CL
FIR TREE HILL
The Grove Park
The Grove Mill
Charlotte's Vale
ROUGHWOOD CL
GLEN WAY
DOWRY WLK
LINGFIELD WAY
BROWNE CL
NASCOT WOOD RD
BAY TREE WLK
FARM FIELD
WD3
Lees Wood
GROVE MILL LA
River Gade
WENTWORTH CL
MANDEVILLE CL
HAWTHORN CL
BIRCHMEAD
Rough Wood
CASSIOBURY DR
HARFORD DR
DEVEREUX DR
MELROSE PL
ELIZABETH CT
FAIRLAWNS
Sch
LANGLEY RD
Sports Gd
A411
30

166
154

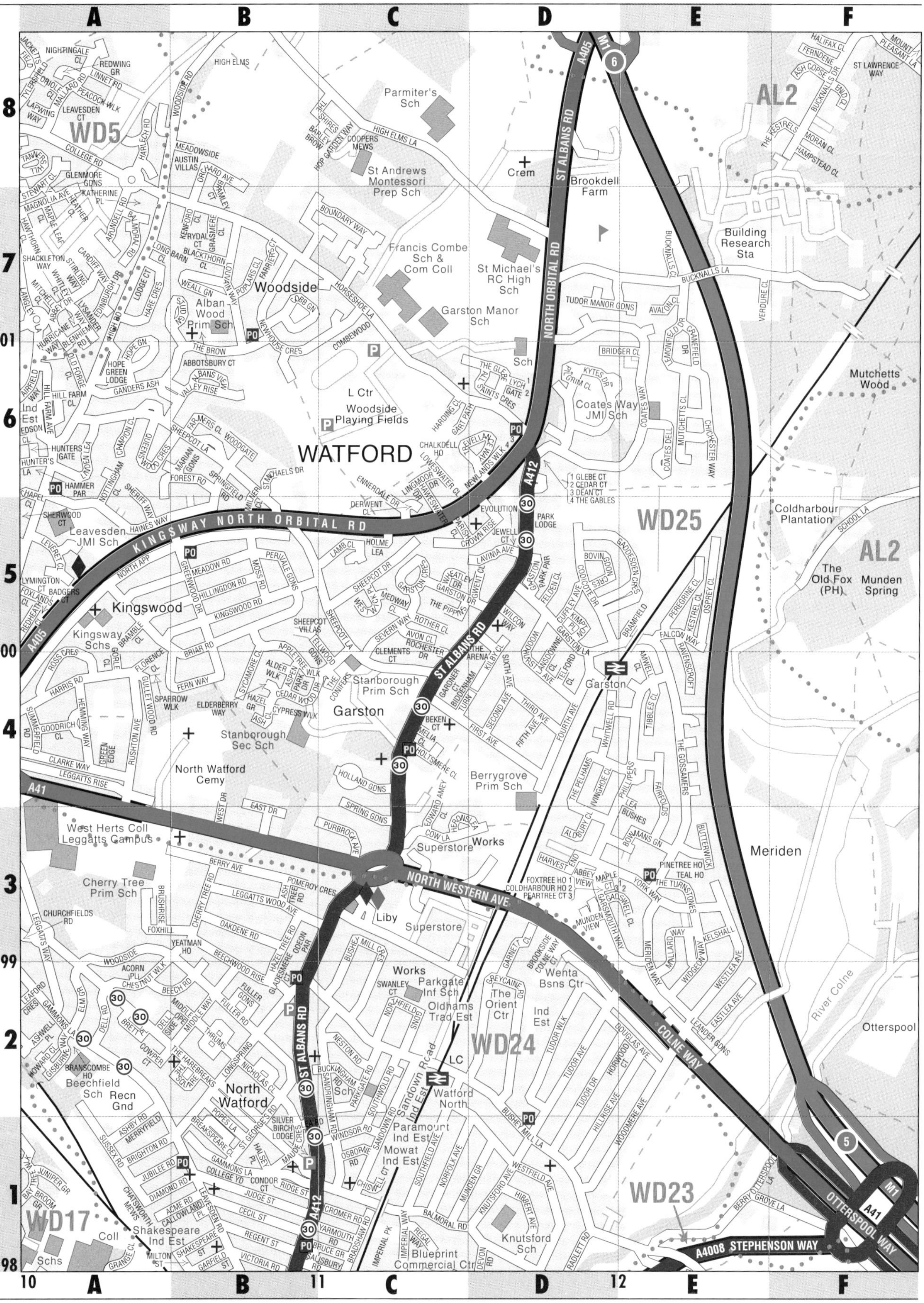

A B C D E F

8 7 01 6 5 00 4 3 99 2 1 98

WD5
AL2
WD25
WD24
WD23
WD17

WATFORD
Woodside
Kingswood
Garston
North Watford
Meriden
Otterspool
Mutchetts Wood
Coldharbour Plantation
The Old Fox (PH)
Munden Spring
Building Research Sta
Brookdell Farm
Crem
Parmiter's Sch
St Andrews Montessori Prep Sch
Francis Combe Sch & Com Coll
St Michael's RC High Sch
Garston Manor Sch
Alban Wood Prim Sch
L Ctr
Woodside Playing Fields
Coates Way JMI Sch
Leavesden JMI Sch
Kingsway Schs
Stanborough Prim Sch
Stanborough Sec Sch
North Watford Cemy
Berrygrove Prim Sch
West Herts Coll Leggatts Campus
Cherry Tree Prim Sch
Superstore
Works
Liby
Parkgate Inf Sch
Oldhams Trad Est
The Orient Ctr
Wenta Bsns Ctr
Ind Est
Watford North
LC
Paramount Ind Est
Mowat Ind Est
Blueprint Commercial Ctr
Knutsford Sch
Beechfield Sch
Recn Gnd
Shakespeare Ind Est
Coll
Schs

KINGSWAY NORTH ORBITAL RD
NORTH ORBITAL RD
ST ALBANS RD
NORTH WESTERN AVE
COLNE WAY
OTTERSPOOL WAY
STEPHENSON WAY
A405
A412
A41
A4008
M1
River Colne

A B C D E F

10 11 12

141
156

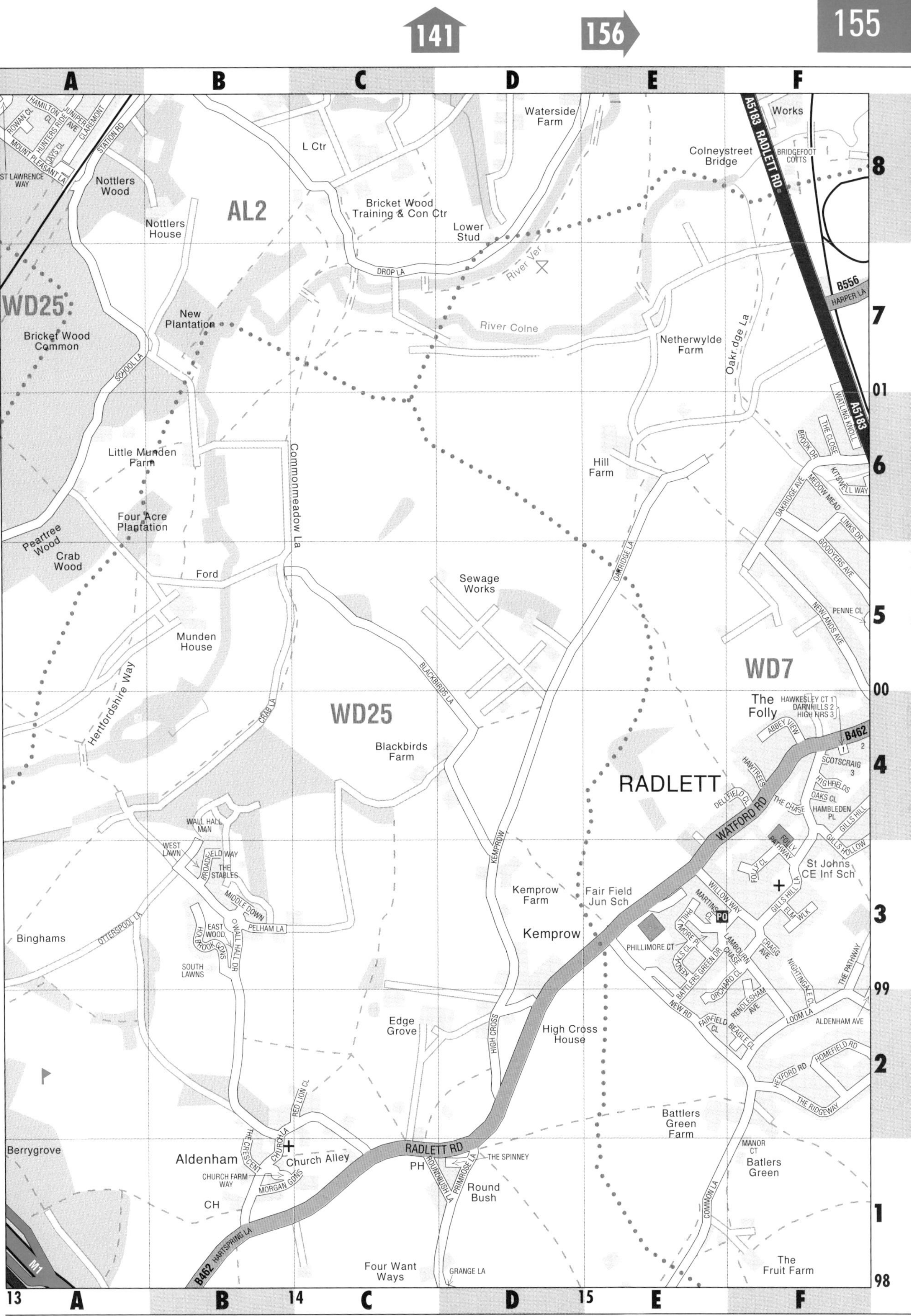

168
156

155
142

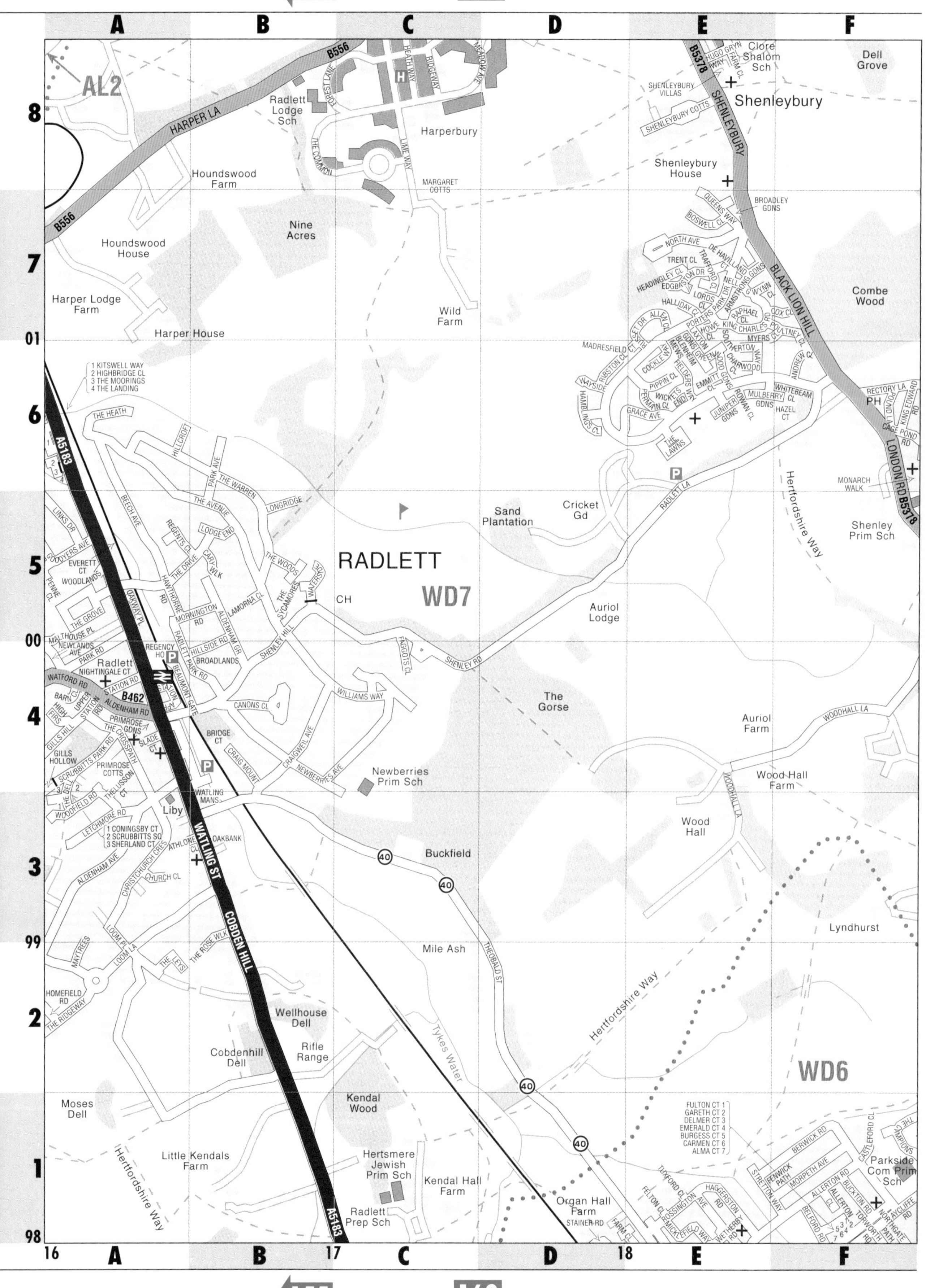

155
169

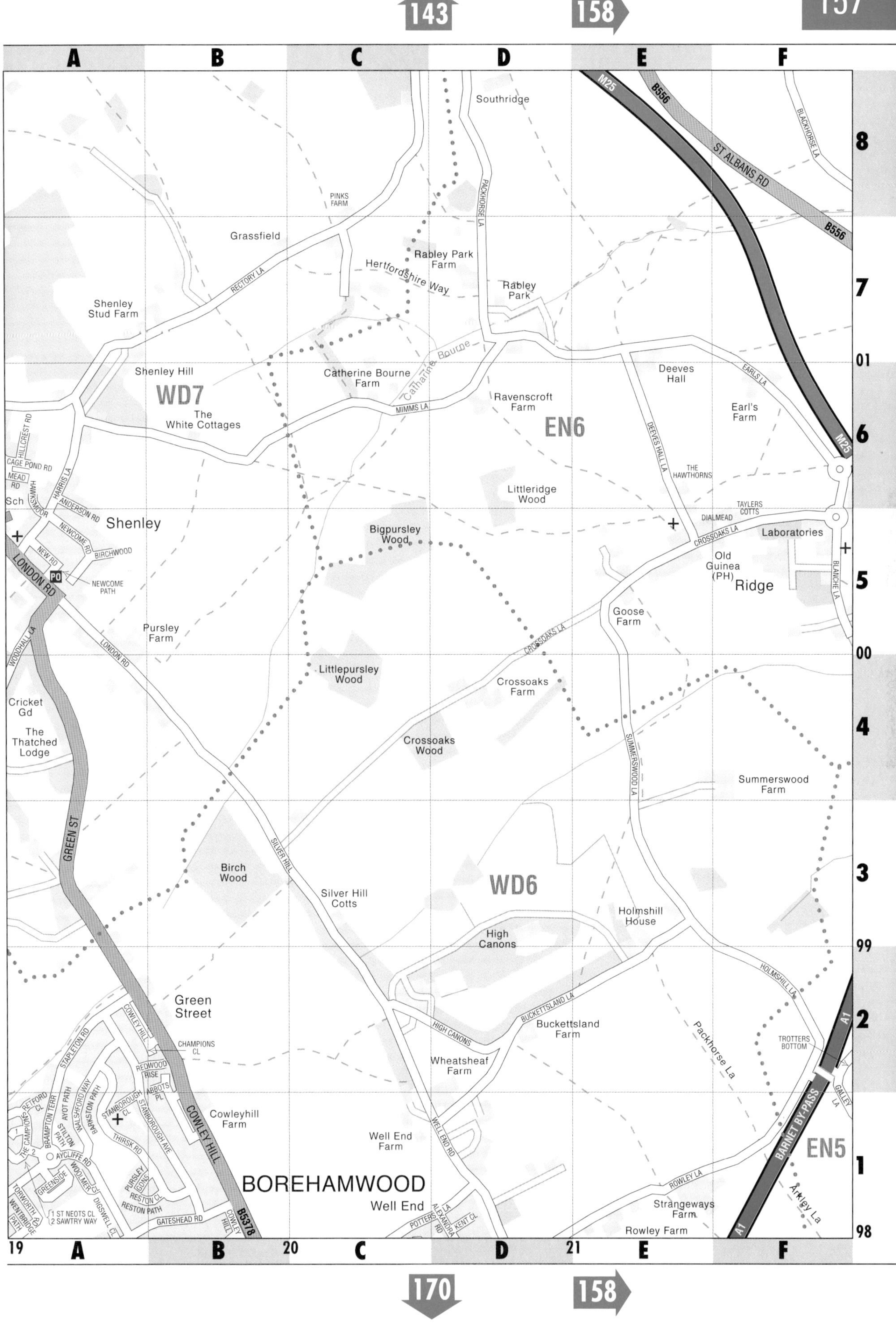
A
B
C
D
E
F
8
7
01
6
5
00
4
3
99
2
1
98
19
20
21
Southridge
M25
B556
ST ALBANS RD
BLACKHORSE LA
PINKS FARM
PACKHORSE LA
Grassfield
Rabley Park Farm
Hertfordshire Way
Rabley Park
RECTORY LA
Shenley Stud Farm
Shenley Hill
WD7
The White Cottages
Catherine Bourne Farm
Catharine Bourne
MIMMS LA
Ravenscroft Farm
Deeves Hall
EARLS LA
Earl's Farm
EN6
DEEVES HALL LA
THE HAWTHORNS
HILLCREST RD
CAGE POND RD
MEAD RD
HARRIS LA
HAWKSMOOR
Sch
ANDERSON RD
Shenley
NEWCOME RD
NEW RD
BIRCHWOOD
PO
NEWCOME PATH
LONDON RD
Littleridge Wood
TAYLERS COTTS
DIALMEAD
CROSSOAKS LA
Laboratories
Bigpursley Wood
Old Guinea (PH)
Ridge
BLANCHE LA
Goose Farm
Pursley Farm
WOODHALL LA
Littlepursley Wood
Crossoaks Farm
Cricket Gd
The Thatched Lodge
Crossoaks Wood
SUMMERSWOOD LA
Summerswood Farm
GREEN ST
SILVER HILL
Birch Wood
Silver Hill Cotts
WD6
Holmshill House
High Canons
HOLMSHILL LA
Green Street
COWLEY HILL
CHAMPIONS CL
STAPLETON RD
HIGH CANONS
BUCKETTSLAND LA
Buckettsland Farm
Packhorse La
TROTTERS BOTTOM
A1
Wheatsheaf Farm
REDWOOD RISE
ABBOTS PL
RETFORD CL
BRAMPTON TERR
AYOT PATH
WALSHFORD WAY
BARKSTON PATH
STANBOROUGH CL
STANBOROUGH AVE
STILTON PATH
THE CAMPIONS
THIRSK RD
AYCLIFFE RD
WOOLMER CL
GREENSIDE
PURSLEY GDNS
RESTON CL
RESTON PATH
DIGSWELL CL
TORWORTH RD
WENTBRIDGE PATH
1 ST NEOTS CL
2 SAWTRY WAY
GATESHEAD RD
B5378
Cowleyhill Farm
Well End Farm
WELL END RD
BOREHAMWOOD
Well End
POTTERS LA
ALEXANDRA RD
KENT CL
ROWLEY LA
Strangeways Farm
Rowley Farm
BARNET BY-PASS
GALLEY LA
EN5
Arkley La

A B C D E F

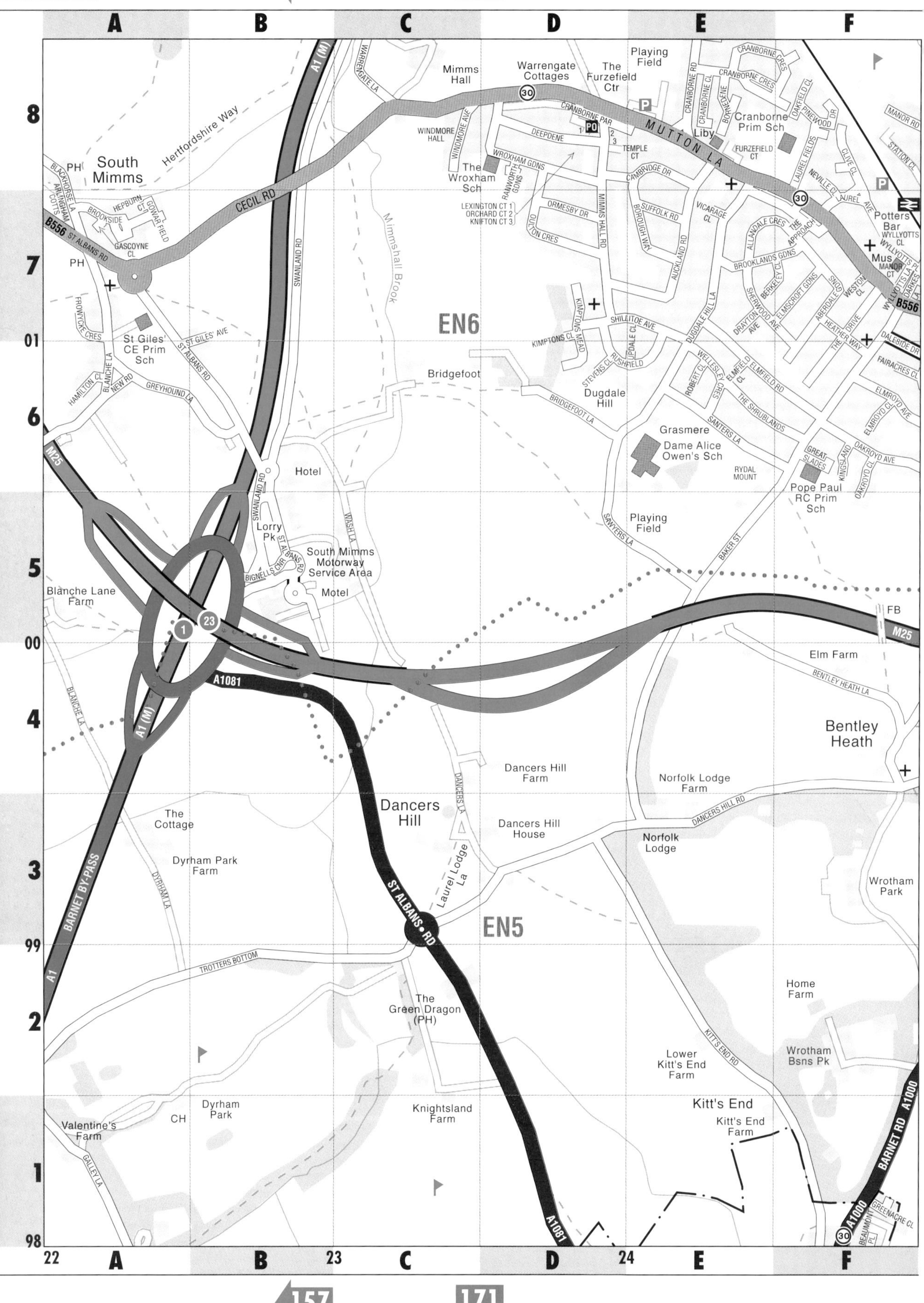

22 A B 23 C D 24 E F

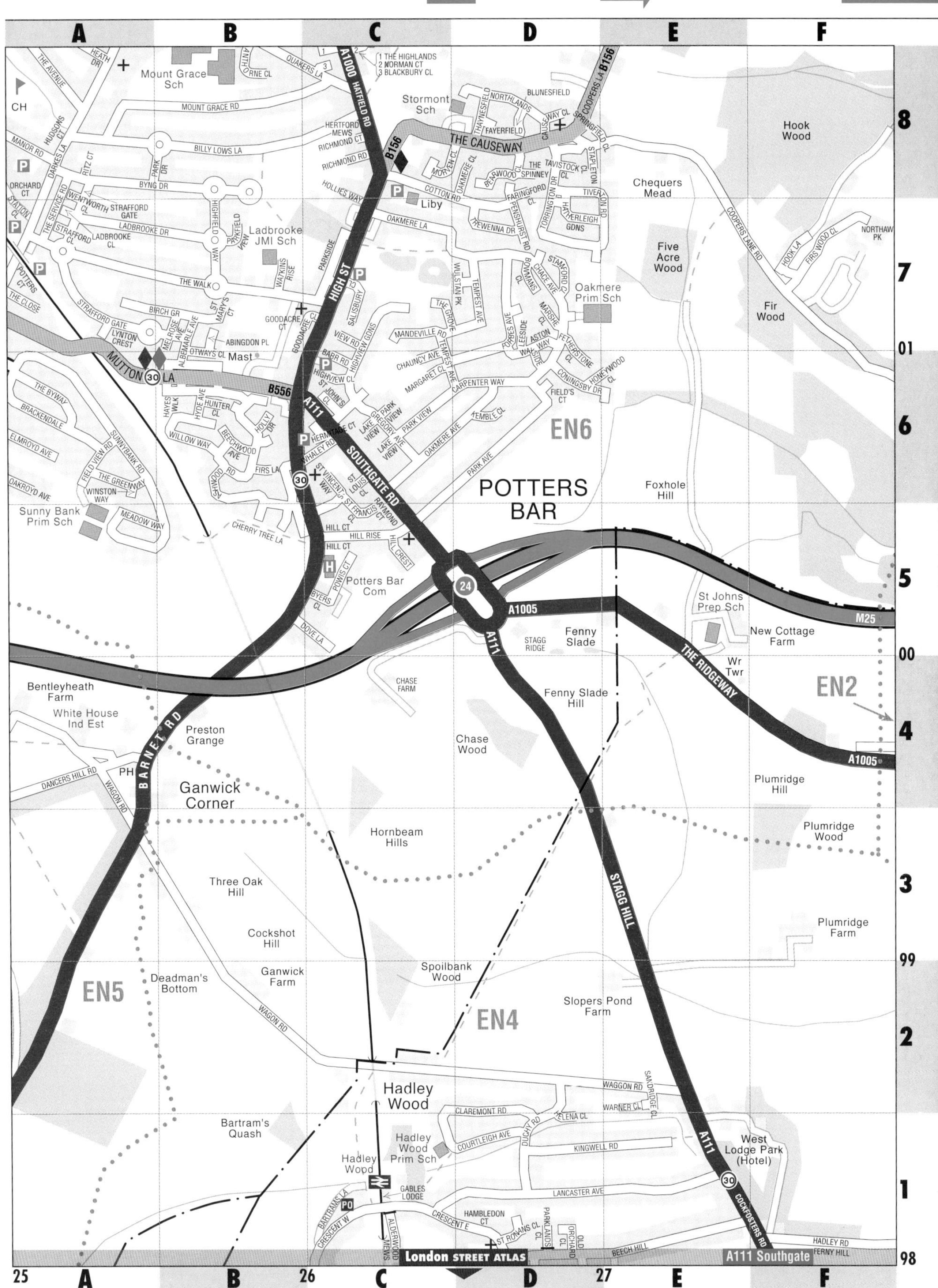
A
B
C
D
E
F
Mount Grace Sch
MOUNT GRACE RD
Stormont Sch
THE CAUSEWAY
Hook Wood
Chequers Mead
Five Acre Wood
Fir Wood
Oakmere Prim Sch
Ladbrooke JMI Sch
Liby
HIGH ST
HATFIELD RD
A1000
B156
MUTTON LA
B556
Mast
SOUTHGATE RD
A111
EN6
POTTERS BAR
Foxhole Hill
Sunny Bank Prim Sch
Potters Bar Com
A1005
M25
St Johns Prep Sch
New Cottage Farm
Fenny Slade
Wr Twr
THE RIDGEWAY
EN2
Bentleyheath Farm
White House Ind Est
Fenny Slade Hill
Chase Wood
Preston Grange
BARNET RD
Ganwick Corner
Plumridge Hill
Plumridge Wood
Hornbeam Hills
Three Oak Hill
Cockshot Hill
STAGG HILL
Plumridge Farm
Spoilbank Wood
Deadman's Bottom
Ganwick Farm
EN5
EN4
Slopers Pond Farm
WAGON RD
Hadley Wood
WAGGON RD
Bartram's Quash
Hadley Wood Prim Sch
West Lodge Park (Hotel)
KINGWELL RD
LANCASTER AVE
COCKFOSTERS RD
London STREET ATLAS
A111 Southgate
8
7
01
6
5
00
4
3
99
2
1
98
25
26
27

160

159 146

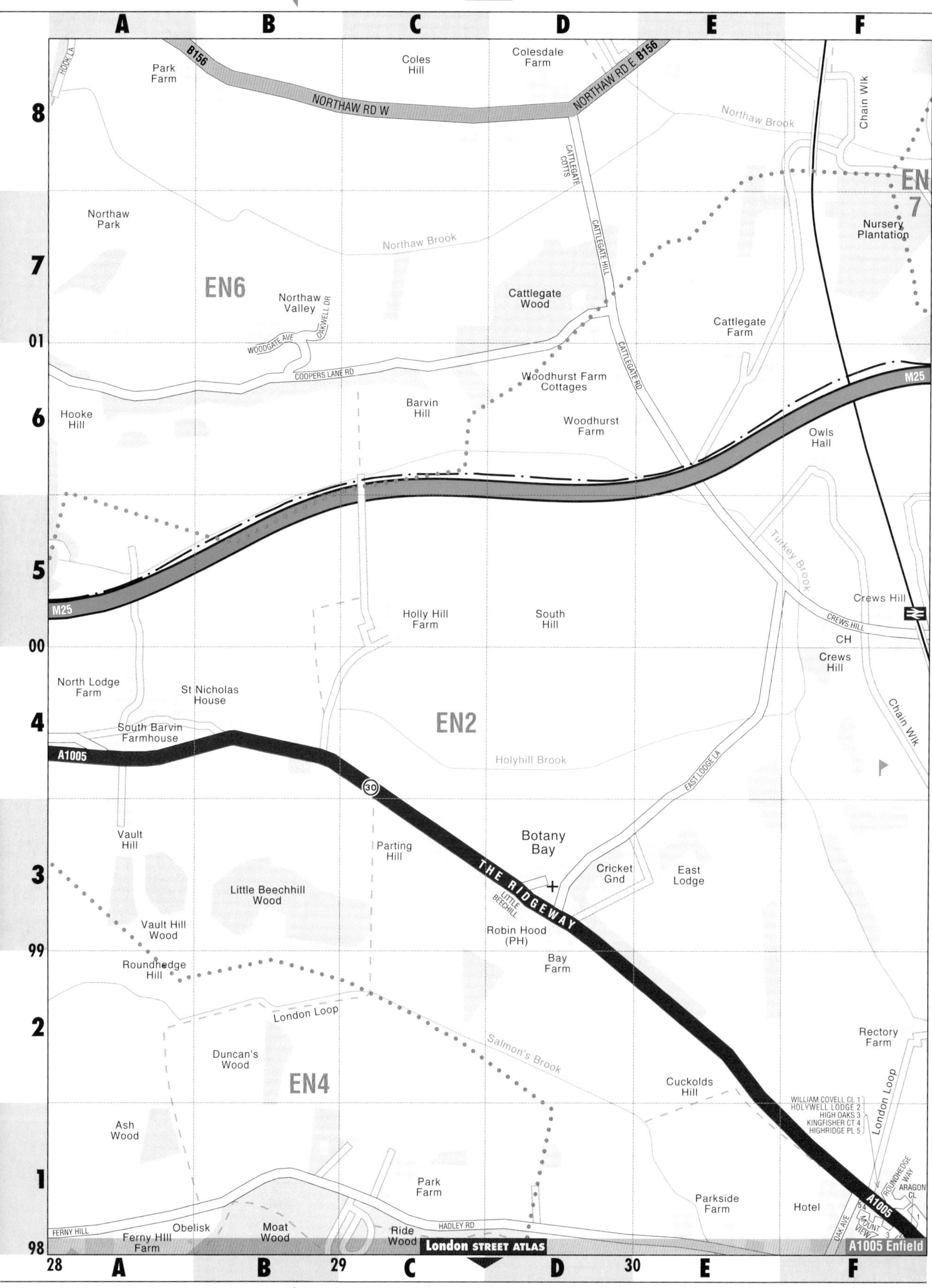
A
B
C
D
E
F
8
7
01
6
5
00
4
3
99
2
1
98
28
29
30
Park Farm
B156
NORTHAW RD W
Coles Hill
Colesdale Farm
NORTHAW RD E
HOOK LA
Northaw Brook
Chain Wlk
CATTLEGATE COTTS
EN 7
Northaw Park
Nursery Plantation
CATTLEGATE HILL
EN6
Northaw Valley
OAKWELL DR
Cattlegate Wood
Cattlegate Farm
WOODGATE AVE
COOPERS LANE RD
Woodhurst Farm Cottages
M25
Hooke Hill
Barvin Hill
Woodhurst Farm
Owls Hall
Turkey Brook
Crews Hill
CREWS HILL
Holly Hill Farm
South Hill
CH
Crews Hill
North Lodge Farm
St Nicholas House
EN2
Chain Wlk
South Barvin Farmhouse
A1005
Holyhill Brook
EAST LODGE LA
30
Vault Hill
Parting Hill
Botany Bay
THE RIDGEWAY
Cricket Gnd
East Lodge
Little Beechhill Wood
LITTLE BEECHILL
Vault Hill Wood
Robin Hood (PH)
Roundhedge Hill
Bay Farm
London Loop
Salmon's Brook
Rectory Farm
Duncan's Wood
EN4
Cuckolds Hill
WILLIAM COVELL CL 1
HOLYWELL LODGE 2
HIGH OAKS 3
KINGFISHER CT 4
HIGHRIDGE PL 5
London Loop
Ash Wood
ROUNDHEDGE WAY
ARAGON CL
Park Farm
Parkside Farm
Hotel
OAK AVE
MOUNT VIEW
FERNY HILL
Obelisk
Moat Wood
HADLEY RD
Ferny Hill Farm
Ride Wood
London STREET ATLAS
A1005 Enfield

159

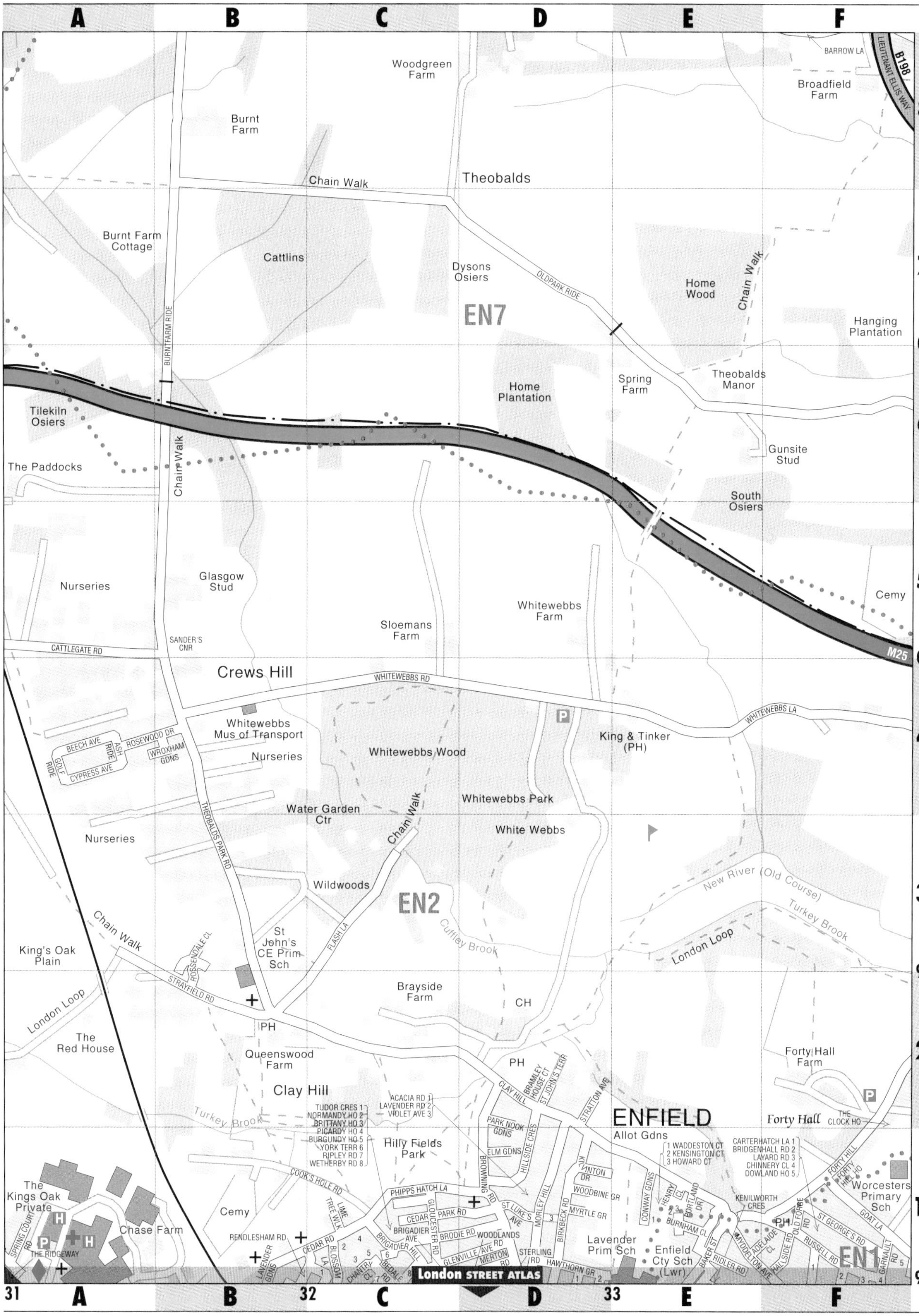

A B C D E F

Woodgreen Farm
Burnt Farm
BARROW LA
LIEUTENANT ELLIS WAY
B198
Broadfield Farm
8
Chain Walk
Theobalds
Burnt Farm Cottage
Cattlins
Dysons Osiers
OLDPARK RIDE
Home Wood
Chain Walk
7
EN7
Hanging Plantation
BURNTFARM RIDE
01
Home Plantation
Spring Farm
Theobalds Manor
Tilekiln Osiers
6
Gunsite Stud
The Paddocks
Chain Walk
South Osiers
Nurseries
Glasgow Stud
5
Cemy
Whitewebbs Farm
Sloemans Farm
SANDER'S CNR
CATTLEGATE RD
M25
00
Crews Hill
WHITEWEBBS RD
Whitewebbs Mus of Transport
WHITEWEBBS LA
King & Tinker (PH)
4
BEECH AVE
ROSEWOOD DR
ASH RIDE
WROXHAM GDNS
GOLF RIDE
CYPRESS AVE
Nurseries
Whitewebbs Wood
Whitewebbs Park
Water Garden Ctr
Chain Walk
White Webbs
Nurseries
THEOBALDS PARK RD
New River (Old Course)
Wildwoods
3
EN2
Turkey Brook
Chain Walk
St John's CE Prim Sch
FLASH LA
Cuffley Brook
London Loop
King's Oak Plain
ROSSENDALE CL
99
STRAYFIELD RD
Brayside Farm
CH
London Loop
PH
The Red House
Queenswood Farm
PH
Forty Hall Farm
2
Clay Hill
CLAY HILL
BRAMLEY HOUSE CT
ST JOHN'S TERR
STRATTON AVE
ACACIA RD 1
LAVENDER RD 2
VIOLET AVE 3
TUDOR CRES 1
NORMANDY HO 2
BRITTANY HO 3
PICARDY HO 4
BURGUNDY HO 5
YORK TERR 6
RIPLEY RD 7
WETHERBY RD 8
Turkey Brook
PARK NOOK GDNS
ENFIELD
Forty Hall
THE CLOCK HO
Allot Gdns
1 WADDESTON CT
2 KENSINGTON CT
3 HOWARD CT
CARTERHATCH LA 1
BRIDGENHALL RD 2
LAYARD RD 3
CHINNERY CL 4
DOWLAND HO 5
Hilly Fields Park
ELM GDNS
HILLSIDE CRES
KINTON DR
FORTY HILL
FORTY HILL HO
COOK'S HOLE RD
BROWNING RD
WOODBINE GR
CONWAY GDNS
HENRY CL
PORTLAND DR
The Kings Oak Private
PHIPPS HATCH LA
KENILWORTH CRES
Worcesters Primary Sch
1
Cemy
ST LUKE'S AVE
MORLEY HILL
MYRTLE GR
BURNHAM CL
PH
ST GEORGE'S RD
GOAT LA
CEDAR RD
PARK RD
LIME TREE WLK
GLOUCESTER RD
Chase Farm
BIRKBECK RD
OLD FORGE RD
RENDLESHAM RD
BRIGADIER AVE
BRODIE RD
WOODLANDS RD
Lavender Prim Sch
Enfield Cty Sch (Lwr)
SPRING COURT RD
CEDAR RD
BRIGADIER HILL
GLENVILLE AVE
MERTON RD
STERLING RD
BAKER ST
HALLSIDE RD
RUSSELL RD
THE RIDGEWAY
LAVENDER GDNS
BLOSSOM LA
CHANTRY CL
BEDALE RD
HAWTHORN GR
RIDLER RD
MYDDELTON AVE
ADELAIDE CL
EN1
GARNAULT RD
98

31 A B 32 C D 33 E F

161
148

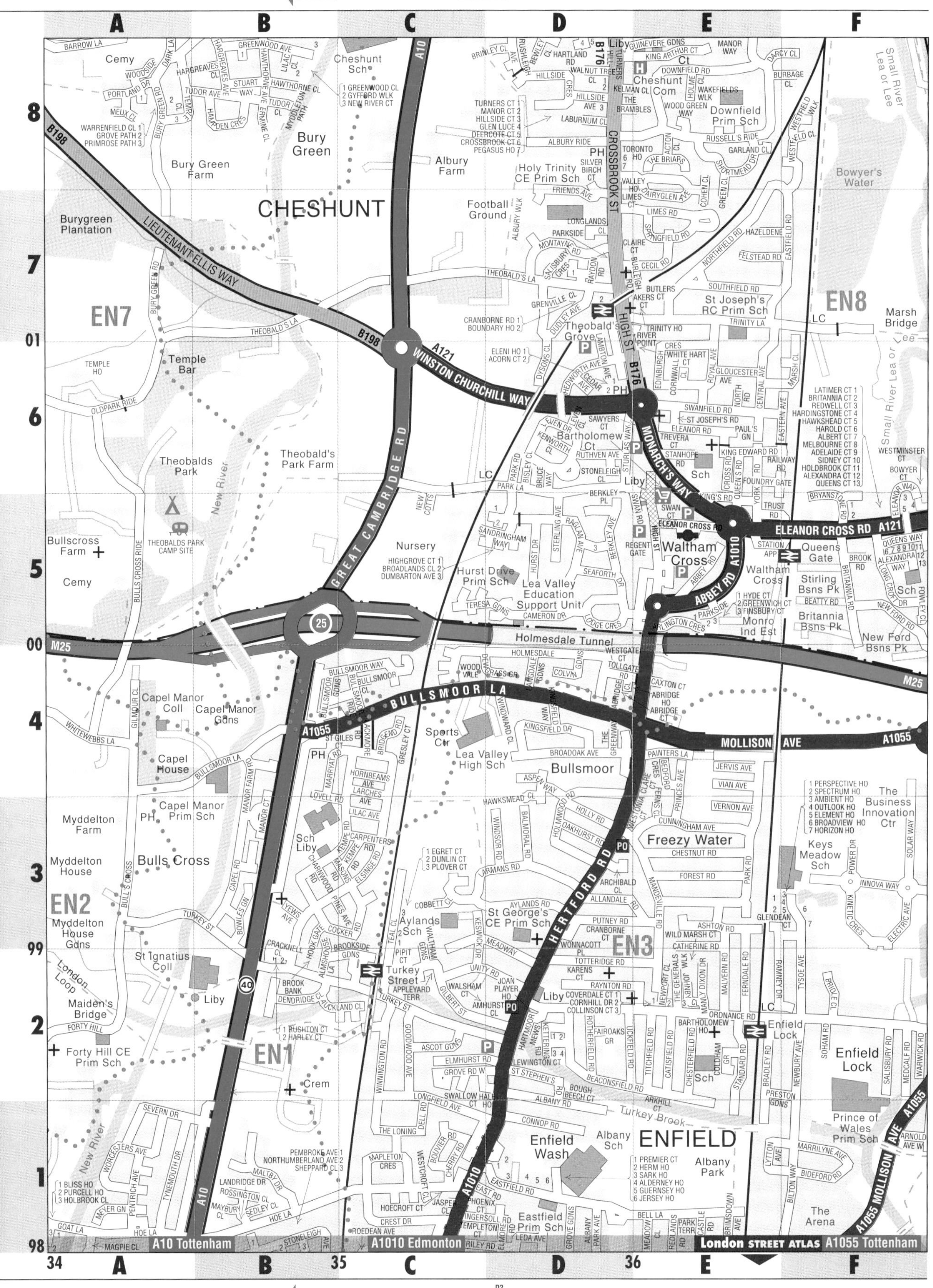

161

D2
1 WOOLPACK HO
2 WELCH HO
3 DORSET HO
4 KEYS HO

149

B6
1 CANNON MEWS
2 POWDERMILL MEWS
3 PLANTAGANET PL
4 NORTH PL
5 HIGHBRIDGE CT
6 HIGHBRIDGE HO
7 FRANCIS GREEN HO
8 WINCHESTER CL

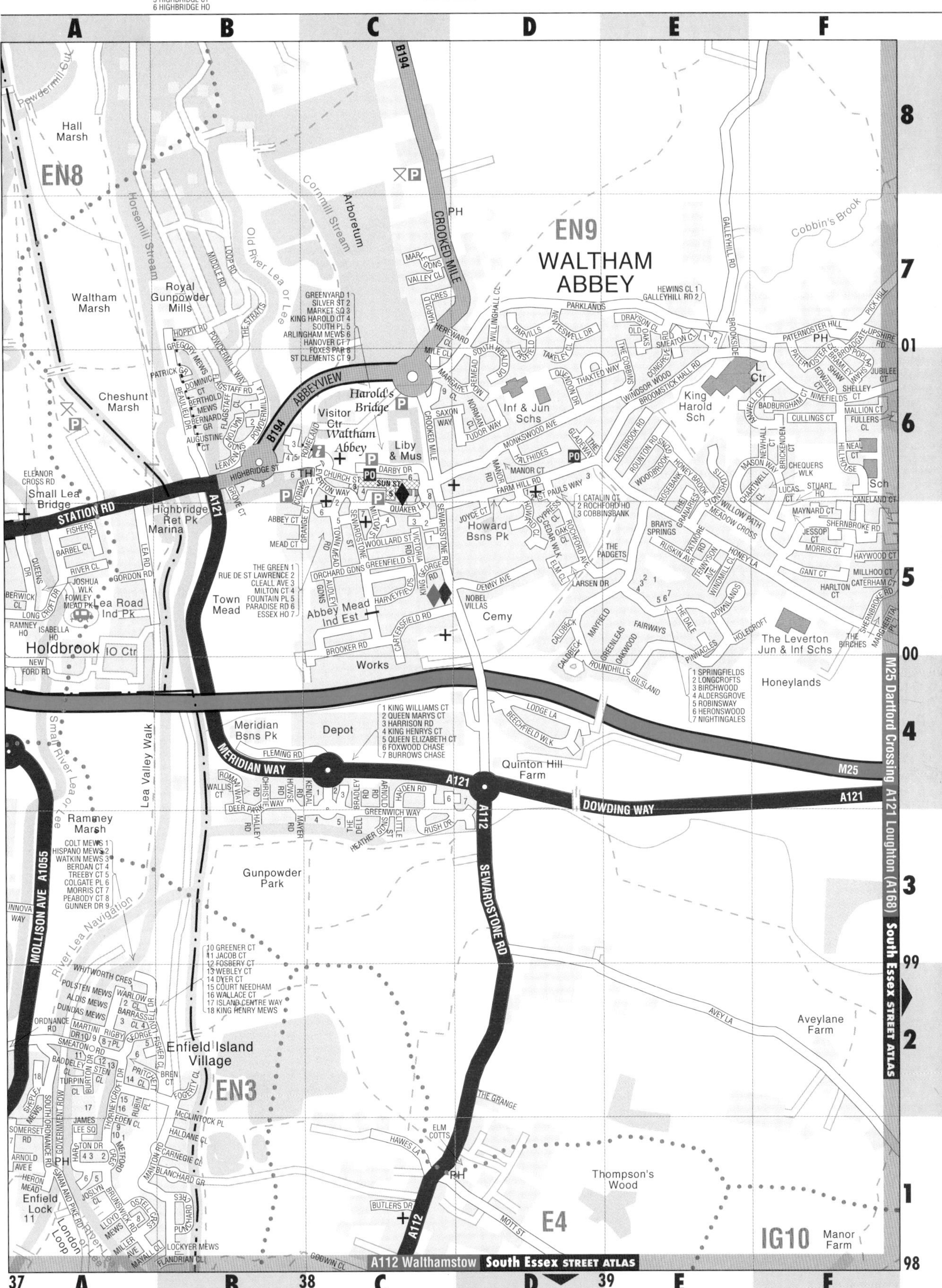

151

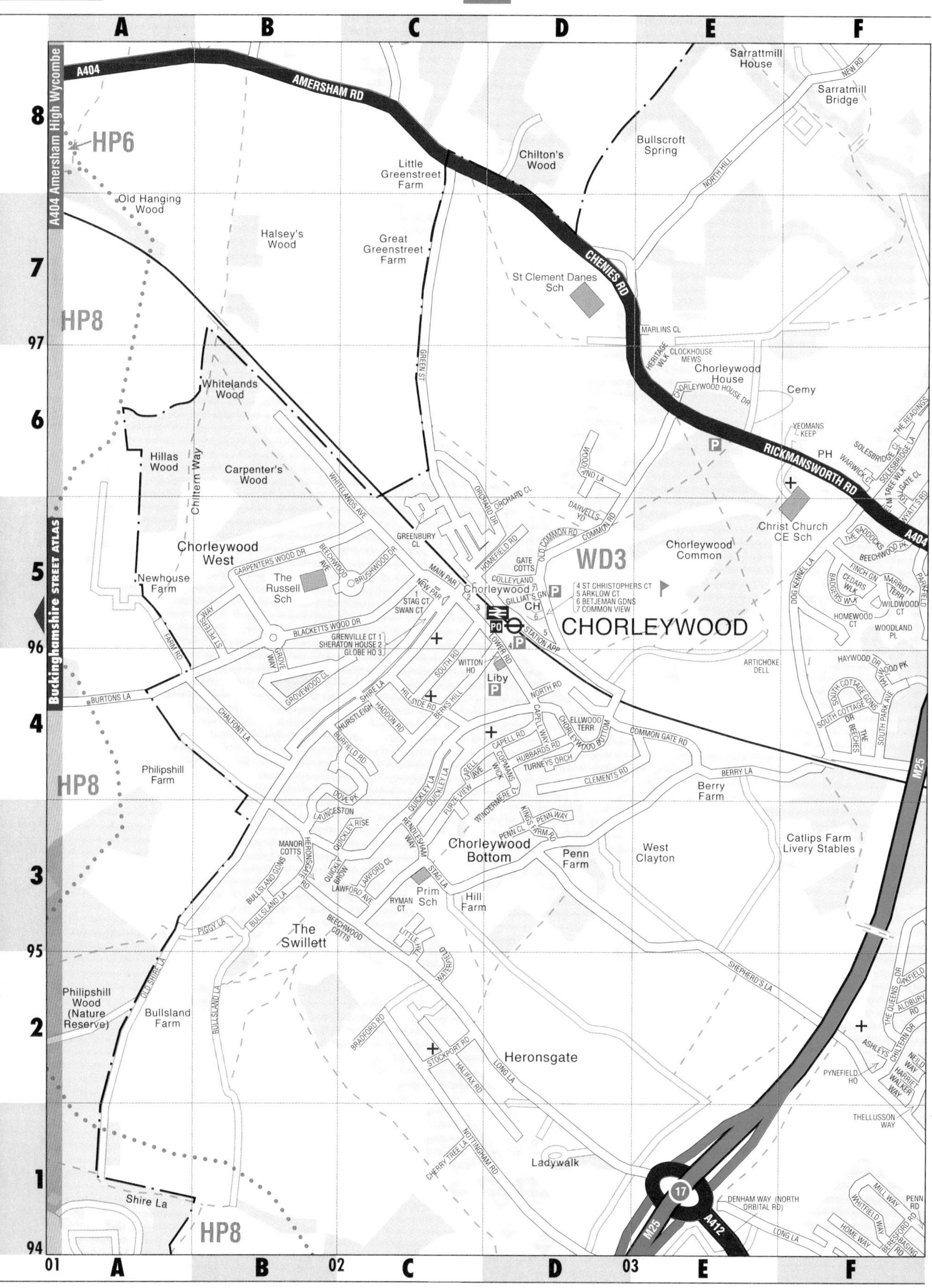
A
B
C
D
E
F
A404
AMERSHAM RD
HP6
Old Hanging Wood
Halsey's Wood
Little Greenstreet Farm
Great Greenstreet Farm
Chilton's Wood
St Clement Danes Sch
CHENIES RD
Sarrattmill House
Sarratmill Bridge
NEW RD
Bullscroft Spring
NORTH HILL
HP8
Whitelands Wood
Hillas Wood
Chiltern Way
Carpenter's Wood
GREEN ST
MARLINS CL
HERITAGE WLK
CLOCKHOUSE MEWS
Chorleywood House
CHORLEYWOOD HOUSE DR
Cemy
YEOMANS KEEP
PH
RICKMANSWORTH RD
Christ Church CE Sch
A404
Chorleywood West
Newhouse Farm
The Russell Sch
WHITELANDS AVE
GREENBURY CL
ORCHARD DR
ORCHARD CL
HOMEFIELD RD
GATE COTTS
OLD COMMON RD
COMMON RD
DARVELLS YD
WOODLAND LA
WD3
Chorleywood Common
CARPENTERS WOOD DR
BEECHWOOD AVE
BRUSHWOOD DR
MAIN PAR
NEW PAR
STAG CT
SWAN CT
Chorleywood
COLLEYLAND
GILLIAT'S GN
CH
4 ST CHRISTOPHERS CT
5 ARKLOW CT
6 BETJEMAN GDNS
7 COMMON VIEW
CHORLEYWOOD
BLACKETTS WOOD DR
GRENVILLE CT 1
SHERATON HOUSE 2
GLOBE HO 3
ST PETERS WAY
GROVE WAY
GROVEWOOD CL
FARM RD
STATION APP
LOWER RD
SOUTH RD
WITTON HO
Liby
NORTH RD
BERKS HILL
HILLSIDE RD
HADDON RD
SHIRE LA
HURSTLEIGH
BURFIELD RD
BURTONS LA
CHALFONT LA
CAPELL WAY
CHORLEYWOOD BOTTOM
ELLWOOD TERR
COMMON GATE RD
CAPELL RD
HUBBARDS RD
TURNEYS ORCH
CLEMENTS RD
BERRY LA
Berry Farm
Philipshill Farm
DOVE PK
LAUNCESTON
QUICKLEY RISE
QUICKLEY LA
FURZE VIEW
ISELL AVE
COPMANS WICK
WINDERMERE CL
KINGS FARM RD
PENN WAY
PENN CL
Chorleywood Bottom
Penn Farm
West Clayton
Catlips Farm Livery Stables
MANOR COTTS
HERONSGATE RD
RENDLESHAM WAY
QUICKLEY BROW
LAWFORD CL
LAWFORD AVE
STAG LA
Prim Sch
RYMAN CT
Hill Farm
BULLSLAND GDNS
BULLSLAND LA
PIGGY LA
The Swillett
BEECHWOOD COTTS
LITTLE HL
WATERFIELD
SHEPHERD'S LA
Philipshill Wood (Nature Reserve)
Bullsland Farm
OLD SHIRE LA
BULLSLAND LA
BRADFORD RD
STOCKPORT RD
HALIFAX RD
LONG LA
Heronsgate
CHERRY TREE LA
NOTTINGHAM RD
Ladywalk
Shire La
HP8
M25
A412
17
DENHAM WAY (NORTH ORBITAL RD)
LONG LA
M25
PYNEFIELD HO
THELLUSSON WAY
ASHLEYS
THE QUEENS DR
OAKFIELD
ALDBURY RD
CHILTERN DR
NEILD WAY
HARRIET WALKER WAY
MILL WAY
WHITEFIELD WAY
HOME WAY
BERESFORD RD
BASING RD
PENN RD
SOLESBRIDGE CL
SOLESBRIDGE LA
WARWICK CT
ELM TREE WLK
GATE CL
WYATT'S RD
THE READINGS
THE PADDOCKS
BEECHWOOD PK
FINCH GN
CEDARS WLK
MARRIOTT TERR
BADGERS WLK
WILDWOOD CT
HOMEWOOD CT
WOODLAND PL
PARK LA
DOG KENNEL LA
ARTICHOKE DELL
HAYWOOD DR
WOOD PK
SOUTH COTTAGE GDNS
SOUTH COTTAGE DR
THE BEECHES
SOUTH PARK AVE
Buckinghamshire STREET ATLAS
A404 Amersham High Wycombe
8
7
97
6
5
96
4
3
95
2
1
94
01
02
03

172

152
166

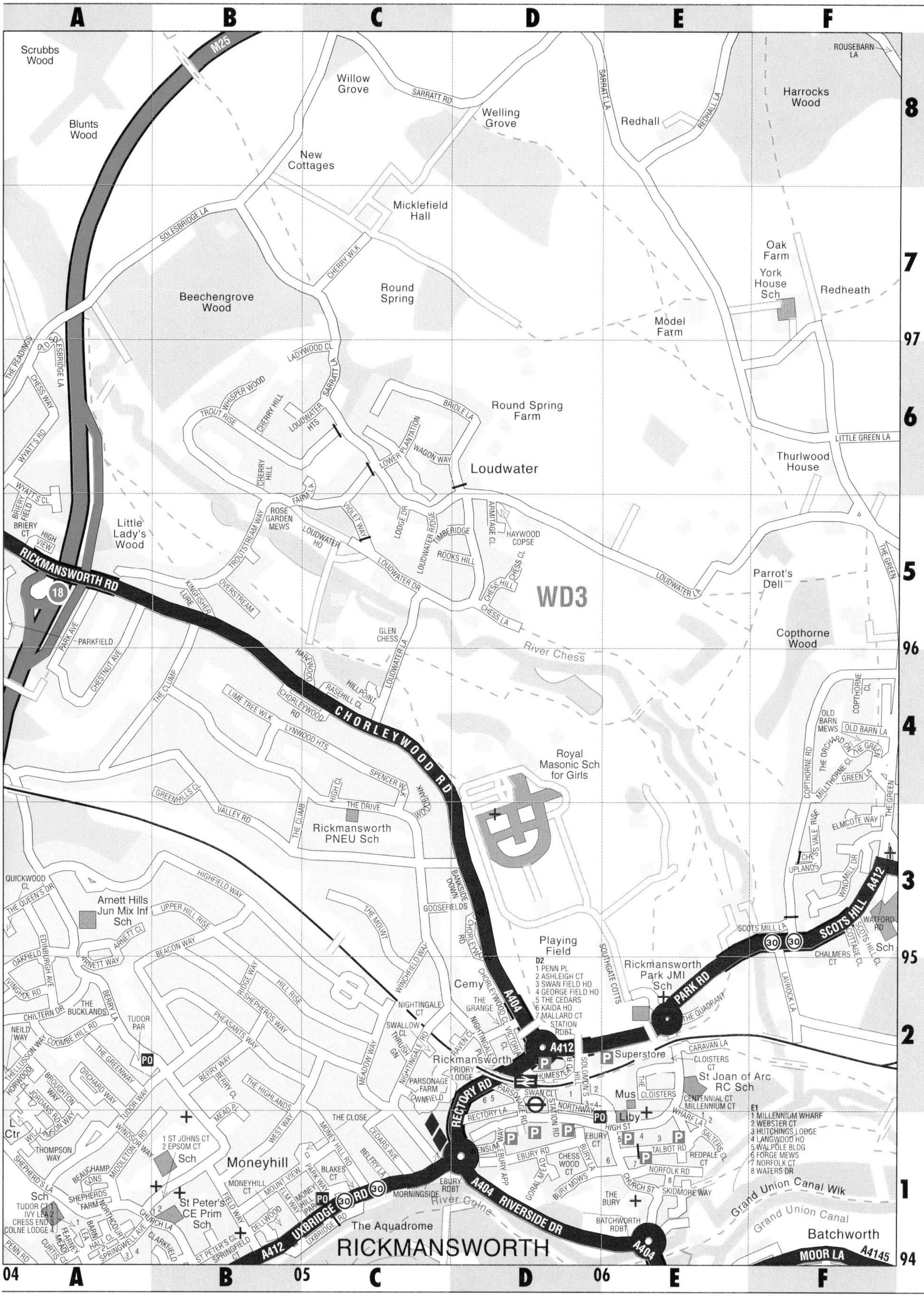
A
B
C
D
E
F
8
7
97
6
5
96
4
3
95
2
1
94
04
05
06
Scrubbs Wood
Blunts Wood
M25
Willow Grove
SARRATT RD
Welling Grove
SARRATT LA
Redhall
REDHALL LA
ROUSEBARN LA
Harrocks Wood
New Cottages
Micklefield Hall
SOLESBRIDGE LA
CHERRY WLK
Round Spring
Beechengrove Wood
Oak Farm
York House Sch
Redheath
Model Farm
THE READINGS
OLD SOLESBRIDGE LA
CHESS WAY
LADYWOOD CL
SARRATT LA
WHISPER WOOD
TROUT RISE
CHERRY HILL
LOUDWATER HTS
BRIDLE LA
Round Spring Farm
LOWER PLANTATION
WAGON WAY
Loudwater
LITTLE GREEN LA
Thurlwood House
WYATT'S RD
WYATT'S CL
BRIERY FIELD
BRIERY CT
HIGH VIEW
CHERRY HILL
FARM LA
ROSE GARDEN MEWS
VIOLET WAY
LODGE DR
LOUDWATER RIDGE
TIMBERIDGE
ARMITAGE CL
HAYWOOD COPSE
Little Lady's Wood
TROUTSTREAM WAY
LOUDWATER HO
ROOKS HILL
CHESS CL
CHESS HILL
RICKMANSWORTH RD
18
KINGFISHER LURE
OVERSTREAM
LOUDWATER DR
WD3
LOUDWATER LA
Parrot's Dell
THE GREEN
CHESS LA
PARK AVE
PARKFIELD
CHESTNUT AVE
GLEN CHESS
LOUDWATER LA
River Chess
Copthorne Wood
HAREWOOD
RASEHILL CL
HILLPOINT
THE CLUMP
CHORLEYWOOD RD
LIME TREE WLK
CHORLEYWOOD RD
LYNWOOD HTS
COPTHORNE CL
OLD BARN MEWS
OLD BARN LA
COPTHORNE RD
THE ORCHARD
ON THE GREEN
MILLTHORNE CL
GREEN LA
Royal Masonic Sch for Girls
SPENCER WLK
GREENHILLS CL
VALLEY RD
HIGH CL
THE DRIVE
WOODBANK
THE CLIMB
Rickmansworth PNEU Sch
ELMCOTE WAY
SWISS VALE
CHESS RISE
UPLANDS
WINDMILL DR
A412
QUICKWOOD CL
THE QUEEN'S DR
HIGHFIELD WAY
Arnett Hills Jun Mix Inf Sch
UPPER HILL RISE
ARNETT CL
ARNETT WAY
BEACON WAY
THE MOUNT
BANKSIDE DOWN
GOOSEFIELDS
CHORLEYWOOD RD
SCOTS MILL LA
30
SCOTS HILL
WATFORD RD
SCOTS HILL CL
COTTAGE CL
CHALMERS CT
Sch
OAKFIELD
EDINBURGH AVE
IVINGHOE RD
BERRY LA
RIDGE WAY
HILL RISE
SHEPHERDS WAY
WINCHFIELD WAY
Playing Field
D2
1 PENN PL
2 ASHLEIGH CT
3 SWAN FIELD HO
4 GEORGE FIELD HO
5 THE CEDARS
6 KAIDA HO
7 MALLARD CT
SOUTHGATE COTTS
Rickmansworth Park JMI Sch
PARK RD
LAVROCK LA
THE QUADRANT
Cemy
A404
THE GRANGE
NIGHTINGALE PL
VICTORIA CL
CHILTERN DR
THE BUCKLANDS
TUDOR PAR
PHEASANTS WAY
NIGHTINGALE CT
SWALLOW CL
THRUSH GN
NIGHTINGALE RD
STATION RDBT
A412
Superstore
CARAVAN LA
CLOISTERS CT
NEILD WAY
COOMBE HILL RD
THE GREENWAY
PO
MEADOW WAY
RAVEN CL
Rickmansworth
PRIORY LODGE
HOMESTEAD RD
SOLOMON'S HILL
St Joan of Arc RC Sch
THE LLUSSON WAY
HORWOOD CL
BROUGHTON WAY
ORCHARD WAY
TUDOR WAY
BERRY WAY
BERRY CL
THE HIGHLANDS
PARSONAGE FARM
TOWNFIELD
RECTORY RD
PARSONAGE RD
SWAN CL
STATION RD
NORTHWAY
Mus
THE CLOISTERS
CENTENNIAL CT
MILLENNIUM CT
WHARF LA
JORDANS WAY
L Ctr
THOMPSON WAY
WINDSOR RD
MIDDLETON RD
MEAD PL
WEST WAY
THE CLOSE
MONEY HILL RD
CEDARS AVE
RECTORY LA
Liby
HIGH ST
EBURY CT
TALBOT RD
REDPALE CT
SALTERS CL
E1
1 MILLENNIUM WHARF
2 WEBSTER CT
3 HUTCHINGS LODGE
4 LANGWOOD HO
5 WALPOLE BLDG
6 FORGE MEWS
7 NORFOLK CT
8 WATERS DR
SHEPHERD'S LA
1 ST JOHNS CT
2 EPSOM CT
Sch
BEAUCHAMP GDNS
Moneyhill
MONEYHILL CT
MOUNT VIEW
PARK WAY
BLAKES CT
BELFRY LA
WENSUM WAY
EBURY APP
EBURY RD
GORAL MEAD
CHESS WOOD CT
BURY LA
NORFOLK RD
Sch
TUDOR CT 1
IVY LEA 2
CRESS END 3
COLNE LODGE 4
SHEPHERDS FARM
NORTHCOURT
St Peter's CE Prim Sch
CHURCH LA
FIELD WAY
ELM WAY
MONEY HILL PDE
UXBRIDGE RD
MORNINGSIDE
EBURY RDBT
River Colne
RIVERSIDE DR
BURY MDWS
CHURCH ST
SKIDMORE WAY
THE BURY
Grand Union Canal Wlk
Grand Union Canal
Batchworth
BARN LEA
FEARNLEY MEAD
HALL CL
SPRINGWELL AVE
CLARKFIELD
ST PETER'S CL
SPRINGFIELD CT
DELLWOOD
The Aquadrome
RICKMANSWORTH
BATCHWORTH RDBT
MOOR LA
A4145
PENN RD
CURTIS

173
166

165
153

E4
1 REDFERN CT
2 LUCIDA CT
3 VERDANA CT
4 PRINTERS AVE
5 OMEGA CT
6 ROCKWELL CT
7 COPPERDALE CT

E5
1 MALKIN WAY
2 MONET HO
3 BLANCHARD DR
4 RENOIR HO
5 MATISSE HO
6 DUMAS WAY
7 TOULOUSE HO
8 MERCURY HO
9 MANHATTAN HO
10 METROPOLITAN MEWS
11 EMPIRE PL
12 SILVER PL
13 MODENA MEWS
14 CAVALLI APARTMENTS
15 TURIN HO
16 FLORENCE HO
17 PISA HO

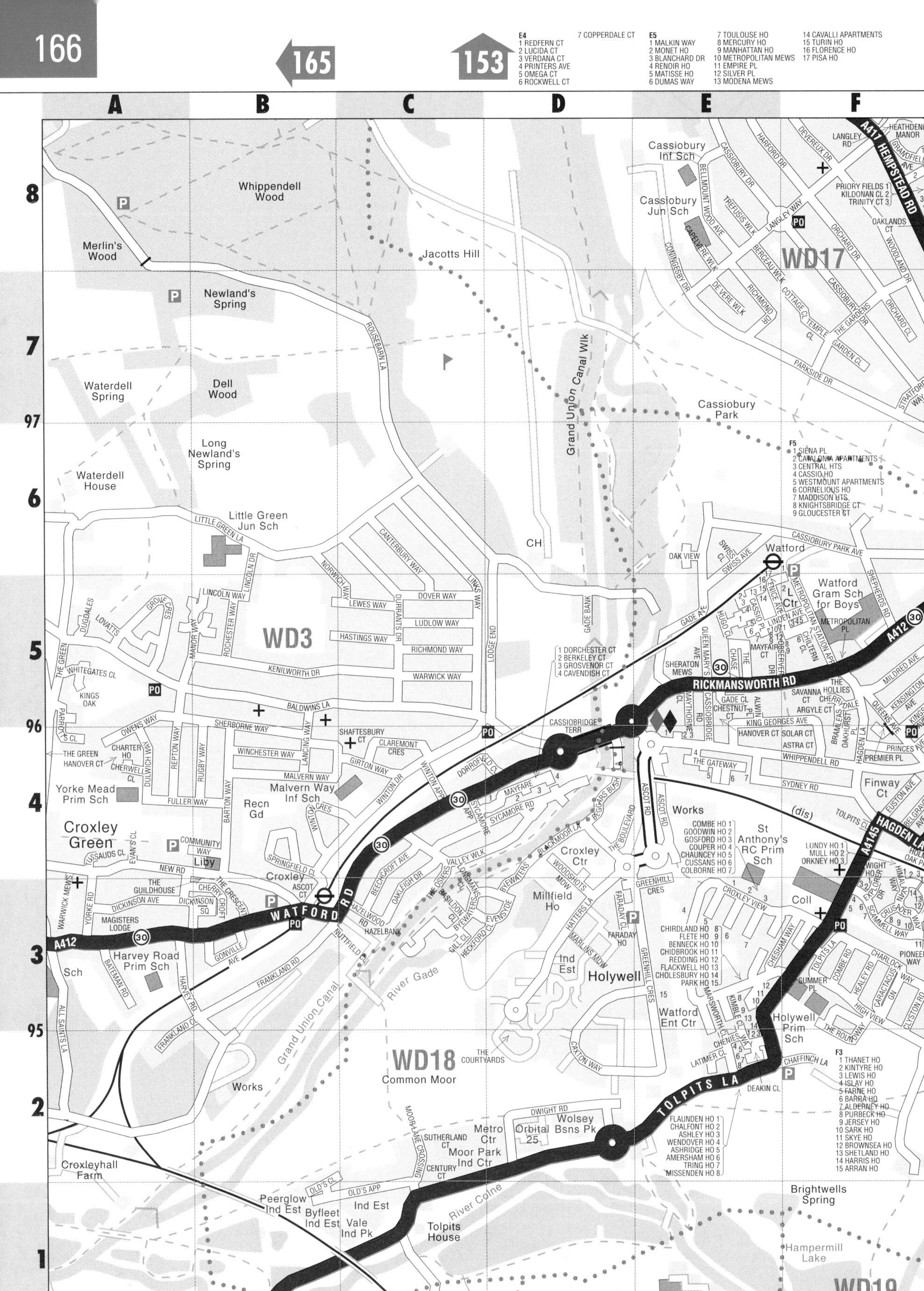

165
174

A8
1 CURZON GATE CT
2 BLOCK 14
3 BLOCK 12
4 BLOCK 10
5 BEECHFIELD CT
6 LANGWOOD
7 PRIORY FIELDS
8 REGENCY CT

B6
1 BALLINGER CT
2 THE BEECHES
3 BURVALE CT
4 CRAKERS MEAD
5 BRIDGEFORD HO
6 FAIRCROSS HO

C6
1 OTTOMAN TERR
2 VICTORIA CT
3 THE BROADWAY
4 QUEENS CT
5 TANTIVY CT
6 ASHLEIGH CT
7 QUEENS GATE
8 ALPHA CT

C7
1 WELLINGTON HO
2 CHELTENHAM HO
3 ROEDEAN HO
4 CANTERBURY HO
5 LANCING HO
6 WESTMINSTER HO

154

C7
7 ELIZABETH HO
8 BADMINTON HO
9 ETON HO
10 ANDREW REED CT
11 ALEXANDRA CT
12 REEDS CHAPEL

168

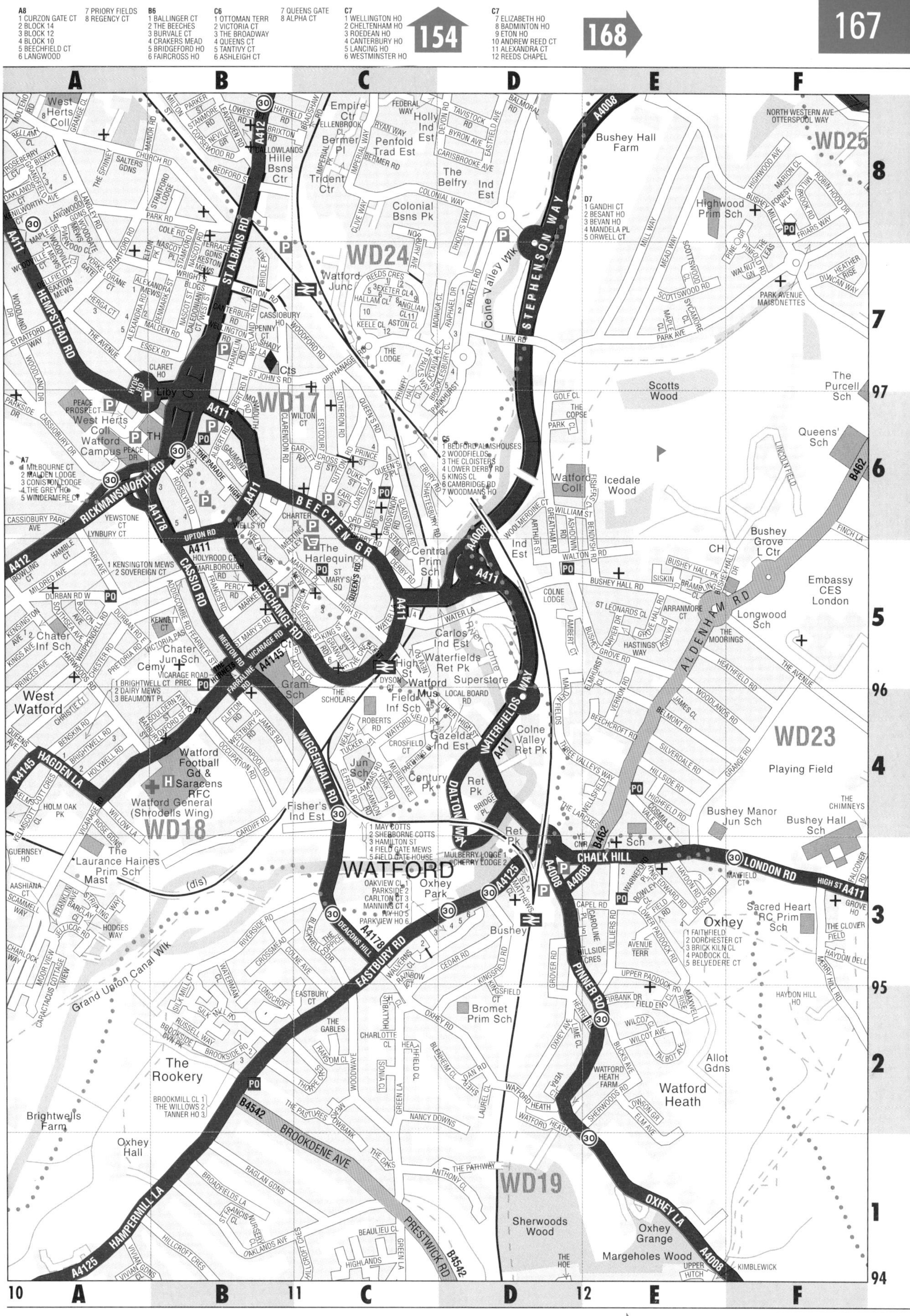

175
168

167
155

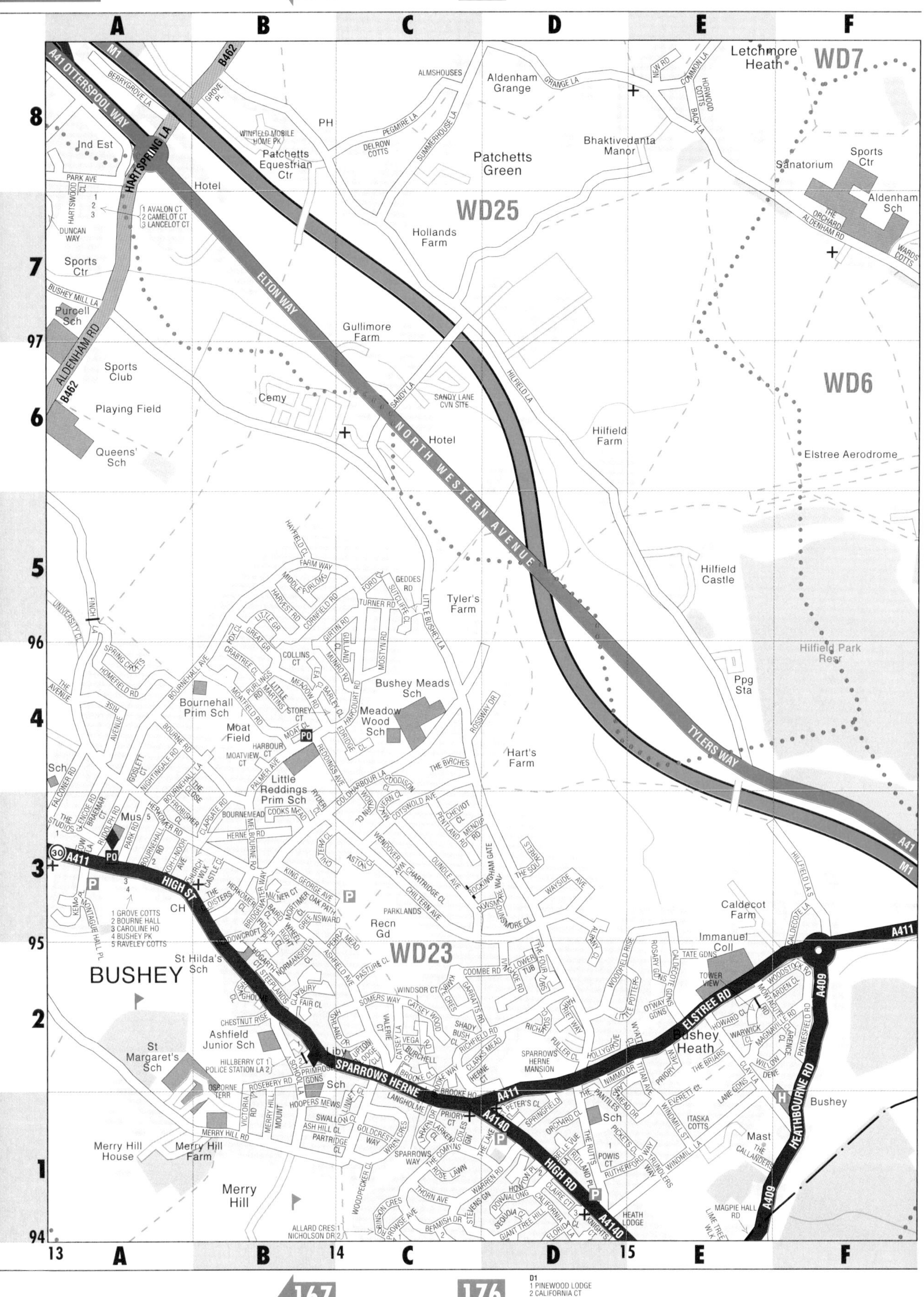

167
176

D1
1 PINEWOOD LODGE
2 CALIFORNIA CT
3 UPLANDS CT

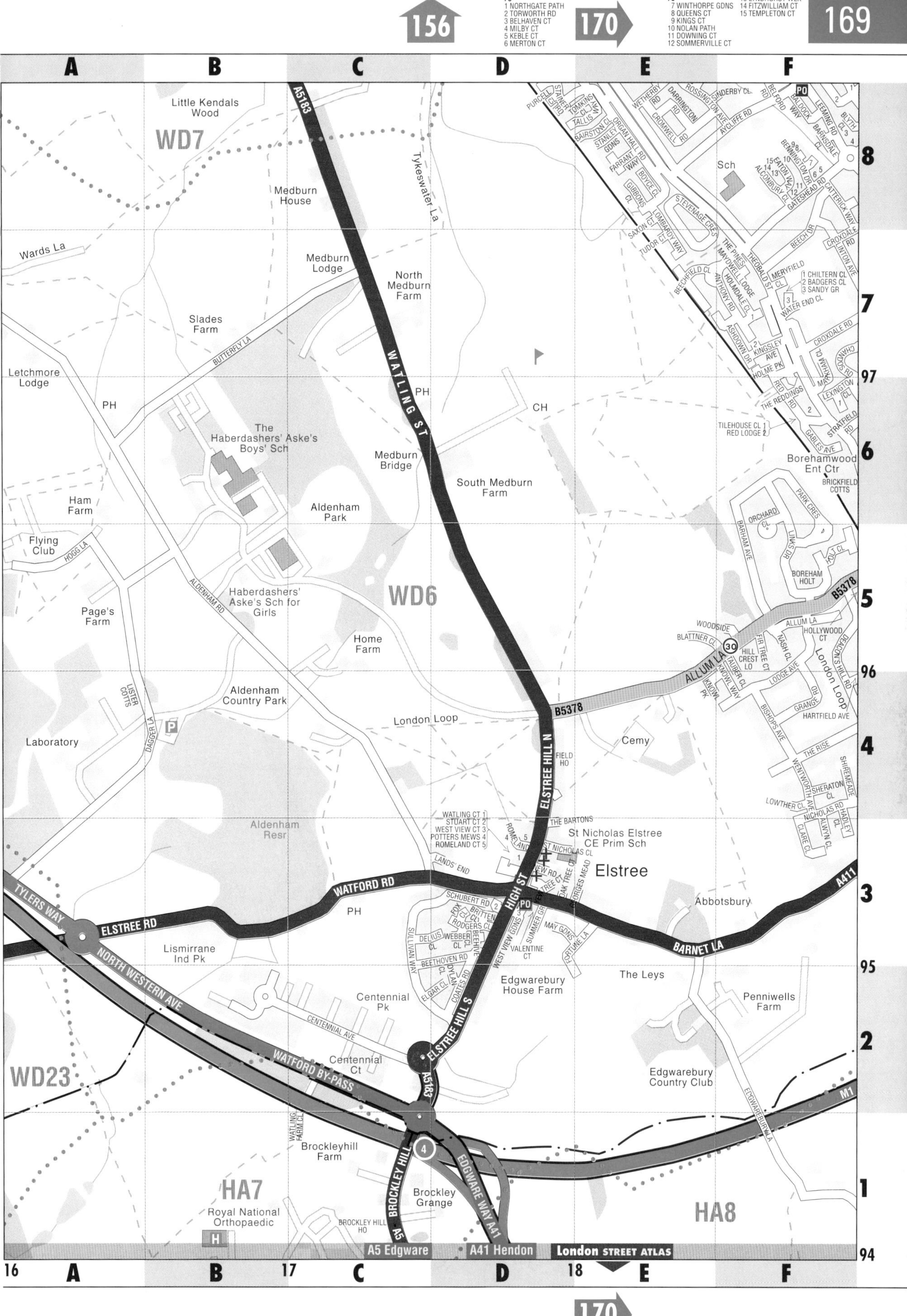
A B C D E F
Little Kendals Wood
WD7
Medburn House
Tykeswater La
Wards La
Medburn Lodge
North Medburn Farm
Slades Farm
Butterfly La
Letchmore Lodge
PH
WATLING ST
CH
The Haberdashers' Aske's Boys' Sch
Medburn Bridge
South Medburn Farm
Ham Farm
Aldenham Park
Flying Club
Hogg La
Haberdashers' Aske's Sch for Girls
WD6
Page's Farm
Aldenham Rd
Home Farm
Lister Cotts
Aldenham Country Park
London Loop
B5378
Laboratory
Dagger La
Cemy
Field Ho
ELSTREE HILL N
Aldenham Resr
St Nicholas Elstree CE Prim Sch
Elstree
WATFORD RD
HIGH ST
Abbotsbury
ELSTREE RD
TYLERS WAY
PH
Lismirrane Ind Pk
NORTH WESTERN AVE
BARNET LA
A411
Edgwarebury House Farm
The Leys
Penniwells Farm
Centennial Pk
Centennial Ave
ELSTREE HILL S
WATFORD BY-PASS
Centennial Ct
A5183
WD23
Edgwarebury Country Club
M1
Brockleyhill Farm
BROCKLEY HILL
EDGWARE WAY A41
Brockley Grange
HA7
Royal National Orthopaedic
Brockley Hill Ho
HA8
A5 Edgware
A41 Hendon
Sch
Borehamwood Ent Ctr
Brickfield Cotts
Boreham Holt
Allum La
Woodside
London Loop
1 CHILTERN CL
2 BADGERS CL
3 SANDY GR
Tilehouse Cl 1
Red Lodge 2
Watling Ct 1
Stuart Ct 2
West View Ct 3
Potters Mews 4
Romeland Ct 5
8 7 97 6 5 96 4 3 95 2 1 94
16 17 18

A7
1 THIRSTON PATH
2 GOODWOOD PATH
3 BADMINTON CL
4 LICHFIELD HO
5 NORWICH HO
6 GLOUCESTER HO
7 EXETER HO
8 OXFORD HO
9 PETERBOROUGH HO
10 CANTERBURY HO
11 SOUTHWARK HO
12 WORCESTER HO
13 YORK HO
14 DURHAM HO
15 CARLISLE HO
16 BRISTOL HO

169
157

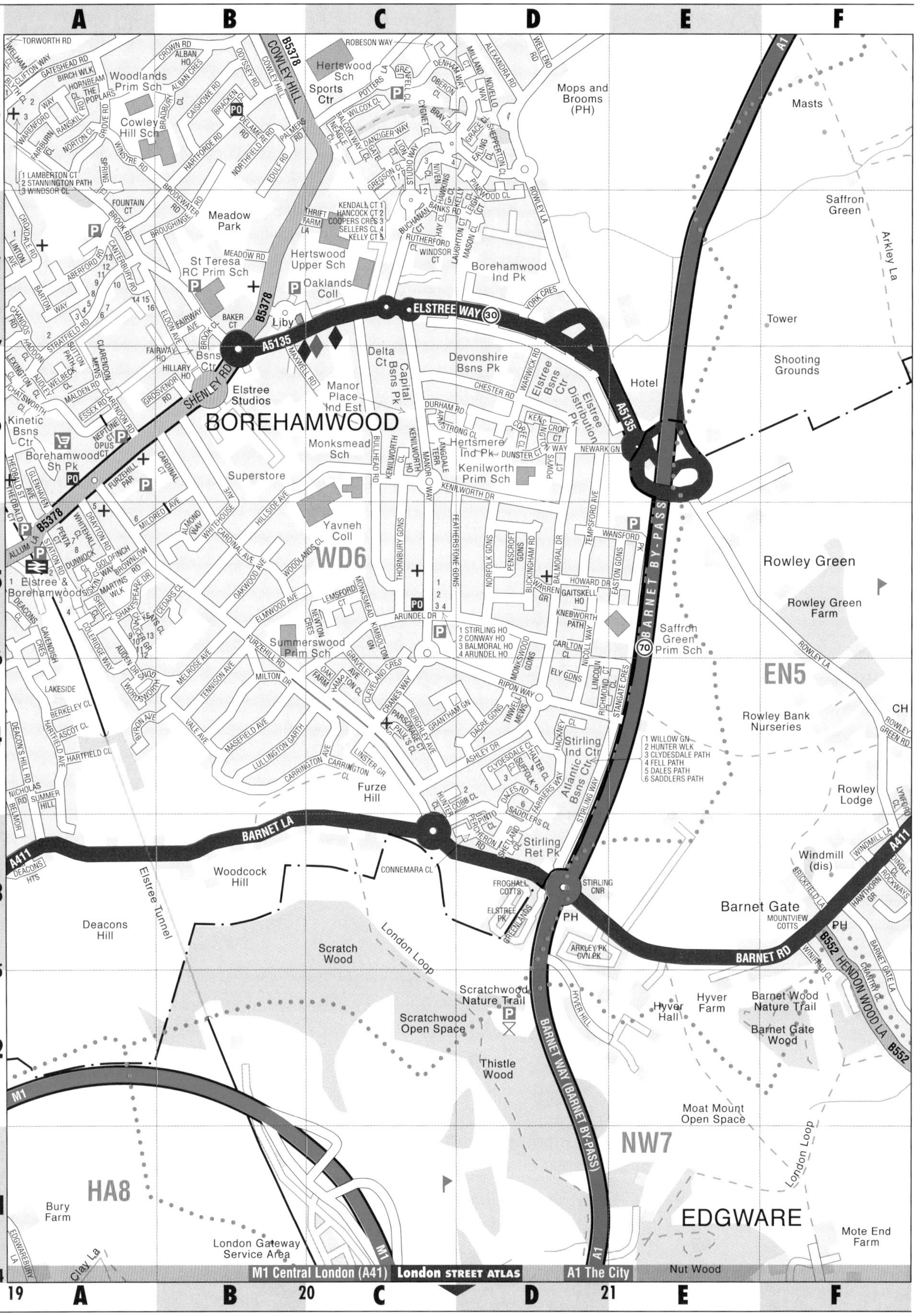

A B C D E F

8 7 97 6 5 96 4 3 95 2 1 94

BOREHAMWOOD
WD6
EN5
NW7
HA8
EDGWARE

Woodlands Prim Sch
Cowley Hill Sch
Hertswood Sch
Sports Ctr
Mops and Brooms (PH)
Masts
Meadow Park
St Teresa RC Prim Sch
Hertswood Upper Sch
Oaklands Coll
Borehamwood Ind Pk
Saffron Green
Arkley La
Tower
Shooting Grounds
Hotel
Elstree Studios
Delta Ct
Capital Bsns Pk
Manor Place Ind Est
Devonshire Bsns Pk
Elstree Bsns Ctr
Elstree Distribution Pk
Kinetic Bsns Ctr
Borehamwood Sh Pk
Monksmead Sch
Hertsmere Ind Pk
Kenilworth Prim Sch
Superstore
Yavneh Coll
Elstree & Borehamwood
Rowley Green
Rowley Green Farm
Saffron Green Prim Sch
Summerswood Prim Sch
Rowley Bank Nurseries
Stirling Ind Ctr
Atlantic Bsns Ctr
Furze Hill
Rowley Lodge
Stirling Ret Pk
Windmill (dis)
Woodcock Hill
Deacons Hill
Elstree Tunnel
Barnet Gate
Scratch Wood
London Loop
Scratchwood Nature Trail
Scratchwood Open Space
Hyver Hall
Hyver Farm
Barnet Wood Nature Trail
Barnet Gate Wood
Thistle Wood
Moat Mount Open Space
Bury Farm
London Gateway Service Area
Mote End Farm
Nut Wood

ELSTREE WAY
SHENLEY RD
BARNET LA
BARNET RD
BARNET BY-PASS
BARNET WAY (BARNET BY-PASS)
COWLEY HILL
HENDON WOOD LA
A1 A5135 B5378 A411 B552 M1

1 LAMBERTON CT
2 STANNINGTON PATH
3 WINDSOR CL

KENDALL CT 1
HANCOCK CT 2
COOPERS CRES 3
SELLERS CL 4
KELLY CT 5

1 STIRLING HO
2 CONWAY HO
3 BALMORAL HO
4 ARUNDEL HO

1 WILLOW GN
2 HUNTER WLK
3 CLYDESDALE PATH
4 FELL PATH
5 DALES PATH
6 SADDLERS PATH

M1 Central London (A41) London STREET ATLAS A1 The City

19 A B 20 C D 21 E F

A5
1 HOLLYWOOD CT
2 TRINITY HO
3 PEMBROKE HO
4 ACADEMY HO
5 MAPLE CT
6 FAIRLANDS LODGE
7 GRANGER CT
8 WILDING CT
9 BROWNING CT
10 HARDY CT
11 BRONTE CT
12 PARSONS CT
13 HOLLAND CT

169

E5
1 COE'S ALLEY
2 HERTSWOOD CT
3 SUNBURY CT
4 MERIDEN HO
5 NORFOLK CT
6 VANBURGH CT
7 MORRISON CT
8 KINGSHILL CT
9 BARONSMERE CT
10 CHARTWELL CT

E6
1 RICHARD CT
2 ALSTON CT
3 RIDGELEIGH CT
4 BARLETTS COTTS
5 NURSERY ROW
6 HADLEY PAR
7 EXCHANGE BLDGS
8 CHIPPING CL
9 BRUCE RD
10 HART LODGE
11 HOLKHAM HO
12 LEATHERSELLERS CL
13 BRADDON CT
14 LEINSTER MEWS

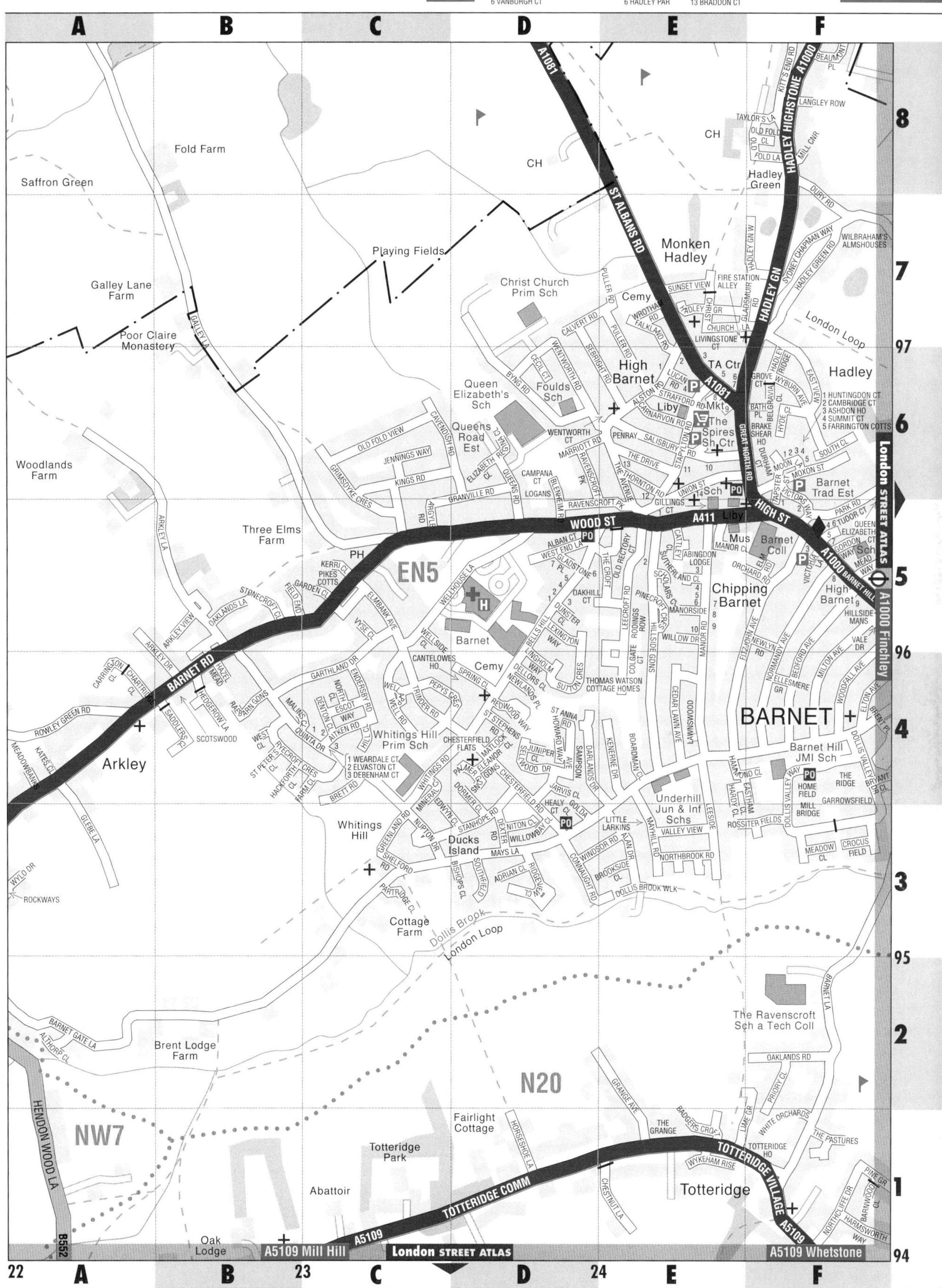
A
B
C
D
E
F
8
7
97
6
5
96
4
3
95
2
1
94
22
23
24
Fold Farm
Saffron Green
CH
Hadley Green
Monken Hadley
Playing Fields
Galley Lane Farm
Poor Claire Monastery
Christ Church Prim Sch
Cemy
High Barnet
Hadley
Queen Elizabeth's Sch
Foulds Sch
Queens Road Est
The Spires Sh Ctr
Barnet Trad Est
Woodlands Farm
Three Elms Farm
EN5
WOOD ST
A411
HIGH ST
Mus
Barnet Coll
Chipping Barnet
High Barnet
Barnet
BARNET RD
Arkley
Whitings Hill Prim Sch
BARNET
Barnet Hill JMI Sch
Underhill Jun & Inf Schs
Whitings Hill
Ducks Island
Cottage Farm
Dollis Brook
London Loop
The Ravenscroft Sch a Tech Coll
Brent Lodge Farm
N20
NW7
Fairlight Cottage
Totteridge Park
Abattoir
Totteridge
Oak Lodge
TOTTERIDGE COMM
TOTTERIDGE VILLAGE
HENDON WOOD LA
A5109 Mill Hill
London STREET ATLAS
A5109 Whetstone
A1000 Finchley
ST ALBANS RD
HADLEY GN
HADLEY HIGHSTONE
GREAT NORTH RD

D5
1 BIRNBECK CT
2 WILBURY LODGE
3 CHAUCER HO
4 PINERIDGE CT
5 BYFORD HO
6 OAKMEDE
7 WESSEX CT

F5
1 OLIVIA CT
2 VANTAGE CT
3 GRASEBY HO
4 WINCHESTER CT
5 MONTAGUE CL
6 ROCHESTER CT
7 GORDON MANS
8 LAWN MANS
9 AVENUE MANS

164

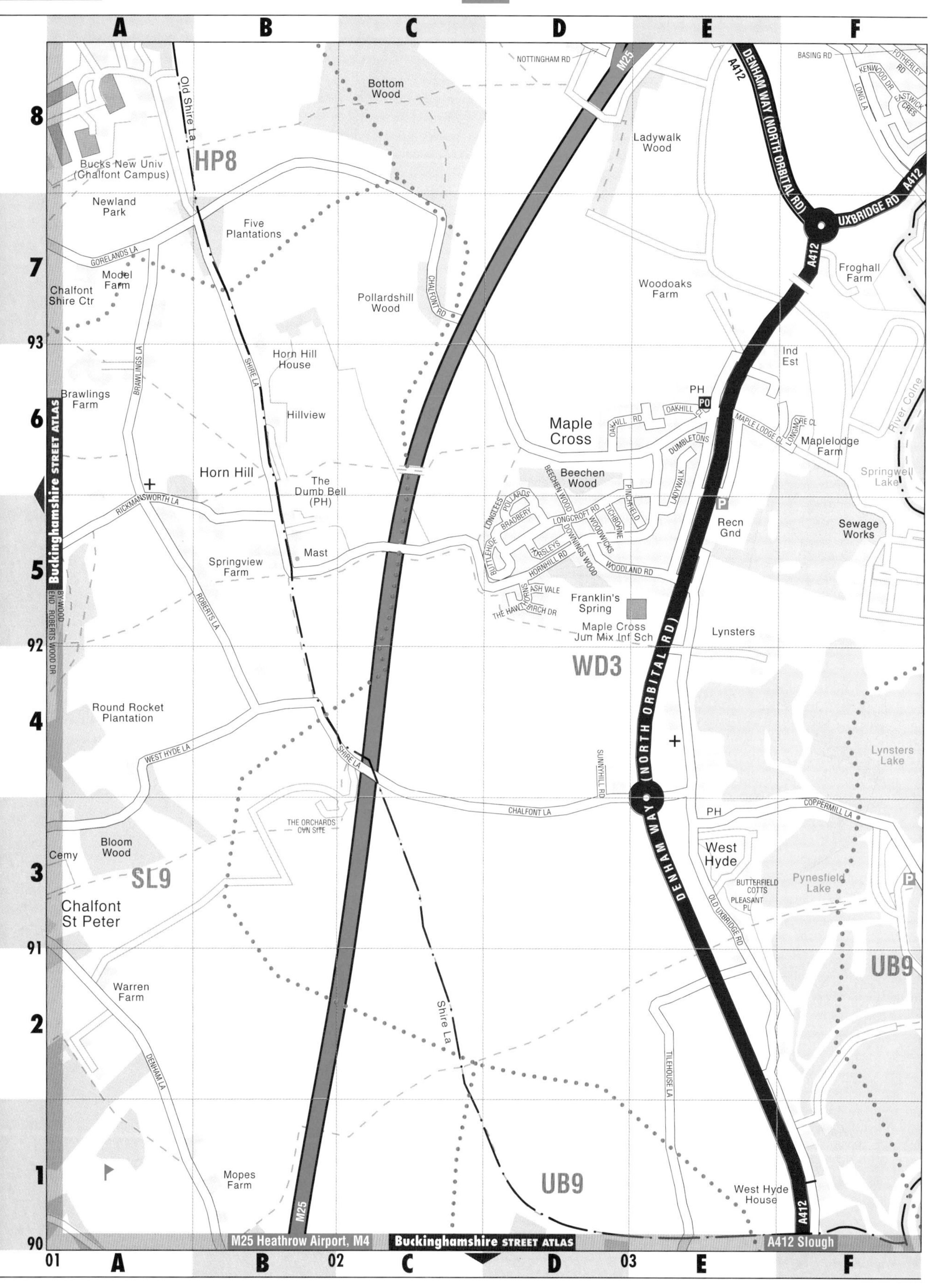
A
B
C
D
E
F
8
7
93
6
5
92
4
3
91
2
1
90
01
02
03
Old Shire La
HP8
Bucks New Univ
(Chalfont Campus)
Newland
Park
Bottom
Wood
NOTTINGHAM RD
M25
DENHAM WAY (NORTH ORBITAL RD)
A412
BASING RD
FOTHERLEY RD
KENWOOD DR
LONG LA
EASTWICK CRES
Ladywalk
Wood
UXBRIDGE RD
Five
Plantations
GORELANDS LA
Model
Farm
Chalfont
Shire Ctr
Pollardshill
Wood
CHALFONT RD
Woodoaks
Farm
Froghall
Farm
Horn Hill
House
SHIRE LA
BRAWLINGS LA
Brawlings
Farm
Hillview
Ind
Est
PH
PO
OAKHILL RD
OAKHILL CL
MAPLE LODGE CL
LONGMORE CL
Maplelodge
Farm
River Colne
Maple
Cross
DUMBLETONS
Beechen
Wood
Springwell
Lake
Horn Hill
The
Dumb Bell
(PH)
RICKMANSWORTH LA
BEECHEN WOOD
POLLARDS
LONGLEES
BRADBERY
LONGCROFT RD
TICHBORNE
PINEFIELD
LADYWALK
P
Recn
Gnd
Sewage
Works
Mast
BUTTLEHIDE
HORSLEYS
HORNHILL RD
DOWNINGS WOOD
WOODWICKS
WOODLAND RD
Springview
Farm
ASH VALE
THE HAWTHORNS
BIRCH DR
Franklin's
Spring
Maple Cross
Jun Mix Inf Sch
Lynsters
ROBERTS LA
Buckinghamshire STREET ATLAS
BY-WOOD END
ROBERTS WOOD DR
WD3
Round Rocket
Plantation
WEST HYDE LA
SHIRE LA
SUNNYHILL RD
Lynsters
Lake
DENHAM WAY (NORTH ORBITAL RD)
CHALFONT LA
THE ORCHARDS
CVN SITE
PH
COPPERMILL LA
Bloom
Wood
Cemy
SL9
West
Hyde
BUTTERFIELD
COTTS
PLEASANT
PL
Pynesfield
Lake
Chalfont
St Peter
OLD UXBRIDGE RD
UB9
Warren
Farm
Shire La
DENHAM LA
TILEHOUSE LA
Mopes
Farm
UB9
West Hyde
House
M25 Heathrow Airport, M4
Buckinghamshire STREET ATLAS
A412 Slough

A B C D E F

8
Mill End
BASING RD
PENN RD
SPRINGWELL AVE
GROVE RD
COLNE AVE
MAXWELL CL
CLARKFIELD
UXBRIDGE RD
A412
VINE TREE CT
WATERDELL PL
CHURCH LA
MILL STREAM LODGE
COLNE MEAD
THE WILLOWS
1 CURTIS CL
2 DELL CT
3 ARDEN CT
4 SPRINGWELL CT
5 FOTHERLEY RD
6 EASTWICK CRES
River Colne
Bury Lake
The Aquadrome
Batchworth Lake
Superstore
CHURCH ST
A404
MOOR LA
LONDON RD
A4145
LONDON RD/MOOR LA RDBT
CH
FROGMOOR LA
FROGMOOR CT
MOSS CL
HERON CL
MALM CL
RUSHMOOR CL
SHERFIELD AVE
PLAITFORD CL
LANDFORD CL
THE BYEWAY
BATCHWORTH HILL
The Grove

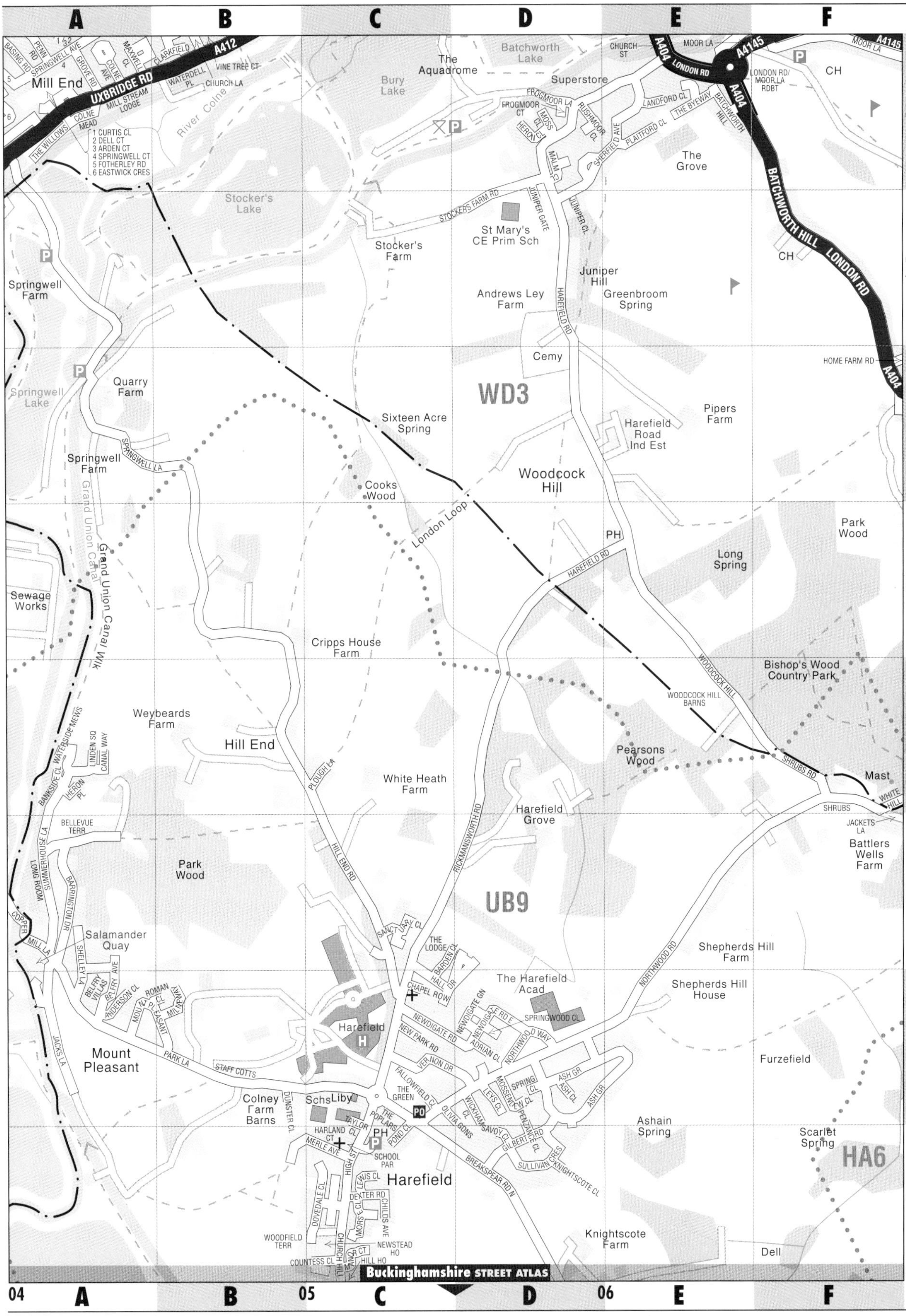

7
Stocker's Lake
STOCKERS FARM RD
St Mary's CE Prim Sch
JUNIPER GATE
JUNIPER CL
Stocker's Farm
Springwell Farm
Juniper Hill
Greenbroom Spring
Andrews Ley Farm
HAREFIELD RD
BATCHWORTH HILL
LONDON RD
CH
Cemy

93
HOME FARM RD
A404
Springwell Lake
Quarry Farm
WD3

6
Sixteen Acre Spring
Harefield Road Ind Est
Pipers Farm
Springwell Farm
SPRINGWELL LA
Woodcock Hill
Cooks Wood
Grand Union Canal
Park Wood
PH
London Loop
Long Spring

5
Grand Union Canal Wlk
Sewage Works
HAREFIELD RD
Cripps House Farm

92
WOODCOCK HILL
Bishop's Wood Country Park
WOODCOCK HILL BARNS
Weybeards Farm

4
WATERSIDE MEWS
LINDEN SQ
CANAL WAY
BANKSIDE CL
HERON PL
Hill End
Pearsons Wood
SHRUBS RD
Mast
PLOUGH LA
White Heath Farm
WHITE HILL
SHRUBS
Harefield Grove
JACKETS LA
BELLEVUE TERR
RICKMANSWORTH RD
Battlers Wells Farm
HILL END RD
Park Wood

3
SUMMERHOUSE LA
LONG ROOM
BARRINGTON DR
UB9
COPPER MILL LA
Salamander Quay
SANCTUARY CL
THE LODGE
BARDEN CL
Shepherds Hill Farm
SHELLEY LA
HALL DR
NORTHWOOD RD

91
The Harefield Acad
Shepherds Hill House
BELFRY VILLAS
BELFRY AVE
ANDERSON CL
CHAPEL ROW
ROMAN CL
MOUNT PLEASANT
MILLWAY
NEWDIGATE GN
NEWDIGATE RD E
SPRINGWOOD CL
Harefield
H
NEWDIGATE RD
NEW PARK RD
ADRIAN CL
NORTHWOOD WAY

2
JACKS LA
Mount Pleasant
PARK LA
STAFF COTTS
VERNON DR
Furzefield
FALLOWFIELD CL
ASH GR
ASH CL
MOSSENDEW CL
SPRING CL
LEYS CL
THE GREEN
Colney Farm Barns
DUNSTER CL
Schs
Liby
PO
WICKHAM CL
OLIVIA GDNS
SAVOY CL
PENZANCE CL
THE POPLARS
TAYLOR CL
PH
POND CL
Ashain Spring
GILBERT RD
Scarlet Spring
HARLAND CT
MERLE AVE
SCHOOL PAR
SULLIVAN CRES
KNIGHTSCOTE CL
HA6
BREAKSPEAR RD N
HIGH ST
LEWIS CL

1
Harefield
DOVEDALE CL
DEXTER RD
CHILDS AVE
MORSE CL
WOODFIELD TERR
CHURCH HILL
MANOR CT
NEWSTEAD HO
Knightscote Farm
Dell
COUNTESS CL
HILL HO
90

173
166

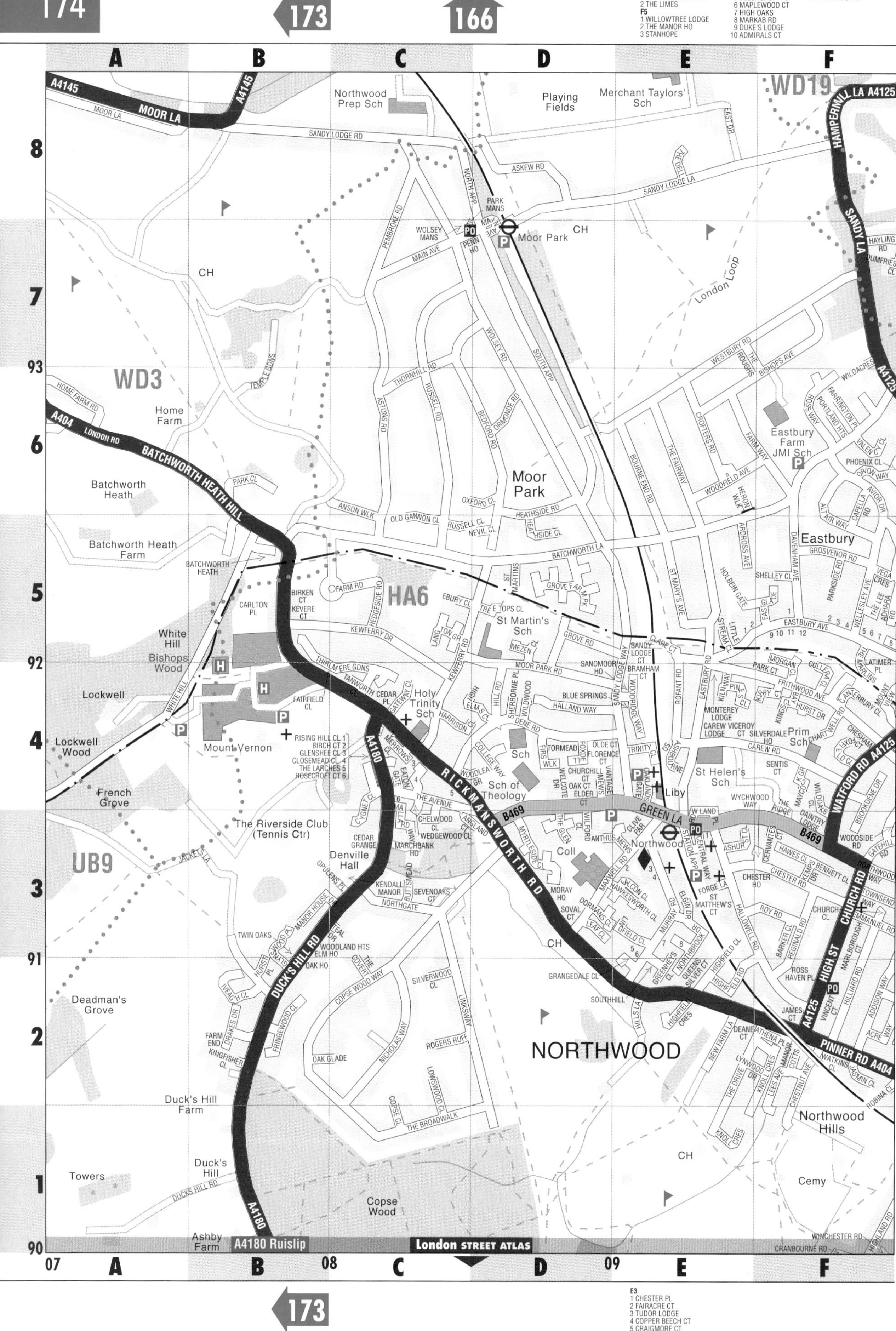

173

E3
1 CHESTER PL
2 FAIRACRE CT
3 TUDOR LODGE
4 COPPER BEECH CT
5 CRAIGMORE CT
6 MANSION HO
7 ST JOHN'S CT
8 DRYSDALE CL

C7
1 KIRKCALDY GN
2 HARROGATE RD
3 SWANSTON PATH
4 LALSHAM HO
5 GOSFORTH LA
6 ALDERWOOD HO
7 FORFAR HO
8 ENVILLE HO
9 DUNFERMLINE HO
10 DENTON HO
11 LINDRICK HO
12 PADGATE HO
13 OFFERTON HO
14 PENN HO
15 MALDEN HO

D7
1 LUFFENHAM HO
2 ST ANDREWS RD
3 PENNARD HO
4 LAWRENCE CT
5 ERSKINE HO
6 FILTON HO
7 HARTCRAN HO
8 MANSCOTT HO
9 Carpenders Park Bsns Ctr

167

176

E8
1 CHOLESBURY
2 PRESTWOOD
3 CHAMPNEYS

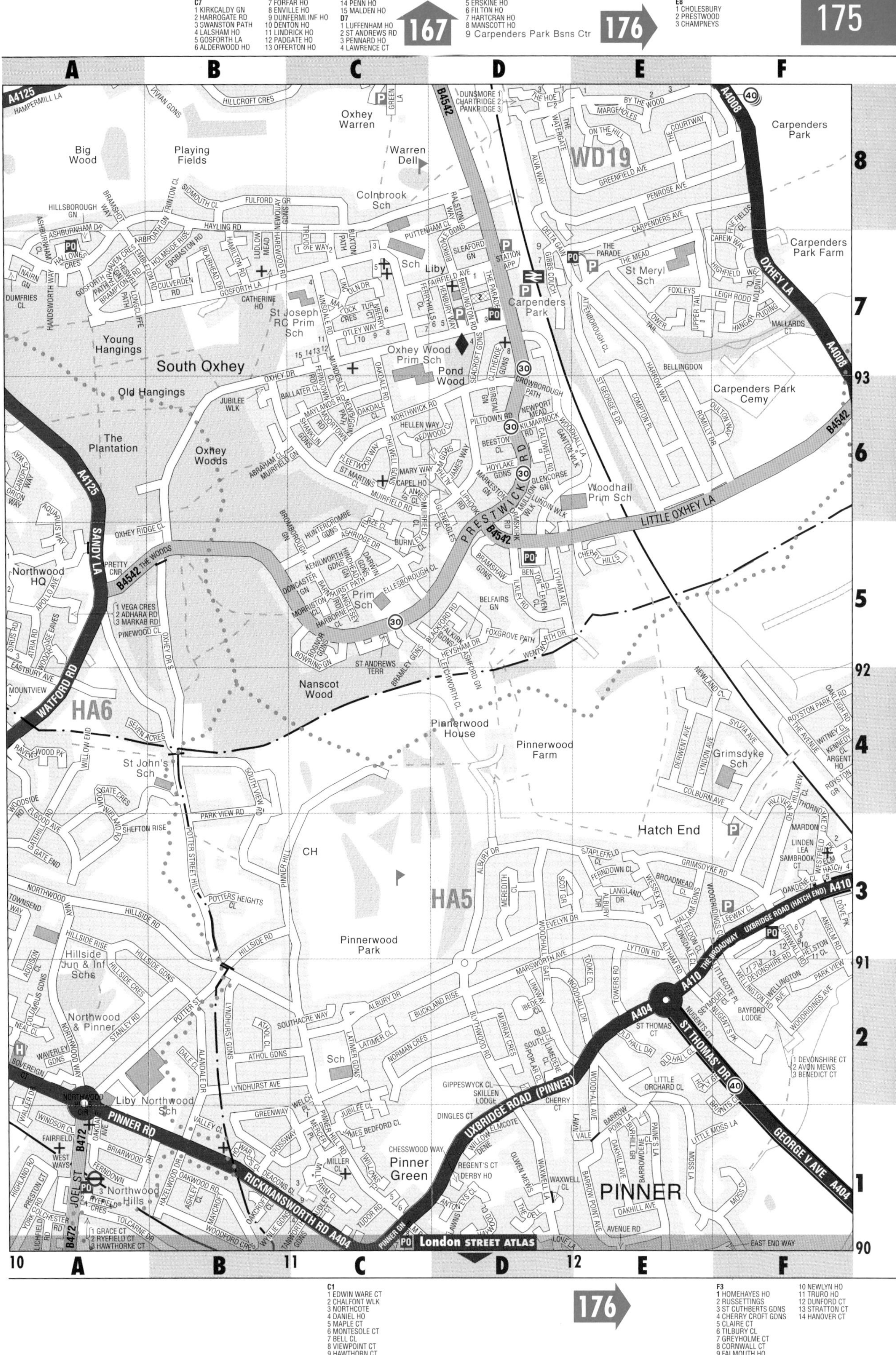

C1
1 EDWIN WARE CT
2 CHALFONT WLK
3 NORTHCOTE
4 DANIEL HO
5 MAPLE CT
6 MONTESOLE CT
7 BELL CT
8 VIEWPOINT CT
9 HAWTHORN CT

176

F3
1 HOMEHAYES HO
2 RUSSETTINGS
3 ST CUTHBERTS GDNS
4 CHERRY CROFT GDNS
5 CLAIRE CT
6 TILBURY CL
7 GREYHOLME CT
8 CORNWALL CT
9 FALMOUTH HO
10 NEWLYN HO
11 TRURO HO
12 DUNFORD CT
13 STRATTON CT
14 HANOVER CT

175

168

BUSHEY
WD23
WD19
Hartsbourne Ctry Club
Hartsbourne Prim Sch
Stanmore Common
THE COMMON A4140
Harrow Weald Common
Bentley Priory
Mutton Wood
Levels Wood
Mast
Grimsdyke Hotel
Valley View Farm
HA7
Deer Park
Heriot's Wood
The Kiln
Weald Wood
OLD REDDING
Priory House
Burnt Oak Farm
PH
CH
Stony Wood
Copse Farm
Lower Priory Farm
STANMORE
Oxheylane Farm
OXHEY LA
Hillside
BROOKSHILL
Bentley Wood High Sch
HA5
HA3
Harrow Coll Harrow Weald Campus
Harrow Weald Cemy
COMMON RD
The Bannister Sports Ctr
UXBRIDGE RD (HARROW WEALD)
UXBRIDGE RD (HATCH END)
A410
A4008
Hatch End
Superstore
Hatch End High Sch
Kingsley High Sch
Recn Gd
Weald Fst & Mid Schs
Playing Field
Shaftesbury High Sch
St Teresa's RC Fst & Mid Sch
Cedars Manor Sch
Harrow Weald
Superstore
HIGH RD
Headstone Lane
HA2
Pinner Park Farm
Sports Gd
HARROW
Coll
Whitefriars Trad Est
Belmont Fst & Mid Schs
A409 HIGH ST

A4140 Stanmore
A410 Stanmore
A404 Harrow
A409 Harrow

13 A B 14 C D 15 E F

A3
1 ASHWOOD HO
2 ROSEMARY CT
3 RANDOLPH CT
4 AVON CT
5 CHERRY CROFT GDNS
6 ALDEN MEAD
7 ELMWOOD

175

E1
1 DAUPHINE CT
2 LAMORNA CT
3 PENGELLY CT
4 LOCKET ROAD MEWS

F3
1 CASTELLANE CL
F4
1 CYGNET HO
2 CORONET HO
3 AMBERDENE
4 SINCLAIR HO
5 ROWAN CL
6 KENNETH GDNS

Index

Place name May be abbreviated on the map
Location number Present when a number indicates the place's position in a crowded area of mapping
Locality, town or village Shown when more than one place has the same name
Postcode district District for the indexed place
Page and grid square Page number and grid reference for the standard mapping

Church Rd 6 Beckenham BR2..........**53** C6

Cities, towns and villages are listed in CAPITAL LETTERS
Public and commercial buildings are highlighted in **magenta** **Places of interest** are highlighted in blue with a star★

Abbreviations used in the index

Acad	**Academy**	Comm	**Common**	Gd	**Ground**	L	**Leisure**	Prom	**Promenade**
App	**Approach**	Cott	**Cottage**	Gdn	**Garden**	La	**Lane**	Rd	**Road**
Arc	**Arcade**	Cres	**Crescent**	Gn	**Green**	Liby	**Library**	Recn	**Recreation**
Ave	**Avenue**	Cswy	**Causeway**	Gr	**Grove**	Mdw	**Meadow**	Ret	**Retail**
Bglw	**Bungalow**	Ct	**Court**	H	**Hall**	Meml	**Memorial**	Sh	**Shopping**
Bldg	**Building**	Ctr	**Centre**	Ho	**House**	Mkt	**Market**	Sq	**Square**
Bsns, Bus	**Business**	Ctry	**Country**	Hospl	**Hospital**	Mus	**Museum**	St	**Street**
Bvd	**Boulevard**	Cty	**County**	HQ	**Headquarters**	Orch	**Orchard**	Sta	**Station**
Cath	**Cathedral**	Dr	**Drive**	Hts	**Heights**	Pal	**Palace**	Terr	**Terrace**
Cir	**Circus**	Dro	**Drove**	Ind	**Industrial**	Par	**Parade**	TH	**Town Hall**
Cl	**Close**	Ed	**Education**	Inst	**Institute**	Pas	**Passage**	Univ	**University**
Cnr	**Corner**	Emb	**Embankment**	Int	**International**	Pk	**Park**	Wk, Wlk	**Walk**
Coll	**College**	Est	**Estate**	Intc	**Interchange**	Pl	**Place**	Wr	**Water**
Com	**Community**	Ex	**Exhibition**	Junc	**Junction**	Prec	**Precinct**	Yd	**Yard**

Index of towns, villages, streets, hospitals, industrial estates, railway stations, schools, shopping centres, universities and places of interest

A

Aashiana Ct WD18 ...... **167** A3
Abbey Ave AL3 .... **127** B1
Abbey CE Prim Sch The AL1 .... **127** D2
Abbey Ct
St Albans AL1 .... **127** D2
Waltham Abbey EN9 ..... **163** B5
Abbey Dr
Abbots Langley WD5 ..... **154** A7
Luton LU2 .... **46** A1
Abbeyfield Ho HA3...... **176** E3
Abbeygate Bsns Ctr The 6 LU2.................... **63** F8
Abbey Mead Ind Est EN9.................. **163** C5
Abbey Mill End AL3 ..... **127** C2
Abbey Mill La AL3....... **127** C2
Abbey Rd EN8 .... **162** E5
Abbey Sta AL1.......... **127** D1
Abbey Theatre AL1...... **127** C1
Abbeyview EN9......... **163** C6
Abbey View
Radlett WD7 .... **155** F4
St Albans AL1 .... **127** D1
Watford WD25.......... **154** D3
Abbey View Rd AL3 ..... **127** C3
Abbis Orch SG5.......... **21** E5
Abbot John Mews 4 AL4.................... **87** D1
Abbots Ave AL1......... **141** E8
Abbots Ave W AL1 ...... **141** D8
Abbotsbury Ct WD25.... **154** B7
Abbots Cl SG3 .... **69** D1
Abbots Ct LU2 .... **46** A1
Abbotsford Lo 1 HA6 .... **174** E5
Abbots Gr SG1........... **50** F5
Abbot's Hill Sch HP3.... **139** B5
ABBOTS LANGLEY **153** F7
Abbots Langley Sch WD5 .... **139** F1
Abbots Pk AL1.......... **128** A1
Abbots Pl WD6 .... **157** B2
Abbots Rd WD5......... **139** E1
Abbots Rise WD4 .... **138** F5
Abbots View WD4....... **138** F4
Abbotswood Par LU2..... **46** A1
Abbots Wood Rd LU2 .... **64** A8
Abbotts Ct SG12 .... **115** D4
Abbottsfield Cotts SG12 .... **94** E5
Abbotts La SG12......... **95** D3
Abbotts Rd SG6.......... **22** D6
Abbotts Rise SG12 ...... **115** D4
Abbotts Way
Bishop's Stortford CM23 .... **76** E3
Stanstead Abbotts SG12................ **115** D4
Wingrave HP22.......... **60** A4
Abbotts Yd 1 SG8 .... **7** D6
Abdale La AL9.......... **144** C4
Abel Cl HP2 .... **125** A3
Abel Smith Sch SG13 ... **113** D6
Abercorn Dell WD23 .... **176** C8
Aberdale Gdns EN6 ..... **158** F7
Aberdeen Rd HA3....... **176** F1
Aberford Rd WD6....... **170** A7
Abigail Cl LU3 .... **45** D3
Abigail Ct LU3 .... **45** D3
Abingdon Lo EN5 .... **171** E5
Abingdon Pl EN6 .... **159** B7
Abingdon Rd LU4 .... **44** C3
Abinger Cl SG1 .... **50** E3
Aboyne Lodge Jun Mix Inf Sch AL3.............. **127** D4
Abraham Cl WD19 ...... **175** B6
Abridge Cl EN8 .... **162** D4
Abridge Ct EN8 .... **162** D4
Abridge Ho EN8 .... **162** D4
Abstacle Hill HP23 .... **99** F3
Acacia Cl
Hammond Street EN7 .... **147** E4
Stanmore HA7.......... **176** E4
Acacia Gr HP4.......... **122** B3
Acacia Rd EN2.......... **161** D1
Acacias Ct 12 EN11..... **135** A6
Acacia St AL10.......... **130** A2
Acacia Wlk
Harpenden AL5 .... **107** D6
Tring HP23.............. **99** E3
Academy Ct AL2 .... **142** B5
Academy Ho 4 WD6.... **170** A5
Academy The 11 LU1..... **63** E6
Acers AL2 .... **141** C3
Achilles Cl HP2 .... **124** F5
Ackroyd Rd SG8 .... **7** E8
Acme Rd WD24 .... **154** B1
Acorn Cl LU2 .... **45** F3
Acorn Ct
Cheshunt EN8 .... **162** D6
London Colney AL2 ...... **142** B4
Acorn Glade AL6......... **89** F4
Acorn La EN6........... **146** E2
Acorn Pl WD24 .... **154** A2
Acorn Rd HP3 .... **125** A2
Acorn St SG12.......... **116** D8
Acorns The
1 Luton LU2............ **45** D1
St Albans AL4 .... **128** D3
Acremore St SG11 .... **75** C7
Acre Piece SG4.......... **35** A6
Acre Way HA6 .... **174** F2
Acre Wood HP2......... **124** E2
Acrewood Way AL4 ..... **128** F3
Acton Cl EN8 .... **162** E8
Acworth Cres LU4 .... **44** C5
Acworth Ct 2 LU4 .... **44** C5
Adamsfield EN7 .... **148** A5
Adams Ho CM20 .... **117** D1
Adams Way HP23 .... **100** B6
Adam's Yd 1 SG14 ..... **113** D6
Adderley Rd
Bishop's Stortford CM23 .... **76** F7
Harrow HA3............ **176** F2
Addington Way LU4...... **44** D3
Addiscombe Rd WD18................. **167** B5
Addison Cl HA6......... **175** A2
Addison Way HA6....... **174** F2
Adelaide Cl EN1 .... **161** F1
Adelaide Ct EN8 .... **162** F5
Adelaide St
Luton LU1 .... **63** D7
St Albans AL3 .... **127** D4
Adele Ave AL6........... **89** F3
ADEYFIELD **125** A3
Adeyfield Gdns HP2..... **124** F4
Adeyfield Rd HP2 .... **124** F3
Adeyfield Sch HP2...... **125** A3
Adhara Rd HA6 .... **175** A5
Adingtons CM20 .... **117** F2
Adlington Ct LU4 .... **44** C4
Admirals Cl AL4 .... **143** E8
Admirals Ct 10 HA6 ..... **174** F5
Admiral St SG13 .... **114** A6
Admirals Wlk
Hoddesdon EN11........ **135** B4
St Albans AL1 .... **142** A8
Admiral Way HP4....... **121** F6
Adrian Cl
Barnet EN5 .... **171** D3
Harefield UB9 .... **173** D2
Adrian Ho WD5 .... **153** E8
Adrian Rd WD5 .... **153** E8
Adstone Rd LU1 .... **62** F3
Ailsworth Rd LU3 .... **45** A7
AIMES GREEN **149** F2
Ainsdale Rd WD19 ...... **175** C7
Ainsland Ct LU4 .... **44** B2
Aintree Rd SG8 .... **7** F6
Aintree Way SG1......... **51** C8
Airedale
Hemel Hempstead HP2................. **124** E6
7 Luton LU4............ **44** C5
Airfield Way WD25...... **153** F5
Airport Approach Rd
Luton LU2 .... **64** D7
Luton LU2 .... **64** D8
Airport Executive Pk LU2.................... **64** D8
Airport Way LU1, LU2..... **64** A5
Aitken Rd EN5.......... **171** C4
Akeman Cl AL3 .... **126** F1
Akeman St HP23........ **100** A3
Akers Ct EN8 .... **162** E7
Akrill Ho AL5 .... **86** A3
Alamein Cl EN10........ **134** E3
Alandale Dr HA5........ **175** B2
Alan Dr EN5 .... **171** E3
Alban Ave AL3.......... **127** D5
Alban Cres WD6 .... **170** B8
Alban Ct
Barnet EN5 .... **171** D5
St Albans AL1 .... **128** C3
Alban Ho WD6.......... **170** B8
Albanian Ct 4 AL1...... **128** A2
Alban Pk Ind Est AL4.... **128** F3
Alban Rd SG6............ **23** C3
Albans View WD25...... **154** B6
Alban Wood Prim Sch WD25 .... **154** B7
Albany Cl WD23......... **168** D3
Albany Ct
Harpenden AL5 .... **107** C8
Luton LU1 .... **63** B8
Albany Mews
Chiswell Green AL2...... **141** A4
3 Ware SG12........... **93** E1
Albany Park Ave EN3.... **162** D1
Albany Pl AL7 .... **110** E6
Albany Rd EN3.......... **162** D1
Albany Sch EN3 .... **162** D1
Albany Terr HP23 .... **100** B6
Alba Rd CM17 .... **118** C1
Albatross Ct SG13....... **114** B7
Albemarle Ave
Cheshunt EN8 .... **148** C3
Potters Bar EN6 .... **159** B7
Albeny Gate AL1........ **127** D2
Albert Ct EN8........... **162** F5
Albert Rd
Arlesey SG15............ **11** A4
Luton LU1 .... **63** E6
Albert Rd N WD17....... **167** B6
Albert Rd S WD17....... **167** B6
Albert St
Markyate AL3 .... **83** E5
St Albans AL1 .... **127** D2
Stevenage SG1 .... **50** D7
Tring HP23............. **100** A3
Albion Cl SG13.......... **113** E7
Albion Ct 4 LU2.......... **63** E8
Albion Hill HP2 .... **124** D2
Albion Rd
Luton LU2 .... **63** E8
Pitstone LU7 .... **80** D5
St Albans AL1 .... **127** F3
Albion The 9 SG12 ...... **93** D2
Albright Ho AL4 .... **128** A7
ALBURY **57** A6
Albury CE Prim Sch SG11.................... **57** A6
Albury Cl LU3............ **31** A1
Albury Dr
Pinner HA5 .... **175** D3
Pinner HA5 .... **175** E3
ALBURY END **56** F4
Albury Grove Rd EN8.... **148** D1
Albury Hall Cotts SG11... **56** F7
Albury Rd SG11.......... **57** C2
Albury Ride EN8 .... **162** D8
Albury Wlk EN8......... **148** C1
Albyn Ho 2 HP2........ **124** D3
Alconbury
Bishop's Stortford CM23 .... **59** B1
Welwyn Garden City AL7.................. **111** E6
Alconbury Cl WD6 ...... **169** F8
Alcorns The CM24 .... **59** E7
ALDBURY **101** C5
Aldbury CE Prim Sch HP23.................. **101** C6
Aldbury Cl
St Albans AL4 .... **128** C8

Aldbury Cl *continued*
Watford WD25 154 D3
Aldbury Gdns HP23 100 B6
Aldbury Gr AL7 111 B6
Aldbury Rd WD3 164 F2
Aldeburgh Cl SG1 36 A1
ALDENHAM 155 B1
Aldenham Ave WD7 156 A3
Aldenham Ctry Pk*
WD6 169 B4
Aldenham Gr WD7 156 B5
Aldenham Rd
Bushey WD23 168 A6
Elstree WD6, WD25 169 B5
Radlett WD7 156 A4
Watford WD23 167 E5
Aldenham Sch WD6 168 F7
Alden Mead 6 HA5 176 A3
Alderbury Rd CM24 59 E8
Alder Cl
Baldock SG7 23 F7
Bishop's Stortford CM23 76 D4
Chiswell Green AL2 141 C3
Hoddesdon EN11 135 B8
Alder Cres LU3 45 A3
Alder Ct LU3 45 B3
Alderley Ct HP4 122 C3
Alderman Cl AL9 144 C7
Alderney Ho
Enfield EN3 162 D1
7 Watford WD18 166 F3
Alders Ct AL7 111 A6
Alders End La AL5 85 F2
Aldersgrove EN9 163 E5
Alders Wlk CM21 97 E2
Alderton Cl 5 LU2 46 D1
Alderton Dr HP4 102 B8
Alder Wlk WD25 154 B4
Alderwood Ho 6
WD19 175 C7
Alderwood Mews
EN4 159 C1
Aldhous Cl LU3 45 B5
Aldis Mews EN3 163 A2
Aldock AL7 111 A3
Aldock Rd SG1 50 E7
Aldridge Ave 7 EN3 163 A1
Aldridge Ct SG7 12 E1
Aldwick AL1 128 B1
Aldwickbury Cres AL5 86 D1
Aldwickbury Sch AL5 107 E8
Aldwick Ct AL1 128 B1
Aldwick Rd AL5 107 E8
Aldwyck Ct HP1 124 C4
Aldwyck Ho 4 LU1 63 D7
Aldwyke Rise SG12 93 C3
Aldykes AL10 129 F5
Alesia Rd LU3 44 F6
Alexander Ct 2 EN8 148 D1
Alexander Gate SG1 51 C8
Alexander Rd
Hertford SG14 113 A6
London Colney AL2 142 D6
Stotfold SG5 11 F6
Alexandra Ave LU3 45 C2
Alexandra Ct
Cheshunt EN8 162 F5
11 Watford WD24 167 C7
Alexandra Mews
WD17 167 A7
Alexandra Rd
Borehamwood WD6 170 D8
Chipperfield WD4 138 A1
Harlow CM17 118 C2
Hemel Hempstead HP2 124 D4
Hitchin SG5 21 F1
Kings Langley WD4 139 B1
Sarratt WD3 152 A3
St Albans AL1 127 E3
Watford WD17 167 A7
Alexandra Way EN8 162 F5
Alex Ct HP2 124 D4
ALEY GREEN 62 E1
Aleyn Way SG7 13 B1
Alfriston Cl LU2 46 C3
Algar Cl HA7 176 F5
Alington La SG6 22 F3
Alison Ct HP2 125 C4
Allandale
Hemel Hempstead
HP2 124 D5
St Albans AL3 141 B8
Allandale Cres EN6 158 E7
Allandale Rd EN3 162 D3
Allard Cl EN7 147 F4
Allard Cres WD23 168 C1
Allard Way EN10 134 E2
Alldicks Rd HP3 124 F1
Allenby Ave LU5 44 A1
Allen Cl
Shenley WD7 156 E7
Wheathampstead AL4 108 D7
Allen Ct 2 AL10 130 B3
Allendale LU3 31 A1
Allen Ho CM21 97 F2
ALLEN'S GREEN 96 F6
Allerton Cl WD6 156 F1
Allerton Rd WD6 156 F1
Alleyns Rd SG1 50 D7
Allied Bsns Ctr AL5 86 C3
Allis Mews 5 CM17 118 C1
Allison SG6 23 C5
All Saints CE Prim Sch
Bishop's Stortford
CM23 77 B8
All Saints CE Prim Sch
continued
Datchworth SG3 69 D3
All Saints Cl CM23 77 A8
All Saints Cres WD25 154 D6
All Saints La WD3 166 A3
All Saints Mews HA3 176 E4
Allton Rd SG16 10 A4
Allum La WD6 169 E5
Allwood Rd EN7 147 F4
Alma Ct
Borehamwood WD6 156 F1
Potters Bar EN6 145 C1
Alma Cut AL1 127 E2
Alma Link 3 LU1 63 D7
Alma Rd
Berkhamsted HP4 121 E6
St Albans AL1 127 E2
Alma Row HA3 176 D2
Alma St LU1 63 D7
Almond Cl LU3 45 B4
Almond Hill Jun Sch
SG1 50 E8
Almonds La SG1 50 E8
Almonds The AL1 142 B7
Almond Way
Borehamwood WD6 170 B5
Harrow HA2 176 C1
Almond Wlk 1 AL10 130 A2
Almshoebury Cotts
SG4 49 D8
Almshouse La EN1 162 B2
Almshouses
Radlett WD25 168 C8
Stevenage SG1 50 C7
Alms La SG7 4 D4
Alnwick Dr HP23 78 F7
Alpha Bsns Pk AL9 144 C8
Alpha Ct 8 WD17 167 C6
Alpha Pl 4 CM23 76 F8
Alpine Cl SG4 35 A5
Alpine Terr 16 LU1 63 D6
Alpine Way LU3 44 D8
Alpine Wlk HA7 176 E8
Alsford Wharf 1 HP4 122 C4
Alsop Cl AL2 142 E3
Alston Ct 2 EN5 171 E6
Alston Rd
Barnet EN5 171 E6
Hemel Hempstead HP1 124 A2
Alswick Hall Cotts SG9 41 B8
Altair Way HA6 174 F5
Altham Gdns WD19 175 D6
Altham Gr CM20 117 F3
Altham Rd HA5 175 E3
Althorp Cl EN5 171 A2
Althorp Rd
Luton LU3 45 C1
St Albans AL1 127 F4
Alton Ave HA7 176 F3
Alton Gdns LU1 63 F5
Alton Rd LU1 63 F5
Altwood AL5 86 D1
Alva Way WD19 175 D8
Alverton AL3 127 C6
Alwin Pl WD18 166 E5
Alwyn Cl
Borehamwood WD6 169 F3
Luton LU2 45 E2
Alyngton HP4 121 E7
Alzey Gdns AL5 107 D8
Amberdene 3 HA7 176 F4
Amberley Cl
Harpenden AL5 86 B2
Luton LU2 46 D4
Amberley Gn SG12 93 C4
Amberry Ct CM20 117 D1
Amberside Ct HP3 138 B8
Ambient Ho EN3 162 F3
Ambleside
Harpenden AL5 86 D2
Luton LU3 44 F5
Ambrose La AL5 85 F4
Amenbury Ct 7 AL5 86 A1
Amenbury La AL5 86 A1
Amersham Ho WD18 166 E2
Amersham Rd WD3 164 B8
Ames Cl
Luton LU3 31 A1
Luton LU3 44 F8
Amethyst Wlk AL8 110 B4
Amherst Lo 6 CM20 117 C1
Amhurst Cl EN3 162 D2
Amor Way SG6 23 B6
AMWELL 115 A6
Amwell Cl WD25 154 E4
Amwell Comm AL7 111 C5
Amwell Ct
Hoddesdon EN11 135 A7
Waltham Abbey EN9 163 E6
Amwell End SG12 93 D1
Amwell Hill SG12 114 F6
Amwell La
Stanstead Abbotts
SG12 115 B5
Wheathampstead AL4 108 B7
Amwell Pl SG13 114 C4
Amwell St EN11 135 A7
Amwell View Sch
SG12 115 B4
Anchor Cl EN8 148 D3
Anchor Cotts SG12 93 D7
Anchor La
Hemel Hempstead
HP1 124 B1
Hemel Hempstead HP1 124 C2
Tonwell SG12 93 B6
Anchor Rd SG7 23 F7
Anchor St CM23 77 A6
Ancient Almhos 4
EN8 148 D1
Anderson Cl UB9 173 A2
Anderson Ho AL4 128 D2
Anderson Rd
Shenley WD7 157 A6
Stevenage SG2 51 D6
Anderson's Ho 3 SG5 34 F8
Anderson's La SG9 29 A1
Andover Cl LU4 44 C6
Andrew Cl WD7 156 F6
Andrew Reed Ct 10
WD24 167 C7
Andrews Cl HP2 124 D5
Andrewsfield AL7 111 C6
Andrew's La
Cheshunt EN7 148 B3
Goff's Oak EN7 147 F3
Andrews Lane Prim Sch
EN7 148 B3
Anelle Rise HP3 138 F7
Anershall HP22 60 B3
Angel Cl LU4 44 D3
Angel Cotts SG5 33 D2
Angell's Mdw SG7 4 D4
Angel Pavement 7 SG8 7 D6
Anglefield Rd HP4 122 A4
Anglesey Cl CM23 76 C7
Anglesey Rd WD19 175 C5
Angle The 5 CM20 117 C1
Angle Ways SG2 51 B1
Anglian Bsns Pk SG8 7 C7
Anglian Cl WD24 167 C7
Angotts Mead SG1 50 B6
Angus Cl LU4 44 A3
Anmer Gdns LU4 44 B4
Annables Ct 8 AL1 127 E3
Annables La AL5 85 A4
Annette Cl HA3 176 E1
Anns Cl HP23 99 E3
Ansell Ct SG1 36 B1
ANSELLS END 65 F2
Anselm Rd HA5 175 F3
Anson Cl
Bovingdon HP3 136 F4
Sandridge AL4 108 C1
St Albans AL1 128 B1
Anson Wlk HA6 174 C6
Anstee Rd LU4 44 B6
ANSTEY 29 B6
Anstey Fst Sch SG9 29 A6
Anthony Cl WD19 167 D1
Anthony Gdns LU1 63 D6
Anthony Rd WD6 169 F7
Anthorne Cl EN6 159 B8
Anthus Mews HA6 174 E3
Antoinette Ct WD5 139 F2
Antoneys Cl HA5 175 D1
Antonine Gate AL3 127 A2
Anvil Cl HP3 137 B3
Anvil Ct
Buntingford SG9 40 E8
Luton LU3 44 E5
Anvil Ho 8 AL5 86 A2
Apex Point AL9 130 C1
Aplins Cl AL5 86 A2
Apollo Ave HA6 175 A5
Apollo Way
Hemel Hempstead
HP2 124 F5
Stevenage SG2 51 C8
Appleby St EN7 147 E5
Apple Cotts HP3 137 A4
Applecroft
Berkhamsted HP4 121 E6
Chiswell Green AL2 141 B3
Lower Stondon SG16 10 B3
Applecroft Rd
Luton LU2 46 C4
Welwyn Garden City
AL8 110 B6
Applecroft Sch AL8 110 B5
Appleford's Cl EN11 134 F8
Apple Orch The HP2 124 F5
Appleton Ave SG12 94 E5
Appleton Fields CM23 76 E4
Appletree Gr AL3 106 B6
Appletrees SG5 34 D6
Appletree Wlk WD25 154 B4
Applewood Cl AL5 85 E3
Appleyard Terr EN3 162 C2
Approach Rd AL1 127 E2
Approach The EN6 158 F7
Appspond La AL2 140 C8
April Pl CM21 97 F3
APSLEY 138 D7
Apsley Cl CM23 76 F4
APSLEY END 19 E7
Apsley End Rd SG5 19 E6
Apsley Grange HP3 138 E6
Apsley Ind Est HP3 138 D7
Apsley Manor Farm Barns
HP3 138 D5
Apsley Mills Ret Pk
HP3 138 E7
Apsley Sta HP3 138 E6
Apton Ct CM23 76 F7
Apton Fields 7 CM23 76 F6
Apton Rd CM23 76 F7
Aquarius Way HA6 175 A6
Aragon Cl
Enfield EN2 160 F1
Hemel Hempstead HP2 125 C8
Aran Cl AL5 107 D6
Arbour Cl LU3 31 A1
Arbour The SG13 113 D4
Arbroath Gn WD19 175 B7
Arcade 5 SG5 34 E7
Arcade The
Hatfield AL10 130 B6
Letchworth Garden City
SG6 22 F6
Luton LU4 45 C1
Arcade Wlk 4 SG5 34 E7
Arcadian Ct AL5 86 A2
Archer Cl WD4 138 F2
Archer Rd SG1 51 A6
Archers SG9 40 F8
Archers Cl
Hertford SG14 113 C7
Redbourn AL3 106 B5
Archers Fields AL1 127 F5
Archers Green La
AL6 111 E8
Archers Ride AL7 111 B4
Archers Way SG6 22 D6
Arches Hall Cotts SG11 73 E5
Archfield AL7 89 E1
Archibald Cl EN3 162 D3
Arch Rd SG4 35 E4
Archway Ho AL9 130 C6
Archway Par LU3 44 F4
Archway Rd LU3 44 E4
Arckle Ho 2 EN10 148 F5
ARDELEY 38 F3
Ardeley St Lawrence CE
Prim Sch SG2 38 F3
Arden Cl
Bovingdon HP3 137 A3
Bushey WD23 168 F2
Arden Ct WD3 173 A8
Arden Gr AL5 86 B1
Arden Pl LU2 45 E1
Arden Press Way SG6 23 B6
Ardens Way AL4 128 D6
Ardentinny 10 AL1 127 E2
Ardleigh Gn LU2 46 E1
Ardross Ave HA6 174 E5
Arena Par SG6 22 F6
Arena The EN3 162 F1
Arena The WD25 154 D5
Argent Ho HA5 175 F4
Argent Way EN7 147 D5
Argyle Ct WD18 166 F5
Argyle Rd EN5 171 C5
Argyle Way SG1 50 C5
Argyle Way Trad Est
SG1 50 C5
Argyll Ave LU3 45 C2
Argyll Rd HP2 124 E8
Arkhill Ct EN3 162 E2
ARKLEY 171 A4
Arkley Ct HP2 125 B8
Arkley Dr EN5 171 B4
Arkley La EN5 171 B5
Arkley Pk Cvn Pk
EN5 170 D3
Arkley Rd HP2 125 B8
Arkley View EN5 171 B5
Arklow Ct WD3 164 D5
Arkwrights CM20 117 F1
ARLESEY 11 A4
Arlesey Ho SG15 11 A8
Arlesey New Rd SG15, SG5,
SG6 22 B7
Arlesey Rd
Henlow SG16 10 D8
Henlow SG16 10 E8
Ickleford SG5 21 F5
Stotfold SG5 11 E6
Arlesey Sta SG15 11 A8
Arlingham Cotts EN6 158 A7
Arlingham Mews EN9 163 C6
Arlington Bsns Pk SG1 50 D2
Arlington Cres EN8 162 E5
Arlington Ct SG1 50 D2
Armand Cl WD17 153 F1
Armitage Cl WD3 165 D5
Armitage Gdns LU4 44 D1
Armourers Cl CM23 76 B4
Armour Rise SG4 22 B2
Armstrong Cl
Borehamwood WD6 170 C6
London Colney AL2 142 E4
Armstrong Gdns WD7 156 E7
Armstrong Pl 1 HP1 124 D4
Arncliffe Cres LU2 45 E1
Arndale Ct LU2 63 F8
Arndale Ctr LU1 63 E7
Arnett Cl WD3 165 A3
Arnett Hills Jun Mix Inf
Sch WD3 165 A3
Arnett Way WD3 165 A2
Arnold Ave E EN3 163 A1
Arnold Ave W EN3 162 F1
Arnold Cl
Hitchin SG4 35 B8
Luton LU2 46 A3
Stevenage SG1 36 D2
Arnold Rd EN9 163 C4
Arnolds La SG7 3 D6
Arran Cl HP3 125 C1
Arran Ct LU1 63 D7
Arran Ho 15 WD18 166 F3
Arranmore Ct WD23 167 E5
Arretine Cl AL3 126 F1
Arrewig La HP5, HP23 119 D1
Arrow Cl LU3 44 E6
Arthur Gibbens Ct SG1 37 A1
Arthur Rd AL1 128 B3
Arthur St
Luton LU1 63 E6
Watford WD23 167 D5
Artichoke Dell WD3 164 E4
Artillery Pl HA3 176 C3
Artisan Cres AL3 127 C4
Art School Yd 10 AL1 127 D3
Arts Educational Sch
HP23 100 B3
Arundel Cl
Aston SG2 51 E3
Cheshunt EN8 148 C3
Hemel Hempstead HP2 125 B4
Arundel Dr WD6 170 C5
Arundel Gr AL3 127 D7
Arundel Ho WD6 170 C5
Arundell Rd WD5 154 A7
Arundel Rd LU4 44 F2
Arwood Mews SG7 23 F7
Ascent Pk CM20 118 B5
Ascot Cl
Bishop's Stortford
CM23 77 C8
Borehamwood WD6 170 A4
Ascot Cres SG1 37 B1
Ascot Ct WD3 166 B3
Ascot Gdns EN3 162 C2
Ascot Ind Est SG6 23 B7
Ascot Rd
Luton LU3 45 B2
Royston SG8 7 F6
Watford WD18 166 E4
Ascots La AL7 110 F2
Ascot Terr SG12 114 F7
Ashanger La SG7 24 D4
Ashbourne Cl SG6 23 B3
Ashbourne Ct AL4 142 C8
Ashbourne Gdns
SG13 113 E5
Ashbourne Rd EN10 134 F2
Ashbourne Sq HA6 174 E4
Ashbrook La SG4 35 B3
Ashburnam Wlk SG2 50 F1
Ashburnham Cl
WD19 175 A7
Ashburnham Dr
WD19 175 A7
Ashburnham Rd LU1 63 C7
Ashbury Cl AL10 129 E5
Ashby Ct HP2 105 B1
Ashby Gdns AL1 141 D7
Ashby Rd
Berkhamsted HP4 121 D7
Watford WD24 154 A1
Ashby Rise CM23 59 B1
Ash Cl
Abbots Langley WD5 153 D7
Brookmans Park AL9 145 A6
Harefield UB9 173 D2
Harrow HA7 176 F4
Watford WD25 154 B4
Ashcombe AL8 89 E2
Ash Copse AL2 154 F8
Ashcroft HA5 176 A4
Ashcroft Cl AL5 107 E8
Ashcroft Ct EN10 134 F1
Ashcroft High Sch LU2 46 C2
Ashcroft Rd LU2 46 B3
Ashdale CM23 76 D4
Ashdale Gdns LU3 31 A1
Ashdale Gr HA7 176 F4
Ashdales AL1 141 D7
Ashdon Ho EN5 171 F6
Ashdown SG6 11 F1
Ashdown Cres EN8 148 E3
Ashdown Dr WD6 169 F7
Ashdown Rd
Stevenage SG2 69 B8
Watford WD23 167 D6
Ash Dr
Hatfield AL10 130 A2
Hitchin SG4 35 A4
Ashendene Rd SG13 132 F4
Ashfield Ave WD23 168 C2
Ashfield Jun Sch
WD23 168 B2
Ashfields WD24, WD25 153 F4
Ashfield Way LU3 45 A6
Ashford Gn WD19 175 D5
Ashfords SG9 40 E8
Ash Gr
Harefield UB9 173 D2
Hemel Hempstead HP3 138 F7
Wheathampstead AL4 87 C1
Ash Groves CM21 98 A2
Ash Hill Cl WD23 168 B1
Ashleigh SG2 51 B4
Ashleigh Ct
Hoddesdon EN11 135 A5
2 Rickmansworth
WD3 165 D2
6 Watford WD17 167 C6
Ashleigh Cvn Pk SG11 73 C3
Ashley Cl
Cheddington LU7 80 A8
Hemel Hempstead HP3 124 F1
Pinner HA5 175 B1
Welwyn Garden City
AL8 110 C8
Ashley Ct AL10 130 B6
Ashley Dr WD6 170 D4
Ashley Gdns AL5 85 D3
ASHLEY GREEN 136 A7
Ashley Ho WD18 166 E2
Ashley Rd
Hertford SG14 113 B5
St Albans AL1 128 C2
Ashleys WD3 164 F2
Ashlyn Cl WD23 167 E5
Ashlyns Ct HP4 122 B3
Ashlyns Rd HP4 122 B3
Ashlyns Sch HP4 122 C2
Ash Mdw SG10 74 F2

Ash Mill SG8 17 C3
Ashmore Gdns HP3 125 B2
Ashok Ho AL1 142 A8
Ash Rd
  Luton LU4 63 B8
  Tring HP23 99 F4
  Ware SG12 94 A3
Ash Ride EN2 161 A4
Ashridge Bsns Sch
  HP4 102 C5
Ashridge Cl HP3 137 A3
Ashridge Cotts HP4 102 E5
Ashridge Dr
  Bricket Wood AL2 140 F1
  South Oxhey WD19 175 C5
Ashridge Estate Visitor
  Ctr* HP4 101 E6
Ashridge Gdns* HP4 102 D5
Ashridge Ho WD18 166 E2
Ashridge La HP5 150 D7
Ashridge Rise HP4 121 F5
Ash Shams Sch LU1 63 D6
Ashton Rd
  Enfield EN3 162 E3
  Luton LU1 63 E5
Ashton's La SG7 23 F6
Ashtree Ct AL1 127 F3
Ash Tree Field CM20 117 A2
Ashtree Prim Sch SG2 51 C4
Ash Tree Rd WD24 154 B3
Ashtree Way HP1 124 A2
Ashurst Cl HA6 174 E3
Ash Vale WD3 172 D5
Ashville Trad Est SG7 12 F1
Ashville Way SG7 13 A1
Ash Way SG8 7 F6
ASHWELL 4 D3
Ashwell SG1 36 C2
Ashwell Ave LU3 44 C8
Ashwell Cl SG4 36 B4
Ashwell Comm SG4 36 B4
ASHWELL END 4 A5
Ashwell & Morden Sta
  SG7 5 D2
Ashwell Par LU3 44 C8
Ashwell Pk AL5 86 D1
Ashwell Pl WD24 154 A2
Ashwell Prim Sch SG7 4 D4
Ashwell Rd
  Bygrave SG7 13 C4
  Guilden Morden SG8 1 F1
  Hinxworth SG7 3 E5
  Newnham SG7 12 F8
Ashwell St
  Ashwell SG7 4 D4
  Kneesworth SG8 2 A3
  St Albans AL3 127 D4
Ashwell Village Mus*
  SG7 4 D4
Ashwood Ho 1 HA5 176 A3
Ashwood Mews AL1 127 D1
Ashwood Pl SG4 35 A5
Ashwood Rd EN6 159 B6
Askew Rd HA6 174 D8
Aspasia Cl AL1 127 F2
Aspen Cl
  Bricket Wood AL2 140 E1
  Stevenage SG2 69 B7
ASPENDEN 40 D5
Aspenden Ho SG9 40 D5
Aspenden Rd SG9 40 E6
Aspen Park Dr WD25 154 B4
Aspens Pl HP3 137 F8
Aspens The
  Bishop's Stortford
    CM23 59 B3
  Hitchin SG4 35 A6
Aspen Way
  Enfield EN3 162 D4
  Welwyn Garden City
    AL7 111 C5
Aspfield Row HP1 124 B5
Asquith Ct SG2 69 C7
Asquith Ho AL8 110 D7
Ass House La HA3 176 B6
Astall Cl HA3 176 E2
Aster Cl CM23 76 D6
Asters The EN7 147 D3
Astley Cooper Sch The
  HP2 125 A8
Astley Gn LU2 46 D2
Astley Rd HP1 124 C3
ASTON 51 E2
Aston Bury SG2 69 F8
Aston Cl
  Bushey WD23 168 C3
  Stevenage SG1 36 C2
  Watford WD24 167 C7
ASTON CLINTON 99 A3
ASTON END 51 E5
Aston End Rd SG2 51 E3
Aston Grange SG14 113 D8
Astonia Ho SG7 23 F7
Aston La SG2 69 E8
Aston Rd SG11 55 D2
Aston Rise SG4 35 B6
Aston St Mary's CE Prim
  Sch SG2 51 E2
Astons Rd HA6 174 C6
Aston View HP2 105 A1
Aston Way EN6 159 D7
Astra Ct
  Luton LU2 45 F2
  Watford WD18 166 F4
Astra Ctr CM20 117 F4
Astral Cl SG16 10 B3
ASTROPE 79 A3
Astrope La HP23 79 B3
Astwick Ave AL10 129 F8
Astwick Manor AL10 129 C8
Astwick Rd
  Stotfold SG5 3 A2
  Stotfold SG5 11 F8
Athelstan Rd HP3 138 F8
Athelstan Wlk N AL7 110 E5
Athelstan Wlk S AL7 110 D5
Athelstone Rd HA3 176 D1
Athena Est CM20 118 B4
Athena Pl HA6 174 F2
Athenia Cl EN7 147 B2
Atherstone Rd LU4 44 D1
Atherton End CM21 97 E3
Athlone Cl WD7 156 B3
Athol Cl HA5 175 B2
Athol Gdns HA5 175 B2
Atholl Cl LU3 44 D8
Atlantic Bsns Ctr
  WD6 170 D4
Atlantic Lo 2 SG4 35 A8
Atria Rd HA6 175 A5
Attenborough Cl
  WD19 175 E7
Attimore Cl AL8 110 B5
Attimore Rd AL8 110 B5
Auber Cl EN11 114 F1
Aubretia Ho AL7 111 B4
Aubrey Ave AL2 142 C5
Aubrey Gdns LU4 44 B6
Aubrey La AL3 105 E2
Aubreys SG6 23 A2
Aubreys Rd HP1 123 E3
Aubries SG2 38 B1
Auckland Cl EN1 162 B2
Auckland Rd EN6 158 E7
Auction House Ctyd 10
  LU1 63 E7
Auden Dr WD6 170 A4
Audley Cl WD6 170 A6
Audley Ct HA5 175 C1
Audley Gdns EN9 163 C5
Audrey Gdns CM23 76 F4
Audwick Cl EN8 148 E3
Augustine Ct EN9 163 B6
Augustine Rd HA3 176 C2
Augustus Cl AL3 127 A1
Augustus Gate SG2 51 D8
Augustus Smith Ho 8
  HP4 122 D4
Austen Paths SG2 51 C6
Austin Mews 6 HP1 124 D4
Austin Rd LU3 45 C4
Austins Mead HP3 137 B3
Austins Pl HP2 124 D4
Austin Villas WD25 154 B8
Autumn Glades HP3 125 C1
Autumn Gr AL7 111 B4
Avalon Cl WD25 154 E7
Avalon Ct WD23 168 A7
Avebury Ave LU2 45 D4
Avebury Ct HP2 125 A5
Aventine Ct AL1 127 D2
Avenue App WD4 139 A1
Avenue Ct AL6 89 E7
Avenue Grimaldi LU3 45 A3
Avenue Mans 9 EN5 171 F5
Avenue One SG6 23 C6
Avenue Rd
  Bishop's Stortford
    CM23 77 B6
  Hoddesdon EN11 135 D5
  Pinner HA5 175 E1
  St Albans AL1 127 E4
Avenue Rise WD23 168 A4
Avenue St Nicholas
  AL5 86 A1
Avenue Terr WD19 167 E3
Avenue The
  Barnet EN5 171 E6
  Bushey WD23 167 F5
  Harrow HA3 176 F2
  Hemel Hempstead HP1 123 E4
  Hertford SG14 113 B8
  Hitchin SG4 35 A7
  Hoddesdon EN11 135 A4
  Luton LU4 44 D5
  Northwood HA6 174 C4
  Oaklands AL6 89 D7
  Pinner HA5 175 F4
  Potters Bar EN6 145 A1
  Radlett WD7 156 B5
  Stevenage SG1 50 D8
  Stotfold SG5 11 F6
  Watford WD17 167 A7
Avey La EN9 163 E2
Avia Cl HP3 138 D7
Avior Dr HA6 174 F6
Avocet SG6 11 E1
Avocet Cl AL3 127 C6
Avon Chase SG16 10 C4
Avon Cl WD25 154 C5
Avon Cotts LU2 46 B3
Avon Ct
  17 Harpenden AL5 86 B1
  Luton LU1 63 C8
  4 Pinner HA5 176 A3
Avondale Ct AL1 127 E3
Avondale Rd LU1 63 C8
Avon Dr SG1 37 A3
Avon Mews HA5 175 F2
Avon Rd SG16 10 B4
Avon Sq HP2 124 F8
Axe Cl LU3 44 E6
Aycliffe Dr HP2 124 E7
Aycliffe Drive Prim Sch
  HP2 124 E7
Aycliffe Rd WD6 156 F1
Aydon Rd LU3 45 B6
Aylands Rd EN3 162 D3
Aylands Sch EN3 162 C3
Aylesbury Rd HP23 99 E3
Aylott Ct SG14 70 D4
Aylotts Cl SG9 40 D8
Aylsham Rd EN11 135 C8
Aylward Dr SG2 51 B4
Aynho St WD18 167 B4
Aynsworth Ave CM23 59 B2
Ayot Gn
  Ayot St P AL6 89 A1
  Hatfield AL6 109 F8
  Welwyn Garden City
    AL6 109 F8
AYOT GREEN 89 A1
Ayot Ho AL6 88 A6
Ayot Little Green La
  AL6 88 F1
Ayot Path WD6 157 A1
AYOT ST LAWRENCE 88 B6
AYOT ST PETER 88 F3
Ayot St Peter Rd AL6 88 E3
Ayr Cl SG1 51 C8
AYRES END 107 E5
Ayres End La AL3, AL5 107 E5
Aysgarth Cl AL5 107 B8
Aysgarth Rd AL3 106 A6
Azalea Cl AL2 142 B4
Azure Appartments
  HA3 176 E2

B

Baas Hill EN10 134 D2
Baas Hill Cl EN10 134 E2
Baas La EN10 134 E3
Babbage Rd SG1 50 B5
BABBS GREEN 94 E5
Back La
  Buckland SG9 27 D8
  Little Hallingbury CM22 98 B7
  Preston SG4 48 D6
  Radlett WD25 168 E8
  Sheering CM22 98 B1
  Tewin AL6 90 E2
Back St
  Ashwell SG7 4 C3
  Luton LU2 63 E8
Back The HP4 123 B7
Bacons Dr EN6 146 E2
Bacon's Yd SG7 4 D4
Badburgham Ct EN9 163 F6
Baddeley Cl
  Holdbrook EN3 163 A2
  Stevenage SG2 51 B2
Bader Cl
  Stevenage SG1 36 F1
  Welwyn Garden City
    AL7 111 C6
Badger Cl SG3 69 A6
Badgers CM23 76 E5
Badgers Cl
  Borehamwood WD6 169 F7
  Hertford SG13 114 B6
  Stevenage SG1 50 E4
Badgers Croft
  Hemel Hempstead
    HP2 125 D2
  Hoddesdon EN10 134 E2
  Totteridge N20 171 E1
Badgers Ct WD25 154 A5
Badgers Wlk
  Burnham Green AL6 90 C5
  Chorleywood WD3 164 F5
Badger Way AL10 130 B3
Badingham Dr AL5 85 E1
Badminton Cl
  3 Borehamwood
    WD6 170 A7
  Stevenage SG2 69 B7
Badminton Ho 8
  WD24 167 C7
Badminton Pl EN10 134 E3
Bagenal Ho WD5 153 F7
Bagwicks Cl LU3 44 E7
Bailey Hill Ct 1 LU1 63 E5
Baileys Mews HP1 124 D4
Bailey St LU1 63 F6
Baines La SG3 69 C4
Baird Cl WD23 168 B3
Bairstow Cl WD6 169 E8
Baisley Ho EN7 148 A3
Bakehouse Ct SG9 40 E8
Baker Ct WD6 170 B7
Bakerscroft 1 EN8 148 E3
Bakers Ct 6 CM23 77 A7
BAKER'S END 94 E7
Bakers Gr AL7 111 C7
Bakers La
  Barley SG8 8 F2
  Kensworth Common LU6 82 E8
Baker's La SG4 67 F1
Bakers Rd EN7 148 B1
Baker St
  Enfield EN1 161 E1
  Hertford SG13 113 E6
  Luton LU1 63 E5
  Potters Bar EN6 158 E5
  2 Stevenage SG1 50 C7
Bakers Wlk CM21 97 E2
Bakery Ct CM24 59 D6
Bakery The 2 SG12 93 D2
Bakewell Cl LU4 44 C1
Balcary Gdns HP4 121 F4
Balcombe Cl LU2 46 D4
Balcon Way WD6 170 C8
BALDOCK 23 E8
Baldock Ind Est SG7 23 F7
Baldock La SG6 23 D4
Baldock Rd
  Aspenden SG9 40 B8
  Letchworth Garden City
    SG6 23 B5
  Royston SG8 6 C4
  Stotfold SG5 12 A5
Baldock St
  Royston SG8 7 C6
  Ware SG12 93 D2
Baldock Sta SG7 12 F1
Baldock Way WD6 169 F8
Baldways Cl HP22 60 C3
Baldwins AL7 111 C6
Baldwins La WD3 166 B5
Balfour Ct AL5 86 C3
Balfour Mews HP3 137 A4
Balfour St SG14 113 C7
Baliol Rd SG5 34 F8
Ballater Cl WD19 175 C6
BALLINGDON BOTTOM
  82 F1
Ballinger Ct
  Berkhamsted HP4 122 B3
  1 Watford WD18 167 B6
Balloon Cnr AL9 144 B8
Ballslough Hill SG4 66 D1
Balmoral Cl
  Chiswell Green AL2 141 C3
  Stevenage SG2 69 C7
Balmoral Dr WD6 170 D5
Balmoral Ho WD6 170 C5
Balmoral Rd
  Abbots Langley WD5 154 A7
  Enfield EN3 162 D3
  Hitchin SG5 21 E1
  Watford WD24 154 C1
Balmore Wood LU3 31 B1
Balsams Cl SG13 113 D4
Bampton Rd LU4 44 B2
Bamville Wood AL5 107 C5
Banbury Cl LU4 44 F4
Banbury St WD18 167 B4
Bancroft SG5 34 F7
Bancroft Gdns HA3 176 C2
Bancroft Rd
  Harrow HA3 176 C1
  Luton LU3 45 B5
Bandley Rise SG2 51 C3
Banes Down EN9 135 E1
Bank Cl LU4 44 C4
Bank Ct HP1 124 C2
Bank Mill HP4 122 E4
Bank Mill La HP4 122 E3
Bankside Cl UB9 173 A4
Bankside Down WD3 165 D3
Banks Rd WD6 170 C7
Bannister Gdns SG8 7 E8
Bantel Villas EN11 135 C8
Barbel Cl EN8 163 A5
Barberry Rd HP1 124 A3
Barbers La 2 LU1 63 E7
Barbers Wlk HP23 99 F3
Barchester Rd HA3 176 D1
Barclay Cl
  Hertford Heath SG13 114 B4
  Watford WD18 167 A3
Barclay Cres SG1 50 E7
Barclay Ct
  Hoddesdon EN11 135 A5
  Luton LU2 63 F8
Barclay Sch SG1 50 D8
Barden Cl UB9 173 C3
Bards Cnr HP1 124 B4
Bardwell Ct 6 AL1 127 D2
Bardwell Rd AL1 127 D2
Barfolds AL9 144 C8
Barford Rise LU2 46 D1
Barge Ho HP3 138 E7
Bargrove Ave HP1 124 A2
Barham Ave WD6 169 F5
Barham Rd SG2 51 C5
Barker Cl HA6 174 F3
Barkers Mead CM22 77 B1
Barkham Cl LU7 79 F7
Barking Cl LU4 44 B6
Barkston Path WD6 157 A1
BARKWAY 17 D4
Barkway CE Fst Sch
  SG8 17 C4
Barkway Hill SG8 17 E6
Barkway Rd SG8 7 E5
Barkway St SG8 7 D5
BARLEY 8 F1
Barley Brow WD25 154 C8
Barley CE Fst Sch SG8 9 A1
Barley Cl WD23 168 B4
Barleycorn The 1 LU3 63 D8
Barleycroft
  Buntingford SG9 40 E6
  Stevenage SG2 51 D3
  Tonwell SG12 92 F7
Barley Croft
  Hemel Hempstead
    HP2 125 C3
  Hertford SG14 113 D8
  Stapleford SG14 92 A3
BARLEYCROFT END 43 B4
Barleycroft Gn AL8 110 C6
Barleycroft Rd AL8 110 C5
Barley Ct
  Cheshunt EN7 148 B1
  2 Hoddesdon EN11 135 D8
Barley Hills CM23 76 E4
Barley La LU4 44 C5
Barley Mow Cvn Site The
  AL4 128 F1
Barley Mow La AL4 142 F8
Barley Ponds Cl SG12 93 F1
Barley Ponds Rd SG12 93 F1
Barley Rd
  Barley SG8 9 A7
  Great Chishill SG8 9 C2
Barley Rise
  Baldock SG7 24 B8
  Harpenden AL5 86 C4
Barleyvale LU3 45 A8
Barlings Rd AL5 107 B5
Barlow Cl AL10 129 D7
Barmor Cl HA2 176 B1
Barmouth Row 6
  HP2 124 E6
Barnack Gr SG8 7 C7
Barnacres Rd HP3 139 A8
Barnard Acres EN9 149 E8
Barnard Gn AL7 110 F5
Barnard Rd
  Luton LU1 63 A7
  Sawbridgeworth CM21 97 E4
Barnard Way HP3 124 E1
Barn Cl
  Hemel Hempstead
    HP3 138 F8
  Radlett WD7 156 A4
  Welwyn Garden City
    AL8 110 C6
Barncroft SG11 57 C7
Barncroft Prim Sch
  HP2 124 D8
Barncroft Rd HP4 121 F3
Barncroft Way AL1 128 A2
Barn Ct
  Luton LU1 63 E7
  Sawbridgeworth CM21 97 E3
Barndell Cl SG5 11 F6
Barndicott AL7 111 C6
Barndicott Ho AL7 111 C6
Barnes La WD4 138 D3
Barnes Rise WD4 138 F4
BARNET 171 F4
Barnet By-Pass
  Borehamwood WD6 170 E5
  Dancers Hill EN5 158 A3
Barnet Coll EN5 171 F5
BARNET GATE 170 F3
Barnet Gate La EN5 170 F3
Barnet Hill EN5 171 F5
Barnet Hill Jun Mix Inf
  Sch EN5 171 F4
Barnet Hospl EN5 171 D5
Barnet La
  Borehamwood WD6 170 B3
  Totteridge EN5, N20 171 F2
Barnet Mus* EN5 171 E5
Barnet Rd
  Barnet EN5 170 E3
  Ganwick Corner EN6,
    EN5 159 A4
  London Colney AL2 142 F4
Barnet Stall Market
  EN5 171 E6
Barnett Ho HP4 121 E7
Barnet Trad Est EN5 171 F6
Barnet Way (Barnet By-
  Pass) NW7 170 D2
Barnet Wood Nature
  Trail* EN5 170 F2
Barnfield HP3 138 F8
Barnfield Ave LU2 45 D5
Barnfield Cl
  Hoddesdon EN11 135 A8
  Lower Nazeing EN9 135 F1
Barnfield Coll (New
  Bedford Rd Campus)
  LU2 45 D5
Barnfield Coll (Rotherham
  Avenue Campus) LU1 63 B5
Barnfield Coll (York Street
  Campus) LU2 63 F8
Barnfield Ct AL5 107 C8
Barnfield Rd
  Harpenden AL5 107 C8
  St Albans AL4 128 C5
  Welwyn Garden City
    AL7 110 E4
Barnfield South Acad
  LU1 63 F5
Barnfield Tech Coll
  LU3 45 B8
Barnfield West Acad
  LU4 44 A3
Barnhurst Path WD19 175 C5
Barn Lea WD3 165 A1
Barnsdale Cl WD6 169 F8
Barns Dene AL5 85 E2
Barnside Ct AL8 110 C6
Barns The HP23 99 F1
Barnston Cl LU2 46 D1
Barnsway WD4 138 E3
Barn The
  Stevenage SG1 50 C6
  9 Wheathampstead
    AL4 87 D1
Barnview Lo HA3 176 E2
Barnwell SG2 51 B2
Barnwell Sch East Campus
  SG2 51 C4
Barnwell Sch West
  Campus SG2 51 B2
Barnwood Cl N20 171 F1

Baron Ct SG1 . . . 36 B1
Barons Ct [10] LU2 . . . 45 D1
Baronsmere Ct [9]
EN5 . . . 171 E5
Barons The CM23 . . . 76 D5
Barra Cl HP3 . . . 139 C8
Barra Ho [6] WD18 . . . 166 F3
Barrass Cl EN3 . . . 163 A2
Barratt Ind Pk LU2 . . . 64 C6
Barratt Way HA3 . . . 176 D1
Barrells Down Rd
CM23 . . . 58 E1
Barrett La [5] CM23 . . . 76 F7
Barrington Dr UB9 . . . 173 A3
Barrington Mews AL7 . . . 111 B5
Barrington Rd SG6 . . . 22 F4
Barrons Row AL5 . . . 107 D7
Barrowby Cl LU2 . . . 46 D1
Barrowdene Cl HA5 . . . 175 E1
Barrow La EN7 . . . 147 F1
Barrow Point Ave
HA5 . . . 175 E1
Barrow Point La HA5 . . . 175 E1
Barr Rd EN6 . . . 159 C6
Barry Cl AL2 . . . 141 B6
Barry Ct SG1 . . . 50 B8
Bartel Cl HP3 . . . 125 D1
Bartholomew Court Sh
Pavilion EN8 . . . 162 E6
Bartholomew Gn AL3 . . . 83 E5
Bartholomew Ho EN3 . . . 162 E2
Bartholomew Rd [8]
CM23 . . . 76 F6
Bartletts Cotts [4]
EN5 . . . 171 E6
Bartletts Mead SG14 . . . 92 D1
Barton Cl AL5 . . . 86 C3
Barton Rd
Hexton SG5 . . . 19 A1
Luton LU3 . . . 45 C7
Wheathampstead AL4 . . . 108 C8
Bartons The WD6 . . . 169 D3
Barton Way
Borehamwood WD6 . . . 170 A7
Croxley Green WD3 . . . 166 B4
Bartrams La EN4 . . . 159 C1
Bartrop Cl EN7 . . . 147 D3
Bartrum Villas [4]
HP4 . . . 122 D4
BARWICK . . . 73 C3
Barwick La SG11 . . . 73 C3
Basbow La [2] CM23 . . . 76 F7
Basildon Cl WD18 . . . 166 C3
Basildon Sq HP2 . . . 124 F7
Basil Mews [1] CM17 . . . 118 C1
Basils Rd SG1 . . . 50 D7
Baslow Cl HA3 . . . 176 D2
Bassett Cl AL3 . . . 106 B5
Bassil Rd HP2 . . . 124 D2
Bassingbourne Cl
EN10 . . . 134 F3
Bassingburn Wlk AL7 . . . 110 F5
BASSUS GREEN . . . 52 F8
Batchelors SG11 . . . 55 E2
Batchwood Dr AL3 . . . 127 C6
Batchwood Gdns AL3 . . . 127 D6
Batchwood Sch AL3 . . . 127 D6
Batchwood View AL3 . . . 127 D5
BATCHWORTH . . . 165 F1
Batchworth Heath
WD3 . . . 174 B5
Batchworth Heath Hill
WD3 . . . 174 A6
Batchworth Hill WD3 . . . 173 F7
Batchworth La HA6 . . . 174 D5
Batchworth Rdbt
WD3 . . . 165 E1
Bateman Rd WD3 . . . 166 A3
BATFORD . . . 86 D3
Batford Cl AL7 . . . 111 B5
Batford Mill Ind Est
AL5 . . . 86 D2
Batford Rd AL5 . . . 86 D3
Bath Pl EN5 . . . 171 F6
Bath Rd LU3 . . . 45 D2
Bathurst Rd HP2 . . . 124 E6
Batterdale AL9 . . . 130 C6
Battlefield Rd AL1 . . . 127 F5
Battlers Green Dr
WD7 . . . 155 E3
Battleview AL4 . . . 108 E8
Baud Cl SG11 . . . 57 E2
Baulk The
Cheddington LU7 . . . 79 F7
Ivinghoe LU7 . . . 80 F5
Lilley LU2 . . . 32 D2
Bawdsey Cl [1] SG1 . . . 50 B8
Bay Cl LU4 . . . 44 B6
Bay Ct HP4 . . . 122 B4
BAYFORD . . . 133 F6
Bayford CE Prim Sch
SG13 . . . 132 F5
Bayford Cl
Hemel Hempstead
HP2 . . . 125 C8
Hertford SG13 . . . 113 C4
Bayford Gn SG13 . . . 133 A6
Bayford La SG13 . . . 132 F7
Bayford Lo HA5 . . . 175 F2
Bayford Sta SG13 . . . 133 B5
Bayhurst Dr HA6 . . . 174 F4
Baylam Dell LU2 . . . 46 E1
Bayley Hall Mews
SG14 . . . 113 D5
Baylie Ct HP2 . . . 124 E4
Baylie La HP2 . . . 124 E4
Bay Tree Cl
Chiswell Green AL2 . . . 141 C3
Hammond Street EN7 . . . 147 F4
Bay Tree Wlk WD17 . . . 154 A1
Bayworth SG6 . . . 23 B5
Beacon Ct SG13 . . . 114 C3
Beacon Ho AL1 . . . 127 F3
Beacon Rd
Ringshall HP4 . . . 81 A1
Ware SG12 . . . 94 A2
Beaconsfield LU2 . . . 64 B8
Beaconsfield Rd
Enfield EN3 . . . 162 D2
Hatfield AL10 . . . 130 C6
St Albans AL1 . . . 127 E3
Tring HP23 . . . 99 E3
Beacons The AL10 . . . 130 C6
Beacons The SG1 . . . 37 B3
Beacon Way
Rickmansworth WD3 . . . 165 B3
Tring HP23 . . . 100 C5
Beadles The CM22 . . . 98 B8
Beadlow Rd LU4 . . . 44 A4
Beagle Cl WD7 . . . 155 F2
Beale Cl SG2 . . . 51 C6
Beamish Dr WD23 . . . 168 C1
Beane Ave SG2 . . . 51 D6
Beane Rd
Hertford SG14 . . . 113 B7
Watton at S SG14 . . . 70 D4
Beane River View
SG14 . . . 113 C6
Beaneside The SG14 . . . 70 D4
Beane Wlk SG2 . . . 51 D6
Beanfield Rd CM21 . . . 97 A4
Beanley Cl LU2 . . . 46 E2
Bear La SG7 . . . 4 D4
Bearton Ave SG5 . . . 34 E8
Bearton Cl SG5 . . . 21 E1
Bearton Ct SG5 . . . 21 E1
Bearton Gn SG5 . . . 21 D1
Bearton Rd SG5 . . . 21 E1
Bearwood Cl EN6 . . . 159 D8
Beatty Rd EN8 . . . 162 F5
Beauchamp Gdns
WD3 . . . 165 A1
Beauchamps AL7 . . . 111 B5
Beaulieu Cl WD19 . . . 167 C1
Beaulieu Dr EN9 . . . 163 B6
Beaumayes Cl HP1 . . . 124 B2
Beaumonds [3] AL1 . . . 127 E3
Beaumont Ave AL1 . . . 128 B4
Beaumont Cl [3] SG5 . . . 34 D8
Beaumont Ct
[10] Harpenden AL5 . . . 86 B1
Welwyn Garden City
AL7 . . . 110 F4
Beaumont Gate WD7 . . . 156 A4
Beaumont Hall La
AL3 . . . 106 C2
Beaumont Pl
Barnet EN5 . . . 171 F8
Watford WD18 . . . 167 A4
Beaumont Rd
Hammond Street EN7 . . . 147 F7
Luton LU3 . . . 45 B2
Beaumont Sch AL4 . . . 128 C4
Beaumont View EN7 . . . 147 D5
Beazley Cl SG12 . . . 93 E2
Beckbury Cl LU2 . . . 46 E2
Becket Gdns AL6 . . . 89 C4
Beckets Sq HP4 . . . 122 A6
Beckets Wlk [14] SG12 . . . 93 D1
Becketts SG14 . . . 113 A5
Beckett's Ave AL3 . . . 127 C6
Beckfield La SG9 . . . 26 D7
Beckham Cl LU2 . . . 45 D7
Becks Cl AL3 . . . 83 D5
Bedale Rd EN2 . . . 161 C1
Bede Cl HA5 . . . 175 D2
Bede Ct HP4 . . . 102 C8
Bedford Almshouses [1]
WD18 . . . 167 C5
Bedford Ave EN5 . . . 171 F4
Bedford Cl WD3 . . . 151 B1
Bedford Cres EN3 . . . 162 E4
Bedford Gdns [4] LU2 . . . 63 D8
Bedford Park Rd AL1 . . . 127 E3
Bedford Rd
Hitchin SG5 . . . 34 E7
Ickleford SG5 . . . 21 D5
Letchworth Garden City
SG6 . . . 22 D7
Lower Stondon SG16 . . . 10 B3
Moor Park HA6 . . . 174 D6
St Albans AL1 . . . 127 E2
Bedford St
Berkhamsted HP4 . . . 122 D4
Hitchin SG5 . . . 34 D7
Watford WD24 . . . 167 B8
BEDMOND . . . 139 F4
Bedmond La
Bricket Wood AL3,
WD5 . . . 140 B6
St Albans AL3 . . . 126 F1
Bedmond Rd
Abbots Langley WD5 . . . 139 F2
Hemel Hempstead HP3 . . . 125 D1
Pimlico HP3 . . . 139 E7
Bedmond Village Prim
Sch WD5 . . . 139 F3
BEDWELL . . . 50 F5
Bedwell Ave AL9,
SG13 . . . 132 A7
Bedwell Cl AL7 . . . 110 E5
Bedwell Cres SG1 . . . 50 F5
Bedwell Prim Sch SG1 . . . 51 A5
Bedwell Rise SG1 . . . 50 E5
Beech Ave
Crews Hill EN2 . . . 161 A4
Radlett WD7 . . . 156 A5
Beech Bottom AL3 . . . 127 D6
Beech Cl
Harpenden AL5 . . . 107 C5
Hatfield AL10 . . . 130 A4
Ware SG12 . . . 114 D7
Beech Cres AL4 . . . 108 D7
Beechcroft
Berkhamsted HP4 . . . 122 C3
Datchworth SG3 . . . 69 D1
Beechcroft Ave WD3 . . . 166 C4
Beechcroft Pl [5] HA6 . . . 174 F5
Beechcroft Rd WD23 . . . 167 E4
Beech Ct
Harpenden AL5 . . . 85 F3
Hoddesdon EN10 . . . 135 A3
Beech Dr
Berkhamsted HP4 . . . 122 C3
Borehamwood WD6 . . . 169 F7
Sawbridgeworth CM21 . . . 118 C8
Stevenage SG2 . . . 51 B3
Beechen Gr WD17 . . . 167 C6
Beechen Wood WD3 . . . 172 D5
Beeches The
Chorleywood WD3 . . . 164 F4
Hemel Hempstead HP1 . . . 124 B2
Hitchin SG4 . . . 35 A6
Park Street AL2 . . . 141 D4
Royston SG8 . . . 7 D6
Tring HP23 . . . 100 C4
[2] Watford WD18 . . . 167 B6
Welwyn AL6 . . . 89 C4
Beech Farm Dr AL4 . . . 128 F7
Beechfield
Hoddesdon EN11 . . . 115 A2
Kings Langley WD4 . . . 138 F1
Sawbridgeworth CM21 . . . 97 F2
Beechfield Cl
Borehamwood WD6 . . . 169 E7
Redbourn AL3 . . . 106 B5
Beechfield Ct [5]
WD17 . . . 167 A8
Beechfield Rd
Hemel Hempstead
HP1 . . . 124 B2
Ware SG12 . . . 93 F2
Welwyn Garden City
AL7 . . . 110 E5
Beechfield Sch WD24 . . . 154 A2
Beechfield Wlk EN9 . . . 163 D4
Beech Gr HP23 . . . 100 C4
Beech Hill
Hadley Wood EN4 . . . 159 E1
Letchworth Garden City
SG6 . . . 22 D7
Luton LU2 . . . 46 D8
Beech Hill Com Prim Sch
LU4 . . . 45 B1
Beech Hill Ct HP4 . . . 122 D4
Beech Ho EN11 . . . 134 F6
Beech Hyde La AL4 . . . 108 F6
Beech Hyde Prim Sch
AL4 . . . 108 D7
Beech Ind Ctr [2] AL3 . . . 127 F7
Beeching Cl AL5 . . . 86 B4
Beechlands CM23 . . . 76 F5
Beecholm Mews [8]
EN8 . . . 148 E3
Beechpark Way
WD17 . . . 153 E2
Beech Pk
Cholesbury HP23 . . . 120 F5
Little Chalfont HP6 . . . 150 B1
Beech Pl AL3 . . . 127 D6
Beech Rd
Luton LU1 . . . 63 C8
St Albans AL3 . . . 127 E6
Watford WD24 . . . 154 B2
Beech Ridge
Baldock SG7 . . . 23 F6
Harpenden AL5 . . . 85 B5
Beechtree La AL3 . . . 126 B2
Beech Way AL4 . . . 87 B6
Beech Wlk
Hoddesdon EN11 . . . 134 F6
Tring HP23 . . . 100 C4
Beechwood Ave
Chorleywood WD3 . . . 164 B5
Little Chalfont HP6 . . . 150 C1
Potters Bar EN6 . . . 159 B6
St Albans AL1 . . . 128 C4
Beechwood Cl
Baldock SG7 . . . 23 F5
Hammond Street EN7 . . . 147 E5
Hertford SG13 . . . 113 F6
Hitchin SG5 . . . 21 D2
Beechwood Cotts
WD3 . . . 164 C3
Beechwood Ct HP22 . . . 99 A4
Beechwood Dr HP23 . . . 101 D5
Beechwood Park Sch
AL3 . . . 83 B1
Beechwood Pk
Chorleywood WD3 . . . 164 F5
Hemel Hempstead HP3 . . . 137 F7
Beechwood Prim Sch
LU4 . . . 44 E4
Beechwood Rd LU4 . . . 44 E3
Beechwood Rise
WD24 . . . 154 B2
Beecroft La SG2 . . . 38 C2
Beehive Cl WD6 . . . 169 D3
Beehive Gn AL7 . . . 111 A4
Beehive La AL7 . . . 111 A3
Beehive Rd EN7 . . . 147 B3
Beesonend Cotts AL5 . . . 107 B4
Beesonend La AL3,
AL5 . . . 106 F3
Beeston Cl WD19 . . . 175 D6
Beeston Dr EN8 . . . 148 D4
Beetham Ct SG12 . . . 92 E4
Beethoven Rd WD6 . . . 169 D3
Beeton Cl HA5 . . . 176 A3
Beggarman's La SG11 . . . 72 D8
Beggars Bush La WD18,
WD3 . . . 166 D4
Beggars La HP23 . . . 101 A3
Beken Ct WD25 . . . 154 C4
Belcher Rd [6] EN11 . . . 135 A7
Belcon Ind Est EN11 . . . 135 C6
Beldam Ave SG8 . . . 7 E5
Beldams Gate CM23 . . . 77 B5
Beldams La CM23 . . . 77 B5
Belfairs Gn WD19 . . . 175 D5
Belford Rd WD6 . . . 156 F1
Belfry Ave UB9 . . . 173 A2
Belfry La WD3 . . . 165 C1
Belfry The LU2 . . . 45 E6
Belfry The WD24 . . . 167 D8
Belfry Villas UB9 . . . 173 A2
Belgrave Ave WD18 . . . 166 F4
Belgrave Cl AL4 . . . 128 C7
Belgrave Dr WD4 . . . 139 C3
Belgrave Ho [6] CM23 . . . 77 B8
Belgrave Mews SG2 . . . 69 A8
Belgrave Rd LU4 . . . 44 D5
Belgravia Cl EN5 . . . 171 F6
Belham Rd WD4 . . . 139 A3
Belhaven Ct [3] WD6 . . . 169 F8
Bell Acre SG6 . . . 23 B4
Bell Acre Gdns SG6 . . . 23 B4
Bellamy Cl
Knebworth SG3 . . . 68 F5
Watford WD17 . . . 167 A8
Bellamy Rd EN8 . . . 148 E2
BELL BAR . . . 145 A7
Bellchambers Cl AL2 . . . 142 C5
Bell Cl
Bedmond WD5 . . . 139 F4
Hitchin SG4 . . . 35 B6
Knebworth SG3 . . . 69 A5
[7] Pinner HA5 . . . 175 C1
Bellerby Rise LU4 . . . 44 B6
Belle Vue La WD23 . . . 168 D1
Belle Vue Rd SG12 . . . 93 F1
Bellevue Terr UB9 . . . 173 A3
Bell Farm Ind Pk SG8 . . . 18 A2
Bellfield Ave HA3 . . . 176 D4
Bellgate HP2 . . . 124 E6
Bellgate Prim Sch
HP2 . . . 124 E5
Bell Gn HP3 . . . 137 B4
Bell Ho SG1 . . . 37 B3
Bellingdon WD19 . . . 175 E7
Bellis Ho AL7 . . . 111 B4
Bell La
Abbots Langley WD5 . . . 140 A4
Berkhamsted HP4 . . . 121 E5
Brookmans Park AL9 . . . 145 A7
Enfield EN3 . . . 162 E1
Hertford SG14 . . . 113 D6
Hoddesdon, Broxbourne
EN11 . . . 134 E2
Hoddesdon EN11 . . . 135 A6
Little Chalfont HP6 . . . 150 C1
Nuthampstead SG8 . . . 18 B2
Shenley AL2 . . . 142 E2
Stevenage SG1 . . . 50 C7
Widford SG12 . . . 95 D4
Bell Lane Comb Sch
HP6 . . . 150 B1
Bell Leys HP22 . . . 60 B3
Bell Mead CM21 . . . 97 E2
Bellmount Wood Ave
WD17 . . . 166 E8
Bell Rdbt The AL2 . . . 142 F4
Bell Row [3] SG7 . . . 23 E8
Bells Hill
Barnet EN5 . . . 171 D5
Bishop's Stortford CM23 . . . 76 E7
Bell St CM21 . . . 97 E2
Bells Wlk CM21 . . . 97 E2
Bell View AL4 . . . 128 D3
Bell Wlk HP22 . . . 60 B3
Belmers Rd HP23 . . . 100 D1
Belmont Ct [7] AL1 . . . 127 D2
Belmont Fst Sch HA3 . . . 176 F1
Belmont Hill AL1 . . . 127 D2
Belmont Lo HA3 . . . 176 D3
Belmont Mid Sch
HA3 . . . 176 F1
Belmont Rd
Hemel Hempstead
HP3 . . . 138 E8
Luton LU1 . . . 63 C7
Watford WD23 . . . 167 E4
Belmor WD6 . . . 170 A3
Belper Rd LU4 . . . 44 D2
Belsham Pl LU2 . . . 46 E2
BELSIZE . . . 151 E6
Belsize Cl
Hemel Hempstead
HP3 . . . 125 A2
St Albans AL4 . . . 128 C8
Belsize Cotts WD3 . . . 151 E6
Belsize Rd
Harrow HA3 . . . 176 D3
Hemel Hempstead HP3 . . . 125 A2
Belswains Gn HP3 . . . 138 E8
Belswains La HP3 . . . 138 F7
Belswains Prim Sch
HP3 . . . 138 F7
Beltona Gdns EN8 . . . 148 D4
Belton Rd HP4 . . . 122 A5
Belvedere Ct
Hoddesdon EN11 . . . 135 A5
Watford WD19 . . . 167 E3
Belvedere Gdns AL2 . . . 141 A4
Belvedere Rd LU3 . . . 45 B5
Bembridge Gdns LU3 . . . 44 F7
Ben Austins AL3 . . . 106 A4
Benbow Cl AL1 . . . 128 B1
Benbroke Pl SG1 . . . 37 B4
Benchley Hill SG4 . . . 35 C8
Benchleys Rd HP1 . . . 123 F2
Bencroft EN7 . . . 148 A5
Bencroft Rd HP2 . . . 124 E3
Bencroft Wood ★
EN10 . . . 133 D1
BENDISH . . . 66 A7
Bendish La SG4 . . . 66 C7
Bendysh Rd WD23 . . . 167 E5
Benedict Ct HA5 . . . 175 F2
Benedict Ho [8] AL3 . . . 127 D4
Benedictine Gate
EN8 . . . 148 E4
Benedictine Pl [12]
AL1 . . . 127 D3
Benford Rd EN11 . . . 134 F4
Bengarth Dr HA3 . . . 176 D1
BENGEO . . . 113 C8
Bengeo Ho SG14 . . . 92 C1
Bengeo Mdws SG14 . . . 92 C1
Bengeo Mews SG14 . . . 92 C1
Bengeo Prim Sch
SG14 . . . 92 C1
Bengeo St SG14 . . . 113 C8
Benhooks Ave CM23 . . . 76 E5
Benhooks Pl [1] CM23 . . . 76 E5
Beningfield Dr AL2 . . . 142 B4
BENINGTON . . . 52 E4
Benington CE Prim Sch
SG2 . . . 52 D4
Benington Cl LU2 . . . 45 F5
Benington Lordship
Gdns ★ SG2 . . . 52 D4
Benington Rd
Aston SG2 . . . 51 F2
Benington SG2 . . . 52 A7
Benneck Ho WD18 . . . 166 E3
Bennett Cl
Northwood HA6 . . . 174 F3
Welwyn Garden City
AL7 . . . 110 F2
Bennett Ct
Letchworth Garden City
SG6 . . . 22 F6
Letchworth Garden City
SG6 . . . 23 A5
Bennetts Cl AL4 . . . 143 D8
BENNETTS END . . . 139 A8
Bennetts End Cl HP3 . . . 124 F1
Bennetts End Rd HP3 . . . 125 A1
Bennettsgate HP3 . . . 139 A8
Bennetts La SG9 . . . 25 F4
Benningfield Cl SG12 . . . 95 D5
Benningfield Gdns
HP4 . . . 122 E6
Benningfield Rd SG12 . . . 95 D4
Benington Dr WD6 . . . 169 F8
Benskin Rd WD18 . . . 167 A4
Benslow La SG4 . . . 35 A7
Benslow Rise SG4 . . . 35 A8
Benson Cl LU3 . . . 44 F7
Benson Ct [4] EN3 . . . 163 A1
Benstede SG2 . . . 69 C8
Benstede Ct [9] EN11 . . . 135 A6
BENTFIELD BOWER . . . 59 C8
Bentfield Bower CM24 . . . 59 C8
Bentfield End Cswy
CM24 . . . 59 D7
Bentfield Gdns CM24 . . . 59 D7
Bentfield Gn CM24 . . . 59 D8
BENTFIELD GREEN . . . 59 D8
Bentfield Pl CM24 . . . 59 D7
Bentfield Prim Sch
CM24 . . . 59 D8
Bentfield Rd CM24 . . . 59 D7
Bentham Ho [4] CM20 . . . 117 C1
Bentick Way SG4 . . . 67 F2
Bentley Cl CM23 . . . 76 F5
Bentley Ct [2] LU1 . . . 63 C8
BENTLEY HEATH . . . 158 F4
Bentley Heath La EN5 . . . 158 F4
Bentley Lo WD23 . . . 176 E8
Bentley Rd SG14 . . . 112 F7
Bentley Wood High Sch
HA7 . . . 176 F5
Benton Rd WD19 . . . 175 D5
Bentons The HP4 . . . 121 F6
Bentsley Cl AL4 . . . 128 C7
Berceau Wlk WD17 . . . 166 E8
Berdan Ct EN3 . . . 163 A2
Berefeld HP2 . . . 124 D5
Beresford Rd
Luton LU4 . . . 45 A1
Rickmansworth WD3 . . . 164 F1
St Albans AL1 . . . 128 C2
Bericot Gn AL9 . . . 111 E7
Bericot Way AL7 . . . 111 D6
Berkeley SG6 . . . 23 A4
Berkeley Cl
Abbots Langley WD5 . . . 153 F8
Borehamwood WD6 . . . 170 A4
[6] Hitchin SG5 . . . 34 D8
Potters Bar EN6 . . . 158 F7
Stevenage SG2 . . . 69 A8
Ware SG12 . . . 93 C2
Berkeley Ct
Croxley Green WD3 . . . 166 D4
[6] Harpenden AL5 . . . 86 A2

Berkeley Mews AL1 ..... 128 B2
Berkeley Path 2 LU2 ..... 63 E8
Berkeley Sq HP2 ..... 105 C1
BERKHAMSTED 122 C6
Berkhamsted Castle* HP4 ..... 122 D5
Berkhamsted Collegiate Sch
  Berkhamsted HP4 ..... 122 B4
  Berkhamsted HP4 ..... 122 C4
Berkhamsted Rd HP1 ..... 123 E5
Berkhamsted Sta HP4 ..... 122 C5
Berkley Ave EN8 ..... 162 D5
Berkley Cl
  Pitstone LU7 ..... 80 D3
  St Albans AL4 ..... 128 C7
Berkley Ct 2 HP4 ..... 122 C4
Berkley Pl EN8 ..... 162 D5
Berks Hill WD3 ..... 164 C4
Bermer Pl WD24 ..... 167 C8
Bermer Rd WD24 ..... 167 C8
Bernard Gr EN9 ..... 163 B6
BERNARD'S HEATH 127 F6
Bernards Heath Inf Sch AL1 ..... 127 F5
Bernards Heath Jun Sch AL3 ..... 127 E6
Bernard St AL3 ..... 127 D4
Berners Dr AL1 ..... 141 E8
Berners Way EN10 ..... 148 F8
Bernhardt Cres SG2 ..... 51 C6
Berries The AL4 ..... 128 A7
Berrow Cl LU2 ..... 46 E2
Berry Ave WD24 ..... 154 B3
Berry Cl WD3 ..... 165 B2
Berryfield LU7 ..... 79 F7
Berrygrove La WD25 ..... 168 A8
Berry Grove La WD24, WD25 ..... 154 E1
Berrygrove Prim Sch WD25 ..... 154 D4
Berry La WD3 ..... 165 A2
Berry Leys LU3 ..... 44 E7
Berrymead HP2 ..... 124 F5
Berry Way WD3 ..... 165 B2
Bert Collins Ct LU1 ..... 63 C7
Berthold Mews EN9 ..... 163 B6
Berwick Cl
  Harrow HA7 ..... 176 F4
  Holdbrook EN8 ..... 163 A5
  Stevenage SG1 ..... 50 A8
Berwick Pl AL7 ..... 110 D3
Berwick Rd WD6 ..... 156 F1
Besant Ho 2 WD24 ..... 167 D7
Besford Cl LU2 ..... 46 E2
Bessemer Cl SG5 ..... 21 E2
Bessemer Dr SG1 ..... 50 B4
Bessemer Rd AL7, AL8 ..... 89 E2
Bethune Cl LU1 ..... 63 B6
Bethune Ct LU1 ..... 63 B6
Betjeman Cl
  Cheshunt EN7 ..... 148 A3
  Harpenden AL5 ..... 86 C1
Betjeman Gdns WD3 ..... 164 D5
Betjeman Rd SG8 ..... 2 D1
Betjeman Way HP1 ..... 124 B4
Betony Vale SG8 ..... 7 E5
Bettespol Mdws AL3 ..... 106 A6
Betty Entwistle Ho AL1 ..... 141 E8
Betty's La HP23 ..... 100 A4
Bevan Cl HP3 ..... 124 E1
Bevan Ho 3 WD24 ..... 167 D7
Beverley Cl SG8 ..... 7 B8
Beverley Gdns
  Cheshunt EN7 ..... 148 A1
  St Albans AL4 ..... 128 D7
  Welwyn Garden City AL7 ..... 111 C6
Beverley Rd
  Luton LU4 ..... 44 F1
  Stevenage SG1 ..... 37 B2
Beverly Cl EN10 ..... 134 E2
Bevil Ct EN11 ..... 115 A1
Bewdley Cl AL5 ..... 107 D6
Bewley Cl EN8 ..... 162 D8
Bexhill Rd LU2 ..... 46 D2
Beyers Gdns 5 EN11 ..... 115 A1
Beyers Prospect EN11 ..... 115 A1
Beyers Ride 3 EN11 ..... 115 A1
Bibbs Hall La SG4, AL6 ..... 87 E6
Biddenham Turn WD25 ..... 154 C4
Bideford Gdns LU3 ..... 45 D4
Bideford Rd EN3 ..... 162 F1
Bidwell Cl SG6 ..... 23 B5
Biggin Hill SG9 ..... 28 D7
Biggin La SG5 ..... 34 F7
Biggs Grove Rd EN7 ..... 147 E4
Bignells Cnr EN6 ..... 158 B5
Billet La HP4 ..... 122 A6
Bill Miller Ct SG6 ..... 22 F8
Billy Lows La EN6 ..... 159 B8
Bilton Ct LU1 ..... 44 F1
Bilton Rd SG4 ..... 21 F2
Bilton Way
  Enfield EN3 ..... 162 F1
  Luton LU1 ..... 44 F1
Bilton Way Ind Est LU1 ..... 62 F8
Bingen Rd SG5 ..... 21 C1
Bingham Cl HP1 ..... 123 F5
Bingham's Park Childrens Farm* HP1 ..... 123 E8
Bingley Rd EN11 ..... 135 C6
Binham Cl LU2 ..... 45 D7
Binyon Cres HA7 ..... 176 F5
Birchall La SG14 ..... 111 E4
Birchalls CM24 ..... 59 E8
Birchall Wood AL7 ..... 111 C5
BIRCHANGER 59 E2
Birchanger CE Prim Sch CM23 ..... 59 D2
Birchanger Ind Est CM23 ..... 59 B2
Birchanger La CM23 ..... 59 D2
Birch Copse AL2 ..... 140 E1
Birch Ct HA6 ..... 174 C4
Birch Dr
  Hatfield AL10 ..... 130 A4
  Maple Cross WD3 ..... 172 D5
Birchen Gr LU2 ..... 45 F3
Bircherley Ct 14 SG14 ..... 113 D6
Bircherley Green Ctr The 9 SG14 ..... 113 D6
Bircherley St SG14 ..... 113 D6
Birches The
  Bushey WD23 ..... 168 C4
  Codicote SG4 ..... 89 A8
  Hemel Hempstead HP3 ..... 137 F8
  Letchworth Garden City SG6 ..... 22 E8
  London Colney AL2 ..... 142 C4
  Waltham Abbey EN9 ..... 163 F5
Birchfield Rd EN8 ..... 148 C2
Birch Gn
  Hemel Hempstead HP1 ..... 123 F5
  Hertingfordbury SG14 ..... 112 C4
Birch Gr
  Lower Stondon SG16 ..... 10 B3
  Oaklands AL6 ..... 89 E8
  Potters Bar EN6 ..... 159 B7
BIRCH GREEN 112 C3
Birch La HP3 ..... 151 B7
Birch Leys HP2 ..... 125 C8
Birch Link LU4 ..... 45 C1
Birchmead WD17 ..... 153 F1
Birchmead Cl AL3 ..... 127 D6
Birch Pk HA3 ..... 176 C3
Birch Rd
  Berkhamsted HP4 ..... 121 D7
  Woolmer Green SG3 ..... 69 B1
Birch Tree Gr HP5 ..... 136 B1
Birch Tree Wlk WD17 ..... 153 F2
Birchway AL10 ..... 130 B7
Birch Way
  Harpenden AL5 ..... 107 C8
  London Colney AL2 ..... 142 D4
Birch Wlk WD6 ..... 170 A8
BIRCHWOOD 130 B7
Birchwood
  Birchanger CM23 ..... 59 D2
  Shenley WD7 ..... 157 A5
  Waltham Abbey EN9 ..... 163 E5
Birchwood Ave AL10 ..... 130 A7
Birchwood Avenue Prim Sch AL10 ..... 130 B7
Birchwood Cl AL10 ..... 130 A7
Birchwood High Sch CM23 ..... 77 C8
Birchwood Ho AL7 ..... 111 B6
Birchwood Way AL2 ..... 141 B3
Birdcroft Rd AL8 ..... 110 D5
Birdie Way SG13 ..... 114 B7
Birds Cl AL7 ..... 111 B4
Birdsfoot La LU3 ..... 45 B6
Birds Hill SG6 ..... 23 A6
Birkbeck Rd EN2 ..... 161 D1
Birkdale Gdns WD19 ..... 175 D7
Birken Ct HA6 ..... 174 B5
Birklands AL1 ..... 142 B7
Birklands La AL1 ..... 142 B7
Birling Dr LU2 ..... 46 C4
Birnbeck Ct 1 EN5 ..... 171 D5
Birstal Gn WD19 ..... 175 D6
Birtley Croft LU2 ..... 46 E1
BISCOT 45 C2
Biscot Rd LU3 ..... 45 C2
Bishop Ct WD5 ..... 153 F8
Bishop Ken Rd HA3 ..... 176 F2
Bishops Ave
  Borehamwood WD6 ..... 169 F4
  Moor Park HA6 ..... 174 F7
Bishop's Ave CM23 ..... 76 F3
Bishops Cl
  Barnet EN5 ..... 171 D3
  Hatfield AL10 ..... 129 F5
Bishop's Cl AL4 ..... 128 A7
Bishopscote Rd LU3 ..... 45 B3
Bishops Ct
  Cheshunt EN8 ..... 148 B1
  9 Luton LU3 ..... 45 D1
Bishops Field HP22 ..... 99 A4
Bishop's Garth AL4 ..... 128 A7
Bishop's Hatfield Girls' Sch AL10 ..... 130 A5
Bishops Mead HP1 ..... 124 B1
Bishop's Palace (rem of)* AL9 ..... 130 D6
BISHOP'S PARK 76 C6
Bishops Park Way CM23 ..... 76 B7
Bishop Sq Bsns Pk AL10 ..... 129 E5
Bishops Rd AL6 ..... 90 D6
Bishops Rise AL10 ..... 129 F2
BISHOP'S STORTFORD 76 D7
Bishop's Stortford Bsns Ctr CM23 ..... 77 A6
Bishop's Stortford Coll CM23 ..... 76 E7
Bishop's Stortford High Sch The CM23 ..... 76 F4
Bishop's Stortford Sta CM23 ..... 77 A6
Bishop's Wood Ctry Pk* WD3 ..... 173 F4
Bishops Wood Hospl HA6 ..... 174 B4
Bishop Wood CE Jun Sch HP23 ..... 100 A3
Biskra WD17 ..... 167 A8
Bisley Cl EN8 ..... 162 D6
Bittern Cl
  Hammond Street EN7 ..... 147 C6
  Hemel Hempstead HP3 ..... 138 F6
  Stevenage SG2 ..... 51 D2
Bittern Way SG6 ..... 11 E1
Bit The HP23 ..... 100 D1
Black Adder Cotts EN9 ..... 149 D8
Blackberry Mead SG2 ..... 51 D3
Blackbirds La WD25 ..... 155 C5
Black Boy Wood AL2 ..... 141 A1
Blackbridge La SG10 ..... 95 E7
Blackbury Cl EN6 ..... 159 C8
Blackbushe CM23 ..... 59 C1
Blackbush Spring CM20 ..... 118 A1
Black Cut 3 AL1 ..... 127 E2
Blackdale EN7 ..... 148 A4
Blackdown Cl SG1 ..... 37 B3
Blackett-Ord Ct SG8 ..... 7 D7
Blacketts Wood Dr WD3 ..... 164 B5
Black Fan Rd
  Welwyn Garden City AL7 ..... 110 F7
  Welwyn Garden City AL7 ..... 111 B6
Blackford Rd WD19 ..... 175 D5
Black Green Wood Cl AL2 ..... 141 B2
BLACKHALL 30 B4
Blackhorse Cl SG4 ..... 35 A5
Blackhorse La
  Hitchin SG4 ..... 35 A5
  Redbourn AL3 ..... 106 A6
  Ridge EN6 ..... 157 F8
Blackhorse Rd SG6 ..... 23 C8
Blackley Cl WD17 ..... 153 F2
Black Lion Ct CM17 ..... 118 C4
Black Lion Hill WD7 ..... 156 F7
Blackmoor La WD18 ..... 166 D4
Blackmore SG6 ..... 23 B3
BLACKMORE END 87 C6
Blackmore Gate HP22 ..... 99 A4
Blackmore Manor AL4 ..... 87 B6
Blackmore Way AL4 ..... 87 B6
Blacksmith Cl SG5 ..... 11 F7
Blacksmiths Cl CM23 ..... 76 B5
Black Smiths Cl SG12 ..... 115 A7
Blacksmiths Hill SG2 ..... 52 E4
Blacksmith's La
  Reed SG8 ..... 16 D5
  St Albans AL3 ..... 127 B3
Blacksmiths Way CM21 ..... 97 A1
Black Swan Ct 1 SG12 ..... 93 D1
Black Swan La LU3 ..... 45 A5
Blackthorn Cl
  St Albans AL4 ..... 128 C6
  Watford WD25 ..... 154 B7
Blackthorn Dr LU2 ..... 46 C4
Blackthorne Cl AL10 ..... 129 F2
Blackthorn Rd AL7 ..... 111 A5
Blackwater La HP3 ..... 125 E1
Blackwell Cl HA3 ..... 176 D3
Blackwell Dr WD19 ..... 167 C3
Blackwell Hall La HP5 ..... 150 C6
Blackwell Rd WD4 ..... 139 A2
Blackwells HP23 ..... 101 D2
Blackwood Ct EN7 ..... 148 F5
Bladon Cl SG4 ..... 35 F3
Blaine Cl HP23 ..... 100 A6
Blair Cl
  Bishop's Stortford CM23 ..... 76 C7
  Hemel Hempstead HP2 ..... 105 B1
  Stevenage SG2 ..... 50 F1
Blairhead Dr WD19 ..... 175 B7
Blake Cl
  Royston SG8 ..... 2 D1
  St Albans AL1 ..... 142 A8
Blakedown LU2 ..... 45 E1
Blakemere Rd AL8 ..... 110 D8
Blakemore End Rd SG4 ..... 35 D3
Blakeney Dr LU2 ..... 45 C7
Blakeney Ho SG1 ..... 50 A7
Blakeney Rd SG1 ..... 50 A7
Blakes Ct
  Rickmansworth WD3 ..... 165 C1
  Sawbridgeworth CM21 ..... 97 E2
Blakesware Manor SG12 ..... 95 B5
Blakes Way AL6 ..... 89 C6
Blanchard Dr 3 WD18 ..... 166 E5
Blanchard Gr EN3 ..... 163 B1
Blanche La EN6 ..... 157 F5
Blandford Ave LU2 ..... 45 D6
Blandford Rd AL1 ..... 128 A3
Blanes The SG12 ..... 93 C3
Blattner Cl WD6 ..... 169 E5
Blaxland Terr 9 EN8 ..... 148 D3
Blaydon Rd LU2 ..... 64 A8
Bleak House Mews 9 AL3 ..... 127 D4
Blegberry Gdns HP4 ..... 121 E4
Blenheim Cl
  Cheddington LU7 ..... 79 F8
  Sawbridgeworth CM21 ..... 118 C8
  Watford WD19 ..... 167 D2
Blenheim Cres LU3 ..... 45 C2
Blenheim Ct
  Bishop's Stortford CM23 ..... 76 C7
  Welwyn Garden City AL7 ..... 110 F7
Blenheim Mews WD7 ..... 156 E6
Blenheim Rd
  Barnet EN5 ..... 171 D5
  St Albans AL1 ..... 127 F4
Blenheim Way SG2 ..... 69 D7
Blenhiem Rd WD5 ..... 154 A7
Blenkin Cl AL3 ..... 127 C7
Blind La SG2, SG9 ..... 38 F5
Blindman's La EN8 ..... 148 D2
Bliss Ho EN1 ..... 162 A1
Block 10 4 WD17 ..... 167 A8
Block 12 3 WD17 ..... 167 A8
Block 14 2 WD17 ..... 167 A8
Bloomfield Ave LU2 ..... 46 A1
Bloomfield Rd
  Hammond Street EN7 ..... 147 C6
  Harpenden AL5 ..... 85 F3
Blossom La EN2 ..... 161 C1
Bluebell Cl
  Hemel Hempstead HP1 ..... 123 E2
  Hertford SG13 ..... 114 A6
Bluebell Dr
  Bedmond WD5 ..... 139 F4
  Goff's Oak EN7 ..... 147 D3
  Lower Stondon SG16 ..... 10 A3
Bluebells AL6 ..... 89 D7
Bluebell Way AL10 ..... 109 F1
Bluebell Wood Cl LU1 ..... 63 A7
Blueberry Cl AL3 ..... 127 D7
Bluebird Way AL2 ..... 140 E1
Bluebridge Ave AL9 ..... 144 F4
Blue Bridge Rd AL9 ..... 144 E4
Bluecoat Ct 18 SG14 ..... 113 D6
Bluecoats Ave SG14 ..... 113 D6
Bluecoat Yd SG12 ..... 93 D1
Bluehouse Hill AL3 ..... 127 B3
Blueprint Commercial Ctr WD24 ..... 154 C1
Blue Springs HA6 ..... 174 E4
Bluett Rd AL2 ..... 142 D4
Blundell Cl AL3 ..... 127 D7
Blundell Rd LU3 ..... 45 A4
Blunesfield EN6 ..... 159 D8
Blunts La AL2 ..... 140 D5
Blyth Cl
  Borehamwood WD6 ..... 170 A8
  Stevenage SG1 ..... 50 A7
Blythe Rd EN11 ..... 135 D5
Blytheswood HP3 ..... 138 A8
Blyth Pl 18 LU1 ..... 63 D6
Blythway AL7 ..... 89 F1
Blythway Ho AL7 ..... 89 F1
Blythwood Gdns CM24 ..... 59 D6
Blythwood Rd HA5 ..... 175 D2
Boardman Cl EN5 ..... 171 E4
Bockings SG2 ..... 38 C1
Bodmin Rd LU4 ..... 44 F3
Bodwell Cl HP1 ..... 124 A4
Bogmoor Rd SG8 ..... 18 A8
Bognor Gdns WD19 ..... 175 C5
Bohemia HP2 ..... 124 E4
Boissy Cl AL4 ..... 128 E2
Boleyn Cl HP2 ..... 125 C8
Boleyn Ct EN10 ..... 134 E2
Boleyn Dr AL1 ..... 127 D1
Bolingbroke Rd LU1 ..... 63 B6
Boling Brook AL4 ..... 128 A7
Bolney Gn LU2 ..... 46 D3
Bolton Rd LU1 ..... 63 F7
Boltons Park (Royal Veterinary Coll) EN6 ..... 145 A2
Bond Ct AL5 ..... 85 F3
Bondor Bsns Ctr SG7 ..... 23 F7
Boniface Gdns HA3 ..... 176 B3
Boniface Wlk HA3 ..... 176 B3
Bonks Hill CM21 ..... 97 D1
Bonney Gr EN7 ..... 148 A1
Bonneygrove Prim Sch EN7 ..... 148 A1
Bonnick Cl LU1 ..... 63 C6
Bonnick Ct LU1 ..... 63 C6
Booths Cl AL9 ..... 144 D7
Boreham Holt WD6 ..... 169 F5
Boreham Mews 1 EN11 ..... 115 A1
BOREHAMWOOD 170 B6
Borehamwood Ent Ctr WD6 ..... 169 F6
Borehamwood Ind Pk WD6 ..... 170 D7
Borehamwood Sh Pk WD6 ..... 170 A6
Bornedene EN6 ..... 158 E8
Borodale AL5 ..... 86 A1
Borough Ind Est The LU3 ..... 45 B2
Borough Way EN6 ..... 158 E7
Borrell Cl EN10 ..... 134 F3
Borrowdale Ct 4 HP2 ..... 124 E6
Borton Ave SG16 ..... 10 B4
Bosanquet Rd EN11 ..... 135 C8
Boscombe Ct SG6 ..... 23 B6
Bosmore Rd LU3 ..... 44 F5
Boswell Cl WD7 ..... 156 E7
Boswell Dr SG5 ..... 21 E4
Boswell Gdns SG1 ..... 36 D1
Boswick La HP4 ..... 121 D8
BOTANY BAY 160 D3
Botany Lo SG1 ..... 37 B3
BOTLEY 136 A1
Botley La HP5 ..... 136 A1
Botley Rd
  Botley HP5 ..... 136 A1
  Hemel Hempstead HP2 ..... 125 B8
Bottom House La HP23 ..... 101 A1
Bottom La WD3, WD4 ..... 152 C4
Bottom Rd HP23 ..... 119 F3
Bough Beech Ct EN3 ..... 162 D2
Boughton Way HP6 ..... 150 C1
Boulevard The
  Watford WD18 ..... 166 D4
  Welwyn Garden City AL7 ..... 110 F8
Boulton Rd SG1 ..... 37 C2
Bounce The HP2 ..... 124 D5
Boundary Cl
  Barnet EN5 ..... 171 F8
  Bishop's Stortford CM23 ..... 77 A5
Boundary Cotts HP3 ..... 137 D2
Boundary Ct AL7 ..... 110 F2
Boundary Dr SG14 ..... 113 D8
Boundary Ho
  Cheshunt EN8 ..... 162 D7
  Welwyn Garden City AL7 ..... 110 D3
Boundary La AL7 ..... 110 E2
Boundary Pk HP2 ..... 125 C5
Boundary Rd
  Bishop's Stortford CM23 ..... 77 A5
  St Albans AL1 ..... 127 E5
Boundary Way
  Hemel Hempstead HP2 ..... 125 C5
  Watford WD25 ..... 154 C7
Bounds Field SG11 ..... 75 F8
Bourne Apartments The 2 AL5 ..... 85 F2
Bourne Cl
  Hoddesdon EN10 ..... 134 F3
  Ware SG12 ..... 93 D2
BOURNE END 123 B1
Bourne End Cotts HP1 ..... 123 C1
Bourne End Mills Ind Est HP1 ..... 137 B8
Bourne End Rd HA6 ..... 174 E6
Bourne Hall WD23 ..... 168 A3
Bournehall Ave WD23 ..... 168 A4
Bournehall La WD23 ..... 168 A4
Bournehall Prim Sch WD23 ..... 168 B4
Bournehall Rd WD23 ..... 168 A3
Bourne Honour SG12 ..... 92 E7
Bourne La SG10 ..... 96 A6
Bournemead WD23 ..... 168 B3
Bournemouth Rd 3 SG1 ..... 50 B8
Bourne Rd
  Berkhamsted HP4 ..... 121 F5
  Bushey WD23 ..... 168 A4
Bourne The
  Bishop's Stortford CM23 ..... 77 A8
  Bovingdon HP3 ..... 137 A4
  Clapgate SG11 ..... 57 C6
  3 Harpenden AL5 ..... 85 F2
  Ware SG12 ..... 93 D2
Bouvier Rd EN3 ..... 162 C1
BOVINGDON 137 B3
Bovingdon Cres WD25 ..... 154 D5
Bovingdon Ct HP3 ..... 137 A3
BOVINGDON GREEN 137 A2
Bovingdon Prim Sch HP3 ..... 137 B4
Bowbrookvale LU2 ..... 46 F1
Bowcock Wlk SG1 ..... 50 E3
Bower Heath La AL5 ..... 86 C6
Bowershott SG6 ..... 23 A4
Bower's Par AL5 ..... 86 A1
Bowers Way AL5 ..... 86 A1
Bowes Lyon Mews AL3 ..... 127 D3
Bowgate AL1 ..... 127 E4
Bowlers Mead SG9 ..... 40 D7
Bowles Gn EN1 ..... 162 B3
Bowling Cl
  14 Bishop's Stortford CM23 ..... 76 F6
  Harpenden AL5 ..... 107 C7
Bowling Ct WD18 ..... 167 A5
Bowling Gn SG1 ..... 50 C8
Bowling Green La
  Buntingford SG9 ..... 40 D8
  Luton LU2 ..... 45 E2
Bowling Rd SG12 ..... 93 E1
Bowmans Ave SG4 ..... 35 B6
Bowmans Cl
  Potters Bar EN6 ..... 159 D7
  Welwyn AL6 ..... 89 C6
Bowmans Ct HP2 ..... 124 E5
Bowmans Gn WD25 ..... 154 E3
Bowmansgreen Prim Sch AL2 ..... 142 C4
Bowman Trad Est SG1 ..... 50 B5

Bowring Gn WD19 . . . . . . 175 C5
Bowsher Ct 5 SG12. . . . . . 93 E1
Bowyer Ct EN8 . . . . 162 F6
Bowyers 6 HP2 . . . . 124 D5
Bowyer's Cl SG5 . . . . 21 D1
Boxberry Cl SG1 . . . . 50 E6
Boxfield AL7. . . . . 111 B3
Boxfield Gn SG2 . . . . 51 D8
Boxgrove Cl LU2 . . . . 46 C5
Boxhill 3 HP2. . . . . 124 D5
Box La
 Hemel Hempstead
 HP3. . . . . 137 E7
 Hoddesdon EN11. . . . . 134 E6
BOXMOOR 124 B1
Boxmoor Prim Sch
 HP1. . . . . 124 A2
Boxted Cl LU4 . . . . 44 C5
Boxted Rd HP1 . . . . 123 F5
Boxtree La HA3. . . . . 176 D3
Boxtree Rd HA3. . . . . 176 D3
Boxwell Rd HP4 . . . . 122 B4
Boyce Cl WD6 . . . . 169 E8
Boyd Cl 1 CM23 . . . . 77 B8
Boyes Cres AL2. . . . . 142 B5
Boyle Cl LU2. . . . . 63 E8
Braceby Cl LU3 . . . . 44 F6
Brace Cl EN7 . . . . 147 B6
Braceys SG2. . . . . 52 F2
Brache Cl AL3 . . . . 106 A5
Brache Ct LU1 . . . . 63 F6
Bracken Cl WD6 . . . . 170 B8
Bracken Ct AL10 . . . . 109 F1
Brackendale EN6 . . . . 159 A6
Brackendale Gr
 Harpenden AL5 . . . . 85 D3
 Luton LU3 . . . . 45 B5
Brackendene AL2. . . . . . . 140 F1
Bracken Hill HP4 . . . . 122 F5
Bracken La AL6. . . . . 89 F7
Brackens The HP2 . . . . . . 124 D4
Bracklesham Gdns
 LU2 . . . . 46 D3
Bracknell Pl HP2 . . . . 124 F7
Bradbery WD3. . . . . 172 D5
Bradbury Cl WD6 . . . . 170 B8
Bradcot Cotts SG2 . . . . 39 C2
Bradden Cotts HP2 . . . . . 103 F8
Bradden La HP1, HP2 . . . . . 103 E7
Bradden Villas HP2 . . . . . 103 F8
Braddon Ct 13 EN5. . . . . . 171 E6
Bradfordbury Mansion
 SG13 . . . . 113 B1
Bradford Rd WD3. . . . . . . 164 C2
Bradgate EN6 . . . . 146 D4
Bradgate Cl EN6. . . . . 146 D3
Bradgers Hill Rd LU2. . . . . 45 E4
Bradley Comm CM23. . . . . 59 C3
Bradley Rd
 Enfield EN3 . . . . 162 E2
 Luton LU4 . . . . 44 D1
 Waltham Abbey EN9 . . . . . 163 C4
Bradleys Cnr SG4 . . . . 35 C8
Bradman Way SG1. . . . . . . 37 A1
Bradmore Gn AL9. . . . . . . 144 E5
Bradmore La AL9 . . . . 144 C5
Bradmore Way AL9 . . . . . . 144 E5
Bradshaw Rd WD24 . . . . . 154 C1
Bradshaws AL10 . . . . 129 F1
Bradway SG4 . . . . 66 E6
Braeburn Wlk SG8 . . . . 7 C7
Braemar Cl SG2 . . . . 69 B7
Braemar Ct WD23. . . . . . . 168 A3
Braemar Turn HP2. . . . . . . 105 B1
Braeside Cl HA5 . . . . 176 A3
Bragbury Cl SG2 . . . . 69 D7
BRAGBURY END 69 D6
Bragbury La SG2, SG3 . . . . 69 D5
Bragmans La WD3 . . . . . . 151 E6
Braham Ct 2 SG5 . . . . 34 E7
Brain Cl AL10. . . . . 130 B6
Braithwaite Ct 19 LU3 . . . . 45 D1
Brake Shear Ho EN5 . . . . 171 F6
Brakynbery HP4 . . . . 121 E7
Bramble Cl
 Harpenden AL5 . . . . 85 F3
 Luton LU4 . . . . 44 C4
 Watford WD25. . . . . 154 A5
Bramble Rd
 Hatfield AL10. . . . . 129 D5
 Luton LU4 . . . . 44 C4
Bramble Rise CM20 . . . . . 117 C1
Brambles The
 Bishop's Stortford
 CM23 . . . . 76 C6
 Cheshunt EN8 . . . . 162 D8
 Oaklands AL6. . . . . 89 E8
 Royston SG8 . . . . 7 E5
 St Albans AL1 . . . . 127 D1
 Stevenage SG1 . . . . 36 D2
 Ware SG12 . . . . 93 C3
Brambling Cl WD23 . . . . . 167 E5
Brambling Rise HP2 . . . . 124 E6
BRAMFIELD 91 C4
Bramfield
 Hitchin SG4 . . . . 35 B6
 Watford WD25. . . . . 154 E5
Bramfield Ct SG14 . . . . . . 113 A7
Bramfield La SG14 . . . . 91 F3
Bramfield Pl HP2 . . . . 105 A1
Bramfield Rd
 Datchworth SG3 . . . . 90 E8
 Hertford SG14. . . . . 112 F8
Bramham Ct HA6 . . . . 174 E4
Bramhanger Acre LU3 . . . 44 D7
Bramingham Bsns Pk
 LU3. . . . . 45 B8
Bramingham Prim Sch
 LU3. . . . . 45 B8
Bramingham Rd LU3 . . . . . 44 F6
Bramleas WD18. . . . . 166 F5
Bramley Cl SG7. . . . . 12 F1
Bramley Ct WD25 . . . . 154 B8
Bramley Gdns WD19 . . . . 175 C5
Bramley House Ct
 EN2 . . . . 161 D2
Bramley Shaw EN9. . . . . . 163 F6
Bramley Way AL4 . . . . 128 C2
Brampton Cl
 Cheshunt EN7 . . . . 148 A3
 Harpenden AL5 . . . . 86 D1
Brampton Park Rd
 SG5 . . . . 21 E1
Brampton Rd
 Royston SG8 . . . . .7 F6
 South Oxhey WD19 . . . . . . 175 A7
 St Albans AL1 . . . . 128 A4
Brampton Terr WD6 . . . . 157 A1
Bramshaw Gdns
 WD19. . . . . 175 D5
Bramshott Cl SG4. . . . . 34 F5
Bramshott Way WD19. . . . 175 A8
Branch Cl AL10 . . . . 130 C7
Branch Rd
 Park Street AL2. . . . . 141 D4
 St Albans AL3 . . . . 127 B4
Brandles Rd SG6. . . . . 23 A3
Brandles Sch SG7 . . . . 23 E7
Brandon Cl EN7. . . . . 147 F5
Brandon Ct HP23 . . . . 78 D7
Brandon Mobile Home Pk
 AL4. . . . . 128 D2
Brand St SG5. . . . . 34 E7
Branksome Cl HP2. . . . . . 125 A4
Branscombe Ho
 WD24. . . . . 154 A2
Branton Cl LU2 . . . . 46 E2
Brantwood Rd LU1. . . . . . . 63 C7
BRAUGHING 55 F6
BRAUGHING FRIARS 56 D5
Brawlings La SL9 . . . . 172 A6
Bray Cl WD6. . . . . 170 C8
Bray Dr SG1 . . . . 37 A3
Brayes Manor SG5 . . . . 11 F6
Bray Lo 3 EN8 . . . . 148 E3
Brays Ct LU2 . . . . 46 B3
Brays Rd LU2. . . . . 46 B3
Brays Springs EN9 . . . . . . 163 E5
Braziers End HP5 . . . . 120 C1
Braziers Field SG13. . . . . . 113 F6
Braziers Quay CM23. . . . . . 77 A6
Breach Barns La EN9. . . . 149 F1
BREACHWOOD GREEN
 . . . . 47 E1
Breachwood Green Jun
 Mix & Inf Sch SG4 . . . . . . 47 E1
Bread & Cheese La
 EN7 . . . . 147 D6
Breadcroft La AL5 . . . . 86 B1
Breakmead AL7. . . . . 111 B4
Breakspear SG2 . . . . 51 C3
Breakspear Ave AL1 . . . . 127 F2
Breakspear Ct WD5 . . . . . 139 F1
Breakspeare Cl WD24 . . . 154 B1
Breakspeare Rd WD5 . . . 153 E8
Breakspeare Sch
 WD5 . . . . 153 E8
Breakspear Pl WD5 . . . . . 139 F1
Breakspear Rd N UB9 . . . 173 D1
Breakspear Way HP2. . . . 125 C4
Breaks Rd AL10. . . . . 130 B6
Brecken Cl AL4 . . . . 128 A7
Brecon Cl 14 LU1 . . . . 63 D6
Breeze Terr 5 EN8 . . . . . 148 D3
Bren Ct EN3 . . . . 163 A2
Brendon Ave LU2 . . . . 46 C1
Brent Ct SG1 . . . . 50 E5
BRENT PELHAM 30 B2
Brent Pl EN5 . . . . 171 F4
Brett Pl WD24 . . . . 154 A2
Brett Rd EN5 . . . . 171 C4
Bretts Mead LU1. . . . . 63 C5
Bretts Mead Ct LU1 . . . . . . 63 C5
Brewers Cl CM23 . . . . 76 C5
Brewery Cotts SG7. . . . . . . 12 E1
Brewery La
 1 Baldock SG7. . . . . 23 E8
 Stansted Mountfitchet
 CM24 . . . . 59 E7
Brewery Rd EN11 . . . . 135 B6
Brewery Yd CM24. . . . . 59 F7
Brewhouse Hill AL4. . . . . 108 C8
Brewhouse La SG14. . . . . 113 C6
Briants Cl HA5. . . . . 175 F1
Briar Cl
 Cheshunt EN8 . . . . 148 C2
 Luton LU2 . . . . 46 C4
 Potten End HP4. . . . . 123 A7
Briarcliff HP1. . . . . 123 E4
Briardale
 Stevenage SG1 . . . . 50 E4
 Ware SG12 . . . . 93 C3
Briarley Cl EN10 . . . . 134 F1
Briar Patch La SG6. . . . . . . 22 D3
Briar Rd
 St Albans AL4 . . . . 128 D6
 Watford WD25. . . . . 154 B8
Briars Cl AL10 . . . . 130 A5
Briars La AL10. . . . . 130 A5
Briars The
 Bushey WD23 . . . . 168 E2
 Cheshunt EN8 . . . . 162 E8
 Hertford SG13. . . . . 114 A6
Briars The continued
 Sarratt WD3. . . . . 152 A3
Briarswood EN7 . . . . 147 E3
Briars Wood AL10. . . . . . . 130 A5
Briar Way HP4. . . . . 122 D3
Briarwood Dr HA6 . . . . . . 175 A1
Briary La SG8. . . . . 7 C5
Briary Wood End AL6 . . . . 89 F8
Briary Wood La AL6. . . . . . 89 F8
Brick Cotts SG9. . . . . 27 D8
Brickcroft EN10. . . . . 148 E5
Brickenden Ct EN9. . . . . . 163 F6
BRICKENDON 133 C4
Brickendon Ct EN11. . . . . 135 A5
Brickendon La
 Brickendon SG13. . . . . 133 D6
 Hertford SG13. . . . . 113 C3
Bricket Rd AL1 . . . . 127 D3
BRICKET WOOD 140 F1
Bricket Wood Sta
 AL2. . . . . 141 A1
Brickfield AL10 . . . . 130 A2
Brickfield Ave HP3. . . . . . 125 B2
Brickfield Cotts WD6. . . . 169 F6
Brickfield Ct AL10 . . . . . . 130 B2
Brickfield La EN5 . . . . 170 F3
Brickfields Ind Est
 HP2. . . . . 125 B7
Brickfields The SG12. . . . . 93 B2
Brickhill Pk LU1 . . . . 84 C8
Brick Kiln Cl WD19. . . . . . 167 E3
Brick Kiln La SG4 . . . . 34 E5
Brick Kiln Rd
 Cockernhoe LU2 . . . . 47 A3
 Stevenage SG1 . . . . 50 C6
Brick Knoll Pk AL1. . . . . . 128 C2
Brickley Rd LU4 . . . . 44 C5
Brickmakers La HP3 . . . . 125 B2
Brickwall Cl AL6 . . . . 110 A8
Brickyard La SG8 . . . . 16 E5
Bride Hall La AL6 . . . . 88 A5
Bridewell Cl SG9. . . . . 40 E8
Bridewell Mews 24
 SG14 . . . . 113 D6
Bridge Ct
 1 Berkhamsted HP4 . . . . 122 D4
 Harpenden AL5 . . . . 85 F3
 Radlett WD7 . . . . 156 B4
 Welwyn Garden City
 AL7 . . . . 110 F6
Bridge End SG9. . . . . 40 E8
Bridgefields AL7. . . . . 110 F7
Bridgefoot SG9 . . . . 40 E7
Bridgefoot SG12. . . . . 93 D1
Bridgefoot Cotts AL2. . . . 155 F8
Bridgefoot La EN6 . . . . . . 158 D6
Bridgeford Ho
 13 Bishop's Stortford
 CM23 . . . . 76 F6
 5 Watford WD18. . . . . . . 167 B6
Bridgegate Bsns Ctr
 AL7 . . . . 110 F6
Bridgend Rd EN1 . . . . 162 C4
Bridgenhall Rd EN1 . . . . . 161 F1
Bridge Pk AL7 . . . . 110 E7
Bridge Pl WD17. . . . . 167 D4
Bridger Cl WD25 . . . . 154 E6
Bridge Rd
 Abbots Langley WD4 . . . . . 153 C6
 Letchworth Garden City
 SG6. . . . . 22 F6
 Stevenage SG1 . . . . 50 C7
 Welwyn Garden City
 AL8 . . . . 110 C7
 Woolmer Green SG3 . . . . . . 69 A2
Bridge Rd E AL7 . . . . 110 F6
Bridge Rd W SG1 . . . . 50 B7
Bridges Ct SG14 . . . . 113 C6
Bridges Rd HA7. . . . . 176 F5
Bridge St
 Berkhamsted HP4 . . . . 122 D4
 Bishop's Stortford CM23. . . 76 F7
 Hemel Hempstead HP1 . . . 124 C2
 Hitchin SG5 . . . . 34 E6
 Kneesworth SG8 . . . . 2 B8
 Luton LU1 . . . . 63 E8
Bridgewater Ct HP4. . . . . 102 C8
Bridgewater Hill HP4 . . . 121 F7
Bridgewater Mid Sch
 HP4. . . . . 122 A6
Bridgewater Monument
 The* HP4. . . . . 101 E7
Bridgewater Rd HP4 . . . . 122 B5
Bridgewater Way
 WD23. . . . . 168 B3
Bridgeways EN11 . . . . 135 B6
Bridle Cl
 Enfield EN3 . . . . 162 F2
 Hoddesdon EN11. . . . . 115 A2
 St Albans AL3 . . . . 127 E5
Bridle La WD3. . . . . 165 D6
Bridle Path WD17. . . . . . . 167 B7
Bridleway HP23. . . . . 119 E5
Bridle Way
 Berkhamsted HP4 . . . . 122 A6
 Great Amwell SG12. . . . . . 115 A6
 4 Hoddesdon EN11 . . . . . 115 A1
Bridle Way (N) EN11 . . . . 115 B2
Bridle Way (S) EN11 . . . . 115 A1
Bridlington Rd WD19. . . . 175 D7
Brierley Cl LU2 . . . . 46 D2
Briery Ct WD3 . . . . 165 A5
Briery Field WD3 . . . . 165 A5
Briery Way HP2. . . . . 125 A4
Brigadier Ave EN2 . . . . . . 161 C1
Brigadier Hill EN2 . . . . . . 161 C1
Brightman Cotts 2
 LU3 . . . . 45 A7
Brighton Rd WD24 . . . . . . 154 A1
Brighton Way SG1 . . . . 50 A8
Brightview Cl AL2. . . . . . . 140 E2
Brightwell Ct WD18. . . . . 167 A4
Brightwell Rd WD18 . . . . 167 A4
Brill Cl LU2. . . . . 46 D2
Brimfield Cl LU2. . . . . 46 D2
Brimsdown Ave EN3 . . . . 162 E1
Brimstone Way HP4. . . . . 121 F6
Brindley Way HP3 . . . . . . 138 F6
Brinklow Ct AL3 . . . . 141 B8
Brinley Cl EN8 . . . . 162 D8
Brinsley Rd HA3 . . . . 176 D1
Brinsmead AL2 . . . . 141 E4
Briscoe Cl EN11 . . . . 134 F8
Briscoe Rd EN11. . . . . 134 F8
Bristol Ho 16 WD6 . . . . . . 170 A7
Bristol Rd LU3 . . . . 45 B4
Britannia SG11 . . . . 55 E2
Britannia Ave LU3 . . . . 45 B4
Britannia Bsns Pk
 EN8. . . . . 162 F5
Britannia Ct EN8. . . . . 162 F5
Britannia Est LU3. . . . . 45 B2
Britannia Hall LU2 . . . . 64 C8
Britannia Pl 3 CM23. . . . . 76 E5
Britannia Rd EN8 . . . . 162 F5
Brittain Way SG2 . . . . 51 B4
Brittany Ho EN2 . . . . 161 C1
Britten Cl WD6 . . . . 169 D3
Britton Ave AL3. . . . . 127 D3
Britwell Dr HP4. . . . . 122 E6
Brixham Cl SG1. . . . . 50 B7
Brixton Rd WD24 . . . . 167 B8
Broad Acre AL2. . . . . 140 E1
Broadacres LU2 . . . . 45 D6
Broad Acres AL10. . . . . . . 129 F8
Broad Baulk SG9 . . . . 40 D8
Broadcroft
 2 Hemel Hempstead
 HP2. . . . . 124 D5
 Letchworth Garden City
 SG6. . . . . 22 F2
Broad Ct AL7 . . . . 110 E6
Broadfield
 Bishop's Stortford
 CM23 . . . . 58 F2
 Harlow CM20. . . . . 117 E1
Broadfield Cl SG10. . . . . . . 74 E1
Broadfield Ct WD23. . . . . 176 E8
Broadfield Pl AL8. . . . . . . 110 B5
Broadfield Prim Sch
 HP2. . . . . 124 F3
Broadfield Rd
 Hemel Hempstead
 HP2. . . . . 124 F3
 Woolmer Green SG3 . . . . . . 69 B1
Broadfields
 Goff's Oak EN7 . . . . 147 B2
 Harpenden AL5 . . . . 85 F2
 Harrow HA2. . . . . 176 B1
 High Wych CM21 . . . . 97 B1
Broadfields La WD19. . . . 167 B1
Broadfields Prim Sch
 CM20 . . . . 117 E1
Broadfield Way
 Much Hadham SG10 . . . . . . 74 F1
 Radlett WD25 . . . . 155 B3
Broadgate EN9 . . . . 163 F7
Broad Gn SG13 . . . . 132 F8
Broadgreen Rd EN7. . . . . 147 D5
BROADGREEN WOOD
 . . . . 132 F8
Broad Green Wood
 SG13 . . . . 133 A8
Broadhall Way SG2 . . . . . . 51 B2
Broadlake Cl AL2 . . . . 142 D4
Broadlands WD7. . . . . 156 B4
Broadlands Cl EN8. . . . . . 162 D5
Broadlawns Ct HA3 . . . . . 176 F2
Broadleaf Ave CM23 . . . . . 76 D4
Broadleaf Gr AL8 . . . . 89 B1
Broadley Gdns WD7. . . . . 156 E7
Broadmead SG4 . . . . 35 B5
Broad Mead LU3. . . . . 45 A3
Broadmead Cl HA5. . . . . . 175 E3
Broadmeadow Ride
 SG4 . . . . 35 A4
Broadmeads SG12 . . . . 93 D1
Broadoak Ave EN3 . . . . . . 162 D4
Broad Oak Ct LU2. . . . . 46 D3
BROADOAK END 112 F8
Broad Oak La SG14 . . . . . . 112 F8
Broad Oak Way SG2. . . . . . 50 F1
Broad St HP2 . . . . 124 D4
Broadstone Rd AL5 . . . . . 107 D7
Broadview SG1 . . . . 50 E6
Broadview Ho EN3 . . . . . . 162 F3
Broadwalk The HA6. . . . . . 174 C1
BROADWATER 51 A1
Broadwater
 Berkhamsted HP4 . . . . 122 C5
 Potters Bar EN6 . . . . 145 B1
Broadwater Ave SG6. . . . . 22 E5
Broadwater Cres
 Stevenage SG2 . . . . 69 C8
 Welwyn Garden City
 AL7 . . . . 110 D5
Broadwater Dale SG6 . . . . 22 E5
Broadwater La SG2 . . . . . . 51 D1
Broadwater Rd AL7 . . . . . 110 E6
Broadway SG6. . . . . 22 F5
Broadway Ave CM17 . . . . 118 B4
Broadway Ct SG6 . . . . 22 E3
Broadway The
 Blackmore End AL4 . . . . 87 B5
 Harrow HA3. . . . . 176 F1
 Hatfield AL9. . . . . 130 C6
Broadway The continued
 Pinner HA5 . . . . 175 F3
 2 St Albans AL1. . . . . 127 D3
 3 Watford WD17 . . . . 167 C6
Broad Wlk CM20. . . . . 117 D1
Brocket Cnr AL8. . . . . 109 F4
Brocket Ct
 15 Hoddesdon EN11 . . . . . 135 A6
 Luton LU4 . . . . 44 D5
Brocket Rd
 Hatfield AL8. . . . . 110 A3
 Hoddesdon EN11. . . . . 135 A6
Brockett Cl AL8. . . . . 110 B6
Brocket View AL4. . . . . . . 108 D8
Brockhurst Cl HA7 . . . . . . 176 F4
Brocklesbury Cl
 WD24. . . . . 167 D7
Brockley Hill HA7. . . . . . . 169 C1
Brockley Hill Ho HA7. . . . 169 C1
Brockswood La AL8. . . . . 110 B7
Brockswood Prim Sch
 HP2. . . . . 105 C1
Brockton Cl LU1 . . . . 63 A7
Brockwell Shott SG2. . . . . 38 B1
Brodewater Rd WD6 . . . . 170 B7
Brodie Rd EN2. . . . . 161 C1
Broken Green Cotts
 SG11 . . . . 56 C2
Bromborough Gn
 WD19. . . . . 175 C5
Bromet Cl WD17. . . . . 153 F1
Bromet Prim Sch
 WD19 . . . . 167 D2
Bromleigh Cl EN8. . . . . . . 148 E3
Bromley HP23 . . . . 79 A4
Bromley Cl CM20 . . . . 118 B4
Bromley La SG10, SG11 . . . 74 D6
Brompton Cl LU3 . . . . 44 F8
Brompton Gdns LU3 . . . . . 44 F8
Bronte Ave SG5. . . . . 11 C2
Bronte Cres HP2. . . . . 105 B1
Bronte Ct 11 WD6. . . . . . . 170 A5
Bronte Paths SG2. . . . . 51 C6
Brook Bank EN1 . . . . 162 B2
Brookbridge La SG3 . . . . . 69 D2
Brook Cl WD6 . . . . 170 B7
Brook Cotts CM24. . . . . 59 E5
Brook Ct LU3 . . . . 45 D1
Brookdene Ave WD19 . . . 167 C1
Brookdene Dr HA6. . . . . . 174 F4
Brook Dr
 Radlett WD7 . . . . 155 F6
 Stevenage SG2 . . . . 69 B8
Brooke Cl WD23 . . . . 168 C2
Brooke End AL3 . . . . 106 A4
Brooke Gdns CM23. . . . . . . 77 C7
Brooke Ho WD23 . . . . 168 C1
BROOK END 11 E5
Brook End CM21 . . . . 97 D2
Brookend La SG4 . . . . 35 B3
Brooke Rd SG8 . . . . 7 D8
Brooker Rd EN9 . . . . 163 C5
Brooke Way WD23 . . . . . . 168 C2
Brook Farm Cl CM23 . . . . . 76 C3
Brook Field SG2 . . . . 51 E2
Brookfield Cl HP23. . . . . . 100 B4
Brookfield Ctr EN8. . . . . . 148 D4
Brookfield Gdns EN8. . . . 148 D4
Brookfield Ho
 Cheshunt EN8 . . . . 148 D4
 Hemel Hempstead HP2 . . . 124 D2
Brookfield La SG2 . . . . 51 F3
Brookfield La E EN8. . . . . 148 D3
Brookfield La W EN8. . . . 148 C4
Brookfield Ret Pk
 EN8. . . . . 148 D5
Brookfields CM21. . . . . 97 D2
Brookfield View WD4 . . . 139 A3
Brookhill SG2 . . . . 68 F8
Brook Ho 5 EN10. . . . . . . 148 F5
Brookhouse Pl 3
 CM23. . . . . 76 F8
Brook La
 Berkhamsted HP4 . . . . 122 B5
 Sawbridgeworth CM21 . . . . 97 D2
Brookland Inf Sch
 EN8. . . . . 148 E3
Brookland Jun Sch
 EN8. . . . . 148 E3
Brooklands Cl LU4 . . . . 44 C6
Brooklands Ct AL1 . . . . . . 127 E3
Brooklands Gdns EN6. . . . 158 E7
Brookmans Ave AL9. . . . . 144 F5
BROOKMANS PARK 144 E5
Brookmans Park Prim Sch
 AL9 . . . . 144 E5
Brookmans Park Sta
 AL9. . . . . 144 E5
Brookmead Sch LU7 . . . . . 80 E5
Brookmill Cl WD19. . . . . . 167 B2
Brook Rd
 Borehamwood WD6. . . . . . 170 A7
 Cheshunt EN8 . . . . 162 F5
 Sawbridgeworth CM21 . . . . 97 E1
 Stansted Mountfitchet
 CM24 . . . . 59 E6
Brooks Ct SG14 . . . . 112 F7
Brooksfield AL7 . . . . 111 B7
Brookshill HA3 . . . . 176 D5
Brookshill Ave HA3 . . . . . 176 E5
Brookshill Dr HA3 . . . . . . 176 D5
Brookshill Gate HA3 . . . . 176 D5
Brookside
 Buckland SG9. . . . . 27 D5
 Furneux Pelham SG9. . . . . . 43 B4
 Hatfield AL10. . . . . 129 D5
 Hertford SG13. . . . . 113 E5
 Hoddesdon EN11. . . . . 135 A6

Brookside *continued*
Letchworth Garden City SG6 22 F5
South Mimms EN6 158 A7
Waltham Abbey EN9 163 E7
Watford WD24 154 D3
Brookside Cl EN5 171 E3
Brookside Cotts WD4 153 C5
Brookside Cres EN6 146 E4
Brookside Cvn Pk WD19 167 B2
Brookside Gdns EN1 162 C2
Brookside Rd WD19 167 B2
Brook St
Luton LU3 63 D8
Stotfold SG5 11 E6
Tring HP23 100 B4
Brook View
Hitchin SG4 35 C6
Stansted Mountfitchet CM24 59 E5
Broom Barns Jun Mix Inf Sch SG1 50 E4
Broom Cl
Hammond Street EN7 148 A4
Hatfield AL10 129 F2
Broom Cnr AL5 107 C8
Broomer Pl EN8 148 C2
Broomfield
Chiswell Green AL2 141 C4
Harlow CM20 118 B3
Broomfield Ave EN10 148 E5
Broomfield Cl AL6 89 C4
Broomfield Ct 2 AL10 130 A6
Broomfield Rd AL6 89 C4
Broomfield Rise WD5 153 D7
Broom Gr
Knebworth SG3 68 F5
Watford WD17 154 A1
Broom Hill
Hemel Hempstead HP1 123 E2
Welwyn AL6 90 A8
Broomhills AL7 111 B7
Broomleys AL4 128 D6
Brooms Cl AL8 89 D1
Brooms Rd LU2 64 A8
Broomstick Hall Rd EN9 163 E6
Broomstick La HP5 136 A1
Broom Wlk SG1 50 E5
Broughinge Rd WD6 170 B7
Broughton Ave LU3 45 C5
Broughton Hill SG6 23 B6
Broughton Way WD3 165 A2
Brownfields AL7 110 F7
Brownfields Ct AL7 111 A7
Brownfield Way AL4 87 B6
Browning Ct 9 WD6 170 A5
Browning Dr SG4 35 B8
Browning Rd
Enfield EN2 161 D1
Harpenden AL5 86 C2
Luton LU4 44 A2
Brownings La SG4 47 D1
Brownings The AL2 142 B4
Brownlow Farm Barns HP1 123 D5
Brownlow Gate HP4 81 B1
Brownlow La LU7 80 A7
Brownlow Rd
Berkhamsted HP4 122 C5
Borehamwood WD6 170 A5
Brown's Cl LU4 44 D5
Brown's Cnr SG9 27 F3
Brownsea Ho 12 WD18 166 F3
Browns Hedge LU7 80 C3
Brown's La HP23 119 F7
Brown's Rise HP23 119 F3
Browns Spring HP4 123 C7
Brow The WD25 154 B6
BROXBOURNE 134 F3
Broxbournebury Mews EN10 134 C3
Broxbourne CE Prim Sch EN10 134 F2
Broxbourne & Hoddesdon Sta EN10 135 A3
Broxbourne Sch The EN10 134 E2
Broxdell SG1 50 E6
Broxley Mead LU4 44 D5
Bruce Gr WD24 154 C1
Bruce Rd
9 Barnet EN5 171 E6
Harrow HA3 176 E1
Bruce Way EN8 162 D6
Brummell Pl CM17 118 C3
Brunel Ct HP3 124 D1
Brunel Rd SG2 51 B7
Brunel Wk SG5 11 C2
Brunswick Ct EN11 135 A5
Brunswick Rd EN3 163 A1
Brunswick St LU2 63 F8
Brunts Hall AL9 130 F2
Brushrise WD24 154 A3
Brushwood Dr WD3 164 C5
Brussels Way LU3 44 D8
Bryan Rd CM23 76 F8
Bryanstone Rd EN8 162 F5
Bryant Cl EN5 171 F4
Bryant Ct AL5 86 A3
Bryce Cl SG12 93 D3
Bryfield Cotts HP3 137 C1
Buchanan Ct
Borehamwood WD6 170 C7
Buchanan Ct *continued*
Luton LU2 64 B8
Buchanan Dr LU2 64 B8
Buckettsland La WD6 157 D2
Buckingham Ct AL1 127 F4
Buckingham Dr LU2 46 D2
Buckingham Lo 6 EN11 135 A6
Buckingham Rd
Borehamwood WD6 170 D5
Tring HP23 99 E3
Watford WD24 154 C2
BUCKLAND 27 D8
BUCKLAND COMMON 120 B3
Buckland Rd HP22 99 A4
Buckland Rise HA5 175 D2
Bucklands Croft HP23 99 C8
Bucklands The WD3 165 A2
Buckland Wharf Ct HP22 99 A4
Buckle Cl LU3 44 F7
Bucklersbury SG5 34 E6
Bucklers Cl EN10 134 F1
Bucknalls Cl WD25 154 E7
Bucknalls Dr AL2 154 F8
Bucknalls La WD25 154 E7
Bucks Alley SG13 132 D4
Bucks Ave WD19 167 E2
Buck's Head Cotts SG4 35 E3
BUCKS HILL 152 C5
Bucks Hill WD4 152 C5
Bucks New Univ (Chalfont Campus) HP8 172 A8
Buckthorn Ave SG1 50 E4
Buckton Rd WD6 156 F1
Buckwood La LU6 82 C7
Buckwood Rd AL3 83 C6
Buddcroft AL7 111 B7
Bude Cres SG1 50 A7
BULBOURNE 100 C8
Bulbourne Cl
Berkhamsted HP4 121 F6
Hemel Hempstead HP1 124 A2
Bulbourne Ct HP23 100 A7
Bulbourne Rd HP23 100 B7
Bullace Cl HP1 124 A4
Bullbeggars La HP4 123 A4
Bullen's Green La AL4 143 E8
Bullfields CM21 97 E3
Bullhead Rd WD6 170 C6
Bull La
Cottered SG9 39 C8
Wheathampstead AL4 108 A6
Bullock's Hill SG4 49 B1
Bullock's La SG13 113 C4
Bull Plain SG14 113 D6
Bull Rd AL5 107 B8
Bullrush Cl AL10 130 B4
BULLS CROSS 162 A3
Bull's Cross EN2 162 A3
Bulls Cross Ride EN7 162 A5
BULL'S GREEN 90 D7
Bulls La AL9 144 E7
Bullsland Gdns WD3 164 B3
Bullsland La WD3 164 B3
BULLSMOOR 162 D4
Bullsmoor Cl EN8 162 C4
Bullsmoor Gdns EN8 162 B4
Bullsmoor La EN1, EN3 162 C4
Bullsmoor Ride EN8 162 C4
Bullsmoor Way EN8 162 C4
Bull Stag Gn AL9 130 C7
Bullwell Cres EN8 148 E2
BULSTRODE 137 E3
Bulstrode Cl WD4 137 E2
Bulstrode La
Chipperfield WD4 137 F3
Hemel Hempstead HP3 138 A5
Bulwer Link SG1 50 E3
Buncefield La HP2 125 C5
Bungalows The
Essendon AL9 131 F7
Harpenden AL5 86 C3
Bungalow The SG11 41 E1
Bunker's Farm Cotts HP3 139 D8
Bunkers La HP3 139 B7
Bunnsfield AL7 111 C7
Bunstrux HP23 100 A4
BUNTINGFORD 40 F7
Buntingford Bsns Pk SG9 40 C8
Buntingford Rd SG11 55 D4
Bunting Rd LU4 44 A4
Bunyan Cl
Pirton SG5 20 D4
Tring HP23 100 B5
Bunyan Ho 23 LU2 45 D1
Bunyan Rd SG5 34 F8
Bunyans Cl LU3 45 A5
BUPA Bushey Hospl WD23 168 F1
Burbage Cl EN8 162 F8
Burchell Ct WD23 168 C2
Burfield Cl AL10 130 A7
Burfield Ct LU2 46 D3
Burfield Rd WD3 164 C4
Burford Cl LU3 31 A1
Burford Gdns EN11 135 B7
Burford Ho EN11 135 B7
Burford Mews 9 EN11 135 A7
Burford Pl 11 EN11 135 A7
Burford St EN11 135 A7
Burford Way SG5 21 D2
Burgage Ct 12 SG12 93 D1
Burgage La SG12 93 D1
BURGE END 20 D5
Burge End La SG5 20 C5
Burgess Cl EN7 147 C6
Burgess Ct WD6 156 F1
Burghley Ave
Bishop's Stortford CM23 76 C7
Borehamwood WD6 170 C4
Burghley Cl SG2 69 B8
Burgoyne Hatch CM20 118 A1
Burgundy Croft AL7 110 F4
Burgundy Ho EN2 161 C1
Burhill Gr HA5 175 E1
Burleigh Mead AL9 130 C7
Burleigh Prim Sch EN8 148 D1
Burleigh Rd
Cheshunt EN8 162 E7
Hemel Hempstead HP2 125 C2
Hertford SG13 114 A7
St Albans AL1 128 B3
Burleigh Way EN6 146 E1
Burley SG6 11 F2
Burley Ho WD5 153 F7
Burley Rd CM23 77 A4
Burnell Rise SG6 22 D5
Burnells Way CM24 59 E7
Burnell Wlk SG6 22 E5
Burnet Cl HP3 124 E2
Burnett Ave SG16 10 B4
Burnett Sq SG14 112 F7
Burnham Cl
Burnham Green AL6 90 C6
Enfield EN1 161 E1
BURNHAM GREEN 90 C6
Burnham Green Rd AL6, SG3 90 D6
Burnham Rd
Luton LU2 46 B2
St Albans AL1 128 B3
Burnley Cl WD19 175 C5
Burnsall Pl AL5 107 C6
Burns Cl
Hitchin SG4 35 B8
Stevenage SG2 51 C8
Burns Dr HP2 105 B1
BURN'S GREEN 52 F2
Burnside
Hertford SG14 113 A5
Hoddesdon EN11 134 F6
Sawbridgeworth CM21 97 D2
St Albans AL1 128 B1
Burnside Cl AL10 130 A8
Burnside Terr CM17 118 F3
Burns Rd SG8 7 D8
Burnt Cl LU3 44 F7
Burntfarm Ride EN2, EN7 161 B7
Burntmill Cl CM20 117 C3
Burntmill Cnr CM20 117 D4
Burnt Mill Comp Sch CM20 117 E2
Burnt Mill Ind Est CM20 117 C3
Burntmill La CM20 117 D3
Burr Cl AL2 142 E4
Burrowfield AL7 110 D4
Burrows Chase EN9 163 D4
Burrs La SG8 17 C3
Burrs Pl LU1 63 E6
Burr St LU2 63 E8
Bursland SG6 22 D6
Burston Dr AL2 141 C3
Burton Ave WD18 167 A5
Burton Cl AL4 87 C5
Burton Dr EN3 163 A2
Burton Grange EN7 147 E4
Burton La EN7 147 E3
Burtons La WD3 164 A4
Burtons Mill CM21 97 F3
Burvale Ct 3 WD18 167 B6
Burwell Rd SG2 51 B4
Bury Cotts AL3 105 E5
Burycroft AL8 89 E1
Burydale SG2 69 B8
Burydell La AL2 141 D5
Bury End SG5 20 D4
Bury Field SG9 29 B7
Buryfield Maltings SG12 93 C2
Buryfield Terr SG12 93 C1
Buryfield Way SG12 93 C1
Bury Gn
Hemel Hempstead HP1 124 C4
Wheathampstead AL4 108 C8
BURY GREEN
Bishop's Stortford 75 E7
Cheshunt 162 B8
Bury Green Rd
Cheshunt EN7 162 A7
Cheshunt EN7 162 A8
Bury Hill HP1 124 C4
Bury Hill Cl HP1 124 C4
Bury Holme EN10 148 F8
Bury La
Bramfield SG14 91 B4
Codicote SG4 67 F2
Datchworth SG3 69 D3
Rickmansworth WD3 165 D1
Streatley LU3 31 A5
Bury Mdws WD3 165 D1
Burymead SG1 36 C1
Bury Mead SG15 11 A7
Bury Mead Rd SG5 21 F1
BURY PARK 45 B1
Bury Park Ind Est 4 LU1 63 C8
Bury Park Rd LU1 63 C8
Bury Plantation SG8 7 F6
Bury Rd
Harlow CM17 118 D4
Hatfield AL10 130 C6
Hemel Hempstead HP1 124 C3
Bury Rise HP3 137 D6
Bury The
Codicote SG4 67 F2
Rickmansworth WD3 165 E1
Burywick AL5 107 B5
Bushbarns EN7 148 A2
Bushby Ave EN10 134 F1
Bushell Gn WD23 176 D8
Bushel Wharf HP23 100 A6
BUSHEY 168 A2
Bushey Cl AL7 111 B5
Bushey Gn AL7 111 B5
Bushey Grove Rd WD23 167 E5
Bushey Hall Dr WD23 167 E5
Bushey Hall Pk WD23 167 E5
Bushey Hall Rd WD23 167 E5
Bushey Hall Sch WD23 167 F4
BUSHEY HEATH 168 E2
Bushey Heath Prim Sch WD23 168 D1
Bushey Ley AL7 111 B5
Bushey Manor Jun Sch WD23 167 E4
Bushey Meads Sch WD23 168 C4
Bushey Mill Cres WD24 154 C3
Bushey Mill La
Watford, North Watford WD24 154 D1
Watford WD23 167 E8
Bushey Mus* WD23 168 A3
Bushey & Oxhey Inf Sch WD23 167 E4
Bushey Pk WD23 168 A3
Bushey Sta WD19 167 D3
Bushfield Rd HP3 137 C6
Bush Hall La AL9 130 D8
Bushmead Ct LU2 45 E6
Bushmead Prim Sch LU2 45 E5
Bushmead Rd LU2 45 E5
Bushmead Sh Ctr LU2 45 E5
Bush Spring SG7 13 A1
Bushwood Cl AL9 144 B8
Business Ctr E SG6 23 C6
Business Ctr The LU2 64 B6
Business Ctr W SG6 23 C6
Business Innovation Ctr The EN3 162 F3
Butchers La SG4 48 D6
Butely Rd LU4 44 B5
Bute Sq LU1 63 E7
Bute St LU1 63 E7
Butlers Ct EN8 162 E7
Butlers Dr E4 163 C1
Butler's Hall La CM23 76 B3
Butlers Yd SG7 12 E1
Butlin Rd LU1 63 B7
Buttercup Cl AL10 109 F1
Butterfield LU2 46 B7
Butterfield Cotts WD3 172 E3
Butterfield Ct SG7 23 E8
Butterfield Green Rd LU2 46 A6
Butterfield La AL1 141 E7
Butterfield Rd AL4 108 C7
Butterfly La WD6 169 B7
Buttermere Cl AL1 128 B2
Buttersweet Rise CM21 97 E1
Butterwick WD25 154 E3
Butterworth Path 1 LU2 63 E8
Butt Field View AL1 141 C7
Buttlehide WD3 172 D5
Buttondene Cres EN10 135 B1
Butts End HP1 124 A5
BUTTS GREEN 30 E8
Buttsmead HA6 174 C3
Butts The EN10 148 E7
Buttway SG7 4 C5
Buxton Cl AL4 128 D6
Buxton Path WD19 175 C7
Buxton Rd LU1 63 D7
Buxtons La SG8 1 F3
Buzzard Rd LU4 44 A4
Byde St SG14 113 C7
Byers Cl EN6 159 C5
Byewaters WD18 166 C3
Byeway The WD3 173 E8
Bye Way The HA3 176 F2
Byfield AL8 89 E1
Byfield Cl LU4 44 B1
Byfleet Ind Est WD18 166 B1
Byford Ho 5 EN5 171 D5
BYGRAVE 13 C5
Bygrave SG1 36 C2
Bygrave Rd SG7 12 F1
Bylands Cl CM23 76 D6
Bylands Ho AL3 106 A7
Byng Dr EN6 159 A8
Byng Rd EN5 171 D6
Byrd Ct SG1 50 D4
Byrd Wlk SG7 23 F7
Byron Ave
Borehamwood WD6 170 A4
Watford WD24 167 D8
Byron Cl
Hammond Street EN7 147 F4
Hitchin SG4 35 B8
Stevenage SG2 51 C7
Byron Ct EN8 148 B3
Byron Pl HP2 105 B1
Byron Rd
Harpenden AL5 86 A2
Harrow HA3 176 F1
Luton LU4 44 B2
Royston SG8 7 E8
Byslips Rd LU6 82 D5
By The Mount AL7 110 D5
By The Wood WD19 175 E8
Byways HP4 122 E5
Byway The EN6 159 A6
By-Wood End SL9 172 A5

C

Cabot Cl SG2 51 A7
CADDINGTON 62 D3
Caddington Comm AL3 83 E8
Caddington Pk LU1 44 B1
Caddis Cl HA7 176 F3
Cade Cl SG6 12 C1
Cades Cl LU1 63 A6
Cades La LU1 63 A6
Cadia Cl LU1 62 E4
Cadmore Ct
12 Cheshunt EN8 148 D3
Hertford SG14 112 F7
Cadmore La EN8 148 E2
Cadogen Pl AL1 142 A8
CADWELL 21 F5
Cadwell Ct SG4 22 A2
Cadwell Gn SG4 22 A2
Cadwell La SG4 22 A2
Caernarvon Cl
Hemel Hempstead HP2 124 D3
Stevenage SG2 69 B7
Caernarvon Ct HP2 124 D3
Caesars Rd AL4 108 E8
Cage Pond Rd WD7 156 F6
Cain Cl AL1 127 F1
Cain Ct 15 EN8 148 D3
Cairns Cl AL4 128 D2
Cairn Way HA7 176 F4
Caishowe Rd WD6 170 B8
Caister Cl
Hemel Hempstead HP2 124 E2
Stevenage SG1 36 A1
Calais Cl EN7 147 D5
Calbury Cl AL1 128 B2
Caldbeck EN9 163 D5
Caldecot Ave EN7 147 F2
CALDECOTE 3 D1
Caldecote Gdns WD23 168 E2
Caldecote La WD23 168 F3
Caldecote Rd SG7 12 E8
Caldecot Way EN10 134 F1
Calder Ave AL9 145 B5
Calder Way SG1 37 A3
Caldicott Ct 4 SG4 34 F7
Caldwell Rd WD19 175 D6
Caleb Cl LU4 44 F2
Caledonian Ct WD17 167 B7
Caledon Rd AL2 142 D5
California SG7 12 F1
California Ct 2 WD23 168 D1
California La WD23 168 D1
Callaghan Ct HP4 122 D4
Callanders The WD23 168 E1
Callard Ho HP4 122 B4
Callisto Ct HP2 124 F6
Callowland Pl WD24 154 B1
Callowlands WD24 167 B8
Calnwood Ct LU4 44 C3
Calnwood Rd LU4 44 C3
Calton Ave SG14 112 F7
Calton Ct SG14 112 F6
Calton Ho SG14 112 F6
Calverley Cl CM23 76 E4
Calverton Rd LU3 45 A6
Calvert Rd EN5 171 D7
Camberley Pl AL5 107 D6
Camborne Dr HP2 124 E7
Cambrian Way HP2 124 F6
Cambridge Cl EN8 148 C2
Cambridge Cotts SG11 72 E2
Cambridge Cres SG8 2 A8
Cambridge Ct
Barnet EN5 171 F6
Standon SG11 55 C2
Cambridge Dr EN6 158 E8
Cambridge Ho CM17 118 C5
Cambridge Rd
Barkway SG8 17 D5
Barley SG8 9 A3
Harlow CM20 118 C6
Hitchin SG4 22 C2
Sawbridgeworth CM21 97 E4
St Albans AL1 128 B2
Standon SG11 55 C2
Stansted Mountfitchet CM24 59 E8
6 Watford WD18 167 C5

Cambridge St LU1 63 F6
Cambridge Terr 16 HP4 122 D4
Cam Ctr SG4 22 A3
Camden Ho HP1 124 D3
Camelot Ct WD23 168 A7
Cameron Cl SG2 51 B7
Cameron Ct 8 SG12 93 D2
Cameron Dr EN8 162 D5
Camfield AL7 110 F2
Camford Way LU3 44 A8
Camlet Way AL3 127 B4
Campana Ct EN5 171 D6
Campania Gr LU3 45 A8
Campbell Cl
 Buntingford SG9 40 E7
 Hitchin SG4 35 B8
Campers Ave SG6 22 E5
Campers Rd SG6 22 E5
Campers Wlk SG6 22 E5
Campfield Rd
 Hertford SG14 113 B5
 St Albans AL1 128 A3
Campfield Way SG6 22 D5
Campine Cl 1 EN8 148 D3
Campion Cl WD25 154 A6
Campion Ct SG1 50 C8
Campion Rd
 Hatfield AL10 129 F8
 Hemel Hempstead HP1 123 E2
Campions CM17 118 F5
Campions Ct HP4 122 B3
Campions The
 Borehamwood WD6 157 A1
 Stansted Mountfitchet CM24 59 E8
Campion Way SG8 7 E5
Campkin Mead SG2 51 D3
Camp Prim Sch AL1 128 B2
Camp Rd AL1 128 B2
Camps Hill Com Prim Sch SG2 51 C6
CAMP THE 128 B2
Campus Five SG6 23 C7
Campus The AL8 110 D7
Camp View Rd AL1 128 B2
Cam Sq SG4 22 A3
Canada La EN10 148 E6
Canadas The EN10 148 E6
Canal Ct HP4 122 E4
Canalside HP4 121 F6
Canal Way UB9 173 A4
Canberra Cl
 Kneesworth SG8 2 B5
 St Albans AL3 127 F7
Canberra Gdns LU3 45 B6
Candlefield Cl HP3 139 A8
Candlefield Rd HP3 139 A8
Candlefield Wlk HP3 139 A8
Caneland Ct EN9 163 F5
Canfield CM23 76 E8
Cangels Cl HP1 124 A1
Canham Cl SG4 66 D1
Cannix Cl SG2 51 A2
Cannon Ho 1 SG4 34 F6
Cannon La LU2 46 B5
Cannon Mews 1 EN9 163 B6
Cannon Rd WD18 167 C4
Cannons Cl CM23 59 A1
Cannon's Cl SG8 1 F5
Cannons Ct SG11 55 D3
Cannons Mdw AL6 90 E2
Cannons Mead CM24 59 D7
Cannons Mill La CM23 59 A1
Cannon St AL3 127 D4
Canons Cl WD7 156 B4
Canons Field
 Oaklands AL6 89 E8
 Wheathampstead AL6 87 D1
Canonsfield Ct AL6 89 E7
Canonsfield Rd AL6 89 E8
Canons Gate
 Cheshunt EN8 148 F5
 Harlow CM20 117 A2
Canons Rd SG12 93 C2
Canopus Way HA6 175 A6
Canopy La CM17 118 C1
Cantelowes Ho EN5 171 D4
Canterbury Cl
 Luton LU3 44 F4
 Northwood HA6 174 F4
Canterbury Ct AL1 127 F4
Canterbury Ho
 10 Borehamwood WD6 170 A7
 4 Watford WD24 167 C7
Canterbury Rd
 Borehamwood WD6 170 A7
 Watford WD17 167 B7
Canterbury Way
 Croxley Green WD3 166 C6
 Stevenage SG1 36 F2
Capability Gn LU1 63 F4
Capel Ct SG11 57 E2
Capel Ho WD19 175 D6
Capella Rd HA6 174 F6
Capell Ave WD3 164 C4
Capell Rd WD3 164 D4
Capell Way WD3 164 D4
Capel Manor Coll EN1 162 A4
Capel Manor Gdns* EN1, EN7 162 B4
Capel Manor Prim Sch EN1 162 B4
Capel Rd
 Enfield EN1 162 B3
 Watford WD19 167 E3
Capelvere Wlk WD17 166 E8
Cape Rd AL1 128 B3
Capio Rivers Hospl The CM21 97 C1
Capital Bsns Pk WD6 170 C6
Caponfield AL7 111 B4
Cappell La SG12 115 D5
Capron Rd LU4 44 E4
Captains Wlk HP4 122 D3
Caractacus Cottage View WD18 167 A3
Caractacus Gn WD18 166 F3
Caravan La WD3 165 E2
Caravan Site The HP23 79 C4
Carbone Hill EN6, SG13 146 D5
Carde Cl SG14 112 F7
Cardiff Cl SG2 69 B7
Cardiff Gr LU1 63 D7
Cardiff Pl SG8 2 A8
Cardiff Rd
 Luton LU1 63 D7
 Watford WD18 167 B4
Cardiff Way WD5 154 A7
Cardigan Ct 11 LU1 63 D8
Cardigan Gdns 12 LU1 63 D8
Cardigan St LU1 63 D7
Cardinal Ave WD6 170 B5
Cardinal Cl EN7 147 F5
Cardinal Ct
 Borehamwood WD6 170 B6
 6 Luton LU2 45 D1
Cardinal Gr AL3 127 B1
Cardinal Newman RC Sch A Specialist Science Coll LU3 31 C1
Cardinals Gate SG8 7 C6
Cardy Rd HP1 124 B3
Careless Ct 21 CM23 76 F7
Carew Lo HA6 174 E4
Carew Rd HA6 174 F4
Carew Way WD19 175 F7
Careys Croft HP4 122 A7
Carisbrooke Ave WD24 167 D8
Carisbrooke Cl SG2 68 F8
Carisbrooke Rd
 Harpenden AL5 86 C2
 Luton LU4 44 E1
Carisbrook Rd AL2 141 B5
Carleton Rd EN8 148 E4
Carleton Rise AL6 89 C6
Carlisle Ave AL3 127 D4
Carlisle Ho 15 WD6 170 A7
Carlos Ind Est WD17 167 D5
Carlton Bank 2 AL5 86 B1
Carlton Cl
 Borehamwood WD6 170 D5
 Luton LU3 45 C2
Carlton Cres LU3 45 C2
Carlton Ct
 1 Harpenden AL5 86 B1
 Watford WD19 167 C3
Carlton Pl HA6 174 B5
Carlton Rd AL5 86 B2
Carman Ct HP23 99 F3
Carmelite Cl HA3 176 C2
Carmelite Rd
 Harrow HA3 176 C1
 Luton LU4 44 A3
Carmelite Way HA3 176 C1
Carmelite Wlk HA3 176 C2
Carmen Ct WD6 156 F1
Carnaby Rd EN10 134 E3
Carnarvon Rd EN5 171 E6
Carnegie Cl EN3 163 B1
Carnegie Gdns LU3 45 A8
Carnegie Rd AL3 127 D7
CARNELES GREEN 134 B1
Caro La HP3 125 B1
Carol Cl LU3 45 B4
Carole Ct 2 LU1 63 E5
Caroline Ho WD23 168 A3
Caroline Pl WD19 167 E3
Caroline Sharpe Ho AL4 128 C7
Carolyn Ct LU3 45 B4
Caroon Dr WD3 152 B3
Carpenders Ave WD19 175 E8
Carpenders Cl AL5 85 D4
Carpenders Park Bsns Ctr WD19 175 D7
Carpenders Park Sta WD19 175 D7
Carpenters Rd EN1 162 C3
Carpenters The CM23 76 B5
Carpenters Wood Dr WD3 164 B5
Carpenters Yd HP23 100 B3
Carpenter Way EN6 159 D6
Carriages The SG12 114 E8
Carriden Ct SG14 112 F8
Carrigans CM23 76 E8
Carrington Ave WD6 170 C4
Carrington Cl
 Arkley EN5 171 A4
 Borehamwood WD6 170 C4
Carrington Pl HP23 100 C5
Carrington Sq HA3 176 C3
Carsdale Cl LU3 45 A6
Carteret Rd LU2 46 C1
Carterhatch La EN1 161 F1
Carters Cl
 Arlesey SG15 11 A7
Carters Cl *continued*
 Aston SG2 51 D4
Cartersfield Rd EN9 163 C5
Carters La (Wibbly Wobbley La) SG5 34 A6
Carters Leys CM23 76 D8
Carters Way SG15 11 A7
Carters Wlk SG15 11 A7
Carthagena Est EN9 135 C3
Cart Path WD25 154 C6
Cartref SG1 50 A6
Cart Tk The HP3 138 F6
Cartwright Rd
 Royston SG8 7 D5
 Stevenage SG1 37 C2
Carve Ley AL7 111 B5
Carvers Croft SG3 69 B2
Cary Wlk WD7 156 B5
Cashio La SG6 23 A8
Caslon Way SG6 11 F1
Cassandra Gate EN8 148 F4
Cassiobridge Rd WD18 166 E5
Cassiobridge Terr WD3 166 D4
Cassiobury Dr WD17 166 F7
Cassiobury Ho WD17 167 B7
Cassiobury Inf Sch WD17 166 E8
Cassiobury Jun Sch WD17 166 E8
Cassiobury Park Ave WD18 166 F6
Cassio Ho 4 WD18 166 F5
Cassio Pl WD18 166 E5
Cassio Rd WD18 167 B5
Casson Ct AL2 142 A4
Castano Ct WD5 153 E8
Castellane Cl 1 HA7 176 F3
Castile Gdns WD4 138 F2
Castings Ho SG6 23 A7
Castle Cl
 Bushey WD23 168 B3
 Hoddesdon EN11 115 C1
 Pitstone LU7 80 D3
Castle Cotts SG9 29 B7
Castle Croft Rd LU1 63 A6
Castle Ct SG5 21 D1
Castleford Cl WD6 156 F1
Castle Gate 1 SG14 113 C5
Castle Gate Way HP4 122 C6
Castle Hill HP4 122 C6
Castle Hill Ave HP4 122 C5
Castle Hill Cl HP4 122 C5
Castle Hill Ct HP4 122 C6
Castle Mead HP1 124 B1
Castle Mead Gdns 3 SG14 113 C5
Castle Mews 3 HP4 122 D4
Castle Mill HP4 122 C5
Castle Rd
 Enfield EN3 162 E1
 Hoddesdon EN11 115 C1
 St Albans AL1 128 B3
Castle Rise AL4 86 F2
Castle Row HP23 100 A3
Castles Cl SG5 11 F8
Castle St
 Berkhamsted HP4 122 C4
 Bishop's Stortford CM23 76 F6
 Hertford SG14 113 D5
 Luton, High Town LU1 63 E7
 Luton, New Town LU1 63 E6
 Wingrave HP22 60 B3
Castle View CM23 77 A7
Castle Wlk CM24 59 E6
Catalin Ct EN9 163 D6
Catalonia Apartments 2 WD18 166 F5
Caterham Ct EN9 163 F5
Catesby Gn LU3 31 A1
Catham Cl AL1 128 B1
Cathedral & Abbey Church of St Alban* AL3 127 D3
Cathedral Ct AL3 127 B1
Catherall Rd LU3 45 B6
Catherine Cl HP2 125 B8
Catherine Cotts HP23 120 E8
Catherine Ho WD19 175 B7
Catherine Rd EN3 162 E3
Catherine St AL3 127 D4
Catherine Wheel Mews 20 SG12 93 D1
Cathrow Mews 2 EN11 115 A1
Catisfield Rd EN3 162 E2
Catkin Cl HP1 124 B4
Catlin St HP3 138 B8
Catsbrook Rd LU3 45 B6
Catsdell Bottom HP3 139 B8
Catsey La WD23 168 C2
Catsey Wood WD23 168 C2
Catterick Way WD6 169 F8
Cattlegate Cotts EN6 160 D8
Cattlegate Hill EN6 160 D7
Cattlegate Rd
 Crews Hill EN2 161 A5
 Northaw EN6 160 D6
Cattley Cl EN5 171 E5
Cattlins Cl EN7 147 F2
Cattsdell HP2 124 E5
Causeway Cl EN6 159 D8
Causeway Ho WD5 153 E8
Causeway The
 1 Bishop's Stortford CM23 77 A7
 Braughing SG9, SG11 42 D1
 Brent Pelham SG9 30 B1
Causeway The *continued*
 Buntingford SG9 40 F8
 Furneux Pelham SG9 43 A3
 Kneesworth SG8 2 A5
 Potters Bar EN6 159 D8
 Therfield SG8 15 F7
Cautherly La SG12 115 A5
Cavalier Cl LU3 45 A5
Cavalier Ct
 7 Berkhamsted HP4 122 C4
 Stevenage SG1 36 B1
Cavalli Apartments 14 WD18 166 E5
Cavan Ct AL10 130 A4
Cavan Dr AL3 127 D8
Cavan Rd AL3 106 A6
Cave Gate SG9 28 D6
Cavell Ct CM23 77 B6
Cavell Dr CM23 77 B6
Cavell Rd EN7 148 A4
Cavell Wlk SG2 51 C5
Cavendish Cres WD6 170 A5
Cavendish Ct
 Croxley Green WD3 166 D4
 Hemel Hempstead HP3 138 E6
Cavendish Rd
 Barnet EN5 171 C6
 Luton LU3 45 B2
 Markyate AL3 83 D6
 St Albans AL1 127 F3
 Stevenage SG1 50 B5
Cavendish Sch The HP1 124 B4
Cavendish Way AL10 129 F5
Cawkell Cl CM24 59 D7
Caxton Ct
 Enfield EN3 162 E4
 Luton LU3 44 F4
Caxton Ctr AL3 127 F8
Caxton Gate SG1 50 B4
Caxton Hill SG13 113 F6
Caxton Pl SG1 50 B4
Caxton Rd EN11 115 B2
Caxton Way
 Stevenage SG1 50 B4
 Watford WD18 166 D2
Cecil Cl CM23 77 D7
Cecil Cres AL10 130 B7
Cecil Ct EN5 171 D6
Cecil Rd
 Cheshunt EN8 162 E7
 Hertford SG13 113 C3
 Hoddesdon EN11 135 C8
 South Mimms EN6 158 B7
 St Albans AL1 127 F3
Cecil St WD24 154 B1
Cedar Ave
 Cheshunt EN8 162 D6
 Ickleford SG5 21 E4
Cedar Cl
 Hertford SG14 113 B6
 Potters Bar EN6 145 A1
 Sawbridgeworth CM21 97 E1
 Ware SG12 114 D8
Cedar Cres SG8 7 B6
Cedar Ct
 Bishop's Stortford CM23 58 F1
 St Albans AL4 128 D3
 Watford WD25 154 D6
Cedar Dr HA5 176 A4
Cedar Gn EN11 135 A5
Cedar Grange HA6 174 C3
Cedar Lawn Ave EN5 171 E4
Cedar Lo 8 EN8 148 D3
Cedar Park Rd EN2 161 C1
Cedar Pk CM23 76 D4
Cedar Pl HA6 174 C4
Cedar Rd
 Berkhamsted HP4 122 E3
 Enfield EN2 161 C1
 Hatfield AL10 130 A4
 Watford WD19 167 D3
Cedars Ave WD3 165 C1
Cedars Cl WD6 170 B5
Cedars Manor Sch HA3 176 C2
Cedars The
 Berkhamsted HP4 122 E4
 13 Harpenden AL5 86 B1
 5 Rickmansworth WD3 165 D2
 St Albans AL3 127 C5
 Stevenage SG2 69 B8
Cedars Wlk WD3 164 F5
Cedar Way HP4 122 D3
Cedar Wlk
 Hemel Hempstead HP3 124 D1
 Waltham Abbey EN9 163 D5
 Welwyn Garden City AL7 111 B5
Cedarwood Dr AL4 128 D3
Cedar Wood Dr WD25 154 B4
Celandine Dr LU3 45 A8
Celia Ho AL7 110 F6
Cell Barnes Cl AL1 128 B1
Cell Barnes La AL1 128 B1
Cemetery Hill HP1 124 C2
Cemetery Rd CM23 76 F6
Cemmaes Court Rd HP1 124 C3
Cemmaes Mdw HP1 124 C3
Centenary Cl SG10 96 C6
Centennial Ave WD6 169 C2
Centennial Ct WD3 165 E2
Centennial Ct WD6 169 C2
Centennial Pk WD6 169 C2
Central App SG6 22 F6
Central Ave
 Cheshunt EN8 162 E6
 Lower Stondon SG16 10 B3
 Whipsnade LU6 81 E8
Central Dr
 St Albans AL4 128 C4
 Welwyn Garden City AL7 110 F8
Central Hts 3 WD18 166 F5
Central Prim Sch WD18 167 C5
Central Rd CM20 118 A4
Central Way HA6 174 E3
Centrium AL1 127 C1
Centro HP2 125 C5
Centurion Ct 3 AL1 128 A2
Century Cl AL3 127 C4
Century Ct WD18 166 C2
Century Ho HP1 124 C4
Century Pk WD17 167 C4
Century Rd
 Hoddesdon EN11 135 A7
 Ware SG12 93 D2
Cervantes Ct HA6 174 F3
Chace Ave EN6 159 D7
Chace The SG2 50 F1
Chad La AL3 84 C4
Chadwell SG12 114 C8
Chadwell Ave EN8 148 C3
Chadwell Cl LU2 45 F1
Chadwell Rd SG1 50 B3
Chadwell Rise SG12 114 C8
Chaffinches Gn HP3 139 A7
Chaffinch La WD18 166 F2
Chagny Cl SG6 22 E6
Chalet Cl HP4 121 F4
Chalet The EN11 134 E8
Chalfont Cl HP2 125 B8
Chalfont Ho WD18 166 E2
Chalfont La
 Chorleywood WD3 164 B4
 Maple Cross WD3 172 D3
Chalfont Pl AL1 127 E3
Chalfont Rd WD3, SL9, HP8 172 C7
CHALFONT ST PETER 172 A3
Chalfont Shire Ctr* HP8 172 A7
Chalfont Way LU2 46 D2
Chalfont Wlk 2 HA5 175 C1
Chalgrove AL7 111 D7
Chalk Dale AL7 111 B7
Chalkdell Fields AL4 128 A7
Chalkdell Hill HP2 124 E3
Chalkdell Ho WD25 154 C6
Chalkdell Path 8 SG5 34 D8
Chalkdown
 Luton LU2 45 E6
 Stevenage SG2 51 D7
Chalk Field SG6 23 C3
Chalk Hill
 Cockernhoe LU2 47 A5
 Watford WD19 167 E3
Chalk Hills SG7 23 F5
Chalks Ave CM21 97 D3
Challney Boys High Sch & Com Coll LU4 44 D2
Challney Cl LU4 44 D2
Challney Girls High Sch LU4 44 D2
Chalmers Ct WD3 165 F3
Chalton Rd LU4 44 C5
Chamberlaines AL5 85 A5
Chambersbury La HP3 139 A7
Chambersbury Prim Sch HP3 139 B8
Chambers Gate SG1 50 D7
Chambers Gr AL7 110 E3
Chambers La SG5 21 E4
Chambers' St SG14 113 C6
Champions Cl WD6 157 B2
Champions Gn EN11 115 A1
Champions Way EN11 115 A1
Champneys 3 WD19 175 E8
Chancellors SG15 11 B7
Chancellors Rd SG1 36 D1
Chancellor's Sch AL9 145 A6
Chancery Cl AL4 128 D8
Chandlers Cl CM23 76 C4
CHANDLER'S CROSS 152 F1
Chandler's La WD3 152 E2
Chandlers Rd AL4 128 C6
Chandlers Way SG14 113 A6
Chandos Cl HP6 150 C1
Chandos Rd
 Borehamwood WD6 170 A7
 Luton LU4 44 F1
Chantry Cl
 Bishop's Stortford CM23 76 E8
 Edgware NW7 170 F2
 Enfield EN2 161 C1
 Kings Langley WD4 139 A2
Chantry Ct AL10 130 A4
Chantry La
 Hatfield AL10 129 F4
 Hatfield AL10 130 A4
 Little Wymondley SG4 35 F2
 London Colney AL2 142 D5
Chantry Mount CM23 76 E8
Chantry Pl HA3 176 B2

Chantry Rd
Bishop's Stortford CM23 76 E8
Harrow HA3 176 B2
Chantry The
6 Bishop's Stortford CM23 76 F8
Harlow CM20 118 A2
Chaomans SG6 22 F3
Chapel Cl
Brookmans Park AL9 145 D4
Little Gaddesden HP4 102 D6
Luton LU2 45 C8
St Albans AL1 141 D8
Chapel Cotts HP2 124 D4
Chapel Croft WD4 152 A8
Chapel Crofts HP4 121 E6
Chapel Dr SG15 11 A4
CHAPEL END 99 C8
Chapel End
Buntingford SG9 40 E7
Hoddesdon EN11 135 A5
Chapel End La HP23 99 C8
Chapelfields SG12 115 D4
Chapel Fields HP23 99 C8
Chapel Hill CM24 59 E6
Chapel La
Letty Green SG14 112 B3
Little Hadham SG11 75 A8
Long Marston HP23 79 B4
St Leonards HP23 119 D2
Chapel Pl SG5 11 F6
Chapel Rd
Breachwood Green SG4 65 E8
Flamstead AL3 84 B2
Chapel Row
Bendish SG4 66 A8
3 Bishop's Stortford CM23 76 F6
Harefield UB9 173 C2
Hitchin SG5 34 F8
Chapel St
Berkhamsted HP4 122 D4
Hemel Hempstead HP2 124 D4
Hinxworth SG7 3 D6
Luton, High Town LU1 63 E7
Luton, New Town LU1 63 E6
Tring HP23 99 F3
Chapel Viaduct LU1 63 E7
Chapel Way WD5 139 F4
Chapman Ctyd 8 EN8 148 D1
Chapman Rd SG1 36 B1
Chapmans End SG11 55 D3
CHAPMORE END 92 D5
Chappell Ct SG12 92 E7
Chappel Mdw HP23 100 B6
Chapter House Rd LU4 44 A3
Chard Dr LU3 31 B1
Chardia Terr EN8 148 D1
Charding Cres SG8 7 C7
Chardins Cl HP1 123 F4
Charkham Mews AL9 144 C7
Charles Ho 8 EN11 135 D8
Charles St
Berkhamsted HP4 122 B4
Hemel Hempstead HP1 124 C2
Luton LU2 63 F8
Tring HP23 100 A3
Charlesworth Cl 4 HP3 124 D1
Charlock Way WD18 166 F3
Charlotte Cl
St Albans AL4 128 E3
Watford WD19 167 C2
Charlottes Ct 2 LU1 63 D7
CHARLTON 34 D5
Charlton Cl EN11 135 A6
Charlton Mead La EN11 135 D5
Charlton Rd SG5 34 D5
Charlton Way EN11 135 B6
Charlwood Cl HA3 176 E4
Charlwood Rd LU4 44 B1
Charmbury Rise LU2 46 A4
Charmouth Ct AL1 128 A6
Charmouth Rd AL1 128 A5
Charndon Cl LU3 31 B1
Charnwood Rd EN1 162 B3
Charter Ho WD3 166 A4
Charter Pl WD17 167 C6
Chartley Ave HA7 176 F4
Chartridge WD19 175 D8
Chartridge Cl
Arkley EN5 171 A4
Bushey WD23 168 C3
Chartridge Way HP2 125 C3
Chartwell Cl EN9 163 E6
Chartwell Ct 10 EN5 171 E5
Chartwell Dr LU2 45 E3
Chartwell Pl CM23 59 B1
Chartwell Rd HA6 174 F4
Charwood Cl WD7 156 E6
Chasden Rd HP1 123 F5
Chase Cl SG15 11 A8
Chase Farm EN6 159 C4
Chase Farm Hospl EN2 161 A1
Chase Hill Rd SG15 11 A7
Chaseside Cl LU7 80 A7
Chase St LU1 63 E6
Chase The
Arlesey SG15 11 A6
Bishop's Stortford CM23 76 F6
Goff's Oak EN7 147 B3
Great Amwell SG12 115 A6
Harlow CM17 118 C1
Chase The *continued*
Hemel Hempstead HP2 124 E2
Hertford SG13 113 F6
Oaklands AL6 89 F7
Radlett WD7 155 F4
Watford WD18 166 E5
Chaseways CM21 118 C8
Chasten Hill SG6 22 D7
Chater Inf Sch WD18 167 A5
Chater Jun Sch WD18 167 B5
Chatsworth Cl
Bishop's Stortford CM23 76 C7
Borehamwood WD6 170 A6
Chatsworth Ct
St Albans AL1 127 F3
Stevenage SG2 50 F1
Chatsworth Mews WD24 154 A1
Chatsworth Rd LU4 45 B1
CHATTER END 58 C7
Chatter End CM23 58 C7
Chatteris Cl LU4 44 D4
Chatterton SG6 23 C5
Chatton Cl LU2 46 E2
Chaucer Cl HP4 121 F5
Chaucer Ct EN11 115 A1
Chaucer Gr WD6 170 A5
Chaucer Ho 3 EN5 171 D5
Chaucer Rd
Luton LU3 45 C2
Royston SG8 7 C8
Chaucer Way
Hitchin SG4 35 C7
Hoddesdon EN11 115 A2
Chaucer Wlk HP2 105 B1
CHAULDEN 123 E2
Chaulden House Gdns HP1 123 F1
Chaulden Jun & Inf Schs HP1 123 F2
Chaulden La HP1 123 E1
Chaulden Terr HP1 123 F2
CHAUL END 62 C7
Chaul End La LU4 44 E1
Chaul End Rd
Caddington LU1 62 D6
Luton LU1 44 C1
Chauncey Ho WD18 166 E3
Chauncy Ave EN6 159 C6
Chauncy Cl SG12 93 D3
Chauncy Ct 19 SG14 113 D6
Chauncy Gdns SG7 13 B1
Chauncy Ho 3 SG1 50 E6
Chauncy Rd SG1 50 E6
Chauncy Sch The SG12 93 B2
Chaworth Gn 1 LU4 44 C5
CHEAPSIDE 29 B7
Cheapside LU1 63 E7
Cheapside Sq 4 LU1 63 E7
Chedburgh AL7 111 D7
CHEDDINGTON 80 A8
Cheddington Comb Sch LU7 80 A7
Cheddington La HP23 79 C5
Cheddington Rd LU7 80 C4
Cheffins Rd EN11 114 F1
CHELLS 51 B6
Chells Ent Village SG2 51 C6
Chells La SG2 51 D7
Chells Way SG2 51 B6
Chelmsford Rd SG14 113 B5
Chelsea Fields EN11 115 B2
Chelsing Rise HP2 125 C2
Chelsworth Cl 1 LU2 46 D1
Cheltenham Ct 9 AL1 128 A2
Cheltenham Ho 2 WD24 167 C7
Chelveston AL7 111 D7
Chelwood Ave AL10 130 A8
Chelwood Cl HA6 174 C3
Chenduit Way HA7 176 F5
Chene Dr AL3 127 D5
Chene Mews AL3 127 D5
Cheney Rd LU4 44 C5
CHENIES 151 B1
Chenies 4 HA6 174 F5
Chenies Ave HP6 150 D1
CHENIES BOTTOM 151 A2
Chenies Ct HP2 125 B8
Chenies Gn CM23 76 D6
Chenies Manor Ho* WD3 151 A1
Chenies Rd WD3 164 D7
Chenies Sch WD3 151 B1
Chenies Way WD18 166 E2
Chennells AL10 129 F4
Chennells Cl SG4 22 B2
Chepstow AL5 85 F2
Chepstow Cl SG1 51 B8
Chequer Ct LU1 63 F6
Chequer La AL3 106 B4
Chequers
Bishop's Stortford CM23 76 C8
Hatfield AL9 130 D8
Welwyn Garden City AL7 110 D3
Chequers Bridge Rd SG1 50 C6
Chequers Cl
Buntingford SG9 40 D8
Pitstone LU7 80 C4
Standon SG11 55 D4
Stotfold SG5 12 A6
Chequers Cotts
Preston SG4 48 D6
Chequers Cotts *continued*
Whipsnade LU6 82 A8
Chequers End HP2 104 D5
Chequersfield AL7 110 D3
Chequers Hill AL3 84 C2
Chequers La
Abbots Langley WD2 140 C1
Pitstone LU7 80 C5
Preston SG4 48 D7
Chequer St
Luton LU1 63 F6
St Albans AL1 127 D3
Chequers Wlk EN9 163 F6
Cheriton Cl AL4 128 D7
Cherrington Ct LU2 46 A4
Cherry Bank HP2 124 D5
Cherry Blossom Cl 3 CM17 118 C4
Cherry Cl SG3 68 F4
Cherry Croft
Croxley Green WD3 166 B3
Welwyn Garden City AL8 89 D2
Cherry Croft Gdns 4 HA5 175 F3
Cherry Ct HA5 175 D2
Cherrydale WD18 166 F5
Cherry Dr SG8 7 E7
Cherry Gdns
Bishop's Stortford CM23 77 A8
Sawbridgeworth CM21 97 E4
Tring HP23 99 F3
CHERRY GREEN 40 C1
Cherry Green Barns SG9 40 C1
Cherry Green La SG9 40 F3
Cherry Hill
Chiswell Green AL2 141 A6
Harrow HA3 176 E4
Rickmansworth WD3 165 B6
Cherry Hills WD19 175 E5
Cherry Hollow WD5 153 F8
Cherry Orch HP1 124 A5
Cherry Orchard La SG9 28 A3
Cherry Rd EN3 162 C1
Cherry Tree Ave AL2 142 D5
Cherry Tree Cl
Arlesey SG15 11 A4
Luton LU2 46 A1
Cherry Tree Gn SG14 112 F7
Cherrytree La HP2 125 C7
Cherry Tree La
Cholesbury HP23 120 A3
Chorleywood WD3 164 C1
Harlow CM20 117 B1
Potters Bar EN6 159 B5
Wheathampstead AL4 87 A2
Cherry Tree Prim Sch WD24 154 A3
Cherry Tree Rd
Hoddesdon EN11 135 A7
Watford WD24 154 B3
Cherry Tree Rise SG2 38 B1
Cherry Trees SG16 10 B3
Cherry Trees Dr SG2 51 B7
Cherry Way AL10 130 A2
Cherry Wlk WD3 165 C7
Chertsey Cl LU2 64 D8
Chertsey Rise SG2 51 C4
Cherwell Cl WD3 166 A4
Cherwell Dr SG1 37 A3
Chesfield Cl CM23 76 F5
Chesford Ct 16 LU1 63 E6
Chesford Rd LU2 46 C4
Chesham Ct HA6 174 F4
Chesham Prep Sch HP5 136 A4
Chesham Rd
Berkhamsted HP4 122 C3
Bovingdon HP3, HP3 136 E3
Wigginton HP23 120 E7
Chesham Way WD18 166 F3
Cheshire Dr WD25 153 F5
CHESHUNT 148 C1
Cheshunt Centre The EN8 148 D3
Cheshunt Com Hospl EN8 162 E8
Cheshunt Folly EN8 148 B3
Cheshunt Sch EN8 148 C1
Cheshunt Sta EN8 148 F1
Cheshunt Wash EN8 148 E4
Cheslyn Cl LU2 46 E2
Chess Cl
Latimer HP5 150 D3
Rickmansworth WD3 165 D5
Chess Hill WD3 165 D5
Chess La WD3 165 D5
Chess Vale Rise WD3 165 F3
Chess Way WD3 165 A6
Chesswood Ct WD3 165 D1
Chesswood Way HA5 175 D1
Chester Ave LU4 44 E3
Chester Cl
Luton LU4 44 F2
Potters Bar EN6 145 B2
Chesterfield Flats EN5 171 D4
Chesterfield Prim Sch EN3 162 E2
Chesterfield Rd
Barnet EN5 171 D4
Enfield EN3 162 E2
Chester Gibbons Gn AL2 142 D5
Chester Ho HA6 174 F3
Chester Pl 1 HA6 174 E3
Chester Rd
Borehamwood WD6 170 D6
Northwood HA6 174 F3
Stevenage SG1 37 A1
Watford WD18 167 A5
Chesterton Ave AL5 86 D1
Chestnut Ave
Lower Stondon SG16 10 C3
Luton LU3 44 C8
Northwood HA6 174 F2
Rickmansworth WD3 165 A4
Ware SG12 93 F3
Chestnut Cl
Bishop's Stortford CM23 76 E6
Dagnall HP4 81 C5
Hunsdon SG12 95 D1
Potten End HP4 123 B6
Chestnut Ct
4 Hitchin SG5 34 D8
Watford WD18 166 E5
Chestnut Dr
Berkhamsted HP4 122 D3
Harrow HA3 176 F2
Hatfield Heath CM22 98 F3
St Albans AL4 128 C5
Chestnut Gr EN11 115 C2
Chestnut La
Harlow CM20 117 B1
Kneesworth SG8 2 B6
Totteridge N20 171 E1
Chestnut Rd EN3 162 E3
Chestnut Rise WD23 168 B2
Chestnuts The
Codicote SG4 67 F2
Hemel Hempstead HP3 137 F7
Hertford SG13 113 D5
Chestnut Wlk
Hitchin SG4 35 A4
Royston SG8 7 E5
Stevenage SG1 36 D1
Watford WD24 154 A2
Welwyn AL6 90 A8
Cheverells Cl AL3 83 D4
Cheverell's Gn
Cheverell's Green AL3 83 C4
Markyate AL3 83 C4
CHEVERELL'S GREEN 83 C4
Cheviot Cl
Bushey WD23 168 C3
Luton LU3 44 D7
Cheviot Rd LU3 44 D7
Cheviots
Hatfield AL10 130 A3
Hemel Hempstead HP2 124 F6
Cheviot Way SG1 37 A3
Cheyne Cl
Pitstone LU7 80 D4
Ware SG12 93 D3
Cheynes Inf Sch LU3 44 D8
Chicheley Gdns HA3 176 C3
Chicheley Rd HA3 176 C3
Chichester Way WD25 154 E6
Chicken La AL2 142 D4
Chidbrook Ho WD18 166 E3
Chilcott Rd WD24 153 F3
Chilcourt SG8 7 C6
Childs Ave UB9 173 C1
Childwick Ct HP3 139 B8
Childwick Gn AL3 107 C2
CHILDWICK GREEN 107 C2
Childwick Way SG6 22 E8
Chilham Cl HP2 124 E2
Chiltern Ave WD23 168 C3
Chiltern Cl
Berkhamsted HP4 121 F5
Borehamwood WD6 169 F7
Bushey WD23 168 B3
Goff's Oak EN7 147 B4
Ware SG12 93 D3
Watford WD18 166 F5
Chiltern Cnr HP4 122 A5
Chiltern Cotts HP23 120 A2
Chiltern Ct
19 Harpenden AL5 86 B1
St Albans AL4 128 D7
Chiltern Dr WD3 165 A2
Chiltern Gdns LU4 44 F3
CHILTERN GREEN 65 B3
Chiltern Park Ave HP4 122 A6
Chiltern Rd
Baldock SG7 23 F6
Hitchin SG4 35 A7
St Albans AL4 128 C7
Wingrave HP22 60 A3
Chiltern Rise LU1 63 D6
Chilterns
Berkhamsted HP4 121 F6
Hatfield AL10 130 A2
Hemel Hempstead HP2 124 E5
Chilterns The
Hitchin SG4 35 A6
Kensworth Common LU6 82 F8
Stevenage SG1 37 B3
Chiltern View SG6 22 D5
Chiltern Villas HP23 99 E3
Chiltern Way HP23 100 C5
Chilton Ct SG14 112 F8
Chilton Gn AL7 111 C6
Chilvers Bank SG7 23 E7
Chilwell Gdns WD19 175 C6
Chilworth Gate EN10 134 F1
Chime Sq AL3 127 E4
Chimneys The WD23 167 F4
Chindit Cl EN10 134 E3
Chinneck Ho 10 HP4 122 C4
Chinnery Cl EN1 161 F1
Chinnery Hill CM23 76 F5
Chipmunk Chase AL10 129 D7
CHIPPERFIELD 152 B8
Chipperfield Rd
Bovingdon HP3 137 C3
Hemel Hempstead HP3 138 C7
Kings Langley WD4 138 D2
CHIPPING 27 D5
CHIPPING BARNET 171 E5
Chipping Cl 8 EN5 171 E6
Chippingfield CM17 118 C3
Chipping Hall Cotts SG9 27 D4
Chirdland Ho WD18 166 E3
Chishill Rd
Barley SG8 9 A2
Great Chishill SG8 9 F3
Chishill Windmill* SG8 9 C2
Chiswell Ct WD24 154 C1
CHISWELL GREEN 141 A5
Chiswell Green La AL2 140 E6
Chittenden Cl 5 EN11 115 B1
Chivenor Pl AL4 128 C1
CHIVERY 119 C4
Chobham Ct 8 LU1 63 F6
Chobham St LU1 63 F6
Chobham Wlk 5 LU1 63 E6
CHOLESBURY 120 C2
Cholesbury 1 WD19 175 E8
Cholesbury Ho WD18 166 E3
Cholesbury La HP23 120 B2
Cholesbury Rd HP23 120 D5
CHORLEYWOOD 164 D5
CHORLEYWOOD BOTTOM 164 D3
Chorleywood Bottom WD3 164 D4
Chorleywood Cl WD3 165 D2
Chorleywood House Dr WD3 164 E6
Chorleywood Prim Sch WD3 164 C3
Chorleywood Rd WD3 165 C4
Chorleywood Sta WD3 164 D5
CHORLEYWOOD WEST 164 B5
Chouler Gdns SG1 36 C2
Chowns The AL5 107 A5
Christ Church CE Prim Sch SG12 93 E1
Christ Church CE Sch WD3 164 F5
Christchurch Cl AL3 127 D4
Christchurch Cres WD7 156 A3
Christchurch Ho HP23 100 A3
Christ Church La EN5 171 E7
Christchurch Pl SG14 113 C6
Christ Church Prim Sch EN5 171 D7
Christchurch Rd
Hemel Hempstead HP2 124 D4
Tring HP23 99 F4
Christian Cl EN11 114 F2
Christie Cl EN10 134 F3
Christie Ct WD18 167 A4
Christie Rd
Stevenage SG2 51 D5
Waltham Abbey EN9 163 B4
Christies Ct 5 EN11 135 A6
Christina Ct AL3 83 E5
Christopher Ct
Hemel Hempstead HP3 138 D8
13 Ware SG12 93 D1
Christopher Pl 5 AL3 127 D3
Christy's Yd SG7 3 D6
Chrysalis Sch for Autism SG4 67 F2
Church Cl
Codicote SG4 67 F2
Cuffley EN6 146 E2
Little Berkhamsted SG13 132 C4
Northwood HA6 174 F3
Radlett WD7 156 A3
Reed SG8 16 E4
Studham LU6 82 B4
Church Cotts
Essendon AL9 131 E6
Gilston CM20 117 C7
Great Gaddesden HP1 103 D3
Church Cres
Sawbridgeworth CM21 97 F2
St Albans AL3 127 C4
Church Ct
Hoddesdon EN10 135 A3
10 Ware SG12 93 D2
CHURCH END 11 B7
Church End SG15 11 A8
CHURCH END 24 D1
Church End
Barley SG8 9 A1
Braughing SG11 55 F7
CHURCH END 57 D2
Church End AL3 83 D6

CHURCH END
Pitstone 80 D3
Redbourn 105 F4
Church End
Redbourn AL3 106 A4
Sandridge AL4 108 C2
CHURCH END 151 F1
Church End SG2 38 C2
Church End Cotts WD3 151 F1
Church Farm HP23 101 C5
Church Farm La HP23 79 F3
Church Farm Way WD25 155 B1
Churchfield
Barley SG8 9 A1
Harlow CM20 118 B2
Harpenden AL5 107 C8
Church Field SG12 93 B3
Churchfield Ho AL8 110 C6
Church Field Path EN8 148 C2
Churchfield Rd AL6 90 C1
Churchfields
Hertford SG13 113 D5
Hoddesdon EN10 135 A3
Standon SG11 55 E2
Stansted Mountfitchet CM24 59 F6
Churchfields La EN10 135 A3
Churchfields Rd WD24 153 F3
CHURCHGATE 148 A1
Churchgate
Cheshunt EN8 148 B1
7 Hitchin SG5 34 E7
Churchgate CE Prim Sch CM17 118 F3
Churchgate Rd EN8 148 B2
Church Gates 4 HP4 122 C4
Churchgate St CM17 118 E4
CHURCHGATE STREET 118 F3
Church Gn
Benington SG2 52 D4
Great Wymondley SG4 35 E6
Harpenden AL5 86 A1
Church Green Mews 4 AL5 86 A1
Church Green Row 3 AL5 86 A1
Church Hill
Bedmond WD5 139 F4
Cheddington LU7 80 A8
Harefield UB9 173 C1
Hertford Heath SG13 114 C4
Churchill Cres AL9 144 C8
Churchill Ct HA6 174 D4
Churchill Rd
Luton LU4 45 A1
St Albans AL1 128 A4
Church La
Arlesey SG15 11 A7
Ashwell SG7 4 D4
Barkway SG8 17 C4
Berkhamsted HP4 122 C4
Bishop's Stortford CM23 76 D3
Bovingdon HP3 137 B4
Cheddington LU7 80 A8
Cheshunt EN8 148 C2
Colney Heath AL4 143 B8
Dane End SG12 71 F8
Graveley SG4 36 C4
Guilden Morden SG8 1 F5
Harrow HA3 176 F2
Hatfield AL9 130 C5
Hoddesdon EN10 134 C1
Kimpton SG4 66 D1
Kings Langley WD4 139 A2
Letchworth Garden City SG6 12 C1
Marsworth HP23 79 F1
Much Hadham SG10 74 F3
Northaw EN6 146 A1
Preston SG4 48 D6
Radlett WD25 155 B1
Reed SG8 16 E5
Rickmansworth WD3 165 B1
4 Royston SG8 7 D6
Sarratt WD3 152 A2
Stapleford SG14 92 A6
Stevenage SG1 50 D8
Therfield SG8 15 F7
Tring HP23 120 A7
Weston SG4 24 D1
Church Manor CM23 77 B8
Church Mead
Roydon CM19 116 B1
Studham LU6 82 B4
Church Meadow Cotts HP1 103 D3
Church Mill Grange CM17 118 E4
Church Path
Great Amwell SG12 114 F6
Ickleford SG5 21 E4
Little Wymondley SG4 35 F3
Church Pl AL6 89 C5
Church Rd
Flamstead AL3 84 B2
Great Hallingbury CM22 77 D3
Hemel Hempstead HP3 125 C2
Hertford SG14 113 C7
Ivinghoe LU7 80 F5
King's Walden SG4 47 F3

Church Rd *continued*
Little Berkhamsted SG13 132 C4
Little Gaddesden HP4 102 D8
Northwood HA6 174 F3
Pitstone, Church End LU7 80 E3
Potten End HP4 123 B6
Potters Bar EN6 145 B1
Slip End LU1 63 C2
Stansted Mountfitchet CM24 59 F5
Stotfold SG5 11 F6
Streatley LU3 31 A6
Studham LU6 82 B4
Watford WD17 167 B8
Welwyn Garden City AL8 110 D6
Church Row Mews 2 SG12 93 D1
Church St
Baldock SG7 12 E1
Bishop's Stortford CM23 76 F7
Bovingdon HP3 137 B4
Buntingford SG9 40 E8
Essendon AL9 131 E6
Guilden Morden SG8 1 F5
Hatfield AL9 130 C5
Hemel Hempstead HP2 124 D5
Hertford SG14 113 D6
Luton, High Town LU2 63 F8
Luton LU2 63 E7
Rickmansworth WD3 165 E1
Sawbridgeworth CM21 97 E2
Shillington SG5 19 E8
St Albans AL3 127 D4
Waltham Abbey EN9 163 C6
Ware SG12 93 D1
Watford WD18 167 C5
Welwyn AL6 89 C5
Wheathampstead AL4 108 D8
Wingrave HP22 60 B2
Church Street Ind Est SG12 93 D1
Church View
Hoddesdon EN10 134 F3
Long Marston HP23 79 A4
Church Wlk
Bushey WD23 168 A3
Sawbridgeworth CM21 97 F2
Churchyard Wlk 6 SG5 34 E7
Church Yd
Hitchin SG5 34 E7
Tring HP23 100 A3
Cicero Dr LU3 45 A8
Cillocks Cl EN11 135 A7
City Point 7 AL1 127 D4
Claggy Rd SG4 66 B2
Claggy Road Ind Est SG4 66 C2
Claire Ct
Bushey WD23 168 D1
Cheshunt EN8 162 D7
5 Pinner HA5 175 F3
Clamp Hill HA7 176 E5
CLAPGATE 57 C6
Clapgate Rd WD23 168 B3
Clare Cl WD6 169 F3
Clare Cres SG7 23 E6
Clare Ct
Enfield EN3 162 E4
Northwood HA6 174 E5
St Albans AL1 127 F1
Clare Gdns SG4, SG5 34 F7
Claremont
Bricket Wood AL2 155 A8
Goff's Oak EN7 147 F2
Claremont Cres WD3 166 C4
Claremont Rd
Hadley Wood EN4 159 D2
Harrow HA3 176 E1
Luton LU4 45 B1
Clarence Cl WD23 168 F2
Clarence Lo 8 EN11 135 A6
Clarence Rd
Berkhamsted HP4 122 C4
Harpenden AL5 86 A3
St Albans AL1 128 A4
Stansted Mountfitchet CM24 59 E7
Clarendon Cl 1 HP2 124 E4
Clarendon Ct
Harpenden AL5 86 B3
3 Luton LU2 45 D1
12 Northwood HA6 174 F5
Clarendon Fields WD3 152 F1
Clarendon Mews WD6 170 A6
Clarendon Par EN8 148 D2
Clarendon Rd
Borehamwood WD6 170 A6
Cheshunt EN8 148 D2
Harpenden AL5 86 B3
Luton LU2 45 E1
Watford WD17 167 B6
Claret Ho WD17 167 B7
Clarion Cl SG5 33 C2
Clarion Ho SG5 33 C2
Clarke's Rd AL10 130 B7
Clarke's Spring HP23 100 F5
Clarke Way WD25 154 A4
Clarkfield WD3 165 B1
Clarklands Ind Est CM21 97 E5
Clark Rd SG8 7 D7
Clarks Cl SG12 93 D3

Clarks Mead WD23 168 D2
Clarkson Ct AL10 129 E6
Claudian Pl AL3 127 A1
Claughton Ct AL4 128 C2
Claverhambury Rd EN9 149 F2
Claverley Gn LU2 46 E2
Claverton Cl HP3 137 A3
Claybury WD23 168 B2
Claybush Rd SG7 4 D3
Claycroft AL7 111 B7
Claydon Cl LU3 45 C7
Claydown Way LU1 63 B1
CLAY END 52 F7
Claygate Ave AL5 85 E2
Clay Hall Rd LU6 82 F7
Clayhill HP23 120 E7
CLAY HILL 161 B2
Clay Hill EN2 161 D2
Clay La WD23 168 E2
Claymore HP2 124 E7
Claymore Dr SG5 21 F5
Claymores SG1 50 E6
Claypond CM23 77 B7
Clayton Dr HP3 125 D1
Clayton Hill Ctry Pk* EN9 149 D8
Clayton Par 7 EN8 148 D1
Cleall Ave EN9 163 C5
Cleave The AL5 86 D1
Clement Ct 7 AL1 128 A2
Clementine Way 4 HP1 124 B1
Clement Pl HP23 100 A3
Clement Rd EN8 148 E4
Clementsbury SG13 133 C8
Clements Ct WD25 154 C4
CLEMENT'S END 82 D3
Clements End Rd LU6, HP2 82 E2
Clements Rd WD3 164 D4
Clements St SG12 93 E1
Clevedon Rd LU2 46 B2
Cleveland Cres WD6 170 C4
Cleveland Rd
Hemel Hempstead HP2 125 B5
Markyate AL3 83 E5
Cleveland Way
Hemel Hempstead HP2 125 B5
Stevenage SG1 37 C3
Cleves Rd HP2 125 B8
Cleviscroft SG1 50 E4
Clewer Cres HA3 176 D2
Clifford Cres LU4 44 D5
Clifford Ct 10 CM23 77 A7
Cliff Richard Ct 14 EN8 148 D3
Clifton Cl EN8 148 E2
Clifton Ct HP3 124 D1
Clifton Rd
Luton LU1 63 B8
Watford WD18 167 B4
Clifton St AL1 127 E4
Clifton Way
Borehamwood WD6 170 A8
Ware SG12 93 D3
Climb The WD3 165 B3
Clinton Ave LU2 45 F3
Clinton End HP2 125 C3
Clitheroe Gdns WD19 175 D7
Clive Cl EN6 158 F8
Clive Ct LU2 45 E1
Clive Par HA6 174 E3
Clive Way WD24 167 C8
Clock Ho The EN2 161 F2
Clockhouse Mews WD3 164 E6
Clock Tower The AL2 142 B4
Cloister Garth
Berkhamsted HP4 122 C4
St Albans AL1 141 E7
Cloister Lawns SG6 22 F4
Cloisters Ct WD3 165 E2
Cloisters Rd
Letchworth Garden City SG6 23 A4
Luton LU4 44 B3
Cloisters The
Bushey WD23 168 B3
Kings Langley WD4 139 A2
Rickmansworth WD3 165 E2
Slip End LU1 84 C8
3 Watford WD18 167 C5
Welwyn Garden City AL8 110 D6
Cloister Wlk HP2 124 D5
Clonard Way HA5 176 A4
Clore Shalom Sch
London Colney WD7 142 E1
Shenleybury WD7 156 E8
Closemead Cl HA6 174 C4
Close The
Baldock SG7 23 E7
Brookmans Park AL9 144 E5
Bushey WD23 168 A4
Codicote SG4 67 F1
Harpenden AL5 85 D4
Harrow HA2 176 C1
Hinxworth SG7 3 D6
Luton LU3 45 A5
Markyate AL3 83 E5
Potters Bar EN6 159 A7
Radlett WD7 155 F6
Rickmansworth WD3 165 B1
Royston SG8 7 F7
St Albans AL1 141 C8

Close The *continued*
Stevenage SG1 36 C1
Wallington SG9 25 E6
Ware SG12 93 E1
CLOTHALL 24 E4
Clothall Rd
Baldock SG7 23 F8
Clothall SG7 24 C6
Clovelly Way SG1 50 A7
Clover Ave CM23 76 B6
Clover Cl LU4 44 A3
Cloverfield AL7 89 F1
Clover Field The WD23 167 F3
Cloverland AL10 129 F2
Clover Way
Hatfield AL10 129 F8
Hemel Hempstead HP1 124 B4
Club Cotts AL6 90 D6
Clump The WD3 165 B4
Clunbury Ct HP4 122 D4
Cluny Way SG15 11 A5
Clusterbolts SG14 92 A7
Clutterbucks WD3 152 A3
Clyde Rd EN11 135 D5
Clydesdale Cl WD6 170 D4
Clydesdale Ct LU4 44 A3
Clydesdale Path WD6 170 D4
Clydesdale Rd
Luton LU4 44 A3
Royston SG8 7 E6
Clydesdale Wlk 2 EN10 148 F6
Clyde Sq HP2 124 F8
Clyde Terr SG13 114 A6
Clyfton Cl EN10 148 F8
Clyston Rd WD18 166 F3
Coach Dr SG4 34 F5
Coach Ho Cloisters 2 SG7 23 E8
Coach House Cloisters SG7 23 E7
Coachman's La SG7 23 D8
Coach Mews AL1 128 B3
Coanwood Cotts SG12 94 E4
Coates Dell WD25 154 E6
Coates Rd WD6 169 D2
Coates Way WD25 154 E6
Coates Way Jun Mix Inf Sch WD25 154 E6
Cobb Cl WD6 170 C4
Cobbett Cl EN3 162 C3
Cobbetts Ride HP23 99 F3
Cobb Gn WD25 154 B7
Cobbinsbank EN9 163 D6
Cobbins The EN9 163 E6
Cobbins Way CM17 118 E4
Cobblers Wick HP22 60 B3
Cobb Rd HP4 121 F4
Cobden Hill WD7 156 B2
Cobden St LU2 45 F1
Cobham Rd SG12 93 F2
Cob Lane Cl AL6 89 F4
Cobmead AL10 130 B7
Cockbush Ave SG13 114 B7
Cockerell Cl SG1 50 B6
COCKERNHOE 46 F3
Cockernhoe Endowed CE Prim Sch LU2 46 E3
Cocker Rd EN1 162 C3
Cockfosters Rd EN4 159 E1
Cock Gr HP23 121 C4
Cock La
Brent Pelham CB11 30 F3
Hoddesdon EN11 134 D4
Cockle Way WD7 156 E6
Cockrobin La CM20 117 A7
CODICOTE 67 E1
CODICOTE BOTTOM 88 D8
Codicote CE Prim Sch SG4 67 E1
Codicote Dr WD25 154 D5
Codicote Ho SG1 36 C1
Codicote Hts SG4 68 B1
Codicote Innovation Ctr SG4 88 E8
Codicote Rd
Ayot St L AL4, AL6, SG4 88 C3
Welwyn AL6 89 B7
Wheathampstead AL4 87 D1
Whitwell SG4 66 F6
Codicote Row HP2 105 B1
Codmore Wood Rd HP5 150 D6
Coe's Alley 1 EN5 171 E5
Cohen Cl EN8 162 E8
Colborne Ho WD18 166 E3
Colbron Cl SG7 4 C4
Colburn Ave HA5 175 E4
Colchester Rd HA6 175 A1
COLD CHRISTMAS 94 B6
Cold Christmas La SG12 93 E6
Coldham Gr EN3 162 E2
Coldharbour La
Bushey WD23 168 C4
Harpenden AL5 86 C4
Colebrook Ave LU3 44 C7
COLE GREEN
Brent Pelham 29 F3
Letty Green 112 A3
Cole Green Ho AL7 110 F4
Cole Green La AL7 111 B4
Cole Green Way SG14 113 A4
Coleman Bsns ctr SG4 66 C2
Coleman Green La
Sandridge AL4 108 E4

Coleman Green La *continued*
Wheathampstead AL4 109 A7
Colemans Cl SG5 20 D4
COLEMANS GREEN 47 D1
Coleman's La EN9 149 E5
Colemans Rd SG4 47 D1
Cole Rd WD17 167 B8
Coleridge Cl
Hammond Street EN7 147 F4
Hitchin SG4 35 B8
Coleridge Cres HP2 105 B1
Coleridge Ct 9 AL5 86 B1
Coleridge Way WD6 170 A5
Colesdale EN6 146 E1
Coles Gn WD23 168 C1
Coles Hill HP1 124 A5
Colestrete SG1 50 F5
Colestrete Cl SG1 51 A5
Coleswood Rd AL5 107 C7
Colgate Ct EN5 171 E4
Colgate Pl EN3 163 A2
Colgrove AL8 110 C5
Colindale Ave AL1 127 F1
Colin Rd LU2 45 F2
College Ave HA3 176 E2
College Bsns Pk HP22 78 C1
College Cl
Bishop's Stortford CM23 76 D7
Flamstead AL3 84 B1
Harrow HA3 176 E3
Ware SG12 114 D8
College Ct
Cheshunt EN8 148 C1
Hoddesdon EN11 134 F8
College Hill Rd HA3 176 E3
College Ho LU1 63 F7
College La AL10 129 E4
College Lake Wildlife Ctr* HP23 100 C8
College Pl AL3 127 C3
College Rd
Abbots Langley WD5 154 A8
Cheshunt EN8 148 D1
Harrow HA3 176 E2
Hertford Heath SG13 114 D2
Hitchin SG5 34 F8
Hoddesdon EN11 134 F8
St Albans AL1 128 B2
College Rd N HP22 78 C1
College St AL3 127 D3
College Way
Northwood HA6 174 D4
Welwyn Garden City AL8 110 D7
College Yd WD24 154 B1
Collens Rd AL5 107 B5
Collenswood Rd SG2 51 B4
Collet Cl EN8 148 D3
Collet Gdns EN8 148 D3
Collett Rd
Hemel Hempstead HP1 124 C3
Ware SG12 93 D2
Collett Sch The HP1 124 B4
Colleyland WD3 164 D5
COLLIERS END 73 A6
Collingdon Ct 10 LU1 63 D8
Collingdon St LU1 63 D8
Collings Wells Cl LU1 62 E4
Collingtree LU2 46 B4
Collingwood Cl LU4 44 D3
Collingwood Ct SG8 7 D7
Collingwood Dr AL2 142 D6
COLLINS CROSS 77 B8
Collins Cross CM23 59 B1
Collins Ct WD23 168 B4
Collinson Ct EN8 162 E2
Collison Cl SG4 22 C2
Collyer Rd AL2 142 D4
Colmer Pl HA3 176 D3
Colnbrook Cl AL2 142 E4
Colnbrook Sch WD19 175 C7
Colne Ave
Rickmansworth WD3 173 A8
Watford WD19 167 C3
Colne Bridge Ret Pk WD17 167 D4
Colne Gdns AL2 142 E4
Colne Lo
Rickmansworth WD3 165 A1
Watford WD23 167 D5
Colne Mead WD3 173 A8
Colne Valley Ret Pk WD17 167 D4
Colne Way
Hemel Hempstead HP2 124 F8
Watford WD24, WD25 154 E2
Colne Way Ct WD24 154 D3
Colney Fields Shopping Pk AL2 142 F3
COLNEY HEATH 143 D8
Colney Heath Jun Mix Inf Sch AL4 129 C1
Colney Heath La AL4 128 E2
COLNEY STREET 141 E1
Colonial Bsns Pk WD24 167 C8
Colonial Way WD24 167 D8
Colonnade The 7 EN8 148 D3
Colonsay HP3 125 C1
Colston Cres EN7 147 B4
Colt Hatch CM20 117 B1
Colthurst Gdns EN11 135 D8
Colt Mews EN3 163 A2

Colts Cnr SG2 51 B4
Colts Croft SG8 9 E2
Coltsfield CM24 59 E8
Coltsfoot AL7 111 B4
Coltsfoot Dr SG8 7 E6
Coltsfoot Gn LU4 44 A5
Coltsfoot La SG3 90 D7
Coltsfoot Rd SG12 93 E3
Coltsfoot The HP1 123 E2
Colts The CM23 76 E4
Columbia Rd EN10 148 E5
Columbus Cl SG2 51 A7
Columbus Gdns HA6 175 A2
Colvin Gdns EN8 162 D4
Colwell Ct LU2 46 E2
Colwell Rd SG2 51 C3
Colwell Rise LU2 46 E2
Colwyn Cl SG1 50 B7
Colyer Cl AL6 89 F3
Combe Ho WD18 166 E3
Combe Rd WD18 166 F3
Combe St HP1 124 C3
Combewood WD25 154 C7
Comet Cl WD25 153 F5
Comet Rd AL10 129 F6
Comet Way AL10 129 E5
Commerce Way SG6 22 F6
Common Field HP23 100 D1
Commonfields CM20 117 E1
Common Gate Rd
WD3 164 E4
Common Gdns HP4 123 B6
Common La
Ashwell SG7 4 B6
Harpenden AL5 86 D5
Kimpton SG4 66 B1
Kings Langley WD4 138 F3
Radlett WD7, WD25 155 E1
Common Rd
Chorleywood WD3 164 D5
Kensworth Common LU6 82 F8
Stanmore HA7 176 D7
Stotfold SG5 11 F7
Studham LU6 82 B3
Common Rise SG4 22 A1
Commons La HP2 124 E4
Commons The AL7 111 B3
Commonswood Sch
AL7 111 B3
Common The
Chipperfield WD4 152 B8
Harpenden AL5 85 C4
Hatfield AL10 130 A6
London Colney WD7 156 B8
Potten End HP4 123 A6
Redbourn AL3 106 B5
Stanmore HA7 176 F8
Common View
Chorleywood WD3 164 D5
Letchworth Garden City
SG6 23 B8
Common View Sq SG6 23 A8
Common Wharf SG12 93 E1
COMMONWOOD 152 B5
Community Way WD3 166 B4
Compass Point HP4 121 E6
Compton Ave LU4 44 D4
Compton Gdns AL2 141 B5
Compton Pl WD19 175 E6
Comroston 13 EN11 135 A6
Comyne Rd WD24 153 F3
Comyns The WD23 168 C1
Concorde Dr HP2 124 D3
Concorde St LU2 63 F8
Condor Ct WD24 154 B1
Conduit La
Great Hormead SG9 29 B1
Hoddesdon EN11 135 A6
Conduit La E EN11 135 B6
Coney Cl AL10 130 B3
Coneydale AL8 110 D8
Coney Gree CM21 97 D3
Congreve Rd EN9 163 E6
Conifer Cl
Goff's Oak EN7 147 F2
Stevenage SG2 51 D7
Conifer Ct 7 CM23 76 F8
Conifers The
19 Luton LU1 63 D6
Watford WD25 154 C4
Conifer Wlk SG2 51 C7
Coningesby Dr WD17 166 E7
Coningsby Bank AL1 141 D7
Coningsby Cl AL9 144 D7
Coningsby Ct WD7 156 A3
Coningsby Dr EN6 159 D6
Coniston Cl HP3 125 C2
Coniston Lo 3 WD17 167 A7
Coniston Rd
Kings Langley WD4 138 F3
Luton LU3 44 F5
Connaught Cl HP2 125 A5
Connaught Gdns HP4 121 F7
Connaught Rd
Barnet EN5 171 D3
Harpenden AL5 86 B2
Harrow HA3 176 F2
Luton LU4 44 F1
St Albans AL3 127 C6
Connelly La SG5 11 D2
Connemara Cl WD6 170 D3
Connemara Ct 1
EN10 148 F5
Conner's Cl SG8 1 F4
Connop Rd EN3 162 D1
Conquerors Hill AL4 108 E8
Conquest Cl SG4 34 F5
Constable Ct LU4 45 A1
Constantine Cl SG1 36 F1
Constantine Pl SG7 13 B1
Convent Cl SG5 34 F8
Convent Ct HP23 99 F3
Convent Ho 6 EN10 148 F5
Conway Gdns EN2 161 E1
Conway Ho WD6 170 C5
Conway Rd LU4 45 B1
Cony Cl 7 EN7 147 E5
Conyers CM20 117 C2
Cook Rd SG2 51 B7
Cook's Hole Rd EN2 161 C1
Cooks Mead WD23 168 B3
Cooks Spinney CM20 118 A2
Cooks Vennel HP1 124 B5
Cooks Way
Hatfield AL10 130 B3
Hitchin SG4 22 A1
Coombe Gdns HP4 121 F5
Coombe Hill Rd WD3 165 A2
Coombelands Rd SG8 2 E1
Coombe Rd
Bushey WD23 168 D2
Kelshall SG8 6 A1
Coombes Rd AL2 142 C5
Coopers Cl
Aston SG2 51 D4
Bishop's Stortford CM23 76 B4
Cooper's Cl SG4 66 B1
Coopers Cres WD6 170 C8
Coopers Ct SG14 113 D6
Coopers Field SG6 22 D7
Coopers Gate AL4 129 B1
Coopers Green La AL4,
AL10 109 D1
Cooper's Hill SG4 87 B8
Coopers La EN6 145 E1
Coopers Lane Rd EN6 160 B6
Coopers Mdw AL3 106 A6
Coopers Mews
Harpenden AL5 107 A8
9 Luton LU1 63 D7
Watford WD25 154 C8
Coopers Rd EN6 145 C1
Coopers Wlk 10 EN8 148 D3
Cooper Way 10 HP4 122 D4
Cooters End La AL5 85 F5
Copenhagen Cl LU3 44 D8
Copmans Wick WD3 164 D4
Coppens The SG5 12 A5
Copper Beech Cl HP3 137 F8
Copper Beech Ct 4
HA6 174 E3
Copper Beeches
11 Harpenden AL5 86 B1
Oaklands AL6 89 D7
Copper Ct CM21 97 E2
Copperdale Ct 7
WD18 166 E4
Copperfield Cl SG5 11 C2
Copperfields
Luton LU4 44 C3
Royston SG8 7 C6
Welwyn Garden City
AL7 111 C5
Coppermill La WD3,
UB9 172 F3
Copperwood SG13 113 F6
Coppice Cl
Harrow HA7 176 F4
Hatfield AL10 129 F1
Coppice Farm Pk
HP23 119 D4
Coppice Mead SG5 11 E5
Coppice The
Bishop's Stortford
CM23 76 D5
1 Harpenden AL5 85 F2
Hemel Hempstead HP2 125 B4
Watford WD19 167 C3
Wigginton HP23 100 D1
Coppings The EN11 115 A1
Coppins Cl HP4 121 F4
Coppins The
Harrow HA3 176 E4
Hatfield AL8 110 A4
Markyate AL3 83 D5
Copse Cl HA6 174 C1
Copse Hill AL6 90 A8
Copse The
Bishop's Stortford
CM23 77 C8
Hemel Hempstead HP1 123 E5
Hertford SG13 114 A6
Watford WD23 167 D6
Copse Way LU3 44 D8
Copsewood Rd WD24 167 B8
Copse Wood Way
HA6 174 C2
Copthall Cl CM22 77 F4
Copt Hall Cotts LU2 64 E4
Copthorne LU2 46 D3
Copthorne Ave EN10 134 F3
Copthorne Cl WD3 165 F4
Copthorne Rd WD3 165 F4
Coral Gdns HP2 124 F3
Coral Ho CM20 117 A1
Corals Mead AL7 110 D5
Coram Cl HP4 122 C3
Corbridge Dr LU2 46 E1
Corby Cl AL2 141 A6
Cordell Cl EN8 148 E3
Corder Cl AL3 141 A8
COREY'S MILL 36 B2
Coreys Mill La SG1 36 C1
Corfe Cl
Borehamwood WD6 170 D6
Corfe Cl *continued*
4 Hemel Hempstead
HP2 124 E2
Corinium Gate AL3 127 A1
Corinium Gdns LU3 45 A8
Corncastle Rd LU1 63 D6
Corncrake Cl LU2 46 C5
Corncroft AL10 130 B7
Cornel Cl LU1 63 A7
Cornel Ct LU1 63 A7
Cornelia Ct 3 AL5 86 A2
Cornelious Ho 6
WD18 166 F5
Corner Cl SG6 22 E6
Cornerfield AL10 130 B8
Corner Hall HP3 124 D1
Corner Hall Ave HP3 124 D1
Corners AL7 111 A7
Corner View AL9 144 C7
Corner Wood AL3 83 D5
Cornfield Cres HP4 121 D7
Cornfield Rd WD23 168 B5
Cornfields SG2 51 C7
Cornfields The HP1 124 B2
Cornflower Way AL10 129 E8
Cornhill Dr EN3 162 E2
Corn Mead AL8 89 C1
Cornmill EN9 163 B6
Cornwall Cl EN8 162 E6
Cornwall Ct 8 HA6 175 F3
Cornwall Ho CM23 76 E4
Cornwall Rd
Harpenden AL5 86 B2
Pinner HA5 175 F3
St Albans AL1 127 E1
Coronation Ave SG8 7 C5
Coronation Rd
Bishop's Stortford
CM23 76 E5
Ware SG12 93 D2
Coronet Ho 2 HA7 176 F4
Corringham Ct AL1 127 F4
Corton Cl SG1 50 B8
Corvus Cl SG8 7 E8
Cory-Wright Way AL4 87 E1
Cosgrove Way LU1 44 D1
Cosmia Ct WD23 167 E4
Cosne Mews AL5 107 C7
Costins Wlk 12 HP4 122 D4
Cotefield LU4 44 C3
Cotesmore Rd HP1 123 E2
Cotlandswick AL2 142 C5
Cotney Croft SG2 51 D3
Cotsmoor AL1 127 F3
Cotswold HP2 124 E6
Cotswold Ave WD23 168 C3
Cotswold Bsns Pk LU1 62 D2
Cotswold Cl AL4 128 C8
Cotswold Dr SG1 37 A3
Cotswold Gdns LU3 44 C7
Cotswolds AL10 130 A3
Cottage Cl
Croxley Green WD3 165 F3
Watford WD17 166 F7
Cottage Gdns EN8 148 D2
COTTERED 39 C7
Cottered Rd SG9 26 F1
Cotterells HP1 124 C2
Cotterells Hill HP1 124 C3
Cotter Ho SG1 37 A3
Cotton Dr SG13 114 B7
Cotton Field AL10 130 B7
Cottonmill Cres AL1 127 D2
Cottonmill La AL1 127 D1
Cotton Rd EN6 159 C8
Coulser Cl HP1 124 A6
Coulson Ct
London Colney AL2 142 D4
Luton LU1 62 F8
Coulter Cl EN6 146 D4
Council Cotts
Great Wymondley SG4 35 F6
Letchworth Garden City
SG6 23 B2
Radwell SG7 12 C4
Council Hos LU2 32 D3
Counters Cl HP1 124 A3
COUNTER'S END 124 A3
Countess Anne CE Prim
Sch AL9 130 C6
Countess Cl UB9 173 C1
Countess Ct 7 LU2 45 D1
Couper Ho WD18 166 E3
Coursers Farm Cotts
AL4 143 C6
Coursers Rd AL2, AL4 143 C6
Courtaulds WD4 138 B1
Court Cl CM23 76 E5
Courtenay Ave HA3 176 C2
Courtenay Gdns HA3 176 C1
Courtfield Cl EN10 135 A3
Courtfields AL5 86 D1
Courtlands Cl WD24 153 E4
Courtlands Dr WD17 153 E3
Courtleigh Ave EN4 159 D1
Court Needham EN3 163 A2
Courtway The WD19 175 E8
Courtyard Mews SG12 92 E4
Courtyards The
WD18 166 D2
Courtyard The
Harlow CM17 118 D4
Hemel Hempstead HP3 138 D5
Hertingfordbury SG14 112 F5
St Albans AL4 128 F3
Covent Garden Cl LU4 44 F3
Coventry Cl SG1 37 B1
Coverdale
Hemel Hempstead
HP2 124 E6
Luton LU4 44 B6
Coverdale Ct EN3 162 E2
Covert Cl HP4 121 D6
Covert Rd HP4 121 D6
Covert The HA6 174 C2
Cowards La SG4 88 F8
Cowbridge SG14 113 C6
Cowdray Cl LU2 46 C3
Cow La
Bushey WD23 168 A3
Tring HP23 100 D4
Watford WD25 154 C3
Cowles EN7 147 F4
Cowley Hill WD6 157 B1
Cowley Hill Sch WD6 170 A8
Cowlins CM17 118 D4
Cowper Cres SG14 92 B1
Cowper Ct
Markyate AL3 83 D5
Watford WD24 154 A2
Cowper Rd
Berkhamsted HP4 122 B4
Harpenden AL5 86 C1
Hemel Hempstead HP1 124 B2
Markyate AL3 83 D5
Welwyn Garden City
AL7 110 F4
Cowper Rise AL3 83 D5
Cowper St LU1 63 E5
Cowpers Way AL6 90 D5
Cowridge Cres LU2 64 A8
COW ROAST 101 B1
Cowslip Cl SG8 7 F5
Cowslip Hill SG6 22 E7
Cowslips AL7 111 C5
Cox Cl WD7 156 F7
Coxfield Cl HP2 124 E2
COX GREEN 48 A6
Cox's Gdns CM23 76 E5
Cox's Way SG15 11 A6
Coyney Gn LU3 45 C1
Cozens La E EN10 134 F1
Cozens La W EN10 134 F1
Cozens Rd SG12 94 A2
Crabbes Cl SG5 34 E7
CRABB'S GREEN 43 E6
Crabb's La SG9 43 F6
Crab La WD25 155 B4
Crabtree Cl
Bushey WD23 168 B4
Hemel Hempstead HP3 124 D1
Crabtree Ct 3 HP3 124 E1
Crabtree Dell SG6 23 B3
Crabtree Jun & Inf Sch
AL5 86 C1
Crabtree La
Harpenden AL5 86 C1
Hemel Hempstead HP3 124 D1
Crab Tree La SG5 20 D4
Crab Tree Rd SG3 68 F4
Crabtree Wlk EN10 134 E4
Crackley Mdw HP2 125 B8
Cracknell Cl EN1 162 B2
CRADLE END 75 F8
Cradock Rd LU4 44 B1
CRAFTON 60 F4
Crafton Gn CM24 59 E7
Cragg Ave WD7 155 F3
Cragside SG2 69 C7
Craigavon Rd HP2 124 F7
Craiglands AL4 128 D7
Craigmore Ct 5 HA6 174 E3
Craig Mount WD7 156 B4
Craigs Wlk 4 EN8 148 D3
Craigweil Ave WD7 156 B4
Crakers Mead 4
WD18 167 B6
Cranborne Ave SG5 34 D6
Cranborne Cl
Hertford SG13 113 C3
Potters Bar EN6 158 E8
Cranborne Cres EN6 158 E8
Cranborne Ct EN3 162 D3
Cranborne Gdns AL7 110 F5
Cranborne Ind Est
EN6 144 E1
Cranborne Par EN6 158 D8
Cranborne Prim Sch
EN6 158 F8
Cranborne Rd
Cheshunt EN8 162 D7
Hatfield AL10 130 B6
Hoddesdon EN11 135 C7
Cranbourne Ct SG1 36 B1
Cranbourne Dr
Harpenden AL5 107 D6
Hoddesdon EN11 115 C2
Cranbourne Ho EN11 115 C2
Cranbourne Prim Sch The
EN11 115 B2
Cranbourne Rd
Northwood HA6 174 F1
Potters Bar EN6 144 E1
Cranbrook Cl SG12 93 D3
Cranbrook Dr
Luton LU3 44 D8
St Albans AL4 128 E3
Cranefield Dr WD25 154 E6
Crane Mead SG12 114 E8
Crane Mead Bsns Pk
SG12 114 E8
Cranes Way WD6 170 C4
Cranfield Cres EN6 146 E2
Cranford HP2 124 E5
Cranford Ct
Harpenden AL5 86 C1
Hertford SG14 112 F7
Cranleigh Cl EN7 148 A3
Cranleigh Gdns LU3 45 D3
Cranmer Cl EN6 145 C1
Cranmore Ct AL1 127 F4
Cranwell Cl AL4 128 C1
Cranwell Gdns CM23 59 C1
Cravells Ct AL5 107 C7
Cravells Rd AL5 107 C7
Crawford Rd AL10 130 A7
Crawley Cl LU1 63 C1
Crawley Dr HP2 124 F7
Crawley Green Inf Sch
LU2 64 B8
Crawley Green Rd
Luton, Hart Hill LU2 64 A8
Luton, Wigmore LU2 46 D1
Crawley Rd LU1 63 D8
Crawley's La HP23 120 F7
Creamery Ct SG6 23 C3
Creasy Cl WD5 153 F8
Crecy Gdns AL3 106 A6
Creighton Ave AL1 141 D8
Crescent E EN4 159 C1
Crescent Rd
Bishop's Stortford
CM23 77 A6
Hemel Hempstead HP2 124 D3
Luton LU2 63 F8
Crescent Rise LU2 63 F8
Crescent The
Abbots Langley WD5 139 F1
Ardeley SG2 38 F2
Bricket Wood AL2 141 A1
Caddington LU1 62 E3
Cottered SG9 39 D7
Croxley Green WD3 166 B3
Harlow CM17 118 C6
Hitchin SG5 21 D1
Letchworth Garden City
SG6 23 A5
Lower Stondon SG16 10 C4
Marsworth HP23 80 A1
Pitstone LU7 80 C4
Radlett WD25 155 B1
St Ippolyts SG4 35 A3
Watford WD18 167 C5
Welwyn AL6 89 C4
Crescent W EN4 159 C1
Cress End WD3 165 A1
Cresset Cl SG12 115 C3
Cresswell Gdns 4 LU3 31 B1
Cresswick SG4 66 E7
Cresta Cl LU5 44 A2
Crest Dr EN3 162 C1
Crest Pk HP2 125 C4
Crest The
Goff's Oak EN7 147 B4
Luton LU3 45 B7
Oaklands AL6 89 D8
Sawbridgeworth CM21 97 D2
Ware SG12 93 D3
Creswick Ct AL7 110 D5
Creswick Prim Sch
AL7 110 E3
Crew Curve HP4 121 F7
CREWS HILL 161 B4
Crews Hill EN2 160 F5
Crews Hill Sta EN2 160 F5
Crib St SG12 93 D2
Cricketers Cl AL3 127 E4
Cricketer's Rd SG15 11 A4
Cricketfield La CM23 76 E8
Cringle Ct EN6 145 C1
Crispin Field LU7 80 C4
Croasdaile Rd CM24 59 E8
Croasdale Cl CM24 59 E8
Crocus Field EN5 171 F3
Croft Cl WD4 138 A1
Croft Ct
Borehamwood WD6 170 D6
4 Harpenden AL5 86 B1
Hitchin SG5 34 E7
Croft End Rd WD4 138 A1
Crofters CM21 97 E3
Crofters End CM21 97 E3
Crofters Rd HA6 174 E6
Croft Field
Chipperfield WD4 138 A1
Hatfield AL10 130 A5
Croft La
Chipperfield WD4 138 A1
Letchworth Garden City
SG6 12 B1
Croft Mdw WD4 138 A1
Croft Mdws LU7 80 A7
Croft Rd
Luton LU2 46 B3
Ware SG12 93 C2
Crofts Path HP3 125 B1
Crofts The
Hemel Hempstead
HP3 125 B2
Stotfold SG5 11 F6
Croft The
Barnet EN5 171 E5
Chiswell Green AL2 141 A6
Hoddesdon EN10 148 E8
Luton LU3 44 D8
Wareside SG12 94 E4
Welwyn Garden City
AL7 110 F3
Croftwell AL5 107 F8

Croft Wlk EN10 148 E8
Cromdale Wlk SG1 37 B4
CROMER 38 D5
Cromer Cl HP4 102 E5
Cromer Hyde La AL8 109 C5
Cromer Rd WD24 154 C1
Cromer Way
  Luton, Stopsley Common LU2 45 E6
  Luton, Warden Hill LU2 45 D7
Cromer Windmill* SG2 38 E6
Crompton Pl 8 EN3 163 A1
Crompton Rd SG1 50 A6
Cromwell Ave EN7 148 B1
Cromwell Cl
  Bishop's Stortford CM23 76 B7
  St Albans AL4 128 D8
Cromwell Gn SG6 23 B8
Cromwell Hill LU2 45 D1
Cromwell Rd
  Borehamwood WD6 169 E8
  Cheshunt EN7 148 B3
  Hertford SG13 114 A7
  Letchworth Garden City SG6 23 B8
  Luton LU3 45 D1
  Stevenage SG2 51 C5
  Ware SG12 93 F2
Cromwell Way SG5 20 D4
Crooked Mile
  Waltham Abbey EN9 163 C6
  Waltham Abbey EN9 163 C7
Crooked Way EN9 135 E1
Crookhams AL7 90 A1
Crop Comm AL10 130 B7
Crosby Cl
  Luton LU4 45 A2
  St Albans AL4 142 C8
Crosfield Ct WD17 167 D4
Crossbrook AL10 129 E4
Crossbrook Ct EN8 162 D8
Crossbrook St EN8 162 D8
Crossett Gn HP3 125 C1
Cross Farm Mews HP3 137 D2
Crossfell Rd HP3 125 C2
Crossfield Rd EN11 135 B8
Crossfields AL3 141 B8
Crossfields Cl HP4 121 F4
Crossgates SG1 50 E5
Cross La
  Harpenden AL5 107 C5
  Hertford SG14 113 B6
Crosslands LU1 62 E3
Crossleys SG6 11 F2
Crossmead WD19 167 B3
Cross Oak Rd HP4 122 A4
Crossoaks La EN6 157 F5
Crosspaths AL5 85 C4
Crosspath The WD7 156 A4
Cross Rd
  Cheshunt EN8 162 E6
  Hertford SG14 113 C7
  Watford WD19 167 E3
Cross St
  Letchworth Garden City SG6 22 F7
  Luton LU2 63 E8
  4 St Albans AL3 127 D3
  Ware SG12 93 E1
  Watford WD17 167 C6
Crossway
  Pinner HA5 175 B1
  Welwyn Garden City AL8 89 C2
Cross Way
  3 Harlow CM17 118 D1
  Harpenden AL5 86 C3
Crossways
  Barley SG8 8 F1
  Berkhamsted HP4 121 F3
  Hemel Hempstead HP3 125 B3
Crossway The HA3 176 E1
Cross Way The LU1 63 C5
Crosthwaite Ct AL5 86 B2
Crouch Ct CM20 117 C3
Crouchfield
  Hemel Hempstead HP1 124 B2
  Hertford SG14 92 C1
Crouchfield La SG12 92 E4
Crouch Hall Gdns AL3 106 A6
Crouch Hall La AL3 106 A6
Crouch La EN7 147 C4
Crowborough Path WD19 175 D6
Crow Furlong SG5 34 D7
Crow La SG8 16 F5
Crowland Rd LU2 46 C5
Crown Cl CM22 98 C1
Crown Cotts
  Botley HP5 150 B8
  King's Walden SG4 48 A6
Crown Ct 14 LU1 63 D7
Crownfield EN10 135 A2
Crown Lo SG15 11 A4
Crown Rd WD6 170 B8
Crown Rise WD25 154 D5
Crown Rose Ct HP23 100 A3
Crown St AL3 106 B5
Crown Terr CM23 77 A7
Crown Wlk HP3 138 E7
Crown Yd AL3 106 D2
Croxdale Rd WD6 170 A7
Croxley Ctr WD18 166 D4
CROXLEY GREEN 166 A4
Croxley Sta WD3 166 B3
Croxley View WD18 166 E3
Croxton Cl 3 LU3 45 A7
Crozier Ave CM23 76 C8
Crunnell's Gn SG4 48 E5
Crusader Way WD18 166 F3
Cubbington Cl LU3 45 A7
Cubitt Cl SG4 35 C7
Cubitts Cl AL6 89 F3
Cublands SG13 114 B6
Cuckmans Dr AL2 141 A6
CUCKOLDS CROSS 66 D3
Cuckoo's Nest LU2 64 A7
Cucumber La AL9, SG13 132 A1
CUFFLEY 146 E3
Cuffley Ave WD25 154 D5
Cuffley Cl LU3 44 F4
Cuffley Ct HP2 125 C8
Cuffley Hill EN7 147 B2
Cuffley Sch EN6 146 F1
Cuffley Sta EN6 146 F2
Cullera Cl HA6 174 F4
Cullings Ct EN9 163 F6
Culrose Ct SG2 68 F8
Culverden Rd WD19 175 B7
Culverhouse Rd LU3 45 C3
Culver Lo AL1 127 E5
Culver Rd AL1 127 E5
Culworth Cl LU1 62 E3
Cumberland Cl
  Hertford SG14 113 C8
  Pimlico HP3 139 E7
Cumberland Ct
  2 Hoddesdon EN11 135 A7
  St Albans AL3 127 E4
Cumberland Dr AL3 106 B6
Cumberland St LU1 63 E6
CUMBERLOW GREEN 25 E1
Cumberlow Pl HP2 125 C2
Cundalls Rd SG12 93 E2
Cunningham Ave
  Enfield EN3 162 E3
  Hatfield AL10 129 D6
  St Albans AL1 127 F1
Cunningham Ct 4 EN8 148 E3
Cunningham Hill Inf Sch AL1 128 A1
Cunningham Hill Jun Sch AL1 128 A1
Cunningham Hill Rd AL1 128 A1
Cunningham Rd EN8 148 E4
CUPID GREEN 125 B7
Cupid Green La
  Flamstead HP2 104 E3
  Hemel Hempstead HP2 105 A1
Curlew Cl
  Berkhamsted HP4 122 C3
  Letchford Garden City SG6 11 E1
Curlew Cres SG8 7 E8
Curlew Ct EN10 148 F8
Curlew Rd LU2 46 C5
Curo Pk AL2 141 E4
Currie St SG13 113 E6
Curteys CM17 118 D5
Curtis Cl WD3 165 A1
Curtis Rd HP3 125 D2
Curtiss Dr WD25 153 F5
Curtis Way HP4 122 D3
Curzon Gate Ct 1 WD17 167 A8
Curzon Rd LU3 45 C1
Cussans Ho WD18 166 E3
Cussons Cl EN7 148 A2
Cutenhoe Rd LU1 63 E4
Cutforth Rd CM21 97 E3
Cuthbert Cl EN7 147 F2
Cutlers Cl CM23 76 C4
Cutlers Gn LU2 46 F2
Cutmore Dr AL4 129 B1
Cut Throat Ave HP4, LU6 81 E7
Cuttsfield Terr HP1 123 F2
Cutts La SG4 66 D1
Cuttys La SG1 50 E5
Cwmbran Ct HP2 124 F7
Cygnet Cl
  Borehamwood WD6 170 C8
  Northwood HA6 174 C4
Cygnet Ct 11 CM23 76 F6
Cygnet Ho
  Hemel Hempstead HP3 138 F6
  1 Stanmore HA7 176 F4
Cygnet Hospl SG1 36 B2
Cygnet Way CM19 116 A1
Cylers Thicket AL6 89 C6
Cymbeline Ct AL3 127 C4
Cypress Ave
  Crews Hill EN2 161 A4
  Welwyn Garden City AL7 111 C5
Cypress Cl EN9 163 D5
Cypress Rd HA3 176 D1
Cypress Wlk WD25 154 B4
Cyril Dumpleton Ho AL2 142 D5
Cyrils Way AL1 141 D8

D

Dacorum Way HP1 124 C3
Dacre Bldgs EN8 148 F2
Dacre Cres SG4 66 C1
Dacre Gdns WD6 170 D4
Dacre Gn SG8 7 F6
Dacre Ind Est EN8 148 F3
Dacre Rd SG5 35 A8
Daffodil Cl AL10 109 F1
Dagger La WD6 169 B4
Daggs Dell Rd HP1 123 E5
DAGNALL 81 C6
Dagnall Rd
  Great Gaddesden HP1 103 C5
  Whipsnade HP4, LU6 81 D8
Dagnalls SG6 22 F2
Dagnall Sch HP4 81 C5
Dahlia Cl
  Hammond Street EN7 147 C6
  Luton LU2 46 B4
Daintrees SG12 95 E4
Daintry Lo HA6 174 F3
Dairy Cotts SG5 19 B2
Dairyglen Ave EN8 162 E7
Dairy Mews WD18 167 A4
Dairy Way WD5 139 F2
Daisy Ct SG6 23 A8
Daisy Dr AL10 129 F8
Dalby Cl LU4 44 B3
Dale Ave AL4 87 B5
Dale Cl
  Hitchin SG4 34 F4
  Pinner HA5 175 B2
Dale Ct CM21 97 D1
Dale Rd LU1 63 C7
Daleside Dr EN6 158 F6
Dales Path WD6 170 D4
Dales Rd WD6 170 D4
Dale The
  Letchworth Garden City SG6 22 E5
  Waltham Abbey EN9 163 E5
Dalewood
  Harpenden AL5 86 D1
  Welwyn Garden City AL7 111 D5
Dalkeith Rd AL5 86 C1
Dallow Prim Sch LU1 63 C8
Dallow Rd LU1 63 B8
Dalroad Ent Est LU1 63 B8
Dalton Cl LU3 31 B1
Dalton Gdns CM23 76 E4
Dalton St AL3 127 D4
Dalton Way
  Watford WD17 167 D4
  Whitwell SG4 66 E7
Daltry Cl SG1 36 C2
Daltry Rd SG1 36 C2
Damask Cl
  Tring HP23 100 C4
  Weston SG4 37 B8
Damask Gn HP1 123 E2
DAMASK GREEN 37 B8
Damask Green Rd SG4 37 B8
Dame Alice Owen's Sch EN6 158 E6
Dammersey Cl AL3 83 F4
Damson Way AL4 128 C5
Damson Wlk SG7 5 A3
Dancers End La HP23 99 C2
DANCERS HILL 158 C3
Dancers Hill Rd EN5 158 E3
Dancers La EN5 158 C4
Dancote SG3 68 F5
Dane Acres CM23 76 D8
Dane Bridge La SG10 75 B2
Danebridge Rd SG10 75 B2
Dane Cl
  Harpenden AL5 86 C4
  Stotfold SG5 11 F8
Dane Ct AL1 128 B2
DANE END 71 F8
Dane End SG8 16 B4
Dane End Ho SG1 36 C1
Dane End La SG4 37 E5
Dane End Rd SG11 72 E3
Danefield Rd SG5 20 C4
Dane Ho CM23 76 D8
Danemead EN11 115 A1
Dane O'Coys Rd CM23 58 E1
Dane Pk CM23 76 D8
Dane Rd LU3 45 C2
Danesbury La AL6 89 D8
Danesbury Park Rd AL6 89 D8
Danesbury Pk
  Hertford SG14 113 D7
  Welwyn AL6 89 C7
Danesbury Pk Cvn Site AL6 89 D8
Danescroft SG6 12 A1
Danesgate SG1 50 D4
Dane St CM23 77 A7
Danes The AL2 141 C3
Danestrete SG1 50 D5
Daniel Ho 4 HA5 175 C1
Daniells AL7 111 A7
Danvers Croft HP23 100 C5
Danvers Dr LU3 31 C1
Danziger Way WD6 170 C8
Darblay Cl AL4 108 F5
Darby Dr
  Waltham Abbey EN9 163 C6
  Welwyn AL6 68 E3
Darcy Cl EN8 162 E8
Darkes La EN6 159 A8
Dark La
  Cheshunt EN7 148 A1
  Codicote SG4 88 E8
  Harpenden AL5 107 D7
  Sandon SG9 15 B1
  Wingrave HP22 60 C3
Darlands Dr EN5 171 D4
Darleyhall LU2 47 C1
Darley Rd LU2, SG4 47 C2
Darlington Ct 6 CM17 118 C4
Darnhills WD7 155 F4
Darnicle Hill EN7 147 A6
Darrington Rd WD6 169 E8
Darr's La HP4 121 D6
Dartmouth Mews LU4 44 D3
Dartons Ho SG7 12 E1
Dart The HP2 125 A8
Darvells Yd WD3 164 D5
Darwin Cl
  Hemel Hempstead HP2 105 B1
  St Albans AL3 127 E7
Darwin Gdns WD19 175 C5
Darwin Rd SG2 51 B6
Dashes The CM20 117 E1
DASSELS 41 E3
Datchet Cl HP2 125 B8
DATCHWORTH 69 E2
DATCHWORTH GREEN 69 C1
Datchworth Turn HP2 125 C3
Dauphin Ct 8 LU2 45 D1
Dauphine Ct 1 HA3 176 E1
Davenham Ave HA6 174 F5
Daventer Dr HA7 176 F3
David Evans Ct SG6 22 D7
Davidson Ho 11 HP2 124 D4
Davies St SG13 113 E6
Davis Cres SG5 20 D4
Davis Ct AL1 127 E3
Davis Ho 11 HP4 122 C4
Davison Cl EN8 148 D3
Davison Dr EN8 148 D3
Davis' Row SG15 11 A4
Davys Cl AL4 108 E7
Dawes La
  Sarratt WD3 151 F3
  Wheathampstead AL4 87 D1
Dawley AL7 89 F1
Dawley Ct HP2 125 A7
Dawlish Cl SG2 69 C7
Dawlish Rd LU4 44 F3
Dawn Ct 6 AL1 128 A2
Dawson Cl SG16 10 C5
Dayemead AL7 111 B3
Days Cl AL10 129 F5
Day's Cl SG8 7 C5
Days Mead AL10 129 F5
Deacon Cl AL1 141 D7
Deacons Cl
  Borehamwood WD6 170 A5
  Pinner HA5 175 B1
Deacons Ct 7 LU2 63 D8
Deaconsfield Rd HP3 138 E8
Deacons Hill WD19 167 C3
Deacon's Hill Rd WD6 170 A4
Deacons Hts WD6 170 A3
Deacons Way SG5 21 D1
Deadman's Ash La WD3 152 B3
Dead Woman's La SG4 48 C7
Deakin Cl WD18 166 E2
Dean Ct WD25 154 D6
Deane Ct HA6 174 E2
Dean Field HP3 137 A4
Dean Ho CM23 76 F5
Dean Moore Cl AL1 127 D2
Deans Cl
  Abbots Langley WD5 153 D7
  Tring HP23 100 A4
Deanscroft SG3 68 F5
Deans Furlong HP23 100 A4
Dean's Gdns AL4 128 A7
Deans Lawn 8 HP4 122 C4
Deans Mdw HP4 81 C5
Deansway HP3 138 F8
Dean The HP22 60 B3
Deard's End La SG3 68 F6
Deards Wood SG3 68 F5
Debenham Ct EN5 171 C4
Debenham Rd EN7 148 B4
Deepdene EN6 158 D8
Deep Denes LU2 46 A2
Deeping Cl SG3 68 F4
Deer Cl SG13 113 F6
Deercote Ct EN8 162 D8
Deerfield Cl SG12 93 D2
Deerings The AL5 107 A4
Deer Park Way EN9 163 B4
Deerswood Ave AL10 130 B3
Dee The HP2 124 F8
Deeves Hall La EN6 157 E6
de Havilland Aircraft Heritage Mus The* AL2 143 B2
De Havilland Cl AL10 129 F6
De Havilland Ct WD7 156 E7
De Havilland Ho AL10 130 C6
De Havilland Prim Sch AL10 130 A3
De Havilland Way WD5 153 F7
Deimos Dr HP2 125 A6
Delahay Rise HP4 122 B6
Delamare Rd EN8 148 F2
Delamere Rd WD6 170 B8
Delfcroft SG12 93 C2
Delfield Gdns LU1 62 E4
Delius Cl WD6 169 C3
Dell Cl AL5 86 B3
Dellcot Cl LU2 46 B4
Dellcott Cl AL8 110 C7
Dellcroft Way AL5 107 A5
Dell Ct WD3 173 A8
Dellcut Rd HP2 125 A5
Dellfield
  St Albans AL1 127 F2
  Thundridge SG12 93 D8
Dell Field Ave HP4 122 B6
Dellfield Cl
  Berkhamsted HP4 122 A6
  Radlett WD7 155 F4
  Watford WD17 167 A7
Dellfield Ct
  4 Harlow CM17 118 C4
  Luton LU2 46 D2
Dellfield Rd AL10 130 A5
Dell La
  Bishop's Stortford CM23 77 A7
  Spellbrook CM22 98 A8
Dell Mdw HP3 138 E7
Dellmeadow WD5 139 E1
Dellors Cl EN5 171 D4
Dell Rd
  Berkhamsted HP4 121 D7
  Enfield EN3 162 C1
  Watford WD24 154 A2
Dell Rise AL2 141 B5
Dell Side WD24 154 A2
Dellsome La
  Colney Heath AL4 143 E8
  Welham Green AL9 144 B8
Dell Spring SG9 40 E8
Dells The
  11 Bishop's Stortford CM23 76 F7
  Hemel Hempstead HP3 125 B2
Dellswood Cl SG13 113 E5
Dells Wood Cl EN11 114 F1
Dell The
  Baldock SG7 23 E6
  Caddington LU1 62 E3
  Hertford SG13 113 C3
  Luton LU2 46 F1
  Markyate AL3 83 D5
  Moor Park HA6 174 E8
  Pinner HA5 175 D1
  Radlett WD7 156 A4
  Royston SG8 7 C5
  St Albans AL1 128 A4
  Stevenage SG1 50 E5
  Waltham Abbey EN9 163 C3
  Welwyn AL6 90 A4
Dellwood WD3 165 B1
Delmar Ave HP2 125 D2
Delmer Ct WD6 156 F1
Delmerend La AL3 84 C1
Delphine Cl LU1 63 B6
Delrow Cotts WD25 168 C8
Delta Ct WD6 170 C6
Delta Gain WD19 175 D7
Demontfort Rise SG12 93 C3
Denbigh Cl 2 HP2 124 E2
Denbigh High Sch LU3 45 C2
Denbigh Inf Sch LU3 45 B2
Denbigh Jun Sch LU3 45 B2
Denbigh Rd LU3 45 B2
Denby SG6 23 B4
Dencora Ctr The AL1 128 A3
Dencora Way LU3 44 B8
Dendridge Cl EN1 162 B2
Dene La SG2 51 E2
Dene Rd HA6 174 D4
Denes The HP3 138 F7
Denewood Cl WD17 153 F2
Denham Cl
  Hemel Hempstead HP2 125 A8
  Luton LU3 44 E8
Denham La SL9 172 A2
Denham Way WD6 170 C8
Denham Way (North Orbital Rd) WD3 172 E4
Denmark Cl LU3 44 E8
Denmark St WD17 167 B7
Dennis Cl HP22 99 A4
Dennis Ct 2 AL3 127 D4
Denny Ave EN9 163 D5
Denny Ct CM23 59 B2
Denny Gate EN8 148 F4
Denny's La HP4 121 F3
De Novo Pl AL1 127 F3
Densley Cl AL8 110 D8
Denton Cl
  Barnet EN5 171 C4
  Luton LU4 44 B3
Denton Ho 10 WD19 175 C7
Denton Rd SG1 50 E4
Dents Cl SG6 23 C3
Denvers Yd SG11 73 D3
Derby Ave HA3 176 D2
Derby Ho HA5 175 D1
Derby Rd
  Hoddesdon EN11 135 D5
  Luton LU4 44 C2
  Watford WD18 167 C5
Derby Way SG1 51 B8
Derry Leys AL10 129 E7
Derwent Ave
  Luton LU3 45 B7
  Pinner HA5 175 E4

Derwent Cl WD25 154 C5
Derwent Lower Sch SG16 10 B5
Derwent Rd
Harpenden AL5 85 C4
Hemel Hempstead HP3 125 C2
Lower Stondon SG16 10 B4
Luton LU2 64 A8
Desborough Cl
Hertford SG14 92 C1
Welwyn Garden City AL7 111 B3
Desborough Dr AL6 90 D5
Desborough Rd SG4 35 C8
Des Fuller Ct 3 LU1 63 F6
Desmond Rd WD24 153 F3
De Soissons Cl AL8 110 B4
De Tany Ct AL1 127 D2
Deva Cl AL3 127 A1
Devereux Dr WD17 153 E1
De Vere Wlk WD17 166 E7
Devey Way SG14 92 A1
Devoils La 9 CM23 76 F7
Devon Ct 8 AL1 127 E2
Devon Mead AL10 129 E7
Devon Rd
Luton LU2 64 B8
Watford WD24 167 D8
Devonshire Bsns Ctr EN6 144 E1
Devonshire Bsns Pk WD6 170 D6
Devonshire Cl SG2 69 A8
Devonshire Ct HA5 175 F2
Devonshire Rd
5 Harpenden AL5 86 B1
Pinner HA5 175 F2
Dewars Cl AL6 89 C6
DEWES GREEN 30 F1
Dewes Green Rd CM23 30 F1
Dewgrass Gr EN8 162 D4
Dewhurst Rd EN8 148 C2
Dewhurst St Mary CE Prim Sch EN8 148 C2
Dewpond Cl SG1 50 C8
Dewsbury Rd LU3 45 C6
Dexter Cl
Luton LU3 31 B1
St Albans AL1 128 A2
Dexter Rd
Barnet EN5 171 D3
Harefield UB9 173 C1
Dialmead EN6 157 F5
DIAMOND END 65 C6
Diamond Ind Ctr SG6 23 C7
Diamond Rd WD24 154 A1
Dickens Bvd SG5 11 C2
Dickens Cl AL3 127 D4
Dickens Ct
Hatfield AL10 130 B7
Hemel Hempstead HP2 105 B1
Dickenson Way 19 SG12 93 D1
Dicker Mill SG13 113 D7
Dicket Mead AL6 89 C5
Dickins Cl EN7 148 A5
Dickinson Ave WD3 166 A3
Dickinson Quay HP3 138 F7
Dickinsons Field AL5 107 C7
Dickinson Sq WD3 166 A3
Dickson EN7 147 F4
Didsbury Cotts WD4 152 A8
Dig Dag Hill EN7 147 F4
DIGSWELL 89 F4
Digswell Cl WD6 157 A1
Digswell Ct AL8 110 E8
Digswell Hill AL6 89 B2
Digswell Ho AL8 89 D2
Digswell House Mews AL8 89 D2
Digswell La AL7 89 F2
DIGSWELL PARK 89 D1
Digswell Park Rd
Welwyn Garden City AL8 89 D3
Welwyn Garden City AL8 89 E3
Digswell Pl AL8 89 C1
Digswell Rd AL8 89 E1
Digswell Rise AL8 110 E8
Dimmocks La WD3 152 B3
Dimsdale Cotts SG9 29 B7
Dimsdale Cres CM23 77 B6
Dimsdale St SG14 113 C6
Dinant Link Rd EN11 135 B7
Dingle Cl EN5 170 F3
Dingles Ct HA5 175 D1
Dinmore HP3 136 F3
Dione Rd HP2 124 F6
Ditchfield Rd EN11 115 A1
Ditchling Cl LU2 46 C3
Ditchling Ct 1 AL1 127 E3
Ditchmore La SG1 50 D6
Ditton Gn LU2 46 E3
Divine Saviour RC Prim Sch WD5 153 D7
Divot Pl SG13 114 B7
Dixies Cl SG7 4 D3
Dixon Pl SG9 40 E7
Dixon's Ct SG12 114 E8
Dixons Hill Cl AL9 144 B6
Dixons Hill Rd AL9 144 C7
Dobb's Weir Rd EN11 135 D5
Docklands SG5 20 D4
Doctor's Commons Rd HP4 122 B4
Dodds La HP2 104 E1
Dodwood AL7 111 B5
Doggetts Way AL1 127 C1
Dog Kennel La
Chorleywood WD3 164 F5
Hatfield AL10 130 A6
Royston SG8 7 D6
Dognell Gn AL8 110 B7
Dolesbury Dr AL6 89 E8
Dollimore Cl SG4 67 F1
Dollis Brook Wlk EN5 171 E3
Dollis Valley Dr EN5 171 F4
Dollis Valley Way EN5 171 F3
Dolphin Sq HP23 100 A3
Dolphin Way CM23 77 A8
Dolphin Yd
2 Hertford SG14 113 D6
St Albans AL1 127 D3
7 Ware SG12 93 D1
Dominic Ct EN9 163 B6
Doncaster Cl SG1 51 C8
Doncaster Gn WD19 175 C5
Donkey La HP23 99 E2
Donne Cl SG8 7 C8
Dorant Ho AL3 127 D7
Dorcas Ct 9 AL1 127 E2
Dorchester Ave EN11 135 A8
Dorchester Ct
Croxley Green WD3 166 D4
8 St Albans AL1 128 A2
Watford WD19 167 E3
Dordans Rd LU4 44 F4
Dorel Cl LU2 45 F2
Dorian Cl HP23 100 D4
Dormans Cl HA6 174 D3
Dormer Cl EN5 171 D4
Dormie Cl AL3 127 C5
Dornan Ct 4 LU1 63 E5
Dorrien's Croft HP4 121 F7
Dorrington Cl LU3 45 C1
Dorrofield Cl WD3 166 D4
Dorset Cl HP4 121 F5
Dorset Ct 4 LU1 63 F6
Dorset Ho
13 Bishop's Stortford CM23 76 F7
3 Enfield EN3 162 D2
Douglas Ave WD24 154 E2
Douglas Cl AL6 89 E3
Douglas Dr SG1 51 A8
Douglas Ho 11 EN8 148 D3
Douglas Rd
Harpenden AL5 85 F2
Luton LU4 45 A2
Douglas Way AL7 111 C6
Dove Cl
Bishop's Stortford CM23 76 E3
Stansted Mountfitchet CM24 59 E8
Dovecote The SG7 4 D4
Dove Ct AL10 130 A3
Dovedale
Luton LU2 45 E6
Stevenage SG2 51 B4
Ware SG12 93 C3
Dovedale Cl UB9 173 C1
Dovehouse Croft CM20 118 A2
Dove House Dr SG16 10 D8
Dovehouse Hill LU2 46 B1
Dovehouse La LU6 82 D8
Dove La EN6 159 C5
Dove Pk
Chorleywood WD3 164 C4
Pinner HA5 176 A3
Dover Cl
Luton LU3 45 A3
Pitstone LU7 80 D2
Dove Rd SG1 36 F3
Doverfield EN7 147 C2
Dover Way WD3 166 C5
Dowding Way
Waltham Abbey EN9 163 E3
Watford WD25 153 F5
Dower Ct SG4 34 F5
Dower Mews 5 HP4 122 C4
Dowland Ho EN1 161 F1
Dowley Wood AL7 111 B5
Dowling Ct HP3 138 D8
Downalong WD23 168 D1
Downedge AL3 127 B4
Down Edge AL3 105 F5
Downer Dr WD3 152 A3
Downes Rd AL4 128 B7
Downfield Cl SG13 114 C4
Downfield Ct SG12 93 B5
Downfield Prim Sch EN8 162 E8
Downfield Rd
Cheshunt EN8 162 E8
Hertford Heath SG13 114 C5
Downfields AL8 110 B4
Down Green La AL4 108 B7
Downhall Ley SG9 40 E7
Downing Ct 11 WD6 169 F8
Downings Wood WD3 172 D5
Downlands
Baldock SG7 13 A1
Luton LU3 44 C7
Royston SG8 7 C6
Slip End LU1 84 C8
Stevenage SG2 51 D7
Waltham Abbey EN9 163 E5
Downlands Ct LU4 44 A2
Downs Ct LU1 63 C7
Downsfield AL10 130 B2
Downside HP2 124 E4
Downside Inf Sch LU4 44 E1
Downside Jun Sch LU4 44 E1
Downs La AL10 130 A3
Downs Rd LU1 63 C7
Downs The AL10 130 A3
Downs View LU4 44 D4
Downsway Ct SG8 7 C6
Downton Ct 3 LU3 63 D8
Downview LU4 44 B2
Dowry Wlk WD17 153 F1
Dragon Rd AL10 129 D6
Drakes Cl EN8 148 D3
Drakes Dr
Northwood HA6 174 B2
St Albans AL1 128 C1
Stevenage SG2 51 B7
Drakes Mdw CM17 118 E4
Drakes Way AL10 130 B3
Drapers Mews LU3 45 C1
Drapers Way SG1 50 C7
Drayman's Cl CM23 76 B5
Drayson Cl EN9 163 F7
Drayton Ave EN6 158 E7
DRAYTON BEAUCHAMP 99 C5
Drayton Rd
Borehamwood WD6 170 A5
Luton LU4 44 A3
Driftway SG8 16 E4
Driftway The HP2 124 F3
Driftwood Ave AL2 141 B5
Driver's End SG4 68 A4
Driver's End La SG4, SG3 68 A4
Drive The
Barnet EN5 171 E6
Blackmore End AL4 87 B7
Brookmans Park AL9 145 B6
Cheshunt EN7 148 B3
Goff's Oak EN7 147 B3
Harlow CM20 117 E1
Harpenden AL5 86 A1
Hertford SG14 113 C8
Hoddesdon EN11 135 A8
London Colney AL2 142 A6
Northwood HA6 174 E2
Oaklands AL6 69 A1
Potters Bar EN6 158 F7
Radlett WD7 156 A5
Rickmansworth WD3 165 C3
Sawbridgeworth CM21 97 E2
Watford WD17 153 E2
Driveway The
Cuffley EN6 146 E3
Hemel Hempstead HP1 124 B1
Dromey Gdns HA3 176 F3
Drop La AL2 155 C7
Drovers Way
Bishop's Stortford CM23 76 C5
Hatfield AL10 130 B8
St Albans AL1 127 D3
Drummond Dr HA7 176 F3
Drummond Ride HP23 100 A5
Drummonds Fold AL3 83 D8
Drummonds The LU4 44 C2
Drury La SG12 95 E1
Drycroft AL7 110 E2
Dryden Cres SG2 51 C8
Dryden Rd HA3 176 F2
Drysdale Cl 8 HA6 174 E3
Dubbs Knoll Rd SG8 1 F5
Dubrae Cl AL3 127 A1
Duchess Cl CM23 76 C7
Duchy Rd EN4 159 D1
DUCK END 59 E1
Duck End CM23 59 E1
Ducketts La SG10 75 D1
Ducketts Mead CM19 116 B1
Ducketts Wharf 10 CM23 76 F6
Ducketts Wood SG12 93 E6
Duck La SG2 52 E4
Duckling La CM21 97 E2
Duckmore La HP23 99 E2
Duck's Hill Rd HA6 174 B1
Dudley Ave EN8 162 D7
Dudley Hill Cl AL6 89 E8
Dudley Ho HP3 137 A4
Dudley St LU2 63 E8
DUDSWELL 121 D7
Dudswell La HP4 121 D7
Dugdale Ct SG5 21 C1
Dugdale Hill La EN6 158 E7
Dugdales WD3 166 A5
Dukes Ave LU6 81 E8
Dukes Ct 4 LU1 63 D6
Duke's La SG5 34 F8
Duke's Lo 9 HA6 174 F5
Dukes Ride
Bishop's Stortford CM23 76 C7
16 Luton LU2 45 D1
Duke St
Hoddesdon EN11 135 A7
Luton LU2 63 E8
Watford WD17 167 C6
Dukes Way HP4 122 A6
Dulwich Way WD3 166 A4
Dumas Way 6 WD18 166 E5
Dumbarton Ave EN8 162 D5
Dumbletons WD3 172 E6
Dumfries Cl WD19 175 A7
Dumfries Ct 9 LU1 63 D6
Dumfries St LU1 63 D6
Duncan Cl AL7 110 E5
Duncan Ct AL1 127 F1
Duncan Way WD23 167 F7
Duncombe Cl
Hertford SG14 113 C8
Luton LU3 45 C6
Duncombe Rd
Berkhamsted HP4 121 E6
Hertford SG14 113 C8
Duncombe Sch SG14 113 C7
Duncots Cl SG5 21 E3
Dundale Prim Sch HP23 100 A5
Dundale Rd HP23 100 A4
Dundas Mews EN3 163 A2
Dunedin Ho SG8 7 C6
Dunfermline Ho 9 WD19 175 C7
Dunford Ct 12 HA5 175 F3
Dunham's La SG6 23 C6
Dunkerley Ct SG6 23 A6
Dunkirks Mews SG13 113 D4
Dunlin SG6 11 E1
Dunlin Ct EN3 162 C3
Dunlin Rd HP2 124 E8
Dunmow Ct LU3 45 D2
Dunmow Rd CM23 77 C7
Dunn Cl SG1 50 E3
Dunnock Cl WD6 170 A5
Dunny La WD4 151 F7
Dunraven Ave LU1 63 A8
Dunsby Rd LU3 45 A6
Dunsley Pl HP23 100 B3
Dunsmore WD19 175 D8
Dunsmore Cl WD23 168 D3
Dunsmore Rd LU1 63 C6
Dunsmore Way WD23 168 D3
DUNSTABLE 44 A1
Dunstable Cl LU4 45 A1
Dunstable Ct LU4 44 F2
Dunstable Pl 5 LU1 63 D7
Dunstable Rd
Caddington LU1, LU6 62 C3
Dagnall HP4, LU6 81 C7
Luton, Bury Park LU1, LU4 45 B1
Luton LU4 44 D2
Redbourn AL3 106 A7
Studham LU6 82 B6
Dunster Cl
Barnet EN5 171 D5
Harefield UB9 173 B2
Dunster Ct WD6 170 D6
Dunster Rd HP2 105 B1
Dunsters Mead AL7 111 B4
Dunston Hill HP23 100 A4
Dunwich Farm SG1 50 A6
Durban Rd E WD18 167 A5
Durban Rd W WD18 167 A5
Durbar Rd LU4 45 B1
Durham Cl
Sawbridgeworth CM21 97 C1
Stanstead Abbotts SG12 115 B5
Durham Ct EN5 171 F6
Durham Ho 14 WD6 170 A7
Durham Rd
Borehamwood WD6 170 C6
Luton LU2 64 A7
Stevenage SG1 37 A1
Durler Gdns LU1 63 D5
Durrant Ct HA3 176 E2
Durrants Dr WD3 166 C5
Durrants Hill Rd HP3 138 D8
Durrants La HP4 121 F5
Durrants Rd HP4 121 F5
Dury Rd EN5 171 F7
Duxford Cl LU3 45 B7
Duxons Turn HP2 125 B4
Dwight Rd WD18 166 D2
Dyer Ct EN3 163 A2
Dyers Ct CM23 76 C5
DYER'S GREEN 2 B8
Dyes La SG4 49 F3
Dyes Lane Cvn Site SG1 50 A4
Dyke La AL4 108 E7
Dylan Cl WD6 169 D2
Dymoke Gn AL4 128 A7
Dymokes Way EN11 115 A1
Dyrham La EN5 158 A3
Dyson Ct WD17 167 C5
Dysons Cl EN8 162 D6

E

Eagle Centre Way LU4 44 B7
Eagle Cl LU4 44 A4
Eagle Ct
Baldock SG7 12 E1
Hertford SG13 114 B7
Eagle Way AL10 130 A3
Ealing Cl WD6 170 D8
Earleswood Ct HP3 138 D7
Earls Cl CM23 76 D6
Earls Hill Gdns SG8 7 C6
Earls La EN6 157 F6
Earlsmead SG6 22 F3
Earls Meade LU2 45 D1
Earl St WD17 167 C6
Easington Rd SG12 71 E7
Easingwold Gdns LU1 62 F8
Eastbourne Ave SG1 50 A6
Eastbrook Rd EN9 163 E6
Eastbrook Way HP2 124 E3
East Burrowfield AL7 110 D4
EASTBURY 174 F5
Eastbury Ave HA6 174 F5
Eastbury Ct
St Albans AL1 127 F4
Eastbury Ct *continued*
Watford WD19 167 C2
Eastbury Farm Jun Mix Inf Sch HA6 174 F6
Eastbury Pl 11 HA6 174 F5
Eastbury Rd
Northwood HA6 174 E4
Watford WD19 167 C3
Eastcheap SG6 22 F6
East Cl
Chiswell Green AL2 141 B6
Hitchin SG4 22 B1
Stevenage SG1 50 F5
East Comm
Harpenden AL5 107 C7
Redbourn AL3 106 A4
Eastcote Dr AL5 107 D6
Eastcott Cl LU2 46 D1
East Dr
Moor Park WD1 174 E8
Sawbridgeworth CM21 97 E1
St Albans AL4 128 F4
Watford WD25 154 B3
EASTEND 116 E1
EAST END 43 E4
Eastend Cotts CM19 116 D1
EAST END GREEN 112 D2
East End Way HA5 175 F1
Eastern Ave
Cheshunt EN8 162 F6
Lower Stondon SG16 10 C3
Eastern Way SG6 12 A1
Eastfield Ave WD24 167 D8
Eastfield Cl LU2 46 C4
Eastfield Ct AL4 128 D6
Eastfield Prim Sch EN3 162 D1
Eastfield Rd
Cheshunt EN8 162 F7
Enfield EN3 162 D1
Royston SG8 7 E6
East Flint HP1 123 F4
Eastgate SG1 50 D5
East Gate CM20 117 D1
Eastglade HA6 174 F5
East Gn HP3 139 A6
EASTHALL 49 B2
Easthall Cotts SG4 67 C8
Easthall Ho SG1 36 C1
Eastham Cl EN5 171 F4
East Hill LU3 45 B6
Eastholm SG6 23 A8
Eastholm Gn SG6 23 A8
EAST HYDE 85 F8
East La
Abbots Langley WD5 140 A2
Wheathampstead AL4 87 D1
Eastlea Ave WD25 154 E2
East Lodge La EN2 160 E4
Eastman Way
Hemel Hempstead HP2 125 A6
Stevenage SG1 37 C2
East Mead AL7 111 B3
East Mimms 4 HP2 124 E4
Eastmoor Ct AL5 107 C6
Eastmoor Pk AL5 107 C6
East Mount 2 AL4 87 D1
Eastnor HP3 137 A3
Easton Gdns WD6 170 E5
Eastor AL7 90 A1
East Pk
Harlow CM17 118 C3
Sawbridgeworth CM21 97 E1
East Rd
Bishop's Stortford CM23 77 B7
Enfield EN3 162 C1
Harlow CM20 118 B4
East Reach SG2 51 A2
East Ridgeway EN6 146 E3
East Riding AL6 90 D5
East St
Hemel Hempstead HP2 124 D3
Lilley LU2 32 D2
Ware SG12 93 D1
East View
Barnet EN5 171 F6
Essendon AL9 131 F6
St Ippolyts SG4 35 C2
EASTWICK 117 A4
Eastwick Cres WD3 172 F8
Eastwick Hall La CM20 117 A5
Eastwick Rd
Eastwick CM20 117 B4
Gilston CM20 117 E6
Eastwick Row HP2 125 A2
East Wlk CM20 117 D1
East Wood WD25 155 B3
Eastwood Ct HP2 125 A4
Eaton Gate HA6 174 C4
Eaton Gdns EN10 134 E1
Eaton Green Ct LU2 64 C8
Eaton Green Rd LU2 64 C8
Eaton Ho 5 CM23 77 B8
Eaton Pl LU2 46 D1
Eaton Rd
Hemel Hempstead HP2 125 B6
St Albans AL1 128 B3
Eaton Valley Rd LU2 64 B8
Eaton Way WD6 169 F8
Ebberns Rd HP3 138 E8

Ebeneezer Ct SG14 113 C6
Ebenezer St 7 LU1 63 D6
Ebury App WD3 165 D1
Ebury Cl HA6 174 C5
Ebury Ct WD3 165 D1
Ebury Rd
 Rickmansworth WD3 165 D1
 Watford WD17 167 C6
Ebury Rdbt WD3 165 D1
Echo Hill SG8 7 C5
Eddington Cres AL7 110 D3
Eddy St HP4 122 A5
Eden Cl EN3 163 A1
Edenhall Cl HP2 125 D2
Edens Cl CM23 77 B7
Edens Mount CM21 97 F4
Edenvale EN7 148 B2
Edgars Ct AL7 110 E5
Edgbaston Dr WD7 156 E7
Edgbaston Rd WD19 175 B7
Edgcott Cl LU3 31 B1
Edgecote Cl LU1 62 E3
Edgehill Gdns LU3 44 C8
Edgewood Dr LU2 46 C6
Edgeworth Cl SG2 51 C1
EDGWARE 170 E1
Edgwarebury La WD6, HA8 169 F1
Edgware Way HA8 169 D1
Edinburgh Ave WD3 165 A2
Edinburgh Cres EN8 162 E6
Edinburgh Dr WD5 154 A7
Edinburgh Gate CM20 117 D3
Edinburgh Gdns CM23 76 E6
Edinburgh Pl CM20 118 A4
Edinburgh Sq SG8 2 A6
Edinburgh Way CM20 117 E3
Edison Cl AL4 128 C2
Edison Rd SG2 51 B6
Edkins Cl LU2 45 E5
Edlyn Cl HP4 121 F5
Edmonds Dr SG2 51 D4
Edmund Beaufort Dr AL3 127 E5
Edmund Mews WD4 139 A2
Edmunds Rd SG14 112 F7
Edridge Cl WD23 168 C4
Edson Cl WD25 153 F6
Edulf Rd WD6 170 B8
Edward Amey Cl WD25 154 C3
Edward Cl
 Abbots Langley WD5 153 F7
 St Albans AL1 127 F2
Edward Cotts SG11 54 C3
Edward Ct
 Hemel Hempstead HP3 138 D7
 Waltham Abbey EN9 163 F6
Edwards Ct EN8 148 E1
Edward St LU2 45 F1
Edwick Ct EN8 148 D2
Edwinstree CE Mid Sch SG9 40 D8
Edwin Ware Ct 1 HA5 175 C1
EDWORTH 3 A6
Edwyn Cl EN5 171 D3
Egdon Dr LU2 45 D6
Egerton Rd HP4 122 B6
Egerton-Rothesay Sch HP4 121 E4
Egg Farm La WD4 139 B1
Egglesfield Cl HP4 121 E6
Eggleton Dr HP23 100 A5
Egret Ct EN3 162 C3
Eider Ct 1 CM23 77 A6
Eight Acres HP23 100 A4
Eighth Ave LU3 44 D7
Eisenberg Cl SG7 13 B1
Elaine Gdns LU1 63 A1
Elbow La
 Hertford Heath EN11, SG13 134 B7
 Stevenage SG2 51 B1
Eldefield SG6 22 D7
Elderbeck Cl EN7 148 A2
Elderberry Cl LU2 46 B4
Elderberry Dr SG4 35 A4
Elderberry Way WD25 154 B4
Elder Ct
 Bushey WD23 176 E8
 Northwood HA6 174 D4
Elderfield
 Harlow CM17 118 D3
 Welwyn Garden City AL7 111 B6
Elderflower Ct 6 SG5 34 F7
Elder Rd SG12 93 F3
Elder Way SG1 50 E3
Eldon Ave WD6 170 B7
Eldon Rd
 Hoddesdon EN11 135 D4
 Luton LU4 44 C1
Eldrig Turn HP2 124 E7
Eleanor Ave AL3 127 D5
Eleanor Cross Rd
 Cheshunt EN8 162 F5
 Holdbrook EN8 163 A5
Eleanor Gdns EN5 171 D4
Eleanor Rd
 Cheshunt EN8 162 E6
 Hertford SG14 113 C7
Eleanor's Cl SG12 93 D7
Eleanor Way EN8 162 F5
Electric Ave EN3 162 F3
Element Ho EN3 162 F3
Eleni Ho EN8 162 D6
Elfrida Rd WD18 167 C4
Elgar Cl WD6 169 D2
Elgar Path LU2 63 E8
Elgin Dr HA6 174 E3
Elgin Ho SG4 35 A6
Elgin Rd
 Cheshunt EN8 148 C1
 Hoddesdon EN10 148 F8
Elgood Ave HA6 175 A3
Eliot Rd
 Royston SG8 7 D8
 Stevenage SG2 51 C6
Elizabeth Cl
 Barnet EN5 171 D6
 Hertford SG14 112 F6
 Lower Nazeing EN9 149 D8
 Welwyn Garden City AL7 111 C6
Elizabeth Ct
 10 Luton LU1 63 D6
 St Albans AL4 128 D6
 Watford WD17 153 F1
Elizabeth Dr HP23 100 B6
Elizabeth Ho
 12 Hemel Hempstead HP1 124 D4
 7 Watford WD24 167 C7
 Welwyn Garden City AL7 111 C6
Elizabeth Rd CM23 76 E5
Elizabeth St LU1 63 D6
Elizabeth Way CM20 117 B2
Ella Ct LU2 45 F1
Ellenborough Cl CM23 76 D5
ELLENBROOK 129 D5
Ellenbrook Cl WD24 167 C8
Ellenbrook Cres AL10 129 D5
Ellenbrook La AL10 129 D4
Ellen Cl HP2 124 F4
Ellenhall Cl LU3 45 C1
Ellerdine Cl LU3 45 B4
Ellesborough Cl WD19 175 C5
Ellesfield AL6 89 B5
Ellesmere Gr EN5 171 F4
Ellesmere Rd HP4 122 D4
Ellice SG6 23 B4
Elliman Ct HP23 99 F3
Ellingham Cl HP2 125 A5
Ellingham Rd HP2 124 F4
Elliott Cl AL7 110 D3
Elliott Ct CM23 77 A8
Ellis Ave SG1 50 E8
Ellis Cl EN11 114 F2
Ellis Fields AL3 127 E6
Elliswick Rd AL5 86 B2
Ellwood Gdns WD25 154 C5
Ellwood Terr WD3 164 D4
Elm Ave
 Caddington LU1 62 E3
 Watford WD19 167 E2
Elmbank Ave EN5 171 C5
Elmbridge CM17 118 F3
Elmbrook Dr CM23 76 E3
Elm Cl EN9 163 D5
Elmcote HA5 175 D1
Elmcote Way WD3 165 F3
Elm Cotts
 Meesden SG9 29 F6
 Waltham Abbey EN9 163 D1
Elm Dr
 Cheshunt EN8 148 E3
 Hatfield AL10 130 A4
 St Albans AL4 128 C3
Elmfield Cl EN6 158 E6
Elmfield Ct LU2 46 A1
Elmfield Rd EN6 158 E6
Elm Gdns
 Enfield EN2 161 D1
 Welwyn Garden City AL8 110 B6
Elm Gn HP1 123 E5
Elm Gr
 Berkhamsted HP4 122 C4
 Bishop's Stortford CM23 77 B7
 Watford WD24 154 A2
Elm Hatch HA5 175 F3
Elm Ho HA6 174 B3
Elmhurst EN10 135 A4
Elmhurst Cl WD23 167 E5
Elmhurst Rd EN3 162 C2
Elm Lawn Cl 2 AL1 127 E4
Elmoor Ave AL6 89 B5
Elmoor Cl AL6 89 B4
Elmore Rd
 Enfield EN3 162 D1
 Luton LU2 46 A1
Elm Park Rd HA5 175 D1
Elm Pk SG7 23 F8
Elm Rd
 Barnet EN5 171 F5
 Bishop's Stortford CM23 76 F8
Elmroyd Ave EN6 158 F6
Elmroyd Cl EN6 158 F6
Elms Cl SG4 35 E3
Elmscroft Gdns EN6 158 F7
Elmside LU6 82 E8
Elmside Wlk SG5 34 E7
Elms Rd
 Harrow HA3 176 E3
 Ware SG12 94 A2
Elms The
 Codicote SG4 67 F2
Elms The *continued*
 Hertford SG13 114 A6
 Stevenage SG2 69 B8
Elmswell Ct SG14 112 F7
Elm Terr HA3 176 D2
Elmtree Ave LU2 46 E3
Elm Tree Farm Cl SG5 20 D4
Elm Tree Wlk
 Chorleywood WD3 164 F5
 Tring HP23 100 A5
Elm Way WD3 165 B1
Elm Wlk
 Radlett WD7 155 F3
 Royston SG8 7 F7
 Stevenage SG2 51 B3
Elmwood
 7 Pinner HA5 176 A3
 Sawbridgeworth CM21 97 F1
 Welwyn Garden City AL8 110 B5
Elmwood Ave
 Baldock SG7 23 F7
 Borehamwood WD6 170 B5
Elmwood Cres LU2 45 E3
Elmwood Ct SG7 23 F8
Elmwood Gr HP3 138 F8
Elm Yd SG4 35 E3
Elppin Ct EN10 134 F3
Elsinge Rd EN1 162 C3
Elsons Mews AL7 111 B6
ELSTREE 169 E3
Elstree & Borehamwood Sta WD6 170 A5
Elstree Bsns Ctr WD6 170 D6
Elstree Distribution Pk WD6 170 D6
Elstree Hill N WD6 169 D4
Elstree Hill S WD6 169 D2
Elstree Pk WD6 170 D3
Elstree Rd
 Bushey WD23 168 E2
 Elstree WD6 169 A3
 Hemel Hempstead HP2 105 A1
Elstree Way WD6 170 C7
Elton Ave EN5 171 F4
Elton Ct SG14 113 C7
Elton Pk WD17 167 B7
Elton Rd SG14 113 C7
Elton Way WD25 168 B7
Elvaston Ct EN5 171 C4
Elveden Cl LU2 45 E6
Elvington Gdns LU3 31 B1
Ely Cl
 Hatfield AL10 129 F6
 Stevenage SG1 37 B1
Ely Gdns WD6 170 D4
Ely Ho AL7 110 F6
Ely Rd AL1 128 B2
Ely Way LU4 44 D4
Embleton Rd WD19 175 A7
Emerald Ct WD6 156 F1
Emerald Rd LU4 44 A3
Emerton Ct HP4 121 E7
Emerton Garth HP4 121 E7
Emily Ct AL5 107 C7
Emmanuel Lo EN8 148 C1
Emmanuel Rd HA6 174 F3
Emma Rothschild Ct HP23 100 A5
Emma's Cres SG12 115 B4
Emmer Gn LU2 46 F2
Emmerson Ho CM23 77 A5
Emmitt Cl WD7 156 E6
Emperor Cl HP4 121 F7
Emperors Gate SG2 51 D8
Empire Ctr WD24 167 C8
Empire Pl 11 WD18 166 E5
Empress Rd LU3 44 E4
Endeavour Rd EN8 148 E4
Enderby Rd LU3 45 C6
Enderley Cl HA3 176 E2
Enderley Rd HA3 176 E2
Endersby Rd EN5 171 C4
Endymion Ct AL10 130 C6
Endymion Mews AL10 130 C6
Endymion Rd AL10 130 C6
ENFIELD 162 E1
Enfield Cty Sch (Lwr) EN2 161 E1
ENFIELD ISLAND VILLAGE 163 B2
ENFIELD LOCK 162 F2
Enfield Lock Sta EN3 162 E2
ENFIELD WASH 162 D1
Englefield LU2 45 F3
Englehurst AL5 86 D1
Enid Cl AL2 154 F8
Enjakes Cl SG2 69 B7
Ennerdale Cl AL1 128 B1
Ennerdale Dr WD25 154 C5
Ennis Cl AL5 107 D6
Ennismore Cl SG6 23 C3
Ennismore Gn LU2 46 F1
Enslow Cl LU1 62 E3
Enterprise Ctr LU2 64 B6
Enterprise Ctr The EN6 144 E1
Enterprise Way
 Hemel Hempstead HP2 125 C5
 Luton LU3 45 B8
Enville Ho 8 WD19 175 C7
Epping Forest District Mus* EN9 163 C6
Epping Gn HP2 125 B8
EPPING GREEN 132 D2
Epping Way LU3 44 C8
Epsom Cl SG1 51 B8
Epsom Ct WD3 165 B1
Ereswell Rd LU3 45 A7
Eric Steele Ho AL2 141 B4
Erin Cl LU4 45 A2
Erin Ct LU4 45 A2
Ermine Cl
 Cheshunt EN7 162 B8
 Royston SG8 7 D8
 St Albans AL3 127 A2
Ermine Ct SG9 40 E8
Ermine Pl 11 LU2 45 D1
Ermine Point Bsns Pk SG12 93 B3
Ermine St
 Buckland SG9 27 D6
 Thundridge SG12 93 D7
Errington Cl AL10 129 E6
Erskine Ho 5 WD19 175 D7
Escarpment Ave HP4, LU6 81 D8
Escot Way EN5 171 C4
Esdaile Hall EN11 135 A5
Esdaile La EN11 135 A5
Eskdale
 London Colney AL2 142 F4
 Luton LU4 44 C5
Eskdale Ct 3 HP2 124 E6
ESSENDON 131 F6
Essendon CE Prim Sch AL9 131 F6
Essendon Gdns AL7 110 F5
Essendon Hill AL9 131 F7
Essex Cl LU1 63 F6
Essex Ct 7 LU1 63 E6
Essex Ho EN9 163 C5
Essex La WD4 153 D6
Essex Mead HP2 105 A1
Essex Rd
 Borehamwood WD6 170 A6
 Hoddesdon EN11 135 C6
 Stevenage SG1 50 B8
 Watford WD17 167 B7
Essex St AL1 127 E4
Essex Yd HP22 60 C3
Estcourt Rd WD17 167 C6
Estfeld Cl 4 EN11 115 B1
Ethelred Cl AL7 110 F5
Etna Rd AL3 127 D4
Etonbury Mid Sch SG15 11 C7
Eton Ho 9 WD24 167 C7
Europa Rd HP2 124 F6
Euston Ave WD18 166 F4
Evans Ave WD25 153 F4
Evans Cl SG8 7 D7
Evan's Cl WD3 166 A4
Evans Gr AL4 128 C7
Evans Way HP23 100 B4
Evans Wharf HP3 138 E7
Evedon Cl LU3 44 F6
Evelyn Dr HA5 175 D3
Evelyn Rd LU5 44 A1
Evelyn Sharp Ho HP2 125 A2
Evensyde WD18 166 D3
Everall Cl HP1 124 C3
Everard Cl AL1 127 D1
Everest Cl SG15 11 B5
Everest Gdns CM23 76 E6
Everest Way HP2 125 A3
Everett Cl
 Bushey WD23 168 E1
 Hammond Street EN7 147 C6
Everett Ct WD7 156 A5
Evergreen Cl SG3 69 A2
Evergreen Rd SG12 93 F3
Evergreen Way LU3 45 A8
Evergreen Wlk 2 HP3 124 E1
Everlasting La AL3 127 C5
Eversden Ct HP2 105 B1
Eversley Lo 11 EN11 135 A6
Evolution WD25 154 D5
Evron Pl 4 SG14 113 D6
Exchange Bldgs 7 EN5 171 E6
Exchange Rd
 Stevenage SG1 50 F5
 Watford WD18 167 B5
Executive Pk Ind Est AL1 128 B3
Exeter Cl
 Stevenage SG1 37 B2
 Watford WD24 167 C7
Exeter Ho 7 WD6 170 A7
Exhims Mews HP4 121 E6
Explorer Dr WD18 166 F3
Exton Rd SG13 113 F6
Exton Ave LU2 46 A1
EYEWORTH 1 A8
Eynsford Ct SG4 34 F6
Eynsford Rd LU4 44 D3

F

Faggots Cl WD7 156 C4
Faints Cl EN7 147 F2
Fairacre HP3 138 F7
Fairacre Ct 2 HA6 174 E3
Fairacres Cl EN6 158 F6
Fairburn Cl WD6 170 A8
Fair Cl WD23 168 B2
Faircraft CM17 118 C4
Faircross Ho 6 WD17 167 B6
Faircross Way AL1 128 A5
Fairfax Ave LU3 44 D7
Fairfax Rd SG13 113 F7
Fairfield
 Buntingford SG9 40 F6
 Northwood HA6 175 A1
 Pinner HA6 175 A1
Fairfield Ave WD19 175 D7
Fairfield Cl
 Harpenden AL5 86 D1
 Hatfield AL10 130 C8
 Northwood HA6 174 B4
 Radlett WD7 155 E2
Fairfield Cres SG1 37 B4
Fairfield Dr EN10 148 F7
Fair Field Jun Sch WD7 155 E3
Fairfield Lower Sch SG5 11 C2
Fairfield Rd EN11 135 A8
Fairfields Prim Sch EN7 148 A4
Fairfield Way
 Hitchin SG4 35 D8
 Stevenage SG1 37 C3
Fairfield Wlk 9 EN8 148 E3
Fairfolds WD25 154 E4
Fairford Ave LU2 45 E4
Fairgreen Rd LU1 62 F3
Fairhaven AL2 141 D4
Fairhaven Cres WD19 175 A7
Fairhill HP3 138 F7
Fairlands Lo 6 WD6 170 A5
Fairlands Prim Sch SG1 50 D6
Fairlands Way SG1 51 A7
Fairlawns
 Pinner HA5 175 D1
 Watford WD17 153 F1
Fairley Way EN7 148 B3
Fairmead Ave AL5 107 C8
Fair Oak Ct LU2 45 F3
Fair Oak Dr LU2 45 F3
Fairoaks Gr EN3 162 D2
Fairseat Cl WD23 176 E8
Fairshot Ct AL4 108 D2
Fairthorn Cl HP23 99 E3
Fair View EN6 145 B2
Fairview Dr WD17 153 E3
Fairview Rd SG1 50 B7
Fairway
 Bishop's Stortford CM23 77 C6
 Hemel Hempstead HP3 138 F7
 Sawbridgeworth CM21 97 F2
 Ware SG12 114 C8
Fairway Ave WD6 170 B7
Fairway Cl
 Chiswell Green AL2 141 C4
 Harpenden AL5 107 A5
Fairway Ct HP3 138 F7
Fairway Ho WD6 170 B6
Fairways
 Cheshunt EN8 148 D5
 Waltham Abbey EN9 163 E5
Fairway The
 Abbots Langley WD5 153 D7
 Moor Park HA6 174 E6
Faithfield WD19 167 E3
Faith Ho 11 LU1 63 D7
Falcon Cl
 Hatfield AL10 130 A3
 Northwood HA6 174 E3
 Sawbridgeworth CM21 97 C1
 Stevenage SG2 51 D2
Falcon Ct 2 SG12 93 C3
Falconer Rd WD23 168 A3
Falconer Sch WD23 168 A4
Falconers Field AL5 85 E3
Falconers Pk CM21 97 D1
Falconers Rd LU2 46 B1
Falconer St CM23 76 C5
Falcon Ridge HP4 122 C3
Falcon Way
 Watford WD25 154 E5
 Welwyn Garden City AL7 110 E8
Falkirk Gdns WD19 175 D5
Falkland Rd EN5 171 E7
Fallow End AL6 68 D1
Fallowfield
 Luton LU3 45 C4
 Stevenage SG2 51 C3
 Welwyn Garden City AL7 89 F1
Fallowfield Cl UB9 173 C2
Fallowfield Wlk HP1 124 A6
Fallow Rise SG13 113 F6
Fallows Gn AL5 86 B3
Falmouth Ct AL3 127 D5
Falmouth Ho 9 HA5 175 F3
Falstaff Gdns AL1 141 C8
Falstone Gn LU2 46 E1
Fanhams Hall SG12 94 A4
Fanhams Hall Rd SG12 93 F3
Fanhams Rd SG12 93 E2
Fanshaw Ct SG14 113 C7
Fanshawe Cres SG12 93 C2
Fanshawe St SG14 113 B7
Fanshaws La SG13 133 C5
Fantail La HP23 99 F4
Faraday Cl
 Luton LU4 44 C1
 Watford WD18 166 D3
Faraday Gdns SG5 11 C1
Faraday Ho WD18 166 D3
Faraday Rd SG2 51 B6
Fareham Ho HP2 124 D2
Far End AL10 130 B2
Faringdon Rd LU4 44 C3
Faringford Cl EN6 159 D8

Farland Rd HP2 125 B3
Farley Ct LU1 63 C5
Farley Farm Rd LU1 63 B5
FARLEY HILL 63 C6
Farley Hill LU1 63 C5
Farley Jun Sch LU1 63 C6
Farley Lo LU1 63 D5
Farm Ave AL5 85 D4
Farmbrook LU2 45 D7
Farm Cl
Barnet EN5 171 C4
Borehamwood WD6 156 E1
Cheshunt EN8 148 C1
Cuffley EN6 146 E4
Harpenden AL5 85 D4
Hertford SG14 113 A6
Letchworth Garden City SG6 12 A1
London Colney WD7 142 E1
Roydon CM19 116 B1
Shenleybury WD7 156 E8
Stevenage SG1 50 E4
Welwyn Garden City AL8 110 C6
Farm Cotts SG12 93 D5
Farm Cres AL2 142 A5
Farm End HA6 174 B2
Farmers Cl WD25 154 B6
Farmery Ct HP4 122 E6
Farm Field WD17 153 E1
Farm Gn LU1 63 C5
Farm Hill Rd EN9 163 D6
Farmhouse Cl 3 EN10 148 F6
Farmhouse La HP2 125 A5
Farmhouse The HP2 125 A5
Farm La
Hoddesdon EN11 135 C8
Rickmansworth WD3 165 C6
Standon SG11 73 A8
Farm Pl HP4 121 F5
Farm Rd
Little Chalfont WD3 164 A5
Northwood HA6 174 C5
Slip End LU1 85 B7
St Albans AL1 128 B4
Farmstead Rd HA3 176 D1
Farm Way
Bushey WD23 168 B5
Moor Park HA6 174 F6
Farne Ho 5 WD18 166 F3
FARNHAM 58 D6
Farnham CE Prim Sch CM23 58 D6
Farnham Cl
Bovingdon HP3 137 A3
Sawbridgeworth CM21 97 C1
Farnham Gn CM23 58 B7
FARNHAM GREEN 58 B7
Farnley Gr LU2 64 A7
Farquhar St SG14 113 C7
Farraline Rd WD18 167 B5
Farrant Way WD6 169 E8
Farrer Top AL3 83 E5
Farriday Cl AL3 127 E7
Farrier Ct SG8 7 C7
Farriers
Great Amwell SG12 115 A6
Sawbridgeworth CM21 97 E3
Farriers Cl
Baldock SG7 12 E1
Bovingdon HP3 137 B3
Codicote SG4 67 F1
Farriers Ct WD25 154 B7
Farriers End EN10 148 F5
Farriers Way WD6 170 D4
Farringford Cl AL2 141 B5
Farrington Cotts EN5 171 F6
Farrington Pl HA6 174 F6
Farrow Cl LU3 31 C1
Farr's La LU2 65 B1
Farthing Cl WD18 167 C4
Farthing Dr SG6 23 C3
Farthings The HP1 124 B3
Faulkner Ct AL1 127 E5
Faverolle Gn EN8 148 D3
Faversham Cl HP23 100 A4
Fawbert & Barnard's Prim Sch CM17 118 C3
Fawbert & Bernard Inf Sch CM21 97 E2
Fawcett Rd SG2 51 B8
Fawkon Wlk EN11 135 A6
Fawn Ct AL9 130 C7
Fayerfield EN6 159 D8
Fay Gn WD5 153 D6
Fayland Cotts SG9 41 E7
Feacey Down HP1 124 B5
Fearney Mead WD3 165 A1
Fearnhill Sch SG6 22 C5
Fearnley Rd AL8 110 C5
Fearnley St WD18 167 B5
Featherbed La HP3 138 B7
Feather Dell AL10 130 A5
Featherstone Gdns WD6 170 C5
Featherstone Wood Prim Sch SG2 51 C3
Featherston Rd SG2 51 C3
Federal Way WD24 167 C8
Felbrigg Cl LU2 46 F2
FELDEN 138 A8
Felden Cl
Pinner HA5 175 E3
Watford WD25 154 D5
Felden Dr HP3 138 A7
Feldenhurst HP3 138 A7
Felden La HP3 138 A7
Felden Lawns HP3 138 A7
Felix Ave LU2 46 A2
Fellowes La AL4 143 E8
Fellowes Way SG2 51 A2
Fell Path WD6 170 D4
Fells Cl SG5 34 F8
Felmersham Ct LU1 63 B7
Felmersham Rd LU1 63 A7
Felmongers CM20 118 B2
Felstead Cl LU2 45 F3
Felstead Rd EN8 162 E7
Felstead Way LU2 45 F3
Felton Cl
Borehamwood WD6 156 E1
Cheshunt EN10 148 F6
Luton LU2 46 D1
Fen End SG5 11 F8
Fennycroft Rd HP1 124 A6
Fensomes Alley HP2 124 D4
Fensom's Cl HP2 124 D4
Fenwick Cl LU3 45 B5
Fenwick Path WD6 156 F1
Ferguson Gr EN8 148 D2
Fermor Cres LU2 46 C1
Fern Cl EN10 148 F8
Fern Ct HP4 122 B4
Ferndale
7 Harpenden AL5 86 A2
Much Hadham SG10 74 F2
Ferndale Rd
Enfield EN3 162 E2
Luton LU1 63 B7
Fern Dells AL10 129 F4
Ferndene AL2 154 F8
Ferndown HA6 175 A1
Ferndown Cl HA5 175 E3
Ferndown Rd WD19 175 C6
Fern Dr HP3 124 E2
Fernecroft AL1 141 D8
Ferney Rd EN7 147 D5
Fern Gr AL8 89 D2
Fernheath LU3 31 A1
Fernhills WD4 153 D6
Fern Ho HA7 176 F4
Fernleigh Ct HA2 176 B1
Fernleys AL4 128 C5
Ferns Cl EN3 162 E3
Ferns The AL3 127 D7
Fernville La HP2 124 D3
Fern Way WD25 154 B4
Ferny Hill EN4 159 F1
Ferrars Cl LU4 44 B1
Ferrars Inf Sch LU4 44 B3
Ferrars Jun Sch LU4 44 B3
Ferrers La AL4 108 B5
Ferrier Rd SG2 51 C6
Ferryhills Cl WD19 175 C7
Feryngs Cl CM17 118 D4
Fesants Croft CM20 118 B3
Fetherstone Cl EN6 159 D7
Fiddlebridge Ind Ctr AL10 129 F6
Fiddle Bridge La AL10 129 F6
Fidler Pl WD23 168 B3
Field Cl
Harpenden AL5 107 D7
St Albans AL4 128 A7
Field Cres SG8 7 F7
Field End EN5 171 B5
Field End Cl
Luton LU2 46 C4
Watford WD19 167 E2
Wigginton HP23 100 D1
Fielder Ctr (Univ of Herts) AL10 129 D8
Fielders Way WD7 156 E6
Fieldfare
Letchford Garden City SG6 11 E1
Stevenage SG2 51 D3
Fieldfare Gn LU4 44 A5
Fieldfares AL2 142 D4
Fieldfare Way SG8 7 E8
Fieldgate Ho SG1 50 F5
Field Gate Ho WD17 167 C4
Field Gate Mews WD17 167 C4
Fieldgate Rd LU4 44 D2
Field Ho WD6 169 D4
Field Inf Sch WD18 167 C4
Fieldings Rd EN8 148 F2
Field Jun Sch WD18 167 C4
Field La SG6 22 F4
Field Rd
Hemel Hempstead HP2 125 A3
Watford WD19 167 E3
Field's Ct EN6 159 D6
FIELDS END 123 D4
Fields End HP23 100 A6
Fields End La HP1 123 E5
Field View Rd EN6 159 A6
Field View Rise AL2 140 E2
Fieldway
Berkhamsted HP4 122 E2
Stanstead Abbotts SG12 115 B4
Wigginton HP23 100 D1
Field Way
Bovingdon HP3 137 A4
Hoddesdon EN11 115 C2
Rickmansworth WD3 165 B1
Fifth Ave
Letchworth Garden City SG6 23 C6
Watford WD25 154 D4
Fifth Ave / Allende Ave CM20 117 C3
Figtree Hill HP2 124 D4
Filey Cl SG1 50 A7
Filliano Ct 4 LU2 45 D1
Fillingham Way AL10 129 E7
Filmer Rd LU4 44 E4
Filton Ho 6 WD19 175 D7
Finbracks SG1 37 A4
Finch Cl
Hatfield AL10 130 A3
Luton LU4 44 A4
Finchdale HP1 124 A3
Finche's End SG2 52 B8
Finches The
Hertford SG13 114 B6
Hitchin SG4 35 A7
Finch Gn WD3 164 F5
Finch La WD23 168 A5
Finch Rd HP4 122 A4
Finley Rd AL5 86 D3
Finsbury Ct EN8 162 E5
Finsbury Rd LU4 44 D5
Finucane Rise WD23 176 C8
Finway LU1 63 A8
Finway Ct WD18 166 F4
Finway Rd HP2 125 B7
Firbank Dr WD19 167 E2
Firbank Ind Est LU1 63 A8
Firbank Rd AL3 127 F7
Fir Cl SG2 50 F1
Firecrest SG6 11 E1
Fire Station Alley EN5 171 E7
Firlands CM23 76 E6
Firlands Ho CM23 76 E6
Firs Cl
Hatfield AL10 130 B4
Hitchin SG5 34 D8
Firs Dr AL4 87 C5
Firs La EN6 159 B6
Firs Pk The AL9 145 A8
First Ave WD25 154 D4
First Ave / Mandela Ave CM20 117 F2
First Garden City Heritage Mus★ SG6 23 A5
Firs The
Hammond Street EN7 147 E4
Harpenden AL5 86 D2
St Albans AL1 142 B7
Welwyn Garden City AL8 89 C2
Wigginton HP23 100 D1
Firs Wlk
Burnham Green AL6 90 E5
Northwood HA6 174 D4
Firs Wood Cl EN6 159 F7
Firthesden Vinyard★ HP4 123 B8
Fir Tree Cl HP3 125 B2
Fir Tree Ct WD6 169 F5
Fir Tree Hill WD3 153 A2
Firway AL6 89 F7
Firway Cl AL6 89 F7
Firwood Ave AL4 128 E3
Fisher Cl
Holdbrook EN3 163 B2
Kings Langley WD4 139 A2
Fishermans Way EN11 135 D8
Fisher Rd HA3 176 F1
Fishers Cl
Holdbrook EN8 163 A5
Standon SG11 55 D3
Watford WD23 167 E6
Fishers Gn SG1 36 A1
FISHERS GREEN 36 A1
Fisher's Green Rd SG1 50 B8
Fishers Hatch CM20 117 E1
Fisher's Ind Est WD18 167 C4
Fishers Mead SG11 55 D3
Fishery Cotts HP1 124 A1
Fishery Pas HP1 124 B1
Fishery Rd HP1 124 A1
Fish Hill SG8 7 D6
Fishponds Rd SG5 34 E8
Fishpool St AL3 127 C3
Fish St AL3 106 B5
Fish Street Farm AL3 106 B5
Fitzjohn Ave EN5 171 F5
Fitzroy Ave LU3 45 B3
Fitzwarin Cl LU3 44 E8
Fitzwilliam Ct 14 WD6 169 F8
Fitzwilliams Ct CM17 118 E4
Five Acres
Kings Langley WD4 138 F2
London Colney AL2 142 D6
Stansted Mountfitchet CM24 59 E8
Five Acres Ave AL2 140 F2
Five Fields Cl WD19 175 F7
Five Oaks
Caddington LU1 62 F4
Hatfield AL10 130 B2
Five Oaks Mid Sch LU1 62 F3
Five Springs LU3 44 E6
Five Springs Ct LU3 44 E6
Flackwell Ho WD18 166 E3
Flagstaff Cl EN9 163 B6
Flagstaff Rd EN9 163 B6
Flags The HP2 125 B3
Flamingo Cl AL10 129 D6
FLAMSTEAD 84 B1
Flamsteadbury La AL3 106 A4
FLAMSTEAD END 148 B4
Flamstead End Prim Sch EN7 148 A4
Flamstead End Rd EN8 148 B3
Flamstead Village Sch AL3 84 B1
Flandrian Cl EN3 163 B1
Flash La EN2 161 C3
Flatfield Rd HP3 125 A1
FLAUNDEN 151 A6
Flaunden Bottom HP3, HP5 150 E4
Flaunden Hill HP3 151 A6
Flaunden Ho WD18 166 E2
Flaunden La
Bovingdon HP3 137 D3
Sarratt WD3 151 E6
Flaunden Pk HP3 151 A8
Flavian Cl AL3 126 F1
Flax Mews AL3 83 E5
Flecker Cl HA7 176 F5
Fleet The SG8 7 C6
FLEETVILLE 128 B4
Fleetville Inf Sch AL1 128 B3
Fleetville Jun Sch AL1 128 A3
Fleetwood SG6 23 B4
Fleetwood Cres SG1 50 B7
Fleetwood Way WD19 175 C6
Fleming Cl EN7 148 A5
Fleming Cres SG14 113 A6
Fleming Dr SG5 11 D2
Fleming Rd EN9 163 B4
Fletcher Way HP2 124 D6
Flete Ho WD18 166 E3
Flexley Wood AL7 90 A1
Flight Path SG16 10 B3
Flinders Cl
St Albans AL1 128 A1
Stevenage SG2 51 D5
Flint Cl LU3 44 E7
Flint Copse AL3 106 C6
Flint Cotts SG5 33 A2
Flint Ct LU1 63 D5
Flintings The HP2 103 F8
Flint Rd SG6 23 C8
Flint Way AL3 127 C7
Flora Gr AL1 127 F2
Floral Dr AL2 142 D5
Florence Ave LU3 44 D6
Florence Cl WD25 154 A4
Florence Ct HA6 174 E4
Florence Ho 15 WD18 166 E5
Florence Longman Ho HP3 138 D7
Florence St SG5 34 F8
Florence Wlk 8 CM23 76 F8
Florida Cl WD23 176 D8
Flowers Ind Est 18 LU1 63 E6
Flowers Way LU1 63 E7
Flowton Gr AL5 107 A7
Floyds Barns HP22 60 C2
Fog Cotts HP23 101 A5
Fogerty Cl EN3 163 B2
Fold Croft CM20 117 A1
Foldingshott SG3 69 D3
Follett Dr WD5 153 F8
Folly Ave AL3 127 C4
Folly Cl
Hitchin SG4 35 A5
Radlett WD7 155 F3
Folly Fields AL4 87 B2
Folly La
Caddington LU1 62 E4
St Albans AL3 127 C4
Folly Path SG4 35 A5
Folly Pathway WD7 155 F3
Folly The
Buntingford SG9 40 D7
Hertford SG14 113 D6
FOLLY THE
Radlett 155 F4
Wheathampstead 87 B2
Folly View SG12 115 B4
Fontmell Cl AL3 127 E5
Fontwell Cl HA3 176 E3
Football Cl SG7 12 E1
Forbes Ave EN6 159 D7
Ford Cl WD23 168 C5
Ford Cotts SG11 75 B8
FORD END 30 E4
Ford End Watermill★ LU7 80 E6
Ford Field SG11 75 A8
Fordham Cl SG7 4 D4
Fordham Rd SG8 7 E5
Fordhams Terr SG8 15 F7
Fordhams Wood (Nature Reserve)★ SG8 6 E4
Ford Hill SG11 75 B8
Ford La SG2 52 A3
Ford St SG11 55 E6
Fordwich Cl SG14 113 A6
Fordwich Hill SG14 113 A6
Fordwich Rd AL8 110 C5
Fordwich Rise SG14 113 A6
Forebury Ave CM21 97 F2
Forebury Cres CM21 97 F2
Forebury The CM21 97 F2
Forefield AL2 141 A4
Forelands Pl CM21 97 E2
Fore St
Harlow CM17 118 C4
Hatfield AL9 130 C6
Hertford SG14 113 D6
Weston SG4 24 B1
Forest Ave 5 HP3 124 D1
Foresters Cl EN7 147 E4
Foresthall Rd CM24 59 E4
Forest La WD7 156 B8
Forest Rd
Cheshunt EN8 148 D2
Enfield EN3 162 E3
Watford WD25 154 B6
Forest Row SG2 50 F1
Forest Wlk WD23 167 F8
Forfar Ho 7 WD19 175 C7
Forge Cl
Chipperfield WD4 152 A8
5 Hitchin SG5 34 F8
Forge Cotts
Essendon AL9 131 E6
Hatfield Heath CM22 98 F3
Forge End
Chiswell Green AL2 141 A5
Weston SG4 24 C1
Forge La
Northwood HA6 174 E3
Welwyn AL6 89 C5
Forge Mews 6 WD3 165 E1
Forres Cl EN11 135 A8
Forres Prim Sch EN11 115 B1
Forrest Cres LU2 46 A3
Forrester Ho 1 AL1 127 D3
Forresters Dr AL7 111 C5
Fortnums Acre HA7 176 F4
Fortuna Cl SG1 51 C8
Fortune La WD6 169 D3
Forty Hall★ EN2 161 F2
Forty Hill EN2 161 F1
Forty Hill CE Prim Sch EN2 162 A2
Forty Hill Ho EN2 161 F1
Forum Ctr The SG1 50 D5
Forum The
Stevenage SG1 50 D5
Tring HP23 99 E4
Fosbery Ct EN3 163 A2
Fosman Cl 7 SG5 34 D8
Fosse Ho AL3 127 A2
Foster Cl
Cheshunt EN8 148 E1
Stevenage SG1 36 D1
Foster Dr SG4 35 A5
Foster Rd HP1 124 B1
Foston Cl LU3 44 F6
Fotherley Rd WD3 172 F8
Foulds Sch EN5 171 D6
Founceley Ave SG12 71 F8
Founders Rd EN11 115 B1
Foundry Gate EN8 162 E6
Fountain Ct
Borehamwood WD6 170 A7
Cheshunt EN8 148 D1
Fountain Dr SG13 113 F7
Fountain Pl EN9 163 C5
Fountain Row SG4 35 B6
Fountains Rd LU3 45 D3
Fouracres SG6 23 A3
Four Acres
Stevenage SG1 50 D7
Welwyn Garden City AL7 110 F4
Fouracres Dr HP3 124 F1
Four Acres The CM21 98 A2
Fouracres Wlk HP3 124 F1
Fourdrinier Way HP3 138 D8
Four Limes AL4 108 D8
Four Swannes Prim Sch EN8 162 E6
Fourth Ave
Harlow CM20 117 C1
Letchworth Garden City SG6 23 C7
Luton LU3 44 D7
Watford WD25 154 D4
Four Trees AL2 141 B7
Four Tubs The WD23 168 D2
Fourways SG13 133 A5
Fourways Ct 1 EN11 135 A7
Fourways Market AL9 144 C7
Fovant Cl AL5 107 C6
Fovant Ct SG1 36 B1
Fowley Cl EN8 162 F5
Fowley Mead Pk EN8 163 A5
Fowlmere Rd SG8 9 F8
Foxbury Cl LU2 45 D6
Fox Cl
Bushey WD23 168 B5
Elstree WD6 169 D3
Wigginton HP23 100 D1
Fox Cnr SG8 1 F5
Foxcroft AL1 128 A1
Foxdell HA6 174 D4
Foxdell Inf Sch LU1 63 A8
Foxdell Jun Sch LU1 62 E8
Foxdells SG14 112 C3
Foxdells La CM23 58 F2
Foxes Cl SG13 114 B6
Foxes Dr EN7 148 A2
Foxes La EN6 146 E3
Foxes Par EN9 163 C6
Foxfield SG2 51 C3
Foxfield Cl HA6 174 F4
Foxglove Bank SG8 7 F5
Foxglove Cl
Bishop's Stortford CM23 76 C6
Hatfield AL10 130 B4
Hoddesdon EN11 115 C1

Foxgloves The HP1 123 E2
Foxglove Way
Luton LU3 45 D2
Oaklands AL6 89 E8
Foxgrove Path WD19 175 D5
Foxhill
Luton LU2 45 E5
Watford WD24 154 A3
Fox Hill SG8 1 F5
Fox Hill Rd SG8 1 F5
Foxholes Ave SG13 113 F6
Foxhollows
Hatfield AL10 130 B7
London Colney AL2 142 C5
Fox La SG8 15 F7
Foxlands Cl WD25 154 A5
Foxley Dr CM23 77 B8
Foxley Gr AL6 89 F4
Foxleys WD19 175 E7
Fox Rd
Stevenage SG1 50 E4
Wigginton HP23 100 C2
Fox's La AL9 144 F7
Foxton Rd EN11 135 A6
Foxtree Ho WD25 154 E3
Foxwood Chase EN9 163 C4
Foyle Cl SG1 37 C3
Frampton Rd EN6 145 C1
Frampton St SG14 113 D6
Frances Ho HP3 138 E6
Francis Ave AL3 127 D6
Francis Bacon Sch
AL1 142 B8
Francis Cl
Hitchin SG4 35 A5
Stotfold SG5 11 E6
Francis Combe Sch & Com
Coll WD25 154 C7
Francis Ct
Harlow CM20 117 B2
St Albans AL1 127 E2
Francis Green Ho 7
EN9 163 B6
Francis House Prep Sch
HP23 99 F3
Francis Rd
Hinxworth SG7 3 C6
Ware SG12 93 D2
Watford WD18 167 B5
Francis St LU1 63 D8
Francis Wks EN11 135 B6
Frankland Cl WD3 166 A2
Frankland Rd WD3 166 B3
Frank Lester Way LU2 64 D8
Franklin Ave
Cheshunt EN7 148 B1
Watford WD18 167 A3
Franklin Cl
Colney Heath AL4 129 E1
Hemel Hempstead HP3 138 E8
Pirton SG5 20 D4
Franklin Gdns SG4 22 B1
Franklin Rd WD17 167 B7
Franklin's Rd SG1 50 C8
Frank Martin Ct EN7 148 B1
Franks Cl SG16 10 B5
Frank Young Ct SG5 21 D1
Franshams WD23 176 D8
Fraser Rd EN8 148 E3
Fredericks Gate LU2 45 E1
Frederick St LU2 45 E1
Frederick Street Pas
LU2 45 E1
Fred Millard Ct SG1 50 E5
Freeman Ave LU3 45 B8
Freemans Cl SG5 21 D1
Freewaters Cl SG5 21 E4
FREEZY WATER 162 E3
Freezywater St George's
CE Prim Sch EN3 162 D3
Freman Coll SG9 40 D8
Freman Dr SG9 40 D8
French Horn Ct 5
SG12 93 D1
French Horn La AL10 130 B6
French Lo SG5 34 F8
French Row 6 AL3 127 D3
French's Cl SG12 115 B4
French's Yd 21 SG12 93 D1
Frensham EN7 148 A4
Frensham Dr SG4 22 C2
Frere Ct CM23 58 F1
Freshwater Cl LU3 44 F7
Freshwaters CM20 117 E1
Fresson Rd SG1 50 D8
Fretherne Rd AL8 110 D6
Friars Cl LU1 63 B5
Friarscroft EN10 135 A3
Friars Ct LU1 63 B5
Friars Field HP4 121 E7
Friars Rd
Braughing SG11 56 A7
Weston SG4 24 B1
Friars Way
Kings Langley WD4 139 A1
Luton LU1 63 B5
Watford WD23 167 F8
Friars Wlk HP23 100 A4
Friars Wood CM23 77 C8
Friday Furlong SG5 34 C8
Friedberg Ave CM23 76 D4
Friendless La AL3 83 F2
Friends Ave EN8 162 D7
Friern Cl 6 EN7 147 E5
Friesian Cl LU4 44 A3
Frimley Rd HP1 123 E4
Fringewood Cl HA6 174 B2
Frinton Cl WD19 175 B8
Friston Gn LU2 46 D1
FRITHSDEN 123 B8
Frithsden Copse HP4 122 F8
FRITHSDEN GARDENS
102 F1
Frithwood Ave HA6 174 F4
Frithwood Prim Sch
HA6 174 F4
Frobisher Cl WD23 168 A3
Frobisher Dr SG2 51 B7
Frobisher Rd AL1 128 C1
Frobisher Way AL10 129 D8
Froghall Cotts WD6 170 D3
Froghall La SG2 38 B1
Frogmoor Ct WD3 173 D8
Frogmoor La WD3 173 D8
FROGMORE 141 E4
Frogmore AL2 141 E4
Frogmore Bsns Pk
AL2 141 E3
FROGMORE END 138 E7
Frogmore Hill SG14 70 B7
Frogmore Ho SG1 36 C1
Frogmore Home Pk
AL2 141 D4
Frogmore Rd HP3 138 D8
Frogmore Road Ind Est
HP3 138 D8
Frogmore St HP23 100 A3
Frogs Hall La SG11 53 F3
Frome Cl LU4 44 E4
Frome Sq HP2 125 A8
Front St LU1 63 C1
Front The HP4 123 B7
Frost Ho HP4 122 C3
Frowick Cl AL9 144 B8
Frowycke Cres EN6 158 A7
Fry Rd SG2 51 C5
Fryth Mead AL3 127 B4
Fulbeck Way HA2 176 C1
Fulbourne Cl LU4 44 E2
Fulford Gr WD19 175 B8
Fuller Cl WD23 168 D2
Fuller Ct 3 CM23 77 A7
Fuller Gdns WD24 154 B2
Fuller Rd WD24 154 B2
Fuller's Almshouses
CM24 59 F6
Fullers Cl EN9 163 F6
Fullers Ct SG6 22 E7
Fullerton Cl AL3 83 E6
Fuller Way WD3 166 A4
Fulling Mill La AL6 89 B6
Fulmar Cres HP1 124 A3
Fulmore Cl AL5 86 D4
Fulton Cl SG1 50 C5
Fulton Cres CM23 77 C8
Fulton Ct
Borehamwood WD6 156 F1
3 Holdbrook EN3 163 A1
Furham Feild HA5 176 A3
Furlay Cl SG6 22 D7
Furlongs HP1 124 A4
Furlong The HP23 100 A3
Furlong Way SG12 115 A7
Furmston Ct SG6 23 A7
FURNEUX PELHAM 43 A5
Furneux Pelham CE Sch
SG9 43 A4
Furriers Cl CM23 76 C5
Furrowfield AL10 130 B7
Furrows The LU3 45 B7
Furse Ave AL4 128 A7
Furtherfield WD5 153 E7
FURTHER FORD END 30 D6
Furtherground 1
HP2 124 E2
Furzebushes La AL2 140 F6
Furze Cl
Luton LU2 45 D7
South Oxhey WD19 175 C5
Furzedown SG2 51 B4
Furzedown Ct 18 AL5 86 B1
Furzefield EN8 148 B3
Furzefield Ct EN6 158 E8
Furzefield Ctr The
EN6 158 D8
Furzefield Rd AL7 110 E4
Furze Gr SG8 7 E5
Furzehill Par WD6 170 A6
Furzehill Rd WD6 170 B5
Furzen Cres AL10 129 F2
Furze Rd HP1 123 E2
Furze View WD3 164 C4
Fyffes Ct SG5 34 F8

G

Gable Cl
Abbots Langley WD5 153 E7
Pinner HA5 176 A3
Gables Ave WD6 169 F6
Gables Lo EN4 159 C1
Gables The
3 Hemel Hempstead
HP1 124 D4
Sawbridgeworth CM21 97 E2
Watford WD19 167 C2
Watford, Woodside
WD25 154 D6
Gaddesden Cres
WD25 154 E5
Gaddesden Gr AL7 111 B6
Gaddesden La AL3 105 C4
GADDESDEN ROW 104 C6
Gaddesden Row HP2 104 C6
Gaddesden Row Jun Mix
Inf Sch HP2 104 B6
Gade Ave WD18 166 E5
Gade Bank WD1 166 D5
GADEBRIDGE 124 A5
Gadebridge Ct HP1 124 C4
Gadebridge La
Hemel Hempstead,
Gadebridge HP1 124 B5
Hemel Hempstead HP1 124 C5
Gadebridge Rd HP1 124 B4
Gadebury Hts HP1 124 C3
Gade Cl
Hemel Hempstead
HP1 124 B6
Watford WD18 166 E5
Gadeside WD24, WD25 153 E4
Gade Twr HP3 138 F6
Gade Valley Cl WD4 139 A3
Gade Valley Cotts
HP1 103 E4
Gade Valley Jun Mix Inf
Sch HP1 124 B4
Gadeview HP1 124 C3
Gade View Gdns
WD4 153 C7
Gadeview Rd HP3 138 D7
Gadmore La HP23 119 F7
Gadsby Ct 20 LU1 63 D6
Gadswell Cl WD25 154 E3
Gage Cl SG8 7 D7
Gainsborough Ave
AL1 127 F4
Gainsborough Ct LU2 45 F2
Gainsford Cres SG4 22 C2
Gainswood AL7 110 E5
Gaitskell Ho WD6 170 D5
Gall End La CM24 59 F7
Galleria The AL10 129 F5
Gallery The
Letchworth Garden City
SG6 22 F6
7 Luton LU1 63 E7
Galleycroft Ct 4
AL10 130 A6
Galley Gn SG13 115 A2
Galley Hill HP1 124 B6
Galleyhill Rd EN9 163 E7
Galley La EN5 171 B7
Galleywood SG5 21 D4
Galliard Cl LU3 45 B4
Galloway Cl
1 Bishop's Stortford
CM23 76 F8
Cheshunt EN10 148 F5
Galloway Rd CM23 58 F1
Gallows Hill WD4 153 C7
Gallows Hill La WD5 153 D8
Galston Rd LU3 44 D8
Games Yd SG1 50 C6
Gammon Cl HP3 125 A2
Gammons Farm Cl
WD24 153 F3
Gammons La WD17,
WD24 154 A2
Gamnel HP23 100 B6
Gamnel Mews HP23 100 B7
Ganders Ash WD25 154 A6
Gandhi Ct 1 WD24 167 D7
Gangies Hill CM21 97 A4
Gant Ct EN9 163 F5
Ganton Wlk WD19 175 E6
GANWICK CORNER 159 B4
Ganymede Pl HP2 124 F6
Gaping La SG5 34 D7
Garden Ave AL10 130 A2
Garden Cl
Barnet EN5 171 C5
Harpenden AL5 107 A5
Royston SG8 7 E7
St Albans AL1 128 B4
Watford WD17 166 F7
Woolmer Green SG3 69 B2
Garden Cotts
Park Street AL2 141 E4
Standon SG11 73 A8
Garden Ct
Hoddesdon EN10 134 F4
Luton LU3 45 A4
Welwyn Garden City
AL7 110 E7
Wheathampstead AL4 87 D1
Garden Field SG2 51 E2
Garden Field La HP4 122 F2
Garden Fields Jun Mix Inf
Sch AL3 127 D6
Garden Ho SG13 113 C5
Garden Hos The CM21 98 B3
Gardenia Ave LU3 45 A4
Garden La SG8 7 D5
Garden Rd
Abbots Langley WD5 153 E8
Buntingford SG9 40 E8
Woolmer Green SG3 69 B2
Garden Row 6 SG5 34 F8
Gardens of the Rose The*
AL2 140 F5
Gardens The
Baldock SG7 23 E8
Brookmans Park AL9 144 E4
Henlow SG16 10 D8
Stotfold SG5 11 E6
Watford WD17 166 F7
Garden Terr SG12 92 E4
Garden Terrace Rd 2
CM17 118 C4
Garden Wlk
Royston SG8 7 E7
Stevenage SG1 50 E5
Gardiners La SG7 4 D4
Gardner Ct
Luton LU1 63 E4
Watford WD25 154 C4
GARDNERS END 39 B3
Gareth Ct WD6 156 F1
Garfield Ct LU2 46 D3
Garfield St WD24 154 B1
Garland Cl
Cheshunt EN8 162 E8
Hemel Hempstead HP2 124 D4
Garland Ct 6 AL1 127 E3
Garland Rd SG12 93 E1
Garnault Rd EN1 161 F1
Garner Dr EN10 148 E5
Garnett Cl WD24 154 D3
Garnett Dr AL2 140 F2
Garrard Way AL4 108 D8
Garratts Rd WD23 168 C2
Garretts Cl SG14 113 C6
Garretts Mead LU2 46 B3
Garrison Ct 2 SG4 34 F7
Garrowsfield EN5 171 F4
Garsmouth Way
WD25 154 D3
GARSTON 154 C4
Garston Cres WD25 154 C5
Garston Dr WD25 154 C5
Garston La WD25 154 D5
Garston Manor Sch
WD25 154 C7
Garston Park Par
WD25 154 D5
Garston Sta WD25 154 D4
Garter Ct 13 LU2 45 D1
Garthland Dr EN5 171 C4
Garth Rd SG6 22 E3
Garth The WD5 153 D6
Gartlet Rd WD17 167 C6
Gascoyne Cl EN6 158 A7
Gascoyne Way SG13,
SG14 113 D5
Gas La SG8 17 C3
GASTON GREEN 98 B7
Gatcombe Ct 10 AL1 128 A2
Gate Cl WD6 170 C8
Gate Cotts WD3 164 D5
Gatecroft HP3 139 A8
Gate End HA6 175 A3
Gatehill Gdns LU3 31 B1
Gatehill Rd HA6 175 A3
Gatehouse Mews SG9 40 E8
Gate House The AL9 130 D6
Gatesbury Way SG11 55 D3
Gatesdene Cl HP4 102 C8
Gateshead Rd WD6 170 A8
Gates Way SG1 50 C6
Gateway Cl HA6 174 C4
Gateway Ct AL2 140 E1
Gateways The EN7 147 E3
Gateway The WD18 166 E4
Gatwick Cl CM23 59 B1
Gauldie Way SG11 55 D2
Gaumont App WD17 167 B6
Gaunts Way SG6 12 A2
Gaveston Dr HP4 122 B6
Gayland Ave LU2 64 B8
Gayton Cl LU3 45 B4
Gaywood Ave EN8 148 D1
Gazelda Ind Est
WD17 167 D4
Gean Wlk 3 AL10 130 A2
Geddes Rd WD23 168 C5
Geddings Rd EN11 135 B6
Geescroft Wlk AL5 107 A6
Generals Wlk The
EN3 162 E2
Gentle Ct 4 SG7 23 E8
Gentlemens Field
SG12 93 B3
George Field Ho 4
WD3 165 D2
George Gn CM22 77 B1
George Green Villas
CM22 98 B8
George La 5 SG8 7 D6
George Leighton Ct
SG2 51 B4
George Lovell Dr EN3 163 A2
George St W LU1 63 E7
Georges Mead WD6 169 E3
George St
Berkhamsted HP4 122 D4
Hemel Hempstead HP2 124 D4
Hertford SG14 113 C6
Luton LU1 63 E7
Markyate AL3 83 E5
St Albans AL3 127 D3
Watford WD18 167 C5
George Street Prim Sch
HP2 124 D4
George's Wood Rd
AL9 145 B5
George V Ave HA5 175 F1
George V Way WD3 152 B3
George Wlk 9 SG12 93 D1
Georgewood Rd HP3 139 A7
Georgina Ct SG15 11 A3
Gerard Ave CM23 76 E4
Gerard Ct 2 AL5 86 A2
Gernon Rd SG6 22 F5
Gernon Wlk SG6 22 F5
Gew's Cnr EN8 148 D2
Giant Tree Hill WD23 168 D1
Gibbons Cl
Borehamwood WD6 169 E8
Sandridge AL4 108 C1
Gibbons Way SG3 68 F5
Gibbs Cl EN8 148 D2
Gibbs Couch WD19 175 D7
Gibbs Field CM23 76 D5
Gibraltar Lo AL5 86 D3
Gibson Cl SG4 35 B7
Gidian Ct AL2 141 D4
Gifford's La SG11 54 A2
Gilbert Burnet Ho
HP3 124 F1
Gilbert Ct AL5 86 B4
Gilbert Rd UB9 173 D1
Gilbert's Hill HP23 119 E3
Gilbert St EN3 162 C2
Gilbert Way HP4 122 A4
Gilbey Ave CM23 77 B6
Gilbey Cres CM24 59 E8
Gildea Cl HA5 176 A3
Gilden Cl CM17 118 E4
Gilden Way CM17 118 D3
Gilder Cl LU3 45 A8
Gilderdale LU4 44 B6
Gilders CM21 97 D2
Giles Cl AL4 108 C1
Giles Inf Sch The SG1 37 A1
Giles Jun Sch SG1 37 A1
Gilhams Ct HP4 122 B5
Gillam St LU2 63 E8
Gillan Gn WD23 176 C8
Gill Cl WD18 166 C3
Gillian Ave AL1 141 C7
Gillian Ho HA3 176 E4
Gilliat's Gn WD3 164 D5
Gilliflower Ho EN11 135 A5
Gillings Ct EN5 171 E5
Gillison Cl SG6 23 B5
Gills Hill WD7 155 F4
Gills Hill La WD7 155 F3
Gills Hollow WD7 155 F3
Gillsted Ct AL3 127 D7
Gilmour Cl EN2 162 A4
Gilpin Gn AL5 86 C1
Gilpin Rd SG12 114 E8
Gilpin's Gallop SG12 115 B4
Gilpin's Ride HP4 122 E5
Gilroy Rd 10 HP2 124 D4
Gilsland EN9 163 E4
GILSTON 117 E5
Gilston Mews CM20 117 C6
Gilston Park Ho
CM20 117 C6
Gilston Pk CM20 117 C7
Ginns Rd SG9 43 D6
Gippeswyck Cl HA5 175 D2
Gipsy La
Bishop's Stortford CM23,
CM24 59 C4
Knebworth AL6, SG3 68 E4
Luton LU1 64 A6
Girdle Rd SG4 22 A2
Girons Cl SG4 35 B7
Girtin Rd WD23 168 C5
Girton Ct EN8 148 E1
Girton Way WD3 166 C4
Gisburne Way WD24 154 A2
Gladding Rd EN7 147 B6
Gladeside AL4 128 D6
Gladesmere Ct WD24 154 B2
Glades The HP1 123 E4
Glade The
Baldock SG7 23 E7
Letchworth Garden City
SG6 22 F3
Welwyn Garden City
AL8 110 C8
Gladeway The EN9 163 D6
Gladsmuir Rd EN5 171 E7
Gladstone Ave LU1 63 C7
Gladstone Ct SG2 69 A8
Gladstone Dr SG5 11 D2
Gladstone Pl EN5 171 D5
Gladstone Rd
Dane End SG12 71 F8
Hoddesdon EN11 135 B7
Ware SG12 93 C2
Watford WD17 167 C6
Gladwin Way CM20 117 D2
Glaisdale LU4 44 C5
Glamis Cl
Cheshunt EN7 148 A2
Hemel Hempstead HP2 105 B1
Glamis Pl HP2 124 E4
Glanfield HP2 124 E6
Glassmill Ho 6 HP4 122 D4
Gleave Cl AL1 128 B4
Glebe Ave SG15 11 A7
Glebe Cl
Essendon AL9 131 F6
Hemel Hempstead HP3 138 E7
Hertford SG14 113 D8
Pirtone LU7 80 D5
Watton at S SG14 70 D3
Glebe Cotts AL9 131 F6
Glebe Ct
Bishop's Stortford
CM23 77 B8
Cheshunt EN8 148 D2
Hatfield AL10 130 C6
Watford WD25 154 D6
Watton at S SG14 70 E3
Glebe Ho AL9 131 F6
Glebe La EN5 171 A3
Glebeland AL10 130 C5
Glebelands CM20 117 F3

Glebe Rd
Hertford SG14 113 D8
Letchworth Garden City SG6 23 B8
Welwyn AL6 89 B5
Glebe The
Ardeley SG2 38 F3
Harlow CM20 117 E1
Kings Langley WD4 139 A2
Stevenage SG2 51 B6
St Ippolyts SG4 35 C2
Watford WD25 154 D6
Glebe View SG2 38 C2
Gleed Ave WD23 176 D8
Glemsford Cl LU4 44 B6
Glemsford Dr AL5 86 D2
Glenblower Ct AL4 128 D3
Glenbourne SG4 67 F1
Glen Chess WD3 165 C5
Glencoe Rd WD23 168 A3
Glencorse Gn WD19 175 D6
Glendale HP1 124 B3
Glendale Wlk EN8 148 E1
Glendean Ct EN3 162 F3
Gleneagles Cl WD19 175 D6
Gleneagles Dr LU2 45 E6
Glenester Cl EN11 115 A1
Glen Faba CM19 135 E7
Glen Faba Rd CM19 135 F6
Glenferrie Rd AL1 128 A3
Glenfield Ct SG14 112 F7
Glenfield Rd LU3 45 C6
Glengall Pl AL1 141 E8
Glenhaven Ave WD6 170 A6
Glen Luce EN8 148 D1
Glenlyn Ave AL1 128 B2
Glenmire Terr SG12 115 D4
Glenmore Gdns WD5 154 A7
Glenshee Cl HA6 174 C4
Glen The
Caddington LU1 62 E3
Hemel Hempstead HP2 124 F8
Northwood HA6 174 D3
Glenview Gdns HP1 124 B3
Glenview Rd HP1 124 B3
Glenville Ave EN2 161 D1
Glen Way WD17 153 E1
Glenwood
Hoddesdon EN10 134 F4
Welwyn Garden City AL7 111 D5
Glenwood Cl SG2 51 C2
Glevum Cl AL3 126 F1
Globe Cl AL5 86 B1
Globe Cres CM23 58 D6
Globe Ct
Hertford SG14 113 C8
Hoddesdon EN10 148 F8
Globe Ho WD3 164 C5
Glossop Way SG15 11 B7
Gloucester Ave EN8 162 E6
Gloucester Cl SG1 36 E2
Gloucester Ct
Hatfield AL10 129 F6
9 Watford WD18 166 F5
Gloucester Ho 6 WD6 170 A7
Gloucester Rd
Enfield EN2 161 C1
1 Luton LU1 63 F6
Glover Cl EN7 147 F4
Glovers Cl SG13 113 C4
Glovers Ct SG5 21 F1
Glynde The SG2 69 B8
Glynswood Pl HA6 174 B3
Goat La EN1 161 F1
Gobions Way EN6 145 B3
Goblins Gn AL7 110 D5
Goddard End SG2 69 C8
Goddards Cl SG13 132 C4
Godfrey Cl SG2 51 B3
Godfreys Cl LU1 63 B6
Godfreys Ct LU1 63 B6
Godfries Cl AL6 90 E3
Godsafe CM17 118 E4
Godwin Cl E4 163 C1
Goffs Cres EN7 147 C2
Goffs La EN7 148 A2
Goff's La EN7 147 E2
GOFF'S OAK 147 C3
Goff's Oak Ave EN7 147 C3
Goffs Oak Prim Sch EN7 147 B3
Goffs Sch EN7 148 A2
Golda Cl EN5 171 D3
Gold Cl EN10 134 E3
Goldcrest Cl LU4 44 A5
Goldcrest Way WD23 168 C1
Goldcroft HP3 125 A1
Golden Dell AL7 110 F2
Goldens Way SG14 92 A1
Golden Willows SG5 21 E6
Goldfield Inf Sch HP23 99 F3
Goldfield Rd HP23 99 F3
Goldfinch Way WD6 170 A5
Goldings
Bishop's Stortford CM23 77 B8
Hertford SG14 92 A1
Goldings Cres AL10 130 B6
Goldings Hall SG14 91 F1
Goldings Ho AL10 130 B6
Goldings La SG14 92 A2
Goldington Cl EN11 114 F1
Goldon SG6 23 C4
Goldring Way AL2 142 B5
Goldsmith Way AL3 127 C4
Goldstone Cl SG12 93 D2
Golf Cl WD23 167 D6
Golf Club Rd AL9 145 A6
Golf Ride EN2 161 A4
Gombards AL3 127 D4
Gomer Cl SG4 67 E2
Gonnerston AL3 127 B4
Gonville Ave WD3 166 B3
Gonville Cres SG2 51 C2
Goodacre Cl EN6 159 C7
Goodacre Ct EN6 159 B7
Goodey Meade SG2 52 F2
Goodison Cl WD23 168 C4
Goodliffe Pk CM23 59 B2
Goodman Ct 7 EN8 148 E3
Goodrich Cl WD25 154 A4
Goodwin Ho WD18 166 E3
Goodwins Mead LU7 80 A7
Goodwin Stile CM23 76 D5
Goodwood Ave
Enfield EN3 162 C2
Watford WD24 153 E3
Goodwood Cl EN11 135 A7
Goodwood Par WD24 153 E3
Goodwood Path 2 WD6 170 A7
Goodwood Rd SG8 7 F6
Goodyers Ave WD7 155 F5
Gooseacre AL7 110 F4
Goose Acre
Botley HP5 136 A1
Cheddington LU7 80 A7
Gooseberry Hill LU3 45 B7
Goosecroft HP1 123 F4
Goosefields WD3 165 C3
GOOSE GREEN 134 C7
Goose La CM22 98 E7
Goral Mead WD3 165 D1
Gordian Way SG2 37 C1
Gordon Ave HA7 176 F4
Gordon Cl AL1 128 B2
Gordon Ct SG3 69 A5
Gordon Ho AL1 128 B2
Gordon Mans 7 EN5 171 F5
Gordon Rd EN9 163 A5
Gordon St LU1 63 D7
Gordon's Wlk AL5 107 C8
Gordon Way EN5 171 F5
Gore La SG11 73 D3
Gorelands La HP8 172 A7
Gorhambury* AL3 126 C4
Gorham Dr AL1 141 E8
Gorle Cl WD25 154 A4
Gorleston Cl SG1 36 A1
Gorse Cl AL10 129 F2
Gorse Cnr
Harpenden AL5 107 C8
St Albans AL3 127 D5
Gorselands AL5 107 B7
Gorseway AL10 109 F1
Gorst Cl SG6 22 E5
Gosford Ho WD18 166 E3
Gosforth La
South Oxhey WD19 175 B7
5 South Oxhey WD19 175 C7
Gosforth Path WD19 175 A7
Goshawk Cl LU4 44 A4
Goslett Ct WD23 168 A4
Gosling Ave SG5 33 C2
Gosling Ski Ctr* AL8 110 C4
GOSMORE 34 E3
Gosmore SG1 36 C2
Gosmore Ley Cl SG4 34 F3
Gosmore Rd SG4 34 E3
Gossamers The WD25 154 E4
Gosse Cl EN11 114 F1
Gosselin Ho SG14 113 D8
Gosselin Rd SG14 113 C8
Gossoms End HP4 122 A5
Gossoms Ryde HP4 122 A5
Gothic Mede Lower Sch SG15 11 A5
Gothic Way SG15 11 B5
Gould Cl AL9 144 B7
Government Row EN3 163 A2
Gowar Field EN6 158 A7
Gower Rd SG8 7 C7
Gowers The CM20 118 B2
Grace Ave WD7 156 E6
Grace Cl WD6 170 D8
Grace Ct HA6 175 A1
Grace Gdns CM23 76 F4
Graces Maltings HP23 100 A3
Grace Way SG1 50 E7
Graemesdyke Rd HP4 122 A3
Grafton Cl AL4 128 D2
Grafton Pl SG11 55 F1
Graham Ave EN10 134 E2
Graham Cl AL1 127 D1
Graham Ct 3 AL3 127 D4
Graham Gdns LU3 45 C4
Graham Rd HA3 176 E1
Grailands CM23 76 D8
Grammar School Wlk SG5 34 E7
Grampian Pl SG1 37 B4
Grampian Way LU3 44 C8
Granaries The EN9 163 E5
Granary Cl AL4 108 D8
Granary Ct CM21 97 E2
Granary La AL5 86 C1
Granary The
Arlesey SG15 11 A5
Flamstead HP2 104 F4
Hemel Hempstead HP1 124 B7
Roydon CM19 116 B1
Granary The *continued*
Stanstead Abbotts SG12 115 C3
Tewin AL6 90 E4
Granby Ave AL5 86 D2
Granby Ct AL5 86 D2
Granby Rd
Luton LU4 44 E2
Stevenage SG1 36 C2
Grandfield Ave WD17 167 A8
Grandmill Pl 2 EN8 148 E3
Grand Union Way WD4 139 B2
Grange Ave
Luton LU4 44 D4
Totteridge N20 171 E2
Grange Bottom SG8 7 E5
Grange Cl
Hemel Hempstead HP2 125 A2
Hertford SG14 113 B6
Hitchin SG4 35 A4
Markyate AL3 83 D6
Watford WD17 167 A8
Grange Court Rd AL5 107 C6
Grange Ct
Hertford SG14 113 C7
Letchworth Garden City SG6 12 A1
4 St Albans AL3 127 D4
Waltham Abbey EN9 163 C5
Grangedale Cl HA6 174 E2
Grange Dr SG5 11 F5
Grange Gdns SG12 114 E8
Grange Hill AL6 89 C6
Grange Jun Sch SG6 12 A2
Grange La WD25 168 D8
Grange Pk CM23 58 F1
Granger Ct 7 WD6 170 A5
Grange Rd
Bishop's Stortford CM23 77 A7
Borehamwood WD6 169 F4
Letchworth Garden City SG6 22 F8
Pitstone LU7 80 D5
Tring HP23 100 C5
Watford WD23 167 F4
Wilstone HP23 79 D1
Grange Rise SG4 67 F1
Grangeside CM23 59 A2
Grange St AL3 127 D4
Grange Street Mews 1 AL3 127 D4
Grange The
Abbots Langley WD5 153 E8
Bishop's Stortford CM23 58 F1
Hoddesdon EN11 135 A5
Rickmansworth WD3 165 D2
Standon SG11 55 D3
Stevenage SG1 50 C8
Therfield SG8 15 F6
Totteridge N20 171 E1
Waltham Abbey EN9 163 D2
Grange Wlk CM23 77 A7
Grangewood EN6 145 B1
Gransden Cl LU3 45 A7
Grant Gdns AL5 86 B2
Grantham Cl SG8 7 B8
Grantham Gdns SG12 93 E2
Grantham Gn WD6 170 C4
Grantham Mews HP4 122 D4
Grantham Rd LU4 45 B1
Granville Ct AL1 127 F3
Granville Dene HP3 137 A4
Granville Gdns EN11 115 A2
Granville Rd
Barnet EN5 171 D6
Berkhamsted HP4 121 E6
Hitchin SG4 22 C1
Luton LU1 63 B8
St Albans AL1 127 F3
Watford WD18 167 C5
Graseby Ho 3 EN5 171 F5
Grasmere SG1 37 C3
Grasmere Ave
Harpenden AL5 86 C1
Luton LU3 45 B7
Grasmere Cl
Hemel Hempstead HP3 125 B1
Watford WD25 154 B7
Grasmere Rd
Luton LU3 45 C7
St Albans AL1 128 B1
Ware SG12 93 E3
Grassington Cl AL2 141 A1
Grass Mdws SG2 51 D7
Grass Warren AL6 90 E1
Grassy Cl HP1 124 A4
Gravel Dr HP23 99 B3
GRAVELEY 36 C4
Graveley Ave WD6 170 C4
Graveley Cl SG1 36 C2
Graveley Dell AL7 111 B5
Graveley La SG4 36 B5
Graveley Prim Sch SG4 36 B4
Graveley Rd
Graveley SG1 36 B3
Great Wymondley SG4 35 F6
Gravelhill Terr HP1 124 A2
Gravel La HP1 124 A3
Gravelly Dell SG11 55 F8
Gravelly La SG11 55 F8
Gravel Path
Berkhamsted HP4 122 E5
Hemel Hempstead HP1 124 A3
Gravely Ct HP2 125 C2
GRAVESEND 57 B8
Grayling Ct HP4 121 F6
Graylings The WD5 153 D6
Grays Cl SG8 7 C8
Grays Ct CM23 76 E8
Graysfield AL7 111 A3
Gray's La SG5 34 D7
Grazings The HP2 124 F5
GREAT AMWELL 114 F5
GREAT ASHBY 37 D3
Great Ashby Way SG1 37 B3
Great Augur St 4 CM17 118 D1
Great Braitch La AL10 109 F1
Great Bramingham La LU3 31 B2
Great Break AL7 111 B5
Great Cambridge Rd
Cheshunt EN8 148 D4
Enfield EN1 162 C6
GREAT CHISHILL 9 F2
Great Conduit AL7 111 C7
Great Dell AL8 89 D1
Great Eastern Cl CM23 77 A6
Great Elms Rd HP3 138 F7
Greatfield Cl AL5 85 C4
Great Gables SG1 37 B4
GREAT GADDESDEN 103 D3
Great Gaddesden CE Prim Sch HP1 103 D3
Great Ganett AL7 111 C4
GREATGAP 80 D6
Great Gn SG5 20 D4
Great Gr WD23 168 B5
Great Groves EN7 147 E3
Great Hadham Rd CM23 76 C5
GREAT HALLINGBURY 77 E4
Greatham Rd WD23 167 D6
Greatham Road Ind Est WD23 167 D5
Great Havers Ct CM23 76 E5
Great Heart HP2 124 E5
Great Heath AL10 130 B8
GREAT HORMEAD 42 B8
Great Hyde Hall CM21 98 B3
Great Innings N SG14 70 D4
Great Innings S SG14 70 D3
Great Lawne SG3 69 D2
Great Ley AL7 110 E4
Great Leys Ct AL2 142 B4
Great Marlings LU2 46 C6
Great Mdw EN10 135 A1
Great Molewood SG14 92 B1
GREAT MUNDEN 54 C5
Great North Rd
Barnet EN5 171 E6
Brookmans Park AL9, EN6 145 B5
Hatfield AL9 130 C5
Oaklands AL6 89 E7
Radwell SG7 12 D3
Welwyn Garden City AL8 110 A7
GREAT OFFLEY 33 D2
Great Palmers HP2 124 F8
Great Pk WD4 139 A1
Great Plumtree CM20 117 F2
Great Rd HP2 124 F4
Great Slades EN6 158 F6
Great Stockwood Rd EN7 147 D5
Great Sturgess Rd HP1 123 F3
Great Whites Rd HP3 124 F1
Great Wood Ctry Pk* EN6 146 B5
GREAT WYMONDLEY 35 F6
Greenacre Cl EN5 158 F1
Greenacres
Bushey WD23 176 D8
Hemel Hempstead HP2 125 D2
Pitstone LU7 80 C4
Wingrave HP22 60 B2
Green Acres
Lilley LU2 32 D2
Stevenage SG2 51 C1
Welwyn Garden City AL7 110 F3
Greenacres Cvn Pk LU6 82 F8
Greenall Cl EN8 148 E1
Greenbank EN8 148 B3
Greenbank Rd WD17 153 D3
Green Banks AL1 127 F1
Greenbury Cl
Barley SG8 8 F1
Chorleywood WD3 164 C5
Greenbushes LU4 44 D6
Green Cl
Brookmans Park AL9 144 E5
Cheshunt EN8 162 E8
Luton LU4 44 C5
Stevenage SG2 50 F2
Greencoates SG13 113 E5
Green Croft AL10 130 A8
Green Ct 6 LU4 44 C5
Green Dell Way HP3 125 C3
Green Dragon Ct LU1 63 F6
Green Drift SG8 7 C7
Green Edge WD25 154 A4
Greene Field Rd HP4 122 C4
GREEN END 55 E7
Green End SG11 55 E8
GREEN END
Dane End 53 E1
GREEN END *continued*
Hemel Hempstead 124 A2
Sandon 26 D7
Green End AL6 89 B4
GREEN END 24 C2
Green End Bsns Ctr WD3 152 A2
Green End Gdns HP1 124 A2
Green End La HP1 123 F3
Green End Rd HP1 124 A2
Greener Ct EN3 163 A2
Greenes Ct HP4 122 C5
Greene Wlk HP4 122 D3
Greenfield
Hatfield AL9 130 D8
Royston SG8 7 B7
Welwyn Garden City AL8 89 D1
Greenfield Ave
Ickleford SG5 21 D4
South Oxhey WD19 175 E8
Greenfield La SG5 21 E4
Greenfield Rd SG1 50 E7
Greenfields
Cuffley EN6 146 E1
Stansted Mountfitchet CM24 59 E7
Greenfields Prim Sch WD19 175 C5
Greenfield St EN9 163 C5
Greengate LU3 44 C8
Greenheys Cl HA6 174 E2
Greenhill Ave LU2 45 E3
Green Hill Cl SG11 55 F7
Greenhill Cres WD18 166 E3
Greenhill Ct HP1 124 B2
Greenhill Pk CM23 76 D5
Greenhills SG12 93 C3
Greenhills Cl WD3 165 B4
Green La
Ashwell SG7 4 E5
Bovingdon HP3 137 A3
Bovingdon, Pudds Cross HP3 136 F3
Braughing SG11 55 F7
Croxley Green WD3 165 F4
Hemel Hempstead HP2 125 D4
Hitchin SG4 22 B1
Hoddesdon EN10 149 B8
Ivinghoe LU7 80 E5
Kensworth Common LU6 82 E8
Latimer HP5 150 C6
Letchworth Garden City SG6 23 C8
Luton LU2 46 C4
Markyate AL3 83 F5
Northwood HA6 174 E3
St Albans, New Greens AL3 127 D7
St Albans, Sopwell AL1 142 A7
Watford WD19 167 C2
Welwyn Garden City AL7 111 D5
Greenland Rd EN5 171 C3
Greenlands WD6 170 D3
Green Lane Cl AL5 107 E8
Greenlane Ind Est SG6 23 C7
Green Lanes AL10 109 F2
Green Lanes Prim Sch AL10 109 F1
Greenleas EN9 163 E5
Green Leys Cotts SG11 55 F1
Green Man Ct CM20 117 A4
Green Mdw EN6 145 A1
Green Oaks LU2 45 F3
Green Path HP22, HP23 99 D4
Greenriggs LU2 46 F2
Greenside WD6 157 A1
Greenside Dr SG5 34 D8
Greenside Pk LU2 45 E3
Greenside Sch SG2 51 B2
Greensleeves Cl AL4 128 C2
Green St
Chorleywood WD3 164 C6
2 Harlow CM17 118 D1
Royston SG8 7 D8
Shenley WD6, WD7 157 A3
Stevenage SG1 50 C7
Greenstead CM21 97 E1
GREEN STREET
Borehamwood 157 B2
Little Hadham 75 E8
Greensward WD23 168 B3
GREEN THE 81 F8
Green The
Bishop's Stortford CM23 76 F4
Caddington LU1 62 E4
Cheddington LU7 80 A7
Cheshunt EN8 148 C3
Codicote SG4 67 F1
Harefield UB9 173 C2
Kimpton SG4 66 D1
London Colney AL2 142 D4
Luton LU4 44 C5
Mentmore LU7 61 D4
Newnham SG7 12 E7
Old Knebworth SG3 68 C5
Peters Green LU2 65 C3
Pitstone LU7 80 D4
Potten End HP4 123 B6
Royston SG8 7 D6
Sarratt WD3 152 A3
Stotfold SG5 11 F7
Waltham Abbey EN9 163 C5
Ware SG12 93 D3

Green The *continued*
Welwyn AL6 89 B5
Welwyn Garden City AL7 111 A4
Wingrave HP22 60 B2
GREEN TYE 75 D1
Green Vale AL7 111 A5
Green View Cl HP3 137 A2
Greenway
Berkhamsted HP4 122 A4
Bishop's Stortford CM23 77 C6
Harpenden AL5 107 E8
Hemel Hempstead HP2 125 B3
Letchworth Garden City SG6 23 A2
Pinner HA5 175 B1
Walkern SG2 52 B8
Greenway Fst Sch HP4 121 F4
Greenway Gdns HA3 176 E1
Greenways
Abbots Langley WD5 153 E7
Buntingford SG9 40 D8
Goff's Oak EN7 147 B2
Hertford SG14 113 B6
Luton LU2 46 B5
Stevenage SG1 50 E6
Welwyn AL6 89 E3
Greenway The
Enfield EN3 162 D4
Harrow HA3 176 E2
Potters Bar EN6 159 A6
Rickmansworth WD3 165 A2
Tring HP23 99 F5
Greenwich Ct
Cheshunt EN8 162 E5
11 St Albans AL1 128 A2
Greenwich Way EN9 163 C3
Greenwood Ave EN7 162 B8
Greenwood Cl EN7 162 B8
Greenwood Court Ind Est LU2 46 A2
Greenwood Dr WD25 154 B5
Greenwood Gdns WD7 156 E6
Greenyard EN9 163 C6
Greer Rd HA3 176 C2
Gregories Cl LU3 45 D1
Gregory Ave EN6 159 C6
Gregory Mews EN9 163 B7
Gregson Cl WD6 170 C8
Grenadier Cl AL4 128 C2
Grenadine Cl EN7 147 F4
Grenadine Way HP23 100 A5
Greneway Sch The SG8 7 E7
Grenfell Cl WD6 170 C8
Grenville Ave EN10 134 F2
Grenville Cl EN8 162 D7
Grenville Ct WD3 164 C5
Grenville Way SG2 51 A1
Gresford Cl AL4 128 D3
Gresham Cl LU2 64 D8
Gresham Ct HP4 122 B3
Gresley Cl AL8 110 E8
Gresley Ct
Enfield EN1 162 C4
Potters Bar EN6 145 C1
Gresley Way SG2 51 D5
Greville Cl AL9 144 C7
Greycaine Rd WD24 154 D2
Greydells Rd SG1 50 E6
Greyfriars SG12 93 B3
Greyfriars La AL5 107 A7
Greyholme Ct 7 HA6 175 F3
Greyhound La EN6 158 A6
Grey House The 4 WD17 167 A7
Greystoke Cl HP4 122 A3
Griffiths Way AL1 127 C1
Griffon Way WD25 153 F5
Grimsdyke Cres EN5 171 C6
Grimsdyke Fst & Mid Sch HA5 175 F4
Grimsdyke Lo AL1 128 A3
Grimsdyke Rd
Pinner HA5 175 E3
Wigginton HP23 100 D1
Grimstone Rd SG4 35 E4
Grimston Rd AL1 127 F2
Grimthorpe Cl AL3 127 D6
Grindcobbe AL1 141 D8
Grinders End SG4 36 B4
Grinstead La CM22 98 C6
Groom Ct AL1 127 E5
Groom Rd EN10 148 F5
Groomsby Dr LU7 80 E5
Grooms Cotts HP5 136 B1
Grosvenor Ave WD4 139 C3
Grosvenor Cl CM23 76 D4
Grosvenor Ct
Croxley Green WD3 166 D4
Stevenage SG1 50 A7
Grosvenor Ho 4 CM23 77 B8
Grosvenor Rd
Baldock SG7 12 F1
Borehamwood WD6 170 B6
Hoddesdon EN10 134 F3
Luton LU3 45 B5
Moor Park HA6 174 F5
St Albans AL1 127 E2
Watford WD17 167 C6
Grosvenor Rd W SG7 12 F1
Grosvenor Sq WD4 139 C3
Grosvenor Terr HP1 124 A2
Grotto The SG12 114 D8
Ground La AL10 130 B7
Grove Ave AL5 107 D7
Grovebury Gdns AL2 141 C4
Grove Cotts WD23 168 A3
Grove Cres WD3 166 A5
Grove Ct
Arlesey SG15 11 A8
Barnet EN5 171 F6
Waltham Abbey EN9 163 B6
Grovedale Cl EN7 147 F1
Grove End LU1 63 B5
Grove Farm Pk HA6 174 D5
Grove Gdns
Enfield EN3 162 D1
Tring HP23 100 B5
Grove Hall Rd WD23 167 E5
GROVEHILL 124 E8
Grove Hill CM24 59 E7
Grove Ho
Bushey WD23 167 F3
Cheshunt EN8 148 B1
Hitchin SG4 22 A2
12 Luton LU1 63 D7
Grove Inf Sch The AL5 107 D7
Grove Jun Sch The AL5 107 D7
Grove La HP5 136 B5
Grovelands
Chiswell Green AL2 141 B4
Hemel Hempstead HP2 125 C5
Grovelands Ave SG4 22 C2
Grovelands Bsns Ctr HP2 125 C5
Groveland Way SG5 12 A5
Grove Lea AL10 130 A2
Grove Mdw AL7 111 C6
Grove Mead AL10 129 F5
Grove Mill Ct SG4 22 A2
Grove Mill La WD3, WD17 153 C1
Grove Park Rd LU1 63 B3
Grove Path EN7 162 A8
Grove Pk
Bishop's Stortford CM23 76 C8
Tring HP23 100 C5
Grove Pl
19 Bishop's Stortford CM23 76 F7
Bushey WD25 168 B8
Welham Green AL9 144 C7
Grover Cl HP2 124 D4
Grove Rd
Borehamwood WD6 170 A8
Harpenden AL5 107 D7
Hemel Hempstead HP1 124 A1
Hitchin SG4 21 F1
Luton LU1 63 D7
Northwood HA6 174 D5
Rickmansworth WD3 173 A8
Slip End LU1 63 B2
St Albans AL1 127 D2
Stevenage SG1 50 D7
Tring HP23 100 C5
Ware SG12 93 F2
Grove Rd W EN3 162 C2
Grove Road Prim Sch HP23 100 C5
Grover Rd WD19 167 D3
Grove The
Brookmans Park AL9 145 A4
Chipperfield WD4 138 C1
Great Hallingbury CM22 77 F4
Latimer HP5 150 D3
Little Hadham SG11 75 E7
Luton LU1 63 B5
Potters Bar EN6 159 C7
Radlett WD7 156 A5
Tring HP23 100 C5
Woodside LU1 63 B3
Grove Way WD3 164 B4
Grove Wlk SG14 113 C8
Grovewood Cl WD3 164 B4
Grubbs La AL9 145 C8
Gryphon Ind Pk The AL3 127 F8
Guardian Bsns Pk LU1 63 C8
GUBBLECOTE 79 D3
Guernsey Cl LU4 44 A3
Guernsey Ho
Enfield EN3 162 D1
Watford WD18 167 A3
Guessens Ct AL8 110 C6
Guessens Gr AL8 110 C6
Guessens Rd AL8 110 C6
Guessens Wlk AL8 110 C7
GUILDEN MORDEN 1 F4
Guilden Morden CE Prim Sch SG8 1 F5
Guildford Cl SG1 36 F2
Guildford Rd AL1 128 B2
Guildford St LU1 63 E7
Guildhouse The WD3 166 B3
Guilfords CM17 118 D5
Guinevere Gdns EN8 162 E8
Guiver Ct 5 EN8 148 E3
Gulland Cl WD23 168 C4
Gullbrook HP1 124 A3
Gullet Wood Rd WD25 154 A4
Gullicot Way LU7 80 D4
Gulphs The SG13 113 D5
Gun Ho SG3 68 F5
Gun La SG3 68 F4
Gun Meadow Ave SG3 69 A4
Gunnels Wood Ind Est SG1 50 D3
Gunnels Wood Pk SG1 50 B5
Gunnels Wood Rd SG1 50 B5
Gunner Dr EN3 163 A2
Gunpowder Pk* EN9 163 B3
Gun Rd SG3 69 A4
Gun Road Gdns SG3 68 F4
Gurney Court Rd AL1 127 F5
Gurney's La SG5 21 B7
GUSTARD WOOD 87 D4
Gustard Wood AL4 87 C5
Gwent Cl WD25 154 D5
Gwynfa Cl AL6 89 D7
Gwynne Cl HP23 100 A5
Gwynns Wlk SG13 113 E6
Gyfford Wlk EN7 162 B8
Gypsy Cl SG12 114 F4
Gypsy La
Abbots Langley WD4 153 D5
Great Amwell SG12 114 F4
Welwyn Garden City AL7 110 F1
Gypsy Moth Ave AL10 129 E7

H

Haberdashers' Aske's Boys' Sch WD6 169 B6
Haberdashers' Aske's Sch for Girls WD6 169 B5
Hackforth Cl EN5 171 B4
Hackney Cl WD6 170 D4
Haddenham Ct HP2 105 B1
Haddestoke Gate EN8 148 F5
Haddon Cl
Borehamwood WD6 170 A6
Hemel Hempstead HP3 125 A2
Stevenage SG2 69 C7
Haddon Ct 20 AL5 86 B1
Haddon Rd
Chorleywood WD3 164 C4
Luton LU2 63 F8
HADHAM CROSS 74 F2
Hadham Ct CM23 76 E8
HADHAM FORD 75 B8
Hadham Gr CM23 76 C8
Hadham Hall SG11 57 E2
Hadham Rd
Bishop's Stortford CM23 76 D8
Little Hadham SG11 57 F1
Standon SG11 55 F1
Hadland Cl HP3 137 A5
Hadleigh SG6 23 B4
Hadleigh Ct
Harpenden AL5 107 E6
Hoddesdon EN10 134 F1
HADLEY 171 F6
Hadley Cl WD6 169 F3
Hadley Ct LU3 45 D1
Hadley Gn EN5 171 F7
Hadley Gn W EN5 171 F7
Hadley Gr EN5 171 E7
Hadley Green Rd EN5 171 F7
Hadley Highstone EN5 171 F8
Hadley Par 6 EN5 171 E6
Hadley Rd EN2, EN4 160 C1
Hadley Ridge EN5 171 F6
HADLEY WOOD 159 C2
Hadley Wood Prim Sch EN4 159 C1
Hadley Wood Sta EN4 159 C1
Hadlow Down Cl LU3 45 A5
Hadrian Cl AL3 127 A1
Hadrians Wlk SG1 51 C8
Hadrian Way SG7 23 D7
Hadwell Cl SG2 51 A3
Hagdell Rd LU1 63 C5
Hagden La WD18 167 A4
Haggerston Rd WD6 156 E1
Hagsdell Rd SG13 113 D5
Haig Cl AL1 128 B2
Haig Ho AL1 128 B2
HAILEY 114 F2
Hailey Ave EN11 115 A2
Haileybury & Imperial Service Coll SG13 114 D2
Hailey Cl SG13 114 E2
Hailey Hall Sch SG13 114 F2
Hailey La
Hertford Heath SG13 114 E2
Hoddesdon SG13 114 F2
Hailey Pl CM21 97 E2
Haines Way WD25 154 A5
Halcroft Ho EN7 147 F4
Haldane Cl EN3 163 B1
HALDENS 89 F1
Haldens AL7 89 F1
Haldens Ho 3 AL7 89 F1
Hale Ct SG13 113 D5
Hale Ho EN3 162 D2
Hale La HP22 119 A3
Hale Rd SG13 113 D5
Hales Mdw AL5 86 A2
Hales Park Cl HP2 125 C4
Hales Pk HP2 125 C4
Haleswood Rd HP2 125 B4
Half Acre SG5 34 D6
Half Acres CM23 76 F8
Halfhide La EN8 148 D5
Halfhides EN9 163 D6
Half Moon Cotts CM21 97 B1
Half Moon La LU1 84 C8
Half Moon Mdw HP2 125 C8
Half Moon Mews 9 AL1 127 D3
Halford Ct AL10 129 E6
Halfway Ave LU4 44 D1
Halifax Cl
Bricket Wood AL2 154 F8
Watford WD25 153 F5
Halifax Rd WD3 164 C2
Halifax Way AL7 111 E6
Hallam Cl WD24 167 C7
Hallam Gdns HA5 175 E3
Halland Way HA6 174 D4
Hall Barns
Furneux Pelham SG9 42 F4
Stansted Mountfitchet CM24 59 D7
Hall Cl WD3 165 A1
Hall Cotts SG9 29 A1
Hall Dr UB9 173 C2
Halley Rd EN9 163 B3
Halleys Ridge SG14 113 A5
Hall Gdns AL4 143 D8
Hall Gr AL7 111 B4
HALL GROVE 111 B3
Hall Heath Cl AL1 128 B5
Halliday Cl WD7 156 E7
Hallingbury Cl CM22 77 B1
Hallingbury Rd
Bishop's Stortford CM22 77 B4
Sawbridgeworth CM21 98 A4
Halling Hill CM20 117 F2
Hall La
Blackmore End SG4 87 C8
Great Chishill SG8 9 F2
Great Hormead SG9 29 A1
Woolmer Green SG3 69 A2
Hall Mead SG6 22 D6
Hallmores EN10 135 A4
Hallowell Rd HA6 174 E3
Hallowes Cres WD19 175 A7
Hall Park Gate HP4 122 E3
Hall Park Hill HP4 122 E3
Hall Pk HP4 122 E3
Hall Place Cl AL1 127 E4
Hall Place Gdns AL1 127 E4
Hall Rd HP2 125 B5
Halls Cl AL6 89 C4
HALL'S GREEN 37 E6
Hallside Rd EN1 161 F1
Hallwicks Rd LU2 46 B3
Hallworth Dr SG5 11 E6
Hallworth Ho SG5 11 E6
Halsey Dr
Hemel Hempstead HP1 123 F5
Hitchin SG4 35 B7
Halsey Pk AL2 142 F4
Halsey Pl WD24 154 B1
Halsey Rd WD18 167 B6
Halstead Hill EN7 147 E1
Halter Cl WD6 170 D4
Halton Cl AL2 141 C3
Halton Wood (Forest Wlks)* HP23 119 A5
Haltside AL10 129 E4
Halwick Cl 1 HP1 124 B1
Halyard Cl LU3 45 B6
Halyard Ind Est SG6 23 B6
Hamberlins La HP4 121 C7
Hamble Ct WD18 167 A5
Hambleden Pl WD7 155 F4
Hambledon Ct EN4 159 D1
Hamblings Cl WD7 156 D6
Hambridge Way SG5 20 D4
Hambro Cl LU2 85 F7
Hamburgh Ct EN8 148 D3
Hamels Dr SG13 114 B7
Hamels La SG9 55 B7
Hamels Mans SG11 55 B6
Hamels Park Barns SG11 55 B6
Hamer Cl HP3 137 A3
Hamer Ct LU2 45 D8
Hamilton Ave EN11 135 A8
Hamilton Cl
Bricket Wood AL2 155 A8
Dagnall HP4 81 C5
South Mimms EN6 158 A6
Hamilton Ct 3 AL10 130 B3
Hamilton Mead HP3 137 A4
Hamilton Rd
Abbots Langley WD4 153 C6
Berkhamsted HP4 122 B4
South Oxhey WD19 175 B7
St Albans AL1 128 A4
Hamilton St WD18 167 C4
Hamlet Cl AL2 140 F1
Hamlet Hill CM19 135 F4
Hamlet The HP4 123 A7
Hammarsfield Cl SG11 55 D2
Hammarskjold Rd CM20 117 D2
Hammerdell SG6 22 D7
HAMMERFIELD 124 A3
Hammer La HP2 124 F4
Hammer Par WD25 154 A6
Hammers Gate AL2 141 A5
Hammond Cl
Barnet EN5 171 E4
Hammond Street EN7 147 F5
Stevenage SG1 50 D6
Hammond Ct LU1 63 C1
Hammond End La AL5 106 F5
Hammond Prim Sch The HP2 124 F6
Hammonds Hill AL5 106 F4
Hammonds La AL10 109 B3
HAMMOND STREET 147 D5
Hammondstreet Rd EN7 147 D5
Hammondswick AL5 106 F4
Hamonte SG6 23 C4
Hampden SG4 66 C1
Hampden Cl SG6 23 B8
Hampden Cres EN7 162 B8
Hampden Hill SG12 93 F2
Hampden Hill Cl SG12 93 F2
Hampden Pl AL2 141 E2
Hampden Rd
Harrow HA3 176 C1
Hitchin SG4 22 C1
Hampden Rise SG8 7 D4
Hampden Way WD17 153 E3
Hampermill La WD19 167 A1
Hampstead Cl AL2 154 F8
Hampton Cl
Borehamwood WD6 170 C4
Stevenage SG2 69 C7
Hampton Gdns CM21 118 C7
Hampton Ho SG13 113 E6
Hampton Rd LU4 63 B8
Hamstel Rd CM20 117 C1
Hamsworth Ct SG14 112 F7
Hanaper Dr SG8 8 F2
Hanbury Cl
Cheshunt EN8 148 E2
Ware SG12 93 E1
Hanbury Cotts AL9 131 E6
Hanbury Dr SG12 93 C6
Hanbury Mews SG12 93 C5
Hancock Ct WD6 170 C8
Hancock Dr LU2 45 E5
Hancroft Rd HP3 124 F1
Handa Cl HP3 139 B8
Handcross Rd LU2 46 D2
Hand La CM21 97 C1
Handley Gate AL2 140 F2
Handley Page Way AL2 141 F1
Handleys Ct HP2 124 D2
Handpost Lodge Gdns HP2 125 D2
HANDSIDE 110 C5
Handside Cl AL8 110 C6
Handside Gn AL8 110 C7
Handside La AL8 110 C6
Handsworth Way WD19 175 A7
Hangar Ruding WD19 175 F7
Hanger Cl HP1 124 B2
Hangmans La AL6 89 F8
Hanover Cl SG2 50 F1
Hanover Ct
Croxley Green WD3 166 A4
Hoddesdon EN11 135 A7
Luton LU4 44 D5
14 Pinner HA5 175 F3
Sawbridgeworth CM21 97 F1
Waltham Abbey EN9 163 C6
Watford WD18 166 E5
Hanover Gdns WD5 139 F1
Hanover Gn HP1 124 A1
Hanover Grange AL5 85 E3
Hanover Ho AL7 110 F4
Hanover Wlk AL10 129 F2
Hanross Cl AL2 140 E1
HANSCOMBE END 19 D8
Hanscombe End Rd SG5 19 D7
Hanselin Cl HA7 176 F5
Hanswick Cl LU2 46 B2
Hanworth Cl LU2 45 D7
Hanyards End EN6 146 E3
Hanyards La EN6 146 D3
Happy Valley Ind Pk WD4 139 B3
Harbert Gdns AL2 141 C2
Harborne Cl WD19 175 C5
Harbour Ct WD23 168 B4
Harbury Dell LU3 45 B7
Harcourt Rd
Bushey WD23 168 C4
Tring HP23 100 C4
Harcourt St LU1 63 E5
Hardenwick Ct 4 AL5 86 A2
Harding Cl
Luton LU3 44 E7
Redbourn AL3 106 B5
Watford WD25 154 C6
Harding Ct AL5 86 B4
Harding Par 8 AL5 86 B1
Hardings AL7 111 C7
Hardings Cl HP3 138 B8
Hardingstone Ct EN8 162 F5
Hardwick Cl SG2 69 C7
Hardwicke Pl AL2 142 D4
Hardwick Gn LU3 45 B7
Hardy Cl
Barnet EN5 171 E4
Hitchin SG4 35 C7
Hardy Ct 10 WD6 170 A5
Hardy Dr SG8 7 D8
Hardy Rd HP2 124 F4
Harebell AL7 110 E3
Harebell Cl SG13 114 B6
Harebreaks The WD24 154 B2
Hare Cres WD25 154 A7
HAREFIELD 173 C1
Harefield
Harlow CM20 118 A1
Stevenage SG2 51 C3
Harefield Acad The UB9 173 D2
Harefield Ct LU1 62 F8
Harefield Hospl UB9 173 C2

Harefield Inf Sch UB9 173 C2
Harefield Jun Sch UB9 173 C2
Harefield Pl AL4 128 D6
Harefield Rd
Luton LU1 62 F8
Rickmansworth WD3 173 D7
Harefield Road Ind Est WD3 173 E6
Hare La AL10 130 B3
Harepark Cl HP1 123 F4
Haresfoot Sch HP4 122 B1
HARE STREET
Buntingford 41 D7
Cottered 38 F6
Hare Street Rd SG9 41 B8
Harewood WD3 165 C4
Harewood Ct HA3 176 E2
Harewood Rd WD19 175 B7
Harford Dr WD17 166 E8
Harforde Ct SG13 114 A6
Hargrave Cl CM24 59 E8
Hargreaves Ave EN7 162 B8
Hargreaves Cl EN7 162 B8
Hargreaves Rd SG8 7 D5
Harkett Cl HA3 176 F1
Harkett Ct HA3 176 F1
Harkness EN7 148 B2
Harkness Ct SG4 22 B1
Harkness Rd 9 HP2 124 D4
Harkness Way SG4 22 C2
Harland Ct UB9 173 C1
Harlech Rd WD5 154 A8
Harlequin The WD17 167 C5
Harlesden Rd AL1 128 A3
Harlestone Cl LU3 31 A1
Harley Ct
Enfield EN1 162 B2
St Albans AL4 128 D7
Harlings The SG13 114 C2
HARLOW 118 C2
Harlowbury Prim Sch CM17 118 D4
Harlow Coll CM20 117 D1
Harlow Ct HP2 125 A7
Harlow Mill Sta CM20 118 C5
Harlow Rd
Roydon CM19 116 C1
Sawbridgeworth CM21 118 C8
Harlow Ret Pk CM20 117 F4
Harlow Stad (Greyhounds) CM19 116 E1
Harlow Town Sta CM20 117 D3
Harlton Ct EN9 163 F5
Harmer Dell AL6 89 F4
HARMER GREEN 90 B5
Harmer Green La AL6 90 B5
Harmony Cl AL10 130 A7
Harmsworth Way N20 171 F1
Harness Way AL4 128 D6
Harold Cres EN9 163 C7
Harold Ct EN8 162 F5
HARPENDEN 86 B2
HARPENDEN COMMON 107 B7
Harpenden Hospl (private) AL5 86 A4
Harpenden La AL3 106 B6
Harpenden Meml Hospl AL5 86 B2
Harpenden Rd
St Albans AL3 127 E6
Wheathampstead AL5, AL4 108 B8
Harpenden Rise AL5 85 F3
Harpenden Sta AL5 86 B1
Harperbury Hospl WD7 156 C8
Harper Ct SG1 50 F5
Harper La WD7 156 B8
Harpsfield Broadway AL10 129 F6
Harps Hill AL3 83 E5
Harptree Way AL1 128 A5
Harriet Ho HP3 138 E6
Harriet Walker Way WD3 164 F2
Harriet Way WD23 168 D2
Harrington Cl 8 CM23 77 A7
Harrington Ct SG13 114 C3
Harriot Hts AL3 127 C4
Harris Ho 14 WD18 166 F3
Harris La
Great Offley SG5 33 D2
Shenley WD7 157 A6
Harrison Cl
3 Hitchin SG4 34 F7
Northwood HA6 174 C4
Harrison Rd EN9 163 C4
Harrisons CM23 59 D2
Harrison Wlk EN8 148 D1
Harris Rd WD25 154 A4
Harris's La SG12 93 C1
Harrogate Rd 2 WD19 175 C7
HARROW 176 E1
Harrowband Rd 7 CM17 118 C1
Harrow Coll, Harrow Weald Campus HA3 176 E4
Harrow Ct SG1 50 E5
Harrowden Ct LU2 64 C8
Harrowdene SG2 51 C4
Harrowden Rd LU2 64 B8
Harrow View HA2 176 C1
Harrow Way WD19 175 E6
HARROW WEALD 176 D2
Harrow Weald Pk HA3 176 D4
Harrow Yd HP23 100 A3
Harry Scott Ct LU4 44 C6
Harston Dr EN3 163 A1
Hartcran Ho 7 WD19 175 D7
Hartcroft Cl HP3 125 B2
Hartfield Ave WD6 170 A4
Hartfield Cl WD6 170 A4
Hartfield Ct 6 SG12 93 D2
Hartforde Rd WD6 170 B8
Harthall La WD4, HP3 139 D4
HARTHAM 113 D7
Hartham La SG14 113 D6
Hartham Villas SG14 113 C7
HART HILL 46 A1
Hart Hill Dr LU2 63 F8
Hart Hill La LU2 63 F8
Hart Hill Path LU2 63 F8
Hart La LU2 64 A8
Hartland Ct SG5 34 D7
Hartland Rd EN8 148 D1
Hartley Rd LU2 63 F8
Hart Lo 10 EN5 171 E6
Hartmoor Mews EN3 162 D2
Hart Rd
Harlow CM17 118 C6
St Albans AL1 127 D2
Hartsbourne Ave WD23 176 D8
Hartsbourne Cl WD23 176 D8
Hartsbourne Pk WD23 176 E8
Hartsbourne Prim Sch WD23 176 D8
Hartsbourne Rd WD23 176 D8
Hartsbourne Way HP2 125 C2
Hartsfield Jun Mix Inf Sch SG7 12 F1
Hartsfield Rd LU2 46 B2
Hartspring La WD23, WD25 168 A8
Hartswood Cl WD23 168 A8
Hartswood Gn WD23 176 D8
Hartwell Gdns AL5 85 E1
Harvest Cl LU4 44 A3
Harvest Ct
Letchworth Garden City SG6 23 A2
Oaklands AL6 89 E7
St Albans AL4 128 D7
Harvest End WD25 154 D3
Harvest La SG2 51 D7
Harvest Mead AL10 130 B7
Harvest Rd WD23 168 B5
Harveyfields EN9 163 C5
Harvey Rd
Croxley Green WD3 166 A3
London Colney AL2 142 C5
Stevenage SG2 51 B6
Harvey Road Prim Sch WD3 166 A3
Harvey's Hill LU2 45 F5
Harvington Pk LU7 80 D3
Harvingwell Pl HP2 125 B5
Harwood Cl
Tewin AL6 90 E2
Welwyn Garden City AL8 89 E2
Harwood Hill AL8 89 E1
Harwood Hill Jun Mix Inf Sch AL8 89 E2
Harwoods Rd WD18 167 A5
Hasedines Rd HP1 124 A4
Haseldine Mdws AL10 129 F4
Haseldine Rd AL2 142 D5
Haselfoot SG6 22 E6
Hasketon Dr LU4 44 B6
Haslemere CM23 77 A4
Haslemere Est The EN11 135 D6
Haslemere Ind Est
Bishop's Stortford CM23 77 A4
Welwyn Garden City AL7 110 F7
Haslewood Ave EN11 135 A6
Haslingden Cl AL5 85 D3
Hastings Cl SG1 50 A8
Hastings St LU1 63 D6
Hastings Way
Croxley Green WD3 166 C5
Watford WD23 167 E5
HASTOE 119 F7
Hastoe Cross HP23 120 A7
Hastoe Farm Barns HP23 119 F7
Hastoe La HP23 100 A2
HATCH END 175 E3
Hatch End High Sch HA3 176 B2
Hatch End Sta HA5 176 A3
Hatch Gn CM22 98 B8
HATCHING GREEN 107 A6
Hatching Green Cl AL5 107 A6
Hatching Green Cotts AL5 107 A7
Hatch La SG4 24 A3
HATFIELD 130 B8
Hatfield Ave AL10 129 E8
Hatfield Bsns Pk AL10 129 D8
Hatfield Cres HP2 124 F7
HATFIELD GARDEN VILLAGE 129 E8
HATFIELD HEATH 98 F4
Hatfield House & Gdns★ AL9 130 D5
HATFIELD HYDE 110 F3
Hatfield Rd
Essendon AL9 111 E1
Potters Bar EN6 159 C8
St Albans AL1, AL4 128 C3
Watford WD24 167 B8
Hatfield Sta AL9 130 C6
Hatfield Tunnel AL10 129 F6
Hathaway Cl LU4 44 B2
Hathaway Ct AL4 128 E3
Hatherleigh Gdns EN6 159 D7
Hatherley Chase LU2 45 E2
Hatters La WD18 166 D3
Hatters Way LU1, LU4 44 D1
Hatters Way Ret Pk LU4 44 E1
Hatton Pl LU2 63 E8
Hatton Rd EN8 148 D2
HAULTWICK 53 F3
Havelock Rd
Kings Langley WD4 138 F3
Luton LU2 45 E1
Havelock Rise LU2 45 E1
Haven Cl AL10 129 F6
Havensfield WD4 152 B8
Haven The SG5 11 F6
Havercroft Cl AL3 127 C1
Haverdale LU4 44 C4
Havers La CM23 76 F5
Haward Rd EN11 135 C8
Hawbush Cl AL6 89 B4
Hawbush Rise AL6 89 B5
Hawes Cl HA6 174 F3
Hawes La E4 163 C1
Haweswater Dr WD25 154 C6
Hawfield Gdns AL2 141 D5
Hawkes Dr AL3 106 B5
Hawkesley Ct WD7 155 F4
Hawkesworth Cl HA6 174 E3
Hawkfield SG6 22 E8
Hawkfields LU2 45 E6
Hawkings Way HP3 137 A5
Hawkins Cl WD6 170 C7
Hawkins Hall La SG3 69 E2
Hawkshead Ct EN8 162 F5
Hawkshead La AL9 144 D3
Hawkshead Rd EN6 145 B2
Hawkshill AL1 128 A2
Hawkshill Dr HP3 137 F8
Hawksmead Cl EN3 162 D3
Hawksmoor WD7 157 A6
Hawkwell Dr HP23 100 C4
HAWRIDGE 120 E1
Hawridge & Cholesbury CE Sch HP5 120 E2
Hawridge La HP5 120 F1
Hawridge Vale HP5 120 F1
Hawsley Rd AL5 107 A4
Hawthorn Ave LU2 46 B4
Hawthorn Cl
Abbots Langley WD5 154 A7
Harpenden AL5 107 D7
Hertford SG14 113 A7
Hitchin SG5 34 E6
Royston SG8 7 F7
Watford WD17 153 F1
Hawthorn Cres LU1 62 E3
Hawthorn Ct 9 HA5 175 C1
Hawthorne Ave EN7 162 B8
Hawthorne Cl EN7 162 B8
Hawthorne Ct HA6 175 A1
Hawthorne Rd WD7 156 A5
Hawthornes AL10 129 F3
Hawthorn Gr
Barnet EN5 170 F3
Enfield EN2 161 D1
Hawthorn Hill SG6 22 F7
Hawthorn La HP1 123 F4
Hawthorn Rd EN11 135 B8
Hawthorn Rise CM23 76 F3
Hawthorns AL8 110 D8
Hawthorns The
Berkhamsted HP4 122 A5
Hemel Hempstead HP3 137 F7
Maple Cross WD3 172 D5
Ridge EN6 157 E6
Stevenage SG1 51 A4
Ware SG12 93 C3
Hawthorn Way
Chiswell Green AL2 141 A7
Royston SG8 7 F7
Hawtrees WD7 155 F4
Haybluff Dr SG1 37 A4
Haybourn Mead HP1 124 B2
Hay Cl WD6 170 C7
Haycroft
Bishop's Stortford CM23 77 C7
Luton LU2 45 E6
Haycroft Rd SG1 50 E7
Hayden Rd EN9 163 C4
Haydock Rd SG8 7 F6
Haydock Round SG1 37 A4
Haydon Dell WD23 167 F3
Haydon Hill Ho WD23 167 F2
Haydon Rd WD19 167 E3
Hayes Cl LU2 46 C5
Hayes Hill Farm★ EN9 149 C3
Hayes Wlk
1 Cheshunt EN10 148 F6
Potters Bar EN6 159 B6
Hayfield SG2 51 D7
Hayfield Cl WD23 168 B5
Haygarth SG3 69 A4
Hay Gn SG8 15 F6
HAY GREEN 15 F6
Hayhurst Rd LU4 44 B1
Hay La AL5 86 A1
Hayley Bell Gdns CM23 76 F3
Hayley Comm SG2 51 C3
Hayling Dr LU2 46 D3
Hayling Rd WD19 175 B8
Haymeads AL8 89 E1
Haymeads La CM23 77 C6
Haymoor SG6 22 E7
Haynes Cl AL7 111 A5
Haynes Mead HP4 122 A6
Haysman Cl SG6 23 B7
HAY STREET 41 E1
Hayton Cl LU3 31 B2
Hay Wains SG3 69 B2
Haywards The EN10 134 F2
Haywood Cl HA5 175 D1
Haywood Copse WD3 165 D5
Haywood Ct EN9 163 F5
Haywood Dr WD3 164 F4
Haywood Grove Sch HP2 125 A8
Haywood La SG8 16 A6
Haywood Pk WD3 164 F4
Haywoods Dr HP3 137 F8
Haywoods La SG8 7 E7
Hazelbank WD3 166 C3
Hazelbury Ave WD5 153 C7
Hazelbury Cres LU1 63 C8
Hazelbury Ct 3 LU1 63 C8
Hazel Cl
3 Hammond Street EN7 147 E5
Welwyn AL6 89 E3
Hazelcroft HA5 176 B4
Hazel Ct
Hitchin SG4 35 A7
Shenley WD7 156 F6
Hazeldell SG14 70 D3
Hazeldell Link HP1 123 E2
Hazeldell Rd HP1 123 F2
Hazeldene EN8 162 E7
HAZEL END 59 A6
Hazel End CM23 59 A5
Hazelend Rd CM23 59 B4
Hazel Gdns CM21 97 F1
Hazel Gr
Hatfield AL10 129 F2
Stotfold SG5 11 E5
Watford WD25 154 B4
Welwyn Garden City AL7 111 C7
Hazel Grove Ho AL10 129 F3
Hazel Mead EN5 171 B4
Hazelmere Rd
St Albans AL4 128 C6
Stevenage SG2 69 A8
Hazel Rd
Berkhamsted HP4 122 D3
Chiswell Green AL2 141 B3
Hazels The AL6 90 E2
Hazel Tree Rd WD24 154 B3
Hazelwood Cl
Hitchin SG5 34 F8
Luton LU2 46 B4
Hazelwood Dr
Pinner HA5 175 B1
St Albans AL4 128 C4
Hazelwood La WD5 153 D7
Hazelwood Rd WD3 166 C3
Hazely HP23 100 C4
Heacham Cl LU4 44 B4
Headingley Cl
Hammond Street EN7 147 F5
Shenley WD7 156 E7
Stevenage SG1 50 E8
Headlands Dr HP4 122 E5
Headstone La HA3 176 B2
Headstone Lane Sta HA3 176 B2
Healey Rd WD18 166 F3
Healy Ct EN5 171 D3
Hearle Way AL10 129 E7
Heath Ave
Royston SG8 7 C6
St Albans AL3 127 D5
Heathbourne Rd WD23 168 F1
Heath Brow HP1 124 C1
Heathbrow Rd AL6 89 F8
Heath Cl
Harpenden AL5 107 C7
Hemel Hempstead HP1 124 C2
Luton LU1 63 B6
Potters Bar EN6 145 B1
Heathcliff Ave SG5 11 B2
Heathcote Ave AL10 130 A7
Heathcote Sch The SG2 51 A2
Heath Cotts EN6 145 B1
Heathcroft AL7 111 C6
Heathdene Manor WD17 166 F8
Heath Dr
Potters Bar EN6 145 A1
Ware SG12 93 D3
HEATH END 121 A2
Heath End Ct WD23 176 E8
Heather Cl
Abbots Langley WD5 154 A7
Bishop's Stortford CM23 76 D6
Heather Ct AL2 142 D4
Heather Gdns EN9 163 C3
Heathermere SG6 11 F1
Heather Rd AL8 110 C4
Heather Rise WD23 167 F7
Heathers The SG13 113 E6
Heather Way
Harrow HA7 176 F4
Hemel Hempstead HP2 124 D4
Potters Bar EN6 158 F7
Heath Farm Ct WD17 153 D2
Heath Farm La AL1, AL3 127 E5
Heathfield SG8 7 B6
Heathfield Cl
Caddington LU1 62 F4
Potters Bar EN6 145 B1
Watford WD19 167 C2
Heathfield Ct 4 AL1 127 E4
Heathfield Lower Sch LU1 62 E4
Heathfield Rd
Hitchin SG5 21 F1
Luton LU3 45 C4
Watford WD23 167 F5
Heathgate SG13 114 B2
Heath Hall SG7 23 F7
Heath Hill SG4 67 D1
Heath La
Codicote SG4 67 E1
Hemel Hempstead HP1 124 C2
Hertford Heath SG13 114 C2
Heathlands AL6 68 F1
Heathlands Dr AL3 127 E5
Heathlands Sch AL3 127 E6
Heath Lo WD23 168 D1
Heath Mount Sch SG14 71 B2
Heath Park Ho HP1 124 C1
Heath Rd
Breachwood Green SG4 47 D1
Oaklands AL6 68 F1
Potters Bar EN6 145 B1
St Albans AL1 127 E5
Watford WD19 167 E2
Heath Row CM23 59 B1
Heathside
Colney Heath AL4 143 B8
St Albans AL1 127 E5
Heathside Cl HA6 174 D5
Heathside Rd HA6 174 D6
HEATH THE 47 D2
Heath The
Breachwood Green SG4 47 D2
Radlett WD7 156 A6
Heathview AL5 107 B8
Heath Way WD7 156 C8
Heaton Ct EN8 148 D2
Heaton Dell LU2 46 E1
Heay Fields AL7 111 C7
Hebden Cl LU4 44 B4
HEBING END 53 A2
Hebing End SG2 52 F2
Heckford Cl WD18 166 C3
Hedgebrooms AL7 111 C7
Hedge Row HP1 124 A5
Hedgerow Cl SG2 51 D8
Hedgerow La EN5 171 B4
Hedgerows CM21 97 F2
Hedgerows The
Bishop's Stortford CM23 77 B6
Stevenage SG2 51 D8
Hedgerow The LU4 44 D6
Hedgerow Wlk EN8 148 D1
Hedges Cl AL10 130 B6
Hedgeside HP4 123 A7
Hedgeside Rd HA6 174 C5
Hedges The AL3 127 C7
Hedley Cl HP22 99 A4
Hedley Rd AL1 128 B3
Hedley Rise LU2 46 F2
Hedley Villas AL1 128 B3
Hedworth Ave EN8 162 D6
Heights The
Hemel Hempstead HP2 124 F6
Luton LU3 44 E5
Helena Cl EN4 159 D1
Helena Pl 5 HP2 124 D5
Helens Gate EN8 148 F5
Helham Gn SG12 94 F4
Hellards Rd SG1 50 D7
Hellebore Ct SG1 51 B8
Hellen Way WD19 175 D6
Helmsley Cl LU4 44 C5
Helston Cl HA5 175 F3
Helston Gr HP2 124 D8
Helston Pl WD5 153 F7
HEMEL HEMPSTEAD 124 D6
Hemel Hempstead General Hospl HP2 124 D3
Hemel Hempstead Ind Est HP2 125 B5
Hemel Hempstead Montessori Sch HP1 124 B1
Hemel Hempstead Rd
Great Gaddesden HP4 81 F1
Hemel Hempstead HP2, HP3 125 E1
Redbourn AL3, HP2 105 E2
St Albans HP3, AL2, AL3 126 D1
Hemel Hempstead Sch The HP1 124 C2

Hemel Hempstead Sta HP3 138 A8
Hemingford Dr LU2 45 D6
Hemingford Rd WD17 153 E3
Hemmings The HP4 121 F3
Hemming Way WD25 154 A4
Hemp La HP23 100 F1
Hempstall AL7 111 B4
Hempstead La HP4 123 C6
Hempstead Rd
Bovingdon HP3 137 B5
Kings Langley WD4 139 A3
Watford WD17 153 E2
Hemsley Rd WD4 139 B2
Henbury Way WD19 175 D7
Henderson Cl AL3 127 C7
Henderson Pl
Bedmond WD5 139 F4
Little Berkhamsted SG13 132 C2
Hendon Wood La NW7 171 A1
Hendren Ct 2 SG1 51 A8
Henge Way LU3 44 E7
HENLOW 10 D8
Henlow Ind Est SG16 10 B4
Henry Cl EN2 161 E1
Henry St
Hemel Hempstead HP3 138 D7
Tring HP23 100 A3
Hensley Cl
Hitchin SG4 35 B6
Welwyn AL6 89 C6
Henstead Pl LU2 46 D1
Hepburn Ct EN6 158 A7
Hepworth Ct SG2 51 C6
Heracles Cl AL2 141 C3
Herald Cl CM23 76 D6
Herbert St HP2 124 D4
Hercules Way WD25 153 F6
Hereford Rd LU4 44 A3
Hereward Cl EN9 163 C7
Herga Ct WD17 167 A7
Heritage Cl 7 AL3 127 D3
Heritage Gn HP23 120 F5
Heritage Wlk WD3 164 E6
Herkomer Cl WD23 168 B3
Herkomer Rd WD23 168 A3
Herm Ho EN3 162 D1
Hermitage Ct
Potters Bar EN6 159 C6
Stansted Mountfitchet CM24 59 D7
Hermitage Ho CM24 59 D7
Hermitage Rd SG5 34 F7
Hermitage The SG15 11 B8
Herne Ct WD23 168 C2
Herne Rd
Bushey WD23 168 B3
Stevenage SG1 36 B1
Herneshaw AL10 129 F3
Herns La AL7 111 B8
Herns Way AL7 111 A7
Heron Cl
Hemel Hempstead HP3 138 F6
Rickmansworth WD3 173 D8
Sawbridgeworth CM21 97 D1
Heron Ct CM23 77 A7
Heron Dr
Luton LU2 45 E6
Stanstead Abbotts SG12 115 C3
Heronfield EN6 145 C1
Herongate Rd EN8 148 E4
Heron Mead EN3 163 A1
Heron Pl UB9 173 A4
Herons Elm HP4 121 E7
HERONSGATE 164 D2
Heronsgate Rd WD3 164 B3
Heronslea WD25 154 C3
Herons Way AL1 142 B8
Heronswood EN9 163 E5
Herons Wood CM20 117 B2
Heronswood Pl AL7 111 A5
Heronswood Rd AL7 111 A5
Heron Trad Est LU3 44 C7
Heron Way
Hatfield AL10 130 A3
Roydon CM19 116 A1
Royston SG8 7 E8
Stotfold SG5 11 E6
Heron Wlk HA6 174 E6
HERTFORD 113 C5
Hertford Castle* SG14 113 D6
Hertford County Hospl SG14 113 B6
Hertford East Sta SG13 113 E6
HERTFORD HEATH 114 B3
Hertford Heath Prim Sch SG13 114 C4
Hertford Mews EN6 159 C8
Hertford Mus* SG14 113 D6
Hertford North Sta SG14 113 B6
Hertford Rd
Enfield EN3 162 D3
Great Amwell SG12 114 F4
Hatfield AL9 111 B1
Hoddesdon EN11 134 E8
Stevenage SG2 69 B7
Tewin AL6 90 F2
Hertford Rd *continued*
Welwyn AL6 89 D3
Hertford Regional Coll
Cheshunt EN10 148 F6
Ware SG12 114 D8
Hertford St Andrew CE Prim Sch SG14 112 F7
Hertfordshire Bsns Ctr AL2 142 D5
Hertfordshire & Essex High Sch The CM23 77 B7
Hertfordshire Theatre Sch SG4 34 F6
HERTINGFORDBURY 112 E5
Hertingfordbury Cowper Prim Sch SG14 112 C4
Hertingfordbury Rd
Hertford SG14 113 B5
Hertingfordbury SG14 112 F4
Herts & Essex Hospl CM23 77 B6
Hertsmere Ind Pk WD6 170 D6
Hertsmere Jewish Prim Sch WD7 156 C1
Hertswood Ct 2 EN5 171 E5
Hertswood Sch WD6 170 C8
Hertswood Upper Sch WD6 170 C7
Hester Ho CM20 117 C2
Heswall Ct 5 LU1 63 F6
Heswell Gn WD19 175 A7
Hetchleys HP1 124 A6
Hever Cl LU7 80 D2
Hewins Cl EN9 163 E7
Hewitt Cl AL4 108 D7
Hewlett Rd LU3 44 E5
HEXTON 19 B2
Hexton Jun Mix Inf Sch SG5 19 A1
Hexton Rd
Great Offley SG5 33 E8
Lilley LU2 32 C4
Heybridge Ct SG14 112 F7
Heybridge Cl AL3 106 A5
Heydon Rd SG8 9 E3
Heydons Cl AL3 127 D5
Heyford End AL2 141 C3
Heyford Rd WD7 155 F2
Heyford Way AL10 130 C7
Heysham Dr WD19 175 D5
Heywood Dr LU2 45 F2
Hibbert Ave WD24 154 D1
Hibbert Rd HA3 176 F1
Hibberts Ct SG6 22 E7
Hibbert St LU1 63 E6
Hibbert Street Almshouses 13 LU1 63 E6
Hickling Cl LU2 46 D1
Hickling Way AL5 86 C3
Hickman Cl EN10 134 D3
Hickman Ct LU3 44 D8
Hickman's Hill SG7 24 D4
Hicks Rd AL3 83 F6
Hidalgo Ct HP2 124 F6
Hideaway The WD5 153 F8
Hides The CM20 117 D1
Higgins Rd EN7 147 D4
Higgins Wlk SG1 36 C1
High Acres WD5 153 D7
Higham Dr LU2 46 D1
HIGHAM GOBION 19 A6
High Ash Rd AL4 108 C7
High Ave SG6 22 E4
Highbanks Rd HA5 176 B4
HIGH BARNET 171 E6
High Barnet Sta EN5 171 F5
Highbarns HP3 139 A6
High Beeches Prim Sch AL5 86 D1
High Beech Rd LU3 44 D7
Highbourne Ct 2 EN11 135 A6
Highbridge Cl WD7 156 A6
Highbridge Ct 5 EN9 163 B6
Highbridge Ho 6 EN9 163 B6
Highbridge Ret Pk EN9 163 B5
Highbridge St EN9 163 B6
Highbury Ave EN11 135 A8
Highbury Ho (North Herts Music Sch) SG4 35 A7
Highbury Inf Sch SG4 34 F6
Highbury Rd
Hitchin SG4 35 A7
Luton LU3 45 C1
Highbush Rd SG5 11 E5
High Canons WD6 157 D2
High Cl WD3 165 C4
Highclere Ct 6 AL1 127 E4
Highclere Dr HP3 139 B7
Highcroft 2 SG2 50 F1
Highcroft Rd HP3 138 B6
HIGH CROSS 72 F2
High Cross WD25 155 D2
High Dane SG4 22 A2
High Dells AL10 129 F4
High Elms
Harpenden AL5 107 A6
Watford WD25 154 B8
High Elms Cl HA6 174 D4
High Elms La
Abbots Langley WD25, WD5 154 C8
Benington SG2 52 F1
HIGHFIELD 124 F6
Highfield
Bushey WD23 176 E8
Kings Langley WD4 138 E3
Letchworth Garden City SG6 22 E4
Little Hadham SG11 57 C3
Sawbridgeworth CM21 97 E3
South Oxhey WD19 175 F7
Watford WD25 153 F5
Highfield Ave
Bishop's Stortford CM23 77 C6
Harpenden AL5 107 C8
Highfield Cl HA6 174 E2
Highfield Cres HA6 174 E2
Highfield Ct
Hertford SG13 113 D4
Stevenage SG1 50 F7
Highfield Dr EN10 134 E2
Highfield Farm SG13 134 A6
Highfield Hall AL4 142 E7
Highfield Ho HP2 124 F5
Highfield La
Colney Heath AL4 142 E8
Hemel Hempstead HP2 124 F5
Highfield Manor AL4 142 E7
Highfield Oval AL5 86 A4
Highfield Park Dr AL4 142 C8
Highfield Rd
Berkhamsted HP4 122 D4
Hammond Street EN7 147 E5
Hertford SG13 113 D4
Luton LU4 45 B1
Northwood HA6 174 E2
Sandridge AL4 108 B1
Tring HP23 99 E3
Watford WD23 167 E4
Wigginton HP23 100 D1
Highfields
Cuffley EN6 146 E3
Radlett WD7 155 F4
Highfield Sch The SG6 22 D4
Highfields Cl LU5 44 A2
Highfield Way
Potters Bar EN6 159 B7
Rickmansworth WD3 165 B3
High Firs WD7 156 A4
High Firs Cres AL5 107 D8
Highgate Gr CM21 97 D2
High Gr
St Albans AL3 127 D5
Welwyn Garden City AL8 110 C7
Highgrove Ct EN8 162 D5
High House Est CM17 118 F4
High La CM24 59 F8
Highland Dr
Bushey WD23 168 C2
Hemel Hempstead HP3 125 B3
Highland Rd
Bishop's Stortford CM23 76 F3
Lower Nazeing EN9 135 E1
Northwood HA6 175 A1
Highlands
Hatfield AL9 130 C8
Royston SG8 7 E6
Watford WD19 167 C1
Highlands The
Potters Bar EN6 145 C1
Rickmansworth WD3 165 B2
High Leigh Barns EN11 134 E6
Highmead CM24 59 E8
High Mead LU3 45 A3
High Meads AL4 108 C8
Highmill SG12 93 D3
Highmoor AL5 86 A4
High Oak Rd SG12 93 E3
High Oaks
Enfield EN2 160 F1
7 Northwood HA6 174 F5
St Albans AL3 127 D7
High Oaks Rd AL8 110 B7
Highover Cl LU2 46 B1
Highover Jun Mix Inf Sch SG4 22 C1
Highover Rd SG6 22 D5
Highover Way SG4 22 B1
High Plash SG1 50 E5
High Point 15 LU1 63 D6
High Rd
Bushey WD23 168 D1
Essendon AL9 131 E5
Harrow HA3 176 E3
Hoddesdon EN10 134 F3
Shillington SG5 19 E8
Stapleford SG14 92 A2
Watford WD25 154 A7
High Ridge
Cuffley EN6 146 E4
Harpenden AL5 85 E3
Luton LU2 46 C1
High Ridge Cl HP3 138 D6
Highridge Pl EN2 160 F1
High Ridge Rd HP3 138 D7
High Road Broxbourne EN10 134 F1
High Road Turnford EN10 148 E6
High Road Wormley EN10 148 F8
High St
Abbots Langley WD5 139 F1
Arlesey SG15 11 A5
Ashwell SG7 4 D4
Baldock SG7 23 F8
High St *continued*
Barkway SG8 17 C3
Barley SG8 8 F2
Barnet EN5 171 F5
Bedmond WD5 139 F4
Berkhamsted HP4 122 B4
Berkhamsted, Northchurch HP4 121 E6
Bishop's Stortford CM23 76 F7
Bovingdon HP3 137 A4
Buntingford SG9 40 E8
Bushey WD23 168 A3
Cheddington LU7 80 A7
Cheshunt EN8 148 D2
Cheshunt, Waltham Cross EN8 162 D7
Cheshunt, Waltham Cross EN8 162 E5
Codicote SG4 67 F1
Colney Heath AL4 129 B1
Elstree WD6 169 D3
Eyeworth SG19 1 A8
Flamstead AL3 84 B2
Graveley SG4 36 C4
Great Offley SG5 33 C3
Guilden Morden SG8 1 F4
Harefield UB9 173 C1
Harlow CM17 118 C4
Harpenden AL5 86 A1
Harrow HA3 176 E1
Hemel Hempstead HP1, HP3 124 D4
Hinxworth SG7 3 D6
Hitchin, Gosmore SG4 34 F3
Hitchin SG5 34 E7
Hoddesdon EN11 135 A5
Hunsdon SG12 95 D1
Ivinghoe LU7 80 E5
Kimpton SG4 66 C1
Kings Langley WD4 139 A2
London Colney AL2 142 D5
Luton LU4 44 C4
Markyate AL3 83 E5
Much Hadham SG10 74 F3
Northwood HA6 174 F2
Pirton SG5 20 D4
Potters Bar EN6 159 C7
Redbourn AL3 106 B5
Reed SG8 16 E5
Rickmansworth WD3 165 E1
Roydon CM19 116 B1
Royston SG8 7 D6
Sandridge AL4 108 C2
St Albans AL3 127 D3
Standon, Puckeridge SG11 55 D3
Standon SG11 55 F1
Stanstead Abbotts SG12 115 C4
Stevenage SG1 50 C7
Stotfold SG5 11 F6
Tring HP23 100 A3
Walkern SG2 38 B1
Ware SG12 93 D1
Watford WD17 167 B6
Watford WD17 167 C5
Watton at S SG14 70 E3
Welwyn AL6 89 C5
Wheathampstead AL4 87 D1
Whitwell SG4 66 F7
Widford SG12 95 E5
High Street Gn HP2 125 A5
HIGH TOWN 63 E8
High Town Ent Ctr 1 LU2 63 F8
High Town Rd LU2 45 F1
High View
Birchanger CM23 59 D3
Chorleywood WD3 165 A5
Hatfield AL10 130 A2
Hitchin SG5 34 D7
Markyate AL3 83 E5
Watford WD18 166 F3
Highview Cl EN6 159 C6
High View Ct HA3 176 E3
Highview Gdns
Potters Bar EN6 159 C6
St Albans AL4 128 C8
Highway The HA7 176 F2
High Wickfield AL7 111 C5
Highwood Ave WD23 167 F8
High Wood Cl LU1 62 F7
Highwoodhall La HP3 139 A6
Highwood Prim Sch WD23 167 E8
High Wood Rd EN11 114 F1
HIGH WYCH 97 B1
High Wych CE Prim Sch CM21 97 A1
High Wych La CM21 97 A2
High Wych Rd
Gilston CM21 117 F7
High Wych CM21 97 B1
High Wych Way HP2 105 A1
Hilbury AL10 129 F4
Hilfield La WD25 168 D6
Hillary Cl LU3 44 D7
Hillary Cres LU1 63 C6
Hillary Ho WD6 170 B6
Hillary Rd HP2 125 A4
Hillary Rise SG15 11 B5
Hillberry Ct WD23 168 B2
Hillborough Inf Sch LU1 63 C6
Hillborough Jun Sch LU1 63 C6
Hillborough Rd LU1 63 D6
Hillbrow SG6 22 D5
Hill Cl
Barnet EN5 171 C4
Harpenden AL5 86 C4
Luton LU3 45 C7
Hill Comm HP3 139 A8
Hill Cres SG1 50 F5
Hillcrest
Baldock SG7 23 F7
Hatfield AL10 130 A5
St Albans AL3 127 B1
Hill Crest
Potters Bar EN6 159 C5
Whitwell SG4 66 E6
Hillcrest Ave LU2 45 C8
Hillcrest Cl EN7 147 C2
Hillcrest Cvn Pk LU1 62 F2
Hill Crest Lo WD6 169 F5
Hillcrest Rd WD7 157 A6
Hillcroft WD7 156 A6
Hill Croft Cl LU4 44 C6
Hillcroft Cres WD19 175 B8
Hill Ct EN6 159 C5
Hilldown Rd HP1 124 A5
Hill Dyke Rd AL4 108 E7
Hille Bsns Ctr WD24 167 B8
HILL END 173 B4
Hill End La AL4 128 C2
Hill End Rd UB9 173 C3
Hill Farm Ave WD25 154 A6
Hill Farm Cl WD25 154 A6
Hill Farm Ind Est WD25 154 A6
Hill Farm La
Ayot St L AL6 88 C5
Redbourn AL3 106 C1
Hillfield AL10 130 C8
Hillfield Ave SG4 22 A2
Hillfield Ct HP2 124 E3
Hillfield La S WD23 168 F3
Hillfield Rd HP2 124 D3
Hillgate SG4 22 A3
Hillgrove Bsns Pk EN10 135 C1
Hill Head Cotts SG10 75 B1
Hill Ho
Harefield UB9 173 C1
Hertford SG13 113 C5
Hillhouse EN9 163 F6
Hill House Ave HA7 176 F3
Hillhouse CE Prim Sch EN9 163 F6
Hilliard Rd HA6 174 F2
Hillingdon Rd WD25 154 B5
Hill La SG4 35 A2
Hill Ley AL10 129 F5
Hill Leys EN6 146 E3
Hillmead SG1 51 A6
Hill Mead HP4 122 A3
Hillmead Prim Sch CM23 76 C7
Hillpath SG6 23 B6
Hillpoint WD3 165 C4
Hill Rd
Codicote SG4 67 E1
Northwood HA6 174 D4
Hill Rise
Cuffley EN6 146 E3
Luton LU3 44 D7
Potters Bar EN6 159 C5
Rickmansworth WD3 165 B2
Hillrise Ave WD24 154 D2
Hillsborough Gn WD19 175 A7
Hillshott SG6 23 A6
Hillshott Inf Sch SG6 23 A6
Hillside
Codicote SG4 67 F1
Hatfield AL10 130 A5
Hoddesdon EN11 134 F7
Royston SG8 7 D5
St Albans AL4 128 C2
Stevenage SG1 50 F5
Ware SG12 114 D8
Welwyn Garden City AL7 111 B3
Hill Side LU7 79 F7
Hillside Ave
Bishop's Stortford CM23 77 A7
Borehamwood WD6 170 B5
Cheshunt EN8 162 D8
Hillside Cl WD5 153 E7
Hillside Cotts
Birchanger CM23 59 C3
Wareside SG12 94 F4
Hillside Cres
Cheshunt EN8 162 D8
Enfield EN2 161 D1
Northwood HA6 175 A2
Stanstead Abbotts SG12 115 B4
Watford WD19 167 D3
Hillside Ct
Cheshunt EN8 162 D8
10 St Albans AL1 127 E4
Hillside End CM23 59 C3
Hillside Gate 8 AL1 127 E4
Hillside Gdns
Barnet EN5 171 E5
Berkhamsted HP4 122 D3
Pinner HA6 175 B2
Hillside Ho SG1 50 F5
Hillside Jun & Inf Schs HA6 175 A3
Hillside La SG12 115 A5
Hillside Mans EN5 171 F5
Hillside Rd
Chorleywood WD3 164 C4

Hillside Rd continued
Harpenden AL5 85 F3
Luton LU3 45 D1
Pinner HA5 175 B3
Radlett WD7 156 B4
St Albans AL1 127 E4
Watford WD23 167 E4
Hillside Rise HA6 175 A3
Hillside Terr SG13 113 C4
Hillside Way AL6 90 A8
Hills La HA6 174 E2
Hill St AL3 127 C3
Hill The
Harlow CM17 118 C4
Wheathampstead AL4 108 D8
Hilltop AL3 105 F6
Hill Top SG7 23 E7
Hilltop Cl EN7 147 F5
Hilltop Cotts
Great Munden SG11 54 D4
Great Offley SG5 33 C3
Hilltop Ct LU1 63 C7
Hilltop Rd
Bedmond WD4 139 D4
Berkhamsted HP4 122 C3
Hilltop View AL4 108 C7
Hilltop Wlk AL5 107 D8
Hill Tree Cl CM21 97 D1
Hill View
Berkhamsted HP4 122 A6
Buckland SG9 27 D8
Whitwell SG4 66 E6
Hillview Cl HA5 175 F4
Hillview Cres LU2 45 C8
Hillview Gdns EN8 148 E4
Hillview Rd HA5 175 F4
Hilly Fields AL7 111 C7
Hilmay Dr HP1 124 C2
Hilton Cl SG1 50 B7
Himalayan Way WD18 166 F3
Hindhead Gn WD19 175 C5
Hine Ho AL4 128 D2
Hine Way SG5 21 C1
Hinwick Cl SG15 11 B7
HINXWORTH 3 C5
Hinxworth Rd
Ashwell SG7 4 B4
Hinxworth SG7 3 C3
Hipkins CM23 76 E4
Hipkins Pl EN10 134 E3
Hispano Mews EN3 163 A2
Hitchens Cl HP1 123 F4
HITCHIN 34 E8
Hitchin Boys' Sch SG5 34 E8
Hitchin British Schools Mus★ SG5 34 F6
Hitchin Bsns Ctr The SG4 22 A3
Hitchin Girls' Sch SG4 34 F7
HITCHIN HILL 34 E5
Hitchin Hill SG4 34 F5
Hitchin Hill Path SG4 34 F5
Hitchin Hospl SG5 34 D8
Hitchin Mus★ SG5 34 E7
Hitchin Rd
Arlesey SG15 11 A2
Great Wymondley SG4 35 D6
Hexton SG5 19 E1
Hitchin SG4 34 F3
Kimpton SG4 66 D2
Letchworth Garden City SG6 22 E3
Lower Stondon SG16 10 C6
Luton LU2 46 A4
Pirton SG5 20 E2
Preston SG4 48 E6
Stevenage SG1 36 B2
Stotfold SG5 11 E5
Weston SG4 24 B1
Hitchin Road Ind & Bsns Ctr SG15 11 A3
Hitchin St SG7 23 E8
Hitchin Sta SG4 35 A8
Hitchwood Cotts SG4 48 F5
Hitchwood La SG4 49 A4
Hitherbaulk AL7 110 E4
Hither Field SG12 93 E3
Hitherfield La AL5 86 A2
Hitherway AL8 89 D2
Hitherwell Dr HA3 176 D2
Hive Cl WD23 176 D8
Hive Rd WD23 176 E8
Hixberry La AL4 128 E1
Hobart Wlk AL3 127 F7
Hobbs Cl
Cheshunt EN8 148 D2
St Albans AL4 128 E2
Hobbs Cross Rd CM17 118 F3
Hobbs Ct SG1 51 A8
Hobbs Hayes SG8 16 E5
Hobbs Hill AL6 89 C4
Hobbs Hill Rd HP3 138 F8
Hobbs Hill Wood Prim Sch HP3 125 B1
Hobbs Way AL8 110 C5
Hobby Horse Cl EN7 147 D5
Hobletts Manor Inf Sch HP2 125 A4
Hobletts Manor Jun Sch HP2 125 A4
Hobletts Rd HP2 124 F4
Hobsons Cl EN11 114 F1
Hobsons Wlk HP23 99 F5
Hobtoe Rd CM20 117 A1
Hockeridge View HP4 121 F3
HOCKERILL 77 A6
Hockerill SG14 70 E3
Hockerill Anglo-European Coll CM23 77 B7
Hockerill Ct 7 CM23 77 A7
Hockerill St CM23 77 A7
Hocklands AL7 111 C7
Hockwell Ring LU4 44 C4
HODDESDON 135 C7
Hoddesdon Ind Ctr EN11 135 C7
Hoddesdon Rd SG12 115 C3
Hodges Way WD18 167 A3
Hodings Rd CM20 117 C2
Hodson Pl 1 EN3 163 A1
Hodwell SG7 4 D4
Hoecroft EN9 135 F1
Hoecroft Ct EN3 162 C1
Hoe La
Enfield EN1, EN3 162 B1
Lower Nazeing EN9 135 F1
Ware SG12 114 D7
Hoestock Rd CM21 97 D2
Hoe The WD19 175 D8
Hogarth Cl LU2 46 A2
Hogarth Ct WD23 168 B2
Hogg End La AL3 126 C6
Hogges Cl 16 EN11 135 A6
Hogg La WD6 169 A5
Hog Hall La HP4 81 A5
Hog La HP5 121 C1
HOGPITS BOTTOM 151 B7
Hogpits Bottom HP3 151 A7
Hogsdell La SG13 114 B4
Holbeck La EN7 147 F5
Holbein Gate HA6 174 E5
Holborn Cl AL4 128 D8
Holbrook Cl EN1 162 A1
Holbrook Gdns WD25 155 B3
Holcroft Rd AL5 86 D3
HOLDBROOK 163 A5
Holdbrook SG4 35 B7
Holdbrook Ct EN8 162 F5
Holdbrook Prim Sch EN8 162 F5
Holden Cl
Hertford SG13 113 E7
Hitchin SG4 35 C7
Holders La SG2 51 E5
Holdings The AL9 130 D7
Holecroft EN9 163 E5
Holford Way LU3 31 B1
Holgate Dr LU4 44 B3
Holkham Cl LU4 44 A4
Holkham Ho 11 EN5 171 E6
Holland Ct
13 Borehamwood WD6 170 A5
Luton LU3 45 C2
Holland Gdns WD25 154 C4
Holland Rd LU3 45 B2
Holland's Croft SG12 95 D1
Holland Way CM17 118 D1
Holliday St HP4 122 D4
Hollier Ct AL10 130 B6
Holliers Way AL10 130 A5
Hollies Cl SG8 7 E6
Hollies The
Bovingdon HP3 137 A2
St Albans AL3 127 E4
St Albans, Townsend AL3 127 C5
Watford WD18 166 F5
Welwyn Garden City AL8 110 B2
Wigginton HP23 100 D1
Hollies Way EN6 159 C8
Holloway La WD3 151 C2
Holloways La AL9 144 D7
Holloway The HP23, HP22 99 C4
Hollow La SG4 34 F7
Hollybush Ave AL2 141 A7
Hollybush Cl
Harrow HA3 176 E2
Oaklands AL6 89 E8
Potten End HP4 123 D7
Watford WD19 167 C2
Hollybush Hill LU2, SG5 32 F1
Hollybush Ho AL7 110 E4
Hollybush La
Bendish SG4 66 B8
Datchworth SG3 69 C3
Flamstead AL3 84 B3
Harpenden AL5 86 A3
Hemel Hempstead HP1 123 F4
Welwyn Garden City AL7 110 E3
Hollybush Prim Sch SG14 113 A6
Hollybush Rd LU2 46 C1
Hollybush Row HP23 120 D8
Hollybush Way EN7 148 A3
Holly Cl AL10 129 F4
Holly Copse SG1 50 F4
Holly Cotts SG4 48 D6
Holly Croft SG14 113 A7
Hollycross Rd SG12 115 B7
Holly Dell SG13 113 C4
Holly Dr
Berkhamsted HP4 122 D3
Potters Bar EN6 159 B6
Holly Farm Cl LU1 62 E3
Hollyfield
Hatfield AL10 130 A2
Tring HP23 100 C5
Hollyfield Cl HP23 100 C5
Hollyfields EN10 148 E5
Holly Gr HA5 175 E2
Hollygrove WD23 168 D2
Holly Grove Rd SG14 91 C3
Holly Hall Ct AL6 89 C5
Holly Hedges La HP3 151 C8
Hollyhock Cl HP1 123 E4
Holly Ind Est WD24 167 C8
Holly La AL5 86 E6
Holly Leys SG2 69 C8
Holly Rd
Enfield EN3 162 D3
Woolmer Green SG3 69 B1
Holly Shaws SG2 51 B1
Holly St LU1 63 E6
Holly Street Trad Est 19 LU1 63 E6
Hollytree Cl HP5 150 B8
Holly Tree Ct HP2 125 B3
Hollytree Ho WD24 153 E3
Holly Wlk
Harpenden AL5 86 D1
Welwyn Garden City AL8 89 C2
Hollywood Ct WD6 169 F5
Holmbrook Ave LU3 45 C5
Holmbury Cl WD23 176 E8
Holmbury St Mary Ct AL1 128 B2
Holmdale SG6 23 B5
Holmdale Cl WD6 169 F7
Holme Cl
Cheshunt EN8 162 E8
Hatfield AL10 129 F8
Holme Lea WD25 154 C5
Holme Pk WD6 169 F7
Holme Pl HP2 125 C4
Holme Rd AL10 129 F8
Holmes Ct AL3 127 E4
Holmesdale EN8 162 D4
Holme Way HA7 176 F4
Holmfield Cl LU1 63 D5
Holm Oak Pk WD18 167 A4
Holmscroft Rd LU3 44 F6
Holmshill La EN5, WD6 157 F2
Holmside Rise WD19 175 B7
Holmwood Rd EN3 162 D3
Holroyd Cres SG7 23 F7
Holt Cl WD6 169 F5
Holt Cotts The SG4 66 C4
Holt Ho EN8 148 B3
Holts Mdw AL3 106 B6
Holtsmere Cl
Luton LU2 46 D1
Watford WD25 154 C4
Holtsmere End Inf Sch HP2 125 B8
Holtsmere End Jun Sch HP2 125 B8
Holtsmere End La HP2 105 C1
Holt The
Hemel Hempstead HP2 124 E2
Welwyn Garden City AL7 111 D5
HOLWELL 21 B7
Holwell SG1 36 C2
Holwell Ct AL9 111 F1
Holwell Cvn Pk AL9 111 E1
Holwell Hyde AL7 111 C4
Holwell Hyde La AL7 111 C3
Holwell La AL9 131 F8
Holwell Prim Sch AL7 110 F5
Holwell Rd
Holwell SG5 21 C7
Pirton SG5 20 E6
Welwyn Garden City AL7 110 E5
Holy Acre CM19 116 A1
Holy Cross Hill EN10 148 A8
Holy Family RC Jun Mix & Inf Sch The AL7 90 A1
HOLYFIELD 149 C3
Holyfield Hall Farm★ EN9 149 C4
Holyfield Rd EN9 149 D2
Holyrood Cres AL1 141 D7
Holyrood Ct WD18 167 B5
Holy Rood RC Prim Sch WD17 153 D3
Holy Trinity CE Prim Sch
Cheshunt EN8 162 D7
Northwood HA6 174 C4
HOLYWELL 166 D3
Holywell Cl LU6 82 C6
Holywell Ct LU3 45 B4
Holywell Hill AL1 127 D2
Holywell Lo EN2 160 F1
Holywell Prim Sch WD18 166 F3
Holywell Rd
Studham LU6 82 B6
Watford WD18 167 A4
Home Cl
Cheshunt EN10 148 F7
Luton LU4 44 C4
Stotfold SG5 11 F7
Homedale Dr LU4 44 D2
Homedell Ho AL5 85 E3
Home Farm HP23 100 A2
Home Farm Cotts
Newgate Street SG13 146 F8
Slip End LU1 85 A8
Home Farm Ct
Bovingdon HP3 136 F1
Cockernhoe LU2 46 D5
Standon SG11 55 D3
Home Farm Ind Pk SG12 115 F5
Home Farm Rd
Berkhamsted HP4 121 D7
Brookmans Park AL9 144 B5
Rickmansworth WD3 174 A6
Home Farm Youngsbury SG12 94 A8
Homefield
Bovingdon HP3 137 B3
Hinxworth SG7 3 D6
Potten End HP4 123 B7
Home Field EN5 171 F4
Homefield La SG4 49 F2
Homefield Rd
Bushey WD23 168 A4
Chorleywood WD3 164 D5
Hemel Hempstead HP2 125 A2
Radlett WD7 155 F2
Ware SG12 93 E2
Homehayes Ho 1 HA5 175 F3
Homeleigh Ct EN8 148 B1
Homeleigh St EN8 148 B1
Home Ley AL7 110 E6
Home Mdw AL7 110 F6
Homepark Cotts WD4 139 B1
Home Park Ind Est WD4 139 B1
Home Park Mill Link Rd WD4 139 B1
Home Pastures CM22 98 F3
Homerfield AL8 110 C7
Homerswood La AL6 89 A2
Homerswood Prim Sch AL8 89 D2
Homerton Rd LU3 45 A6
Homestead Cl AL2 141 C4
Homestead Ct AL7 110 F4
Homestead La AL7 110 F4
Homestead Moat SG1 50 E4
Homestead Rd
Hatfield AL10 130 B8
Rickmansworth WD3 165 D2
Homesteads The SG12 116 D8
Homestead Way LU1 63 C5
Home Way WD3 164 F1
Homewood Ct WD3 164 F5
Homewood Ind Sch AL2 141 B3
Homewood La EN6 146 C4
Homewood Rd AL1 128 B5
Homewood Venue EN6 146 E4
Honeybourne CM23 76 E4
Honey Brook EN9 163 E6
Honeycroft AL8 110 C5
Honeycroft Dr AL4 142 C8
Honeycross Rd HP1 123 E2
Honeygate LU2 45 E4
Honey La
Brent Pelham CB11 30 F3
Buntingford SG9 40 E8
5 Hertford SG14 113 D6
Waltham Abbey EN9 163 E5
Honeymead AL6 89 F3
Honeymeade CM21 118 C7
Honeysuckle Cl
Bishop's Stortford CM23 76 C6
Hertford SG13 114 A6
Honeysuckle Gdns AL10 130 B4
Honeyway SG8 7 E6
Honeywood Cl EN6 159 D6
Honilands Prim Sch EN1 162 B3
Honiton Mews LU3 44 E6
Honor St 7 CM17 118 D1
Honours Mead HP3 137 A4
Hoo Cotts SG5 33 D1
HOO END 66 E4
Hoo Farm Cotts SG5 33 D1
Hook Gate EN1 162 B3
Hook La
Northaw EN6 159 F7
Northaw EN6 160 A8
HOOK'S CROSS 69 F6
Hook's Cross SG14 69 F6
Hoopers Mews WD23 168 B1
Hoops La SG8 15 F6
Hoo St LU1 63 E5
Hoo The CM17 118 C5
Hope Gn WD25 154 A6
Hope Green Lo WD25 154 A6
Hopewell Rd SG7 23 D8
Hop Garden Way WD25 154 C8
Hopground Cl AL1 128 A1
Hopkins Cres AL4 108 B1
Hopkins Yd AL1 127 E2
Hoppit Rd EN9 163 B7
Hopps Ho 4 EN11 135 A6
Hopton Rd SG1 50 A8
Hopwood Cl WD17 153 E3
Horace Brightman Cl LU3 45 A7
Horace Gay Gdns SG6 22 E6
Hordle Gdns AL1 127 F2
Horizon Ho EN3 162 F3
Hormead CE Prim Sch SG9 41 F8
Hornbeam Cl
Borehamwood WD6 170 A8
Hertford SG14 113 B7
Hornbeam Ct SG4 35 E5
Hornbeam La AL9 131 E2
Hornbeams
Bricket Wood AL2 140 F1
Hornbeams continued
Welwyn Garden City AL7 111 B5
Hornbeams Ave EN1 162 C4
Hornbeam Spring SG3 68 F4
Hornbeams The
Harlow CM20 117 C2
Stevenage SG2 51 B4
Hornbeam Way EN7 147 F2
Hornets The WD18 167 B5
HORN HILL 172 B6
Horn Hill SG4 66 E6
Hornhill Rd WD3 172 D5
Hornsby Cl LU2 46 C1
Horns Cl SG13 113 C4
Hornsfield AL7 111 C7
Horns Mill Rd SG13 113 C3
Horns Rd SG13 113 C5
Horrocks Cl SG12 93 D3
Horsa Gdns AL10 129 E7
Horseblock La HP5 120 E2
Horsecroft Rd HP1 124 A1
Horse Cross SG11 56 D3
Horse Hill HP5 150 D7
Horselers HP3 139 A8
Horsemans Dr AL2 141 B6
Horseshoe Bsns Pk AL2 141 B1
Horseshoe Cl
Barley SG8 8 F1
Cheddington LU7 80 A7
Horseshoe Ct
Hitchin SG4 34 E6
Stanstead Abbotts SG12 115 D4
Horseshoe Hill SG9 42 A8
Horseshoe La
Great Hormead SG9 42 A8
Totteridge N20 171 D1
Watford WD25 154 C7
Horseshoe The HP3 125 C1
Horsham Cl LU2 46 D2
Horsleys WD3 172 D5
Horton Gdns HP2 105 A1
Horwood Cl WD3 165 A2
Horwood Cotts WD25 168 E8
Horwood Ct WD24 154 E2
Hospital Rd SG15 11 A4
Houghton Mews 12 LU1 63 D6
Housden Cl AL4 108 E7
Housefield Way AL4 142 C8
House La
Arlesey SG15 11 A7
Sandridge AL4 108 C1
St Albans AL4 128 D7
House On The Hill Toy Mus★ CM24 59 F6
Housewood End HP1 124 B6
Housman Ave SG8 2 C1
Howard Agne Cl HP3 137 A4
Howard Bsns Pk EN9 163 D6
Howard Cl
Bushey WD23 168 E2
Luton LU3 45 A4
St Albans AL1 128 C1
Stotfold SG5 11 E5
Waltham Abbey EN9 163 D5
Watford WD24 154 A2
Howard Ct
Enfield EN1 161 E1
Letchworth Garden City SG6 23 B4
Howard Ctr The AL8 110 D6
Howard Dr
Borehamwood WD6 170 D5
Letchworth Garden City SG6 23 B3
Howarde Ct SG1 50 C6
Howard Gate SG6 23 B4
Howard Park Cnr SG6 23 A6
Howards Cl HA5 175 B1
Howards Dr HP1 124 A5
Howardsgate AL8 110 D6
Howards Wood SG6 23 B3
Howard Way
Barnet EN5 171 D4
Harlow CM20 117 F2
Howberry Gn SG15 11 A3
Howe Cl WD7 156 E7
Howe Dell AL10 130 B5
Howe Dell Prim Sch AL10 130 B5
HOWE GREEN 77 D2
Howe Green House Sch CM22 77 D2
Howell Hill Cl LU7 61 D5
Howe Rd HP3 125 A1
How Field AL5 85 E3
Howfield Gn EN11 115 A1
Howicks Gn AL7 111 A3
Howland Garth AL1 141 C7
Howlands AL7 111 B3
Howlands Ho AL7 111 A3
Howse Rd EN9 163 B4
Howton Pl WD23 168 D1
HOW WOOD 141 B3
How Wood AL2 141 B3
How Wood Prim Sch AL2 141 C4
How Wood Sta AL2 141 C3
Hoylake Ct LU1 63 F5
Hoylake Gdns WD19 175 D6
Hubbards Rd WD3 164 D4
Huckleberry Cl LU3 45 A8

HUDNALL 102 F7
HUDNALL CORNER 103 B7
Hudnall La HP4 102 E7
Hudscroft Ct 6 EN8 148 E3
Hudson Cl
St Albans AL1 141 D8
Watford WD24 153 F3
Hudson Rd SG2 51 B7
Hudsons Ct EN6 159 A8
Huggins La AL9 144 C8
Hughenden Rd AL4 128 C6
Hugh's Twr 4 CM20 117 D1
Hugh Villas CM23 77 A5
Hugo Cl WD18 166 E5
Hugo Gryn Way WD7 156 E8
Hull Cl EN7 147 D5
Hull La SG11 55 E7
Humber Ct SG1 36 F3
Humberstone Cl LU4 44 E2
Humberstone Rd LU4 44 E2
Humphrey Talbot Ave LU6 81 F7
HUNSDON 95 D1
Hunsdon AL7 111 D6
HUNSDONBURY 116 C7
Hunsdon Jun Mix Inf Sch SG12 95 D1
Hunsdon Rd
Stanstead Abbotts SG12 115 E5
Widford SG12 95 E3
Hunsdon Road Cotts SG12 115 E5
Hunston Cl LU4 44 B5
Hunt Cl AL4 128 D6
Hunter Cl
Borehamwood WD6 170 C4
Potters Bar EN6 159 B6
Huntercrombe Gdns WD19 175 C5
Hunters Cl
Bovingdon HP3 137 A2
Stevenage SG2 51 D7
Stotfold SG5 11 E6
Tring HP23 100 B5
Hunters Gate WD25 154 A6
Hunter's La WD25 153 F6
Hunters Oak HP2 125 B8
Hunters Pk HP4 122 E5
Hunters Reach EN7 147 F2
Hunters Ride AL2 155 A8
Hunters Way
Royston SG8 7 E6
Welwyn Garden City AL7 110 F3
Hunter Wlk WD6 170 D4
Huntingdon Cl EN10 148 E7
Huntingdon Ct EN5 171 F6
Huntingdon Rd SG1 50 B8
Hunting Gate
Hemel Hempstead HP2 124 E7
Hitchin SG4 22 A3
Hunting Hall LU2 64 C8
HUNTON BRIDGE 153 B6
Hunton Bridge Hill WD4 153 C6
Hunts Cl LU1 63 C6
Huntsman Cl SG11 55 D3
Huntsmans Cl HP4 81 C5
Huntsmill Rd HP1 123 E2
Hurlock Way LU4 44 C5
Hurn Gr CM23 59 C1
Huron Rd EN10 148 E5
Hurricane Way WD5 154 A7
Hurst Cl
Baldock SG7 13 A1
Bishop's Stortford CM23 76 E7
Welwyn Garden City AL7 111 C5
Hurst Dr EN8 162 D5
Hurst Drive Prim Sch EN8 162 D5
Hurstleigh WD3 164 C4
Hurstlings AL7 111 B5
Hurst Pl HA6 174 B2
Hurst Way LU3 44 F5
Hutchings Lo 3 WD3 165 E1
Hutton Cl
Hertford SG14 113 A6
Luton LU4 44 E3
Hutton Gdns HA3 176 C3
Hutton La HA3 176 D3
Hutton Wlk HA3 176 C3
Hyatt Ind Est SG1 50 A5
Hyburn Cl
Bricket Wood AL2 140 F1
Hemel Hempstead HP3 125 B2
Hydean Way SG2 51 B3
Hyde Ave
Potters Bar EN6 159 B6
Stotfold SG5 11 E5
Hyde Cl
Barnet EN5 171 F6
Harpenden AL5 86 B4
Hyde Ct
Cheshunt EN8 162 E5
London Colney AL2 142 B4
Hyde Gn E SG2 51 B3
Hyde Gn N SG2 51 B3
Hyde Gn S SG2 51 B3
Hyde Ho 5 LU2 63 F8
Hyde La
Bedmond HP3 139 D5
Bovingdon HP3 137 A3
Hyde La *continued*
Park Street AL2 141 D3
Peters Green LU2 65 C2
Hyde Mdws HP3 137 A4
Hyde Mead EN9 149 E8
Hyde Mead Ho EN9 149 E8
Hyde Rd
Caddington LU1 62 F4
Watford WD17 167 A7
Hyde Terr HP3 139 E7
Hyde The
Stevenage SG2 51 C3
Ware SG12 93 B2
Hyde Valley AL7 110 F4
Hyde View Rd AL5 86 B4
Hyde Way AL7 110 E6
Hyperion Ct HP2 124 F6
Hyver Hill NW7 170 D2

I

Ibberson Way SG4 35 A7
Iceni Ct SG6 23 B7
ICKLEFORD 21 E4
Ickleford Bury SG5 21 E3
Ickleford Gate SG5 21 D3
Ickleford Prim Sch SG5 21 E4
Ickleford Rd SG5 34 F8
Ickley Cl LU4 44 B5
Icknield Cl
Ickleford SG5 21 E4
St Albans AL3 126 F1
Icknield Gn
Letchworth Garden City SG6 22 E6
Tring HP23 100 A6
Icknield High Sch LU3 45 C5
Icknield Inf Sch SG6 22 D6
Icknield Prim Sch LU3 45 B5
Icknield Rd LU3 44 F4
Icknield Walk Fst Sch SG8 7 E7
Icknield Way
Baldock SG7 12 E1
Dagnall LU6 81 A8
Letchworth Garden City SG6 22 E6
Luton LU3 45 B7
Tring HP23 99 E4
Icknield Way E SG7 12 F1
Icknield Way Ind Est HP23 99 E4
Icknield Wlk SG8 7 F7
Idenbury Ct LU1 63 C7
Ilex Ct HP4 122 B4
Ilford Cl LU2 46 D3
Ilkley Rd WD19 175 D5
Imberfield LU4 44 C3
Immanuel Coll WD23 168 E2
Imperial Pk
Watford WD24 154 C1
Watford WD24 167 C8
Imperial Way
Hemel Hempstead HP3 138 E7
Watford WD24 167 C8
Impresa Pk EN11 135 C7
Indells AL10 129 F4
Ingelheim Ct SG1 50 D7
Ingersoll Rd EN3 162 C1
Inglefield EN6 145 A1
Ingles AL8 89 E2
Ingleside Dr SG1 36 B1
Inglewood Gdns AL2 141 E6
Ingram Gdns LU2 45 D7
Inkerman Rd AL1 127 E2
Inkerman St LU1 63 D7
Innes Ct HP3 138 D8
Innova Way EN3 162 F3
Inn's Cl SG1 50 D6
Inskip Cres SG1 50 E5
IO Ctr
Holdbrook EN9 163 A5
Stevenage SG1 50 D2
Iona Cl SG1 36 F2
Ionian Way 2 HP2 124 F6
Iredale View SG7 13 A1
Irene Stebbings Ho AL4 128 C4
Ireton Ct SG1 50 C6
Iron Dr SG13 114 B7
Irving Cl CM23 76 D4
Irving Cres LU7 80 A8
Isabel Ct EN11 135 B8
Isabel Gate EN8 148 F5
Isabella Ho EN8 163 A5
Isabelle Cl EN7 147 C2
Isenburg Way HP2 124 D8
Isherwood Cl SG8 7 C8
Island Centre Way EN3 163 A2
Island Ct CM23 77 A5
Islay Ho 4 WD18 166 F3
Italstyle Bldg The CM20 118 C6
Itaska Cotts WD23 168 E1
Ivatt Ct SG4 35 C7
Iveagh Cl HA6 174 B2
Iveagh Ct HP2 124 D4
Ivel Ct SG6 23 C4
Ivel Rd SG1 50 C7
Ivel Way
Baldock SG7 24 A6
Stotfold SG5 11 F8
Ives Rd SG14 113 B7
IVINGHOE 80 F5
Ivinghoe Cl
St Albans AL4 128 C8
Watford WD25 154 D4
Ivinghoe Rd
Bushey WD23 168 D2
Rickmansworth WD3 165 A2
Ivory Cl AL4 128 C1
Ivory Ct HP3 138 E8
Ivybridge EN10 135 A4
Ivy Ct LU1 63 B8
Ivy Ho WD19 167 D3
Ivy House La HP4 122 E4
Ivy Lea WD3 165 A1
Ivy Rd LU1 63 C8
Ivy Terr EN11 135 C8
Ivy Wlk AL10 129 F8

J

Jackdaw Cl SG2 51 D4
Jackdaws AL7 111 C6
Jackets La HA6 174 B3
Jacketts Field WD5 153 F8
Jackman's Pl SG6 23 B5
Jacks Hill Pk SG4 36 C7
Jacks La UB9 173 A2
Jacksons Ct SG9 40 E8
Jacksons Dr EN7 148 A3
Jackson's La SG8 16 E5
Jackson Sq 10 CM23 76 F7
Jackson St SG7 12 E1
Jackson Wharf 24 CM23 76 F7
Jacob Ct
Holdbrook EN3 163 A2
St Albans AL4 128 C1
Jacobs Ladder AL9 130 C5
Jakes View AL2 141 C4
James Bedford Cl HA5 175 C1
James Cl WD23 167 E4
James Ct
London Colney AL2 142 B4
Luton LU4 44 B2
14 Luton, New Town LU1 63 E6
Northwood HA6 174 F2
James Foster Ho SG5 21 E1
James Lee Sq EN3 163 A1
James Marshall Commercial Ctr AL5 86 A1
Jameson Ct AL1 127 F4
Jameson Rd AL5 86 B3
James Way
South Oxhey WD19 175 D6
Stevenage SG1 50 C7
Jane Cl HP2 125 B8
Jarden SG6 23 C4
Jardine Ct 1 SG1 51 A8
Jarman Cl HP3 124 E1
Jarman Way
Hemel Hempstead HP2 124 F2
Royston SG8 7 B7
Jarvis Cl EN5 171 D4
Jarvis Cleys EN7 147 F5
Jasmin Cl
Bishop's Stortford CM23 76 C6
Northwood HA6 174 F2
Jasmine Ct SG5 11 F7
Jasmine Dr SG13 114 A6
Jasmine Gdns AL10 130 A7
Jasmin Way HP1 123 E4
Jasons Hill HP5 136 B2
Jasper Cl EN3 162 C1
Jay Cl SG6 22 E8
Jays Cl AL2 155 A8
Jaywood LU2 46 C6
J Ct CM20 117 F1
Jeans La CM23 76 E7
Jeans Way LU5 44 A1
Jeeves Yd 7 SG4 34 F6
Jeffrey Cl SG8 7 C8
Jeffries Rd SG12 93 E1
Jellicoe Gdns HA7 176 F4
Jellicoe Rd WD18 167 A3
Jenkins Ave AL2 140 E1
Jenkins Ct HP22 60 C3
Jenkins La
Bishop's Stortford CM22 77 C5
St Leonards HP23 119 E3
Jenningsbury Ct SG13 114 A4
Jennings Cl SG1 50 E3
Jennings Rd AL1 128 A4
Jennings Way
Barnet EN5 171 C6
Hemel Hempstead HP3 124 E1
Jenning Wood AL6 89 F7
Jenyns Sch SG11 55 F7
Jephson Ct 10 LU1 63 E6
Jepps Cl EN7 147 E4
Jepps La SG8 7 D6
Jerome Dr AL3 127 A1
Jersey Cl EN11 135 A7
JERSEY FARM 128 E7
Jersey Ho
Enfield EN3 162 D1
9 Watford WD18 166 F3
Jersey La
St Albans AL4 128 C8
St Albans, Marshalswick AL4 128 B5
Jersey Rd LU4 44 A3
Jervis Ave EN3 162 E4
Jervis Rd CM23 76 F6
Jessop Ct EN9 163 F5
Jessop Rd SG1 37 A1
Jeve Cl SG7 13 A1
Jewell Ct WD25 154 D5
Jill Grey Pl SG4 34 F6
Jillifer Rd LU4 44 A2
Jim Desormeaux Bglws CM20 117 E2
Jinnings The AL7 111 B3
Joan Player Ho EN3 162 D2
Jocelyns CM17 118 C4
Jocketts Hill HP1 123 F3
Jocketts Rd HP1 123 F2
JOCKEY END 103 F8
Jodies Ct AL4 128 C5
Joel St HA6 175 A1
John Barker Pl SG5 21 C1
Johnby Cl EN3 162 E2
John Ct EN11 115 A1
John Dyde Cl 2 CM23 77 A6
John Eccles Ho AL7 110 F5
John Eliot Cl EN9 135 E2
John F Kennedy RC Sch HP1 123 F4
John Hall Ct SG5 33 C3
John Henry Newman RC Sch The SG1 36 B1
John Howland Cl SG16 10 D8
John Lamb Ct HA3 176 E2
John Rix Ho SG15 11 A4
John Sale Cl SG7 4 C4
Johns La HP5 121 E1
Johnson Ct HP3 124 E1
Johns Rd CM23 59 A1
John St
Luton LU1 63 E7
3 Royston SG8 7 D6
John Tate Rd SG13 113 F6
John Warner Sch The EN11 115 B1
Joiner's Cl HP5 136 B1
Joint The SG8 16 E6
Jones Cl SG1 50 C7
Jones Rd EN7 147 B1
Jonquil Cl AL7 111 B4
Jordan Cl WD25 153 F4
Jordans AL7 111 C7
Jordans Rd WD3 165 A1
Jordan's Way AL2 140 F1
Joscelyn's Yd 14 CM23 77 A7
Joseph Ct 2 AL1 128 B2
Joshua Wlk EN8 163 A5
Joslyn Cl EN3 163 A1
Jowitt Ho 1 SG1 50 E6
Joyce Ct EN9 163 D5
Jubilee Ave
London Colney AL2 142 D5
Ware SG12 93 F2
Jubilee Cl
Lower Stondon SG16 10 B3
Pinner HA5 175 C1
Jubilee Cott 13 CM23 77 A7
Jubilee Cotts
Aspenden SG9 40 D5
Great Hormead SG9 42 A8
Jubilee Cres SG15 11 A2
Jubilee Ct
Harpenden AL5 86 C3
Hatfield AL10 130 B8
Waltham Abbey EN9 163 F6
Jubilee Meml Ave SG1 50 D8
Jubilee Rd
Letchworth Garden City SG6 23 D7
Stevenage SG1 50 B8
Watford WD24 154 A1
Jubilee St LU2 45 F1
Jubilee Trad Ctr SG6 23 D7
Jubilee Wlk
Kings Langley WD4 139 A1
South Oxhey WD19 175 B6
Judge's Hill EN6 145 F2
Judge St WD24 154 B1
Julia Ct LU3 45 B4
Julia Gate SG2 51 C8
Julian's Cl SG1 50 C8
Julian's Rd SG1 50 B8
Julie Ho EN11 135 C8
Julius Gdns LU3 44 F7
Junction Cotts AL8 110 D7
Juniper Ave AL2 155 A8
Juniper Cl
Barnet EN5 171 D4
Cheshunt EN10 148 F6
Luton LU4 44 E2
Rickmansworth WD3 173 D7
Juniper Ct HA3 176 F2
Juniper Gate WD3 173 D8
Juniper Gdns
Oaklands AL6 89 E7
Shenley WD7 156 E6
Juniper Gn HP1 123 E3
Juniper Gr WD17 154 A1
Juniper Ho EN10 148 F6
Juno Rd HP2 124 F6
Jupiter Ct AL10 129 E6
Jupiter Dr HP2 124 F5
Jupiter Drive Jun Mix & Inf Sch HP2 124 F5
Jupiter Gate SG2 51 D8
Juxon Cl HA3 176 B2

K

Kaida Ho 6 WD3 165 D2
Kardwell Cl SG4 35 A6
Karen Ho SG16 10 A4
Karens Ct EN3 162 D2
Katemon Ct SG12 115 D4
Kates Cl EN5 171 A4
Katescroft AL7 110 E2
Katherine Cl HP3 138 E8
Katherine Pl WD5 154 A7
Kathleen Ct LU3 44 E4
Katrine Sq HP2 124 E7
Kay Cl HP23 100 A5
Kay Wlk AL4 128 D3
Keats Cl
Borehamwood WD6 170 A5
Hemel Hempstead HP2 105 B1
Royston SG8 7 C8
Stevenage SG2 51 C7
Keats Ho 15 AL5 86 B1
Keats Way SG4 35 C7
Keble Ct 5 WD6 169 F8
Keble Terr WD5 153 F7
Kecksy's CM21 97 F4
Keeble Cl LU2 46 E1
Keele Cl WD24 167 C7
Keepers Cl
Cheddington LU7 80 A7
Luton LU2 46 C2
Keiths Rd HP3 125 A2
Keiths Wood SG3 68 F5
Kelbys AL7 111 C7
Keller Cl SG2 51 B4
Kelling Cl LU2 45 C8
Kelly Cl WD6 170 D7
Kelly Ct WD6 170 C7
Kelman Cl EN8 162 D8
Kelmscott Cl WD18 167 A4
Kelmscott Cres WD18 167 A4
KELSHALL 15 D5
Kelshall WD25 154 E3
Kelshall St SG8 15 E5
Kelvin Cl LU1 63 E6
Kelvin Cres HA3 176 E3
Kemble Cl EN6 159 D6
Kemble Ho HA7 176 F5
Kempe Cl AL1 141 C7
Kempe Rd EN1 162 C3
Kemp Pl WD23 168 A3
KEMPROW 155 D3
Kemprow WD25 155 D3
Kemps Dr HA6 174 F3
Kempsey Cl LU2 46 D2
Kendal Cl LU3 44 D7
Kendale HP3 125 B2
Kendale Rd
5 Hitchin SG4 34 F6
Luton LU4 44 B2
Kendall Cl AL7 110 F2
Kendall Ct WD6 170 C8
Kendall Manor HA6 174 C3
Kendal Rd EN9 163 C4
Kendals Cl WD7 155 E3
Ken Davies Ct AL3 127 F7
Kenerne Dr EN5 171 E4
Kenford Cl WD25 154 B7
Kenilworth Cl
Borehamwood WD6 170 C6
Hemel Hempstead HP2 124 E2
Stevenage SG2 69 C7
Kenilworth Cres EN1 161 E1
Kenilworth Ct WD17 167 A8
Kenilworth Dr
Borehamwood WD6 170 D6
Croxley Green WD3 166 B5
Kenilworth Gdns WD19 175 C5
Kenilworth Ho WD6 170 C6
Kenilworth Prim Sch WD6 170 D6
Kenilworth Rd LU1 63 C8
Kenmare Cl SG1 36 F3
Kennedy Ave EN11 134 F6
Kennedy Cl
Cheshunt EN8 148 E3
London Colney AL2 142 D5
Pinner HA5 175 F4
Kennedy Ct WD23 176 D8
Kennedy Rd SG12 71 E7
Kennel La AL5 85 A5
Kennelwood La AL10 130 B6
Kennesbourne Ct AL5 85 D4
Kenneth Gdns 6 HA7 176 F4
Kenneth Rd LU2 46 A1
Kennett Way SG1 36 F3
Kenning Rd EN11 135 B8
Kennington Rd LU3 45 B3
Kensington Ave WD18 166 F5
Kensington Cl AL1 128 A1
Kensington Ct EN1 161 E1
Kensington Mews WD18 167 A5
Kensington Way WD6 170 D6
KENSWORTH COMMON 82 F8
Kensworth Lower Sch LU6 82 F8
KENSWORTH LYNCH 62 A1
Kensworth Rd LU6 82 D4
Kent Cl WD6 157 D1
Kent Cres CM23 76 E4
Kentish La AL9 145 C7
Kenton Gdns AL1 127 F2
Kenton La HA3 176 F3
Kent Pl SG5 34 D8

Kent Rd LU1 62 F8
Kents Ave HP3 138 D7
Kents La SG11 55 E2
Kenwood Dr WD3 172 F8
Kenworth Cl EN8 162 D6
Kenyon Pl AL7 110 E3
Kerdistone Cl EN6 145 B1
Kernow Ct LU2 46 A1
Kerr Cl SG3 68 F5
Kerri Cl EN5 171 C5
Kerril Croft CM20 117 A1
Kershaw Cl LU3 45 A8
Kershaw's Hill SG4 34 F6
Kessingland Ave SG1 36 A1
Keston Mews WD17 167 B7
Kestrel Cl
  Berkhamsted HP4 122 C3
  Stevenage SG2 51 D2
  Watford WD25 154 E5
Kestrel Ct 4 SG12 93 C3
Kestrel Gdns CM23 76 C6
Kestrel Gn AL10 130 A4
Kestrels The AL2 154 F8
Kestrel Way
  Luton LU4 44 A5
  Royston SG8 7 E8
  Welwyn Garden City AL7 110 F8
Kestrel Wlk SG6 23 B3
Keswick Cl AL1 128 B1
Keswick Dr EN3 162 C3
Kettering Rd EN3 162 D2
KETTLE GREEN 74 D1
Kettle Green Rd SG10 74 E2
Ketton Cl LU2 64 A7
Ketton Ct LU2 64 A7
Kevere Ct HA6 174 B5
Kewferry Dr HA6 174 C5
Kewferry Rd HA6 174 C5
Keyfield Terr AL1 127 D2
Keymer Cl LU2 46 C3
Keynton Cl SG14 112 F7
KEYSERS ESTATE 135 B1
Keysers Rd EN10 135 B1
Keys Ho 4 EN3 162 D2
Kibes La SG12 93 E1
Kidner Cl LU2 45 E5
Kilbride Ct HP2 124 F7
Kilby Cl WD25 154 D4
Kilby Rd SG1 50 C5
Kildonan Cl WD17 166 F8
Kilfillan Gdns HP4 122 A4
Kilfillan Pk HP4 122 A4
Killigrew Inf Sch AL2 141 B6
Killigrew Jun Sch AL2 141 B6
Kilmarnock Dr LU2 45 E5
Kilmarnock Rd WD19 175 D6
Kiln Ave HP6 150 C1
Kiln Cl HP4 123 B6
Kiln Cotts HP2 125 B4
Kilncroft HP3 125 B1
Kilnfield AL7 89 F1
Kiln Ground HP3 125 A1
Kiln House Cl SG12 93 E2
Kiln House Yd SG8 7 C6
Kiln La HP5 150 B8
Kiln Rd HP23 120 B6
Kiln Way
  Dunstable LU5 44 A1
  Northwood HA6 174 E4
Kilsmore La EN8 148 D2
Kilvinton Dr EN2 161 D1
Kilworth Cl AL7 111 B4
Kimberley SG6 11 F2
Kimberley Cl CM23 77 A5
Kimberley Rd AL3 127 D4
Kimble Cl WD18 166 E2
Kimble Cres WD23 168 C2
Kimblewick WD19 167 E1
Kimbolton Cres SG2 69 A7
Kimbolton Gn WD6 170 C5
Kimps Way HP3 139 A8
KIMPTON 66 C1
Kimpton Bottom AL5, SG4 86 E7
Kimpton Cl
  Hemel Hempstead HP2 125 B8
  Woolmer Green SG3 69 A2
Kimpton Pl WD25 154 D5
Kimpton Prim Sch SG4 66 C1
Kimpton Rd
  Ayot St P AL6 89 A6
  Blackmore End SG4, AL4 87 C7
  Codicote SG4 67 B1
  Luton LU1, LU2 64 A6
  Peters Green LU2, SG4 65 E2
Kimptons Cl EN6 158 D7
Kimptons Mead EN6 158 D7
Kinderscout HP3 125 A1
Kindersley Cl AL6 89 C6
Kindersley Way WD5 153 D8
Kinetic Bsns Ctr WD6 170 A6
Kinetic Cres EN3 162 F3
King Arthur Ct EN8 162 E8
King Charles Rd WD7 156 E7
Kingcroft Rd AL5 107 D7
King Edward Pl AL4 87 D1
King Edward Rd
  Cheshunt EN8 162 E6
  Shenley WD7 156 F6
  Watford WD19 167 E3
King Edward's Rd SG12 93 E2
King Edward St HP3 138 D7
Kingfisher Cl
  Harrow HA3 176 F3
Kingfisher Cl *continued*
  Northwood HA6 174 B2
  Stanstead Abbotts SG12 115 C3
  Wheathampstead AL4 87 D1
Kingfisher Ct
  Enfield EN2 160 F1
  Hitchin SG4 35 A6
  Letchworth Garden City SG6 22 E8
Kingfisher Dr HP3 138 F6
Kingfisher Lure
  Kings Langley WD4 139 B2
  Rickmansworth WD3 165 B5
Kingfisher Rise SG2 51 D2
Kingfisher Way
  Bishop's Stortford CM23 77 A7
  Roydon CM19 116 A1
King George Ave WD23 168 B3
King George Cl SG1 50 E6
King George Rd
  Waltham Abbey EN9 163 C5
  Ware SG12 93 E2
King Georges Ave WD18 166 E5
King Georges Cl SG5 21 D1
King George's Way SG4 66 E6
Kingham Rd SG12 94 E5
Kingham Way LU2 45 E1
King Harold Ct EN9 163 C6
King Harold Sch EN9 163 E6
King Harry La AL3 127 B1
King Harry St HP2 124 D2
King Henry Ct LU3 45 B2
King Henrys Ct EN9 163 C3
King Henry's Mews EN3 163 A2
King James Ave EN6 146 E2
King James Way SG8 7 D6
Kingley Pk WD4 139 B2
Kings Ave
  Hemel Hempstead HP3 138 F7
  Watford WD18 167 A5
Kingsbridge Rd CM23 77 A8
Kingsbury Ave AL3 127 C4
Kingsbury Watermill* AL3 127 B4
Kings Cl
  Chipperfield WD4 152 B8
  Northwood HA6 174 F4
  5 Watford WD18 167 C5
King's Cotts CM23 77 A6
Kingscroft AL7 111 B7
Kings Ct
  Berkhamsted HP4 122 C5
  Bishop's Stortford CM23 77 A8
  9 Borehamwood WD6 169 F8
  Harpenden AL5 107 B8
Kingsdale Ho AL6 89 B3
Kingsdale Rd HP4 122 A3
Kingsdown SG4 35 B6
Kingsdown Ave LU2 45 D5
Kings Farm Rd WD3 164 D3
Kingsfield EN11 135 A8
Kings Field Cotts WD5 153 F8
Kingsfield Ct WD19 167 D2
Kingsfield Dr EN3 162 D4
Kingsfield Rd
  Dane End SG12 71 E8
  Watford WD19 167 D3
Kingsfield Way EN3 162 D4
Kingsgate AL3 127 B1
Kings Head Ct CM21 97 E2
Kings Heath Pk AL5 86 C6
Kings Hedges SG5 34 C8
Kingshill Ave AL4 128 B6
Kingshill Ct 8 EN5 171 E5
Kingshill Inf Sch SG12 93 D3
Kingshill Way HP4 122 B2
Kingshott Sch SG4 35 B5
King's La WD4 152 B8
Kingsland EN6 158 F6
Kingsland Ct 7 LU1 63 F6
Kingsland Rd
  Hemel Hempstead HP1 124 A1
  Luton LU1 63 F6
Kingsland Way SG7 4 D4
KINGS LANGLEY 139 A1
Kings Langley Prim Sch WD4 138 F3
Kings Langley Sch WD4 138 E3
Kings Langley Sta WD4 139 C1
Kingsley Ave
  Borehamwood WD6 169 F7
  Cheshunt EN8 148 C2
Kingsley Ct AL7 110 F2
Kingsley High Sch HA3 176 C3
Kingsley Rd LU3 45 A5
Kingsley Wlk HP23 100 A4
Kings Mdw WD4 139 A3
Kingsmead
  Cheshunt EN8 148 D3
  Cuffley EN6 146 E3
  Lower Nazeing EN9, EN10 135 C1
  Sawbridgeworth CM21 97 E1
  St Albans AL4 128 D6
Kingsmead Rd CM23 77 A8
Kings Mews CM21 97 E2
King's Mews 7 HP2 124 D4
Kingsmill Ct 1 AL10 130 B3
Kings Oak WD3 166 A5
Kings Oak Private Hospl The EN2 161 A1
Kings Park Ind Est WD4 139 B2
Kings Pl AL9 130 C7
Kings Rd
  Barnet EN5 171 C6
  Berkhamsted HP4 122 B3
  Stevenage SG1 50 D4
King's Rd
  Cheshunt EN8 162 E5
  Hertford SG13 114 A7
  Hitchin SG5 34 F8
  London Colney AL2 142 C5
  St Albans AL3 127 C3
Kings Sch The AL5 85 F4
King St
  Bishop's Stortford CM23 76 F7
  Luton LU1 63 E7
  Markyate AL3 83 E5
  2 Royston SG8 7 D6
  Tring HP23 100 A3
  Watford WD18 167 C5
Kingston Ct LU2 45 F1
Kingston Pl HA3 176 F3
Kingston Rd LU2 45 F1
Kingston Vale SG8 7 E5
King Street Mews 1 CM23 76 F7
KING'S WALDEN 48 A3
King's Walden Rd SG5 33 D2
Kings Walden Rise SG2 51 C8
Kingsway
  Cuffley EN6 146 E1
  Luton LU4 45 A1
  Royston SG8 7 C8
  Stotfold SG5 11 F7
  Ware SG12 93 D3
Kingsway Gdns SG5 11 F7
Kingsway Ind Est LU1 63 A8
Kingsway Inf Sch WD25 154 A5
Kingsway Jun Sch WD25 154 A5
Kingsway North Orbital Rd WD25 154 B5
Kingswell Ride EN6 146 E1
King's Wlk SG8 7 D5
KINGSWOOD 154 A5
Kingswood Ave SG4 35 D8
Kingswood Rd WD25 154 B5
Kingwell Rd EN4 159 D1
King Williams Ct EN9 163 C4
Kinloch Ct 6 AL5 86 B1
Kinross Cres LU3 44 D8
Kinsbourne Cl AL5 85 C4
Kinsbourne Cres AL5 85 D4
Kinsbourne Ct AL5 85 E3
KINSBOURNE GREEN 85 C5
Kinsbourne Green La AL5 85 B3
Kintyre Ho 2 WD18 166 F3
Kipling Cl SG4 35 C7
Kipling Gr HP2 105 B1
Kipling Pl HA7 176 F4
Kipling Rd SG8 2 E1
Kipling The LU3 45 B6
Kipling Way AL5 86 B1
Kirby Cl HA6 174 F4
Kirby Dr LU3 45 A8
Kirkcaldy Gn 1 WD19 175 C7
Kirkdale Ct 8 LU1 63 E6
Kirkdale Rd AL5 86 A2
Kirklands AL8 89 D2
Kirkwick Ave AL5 86 A1
Kitchener Cl AL1 128 B2
Kitcheners La SG2 38 B1
Kitchen Garden Ct SG5 34 E6
Kitching La
  Stevenage SG1 50 A5
  St Ippolyts SG4 49 F5
Kite Field HP4 121 E7
Kite Way SG6 22 E8
Kitsbury Ct HP4 122 B4
Kitsbury Rd HP4 122 B4
Kitsbury Terr HP4 122 B4
Kit's La SG7 25 C8
Kitson Way CM20 117 C1
Kitswell Way WD7 156 A6
KITT'S END 158 E1
Kitt's End Rd EN5 158 E2
Kiwi Ct SG5 21 F1
Klondyke AL5 85 D4
Knap Cl SG6 23 D8
KNEBWORTH 69 A5
Knebworth Ct CM23 76 D6
Knebworth Ctry Pk* SG3 68 C7
Knebworth Gate SG2 68 F8
Knebworth Ho* SG3 68 B6
Knebworth Path WD6 170 D5
Knebworth Prim Sch SG3 69 A5
Knebworth Sta SG3 68 F5
KNEESWORTH 2 A5
Kneesworth House Hospl SG8 2 C5
Kneesworth Rd SG8 2 F8
Kneesworth St SG8 7 C6
Knella Gn AL7 111 A6
Knella Rd AL7 111 A6
Knifton Ct EN6 158 D8
Knightsbridge Ct 8 WD18 166 F5
Knightsbridge Way HP2 124 E4
Knights Cl
  Bishop's Stortford CM23 76 C8
  Buntingford SG9 40 E6
Knightscote Cl UB9 173 D1
Knights Ct
  Bushey WD23 168 D1
  Standon SG11 55 F1
Knight's Ct CM21 97 E2
Knightsfield AL8 89 D2
Knights Field LU2 45 D1
Knightsfield Sch AL8 89 D3
Knights Orch
  Hemel Hempstead HP1 123 F5
  St Albans AL3 127 C3
Knights Properties EN11 135 B6
Knights Row CM23 76 E6
Knight St CM21 97 E2
Knights Templar Sch The SG7 23 E8
Knights Templars Gn SG2 51 C8
Knocking Hoe National Nature Reserve* SG5 20 A2
Knoll Cres HA6 174 F2
Knolles Cres AL9 144 B7
Knoll Gn HP2 124 E5
Knoll Rise LU2 45 E4
Knolls Cl HP22 60 B3
Knoll The SG13 114 B7
Knott Cl SG1 37 B3
Knowle Ct SG1 36 B1
Knowle Dr AL5 107 D7
Knowle Ho EN11 135 A5
Knowle The EN11 135 A5
Knowl Piece SG4 22 A3
Knowl Pk WD6 169 E4
Knowl Way WD6 169 F4
Knutsford Ave WD24 154 D1
Knutsford Sch WD24 154 D1
Koh-I-Noor Ave WD23 168 A3
Kristiansand Way SG6 23 C8
Kymswell Rd SG2 51 C3
Kynance Cl LU2 46 A2
Kynaston Cl HA3 176 D3
Kynaston Wood HA3 176 D3
Kyrkeby SG6 23 C4
Kytes Dr WD25 154 D6

L

LABBY GREEN 112 A3
Laburnham Cotts SG12 94 F4
Laburnum Cl
  Cheshunt EN8 162 D8
  Luton LU3 45 C7
Laburnum Gr
  Chiswell Green AL2 141 B6
  Luton LU3 45 B7
Laburnum Rd EN11 135 B8
Laburnum Way EN7 147 B3
Lachbury Cl LU1 63 A6
Lackmore Rd EN1 162 C4
Lacre Way SG6 23 C7
Ladbrooke Cl EN6 159 A7
Ladbrooke Dr EN6 159 A7
Ladbrooke JMI Sch EN6 159 B7
Ladies Gr AL3 127 C5
Lady Cooper Ct HP4 122 E6
Lady Gr AL7 110 E2
Ladygrove Cotts SG4 48 F5
Ladygrove Ct SG4 48 F5
Ladyhill LU4 44 B6
Lady Mdw HP3 138 D4
Lady St John Sq SG14 92 A1
Lady's Cl WD18 167 C5
Ladyshot CM20 118 B1
Ladysmith Rd
  Harrow HA3 176 E1
  Ivinghoe LU7 80 E5
  St Albans AL3 127 D4
Lady Spencer's Gr AL1 127 C2
Ladywalk WD3 172 E6
Ladywell Prospect CM21 98 A1
Ladywood Cl WD3 165 C6
Ladywood Rd SG14 112 F6
Lady Zia Wernher Sch LU2 46 B3
Laelia Ho AL1 128 A2
Lagley Ho HP4 122 A5
Laguna Ct 4 AL1 127 E3
Laidon Sq HP2 124 D7
Lake Dr WD23 176 D8
Lakeland Cl HA3 176 D4
Lake Rd EN9 135 E2
Lakes Ct SG12 115 B4
Lakeside
  Borehamwood WD6 170 A4
  Tring HP23 100 A5
Lakeside Pl AL2 142 D4
Lakeside Rd EN8 148 C3
Lakeside Sch AL8 110 B4
Lake The WD23 168 D1
Lakeview LU3 45 D2
Lake View
  Bishop's Stortford CM23 76 C3
  Potters Bar EN6 159 C6
Lake Villas SG9 43 B4
Lalleford Rd LU2 46 D1
Lalsham Ho 4 WD19 175 C7
Lamb Cl
  Hatfield AL10 130 B4
  Watford WD25 154 C5
Lamb Ct AL4 108 E7
Lambert Ct WD23 167 D5
Lamberton Ct WD6 170 A8
Lamb La AL3 106 B5
Lamb Mdw SG15 11 A3
Lambourn Chase WD7 155 F3
Lambourn Dr LU2 45 E6
Lambourn Gdns AL5 85 F3
Lambs Cl
  Cuffley EN6 146 F2
  Dunstable LU5 44 A1
Lambs Gdns SG12 95 D4
Lambton Ave EN8 162 D6
Lamer La AL4 87 D3
Lamers Rd LU2 46 B2
Lammasmead EN10 148 F8
Lammas Mead SG5 21 E2
Lammas Path SG2 51 B4
Lammas Rd
  Cheddington LU7 80 A7
  Watford WD18 167 C4
  Watton at S SG14 70 D4
Lammas Way SG6 22 F8
Lamorna Cl
  Luton LU3 44 F6
  Radlett WD7 156 B5
Lamorna Ct 2 HA3 176 E1
Lampits EN11 135 B6
Lamsey Rd HP3 124 D1
Lancaster Ave
  Hadley Wood EN4 159 D1
  Hitchin SG5 34 E8
  Luton LU2 45 C8
Lancaster Cl SG1 36 E2
Lancaster Dr HP3 136 F4
Lancaster Rd
  Hitchin SG5 34 E8
  St Albans AL1 127 F5
Lancaster Way
  Abbots Langley WD5 153 F8
  Bishop's Stortford CM23 76 C8
  Welwyn AL6 89 C3
Lance Ho SG13 114 B8
Lancelot Ct WD23 168 A7
Lancing Ho 5 WD24 167 C7
Lancing Rd LU2 46 D3
Lancing Way WD3 166 B4
Landau Way EN10 148 F5
Landford Cl WD3 173 E8
Landing The WD7 156 A6
Landmead Rd EN8 148 E2
Landridge Dr EN1 162 B1
Lands' End WD6 169 D3
Lane End
  Berkhamsted HP4 121 F4
  Hatfield AL10 129 F2
Lanefield Wlk AL8 110 C6
Lane Gdns WD23 168 E2
Lanercost Cl AL6 90 A7
LANES END 119 C4
Langbridge Cl SG4 35 A4
Langdale Ave AL5 86 D2
Langdale Ct 2 HP2 124 E6
Langdale Gdns EN3 162 D4
Langdale Terr WD6 170 C6
Langdon St HP23 100 A3
Langfield Cl EN9 135 E1
Langford Cl AL4 128 C5
Langford Dr LU2 46 A3
Langham Cl
  Luton LU2 45 D7
  St Albans AL4 128 D8
Langham Ho 9 LU1 63 D8
Langholme WD23 168 C1
Langland Ct HA6 174 D3
Langland Dr HA5 175 E3
Langleigh SG6 11 F1
LANGLEY 49 F1
Langley Ave HP3 138 F8
LANGLEYBURY 153 B4
Langleybury La WD4 153 B4
Langley Cres
  Kings Langley WD4 139 A1
  St Albans AL3 127 C5
Langley Ct EN7 147 C3
Langley Gn EN9 135 D1
Langley Gr AL4 108 C2
Langley Hill WD4 138 F2
Langley Hill Cl WD4 139 A2
Langley La
  Abbots Langley WD5 153 F7
  Langley SG4 49 E2
Langley Lodge La WD4 153 A8
Langley Par WD5 153 E8
Langley Rd
  Abbots Langley WD5 153 F8
  Chipperfield WD4 138 B1
  Watford WD17 167 A8
Langley Row EN5 171 F8
Langley Sidings SG1 50 D2
Langley St LU1 63 E6
Langley Terrace Ind Pk 17 LU1 63 E6

Langley Way WD17 166 F8
Langley Wharf WD4 139 A4
Langmead Dr WD23 168 D1
Langstone Ley AL7 111 B5
Langthorne Ave SG1 50 E6
Langton Gr HA6 174 C5
Langton Ho EN11 134 F6
Langton Rd
Harrow HA3 176 C3
Hoddesdon EN11 134 F6
Langwood 6 WD17 167 A8
Langwood Gdns WD17 167 A8
Langwood Ho 4 WD3 165 E1
Langworthy HA5 176 A4
Lankester Rd SG8 7 C5
Lannock SG6 23 D4
Lannock Hill SG4 23 E1
Lannock Prim Sch SG6 23 C4
Lanrick Copse HP4 122 E5
Lansdowne Cl WD25 154 D4
Lansdowne Ct EN10 135 A3
Lansdowne Pl AL1 142 A8
Lansdowne Rd LU3 45 D1
Lanterns La SG2 51 D5
Lanthony Ct SG15 11 A4
Lanthorn Cl EN10 134 E4
Laporte Way LU4 44 F1
Lapwing Cl HP2 124 E6
Lapwing Dell SG6 23 B3
Lapwing Rd LU4 44 A4
Lapwing Rise SG2 51 D3
Lapwing Way WD5 154 A8
Larch Ave
Bricket Wood AL2 140 E1
Hitchin SG4 35 A4
Larch Cl EN7 147 E4
Larches Ave EN1 162 C4
Larches The
Berkhamsted HP4 121 D5
Little Chalfont HP6 150 B1
Luton LU2 45 D1
Northwood HA6 174 C4
St Albans AL4 128 D7
Ware SG12 93 C4
Watford WD23 167 E4
Larch La AL6 89 F8
Larch Rise HP4 122 A5
Larch View HP1 124 B2
Larchwood CM23 76 D5
Larchwood Rd HP2 124 F5
Larken Cl WD23 168 C1
Larken Dr WD23 168 C1
Larkens Cl SG11 55 D3
Larkin Pl SG8 2 D1
Larkins Cl SG7 12 F1
Larkins La SG10 74 F1
Larkinson SG1 50 C7
Lark Rise AL10 130 A3
Larksfield SG12 93 E3
Larkspur Cl
Bishop's Stortford CM23 76 D6
Hemel Hempstead HP1 123 E4
Larkspur Gdns LU4 44 F2
Larks Ridge AL2 141 A4
Larksway CM23 76 C6
Larkswood Rise AL4 128 C8
Larmans Rd EN3 162 D3
Larsen Dr EN9 163 D5
Larwood Gr SG1 51 A8
Larwood Sch SG1 50 F7
LATCHFORD 73 F5
Latchford Mews 8 AL4 87 D1
Latchford Pl HP1 124 A2
LATCHMORE BANK 77 B2
Latchmore Bank
Bishop's Stortford CM22 77 B2
Little Hallingbury CM22 98 B8
Latchmore Cl SG4 34 F5
Lathwell Ct LU2 45 E1
LATIMER 150 E3
Latimer Cl
Hemel Hempstead HP2 125 B8
Pinner HA5 175 C2
Watford WD18 166 E2
Latimer Ct EN8 162 F5
Latimer Gdns
Pinner HA5 175 C2
Welwyn Garden City AL7 111 B6
Latimer Pl HA6 174 F5
Latimer Rd
Little Chalfont HP6, HP5 150 C2
Luton LU1 63 E6
Latium Cl AL1 127 D2
Lattimore Ho 9 AL1 127 E3
Lattimore Rd
St Albans AL1 127 E3
Wheathampstead AL4 108 C8
Latton Hall Cl CM20 118 A1
Lauderdale Rd WD4 153 C6
Laughton Ct WD6 170 D7
Launceston WD3 164 B3
Laundry La EN9 149 E6
Launton Cl LU3 31 B1
Laura Ct HA2 176 C1
Laural Ct EN6 146 F2
Laurance Haines Prim Sch The WD18 167 A3
Laureate Way HP1 124 B5
Laurel Ave EN6 158 F7
Laurel Bank HP3 137 F8
Laurel Cl
Hemel Hempstead HP2 124 F4
Watford WD19 167 D2
Laurel Ct EN6 146 F1
Laureldene SG10 74 F1
Laurel Fields EN6 158 F8
Laurel Mews SG7 12 F1
Laurel Pk HA3 176 F3
Laurel Rd AL1 127 F3
Laurelsfield AL3 141 B8
Laurelside Wlk LU5 44 A2
Laurels The
Bushey WD23 176 E8
Chiswell Green AL2 141 A3
Hammond Street EN7 147 E5
Potten End HP4 123 C6
Laurel Way SG5 21 E3
Lauries Cl HP1 123 C1
Laurino Pl WD23 176 C8
Lavender Cl
Bishop's Stortford CM23 76 D6
Hammond Street EN7 147 F4
Harlow CM20 117 E1
Hatfield AL10 129 F8
Luton LU2 45 E7
Lavender Cres AL3 127 C5
Lavender Croft SG4 35 B6
Lavender Ct SG7 12 E1
Lavender Gdns
Enfield EN2 161 B1
Harrow HA3 176 E4
Lavender Prim Sch EN2 161 E1
Lavender Rd EN2 161 D1
Lavender Way SG5 34 D7
Lavender Wlk HP2 124 D5
Lavinia Ave WD25 154 D5
Lavrock La WD3 165 F2
Lawford Ave WD3 164 C3
Lawford Cl
Chorleywood WD3 164 C3
Luton LU1 63 C7
Law Hall La SG4 66 A8
Law Hall Lane Cotts SG4 66 A8
Lawn Ave SG4 66 C1
Lawn Gdns LU1 63 D5
Lawn La HP3 138 D8
Lawn Mans 8 EN5 171 F5
Lawns Cl SG5 33 C2
Lawns Ct SG8 7 D5
Lawns Dr The EN10 134 F2
Lawns The
Harrow HA5 176 B3
Hemel Hempstead HP1 123 E4
Shenley WD7 156 E6
St Albans AL3 127 C4
Stevenage SG2 51 D4
Welwyn Garden City AL8 89 D1
Lawnswood EN5 171 E4
Lawn The CM20 118 B3
Lawn Vale HA5 175 E1
Lawrance Gdns EN8 148 D3
Lawrance Rd AL3 127 C7
Lawrence Ave
Letchworth Garden City SG6 23 A4
Sawbridgeworth CM21 97 E4
Stanstead Abbotts SG12 115 C4
Stevenage SG1 50 E7
Lawrence Cl SG14 112 E7
Lawrence Ct 4 WD19 175 D7
Lawrence End Rd LU2 65 D4
Lawrence Hall 11 LU1 63 E7
Lawrence Hall End AL7 110 E3
Lawrence Moorings CM21 97 F2
Lawrie Ct HA3 176 F3
Laxton Cl LU2 46 E1
Laxton Gdns
Baldock SG7 24 A7
Shenley WD7 156 E7
Layard Rd EN1 161 F1
Lay Brook AL4 128 A7
Layham Dr LU2 46 E1
Layhill HP2 124 D5
Layston CE Fst Sch SG9 40 F8
Layston Mdw SG9 40 F6
Layston Pk SG8 7 D5
Layton St AL7 110 E3
Lea Bank LU3 44 E6
Lea Bank Ct LU3 44 E6
Lea Bushes WD25 154 E4
Lea Cl
Bishop's Stortford CM23 59 B1
Bushey WD23 168 B4
Leacroft AL5 86 D3
Lea Ct AL5 86 A3
Leaders Cl HP22 60 B3
Leaf Cl HA6 174 D3
Leafield LU3 44 F4
Leaford Cres WD24 153 F2
Leaford Ct WD24 153 F3
Leaforis Rd EN7 148 A3
Leaf Way AL1 141 D8
Leafy La HP23 99 E1
Lea Gn AL9 130 E8
Lea Gr CM23 59 B1
LEAGRAVE 44 D5
Leagrave High St LU4 44 B3
Leagrave Prim Sch LU4 44 C4
Leagrave Rd LU4 45 B2
Leagrave Sta LU4 44 E5
Leahoe Gdns SG13 113 C5
Lea Ind Est AL5 86 C4
Lealands High Sch LU3 44 C8
Lea Manor High Sch LU3 44 F8
Leamington Rd LU3 45 A7
Lea Mount EN7 147 E3
Leander Gdns WD25 154 E2
Lea Prim Sch The AL5 86 B4
Lea Rd
Harpenden AL5 86 B3
Hoddesdon EN11 135 C8
Holdbrook EN9 163 A5
Luton LU1 63 F7
Watford WD24 154 B1
Lea Road Ind Pk EN9 163 A5
Leasey Bridge La AL4 87 A1
Leasey Dell Dr AL4 87 A2
Leaside HP2 125 C2
Leaside Ct AL5 86 C3
Leaside Lo 6 EN11 135 D8
Leaside Wlk 6 SG12 93 D1
Leas The
Baldock SG7 23 E7
Hemel Hempstead HP3 139 A7
Watford WD23 167 F7
Leat Cl CM21 97 F3
Leathersellers Cl 12 EN5 171 E6
Leathwaite Cl LU3 45 A6
LEA VALLEY 86 F2
Lea Valley Education Support Unit EN8 162 D5
Lea Valley High Sch EN3 162 C4
Leavesden Ct WD5 154 A8
Leavesden Film Studios WD4 153 E5
LEAVESDEN GREEN 153 E5
Leavesden Jun Mix Inf Sch WD25 154 A5
Leavesden Rd WD24 154 B1
Leaves Spring SG2 51 A2
Leaview EN9 163 B6
Lea Wlk AL5 86 C4
Lebanon Cl WD17 153 D3
Le Corte Cl WD4 138 F2
Lectern La AL1 141 E7
Leda Ave EN3 162 D1
LEDBURN 61 C8
Ledgemore La HP1, HP2 103 F5
Ledwell Rd LU1 62 F3
Lee Bridge Cnr LU2 85 F7
Leeches Way LU7 80 A7
Lee Cl
Hertford SG13 113 C4
Stanstead Abbotts SG12 115 C4
Leecroft Rd EN5 171 E5
Lee Farm Cl HP5 136 A1
Leefe Way EN6 146 D3
Leeming Rd WD6 169 F8
Lees Ave HA6 174 F2
Leeside
Barnet EN5 171 E3
Potters Bar EN6 159 D7
Leeside Works SG12 115 C4
Leeswood Ct SG14 112 F7
Leete Pl SG8 7 D7
Lee The HA6 174 F5
Lee Valley Ctry Pk* EN10 135 B3
Lee Valley Park Farms Visitor Ctr* EN9 149 C3
Lee Valley Park Vst Ctr* EN9 163 C6
Leeway Cl HA5 175 F3
Leggatts Cl WD24 153 F3
Leggatts Rise WD25 154 A4
Leggatts Way WD24 154 A3
Leggatts Wood Ave WD24 154 B3
Leggett Gr SG1 50 E8
Leggfield Terr HP1 123 F3
Leghorn Cres LU4 44 A3
Legions Way CM23 77 A8
Legra Ave EN11 135 A6
Leicester Cl LU4 44 E1
Leicester Rd LU4 44 E1
Leigh Comm AL7 110 F4
Leigh Ct WD6 170 D7
Leigh Rodd WD19 175 F7
Leighton Buzzard Rd
Great Gaddesden HP1 103 E2
Hemel Hempstead HP1 124 C5
Leighton Ct EN8 148 D2
Leighton Rd
Harrow HA3 176 D1
Wingrave HP22 60 C3
Leinster Mews 14 EN5 171 E6
Lemonfield Dr WD25 154 E6
LEMSFORD 110 A5
Lemsford Ct WD6 170 C5
Lemsford La AL8 110 B4
Lemsford Rd
Hatfield AL10 130 A6
St Albans AL1 127 F4
Lemsford Springs (Nature Reserve)* AL8 110 A5
Lemsford Village AL8 109 F5
Lennon Ct LU1 63 D7
Lennox Gn LU2 46 F2
Lensbury Cl EN8 148 E3
Leonard Ct HA3 176 E3
Leonard's Cl AL6 89 E8
Lesbury Cl LU2 46 E1
Leslie Cl SG2 51 C2
Letchfield HP5 150 B8
LETCHFORD GARDEN CITY 22 C5
Letchmore Cl SG1 50 D6
LETCHMORE HEATH 168 E8
Letchmore Inf Sch SG1 50 D7
Letchmore Rd
Radlett WD7 156 A3
Stevenage SG1 50 D7
Letchworth Bsns & Ret Pk SG6 23 C6
Letchworth Cl WD19 175 D5
Letchworth Gate SG6 23 B4
Letchworth La SG6 22 F3
Letchworth Mus & Art Gall* SG6 22 F5
Letchworth Rd
Baldock SG7 23 D7
Luton LU3 45 A4
Letchworth Sta SG6 22 F6
Letter Box Row SG4 34 F3
LETTY GREEN 112 A2
Level's Gn CM23 58 C5
LEVEL'S GREEN 58 C5
Levenage La SG12 95 E3
Leven Cl
Cheshunt EN8 162 D6
South Oxhey WD19 175 D5
Levendale LU4 44 C5
Leven Dr EN8 162 D6
LEVENS GREEN 54 C1
Leventhorpe Sch The CM21 97 E4
Leven Way HP2 124 D7
Leveret Cl WD25 154 A5
LEVERSTOCK GREEN 125 C2
Leverstock Green CE Prim Sch HP2 125 D2
Leverstock Green Rd
Hemel Hempstead HP2 125 B3
Hemel Hempstead HP2, HP3 125 C2
Leverstock Green Way HP2, HP3 125 C3
Leverton Inf Sch The EN9 163 F5
Leverton Jun Sch The EN9 163 F5
Leverton Way EN9 163 C6
Lewes Way WD3 166 C5
Lewington Ct EN3 162 D2
Lewis Cl UB9 173 C1
Lewisham Ct 9 EN3 163 A1
Lewis Ho 3 WD18 166 F3
Lewis La SG15 11 A6
Lewsey Park Ct LU4 44 A4
Lewsey Rd LU4 44 B2
Lexington Cl WD6 169 F6
Lexington Ct EN6 158 D8
Lexington Way EN5 171 D5
Leyburne Cl LU7 61 C8
Leyburne Rd LU3 45 B6
Leycroft Way AL5 107 E7
Leyden Rd SG1 50 D2
LEY GREEN 47 F5
Leygreen Cl LU2 64 A8
LEY HILL 136 B1
Leyhill Dr LU1 63 B4
Ley Hill Sch HP5 136 B1
Ley Ho AL7 111 C6
Leyland Ave AL1 127 D1
Leyland Cl EN8 148 C2
Ley Park Prim Sch EN10 134 F1
Leys Ave SG6 22 F6
Leys Cl UB9 173 D2
Leysdown AL7 111 D6
Leys Prim Sch The SG1 37 A2
Leys Rd HP3 124 F1
Leys The
Radlett WD7 156 A2
St Albans AL4 128 D6
Tring HP23 100 B4
Leyton Gn AL5 86 A1
Leyton Rd AL5 86 A1
Ley Wlk AL7 111 C6
Liberty Cl SG13 113 C3
Liberty Wlk AL1 128 C2
Library Rd LU1 63 E7
Lichfield Ho 4 WD6 170 A7
Lichfield Rd HA6 175 A1
Lichfield Way EN10 134 F1
Liddel Cl LU3 45 B3
Liddell Hall 6 LU1 63 E8
Lidgate Cl LU4 44 B6
Lieutenant Ellis Way EN7, EN8 162 A7
Lightcroft Cotts HP2 124 E3
Lighthorne Rise LU3 45 A7
Lightswood Cl EN7 147 D4
Lilac Ave EN1 162 C3
Lilac Cl EN7 162 B8
Lilac Gr LU3 44 C8
Lilac Rd EN11 135 B8
Lilac Way AL5 107 D6
Lilbourne Dr SG13 114 A7
LILLEY 32 D2
Lilley Bottom LU2, SG4 47 C5
Lilley Bottom Rd SG4 48 B1
Lilleyhoo La LU2, SG5 32 F2
Lilley Old School Ct LU2 32 D2
Lilliard Cl EN11 115 B2
Lilly La HP2 125 D7
Lily Wlk SG16 10 A3
Limberlost The AL6 89 B7
Limbrick Rd AL5 107 C6
LIMBURY 44 F5
Limbury Rd LU3 44 F4
Lime Ave
Blackmore End AL4 87 B7
Luton LU4 44 C3
Lime Cl
Aston SG2 51 D4
Harrow HA3 176 F1
Ware SG12 93 E2
Watford WD19 167 D2
Limedene Cl HA5 175 D2
Lime Gr
Royston SG8 7 E8
Totteridge N20 171 F1
Limekiln Cl SG8 7 E5
Limekiln La
Baldock SG7 23 F7
Stansted Mountfitchet CM24 59 C5
Lime Pk CM23 77 A6
Limes Cres 4 CM23 77 A7
Limes Ct
Cheshunt EN8 162 D7
17 Hoddesdon EN11 135 A6
Limes Rd EN8 162 E7
Limes The
Buckland SG9 27 D8
Cheshunt EN10 148 F7
Hertford SG14 113 C6
Hitchin SG5 34 D6
5 Luton LU1 63 E5
2 Northwood HA6 174 E5
St Albans AL1 127 E5
Welwyn Garden City AL7 111 A4
Limetree Ave LU1 85 A7
Limetree Ct HA5 176 A3
Lime Tree Ct AL2 142 B5
Lime Tree Pl AL1 127 E2
Lime Tree Wlk
Bushey WD23 176 E8
Enfield EN2 161 C1
Rickmansworth WD3 165 B4
Lime Walk Prim Sch HP3 124 F1
Lime Way WD7 156 C8
Lime Wlk HP3 124 F1
Limit Home Pk HP4 121 D7
Linacres LU4 44 D4
Linbridge Way LU2 46 E2
Linces Way AL7 111 B4
Lincoln Cl
Bishop's Stortford CM23 76 D5
Welwyn Garden City AL7 111 D6
Lincoln Ct
Berkhamsted HP4 122 B4
Borehamwood WD6 170 D4
Lincoln Dr
Croxley Green WD3 166 B6
South Oxhey WD19 175 C7
Lincoln Field WD23 167 F6
Lincoln Hill SG9 29 A5
Lincoln Mews AL3 127 C2
Lincoln Rd
Luton LU4 45 B1
Stevenage SG1 37 B2
Lincoln's Cl AL4 128 D8
Lincoln Way WD3 166 B5
Lindbergh AL7 111 C6
Linden Ave WD18 166 F5
Linden Cl EN7 148 B1
Linden Cres AL1 128 C3
Lindencroft SG6 12 A1
Linden Ct
Harpenden AL5 107 B8
4 Luton LU2 63 F8
Linden Glade HP1 124 A2
Linden Gn SG6 23 A8
Linden Lea WD25 154 A6
Linden Rd
Luton LU4 44 E4
Redbourn AL3 106 A6
Linden Sq UB9 173 A4
Lindens The
Bishop's Stortford CM23 76 F6
Hatfield AL10 129 F6
Hemel Hempstead HP3 137 F8
Stevenage SG1 50 E4
Lindley Cl AL5 86 A4
Lindlings HP1 123 E2
Lindrick Ho 11 WD19 175 C7
Lindsay Ave SG4 35 B5
Lindsay Cl SG8 2 C1
Lindsay Pl EN7 148 B1
Lindsey Cl CM23 58 F1
Lindsey Rd
Bishop's Stortford CM23 58 F1
Luton LU2 46 D1
Lindum Pl AL3 127 A1
Linfield Ct SG14 112 F7
Lingfield Cl HA6 174 E3

Lingfield Rd
Royston SG8 7 F6
Stevenage SG1 37 C1
Lingfield Way WD17 153 F1
Lingholm Way EN5 171 D4
Lingmoor Dr WD25 154 C6
Linington Ave HP5 136 A1
Link Cl AL10 130 B5
Link Dr AL10 130 B5
Linkfield AL7 110 E2
Link Rd
Bishop's Stortford CM23 76 F8
Hemel Hempstead HP1 124 C6
Oaklands AL6 89 F8
Watford WD24 167 D7
Links Ave SG13 114 B7
Links Bsns Ctr The CM23 77 C7
Links Dr
Borehamwood WD6 169 F5
Radlett WD7 155 F6
Linkside Rd CM23 77 C6
Links The
Cheshunt EN8 148 D5
Welwyn Garden City AL8 110 B6
Links View AL3 127 C5
Linksway HA6 174 C2
Links Way
Croxley Green WD3 166 C5
Luton LU2 45 D8
Link The SG6 12 A1
Linkway HA5 175 D2
Link Way CM23 76 E6
Linkways Ct [1] SG1 50 F5
Linkways E SG1 50 F5
Linkways W SG1 50 F5
Link Wlk AL10 130 B6
Linley Ct AL3 127 F6
Linley Dell LU2 46 D2
Linnet Cl
Bushey WD23 168 C1
Letchworth Garden City SG6 22 E8
Luton LU4 44 A4
Linnet Rd WD5 154 A8
Linnet Wlk [1] AL10 130 A3
Linnins Pond AL3 84 B1
Linsey Cl HP3 139 A7
Linster Gr WD6 170 C4
Linten Cl SG4 35 C6
Linton Ave WD6 169 F7
Lintons Cl EN11 135 B7
Lintott Cl SG1 50 D6
Linwood CM21 97 E2
Linwood Rd
Harpenden AL5 107 C7
Ware SG12 93 F3
Lion Ct WD6 170 C8
Lion Yd SG4 66 D1
Liphook Rd WD19 175 D6
Lippitts Hill LU2 45 E5
Lismirrane Ind Pk WD6 169 B3
Lismore
Hemel Hempstead HP3 125 C1
Stevenage SG2 51 C1
Lister Ave SG4 34 F5
Lister Cl SG1 36 C2
Lister Cotts WD6 169 A4
Lister Hospl SG1 36 B2
Liston Cl LU4 44 B5
Little Acre AL3 127 D6
Little Acres SG12 114 D8
LITTLE ALMSHOE 49 B8
Little Almshoe La
St Ippolyts SG4 35 C1
St Ippolyts SG4 49 B8
Little Almshoe Rd SG4 49 A8
Little Beechill EN2 160 D3
LITTLE BERKHAMSTED 132 C4
Little Berkhamsted La AL9, SG13 132 B3
Little Berries LU3 44 E7
Little Bridge Rd [17] HP4 122 D4
Littlebrook Gdns EN8 148 D1
Little Burrow AL7 110 D4
Littlebury Cl SG5 12 A5
Little Bushey La WD23 168 C5
Little Catherells HP1 123 F5
LITTLE CHALFONT 150 B1
LITTLE CHISHILL 18 E7
Little Chishill Rd SG8 18 C8
Little Church Rd LU2 46 B3
Littlecote Pl HA5 175 E2
Little Croft Ct AL2 142 A4
Little Dell AL8 110 D8
Littlefield Rd LU2 46 B2
LITTLE GADDESDEN 102 D7
Little Gaddesden CE Prim Sch HP4 102 C8
Little Gaddesden Ho HP4 102 E6
Little Ganett AL7 111 C4
Little Gr WD23 168 B5
Little Graylings WD5 153 E6
Little Green Jun Sch WD3 166 B6
Littlegreen La LU1 62 E3
Little Green La WD3 166 B6
Little Grove Ave EN7 147 E4
LITTLE HADHAM 57 C2
Little Hadham Prim Sch SG11 57 C2
LITTLE HALLINGBURY 98 D8
Little Hallingbury CE Prim Sch CM22 98 C7
Little Hardings AL7 111 C7
Little Hayes WD4 139 A2
Little Heath CM22 98 F3
LITTLE HEATH
Potten End 123 B5
Potters Bar 145 B2
Little Heath Cotts HP4 123 B4
Little Heath La HP4 123 B4
Little Heath Prim Sch EN6 145 C1
Little Heath Spinney AL3 127 E5
Little Henleys SG12 95 D1
Little Hill WD3 164 C3
Little Hoo HP23 99 F4
LITTLE HORMEAD 42 A6
Little How Croft WD5 153 C8
Little Hyde SG2 51 B4
Little La
Harpenden AL5 107 C6
Pirton SG5 20 D5
Little Lake AL7 111 B3
Little Larkins EN5 171 E3
Little Ley AL7 110 E3
Little Martins WD23 168 B4
Little Mdw LU1 63 B3
Little Mead AL10 130 B8
Little Mimms [2] HP2 124 E4
Little Mollards HP22 60 A3
Little Moss La HA5 175 E1
Little Mundells AL7 110 F8
Little Munden CE Prim Sch SG12 71 E8
Little Orch HP2 125 A5
Little Orchard Cl
Abbots Langley WD5 153 D7
Pinner HA5 175 E1
Little Oxhey La WD19 175 E6
LITTLE PARNDON 117 B1
Little Parndon Sch CM20 117 B1
Little Piper's Cl EN7 147 B2
Little Pk HP3 137 A3
Little Potters WD23 168 E2
Little Rd HP2 124 F4
Little Reddings Prim Sch WD23 168 B4
Little Ridge AL7 111 A6
Little Rivers AL7 111 A7
Little St EN9 163 C3
Little Stock Rd EN7 147 D5
Little Stream Cl HA6 174 E5
Little Thistle AL7 111 C4
LITTLE TRING 99 F6
Little Tring Rd HP23 99 F6
Little Twye HP23 119 F3
Little Twye Rd HP23 119 F3
Little Wade AL7 110 F3
Little Widbury SG12 93 F1
Little Widbury La SG12 93 F1
Little Windmill Hill WD4 151 F7
Little Wlk [7] CM20 117 D1
Little Wood Croft LU3 44 E7
LITTLE WYMONDLEY 35 E3
Little Youngs AL8 110 C6
Liverpool Rd
Luton LU1 63 D7
St Albans AL1 127 E3
Watford WD18 167 B4
Livingstone Ct EN5 171 E7
Livingstone Link SG2 51 B8
Livingstone Wlk HP2 124 F7
Lloyd Mews EN3 163 A1
Lloyd Taylor Cl SG11 57 B2
Lloyd Way SG4 66 C1
Loates La WD17 167 C6
Loates Pasture CM24 59 D8
Local Board Rd WD17 167 D4
Locarno Ave LU4 44 C6
Lochinver House Sch EN6 145 B1
Lochnell Rd HP4 121 F6
Lockers Park La HP1 124 B3
Lockers Park Sch HP1 124 B3
Locket Rd HA3 176 F1
Locket Road Mews [4] HA3 176 E1
Lock Ho HP3 138 E7
Lockley Cres AL10 130 B7
Lockleys Dr AL6 89 C5
Lock View CM21 97 F2
Lockyer Mews EN3 163 B1
Lodge Ave WD6 169 F4
Lodge Cl
Cheddington LU7 80 A7
Hertford SG14 113 C8
Lodge Cres EN8 162 D5
Lodge Ct
Abbots Langley WD25 154 A7
Ickleford SG5 21 E3
Lodge Dr
Hatfield AL9 130 D8
Rickmansworth WD3 165 C5
Lodge End
Croxley Green WD3 166 D5
Radlett WD7 156 B5
Lodge Farm SG4 67 E1
Lodge Farm Prim Sch SG2 51 C7
Lodge Field AL7 89 E1
Lodge Gdns AL5 86 A2
Lodge La EN9 163 D4
Lodge The
Harefield UB9 173 C3
Watford WD24 167 C7
Lodge Way SG2 51 A1
Loftus Cl LU4 44 B3
Logan Ct AL2 142 B4
Logans EN5 171 D6
Loire Mews AL5 107 C7
Lombardy Cl HP2 125 D2
Lombardy Dr HP4 122 D3
Lombardy Way WD6 169 E7
Lomond Rd HP2 124 D7
Lomond Way SG1 37 C3
London Coll of Professional Studies LU1 63 D7
LONDON COLNEY 142 E5
London Colney Jun Mix Inf Sch AL2 142 D6
London Luton Airport LU2 64 D7
London Rd
Aston Clinton HP22 99 A4
Baldock SG7 23 F6
Barkway SG8 17 D1
Barley SG8 8 F1
Berkhamsted HP4 122 E3
Bishop's Stortford CM23 77 A5
Buntingford SG9 40 F6
Bushey WD23 167 F3
Harlow CM17 118 C2
Hemel Hempstead HP1, HP3 124 A1
Hertford Heath SG13 114 B3
Hertford SG13 113 E5
Hitchin SG4 34 F5
Knebworth SG3 69 A3
Langley SG4 49 D5
Luton LU1 84 F7
Luton, New Town LU1 63 E4
Markyate AL3 83 F5
Rickmansworth WD3 173 F7
Royston SG8 7 D5
Sawbridgeworth CM21 97 E2
Shenley WD7 157 A5
Spellbrook CM23 97 F7
St Albans AL1 142 C7
Stevenage SG1, SG2 50 D3
Stotfold SG5 3 A2
Tring HP23 100 C3
Ware SG12 114 E7
Welwyn AL6 89 C4
London Rd/ Moor La Rdbt WD3 173 E8
London Row SG15 11 A3
London School of Theology HA6 174 D4
Londrina Ct [14] HP4 122 D4
Londrina Terr [15] HP4 122 D4
Long Acre CM17 118 B4
Longacres AL4 128 D3
Long Arrotts HP1 124 B5
Long Barn Cl WD25 154 A7
Longbridge Cl HP23 100 A6
Long Buftlers AL5 107 F8
Long Chaulden HP1 123 E3
Long Cl LU2 46 C3
Longcliffe Path WD19 175 A7
Longcroft WD19 167 B2
Long Croft CM24 59 D8
Longcroft Ave AL5 85 F1
Long Croft Dr EN8 163 A5
Longcroft Gdns AL8 110 D5
Longcroft Gn AL8 110 D5
Longcroft Ho AL8 110 D6
Longcroft La
Bovingdon HP3 137 D5
Welwyn Garden City AL8 110 D5
Longcroft Rd
Luton LU1 63 A7
Maple Cross WD3 172 D5
Stevenage SG1 50 E7
Longcrofts EN9 163 E5
Long Cutt AL3 106 A6
Longdean Pk HP3 139 A7
Longdean Sch HP3 139 B8
Long Elmes HA3 176 C2
Long Elms WD5 153 D6
Long Elms Cl WD5 153 D6
Long Fallow AL2 141 A4
Longfield HP3 125 B1
Longfield Ave EN3 162 C1
Longfield Ct SG6 22 D7
Longfield Dr LU4 44 D1
Longfield Gdns HP23 99 E3
Longfield La EN7 148 A4
Longfield Rd
Harpenden AL5 107 C7
Tring HP23 99 F3
Longfields SG2 51 C1
Long Grove Cl EN10 134 E4
Long Hale LU7 80 C3
Long Hedge LU7 80 C4
Long Hyde SG2 51 B4
Long John HP3 124 F1
Long La
Aston SG2 51 E5
Bendish SG4 66 A7
Bovingdon HP3 150 F8
Chorleywood WD3 164 D2
Rickmansworth WD3 172 F8
Longlands HP2 125 A3
Longlands Cl EN8 162 D7
Longlands Prim Sch EN10 148 F6
Longlands Rd AL7 110 F5
Long Leaves SG2 51 A2
Longlees WD3 172 D5
Long Ley
Cheddington LU7 80 A7
Harlow CM20 117 F1
Welwyn Garden City AL7 111 C6
Longman Ct HP3 138 E6
Longmans SG11 55 F7
Longmans Cl WD18 166 C3
LONG MARSTON 79 B4
Long Marston CE Prim Sch HP23 79 B4
Long Marston Rd
Cheddington HP23, LU7 79 E7
Marsworth HP23 79 F2
Long Mdw
Bishop's Stortford CM23 76 D6
Markyate AL3 83 F5
Watton at S SG14 70 D4
Longmead
Buntingford SG9 40 D7
Hatfield AL10 130 B8
Letchworth Garden City SG6 22 E7
Woolmer Green SG3 69 A2
Longmeadow Dr SG5 21 F5
Longmeadow Gn SG2 51 C1
Longmeadow Prim Sch SG2 51 B1
Long Mimms [3] HP2 124 E4
Long Moor EN8 148 E2
Longmore Cl WD3 172 F6
Longmore Gdns AL7 110 F6
Long Pightle Mobile Home Pk WD3 152 F2
Longridge WD7 156 B5
Long Ridge SG2 51 D1
Long Room UB9 173 A3
Long Row SG5 19 D1
Longspring WD24 154 B2
Long Spring AL3 127 F7
Longstanton Ct HP2 105 B1
Long View HP4 122 A6
Long Wlk EN8 149 A1
Longwood Rd SG14 112 F8
Longwood Sch WD23 167 F5
Loning The EN3 162 C1
Lonsdale HP2 124 E6
Lonsdale Cl
Luton LU3 45 B5
Pinner HA5 175 E2
Lonsdale Ct SG1 50 F7
Lonsdale Rd SG1 50 F7
Lonsdale Sch SG1 50 F7
Loom La WD7 156 A2
Loom Pl WD7 156 A3
Loop Rd EN9 163 B7
Loppys Hill CM24 59 E6
Lorane Ct WD17 167 A7
Lord Mead La AL6, SG4 88 C7
Lords Ave CM23 76 B7
Lords Cl WD7 156 E7
Lordship Ctr SG6 23 A3
Lordship Farm SG6 23 B2
Lordship Farm Prim Sch SG6 23 A3
Lordship La SG6 23 B4
Lordship Rd EN7 148 B1
Lords Mdw AL3 106 A5
Lords Pl [15] LU2 45 D1
Lord St
Hoddesdon EN11 134 D6
Watford WD17 167 C6
Lords Wood AL7 111 C6
Loreto Coll AL1 127 E3
Lorimer Cl LU2 45 E6
Loring Rd HP4 122 C3
Lorne Rd HA3 176 F1
Lorraine Pk HA3 176 E3
Lothair Ct [3] AL10 130 A6
Lothair Rd LU2 46 A4
LOUDWATER 165 D6
Loudwater Dr WD3 165 C5
Loudwater Ho WD3 165 C5
Loudwater Hts WD3 165 C6
Loudwater La WD3 165 E5
Loudwater Ridge WD3 165 C5
Louisa Cotts HP23 100 A3
Louise Wlk HP3 137 A3
Louisville Cl SG12 115 C4
Louvain Way WD25 154 B7
Lovatts WD3 166 A5
Love La
Abbots Langley WD5 139 F1
Ashwell SG7 4 A4
Kings Langley WD4 138 E3
Pinner HA5 175 E1
Lovel Cl HP1 124 A3
Lovell Cl SG4 35 A6
Lovell Rd EN1 162 B3
Lovering Rd EN7 147 C6
Lovett Rd AL2 142 A5
Lowbell La AL2 142 E4
Lower Adeyfield Rd HP2 124 D4
Lower Barn HP3 138 F8
Lower Bourne Cl [5] SG12 93 C3
Lower Bourne Gdns SG12 93 C3
Lower Clabdens SG12 93 F1
Lower Cotts SG9 30 B2
Lower Dagnall St AL3 127 C3
Lower Derby Rd [4] WD17 167 C5
Lower Emms HP2 125 C8
LOWER END 79 F3
Lower End HP22 60 B2
Lower Farm Cotts SG18 3 B7
Lowerfield AL7 111 A5
Lower Gn AL6 90 E2
Lower Gower Rd SG8 7 D8
LOWER GREEN
Ickleford 21 E5
Meesden 29 E6
Lower Harpenden Rd LU1, LU2 64 C3
Lower Hatfield Rd SG13 112 F1
Lower High St WD17 167 D4
Lower Icknield Way
Marsworth HP23 80 A1
Wilstone HP22, HP23 99 C7
Lower Innings SG5 34 D8
Lower Kings Rd HP4 122 C5
Lower King St SG8 7 D6
Lower Luton Rd AL4, AL5 86 C3
Lower Mardley Hill AL6 89 F8
Lower Margaret Gdns SG12 93 F3
Lower Mdw EN8 148 D4
LOWER NAZEING 149 E8
Lower Paddock Rd WD19 167 E3
Lower Park Cres CM23 76 F5
Lower Paxton Rd AL1 127 E2
Lower Plantation WD3 165 C6
Lower Rd
Breachwood Green SG4 47 F1
Chorleywood WD3 164 D5
Great Amwell SG12 114 F6
Hemel Hempstead HP3 139 A5
Little Hallingbury CM22 98 C7
Lower Sales HP1 123 F2
Lower Sean SG2 51 A3
LOWER SHEERING 98 A1
Lower Sheering CM21 98 A3
Lower Shott EN7 147 F5
Lower St CM24 59 F7
LOWER STONDON 10 A3
Lower Tail WD19 175 E7
Lower Titmore Gn SG4 35 E1
LOWER TITMORE GREEN 35 F1
Lower Tub WD23 168 D2
Lower Yott HP2 124 F2
Lowes Cl SG1 37 C2
Lowestoft Rd WD24 167 B8
Loweswater Cl WD25 154 C6
Lowewood Mus* EN11 135 A5
Lowfield CM21 97 E1
Lowfield Ct [14] EN11 135 A6
Lowfield La EN11 135 A6
Lowgate La
Dane End SG12 72 A4
Thundridge SG12 72 C5
Low Hill Rd CM19 135 F6
Lowlands AL9 130 C8
Low Rd AL9 131 F8
Lowson Gr WD19 167 E2
Lowswood Cl HA6 174 C2
Lowther Cl WD6 169 F4
Loxley Ct SG12 93 E1
Loxley Rd HP4 121 F6
Loxwood Cl HP3 137 F8
Loyd Ct AL4 128 C1
Lucan Rd EN5 171 E6
Lucas Ct EN9 163 F6
Lucas Gdns LU3 45 B8
Lucas La
Ashwell SG7 4 E4
Hitchin SG5 34 D7
Lucern Cl EN7 147 E4
Lucerne Way LU3 45 C4
Lucida Ct [2] WD18 166 E4
Lucks Hill HP1 123 E3
Ludgate HP23 99 F4
Ludlow Ave LU1 63 E4
Ludlow Mead WD19 175 B7
Ludlow Way WD3 166 C5
Ludwick Cl AL7 110 F4
Ludwick Gn AL7 110 F5
Ludwick Way AL7 110 F5
LUFFENHALL 38 C7
Luffenham Ho [1] WD19 175 D7
Lukes La HP23 79 D3
Lukes Lea HP23 80 A1
Lullington Cl LU2 46 C3
Lullington Garth WD6 170 B4
Lulworth Ave EN7 147 B2
Lumbards AL7 90 A1
Lumen Rd SG8 7 D7
Luna Pl AL1 128 A3
Lunardi Ct SG11 55 C3
Lundin Wlk WD19 175 D6
Lundy Ho WD18 166 F4
LUTON 63 F7
Luton Airport Parkway Sta LU1 64 B5

Luton Dr The LU1 64 B3
Luton & Dunstable Hospl LU4 44 C2
Luton Ent Pk LU3 44 B8
Luton La
Harpenden AL3 85 B1
Redbourn AL3 106 A8
Luton Maternity Hospl LU4 44 C2
Luton Rd
Caddington LU1 63 A4
Cockernhoe LU2 46 E3
Dunstable LU5 44 A1
Great Offley SG5 33 B2
Harpenden AL5 85 D4
Kimpton SG4 66 B2
Luton LU4 44 A7
Markyate AL3 83 F7
Streatley LU3 31 A6
Luton Ret Pk LU1 64 A6
Luton Sixth Form Coll LU2 45 E4
Luton Sta LU2 63 E8
Luton Town FC LU1 63 C8
Luton Univ, Putteridge Bury LU2 46 D6
Luton White Hill SG5 33 B2
Luxembourg Cl LU3 44 D8
Luxford Pl CM21 97 F1
Luynes Rise SG9 40 E6
Lybury La AL3 105 F7
Lycaste Cl AL1 128 A2
Lych Gate WD25 154 D6
Lychgate Cotts HP3 137 B4
Lydekker Mews 1 AL5 86 A2
Lydia Ct AL9 144 C7
Lydia Mews AL9 144 C7
Lye Hill SG4 65 D7
Lye La AL2 141 A2
Lye The HP4 102 D6
Lygean Ave SG12 93 E1
Lygetun Dr LU3 44 F7
Lygrave SG2 69 C8
Lyles La AL8 110 E8
Lyle's Row SG4 34 F6
Lymans Rd SG15 11 A6
Lyme Ave HP4 121 D7
Lymington Ct WD25 154 A5
Lymington Rd SG1 50 B8
Lynbury Ct WD18 167 A6
Lynch Ct AL4 128 D2
Lynch Hill LU6 83 A8
Lynch The EN11 135 B6
Lyndale SG1 50 E4
Lyndhurst Ave HA5 175 B2
Lyndhurst Cl AL5 86 C2
Lyndhurst Dr AL5 86 C2
Lyndhurst Gdns HA5 175 B2
Lyndhurst Rd LU1 63 C7
Lyndhurst Wlk 13 WD6 169 F8
Lyndon Ave HA5 175 E4
Lyndon Mead AL4 108 C2
Lyneham Rd LU2 46 C1
Lyne Way HP1 123 F5
Lynford Cl EN5 170 F4
Lynmouth Rd AL7 110 F6
Lynn Cl HA3 176 D1
Lynsey Cl AL3 106 A6
Lynton Ave
Arlesey SG15 11 A5
St Albans AL1 128 C2
Lynton Crest EN6 159 A7
Lynton Ct CM23 76 E4
Lynton Par EN8 148 D1
Lynwood Ave LU2 46 A3
Lynwood Dr HA6 174 F2
Lynwood Hts WD3 165 C4
Lyon Way AL4 129 A3
Lyrical Way HP1 124 B5
Lysander Cl HP3 137 A4
Lysander Way
Abbots Langley WD5 154 A7
Welwyn Garden City AL7 111 D7
Lys Hill Gdns SG14 113 B8
Lysley Pl AL9 145 C4
Lytham Ave WD19 175 D5
Lytton Almshouses SG3 68 B5
Lytton Ave
Enfield EN3 162 E1
Letchworth Garden City SG6 22 F5
Lytton Fields SG3 68 F5
Lytton Gdns AL8 110 D6
Lytton Rd HA5 175 E3
Lyttons Way EN11 115 A1
Lytton Way SG1 50 C6

M

Mabbutt Cl AL2 140 E1
Mabey's Wlk CM21 97 B1
McAdam Cl EN11 135 A8
Macaulay Rd LU4 44 A2
McClintock Pl EN3 163 B2
McDonald Ct AL10 130 A3
Macdonnell Gdns WD25 153 F4
McDougall Rd 13 HP4 122 D4
Macers Ct EN10 148 F7
Macer's La EN10 148 F7
Macfadyen Webb Ho SG6 23 A7
McGredy EN7 148 B2
Macintosh Cl EN7 147 D5
MacIntyre Sch HP22 60 C3
McKellar Cl WD23 176 C8
McKenzie Rd EN10 135 A3
Mackenzie Sq SG2 51 B3
Mackerel Hall SG8 7 B6
MACKERYE END 86 F4
Maddison Hts 7 WD18 166 F5
Maddles SG6 23 D4
Maddox Rd
Harlow CM20 117 E1
Hemel Hempstead HP2 125 B3
Made Feld SG1 50 F5
Madford Ret Pk LU4 44 F2
Madgeways Cl SG12 114 F5
Madgeways La SG12 114 F5
Madrassa Islamia Sch LU3 45 C2
Madresfield Ct WD7 156 E6
Magdalene Ct SG7 12 F1
Magellan Cl SG2 51 D5
Magisters Lo WD3 166 A3
Magna Cl AL5 107 D6
Magnaville Rd
Bishop's Stortford CM23 76 E4
Bushey WD23 168 F2
Magnolia Ave WD5 154 A7
Magnolia Cl
Hertford SG13 114 A6
Park Street AL2 141 D5
Magpie Cl EN1 162 A1
Magpie Cres SG2 51 D4
Magpie Hall Rd WD23 176 E8
Magpies The LU2 45 E6
Magpie Wlk 2 AL10 130 A3
Maidenhall Prim Sch LU4 45 A2
Maidenhall Rd LU4 45 A2
Maidenhead St 3 SG14 113 D6
Maidenhead Yd SG14 113 D6
Maidensfield AL8 89 D1
Maiden St SG4 24 C1
Main Ave HA6 174 C7
Main Par WD3 164 C5
Main Rd SG14 91 D3
Main Rd N HP4 81 A6
Main Rd S HP4 81 D4
Maison Alfont HA3 176 E2
Maitland Ho 1 HP1 124 D3
Maitland Rd CM24 59 E6
Major Haddock Cl SG8 7 C7
Malden Fields WD23 167 D4
Malden Ho 15 WD19 175 C7
Malden Lodge 2 WD17 167 A7
Malden Rd
Borehamwood WD6 170 A6
Watford WD17 167 B7
Maldon Ct AL5 86 B2
Malham Cl LU4 44 F2
Malin Ct HP3 138 C8
Malins Cl EN5 171 C4
Malkin Way 1 WD18 166 E5
Mallard Ct
3 Bishop's Stortford CM23 77 A6
7 Rickmansworth WD3 165 D2
Mallard Gdns LU3 45 A5
Mallard Mews AL5 86 C3
Mallard Rd
Royston SG8 7 C6
Stevenage SG2 51 D2
Watford WD5 154 A8
Mallards Ct WD19 175 F7
Mallards The HP3 138 F6
Mallard Way
Northwood HA6 174 C3
Roydon CM19 116 A1
Watford WD25 154 E3
Mallion Ct EN9 163 F6
Mallories CM20 117 F2
Mallow The LU3 44 F3
Mallow Wlk
Goff's Oak EN7 147 D3
Royston SG8 7 E5
Mall The AL2 141 C4
Malm Cl WD3 173 D8
Malmes Croft HP3 125 C1
Malmsdale AL8 89 D2
Maltby Dr EN1 162 B1
Malthouse Ct 5 AL1 127 D2
Malthouse Gn LU2 46 F1
Malthouse La SG5 12 A7
Malthouse Pl WD7 156 A5
Malthouse The 15 SG14 113 D6
Malting Cotts SG9 40 D5
Malting La
Aldbury HP23 101 D5
Braughing SG11 55 E7
Dagnall HP4 81 C5
Much Hadham SG10 74 F2
Malting Mead AL10 130 C6
Maltings Cl
Baldock SG7 13 B1
Royston SG8 7 C7
Maltings Ct 2 SG7 23 F8
Maltings Dr AL4 108 C8
Maltings Ind Est The SG12 115 D4
Maltings La SG8 9 E2
Maltings Mews SG13 113 C5
Maltings Orch SG5 20 D3
Maltings The
Abbots Langley WD4 153 C5
Ashwell SG7 4 E4
Hemel Hempstead HP2 124 D4
Letchworth Garden City SG6 12 C1
Pitstone LU7 80 D2
Royston SG8 7 C7
St Albans AL1 127 D3
Walkern SG2 52 B8
Maltsters Lo 9 EN11 135 D8
Malus Cl HP2 125 A4
Malvern Cl
Bushey WD23 168 C3
Hatfield AL10 129 F6
St Albans AL4 128 C7
Malvern Rd
Enfield EN3 162 E2
Luton LU1 63 B7
Malvern Way
Croxley Green WD3 166 B4
Hemel Hempstead HP2 124 F6
Malvern Way Inf Sch WD3 166 C4
Malzeard Ct 20 LU3 45 D1
Malzeard Rd LU3 45 D1
Manan Cl HP3 125 C1
Manchester Cl SG1 36 F3
Manchester St LU1 63 E7
Mancroft Rd LU1 62 E2
Mandela Pl 4 WD24 167 D7
Mandelyns HP4 121 E7
Mandeville SG2 69 C8
Mandeville Cl
Hertford SG13 113 C3
Hoddesdon EN10 134 F3
Watford WD17 153 F1
Mandeville Dr AL1 141 D8
Mandeville Prim Sch
Sawbridgeworth CM21 97 D3
St Albans AL1 141 D8
Mandeville Rd
Enfield EN3 162 E3
Hertford SG13 113 C3
Potters Bar EN6 159 C7
Mandeville Rise AL8 110 D8
Mangrove Dr SG13 113 E4
MANGROVE GREEN 46 E4
Mangrove La SG13 113 E2
Mangrove Rd
Cockernhoe LU2 46 E4
Hertford SG13 113 E5
Luton LU2 46 C2
Manhattan Ave WD18 166 F5
Manhattan Ho 9 WD18 166 E5
Manland Ave AL5 86 C2
Manland Prim Sch AL5 86 B3
Manland Way AL5 86 C3
Manley Highway SG5 34 B7
Manley Highway Cotts SG5 34 A7
Manley Rd HP2 124 E4
Manly Dixon Dr EN3 162 E2
Mannicotts AL8 110 B6
Manning Ct WD19 167 D3
Manning Pl LU2 46 E2
Manor Ave HP3 138 D8
Manor Cl
Barnet EN5 171 E5
Berkhamsted HP4 122 C4
Harpenden AL5 107 A6
Hatfield AL10 129 F8
Hertford SG14 113 D8
Ickleford SG5 21 E3
Letchworth Garden City SG6 22 F3
Manor Cotts
Chorleywood WD3 164 B3
Northwood HA6 174 F2
Nuthampstead SG8 18 D7
Manor Cres SG4 35 B6
Manorcroft Par 6 EN8 148 D1
Manor Ct
Caddington LU1 62 F4
Cheshunt EN8 162 D8
Enfield EN1 162 B3
Harefield UB9 173 C1
Potters Bar EN6 158 F7
Radlett WD7 155 F1
Waltham Abbey EN9 163 D6
Manor Dr AL2 141 A4
Manor Farm Bsns Pk SG5 19 A6
Manor Farm Cl LU4 44 C3
Manor Farm La LU7 61 C8
Manor Farm Rd EN1 162 B4
Manor Farm Stables SG3 68 C5
Manor Fields Prim Sch CM23 76 D5
Manor Ho The 2 HA6 174 F5
Manor House Dr
Northwood HA6 174 B3
Stevenage SG2 51 D7
Manor House Gdns WD5 153 D8
Manor Links CM23 77 C7
Manor Lodge Sch WD7 143 C1
Manor Par AL10 129 F8
Manor Place Ind Est WD6 170 C6
Manor Pound Rd LU7 80 A7
Manor Rd
Barnet EN5 171 E5
Bishop's Stortford CM23 77 A7
Caddington LU1 62 F2
Cheddington LU7 79 F7
Harlow CM17 118 C5
Hatfield AL10 129 F8
Hoddesdon EN11 135 A7
Lea Valley AL4 86 F2
London Colney AL2 142 C5
Luton LU1 63 F6
Potters Bar EN6 159 A8
St Albans AL1 127 E4
Stansted Mountfitchet CM24 59 E5
Tring HP23 100 A4
Waltham Abbey EN9 163 D6
Watford WD17 167 B8
Manorside EN5 171 E5
Manor St HP4 122 D4
Manor View SG2 51 B1
Manorville Rd HP3 138 C7
Manor Way
Borehamwood WD6 170 C6
Cheshunt EN8 148 E1
Croxley Green WD3 166 B5
Letchworth Garden City SG6 22 F3
Potters Bar EN6 145 A1
Mansard Cl HP23 100 A3
Mansards The AL1 127 F4
Manscroft Ho 8 WD19 175 D7
Manscroft Rd HP1 124 B5
Mansdale Rd AL3 105 F4
Manse Ct AL3 83 F5
Mansells La SG4 67 F3
Mansfield CM21 97 A1
Mansfield Ct SG14 113 C8
Mansfield Gdns SG14 113 C8
Mansfield Mews 1 SG7 23 F8
Mansfield Rd
Baldock SG7 23 E8
Luton LU4 45 B1
Mansion Dr HP23 100 B3
Mansion Ho 6 HA6 174 E3
Mansion The HP4 122 E6
Manston Cl EN8 148 C1
Manston Dr CM23 59 B1
Manston Way AL4 128 D2
Manton Dr LU2 45 D3
Manton Rd
Hitchin SG4 35 B6
Holdbrook EN3 163 A1
Manx Cl LU4 45 A2
Maple Ave
Bishop's Stortford CM23 76 D8
St Albans AL3 127 C7
Maple Cl
Bishop's Stortford CM23 76 D8
Hatfield AL10 130 A4
Watford WD23 167 E7
Maple Cotts AL5 107 B5
Maplecroft La EN9 135 E2
MAPLE CROSS 172 D6
Maple Cross Jun Mix Inf Sch WD3 172 E5
Maple Ct
5 Borehamwood WD6 170 A5
17 Luton LU1 63 D6
5 Pinner HA5 175 C1
Stanstead Abbotts SG12 115 D3
Watford WD25 154 D3
Maplefield AL2 141 C2
Maple Flats AL5 86 A3
Maple Gn HP1 123 E5
Maple Gr
Bishop's Stortford CM23 76 D8
Watford WD17 167 A8
Welwyn Garden City AL7 89 F1
Maple Grove Prim Sch HP2 125 A8
Maple Leaf Cl
Abbots Langley WD5 154 A7
Stanstead Abbotts SG12 115 D4
Mapleleaf Villas EN8 148 D4
Maple Lo SG14 113 C5
Maple Lodge Cl WD3 172 E6
Maple Pk EN11 135 C6
Maple Pk AL7 111 A6
Maple Prim Sch AL1 127 E4
Maple Rd AL5 85 F1
Maple Rd E LU4 63 B8
Maple Rd W LU4 63 B8
Maple River Ind Est CM20 118 B6
Maples Ct 1 SG5 34 E7
Maple Spring CM23 76 D8
Maples The
Goff's Oak EN7 147 E3
Hitchin SG4 34 F5
St Albans AL1 127 F3
Maplethorpe Ct SG12 93 C1
Mapleton Cres EN3 162 C1
Maple Way
Kensworth Common LU6 82 E8
Royston SG8 7 E8
Maplewood SG12 93 C3
Maplewood Ct 6 HA6 174 F5
Maran Ave AL6 89 C4
Marbury Pl LU3 44 F4
Marchbank Ho HA6 174 C3
Marchmont Gn HP2 124 D5
Marconi Way AL4 128 D3
Marcus Cl 1 SG1 51 C8
Marden Hill Ho AL6 111 F8
Mardle Cl LU1 62 E2
Mardley Ave AL6 90 A8
MARDLEYBURY 69 C2
Mardleybury Ct SG3 69 A1
Mardleybury Rd SG3 69 B1
Mardley Dell AL6 68 F1
Mardley Hill AL6 69 A1
Mardley Hts AL6 69 A1
Mardley Wood AL6 68 F1
Mardon HA5 175 F3
Mardyke Rd CM20 118 A2
Marford Rd
Hatfield AL4, AL6 109 C7
Wheathampstead AL4 108 E8
Margaret Ave AL3 127 D5
Margaret Cl
Abbots Langley WD5 153 F7
Potters Bar EN6 159 C6
Waltham Abbey EN9 163 D6
Margaret Cotts WD7 156 C8
Margaret Wix Prim Sch AL3 127 C7
Margeholes WD19 175 E8
Margery Wood AL7 90 A1
Margherita Pl EN9 163 F5
Margrave Gdns 4 CM23 76 E5
Marguerite Way CM23 76 C6
Marian Gdns WD25 154 B6
Maricas Ave HA3 176 D2
Marigold Pl CM17 118 B4
Marina Gdns EN8 148 C1
Mariner Way 2 HP2 125 A2
Marion Cl WD23 167 F8
Marion Wlk 4 HP2 124 F8
Markab Rd HA6 175 A5
Markeston Gn WD19 175 D6
Market Hill
Buntingford SG9 40 E7
Royston SG8 7 D5
6 Royston SG8 7 D6
Market Ho 2 CM20 117 D1
Market Oak La HP3 139 A7
Market Pl
Hatfield AL10 130 B6
6 Hertford SG14 113 D6
Hitchin SG5 34 F7
St Albans AL3 127 D3
Stevenage SG1 50 D5
Watford WD17 167 C5
Market Sq
6 Bishop's Stortford CM23 76 F7
Luton LU1 63 B6
Stevenage SG1 50 D5
Waltham Abbey EN9 163 C6
Market St
7 Bishop's Stortford CM23 76 F7
Harlow CM17 118 C4
Hertford SG14 113 D6
Watford WD18 167 B5
Markfield Cl LU3 45 C7
Mark Hall Moors CM20 118 B3
MARK HALL NORTH 118 A3
Mark Hall Sch CM17 118 C3
MARK HALL SOUTH 118 A1
Markham Cl WD6 169 F6
Markham Rd
Hammond Street EN7 147 C6
Luton LU3 45 C8
Mark Rd HP2 125 B5
MARKYATE 83 E6
Markyate Rd LU1 63 B1
Markyate Village Sch AL3 83 D6
Marlands CM21 97 E4
Marlborough Bldgs 2 AL1 127 E3
Marlborough Cl
Bishop's Stortford CM23 76 F5
Oaklands AL6 89 F8
Weston SG4 37 B8
Marlborough Ct
13 Luton LU1 63 D7
Northwood HA6 174 F3
Marlborough Gate AL1 127 E3
Marlborough Ho HP4 122 B3
Marlborough Pk AL5 107 C7
Marlborough Rd
Luton LU3 45 D1
St Albans AL1 127 E3
Stevenage SG2 51 C5
Watford WD18 167 B5
Marlborough Rise HP2 124 E6
Marlborough Sch AL1 141 C8
Marlborough Wks LU3 44 F4
Marle Gdns EN9 163 C7
Marley Ct EN10 148 F8
Marley Rd AL7 111 A4
Marlin Cl HP4 121 F5
Marlin Copse HP4 122 A3
Marlin Hill HP23 120 A8
Marlins Cl WD3 164 E7
Marlins End HP4 121 F3
Marlins Mdw WD18 166 D3

Marlin Sq WD5 153 F8
Marlins The HA6 174 F5
Marlins Turn HP1 124 B6
Marlow Ave LU1 63 A8
Marlowe Cl SG2 51 C8
Marlowes HP1 124 D3
Marlow Ho LU1 63 A8
Marlows Ctr The HP2 124 D2
Marmet Ave SG6 22 E6
Marnham Rise HP1 124 A5
Marquis Bsns Ctr SG7 13 A1
Marquis Cl
Bishop's Stortford CM23 76 B7
Harpenden AL5 86 D2
Marquis Ct
Hoddesdon EN11 135 C8
12 Luton LU2 45 D1
Marquis La AL5 86 D2
Marrilyne Ave EN3 162 F1
Marriott Rd
Barnet EN5 171 D6
Luton LU3 45 B6
Marriotts CM17 118 C5
Marriotts Sch SG2 51 A6
Marriotts Way HP3 124 D1
Marriott Terr WD3 164 F5
Marryat Rd EN1 162 B4
Marschefield SG5 11 E6
Marsden Cl AL8 110 B4
Marsden Gn AL8 110 B4
Marsden Rd AL8 110 C5
Marshall Ave AL3 127 F6
Marshall Rd LU2 46 C2
Marshalls Heath La AL4, AL5 87 A4
Marshall's La SG12, SG11 72 C2
Marshalls Way AL4 86 F2
Marshals Ct AL1 128 B5
Marshal's Dr AL1 128 A6
MARSHALSWICK 128 B6
Marshalswick La AL1 128 B6
Marshbarns CM23 76 C8
Marsh Cl EN8 162 F6
Marshcroft Dr EN8 148 F1
Marshcroft La HP23 100 D6
Marshe Cl EN6 159 D7
MARSH FARM 44 E7
Marshgate SG1 50 D5
Marshgate Dr SG13 113 E7
Marshgate Trad Est SG13 113 E7
Marsh Hill EN9 149 E4
Marsh Ho LU3 44 F4
Marsh La
Harlow CM17 118 E5
Stanstead Abbotts SG12 115 D4
Ware SG12 114 E8
MARSHMOOR 130 D1
Marshmoor Cres AL9 130 D1
Marshmoor La AL9 144 D8
Marsh Rd LU3 44 F4
Marsom Gr LU3 45 B8
Marston Cl HP3 125 A2
Marston Ct HP23 79 B4
Marston Gdns LU2 45 D4
Marston Rd EN11 135 B7
MARSWORTH 80 A1
Marsworth Ave HA5 175 D2
Marsworth CE Inf Sch HP23 80 A2
Marsworth Cl WD18 166 E2
Marsworth Rd LU7 80 D4
Marsworth Resr Nature Reserve* HP23 100 A8
Marten Gate AL4 128 A7
Martham Ct AL5 86 C3
Marthorne Cres HA3 176 D1
Martian Ave HP2 124 F6
Martin Cl AL10 130 A3
Martindale Ct SG7 23 F6
Martindale Prim Sch HP1 123 F4
Martindale Rd HP1 123 F4
Martindales The LU2 63 F7
Martinfield AL7 110 F7
Martinfield Bsns Ctr AL7 110 F7
Martingale Rd SG8 7 E6
Martini Dr EN3 163 A2
Martins Cl WD7 155 E3
Martins Dr
Cheshunt EN8 148 E3
Hertford SG13 114 B6
Martins Way SG1 36 E1
Martins Wlk WD6 170 A5
Martins Wood Prim Sch SG1 37 B1
Martin Way SG6 22 D5
Martlesham AL7 111 E6
Martyr Cl AL1 141 D7
Marwood Cl WD4 138 F2
Mary Barfield Ho SG8 7 D8
Mary Brash Ct LU2 46 C3
Mary Cross Cl HP23 100 D1
Mary Exton Jun Mix Inf Sch SG4 35 C7
Maryland AL10 129 F5
Mary McArthur Pl CM24 59 E8
Marymead Ct SG2 69 A8
Marymead Dr SG2 69 A8
Marymead Ind Est SG2 69 B8
Mary Park Gdns CM23 76 F4
Maryport Rd LU4 45 A2
Mary Proud Ct AL6 89 E7
Mary Way WD19 175 C6
Masefield SG4 35 C7
Masefield Ave
Borehamwood WD6 170 B4
Stanmore HA7 176 F5
Masefield Ct AL5 86 B4
Masefield Rd AL5 86 B4
Masefield Way SG8 2 D1
Maslen Rd AL4 128 C1
Mason Cl WD6 170 D7
Masons Ct CM23 76 E7
Masons Rd
Enfield EN1 162 C3
Hemel Hempstead HP2 125 B4
Mason's Yd 2 HP4 122 D4
Mason Way EN9 163 F6
Massey Ho HP23 100 B5
Masterman Wharf 12 CM23 76 F7
Masters Cl LU1 63 B5
Matching La CM23 76 D8
Mathams Dr CM23 76 D5
Mathews Cl SG1 36 D1
Matisse Ho 5 WD18 166 E5
Matlock Cl EN5 171 D4
Matlock Cres
Luton LU4 44 C1
South Oxhey WD19 175 C7
Matthew Gate SG4 35 A5
Mattocke Rd SG5 21 C1
Maude Cres WD24 154 B1
Maud Jane's Cl LU7 80 E5
Maulden Cl LU2 46 C1
Maxted Cl HP2 125 C5
Maxted Cnr HP2 125 B6
Maxted Rd HP2 125 C6
Maxwell Cl WD3 173 A8
Maxwell Rd
Borehamwood WD6 170 B6
Northwood HA6 174 E3
St Albans AL1 128 B2
Stevenage SG1 50 B5
Maxwell Rise WD19 167 E2
Maxwell's Path SG5 34 D8
Mayall Cl EN3 163 A1
Maybury Ave EN8 148 B3
Maybury Cl EN1 162 B1
May Cl AL3 127 D5
Maycock Gr HA6 174 F4
May Cotts WD18 167 C4
Maycroft
Letchworth Garden City SG6 12 A1
Pinner HA5 175 B1
Maycroft Rd EN7 147 E5
Maydencroft La SG4 34 E3
Maydwell Lo WD6 169 F7
Mayer Rd EN9 163 B3
Mayes Cl CM23 77 D8
Mayfair Cl AL4 128 C8
Mayfair Ct WD18 166 E5
Mayfare WD3 166 D4
Mayfield
Waltham Abbey EN9 163 D5
Welwyn Garden City AL8 89 C2
Mayfield Cl
Harlow CM17 118 F4
Harpenden AL5 85 E3
Mayfield Ct WD23 167 F3
Mayfield Inf Sch EN8 148 E4
Mayfield Pk CM23 76 D3
Mayfield Rd LU2 46 B4
Mayflower Ave HP2 124 D3
Mayflower Cl
Codicote SG4 67 F1
Hertingfordbury SG14 112 E4
Lower Nazeing EN9 149 E8
Mayflower Gdns CM23 76 B6
Mayflower Rd AL2 141 B4
May Gdns WD6 169 D3
Mayhill Rd EN5 171 E3
Maylands Ave HP2 125 B5
Maylands Ct HP2 125 B4
Maylands Rd WD19 175 C6
Mayles Cl SG1 50 B7
Maylin Cl SG4 35 C8
Maylins Dr CM21 97 D2
Maynard Ct
2 Holdbrook EN3 163 A1
Waltham Abbey EN9 163 F5
Maynard Dr AL1 141 D8
Maynard Pl EN6 146 E2
Maynard Rd HP2 124 D2
Mayne Ave
Luton LU4 44 C4
St Albans AL3 127 A2
Mayo Cl EN8 148 C3
Mayo Gdns HP1 124 B2
Maypole St CM17 118 C1
Mayshades Cl SG3 69 A2
Mays La EN5 171 D3
May St
Great Chishill SG8 9 E2
Luton LU1 63 E5
Maythorne Cl WD18 166 E5
Maytree Cres WD24 153 F4
Maytree La HA7 176 F3
Maytrees
Hitchin SG4 35 A6
Radlett WD7 156 A2
Maze Green Hts CM23 76 C7
Maze Green Rd CM23 76 D7
Mazoe Cl CM23 76 F5
Mazoe Rd CM23 76 F5
Mead Bsns Ctr SG13 113 E7
Mead Cl
Harrow HA3 176 D2
Stevenage SG1 50 F6
Mead Ct
Stansted Mountfitchet CM24 59 D7
Waltham Abbey EN9 163 B5
Meadgate Rd EN9 135 C3
Mead Ho AL10 130 B8
Mead La SG13 113 E7
Mead Lo 3 EN11 135 D8
Meadow Ave WD7 156 C8
Meadowbank
Hitchin SG4 22 B1
Kings Langley WD4 139 A1
Watford WD19 167 C2
Meadowbank Cl HP3 137 B3
Meadowbanks EN5 171 A4
Meadowbrook HP23 100 B6
Meadow Cl
Barnet EN5 171 F3
Bricket Wood AL2 141 A2
Datchworth SG3 69 D1
Enfield EN3 162 E1
Hertford SG13 113 F7
London Colney AL2 142 D4
Radlett WD7 142 C1
St Albans AL4 128 C6
Tring HP23 100 A4
Welham Green AL9 144 D7
Meadowcroft
Berkhamsted HP4 121 D7
Bushey WD23 168 B3
St Albans AL1 142 A8
Stansted Mountfitchet CM24 59 E7
Meadow Croft
Caddington LU1 62 F4
Hatfield AL10 129 F5
Meadow Cross EN9 163 E5
Meadow Dell AL10 129 F5
Meadow Gn AL8 110 C6
Meadow La LU7 80 E3
Meadowlands CM23 59 A2
Meadow Rd
Berkhamsted HP4 122 B6
Borehamwood WD6 170 B7
Bushey WD23 168 B4
Hemel Hempstead HP3 139 A7
Luton LU3 45 B4
Watford WD25 154 B5
Meadowside WD25 154 B8
Meadows The
Bishop's Stortford CM23 76 E5
Breachwood Green SG4 47 E1
Hemel Hempstead HP1 123 E4
Sawbridgeworth CM21 98 A2
Meadows View Cotts SG12 94 C7
Meadowsweet Cl CM23 76 C6
Meadow The
Hertford Heath SG13 114 E2
Welwyn Garden City AL7 111 C6
Meadow View
Buntingford SG9 40 D6
Redbourn AL3 106 A8
Meadow Way
Bedmond WD5 139 F4
Caddington LU1 62 E4
Codicote SG4 67 E1
Great Offley SG5 33 C3
Hitchin SG5 34 D6
Kings Langley WD4 139 A1
Letchworth Garden City SG6 22 F5
Potters Bar EN6 159 A5
Rickmansworth WD3 165 C2
Sawbridgeworth CM21 98 A1
Stevenage SG1 50 F5
Stotfold SG5 11 F6
Therfield SG8 16 A6
Meadow Way The HA3 176 E2
Meadow Wlk
Harpenden AL5 107 C8
Standon SG11 55 E2
Meadow Wood Sch WD23 168 C4
Mead Park Ind Est CM20 117 F4
Mead Pl WD3 165 B1
Mead Rd WD7 157 A6
Meads Ind Est AL4 87 D1
Meads La AL4 87 D1
Meads Prim Sch The LU3 45 A6
Meads The
Berkhamsted HP4 121 F6
Bricket Wood AL2 140 F2
Letchworth Garden City SG6 22 E6
Luton LU3 45 A3
Stansted Mountfitchet CM24 59 F6
Tring HP23 100 B4
Mead The
Cheshunt EN8 148 C2
Hitchin SG5 21 F2
Hoddesdon EN10 135 B2
South Oxhey WD19 175 E7
Mead View SG9 43 E6
Meadview Rd SG12 114 D8
Meadway
Barnet EN5 171 F5
Berkhamsted HP4 122 E5
Colney Heath AL4 143 D8
Enfield EN3 162 D3
Harpenden AL5 107 E8
Meadway *continued*
Hoddesdon EN11 135 A4
Knebworth SG3 68 F4
Stevenage SG1 50 A6
Stevenage SG1 50 B7
Welwyn Garden City AL7 110 F4
Mead Way WD23 167 E7
Meadway Cl HA5 176 B4
Meadway Ct SG1 50 B6
Meadway The EN6 146 F2
Meautys AL3 127 A1
Medalls Link SG2 51 A3
Medalls Path SG2 51 A3
Medcalf Rd EN3 162 F2
Medina Rd LU4 45 A1
Medlows AL5 85 E2
Medow Mead WD7 155 F6
Medway Cl WD25 154 C5
Medway Rd HP2 124 F8
Medwick Mews HP2 125 B8
Mees Cl LU3 31 A1
MEESDEN 29 F6
Meeting Alley WD17 167 C5
Meeting House La
Baldock SG7 12 E1
Buntingford SG9 40 E7
Megg La WD4 138 B1
Melbourne Cl
St Albans AL3 127 F7
Stotfold SG5 11 F6
Melbourne Ct
Cheshunt EN8 162 F5
Welwyn Garden City AL8 110 B5
Melbourne Rd WD23 168 B3
Melbourn Rd SG8 7 D7
Melbourn St SG8 7 D6
MELDRETH 2 F8
Melford Cl 3 LU2 46 D1
Melia Cl WD25 154 C4
Melings The HP2 125 B8
Melne Rd SG2 69 B8
Melrose Ave
Borehamwood WD6 170 B4
Potters Bar EN6 159 B7
Melrose Ct EN8 148 D2
Melrose Pl WD17 153 F1
Melson Sq 8 LU1 63 E7
Melson St LU1 63 E7
Melsted Rd HP1 124 B3
Melvern Cl SG2 69 B7
Melvyn Cl EN7 147 B3
Memorial Ct LU3 44 F4
Memorial Rd LU3 44 F4
Mendip Cl AL4 128 C8
Mendip Rd WD23 168 C3
Mendip Way
Hemel Hempstead HP2 124 E6
Luton LU3 44 C8
Stevenage SG1 37 B4
Mendlesham AL7 111 E6
Mentley La SG11 54 E4
Mentley La E SG11 55 D4
Mentley La W SG11 55 C4
MENTMORE 61 D4
Mentmore* LU7 61 C4
Mentmore Cross Rds LU7 60 F6
Mentmore Rd
Cheddington LU7 79 F8
St Albans AL1 127 E1
Mentmore View HP23 99 F5
Mepham Cres HA3 176 C3
Mepham Gdns HA3 176 C3
Mercer Pl HA5 175 C1
Mercers HP2 124 E5
Mercers Ave CM23 76 C4
Mercers Row AL1 127 C1
Merchant Dr SG13 113 F7
Merchants Wlk SG7 13 B1
Merchant Taylors' Sch HA6 166 E1
Mercia Rd SG7 24 A8
Mercury Ct AL10 129 E6
Mercury Ho 8 WD18 166 E5
Mercury Wlk 1 HP2 124 F6
Mereden Ct AL1 141 C8
Meredews SG6 23 B7
Meredith Cl HA5 175 D3
Meredith Rd SG1 51 A8
Merefield CM21 97 E1
MERIDEN 154 E3
Meriden Ho 4 EN5 171 E5
Meriden Way WD25 154 E2
Meridian Bsns Pk EN9 163 B4
Meridian Ho EN10 135 C2
Meridian Sch SG8 7 E7
Meridian Way
Stanstead Abbotts SG12 115 B5
Waltham Abbey EN9 163 B4
Merle Ave UB9 173 C1
Merlin Ctr The AL4 128 F3
Merling Croft HP4 121 E7
Merlin Way WD25 153 F5
Mermaid Cl SG4 35 B7
Merrick Cl SG1 37 B4
Merrifield Ct AL7 110 D3
Merrill Pl 2 CM23 76 E5
Merritt Wlk AL9 144 B8
Merrow Dr HP1 123 E4
Merrows Cl HA6 174 C4
Merryfield WD17 154 A1
Merryfields AL4 128 E3
MERRY HILL 168 B1
Merry Hill Inf Sch WD23 168 B2
Merry Hill Mount WD23 168 B1
Merry Hill Rd WD23 168 B1
Mersey Pl
Hemel Hempstead HP2 124 F8
1 Luton LU1 63 D7
Merton Ct 6 WD6 169 F8
Merton Rd
Enfield EN2 161 D1
Watford WD18 167 B5
Meryfield Cl WD6 169 F7
Meryfield Prim Sch WD6 169 F8
Metford Cres EN3 163 A1
Metro Ctr
St Albans AL4 127 F7
Watford WD18 166 D2
Metropolitan Mews 10 WD18 166 E5
Metropolitan Pl WD18 166 F5
Metropolitan Station App WD18 166 F5
Meux Cl EN7 162 A8
Mews The
Bishop's Stortford CM22 77 A3
3 Harpenden AL5 86 B1
Letchworth Garden City SG6 12 C1
Sawbridgeworth CM21 97 E3
St Albans AL1 127 E5
Stansted Mountfitchet CM24 59 F7
Meyer Gn EN1 162 A1
Meyrick Ave LU1 63 C6
Meyrick Ct
Luton LU1 63 D6
St Albans AL1 128 B3
Mezen Cl HA6 174 D5
Michael Muir Ho SG5 21 D1
Michaels Rd CM23 59 A2
Michigan Cl EN10 148 E5
MICKLEFIELD GREEN 152 B1
Micklefield Green Cotts WD3 152 B2
Micklefield Rd HP2 125 C3
Micklefield Way WD6 156 E1
Micklem Dr HP1 123 F4
Micklem Prim Sch HP1 124 A4
Midcot Way HP4 121 F6
Midcroft Ho HP23 100 A3
Middle Down WD25 155 B3
Middle Drift SG8 7 C6
Middlefield
Hatfield AL10 130 A6
Welwyn Garden City AL7 110 E3
Middlefield Ave EN11 135 A8
Middlefield Cl
Hoddesdon EN11 135 A8
St Albans AL4 128 C6
Middlefield La SG16 10 C7
Middlefield Rd EN11 135 A8
Middlefields SG6 11 F1
Middlefields Ct SG6 11 F1
Middle Furlong WD23 168 B5
Middle Hill HP1 123 E3
Middleknights Hill HP1 124 A6
Middle La HP3 137 A1
Middlemarch SG5 11 C3
Middle Ope WD24 154 B2
Middle Rd
Berkhamsted HP4 122 B4
Waltham Abbey EN9 163 B7
Middle Row
5 Bishop's Stortford CM23 76 F6
1 Stevenage SG1 50 C7
Middlesborough Cl SG1 36 F2
Middle St EN9 149 F8
Middleton Rd
Luton LU2 46 D4
Rickmansworth WD3 165 A1
Middleton Sch SG12 114 D7
Middle Way WD24 154 B2
Middle Way The HA3 176 F1
Midhurst SG6 22 F8
Midhurst Gdns LU3 45 C4
Midland Cotts SG5 22 A1
Midland Ho 7 AL1 127 E3
Midland Rd
Hemel Hempstead HP2 124 D3
Luton LU2 63 E8
Midland Way SG16 10 B3
Midway AL3 141 B8
Mike Mably Ho AL10 129 F7
Milbourne Ct 1 WD17 167 A7
Milburn Cl LU3 31 B1
Milby Ct 4 WD6 169 F8
Mildmay Rd SG1 37 B1
Mildred Ave
Borehamwood WD6 170 B5
Watford WD18 167 A5
Mile Cl EN9 163 C6
Mile House Cl AL1 142 A8

Mile House La AL1 142 A8
Milestone Cl SG2 51 D4
Milestone Rd
Harlow CM17 118 C2
Hitchin SG5 21 D2
Knebworth SG3 69 A5
Milford Cl AL4 128 D7
Milford Hill AL5 86 D4
Milksey La SG4 36 C5
Millacres 1 SG12 93 E1
Milland Ct WD6 170 D8
Millard Way SG4 22 C1
Millbank HP3 138 D7
Mill Bridge
Barnet EN5 171 F3
Hertford SG14 113 C6
Millbridge Mews 2
SG14 113 C6
Millbrook Ct SG12 93 D2
Millbrook Rd WD23 167 F8
Millbrook Sch EN8 148 D2
Mill Cl
Buntingford SG9 40 E7
Hatfield AL8 110 A5
Hemel Hempstead, Nash Mills HP3 139 A6
Hemel Hempstead, Piccotts End HP1 124 B7
Hitchin SG4 35 C8
Stotfold SG5 12 A6
Ware SG12 93 D1
Wingrave HP22 60 A3
Mill Cnr
Barnet EN5 171 F8
Roydon CM19 116 A1
Mill Cotts
Barkway SG8 17 C5
Wingrave LU7 60 D8
Millcrest Rd EN7 147 B3
Millcroft CM23 59 A1
Mill Ct CM20 117 D3
MILL END
Rickmansworth 173 A8
Rushden 25 E4
Sandon 26 E6
Mill End SG11 55 F2
Millennium Ct WD3 165 E2
Millennium Wharf 1
WD3 165 E1
Miller Ave EN3 163 A1
Miller Cl
Pinner HA5 175 C1
Redbourn AL3 106 B5
Millers Cl CM23 76 C5
Millers Ct SG14 113 D5
Millers Ho The SG12 115 D4
Millers La SG12 115 C4
Millers Rise AL1 127 E2
Millers View SG10 74 E1
Miller Way SG1 50 E6
Mill Farm Cl HA5 175 C1
Millfield
Berkhamsted HP4 122 D5
Thundridge SG12 93 E8
Welwyn Garden City AL7 111 C7
Mill Field CM17 118 C4
Millfield Cl AL2 142 D5
Millfield Fst Sch SG9 40 E7
Millfield Ho WD18 166 D3
Millfield La
Caddington LU1 62 D2
Hitchin SG4 34 F4
Little Hadham SG11 75 D8
Millfield Rd LU3 45 B3
Millfields
Sawbridgeworth CM21 97 F3
Stansted Mountfitchet CM24 59 E6
Millfield Way LU1 62 D3
Millfield Wlk HP3 139 A8
Mill Gdns HP23 100 A4
MILL GREEN 130 E8
Millgreen Cotts AL9 131 F8
Mill Green La AL9 110 E1
Mill Green Rd AL7 110 E5
Mill Green Watermill & Mus* AL9 130 D8
Mill Ground Cotts SG4 24 C1
Mill Hatch CM20 118 A4
Mill Hill
Farnham CM23 58 E5
Royston SG8 7 E4
Stansted Mountfitchet CM24 59 E6
Millhoo Ct EN9 163 F5
Millhouse La WD5 140 A4
Millhurst Mews CM17 118 E4
Milligan Cl LU4 44 D4
Milliners Ct
Luton LU3 45 C1
St Albans AL1 127 E3
Milliners Way
Bishop's Stortford CM23 76 C4
Luton LU3 45 C1
Mill La
Albury SG11 57 C6
Arlesey SG15 10 F4
Cheshunt EN8 148 E3
Flamstead AL3 84 A1
Harlow CM17 118 E4
Hatfield Heath CM22 98 F3
Hexton SG5 19 C3
Hitchin SG4 34 F3
Mill La *continued*
Hoddesdon EN10 135 A2
Kings Langley WD4 139 A2
Meesden SG9 30 A5
Sawbridgeworth CM21 97 F3
Stotfold SG5 12 A6
Therfield SG8 15 F8
Watton at S SG12 71 A6
Welwyn AL6 89 C5
Weston SG4 24 C1
Wingrave HP22 60 C2
Mill Lane Cl EN10 134 F2
Mill Mead Prim Sch SG14 113 C6
Millmead Way SG14 113 B6
Mill Race SG12 115 D4
Mill Rd
Hertford SG14 113 D6
Royston SG8 7 D7
St Ippolyts SG4 35 A3
Millside CM23 77 A5
Mill Side CM24 59 E6
Mill St
Ashwell SG7 4 D4
Berkhamsted HP4 122 C4
Bishop's Stortford CM23 77 A5
Hemel Hempstead HP3 138 D8
Luton LU1 63 D8
Millstream Cl
Hertford SG14 113 B6
Hitchin SG4 22 A1
Mill Stream Lo WD3 173 A8
Mill Studio Bsns Ctr 6 SG12 93 E1
Mill The HP23 79 C1
Millthorne Cl WD3 165 F4
Mill View AL2 141 D4
Mill View Rd HP23 99 F4
Millwards AL10 130 B2
Mill Way
Breachwood Green SG4 47 D2
Rickmansworth WD3 164 F1
Watford WD23 167 E8
Mill Wlk 11 AL4 87 D1
Millwood Ct SG5 11 F6
Millwright Wlk HP3 138 F6
Milne Cl SG6 23 B3
Milne Field HA5 176 A3
Milner Cl WD25 154 B6
Milner Ct
Bushey WD23 168 B3
Luton LU2 63 E8
Milneway UB9 173 B2
Milton Ave EN5 171 F4
Milton Cl SG8 2 C1
Milton Ct
Hammond Street EN7 147 F5
12 Harpenden AL5 86 B1
Hemel Hempstead HP2 105 B1
Waltham Abbey EN9 163 C5
Milton Dene HP2 125 B8
Milton Dr WD6 170 B4
Milton Rd
Harpenden AL5 86 B1
Luton LU1 63 C6
Ware SG12 93 D2
Milton St
Waltham Abbey EN9 163 C5
Watford WD24 167 B8
Milton View SG4 35 C7
Milverton Gn LU3 45 A7
Mimms Hall Rd EN6 158 D7
Mimms La EN6, WD7 157 C6
Mimram Cl SG4 66 E7
Mimram Pl AL6 89 C5
Mimram Rd
Hertford SG14 113 B5
Welwyn AL6 89 C5
Mimram Wlk AL6 89 C5
Minall Cl HP23 99 F4
Minchen Rd CM20 118 A1
Minderhall Ct SG1 50 C7
Minehead Way SG1 50 A7
Mineral Cl EN5 171 C4
Minerva Cl 3 SG1 51 C8
Minerva Dr WD24 153 E3
Minims The AL10 130 A7
Minister Ct AL2 141 E3
Minoan Dr HP3 138 E7
Minorca Way LU4 44 A3
Minsden Rd SG2 51 D3
Minster Cl AL10 130 A3
Minster Ho AL10 130 A3
Minster Rd SG8 7 C8
Minstrel Cl HP1 124 B4
Minstrel Ct HA3 176 E1
Missden Dr HP3 125 C1
Missenden Ho WD18 166 E2
Miss Joans Ride HP4, LU6 81 E7
Mistletoe Ct LU2 64 C8
Mistletoe Hill LU2 64 C8
Mistley Rd CM20 118 A2
Mistral Ct 5 AL1 128 A2
Miswell La HP23 99 F3
Mitchell Cl
Abbots Langley WD5 154 A7
Bovingdon HP3 136 F4
St Albans AL1 141 D7
Welwyn Garden City AL7 111 C6
Mitre Bldgs 3 CM20 117 C1
Mitre Ct 20 SG14 113 D6
Mitre Gdns CM23 77 A4
Mixes Hill Ct LU2 46 A4
Mixes Hill Rd LU2 45 F4
Mixies The SG5 11 E6
Moakes The LU3 44 E7
Moat Cl WD23 168 B4
Moatfield Rd WD23 168 B4
Moat La
Luton LU3 45 B4
Wingrave HP22 60 B2
Moatside SG9 29 B7
Moat The SG11 55 D3
Moatview Ct WD23 168 B4
Moatwood Gn AL7 110 E5
Mobbsbury Way SG2 51 C7
Mobley Gn LU2 46 B3
Modena Mews 13
WD18 166 E5
Moffats Cl AL9 145 A5
Moffats La AL9 144 F5
Moira Cl LU3 44 D7
Molescroft AL5 85 D4
Moles La SG9 28 A3
Molesworth EN11 115 A2
Molewood Rd SG14 113 B7
Mollison Ave EN3 163 A3
Molteno Rd WD17 167 A8
Molyneaux Ave HP3 136 F4
Momples Rd CM20 118 B1
Monarch Hall LU2 64 C8
Monarch's Way EN8 162 E6
Monarch Wlk WD7 156 F6
Monastery Cl AL3 127 C3
Monet Ho 2 WD18 166 E5
MONEYHILL 165 B1
Moneyhill Ct WD3 165 B1
Money Hill Par WD3 165 C1
Money Hill Rd WD3 165 C1
Money Hole La AL6 111 E7
Monica Cl WD24 167 D7
MONKEN HADLEY 171 E7
Monkhams Hall EN9 149 C2
Monklands SG6 22 D6
Monks Cl
Hoddesdon EN10 135 A3
Letchworth Garden City SG6 22 C6
Redbourn AL3 106 B5
St Albans AL1 127 E1
Monks Gate AL1 127 E1
Monks Horton Way
AL1 128 A4
Monksmead WD6 170 C5
Monksmead Sch WD6 170 C6
Monks Rise AL8 89 D2
Monks Row 7 SG12 93 D2
Monks View SG2 50 F2
Monks Walk Sch AL8 89 C3
Monkswick Rd CM20 117 F1
Monks Wlk SG9 40 E7
Monkswood AL8 89 C2
Monkswood Ave EN9 163 D6
Monkswood Dr CM23 76 D6
Monkswood Gdns
WD6 170 D5
Monkswood Ret Pk SG1 50 E3
Monkswood Way SG1 50 E3
Monmouth Rd WD17 167 B6
Monro Gdns HA3 176 E3
Monro Ind Est EN8 162 E5
Mons Ave SG7 23 F6
Mons Cl AL5 107 D6
Monson Rd EN10 134 F3
Montacute Rd WD23 168 E2
Montague Ave LU4 44 C6
Montague Cl 5 EN5 171 F5
Montague Hall Pl
WD23 168 A3
Montague Rd HP4 122 B4
Montayne Rd EN8 162 D7
Monterey Lo HA6 174 E4
Montesole Ct 6 HA5 175 C1
Montessori At Little Cheverells AL3 83 D4
Montfitchet Wlk SG2 51 D7
Montgomerie Cl HP4 122 A6
Montgomery Ave
HP2 125 A4
Montgomery Dr EN8 148 E3
Monton Cl LU3 44 F6
Montrose Ave LU3 45 C3
Montrose Rd HA3 176 F1
Monument Pl AL3 127 D4
Moon La EN5 171 F6
Moorend AL7 111 A3
Moor End Rd HP1 124 C2
Moore Rd HP4 121 F6
Moorfields SG9 41 E8
MOOR GREEN 39 D2
Moor Hall La CM23 76 B3
Moor Hall Rd CM17 118 F4
Moorhen Way CM19 116 A1
Moorhurst Ave EN7 147 B2
Moorings The
Bishop's Stortford CM23 77 A5
Radlett WD7 156 A6
St Albans AL1 127 F4
Watford WD23 167 E5
Moor La
Moor Park WD3 174 A8
Sarratt WD3 151 E3
Moorland Gdns LU2 63 D8
Moorland Rd
Harpenden AL5 86 B4
Hemel Hempstead HP1 124 A1
Moorlands
Park Street AL2 141 E3
Welwyn Garden City AL7 111 A3
Moorlands Reach
CM21 98 A1
Moorlands Sch LU4 44 C3
Moor Lane Crossing
WD18 166 C2
Moormead Cl SG5 34 D6
Moormead Hill SG5 34 D6
Moor Mill La AL2 141 E2
MOOR PARK 174 D6
Moor Park Rd HA6 174 D4
Moor Park Sta HA6 174 D7
Moor Pk Ind Ctr WD18 166 C2
Moor's Farm Cotts
HP5 136 B4
Moorside
Hemel Hempstead HP3 138 B8
Welwyn Garden City AL7 111 A3
Moors Ley SG2 38 B1
Moor St LU1 63 C8
Moors The AL7 111 A7
Moors Wlk AL7 111 C6
Moortown Rd WD19 175 C6
Moor View WD18 167 A3
Moorview Ho HP2 124 D1
Moorymead Cl SG14 70 D3
Moran Cl AL2 154 F8
Moray Ho HA6 174 D3
Morecambe Cl
Luton LU4 44 B3
Stevenage SG1 50 B7
Morefields HP23 100 A6
Moremead EN9 163 D6
Moreton Ave AL5 85 F2
Moreton Cl EN7 148 B4
Moreton End Cl AL5 85 F2
Moreton End La AL5 85 F2
Moreton Pk Ind Est LU2 46 A2
Moreton Pl AL5 85 F3
Moreton Rd N LU2 46 A2
Moreton Rd S LU2 46 A2
Morgan Cl
Luton LU4 44 E3
Northwood HA6 174 F4
Stevenage SG1 36 D1
Morgan Gdns WD25 155 B2
Morgans Cl SG13 113 D4
Morgans Jun Mix & Inf Sch SG13 113 D4
Morgan's Rd SG13 113 D4
Morgan's Wlk SG13 113 D3
Morice Rd EN11 134 F8
Morland Way EN8 148 E3
Morley Gr CM20 117 C2
Morley Hill EN2 161 D1
Morningside WD3 165 C1
Mornington AL6 90 A4
Mornington Rd WD7 156 B5
Morpeth Ave WD6 156 F1
Morpeth Cl 3 HP2 124 E2
Morrell Cl LU3 45 A7
Morrell Ct AL7 110 F7
Morrello Gdns SG4 35 A5
Morris Cl
Lower Stondon SG16 10 C5
Luton LU3 44 E8
Morris Ct
Holdbrook EN3 163 A2
Waltham Abbey EN9 163 F5
Morrison Ct 7 EN5 171 E5
Morriston Cl WD19 175 C5
Morris Way AL2 142 D5
Morse Cl UB9 173 C1
Mortain Dr HP4 121 F6
Mortimer Cl
Bushey WD23 168 B3
Luton LU1 63 A7
Mortimer Gate EN8 148 F4
Mortimer Hill HP23 100 B4
Mortimer Rd SG8 7 E7
Mortimer Rise HP23 100 B4
Morton Cl LU7 80 C4
Morton St SG8 7 D7
Morven Cl EN6 159 C8
Mosquito Way AL10 129 E7
Mossbank Ave LU2 64 C8
Moss Bury Prim Sch SG1 51 A7
Moss Cl
Pinner HA5 175 F1
Rickmansworth WD3 173 D8
Mossdale Ct 3 LU4 44 C5
Mossendew Cl UB9 173 D2
Moss Gn AL7 110 E4
Moss La HA5 175 E1
Mossman Dr LU1 62 E4
Moss Rd WD25 154 B5
Moss Side AL2 140 F1
Moss Way SG5 21 C1
Mostyn Rd
Bushey WD23 168 C4
Luton LU3 44 E4
Motts Cl SG14 70 D4
MOTT'S GREEN 98 D6
Mott St EN9 163 D1
Moules Yd SG7 4 D3
Moulton Ct 3 LU2 63 F8
Moulton Rise LU2 63 F8
Mountbatten Cl AL1 142 B8
Mount Cl HP1 123 F3
Mount Dr
Park Street AL2 141 D6
Stansted Mountfitchet CM24 59 E5
Mounteagle SG8 7 D5
Mountfield Rd
Hemel Hempstead HP2 124 E3
Luton LU2 45 E2
Mountfitchet Castle & Norman Village* CM24 59 F6
Mountfitchet Maths & Computing Coll The CM24 59 F4
Mountfitchet Rd CM24 59 E5
Mount Garrison SG4 34 F7
Mountgrace Rd LU2 46 C6
Mount Grace Rd EN6 159 B8
Mount Grace Sch EN6 159 B8
Mountjoy SG4 22 C1
Mount Keen SG1 37 C3
MOUNT PLEASANT 173 A2
Mount Pleasant
Harefield UB9 173 A2
Hertford Heath SG13 114 C4
Hitchin SG5 34 D6
St Albans AL3 127 C3
Mount Pleasant Cl
AL9 130 D8
Mount Pleasant Flats
SG1 50 E8
Mount Pleasant La
Bricket Wood AL2 140 E1
Hatfield AL9 130 C8
Mount Pleasant Lane Jun Mix & Inf Sch AL2 140 E1
Mount Pleasant Rd
LU3 44 E5
Mount Rd
Hertford SG14 113 A5
Wheathampstead AL4 87 D1
Mountside HA7 176 F2
Mount Sorrel SG13 113 F6
Mount The
Barley SG8 8 F1
Hammond Street EN7 147 D5
5 Luton LU3 63 D8
Potters Bar EN6 145 B1
Rickmansworth WD3 165 C3
Mount Vernon Hospl HA6 174 B4
Mountview HA6 174 F4
Mount View
Enfield EN2 160 F1
London Colney AL2 142 F4
Rickmansworth WD3 165 B1
Mountview Cotts EN5 170 F3
Mountview Rd EN7 147 E5
Mountway EN6 145 A1
Mount Way AL7 110 F3
Mountway Cl AL7 110 F3
Mowat Ind Est WD24 154 C1
Mowbray Cres SG5 11 F7
Mowbray Gdns SG4 35 A5
Mowbray Rd CM20 118 A3
Mowbrays The SG5 11 F7
Moxes Wood LU3 44 E7
Moxom Ave EN8 148 E1
Moxon St EN5 171 F6
Mozart Ct SG1 50 C5
MUCH HADHAM 74 F3
Muddy La SG6 22 F3
Muirfield LU2 45 E6
Muirfield Cl WD19 175 C6
Muirfield Gn WD19 175 C6
Muirfield Rd WD19 175 C6
Muirhead Way SG3 68 F5
Mulberry Cl
Cheshunt EN10 148 F7
Chiswell Green AL2 141 B3
Luton LU1 63 B7
Stotfold SG5 11 F5
Tring HP23 100 A5
Watford WD17 153 E3
Mulberry Ct
Bishop's Stortford CM23 77 A5
5 Hemel Hempstead HP1 124 D4
Royston SG8 7 D5
Mulberry Gdns WD7 156 E6
Mulberry Gn CM17 118 D4
Mulberry Lo WD19 167 D3
Mulberry Mead AL10 109 F1
Mulberry Pl AL3 106 B4
Mulberry Terr CM17 118 B4
Mulberry Way SG5 21 D2
Mull Ho WD18 166 F4
Mullion Cl
Harrow HA3 176 B2
Luton LU2 46 B5
Mullion Wlk WD19 175 D6
Mullway SG6 22 C6
Mulready Wlk HP3 138 E7
Mundells
Hammond Street EN7 148 A4
Welwyn Garden City AL7 111 A8
Mundells Ct AL7 110 F8
Munden Gr WD24 154 D1
Munden Rd SG12 71 E7
Munden View WD25 154 D3
Mundesley Cl
South Oxhey WD19 175 C6
Stevenage SG1 36 B1
Mungo-Park Cl
WD23 176 C8
Munro Rd WD23 168 C4
Muntings The SG2 51 A3
Munts Mdw SG4 24 C1
Murchison Rd EN11 115 B1

Muriel Ave WD18 167 C4
Murray Cres HA5 175 D2
Murray Rd
Berkhamsted HP4 122 C6
Northwood HA6 174 E3
Murrell La SG5 12 A5
Murton Ct AL1 127 E4
Museum Ct HP23 100 A3
Museum of St Albans* AL1 127 E3
Musgrave Cl EN7 147 F4
Muskalls Cl EN7 148 A4
Muskham Rd CM20 118 B3
Musk Hill HP1 123 E2
Musleigh Manor SG12 93 F1
Musley Hill SG12 93 E2
Musley La SG12 93 E2
Mus of Harlow* CM20 118 B3
Mussons Path LU2 45 E1
Muswell Cl LU3 45 B6
Mutchetts Cl WD25 154 E6
Mutford Croft 2 LU2 46 D1
Mutton La EN6 158 E8
Myddelton Ave EN1 161 E1
Myddelton House Gdns* EN2 162 A3
Myddleton Path EN7 162 B8
Myddleton Rd SG12 114 D8
Myers Cl WD7 156 E7
Myles Ct EN7 147 C2
Mylne Cl EN8 148 C4
Mylne Ct EN11 135 A8
Mymms Dr AL9 145 B4
Mymms Ho AL9 144 C8
Mymwood Cl AL9 145 C4
Myrtle Cotts
Sarratt WD3 152 A3
Tring HP23 100 C8
Myrtle Gdns SG16 10 A3
Myrtle Gn HP1 123 E4
Myrtle Gr EN2 161 D1
Myrtleside Cl HA6 174 D3
Myson Way CM23 77 B7

N

Nags Head Cl SG13 114 B7
Nails La 15 CM23 76 F7
Nairn Cl AL5 107 D6
Nairn Gn WD19 175 A7
Nan Aires HP22 60 A3
Nancy Downs WD19 167 C2
Napier Cl AL2 142 D6
Napier Ct
Cheshunt EN8 148 B3
Luton LU1 63 D7
Napier Dr WD23 167 E5
Napier Hall LU2 64 C8
Napier Rd LU1 63 D7
Nappsbury Rd LU4 44 D5
Napsbury Ave AL2 142 C5
Napsbury La AL1 142 A7
NAPSBURY PARK 142 B5
Nap The WD4 139 A2
Nascot Pl WD17 167 B7
Nascot Rd WD17 167 B7
Nascot St WD17 167 B7
Nascot Wood Inf Sch WD17 154 A1
Nascot Wood Jun Sch WD17 154 A1
Nascot Wood Rd WD17 153 F1
Naseby Rd LU1 63 B7
Nash Cl
Borehamwood WD6 169 F5
Datchworth SG3 69 E2
Stevenage SG2 51 B6
Welham Green AL9 144 D8
Nashe's Farm La AL4 128 E8
Nash Gn HP3 138 F6
NASH MILLS 139 A6
Nash Mills CE Prim Sch HP3 138 F6
Nash Mills La HP3 138 F5
Nash Rd SG8 7 D5
NASTY 54 D6
Nathaniel Wlk HP23 100 A5
Nathans Cl AL6 89 C6
Navigation Ho 23 CM23 76 F7
Nayland Cl LU2 46 E1
Nazeingbury Cl EN9 135 D1
Nazeingbury Par EN9 135 D1
Nazeing Glass Works EN10 135 C2
NAZEING MEAD 135 D3
Nazeing New Rd EN10 135 B2
Nazeing Prim Sch EN9 149 E8
Nazeing Rd EN9 135 D1
Neagh Cl SG1 37 C3
Neagle Cl WD6 170 C8
Neal Cl HA6 175 A2
Neal Ct
Hertford SG14 113 C6
Waltham Abbey EN9 163 F6
Neal St WD18 167 C4
Nectar Ct 1 EN11 135 D8
Necton Rd AL4 108 E8
Needham Rd LU4 44 B6
Neighbourhood Ctr The SG1 37 B3
Neild Way WD3 164 F2
Nell Gwynn Cl WD7 156 E7
Nelson Ave AL1 142 B8
Nelson Rd
Bishop's Stortford CM23 77 A5
Dagnall HP4 81 C5
Nelson St SG14 113 B7
Nene Rd SG16 10 B4
Neptune Ct WD6 170 A6
Neptune Dr HP2 124 E5
Neptune Gate SG2 51 D8
Neston Rd WD24 154 C2
Netherby Cl HP23 100 C6
Nethercott Cl LU2 46 C1
Netherfield Ct SG12 115 D3
Netherfield La SG12 115 E3
Netherfield Rd AL5 107 B4
Netherhall Rd CM19 135 F5
Nether St SG12 95 E4
Netherstones SG5 11 F7
NETHER STREET 95 E5
Netherway AL3 141 A8
Netley Dell SG6 23 B3
NETTESWELL 117 F1
Netteswell Cross CM20 117 E2
Netteswell Orch CM20 117 D1
Netteswell Rd CM20 117 F3
Netteswell Twr 5 CM20 117 D1
Nettlecroft
Hemel Hempstead HP1 124 B2
Welwyn Garden City AL7 111 B7
NETTLEDEN 103 B1
Nettleden Rd
Little Gaddesden HP4 102 E4
Nettleden HP1 103 C1
Potten End HP4 123 B8
Nevell's Gn SG6 22 F6
Nevells Rd SG6 22 F6
Nevil Cl HA6 174 D5
Neville Cl EN6 158 F8
Neville Rd LU3 45 A5
Neville Road Pas LU3 45 A5
Neville's Ct SG6 23 B7
Nevill Gr WD24 167 B8
Nevis Rd SG1 37 A4
Newark Cl SG8 7 C8
Newark Gn WD6 170 D6
Newark Rd LU4 45 A2
New Barnes Ave AL1 142 A8
New Barn La CM22 77 D1
New Barns La SG10 74 E4
New Bedford Rd
Luton, High Town LU1 63 D8
Luton LU3 45 D3
Newberries Ave WD7 156 B4
Newberries Prim Sch WD7 156 C4
Newbiggin Path WD19 175 C6
Newbold Rd LU3 45 B7
Newbolt SG8 7 D8
Newbolt Rd HA7 176 F5
Newbury Ave EN3 162 F2
Newbury Cl
Bishop's Stortford CM23 76 E8
Luton LU4 44 E2
Stevenage SG1 36 D1
Newcastle Cl SG1 36 F3
New Cl SG3 68 F6
Newcombe Rd LU1 63 C7
Newcome Path WD7 157 A5
Newcome Rd WD7 157 A5
New Cotts
Bendish SG4 66 A7
Brookmans Park AL9 144 D3
Cheshunt EN8 162 C5
Markyate AL3 83 E6
New Ct SG3 69 A2
Newdigate Gn UB9 173 D2
Newdigate Rd UB9 173 C2
Newdigate Rd E UB9 173 D2
Newell La SG2 38 D7
Newell Rd HP3 138 E8
Newell Rise HP3 138 E8
Newells SG6 23 D4
Newells Hedge LU7 80 D5
New England Cl SG4 34 F4
New England Est EN11 135 C7
New England St AL3 127 C3
New Farm SG8 2 A8
New Farm La HA6 174 E2
Newfield La HP2 124 F3
Newfields AL8 110 B5
Newfield Way AL4 128 D1
New Ford Bsns Pk EN8 162 F5
Newford Cl HP2 125 B4
New Ford Rd EN8 162 F5
New Forge Pl AL3 106 B5
Newgate SG2 51 A4
Newgate Cl AL4 128 D6
NEWGATE STREET 146 E7
Newgatestreet Rd EN7 147 B4
Newgate Street Village SG13 146 E6
NEW GREENS 127 D7
New Greens Ave AL3 127 D7
NEW GROUND 101 A2
Newground Rd HP23 101 B3
New Hall Cl HP3 137 A4
Newhall Ct EN9 163 F6
Newhouse Cres WD25 154 B6
New House Pk AL1 142 B7
Newhouse Rd HP3 137 A4
New Inn Rd SG7 3 D5
New Kent Rd AL1 127 D3
Newland Cl
Pinner HA5 175 F4
St Albans AL1 142 A8
Newland Gdns SG13 113 E6
Newlands
Hatfield AL9 130 C7
Letchworth Garden City SG6 23 A3
Newlands Ave WD7 155 F5
Newlands Cl E SG4 34 F4
Newlands Cl W SG4 34 F4
Newlands Cvn Site WD5 139 F5
Newlands La SG4 34 F3
Newlands Pl EN5 171 D4
Newlands Rd
Hemel Hempstead HP1 123 E3
Luton LU1 63 C3
Newlands Way EN6 145 B1
Newlands Wlk WD25 154 D6
Newlyn Cl
Bricket Wood AL2 140 E1
Stevenage SG1 50 A6
Newlyn Ho 10 HA5 175 F3
Newlyn Rd EN5 171 F5
Newman Ave SG8 7 F6
Newmans Ct SG14 70 D3
Newmans Dr AL5 85 F2
Newmarket Ct AL3 127 C4
Newmarket Rd SG8 7 E6
NEW MILL 100 A6
NEW MILL END 64 D1
New Mill Terr HP23 100 B6
NEWNHAM 12 E8
Newnham Cl LU2 46 D1
Newnham Par 5 EN8 148 D1
Newnham Rd SG7 12 E6
Newnham Way SG7 4 B2
New Par WD3 164 C5
New Park Dr HP2 125 B3
New Park La SG2 51 F2
New Park Rd
Harefield UB9 173 C2
Newgate Street SG13 146 D7
New Path CM23 76 F6
New Pl AL6 89 B4
Newport Cl EN3 162 E2
Newport Mead WD19 175 D6
Newports CM21 97 C1
New Provident Pl 7 HP4 122 D4
Newquay Gdns WD19 175 B8
New Rd
Berkhamsted HP4 122 D6
Berkhamsted, Northchurch HP4 121 F7
Chipperfield WD4 137 F1
Croxley Green WD3 166 A4
Elstree WD6 169 D3
Great Chishill SG8 9 D6
Harlow CM17 118 D4
Hatfield AL8 110 A3
Hertford SG14 113 D8
Hoddesdon EN10 135 A4
Little Hadham SG11 75 A7
Lower Stondon SG17 10 A8
Radlett, Letchmore Heath WD25 168 E8
Radlett WD7 155 E2
Sarratt WD3 151 F1
Shenley WD7 157 A5
South Mimms EN6 158 A6
Tring HP23 100 B6
Ware SG12 93 D1
Watford WD17 167 C5
Welwyn AL6 89 F3
Woolmer Green SG3 69 B3
New River Ave SG12 115 B4
New River Cl EN11 135 B7
New River Ct EN7 162 B8
New River Trad Est EN8 148 D5
NEWSELLS 17 D7
New St
Berkhamsted HP4 122 D4
Cheddington LU7 79 F7
5 Luton LU1 63 D6
Sawbridgeworth CM21 97 E3
Slip End LU1 63 C1
Watford WD18 167 C5
New Station Cotts EN10 135 A3
Newstead AL10 129 F2
Newstead Ho UB9 173 C1
Newteswell Dr EN9 163 D7
Newton Cl
Harpenden AL5 107 D6
Hoddesdon EN11 115 B2
Newton Cres WD6 170 C5
Newtondale LU4 44 C5
Newton Dr CM21 97 D1
Newton Rd
Harrow HA3 176 E1
Stevenage SG2 51 B6
Newtons Way SG4 34 F6
NEWTOWN 40 F8
NEW TOWN 76 F5
New Town SG4 67 F1
NEW TOWN 63 E5
Newtown Rd CM23 76 F6
New Town Rd 9 LU1 63 E6
New Town St LU1 63 E6
New Wood AL7 111 C7
Nexus Ct AL1 127 D2
Niagara Cl EN8 148 D2
Nicholas Breakspear RC Sch AL4 128 E2
Nicholas Cl
St Albans AL3 127 D6
Watford WD24 154 B2
Nicholas La 26 SG14 113 D6
Nicholas Pl SG1 36 D1
Nicholas Rd WD6 169 F4
Nicholas Way
Hemel Hempstead HP2 124 F5
Northwood HA6 174 C2
Nicholls Cl AL3 105 F5
Nicholls Yd SG8 16 F5
Nichols Cl LU2 46 C2
Nicholson Ct EN11 135 B6
Nickelby Way SG5 11 C2
Nickmar Ct LU3 45 D2
Nicola Cl HA3 176 D1
Nicoll Way WD6 170 D5
Nicolson Dr WD23 176 C8
Nidderdale HP2 124 F6
Nightingale Ave SG8 2 A5
Nightingale Cl
Kneesworth SG8 2 A6
Luton LU2 46 C6
Radlett WD7 155 F3
Watford WD5 154 A8
Nightingale Ct
Hertford SG14 113 C6
Hitchin SG5 35 A8
1 Luton LU3 63 C8
Radlett WD7 156 A4
Rickmansworth WD3 165 C2
Nightingale La AL1, AL4 142 C7
Nightingale Lo HP4 122 B4
Nightingale Pl WD3 165 D2
Nightingale Rd
Bushey WD23 168 A4
Hammond Street EN7 147 C6
Hitchin SG5 34 F8
Rickmansworth WD3 165 C2
Nightingales
Bishop's Stortford CM23 77 B7
Waltham Abbey EN9 163 E5
Nightingale Terr SG15 11 A3
Nightingale Way
Baldock SG7 23 F6
Royston SG8 7 E8
Nightingale Wlk
Hemel Hempstead HP2 105 C1
Stevenage SG2 51 C5
Nimbus Way SG4 35 C7
Nimmo Dr WD23 168 D2
Nimrod Cl AL4 128 C5
Nimrod Dr AL10 129 D6
Nine Acre La AL10 129 F4
Nine Ashes SG12 116 D7
Ninefields EN9 163 F6
Ninesprings Way SG4 35 B6
Ninfield Ct LU2 46 C3
Ninian Rd HP2 124 E8
Ninnings Cotts AL5 107 A8
Ninning's La AL6 68 D2
Ninth Ave LU3 44 D7
Niton Cl EN5 171 D3
Niven Cl WD6 170 C8
Noahs Court Gdns SG13 113 E5
Noake Mill La HP1 124 A8
Nobel Sch The SG2 51 C7
Nobel Villas EN9 163 D5
NOBLAND GREEN 95 A8
Nobles The CM23 76 D6
Nodes Dr SG2 51 A1
Node Way Gdns AL6 89 C3
Noke La AL2 140 E4
Noke Lane Bsns Ctr AL2 140 F4
Noke Shot AL5 86 C4
Nokeside SG2 69 B8
Noke Side AL2 141 A4
Nokes The HP1 124 A5
Noke The SG2 69 B8
Nolan Path 10 WD6 169 F8
Nook The SG12 115 B4
Norbury Ave WD24 167 C7
NORCOTT HILL 101 D2
Norfolk Ave WD24 154 C1
Norfolk Ct
5 Barnet EN5 171 E5
7 Rickmansworth WD3 165 E1
Norfolk Gdns WD6 170 D5
Norfolk Rd
Buntingford SG9 40 E8
Luton LU2 64 A7
Rickmansworth WD3 165 E1
Norfolk Way CM23 76 F5
Norman Ave CM23 76 D6
Norman Cl
St Albans AL1 141 E8
Waltham Abbey EN9 163 D6
Norman Cres HA5 175 C2
Norman Ct
Potters Bar EN6 145 C1
Stansted Mountfitchet CM24 59 E7
Stevenage SG1 36 F1
Normandy Ave EN5 171 F5
Normandy Ct HP1 124 D4
Normandy Dr HP4 122 B6
Normandy Ho EN2 161 C1
Normandy Rd AL3 127 D4
Normandy Way EN11 135 D8
Norman Rd
Luton LU3 45 B2
Welwyn AL6 89 B3
Normans Cl SG6 11 F1
Normansfield Cl WD23 168 B2
Normans La AL6 68 E2
Norman's La SG8 7 D5
Norman's Way CM24 59 E7
Norrington End AL3 84 E1
Norris Cl
Bishop's Stortford CM23 77 C7
London Colney AL2 142 B5
Norris Gr EN10 134 E3
Norris La EN11 135 A7
Norris Rd EN11 135 A6
Norris Rise EN11 134 F7
Norris Works 23 SG14 113 D6
North App
Moor Park HA6 174 C8
Watford WD25 154 A5
North Area Pupil Referral Unit SG6 22 D3
North Ave
Letchworth Garden City SG6 23 B8
Shenley WD7 156 E7
NORTHAW 146 A1
Northaw CE Prim Sch EN6 146 A1
Northaw Cl HP2 125 B8
Northaw Pk EN6 159 F7
Northaw Rd E EN6 146 E1
Northaw Rd W EN6 160 C8
North Barn EN10 135 B1
Northbridge Rd HP4 122 A6
Northbrook Dr HA6 174 E3
Northbrook Rd EN5 171 E3
NORTHCHURCH 121 D6
Northchurch La HP4, HP5 121 D2
Northchurch St Mary's CE Fst Sch HP4 121 E6
North Cl
Barnet EN5 171 C4
Chiswell Green AL2 141 B6
Royston SG8 7 C7
Northcliffe Dr N20 171 F1
North Comm AL3 106 A5
North Common Rd AL3 106 A4
Northcote 3 HA5 175 C1
Northcotts AL9 130 C6
North Cotts AL2 142 A6
Northcourt WD3 165 A1
North Ct AL3 83 E5
Northdown Rd AL10 130 A2
North Dr
Hatfield AL10 130 C7
High Cross SG11 72 E1
Letchford Garden City SG5 11 C3
St Albans AL4 128 E5
North Drift Way LU1 63 B6
Northend HP3 125 C1
NORTH END 15 D6
North End SG8 15 D6
Northern Ave SG16 10 C3
Northern Ho
Hitchin SG4 35 B7
Hitchin SG4 35 B7
Northfield
Braughing SG11 55 F7
Hatfield AL10 130 B8
Standon SG11 55 E2
Northfield Gdns WD24 154 C2
Northfield Rd
Aldbury HP23 100 F7
Borehamwood WD6 170 B8
Cheshunt EN8 162 E7
Guilden Morden SG7 1 C2
Harpenden AL5 86 C4
Sawbridgeworth CM21 97 E4
Northfields
Letchford Garden City SG6 11 F1
Stansted Mountfitchet CM24 59 E7
Northfields Inf Sch SG6 11 F1
Northgate HA6 174 C3
North Gate CM20 117 C1
Northgate End CM23 76 F8
Northgate Ho EN8 148 D2
Northgate Path 1 WD6 169 F8
Northgate Prim Sch CM23 76 E8
North Gn SG14 91 F1
North Hertfordshire Coll SG1 50 D4
North Hertfordshire Coll (Goldsmith Ctr) SG6 22 F5
North Hertfordshire Coll (Hitchin Ctr) SG4 35 B8
North Hill WD3 164 E8
Northlands EN6 159 D8

North Luton Ind Est LU4 ... 44 B7
NORTH MYMMS ... 144 A5
Northolt Ave CM23 ... 59 B1
North Orbital Commercial Pk AL1 ... 142 A7
North Orbital Rd
Bricket Wood AL2 ... 140 E2
Chiswell Green AL2 ... 141 B5
Colney Heath AL4 ... 129 C2
London Colney AL1, AL2, AL4 ... 142 D6
Park Street AL2 ... 141 E6
Watford WD25 ... 154 D7
North Pl
Harlow CM20 ... 118 B5
Hitchin SG5 ... 21 D1
4 Waltham Abbey EN9 ... 163 B6
North Rd
Baldock SG7 ... 12 E2
Berkhamsted HP4 ... 122 B4
Cheshunt EN8 ... 162 E6
Chorleywood WD3 ... 164 D4
Hertford, Broadoak End SG14 ... 113 A7
Hertford SG14 ... 113 C6
Hoddesdon EN11 ... 135 A7
Stevenage SG1 ... 36 C2
North Ride AL6 ... 89 C6
Northridge Way HP1 ... 124 A3
North Riding AL2 ... 141 A1
North Road Ave SG14 ... 113 A7
North Road Gdns SG14 ... 113 B6
Northside AL4 ... 108 B1
North St
4 Bishop's Stortford CM23 ... 76 F7
Lower Nazeing EN9 ... 135 E1
Luton, Hart Hill LU2 ... 45 E1
Luton, High Town LU2 ... 63 E8
North Terr 5 CM23 ... 76 F8
Northumberland Ave EN1 ... 162 B1
North View Cotts SG12 ... 95 D4
Northview Rd LU2 ... 45 F2
NORTH WATFORD ... 154 B2
Northway
Rickmansworth WD3 ... 165 D2
1 Welwyn Garden City AL7 ... 89 F1
Northwell Dr LU3 ... 44 F7
North Western Ave
Bushey WD23, W25 ... 168 C6
Stanmore WD6 ... 169 A2
Watford, Garston WD24 ... 154 C3
Watford, Leavesden Green WD2 ... 153 D4
Northwick Rd WD19 ... 175 C6
NORTHWOOD ... 174 D2
Northwood AL7 ... 111 D6
Northwood Cl EN7 ... 147 F4
Northwood Coll HA6 ... 174 D3
NORTHWOOD HILLS ... 174 F1
Northwood Hills Cir HA6 ... 175 A2
Northwood Hills Sta HA6 ... 175 A1
Northwood & Pinner Hospl HA6 ... 175 A2
Northwood Prep Sch WD3 ... 174 C8
Northwood Rd UB9 ... 173 E3
Northwood Sch HA6 ... 175 B2
Northwood Sta HA6 ... 174 E3
Northwood Way
Harefield UB9 ... 173 D2
Northwood HA6 ... 175 A3
NORTON ... 12 C1
NORTON BURY ... 12 C2
Norton Bury La SG6 ... 12 D3
Norton Cl WD6 ... 170 A8
Norton Cres SG7 ... 23 E8
NORTON GREEN ... 50 B3
Norton Green Rd SG1 ... 50 C4
Norton Rd
Letchworth Garden City SG5, SG6, SG7 ... 12 C2
Luton LU3 ... 44 F4
Stevenage SG1 ... 50 D4
Norton Road Prim Sch LU3 ... 44 F4
Norton St Nicholas CE Prim Sch SG6 ... 12 C1
Norton Street La SG4 ... 67 B7
Norton Way N SG6 ... 23 A7
Norton Way S SG6 ... 23 A5
Norvic Rd HP23 ... 80 A1
Norwich Cl SG1 ... 37 B1
Norwich Ho 5 WD6 ... 170 A7
Norwich Way WD3 ... 166 B5
Norwood Cl SG14 ... 112 F7
Norwood Rd EN8 ... 148 E1
Nottingham Cl WD25 ... 154 A6
Nottingham Rd WD3 ... 164 C1
Novello Way WD6 ... 170 D8
Nugents Ct HA5 ... 175 E2
Nugent's Pk HA5 ... 175 F2
Numbers Farm WD4 ... 139 C2
Nunfield WD4 ... 152 B8
Nunnery Cl AL1 ... 127 E1
Nunnery La LU3 ... 45 B5
Nunnery Stables AL1 ... 127 D1
Nunsbury Dr EN10 ... 148 E6
Nunsbury Drive Cotts EN10 ... 148 E6
Nun's Cl SG5 ... 34 E7
Nuns La AL1 ... 141 E8
NUP END ... 60 B3
Nup End Bsns Pk SG3 ... 68 B4
Nup End Cl HP22 ... 60 B3
Nup End La HP22 ... 60 B3
Nupton Dr EN5 ... 171 C3
Nurseries Rd AL4 ... 108 E7
Nursery Cl
Bishop's Stortford CM23 ... 76 F6
Stevenage SG2 ... 69 A8
Watford WD19 ... 167 B1
Nursery Cotts SG1 ... 50 A6
Nursery Ct SG6 ... 22 F6
Nursery Fields CM21 ... 97 D2
Nursery Gdns
Goff's Oak EN7 ... 147 D3
Tring HP23 ... 100 B4
Ware SG12 ... 93 E1
Welwyn Garden City AL7 ... 89 E1
Nursery Hill
Hitchin SG4 ... 34 F6
Welwyn Garden City AL7 ... 89 E1
Nursery Par LU3 ... 44 E5
Nursery Rd
Bishop's Stortford CM23 ... 76 F6
4 Cheshunt EN10 ... 148 F6
Hoddesdon EN11 ... 115 B1
Lower Nazeing EN9 ... 135 D2
Luton LU3 ... 44 F5
Nursery Row 5 EN5 ... 171 E6
Nursery Terr HP4 ... 123 B7
Nutcroft SG3 ... 69 D2
Nutfield AL7 ... 90 A1
Nut Gr AL8 ... 89 D1
NUTHAMPSTEAD ... 18 A2
Nuthampstead Rd SG8 ... 17 E2
Nutleigh Gr SG5 ... 21 D1
Nut Slip SG9 ... 40 E6
Nuttfield Cl WD3 ... 166 B3
Nutwood Gdns 5 EN7 ... 147 E5
Nye Way HP3 ... 137 A3
Nymans Cl LU2 ... 46 D3

O

Oak Ave
Bricket Wood AL2 ... 141 A1
Enfield EN2 ... 160 F1
Oakbank WD7 ... 156 B3
Oak Cl
Hemel Hempstead HP3 ... 138 F7
Waltham Abbey EN9 ... 163 D5
Oak Court Bsns Ctr AL3 ... 127 F8
Oakcroft Cl HA5 ... 175 B1
Oak Ct HA6 ... 174 D4
Oakdale AL8 ... 89 D1
Oakdale Ave HA6 ... 175 A1
Oakdale Cl WD19 ... 175 C6
Oakdale Rd WD19 ... 175 C6
Oakdene EN8 ... 148 E1
Oakdene Cl HA5 ... 175 F3
Oakdene Rd
Hemel Hempstead HP3 ... 138 F7
Watford WD24 ... 154 B3
Oakdene Way AL1 ... 128 C3
Oak Dr
Berkhamsted HP4 ... 122 D3
Sawbridgeworth CM21 ... 118 C8
Oak End SG9 ... 40 D7
Oaken Gr AL7 ... 110 E3
Oak Farm WD6 ... 170 C4
OAKFIELD ... 35 B6
Oakfield WD3 ... 165 A2
Oakfield Ave SG4 ... 35 B5
Oakfield Cl EN6 ... 158 F8
Oakfield Rd AL5 ... 107 A5
Oakfields SG2 ... 51 C1
Oakfields Ave SG3 ... 69 A6
Oakfields Cl SG2 ... 51 C1
Oakfields Rd SG3 ... 69 A6
Oak Glade HA6 ... 174 B2
Oak Gn WD5 ... 153 E7
Oak Gr
Hatfield AL10 ... 129 F5
Hertford SG13 ... 113 E4
Oak Green Way WD5 ... 153 E7
Oak Hall CM23 ... 76 E8
Oakhill SG6 ... 23 D4
Oakhill Ave HA5 ... 175 E1
Oakhill Cl WD3 ... 172 E6
Oakhill Ct EN5 ... 171 D5
Oakhill Dr AL6 ... 89 A6
Oakhill Rd WD3 ... 172 D6
Oak Ho HA6 ... 174 B2
Oakhurst HP2 ... 125 B8
Oakhurst Ave AL5 ... 107 A5
Oakhurst Pl WD18 ... 166 F5
Oakhurst Rd EN3 ... 162 D3
Oakington AL7 ... 111 D6
Oak La
Cholesbury HP23 ... 120 B2
Cuffley EN6 ... 146 F3
Graveley SG4 ... 36 C4
OAKLANDS ... 89 F7
Oaklands HP4 ... 122 A4
Oaklands Ave
Brookmans Park AL9 ... 144 E4
Oaklands Ave *continued*
Watford WD19 ... 167 B1
Oaklands Cl CM23 ... 59 B2
Oaklands Coll AL1 ... 127 E3
Oaklands Coll (Borehamwood Campus) WD6 ... 170 C7
Oaklands Coll Smallford Campus AL4 ... 128 E4
Oaklands Coll (Welwyn Garden City Campus) AL8 ... 110 D7
Oaklands Ct
Oaklands AL6 ... 89 E7
Watford WD17 ... 167 A8
Oaklands Dr CM23 ... 59 B2
Oaklands Gate HA6 ... 174 E4
Oaklands Gr EN10 ... 148 E7
Oaklands La
Arkley EN5 ... 171 B5
St Albans AL4 ... 128 F5
Oaklands Pk CM23 ... 59 B2
Oaklands Prim Sch AL6 ... 89 E7
Oaklands Rd
Hammond Street EN7 ... 147 E5
Totteridge N20 ... 171 F2
Oaklands Rise AL6 ... 89 F7
Oaklands Wood AL10 ... 130 A5
Oakland View AL6 ... 89 F7
Oaklawn HP23 ... 100 A3
Oaklea AL6 ... 89 E7
Oaklea Cl AL6 ... 89 E8
Oaklea Wood AL6 ... 89 E7
Oakleigh Ct CM23 ... 76 D8
Oakleigh Dr WD3 ... 166 C3
Oakleigh Rd HA5 ... 175 F4
Oakley Cl LU4 ... 44 D4
Oakley Ct SG8 ... 7 D7
Oakley Rd
Harpenden AL5 ... 107 D7
Luton LU4 ... 44 E3
Oakmeade HA5 ... 176 A4
Oakmede 6 EN5 ... 171 D5
Oakmere Ave EN6 ... 159 C6
Oakmere Cl EN6 ... 159 D8
Oakmere La EN6 ... 159 C7
Oakmere Prim Sch EN6 ... 159 D7
Oak Path WD23 ... 168 B3
Oak Piece AL6 ... 89 E7
Oak Piece Ct AL6 ... 89 E7
Oak Pk SG12 ... 95 B1
Oak Rd
Luton LU4 ... 63 C8
Woolmer Green SG3 ... 69 B1
Oakridge AL2 ... 140 F2
Oakridge Ave WD7 ... 155 F6
Oakridge La WD7 ... 155 E5
Oakroyd Ave EN6 ... 158 F6
Oakroyd Cl EN6 ... 158 F6
Oaks Cl
Hitchin SG4 ... 34 F5
Radlett WD7 ... 155 F4
Oaks Cross SG2 ... 51 B1
Oaks Ret Pk CM20 ... 117 F3
Oak St
Bishop's Stortford CM23 ... 76 F6
Hemel Hempstead HP3 ... 138 F7
Oaks The
Berkhamsted HP4 ... 122 A4
Slip End LU1 ... 63 C1
Watford WD19 ... 167 C1
Oaktree Cl
14 Bishop's Stortford CM23 ... 76 F7
Goff's Oak EN7 ... 147 B3
Oak Tree Cl
Abbots Langley WD5 ... 153 D7
Benington SG2 ... 52 F4
Hatfield AL10 ... 130 A6
Hertford Heath SG13 ... 114 C3
Letchworth Garden City SG6 ... 22 E4
Oaktree Cotts SG12 ... 114 F6
Oak Tree Ct
Elstree WD6 ... 169 D3
Oaklands AL6 ... 89 E8
Oaktree Garth AL7 ... 110 E5
Oak Tree Row LU2 ... 46 A2
Oak View WD18 ... 166 E6
Oakview Cl
Cheshunt EN7 ... 148 B3
Harpenden AL5 ... 106 F5
Watford WD19 ... 167 C3
Oak View Prim Sch AL10 ... 130 B4
Oakway LU6 ... 82 B7
Oak Way AL5 ... 107 A5
Oakway Pl WD7 ... 156 A5
Oakwell Cl SG2 ... 69 D7
Oakwell Dr EN6 ... 160 B7
Oakwood
Berkhamsted HP4 ... 121 F3
Waltham Abbey EN9 ... 163 E5
Oakwood Ave WD6 ... 170 B5
Oakwood Cl SG2 ... 51 C2
Oakwood Dr
Harpenden AL5 ... 106 F5
Luton LU3 ... 44 C8
St Albans AL4 ... 128 C4
Oakwood Est CM20 ... 118 B4
Oakwood Mews 5 CM17 ... 118 C4
Oakwood Prim Sch AL4 ... 128 C4
Oakwood Rd
Bricket Wood AL2 ... 140 F2
Pinner HA5 ... 175 B1
Oban Terr LU1 ... 63 B8
Oberon Cl WD6 ... 170 C8
Obrey Way CM23 ... 76 E3
Observer Dr WD18 ... 166 E5
Occupation Rd WD18 ... 167 B4
Octagon The SG12 ... 93 D2
Octavia Ct WD24 ... 167 C7
Oddfellows Ct 10 SG14 ... 113 D6
Oddy Hill
Tring HP23 ... 100 C3
Wigginton HP23 ... 100 C2
Odeon Par WD24 ... 154 B3
ODSEY ... 5 C1
Odyssey Rd WD6 ... 170 B8
Offa Rd AL3 ... 127 C3
Offas Way AL4 ... 108 D8
Offerton Ho 13 WD19 ... 175 C7
Offley Cross SG5 ... 34 B5
Offley Endowed Prim Sch SG5 ... 33 C3
Offley Hill SG5 ... 33 C3
Offley Rd SG5 ... 34 D6
Ogard Rd EN11 ... 135 C8
Okeford Cl HP23 ... 99 F4
Okeford Dr HP23 ... 99 F4
Okeley La HP23 ... 99 E3
Old Airfield Ind Est HP23 ... 79 E5
Old Bakery SG5 ... 34 E7
Old Barn La WD3 ... 165 F4
Old Barn Mews WD3 ... 165 F4
Old Bedford Rd
Luton LU2 ... 45 E4
Luton, Warden Hill LU2 ... 45 D6
Old Bell Cl CM24 ... 59 D6
Old Bourne Way SG1 ... 37 A3
Old Brewery Cl SG5 ... 11 F7
Old Brewery Pl SG4 ... 66 D1
Old Chantry La SG4 ... 35 F2
Old Chapel Mews SG4 ... 67 F1
Old Charlton Rd SG5 ... 34 E6
Old Chorleywood Rd WD3 ... 165 D3
Old Church La SG12 ... 93 E7
Old Coach Rd The SG14 ... 112 C4
Old Common Rd WD3 ... 164 D5
Old Common The SG9 ... 43 B4
Old Court Ho CM24 ... 59 E6
Old Crabtree La HP2 ... 124 E2
Old Cross SG14 ... 113 C6
Old Cross Wharf 25 SG14 ... 113 D6
Old Dairy Mews The AL1 ... 128 B3
Old Dean HP3 ... 137 A4
Old Dr The AL8 ... 110 B5
Olde Ct HA6 ... 174 E4
Olden Mead SG6 ... 23 B3
Olde Swann Ct SG1 ... 50 C8
Old Farm LU7 ... 80 D4
Oldfield Cl EN8 ... 148 E3
Oldfield Ct AL1 ... 127 E3
Oldfield Dr EN8 ... 148 E3
Oldfield Farm Rd
Lower Stondon SG16 ... 10 B4
Lower Stondon SG16 ... 10 C4
Oldfield Rd
Hemel Hempstead HP1 ... 123 E2
London Colney AL2 ... 142 D6
Oldfield Rise SG4 ... 66 E7
Old Fishery La
Hemel Hempstead HP1 ... 123 F1
Hemel Hempstead HP1 ... 137 F8
Old Fold Cl EN5 ... 171 F8
Old Fold La EN5 ... 171 F8
Old Fold View EN5 ... 171 C6
Old Forge Cl
Abbots Langley WD25 ... 154 A6
Welwyn Garden City AL7 ... 89 F2
Old Forge Rd EN1 ... 161 F1
Old Forge Row SG13 ... 114 B3
Old Forge The HP23 ... 79 B4
Old French Horn La AL10 ... 130 B6
Old Gannon Cl HA6 ... 174 C5
Old Garden Ct AL3 ... 127 C3
Old Gorhanbury Ho* AL3 ... 126 C4
Old Granary The SG7 ... 4 D4
Old Grove Cl EN7 ... 147 D5
Old Hale Way SG5 ... 21 E2
Old Hall Cl HA5 ... 175 E2
Oldhall Ct SG4 ... 66 E7
Old Hall Dr HA5 ... 175 E2
OLD HALL GREEN ... 54 F1
Oldhall St SG14 ... 113 D6
Oldhams Trad Est WD24 ... 154 C2
OLD HARLOW ... 118 D4
Old Harpenden Rd AL3 ... 127 E6
Old Hat Factory The 2 LU2 ... 45 D1
OLD HATFIELD ... 130 D6
Old Herns La AL7 ... 111 C8
Old Hertford Rd AL9 ... 130 C7
Old Highway EN11 ... 135 C8
Oldhill Wood LU6 ... 82 D6
Oldhouse Croft CM20 ... 117 E2
Old House Ct HP2 ... 124 F3
Old House La
Lower Nazeing EN9 ... 149 F8
Sarratt WD4 ... 152 F4
Old House Rd HP2 ... 124 F3
Oldings Cnr AL9 ... 110 B1
OLD KNEBWORTH ... 68 C6
Old Knebworth La SG3, SG2 ... 68 D8
Old La SG3 ... 69 B5
Old Leys AL10 ... 130 A2
Old Library La 27 SG14 ... 113 D6
Old London Rd
Hertford SG13 ... 113 E6
St Albans AL1 ... 127 E2
Old Lyndale Sch 11 AL1 ... 127 E4
Old Maltings Ct The 3 EN11 ... 135 A6
Old Maltings The 2 CM23 ... 77 A7
Old Maple HP2 ... 104 F1
Old Meadow Cl HP4 ... 122 A2
Old Mile House Ct AL1 ... 142 A8
Old Mill Gdns HP4 ... 122 D4
Old Mill La CM22 ... 98 B6
Old Mill Rd WD4 ... 153 C5
Old Nazeing Rd EN10 ... 135 C1
Old North Rd
Kneesworth SG8 ... 2 B4
Royston SG8 ... 7 C8
Old Nursery Way AL6 ... 89 A7
Old Oak AL1 ... 141 E8
Old Oak Cl SG15 ... 11 A8
Old Oak Gdns HP4 ... 121 E7
Old Oak Ind Est SG15 ... 11 A8
Old Oaks EN9 ... 163 E7
Old Orch
Luton LU1 ... 63 D5
Park Street AL2 ... 141 D5
Old Orchard Cl EN4 ... 159 D1
Old Orchard Mews HP4 ... 122 C3
Old Parkbury La AL2 ... 141 F1
Old Park Rd SG5 ... 34 E7
Oldpark Ride EN7 ... 161 D7
Old Priory Pk AL1 ... 127 E2
Old Rd CM17 ... 118 D5
Old Rectory Cl AL5 ... 86 A2
Old Rectory Ct EN5 ... 171 E5
Old Rectory Dr AL10 ... 130 B5
Old Rectory Gdns AL4 ... 108 D8
Old Redding HA3 ... 176 C6
Old River La CM23 ... 76 F7
Old's App WD18 ... 166 C1
Old School Cl SG4 ... 67 F1
Old School Cotts HP5 ... 136 D5
Old School Flats The HP23 ... 99 D8
Old School Gn SG2 ... 52 E5
Old School Orch SG14 ... 70 E3
Old School The
Hertford Heath SG13 ... 114 C4
Shillington SG5 ... 19 E8
Old School Wlk
Arlesey SG15 ... 11 A4
Slip End LU1 ... 63 C1
Old's Cl WD18 ... 166 B1
Old Shire La WD3 ... 164 A2
Old Solesbridge La WD3 ... 165 A6
Old Sopwell Gdns AL1 ... 127 E1
Old South Cl HA5 ... 175 D2
OLD TOWN ... 50 C8
Old Uxbridge Rd WD3 ... 172 E3
Old Vicarage Gdns AL3 ... 83 D6
Old Waddling La 5 AL4 ... 87 D1
Old Walled Gdn The SG1 ... 36 C1
Old Watford Rd AL2 ... 140 E2
Old Watling St AL3 ... 84 B3
Oldwood AL6 ... 89 D7
Old Works The 4 AL1 ... 127 E2
Olive Cl AL1 ... 128 B1
Oliver Cl
Hemel Hempstead HP3 ... 138 E7
Hoddesdon EN11 ... 135 B8
Park Street AL2 ... 141 D4
Oliver Ct SG12 ... 92 E4
Oliver Rd HP3 ... 138 F7
Oliver Rise HP3 ... 138 E7
Olivers Cl HP4 ... 123 C7
Oliver's La SG5 ... 11 F7
Olive Taylor Ct HP2 ... 124 F7
Olivia Ct 1 EN5 ... 171 F5
Olivia Gdns UB9 ... 173 C2
Olivia Mews HA3 ... 176 E3
Olleberrie La HP3, WD3 ... 151 D7
Olwen Mews HA5 ... 175 D1
Olyard Ct LU1 ... 63 B6
Olympus Rd SG16 ... 10 B4
Omega Ct
4 Ware SG12 ... 93 D1
5 Watford WD18 ... 166 E4
Omega Maltings 2 SG12 ... 93 E1
Onslow Cl AL10 ... 130 B5
Onslow Rd LU4 ... 44 D5

Onslow St Audrey's Sch AL10 130 B5
Ontario Cl EN10 148 E6
On The Hill WD19 175 E8
Opening The SG4 88 F8
Openshaw Way SG6 23 A6
Optima Bsns Pk EN11 135 C7
Opulens Pl HA6 174 C3
Opus Ct WD6 170 A6
Oram Pl HP3 138 D8
Orbital 25 Bsns Pk WD18 166 D2
Orbital Cres WD25 153 F4
Orbital Ctr The SG1 50 B6
Orchard Ave
Berkhamsted HP4 122 A4
Harpenden AL5 85 F1
Watford WD25 154 B8
Orchard Cl
Borehamwood WD6 169 F6
Bushey WD23 168 D1
Caddington LU1 62 E4
Chorleywood WD3 164 D5
Cuffley EN6 146 E3
Hemel Hempstead HP2 124 F5
Kneesworth SG8 2 A5
Letchworth Garden City SG6 22 F8
Little Berkhamsted SG13 132 C4
Radlett WD7 155 E3
St Albans AL1 127 F2
Stanstead Abbotts SG12 115 C4
St Ippolyts SG4 34 F3
Ware SG12 93 D2
Watford WD17 166 F7
Wingrave HP22 60 B3
Orchard Cres SG1 50 C7
Orchard Croft CM20 118 A2
Orchard Ct
Bovingdon HP9 137 A4
Potters Bar EN6 158 D8
Potters Bar EN6 159 A8
Orchard Ctr The LU4 44 C4
Orchard Dr
Chiswell Green AL2 141 B5
Chorleywood WD3 164 D5
Standon SG11 55 E2
Watford WD17 166 F8
Orchard Gdns EN9 163 C5
Orchard Ho
Braughing SG11 55 F7
London Colney AL2 142 B5
Orchard House La AL1 127 D2
Orchard Lea CM21 97 C1
ORCHARD LEIGH 136 A3
Orchard Leigh Villas HP5 136 A4
Orchard Mead AL10 129 F5
Orchard On The Green The WD3 165 F4
Orchard Pl EN8 148 D1
Orchard Prim Sch The WD24 153 F3
Orchard Rd
Baldock SG7 12 E1
Barnet EN5 171 F5
Bishop's Stortford CM23 59 B1
Burnham Green AL6 90 C5
Hitchin SG4 22 B1
Royston SG8 7 B7
Stevenage SG1 50 C7
Welwyn AL6 89 C5
Orchards Cvn Site The WD3 172 B3
Orchard Sq EN10 148 F7
Orchard St
Hemel Hempstead HP3 138 D8
St Albans AL3 127 C2
Orchards The
Sawbridgeworth CM21 97 E3
Slip End LU1 63 C2
Tring HP23 99 F3
Orchard The
Baldock SG7 23 F8
Codicote SG4 67 F1
Hertford SG14 92 C1
Kings Langley WD4 139 A2
Radlett WD6 168 F7
Tonwell SG12 92 E7
Welwyn Garden City AL8 110 D8
Orchard View SG7 5 A3
Orchard Way
Bovingdon HP3 137 A3
Breachwood Green SG4 47 E1
Goff's Oak EN7 147 B3
Ivinghoe LU7 80 E5
Knebworth SG3 68 E5
Letchworth Garden City SG6 22 F8
Lower Stondon SG16 10 B3
Luton LU4 44 C4
Potters Bar EN6 145 B2
Rickmansworth WD3 165 A2
Royston SG8 7 C8
Orchid Cl
Goff's Oak EN7 147 C1
Hatfield AL10 109 F1
Luton LU3 44 C6
Orchid Ct HA3 176 E2
Orchid Ho AL1 127 F3
Ordelmere SG6 11 F1
Ordnance Rd EN3 162 E2
Oregon Way LU3 45 A8
Organ Hall Rd WD6 169 E8
Orient Cl AL1 127 E1
Orient Ctr The WD24 154 D2
Orient Lo 1 SG4 35 A8
Oriole Cl WD5 154 A8
Oriole Way CM23 76 C6
Orion Gate SG1 50 F5
Orion Way HA6 175 A6
Orkney Ho WD18 166 F4
Orlando Cl SG4 35 A6
Ormesby Dr EN6 158 D7
Ormonde Rd HA6 174 D6
Ormsby Cl LU1 63 E5
Ormskirk Rd WD19 175 D5
Oronsay HP3 125 B1
Orphanage Rd WD17, WD24 167 C7
Orpington Cl LU4 44 A3
Orton Cl AL4 128 A7
Orwell Ave SG1 36 F3
Orwell Ct 5 WD24 167 D7
Orwell View SG7 13 B1
Osborne Ct
9 Luton LU1 63 F6
Potters Bar EN6 145 B1
Osborne Gdns EN6 145 B1
Osborne Rd
Cheshunt EN8 148 E4
Hoddesdon EN10 135 A4
Luton LU1 63 F6
Potters Bar EN6 145 B1
Watford WD24 154 C1
Osborne Terr WD23 168 B1
Osborne Way HP23 100 D1
Osborn Way AL8 110 D6
Osbourne Ave WD4 138 F3
Osbourne Gdns 5 CM23 76 E5
Osier Ct 9 SG5 34 F8
Osiers The WD3 166 C4
Osmington Pl HP23 99 F4
Osprey Cl WD25 154 E5
Osprey Ct SG6 22 E8
Osprey Gdns SG2 51 D2
Osprey Ho 3 SG12 93 C3
Osprey Wlk LU4 44 A5
Ostell Cres EN3 163 A1
Oster Ho E AL3 127 C5
Osterley Cl SG2 69 C7
Oster St AL3 127 C4
Ostler Cl CM23 76 C4
Oswald Rd AL1 127 E2
Otley Way WD19 175 C7
Ottawa Ct EN10 148 E6
Otter Gdns AL10 130 B4
Otterspool La WD25 154 E1
Otterspool Way WD25 154 F1
Otterton Cl AL5 85 F3
Ottoman Terr 1 WD17 167 C6
Ottway Wlk AL6 89 C4
Otway Gdns WD23 168 E2
Otways Cl EN6 159 B6
Oudle La SG10 74 F2
Oughton Cl SG5 34 C8
Oughtonhead La SG5 34 C8
Oughton Head Way SG5 34 D8
Oughton Prim Sch SG5 21 C1
Oulton Cres EN6 158 D7
Oulton Rise AL5 86 C3
Oulton Way WD19 175 F6
Oundle Ave WD23 168 C3
Oundle Ct SG2 69 C8
Oundle Path SG2 69 C8
Oundle The SG2 69 C8
Our Lady RC Prim Sch
Hitchin SG5 21 E2
Welwyn Garden City AL7 110 E4
Ousden Cl EN8 148 E1
Ousden Dr EN8 148 E1
Ouseley Cl LU4 44 D3
Outlook Ho EN3 162 F3
Oval The
Cheshunt EN10 148 E7
Lower Stondon SG16 10 C3
Stevenage SG1 37 A1
Ovaltine Ct WD4 139 B2
Ovaltine Dr WD4 139 B2
Overfield Rd LU2 46 C1
Overlord Cl EN10 134 E3
Overstone Rd
Harpenden AL5 86 C1
Luton LU4 44 D1
Overstream WD3 165 B5
Overtrees AL5 85 F3
Oving Cl LU2 46 D2
Owen Dr SG8 2 D1
Owen Jones Cl SG16 10 C5
Owens Way WD3 166 A5
Owles La SG9 41 A6
Oxcroft CM23 76 F3
Oxendon Dr EN11 135 A5
Oxen Ind Est LU2 45 F1
Oxen Rd LU2 45 F1
Oxfield Cl HP4 122 A3
Oxford Ave AL1 128 C2
Oxford Cl
Cheshunt EN8 148 D2
Kneesworth SG8 2 A7
Moor Park HA6 174 D6
Oxford Ho 8 WD6 170 A7
Oxford Pl AL10 129 E7
Oxford Rd
Breachwood Green SG4 47 E1
Oxford Rd *continued*
2 Luton LU1 63 E6
Oxford St WD18 167 B4
Oxhey Ave WD19 167 D2
Oxhey La
Pinner HA5 176 A5
South Oxhey WD19 175 F7
Watford WD19 167 D2
Oxhey Rd WD19 167 D2
Oxhey Ridge Cl HA6 175 B5
Oxhey Wood Prim Sch WD19 175 C7
Ox La AL5 86 B3
OXLEASE 130 B5
Oxlease Dr AL10 130 B4
Oxleys Rd SG2 51 B3
Oxleys The CM17 118 E4
Oysterfields AL3 127 C4

P

Pacatian Way SG1 51 C8
Pacific Lo 3 SG4 35 A8
Packhorse Cl AL4 128 C6
Packhorse La EN6 157 D8
Paddick Cl EN11 134 F7
Paddock Cl
Hunsdon SG12 95 D1
Letchworth Garden City SG6 23 A5
Watford WD19 167 E3
Paddock Ho AL7 111 B6
Paddock Rd SG9 40 E8
Paddocks Cl SG2 51 B4
Paddocks The
Blackmore End AL4 87 B6
Chorleywood WD3 164 F5
Codicote SG4 68 A1
Hertford Heath SG13 114 B3
Stevenage SG2 51 B3
Welwyn Garden City AL7 111 B7
Paddock The
Bishop's Stortford CM23 76 D3
Hatfield AL10 130 A6
Hitchin SG4 35 A5
Hoddesdon EN10 135 A3
Paddock Way HP1 123 E3
Paddock Wood AL5 107 E7
Padgate Ho 12 WD19 175 C7
Padgets The EN9 163 E5
Pageant Rd AL1 127 D2
Page Cl SG7 23 F6
Page Hill SG12 93 C2
Page Rd SG13 114 A6
Pages Cl CM23 76 D5
Pages Croft HP4 122 A6
Paget Cotts SG12 71 F7
Paignton Cl LU4 44 D4
Paine's La HA5 175 E1
Paines Orch LU7 80 A8
PAINTER'S GREEN 69 D2
Painters La EN3 162 E4
Paisley Cl LU4 44 D3
Palace Cl WD4 139 A1
Palace Gdns
Bishop's Stortford CM23 76 E5
Royston SG8 7 C6
Palfrey Cl AL3 127 D5
Pallas Rd HP2 124 F5
Pallett Ct EN11 135 B4
Palmer Ave WD23 168 B4
Palmer Cl SG14 113 C8
Palmer Ct SG12 92 E4
Palmer Gdns EN5 171 D4
Palmer Rd SG14 113 D8
Palmers Gr EN9 135 F1
Palmers La 8 CM23 76 F7
Palmers Rd WD6 170 B8
Palmerston Cl AL8 110 C6
Palmerston Ct SG2 51 B7
Palmerston Dr 7 AL4 87 D1
Palmerston Way SG5 11 C2
Palmers Way EN8 148 E2
Pamela Ave HP3 138 F8
Pamela Gdns CM23 76 F3
Pams La SG4 66 D1
Pancake La HP2 125 D2
Pankhurst Cres SG2 51 C5
Pankhurst Pl WD24 167 C6
Pankridge WD19 175 D8
PANSHANGER 111 B7
Panshanger Aerodrome AL7 111 D7
Panshanger Dr AL7 111 C6
Panshanger Prim Sch AL7 111 A7
Pantiles The WD23 168 D1
Panxworth Rd 1 HP3 124 D1
Paper Mill La SG11 55 E1
Parade The
Hatfield AL10 130 C7
Letchford Garden City SG6 11 F1
Parade The LU2 45 E6
Parade The
South Oxhey WD19 175 D7
South Oxhey WD19 175 E7
Watford WD17 167 B6
PARADISE 124 C1
Paradise HP2 124 D2
Paradise Cl EN7 148 B3
Paradise Ind Est HP2 124 D2
Paradise Rd EN9 163 C5
Paradise Wildlife Pk★ EN10 133 F2
Paramount Ind Est WD24 154 C1
Par Cl SG13 114 B7
Parish Cl WD25 154 C5
Parishes Mead SG2 51 D4
Park Ave
Bishop's Stortford CM23 76 F3
Luton LU3 44 C7
Potters Bar EN6 159 D6
Radlett WD7 156 B6
Rickmansworth WD3 165 A5
St Albans AL1 128 A4
Watford WD23 167 E7
Watford, West Watford WD18 167 A5
Park Ave N AL5 85 F1
Park Avenue Maisonettes WD23 167 F7
Park Avenue Trad Est LU3 44 C7
Park Ave S AL5 85 F1
Park Cl
Baldock SG7 23 F7
Brookmans Park AL9 145 A5
Harrow HA3 176 E2
Hatfield AL9 130 C6
Hitchin SG5 34 E6
Markyate AL3 83 D5
Rickmansworth WD3 174 B6
Stevenage SG2 51 B1
Watford WD23 167 D6
Park Cnr AL4 143 B8
Park Cres
Baldock SG7 23 E7
Borehamwood WD6 169 F6
Harrow HA3 176 E2
Park Ct
Harlow CM20 117 D2
Letchworth Garden City SG6 23 A6
Luton LU2 45 D1
Northwood HA6 174 F4
Park Dr
Baldock SG7 23 E7
Potters Bar EN6 159 B8
Standon SG11 55 D3
Stanmore HA3 176 E4
Parker Ave SG14 113 D8
Parker Cl SG6 22 E4
Parker's Field SG2 51 C4
PARKER'S GREEN 53 B7
Parkers La SG7 3 D5
Parker St WD24 167 B8
Park Farm Cl SG16 10 D8
Park Farm Ind Est
Buntingford SG9 40 D8
Nuthampstead SG8 18 C2
Park Farm La SG8 18 C2
Parkfield
Chorleywood WD3 164 F5
Letchworth Garden City SG6 23 D4
Markyate AL3 83 D5
Parkfield Ave HA2 176 C1
Parkfield Cres
Harrow HA2 176 C1
Kimpton SG4 66 D1
Parkfield Ho HA2 176 B2
Parkfields AL8 110 D6
Parkfield View EN6 159 B7
Park Gate SG4 34 F6
Parkgate Inf Sch WD24 154 C2
Parkgate Jun Sch WD24 154 C2
Parkgate Rd WD24 154 C2
Park Gdns SG7 23 E7
Park Hill
Harlow CM17 118 B4
Harpenden AL5 85 F2
Park Hill Rd HP1 124 B3
Park Ho
Berkhamsted HP4 122 B5
Watford WD18 166 E3
Welwyn Garden City AL8 110 D7
Park Homes AL2 142 C6
Parkhurst Rd SG14 113 C7
Park Ind Est AL2 141 E4
Parkins Cl SG11 73 A6
Parkinson Cl AL4 108 D8
Park La
Bishop's Stortford CM23 76 F4
Cheshunt EN7 162 D6
Colney Heath AL4 129 C1
Hammond Street EN7 148 A4
Harefield UB9 173 B2
Harlow CM20 117 D2
Hemel Hempstead HP2 124 D2
Hoddesdon EN10 134 F3
Kimpton SG4 66 C1
Old Knebworth SG3 68 D5
Standon SG11 55 D3
Parkland Cl 3 EN11 115 B1
Parkland Dr LU1 63 D5
Parklands
Bushey WD23 168 C3
Hemel Hempstead HP1 123 F5
Royston SG8 7 E6
Waltham Abbey EN9 163 D7
Parklands Cl EN4 159 D1
Parklands Dr AL3 127 A2
Park Lane Paradise EN7 148 A6
Park Lo
6 Harpenden AL5 86 A1
Watford WD25 154 D5
Park Mans HA6 174 C7
Park Mdw AL9 130 C6
Parkmead 6 LU1 63 F6
Park Mead CM20 117 B1
Park Mews AL9 130 C6
Park Mount AL5 85 F3
Park Nook Gdns EN2 161 D2
Park Pl
Park Street AL2 141 D4
Stevenage SG1 50 D5
Park Place Chambers SG1 50 D5
Park Rd
Barnet EN5 171 F5
Bushey WD23 168 A3
Cheshunt EN8 162 D6
Enfield EN3 162 E3
Hemel Hempstead HP1 124 C1
Hertford SG13 113 E6
Hoddesdon EN11 135 A6
Northaw EN6 146 A1
Radlett WD7 156 A4
Rickmansworth WD3 165 E2
Stansted Mountfitchet CM24 59 E6
Tring HP23 100 A3
Ware SG12 93 B2
Watford WD17 167 B8
Park Rise
Berkhamsted HP4 121 E6
Harpenden AL5 85 E3
Harrow HA3 176 E2
Park Rise Cl AL5 85 E3
Park St W LU1 63 E7
Parkside
Cheshunt EN8 162 D7
Cheshunt, Waltham Cross EN8 162 E5
Potters Bar EN6 159 C7
Watford WD19 167 C3
Welwyn AL6 89 C5
Wyddial SG9 27 D2
Parkside Bsns Ctr EN11 135 C8
Parkside Com Prim Sch WD6 156 F1
Parkside Ct EN7 148 B3
Parkside Dr WD17 166 F7
Parkside Rd HA6 174 F5
Park Sq LU1 63 E7
Park St
Baldock SG7 23 E8
Berkhamsted HP4 122 B5
Hatfield AL9 130 C6
Hitchin SG4 34 E6
Luton LU1 63 F6
Park Street AL2 141 D5
Tring HP23 100 A3
PARK STREET 141 D5
Park Street CE Prim Sch AL2 141 D4
Park Street La AL2 141 C3
Park Street Sta AL2 141 D5
Park Terr
Enfield EN3 162 E1
2 Luton LU1 63 F6
Much Hadham SG10 74 F3
Park The
Redbourn AL3 106 B5
St Albans AL1 128 A5
PARK TOWN 63 F6
Park Viaduct LU1 63 F6
Park View
22 Bishop's Stortford CM23 76 F7
Great Hormead SG9 42 A7
Hatfield AL9 130 C7
Hemel Hempstead HP1 124 B5
Hoddesdon EN11 135 A5
Pinner HA5 175 F2
Potters Bar EN6 159 C6
Stevenage SG2 51 B1
Park View Cl
Luton LU3 44 D6
St Albans AL1 128 A2
Park View Cotts CM23 76 F3
Parkview Ct HA3 176 E3
Park View Ct HP4 122 B4
Park View Dr AL3 83 D6
Parkview Ho WD19 167 D3
Park View Rd
Berkhamsted HP4 122 B4
Pinner HA5 175 B3
Parkway
Sawbridgeworth CM21 97 F1
St Albans AL3 127 F7
Stevenage SG2 51 A1
Welwyn Garden City AL8 110 C6
Park Way
Hitchin SG5 34 E6
Rickmansworth WD3 165 C1
Parkway Cl AL8 110 C6
Parkway Ct AL1 142 B8
Parkway Gdns AL8 110 D5
Parkway Rd LU1 64 B5
Parkwood Cl EN10 134 F4
Parkwood Dr HP1 123 F3
Parliament Sq SG14 113 D6
Parmiter's Sch WD25 154 C8
Parndon Mill La CM20 117 B3

Parnell Cl WD5 139 F1
Parnel Rd SG12 93 F2
Parr Cres HP2 125 B8
Parrotts Cl WD3 166 A4
Parrotts Field EN11 135 B7
Parrott's La HP23 120 A4
Parsonage Cl
Abbots Langley WD5 139 E1
Tring HP23 100 A4
Parsonage Ct
Borehamwood WD6 170 C4
Tring HP23 100 A3
Parsonage Farm
Rickmansworth WD3 165 C2
Wingrave HP22 60 B3
Parsonage Farm Trad Est CM24 59 F3
Parsonage La
Albury SG11 57 A6
Bishop's Stortford CM23 77 C8
King's Walden SG4 48 A5
Stansted Mountfitchet CM24 59 F4
Welham Green AL9 144 B8
Parsonage Pl HP23 100 A3
Parsonage Rd
Rickmansworth WD3 165 D2
Welham Green AL9 144 B8
Parson's Cl AL3 84 B1
Parsons Ct [12] WD6 170 A5
Parsons Green Est SG1 37 C2
Parthia Cl SG8 7 E6
Partridge Cl
Barnet EN5 171 C3
Bushey WD23 168 C1
Luton LU4 44 A5
Partridge Hill SG7 4 C3
Partridge Rd AL3 127 D7
Partridges The HP3 125 A1
Parva Cl AL5 107 D6
Parvills EN9 163 D7
Parys Rd LU3 45 B6
Pascal Way SG6 23 B8
Pasfield EN9 163 D6
Passfield Cotts SG11 72 F1
Passingham Ave SG4 35 A6
Paston Rd HP2 124 E5
Pasture Cl WD23 168 C2
Pasture La SG4 65 E8
Pasture Rd SG6 22 E3
Pastures Ct LU4 44 A3
Pastures The
Chiswell Green AL2 141 A7
Hatfield AL10 130 B4
Hemel Hempstead HP1 123 E4
Stevenage SG2 51 D8
Totteridge N20 171 F1
Ware SG12 93 C3
Watford WD19 167 C2
Welwyn Garden City AL7 111 B4
Pastures Way LU4 44 A4
PATCHETTS GREEN 168 D8
Paternoster Cl EN9 163 F6
Paternoster Hill EN9 163 F7
Pathway The
Radlett WD7 155 F3
Watford WD19 167 D1
PATIENT END 42 F3
Pat Larner Ho [9] AL1 127 D2
Patmore Cl CM23 76 C8
Patmore Heath (Nature Reserve)* SG11 57 D8
Patmore Link Rd HP2 125 C2
Patmore Rd EN9 163 E5
Patricia Gdns CM23 76 E5
Patrick Gr EN9 163 B6
Paul Cl EN7 147 C6
Paul's Gn EN8 162 E6
Pauls La EN11 135 A6
Paxton Dr SG5 11 C2
Paxton Rd
Berkhamsted HP4 122 D4
St Albans AL1 127 E2
Payne End SG9 15 B1
Paynes Cl SG6 12 A1
Paynes Field Cl HP4 121 D7
Paynesfield Rd WD23 168 F2
Paynes La EN9 149 C7
Payne's Pk SG5 34 E7
Peabody Ct EN3 163 A2
Peace Cl EN7 148 B2
Peace Dr WD17 167 A6
Peace Gr AL6 90 A7
Peace Mews LU4 44 B2
Peace Prospect WD17 167 A6
Peach Ct LU1 63 F6
Peacocks Cl HP4 121 F6
Peacock Wlk WD5 154 A8
Peakes La EN7 147 F4
Peakes Pl AL1 127 F3
Peakes Way EN7 147 F4
Pea La HP4 121 D7
Pearces Wlk [4] AL1 127 D2
Pearl Ct
Baldock SG7 12 F1
[10] Hoddesdon EN11 135 A6
Pearman Dr SG12 71 E7
Pearsall Cl SG6 23 B5
Pearson Ave SG13 113 C4
Pearsons Cl SG13 113 C4
PEARTREE 110 F5
Peartree Cl
Hemel Hempstead HP1 124 A4
Welwyn Garden City AL7 110 E6
Pear Tree Cl SG16 10 B3
Peartree Ct
Watford WD24 154 D3
Welwyn Garden City AL7 110 E5
Pear Tree Dell SG6 23 B3
Peartree Farm AL7 110 E6
Peartree La AL7 110 E6
Peartree Prim Sch AL7 110 E5
Peartree Rd
Hemel Hempstead HP1 124 A4
Luton LU2 46 C4
Peartree Spring Inf Sch SG2 51 B3
Peartree Spring Jun Sch SG2 51 B3
Peartree Way SG2 51 A3
Pear Tree Wlk EN7 147 E5
Peascroft Rd HP3 125 B1
Peasecroft SG9 39 C7
Peasleys Yd CM23 77 B7
Peasmead SG9 40 E6
Pebbles The SG7 12 C4
Peck's Hill EN9 135 E2
Peckworth Ind Est SG16 10 A4
Pedlars La SG8 15 E7
Pedley Hill HP4, LU6 82 C1
Peel Cres SG14 113 C8
Peel Pl [6] LU1 63 D7
Peel St LU1 63 D7
Peerglow Ctr SG12 114 E8
Peerglow Ind Est WD18 166 B1
Pegasus Ct WD5 153 F7
Pegasus Ho EN8 162 D8
Pegasus Pl AL3 127 D5
Pegmire La WD25 168 C8
Pegrum Dr AL2 142 B5
PEGSDON 19 D1
Pegsdon Cl LU3 45 B7
Pegsdon Way SG5 19 E1
Pegs La SG12 95 D5
Peg's La SG13 113 D5
Peitley Cotts AL3 84 A1
Pelham Ct
Hemel Hempstead HP2 125 C3
Welwyn Garden City AL7 111 C5
Pelham La WD25 155 B3
Pelham Rd SG11 55 F7
Pelhams The WD25 154 D4
Pelican Way SG6 11 F1
Pemberton Almshouses [5] AL3 127 D4
Pemberton Cl AL1 141 D8
Pembridge Chase HP3 137 A3
Pembridge Cl HP3 136 F3
Pembridge La EN10 133 E2
Pembridge Rd HP3 137 A3
Pembroke Ave
Enfield EN1 162 B1
Luton LU4 44 F3
Pembroke Cl EN10 148 E8
Pembroke Dr EN7 147 B2
Pembroke Ho [3] WD6 170 A5
Pembroke Rd
Baldock SG7 23 F8
Moor Park HA6 174 C7
Pemsel Ct HP3 124 E1
Penda Cl LU3 44 F7
Pendennis Ct AL5 107 D7
Penfold Cl SG7 24 A7
Penfold Trad Est WD24 167 C8
Pengelly Cl EN7 148 B1
Pengelly Ct [3] HA3 176 E1
Penhill LU3 44 E6
Penhill Ct LU3 44 E6
Penman Cl AL2 141 A4
Pennard Ho [3] WD19 175 E7
Penn Cl WD3 164 D3
Penne Cl WD7 156 A5
Penn Ho
Moor Park HA6 174 C7
[14] South Oxhey WD19 175 C7
Pennine Ave LU3 44 D8
Pennine Way HP2 125 A7
Pennington La CM24 59 D8
Penningtons CM23 76 C5
Penn Pl [1] WD3 165 D2
Penn Rd
Chiswell Green AL2 141 C4
Rickmansworth WD3 165 A1
Stevenage SG1 50 E4
Penns The SG8 17 E6
Penn Way
Chorleywood WD3 164 D3
Letchworth Garden City SG6 23 B3
Penny Croft AL5 107 A4
Penny Ct WD17 167 B7
Pennyfather Cl SG3 69 E2
Pennyfathers La AL6 90 B4
Pennymead CM20 118 A1
Penray EN5 171 E6
Penrose Ave WD19 175 E8
Penrose Ct HP2 124 E7
Penscroft Gdns WD6 170 D5
Penshurst CM17 118 C3
Penshurst Cl AL5 85 D4
Penshurst Rd EN6 159 D7
Penta Ct WD6 170 A5
Pentagon Pk HP2 125 C5
Pentland HP2 124 F6
Pentland Rd WD23 168 C3
Pentland Rise SG1 37 C3
Pentley Cl AL8 89 D1
Pentley Pk AL8 89 D1
Penton Dr EN8 148 D2
Pentrich Ave EN1 162 A1
Penzance Cl UB9 173 D1
Peplins Cl AL9 144 E5
Peplins Way AL9 144 E5
Peppard Cl AL3 106 A6
Peppercorn Wlk SG4 35 B7
Pepper Ct SG7 23 F8
Pepper Hill SG12 114 F4
Peppermint Rd SG5 34 F7
PEPPERSTOCK 63 C1
Peppett's Gn HP5 120 D1
Pepsal End SG2 69 B8
Pepsal End Rd LU1 84 C7
Pepys Cres EN5 171 C4
Pepys Ct [4] EN11 135 D8
Pepys Way SG7 23 E8
Percheron Dr LU4 44 A3
Percheron Rd WD6 170 D3
Percival Ct EN8 148 E1
Percival Way LU2 64 C7
Percy Rd WD18 167 B5
Peregrine Cl
Bishop's Stortford CM23 76 D6
Watford WD25 154 E5
Peregrine Ho [1] SG12 93 C3
Peregrine Rd LU4 44 A4
Perham Way AL2 142 D6
Perivale Gdns WD25 154 B5
Periwinkle Cl SG8 17 C5
Periwinkle La SG5 21 F1
Permain Cl WD7 156 E6
Perowne Way SG11 55 E3
Perram Cl EN10 148 E5
Perrett Gdns SG14 112 E7
Perriors Cl EN7 148 A4
Perrycoste Ct AL4 128 A8
Perry Dr SG8 7 E7
Perry Gn HP2 105 A1
PERRY GREEN
Much Hadham 96 B8
Peters Green 65 C3
Perry Hill EN9 149 F8
Perrymead LU2 46 F2
Perry Mead WD23 168 C3
Perrysfield Rd EN8 148 E5
Perrywood AL8 110 D8
Perrywood La SG14 91 B7
Perspective Ho EN3 162 E3
Pescot Hill HP1 124 B5
Petard Cl LU4 44 A2
Peterborough Ho [9] WD6 170 A7
Peterlee Ct [2] HP2 124 F7
Peters Ave AL2 142 C5
Petersfield AL3 127 E7
PETERS GREEN 65 C3
Peterslea WD4 139 B2
Peter's Pl HP4 121 E6
Peters Way SG3 68 F6
Peters Wood Hill SG12 114 E7
Pettys Cl EN8 148 D3
Petunia Ct LU3 45 C1
Petworth Cl SG2 69 C7
Pevensey Cl LU2 46 D4
Pewterers Ave CM23 76 C4
Pheasant Cl
Berkhamsted HP4 122 C3
Tring HP23 100 B6
Pheasants Way WD3 165 B2
Philipshill Wood (Nature Reserve)* WD3 164 A2
Phillimore Ct WD7 155 E3
Phillimore Pl WD7 155 E3
Phillipers WD25 154 E4
Phillips Ave SG8 7 C8
Phipps Hatch La EN2 161 C1
Phoebe Rd [3] HP2 124 F6
Phoenix Cl HA6 174 F6
Phoenix Ct EN3 162 C1
Phoenix Ho [2] AL1 128 A2
Phyllis Courtnage Ho [4] HP2 124 D5
Picardy Ho EN2 161 C1
PICCOTTS END 124 C7
Piccotts End La HP2 124 D7
Piccotts End Rd HP1 124 C7
Pickets Cl WD23 168 E1
Picketts AL8 89 D1
Pickford Hill AL5 86 D4
Pickford Rd
Markyate AL3 83 D5
St Albans AL1 128 B2
Pick Hill EN9 163 F7
Picknage Cnr SG8 9 A2
Picknage Rd SG8 9 A2
Pie Cnr AL3 84 C1
Pie Gdn AL3 84 C1
Pierian Spring HP1 124 B5
Pietley Hill AL3 84 A1
Pigeonwick AL5 86 B3
Piggottshill La AL5 107 D8
Piggotts La LU4 44 D4
Piggotts Way CM23 76 E5
Piggy La WD3 164 B3
Pightle Cl SG8 7 D7
Pightle The LU7 80 D3
Pig La CM22 77 A3
Pike End SG1 50 D6
Pikes Cotts EN5 171 C5
Pikes Leap [6] AL4 87 D1
Pilgrim Cl
Chiswell Green AL2 141 C4
Watford WD25 154 D6
Pilgrims Row SG9 40 F3
Pilgrims Way SG1 37 B2
Pilkington Manor [12] HP4 122 C4
Piltdown Rd WD19 175 D6
PIMLICO 139 E7
Pimlico Ct [2] SG13 113 C5
Pinchfield WD3 172 D5
Pindar Rd EN11 135 C7
Pine Cl
Berkhamsted HP4 122 B4
Cheshunt EN8 148 D3
Pine Crest AL6 89 E8
Pinecroft HP3 138 F7
Pinecroft Cres EN5 171 E5
Pinecroft Ct HP3 138 F7
Pine Gr
Bishop's Stortford CM23 77 B6
Bricket Wood AL2 140 F1
Brookmans Park AL9 145 B6
Totteridge N20 171 F1
Watford WD23 167 F8
Pinehill Hospl SG4 35 A7
PINE HURST 114 B7
Pinehurst Cl WD5 153 E7
Pinelands CM23 58 F1
Pine Ridge AL1 142 A8
Pineridge Ct [4] EN5 171 D5
Pines Ave EN1 162 B3
Pines Cl HA6 174 E4
Pines Hill CM24 59 D5
Pines The
Borehamwood WD6 169 F7
Hemel Hempstead HP3 137 F7
Pine Tree Cl HP2 124 D4
Pinetree Ct SG1 50 D4
Pinetree Gdns [5] HP2 124 E2
Pinetree Ho WD25 154 E3
Pine Wlk HP4 121 D7
Pinewood AL7 110 E4
Pinewood Ave HA5 176 B4
Pinewood Cl
Borehamwood WD6 170 D7
Pinner HA5 176 B4
South Oxhey WD19 175 B5
St Albans AL4 128 C3
Watford WD17 167 A8
Pinewood Dr EN6 158 F8
Pinewood Gdns HP1 124 B3
Pinewood Lo [1] WD23 168 D1
Pinewoods [4] SG2 50 F1
Pinewood Sch SG12 114 D7
Pinfold Rd WD23 167 F7
Pinford Dell [4] LU2 46 D1
PIN GREEN 50 F8
Pin Green Ind Est SG1 37 C2
Pinks Farm WD7 157 C8
Pinnacles EN9 163 E5
Pinnate Pl AL7 110 E2
PINNER 175 E1
Pinner Gn HA5 175 C1
PINNER GREEN 175 C1
Pinner Hill HA5 175 B3
Pinner Hill Rd HA5 175 C1
Pinner Park Ave HA2 176 C1
Pinner Park Gdns HA2 176 C1
Pinner Rd
Northwood HA6 175 A1
Watford WD19 167 E2
Pinner Wood Sch HA5 175 C2
Pinnocks Cl SG7 23 F7
Pinnocks La SG7 23 F8
Pinto Cl WD6 170 D3
Pioneer Way WD18 166 F3
Pipers Ave AL5 107 D7
Pipers Cl AL3 106 A6
PIPER'S END 112 B1
Pipers Hill HP1 103 D3
Pipers La
Caddington AL3, LU1 62 F1
Wheathampstead AL5 107 F7
Pipit Cl SG8 7 E8
Pipit Ct EN3 162 C2
Pippens AL8 89 E1
Pippin Cl WD7 156 E6
Pippin Gr SG8 7 C7
Pippins The WD25 154 C5
PIRTON 20 E4
Pirton Cl
Hitchin SG5 34 D6
St Albans AL4 128 C8
Pirton Cross SG5 34 A7
Pirton Ct HP2 124 F4
Pirton Hill Inf Sch LU4 44 B6
Pirton Hill Jun Sch LU4 44 B6
Pirton Rd
Hitchin SG5 34 C6
Holwell SG5 21 A7
Luton LU4 44 D5
Pirton Sch SG5 20 D4
Pisa Ho [17] WD18 166 E5
Pishiobury Dr CM21 118 D8
Pitsfield AL8 89 D1
Pitsford Terr LU2 46 A1
PITSTONE 80 D4
Pitstone Cl AL4 128 C8
Pitstone Common Forest Trails* HP4 101 E7
Pitstone Green Bsns Pk LU7 80 D2
Pitstone Green Mus* LU7 80 D4
Pitstone Windmill* LU7 80 F4
Pitt Ct SG2 51 B1
Pitt Dr AL4 142 C8
Pitteway Wlk SG14 113 C6
Pittman's Field CM20 117 F1
Pix Ct SG15 11 A8
Pix Farm La HP1 123 C2
Pixies Hill Cres HP1 123 F2
Pixies Hill Prim Sch HP1 123 F2
Pixies Hill Rd HP1 123 F2
Pixmore Ave SG6 23 B6
Pixmore Ind Est SG6 23 A6
Pixmore Jun Sch SG6 23 A5
Pixmore Way SG6 23 A5
Pix Rd
Letchworth Garden City SG6 23 A6
Stotfold SG5 11 E5
Place Farm [10] AL4 87 D1
Plaistow Way SG8 9 E2
Plaiters Cl HP23 100 B4
Plaitford Cl WD3 173 E8
Plantaganet Pl [3] EN9 163 B6
Plantation Rd LU3 44 D7
Plantation Wlk HP1 124 A6
Plash Dr SG1 50 E5
Plashes Cl SG11 55 D2
Plashes Dr SG9 40 F6
Plashets CM22 98 C1
Platt Cl LU4 44 D4
Plaw Hatch Cl CM23 77 B8
Plaw Hatch Cnr CM23 77 D8
Playford Sq LU4 44 D5
Pleasance The AL5 85 D4
Pleasant Pl WD3 172 E3
Pleasant Rd CM23 76 E8
Pleasant Rise AL9 130 C8
Plewes Cl LU6 82 E8
Plomer Ave EN11 114 F1
Plotters Ct [7] EN11 135 D8
Plough Cl SG8 5 B8
Plough Hill EN6 146 E2
Plough La
Harefield UB9 173 C4
King's Walden SG4 48 A5
Potten End HP4 123 B7
Sarratt WD3 151 F6
Ploughmans Cl CM23 76 C5
Ploughmans End AL7 111 C5
Plover Cl HP4 122 C3
Plover Ct EN3 162 C3
Plummers La LU2 65 C2
Plumpton Cl LU2 46 D3
Plumpton Rd EN11 135 C8
Plum Tree Rd SG16 10 B2
Pluto Rise HP2 124 F5
Plymouth Cl LU2 46 B1
Poets Chase HP1 124 B5
Poets Cl HP1 124 B4
Poets Ct AL5 86 B1
Poets Gate
Goff's Oak EN7 147 E3
Widford SG12 95 D4
Poets Gn LU4 44 A2
Polayn Garth AL8 110 C7
Polegate LU2 46 D2
Polehanger La HP1 123 E5
Poles Hill WD3 151 E6
Poles La
Thundridge SG12 93 C6
Ware SG12 93 C3
Poles Pk SG12 93 C6
Police Row SG8 15 F7
Police Station La WD23 168 B2
Pollard Gdns SG1 50 F8
Pollards WD3 172 D5
Pollards Cl EN7 147 C2
Pollards Way
Lower Stondon SG16 10 A3
Pirton SG5 20 D4
Pollicott Cl AL4 128 C8
Pollywick Rd HP23 100 D1
Polsten Mews EN3 163 A2
Polzeath Cl LU2 64 C8
Pomeroy Cres WD24 154 B3
Pomeroy Gr LU2 45 E6
Pomfret Ave LU2 45 F1
Pond Cl
Harefield UB9 173 C1
Luton LU4 44 B5
Stevenage SG1 50 C7
Tring HP23 100 A4
Pond Croft
Hatfield AL10 129 F5
Welwyn Garden City AL7 110 E5
Pondcroft Rd SG3 69 A4
Pond Field AL7 90 A1
Pondfield Cres AL4 128 B7
Pond Gdns SG4 67 F1
Pond La
Baldock SG7 23 E8
Little Gaddesden HP4 102 E7
Stansted Mountfitchet CM24 59 D7

Pond Rd HP3 139 A6
Pondside SG4 36 C4
Pondsmeade AL3 106 B5
Pondwick Rd AL5 85 E2
Pondwicks Cl AL1 127 C2
Pondwicks Rd LU1 63 F7
Ponsbourne St Mary's CE Prim Sch SG13 146 E7
Pooleys La AL9 144 C8
Pope Ct HP23 99 F3
Pope Paul RC Prim Sch EN6 158 F6
Popes Ct LU2 45 D1
Popes La WD24 154 B1
Pope's Rd WD5 153 E8
Popes Row SG12 93 D3
Popis Gdns SG12 93 E2
Poplar Ave
Hatfield AL10 129 D5
Luton LU3 45 C8
Poplar Cl
High Cross SG11 72 F2
Hitchin SG4 35 B6
Pinner HA5 175 D2
Royston SG8 7 E7
Poplar Dr
Royston SG8 7 E7
Stotfold SG5 11 F8
Poplar Rd LU6 82 E8
POPLARS 51 D3
Poplars AL7 111 B7
Poplars Cl
Hatfield AL10 129 D5
Luton LU2 46 B3
Watford WD25 154 B7
Poplar Shaw EN9 163 F6
Poplars The
Arlesey SG15 11 A8
Borehamwood WD6 170 A8
Great Hallingbury CM22 77 F4
2 Hammond Street EN7 147 E5
Harefield UB9 173 C2
Hemel Hempstead HP1 124 B2
Ickleford SG5 21 F5
St Albans AL1 142 B7
Poplar View SG12 92 E4
Popple Way SG1 50 E6
Poppy Cl
Hemel Hempstead HP1 123 E4
Luton LU3 45 D2
Poppy Ct 8 AL5 86 A1
Poppyfields AL7 111 C5
Poppy Mead SG1 50 F4
Poppy Wlk
Goff's Oak EN7 147 D3
Hatfield AL10 129 F8
Porlock Dr LU2 46 C1
Porters Cl SG9 40 E8
PORTER'S END 87 A7
Porters Hill AL5 86 C4
Porter's Mews SG4 67 F1
Porters Park Dr WD7 156 E7
Porters Wood AL3 127 F7
Port Hill SG14 113 C7
Port La CM22 77 B2
Portland Ct 18 EN11 135 A6
Portland Ct LU4 45 A1
Portland Dr
Cheshunt EN7 162 A8
Enfield EN2 161 E1
Portland Hts HA6 174 F6
Portland Ind Est SG15 11 A3
Portland Pl
17 Bishop's Stortford CM23 76 F7
Hertford Heath SG13 114 C4
Portland Rd
Bishop's Stortford CM23 76 F7
Luton LU4 45 A1
Portland St AL3 127 C4
Portman Cl
Hitchin SG5 21 D2
St Albans AL4 128 C7
Portman Hall HA3 176 D5
Portman Ho AL3 127 D6
Portmill La SG5 34 F7
Port Vale SG14 113 C6
Postfield AL7 90 A1
Posting Ho HP23 101 A5
Post Office Cotts CM22 98 C8
Post Office Rd CM20 117 D1
Post Office Row SG4 24 B1
Post Office Wlk 8 SG14 113 D6
Postwood Gn SG13 114 C3
Post Wood Rd SG12 114 E7
Potash La HP23 79 A5
POTTEN END 123 C7
Potten End CE Fst Sch HP4 123 B6
Potten End Hill HP1 123 E8
POTTERS BAR 159 D6
Potters Bar Com Hospl EN6 159 C5
Potters Bar Mus* EN6 158 F7
Potters Bar Sta EN6 158 F7
POTTERS CROUCH 140 D7
Potterscrouch La AL2, AL3 140 E7
Potters Ct EN6 159 A7
Potters Field AL3 127 E7
POTTER'S GREEN 72 C6
POTTERSHEATH 89 D7
Pottersheath Rd AL6 68 D1
Potters Heights Cl HA5 175 B3
Potters La
Borehamwood WD6 170 C8
Stevenage SG1 50 B4
Potters Mews WD6 169 D3
Potter St
Bishop's Stortford CM23 76 F7
Pinner HA5 175 B2
Potter Street Hill HA5 175 B3
Potters Wood Cl SG12 72 C6
Pottery Cl LU3 44 F7
Potton Rd SG8 1 F6
POUCHEN END 123 D2
Pouchen End La HP1 123 D3
Poultney Cl WD7 156 F7
Poultney Rd CM24 59 E8
Pound Ave SG1 50 D6
Pound Cl
Lower Nazeing EN9 149 E8
Sandridge AL4 108 C2
Poundfield WD25 153 F4
Pound Gn SG8 1 F5
Pound La
Heath End HP5 121 A1
Shenley WD7 156 F6
Poundwell AL7 111 A5
Powdermill La EN9 163 B6
Powdermill Mews 2 EN9 163 B6
Powdermill Way EN9 163 B6
Power Ct LU1 63 F7
Power Dr EN3 162 F3
Powis Ct
Bushey WD23 168 D1
Potters Bar EN6 159 C5
Powys Ct WD6 170 D6
Poynders Hill HP2 125 C3
Poynders Mdw SG4 88 F8
Poynings Cl AL5 107 F8
Poynters Rd LU5 44 A2
Prae Cl AL3 127 B3
Praetorian Ct AL1 141 C8
Prae Wood Prim Sch AL3 127 A1
Prebendal Dr LU1 63 B2
Precinct The EN10 134 F3
Premier Bsns Pk LU3 44 B8
Premier Ct EN3 162 D1
Premier Ho SG1 50 C5
Premier Pl WD18 166 F4
Prentice Way LU2 64 D7
Prescott Rd EN8 148 E4
PRESDALES 114 E7
Presdales Ct SG12 114 D8
Presdales Dr SG12 114 E8
Presdales Sch SG12 114 D7
Presentation Ct LU1 63 F6
President Way LU2 64 D8
Prestatyn Cl SG1 50 B8
PRESTON 48 D6
Preston Ct HA6 175 A1
Preston Gdns
Enfield EN3 162 E2
Luton LU2 45 F2
Preston Path LU2 45 F2
Preston Prim Sch SG4 48 D6
Preston Rd
Preston SG4 48 E8
St Ippolyts SG4 34 F1
Prestwick Cl LU2 45 E5
Prestwick Dr CM23 59 B1
Prestwick Rd WD19 175 D6
Prestwood 2 WD19 175 E8
Prestwood Gate AL1 127 E5
Pretoria Rd WD18 167 A5
Pretty Cnr HA6 175 A5
Priestland Gdns HP4 122 E6
Priestleys LU1 63 A7
Priestly Rd SG2 51 B5
Primary Way SG15 11 A4
Primett Rd SG1 50 C7
Primley La CM22 98 C1
Primrose Cl
Arlesey SG15 11 A4
Bishop's Stortford CM23 76 C6
Hatfield AL10 130 B4
Hemel Hempstead HP1 123 E2
Luton LU3 45 D2
Primrose Cotts WD7 156 A4
Primrose Ct SG1 50 D7
Primrose Dr SG13 114 B6
Primrose Gdns
Bushey WD23 168 B2
Radlett WD7 156 A4
Primrose Hill WD4 139 B3
Primrose Hill Rd SG1 50 D7
Primrose La
Arlesey SG15 11 A4
Radlett WD25 155 D1
Primrose Path EN7 162 A8
Primrose View SG8 7 F5
Prince Andrew Dr SG5 12 A6
Prince Andrew's Cl SG8 7 D5
Prince Charles Ave SG5 12 A6
Prince Edward St 6 HP4 122 C4
Prince Edward Way SG5 12 A6
Prince Eugene Pl AL1 141 C8
Prince Harry Cl SG5 12 A6
Prince Of Wales Cl SG15 11 A3
Prince of Wales Prim Sch EN3 162 F2
Prince Pk HP1 124 A2
Princes Ave
Enfield EN3 162 E4
Watford WD18 167 A5
Princes Cl HP4 122 A6
Princes Ct
Bishop's Stortford CM23 76 C7
Hemel Hempstead HP3 138 B8
Princes Gate CM23 76 C7
Princes Gate CM20 117 E3
Princes Mews SG8 7 C6
Princes Pl 18 LU2 45 D1
Princess Alexandra Hospl CM20 117 C1
Princess Diana Dr AL4 128 D2
Princess Helena Coll The SG4 48 E6
Princess Lo 10 LU1 63 D7
Princess St LU1 63 D7
Princes St SG12 93 D2
Prince's St SG5 11 F7
Prince St WD17 167 C6
Prince Way LU2 64 D8
Prince William Cl SG5 12 A5
Printers Ave 4 WD18 166 E4
Printers Ct AL1 127 D2
Printers Way CM20 118 A5
Priors 9 CM23 77 A7
Priors Cl SG13 114 B3
Priors Ct CM22 98 A2
Priors Hill SG5 20 C4
Priors Wood Prim Sch SG12 94 A3
Priors Wood Rd SG13 114 C3
Priory Ave CM17 118 C5
Priory Cl
Cheshunt EN10 148 E7
Hoddesdon EN11 135 A5
Royston SG8 7 E6
Stanmore HA7 176 F7
Totteridge N20 171 F2
Priory Ct
9 Berkhamsted HP4 122 C4
Bishop's Stortford CM23 76 F7
Bushey WD23 168 C1
13 Hertford SG14 113 D6
Hitchin SG4 34 F5
6 St Albans AL1 127 E2
Priory Dell SG1 50 F5
Priory Dr
Stanmore HA7 176 F7
Stansted Mountfitchet CM24 59 E5
Priory End SG4 34 F5
Priory Fields 7 WD17 167 A8
Priory Gate EN8 148 F4
Priory Gdns
Berkhamsted HP4 122 C4
Luton LU2 45 D4
Priory La
Great Wymondley SG4 35 F4
Royston SG8 7 D6
Priory Lo WD3 165 D2
Priory Orch AL3 84 B2
Priory Row SG12 95 E4
Priory Sch The SG5 21 E2
Priory St
Hertford SG14 113 D6
Ware SG12 93 C1
Priory View
Bushey WD23 168 E2
Little Wymondley SG4 35 E4
Priory Way SG4 34 F4
Priory Wharf 12 SG14 113 D6
Priory Wlk AL1 141 E8
Pritchett Cl EN3 163 A2
Proctors Way CM23 77 A4
Proctor Way LU2 64 C7
Progress Ho 21 LU2 45 D1
Progression Ctr HP2 125 A6
Progress Way LU4 44 B7
Prospect La AL5 107 A4
Prospect Pl AL6 89 C5
Prospect Rd
Cheshunt EN8 148 C2
St Albans AL1 127 D1
Prospect Way LU2 64 C7
Protea Way SG6 23 B6
Providence Gr SG1 50 E8
Providence Pl 17 SG14 113 D6
Providence Way SG7 23 F7
Provost Way LU2 64 C8
Prowse Ave WD23 176 C8
Pryor Cl WD5 153 F7
Pryor Ct SG1 50 D7
Pryor Rd SG7 23 F6
Pryors Cl CM23 77 A6
Pryors Ct SG7 12 F1
Pryor Way SG6 23 D5
PUCKERIDGE 55 D3
Puddephat's La AL3 104 D7
Pudding La
Barley SG8 9 A1
Hemel Hempstead HP1 124 A5
Puddingstone Dr AL4 128 C1
PUDDS CROSS 136 E2
Pudgell The SG8 9 E2
Pulham Ave EN10 134 E3
Pullar Meml CE Prim Sch SG11 72 E2
Puller Rd
Barnet EN5 171 E7
Puller Rd *continued*
Hemel Hempstead HP1 124 A2
Pulleys Cl HP1 123 F4
Pulleys La HP1 123 F4
Pullman Cl AL1 127 E1
Pullman Dr SG4 35 B7
Pulter's Way SG4 35 A6
Pump Hill SG9 30 A2
Pump Ho The 12 CM23 77 A7
Pumphouse The SG8 7 D7
Punchard Cres EN3 163 B1
Punch Bowl La AL3 126 B8
Purbeck Ho 8 WD18 166 F3
Purbrock Ave WD25 154 C3
Purcell Cl
Burnham Green AL6 90 E6
Radlett WD6 169 D8
Purcell Ct SG1 50 C8
Purcell Ho EN1 162 A1
Purcell Sch WD23 168 A7
Purdom Rd AL7 110 E3
Purkiss Rd SG13 113 C3
Purley Ctr LU3 44 E7
Purlings Rd WD23 168 B4
Pursley Gdns WD6 157 A1
Purway Cl LU3 44 E7
PURWELL 35 D8
Purwell La SG4 35 C8
Purwell Prim Sch SG4 35 D8
Putney Rd EN3 162 D3
PUTTENHAM 78 E2
Puttenham Cl WD19 175 D8
Puttenham Ct HP23 78 F2
Putteridge High Sch LU2 46 C5
Putteridge Inf Sch LU2 46 C5
Putteridge Jun Sch LU2 46 C5
Putteridge Par LU2 46 B4
Putteridge Rd LU2 46 C4
Putterills The AL5 86 A1
Putters Croft HP2 124 F8
Puttocks Cl AL9 144 C8
Puttocks Dr AL9 144 C8
Pye Cnr CM20 117 D5
Pye Gdns CM23 76 E8
Pyghtle Ct LU1 63 A7
Pyghtle The
Buntingford SG9 40 D7
Luton LU1 63 A7
Pyms Cl SG6 23 B8
Pynchbek CM23 76 E3
Pynchon Paddocks CM22 98 D7
Pynefield Ho WD3 164 F2
Pytchley Cl LU2 45 E5

Q

Quadrangle The AL8 110 C7
Quadrant Pk AL7 110 F8
Quadrant The
Letchworth Garden City SG6 22 F6
Rickmansworth WD3 165 E2
Royston SG8 7 C8
St Albans AL4 128 B6
Stevenage SG1 50 D4
Quail Wlk SG8 7 E8
Quaker La EN9 163 C5
Quaker Rd SG12 93 E3
Quakers La EN6 159 B8
Quantock Cl
Luton LU3 45 B8
St Albans AL4 128 C7
Stevenage SG1 37 D3
Quantock Rise LU3 31 B1
Quantocks HP2 124 F6
Quarry Ct LU7 80 D2
Quarry Rd LU7 80 D2
Quartermass Cl HP1 124 A4
Quartermass Rd HP1 124 A4
Queen Anne's Cl SG5 11 F5
Queen Bee Ct AL10 129 D7
Queen Elizabeth Ct
Barnet EN5 171 F5
4 Cheshunt EN10 148 F5
Waltham Abbey EN9 163 C3
Queen Elizabeth II Hospl AL7 111 A2
Queen Elizabeth's Girls Sch EN5 171 F5
Queen Elizabeth's Sch EN5 171 D6
Queen Hoo La AL6 90 F6
Queen Mary's Ave WD18 166 E5
Queen Marys Ct EN9 163 C4
Queens Ave WD18 166 F5
Queens Cl
4 Luton LU1 63 E6
Stansted Mountfitchet CM24 59 E8
Queen's Cl CM21 97 F4
Queens Cres
Bishop's Stortford CM23 76 E5
St Albans AL4 128 B6
Queens Ct
8 Borehamwood WD6 169 F8
Cheshunt EN8 162 F5
17 Luton LU2 45 D1
4 Watford WD17 167 C6
Queen's Ct
Aspenden SG9 40 D5
Hertford SG13 113 D5
Queen's Ct *continued*
St Albans AL1 128 B3
Queens Dr WD5 153 F7
Queen's Dr EN8 163 A5
Queen's Dr The WD3 165 A3
Queensgate EN8 162 F5
Queens Gate 7 WD17 167 C6
Queensgate Ctr CM20 117 F4
Queens Head Wlk EN10 148 E8
Queen's Pl WD17 167 C6
Queens Rd
Barnet EN5 171 D6
Berkhamsted HP4 122 A5
Royston SG8 7 D7
Ware SG12 93 F2
Queen's Rd
Cheshunt EN8 162 E6
Harpenden AL5 107 B7
Hertford SG13 113 D5
Watford WD17 167 C6
Queens Road Est EN5 171 D6
Queens' Sch WD23 168 A6
Queens Silver Ct HA6 174 E2
Queen's Sq The HP2 124 F4
Queen St
Chipperfield WD4 152 A7
Hitchin SG4, SG5 34 F7
Pitstone LU7 80 D4
St Albans AL3 127 C3
Stotfold SG5 12 A6
Tring HP23 100 A3
Queens Terr HA3 176 E1
Queensway
Hatfield AL10 130 B6
Hemel Hempstead HP1, HP2 124 E4
Royston SG8 7 D7
Stevenage SG1 50 D5
Queens Way
Cheshunt EN8 162 F5
Shenley WD7 156 E7
Queensway Ho 1 AL10 130 A6
Queenswood Cres WD25 154 A6
Queenswood Dr SG4 22 C1
Queenswood Sch AL9 145 D3
Queen Victoria Meml Hospl AL6 89 B4
Quendell Wlk HP2 124 E3
Quendon Dr EN9 163 D6
Quickbeams AL7 90 A1
Quickley La WD3 164 C4
Quickley Rise WD3 164 C3
Quickly Brow WD3 164 B3
Quickmoor La WD4 152 C6
Quickswood LU3 45 A7
Quickwood Cl WD3 165 A3
Quills SG6 23 D4
Quilter Cl LU3 44 F4
Quinces Croft HP1 124 A5
Quincey Rd SG12 93 C4
Quin Ct SG11 55 F7
Quinn Way SG6 23 C5
Quinta Dr EN5 171 C4

R

Raans Rd HP6 150 A1
Raban Cl SG2 51 C1
Raban Ct SG7 12 F1
Rabia Boys Sch LU4 45 B1
Rabia Girls Sch LU4 45 A1
RABLEYHEATH 68 D3
Rabley Heath Rd AL6 68 B2
Rackham Dr LU3 45 C5
Radburn Cnr SG6 23 C5
Radburn Prim Sch SG6 23 C5
Radburn Way SG6 23 C4
Radcliffe Rd SG5 35 A8
RADLETT 156 C5
Radlett La WD7 156 E6
Radlett Lodge Sch WD7 156 B8
Radlett Park Rd WD7 156 A4
Radlett Prep Sch WD7 156 C1
Radlett Rd
London Colney AL2 141 E2
Watford WD24 167 D7
Radlett Sta WD7 156 A4
Radnor Ct HA3 176 F2
Radstone Pl LU2 46 E1
RADWELL 12 C4
Radwell Cotts SG7 12 C4
Radwell La SG7 12 C4
Raeburn Gdns EN5 171 B4
Raffin Cl SG3 69 E3
Raffin Green La SG3 69 F4
Raffin Pk SG3 69 E3
Ragged Hall La AL2 140 E7
Raglan Ave EN8 162 D5
Raglan Gdns WD19 167 B1
Raglan Ho HP4 122 A4
Rags La EN7 147 E4
Railway Cotts HP23 100 F5
Railway Pl SG13 113 E6
Railway Rd EN8 162 F6
Railway St SG13, SG14 113 D6
Railway Terr WD4 139 A4

Railway The SG16 10 B3
Rainbow Cl AL3 105 F6
Rainbow Ct WD19 167 C3
Rainer Cl EN8 148 D2
Rainsborough Ct
SG13 114 A7
Rainsford Rd CM24 59 E8
Raleigh Cres SG2 51 B8
Raleigh Gr LU4 44 D1
Rally The SG15 11 A7
Ralph Sadleir Mid Sch
SG11 55 E3
Ralph Swingler Pl SG6 23 A4
Ralston Way WD19 175 D8
Ramblers La 5 CM17 118 D1
Ramblers Way AL7 111 C5
Rambling Way HP4 123 C6
Ramerick Gdns SG15 11 A2
Ram Gorse CM20 117 B2
Ramney Dr EN3 162 E2
Ramney Ho EN8 163 A5
Ramparts The AL3 127 B2
Ramridge Prim Sch
LU2 46 B2
Ramridge Rd LU2 46 A2
Ramryge Ct AL1 127 D1
Ramsay Cl EN10 134 E2
Ramsbury Rd AL1 127 E2
Ramsdell SG1 50 F5
Ramsey Cl
Brookmans Park AL9 145 D4
St Albans AL1 128 A1
Ramsey Lodge Ct 9
AL1 127 E4
Ramson Rise HP1 123 E2
Ram Yard (Ind Est)
SG15 11 A4
Randalls Ride HP2 124 E5
Randalls Wlk AL2 140 F1
Randals Hill SG2 51 C3
Randolph Ct 3 HA5 176 A3
Randon Cl HA2 176 B1
Rand's Cl SG5 21 B7
Rand's Cotts SG5 21 B7
Rand's Mdw SG5 21 B7
Ranelagh Rd HP2 125 B3
Ranleigh Wlk AL5 107 D6
Rannoch Wlk HP2 124 D7
Rannock Cl LU3 44 D8
Ranskill Rd WD6 170 A8
Ransom Cl
Hitchin SG4 34 F4
Watford WD19 167 C2
Ransom Yd 7 SG5 34 F7
Rant Mdw
Hemel Hempstead
HP3 125 A1
Hemel Hempstead HP3 125 A2
Ranulf Cl CM17 118 C6
Ranworth Ave
Hoddesdon EN11 115 B2
Stevenage SG2 69 C7
Ranworth Cl 2 HP3 124 D1
Ranworth Gdns EN6 158 D8
Raphael Cl WD7 156 E7
Raphael Dr WD24 167 D7
Rapper Ct LU3 63 D8
Rasehill Cl WD3 165 C4
Rathlyn HP3 139 B8
Ratty's La EN11 135 D6
Raveley Cotts WD23 168 A3
Ravenbank Rd LU2 46 C5
Raven Cl WD3 165 D2
Raven Ct AL10 130 A4
Ravenfield Rd AL7 110 F6
Ravenhill Way LU4 44 B4
Ravenscroft
Harpenden AL5 107 D6
Hoddesdon EN10 134 F3
Watford WD25 154 E4
Ravenscroft Pk EN5 171 D5
Ravenscroft Sch a Tech
Coll The N20 171 F2
Ravens Ct
Berkhamsted HP4 122 E6
Long Marston HP23 79 B4
Ravensdell HP1 123 F4
Ravens La HP4 122 D4
Ravensthorpe LU2 46 B4
Ravens Wharf 5 HP4 122 D4
Ravenswood Pk HA6 175 A4
Rawdon Dr EN11 135 A5
Raybarn Rd HP1 124 A5
Raydon Rd EN8 162 D7
Rayfield AL8 89 D1
Rayleigh Ho WD5 153 F7
Raymer Cl AL1 127 E4
Raymer Ct 3 AL1 127 E4
Raymond Cl WD5 153 D7
Raymond Cotts SG5 21 E4
Raymond Ct EN6 159 C5
Raymonds Cl AL7 110 E4
Raymonds Plain AL7 110 E4
Raynham Cl CM23 77 C8
Raynham Rd CM23 77 B8
Raynham St SG13 113 E6
Raynham Way LU2 46 D1
Raynsford Rd SG12 93 E1
Raynton Rd EN3 162 D2
Ray's Hill HP5 120 C2
Readings The WD3 164 F6
Recreation Ground
Stansted Mountfitchet
CM24 59 E6
Wingrave HP22 60 B2
Rectory Cl
Bishop's Stortford
CM23 76 D3
Essendon AL9 131 F6
Hunsdonbury SG12 116 D8
Rectory Croft SG1 36 D1
Rectory Dr CM23 58 D6
Rectory Gdns AL10 130 B5
Rectory La
Berkhamsted HP4 122 C4
Datchworth SG3 69 C2
Farnham CM23 58 D6
Kings Langley WD4 139 A3
Lilley LU2 32 D2
Rickmansworth WD3 165 D1
Shenley WD7 157 B7
Stevenage SG1 36 D1
Watton at S SG14 70 D3
Rectory Rd
Rickmansworth WD3 165 D2
Welwyn Garden City AL8 89 B1
Rectory Wood CM20 117 C1
Redan Rd SG12 93 E3
REDBOURN 106 B6
Redbournbury La
AL3 106 D2
Redbournbury Watermill*
AL3 106 D2
Redbourn Ho AL3 106 A8
Redbourn Ind Est AL3 106 B5
Redbourn Inf Sch
AL3 106 A6
Redbourn Jun Sch
AL3 106 A6
Redbourn La AL3, AL5 106 E6
Redbourn Rd
Hemel Hempstead
HP2 125 B8
St Albans AL3 126 E7
Redbourn Village Mus*
AL3 106 A5
Red Brick Cotts SG11 57 B1
Red Brick Row CM22 98 B8
Redcar Dr SG1 50 A6
Redcote End AL5 107 A7
Red Cottage HP23 100 D1
Red Cow Cotts LU6 83 C8
Redding Ho WD18 166 E3
Redding La AL3 105 F8
Reddings
Hemel Hempstead
HP3 125 A1
Welwyn Garden City
AL8 110 C7
Reddings Ave WD23 168 B4
Reddings Prim Sch The
HP3 125 A1
Reddings The WD6 169 F6
Redditch Ct HP2 124 F7
Redfern Ct 1 WD18 166 E4
Redferns Cl LU1 63 A6
Redferns Ct LU1 63 A6
Redfield Cl AL3 106 A5
Redgrave Gdns LU3 44 F7
Redhall Cl AL10 129 F1
Redhall Dr AL10 129 F1
Redhall La
Colney Heath AL4 129 E1
Sarratt WD3 165 E8
Redheath Cl WD25 153 F4
REDHILL 25 E7
Redhill Rd SG5 34 D8
Redhoods Way E SG6 22 E7
Redhoods Way W SG6 22 E6
Red House Cl SG12 114 E8
Redhouse The EN10 134 F1
Redlands Rd EN3 162 E1
Red Lion Cl WD25 155 C2
Red Lion Cotts SG5 33 D2
Red Lion Ct 5 CM23 77 A7
Red Lion La
Hemel Hempstead
HP3 139 A5
Sarratt WD3 152 A4
Red Lion Yd SG12 94 E4
Red Lo WD6 169 F6
Red Lodge Gdns HP4 122 A3
Redmire Cl LU4 44 B6
Redoubt Cl SG4 22 A1
Redpale Ct WD3 165 E1
Red Rails LU1 63 C5
Red Rails Ct LU1 63 C5
Red Rd WD6 169 F6
Redricks La CM21 118 A6
Redvers Cl CM23 59 A2
Redwell Ct EN8 162 F5
Redwing Cl SG2 51 D4
Redwing Gr WD5 154 A8
Redwing Rise SG8 7 E8
Redwood Cl WD19 175 D6
Redwood Dr
Hemel Hempstead
HP3 124 E1
Luton LU3 44 C8
Redwood Rise WD6 157 B2
Redwoods
Hertford SG14 113 C7
Welwyn Garden City AL8 89 D3
Redwoods The CM23 76 D8
Redwood Way EN5 171 D4
REED 16 E5
Reed Cl AL2 142 E4
REED END 16 C5
Reed Fst Sch SG8 16 E5
Reedham Cl AL2 141 A2
Reedings Jun Sch
CM21 97 E3
Reedings Way CM21 97 F4
Reed Pl AL5 85 F3
Reeds Chapel 12
WD24 167 C7
Reeds Cres WD24 167 C7
Reedsdale LU2 46 F2
Reeds The AL7 110 D5
Reeves Ave LU3 45 B4
Reeves Pightle SG8 9 F3
Regal Cl SG11 55 E2
Regal Ct
Hitchin SG5 34 F8
Tring HP23 100 A3
Regal Way WD24 154 C1
Regency Cl CM23 76 E7
Regency Ct
4 Hemel Hempstead
HP2 124 D3
Hoddesdon EN10 148 F8
St Albans AL1 128 B3
8 Watford WD17 167 A8
Regency Ho WD7 156 A4
Regent Cl
Kings Langley WD4 139 A3
St Albans AL4 128 C7
Welwyn Garden City
AL7 110 E5
Regent Ct
Stotfold SG5 11 F7
Welwyn Garden City
AL7 110 E5
Regent Gate EN8 162 E5
Regents Cl WD7 156 A5
Regents Ct 1 AL1 128 B2
Regent's Ct HA5 175 D1
Regent St
Luton LU1 63 E7
Stotfold SG5 11 F7
Watford WD24 154 B1
Regina Cl EN5 171 D6
Reginald Mews 4
CM17 118 C1
Reginald Rd HA6 174 F3
Reginald St LU2 45 E1
Reiss Ho AL7 110 F6
Remus Cl AL1 141 D7
Rendlesham Ave
WD7 155 F2
Rendlesham Cl SG12 93 B2
Rendlesham Rd EN2 161 B1
Rendlesham Way
WD3 164 C3
Rennie Ct 5 EN3 163 A1
Rennison Cl EN7 147 F4
Renoir Ho 4 WD18 166 E5
Renshaw Cl LU2 46 E2
Repton Cl LU3 44 F6
Repton Gn AL3 127 D6
Repton Way WD3 166 A4
Reson Way HP1 124 B2
Reston Cl WD6 157 B1
Reston Path
Borehamwood WD6 157 A1
Luton LU2 46 E2
Retford Cl WD6 157 A1
Retreat The WD5 153 C8
Revels Cl SG14 113 D8
Revels Rd SG14 113 D8
Rex The HP4 122 C4
Reynard Copse CM23 58 F1
Reynards Rd AL6 89 C7
Reynard's Way AL2 140 F2
Reynard Way SG13 114 B6
Reynolds SG6 11 F1
Reynolds Cl HP1 124 A4
Reynolds Cres AL4 128 B8
Rhee Spring SG7 13 B1
Rhodes Arts Complex &
Bishop's Stortford Mus*
CM23 77 A6
Rhodes Ave CM23 76 F5
Rhodes Way WD24 167 D8
Rhymes HP1 124 B5
Ribbledale AL2 142 F4
Ribblesdale HP2 124 E6
Rib Cl SG11 55 E2
Ribocon Way LU4 44 B7
Ribston Cl WD7 156 D6
Rib Vale SG14 92 D1
Rib Way SG9 40 E7
Riccat La SG1 36 F3
Rice Cl HP2 124 F4
Richard Ct 1 EN5 171 E6
Richard Hale Sch
SG13 113 D5
Richards Cl
Bushey WD23 168 D2
Luton LU1 63 B6
Richards Ct LU1 63 B5
Richardson Cl AL2 142 E4
Richardson Cres EN7 147 B6
Richardson Pl AL4 129 B1
Richards St AL10 129 D7
Richard Stagg Cl AL1 128 C1
Richard Wittington Prim
Sch CM23 76 E4
Richfield Rd WD23 168 C2
Richmond Cl
Bishop's Stortford
CM23 76 C7
Borehamwood WD6 170 D4
Cheshunt EN8 148 C2
Ware SG12 93 B3
Richmond Ct
4 Hatfield AL10 130 B3
Hoddesdon EN10 134 F3
Luton LU2 45 F1
Potters Bar EN6 159 C8
St Albans AL1 128 A3
Richmond Dr WD17 166 E7
Richmond Gdns HA3 176 F3
Richmond Hill LU2 45 F2
Richmond Hill Sch LU2 45 E2
Richmond Rd EN6 159 C8
Richmond Way WD3 166 C5
Richmond Wlk AL4 128 D7
Rickfield Cl AL10 130 A3
RICKMANSWORTH 165 C1
Rickmansworth La
SL9 172 A5
Rickmansworth Park Jun
Mix Inf Sch WD3 165 E2
Rickmansworth PNEU Sch
WD3 165 C3
Rickmansworth Rd
Chorleywood WD3 164 F6
Harefield UB9 173 D3
Northwood HA6 174 D3
Pinner HA5 175 C1
Watford WD18 166 E5
Rickmansworth Sch
WD3 165 F3
Rickmansworth Sta
WD3 165 D2
Rickyard Cl LU2 46 B3
Rickyard Mdw AL3 106 A5
Rickyard The
Ashwell SG7 4 D3
Letchworth Garden City
SG6 12 C1
Riddell Gdns SG7 23 F8
Riddy Hill Cl SG4 35 A6
Riddy La
Hitchin SG4 35 A6
Luton LU3 45 C5
Riddy The SG4 88 F8
RIDGE 157 F5
Ridge Ave
Harpenden AL5 85 E4
Letchworth Garden City
SG6 23 A6
Ridge Ct LU2 46 A1
Ridgedown AL3 106 A5
Ridgefield WD17 153 E2
Ridgehurst Ave WD25 153 F5
Ridge La WD17 153 F2
Ridge Lea HP1 123 F3
Ridgeleigh Ct 3 EN5 171 E6
Ridge Rd SG6 23 A6
Ridge St WD24 154 B1
Ridge The
Barnet EN5 171 F4
Letchworth Garden City
SG6 23 A6
Northwood HA6 174 F3
Ridge View HP23 100 C5
Ridgeview Cl EN5 171 D3
Ridgeway
Berkhamsted HP4 121 F4
Harpenden AL5 85 E4
Kensworth Common LU6 82 E8
Little Hadham SG11 57 B1
London Colney WD7 156 C8
Stevenage SG1 50 F5
Welwyn Garden City
AL7 111 B6
Ridge Way WD3 165 B2
Ridgeway Cl HP3 138 F5
Ridgeway Ct HA5 176 A3
Ridgeway The
Codicote SG4 67 F1
Cuffley EN6 146 A4
Hadley Wood EN2, EN4 160 D3
Hertford SG14 112 F7
Hitchin SG5 34 D6
Radlett WD7 155 F2
St Albans AL4 128 C7
Ware SG12 93 C3
Watford WD17 153 E2
Ridgeway View LU7 80 D4
Ridgewood Dr AL5 85 E4
Ridgewood Gdns AL5 85 E4
Ridgmont Rd AL1 127 E2
Ridgway Rd LU2 45 F1
Ridings The
Bishop's Stortford
CM23 76 D4
Hertford SG14 113 A5
Latimer HP5 150 D3
Luton LU3 45 C1
Markyate AL3 83 E6
Stevenage SG2 51 B3
Ridler Rd EN1 161 E1
Ridlins End SG2 51 C2
Rigby Pl EN3 163 A2
Rigery La SG11 73 A7
Riley Rd EN3 162 C1
Ringmer Ct LU2 46 C3
RINGSHALL 81 B1
Ringshall Dr HP4 102 C8
Ringshall Rd HP4 81 B3
Ringtale Pl SG7 13 B1
Ringway Rd AL2 141 B4
Ringwood Rd LU2 45 D7
Ripley Rd
Enfield EN2 161 C1
Luton LU4 44 C1
Ripley Way
Cheshunt EN7 148 B1
Hemel Hempstead HP1 123 E4
Ripon Rd SG1 37 A2
Ripon Way
Borehamwood WD6 170 D4
St Albans AL4 128 D7
Rise Cotts SG12 95 D2
Risedale Cl HP3 138 E8
Risedale Hill HP3 138 E8
Risedale Rd HP3 138 E8
Rise The
Baldock SG7 23 E7
Borehamwood WD6 169 F4
Harrow HA3 176 C1
Park Street AL2 141 D6
Rising Hill Cl HA6 174 C4
Risingholme Cl
Bushey WD23 168 B2
Harrow HA3 176 E2
Risingholme Rd HA3 176 E1
Ritcroft Cl HP3 125 B2
Ritcroft Dr HP3 125 B2
Ritcroft St HP3 125 B2
Ritz Ct EN6 159 A8
Rivenhall End AL7 111 C6
River Ave EN11 135 B7
Riverbank HP1 124 B7
Riverbanks Cl AL5 86 C4
River Cl EN8 163 A5
River Ct
Ickleford SG5 21 F4
Sacombe SG12 92 E4
Sawbridgeworth CM21 97 F3
Riverfield La CM21 97 E3
Riverford Cl AL5 86 B4
River Gn SG9 40 E8
River Hill AL3 84 B2
River Lee Ctry Pk*
EN9 149 B1
River Mead SG5 21 C2
River Meads SG12 115 C4
Rivermill CM20 117 C2
Rivermill Ct SG8 7 C7
River Park Ind Est
HP4 122 A5
River Pk HP1 124 A1
River Point EN8 162 E7
Riversend Rd HP3 138 C8
Rivershill SG14 70 E3
Riverside
Bishop's Stortford
CM23 76 F7
Buntingford SG9 40 E7
Hemel Hempstead HP3 138 F6
Hertford SG14 113 D6
Hoddesdon EN11 135 C8
London Colney AL2 142 E4
Welwyn AL6 89 B5
Riverside Ave EN10 135 A1
Riverside Bsns Pk
CM24 59 E6
Riverside Cl
Kings Langley WD4 139 B2
St Albans AL1 127 E1
Riverside Club (Tennis
Ctr) The HA6 174 B3
Riverside Cotts SG12 115 C4
Riverside Ct
Harlow CM20 118 C6
St Albans AL1 127 E1
Riverside Dr WD3 165 D1
Riverside Est AL5 86 C4
Riverside Gdns HP4 122 A5
Riverside Ind Est AL2 142 E4
Riverside Mews
Hoddesdon EN10 148 E8
10 Ware SG12 93 D1
Riverside Path EN8 148 C2
Riverside Rd
Luton LU3 45 A5
St Albans AL1 127 E2
Watford WD19 167 B3
Riverside Sh Ctr HP2 124 C1
Riverside Wlk 16 CM23 76 F7
Riversmead EN11 135 A5
Riversmeet SG14 113 B5
River St SG12 93 E1
River View AL7 89 F2
River Way
Harlow CM20 118 B5
Luton LU3 44 E5
Rivett Cl SG7 13 A1
Roan Wlk SG8 7 E6
Roaring Meg Ret Pk
SG1 50 E3
ROAST GREEN 30 F6
Robbery Bottom La
AL6 90 A8
Robbs Cl HP1 124 A5
Robe End HP1 123 F5
Robert Allen Ct 3 LU1 63 E6
Robert Ave AL1 141 C7
Robert Cl EN6 158 E6
Robert Humbert Ho
SG6 23 A5
Robert Saunders Ct
SG6 22 E4
Roberts Cl EN8 148 E1
Roberts Ct SG4 66 F7
Roberts La SL9 172 B5
Robertson Cl EN10 148 E5
Robertson Rd 11 HP4 122 D4
Roberts Rd WD18 167 C4
Roberts Way AL10 129 F3
Roberts Wood Dr SL9 172 A5
Robert Tebbutt Ct SG5 34 E6
Robert Wallace Cl
CM23 58 F1
Robeson Way WD6 170 C8
Robina Cl HA6 174 F2
Robin Cl SG12 115 C3
Robin Ct AL5 86 B4
Robin Hill HP4 122 C3
Robin Hood Dr
Harrow HA3 176 F3
Watford WD23 167 F8
Robin Hood La AL10 130 A6

Robin Hood Mdw HP2 124 F8
Robin Jeffrey Ct 7 CM23 76 F6
Robin Mead AL7 90 A1
Robins Cl AL2 142 E4
Robinsfield HP1 124 A3
Robins Nest Hill SG13 132 C6
Robinson Ave EN7 147 B3
Robinson Cl CM23 76 F5
Robinson Cres WD23 168 C1
Robins Rd HP3 125 A1
Robinsway EN9 163 E5
Robins Way AL10 129 F2
Robinswood LU2 45 E5
Robin Way EN6 146 E3
Robsons Cl EN8 148 C2
Rochdale Ct 6 LU1 63 E6
Rochester Ave LU2 46 C4
Rochester Ct 6 EN5 171 F5
Rochester Dr WD25 154 C4
Rochester Way
Croxley Green WD3 166 B5
Royston SG8 7 D8
Rochford Ave EN9 163 D5
Rochford Cl
Cheshunt EN10 148 E5
Stansted Mountfitchet CM24 59 E5
Rochford Dr LU2 46 E2
Rochford Ho EN9 163 D6
Rochford Rd CM23 59 C1
Rockfield Ave SG12 93 D3
Rockingham Cl LU7 80 D3
Rockingham Gate WD23 168 C3
Rockingham Way SG1 50 E4
Rockleigh SG14 113 C6
Rockley Rd LU1 63 A7
Rockliffe Ave WD4 139 A1
Rock Rd SG8 7 C8
Rockways EN5 170 F3
Rockwell Ct 6 WD18 166 E4
Rodeheath LU4 44 D3
Roden Cl CM17 118 F4
Rodgers Cl WD6 169 D3
Rodings Row EN5 171 E5
Rodney Ave AL1 128 A1
Rodney Cres EN11 135 A8
Rodwell Yd HP23 100 A3
Roebuck Cl
Hertford SG13 114 A6
Luton LU1 63 B6
Roebuck Ct 1 SG2 50 F1
Roebuck Gate SG2 50 F1
Roebuck Prim Sch SG2 50 F2
Roebuck Ret Pk SG1 50 E2
Roe Cl SG5 11 E5
Roecroft Lower Sch SG5 11 F6
Roedean Ave EN3 162 C1
Roedean Cl LU2 46 D3
Roedean Ho 3 WD24 167 C7
Roe End La AL3 83 B4
Roefields Cl HP3 138 A7
ROE GREEN
Hatfield 130 A6
Sandon 26 B8
Roe Green Cl AL10 129 E4
Roe Green Ctr AL10 129 F4
Roe Green La AL10 129 F5
Roe Hill Cl AL10 129 F4
Roehyde Way AL10 129 E2
ROESTOCK 143 E8
Roestock Gdns AL4 129 E1
Roestock La AL4 129 E1
Rofant Rd HA6 174 E4
Rogate Rd LU2 46 C5
Roger de Clare Sch SG11 55 E2
Rogers Cl EN7 147 D4
Roger's La SG9 29 A5
Rogers Ruff HA6 174 C2
Rokewood Mews 3 SG12 93 D2
Roland St AL1 128 B2
Rolleston Cl SG12 93 C3
Rollswood AL7 110 E3
Rollswood Rd AL6 89 B8
Rollys La SG7 4 D4
Roman Cl UB9 173 B2
Roman Gdns WD4 139 B1
Roman Ho AL2 142 D4
Roman La SG7 24 A8
Roman Mews 7 EN11 135 A7
Roman Rd LU4 44 E3
Roman Rise CM21 97 D2
Romans End AL3 127 C1
Roman St 8 EN11 135 A7
Roman Theatre of Verulamium The* AL3 127 A3
Roman Vale CM17 118 C5
Roman Way
Markyate AL3 83 E6
Standon SG11 55 D3
Waltham Abbey EN9 163 B4
Welwyn AL6 89 C6
Roman Way Fst Sch SG8 7 C8
Romany Cl SG6 22 C6
Romany Ct HP2 125 C4
Romeland
Elstree WD6 169 D3
St Albans AL3 127 C3
Waltham Abbey EN9 163 C6
Romeland Ct WD6 169 D3
Romeland Hill AL3 127 C3
Romilly Dr WD19 175 F6
Ronald Ct AL2 140 E2
Rondini Ave LU3 45 B3
Ronsons Way AL4 127 F7
Rookery Dr LU2 45 E6
ROOKERY THE 167 B2
Rookery The
Hatfield AL9 144 D8
Stansted Mountfitchet CM24 59 E8
Westmill SG9 40 F3
Rookery Yd SG1 50 C7
Rookes Cl SG6 23 B3
Rooks Cl AL8 110 D5
Rooks Hill
Rickmansworth WD3 165 D5
Welwyn Garden City AL8 110 C5
Rook's Nest Cotts SG1 36 E2
Rook's Nest Farm Barns SG1 36 E2
Rooks Nest La SG8 16 A5
Rook Tree Cl SG5 12 A6
Rook Tree La SG5 12 A6
Rookwood Dr SG2 51 B1
Rosary Ct EN6 145 B1
Rosary Gdns WD23 168 E2
Rose Acre
Pimlico HP3 139 E6
Redbourn AL3 105 F6
Roseacre Gdns AL7 111 D6
Roseacres CM21 97 D3
Rosebank EN9 163 E6
Rosebarn La HP23 79 D1
Roseberry Ct WD17 167 A8
Rosebery CM23 77 C6
Rosebery Ave AL5 85 F1
Rosebery Mews LU7 61 D4
Rosebery Rd WD23 168 B2
Rosebery Way HP23 100 B5
Rosebriar Wlk WD24 153 F3
Rose Cotts
Arlesey SG15 11 A6
Bricket Wood AL2 141 B1
Meesden SG9 30 A5
Wyddial SG9 28 A3
Rosecroft Ct HA6 174 C4
Rosecroft Dr WD17 153 E3
Rosecroft La AL6 90 A8
Rose Ct
Hammond Street EN7 148 A4
St Albans AL4 128 C5
ROSEDALE 148 A3
Rosedale AL7 89 F2
Rosedale Ave EN7 147 F2
Rosedale Cl
Bricket Wood AL2 140 E1
Luton LU3 44 C7
Rosedale Way EN7 148 A3
Rose Garden Mews WD3 165 B5
Rose Gdns WD18 167 A4
Roseheath HP1 123 E4
Rosehill HP4 122 B4
Rosehill Cl EN11 134 F6
Rosehill Ct HP1 124 A1
Rosehill Gdns WD5 153 C7
Rose La AL4 87 C2
Roselands Ave EN11 114 F1
Roselands Prim Sch EN11 114 F1
Rose Lawn WD23 168 C1
Roseley Cotts CM20 117 B4
Rosemary Cl 1 CM17 118 C4
Rosemary Ct 2 HA5 176 A3
Rosemary Dr AL2 142 A5
Rosemary La SG16 10 A3
Rosemary Lo 5 SG5 34 F7
Rose Mdw SG11 41 E4
Rose Mead EN6 145 C1
Rosemont Cl SG6 22 E6
Rosemoor Cl AL7 110 F5
Rosetta Ho 3 HP1 124 D3
Rose Vale EN11 135 A6
Rose Wlk
Royston SG8 7 C7
St Albans AL4 128 C5
Rose Wlk The WD7 156 B3
Rose Wood Cl LU2 45 F3
Rosewood Ct HP1 123 E4
Rosewood Dr EN2 161 A4
Roslyn Cl EN10 134 E2
Ross Cl
Hatfield AL10 130 A8
Luton LU1 63 B6
Stanmore HA3 176 C3
Ross Cres WD25 154 A4
Ross Ct SG2 51 B7
Rossendale Cl EN2 161 B3
Rossetti Lo SG8 7 D8
Rossfold Rd LU3 44 D8
Rossgate HP1 124 A5
Rossgate Prim Sch HP1 124 A5
Ross Haven Pl HA6 174 F2
Rossington Ave WD6 156 E1
Rossington Cl EN1 162 B1
Rossiter Fields EN5 171 F3
Rosslyn Cres LU3 45 C5
Rosslyn Rd WD18 167 B6
Rossway LU1 63 B1
Ross Way HA6 174 F6
Rossway Dr WD23 168 D4
Rossway La HP4 121 A7
Roswell Cl EN8 148 E1
Rothamsted Ave AL5 86 A1
Rothamsted Ct 2 AL5 86 A1
Rothamsted Experimental Sta AL5 107 A8
Rotheram Ave LU1 63 B5
Rother Cl WD25 154 C5
Rother Field LU2 46 D3
Rotherfield Rd EN3 162 D2
Rothesay Ct HP4 122 A4
Rothesay Rd LU1 63 D7
Roughdown Ave HP3 138 A8
Roughdown Rd HP3 138 B8
Roughdown Villas HP3 138 A8
Roughdown Villas Rd HP3 138 A8
Roughs The HA6 174 E7
Roughwood Cl WD17 153 E1
Roundabout Ho HA6 175 A2
Roundabout La AL6 89 F8
Roundbush La WD25 155 C1
Roundcroft EN7 147 F5
Round Diamond Prim Sch SG1 37 B3
Roundfield Ave AL5 86 D3
ROUND GREEN 45 F2
Roundhaye SG11 55 D3
Roundhedge Way EN2 160 F1
Roundhills EN9 163 E4
Round House Ct 6 EN8 148 D2
Roundings The SG13 114 C2
Round Mead SG2 51 D3
Roundmoor Dr EN8 148 E2
Roundway The WD18 166 F2
Roundwood HP3 138 E4
Roundwood Cl
Hitchin SG4 22 C2
Oaklands AL6 89 D8
Roundwood Ct AL5 85 F3
Roundwood Dr AL8 110 C7
Roundwood Gdns AL5 85 E2
Roundwood La AL5 85 D3
Roundwood Park Sch AL5 85 E2
Roundwood Pk AL5 85 E3
Roundwood Prim Sch AL5 85 E2
Rounton Rd EN9 163 E6
Rousebarn La WD3 166 C7
Rowan Cl
Bricket Wood AL2 155 A8
5 Harrow HA7 176 F4
Luton LU1 63 B7
Shenley WD7 156 E6
St Albans AL4 128 E3
Weston SG4 37 B8
Rowan Cres
Letchworth Garden City SG6 22 E7
Stevenage SG1 50 E7
Rowan Dr EN10 148 F6
Rowan Gr SG4 35 A4
Rowans AL7 90 A1
Rowans Prim Sch AL7 90 A1
Rowans The
Baldock SG7 23 E7
Hemel Hempstead HP1 124 A3
Hoddesdon EN10 134 F4
Rowan Way AL5 107 C8
Rowan Wlk
2 Hatfield AL10 130 A2
Sawbridgeworth CM21 97 E2
Rowbeech Cott LU6 83 C8
Rowbourne Pl EN6 146 D3
Rowcroft HP1 123 E2
Rowel Field LU2 46 C1
Rowington Cl LU2 46 E2
Rowland Cl LU7 80 D3
Rowland Pl HA6 174 E3
Rowland Rd SG1 50 F4
Rowlands Ave HA5 176 B4
Rowlands Cl EN8 148 D1
Rowlands Ct 3 EN8 148 D1
Rowland Way SG6 22 F6
Rowlatt Ct AL1 127 E4
Rowlatt Dr AL3 127 A1
Rowley Cl WD19 167 E3
Rowley Gdns EN8 148 D3
ROWLEY GREEN 170 F5
Rowley Green Rd EN5 171 A4
Rowley La
Barnet EN5 170 F5
Borehamwood WD6 170 D7
Rowley's Rd 2 SG13 113 F7
Rowley Wlk HP2 125 C8
Rowney Gdns CM21 118 C8
Rowney La SG12 72 B5
Rowney Wood CM21 97 C1
Rows The 1 CM20 117 D1
Row The HP5 120 D2
Roxley Cotts SG6 23 B2
Roxley Manor SG6 36 B8
Royal Ave EN8 162 E6
Royal Ct
Aldbury HP23 101 A5
Hemel Hempstead HP3 138 E8
Royal Gunpowder Mills* EN9 163 B7
Royal Masonic Sch for Girls WD3 165 D4
Royal National Orthopaedic Hospl HA7 169 B1
Royal Oak Cl SG9 27 D5
Royal Oak Gdns 6 CM23 76 F6
Royal Oak La SG5 20 D4
Royal Quarter 4 SG5 34 F8
Royal Rd AL1 128 B3
Royal Veterinary Coll (Univ of London) AL9 144 D3
Royce Cl EN10 134 F2
Royce Gr WD25 153 F5
ROYDON 116 C1
Roydon Cl LU4 44 A4
Roydon Ct HP2 105 A1
Roydon Lodge Chalet Est CM19 116 C1
Roydon Mill Leisure Pk CM19 116 A1
Roydon Rd
Harlow CM19 116 E1
Stanstead Abbotts SG12 115 E4
Roydon Sta CM19 116 B2
Roy Rd HA6 174 F3
Royse Gr SG8 7 D4
Roysia Mid Sch SG8 7 D8
ROYSTON 7 C5
Royston Cl SG14 113 B6
Royston & Dist Hospl SG8 7 D4
Royston & District Mus* SG8 7 C6
Royston Gr HA5 176 A4
Royston Park Rd HA5 176 A5
Royston Rd
Baldock SG7 13 D2
Barkway SG8 17 C5
Barley SG8 8 F3
St Albans AL1 128 B2
Royston Sta SG8 7 C7
Rubin Pl EN3 163 A2
Rucklers La WD4 138 C4
RUCKLERS LANE 138 E5
Ruckles Cl SG1 50 E5
Rudd Cl SG2 51 B3
Rudham Gr SG6 23 C3
Rudolf Steiner Sch WD4 138 E2
Rudolph Rd WD23 168 A3
Rudyard Cl LU4 44 D3
Rue De St Lawrence EN9 163 C5
Rueley Dell Rd LU2 32 D2
Rufford Cl WD17 153 F2
Rugby Way WD3 166 B4
Ruins The AL3 106 B5
Rumballs Cl HP3 139 A8
Rumballs Ct CM23 76 C4
Rumballs Rd HP3 139 A8
Rumbold Rd EN11 135 C8
Rumsley EN7 148 A4
Runcie Cl AL4 128 A7
Runcorn Cres HP2 124 F7
Rundells SG6 23 D4
Runfold Ave LU3 45 A5
Runham Cl LU4 44 A4
Runham Rd HP3 124 E1
Runley Rd LU1 62 F7
Runnalow SG6 22 E7
Runsley AL7 90 A1
Runswick Ct SG1 50 A7
Runway The AL10 129 D7
Ruscombe Dr AL2 141 C5
Ruscote HP4 122 A3
Rushall Gn LU2 46 E2
Rushbridge Ct SG6 12 E1
Rushby Mead SG6 23 A5
Rushby Pl SG6 23 A5
Rushby Wlk SG6 23 A6
Rush Cl SG12 115 C4
RUSHDEN 25 F3
Rushden Rd SG9 26 A8
Rush Dr EN9 163 C3
Rushendon Furlong LU7 80 E5
Rushen Dr SG13 114 C3
Rushes Ct CM23 77 A5
Rushfield
Potters Bar EN6 158 E6
Sawbridgeworth CM21 97 E2
Rushfield Rd SG12 93 F3
RUSH GREEN 49 E4
Rushleigh Ave EN8 148 D1
Rushleigh Gn CM23 76 D4
Rush Leys Ct AL2 142 A4
Rushmere Ct 1 HP3 138 E7
Rushmere La HP5 136 B3
Rushmoor Cl WD3 173 D8
Rushmore Cl LU1 62 E4
Rushton Ave WD25 154 A4
Rushton Ct
Cheshunt EN8 148 D2
Enfield EN1 162 B2
Ruskin Ave EN9 163 E5
Ruskin Cl EN7 147 E5
Ruskin La SG4 35 C7
RUSLING END 67 D7
Rusper Gn LU2 46 D3
Russell Ave AL3 127 D3
Russell Cl
Kensworth Common LU6 82 E8
Moor Park HA6 174 C5
Stevenage SG2 51 B2
Russell Cres WD25 153 F4
Russellcroft Rd AL8 110 C7
Russell Ct AL2 141 A1
Russell La WD17 153 D3
Russell Mead HA3 176 F2
Russell Pl HP3 138 B8
Russell Rd
Enfield EN1 161 F1
Moor Park HA6 174 C6
Russell Rise LU1 63 D6
Russell Sch The WD3 164 B5
Russells Nursery WD17 153 D3
Russell's Ride EN8 162 E8
Russell's Slip SG5 34 D6
Russell St
Hertford SG14 113 C6
Luton LU1 63 D6
Russell Way WD19 167 B2
Russet Cl EN7 147 E5
Russet Dr
Shenley WD7 156 E7
St Albans AL4 128 C2
Russett Ho AL7 111 D6
Russettings 2 HA5 175 F3
Russett Wood AL7 111 D5
Rutherford Cl
Borehamwood WD6 170 C7
Stevenage SG1 50 A6
Rutherford Way WD23 168 E1
Ruthin Cl LU1 63 D5
Ruthven Ave EN8 162 D6
Rutland Cres LU2 64 A7
Rutland Ct LU2 64 A7
Rutland Gdns HP2 124 F4
Rutland Hall LU2 64 A7
Rutland Pl WD23 168 D1
Rutts The WD23 168 D1
Ryall Cl AL2 140 E2
Ryans Ct LU2 45 F1
Ryan Way WD24 167 C8
Rydal Ct WD25 154 B7
Rydal Mount EN6 158 E6
Rydal Way LU3 44 F5
Ryder Ave SG5 21 D3
Ryder Cl
Bovingdon HP3 137 A4
Bushey WD23 168 B3
Hertford SG13 114 B7
Ryders Ave AL4 129 E3
Ryder Seed Mews 3 AL1 127 D2
Ryders Hill SG1 37 C3
Ryder Way SG5 21 D3
Ryde Sch The AL9 130 C8
RYDE THE 130 C8
Ryde The AL9 130 C8
Rye Cl
Harpenden AL5 86 B4
Stevenage SG1 36 F3
Ryecroft
Hatfield AL10 129 F3
Stevenage SG1 50 E7
Ryecroft Cl HP2 125 C2
Ryecroft Cres EN5 171 B4
Ryecroft Ct AL4 128 F3
Ryecroft Way LU2 46 A4
Ryefeld Cl EN11 115 B2
Ryefield LU3 31 A1
Ryefield Cres HA6 175 A1
Rye Gdns SG7 13 B1
Rye Hill
Harpenden AL5 86 B4
5 Luton LU2 45 D1
Rye House Gatehouse* EN11 135 D8
Rye House Sta EN11 135 C8
Ryelands AL7 110 F3
Rye Mead Cotts EN11 135 C8
RYE PARK 135 B7
Rye Park Ind Est EN11 135 D7
Rye Rd EN11 135 C8
Rye St CM23 58 F1
Rylands Heath LU2 46 F2
Ryley Cl SG16 10 B5
Ryman Ct WD3 164 C3
Rymill Cl HP3 137 A3
Ryton Cl LU1 63 B6

S

Saberton Cl AL3 105 F4
Sabine Ho WD5 153 F7
SACOMBE 71 E3
Sacombe Gn LU3 31 B1
SACOMBE GREEN 72 A4
Sacombe Green Rd SG12 71 E4
Sacombe Mews SG2 69 D7
Sacombe Pound SG12 71 E3
Sacombe Rd
Hemel Hempstead HP1 123 F5
Hertford SG14 92 C1
Stapleford SG14 92 B4
Sacombes Lane Cotts CM21 96 F7
Sacombs Ash La CM21 96 E7
Sacred Heart Language Coll The HA3 176 E1
Sacred Heart Prim Sch LU2 46 A3
Sacred Heart RC Prim Sch
Bushey WD23 167 F3
Ware SG12 93 D1
Saddlers Cl
Arkley EN5 171 B4
Baldock SG7 23 E8

Saddlers Cl *continued*
Bishop's Stortford CM23 . . . 76 C4
Borehamwood WD6 . . . . . . 170 D3
Pinner HA5 . . . . 176 A4
Saddlers Mews AL3 . . . . . . 83 E5
Saddlers Path WD6 . . . . . 170 D4
Saddlers Pl SG8 . . . . 7 C7
Saddlers Wlk WD4 . . . . . . 139 A2
Sadleir Rd AL1 . . . . 127 E1
Sadler Cl EN7 . . . . 147 C6
Sadlers Way SG14 . . . . 113 A6
Sadlier Rd SG11 . . . . 55 E2
Saffron Cl
Arlesey SG15 . . . . 11 A7
Hoddesdon EN11 . . . . 134 F7
Luton LU2 . . . . 45 D7
Saffron Green Prim Sch WD6 . . . . 170 E5
Saffron Hill SG6 . . . . 22 E6
Saffron La HP1 . . . . 124 B4
Saffron Mdw SG11 . . . . 55 E2
Saffron St SG8 . . . . 7 F5
Sainfoin End HP2 . . . . 125 A5
St Adrian's RC Prim Sch AL1 . . . . 141 C8
St Agnells Ct HP2 . . . . 125 A7
St Agnells La HP2 . . . . 125 A8
ST ALBANS 127 F4
St Alban & St Stephen RC Inf Sch AL1 . . . . 127 F2
St Alban & St Stephen RC Jun Sch AL1 . . . . 128 A3
St Albans City Hospl AL3 . . . . 127 C5
St Albans City Sta AL1 . . . . 127 F3
St Albans City Walls* AL3 . . . . 127 B2
St Albans Dr SG1 . . . . 36 E1
St Albans Girls' Sch AL3 . . . . 127 E7
St Albans High Sch for Girls AL1 . . . . 127 E4
St Albans Highway SG4 . . . . 48 F8
St Albans Hill HP3 . . . . . . 124 F1
St Albans La WD5 . . . . 140 A5
St Albans Link SG1 . . . . . . 36 E1
St Albans Music Sch AL3 . . . . 127 D6
St Albans Organ Mus* AL1 . . . . 128 B2
St Albans RC Prim Sch CM20 . . . . 117 F2
St Albans Rd
Barnet EN5 . . . . 171 E7
Codicote SG4 . . . . 88 F7
Dancers Hill EN5 . . . . 158 C3
Harpenden AL5 . . . . 107 B6
Hemel Hempstead HP2, HP3 . . . . 124 E2
Redbourn AL3 . . . . 106 C3
Ridge EN6 . . . . 157 F8
Sandridge AL4 . . . . 108 B1
St Albans AL4 . . . . 128 A8
St Albans Rd E AL10 . . . . . 130 B6
St Albans Rd W AL10 . . . . 129 D5
St Albans Ret Pk AL1 . . . 127 D1
St Albans Sch AL3 . . . . 127 C3
St Albert the Great RC Prim Sch HP3 . . . . 125 A2
St Aldates Ct LU3 . . . . 45 B3
St Andrew Mews 1 SG14 . . . . 113 C6
St Andrew's Ave AL5 . . . . . 85 F1
St Andrew's CE Prim Sch SG4 . . . . 35 A7
St Andrew's CE Prim Sch
Much Hadham SG10 . . . . . . 74 F2
Stanstead Abbotts SG12 . . . . 115 D4
St Andrew's Cl LU1 . . . . . . 63 B1
St Andrews Dr
St Albans AL1 . . . . 142 B8
Stevenage SG1 . . . . 36 F2
St Andrews Gr LU3 . . . . 45 C3
St Andrews Ho 3 SG4 . . . . 34 F6
St Andrew's Ho CM20 . . . 117 F2
St Andrews Mews LU3 . . . 45 A4
St Andrews Montessori Prep Sch WD25 . . . . 154 C8
St Andrew's Pl 4 SG4 . . . . 34 F6
St Andrews Rd 2 WD19 . . . . 175 D7
St Andrew's Rd HP3 . . . . 138 D7
St Andrew St SG14 . . . . . . 113 C6
St Andrews Terr WD19 . . . . 175 C5
St Andrews Wlk LU1 . . . . . 63 C1
St Anna Rd EN5 . . . . 171 D4
St Annes Cl WD19 . . . . 175 C6
St Anne's Cl EN7 . . . . 148 A3
St Anne's Ct 7 SG5 . . . . . . 34 F8
St Anne's Pk EN10 . . . . 135 A4
St Anne's Rd
Hitchin SG5 . . . . 34 F8
London Colney AL2 . . . . . . 142 D4
St Ann's La LU1 . . . . 63 F7
St Ann's Rd LU1 . . . . 63 F7
St Anthonys Ave HP3 . . . . 125 B1
St Anthonys RC Prim Sch WD18 . . . . 166 E4
St Audreys Cl AL10 . . . . . . 130 B2
St Audreys Gn AL7 . . . . . . 110 F5
St Augusta Ct AL3 . . . . . . 127 D5
St Augustine Ave LU3 . . . . 45 C3
St Augustine Cl 1 SG5 . . . 34 F8
St Augustines Cl EN10 . . . . 134 F3
St Augustines Dr EN10 . . . . 134 F3
St Augustine's RC Prim Sch EN11 . . . . 135 B6
St Barnabas Ct
Harrow HA3 . . . . 176 C2
Hemel Hempstead HP2 . . . 125 A3
St Bartholomew's CE Prim Sch HP23 . . . . 100 D1
St Barts Cl AL4 . . . . 128 D2
St Bernadette RC Prim Sch AL2 . . . . 142 D4
St Bernard's Cl LU3 . . . . . . 45 C3
St Bernard's Rd AL3 . . . . 127 E4
St Brelades Pl AL4 . . . . . . 128 D7
St Catharine's Rd EN10 . . . . 135 A4
St Catherine of Siena RC Prim Sch WD25 . . . . 154 D6
St Catherines Ave LU3 . . . 45 B3
St Catherine's CE Prim Sch SG12 . . . . 93 B2
St Catherines Ct CM23 . . . 76 E7
St Catherine's Hoddesdon CE Prim Sch EN11 . . . . . 135 B6
St Catherine's Rd EN10 . . . . 135 A4
St Christopher Sch SG6 . . . . 22 F3
St Christophers Ct WD3 . . . . 164 D5
St Clement Danes Sch WD3 . . . . 164 D7
St Clement's CE Jun Sch EN8 . . . . 148 E4
St Clements Ct EN9 . . . . . 163 C6
St Columba's Coll AL3 . . . . 127 C1
St Cross Chambers EN10 . . . . 135 A4
St Cross Ct EN11 . . . . 135 A4
St Cross RC Prim Sch EN11 . . . . 135 A4
St Cuthbert Mayne RC Jun Sch HP1 . . . . 124 B4
St Cuthberts Gdns 3 HA5 . . . . 175 F3
St Cuthberts Rd EN11 . . . 115 C1
St Davids Cl SG1 . . . . 36 F2
St David's Cl HP2 . . . . 125 D2
St David's Dr EN10 . . . . . . 134 F4
St Dominic RC Prim Sch AL5 . . . . 107 B8
St Dunstan's Rd SG12 . . . 116 D8
St Edmunds HP4 . . . . 122 C3
St Edmund's Coll SG11 . . . 55 A1
St Edmund's Way CM17 . . . . 118 C4
St Edmunds Wlk AL4 . . . . 128 D2
St Elizabeth's Sch & Coll SG10 . . . . 96 C6
St Elmo Ct SG4 . . . . 34 F5
St Ethelbert Ave LU3 . . . . . 45 C4
St Etheldreda's Dr AL10 . . . . 130 C5
St Evroul Ct 5 SG12 . . . . . 93 D2
St Faiths Cl SG4 . . . . 22 B1
St Francis Cl
Buntingford SG9 . . . . 40 F6
Potters Bar EN6 . . . . 159 C5
Watford WD19 . . . . 167 B1
St Francis' Coll SG6 . . . . . . 22 E4
St George's Dr WD19 . . . . 175 E6
St Georges End SG9 . . . . . 29 A6
St George's Rd
Enfield EN1 . . . . 161 F1
Hemel Hempstead HP3 . . . 138 C7
Watford WD24 . . . . 154 B1
St George's Sch AL5 . . . . . 86 B2
St George's Way SG1 . . . . 50 D5
St Georges Works EN8 . . . . 148 F1
St Giles' Ave EN6 . . . . 158 B7
St Giles' CE Prim Sch EN6 . . . . 158 A7
St Giles Ct EN8 . . . . 162 C4
St Giles Rd SG4 . . . . 67 F2
St Helenas Ct 9 AL5 . . . . . 86 A2
St Helen's CE Prim Sch AL4 . . . . 108 D8
St Helen's Cl AL4 . . . . 108 D8
St Helen's Sch HA6 . . . . . 174 E4
St Heliers Rd AL4 . . . . 128 B8
St Hilda's Sch
Bushey WD23 . . . . 168 B2
Harpenden AL5 . . . . 85 F2
St Hugh's Sch SG11 . . . . . . 73 A8
ST IBBS 35 B2
St Ignatius Coll EN1 . . . . 162 B2
ST IPPOLYTS 35 B3
St Ippolyts CE Prim Sch SG4 . . . . 35 B3
St Ives Cl
Luton LU3 . . . . 45 B3
Welwyn AL6 . . . . 89 F3
St James Ct 15 AL1 . . . . . 128 A2
St James Ctr CM20 . . . . . 118 A4
St James Rd
Harpenden AL5 . . . . 86 B4
Watford WD18 . . . . 167 B4
St James' Rd LU3 . . . . 45 B3
St James's Ct AL5 . . . . 86 B3
St James's Rd EN7 . . . . . . 147 D3
St James Way CM23 . . . . . . 76 C3
St Joan of Arc RC Sch WD3 . . . . 165 E2
St John Cl LU1 . . . . 63 B5
St John Fisher RC Prim Sch AL4 . . . . 128 C6
St John RC Prim Sch SG7 . . . . 23 F7
St Johns SG11 . . . . 55 E3
St John's Ave CM17 . . . . . 118 C4
St Johns CE Inf Sch WD7 . . . . 155 F4
St John's CE Prim Sch
Crews Hill EN2 . . . . 161 B2
Welwyn Garden City AL6 . . . 89 F2
St John's CE Prim Sch AL8 . . . . 109 F5
St Johns Cl
3 Hemel Hempstead HP1 . . . . 124 B1
Welwyn AL6 . . . . 89 C6
St John's Cl EN6 . . . . 159 C6
St John's Cres CM24 . . . . . 59 E7
St Johns Ct
Luton LU1 . . . . 63 B5
Rickmansworth WD3 . . . . . 165 B1
St Albans AL1 . . . . 128 B5
Ware SG12 . . . . 93 F3
St John's Ct
Harpenden AL5 . . . . 107 C7
21 Hertford SG13 . . . . 113 D6
St John's Ct 7 HA6 . . . . . 174 E3
St Johns La SG12 . . . . 115 A6
St John's La CM24 . . . . 59 E7
St John's Path SG4 . . . . . . 34 F5
St Johns Prep Sch EN6 . . . . 159 E5
St John's RC Prim Sch WD3 . . . . 165 B1
St John's Rd
Arlesey SG15 . . . . 11 A4
Harpenden AL5 . . . . 107 C7
Hemel Hempstead HP1 . . . 124 B1
Hitchin SG4 . . . . 34 F6
Stansted Mountfitchet CM24 . . . . 59 E7
Watford WD17 . . . . 167 B7
St John's Sch HA6 . . . . . . 175 B4
St John's St SG13 . . . . 113 D6
St John's Terr EN2 . . . . . . 161 D2
St John's Well Ct HP4 . . . . 122 B5
St John's Well La HP4 . . . . 122 B5
St Johns Wlk CM17 . . . . . 118 C4
St John The Baptist CE Prim Sch SG12 . . . . 115 A5
St Joseph RC Prim Sch WD19 . . . . 175 C7
St Joseph's Cl LU3 . . . . 45 A4
St Josephs Gn AL7 . . . . . . 110 D3
St Joseph's in the Park Sch SG14 . . . . 113 A4
St Joseph's RC Inf Sch LU3 . . . . 45 A4
St Joseph's RC Jun Sch LU3 . . . . 45 A4
St Joseph's RC Prim Sch
Bishop's Stortford CM23 . . . . 76 E6
Cheshunt EN8 . . . . 162 E7
Hertford SG14 . . . . 113 A7
St Joseph's Rd EN8 . . . . . 162 E6
ST JULIANS 141 D8
St Julian's Rd AL1 . . . . . . 127 D1
St Katherines Cl SG5 . . . . . 21 D3
St Katherine's Cotts SG5 . . . . 21 E4
St Katherine's Way HP4 . . . . 121 F7
St Laurence Dr EN10 . . . . 148 F8
St Lawrence Cl
Abbots Langley HP3 . . . . . 139 E1
Bovingdon HP3 . . . . 137 A4
St Lawrence Ct WD5 . . . . 139 E1
St Lawrences Ave LU3 . . . 45 C3
St Lawrence Way AL2 . . . 140 F1
ST LEONARDS 119 E3
St Leonards Cl
Hertford SG14 . . . . 113 E8
Watford WD23 . . . . 167 E5
St Leonards Cres AL4 . . . . 108 C1
St Leonards Ct AL4 . . . . . 108 C1
St Leonards Rd EN9 . . . . . 149 D6
St Leonard's Rd SG14 . . . 113 D8
St Louis Cl EN6 . . . . 159 C6
St Luke's Ave EN2 . . . . . . 161 D1
St Luke's Cl LU4 . . . . 44 E2
St Lukes Ct AL10 . . . . 130 B6
St Lukes Pl 4 AL1 . . . . . . 128 B2
St Luke's Sch AL3 . . . . 106 A6
St Magnus Ct HP3 . . . . . . 125 C1
St Margaret Clitherow RC Prim Sch SG2 . . . . 50 F2
St Margaret of Scotland Jun Sch LU1 . . . . 63 B5
St Margaret of Scotland RC Inf Sch LU1 . . . . 63 B5
ST MARGARETS 115 B4
St Margarets SG2 . . . . 50 F2
ST MARGARET'S 103 C3
St Margarets Ave LU3 . . . . 45 B3
St Margarets Cl LU3 . . . . . 31 A6
St Margaret's Cl HP4 . . . 122 D3
St Margaret's Rd SG12 . . . . 115 B2
St Margaret's Sch WD23 . . . . 168 A2
St Margarets Sta SG12 . . . . 115 C4
St Margarets Way HP2 . . . . 125 D3
St Marks Cl AL4 . . . . 129 B1
St Mark's Cl SG5 . . . . 21 D1
St Martha's Convent Jun Sch EN5 . . . . 171 E5
St Martin de Porres RC Prim Sch LU4 . . . . 44 A4
St Martins HA6 . . . . 174 D5
St Martin's Ave LU2 . . . . . . 45 F2
St Martins Cl
Harpenden AL5 . . . . 86 C4
South Oxhey WD19 . . . . . . 175 C6
St Martins Rd EN11 . . . . . 135 C6
St Martin's Rd SG3 . . . . . . 69 A5
St Martin's Sch HA6 . . . . 174 D5
St Mary RC Prim Sch SG8 . . . . 7 D7
St Mary's Ave
Berkhamsted UB2 . . . . 121 D6
Moor Park HA6 . . . . 174 E5
Stotfold SG5 . . . . 11 F6
St Mary's CE High Sch EN8 . . . . 148 B1
St Mary's CE Jun Sch SG12 . . . . 93 D3
St Mary's CE Prim Sch WD3 . . . . 173 D7
St Mary's CE Prim Sch
Stansted Mountfitchet CM24 . . . . 59 E7
Welham Green AL9 . . . . . . 144 B8
St Mary's CE Prim Sch AL6 . . . . 89 B4
St Marys Church Rd SG4 . . . . 35 F3
St Marys Cl
Aston SG2 . . . . 51 E2
Welwyn AL6 . . . . 89 C5
St Mary's Cl
Letchworth Garden City SG6 . . . . 22 F2
Pirton SG5 . . . . 20 D4
Redbourn AL3 . . . . 106 A4
St Mary's Ct
8 Hemel Hempstead HP2 . . . . 124 D4
Potters Bar EN6 . . . . 159 B7
Welwyn AL6 . . . . 89 C4
St Mary's Ctyd 3 SG12 . . . . 93 D1
St Mary's Dr CM24 . . . . 59 F5
St Mary's Inf Sch SG7 . . . . 23 E6
St Mary's Jun Mix Sch SG7 . . . . 23 E6
St Mary's La SG14 . . . . 112 F3
St Mary's Lower Sch SG5 . . . . 12 A6
St Marys Pk SG8 . . . . 7 D6
Saint Mary's RC Sch CM23 . . . . 76 E7
St Mary's Rd
Cheshunt EN8 . . . . 148 C2
Hemel Hempstead HP2 . . . 124 D4
Luton LU1 . . . . 63 F7
Standon SG11 . . . . 55 D2
Watford WD18 . . . . 167 B5
St Mary's Rise SG4 . . . . 47 D1
St Mary's Sq WD17 . . . . . . 167 C5
St Mary's Way SG7 . . . . 23 E6
St Marys Wlk AL4 . . . . 128 B7
St Matthews Cl
Luton LU2 . . . . 63 E8
Watford WD19 . . . . 167 D3
St Matthew's Ct HA6 . . . . 174 E3
St Matthew's Prim Sch LU2 . . . . 45 E1
St Meryl Sch WD19 . . . . . 175 E7
St Michaels Ave HP3 . . . . 125 B1
St Michael's CE Prim Sch
Bishop's Stortford CM23 . . . . 76 F7
St Albans AL3 . . . . 127 B3
St Michaels Cl
Harlow CM20 . . . . 117 E1
Harpenden AL5 . . . . 107 D7
St Michael's Cres LU3 . . . . 45 D3
St Michaels Ct SG1 . . . . . . 51 B8
St Michael's Ct AL3 . . . . . 127 B3
St Michaels Dr WD25 . . . . 154 B6
St Michaels Ho AL7 . . . . . 110 F5
ST MICHAEL'S MEAD 76 C5
St Michael's Mount SG4 . . . . 35 A8
St Michael's RC High Sch WD25 . . . . 154 D7
St Michaels Rd SG4 . . . . . . 35 B7
St Michael's Rd EN10 . . . . 135 A3
St Michael's St AL3 . . . . . 127 B3
St Michaels View AL10 . . . . 130 B7
St Michaels Way EN6 . . . 145 B1
St Michael's Woolmer Green CE Prim Sch SG3 . . . . 69 A1
St Mildreds Ave LU3 . . . . . 45 C3
St Monicas Ave LU3 . . . . . . 45 B3
St Neots Cl WD6 . . . . 157 A1
ST NICHOLAS 37 A2
St Nicholas CE Prim Sch
Harpenden AL5 . . . . 86 A1
Stevenage SG2 . . . . 50 F4
St Nicholas Cl WD6 . . . . . 169 D3
St Nicholas Ct AL5 . . . . 85 F3
St Nicholas Elstree CE Prim Sch WD6 . . . . 169 D3
St Nicholas Gn 1 CM17 . . . . 118 D1
St Nicholas House Prep Sch HP3 . . . . 139 B6
St Nicholas Mount HP1 . . . . 123 F3
St Nicholas Sch CM17 . . . 118 F3
St Ninian's Ct 8 LU2 . . . . . 63 D8
St Olam's Cl LU3 . . . . 45 B6
St Olives SG5 . . . . 11 E6
St Pancras Ho SG8 . . . . 2 D1
St Paul's CE Prim Sch WD4 . . . . 153 C5
St Paul's CE Prim Sch WD4 . . . . 152 A8
St Pauls Cl AL5 . . . . 107 D8
St Pauls Ct 3 SG2 . . . . 50 F1
St Paul's Gdns LU1 . . . . . . 63 E5
St Pauls Pl AL1 . . . . 128 A3
St Pauls RC Prim Sch EN7 . . . . 148 B4
St Paul's Rd
Hemel Hempstead HP2 . . . . 124 E4
Luton LU1 . . . . 63 E5
St Paul's Walden SG4 . . . . 49 A1
St Paul's Walden Prim Sch SG4 . . . . 66 D7
St Pauls Way
Waltham Abbey EN9 . . . . . 163 D6
Watford WD24 . . . . 167 C7
St Peter's Ave SG15 . . . . . . 11 A7
St Peter's CE Prim Sch WD3 . . . . 165 B1
St Peters Cl AL10 . . . . 130 A6
St Peter's Cl
Barnet EN5 . . . . 171 B4
Bushey WD23 . . . . 168 D1
Rickmansworth WD3 . . . . . 165 B1
St Albans AL1 . . . . 127 D4
St Peters Hill HP23 . . . . . . 100 A4
St Peters Mews 6 AL1 . . . . 127 D4
St Peters Rd LU1 . . . . 63 B7
St Peter's Rd AL1 . . . . 127 E4
St Peter's Sch AL1 . . . . . . 127 E2
St Peter's St AL1 . . . . 127 D4
St Peters Way WD3 . . . . . 164 B5
St Philip Howard RC Prim Sch AL10 . . . . 130 B4
St Raphaels Ct 7 AL1 . . . . 127 E4
St Ronans Cl EN4 . . . . 159 D1
St Rose's RC Inf Sch HP1 . . . . 124 A1
St Saviors View AL1 . . . . . 127 F4
St Saviours's Cres LU1 . . . 63 D6
ST STEPHENS 127 D1
St Stephen's Ave AL3 . . . 141 B8
St Stephen's Cl AL3 . . . . . 141 B8
St Stephens Ct CM24 . . . . . 59 D7
St Stephen's Hill AL1 . . . . 127 C1
St Stephens Rd EN5 . . . . . 171 D4
St Stephen's Rd EN3 . . . . 162 D2
St Teresa RC Prim Sch WD6 . . . . 170 B7
St Teresa's RC Fst & Mid Sch HA3 . . . . 176 C2
St Thomas Ct HA5 . . . . . . 175 E2
St Thomas' Dr HA5 . . . . . . 175 E2
St Thomas More RC Prim Sch
Berkhamsted HP4 . . . . 122 A4
Letchworth Garden City SG6 . . . . 22 D4
St Thomas of Canterbury RC Prim Sch SG11 . . . . 55 C3
St Thomas Pl AL4 . . . . 108 D8
St Thomas's Cl LU2 . . . . . . 46 A4
St Thomas's Rd LU2 . . . . . . 46 A4
St Vincent de Paul RC Prim Sch SG1 . . . . 51 A6
St Vincent Dr AL1 . . . . 128 A1
St Vincent Gdns LU4 . . . . . 44 D3
St Vincent's Way EN6 . . . 159 C6
St Winifreds Ave LU3 . . . . 45 C3
St Yon Ct AL4 . . . . 128 E3
Salamander Quay UB9 . . . . 173 A3
Salar Ho 1 AL1 . . . . 128 A2
Sale Dr SG7 . . . . 12 F1
Salisbury Ave
5 Harpenden AL5 . . . . 86 A1
St Albans AL1 . . . . 128 B4
Salisbury Cl
Bishop's Stortford CM23 . . . . 76 F5
Letchford Garden City SG5 . . . . 11 D2
Potters Bar EN6 . . . . 159 C7
Salisbury Cres EN8 . . . . . 162 D7
Salisbury Gdns AL7 . . . . . 110 F5
Salisbury Hall Dr AL10 . . . . 129 E7
Salisbury Ho AL3 . . . . 127 C2
Salisbury Rd
Baldock SG7 . . . . 12 F1
Barnet EN5 . . . . 171 E6
Enfield EN3 . . . . 162 F2
Harpenden AL5 . . . . 86 D3
Hoddesdon EN11 . . . . 135 C8
Luton LU1 . . . . 63 D6
Stevenage SG1 . . . . 37 A2
Watford WD24 . . . . 154 C1
Welwyn Garden City AL7 . . . . 111 A5
Salisbury Sq
Hatfield AL9 . . . . 130 C6

Salisbury Sq *continued*
 7 Hertford SG14 . . . 113 D6
Sally Deards La AL6 . . . 68 B3
Salmon Cl AL7 . . . 90 A1
Salmons Cl SG12 . . . 93 D4
Saltdean Cl LU2 . . . 46 D4
Salters CM23 . . . 76 C4
Salters Cl WD3 . . . 165 E1
Salter's Cl HP4 . . . 121 F6
Salters Gdns WD17 . . . 167 A8
Saltfield Cres LU4 . . . 44 C4
Salusbury La SG5 . . . 33 C2
Salvatorian RC Coll HA3 . . . 176 E1
Salwey Cres EN10 . . . 134 F3
Sambrook Ct HA5 . . . 175 F3
Samian Gate AL3 . . . 126 F1
Sampson Ave EN5 . . . 171 D4
Samuel Lucas Jun Mix Inf Sch SG5 . . . 34 D7
Samuel Sq 2 AL1 . . . 127 D2
Sancroft Rd HA3 . . . 176 F1
Sanctuary Cl UB9 . . . 173 C3
Sandalls Spring HP1 . . . 123 F5
Sandalwood Cl LU3 . . . 45 B7
Sanday Cl HP3 . . . 125 B1
Sandbrook La HP23 . . . 79 C1
Sandell Cl LU2 . . . 45 F2
Sandeman Gdns SG12 . . . 93 E2
Sanderling Cl SG6 . . . 22 E8
Sanders Cl
 Hemel Hempstead HP3 . . . 138 F7
 London Colney AL2 . . . 142 D4
 Stansted Mountfitchet CM24 . . . 59 D6
Sander's Cnr EN2 . . . 161 B5
Sanders Pl SG4 . . . 35 A8
Sanders Rd HP3 . . . 139 A7
Sandfield Rd AL1 . . . 128 A3
Sandgate Rd LU4 . . . 44 D2
Sandhurst Ct AL5 . . . 107 D6
Sandifield AL10 . . . 130 B2
Sandle Rd CM23 . . . 77 A7
Sandmere Cl HP2 . . . 125 A2
Sandmoor Ho HA6 . . . 174 E4
SANDON . . . 15 B1
Sandon Cl HP23 . . . 99 F4
Sandon Jun Mix & Inf Sch SG9 . . . 15 C1
Sandon Rd EN8 . . . 148 C1
Sandover Cl SG4 . . . 35 B6
Sandown Rd
 Stevenage SG1 . . . 37 C1
 Watford WD24 . . . 154 C1
Sandown Road Ind Est WD24 . . . 154 C2
Sandpiper Ct 15 CM23 . . . 76 F6
Sandpit Hill Cotts HP23 . . . 120 B3
Sandpit La AL1, AL4 . . . 128 C5
Sandpit Rd AL7 . . . 110 E4
SANDRIDGE . . . 108 C1
Sandridgebury La
 Sandridge AL3, AL4 . . . 108 A2
 St Albans AL3 . . . 127 E8
Sandridge Cl
 Hadley Wood EN4 . . . 159 E2
 Hemel Hempstead HP2 . . . 105 A1
Sandridge Ct AL4 . . . 128 D7
Sandridge Gate Bsns Ctr AL1 . . . 127 F7
Sandridge Pk AL3 . . . 127 F8
Sandridge Rd AL1 . . . 127 F5
Sandridge Sch AL4 . . . 108 D1
Sandringham Cres AL4 . . . 128 C8
Sandringham Gdns 6 CM23 . . . 76 E5
Sandringham Lo 7 EN11 . . . 135 A6
Sandringham Rd
 Potters Bar EN6 . . . 145 B1
 Watford WD24 . . . 154 C2
Sandringham Sch AL4 . . . 128 B7
Sandringham Way EN8 . . . 162 D5
Sandy Cl SG14 . . . 113 B6
Sandycroft Rd HP6 . . . 150 C1
Sandy Gr
 Borehamwood WD6 . . . 169 F7
 Hitchin SG4 . . . 34 F6
Sandy La
 Bushey WD25 . . . 168 C6
 Moor Park HA6 . . . 175 A5
Sandy Lane Cvn Site WD25 . . . 168 C6
Sandy Lodge Ct HA6 . . . 174 E5
Sandy Lodge La HA6 . . . 174 E8
Sandy Lodge Rd WD3 . . . 174 C8
Sandy Lodge Way HA6 . . . 174 E4
Sanfoine Cl SG4 . . . 35 C8
Sanfoin Rd LU4 . . . 44 A4
Santers La EN6 . . . 158 E6
Santingfield N LU1 . . . 63 B6
Santingfield S LU1 . . . 63 B6
Sappers Cl CM21 . . . 97 F2
Saracen Est HP2 . . . 125 B5
Saracens Head HP2 . . . 125 A4
Saracens Head Yd 1 AL1 . . . 127 D2
Saracens Mews AL3 . . . 106 B5
Sarbir Ind Pk CM17 . . . 118 C5
Sargents SG11 . . . 55 F1
Sarita Cl HA3 . . . 176 D1
Sark Ho
 Enfield EN3 . . . 162 D1
 10 Watford WD18 . . . 166 F3
SARRATT . . . 152 A4
Sarratt Ave HP2 . . . 125 A8
SARRATT BOTTOM . . . 151 E2
Sarratt CE Prim Sch WD3 . . . 152 A3
Sarratt La
 Rickmansworth WD3 . . . 165 C6
 Sarratt WD3 . . . 165 D8
Sarratt Rd WD3 . . . 165 C8
Sarum Pl HP2 . . . 124 E7
Sarum Rd LU3 . . . 44 F4
Satinwood Ct 1 HP3 . . . 124 E1
Saturn Way HP2 . . . 124 F6
Sauncey Ave AL5 . . . 86 B3
Sauncey Wood AL5 . . . 86 E4
Sauncey Wood La AL5 . . . 86 E6
Sauncey Wood Prim Sch AL5 . . . 86 D4
Saunders Cl
 Cheshunt EN8 . . . 148 D4
 Letchworth Garden City SG6 . . . 23 C7
Savanna Ct WD18 . . . 166 F5
Savill Cl EN7 . . . 147 C6
Savoy Cl UB9 . . . 173 D1
Savoy Mews AL3 . . . 141 B8
SAWBRIDGEWORTH . . . 97 C3
Sawbridgeworth Rd
 Hatfield Heath CM22 . . . 98 D3
 Little Hallingbury CM22 . . . 98 B6
Sawbridgeworth Sta CM21 . . . 98 A3
Sawells EN10 . . . 134 F2
Sawtry Cl LU3 . . . 45 A6
Sawtry Way WD6 . . . 157 A1
Sawyers Ct EN3 . . . 162 E6
Sawyers La EN6 . . . 158 D5
Sawyers Way HP2 . . . 124 F3
Sax Ho SG6 . . . 11 E1
Saxon Ave SG5 . . . 11 F8
Saxon Cl
 Harpenden AL5 . . . 86 C4
 Letchford Garden City SG6 . . . 11 F1
Saxon Ct
 Borehamwood WD6 . . . 169 E8
 Hitchin SG4 . . . 34 F6
Saxon Rd
 Luton LU3 . . . 45 C2
 Welwyn AL6 . . . 89 B3
 Wheathampstead AL4 . . . 108 D7
Saxon Way EN9 . . . 163 C6
Saxtead Cl LU2 . . . 46 D1
Saxton Mews WD17 . . . 167 A7
Sayers Gdns HP4 . . . 122 A6
Sayer Way SG3 . . . 68 F4
Sayesbury Ave CM21 . . . 97 E3
Sayesbury Rd CM21 . . . 97 E2
Sayes Gdns CM21 . . . 97 F2
Sayfield Cotts SG9 . . . 26 B8
Saywell Rd LU2 . . . 46 B1
Scammell Way WD18 . . . 166 F3
Scarborough Ave SG1 . . . 50 B7
Scatterdells La WD4 . . . 138 A2
Scholars Cl EN5 . . . 171 E5
Scholars Ct AL4 . . . 143 C8
Scholar's Hill SG12 . . . 95 A4
Scholars Mews AL8 . . . 110 D8
Scholars The WD18 . . . 167 C4
Scholars Wlk 4 AL10 . . . 130 A2
School Cl
 Essendon AL9 . . . 131 F6
 Stevenage SG2 . . . 51 B3
School Cotts SG4 . . . 47 F6
Schoolfields SG6 . . . 23 C5
School Gdns HP4 . . . 123 B6
School Ho The 1 SG7 . . . 23 F7
School La
 Ardeley SG2 . . . 38 F3
 Aston SG2 . . . 51 E2
 Barley SG8 . . . 9 A1
 Bricket Wood AL2 . . . 155 A7
 Bushey WD23 . . . 168 B2
 Essendon AL9 . . . 131 F6
 Great Offley SG5 . . . 33 C3
 Harlow CM20 . . . 117 E2
 Harpenden AL3 . . . 107 B2
 Hatfield AL10 . . . 130 C6
 Luton LU4 . . . 44 D4
 Preston SG4 . . . 48 E5
 Tewin AL6 . . . 90 E2
 Watton at S SG14 . . . 70 E3
 Welwyn AL6 . . . 89 B4
 Weston SG4 . . . 24 C1
School Mead WD5 . . . 153 D7
School Par UB9 . . . 173 C1
School Rd EN6 . . . 145 C1
School Row HP1 . . . 123 F2
School Wlk SG6 . . . 23 B6
Schubert Rd WD6 . . . 169 D3
Scimitar Pk CM19 . . . 116 F1
Scotfield Ct LU2 . . . 46 D3
Scot Gr HA5 . . . 175 D3
Scotscraig WD7 . . . 155 F4
Scots Hill WD3 . . . 165 F3
Scots Hill Cl WD3 . . . 165 F3
Scots Mill La WD3 . . . 165 F3
Scotswood EN5 . . . 171 B4
Scott Ave SG12 . . . 115 B4
Scott Cl
 Hoddesdon EN11 . . . 135 C6
 Royston SG8 . . . 2 D1
Scott Rd
 Bishop's Stortford CM23 . . . 76 E6
Scott Rd *continued*
 Luton LU3 . . . 44 C7
 Stevenage SG2 . . . 51 B6
Scotts Cl SG12 . . . 114 D8
Scott's Grotto★ SG12 . . . 114 D8
Scott's Rd SG12 . . . 114 D8
Scotts View AL8 . . . 110 C5
Scottswood Cl WD23 . . . 167 E7
Scottswood Rd WD23 . . . 167 E7
Scratchwood Nature Trail★ NW7 . . . 170 D2
Scriveners Cl HP2 . . . 124 E3
Scrubbitts Sq WD7 . . . 156 A4
Scrubbitts Park Rd WD7 . . . 156 A4
Scrubbitts Sq WD7 . . . 156 A3
Seabrook LU4 . . . 44 B3
Seabrook Rd WD4 . . . 139 D4
Seacroft Gdns WD19 . . . 175 D7
Seaford Cl LU2 . . . 46 C3
Seaforth Ct EN11 . . . 135 B4
Seaforth Dr EN8 . . . 162 D5
Seal Cl LU4 . . . 44 D3
Seaman Cl AL2 . . . 141 D6
Seamarks Ct LU4 . . . 45 A1
Searches La WD5 . . . 140 C4
Seaton Rd
 Hemel Hempstead HP3 . . . 124 E1
 London Colney AL2 . . . 142 D5
 Luton LU4 . . . 44 F3
Sebright Rd
 Barnet EN5 . . . 171 D6
 Hemel Hempstead HP1 . . . 124 A1
 Markyate AL3 . . . 83 E5
Secker Cres HA3 . . . 176 C2
Second Ave
 Letchworth Garden City SG6 . . . 23 C6
 Watford WD25 . . . 154 D4
Sedbury Cl LU3 . . . 45 A6
Sedge Gn EN9 . . . 135 E3
Sedgewick Ct HP2 . . . 105 B1
Sedgwick Rd LU4 . . . 44 B7
Sedley Cl EN1 . . . 162 B1
Seebohm Cl SG5 . . . 21 C1
Seeleys CM17 . . . 118 C4
Sefton Ave HA3 . . . 176 D2
Sefton Cl AL1 . . . 127 F4
Sefton Ct AL8 . . . 110 B4
Sefton Rd SG1 . . . 37 B1
Selbourne Rd LU4 . . . 45 A2
Selby Ave AL3 . . . 127 D3
Selden Hill HP2 . . . 124 D2
Sele Mill SG14 . . . 113 B6
Sele Rd SG14 . . . 113 B6
Sele Sch The SG14 . . . 112 F6
Selina Cl LU3 . . . 44 C7
Sell Cl EN7 . . . 147 B5
Sellers Cl WD6 . . . 170 C8
Sells Rd SG12 . . . 93 F2
Sellwood Dr EN5 . . . 171 D4
Selsey Dr LU2 . . . 46 D4
Selwyn Ave AL10 . . . 129 E4
Selwyn Cres AL10 . . . 129 E5
Selwyn Ct SG12 . . . 93 F3
Selwyn Dr AL10 . . . 129 E5
Sempill Rd HP3 . . . 124 E1
Senate Pl SG1 . . . 37 B3
Sentis Ct HA6 . . . 174 F4
Sequoia Cl WD23 . . . 168 D1
Sequoia Pk HA5 . . . 176 B4
Serby Ave SG8 . . . 7 D8
SERGEHILL . . . 140 B5
Sergehill La WD5 . . . 140 A5
Serpentine Ct SG1 . . . 37 C2
Service Industry Bays CM20 . . . 117 F2
Service Rd The EN6 . . . 159 A7
Seven Acres HA6 . . . 175 A4
Sevenoaks Ct HA6 . . . 174 C3
Seven Roe's Malting 5 SG7 . . . 23 E8
Sevens Cl HP4 . . . 122 D4
Severalls The LU2 . . . 46 B3
Severn Dr EN1 . . . 162 A1
Severnmead HP2 . . . 124 E6
Severnvale AL2 . . . 142 F4
Severn Way
 Stevenage SG1 . . . 36 F3
 Watford WD25 . . . 154 C5
Sewardstone Rd
 Sewardstone E4, EN9 . . . 163 D3
 Waltham Abbey EN9 . . . 163 C5
Sewardstone St EN9 . . . 163 C5
Sewell Cl AL4 . . . 128 E3
Sewell Harris Cl CM20 . . . 117 F1
Sewells AL8 . . . 89 E2
Sexton Cl EN7 . . . 147 B6
Seymour Ave LU1 . . . 63 F5
Seymour Cl HA5 . . . 175 F2
Seymour Cres HP2 . . . 124 E3
Seymour Ct
 Berkhamsted HP4 . . . 121 E6
 Tring HP23 . . . 100 A4
Seymour Mews CM21 . . . 118 E7
Seymour Rd
 Berkhamsted HP4 . . . 121 E6
 Luton LU1 . . . 63 F5
 St Albans AL3 . . . 127 E6
Shackledell SG2 . . . 50 F2
Shacklegate La SG4 . . . 66 E5
Shackleton Gdns CM23 . . . 76 E6
Shackleton Spring SG2 . . . 51 A3
Shackleton Way
 Abbots Langley WD5 . . . 154 A7
Shackleton Way *continued*
 Welwyn Garden City AL7 . . . 111 D6
Shady Bush Cl WD23 . . . 168 C2
Shady La WD17 . . . 167 B7
Shafford Cotts
 Hemel Hempstead HP3 . . . 139 A5
 St Albans AL3 . . . 126 F6
SHAFTENHOE END . . . 18 B8
Shaftenhoe End Rd
 Barley SG8 . . . 9 A1
 Nuthampstead SG8 . . . 18 B8
Shaftesbury Ct
 Croxley Green WD3 . . . 166 C4
 Stevenage SG1 . . . 50 E4
Shaftesbury Dr SG5 . . . 11 C3
Shaftesbury High Sch HA3 . . . 176 B2
Shaftesbury Ind Ctr SG6 . . . 23 B7
Shaftesbury Quay 11 SG14 . . . 113 D6
Shaftesbury Rd
 Luton LU4 . . . 45 B1
 Watford WD17 . . . 167 C6
Shaftesbury Way SG8 . . . 7 E5
Shaftsbury Way WD4 . . . 139 C3
Shakespeare SG8 . . . 7 D8
Shakespeare Ct EN11 . . . 115 A2
Shakespeare Dr WD6 . . . 170 A5
Shakespeare Ind Est WD24 . . . 154 A1
Shakespeare Rd
 Harpenden AL5 . . . 86 C1
 Luton LU4 . . . 44 B2
Shakespeare St WD24 . . . 154 B1
Shalcross Dr EN8 . . . 148 F1
Shallcross Cres 6 AL10 . . . 130 A2
Shambrook Rd EN7 . . . 147 B6
Shangani Rd CM23 . . . 76 F5
Shanklin Cl
 Goff's Oak EN7 . . . 147 F2
 Luton LU3 . . . 45 A7
Shanklin Gdns WD19 . . . 175 C6
Shantock Hall La HP3 . . . 136 E1
Shantock La HP3 . . . 136 E1
Sharmans Cl AL6 . . . 89 F4
Sharose Ct AL3 . . . 83 E5
Sharpcroft 1 HP2 . . . 124 D5
Sharp Ct 2 SG1 . . . 50 E6
Sharpenhoe Rd LU3 . . . 31 A5
Sharpes La HP1 . . . 123 B1
Sharples Gn LU3 . . . 45 B8
Shaw Cl
 Bushey WD23 . . . 176 E8
 Cheshunt EN8 . . . 148 C3
SHAW GREEN . . . 25 D5
Shaw's Cnr★ AL6 . . . 88 A6
Shaws The AL7 . . . 111 C5
Shearers The CM23 . . . 76 B4
Sheares Hoppit SG12 . . . 95 D2
Shearwater Cl SG2 . . . 51 D4
Sheepcot Dr WD25 . . . 154 C5
Sheepcote AL7 . . . 111 A3
SHEEPCOTE GREEN . . . 30 F6
Sheepcote La AL4 . . . 87 F1
Sheepcote Rd HP2 . . . 124 F3
Sheepcot La WD25 . . . 154 B6
Sheepcot Villas WD25 . . . 154 C5
Sheepcroft Hill SG2 . . . 51 D3
Sheephouse Rd HP3 . . . 124 F1
SHEERING . . . 98 C1
Sheering CE Prim Sch CM22 . . . 98 D1
Sheering Dr CM17 . . . 118 E4
Sheering Lower Rd
 Harlow CM17, CM21 . . . 118 F7
 Sawbridgeworth CM21 . . . 98 A2
Sheering Mill La CM21 . . . 97 F2
Sheering Rd
 Harlow, Churchgate Street CM17 . . . 118 F4
 Harlow CM17 . . . 118 F5
Sheethanger La HP3 . . . 138 A7
Shefton Rise HA6 . . . 175 A3
Sheldon Cl EN7 . . . 147 E5
Shelford Rd EN5 . . . 171 C3
Shelley Cl
 Borehamwood WD6 . . . 170 A5
 Hitchin SG4 . . . 35 C7
 Moor Park HA6 . . . 174 F5
 Royston SG8 . . . 2 D1
Shelley Ct
 Cheshunt EN7 . . . 148 A3
 16 Harpenden AL5 . . . 86 B1
 Waltham Abbey EN9 . . . 163 F6
Shelley La UB9 . . . 173 A3
Shelley Rd LU4 . . . 44 B2
Shelton Way LU2 . . . 46 A3
Shendish Edge HP3 . . . 138 F6
SHENLEY . . . 157 A5
SHENLEYBURY . . . 156 E8
Shenleybury WD7 . . . 156 E8
Shenleybury Cotts WD7 . . . 156 E8
Shenleybury Farm Cotts WD7 . . . 142 E1
Shenleybury Villas WD7 . . . 156 E8
Shenley Ct HP2 . . . 125 B8
Shenley Hill WD7 . . . 156 B4
Shenley La AL2 . . . 142 C4
Shenley Prim Sch WD7 . . . 156 F5
Shenley Rd
 Borehamwood WD6 . . . 170 B6
 Hemel Hempstead HP2 . . . 105 B1
 Radlett WD7 . . . 156 C4
Shenstone Hill HP4 . . . 122 E5
Shenval Ho CM20 . . . 118 A4
Shenval Ind Est CM20 . . . 118 B4
Shephalbury Park Prim Sch SG2 . . . 51 B1
SHEPHALL . . . 51 B3
Shephall Gn SG2 . . . 51 B2
Shephall La SG2 . . . 50 F1
Shephall View SG1 . . . 51 A5
Shephall Way SG2 . . . 51 C3
Shepherd Cl
 Abbots Langley WD5 . . . 153 F8
 Royston SG8 . . . 7 E5
Shepherd Prim Sch WD3 . . . 165 A1
Shepherds Cl CM23 . . . 76 C4
Shepherds Ct SG14 . . . 92 C1
Shepherds Farm WD3 . . . 165 A1
Shepherds Gn HP1 . . . 123 E2
Shepherds La SG1 . . . 50 A6
Shepherd's La WD3 . . . 164 E2
Shepherds Mead SG5 . . . 21 F2
Shepherds Rd WD18 . . . 166 F5
Shepherd's Row AL3 . . . 106 B5
Shepherds Way
 Brookmans Park AL9 . . . 145 D4
 Harpenden AL5 . . . 85 D4
 Rickmansworth WD3 . . . 165 B2
Shepherds Wlk WD23 . . . 176 D8
Shepley Mews EN3 . . . 163 A2
Sheppard Cl EN1 . . . 162 B1
Sheppards Cl AL3 . . . 127 E6
Sheppards Yd 4 HP1 . . . 124 D4
Shepperton Cl WD6 . . . 170 D8
Sheppey's La WD5 . . . 139 E3
Sheraton Cl WD6 . . . 169 F4
Sheraton Ho WD3 . . . 164 C5
Sheraton Mews WD18 . . . 166 E5
Sherborne Ave LU2 . . . 45 D6
Sherborne Cotts WD18 . . . 167 C4
Sherborne Pl HA6 . . . 174 D4
Sherborne Way WD3 . . . 166 B5
Sherbourne Cl HP2 . . . 124 E2
Sherbourne Ct AL1 . . . 127 F3
Sherd Cl LU3 . . . 44 F7
Sheredes Dr EN11 . . . 134 F4
Sheredes Prim Sch EN11 . . . 134 F4
Sheredes Sch EN11 . . . 134 F5
Sherfield Ave WD3 . . . 173 E8
Sheridan Cl HP1 . . . 124 B2
Sheridan Rd
 Luton LU3 . . . 45 C2
 Watford WD19 . . . 167 D2
Sheriden Wlk EN10 . . . 134 E3
Sheriff Way WD25 . . . 154 A5
Sheringham Ave SG1 . . . 36 B1
Sheringham Cl LU2 . . . 45 C7
Sherington Ave HA5 . . . 176 A3
Sherland Ct WD7 . . . 156 A4
Shernbroke Rd EN9 . . . 163 F5
Sherrards Mans AL8 . . . 89 B1
Sherrards Mews AL8 . . . 89 B1
SHERRARDSPARK . . . 110 C8
Sherrardspark Rd AL8 . . . 110 D8
Sherrardswood Sch AL6 . . . 89 D4
Shervington Gr LU3 . . . 45 C3
Sherwood SG6 . . . 22 F8
Sherwood Ave
 Potters Bar EN6 . . . 158 E7
 St Albans AL4 . . . 128 B6
Sherwood Ct
 20 Bishop's Stortford CM23 . . . 76 F7
 Watford WD25 . . . 154 A5
Sherwood Ho WD5 . . . 153 F8
Sherwood Pl 1 HP2 . . . 124 F7
Sherwood Rd LU4 . . . 45 A2
Sherwoods Rd WD19 . . . 167 E2
Sherwoods Rise AL5 . . . 107 D8
Shetland Cl WD6 . . . 170 D3
Shetland Ho 13 WD18 . . . 166 F3
SHILLINGTON . . . 19 F8
Shillington Rd SG5 . . . 20 B5
Shillitoe Ave EN6 . . . 158 E7
Shingle Cl LU3 . . . 45 A8
Ship La LU7 . . . 80 D3
Shire Cl EN10 . . . 148 F5
Shire Ct
 Hemel Hempstead HP2 . . . 125 A4
 Stevenage SG1 . . . 50 C7
Shire La
 Chalfont St P, Horn Hill WD3 . . . 172 B6
 Chalfont St P, West Hyde WD3 . . . 172 C4
 Chorleywood WD3 . . . 164 C4
 Tring HP23 . . . 120 B4
Shiremeade WD6 . . . 169 F4
Shire Pk AL7 . . . 110 E8
Shires The
 Luton LU2 . . . 45 D1
 Royston SG8 . . . 7 E6
 Watford WD25 . . . 154 C8

- **Shirley Cl**
  - Cheshunt EN8 148 C2
  - Cheshunt, Wormley EN10 148 F7
  - Stevenage SG2 51 C8
- **Shirley Rd**
  - Abbots Langley WD5 153 F7
  - Luton LU1 63 C8
  - St Albans AL1 127 F2
- **Shooters Dr** EN9 135 E1
- **SHOOTERSWAY** 121 F4
- **Shootersway** HP4 121 E4
- **Shootersway La** HP4 121 F4
- **Shootersway Pk** HP4 121 F3
- **Shoplands** AL8 89 D2
- **Shoreham Cl** SG1 50 A8
- **Shortcroft** CM23 77 D7
- **Short Hale** LU7 80 D3
- **Short La**
  - Aston SG2 51 E4
  - Bricket Wood AL2 140 E2
- **Shortlands Gn** AL7 110 F5
- **Shortlands Pl** CM23 76 F8
- **Shortmead Dr** EN8 162 E8
- **Shothanger Way** HP3 137 D6
- **Shottfield Cl** AL4 108 D2
- **Shott La** SG6 23 A5
- **Shrubbery Gr** SG8 7 D4
- **Shrubbery The** HP1 123 E4
- **Shrubhill Rd** HP1 123 F3
- **Shrublands** AL9 145 B5
- **Shrublands Ave** HP4 122 A4
- **Shrublands Rd** HP4 122 A5
- **Shrublands The** EN6 158 E6
- **Shrubs** UB9 173 F4
- **Shrubs Rd** UB9 173 F4
- **Shugars Gn** HP23 100 B5
- **Sibley Ave** AL5 107 E7
- **Sibley Cl** LU2 46 B3
- **Sibthorpe Rd** AL9 144 D7
- **Siccut Rd** SG4 35 E4
- **Sicklefield Cl** EN7 147 F5
- **Siddons Rd** SG2 51 C6
- **Sidford Cl** HP1 123 F3
- **Sidings Ct** SG14 113 C7
- **Sidings The**
  - Hatfield AL10 129 E4
  - Hemel Hempstead HP2 124 D3
  - Hoddesdon EN10 135 A1
  - Lower Stondon SG16 10 B3
- **Siding Way** AL2 142 B5
- **Sidmouth Cl** WD19 175 B8
- **Sidney Ct** EN8 162 F5
- **Sidney Terr** CM23 76 F6
- **Siena Pl** 1 WD18 166 F5
- **Signal Cl** SG16 10 B3
- **Silam Rd** SG1 50 E5
- **Silecroft Rd** LU2 64 B8
- **Silkin Ct** SG2 51 D3
- **Silk Mill Ct** WD19 167 B2
- **Silk Mill Rd**
  - Redbourn AL3 106 B4
  - Watford WD19 167 B2
- **Silk Mill Way** HP23 100 A5
- **Silverbirch Ave** SG5 11 F8
- **Silver Birch Ct** EN8 162 D8
- **Silver Birch Lo** WD24 154 B1
- **Silver Cl** HA3 176 D3
- **Silver Ct**
  - Ashwell SG7 4 D4
  - Hitchin SG5 34 F8
- **Silverdale Ho** HA6 174 F4
- **Silverdale Rd** WD23 167 E4
- **Silver Dell** WD24 153 F4
- **Silverfield** EN10 134 F1
- **Silver Hill** WD6, WD7 157 B3
- **Silver Pl** 12 WD18 166 E5
- **Silver St**
  - Anstey SG9 29 A5
  - Ashwell SG7 4 D4
  - Goff's Oak EN7 147 D1
  - Guilden Morden SG8 1 F4
  - Luton LU1 63 E7
  - Stansted Mountfitchet CM24 59 D6
  - Waltham Abbey EN9 163 C6
- **Silverthorn Dr** HP3 139 B7
- **Silver Trees** AL2 140 F1
- **Silverwood Cl** HA6 174 C2
- **Simmonds Rise** HP3 124 D1
- Simon Balle Sch SG13 113 E5
- **Simon Dean** HP3 137 A4
- **Simplicity La** 6 CM17 118 D1
- **Simpson Cl** LU4 44 D2
- **Simpson Dr** SG7 23 F8
- **Simpsons Ct** 3 SG7 23 F8
- **Sinclair Ho** 4 HA7 176 F4
- **Sinderby Cl** WD6 169 E8
- **Sinfield Cl** SG1 51 A5
- **Singlets La** AL3 84 C2
- Sir Frederic Osborn Sch AL7 111 B7
- **Sir Herbert Janes Village** LU4 44 D4
- Sir John Lawes Sch AL5 86 C3
- **Sir John Newsom Way** AL7 110 E3
- **Sir Joseph's Wlk** AL5 107 A8
- **Sir Peter's Way** HP4 81 E6
- **Sirus Rd** HA6 175 A5
- **Sish Cl** SG1 50 D6
- **Sish La** SG1 50 D6
- **Siskin Cl**
  - Borehamwood WD6 170 A5
  - Royston SG8 7 E8
  - Watford WD23 167 E5
- **Sisson Cl** SG2 51 C2
- **Sitwell Gr** HA7 176 F5
- **Six Acres** HP3 139 A8
- **Six Cotts** SG11 57 C6
- **Six Hills Rdbt** SG1 50 D4
- **Six Hills Way**
  - Stevenage SG1, SG2 50 C4
  - Stevenage SG2 51 B4
- **Sixth Ave**
  - Letchworth Garden City SG6 23 C6
  - Watford WD25 154 D4
- **Skegness Rd** SG1 50 A8
- **Skegsbury La** SG4 65 F1
- **Skelton Cl** LU3 31 B1
- **Skidmore Way** WD3 165 E1
- **Skillen Lo** HA5 175 D2
- **Skimpans Cl** AL9 144 D7
- **Skimpot La** LU1, LU4 44 B1
- **Skimpot Rd** LU4, LU5 44 A1
- **Skinners St** CM23 76 C4
- **Skipton Cl** SG2 68 F8
- **Skua Cl** LU4 44 A5
- **Skye Ho** 11 WD18 166 F3
- **Skylark Cnr** SG2 51 D3
- **Skylark Pl** SG8 7 E8
- Skyswood Prim Sch AL4 128 C6
- **Skys Wood Rd** AL4 128 B7
- **Slade Ct** WD7 156 A4
- **Sleaford Gn** WD19 175 D7
- **Sleapcross Gdns** AL4 129 C2
- **SLEAPSHYDE** 129 C2
- **Sleaps Hyde** SG2 51 C1
- **Sleapshyde La** AL4 129 C2
- **Sleddale** HP2 124 E6
- **Sleets End** HP1 124 B5
- **Slimmons Dr** AL4 128 A7
- **Slipe La** EN10 148 F7
- **SLIP END** 63 C2
- **Slip End** SG7 14 B6
- Slip End Lower Sch LU1 63 B1
- **Slipe The** LU7 80 A7
- **Slip La** SG3, AL6 68 C4
- **Slippers Hill** HP2 124 D4
- **Sloan Ct** SG1 50 F6
- **Sloansway** AL7 90 A1
- **Slowmans Cl** AL2 141 C3
- **Slype The** AL4 87 B5
- **Small Acre** HP1 123 F3
- **Smallcroft** AL7 111 B7
- **SMALLFORD** 129 B4
- **Smallford La** AL4 129 B2
- **Smallford Works** AL4 129 B2
- **Smallwood Cl** AL4 108 E7
- **Smarts Gn** EN7 147 F5
- **Smeathman Ct** HP1 124 C2
- **Smeaton Cl** EN9 163 E7
- **Smeaton Rd** EN3 163 A2
- **Smithfield** HP2 124 D5
- **Smiths Cres** AL4 129 C2
- **SMITH'S END** 18 A8
- **Smith's End La**
  - Barley SG8 17 F8
  - Nuthampstead SG8 18 A8
- **Smiths La** EN7 147 D5
- **Smiths Lane Mall** 5 LU1 63 E7
- **Smiths Sq** 6 LU1 63 E7
- **Smith St** WD18 167 C5
- **Smithy The**
  - Little Hadham SG11 57 B2
  - Sawbridgeworth CM21 97 E3
- **SMUG OAK** 141 B1
- Smug Oak Bsns Ctr AL2 141 B1
- **Smug Oak La** AL2 141 D1
- **SNAILSWELL** 21 E6
- **Snailswell La** SG5 21 E5
- **Snatchup** AL3 106 A5
- **Snells Mead** SG9 40 F7
- **Snipe The** SG4 24 B1
- **Snowdonia Way** SG1 37 A4
- **Snowdrop Cl** CM23 76 C6
- **SNOW END** 29 A6
- **Snowford Cl** 1 LU3 45 A7
- **Snowley Par** CM23 59 B1
- **Soham Rd** EN3 162 F2
- **Solar Ct** WD18 166 F4
- **Solar Way** EN3 162 F3
- **Solesbridge Cl** WD3 164 F6
- **Solesbridge La** WD3 165 B7
- **Sollershott E** SG6 22 F4
- **Sollershott Hall** SG6 22 F4
- **Sollershott W** SG6 22 E4
- **Solomon's Hill** WD3 165 D2
- **Solway** HP2 124 F5
- **Solway Rd N** LU3 45 A4
- **Solway Rd S** LU3 45 A3
- **Somerby Cl** EN10 135 A2
- Someries Inf Sch LU2 46 C3
- Someries Jun Sch LU2 46 C3
- **Someries Rd**
  - Harpenden AL5 86 C4
  - Hemel Hempstead HP1 123 F5
- **Somersby Cl** LU1 63 E5
- **Somerset Ave** LU2 46 A1
- **Somerset Rd** EN3 163 A1
- **Somersham** AL7 111 D6
- **Somers Rd** AL9 144 C7
- **Somers Sq** AL9 144 C8
- **Somers Way** WD23 168 C2
- **Sommer's Ct** SG12 114 E8
- **Sommerville Ct** 12 WD6 169 F8
- **Sonia Cl** WD19 167 C2
- **Soothouse Spring** AL3 127 F7
- **Soper Mews** 6 EN3 163 A1
- **Soper Sq** 2 CM17 118 C1
- **Sopers Rd** EN6 146 F2
- **SOPWELL** 141 F8
- **Sopwell La** AL1 127 D2
- **Sorrel Cl**
  - Luton LU3 45 B8
  - Royston SG8 7 F5
- **Sorrel Garth** SG4 35 A6
- **Sotheron Rd** WD17 167 C6
- **Souberie Ave** SG6 22 F5
- **Souldern St** WD18 167 B4
- **Southacre Way** HA5 175 C2
- **Southall Cl** SG12 93 D2
- **South App** HA6 174 D7
- **South Bank Rd** HP4 121 F6
- **South Block** CM21 97 F2
- **Southbrook** CM21 97 E1
- **Southbrook Dr** 2 EN8 148 D3
- **South Charlton Mead La** EN11 135 D5
- **South Cl**
  - Baldock SG7 23 F7
  - Barnet EN5 171 F6
  - Chiswell Green AL2 141 B6
  - Royston SG8 7 B7
- **South Comm** AL3 106 B5
- **South Cottage Dr** WD3 164 F4
- **South Cottage Gdns** WD3 164 F4
- **South Dene** HP2 104 A8
- **Southdown Ct** AL10 130 A2
- **Southdown Ho** AL5 107 C8
- Southdown Ind Est AL5 107 C8
- **Southdown Rd**
  - Harpenden AL5 107 B8
  - Hatfield AL10 130 A2
- **South Dr**
  - Cuffley EN6 146 E1
  - St Albans AL4 128 E4
- **South Drift Way** LU1 63 B5
- **SOUTH-END** 96 B6
- **Southend Cl** SG1 50 D7
- **Southern Ave** SG16 10 C3
- **SOUTHERN GREEN** 26 A4
- **Southern Rise** LU2 85 F7
- **Southern Terr** 2 EN11 115 B1
- **Southern Way**
  - Letchworth Garden City SG6 22 E8
  - Studham LU6 82 C4
- **Southernwood Cl** HP2 125 A4
- **Southerton Way** WD7 156 E6
- **South Farm Cotts** AL2 142 C3
- **Southfield**
  - Barnet EN5 171 D3
  - Braughing SG11 55 F7
  - Welwyn Garden City AL7 110 D4
- **Southfield Ave** WD24 154 C1
- **Southfield Rd**
  - Cheshunt EN8 162 E7
  - Hoddesdon EN11 135 A7
- **Southfields**
  - Letchford Garden City SG6 11 F1
  - Standon SG11 55 E2
- **Southfield Sch** AL10 130 B1
- **Southfield Way** AL4 128 D6
- **Southgate** SG1 50 D4
- **Southgate Cotts** WD3 165 E2
- **Southgate Ct** 5 AL5 86 A2
- **Southgate Ho** 1 EN8 148 D1
- **Southgate Rd** EN6 159 C6
- **SOUTH HATFIELD** 130 B2
- **Southhill** HA6 174 E2
- **South Hill Cl** SG4 35 A6
- South Hill Prim Sch HP1 124 C2
- **South Hill Rd** HP1 124 C3
- **South Lawns** WD25 155 B3
- **South Ley** AL7 110 E3
- **South Ley Ct** AL7 110 E3
- **South Lodge Mews** 2 SG7 23 F7
- **Southlynn Ho** 2 LU2 63 F8
- **Southmead Cres** EN8 148 F1
- **Southmill Ct** CM23 77 A6
- **Southmill Rd** CM23 77 A5
- Southmill Trad Ctr CM23 77 A6
- **SOUTH MIMMS** 158 A8
- **South Mundells** AL7 110 F7
- **South Ordnance Rd** EN3 163 A2
- **SOUTH OXHEY** 175 B7
- **South Park Ave** WD3 164 F4
- **South Park Gdns** HP4 122 B5
- **South Pl**
  - Harlow CM20 118 A4
  - Hitchin SG5 34 D8
  - Waltham Abbey EN9 163 C6
- **South Rd**
  - Baldock SG7 24 A7
  - Bishop's Stortford CM23 77 A5
  - Chorleywood WD3 164 C4
  - Harlow CM20 118 A4
- **South Rd** *continued*
  - Luton LU1 63 D6
  - Standon SG11 55 D2
- **South Riding** AL2 141 A1
- **Southsea Ave** WD18 167 A5
- **Southsea Rd** SG1 50 B8
- **Southside** SG9 28 A3
- **South St**
  - Bishop's Stortford CM23 76 F6
  - Hertford SG14 113 D6
  - Stanstead Abbotts SG12 115 C4
- South Street Commercial Ctr 1 CM23 76 F6
- **South View** SG6 22 F5
- **Southview Cl** 1 EN7 147 E5
- **Southview Rd** AL5 86 D3
- **South View Rd** HA5 175 B4
- **Southwark Cl** SG1 37 B2
- **Southwark Ho** 11 WD6 170 A7
- **South Way**
  - Abbots Langley WD5, WD25 153 E6
  - Hatfield AL10 130 B2
- **South Weald Dr** EN9 163 D6
- **Southwold Cl** SG1 50 A6
- **Southwold Rd** WD24 154 C2
- **Soval Ct** HA6 174 D3
- **Sovereign Ct**
  - Northwood HA6 175 A2
  - Watford WD18 167 A5
- **Sovereign Pk**
  - Hemel Hempstead HP2 125 B5
  - Luton LU4 44 F1
- **Sovereign Pk** AL4 128 D2
- **Sowerby Ave** LU2 46 C3
- **Spandow Ct** 21 LU1 63 D6
- **Sparhawke** SG6 12 A1
- **Sparrow Cl** LU4 44 A4
- **Sparrow Dr** SG2 51 D4
- **Sparrows Herne** WD23 168 C2
- Sparrows Herne Mansion WD23 168 D2
- **Sparrows Way** WD23 168 C1
- **Sparrowswick Ride** AL3 127 C8
- **Sparrow Wlk** WD25 154 A4
- **Spayne Cl** LU3 45 B8
- **Spear Cl** LU3 44 E6
- **Spectrum Ho** EN3 162 E3
- **Speedwell Cl**
  - Hemel Hempstead HP1 123 E2
  - Luton LU3 45 A8
- **Speke Cl** SG2 51 D5
- **SPELLBROOK** 97 F8
- **Spellbrooke** 5 SG5 34 D8
- **Spellbrook La E** CM22 97 F8
- **Spellbrook La W** CM23 97 E7
- Spellbrook Prim Sch CM23 97 F7
- **Spencer Ave** EN7 147 E5
- **Spencer Cl** CM24 59 E6
- **Spencer Gate** AL1 127 E5
- **Spencer Ho** SG5 11 F6
- **Spencer Pl** AL4 108 C2
- **Spencer Rd**
  - Harrow HA3 176 E1
  - Luton LU3 45 C2
- **SPENCERSGREEN** 119 C7
- **Spencer St**
  - Hertford SG13 113 E7
  - St Albans AL3 127 D3
- **Spencer Way**
  - Hemel Hempstead HP1 124 A6
  - Letchworth Garden City SG6 22 F8
- **Spencer Wlk** WD3 165 C4
- **Spenser Cl** SG8 2 D1
- **Spenser Rd** AL5 86 C1
- **Sperberry Hill** SG4 35 B2
- **Speyhawk Pl** EN6 145 B1
- **Sphere Ind Est** AL1 128 A2
- **Spicersfield** EN7 148 A4
- **Spicer St** AL3 127 C3
- **Spielplatz** AL2 141 A3
- **Spindle Berry Cl** AL6 90 A7
- **Spinney Cl** SG4 35 B6
- **Spinney Ct** CM21 97 E2
- Spinney Inf Sch CM20 118 A1
- Spinney Jun Sch CM20 118 A1
- **Spinney La** AL6 68 E3
- **Spinney Rd** LU3 44 D7
- **Spinney Row** AL2 142 A4
- **Spinneys Dr** AL3 127 B1
- **Spinney St** SG13 114 A6
- **Spinney The**
  - Baldock SG7 23 E7
  - Berkhamsted HP4 121 F3
  - Cheshunt EN7 148 B1
  - 1 Harlow CM20 118 A1
  - Harpenden AL5 85 E3
  - Hertford SG13 113 F6
  - Hoddesdon EN10 134 F4
  - Potters Bar EN6 159 D8
  - Radlett WD25 155 D1
  - Stansted Mountfitchet CM24 59 E6
  - Stevenage SG2 51 D7
  - Watford WD17 167 A8
- **Spinney The** *continued*
  - Welwyn Garden City AL7 110 E5
- **Spires Sh Ctr The** EN5 171 E6
- **Spires The**
  - Bishop's Stortford CM23 76 D7
  - Hemel Hempstead HP2 124 D2
- **SPITALBROOK** 135 B4
- **Spittlesea Rd** LU2 64 C7
- **Spooners Dr** AL2 141 C4
- **Spratts La** LU6 82 F8
- **Spreckley Cl** SG16 10 B5
- **Spring Cl**
  - Barnet EN5 171 D4
  - Borehamwood WD6 170 A8
  - Harefield UB9 173 D2
  - Latimer HP5 150 D3
- **Spring Court Rd** EN2 161 A1
- **Spring Crofts** WD23 168 A4
- **Spring Dr** SG2 69 B8
- **Springfield** WD23 168 D1
- **Springfield Cl**
  - Croxley Green WD3 166 B4
  - Potters Bar EN6 159 E8
- **Springfield Cres** AL5 86 B5
- **Springfield Ct**
  - Bishop's Stortford CM23 76 E8
  - Rickmansworth WD3 165 B1
- **Springfield Lo** SG13 113 E5
- **Springfield Rd**
  - Cheshunt EN8 162 E7
  - Hemel Hempstead HP2 124 F4
  - Luton LU3 45 C6
  - St Albans AL4 129 B3
  - St Albans, The Camp AL1 128 A2
  - Watford WD25 154 B6
- **Spring Field Rd** HP4 122 A6
- **Springfields**
  - Hoddesdon EN10 134 F4
  - Waltham Abbey EN9 163 E5
  - Welwyn Garden City AL8 110 B4
- **Springfields Ho** AL8 110 C4
- **Spring Gdns** WD25 154 C3
- **Spring Glen** AL10 129 F4
- **Springhall Ct** CM21 97 E2
- **Springhall La** CM21 97 E1
- **Springhall Rd** CM21 97 E2
- **Springhead** SG7 4 D4
- **Spring Hills** CM20 117 B1
- **Spring Hills Twr** CM20 117 A1
- **Spring La**
  - Cottered SG9 39 C5
  - Hemel Hempstead HP1 124 A4
- **Springle La** SG13 114 F2
- Springmead Jun Mix Inf Sch AL7 111 C7
- **Spring Mews** CM21 97 E2
- **Spring Pl** 6 LU1 63 D6
- **Spring Rd**
  - Harpenden AL5 85 A4
  - Letchworth Garden City SG6 22 E4
  - Letchworth Garden City SG6 22 E6
- **Springs Cotts** EN10 148 E7
- **Springshott** SG6 22 E5
- **Springs The**
  - Cheshunt EN10 148 E6
  - Hertford SG13 113 F7
- Spring Valley Ent Ctr AL3 127 E7
- **Spring View Rd** SG12 114 C8
- **Spring Way** HP2 125 C5
- **Springwell Ave** WD3 173 A8
- **Springwell Ct**
  - Rickmansworth WD3 173 A8
  - Stanstead Abbotts SG12 115 C3
- **Springwell La** WD3 173 A6
- **Spring Wlk** EN10 134 C2
- **Springwood** EN7 148 A5
- **Springwood Cl** UB9 173 D2
- **Springwood Wlk** AL4 128 D6
- **Spruce Way** AL2 141 B4
- **Spur Cl** WD5 153 D6
- **Spurcroft** LU3 31 C1
- Spurling Wks EN11 135 C7
- **Spurrs Cl** SG4 35 B7
- **Spur The**
  - 3 Cheshunt EN8 148 D3
  - Stevenage SG1 50 E4
- **Square St** 3 CM17 118 C1
- **Square The**
  - Braughing SG11 55 F7
  - Buckland SG9 27 D5
  - Hemel Hempstead HP1 124 C3
  - Hoddesdon EN10 148 E8
  - Much Hadham SG10 74 F3
  - Potten End HP4 123 B7
  - Redbourn AL3 105 F6
  - Sawbridgeworth CM21 97 E2
  - Watford WD24 154 B2
- **Squires Cl** CM23 76 C8
- **Squires Ct** EN11 135 A5
- **Squires Ride** HP2 104 F1
- **Squirrel Chase** HP1 123 E4
- **Squirrels Cl** 2 CM23 76 F8
- **Squirrels The**
  - Bushey WD23 168 D3
  - Hertford SG13 114 B6
  - Welwyn Garden City AL7 111 C5

Stable Block The AL6 .... 90 B2
Stable Cotts SG11 .... 57 E2
Stable Ct AL1 .... 127 E5
Stable Mews
Northaw AL9 .... 145 E3
St Albans AL1 .... 127 E4
Stables The
Radlett WD25 .... 155 B3
Sawbridgeworth CM21 .... 98 B3
Stacey Ct 9 CM23 .... 76 F6
Stackfield CM20 .... 118 A3
Stacklands AL8 .... 110 B4
Staddles CM22 .... 98 B8
Stadium Est The LU4 ...... 44 B1
Stadium Way CM19 ..... 116 F1
Staff Cotts
Harefield UB9 .... 173 B2
London Colney WD7 ...... 142 C1
Stafford Cl EN8 .... 148 B2
Stafford Ct EN10 .... 135 A3
Stafford Dr EN10 .... 135 A3
Stafford Ho
Bishop's Stortford
CM23 .... 76 F5
Hoddesdon EN10 .... 135 A3
Stafford Rd HA3 .... 176 C3
Staffords CM17 .... 118 E4
Stag Ct WD3 .... 164 C5
Stagg Hill EN4 .... 159 E3
Stag Green Ave AL9 ..... 130 C7
Stagg Ridge EN6 .... 159 D5
Stag La
Berkhamsted HP4 .... 122 B5
Chorleywood WD3 .... 164 C3
Stainer Rd
Borehamwood WD6 ...... 156 D1
Radlett WD6 .... 169 D8
Stainers CM23 .... 76 C5
STAINES GREEN 112 D4
Stains Cl EN8 .... 148 F3
Stake Piece Rd SG8 .... 7 C5
Stakers Ct AL5 .... 86 B1
Stamford Ave SG8 .... 7 D7
Stamford Cl
Harrow HA3 .... 176 E3
Potters Bar EN6 .... 159 D7
Stamford Ct SG8 .... 7 D7
Stamford Rd WD17 .... 167 B7
Stamford Yd SG8 .... 7 C6
STANBOROUGH 110 A3
Stanborough Ave
WD6 .... 157 B1
Stanborough Cl
Borehamwood WD6 ...... 157 A1
Welwyn Garden City
AL8 .... 110 C5
Stanborough Gn AL8 .... 110 C4
Stanborough La AL8 .... 110 C4
Stanborough Mews
AL8 .... 110 D4
Stanborough Prim Sch
WD25 .... 154 C4
Stanborough Rd AL8 .... 110 C4
Stanborough Sch AL8 ... 110 B4
Stanborough Sec Sch
WD25 .... 154 B4
Stanbury Ave WD17 ..... 153 E2
Standalone Farm*
SG6 .... 22 D8
Standard Rd EN3 .... 162 E2
Standfield WD5 .... 139 E1
Standhill Cl SG4 .... 34 F6
Standhill Rd SG4 .... 34 F6
STANDON 55 E1
Standon Bsns Pk SG11 ... 55 E1
Standon Ct SG11 .... 55 F1
STANDON GREEN END
.... 72 E4
Standon Hill SG11 .... 55 D2
Standon Mill SG11 .... 55 F2
Standon Rd SG11 .... 56 E3
Standring Rise HP3 ..... 138 B8
Stane Cl CM23 .... 58 F1
Stane Field SG6 .... 23 B3
Stanelow Cres SG11 ..... 55 D2
Stane St SG7 .... 13 A1
Stanford Rd LU2 .... 46 A1
Stangate Cres WD6 ...... 170 E4
Stanhope 3 HA6 .... 174 F5
Stanhope Ave HA3 ...... 176 D2
Stanhope Rd
Barnet EN5 .... 171 D3
Cheshunt EN8 .... 162 E6
St Albans AL1 .... 127 F3
Stanier Rise HP4 .... 121 F7
Stanley Ave AL2 .... 141 A6
Stanley Dr AL10 .... 130 B3
Stanley Gdns
Borehamwood WD6 ...... 169 E8
Tring HP23 .... 99 F3
Stanley Livingstone Ct 2
LU1 .... 63 D6
Stanley Lodge 12 AL1 ... 127 E4
Stanley Rd
Hertford SG13 .... 113 E5
Northwood HA6 .... 175 A2
Stevenage SG2 .... 51 B7
Streatley LU3 .... 31 A5
Watford WD18 .... 167 C5
Stanley St LU1 .... 63 D6
STANMORE 176 F5
Stanmore Chase AL4 .... 128 D2
Stanmore Cres LU3 ...... 44 F4
Stanmore Rd
Stevenage SG1 .... 50 D7
Watford WD24 .... 167 B8
Stanmount Rd AL2 ...... 141 A6
Stannington Path
WD6 .... 170 A8
STANSTEAD ABBOTTS
.... 115 E4
Stanstead Dr EN11 ...... 135 B8
Stanstead Rd
Hertford Heath SG13 ..... 114 D5
Hertford SG13 .... 114 A6
Hoddesdon EN11 .... 115 B1
Stansted Hill SG10 .... 75 A1
STANSTED MOUNTFITCHET 59 D6
Stansted Mountfitchet Sta
CM24 .... 59 E6
Stansted Mountfitchet Windmill* CM24 .... 59 D6
Stansted Rd
Birchanger CM23,
CM24 .... 59 C4
Bishop's Stortford CM23 ... 59 B2
Stanta Bsns Ctr 3
AL3 .... 127 F7
Stanton Cl AL4 .... 128 D7
Stanton Rd LU4 .... 44 C1
Stantons CM20 .... 117 B1
Stants View 1 SG13 .... 113 F7
Staplefield Cl HA5 ...... 175 E3
STAPLEFORD 92 A7
Stapleford AL7 .... 111 D6
Stapleford Prim Sch
SG14 .... 92 A6
Stapleford Rd LU2 .... 46 C4
Stapleton Cl EN6 .... 159 D8
Stapleton Rd WD6 ...... 157 A2
Stapley Rd AL3 .... 127 D4
Stapylton Rd EN5 .... 171 E6
Star Holme Ct SG12 ...... 93 E1
Starkey Cl EN7 .... 147 C6
Starlight Way AL4 ...... 128 C1
Starling Ct 16 CM23 ...... 76 F6
Starling La EN6 .... 146 F3
Starling's Bridge SG5 .... 34 F8
STARLING'S GREEN 30 F3
Star St SG12 .... 93 E1
STARTOP'S END 79 F1
Startpoint LU1 .... 63 C7
Stately Ct 22 LU3 .... 45 D1
Statham Cl LU3 .... 31 B1
Stathams Ct AL3 .... 106 A3
Station App
Cheshunt EN8 .... 162 E5
Chorleywood WD3 .... 164 D5
Harlow CM20 .... 118 C5
Harpenden AL5 .... 86 B1
Hitchin SG4 .... 35 A8
Kings Langley WD4 ...... 139 B1
Knebworth SG3 .... 68 F5
Northwood HA6 .... 174 E3
Radlett WD7 .... 156 A4
South Oxhey WD19 ...... 175 D7
Station Cl
Brookmans Park AL9 ..... 144 E5
Lower Stondon SG16 ...... 10 B3
Potters Bar EN6 .... 158 F8
Station Ct 15 SG12 .... 93 D1
Stationers Pl HP3 .... 138 E6
Station Footpath
WD4 .... 139 B1
Station Par SG6 .... 22 F6
Station Pl SG6 .... 22 F6
Station Rd
Aldbury HP23 .... 101 B5
Arlesey SG15 .... 11 A4
Ashwell SG7 .... 4 F4
Baldock SG7 .... 12 F1
Berkhamsted HP4 .... 122 D4
Bishop's Stortford CM23 ... 77 A7
Borehamwood WD6 ...... 170 A5
Braughing SG11 .... 55 E5
Bricket Wood AL2 .... 155 A8
Brookmans Park AL9 ..... 144 D6
Buntingford SG9 .... 40 E7
Cheddington LU7 .... 79 F8
Cuffley EN6 .... 146 F2
Harlow CM17 .... 118 C4
Harpenden AL5 .... 86 C2
Hemel Hempstead HP1 ... 124 C1
Hoddesdon EN10 .... 135 A3
Holdbrook EN9 .... 163 A5
Ivinghoe LU7 .... 80 E5
Kings Langley WD4 ...... 139 B1
Knebworth SG3 .... 69 A5
Letchworth Garden City
SG6 .... 22 F6
Letty Green SG14 .... 112 B3
Long Marston HP23 .... 79 B4
Lower Stondon SG16 ...... 10 A4
Luton, High Town LU1 .... 63 E8
Luton, Leagrave LU4 ...... 44 E5
Much Hadham SG10 .... 74 E1
Radlett WD7 .... 156 A4
Rickmansworth WD3 ..... 165 D2
Sawbridgeworth CM21 ..... 97 F3
St Albans AL4 .... 129 B3
Standon SG11 .... 55 E2
Stanstead Abbotts
SG12 .... 115 C4
Stansted Mountfitchet
CM24 .... 59 E6
Steeple Morden SG7, SG8 ... 5 C5
Tring HP23 .... 100 D4
Ware SG12 .... 93 E1
Watford WD17 .... 167 B7
Watton at S SG14 .... 70 D3
Welwyn AL6 .... 89 E3
Wheathampstead AL4 ..... 87 D1
Station Rdbt WD3 .... 165 D2
Station Terr
Hitchin SG4 .... 35 A8
Park Street AL2 .... 141 D5
Station Way
Letchworth Garden City
SG6 .... 22 E6
St Albans AL1 .... 127 F3
Staveley Rd LU4 .... 44 C1
Steed Yd 6 SG7 .... 23 E8
Steeplands WD23 .... 168 B2
Steeple View CM23 ...... 76 F8
Sten Cl EN3 .... 163 A2
Stephens Cl LU2 .... 46 A3
Stephens Gdns LU2 ...... 46 A2
Stephenson Cl
Hoddesdon EN11 .... 135 C6
Hoddesdon EN11 .... 135 D6
Royston SG8 .... 7 B7
Stephenson Mews SG2 ... 51 B4
Stephenson Way WD23,
WD24 .... 167 D7
Stephenson Wharf
HP3 .... 138 F6
Stephenson Wk SG5 ..... 11 C2
Stephens Way AL3 ...... 105 F5
Stephyns Chambers
HP1 .... 124 C2
Stepnells HP23 .... 80 A1
Stepping Stones The
LU3 .... 44 E5
Sterling Ave EN8 .... 162 D5
Sterling Rd EN2 .... 161 D1
STEVENAGE 50 D8
Stevenage Bsns Pk
SG1 .... 37 C2
Stevenage Cres WD6 .... 169 E8
Stevenage Enterprise Ctr
SG1 .... 50 B7
Stevenage L Pk SG1 ..... 50 C4
Stevenage Mus* SG1 ..... 50 E5
Stevenage Rd
Hitchin SG4 .... 34 F5
Knebworth SG2, SG3 ...... 68 F7
Little Wymondley SG4 ..... 35 E3
Little Wymondley, Titmore
Green SG4 .... 35 E2
St Ippolyts SG4 .... 35 C2
Walkern SG2 .... 51 E8
Stevenage Rise HP2 .... 124 F7
Stevenage Sta SG1 ...... 50 C5
Stevens Cl EN6 .... 158 D6
Stevens Gn WD23 .... 168 C1
Steward Cl EN8 .... 148 E1
Stewart Cl WD5 .... 154 A7
Stewart Pl 4 SG12 .... 93 E1
Stewart Rd AL5 .... 86 B2
Stewarts The CM23 ...... 76 E6
Stile Plantation SG8 .... 7 E6
Stilton Path WD6 .... 157 A1
Stirling Bsns Pk EN8 .... 162 F5
Stirling Cl
Hitchin SG4 .... 35 C7
Stevenage SG2 .... 69 D7
Stirling Cnr EN5 .... 170 D3
Stirling Ho WD6 .... 170 C5
Stirling Ind Ctr WD6 .... 170 D4
Stirling Ret Pk WD6 .... 170 D3
Stirling Way
Borehamwood WD6 ...... 170 D4
Watford WD5 .... 154 A7
Welwyn Garden City
AL7 .... 111 E6
Stoat Cl SG13 .... 114 A6
Stobarts Cl SG3 .... 68 F6
Stock Bank SG8 .... 8 D1
Stockbreach Cl AL10 .... 130 A6
Stockbreach Rd AL10 ... 130 A6
Stockbridge Cl EN7 ..... 147 E5
Stockens Dell SG3 .... 68 F4
Stockens Gn SG3 .... 68 F4
Stockers Farm Rd
WD3 .... 173 D8
Stockfield Ave EN11 .... 135 B8
Stockholm Way LU3 ..... 44 E8
Stocking Hill SG9 .... 39 B8
Stocking La SG8 .... 18 C1
STOCKING PELHAM 43 E7
Stockings La SG13 ...... 132 D6
Stockingstone Rd LU2 ... 45 E3
Stockmen Field CM23 .... 76 C5
Stockport Rd WD3 ...... 164 C2
Stocks Farm Barns
HP23 .... 101 C7
Stocks Mdw HP2 .... 125 A4
Stocks Rd HP23 .... 101 D7
Stockwell Cl EN7 .... 148 E3
Stockwell La EN7 .... 148 B3
Stockwood Craft Mus & Gdns* LU1 .... 63 D4
Stockwood Cres LU1 .... 63 D6
Stockwood Ct 18 LU1 .... 63 D6
Stockwood Pk* LU1 ..... 63 D3
Stonecroft SG3 .... 68 F5
Stonecroft Cl EN5 ...... 171 B5
Stonecross AL1 .... 127 E4
Stone Cross 3 CM20 .... 117 D1
Stonecross Cl 1 AL1 .... 127 E4
Stonecross Rd AL10 ..... 130 B7
Stonehill Jun Mix Inf Sch
SG6 .... 11 E1
Stonehills AL8 .... 110 D7
Stonelea Rd HP3 .... 138 F8
Stoneleigh CM21 .... 97 D3
Stoneleigh Ave EN1 ..... 162 B1
Stoneleigh Cl
Cheshunt EN8 .... 162 D6
Luton LU3 .... 45 B7
Stoneleigh Dr EN11 ..... 115 B1
Stoneley SG6 .... 11 F1
Stonemason Cl AL5 ...... 86 A3
Stonemead AL8 .... 89 D3
Stonesdale LU4 .... 44 C4
Stoneways Cl LU4 .... 44 C6
Stoney Cl HP4 .... 121 F6
Stoney Comm CM24 ...... 59 E5
Stoney Common Rd
CM24 .... 59 D5
Stoneycroft
Aldbury HP23 .... 101 C5
Hemel Hempstead HP1 ... 124 A3
Welwyn Garden City
AL7 .... 111 A7
Stoneyfield Dr CM24 ..... 59 E6
Stoneygate Rd LU4 ...... 44 D3
Stoney La
Bovingdon HP3 .... 137 C5
Chipperfield WD4 .... 137 E1
Cholesbury HP5 .... 120 F1
Hemel Hempstead HP1 ... 137 B8
Stoney Pl CM24 .... 59 E5
Stonnells Cl SG6 .... 22 F8
Stony Croft SG1 .... 50 E6
Stony Hills SG12 .... 92 C7
Stony La
Chenies HP5, HP6 .... 150 E1
Great Offley LU2, SG4 ..... 47 C4
Stonyshotts EN9 .... 163 E6
Stookslade HP22 .... 60 A3
STOPSLEY 46 B4
STOPSLEY COMMON 45 F6
Stopsley Com Prim Sch
LU2 .... 46 A4
Stopsley High Sch LU2 ... 45 F4
Stopsley Mobile Home Pk
LU2 .... 45 F4
Stopsley Way LU2 .... 46 A3
Storehouse La SG4 ...... 34 F6
Storey Ct WD23 .... 168 B4
Storey St HP3 .... 138 D7
Stormont Rd SG5 .... 21 F1
Stormont Sch EN6 ...... 159 D8
Stornoway HP3 .... 125 B1
Stortford Hall Ind Pk
CM23 .... 77 B7
Stortford Hall Pk CM23 ... 77 B8
Stortford Hall Rd 3
CM23 .... 77 B8
STORTFORD PARK 76 C8
Stortford Rd
Hatfield Heath CM22 ...... 98 E4
Hoddesdon EN11 .... 135 C7
Little Hadham SG11 .... 57 C2
Standon SG11 .... 55 F2
Stort Lo CM23 .... 76 D8
Stort Mill CM20 .... 118 B6
Stort Rd CM23 .... 76 F6
Stort Valley Ind Pk
CM23 .... 59 B2
STOTFOLD 11 E7
Stotfold Ho SG5 .... 11 F6
Stotfold Rd
Arlesey SG15 .... 11 C7
Hinxworth SG7 .... 3 C1
Hitchin SG4, SG6 .... 22 C4
Letchworth Garden City
SG6 .... 11 D1
Stow The CM20 .... 117 F2
Stox Mead HA3 .... 176 D2
Straffan Ct LU3 .... 44 F4
Strafford Cl EN6 .... 159 A7
Strafford Ct SG3 .... 69 A5
Strafford Gate EN6 ..... 159 A7
Strafford Rd EN5 .... 171 E6
Straits The EN9 .... 163 B7
Strandburgh Pl HP3 .... 125 B1
Strangers Way LU4 ...... 44 C4
Strangeways WD17 ..... 153 E3
Stratfield Dr EN10 ...... 134 E4
Stratfield Rd WD6 ...... 170 A7
Stratford Lo WD17 ...... 167 B8
Stratford Rd
Luton LU4 .... 45 B1
Watford WD17 .... 167 A7
Stratford Way
Bricket Wood AL2 .... 140 F2
Hemel Hempstead HP3 ... 138 B8
Watford WD17 .... 167 A7
Strathmore Ave
Hitchin SG5 .... 21 F1
Luton LU1 .... 63 F5
Strathmore Ct SG5 .... 21 F1
Strathmore Inf Sch
SG5 .... 21 E2
Strathmore Rd SG4 ...... 66 E6
Strathmore Wlk LU1 ..... 63 F6
Stratton Ave EN2 .... 161 D2
Stratton Ct 13 HA5 ...... 175 F3
Stratton Gdns LU2 .... 45 D4
Strawberry Cres AL2 .... 142 B5
Strawberry Field
8 Hatfield AL10 .... 130 A2
Luton LU3 .... 44 E7
Strawberry Fields
SG12 .... 93 B2
Strawfields AL7 .... 111 B7
Strawmead AL10 .... 130 B7
Strawplaiters Cl SG3 ..... 69 A2
Straw Plait Way SG15 .... 10 F4
Straws Hadley Ct HP22 ... 60 B2
Strayfield Rd EN2 .... 161 B2
STREATLEY 31 A5
Street The
Braughing SG11 .... 55 F7
Chipperfield WD4 .... 152 A8
Dane End SG11 .... 53 F3
Furneux Pelham SG9 ...... 43 A4
Street The *continued*
Sheering CM22 .... 98 E1
Wallington SG7 .... 25 C8
Stretton Way WD6 ...... 156 E1
Stringers La SG2 .... 51 E2
Stripling Way WD18 ..... 167 A3
Stroma Cl HP3 .... 125 C1
Stronnell Cl LU2 .... 46 B3
Stronsay Cl HP3 .... 125 C1
Stroud Wood Bsns Ctr
AL2 .... 141 E4
Stuart Ct WD6 .... 169 D3
Stuart Dr
Hitchin SG4 .... 35 B7
Royston SG8 .... 7 D8
Stuart Ho EN9 .... 163 F6
Stuart Pl 8 LU1 .... 63 D7
Stuart Rd AL6 .... 89 B3
Stuart St Pas 7 LU1 ..... 63 D7
Stuarts Cl 3 HP3 .... 124 D1
Stuart St LU1 .... 63 D7
Stuart Way EN7 .... 162 B8
Stud Gn WD25 .... 154 B7
STUDHAM 82 C4
Studham CE Lower Sch
LU6 .... 82 B4
Studham La
Dagnall HP4 .... 81 D4
Whipsnade LU6 .... 82 A7
Studios The WD23 ...... 168 A3
Studio Way WD6 .... 170 C8
Studlands Rise SG8 .... 7 E6
Studlands Rise Fst Sch
SG8 .... 7 E5
Studley Rd LU3 .... 45 D1
Stump Cross SG8 .... 15 C6
Sturgeon's Way SG4 ..... 22 B2
Sturla Cl SG14 .... 113 B7
Sturlas Way EN8 .... 162 D6
Sturmer Cl AL4 .... 128 C2
Sturrock Way SG4 .... 35 C6
Styles Cl LU2 .... 46 C2
Such Cl SG6 .... 23 B7
Sudbury Ct 2 AL1 ...... 127 E2
Sudbury Rd LU4 .... 44 B6
Suffolk Cl
Borehamwood WD6 ...... 170 D4
London Colney AL2 ...... 142 C6
Luton LU4 .... 44 A3
Suffolk Rd
Potters Bar EN6 .... 158 E7
Royston SG8 .... 7 E6
Sugar La HP1 .... 123 B1
Sulgrave Cres HP23 ..... 100 C5
Sullivan Cres UB9 ...... 173 D1
Sullivan Way WD6 ...... 169 C3
Summercroft Prim Sch
CM23 .... 77 C8
Summer Ct HP2 .... 124 D5
Summer Dale AL8 .... 89 D1
Summerfield AL10 ...... 130 A2
Summerfield Cl AL2 ..... 142 C5
Summerfield Rd
Luton LU1 .... 62 F8
Watford WD25 .... 154 A4
Summer Gr WD6 .... 169 D3
Summer Hill WD6 .... 170 A4
Summerhill Ct AL1 ...... 127 F4
Summerhouse La
Harefield UB9 .... 173 A3
Radlett WD25 .... 168 C8
Summerhouse Way
WD5 .... 139 F1
Summerlands Rd AL4 ... 128 C7
Summerleas Cl HP2 ..... 124 E3
Summer Pl WD18 .... 166 F3
Summers Lo SG6 .... 22 D6
Summers Rd LU2 .... 46 C1
Summer St LU1 .... 63 C1
Summers Way AL2 ...... 142 E4
Summerswood La EN6,
WD6 .... 157 E4
Summerswood Prim Sch
WD6 .... 170 B5
Summer Wlk AL3 .... 83 E5
Summit Ct EN5 .... 171 F6
Summit Rd EN6 .... 144 E1
Sumpter Yd AL1 .... 127 D3
Sunbury Ct
3 Barnet EN5 .... 171 E5
St Albans AL1 .... 128 B2
Sundale AL1 .... 127 E4
Sunderland Ave AL1 .... 128 A4
Sunderland Est WD4 .... 139 B2
Sunderland Gr WD25 .... 153 F5
Sundew Rd HP1 .... 123 E2
Sundon Bsns Pk LU3 ..... 44 B8
SUNDON PARK 44 C7
Sundon Park Jun Sch
LU3 .... 44 C8
Sundon Park Par LU3 .... 44 C7
Sundon Park Rd LU3 ..... 44 C7
Sun Hill SG8 .... 7 C5
Sun La AL5 .... 86 A2
Sunmead Rd HP2 .... 124 D5
Sunningdale
Bishop's Stortford
CM23 .... 76 E6
Luton LU2 .... 45 F3
Sunningdale Mews
AL7 .... 89 F2
Sunnybank LU7 .... 79 F7
Sunny Bank Prim Sch
EN6 .... 159 A5
Sunnybank Rd EN6 ..... 159 A6

Sunnydell AL2 141 B5
Sunnyfield AL9 130 D8
Sunny Hill SG9 40 F7
Sunnyhill Rd
Hemel Hempstead HP1 124 B3
Maple Cross WD3 172 D4
Sunnymead Orch SG7 5 A3
Sunnyside
Lower Nazeing EN9 135 F1
Stansted Mountfitchet CM24 59 E6
Sunnyside Cotts HP5 136 A5
Sunnyside Rd SG4 35 A5
Sunridge Ave LU2 45 E2
Sunrise Cres HP3 138 F8
Sunrise Ind Est LU2 46 A2
Sunset Dr LU2 45 F3
Sunset View EN5 171 E7
Sunshine House Sch HA6 174 D4
Sun Sq 2 HP1 124 D4
Sun St
Baldock SG7 23 E8
Hitchin SG5 34 E6
Sawbridgeworth CM21 97 F1
Waltham Abbey EN9 163 C6
Surrey Pl HP23 100 A3
Surrey St LU1 63 E6
Surrey Street Prim Sch LU1 63 F6
Sursham Ct AL3 83 E5
Sussex Cl EN11 135 A7
Sussex Pl LU2 46 D2
Sussex Rd WD24 154 A1
Sutcliffe Cl
Bushey WD23 168 C5
Stevenage SG1 51 A8
Sutherland Ave EN6 146 D3
Sutherland Cl EN5 171 E5
Sutherland Ct
Watford WD18 166 C2
Welwyn Garden City AL7 110 F7
Sutherland Pl LU1 63 D5
Sutherland Way EN6 146 E3
Sutton Acres CM22 98 D7
Sutton Cl
Hoddesdon EN10 134 E4
Tring HP23 100 B6
Sutton Cres EN5 171 D4
Sutton Ct SG12 114 E8
Sutton Gdns
Caddington LU1 62 E3
Luton LU3 44 D6
Sutton Ho HP2 124 E7
Sutton Path WD6 170 A6
Sutton Rd
St Albans AL1 128 B3
Watford WD17 167 C6
Swale Cl SG1 37 A3
Swallow Cl
Bushey WD23 168 C1
Luton LU4 44 A4
Rickmansworth WD3 165 C2
Swallow Ct
4 Bishop's Stortford CM23 77 A6
Enfield EN3 162 C2
Hertford SG14 113 C6
Welwyn Garden City AL7 110 F6
Swallowdale La HP2 125 B6
Swallow Dell Prim Sch AL7 111 A5
Swallow End AL7 110 F6
Swallowfields AL7 110 F6
Swallow Gdns AL10 130 A3
Swallow La AL1 142 B8
Swallow Oaks WD5 153 F7
Swallow Pk HP2 125 B7
Swallows CM17 118 C4
Swallows The AL7 89 F2
Swallowtail Wlk HP4 121 F7
Swan Cl WD3 165 D2
Swan Ct
2 Bishop's Stortford CM23 76 F6
Cheshunt EN8 162 E5
Chorleywood WD3 164 C5
Swanells Wood LU6 82 C4
Swan Field Ct AL6 89 A4
Swan Field Ho 3 WD3 165 D2
Swanfield Rd EN8 162 E6
Swangley's La SG3 69 B4
Swanhill AL7 90 A1
Swan La SG8 1 F4
Swanland Rd
South Mimms EN6 158 B5
Welham Green AL9, EN6 144 B3
SWANLEY BAR 145 B2
Swanley Bar La EN6 145 B3
Swanley Cres EN6 145 B2
Swanley Ct WD24 154 C2
Swan Mead
Hemel Hempstead HP3 138 F6
Luton LU4 44 B4
Swan & Pike Rd EN3 163 A1
Swan Rd EN8 162 E5
Swans Cl AL4 128 E2
Swan St SG7 4 D4
Swanstand SG6 23 D4
Swanston Grange LU4 44 B2
Swanston Path 3 WD19 175 C7
Swan Way CM19 116 A1
Swasedale Rd LU3 45 A6
Sweet Briar
Bishop's Stortford CM23 76 B6
Welwyn Garden City AL7 111 A5
Sweetbriar Cl HP1 124 A6
Sweyns Mead SG2 51 C7
Swift Cl
Letchworth Garden City SG6 22 E8
Royston SG8 2 D1
Stanstead Abbotts SG12 115 C3
Swiftfields AL7 111 A7
Swifts Green Cl LU2 46 B5
Swifts Green Rd LU2 46 B5
SWILLETT THE 164 B3
Swinburne Ave SG5 21 C1
Swinburne Cl SG8 2 D1
Swingate SG1 50 D5
Swing Gate Fst Sch HP4 122 D3
Swing Gate La HP4 122 D2
Swinnell Cl SG8 2 B5
Swiss Ave WD18 166 E6
Swiss Cl WD18 166 E6
Sword Cl EN10 134 D3
Sworders Yd 3 CM23 76 F7
Sycamore App WD3 166 C4
Sycamore Ave AL10 130 A4
Sycamore Cl
Hammond Street EN7 147 F4
Hitchin SG4 35 A4
Watford, Garston WD25 154 B4
Watford WD23 167 E7
Sycamore Dr
Park Street AL2 141 D4
Tring HP23 100 B4
Sycamore Ho HP2 124 E4
Sycamore Rd WD3 166 D4
Sycamore Rise HP4 122 D3
Sycamores The
Baldock SG7 23 E8
Bishop's Stortford CM23 77 B6
Hemel Hempstead HP3 137 F8
Radlett WD7 156 B5
8 St Albans AL1 127 D2
Sydney Chapman Way EN5 171 F7
Sydney Rd WD18 166 F4
Sylam Cl LU3 44 E7
Sylvan Cl HP3 125 A2
Sylvandale AL7 111 C5
Sylvan Hts AL1 128 A1
Sylvan Way AL7 111 C5
Sylvia Ave HA5 175 F4
Symonds Ct 13 EN8 148 D3
SYMONDS GREEN 50 A7
Symonds Green La SG1 50 A6
Symonds Green Rd SG1 50 A7
Symonds Rd SG5 34 D8
Syon Ct 14 AL1 128 A2

T

Tabbs Cl SG6 23 B7
Tabor Ct SG6 22 D7
Tacitus Cl 2 SG1 51 C8
Tailors CM23 76 B5
Takeley Cl EN9 163 D6
Talbot Ave WD19 167 E2
Talbot Ct HP3 124 D1
Talbot Rd
Harrow HA3 176 F1
Hatfield AL10 130 A8
Luton LU2 45 F2
Rickmansworth WD3 165 E1
Talbot St
Hertford SG13 113 E6
Hitchin SG5 34 C8
Talbot Way SG6 12 B1
Talisman St SG4 35 C6
Tallack Cl HA3 176 E3
Tallents Cres AL5 86 D3
Tallis Way WD6 169 E8
Tall Trees
Hitchin SG4 35 A4
Royston SG8 7 E6
Tamar Cl SG1 37 A3
Tamar Gn HP2 124 F8
Tamarisk Cl AL3 127 D7
Tamarix Cres AL2 142 A5
Tameton Cl LU2 46 F2
Tamworth Rd SG13 113 F7
Tancred Rd LU2 46 A4
Tanfield Cl EN7 148 A4
Tanfield Gn LU2 46 E1
Tanglewood
Harpenden AL5 85 F2
Welwyn AL6 90 A7
Tanglewood Cl HA7 176 E8
Tankerfield Pl AL3 127 C3
Tanner Ho WD19 167 B2
Tanners Cl AL3 127 C4
Tanners Cres SG13 113 C4
Tanners Hill WD5 154 A8
Tanners Way SG12 116 D8
Tanners Wood Cl WD5 153 E7
Tanners Wood Ct WD5 153 E7
Tanners Wood Jun Mix Inf Sch WD5 153 E7
Tanners Wood La WD5 153 E7
Tannery Cl SG8 7 C6
Tannery Drift SG8 7 C6
Tannery Drift Sch SG8 7 C6
Tannery The SG9 40 E7
Tannery Yd SG4 66 F6
Tannsfield Dr 1 HP2 124 F5
Tannsmore Cl 2 HP2 124 F5
Tansycroft AL7 111 B7
Tantivy Ct 5 WD17 167 C6
Tanworth Cl HA6 174 C4
Tanworth Gdns HA5 175 C1
Tanyard La AL6, SG4 88 B8
Tanys Ct CM20 117 F3
Tany's Dell CM20 118 A3
Tany's Dell Com Prim Sch CM20 118 A3
Tapster St EN5 171 F6
Taransey HP3 125 B1
Tarlings CM20 117 F3
Tarpan Way EN10 148 F6
Tarrant Ct SG1 36 B1
Tarrant Dr AL5 107 D7
Tassell Hall AL3 105 F6
Tate Gdns WD23 168 E2
Tates Way SG1 36 B2
Tatlers La SG2 51 E4
Tatsfield Ave EN9 149 E8
Tatsford Villas EN9 135 C1
Tattershall Dr HP2 105 B1
Tattle Hill SG14 91 E2
Tattlers Hill HP22 60 B3
Tatton St 6 CM17 118 C1
Tauber Cl WD6 169 F5
Taunton Ave LU2 46 B1
Taverners HP2 124 E5
Taverners Way EN11 135 A6
Tavistock Ave AL1 141 D8
Tavistock Cl
Potters Bar EN6 159 D8
St Albans AL1 141 D8
Tavistock Cres LU1 63 E5
Tavistock Ct 3 LU1 63 E5
Tavistock Rd WD24 167 D8
Tavistock St LU1 63 E6
Taylers Cotts EN6 157 F5
Taylor Cl
Harefield UB9 173 C1
St Albans AL4 128 A8
Taylors Ave EN11 135 A5
Taylor's Hill SG4 34 F6
Taylors La HP23 119 C3
Taylor's La EN5 171 F8
Taylor's Rd SG5 11 F8
Taylor St LU2 63 F8
Taylor Trad Est SG13 114 B7
Taywood Cl SG2 51 B2
TEA GREEN 47 B3
Teal Cl EN3 162 C3
Teal Dr HA6 174 C3
Teale Ho 5 EN11 135 D8
Teal Ho WD25 154 E3
Teal Way HP3 138 F6
Teasdale Cl SG8 2 D1
Teasel Cl SG8 7 E5
Tebbutt Ct AL6 90 C6
Tedder Ave SG16 10 B5
Tedder Rd HP2 125 A4
Tees Cl SG1 36 F3
Teesdale
Hemel Hempstead HP2 124 E6
Luton LU4 44 C5
Tee Side SG13 114 B7
Telford Ave SG2 51 B6
Telford Cl WD25 154 D4
Telford Ct
Hatfield AL10 129 F3
St Albans AL1 127 E2
Telford Rd AL2 142 C4
Telford Way LU1 63 D8
Telmere Ind Est 20 LU1 63 E6
Telscombe Way LU2 46 C3
Temperance St AL3 127 C3
Tempest Ave EN6 159 D7
Templar Ave SG7 23 F6
Templars Dr HA3 176 D4
Templars La SG4 48 D6
Temple Bank CM20 118 B5
Temple Cl
Cheshunt EN7 162 A8
Luton LU2 45 E5
Preston SG5 34 B4
Watford WD17 166 F7
Temple Ct
Hertford SG14 92 D1
Potters Bar EN6 158 D8
TEMPLE DINSLEY 48 E6
TEMPLE FIELDS 118 A4
Temple Fields SG14 92 D1
Templefields Ent Ctr CM20 118 A3
Temple Gdns
Letchworth Garden City SG6 23 C8
Moor Park WD3 174 B6
Temple Ho EN7 162 A6
Temple La SG12 92 F8
Temple Mead
Hemel Hempstead HP2 124 D5
Roydon CM19 116 B1
Templepan La WD3 152 E2
Templeton Ct
15 Borehamwood WD6 169 F8
Enfield EN1 162 C1
Temple View AL3 127 C5
Templewood AL8 89 D1
Templewood Prim Sch AL8 110 D8
Tempsford AL7 111 D6
Tempsford Ave WD6 170 D5
Temsford Cl HA2 176 C1
Tenby Dr LU4 44 F3
Tenby Mews LU4 44 E3
Tene The SG7 23 F8
Tennand Cl EN7 147 F5
Tennison Ave WD6 170 B4
Tennyson Ave
Hitchin SG4 35 C7
Waltham Abbey EN9 163 E5
Tennyson Cl SG8 2 E1
Tennyson Ct SG8 2 D1
Tennyson Ho 6 LU1 63 E5
Tennyson Rd
Chiswell Green AL2 141 B5
Harpenden AL5 86 A2
Luton LU1 63 E5
Tennyson Road Prim Sch LU1 63 E5
Tenterfield Ho AL6 89 C4
Tenth Ave LU3 44 C7
Tenzing Gr LU1 63 C6
Tenzing Rd HP2 125 A3
Teresa Gdns EN8 162 D5
Terlings Pk CM20 117 D1
Terminus St 6 CM20 117 D1
Terrace Gdns WD17 167 B7
Terrace The
Essendon AL9 131 E6
Redbourn AL3 106 A5
Tring HP23 100 A3
Westmill SG9 40 F2
Tethys Rd HP2 124 F6
TEWIN 90 E2
Tewin Cl
St Albans AL4 128 C7
Tewin AL6 90 C5
Tewin Cowper CE Prim Sch AL6 90 E2
Tewin Ct AL7 110 F7
Tewin Hill AL6 90 F5
Tewin Rd
Hemel Hempstead HP2 125 C3
Welwyn Garden City AL7 110 F7
Tewin Water Ho AL6 90 B2
TEWIN WOOD 90 D5
Thackeray Cl SG8 2 D1
Thames Ave HP2 124 F8
Thames Ct LU3 45 B3
Thamesdale AL2 142 F4
Thanet Ho 1 WD18 166 F3
Thatched Cotts AL5 107 A7
Thatchers Croft HP2 124 E7
Thatchers End SG4 35 D8
Thatchers The CM23 76 C5
Thaxted Cl LU2 46 F2
Thaxted Way EN9 163 D6
Thaynesfield EN6 159 D8
Thelby Cl LU3 44 F6
Thele Ave SG12 115 D4
Thele Est SG12 115 E4
Thele Ho SG12 115 D4
Theleway Cl EN11 115 B1
Thellusson Way WD3 165 A2
Thelusson Ct WD7 156 A3
Theobald Bsns Ctr SG4 22 A3
Theobald Cres HA3 176 C2
Theobald Ct WD6 170 A6
THEOBALDS 161 D8
Theobalds Cl EN6 146 F1
Theobald's Grove Sta EN8 162 D7
Theobald's La
Cheshunt EN8 162 B7
Cheshunt EN8 162 D7
Theobalds Park Camp Site EN7 162 A5
Theobalds Park Rd EN2 161 B3
Theobald's Rd EN6 146 F1
Theobald St
Borehamwood WD6 169 F7
Radlett WD6, WD7 156 D2
THERFIELD 15 F7
Therfield Fst Sch SG8 15 F7
Therfield Heath Nature Reserve★ SG8 7 A5
Therfield Rd AL3 127 D6
Thetford Gdns LU2 45 E6
Thieves' La
Hertford SG14 112 F7
Hertingfordbury SG14 112 F6
Third Ave
Letchworth Garden City SG6 23 C7
Luton LU3 44 D7
Watford WD25 154 D4
Thirlestane AL1 127 F4
Thirlestone Rd LU4 44 D1
Thirlmere SG1 37 C2
Thirlmere Dr AL1 128 B1
Thirlmere Gdns HA6 174 C4
Thirsk Rd WD6 157 A1
Thirston Path 1 WD6 170 A7
Thistle Cl HP1 123 E2
Thistlecroft HP1 124 B2
Thistle Dr AL10 129 F8
Thistle Gr AL7 111 C3
Thistle Rd LU1 63 F7
Thistles The HP1 124 B4
Thistley La SG4 34 F1
Thomas Alleyne Sch The SG1 50 C8
Thomas Bourne Ho 9 HP4 122 D4
Thomas Coram CE Mid Sch The HP4 122 D2
Thomas Ct HP4 121 F5
Thomas Gould Ho AL2 142 D4
Thomas Heskin Ct 11 CM23 77 A7
Thomas Rochford Way EN8 148 F4
Thomas Sparrow Ho AL4 108 D8
Thomas Watson Cottage Homes EN5 171 E4
Thomas Way SG8 2 D1
Thompsons Cl
Goff's Oak EN7 147 F2
1 Harpenden AL5 86 A1
Thompsons Mdw SG8 1 F4
Thompson Way WD3 165 A1
THORLEY 76 D2
Thorley Hall Stables CM23 76 D2
Thorley High CM23 76 F2
Thorley Hill CM23 76 F5
Thorley Hill Prim Sch CM23 76 F4
THORLEY HOUSES 76 A5
Thorley La CM23 76 F3
Thorley La E CM23 76 D3
Thorley La W CM23 76 B4
Thorley Neighbourhood Ctr CM23 76 D4
THORLEY PARK 76 D5
Thorley Park Rd CM23 76 F4
THORLEY STREET 76 F3
Thornage Cl LU2 45 D7
Thorn Ave WD23 168 C1
Thornbera Cl CM23 76 F4
Thornbera Gdns CM23 76 F4
Thornbera Rd CM23 76 F4
Thornbury AL5 86 D1
Thornbury Cl
Hoddesdon EN11 115 B2
Stevenage SG2 69 A8
Thornbury Gdns WD6 170 C5
Thorncroft HP3 125 B1
Thorndyke Ct HA5 175 F3
Thorne Cl 6 HP1 124 B1
Thorne Ho AL1 127 E4
Thorne Way HP22 99 B4
Thorneycroft Cl LU3 44 F4
Thorneycroft Dr EN3 163 A2
Thornfield Rd CM23 76 E8
Thorn Gr CM23 77 B6
Thorn Grove Prim Sch CM23 77 B6
Thornhill Rd
Luton LU4 44 F2
Moor Park HA6 174 C6
Thorntondale 5 LU4 44 C5
Thornton Gr HA5 176 A4
Thornton Rd
Barnet EN5 171 E6
Potters Bar EN6 145 C1
Thornton St
Hertford SG14 113 D6
St Albans AL3 127 C4
Thorn Tree Dr HP23 99 F4
Thorpe Cres WD19 167 C2
Thorpefield Cl AL4 128 D6
Thorpe Rd AL1 127 D2
Thrales Cl LU3 44 E7
THRALES END 85 E5
Thrales End La AL5 85 E5
Three Cherry Trees La HP2 125 B7
Three Close La HP4 122 C4
Three Closes SG5 20 C4
Three Corners HP3 125 A1
Three Houses La SG4 67 D5
Three Meadows Mews HA3 176 F2
Three Rivers Mus of Local History★ WD3 165 E1
Three Star Cvn Pk SG16 10 A3
Three Stiles SG2 52 E4
Three Valleys Way WD23 167 E4
Thremhall Ave CM23 77 F8
Thresher Cl CM23 76 C5
Thricknells Cl LU3 44 E7
Thrift Farm La WD6 170 C7
Thriftfield HP2 124 D5
Thrimley La CM23 58 C6
Thristers Cl SG6 23 B3
THROCKING 26 F1
Throcking La SG9 27 C1
Throcking Rd SG9 39 D8
Thrums WD24 154 B2
Thrush Ave AL10 130 A3
Thrush Gn WD3 165 C2
Thrush La EN6 146 F3
Thumbswood AL7 111 A3
Thumpers HP2 124 E5
Thundercourt SG12 93 D2
Thunder Hall 1 SG12 93 D2

THUNDRIDGE 93 E7
Thundridge Bsns Pk SG12 93 D7
Thundridge CE Prim Sch SG12 93 D7
Thundridge Cl AL7 111 B5
Thurgood Rd EN11 135 A8
Thurlow Cl SG1 36 D2
Thurnall Ave SG8 7 D5
Thurnall Cl SG7 23 F8
Thyme Cl LU2 45 E7
Tibbles Cl WD25 154 E4
Tibbs Hill Rd WD5 139 F1
Tiberius Rd LU3 44 F6
Tichborne WD3 172 D5
Tiger Moth Way AL10 129 D6
Tilbury Cl 6 HA6 175 F3
Tilecroft AL8 89 D1
Tilehouse Cl WD6 169 F6
Tilehouse La UB9 172 E2
Tilehouse St SG5 34 E6
Tilekiln Cl EN7 147 F2
Tile Kiln Cl HP3 125 B2
Tile Kiln Cres HP3 125 B2
Tile Kiln La HP3 125 B2
Tilgate LU2 46 D3
Tillers Link SG2 51 A2
Tillotson Rd HA3 176 B3
Tilsworth Wlk AL4 128 C8
Timbercroft AL7 89 F1
Timberidge WD3 165 D5
Timber Orch SG14 92 A2
Timbers Ct AL5 85 F2
Times Cl SG5 21 D2
Timplings Row HP1 124 B5
Timworth Cl LU2 46 D1
Tingeys Cl AL3 106 A5
Tinkers La HP23 121 A6
Tinsley Cl LU1 63 B5
Tintagel Cl
Hemel Hempstead HP2 124 D8
Luton LU3 45 B4
Tintern Cl
Harpenden AL5 85 C4
Stevenage SG2 69 A7
Tinwell Mews WD6 170 D4
Tippendell La AL2 141 C5
Tippet Ct SG1 50 D3
Tiree Cl HP3 125 B1
Titan Ct LU4 44 F1
Titan Rd HP2 124 F6
Titchfield Rd EN3 162 E2
Titchmarsh Cl SG8 7 D7
Tithe Barn Cl AL1 141 C8
Tithe Barn Ct WD5 139 F2
Tithe Cl SG4 67 F1
Titian Ave WD23 168 E2
TITMORE GREEN 35 E2
Titmus Cl SG1 50 E6
Tittendell La SG4 35 C2
Tiverton Ct AL5 107 E6
Tiverton Rd EN6 159 E8
Toddington Rd LU4 44 C6
TODD'S GREEN 36 A2
Toland Cl LU4 44 C1
Tolcarne Dr HA5 175 A1
Tollgate Cl WD3 164 F5
Tollgate Rd
Colney Heath AL4, AL9 143 E7
Enfield EN3 162 D4
Welham Green AL9 144 A6
Tollhouse Point 7 AL1 127 E2
Tollpit End HP1 124 A6
Tollsworth Way SG11 55 D3
Tolmers Ave EN6 146 E3
Tolmers Gdns EN6 146 F2
Tolmers Mews SG13 146 E6
Tolmers Rd EN6 146 E3
Tolpits Cl WD18 166 F4
Tolpits La WD18 166 E2
Tomkins Cl WD6 169 E8
Tomlins Cl SG8 8 F1
Toms Croft HP2 124 E2
Toms Field AL10 129 E4
Toms Hill Cl HP23 101 D5
Toms Hill Rd HP23 101 D5
Toms La WD4, WD5 139 D3
TONWELL 92 F7
Tonwell St Mary's CE Prim Sch SG12 92 E7
Tooke Cl HA5 175 E2
Toorack Rd HA3 176 D1
Tooveys Mill Cl WD4 139 A2
Topstreet Way AL5 107 C8
Tormead HA6 174 D4
Toronto Ho EN8 162 D8
Torquay Cres SG1 50 B7
Torquay Dr LU4 44 D4
Torridge Wlk 2 HP2 124 F8
Torrington Dr EN6 159 D7
Torrington Rd HP4 122 B4
Tortoiseshell Way HP4 121 F6
Torwood Cl HP4 121 F4
Torworth Rd WD6 157 A1
Tot La CM23, CM24 59 D4
TOTTERIDGE 171 E1
Totteridge Comm N20 171 D1
Totteridge Ho N20 171 F1
Totteridge Pk N20 171 C1
Totteridge Rd EN3 162 D2
Totteridge Village N20 171 F1
Totton Mews AL3 106 B5
Totts La SG2 38 C1
Toulmin Dr AL3 127 C7
Toulouse Ho 7 WD18 166 E5
Tovey Ave EN11 135 A8
Tovey Cl
London Colney AL2 142 D5
Lower Nazeing EN9 149 E8
Tower Cl
Berkhamsted HP4 122 A3
Hertford Heath SG13 114 C2
Kneesworth SG8 2 A5
Little Wymondley SG4 35 F3
Tower Ct LU2 46 A1
Tower Ctr 1 EN11 135 A6
TOWER HILL 137 F2
Tower Hill
Chipperfield WD4 137 F1
Much Hadham SG10 74 F2
Tower Hill La AL4 108 F4
Tower Hts 10 EN11 135 A7
Tower Prim Sch SG12 93 E3
Tower Rd
Codicote SG4 67 F2
Luton LU2 64 A8
Ware SG12 93 F2
Towers Rd
Hemel Hempstead HP2 124 E4
Pinner HA5 175 E2
Stevenage SG1 50 D4
Tower St SG14 113 C8
Towers The SG1 50 D4
Tower View
Bushey WD23 168 E2
Hemel Hempstead HP1 124 D4
Whitwell SG4 66 D6
Tower Way LU2 64 A8
Town Ctr AL10 130 A6
Towne Rd SG8 7 D5
Town Farm
Cheddington LU7 80 A7
Wheathampstead AL4 108 D8
Town Farm Cl SG8 1 F4
Town Farm Cres SG11 55 F2
Townfield WD3 165 C2
Town Fields AL10 130 A6
Town La SG2 52 E4
Townley SG6 23 D4
Town Mead Rd EN9 163 C5
Town Mill Mews 3 SG14 113 C6
TOWN PARK 117 E2
TOWNSEND 127 C6
Townsend HP2 124 D5
Townsend Ave AL1 127 E4
Townsend CE Sch AL3 127 C8
Townsend Cl
Barkway SG8 17 C3
Harpenden AL5 85 F1
St Ippolyts SG4 35 A3
Townsend Dr AL3 127 D5
Townsend La AL5 85 F1
Townsend Rd AL5 86 A2
Townsend Way HA6 175 A3
Townshend St SG13 113 E6
Townsley Cl LU1 63 E6
Town Sq SG1 50 D5
Tracey Ct 15 LU1 63 E6
Trafalgar Ave EN10 134 F2
Trafford Cl
Shenley WD7 156 E7
Stevenage SG1 36 E1
Traherne Cl SG4 34 F5
Trajan Gate SG2 37 D1
Trapstyle Rd SG12 93 A2
Travellers Cl AL9 144 C8
Travellers Encampment EN10 148 D5
Travellers La
Hatfield AL10 130 B2
Welham Green AL9 130 C1
Treacle La SG9 25 F3
Treacy Cl WD23 176 C8
Trebellan Dr HP2 124 F4
Treeby Ct EN3 163 A2
Treehanger Cl HP23 100 B4
Treetop Cl LU2 45 F1
Treetops
Luton LU2 45 F1
Oaklands AL6 89 E7
Treetops Cl HA6 174 D5
Trefoil Cl LU4 44 A4
Trefusis Wlk WD17 166 E8
Tregelles Rd EN11 135 A8
Tremaine Gr HP2 124 E7
Trent Cl
Shenley WD7 156 E7
Stevenage SG1 50 E8
Trent Rd LU3 45 B4
Tresco Rd HP4 121 F5
Trescott Cl LU2 46 E2
Tresilian Sq HP2 125 A8
Treslian Sq 1 HP2 124 F8
Trevalga Way HP2 124 E7
Trevellance Way WD25 154 D6
Trevelyan Pl AL1 127 C1
Trevelyan Way HP4 122 B6
Trevera Ct
Cheshunt EN8 162 E6
Hoddesdon EN11 135 A7
Trevor Cl HA3 176 F3
Trevor Rd SG4 35 A8
Trevose Way WD19 175 C7
Trewenna Dr EN6 159 D7
Triangle The SG4 34 F6
Trident Ctr WD24 167 C8
Trident Ind Est EN11 135 C7
Trident Rd WD25 153 F5
Triggs Way LU2 46 E3
Trigg Terr SG1 50 E6
Trimley Cl LU4 44 B5
TRIMS GREEN 97 C7
Trinder Rd EN5 171 C4
TRING 100 B4
Tring Bsns Ctr HP23 99 E4
TRINGFORD 99 F7
Tring Ford Rd HP23 100 A7
Tring Hill HP23 99 C3
Tring Ho WD18 166 E2
Tring Rd
Berkhamsted HP4 121 D7
Long Marston HP23 79 C3
Wingrave HP22 60 C1
Tring Sch HP23 100 B4
Tring Sta HP23 101 A5
TRING WHARF 100 B6
Trinity Cl
Bishop's Stortford CM23 76 F6
Northwood HA6 174 E4
Trinity Ct
Hertford SG14 113 C8
Watford WD17 166 F8
Trinity Gr SG14 113 C8
Trinity Hall Cl WD24 167 C6
Trinity Ho
2 Borehamwood WD6 170 A5
Cheshunt EN8 162 E7
Trinity La EN8 162 E7
Trinity Mews HP2 125 D2
Trinity Pl SG1 50 D6
Trinity Rd
Hertford Heath SG13 114 C3
Luton LU3 45 A4
Stevenage SG1 50 C6
Stotfold SG5 11 F7
Ware SG12 93 E2
Trinity St CM23 76 F6
Trinity Way CM23 76 F6
Trinity Wlk
Hemel Hempstead HP2 125 D2
Hertford Heath SG13 114 C3
Tristram Rd SG4 22 B2
Triton Way HP2 124 F5
Triumph Ct 12 LU1 63 E6
Trojan Terr CM21 97 E3
Troon Gdns LU2 45 E7
Trooper Rd HP23 101 C5
Trotters Bottom EN5 158 B2
Trotter's Gap SG12 115 E4
Trotts Hill Prim Sch SG1 36 F1
Trout Rise WD3 165 B6
Troutstream Way WD3 165 B5
Trouvere Pk HP1 124 B5
Trowbridge Gdns LU2 45 E3
TROWLEY BOTTOM 105 B8
Trowley Bottom AL3 105 B8
Trowley Hts AL3 84 B2
Trowley Rise WD5 153 F8
Truemans Rd SG5 21 D2
Trumper Rd SG1 36 F1
Trumpington Dr AL1 141 D8
Truncalls LU1 63 D5
Trundlers Way WD23 168 E1
Truro Gdns LU3 45 C5
Truro Ho 11 HA5 175 F3
Trust Cotts HP4 81 A1
Trust Ind Est SG4 22 A2
Trust Rd EN8 162 E5
Tubbs Croft AL7 111 B5
Tucker's Row 4 CM23 76 F6
Tucker St WD18 167 C4
Tudor Ave
Cheshunt EN7 162 B8
Watford WD24 154 D2
Tudor Cl
Cheshunt EN7 162 B8
Hatfield AL10 129 F2
Hunsdonbury SG12 116 D8
Stevenage SG1 36 C1
Tudor Cres EN2 161 C1
Tudor Ct
Barnet EN5 171 F5
Borehamwood WD6 169 E7
Hitchin SG5 34 D6
Kneesworth SG8 2 B4
London Colney AL2 142 D5
Rickmansworth WD3 165 A1
Sawbridgeworth CM21 97 E3
Tudor Dr WD24 154 D2
Tudor Gdns HA3 176 D1
Tudor Lo 3 HA6 174 E3
Tudor Manor Gdns WD25 154 D7
Tudor Par WD3 165 A2
Tudor Prim Sch HP3 124 E1
Tudor Rd
Harrow HA3 176 D1
Luton LU3 45 B2
Pinner HA5 175 C1
St Albans AL3 127 E7
Welwyn AL6 89 B3
Wheathampstead AL4 108 E8
Tudor Rise EN10 134 E2
Tudor Sq 18 SG12 93 D1
Tudor Way
Hertford SG14 113 A7
Rickmansworth WD3 165 A2
Waltham Abbey EN9 163 D6
Tudor Wlk
17 Ware SG12 93 D1
Watford WD24 154 D2
Tuffnells Way AL5 85 D4
Tunfield Rd EN11 115 B1
Tunnel Way LU7 80 C3
Tunnel Wood Cl WD17 153 F2
Tunnel Wood Rd WD17 153 F2
Tunnmeade CM20 118 A1
Turf La SG4 36 B4
Turin Ho 15 WD18 166 E5
Turkey St EN1, EN3 162 C2
Turkey Street Sta EN3 162 C2
Turmore Dale AL8 110 C5
Turnberry Ct WD19 175 C7
Turnberry Dr AL2 140 E1
Turner Cl SG1 36 C2
Turner Ct HP4 122 A5
Turner Rd WD23 168 C5
Turners Cl
Bramfield SG14 91 C4
Harpenden AL5 86 C4
Turners Cres CM23 76 C4
Turners Ct EN8 162 D8
Turners Hill
Cheshunt EN8 148 D1
Hemel Hempstead HP2 124 E2
Turners Rd N LU2 46 A2
Turners Rd S LU2 46 A2
Turneys Orch WD3 164 D4
TURNFORD 148 E5
Turnford Cotts 3 EN10 148 F5
Turnford Sch EN8 148 E3
Turnford Villas EN8 148 F5
Turnpike Dr LU3 31 C1
Turnpike Gn HP2 124 F7
Turnpike La SG5 21 E3
Turnstones The WD25 154 E3
Turpin Cl EN3 163 A2
Turpins Chase AL6 89 F7
Turpins Cl SG14 112 F6
Turpins Ride AL6 89 F7
Turpin's Ride SG8 7 D5
Turpin's Rise SG2 50 F1
Turpin's Way SG7 23 F7
Tussauds Cl WD3 166 A4
Tuthill Ct SG8 15 E7
Tuxford Cl WD6 156 E1
Tweed Cl HP4 122 B5
Twelve Acres AL7 110 E4
Twelve Leys HP22 60 B3
Twickenham Gdns HA3 176 E3
Twigden Ct LU3 44 E5
Twin Foxes SG3 69 A1
Twin Oaks HA6 174 B3
Twinwoods SG1 50 F4
Twist The HP23 100 D2
Twitchell The SG7 23 F8
Two Acres AL7 110 F3
Two Beeches HP2 124 F8
Two Dells La HP5 136 A4
Two Oaks Dr AL6 90 C6
TWO WATERS 138 C8
Two Waters Prim Sch HP3 138 D6
Two Waters Rd
Hemel Hempstead HP3 124 C1
Hemel Hempstead HP3 138 D8
Twyford Bsns Ctr The CM23 77 A4
Twyford Bury La CM22, CM23 77 A4
Twyford Cl CM23 77 A5
Twyford Dr LU2 46 D1
Twyford Gdns CM23 76 F4
Twyford Ind Est CM23 77 A5
Twyford Mews CM22 77 A3
Twyford Mill CM22 77 A3
Twyford Rd
Bishop's Stortford CM23 77 A5
St Albans AL4 128 C7
Twysdens Terr AL9 144 C7
Tye End SG2 69 B8
Tyfield Cl EN8 148 C1
Tylers AL5 86 D1
TYLERS CAUSEWAY 132 D1
Tylers Cl
Buntingford SG9 40 D7
Kings Langley WD4 138 F3
Tylers Cswy SG13 132 C1
Tylersfield WD5 154 A8
TYLER'S HILL 150 A8
Tylers Hill Rd HP5 150 A8
Tylers Mead LU2 45 E5
Tylers Way WD23, WD25 168 E4
Tylers Wood AL6 90 C6
Tynedale AL2 142 F4
Tynemouth Dr EN1 162 A1
Typleden Cl HP2 124 D5
Tysoe Ave EN3 162 F2
Tythe Rd LU4 44 C6
Tyttenhanger Gn AL4 142 E8

U

Uckfield Rd EN3 162 D2
Ufford Cl HA3 176 B3
Ufford Rd HA3 176 B3
Ullswater Cl SG1 37 C2
Ullswater Rd HP3 125 C1
Ulverston Cl AL1 127 F3
Underacres Cl HP2 125 A4
Underhill Inf Sch EN5 171 E4
Underhill Jun Sch EN5 171 E4
Underwood Rd SG1 36 C2
Union Chapel Ho 1 LU1 63 E6
Union Ct 19 HP4 122 D4
Union Gn HP2 124 D4
Union St
Barnet EN5 171 E6
Luton LU1 63 E6
Union Terr SG9 40 E7
Units D1-D2 CM21 97 F2
Unity Rd EN3 162 D2
University Cl WD23 168 A5
Univ of Bedfordshire LU1 63 E7
Univ of Hertfordshire AL10 129 F3
Unwin Cl SG6 22 E4
Unwin Pl SG2 51 C3
Unwin Rd SG2 51 C3
Updale Cl EN6 158 E6
Upland Dr AL9 145 B6
Uplands
Braughing SG11 55 F6
Croxley Green WD3 165 F3
Luton LU3 44 D8
Stevenage SG2 51 D7
Ware SG12 93 F2
Welwyn Garden City AL8 89 C2
Uplands Ave SG4 35 B6
Uplands Ct
3 Bushey WD23 168 D1
Luton LU1 63 E4
Uplands The
Bricket Wood AL2 140 E1
Harpenden AL5 107 A4
Upper Ashlyns Rd HP4 122 B3
Upper Barn HP3 138 F8
Upper Bourne End La HP1 137 B8
Upper Clabdens SG12 93 F2
Upper Culver Rd AL1 127 F5
Upper Dagnall St AL3 127 D3
UPPER DUNSLEY 100 C4
Upperfield Rd AL7 110 F5
Upper George St LU1 63 D7
Upper Gn
Ickleford SG5 21 E4
Tewin AL6 90 D3
Upper Green Rd AL6 90 E3
Upper Hall Pk HP4 122 E2
Upper Heath Rd AL1 127 F5
Upper Highway WD5 153 D6
Upper Hill Rise WD3 165 B3
Upper Hitch WD19 167 E1
Upper Icknield Way
Aldbury LU7 80 E1
Aston Clinton HP22 99 A3
Tring HP23 100 D8
Upper King St SG8 7 D6
Upper Lattimore Rd AL1 127 E3
Upper Marlborough Rd AL1 127 E3
Upper Marsh La EN11 135 A5
Upper Maylins SG6 23 C3
Upper Paddock Rd WD19 167 E3
Upper Pk CM20 117 B1
Upper Sales HP1 123 F2
Upper Sean SG2 51 A3
Upper Shot AL7 111 A7
Upper Shott EN7 147 F5
Upper Station Rd WD7 156 A4
Upperstone Cl SG5 11 F6
Upper Tail WD19 175 E7
Upper Tilehouse St SG5 34 E7
Upshire Rd EN9 163 F7
Upton Ave AL3 127 D4
Upton Cl
Luton LU2 45 D6
Park Street AL2 141 D6
Upton Lodge Cl WD23 168 C2
Upton Rd WD18 167 B6
Upwell Rd LU2 46 B2
UPWICK GREEN 57 E5
Uranus Rd HP2 124 F5
Urban Hive LU3 44 C8
Urban Rd CM23 77 B7
Uxbridge Rd WD3 173 A8
Uxbridge Rd (Harrow Weald) HA3 176 D3
Uxbridge Rd (Hatch End) HA5 175 F3
Uxbridge Rd (Pinner) HA5 175 D2
Uxbridge Rd (Stanmore) HA7 176 F4

V

Vadis Cl LU3 44 E7
Vale Ave WD6 170 B4
Vale Cl AL5 85 D4
Vale Cotts SG11 54 D5
Vale Ct AL4 108 D7
Vale Dr EN5 171 F5
Vale Ind Pk WD18 166 C1
Valence Dr EN7 148 A3
Valency Cl HA6 174 F6
Valentine Ct WD6 169 D3
Vale Rd WD23 167 E4
Valerian Way SG2 51 D8
Valerie Cl AL1 128 B3
Valerie Ct WD23 168 C2
Valeside SG14 113 A5
Vallance Pl AL5 107 C7
Vallans Cl SG12 93 D3
Vallansgate SG2 51 B1
Valley Cl
  Hertford SG13 113 D5
  Pinner HA5 175 B1
  Studham LU6 82 B4
  Waltham Abbey EN9 163 C7
  Ware SG12 93 B2
  Whipsnade HP4 81 E7
Valley Ct CM23 76 E5
Valley Gn HP2 105 B1
Valley Gn The AL8 110 C7
Valley Ho EN8 162 D8
Valley La AL3 83 E1
Valley Rd
  Berkhamsted HP4 121 F6
  Codicote SG4 67 F1
  Letchworth Garden City SG6 22 D7
  Rickmansworth WD3 165 B3
  St Albans AL3 127 F7
  Studham LU6 82 B3
  Welwyn Garden City AL8 110 B6
Valley Rise
  Lea Valley AL4 86 F2
  Royston SG8 7 E6
  Watford WD25 154 B6
Valley Road S SG4 88 F8
Valley Sch The SG2 50 F2
Valleyside HP1 123 F3
Valley The SG4 66 E7
Valley View
  Barnet EN5 171 E3
  Goff's Oak EN7 147 C3
Valley Way SG2 51 A3
Valley Wlk WD3 166 C4
Valpy Cl HP23 100 D1
Vanburgh Ct 6 EN5 171 E5
Vancouver Rd EN10 148 E6
Vanda Cres AL1 127 F2
Vantage Ct 2 EN5 171 F5
Vantage Mews HA6 174 D4
Vantorts Cl CM21 97 E2
Vantorts Rd CM21 97 E2
Vardon Rd SG1 50 F8
Varna Cl LU3 45 A3
Varney Cl
  Hammond Street EN7 148 A4
  Hemel Hempstead HP1 123 F3
Varney Rd HP1 123 F3
Vaughan Mead AL3 106 A4
Vaughan Rd
  Harpenden AL5 86 B1
  Stotfold SG5 11 E7
Vauxhall Rd
  Hemel Hempstead HP2 125 B3
  Luton LU1, LU2 64 B5
Vauxhall Way LU2 46 B1
Vega Cres HA6 175 A5
Vega Rd WD23 168 C2
Velizy Ave CM20 117 D1
Venables Terr SG1 50 D7
Venetia Rd LU2 46 A4
Venice Ave WD18 166 E5
Ventnor Gdns LU3 45 A7
Ventura Pk AL2 141 F2
Venus Ct AL10 129 E6
VENUS HILL 151 B8
Venus Hill HP3 151 A8
Vera Ct WD19 167 D2
Vera La AL6 90 B4
Verdana Ct 3 WD18 166 E4
Verdure Cl WD25 154 E7
Veritys AL10 130 A5
Verity Way SG1 51 B8
Ver Mdw Cvn Site AL3 106 C5
Verney Cl
  Berkhamsted HP4 121 F5
  Tring HP23 100 C5
Vernon Ave EN3 162 E3
Vernon Ct CM23 76 E4
Vernon Dr UB9 173 C2
Vernon Rd
  Luton LU1 63 C8
  Watford WD23 167 E4
Vernon's Cl AL1 127 E2
Veronica Ho AL7 111 B4
Ver Rd
  Redbourn AL3 106 C6
  St Albans AL3 127 C3
Verulam Cl AL7 110 F6
Verulam Gdns LU3 44 F6
Verulam Ind Est AL1 127 F1
Verulamium Mus★ AL3 127 B3
Verulamium Roman Town★ AL3 127 A3
Verulam Rd
  Hitchin SG5 34 F8
  St Albans AL3 127 C4
Verulam Sch AL1 128 A4
Verwood Rd HA2 176 C1
Vespers Cl LU4 44 A2
Vesta Ave AL1 141 C8
Vesta Rd HP2 124 F5
Vestry Cl LU1 63 D7
Veysey Cl 2 HP1 124 B1
Viaduct Cotts LU1 85 F8
Viaduct Rd SG12 114 F8
Viaduct Way AL7 89 F2
Vian Ave EN3 162 E4
Vicarage Cl
  Arlesey SG15 11 A8
  18 Bishop's Stortford CM23 76 F7
  Hemel Hempstead HP1 124 C2
  Northaw EN6 145 F1
  Potters Bar EN6 158 E7
  Shillington SG5 19 F8
  St Albans AL1 141 C8
  Standon SG11 55 E2
Vicarage Cswy SG13 114 B4
Vicarage Gdns
  Flamstead AL3 84 B1
  Marsworth HP23 80 A2
  Potten End HP4 123 B7
Vicarage Ho AL7 110 F5
Vicarage La
  Bovingdon HP3 137 B4
  Ivinghoe LU7 80 F5
  Kings Langley WD4 138 F2
  Stapleford SG14 92 B2
Vicarage Rd
  Buntingford SG9 40 E8
  Marsworth HP23 80 A2
  Pitstone LU7 80 D3
  Potten End HP4 123 A7
  Ware SG12 93 E1
  Watford WD18 167 A4
  Wigginton HP23 100 D1
Vicarage Road Prec WD18 167 B5
Vicarage St LU1 63 F7
Vicarage Wood CM20 118 A1
Vicerons Pl CM23 76 D4
Viceroy Ct HA6 174 E4
Victoria CE Fst Sch HP4 122 C4
Victoria Cl
  Rickmansworth WD3 165 D2
  Stevenage SG1 50 D7
Victoria Cres SG8 7 D7
Victoria Ct
  Harlow CM20 117 E1
  2 Watford WD17 167 C6
Victoria Dr SG5 12 A5
Victoria La EN5 171 F5
Victoria Mews SG13 113 A1
Victoria Pas WD18 167 B5
Victoria Pl HP2 124 D3
Victoria Rd
  Berkhamsted HP4 122 C4
  Bushey WD23 168 B1
  7 Harpenden AL5 86 B1
  Hitchin SG5 34 D8
  Waltham Abbey EN9 163 C5
  Watford WD24 154 B1
Victoria Sq AL1 127 F2
Victoria St
  Luton LU1 63 E6
  St Albans AL1 127 E3
Victoria Terr 9 SG5 34 D8
Victors Way EN5 171 F6
Victory Ct
  Royston SG8 7 E5
  St Albans AL1 128 B3
Victory Rd HP4 122 A5
View Point SG1 50 A5
Viewpoint Ct 8 HA5 175 C1
View Rd EN6 159 C7
Vigors Croft AL10 129 F4
Villa Ct 6 LU2 63 D8
Village Arc 8 AL1 127 D3
Village Ct EN11 135 D8
Village Ct AL4 128 D7
Village Mews HP3 137 A4
Village St SG4 49 F1
Village Way SG7 5 A3
Villa Rd LU2 63 D8
Villiers Cl LU4 44 D3
Villiers Cres AL4 128 D6
Villiers Rd WD19 167 E3
Villiers St SG13 113 E6
Villiers-Sur-Marne Ave CM23 76 D4
Vincent SG6 23 C4
Vincent Cl EN8 148 E3
Vincent Ct
  Northwood HA6 174 F2
  Stevenage SG1 50 B8
Vincent Rd LU4 44 D5
Vincenzo Cl AL9 144 C8
Vine Cl AL8 110 E8
Vine Ct 11 SG12 93 D2
Vine Gr CM20 117 E5
Vines The SG5 11 E6
Vine Tree Ct WD3 173 B8
Vineyards Hill EN6 146 B2
Vineyards Rd EN6 146 A2
Vineyard The
  Hertford SG14 113 D8
  Ware SG12 94 A2
  Welwyn Garden City AL8 110 E8
Vintage Ct SG11 55 C2
Vinters Ave SG1 50 F5
Violet Ave EN2 161 D1
Violets La SG9 43 B5
Violet Way WD3 165 C5
Virgil Dr EN10 148 F8
Virginia Cl LU2 45 F3
Viscount Cl LU3 45 A5
Viscount Ct 14 LU2 45 D1
Vivian Cl WD19 167 A1
Vivian Gdns WD19 167 A1
Vixen Cl AL10 130 B7
Vixen Dr SG13 114 A6
Vyse Cl EN5 171 C5

W

Wacketts EN7 148 A4
Waddesdon Cl LU2 46 D2
Waddeston Ct EN2 161 E1
Waddington Rd 3 AL3 127 D3
Waddling La AL4 87 D1
WADESMILL 93 D8
Wadesmill Rd
  Tonwell SG12, SG14 92 D3
  Ware SG12 93 D2
Wades The AL10 130 A2
Wade The AL7 111 A3
Wadham Rd WD5 153 F8
Wadhurst Ave LU3 45 C4
Wadley Cl 1 HP2 124 F2
Wadnall Way SG3 68 F3
Waggoners Yd 4 SG12 93 D2
Waggon Rd EN4 159 E2
Wagon Rd
  Ganwick Corner EN5 159 A4
  Hadley Wood EN4 159 B2
Wagon Way WD3 165 C6
Waight Cl AL10 129 E7
Wain Cl EN6 145 B2
Wainwright St CM23 76 C5
Wakefields Wlk EN8 162 E8
Walace Ct EN3 163 A2
Walcot Ave LU2 46 B1
Waldeck Rd LU3 63 C8
Waldegrave Pk AL5 86 D1
Walden End SG1 50 E4
Walden Pl AL8 110 D8
Walden Rd AL8 110 D8
Waleran Cl HA7 176 F4
Waleys Cl LU3 44 E8
Walfords Cl CM17 118 C3
Walkden's SG7 4 E4
Walker Gr AL10 129 D6
WALKERN 38 B1
Walkern Prim Sch SG2 52 B8
Walkern Rd
  Benington SG2 52 D5
  Stevenage SG1 50 D8
  Watton at S SG14 70 C6
Walkers Cl AL5 107 C7
Walkers Ct AL5 107 C7
Walkers' Ct SG7 23 F8
Walkers Rd AL5 107 B7
Walk The
  Hertford SG14 113 A5
  Potters Bar EN6 159 B7
Wallace Ct 10 SG5 34 F8
Wallace Way SG4 22 A2
Walled Garden The SG14 92 A1
Walled Gdn The AL6 90 B2
Waller Ave LU4 44 F3
Waller Dr HA6 175 A2
Waller's Cl SG8 9 F2
Waller Street Mall 3 LU1 63 E7
Wallers Way EN11 115 B1
Wall Hall Dr WD25 155 B3
Wall Hall Man WD25 155 B4
Wallingford Wlk AL1 141 D8
WALLINGTON 25 D8
Wallington Rd SG7 13 D1
Wallis Ct EN9 163 B4
Walnut Ave SG7 24 A7
Walnut Cl
  Chiswell Green AL2 141 B4
  Hitchin SG4 35 A6
  Luton LU2 46 B4
  Much Hadham SG10 74 F2
  Royston SG8 7 D6
  Stotfold SG5 11 F6
Walnut Cotts CM21 97 E3
Walnut Ct
  Welwyn Garden City AL7 110 E3
  Wheathampstead AL4 108 D8
Walnut Dr CM23 76 D3
Walnut Gn WD23 167 F7
Walnut Gr
  Harlow CM20 117 B1
  Hemel Hempstead HP2 124 D3
  Welwyn Garden City AL7 110 E3
Walnut Ho AL7 110 F3
Walnut Tree Ave CM21 97 E4
Walnut Tree Cl
  Aston SG2 51 D4
  Cheshunt EN8 162 D8
  Hoddesdon EN11 135 A6
Walnut Tree Cres CM21 97 E3
Walnut Tree Rd SG5 20 D3
Walnut Tree Wlk SG12 114 E6
Walnut Way SG5 21 E4
Walpole Bldg 5 WD3 165 E1
Walpole Cl HA5 176 A4
Walpole Ct SG2 69 C7
Walsham Cl SG2 69 C7
Walsham Ct EN3 162 C2
Walsh Cl SG5 34 D7
Walshford Way WD6 157 A1
Walsingham Cl
  Hatfield AL10 129 F6
  Luton LU2 45 D7
Walsingham Way AL2 142 C4
WALSWORTH 22 A1
Walsworth Rd SG4 35 A8
Walter Rothschild Zoological Mus The★ HP23 100 A3
Walters Cl EN7 147 B6
WALTHAM ABBEY 163 D7
Waltham Abbey★ EN9 163 C6
WALTHAM CROSS 162 E5
Waltham Cross Sta EN8 162 F5
Waltham Ct LU2 46 C3
Waltham Gate EN8 148 F5
Waltham Gdns EN3 162 C2
Waltham Holy Cross Inf Sch EN9 163 D6
Waltham Holy Cross Jun Sch EN9 163 D6
Waltham Rd
  6 Hitchin SG4 34 F6
  Waltham Abbey EN9 149 F5
Walton Ct EN11 135 C8
Walton Gdns EN9 163 B6
Walton Rd
  Hoddesdon EN11 135 C8
  Ware SG12 114 D8
  Watford WD23 167 E5
Walton St AL1 127 F5
Walverns Cl WD19 167 C3
Wander Wharf WD4 139 B1
Wandon Cl LU2 46 C4
WANDON END 47 B1
Wannions Cl HP5 136 A1
Wansbeck Cl SG1 37 A3
Wansford Pk WD6 170 E5
Warburton Cl HA3 176 D4
Ward Cl
  Hammond Street EN7 148 A4
  Ware SG12 93 C2
Ward Cres CM23 76 E6
Warden Ct 5 LU2 63 E8
WARDEN HILL 45 D7
Warden Hill Cl LU2 45 C8
Warden Hill Gdns LU2 45 C8
Warden Hill Inf Sch LU3 45 C7
Warden Hill Jun Sch LU3 45 C7
Warden Hill Rd LU2 45 C8
Ward Hatch CM20 118 A3
Wardown Cres LU2 45 E2
Wardown Ct LU3 45 D2
Wardown Park Mus★ LU3 45 D2
Wards Cotts WD6 168 F7
Wards Dr WD3 151 F3
WARE 93 F2
Wareham's La SG14 113 C5
Ware Mus★ SG12 93 D1
Warenford Way WD6 170 A8
Ware Park Manor SG12 92 E2
Ware Park Rd SG12, SG14 113 E8
Ware Rd
  Hertford SG13 113 E6
  Hoddesdon EN11 115 A1
  Tonwell SG12 92 F6
  Watton at S SG14, SG12 71 C3
  Widford SG12 95 D4
WARESIDE 94 E4
Wareside HP2 105 A1
Wareside CE Prim Sch SG12 94 E3
Wareside Cl AL7 111 B5
Ware Sta SG12 114 E8
Warham Rd HA3 176 F1
Warlow Cl EN3 163 A2
Warmark Rd HP1 123 E5
Warminster Cl LU2 46 F1
Warneford Pl WD19 167 E3
Warner Cl EN4 159 E2
Warner Rd SG12 114 D8
Warners Ave EN11 134 F4
Warners Cl SG2 51 C3
WARNERS END 123 F4
Warners End Rd HP1 124 B4
Warren Cl
  Hatfield AL10 130 B8
  Letchworth Garden City SG6 22 D7
Warren Cotts SG8 9 A1
Warren Ct
  Cheshunt EN8 148 E1
  Royston SG8 7 D5
Warren Dale AL8 89 D1
Warren Dell Prim Sch WD19 175 C7
Warren Dr The LU1 64 C1
Warrenfield Cl EN7 162 A8
Warrengate La EN6 158 C8
Warrengate Rd AL9 144 C4
Warren Gn AL10 130 B8
Warren Gr WD6 170 D5
Warren La
  Clothall SG7 24 D7
  Cottered SG9 39 B6
  Stanmore HA7 176 F8
Warren Park Rd SG14 113 D7
Warren Pl 16 SG14 113 D6
Warren Rd
  Bushey WD23 168 D1
  Luton LU1 62 F8
  St Albans AL1 141 C7
WARREN'S GREEN 37 D6
Warrensgreen La SG4 37 D5
Warren Terr SG14 113 D8
Warren The
  Harpenden AL5 107 A6
  Kings Langley WD4 138 F2
  Radlett WD7 156 B6
  Royston SG8 7 D5
Warren Way AL6 89 E4
Warren Wood Ind Est SG14 91 F6
Warton Gn LU2 46 E2
Warwick Ave EN6 146 D4
Warwick Cl
  Bushey WD23 168 E2
  Cuffley EN6 146 D4
  Hertford SG13 113 C4
Warwick Ct
  Chorleywood WD3 164 F6
  Luton LU4 63 B8
Warwick Dr EN8 148 D3
Warwick Ho 11 AL1 127 D3
Warwick Mews WD3 166 A3
Warwick Rd
  Bishop's Stortford CM23 77 B6
  Borehamwood WD6 170 D6
  Enfield EN3 162 F2
  Pitstone LU7 80 D3
  St Albans AL1 127 F5
  Stevenage SG2 51 C6
Warwick Rd E LU4 63 B8
Warwick Rd W LU4 63 B8
Warwick Way WD3 166 C5
WASHALL GREEN 30 C1
Washington Ave HP2 124 E8
Wash La
  Dancers Hill EN6 158 C3
  South Mimms EN6 158 C5
Wash The
  Furneux Pelham SG9 43 D5
  Hertford SG14 113 D6
Watchlytes AL7 111 C6
Watchlytes Jun Mix Inf Sch AL7 111 C6
Watchmead AL7 111 A6
Waterbeach AL7 111 D6
Watercress Cl SG2 51 D5
Watercress Rd EN7 147 D5
WATERDALE 140 C1
Waterdale SG13 113 C4
Waterdell La SG4 35 A2
Waterdell Pl WD3 173 B8
WATER END
  Brookmans Park 144 C5
  Hemel Hempstead 103 F1
Water End Cl WD6 169 F7
Waterend La
  Ayot St P AL4, AL6 88 E1
  Redbourn AL3 106 B5
Water End Rd HP4 123 C7
Waterfall Cl EN11 134 F7
Waterfield
  Chorleywood WD3 164 C2
  Welwyn Garden City AL7 111 B7
Waterfields Ret Pk WD17 167 D5
Waterfields Way WD17, WD23 167 D4
WATERFORD 92 A2
Waterford Comm SG14 92 B2
Waterford Gn AL7 111 B6
Waterfront The 22 SG14 113 D6
Watergate The WD19 175 D8
Waterhall Cotts SG13 132 D7
Water Hall Farm & Craft Ctr★ SG4 66 F7
Waterhouse Gdns 7 LU1 63 E5
Waterhouse St HP1 124 C2
Waterhouse The HP1 124 C3
Water La
  Abbots Langley WD4 139 B2
  Berkhamsted HP4 122 C4
  Bishop's Stortford CM23 76 F8
  Bovingdon HP3 137 B1
  Hertford SG14 113 C5
  Hitchin SG5 21 F1
  Stansted Mountfitchet CM24 59 E6
  Watford WD17 167 D5
Waterloo Ct 3 AL1 128 B2
Waterloo La SG5 21 A6
Waterlow Mews SG4 35 E3
Waterman Cl WD19 167 B3
Watermark Way SG13 113 F6
Water Mdws AL2 141 E3
Watermead Rd LU3 44 F6
Watermill Ind Est SG9 40 E6
Watermill La
  Hertford SG14 113 D8

Watermill La *continued*
Stansted Mountfitchet CM24 59 C6
Water Row 11 SG12 93 D1
Waters Dr 8 WD3 165 E1
Waters End SG5 11 E6
Waterside
Berkhamsted HP4 122 D4
Harpenden AL5 86 C3
Kings Langley WD4 139 A2
London Colney AL2 142 E4
Radlett WD7 156 B5
Stansted Mountfitchet CM24 59 E6
Welwyn Garden City AL7 90 B1
Waterside Cotts AL9 130 E8
Waterside Ct
2 Hemel Hempstead HP3 138 E7
Kings Langley WD4 139 B2
Waterside Ind Est EN11 135 D5
Waterside Mews UB9 173 A4
Waterside Pl CM22 98 A2
Waterslade Gn LU3 45 B6
Watersplash Ct AL2 142 F4
Waterways Bsns Ctr 11 EN3 163 A1
Watery La
Flamstead AL3, AL5 84 E3
Hatfield AL10 129 E4
Marsworth HP23 79 F1
WATFORD 167 C3
Watford Arches Ret Pk WD17 167 D4
Watford By-pass WD6 169 C2
Watford Coll (annex) WD23 167 D6
Watford County Ct WD18 167 C5
Watford Ent Ctr WD18 166 E3
Watford Field Rd WD18 167 C4
Watford Football Gd & Saracens RFC WD18 167 B4
Watford General Hospl (Shrodells Wing) WD18 167 B4
Watford Gram Sch for Boys WD18 166 F5
Watford Gram Sch for Girls WD18 167 B5
WATFORD HEATH 167 E2
Watford Heath WD19 167 D2
Watford Heath Farm WD19 167 D2
Watford High Street Sta WD17 167 C5
Watford Junction Sta WD17 167 C7
Watford Mus* WD17 167 C5
Watford North Sta WD24 154 C2
Watford Rd
Abbots Langley WD4 153 C6
Chiswell Green AL2 141 A6
Croxley Green WD3 166 B3
Elstree WD6 169 C3
Kings Langley WD4 139 A1
Moor Park HA6 175 A4
Radlett WD7 155 F4
Watford Sch of Music WD17 154 A1
Watford Sta WD18 166 F6
Watkin Mews EN3 163 A2
Watkins Cl HA6 174 F2
Watkins Rise EN6 159 B7
Watling Cl 1 HP2 124 E6
Watling Ct WD6 169 D3
Watling Farm Cl HA7 169 C1
Watling Knoll WD7 155 F6
Watling Mans WD7 156 B3
Watling St
Elstree WD6 169 C6
Park Street AL2 141 D6
Radlett WD7 156 B3
St Albans AL1 141 C8
Watlington Rd CM17 118 D4
Watling View AL1 141 C8
Watling View Sch AL1 141 D7
Watson Ave AL3 127 F6
Watson Rd SG1 50 C5
Watson's Wlk AL1 127 E2
Watsons Yd 9 CM23 76 F8
WATTON AT STONE 70 E4
Watton-at-Stone Prim Sch SG14 70 D3
Watton at Stone Sta SG14 70 D3
Watton Ho SG14 70 F3
Watton Rd
Knebworth SG3 69 A5
Ware SG12 93 C2
Watton at S SG3, SG14 70 B2
Watts Cl SG11 57 C2
Waulud Prim Sch LU3 44 E7
Wauluds Bank Dr LU3 44 E7
Wavell Cl EN8 148 E4
Wavell Ho AL1 128 A2
Waveney HP2 124 F8
Waveney Rd AL5 86 C3
Waverley Cl SG2 69 A8
Waverley Gdns HA6 175 A2
Waverley Lodge AL3 127 D5
Waverley Rd AL3 127 D5
Waxhouse Gate AL1 127 D3
Waxwell Cl HA5 175 D1
Waxwell La HA5 175 D1
Wayfarers Pk HP4 121 F4
Wayletts Dr CM23 77 B7
Waynes Ct 9 LU1 63 E7
Wayre St CM17 118 C4
Wayre The CM17 118 C4
Waysbrook SG6 23 B5
Wayside
Chipperfield WD4 138 B1
Potters Bar EN6 159 D6
Shenley WD7 156 D6
Wayside Ave WD23 168 D3
Wayside Ct AL2 140 F1
Wayside The HP3 125 C2
Waysmeet SG6 23 B4
Waytemore Rd CM23 76 E6
Weald Fst Sch HA3 176 F3
Weald La HA3 176 D2
Weald Mid Sch HA3 176 F3
Weald Rise HA3 176 F2
Wealdwood Gdns HA5 176 B4
Weall Gn WD25 154 B7
Weardale Ct EN5 171 C4
Weatherby Rd LU4 44 D2
Weavers Orch SG15 11 A4
Weavers Rd HP23 99 E4
Weaver St CM23 76 C4
Weavers Way SG7 24 A8
Webb Cl SG6 23 C5
Webber Cl WD6 169 D3
Webb Rise SG1 50 F7
Webley Ct EN3 163 A2
Webster Ct 2 WD3 165 E1
Wedgewood Cl HA6 174 C4
Wedgewood Rd SG4 35 B7
Wedgewood Way SG1 37 B2
Wedgwood Ct SG1 37 C2
Wedgwood Gate Ind Est SG1 37 B2
Wedmore Rd SG4 35 A6
Wedon Way SG7 13 C4
Weedon Cl SG16 10 C5
Weighton Rd HA3 176 D2
Welbeck Cl WD6 170 A6
Welbeck Rd 3 LU2 63 E8
Welbeck Rise AL5 107 D6
Welbury Ave LU3 45 C7
Welch Ho 2 EN3 162 D2
Welch Pl HA5 175 C2
Welclose St AL3 127 C3
Welcote Dr HA6 174 D4
Weldon Cl LU2 46 E1
Welham Cl
Borehamwood WD6 170 A8
Welham Green AL9 144 C7
Welham Ct AL9 144 C7
WELHAM GREEN 144 C7
Welham Green Sta AL9 144 D8
Welham Manor AL9 144 C7
Welkin Gn HP2 125 C4
Wellands AL10 130 A7
Well App EN5 171 C4
Wellbrook Mews HP23 100 B4
Wellbury Terr HP2 125 C3
Wellcroft LU7 80 F5
Well Croft HP1 124 B4
Wellcroft Cl AL7 111 A4
Wellcroft Rd AL7 111 A4
WELL END 157 C1
Well End Rd WD6 157 D1
Wellen Rise HP3 138 E8
Wellers Gr EN7 148 A3
Wellesley Ave HA6 174 F5
Wellesley Cres EN6 158 E6
Wellfield Ave LU3 44 C8
Wellfield Cl AL10 130 A6
Wellfield Ct SG1 37 B1
Wellfield Rd AL10 130 A7
Well Garth AL7 110 E5
Wellgate Rd LU4 44 D2
Well Gn SG14 91 C4
Wellhouse Cl LU1 63 A7
Wellhouse La EN5 171 D5
Wellingham Ave SG5 21 D1
Wellington Ave HA5 175 F2
Wellington Cl WD19 175 F7
Wellington Cotts SG11 73 B7
Wellington Ct 3 LU1 63 D6
Wellington Dr AL7 111 C6
Wellington Ho 1 WD24 167 C7
Wellington Pl
Cheshunt EN10 148 C8
Kneesworth SG8 2 B5
Wellington Rd
London Colney AL2 142 D5
Pinner HA5 175 F2
St Albans AL1 128 B2
Stevenage SG2 51 C5
Watford WD17 167 B7
Wellington St
Hertford SG14 113 B7
Luton LU1 63 D7
Well La
Harlow CM19 117 A1
Mentmore LU7 61 B8
WELLPOND GREEN 56 D1
Well Rd
Barnet EN5 171 C4
Northaw EN6 145 E2
Well Row SG13 132 F6
Wells Cl
Hammond Street EN7 147 C6
Wells Cl *continued*
Harpenden AL5 85 E4
St Albans AL3 127 C4
Wellsfield WD23 167 E4
Wellside Cl EN5 171 C5
Wellstones WD18 167 B5
Wellswood Cl HP2 125 B4
Wells Yd
8 Ware SG12 93 D1
Watford WD17 167 B6
Welsummer Way EN8 148 D3
Weltmore Rd LU3 44 F6
WELWYN 89 B4
Welwyn By Pass Rd AL6 89 C5
Welwyn Ct HP2 124 F7
WELWYN GARDEN CITY 110 E7
Welwyn Garden City Sta AL8 110 D6
Welwyn Hall Gdns AL6 89 C5
Welwyn North Sta AL6 89 F3
Welwyn Rd SG14 112 F7
Wendover Cl
Harpenden AL5 86 D1
St Albans AL4 128 C8
Wendover Ct AL6 89 C5
Wendover Dr AL6 89 C5
Wendover Ho WD18 166 E2
Wendover Way
Bushey WD23 168 C3
Luton LU2 45 F3
Wengeo La SG12 93 B2
Wenham Ct SG2 52 B8
Wenham Pl AL10 130 A6
Wenlock CE Jun Sch LU2 64 B8
Wenlock St LU2 63 E8
Wensley Cl AL5 107 D6
Wensleydale
Hemel Hempstead HP2 124 F6
Luton LU2 45 E1
Wensum Rd SG1 36 F3
Wensum Way WD3 165 D1
Wenta Bsns Ctr WD24 154 D2
Wentbridge Path WD6 157 A1
Wentworth Ave
Borehamwood WD6 169 F4
Luton LU4 44 C6
Wentworth Cl
Potters Bar EN6 159 A8
Watford WD17 153 F1
Wentworth Cotts
Dane End SG11 53 F2
Hoddesdon EN10 134 E1
Wentworth Ct EN5 171 E6
Wentworth Dr
Bishop's Stortford CM23 76 D6
South Oxhey WD19 175 D5
Wentworth Rd
Barnet EN5 171 D6
Hertford SG13 113 C3
Wenwell Cl HP22 99 A3
Wesley Cl
Arlesey SG15 11 A4
Goff's Oak EN7 147 C3
Wesley Rd AL3 83 E5
Wessex Ct 7 EN5 171 D5
Wessex Dr HA5 175 E3
Westall Cl SG13 113 C5
West Alley 3 SG5 34 E7
Westall Mews SG13 113 C5
West Ave
Baldock SG7 23 E8
Chiswell Green AL2 141 B6
Westbourne Mews AL1 127 D3
Westbourne Mobile Home Pk LU3 44 F5
Westbourne Rd LU4 45 B1
Westbrook Cl SG8 5 B8
Westbrook Ct SG4 34 F5
Westbrook Hay Prep Sch HP1 137 D7
West Burrowfield AL7 110 D4
Westbury EN8 148 D1
Westbury Cl SG5 34 D8
Westbury Farm Cl SG5 33 C3
Westbury Gdns LU2 45 E3
Westbury Pl SG6 22 E5
Westbury Prim Sch SG6 22 E5
Westbury Rd
Moor Park HA6 174 E7
Watford WD18 167 B4
Westbush Cl EN11 114 F1
West Chantry HA3 176 B2
West Cl
Barnet EN5 171 B4
Hitchin SG4 22 B1
Hoddesdon EN11 135 A8
Stevenage SG1 50 F5
West Comm
Harpenden AL5 107 B6
Redbourn AL3 106 A4
West Common Cl AL5 107 B5
West Common Gr AL5 107 B5
West Common Way AL5 107 A5
Westcott AL7 111 D7
Westcroft HP23 100 A3
Westcroft Cl EN3 162 C1
Westcroft Ct EN10 135 A4
West Ct CM21 97 E3
West Dene HP2 104 A8
West Dr
Arlesey SG15 11 B4
Stanmore HA3 176 D4
Watford WD25 154 B3
West Drive Gdns HA3 176 D4
Westell Cl SG7 24 A8
WEST END 131 C5
West End SG7 4 C3
West End La
Barnet EN5 171 D5
Essendon AL9 131 C5
West End Rd EN7 147 F8
Westerdale
Hemel Hempstead HP2 124 E6
Luton LU4 44 B5
Western Ave SG16 10 B3
Western Cl SG6 11 E1
Western House Hospl SG12 93 E2
Western Rd
Lower Nazeing EN9 135 E1
Luton LU1 63 D6
Tring HP23 99 F3
Western Terr 1 EN11 115 B1
Western Way SG6 11 E1
Westfield
Welham Green AL9 144 F8
Welwyn Garden City AL7 111 A7
Westfield Ave
Harpenden AL5 86 A3
Watford WD24 154 D1
Westfield Cl
Bishop's Stortford CM23 76 E8
Cheshunt EN8 162 F8
Hitchin SG5 34 D7
Westfield Com Prim Sch EN11 134 F7
Westfield Com Tech Coll WD18 166 F3
Westfield Ct AL4 128 D6
Westfield Dr AL5 86 B4
Westfield Fst Sch HP4 121 F5
Westfield La SG5 34 D7
Westfield Pk HA5 175 F3
Westfield Pl AL5 86 B4
Westfield Rd
Berkhamsted HP4 121 F5
Bishop's Stortford CM23 76 E8
Harpenden AL5 86 B4
Hertford SG14 113 C8
Hoddesdon EN11 134 F7
Pitstone LU7 80 C3
Westfields AL3 141 A8
Westfield Wlk EN8 162 F8
Westgate SG1 50 D5
West Gate 1 CM20 117 C1
Westgate Ct EN3 162 D4
West Herts Bsns Ctr WD6 170 B6
West Herts Coll Cassio Campus WD17 154 A1
West Herts Coll (Dacorum Campus) HP1 124 C4
West Herts Coll Leggatts Campus WD24 154 A3
West Herts Coll Watford Campus WD17 167 A6
West Hill SG5 34 D7
West Hill Rd
Hoddesdon EN11 134 F8
Luton LU1 63 E5
Westholm SG6 22 F8
WEST HYDE 172 E3
West Hyde La SL9 172 A4
West La
Great Offley SG5 33 C2
Pirton SG5 20 D5
Westland Cl WD25 153 F5
Westland Dr AL9 144 E4
WESTLAND GREEN 56 E1
Westland Rd
Knebworth SG3 69 A5
Watford WD17 167 B7
West Lawn WD25 155 B3
Westlea Ave WD25 154 E2
Westlea Cl EN10 148 F8
Westlea Rd EN10 148 F8
Westlecote Gdns LU2 45 D4
WEST LEITH 99 E1
West Leith HP23 99 F1
West Lodge Cotts LU2 46 D5
Westly Wood AL7 111 A7
West Mead AL7 111 B3
Westmeade Cl EN7 148 B2
WESTMILL
Buntingford 40 F3
Hitchin 21 C1
Westmill La
Hitchin SG5 21 C2
Ickleford SG5 21 C3
Westmill Lawns SG5 21 D1
Westmill Rd
Hitchin SG5 21 D1
Thundridge SG12 93 A3
Westminster Ct
Cheshunt EN8 162 F6
St Albans AL1 127 C1
Westminster Ho 6 WD24 167 C7
Westmorland Ave LU3 44 F5
Westmount Apartments 5 WD18 166 F5
WESTON 24 C1
Weston Ave SG8 7 C7
Weston Cl EN6 158 F7
Westonia Ct EN3 162 E3
Weston Prim Sch SG4 24 C1
Weston Rd
Stevenage SG1 36 E1
Stevenage SG1 36 F2
Weston Way SG7 23 E7
West Pas HP23 100 A3
West Pl CM20 118 A3
Westray HP3 125 C1
West Rd
Berkhamsted HP4 122 A5
Bishop's Stortford CM23 76 E6
Harlow CM20 118 A4
Sawbridgeworth CM21 97 C3
Stansted Mountfitchet CM24 59 E6
West Reach SG2 50 F2
Westridge Cl HP1 123 F3
West Riding
Bricket Wood AL2 140 F1
Burnham Green AL6 90 D5
Westron Gdns HP23 100 B4
West Side EN10 148 E6
West Sq 2 CM20 117 C1
West St
Hertford SG13 113 C5
Lilley LU2 32 D1
Ware SG12 93 D1
Watford WD17 167 B7
West Valley Rd HP3 138 D7
West View
Hatfield AL10 130 A7
Letchworth Garden City SG6 22 E5
Standon SG11 73 A6
West View Ct WD6 169 D3
West View Gdns WD6 169 D3
West View Rd AL3 127 D4
Westview Rise HP2 124 D4
WEST WATFORD 167 A4
West Way
Harpenden AL5 86 C2
Luton LU2 46 C4
Rickmansworth WD3 165 B1
West Ways HA6 175 A1
Westwick Cl HP2 125 D2
Westwick Pl WD25 154 C5
WESTWICK ROW 125 E2
Westwick Row HP2 125 E2
Westwood Ave SG4 35 A6
Westwood Cl EN6 145 A1
Westwood Sch WD23 176 D8
Wetherall Mews 1 AL1 127 E2
Wetherby Cl SG1 51 C8
Wetherby Rd
Borehamwood WD6 169 E8
Enfield EN2 161 C1
Wetherfield CM24 59 D7
Wetherly Cl CM17 118 F4
Wetherne Link LU4 44 C5
Wexham Cl LU3 44 E8
Weybourne Cl AL5 86 D2
Weybourne Dr LU2 45 C7
Weymouth St HP3 138 D7
Weyver Ct 5 AL1 127 E4
Whaley Rd EN6 159 C6
Wharfedale
Hemel Hempstead HP2 124 E6
8 Luton LU4 44 C5
Wharf La
Berkhamsted HP4 121 C8
Rickmansworth WD3 165 E1
Wharf Pl CM23 77 A6
Wharf Rd
12 Bishop's Stortford CM23 76 F6
Hemel Hempstead HP1 124 B1
Hoddesdon EN10 148 F8
Wharf Row HP22 99 B4
Wharf Villas 5 HP1 124 B1
Wheatbarn AL7 111 B7
Wheat Cl AL4 128 A7
Wheatcotes SG3 69 C1
Wheatcroft EN7 148 B3
Wheat Croft CM23 76 E4
Wheatcroft Prim Sch SG13 114 A7
Wheatfield
Hatfield AL10 130 B6
Hemel Hempstead HP2 124 D5
Wheatfield Ave AL5 107 A5
Wheatfield Cres SG8 7 E6
Wheatfield Rd AL5 107 A4
Wheatfields CM17 118 D6
Wheatfields Inf Sch AL4 128 B7
Wheatfields Jun Mix Sch AL4 128 B7
WHEATHAMPSTEAD 108 C7
Wheathampstead Rd
Harpenden AL5 107 E8
Wheathampstead AL5, AL4 108 A8
Wheat Hill SG6 22 F8
Wheatlands SG2 51 C7
Wheatley Cl
Sawbridgeworth CM21 97 C1

Wheatley Cl *continued*
Welwyn Garden City AL7 111 A4
Wheatley Dr WD25 154 C5
Wheatley Rd AL7 111 A4
Wheatleys AL4 128 C5
Wheatlock Mead AL3 106 A5
Wheatsheaf Cotts WD3 152 A4
Wheatsheaf Dr SG12 93 B3
Wheatsheaf Rd SG12 95 D1
Wheelers Cl EN9 135 F1
Wheelers La HP3 124 E1
Wheelers Yd HP23 79 B4
Wheelright Cl WD23 168 B3
Wheelwrights SG4 66 C1
Wheelwrights Cl CM23 76 C4
WHELPLEY HILL 136 D5
Whelpley Hill Pk HP5 136 D5
WHEMPSTEAD 71 B7
Whempstead La SG12 71 B6
Whempstead Rd SG12 71 B7
Whernside Dr SG1 37 B4
Whetstone Cl AL6 89 E8
Whetstone Ct AL6 89 E8
Whinbush Gr 8 SG5 34 F8
Whinbush Rd SG5 34 F8
WHIPPENDELL BOTTOM 138 C1
Whippendell Hill WD4 138 C1
Whippendell Rd WD18 166 F4
Whipperley Ct LU1 63 C5
Whipperley Inf Sch LU1 63 A6
Whipperley Ring LU1 63 A6
Whipperley Way LU1 63 C5
WHIPSNADE 82 A8
Whipsnade Wild Animal Pk* LU6 81 E7
Whisper Mews LU4 44 D4
Whisper Wood WD3 165 B6
Whisperwood Cl HA3 176 E3
Whitby Rd LU3 45 C1
Whitebarns SG9 43 A5
Whitebarns La SG9 43 A6
Whitebeam Cl
4 Hammond Street EN7 147 E5
Shenley WD7 156 F6
Whitebeams AL10 130 A2
White Beams AL2 141 C3
White Bear CM24 59 E8
Whitebroom Rd HP1 123 E5
Whitechurch Cl LU2 46 D2
Whitechurch Gdns SG6 23 C3
White Craig Cl HA5 176 A5
Whitecroft AL1 142 B8
Whitecroft Rd LU2 64 A8
Whitecrofts SG5 11 F6
Whitefield Ave LU3 44 C7
Whitefield Ho AL10 130 C7
Whitefield Inf Sch LU3 44 E8
Whitefield Jun Sch LU3 44 E8
Whitefields Rd EN8 148 C3
Whitefriars Ave HA3 176 E1
Whitefriars Dr HA3 176 E1
Whitefriars Fst & Mid Sch HA3 176 E1
Whitefriars Trad Est HA3 176 D1
Whitegale Cl SG4 35 A6
White Gate Gdns HA3 176 F3
Whitegates Cl WD3 166 A5
Whitehall Cl
Borehamwood WD6 170 A5
Lower Nazeing EN9 135 E1
Whitehall Coll CM23 58 E1
Whitehall Cotts SG12 116 D8
White Hall Farm SG14 70 B8
Whitehall La
Bishop's Stortford CM23 58 F1
King's Walden SG4 48 B4
Whitehall Rd
Bishop's Stortford CM23 58 E1
King's Walden SG4 48 A4
Whitehands Cl EN11 134 F6
White Hart Cl SG9 40 E8
Whitehart Cross HP3 136 F3
White Hart Ct
Cheshunt EN8 162 E6
Hemel Hempstead HP2 125 A2
White Hart Dr HP2 124 F2
White Hart Rd HP2 125 A2
Whitehaven Cl EN7 147 E3
White Hedge Dr AL3 127 C5
Whitehicks SG6 12 A1
Whitehill HP4 122 D5
White Hill
Ashley Green HP3, HP5 136 C7
Flamstead AL3 105 B8
Hemel Hempstead HP1 123 F2
Rickmansworth WD3 174 A4
Walkern SG2 38 C2
Welwyn AL6 89 A3
Whitehill Ave LU1 63 D5
Whitehill Cl SG4 35 A6
Whitehill Cotts AL6 89 A3
Whitehill Ct HP4 122 D5
Whitehill Jun Sch SG4 35 A5
Whitehill La LU7 80 D3
Whitehill Rd SG4 35 A6
Whitehorse La SG1 37 B3
White Horse La
Burnham Green AL6 90 C7
London Colney AL2 142 E5
Whitehorse St SG7 23 F8
Whitehorse Vale LU3 31 A1
White Ho The 6 EN8 148 D3
Whitehouse Ave WD6 170 B5
White House Cl SG14 70 E3
Whitehouse Ct SG8 17 D4
White House Ind Est EN5 159 A4
Whitehouse La WD5 140 C4
White House The SG6 23 B5
Whitehurst Ave SG5 21 F1
White La SG4 49 C7
Whitelands Ave WD3 164 C5
Whiteleaf Rd HP3 138 C8
Whiteley Cl SG12 71 E7
Whiteley La SG9 27 C8
White Lion Ho 5 AL10 130 A6
White Lion St HP3 138 D7
White Orchards N20 171 F1
Whitepost Ct CM23 77 A5
White Post Field CM21 97 D2
White Shack La WD3 152 F2
Whitesmead Rd SG1 50 E7
Whitestone Wlk HP1 124 A6
White Stubbs Farm EN10 134 A2
White Stubbs La EN10, SG13 133 C2
Whitethorn AL7 111 B5
Whitethorn La SG6 23 A4
Whitethorn Way LU1 63 A6
Whitewaits CM20 117 E1
Whiteway SG6 23 C4
Whitewaybottom La LU2, SG4 66 A3
White Way The SG2 51 C7
Whitewebbs La EN2 161 F4
Whitewebbs Mus of Transport* EN2 161 B4
Whitewebbs Pk* EN2 161 D4
Whitewebbs Rd EN2 161 C4
Whitewood Rd HP4 122 A4
Whitfield Way WD3 164 F1
Whit Hern Ct EN8 148 C1
Whitings Cl AL5 86 D4
Whitings Hill Prim Sch EN5 171 C4
Whitings Rd EN5 171 C4
Whitlars Dr WD4 138 F3
Whitley Cl WD5 154 A7
Whitley Ct EN11 135 B8
Whitley Gn LU2 46 D2
Whitley Rd EN11 135 B8
Whitmores Wood HP2 125 B4
Whitney Dr SG1 36 C1
Whittingham Cl LU2 46 F1
Whittingstall Rd EN11 135 C8
Whittington La SG1 50 E4
Whittington Way CM23 76 F3
Whittle Cl
Lower Stondon SG16 10 B4
Watford WD25 153 F5
Whittlesea Cl HA3 176 C3
Whittlesea Path HA3 176 C2
Whittlesea Rd HA3 176 C2
Whittle Way SG1 50 D2
WHITWELL 66 E6
Whitwell Cl LU3 45 B8
Whitwell Rd WD25 154 D4
Whitworth Cres EN3 163 A2
Whitworth Jones Ave SG16 10 C5
Whitworth Rd SG1 37 B3
Whomerley Rd SG1 50 E4
Whybrow Gdns HP4 122 E6
Whydale Rd SG8 7 E5
Whytingham Rd HP23 100 C4
Wick Ave AL4 108 D8
Wicken Fields SG12 93 C3
Wickets End WD7 156 E6
Wickets The LU2 45 E1
Wickfield SG3 69 A2
Wickfield Cl SG3 69 A2
Wickham Cl UB9 173 D2
Wickham Rd HA3 176 D1
Wickhams Wharf SG12 93 E1
Wickham Way SG11 55 E3
Wick Hill LU6 82 F8
Wicklands Rd SG12 116 D8
Wickmere Cl LU2 45 C7
Wick Rd HP23 120 D8
Wickstead Ave LU4 44 E4
Wick The
Hertford SG14 92 C1
Kimpton SG4 66 D1
Wickwood Ct AL1 128 B5
Widbury Gdns SG12 93 F1
Widbury Hill SG12 93 F1
Widbury Ho SG12 94 A1
WIDFORD 95 E4
Widford Rd
Hunsdon SG12 95 D2
Much Hadham SG10 95 F7
Welwyn Garden City AL7 111 B6
Widford Sch SG12 95 D4
Widford Terr HP2 105 A1
Widgeon Way WD25 154 E2
Widmore Dr HP2 125 A5
Wieland Rd HA6 175 A3
Wiggenhall Rd WD18 167 C4
WIGGINTON 100 D1
WIGGINTON BOTTOM 120 D8
Wigginton Bottom HP23 120 E8
Wiggles La HP23 99 F7
Wight Ho WD18 166 F4
WIGMORE 46 E2
Wigmore La LU2 46 D2
Wigmore Park Sh Ctr LU2 46 E1
Wigmore Pl LU2 46 E1
Wigmore Prim Sch LU2 46 E2
Wigmores N AL8 110 D7
Wigmores S AL8 110 D6
Wigram Way SG2 51 B3
Wilbraham's Almshouses EN5 171 F7
Wilbury Cl SG6 22 C7
Wilbury Hills Rd SG6 22 C7
Wilbury Jun Sch SG6 22 D6
Wilbury Lo 2 EN5 171 D5
Wilbury Rd SG6 22 E8
Wilbury Way SG4 22 A3
Wilcon Way WD25 154 D5
Wilcot Ave WD19 167 E2
Wilcot Cl WD19 167 E2
Wilcox Cl WD6 170 C8
Wilcox Ct 4 SG1 50 E6
Wildacres HA6 174 F7
Wild Cherry Dr LU1 63 D5
Wilde Ct AL2 142 B4
Wilderness The
3 Berkhamsted HP4 122 C4
Hertford SG14 92 A1
Stapleford SG14 91 F1
WILDHILL 131 D2
Wildhill Rd AL9 131 B2
Wilding Ct 8 WD6 170 A5
Wildman Ct SG13 114 A7
Wild Marsh Ct EN8 162 E2
Wildoaks Cl HA6 174 F4
Wildwood HA6 174 D4
Wildwood Ave AL2 140 F1
Wildwood Ct WD3 164 F5
Wildwood La SG1 50 E3
Wilford Cl HA6 174 D3
Wilga Rd AL6 89 B5
Wilkins Gr AL8 110 D5
Wilkin's Green La AL4 129 C4
Wilkinsgreen Terr AL4 129 B3
Wilkinson Cl EN7 147 C6
Willenhall Cl LU3 45 A7
Willetts Mews EN11 135 A7
William Austin Inf Sch LU3 45 C4
William Austin Jun Sch LU3 45 C4
William Covell Cl EN2 160 F1
William Crook Ho HP1 123 F3
William Ct HP3 138 D7
William Fiske Ho 13 HP4 122 C4
William Gray Ct AL10 129 F6
William Pl SG2 51 A3
William Ransom Prim Sch SG4 35 B7
William Ransom Way SG5 34 F7
Williams Ct LU7 80 C2
Williamson St 1 LU1 63 E7
Williamson Way WD3 165 A1
William St
18 Berkhamsted HP4 122 D4
Luton LU2 45 E1
Markyate AL3 83 E5
Watford WD23 167 D6
William Sutton Ct LU2 46 B5
Williams Way WD7 156 C4
WILLIAN 23 B2
Willian Church Rd SG6 23 A2
Willian Rd
Baldock SG7 23 E6
Great Wymondley SG4, SG6 35 F7
Hitchin SG4, SG6 22 E1
Willian Way
Baldock SG7 23 E6
Letchworth Garden City SG6 23 A3
Willinghall Cl EN9 163 D7
Williton Rd LU2 46 C2
Willoughby Cl EN10 134 E2
Willoughby Ct AL2 142 D5
Willoughby Rd AL5 86 B4
Willoughby Way SG4 35 A6
Willowbay Cl EN5 171 D3
Willow Cl
Bishop's Stortford CM23 76 E8
Great Hormead SG9 42 A8
Hammond Street EN7 147 E5
Reed SG8 16 D5
Willow Cnr SG13 132 F5
Willow Cres AL1 128 C3
Willow Ct
Harrow HA2 176 C1
Harrow HA3 176 F2
3 Hemel Hempstead HP3 138 E7
Willow Ct *continued*
Letchworth Garden City SG6 23 B2
Luton LU3 44 E5
Willowdene EN8 148 E4
Willow Dene
Bushey WD23 168 E2
Pinner HA5 175 D1
Willow Dr EN5 171 E5
Willow Edge WD4 139 A2
Willow End HA6 175 A4
Willowfield Lower Sch LU1 62 F4
Willowgate Trad Est LU3 44 B8
Willow Gn WD6 170 D4
Willow Gr AL8 89 D3
Willow La
Hitchin SG5 34 D6
St Ippolyts SG4 35 B2
Watford WD18 167 A4
Willowmead SG14 113 B5
Willow Mead CM21 97 E2
Willow Path EN9 163 E5
Willows Cl HA5 175 C1
Willowside AL2 142 E4
Willowside Way SG8 7 C8
Willows La HP1 103 F1
Willows Link SG2 51 A1
Willows The
Buntingford SG9 40 D8
Hemel Hempstead HP2 125 B5
Hitchin SG4 35 A5
Rickmansworth WD3 173 A8
St Albans AL1 142 B7
Stevenage SG2 51 A1
Watford WD19 167 B2
Willowtree Lo
Moor Park HA6 174 F5
1 Northwood HA6 174 F5
Willow Trees Cvn Site SG16 10 A4
Willow Tree Way SG5 21 F2
Willow View SG12 114 E8
Willow Way
Chiswell Green AL2 141 A4
Harpenden AL5 86 C4
Hatfield AL10 129 F2
Hemel Hempstead HP1 124 B5
Luton LU3 44 E5
Potters Bar EN6 159 B6
Radlett WD7 155 E3
Willow Wlk AL6 89 C8
Wilsden Ave LU1 63 C6
Wilshere Ave AL1 127 C1
Wilshere Cres SG4 35 C8
Wilshere Ct 2 SG4 34 F6
Wilshere-Dacre Jun Sch SG5 34 E8
Wilshere Rd AL6 89 A5
Wilsmere Dr HA3 176 E3
Wilson Cl
Bishop's Stortford CM23 76 F5
Stevenage SG1 36 D1
Wilsons La SG7 4 C4
WILSTONE 79 D1
Wilstone Dr AL4 128 C8
WILSTONE GREEN 99 D8
Wilstone Resr Nature Reserve* HP23 99 D7
Wilton Cl CM23 77 B7
Wilton Cres SG13 113 C4
Wilton Ct WD17 167 C6
Wilton Rd SG5 21 E1
Wilton Way SG13 113 C4
Wiltshire Rd SG2 51 A4
Wimborne Cl CM21 97 D2
Wimborne Gr WD17 153 E2
Wimborne Rd LU1 63 C8
Wimple Rd LU4 44 A2
Winch Cl SG4 88 F8
Winchdells HP3 139 A8
Winchester Cl
Bishop's Stortford CM23 76 D4
Stevenage SG1 37 B2
8 Waltham Abbey EN9 163 B6
Winchester Ct 4 EN5 171 F5
Winchester Ho AL3 127 C2
Winchester Rd HA6 174 F1
Winchester Way WD3 166 B4
Winchfield LU1 62 E4
Winchfield Way WD3 165 C2
Winch St LU2 45 F1
Windermere Ave AL1 128 B1
Windermere Cl
Chorleywood WD3 164 D4
Hemel Hempstead HP3 125 C2
Stevenage SG1 37 D2
Windermere Cres LU3 44 F5
Windermere Ct 5 WD17 167 A7
Windermere Prim Sch AL1 128 B1
Windhill
Bishop's Stortford CM23 76 E7
Welwyn Garden City AL7 111 A7
Windhill Old Rd CM23 76 E7
Windhill Prim Sch CM23 76 E6
Winding Hill SG10 75 A4
Winding Shot HP1 124 A4
Winding Shott SG14 91 C4
Windmill Ave AL4 128 C7
Windmill Cl
Barkway SG8 17 C5
Ivinghoe LU7 80 F5
Stansted Mountfitchet CM24 59 D6
Waltham Abbey EN9 163 E5
Windmill Cotts SG12 93 D6
Windmill Dr WD3 165 F3
Windmill Field SG12 114 D8
Windmill Fields CM17 118 F4
Windmill Hill
Buntingford SG9 40 F6
Chipperfield WD4 151 F7
Hitchin SG4 34 F7
Windmill La
Barnet EN5 170 F3
Bushey WD23 168 E1
Cheshunt EN8 148 E1
Windmill Rd
Breachwood Green SG4 47 D2
Hemel Hempstead HP2 124 F2
Luton LU1 63 F6
Markyate AL3, LU1 84 B6
Windmills SG12 71 E8
Windmill St WD23 168 E1
Windmill Trad Est LU1 63 F7
Windmill Way
Much Hadham SG10 74 E1
Tring HP23 99 F4
Windmore Ave EN6 158 C8
Windmore Hall EN6 158 C8
Windridge Cl AL3 127 A1
Windrush Cl SG1 37 A3
Winds End Cl HP2 125 A5
Windsor Cl
Borehamwood WD6 170 A8
Bovingdon HP3 137 A3
Cheshunt EN7 148 A1
Hemel Hempstead HP3 124 E2
Northwood HA6 175 A1
Stevenage SG2 69 B7
Welwyn AL6 89 B3
Windsor Ct
Borehamwood WD6 170 C7
Bushey WD23 168 C2
Kings Langley WD4 139 B2
11 Luton LU1 63 D6
13 St Albans AL1 128 A2
Windsor Dr SG14 112 F7
Windsor Gdns CM23 76 C7
Windsor Ind Est SG13 114 B8
Windsor Rd
Barnet EN5 171 E3
Enfield EN3 162 D3
Harrow HA3 176 D2
Pitstone LU7 80 D3
Royston SG8 7 F6
Watford WD24 154 C1
Welwyn AL6 89 B3
Windsor St LU1 63 D6
Windsor Way WD3 165 A1
Windsor Wlk 8 LU1 63 D6
Windsor Wood EN9 163 E6
Windward Cl EN3 162 D4
Windy Rise SG12 71 F7
Winfield Mobile Home Pk WD25 168 B8
Winford Dr EN10 134 F1
Wingate Ct LU4 44 F2
Wingate Gdns AL6 89 B5
Wingate Ho 16 AL1 128 A2
Wingate Rd LU4 44 F2
Wingate Way AL1 128 A2
WINGRAVE 60 C3
Wingrave CE Comb Sch HP22 60 A3
Wingrave Rd
Tring HP23 100 B6
Wilstone HP23 79 D1
Winifred Cl EN5 170 F3
Winifred Rd HP3 138 D7
Winkfield Cl LU4 44 B1
Winnington Rd EN3 162 C2
Winnipeg Way EN10 148 E6
Winsdon Ct 1 LU1 63 D6
WINSDON HILL 63 B7
Winsdon Rd LU1 63 D6
Winslow Cl LU3 45 C4
Winslow Rd HP22 60 B3
Winston Churchill Way EN8 162 D6
Winston Cl
Harrow HA3 176 F4
Hitchin SG5 34 D7
Winston Ct HA3 176 B3
Winston Gdns HP4 121 F4
Winston Way EN6 159 A6
Winstre Rd WD6 170 A8
Winterscroft Rd EN11 134 F7
Winters La SG2 38 C1
Winthorpe Gdns 7 WD6 169 F8
Winton App WD3 166 C4
Winton Cl
Letchworth Garden City SG6 23 D8
Luton LU2 45 D6
Winton Cres WD3 166 B4
Winton Dr
Cheshunt EN8 148 E2
Croxley Green WD3 166 C4
Winton Rd SG12 93 F1
Winton Terr 5 AL1 127 E2
Wisden Rd SG1 36 F1
Wisdom Dr SG13 113 E6
Wiseman Cl LU2 45 E7
Wisemans Gdns CM21 97 C1

Wistaria Dr AL2 142 B5
Wistlea Cres AL4 129 B1
Wistow Rd LU3 45 A6
Witchford AL7 111 D6
Withy Cl LU4 44 B4
Withy Pl AL2 141 C3
Witney Cl HA5 175 F4
Witter Ave SG5 21 E4
Witton Ho WD3 164 D4
Wiveton Cl LU2 45 D7
Woburn Ave CM23 76 C7
Woburn Cl
Bushey WD23 168 C3
Stevenage SG2 69 C7
Woburn Ct LU4 44 D5
Wodecroft Rd LU3 45 B6
Wodson Park Sports & L Ctr SG12 93 D4
Wolfsburg Ct 4 LU4 44 C5
Wolsey Ave EN7 147 F2
Wolsey Bsns Pk WD18 166 D2
Wolsey Mans HA6 174 C7
Wolsey Rd
Hemel Hempstead HP2 124 D2
Moor Park HA6 174 D7
Wolston Cl LU1 63 C7
Wolverley Ho SG7 4 D4
Wolvescroft SG3 69 A2
Wolves Mere SG3 69 A2
Wonnacott Pl EN3 162 D3
Woodacre Dr AL6 90 A8
Woodbank WD3 165 C3
Woodbine Gr EN2 161 D1
Woodbridge Cl LU4 44 E4
Woodbrook Gdns EN9 163 E6
Woodbury Hill LU2 45 E2
Wood Cl AL10 130 B5
WOODCOCK HILL 173 D6
Woodcock Hill
Rickmansworth WD3 173 E4
Sandridge AL4 108 E1
Woodcock Hill Barns WD3 173 E4
Woodcock Lo SG13 132 C2
Woodcock Rd
Luton LU1 63 A7
Royston SG8 7 E8
Stevenage SG2 51 D2
Wood Comm AL10 130 B8
Woodcote Cl EN8 148 C1
Woodcote Ho 1 SG4 34 F7
Wood Cres HP3 124 E1
Woodcroft SG5 34 E6
Woodcroft Ave SG12 115 E4
Woodcutter Pl AL2 141 C4
Wood Dr SG2 51 B2
WOOD END 53 D7
Wood End AL2 141 C3
Wood End Cl HP2 125 C4
Wood End Hill AL5 85 D4
Wood End La AL3 104 E8
Wood End Rd AL5 85 D3
Wood End Sch AL5 85 D3
Woodfall Ave EN5 171 F4
Wood Farm Rd HP2 124 E2
Woodfield Ave HA6 174 E6
Woodfield Cl CM24 59 E6
Woodfield Dr HP3 125 D1
Woodfield Gdns HP3 125 D1
Woodfield La AL9 145 E8
Woodfield Rd
Radlett WD7 156 A3
Stevenage SG1 36 C1
Welwyn Garden City AL7 110 F6
Woodfield Rise WD23 168 D2
Woodfields
Stansted Mountfitchet CM24 59 E6
2 Watford WD18 167 C5
Woodfield Sch HP3 125 C1
Woodfield Terr
Harefield UB9 173 B1
Stansted Mountfitchet CM24 59 E6
Woodfield Way AL4 128 C6
Woodford Cres HA5 175 B1
Woodforde Cl SG7 4 E4
Woodford Rd WD17 167 C7
Woodgate WD25 154 B6
Woodgate Ave EN6 160 B7
Woodgate Cres HA6 175 A4
Woodgate Mews WD17 167 A8
Woodgrange Ct EN11 135 A5
Wood Green Cl LU2 46 B5
Wood Green Rd LU2 46 C5
Wood Green Way EN8 162 E8
WOODHALL 110 E4
Woodhall Ave HA5 175 E2
Woodhall Cl SG14 113 C8
Woodhall Ct AL7 110 E5
Woodhall Dr HA5 175 E2
Woodhall Gate HA5 175 D2
Woodhall Gr CM23 76 D6
Woodhall Ho AL7 110 F4
Woodhall La
Hemel Hempstead HP2 124 E4
Shenley WD7 156 F4
South Oxhey HA6 175 E6
Welwyn Garden City AL7 110 E4
Woodhall Prim Sch WD19 175 E6
Woodham Way SG12 115 C4
Woodhill Ho AL9 145 D8
Woodhouse Eaves HA6 175 A5
Wood House La EN10 134 A2
Woodhurst SG6 22 F8
Woodhurst Ave WD25 154 D4
Wood La
Birchanger CM23 59 E2
Hemel Hempstead HP2 124 D2
Meesden SG9 30 A6
Woodland Ave
Hemel Hempstead HP1 124 B2
Luton LU3 45 B2
Woodland Cl
Hemel Hempstead HP1 124 B2
Tring HP23 99 F2
Woodland Ct LU2 64 A7
Woodland Ct 1 AL3 127 F7
Woodland Dr
St Albans AL4 128 C4
Watford WD17 166 F8
Woodland Hts HA6 174 B3
Woodland La WD3 164 D6
Woodland Mount SG13 113 F6
Woodland Pl
Chorleywood WD3 164 F5
Hemel Hempstead HP1 124 B2
Woodland Rd
Hertford Heath SG13 114 C3
Maple Cross WD3 172 D5
Woodland Rise
Studham LU6 82 B7
Welwyn Garden City AL8 110 C8
Woodlands
Bishop's Stortford CM23 77 C8
Brookmans Park AL9 145 B4
Caddington LU1 62 E3
Chiswell Green AL2 141 C4
Harpenden AL5 85 E3
Radlett WD7 156 A5
Royston SG8 7 E6
Woodlands Ave HP4 122 D3
Woodlands Cl
Borehamwood WD6 170 B5
Hoddesdon EN11 135 A5
Woodlands Dr
Bedmond WD4 139 C3
Harrow HA7 176 F4
Hoddesdon EN11 135 A4
Woodlands Meade SG4 37 B8
Woodlands Prim Sch WD6 170 A8
Woodlands Rd
Enfield EN2 161 D1
Hertford SG13 113 F6
Kings Langley HP3 139 A4
Thundridge SG12 93 D6
Thundridge SG12 93 E7
Watford WD23 167 E4
Woodlands Sec Sch LU3 44 F7
Woodland Terr SG13 114 B3
Woodland Way
Baldock SG7 23 F6
Bedmond WD5 139 F4
Goff's Oak EN7 147 B3
Stevenage SG2 51 A1
Welwyn AL6 90 A7
Wood Lane End HP2 125 B4
Woodlea AL2 141 A6
Woodlea Gr HA6 174 C4
Woodley Rd SG12 93 F2
Woodleys CM20 118 A1
Woodman Rd 4 HP3 124 E1
Woodmans Ho 7 WD17 167 C5
Woodmere LU3 31 A1
Woodmere Ave WD24 154 E1
Woodmill Mews EN11 135 B8
Woodpecker Cl
Bishop's Stortford CM23 76 C6
Bushey WD23 168 C1
Harrow HA3 176 F2
Hatfield AL10 129 F2
Woodridge Way HA6 174 E4
Woodridings Ave HA5 175 F2
Woodridings Cl HA5 175 F3
Woods Ave AL10 130 B4
Woodshots Mdw WD18 166 D4
Woodside
Bishop's Stortford CM23 77 D8
Borehamwood WD6 169 F5
Cheshunt EN7 162 A8
Hertford Heath SG13 114 C2
WOODSIDE
Slip End 63 A2
Watford 154 B7
Woodside WD24 154 A3
WOODSIDE 131 A2
Woodside Farm & Wildfowl Pk★ LU1 84 A8
Woodside Gdns SG4 34 F7
WOODSIDE GREEN 77 F1
Woodside Ho AL8 110 C7
Woodside Ind Pk SG6 23 B7
Woodside La AL9 131 A1
Woodside Pk LU1 63 B3
Woodside Prim Sch EN7 147 B2
Woodside Rd
Abbots Langley WD25 154 B8
Bricket Wood AL2 140 F2
Welwyn AL6 89 F3
Woodside LU1 63 B3
Woods Pl HP23 100 A3
Wood St
Barnet EN5 171 D5
Luton LU1 63 F6
Woods The
Radlett WD7 156 B5
South Oxhey HA6 175 A5
Woodstock SG3 68 F3
Woodstock Cl SG13 114 B4
Woodstock Rd
Bushey WD23 168 F2
Hoddesdon EN10 134 E4
Woodstock Rd N AL1 128 B4
Woodstock Rd S AL1 128 B3
Woodvale EN8 162 C4
Wood Vale AL10 130 B5
Woodvale Pk AL1 128 B3
Wood View
Cuffley EN6 146 E4
Hemel Hempstead HP1 124 B5
Woodville Court Mews WD17 167 A7
Woodville Ct WD17 167 A7
Woodville Pl SG14 113 B8
Woodward Gdns HA7 176 F3
Woodwaye WD19 167 C2
Woodwicks WD3 172 D5
Woolenwick Inf Sch SG1 50 B6
Woolenwick Jun Sch SG1 50 B6
Woolgrove Ct SG4 22 B1
Woolgrove Rd SG4 22 B1
Woolgrove Sch SG6 23 D5
Woollam Cres AL3 127 C7
Woollams AL3 106 A4
Woollard St EN9 163 C5
WOOLLENSBROOK 134 E8
Woolmans Cl EN10 134 F1
Woolmer Cl WD6 157 A1
Woolmerdine Ct WD23 167 D6
Woolmer Dr HP2 125 C3
WOOLMER GREEN 69 B2
Woolmers La SG14 112 B2
Woolmer's Park Mews SG14 112 B1
Woolners Way SG1 50 C6
Woolpack Ho 1 EN3 162 D2
Woolston Ave SG6 23 A4
Woolwich Ct 10 EN3 163 A1
Wootton Cl LU3 45 B7
Wootton Dr HP2 124 F8
Worboys Ct SG8 1 F5
Worcester Ct 12 AL1 128 A2
Worcester Ho 12 WD6 170 A7
Worcester Rd AL10 129 F6
Worcesters Ave EN1 162 A1
Worcesters Prim Sch EN1 161 F1
Wordsworth Cl SG8 2 D1
Wordsworth Ct AL10 130 A6
Wordsworth Gdns WD6 170 A4
Wordsworth Rd
Harpenden AL5 86 A3
Luton LU4 44 A2
Works Rd SG6 23 C7
Worley Rd AL3 127 D4
WORMLEY 148 E8
Wormleybury EN10 148 D8
Wormley Ct EN10 148 F7
Wormley Lodge Cl EN10 148 F8
Wormley Prim Sch EN10 148 E8
WORMLEY WEST END 147 F8
Wornham Ave SG1 50 E6
Worsdell Way SG4 35 B7
Worsted La SG9 41 E7
Wortham Rd SG8 7 E4
Wortham Way SG2 51 B3
Wraglings The CM23 77 B5
Wratten Cl SG5 34 E6
Wratten Rd E SG5 34 E6
Wratten Rd W SG5 34 E6
Wrayfields SG5 12 B8
Wraysbury Cl LU4 44 D3
Wrenbrook Rd CM23 76 F6
Wren Cl
Kimpton SG4 66 B1
Luton LU2 46 C6
Stevenage SG2 51 B6
Wren Cres WD23 168 C1
Wrensfield HP1 124 B3
Wren Wood AL7 111 B7
Wrestlers Cl AL10 130 C7
Wrexham Terr SG8 7 D7
Wright Cl AL4 108 E7
Wright's Bldgs WD17 167 B7
WRIGHT'S GREEN 98 D7
Wright's Green La CM22 98 D7
Wrights Mdw SG2 52 B8
Wrights Orch SG2 51 E2
Wrotham Bsns Pk EN5 158 F2
Wrotham Pk★ EN5 158 F3
Wrotham Rd EN5 171 E7
Wroxham Ave HP3 124 D1
Wroxham Gdns
Crews Hill EN2 161 B4
Potters Bar EN6 158 D8
Wroxham Sch The EN6 158 D8
Wroxham Way AL5 86 C3
Wulfrath Way SG12 93 C3
Wulstan Pk EN6 159 D7
Wulwards Cl LU1 63 B6
Wulwards Ct LU1 63 B6
Wyatt Cl
Bushey WD23 168 E2
Ickleford SG5 21 D4
Wyatt's Cl WD3 165 A6
Wyatt's Rd WD3 165 A6
Wyburn Ave EN5 171 F6
Wychdell SG2 69 C8
Wych Elm CM20 117 C1
Wych Elm La AL6, SG3 68 F2
Wych Elms AL2 141 B3
Wychford Dr CM21 97 C1
Wychwood Ave LU2 45 E3
Wychwood Way HA6 174 F3
Wycklond Cl SG5 11 E6
Wycliffe Cl
7 Cheshunt EN8 148 D2
Luton LU3 45 C6
Wycliffe Ct WD5 153 E7
Wycombe Pl AL4 128 B6
Wycombe Way
Luton LU3 45 C8
St Albans AL4 128 B6
WYDDIAL 28 A3
Wyddial Gn AL7 111 B6
Wyddial Rd SG9 40 E8
Wyedale AL2 142 F4
Wye The HP2 125 A8
Wykeham Rise N20 171 E1
Wyken Cl LU3 45 A7
Wyldwood Cl CM17 118 C6
Wyllyotts Cl EN6 158 F7
Wyllyotts La EN6 158 F7
Wyllyotts Pl EN6 158 F7
Wylo Dr EN5 171 A3
Wymondley Cl SG4 35 A7
Wymondley Ho SG4 35 E3
Wymondley Jun Mix Inf Sch SG4 35 E4
Wymondley Rd
Hitchin SG4 35 B6
Letchworth Garden City SG6 23 A1
Wynches Farm Dr AL4 128 D3
Wynchgate HA3 176 E3
Wynchlands Cres AL4 128 D3
Wyndham Rd LU4 44 C2
Wyndhams End AL7 110 F2
Wynd The SG6 22 F6
Wynlie Gdns HA5 175 B1
Wynn Cl SG7 13 A1
Wyrley Dell SG6 23 A3
Wysells Ct SG6 22 D7
Wyton AL7 111 D6
Wyvern Cl LU4 44 E3

Y

Yardley SG6 23 C4
Yardley Ave LU7 80 D4
Yardley Ct 14 AL5 86 B1
Yarmouth Rd
Stevenage SG1 50 A7
Watford WD24 154 C1
Yarra Ho 5 AL1 127 E3
Yately Cl LU2 45 D7
Yavneh Coll WD6 170 C5
Yearling Cl SG12 114 F7
Yeatman Ho WD24 154 B3
Yeats Cl SG8 2 D1
Ye Cnr WD19 167 E3
Yeomanry Dr SG7 13 A1
Yeomans Ave AL5 85 D3
Yeomans Cl CM23 76 D6
Yeomans Ct HP2 105 A1
Yeomans Dr SG2 51 E2
Yeomans Keep WD3 164 F6
Yeomans Ride HP2 105 A1
Yeovil Ct LU2 46 B2
Yeovil Rd LU2 46 B2
Yew Cl EN7 147 E4
Yew Gr AL7 111 C5
Yewlands
Hoddesdon EN11 135 A5
Sawbridgeworth CM21 97 E1
Yewlands Dr EN11 135 A5
Yews Ave EN1 162 B3
Yewstone Ct WD18 167 A6
Yewtree Cl LU7 80 E5
Yew Tree Cl HP5 136 A1
Yew Tree Ct
Elstree WD6 169 D3
Hemel Hempstead HP1 124 A1
Yew Tree Dr HP3 137 B3
Yewtree End AL2 141 B4
Yew Tree Pl CM23 76 F8
Yew Wlk EN11 135 A5
York Cl WD4 139 A2
York Cres WD6 170 D7
Yorke Gate WD17 167 A7
Yorke Mead Prim Sch WD3 166 A4
Yorke Rd WD3 166 A3
Yorkes Mews 16 SG12 93 D1
York Ho
13 Borehamwood WD6 170 A7
Hatfield AL9 130 C7
St Albans AL3 127 C2
York House Sch WD3 165 F7
York Rd
Cheshunt EN8 162 E6
Hitchin SG5 34 E8
Northwood HA6 175 A1
St Albans AL1 127 F4
Stevenage SG1 36 F1
Watford WD18 167 C4
York St LU2 63 F8
York Terr EN2 161 C1
York Way
Hemel Hempstead HP2 124 E2
Royston SG8 7 B8
Watford WD25 154 E3
Welwyn AL6 89 C3
Youngfield Rd HP1 123 F4
Youngsbury La SG12 93 E8
Youngs Mews SG14 113 C6
Youngs Rise AL8 110 C6
Yukon Rd EN10 148 E6
Yule Cl AL2 140 F1

Z

Zambesi Rd CM23 76 F5

Addresses

Name and Address	Telephone	Page	Grid reference

Using the Ordnance Survey National Grid

Any feature in this atlas can be given a unique reference to help you find the same feature on other Ordnance Survey maps of the area, or to help someone else locate you if they do not have a Street Atlas.

The grid squares in this atlas match the Ordnance Survey National Grid and are at 500 metre intervals. The small figures at the bottom and sides of every other grid line are the National Grid kilometre values (**00** to **99** km) and are repeated across the country every 100 km (see left).

To give a unique National Grid reference you need to locate where in the country you are. The country is divided into 100 km squares with each square given a unique two-letter reference. Use the administrative map to determine in which 100 km square a particular page of this atlas falls.

The bold letters and numbers between each grid line (**A** to **F**, **1** to **8**) are for use within a specific Street Atlas only, and when used with the page number, are a convenient way of referencing these grid squares.

Example The railway bridge over DARLEY GREEN RD in grid square B1

Step 1: Identify the two-letter reference, in this example the page is in **SP**

Step 2: Identify the 1 km square in which the railway bridge falls. Use the figures in the southwest corner of this square: Eastings **17**, Northings **74**. This gives a unique reference: **SP 17 74**, accurate to 1 km.

Step 3: To give a more precise reference accurate to 100 m you need to estimate how many tenths along and how many tenths up this 1 km square the feature is (to help with this the 1 km square is divided into four 500 m squares). This makes the bridge about **8** tenths along and about **1** tenth up from the southwest corner.

This gives a unique reference: **SP 178 741**, accurate to 100 m.

Eastings (read from left to right along the bottom) come before Northings (read from bottom to top). If you have trouble remembering say to yourself "Along the hall, THEN up the stairs"!

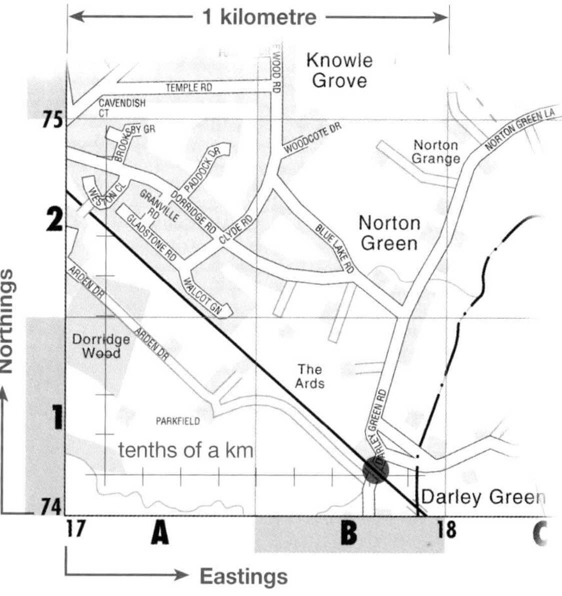